Citroën Saxo
Service and Repair Manual

Spencer Drayton, Louise Brown and RM Jex

Models covered *(3506 - 328 - 4AG3)*

Citroën Saxo models with petrol and diesel engines, including special/limited editions;
3- and 5-door Hatchbacks

1.0 litre (954 cc), 1.1 litre (1124 cc), 1.4 litre (1360 cc), and 1.6 litre (1587 cc, inc. 16-valve) petrol engines
1.5 litre (1527 cc) diesel engine

ABCDE
FGHIJ
KLM

A book in the **Haynes Service and Repair Manual Series**

ISBN **1 85960 766 7**

British Library Cataloguing in Publication Data
A catalogue record for this book is available from the British Library.

Printed in the USA

Haynes Publishing
Sparkford, Yeovil, Somerset BA22 7JJ, England

Haynes North America, Inc
861 Lawrence Drive, Newbury Park, California 91320, USA

Editions Haynes
4, Rue de l'Abreuvoir
92415 COURBEVOIE CEDEX, France

Haynes Publishing Nordiska AB
Box 1504, 751 45 UPPSALA, Sverige

Contents

LIVING WITH YOUR CITROËN SAXO

MAINTENANCE

Routine maintenance and servicing

Contents

REPAIRS & OVERHAUL

The Citroën Saxo range covered by this Manual was introduced to the UK market in May 1996. Originally, the Saxo was available with a choice of 1.1 litre (1124 cc) or 1.4 litre (1360 cc) petrol engines, in three-door and five-door Hatchback form. The range is derived and developed from the very successful Peugeot 106 range, and it attracted very favourable press reports at its launch.

In October 1996, the 1.5 litre (1527 cc) diesel engine was added to the range, together with the 1.6 litre automatic.

January 1997 saw the introduction of the sporty 1.6 litre VTR and 1.6 litre 16-valve VTS models. Both were hailed as fine examples of the new breed of "GTi", marking a welcome return of the "hot hatch".

In June 1997, a 1.0 litre petrol model was added to the range, initially in the form of the limited-edition "Mischief". Further limited editions using this, and the other engine sizes in the range, soon followed.

The range received a minor facelift in January 1998, with cosmetic modifications to the front and rear of the car, and a revised anti-theft immobiliser.

All engines are derived from the well-proven engines which have appeared in many Citroën and Peugeot vehicles. The engine is of four-cylinder overhead camshaft design, mounted transversely, with the transmission mounted on the left-hand side. All models have a five-speed manual transmission or three-speed automatic transmission.

All models have fully-independent front suspension. The rear suspension is semi-independent, with trailing arms and a torsion bar axle.

A wide range of standard and optional equipment is available within the Saxo range to suit most tastes, including central locking, immobiliser, electric windows, and driver's airbag; ABS, air conditioning and a passenger airbag were available as options.

Provided that regular servicing is carried out in accordance with the manufacturer's recommendations, the Citroën Saxo should prove a reliable and economical small car. The engine compartment is well-designed, and most of the items needing frequent attention are easily accessible.

Citroën Saxo 1.1 LX (1996 model)

Citroën Saxo 1.6 VTR (1998 model)

The Citroën Saxo Team

Haynes manuals are produced by dedicated and enthusiastic people working in close co-operation. The team responsible for the creation of this book included:

Authors	**Spencer Drayton** **R. M. Jex** **Louise Brown**
Sub-editor	**Sophie Yar**
Editor & Page Make-up	**Steve Churchill**
Workshop manager	**Paul Buckland**
Photo Scans	**Steve Tanswell** **John Martin**
Cover illustration & Line Art	**Roger Healing**
Wiring diagrams	**Matthew Marke**

We hope the book will help you to get the maximum enjoyment from your car. By carrying out routine maintenance as described you will ensure your car's reliability and preserve its resale value.

Your Citroën Saxo manual

The aim of this manual is to help you get the best value from your vehicle. It can do so in several ways. It can help you decide what work must be done (even should you choose to get it done by a garage). It will also provide information on routine maintenance and servicing, and give a logical course of action and diagnosis when random faults occur. However, it is hoped that you will use the manual by tackling the work yourself. On simpler jobs it may even be quicker than booking the car into a garage and going there twice, to leave and collect it. Perhaps most important, a lot of money can be saved by avoiding the costs a garage must charge to cover its labour and overheads.

The manual has drawings and descriptions to show the function of the various components so that their layout can be understood. Tasks are described and photographed in a clear step-by-step sequence. The illustrations are numbered by the Section number and paragraph number to which they relate - if there is more than one illustration per paragraph, the sequence is denoted alphabetically.

References to the "left" or "right" of the vehicle are in the sense of a person in the driver's seat, facing forwards.

Acknowledgements

Thanks are also due to Draper Tools Limited, who provided some of the workshop tools, and to all those people at Sparkford who helped in the production of this manual.

We take great pride in the accuracy of information given in this manual, but vehicle manufacturers make alterations and design changes during the production run of a particular vehicle of which they do not inform us. No liability can be accepted by the authors or publishers for loss, damage or injury caused by any errors in, or omissions from, the information given.

Working on your car can be dangerous. This page shows just some of the potential risks and hazards, with the aim of creating a safety-conscious attitude.

General hazards

Scalding

- Don't remove the radiator or expansion tank cap while the engine is hot.
- Engine oil, automatic transmission fluid or power steering fluid may also be dangerously hot if the engine has recently been running.

Burning

- Beware of burns from the exhaust system and from any part of the engine. Brake discs and drums can also be extremely hot immediately after use.

Crushing

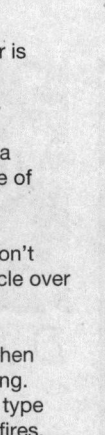

- When working under or near a raised vehicle, always supplement the jack with axle stands, or use drive-on ramps. ***Never venture under a car which is only supported by a jack.***
- Take care if loosening or tightening high-torque nuts when the vehicle is on stands. Initial loosening and final tightening should be done with the wheels on the ground.

Fire

- Fuel is highly flammable; fuel vapour is explosive.
- Don't let fuel spill onto a hot engine.
- Do not smoke or allow naked lights (including pilot lights) anywhere near a vehicle being worked on. Also beware of creating sparks (electrically or by use of tools).
- Fuel vapour is heavier than air, so don't work on the fuel system with the vehicle over an inspection pit.
- Another cause of fire is an electrical overload or short-circuit. Take care when repairing or modifying the vehicle wiring.
- Keep a fire extinguisher handy, of a type suitable for use on fuel and electrical fires.

Electric shock

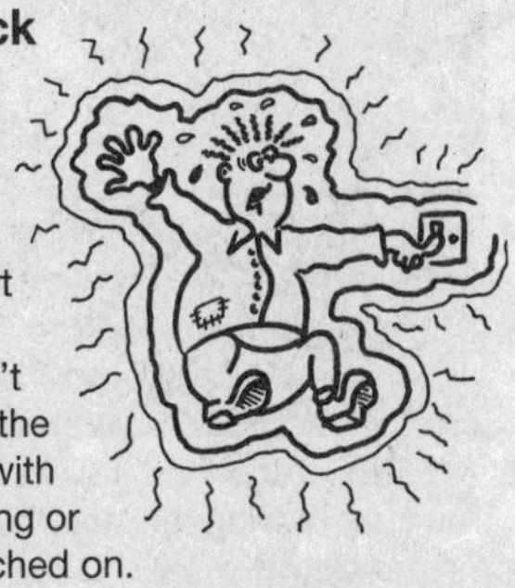

- Ignition HT voltage can be dangerous, especially to people with heart problems or a pacemaker. Don't work on or near the ignition system with the engine running or the ignition switched on.
- Mains voltage is also dangerous. Make sure that any mains-operated equipment is correctly earthed. Mains power points should be protected by a residual current device (RCD) circuit breaker.

Fume or gas intoxication

- Exhaust fumes are poisonous; they often contain carbon monoxide, which is rapidly fatal if inhaled. Never run the engine in a confined space such as a garage with the doors shut.
- Fuel vapour is also poisonous, as are the vapours from some cleaning solvents and paint thinners.

Poisonous or irritant substances

- Avoid skin contact with battery acid and with any fuel, fluid or lubricant, especially antifreeze, brake hydraulic fluid and Diesel fuel. Don't syphon them by mouth. If such a substance is swallowed or gets into the eyes, seek medical advice.
- Prolonged contact with used engine oil can cause skin cancer. Wear gloves or use a barrier cream if necessary. Change out of oil-soaked clothes and do not keep oily rags in your pocket.
- Air conditioning refrigerant forms a poisonous gas if exposed to a naked flame (including a cigarette). It can also cause skin burns on contact.

Asbestos

- Asbestos dust can cause cancer if inhaled or swallowed. Asbestos may be found in gaskets and in brake and clutch linings. When dealing with such components it is safest to assume that they contain asbestos.

Special hazards

Hydrofluoric acid

- This extremely corrosive acid is formed when certain types of synthetic rubber, found in some O-rings, oil seals, fuel hoses etc, are exposed to temperatures above 400°C. The rubber changes into a charred or sticky substance containing the acid. *Once formed, the acid remains dangerous for years. If it gets onto the skin, it may be necessary to amputate the limb concerned.*
- When dealing with a vehicle which has suffered a fire, or with components salvaged from such a vehicle, wear protective gloves and discard them after use.

The battery

- Batteries contain sulphuric acid, which attacks clothing, eyes and skin. Take care when topping-up or carrying the battery.
- The hydrogen gas given off by the battery is highly explosive. Never cause a spark or allow a naked light nearby. Be careful when connecting and disconnecting battery chargers or jump leads.

Air bags

- Air bags can cause injury if they go off accidentally. Take care when removing the steering wheel and/or facia. Special storage instructions may apply.

Diesel injection equipment

- Diesel injection pumps supply fuel at very high pressure. Take care when working on the fuel injectors and fuel pipes.

Warning: Never expose the hands, face or any other part of the body to injector spray; the fuel can penetrate the skin with potentially fatal results.

Remember...

DO

- Do use eye protection when using power tools, and when working under the vehicle.
- Do wear gloves or use barrier cream to protect your hands when necessary.
- Do get someone to check periodically that all is well when working alone on the vehicle.
- Do keep loose clothing and long hair well out of the way of moving mechanical parts.
- Do remove rings, wristwatch etc, before working on the vehicle – especially the electrical system.
- Do ensure that any lifting or jacking equipment has a safe working load rating adequate for the job.

DON'T

- Don't attempt to lift a heavy component which may be beyond your capability – get assistance.
- Don't rush to finish a job, or take unverified short cuts.
- Don't use ill-fitting tools which may slip and cause injury.
- Don't leave tools or parts lying around where someone can trip over them. Mop up oil and fuel spills at once.
- Don't allow children or pets to play in or near a vehicle being worked on.

The following pages are intended to help in dealing with common roadside emergencies and breakdowns. You will find more detailed fault finding information at the back of the manual, and repair information in the main chapters.

If your car won't start and the starter motor doesn't turn

- ☐ If it's a model with automatic transmission, make sure the selector is in 'P' or 'N'.
- ☐ Open the bonnet and make sure that the battery terminals are clean and tight.
- ☐ Switch on the headlights and try to start the engine. If the headlights go very dim when you're trying to start, the battery is probably flat. Get out of trouble by jump starting (see next page) using a friend's car.

If your car won't start even though the starter motor turns as normal

- ☐ Is there fuel in the tank?
- ☐ Is there moisture on electrical components under the bonnet? Switch off the ignition, then wipe off any obvious dampness with a dry cloth. Spray a water-repellent aerosol product (WD-40 or equivalent) on ignition and fuel system electrical connectors like those shown in the photos. Pay special attention to the ignition coil wiring connector and HT leads. (Note that Diesel engines don't normally suffer from damp.)

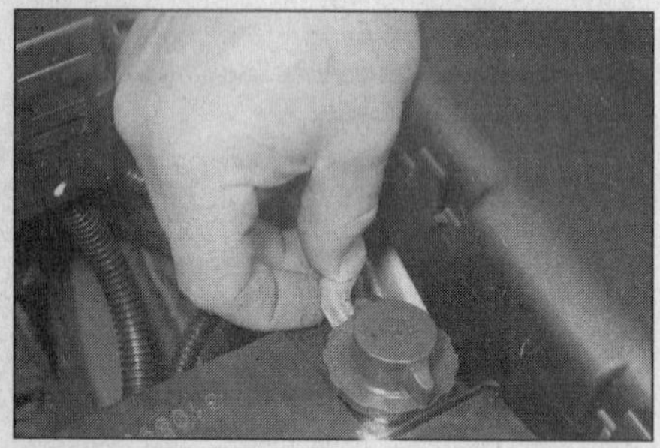

A Check the security and condition of the battery terminals.

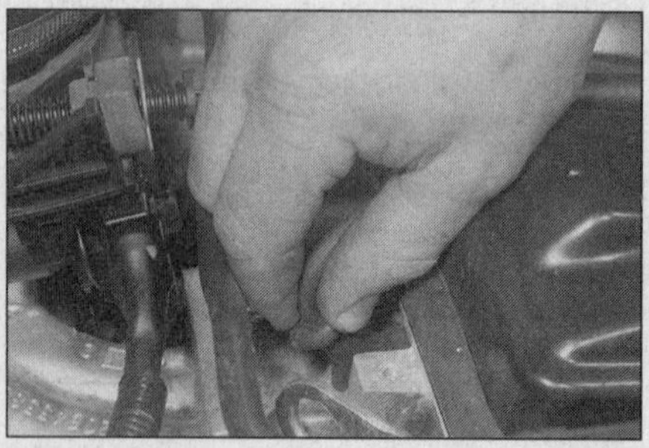

B Check that the HT leads are securely connected to the spark plugs (petrol engine models).

C Also check the four HT lead connections to the ignition coil (petrol engine models).

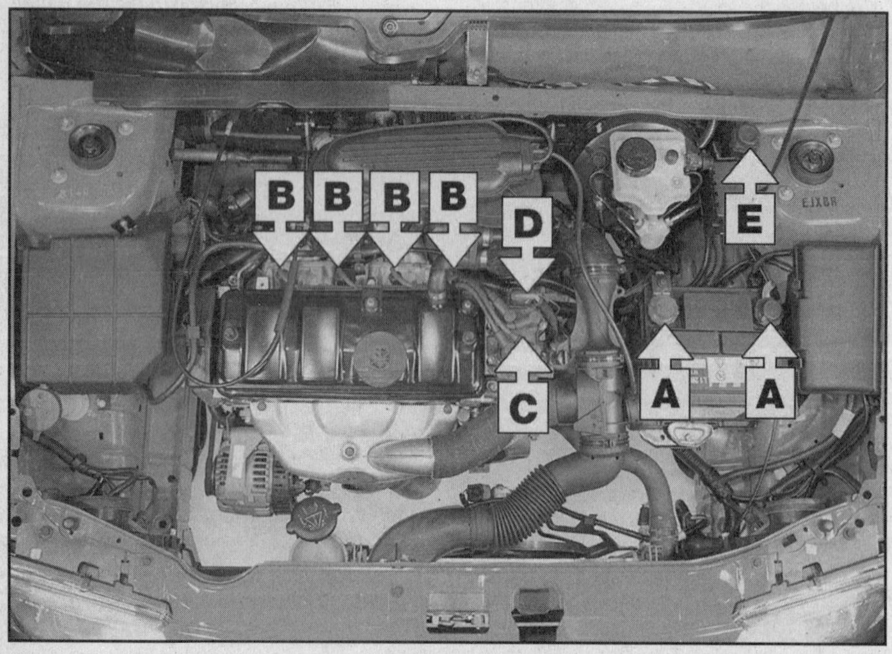

Check that electrical connections are secure (with the ignition switched off) and spray them with a water dispersant spray like WD40 if you suspect a problem due to damp

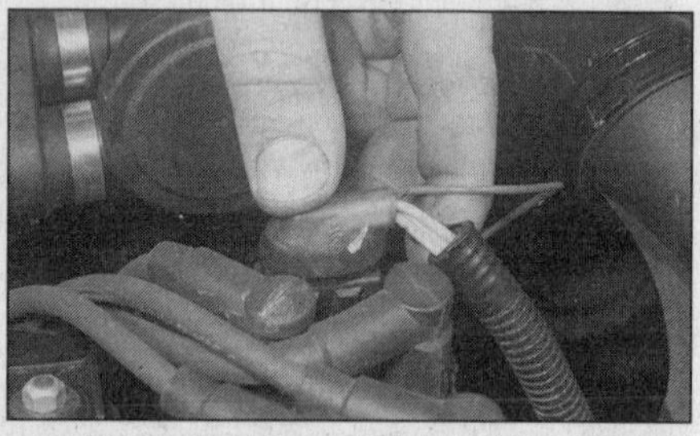

D Check that the ignition coil LT wiring is securely connected (petrol engine models).

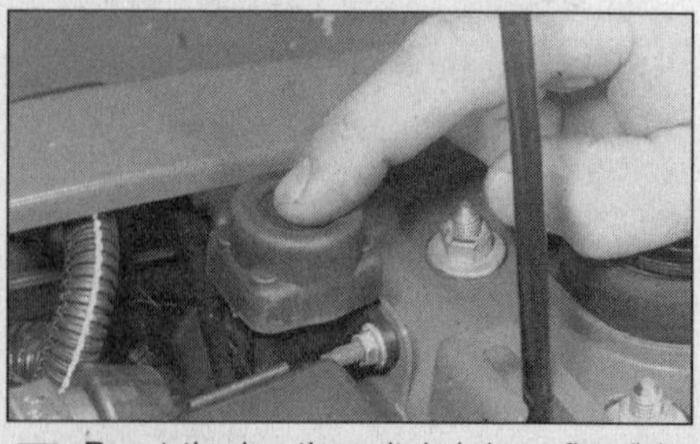

E Reset the inertia switch (where fitted) by depressing the large button on top of the unit.

Jump starting

HAYNES HiNT *Jump starting will get you out of trouble, but you must correct whatever made the battery go flat in the first place. There are three possibilities:*

***1** The battery has been drained by repeated attempts to start, or by leaving the lights on.*

***2** The charging system is not working properly (alternator drivebelt slack or broken, alternator wiring fault or alternator itself faulty).*

***3** The battery itself is at fault (electrolyte low, or battery worn out).*

When jump-starting a car using a booster battery, observe the following precautions:

- ✔ Before connecting the booster battery, make sure that the ignition is switched off.
- ✔ Ensure that all electrical equipment (lights, heater, wipers, etc) is switched off.
- ✔ Take note of any special precautions printed on the battery case.
- ✔ Make sure that the booster battery is the same voltage as the discharged one in the vehicle.
- ✔ If the battery is being jump-started from the battery in another vehicle, the two vehicles MUST NOT TOUCH each other.
- ✔ Make sure that the transmission is in neutral (or PARK, in the case of automatic transmission).

1 Connect one end of the red jump lead to the positive (+) terminal of the flat battery

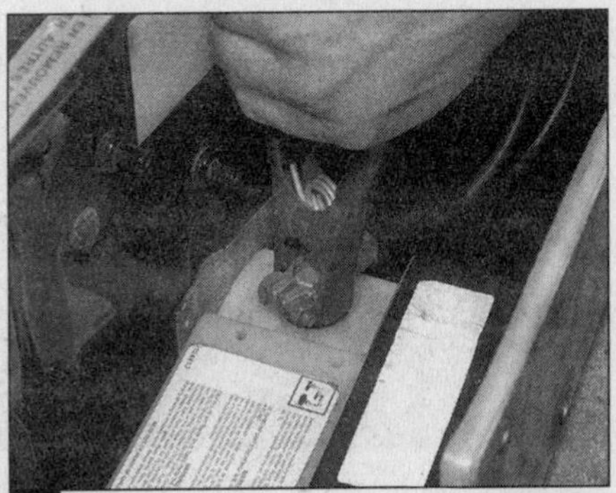

2 Connect the other end of the red lead to the positive (+) terminal of the booster battery.

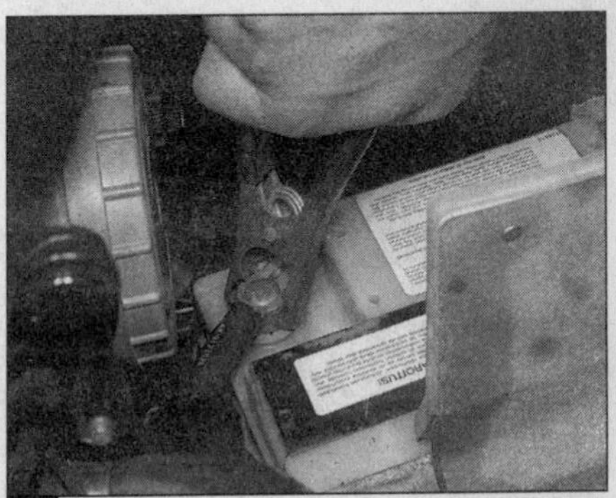

3 Connect one end of the black jump lead to the negative (-) terminal of the booster battery

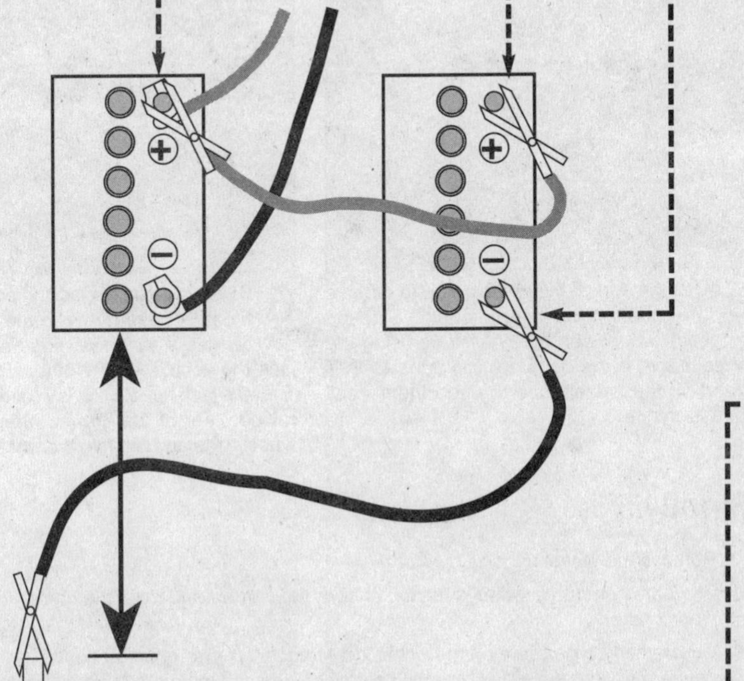

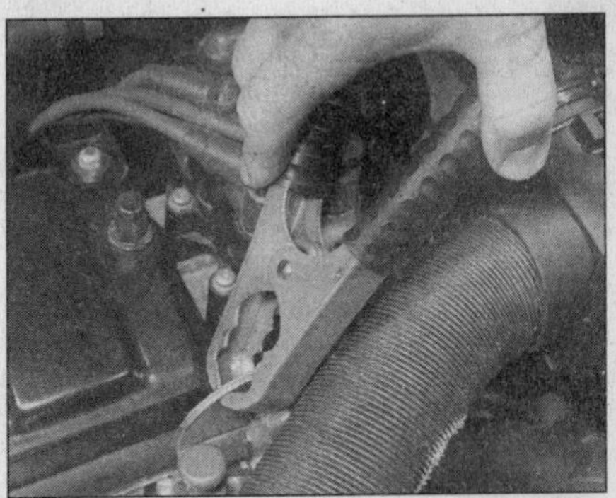

4 Connect the other end of the black jump lead to a bolt or bracket on the engine block, well away from the battery, on the vehicle to be started.

5 Make sure that the jump leads will not come into contact with the fan, drive-belts or other moving parts of the engine.

6 Start the engine using the booster battery and run it at idle speed. Switch on the lights, rear window demister and heater blower motor, then disconnect the jump leads in the reverse order of connection. Turn off the lights etc.

Wheel changing

Note: *Early Saxos had three wheel bolts per wheel; later models, or those with ABS or power steering, had four bolts per wheel. Models fitted with alloy wheels may need a special socket to remove one of the wheel bolts - this socket should be provided in the glove compartment.*

Warning: Do not change a wheel in a situation where you risk being hit by another vehicle. On busy roads, try to stop in a lay-by or a gateway. Be wary of passing traffic while changing the wheel - it is easy to become distracted by the job in hand.

Preparation

- ☐ When a puncture occurs, stop as soon as it is safe to do so.
- ☐ Park on firm level ground, if possible, and well out of the way of other traffic.
- ☐ Use hazard warning lights if necessary.
- ☐ If you have one, use a warning triangle to alert other drivers of your presence.
- ☐ Apply the handbrake and engage first or reverse gear (or Park on models with automatic transmission.
- ☐ Chock the wheel diagonally opposite the one being removed – a couple of large stones will do for this.
- ☐ If the ground is soft, use a flat piece of wood to spread the load under the jack.

Changing the wheel

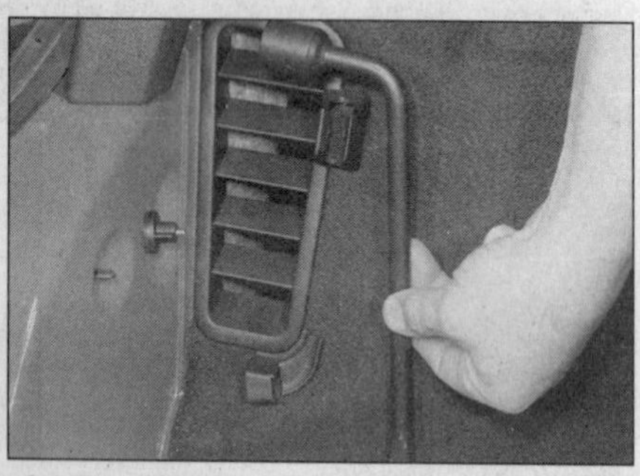

1 The spare wheel and jack are stored in a carrier under the luggage compartment floor. The wheelbrace is clipped to the left-hand side of the luggage compartment, next to the rear light unit.

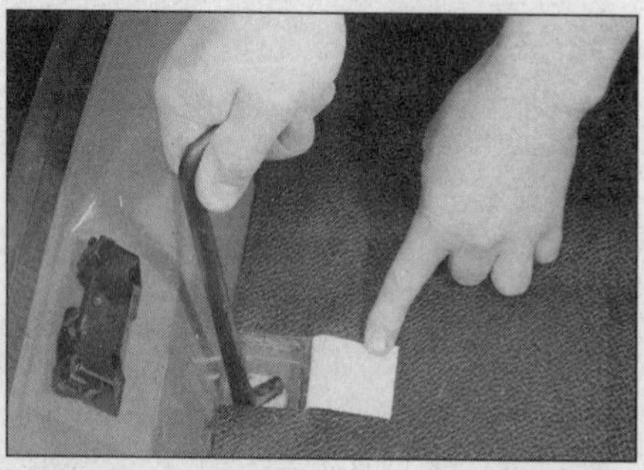

2 Lift up the flap in the boot floor covering, and use the flat end of the wheelbrace to turn the spare wheel carrier bolt. Only turn the bolt a few turns, or the spare wheel will drop to the ground.

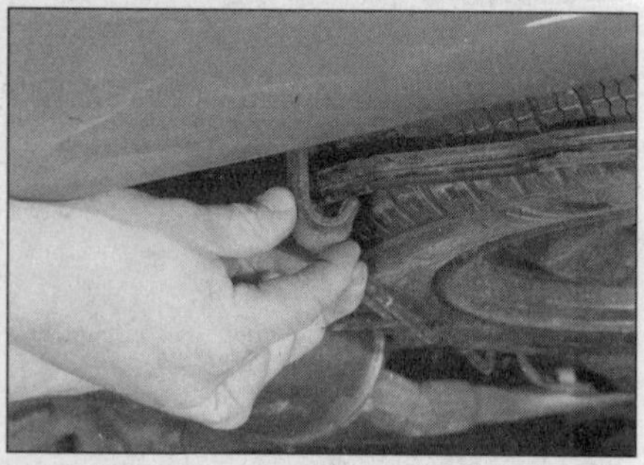

3 Lift the carrier upwards to unhook it, then lower it to the ground and remove the spare wheel. Hook the carrier back up while the wheel is removed.

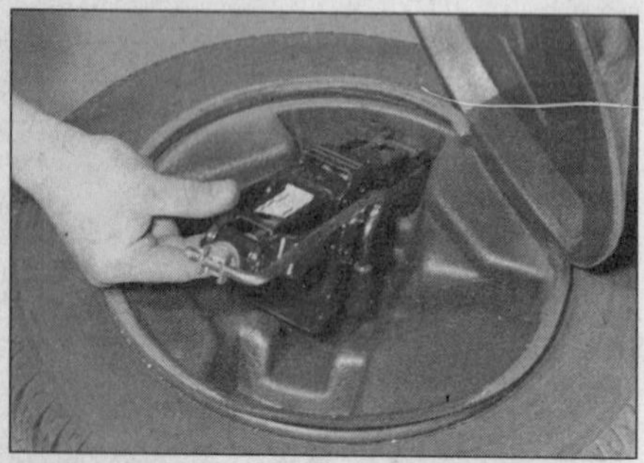

4 Lift off the cover, then remove the jack from the centre of the spare wheel.

5 Use the end of the wheelbrace to remove the wheel trim, if applicable. Slacken each wheel bolt by a half turn, using the wheelbrace. If the bolts are too tight, DON'T stand on the wheelbrace to undo them - call for assistance.

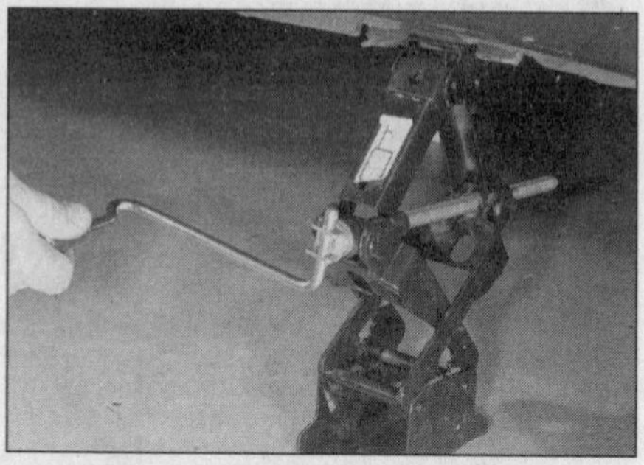

6 Select the nearest jacking point, then place the jack head between the two horizontal flanges in the lower edge of the sill (don't jack the vehicle at any other point of the sill). Turn the jack handle clockwise until the wheel is raised clear of the ground, then unscrew the wheel bolts and remove the wheel.

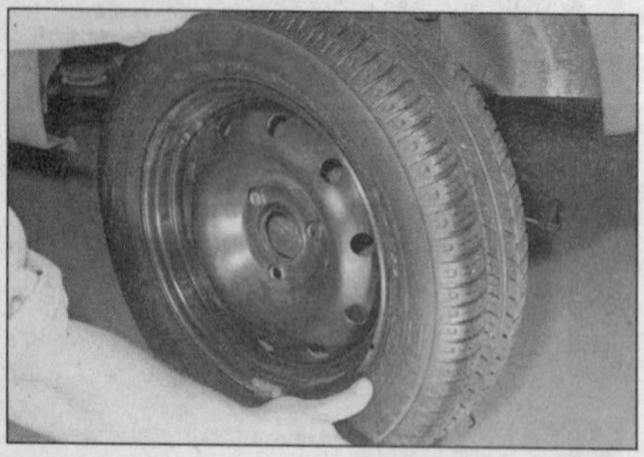

7 Fit the spare wheel, and screw in the bolts. Lightly tighten the bolts with the wheelbrace, then lower the vehicle to the ground. Securely tighten the wheel bolts, then refit the wheel trim, if applicable.

Finally...

- ☐ Remove the wheel chocks.
- ☐ Stow the punctured wheel and jack back in the carrier, and raise the carrier fully with the wheelbrace.
- ☐ Check the tyre pressure on the wheel just fitted. If it is low, or if you don't have a pressure gauge with you, drive slowly to the nearest garage and inflate the tyre to the right pressure.
- ☐ The wheel bolts should be slackened and retightened to the specified torque at the earliest possible opportunity.
- ☐ Have the damaged tyre or wheel repaired as soon as possible.

Identifying leaks

Puddles on the garage floor or drive, or obvious wetness under the bonnet or underneath the car, suggest a leak that needs investigating. It can sometimes be difficult to decide where the leak is coming from, especially if the engine bay is very dirty already. Leaking oil or fluid can also be blown rearwards by the passage of air under the car, giving a false impression of where the problem lies.

Warning: Most automotive oils and fluids are poisonous. Wash them off skin, and change out of contaminated clothing, without delay.

HAYNES HiNT ***The smell of a fluid leaking from the car may provide a clue to what's leaking. Some fluids are distictively coloured. It may help to clean the car carefully and to park it over some clean paper overnight as an aid to locating the source of the leak. Remember that some leaks may only occur while the engine is running.***

Sump oil

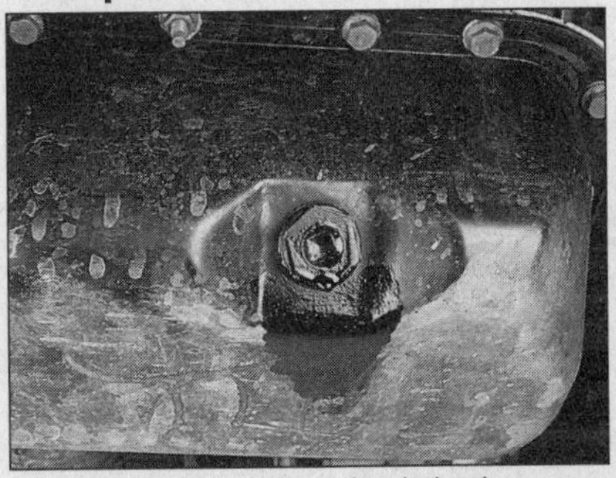

Engine oil may leak from the drain plug...

Oil from filter

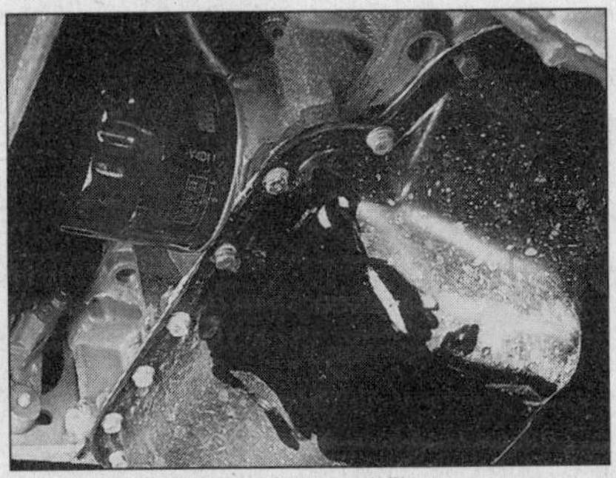

...or from the base of the oil filter.

Gearbox oil

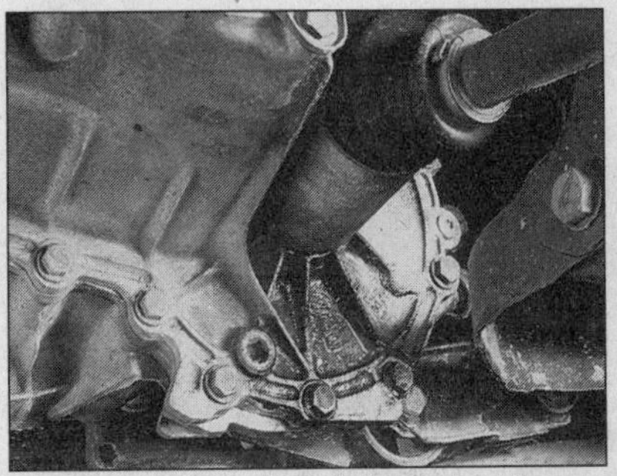

Gearbox oil can leak from the seals at the inboard ends of the driveshafts.

Antifreeze

Leaking antifreeze often leaves a crystalline deposit like this.

Brake fluid

A leak occurring at a wheel is almost certainly brake fluid.

Power steering fluid

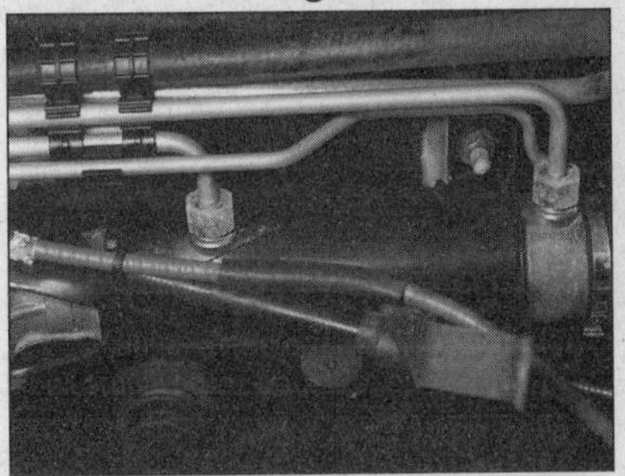

Power steering fluid may leak from the pipe connectors on the steering rack.

Towing

When all else fails, you may find yourself having to get a tow home – or of course you may be helping somebody else. Long-distance recovery should only be done by a garage or breakdown service. For shorter distances, DIY towing using another car is easy enough, but observe the following points:

☐ Use a proper tow-rope – they are not expensive. The vehicle being towed must display an 'ON TOW' sign in its rear window.

☐ Always turn the ignition key to the 'on' position when the vehicle is being towed, so that the steering lock is released, and that the direction indicator and brake lights will work.

☐ A towing eye is provided below each bumper. Where no front towing eye is fitted, a screw-fit eye is provided under the rear seat cushion **(see illustration)**; this towing eye is screwed into the front bumper, after prising out the round trim cover.

☐ Before being towed, release the handbrake and select neutral on the transmission.

☐ Note that greater-than-usual pedal pressure will be required to operate the brakes, since the vacuum servo unit is only operational with the engine running.

☐ On models with power steering, greater-than-usual steering effort will also be required.

☐ The driver of the car being towed must keep the tow-rope taut at all times to avoid snatching.

☐ Make sure that both drivers know the route before setting off.

☐ Only drive at moderate speeds and keep the distance towed to a minimum. Drive smoothly and allow plenty of time for slowing down at junctions.

☐ On models with automatic transmission, special precautions apply. If in doubt, do not tow, or transmission damage may result.

Screw-in towing eye is stored under the rear seat cushion

Introduction

There are some very simple checks which need only take a few minutes to carry out, but which could save you a lot of inconvenience and expense.

These "Weekly checks" require no great skill or special tools, and the small amount of time they take to perform could prove to be very well spent, for example;

☐ Keeping an eye on tyre condition and pressures, will not only help to stop them wearing out prematurely, but could also save your life.

☐ Many breakdowns are caused by electrical problems. Battery-related faults are particularly common, and a quick check on a regular basis will often prevent the majority of these.

☐ If your car develops a brake fluid leak, the first time you might know about it is when your brakes don't work properly. Checking the level regularly will give advance warning of this kind of problem.

☐ If the oil or coolant levels run low, the cost of repairing any engine damage will be far greater than fixing the leak, for example.

Underbonnet check points

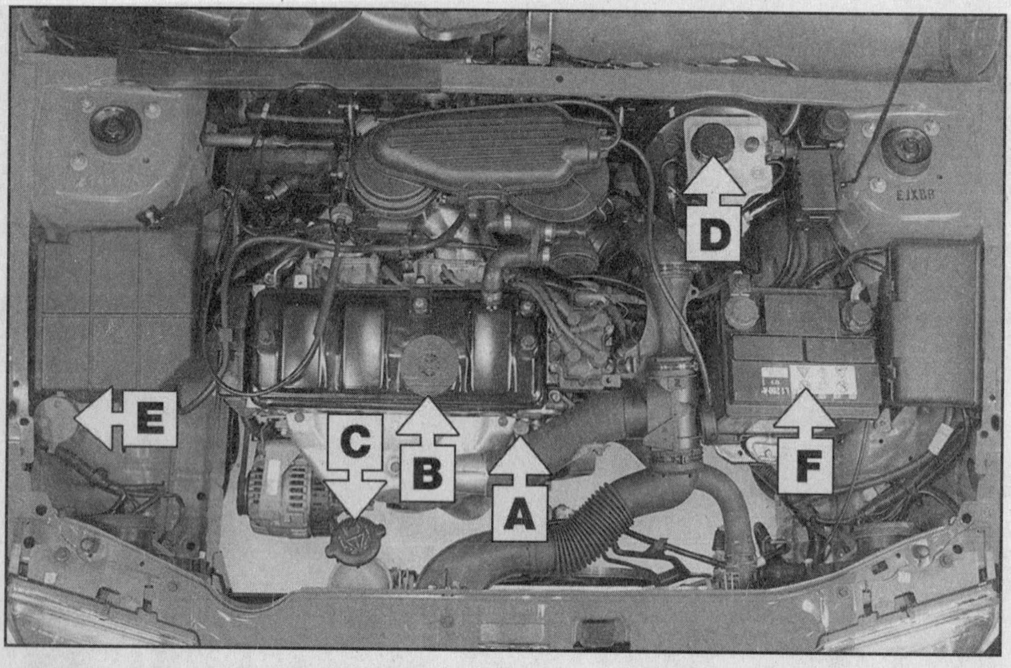

◀ **1.1 litre petrol**

A *Engine oil level dipstick*
B *Engine oil filler cap*
C *Coolant expansion tank*
D *Brake fluid reservoir*
E *Screen washer fluid reservoir*
F *Battery*

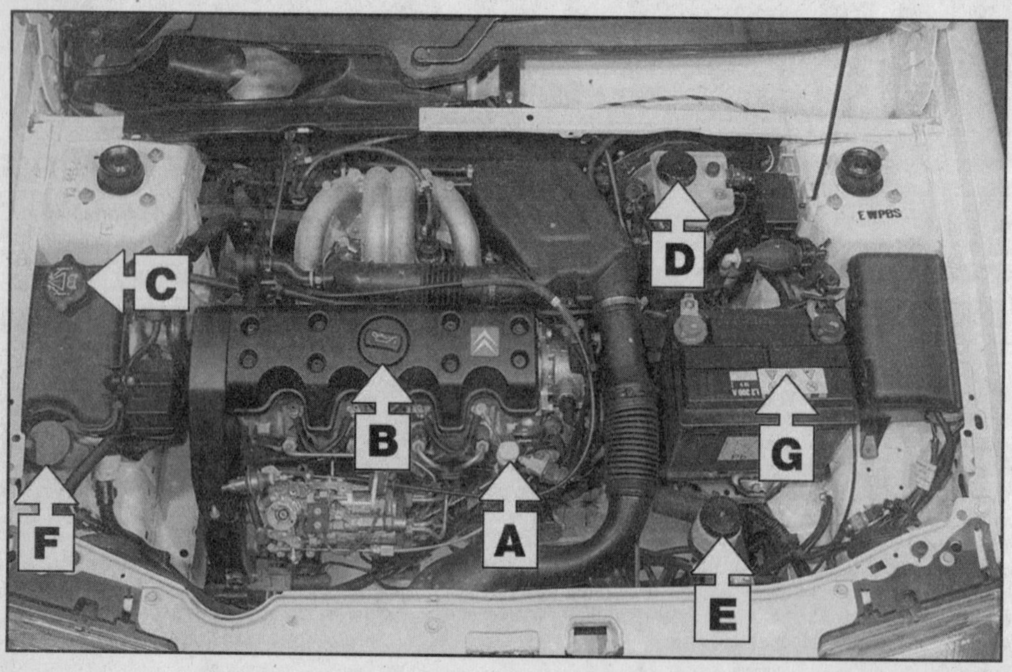

◀ **1.5 litre diesel**

A *Engine oil level dipstick*
B *Engine oil filler cap*
C *Coolant expansion tank*
D *Brake fluid reservoir*
E *Power steering fluid reservoir*
F *Screen washer fluid reservoir*
G *Battery*

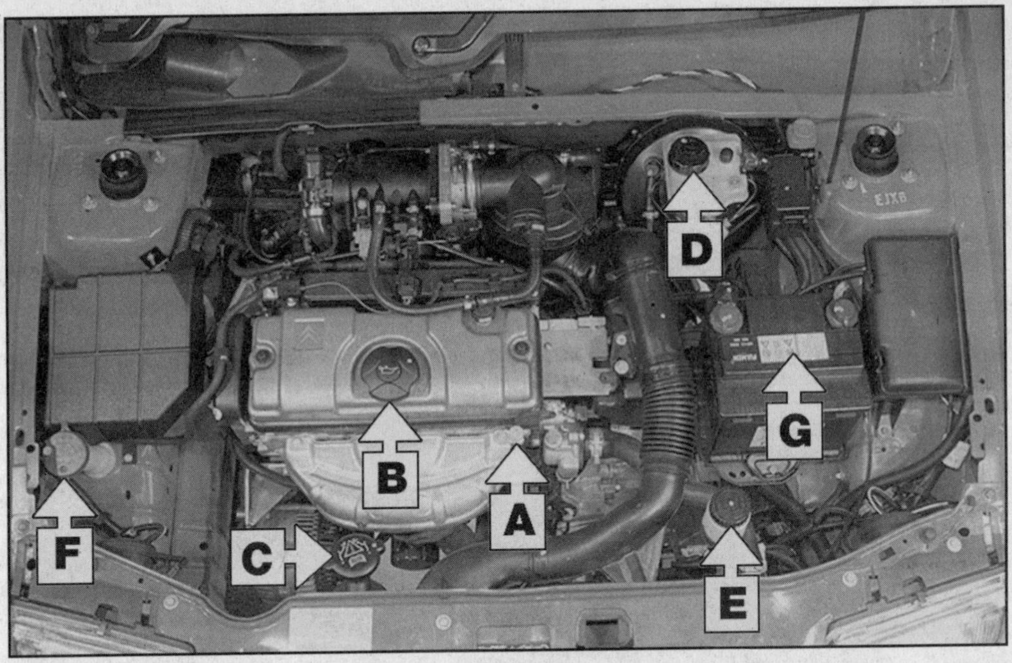

◀ 1.6 litre petrol

A *Engine oil level dipstick*
B *Engine oil filler cap*
C *Coolant expansion tank*
D *Brake fluid reservoir*
E *Power steering fluid reservoir*
F *Screen washer fluid reservoir*
G *Battery*

Engine oil level

Before you start

✔ Make sure that your car is on level ground.
✔ Check the oil level before the car is driven, or at least 5 minutes after the engine has been switched off.

HAYNES HiNT ***If the oil is checked immediately after driving the vehicle, some of the oil will remain in the upper engine components, resulting in an inaccurate reading on the dipstick!***

The correct oil

Modern engines place great demands on their oil. It is very important that the correct oil for your car is used (See "Lubricants and fluids").

Car Care

- If you have to add oil frequently, you should check whether you have any oil leaks. Place some clean paper under the car overnight, and check for stains in the morning. If there are no leaks, the engine may be burning oil.
- Always maintain the level between the upper and lower dipstick marks (see photo 3). If the level is too low severe engine damage may occur. Oil seal failure may result if the engine is overfilled by adding too much oil.
- On models equipped with an oil level gauge, don't be tempted to rely on the gauge alone - verify the level using the dipstick on a regular basis. Equally, don't ignore the gauge if it warns of low oil level.

1 The dipstick top is often brightly coloured for easy identification (see *"Underbonnet check points"* on pages 0•10 and 0•11 for exact location). Withdraw the dipstick.

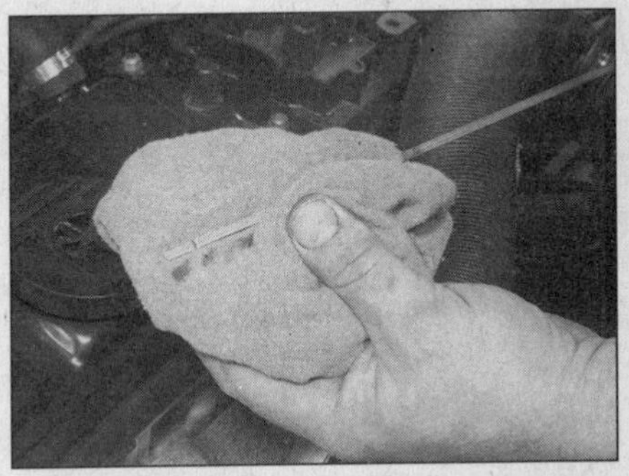

2 Using a clean rag or paper towel remove all oil from the dipstick. Insert the clean dipstick into the tube as far as it will go, then withdraw it again.

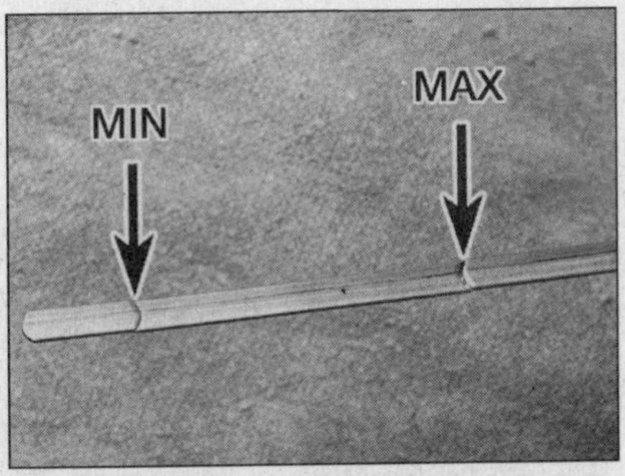

3 Note the oil level on the end of the dipstick, which should be between the "MAX" and "MIN" marks. If the oil level is only just above, or below, the "MIN" mark, topping-up is required.

4 Oil is added through the filler cap. Unscrew the cap and top-up the level; a funnel may be useful in reducing spillage. Add the oil slowly, checking the level on the dipstick often, and allowing time for the oil to fall to the sump. Add oil until the level is just up to the "MAX" mark on the dipstick - don't overfill (see *"Car care"* left).

Coolant level

Warning: DO NOT attempt to remove the expansion tank pressure cap when the engine is hot, as there is a very great risk of scalding. Do not leave open containers of coolant about, as it is poisonous.

Car Care

- With a sealed-type cooling system, adding coolant should not be necessary on a regular basis. If frequent topping-up is required, it is likely there is a leak. Check the radiator, all hoses and joint faces for signs of staining or wetness, and rectify as necessary.

- It is important that antifreeze is used in the cooling system all year round, not just during the winter months. Don't top-up with water alone, as the antifreeze will become too diluted.

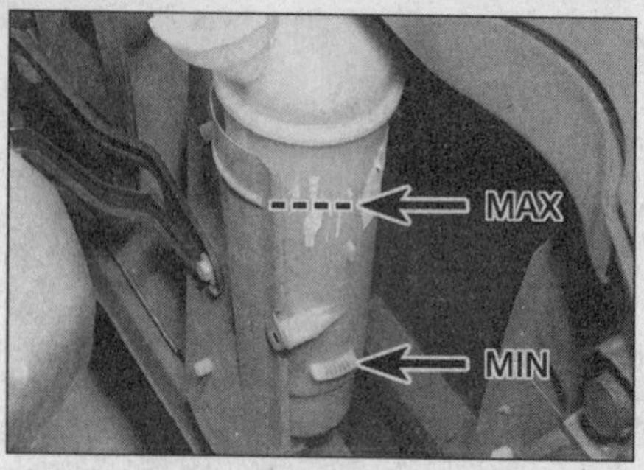

1 The coolant level varies with the temperature of the engine. A "MAX" mark may not be provided on all petrol models - use the "MAX" level shown as a guide. The coolant level must be maintained above the "MIN" level at all times.

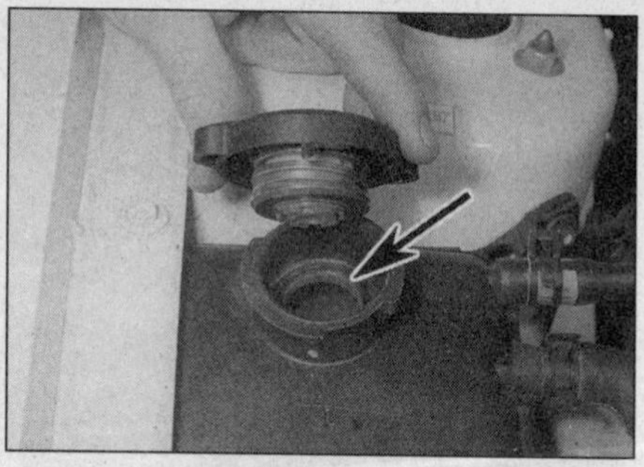

2 On diesel engine models, the "MAX" level is indicated by a red marker visible inside the expansion tank once the pressure cap has been removed.

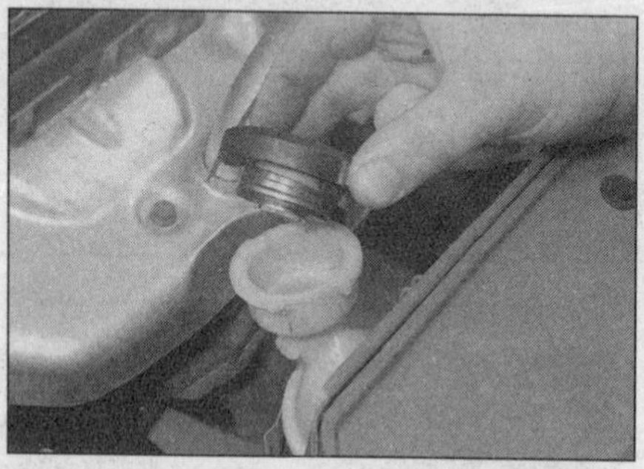

3 If topping up is necessary, **wait until the engine is cold**. Slowly unscrew the expansion tank cap, to release any pressure present in the cooling system, and remove it.

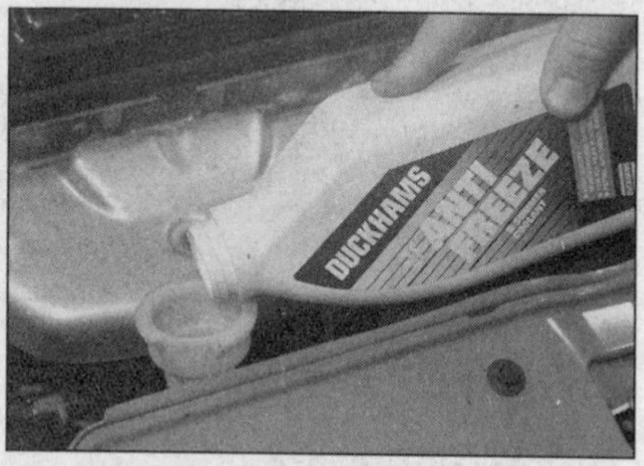

4 Add a mixture of water and antifreeze to the expansion tank until the coolant level is correct. Refit the cap and tighten it securely.

Brake fluid level

Warning:

- ***Brake fluid can harm your eyes and damage painted surfaces, so use extreme caution when handling and pouring it.***
- ***Do not use fluid that has been standing open for some time, as it absorbs moisture from the air, which can cause a dangerous loss of braking effectiveness.***

HAYNES HiNT

- ***Make sure that your car is on level ground.***
- ***The fluid level in the reservoir will drop slightly as the brake pads wear down, but the fluid level must never be allowed to drop below the "MIN" mark.***

Safety First!

- If the reservoir requires repeated topping-up this is an indication of a fluid leak somewhere in the system, which should be investigated immediately.
- If a leak is suspected, the car should not be driven until the braking system has been checked. Never take any risks where brakes are concerned.

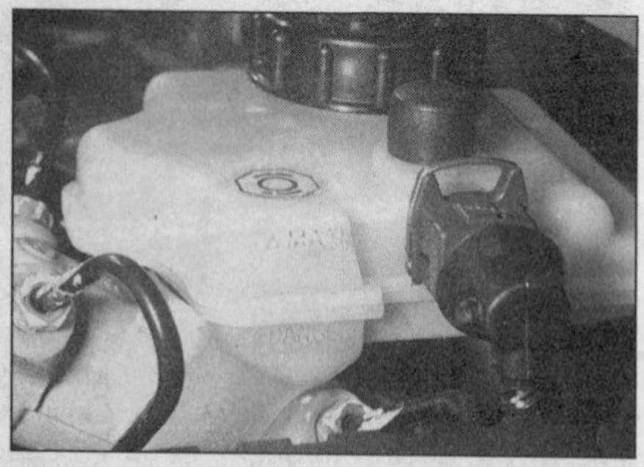

1 The brake fluid reservoir is located on the left-hand side of the engine compartment, next to the suspension strut top mounting. The "MAXI" and "DANGER" marks are indicated on the front of the reservoir. The fluid level must be kept between the marks at all times.

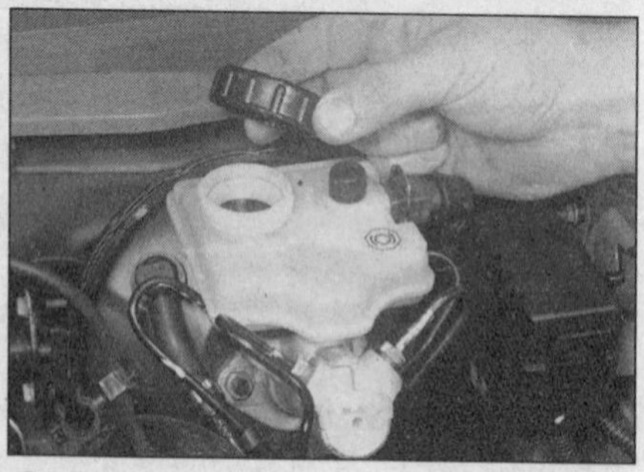

2 Unscrew the reservoir cap and carefully lift it out of position, taking care not to damage the level switch float. Place the cap and float on a piece of clean rag. Inspect the reservoir; if the fluid is dirty, the hydraulic system should be drained and refilled (see Chapter 1A or 1B).

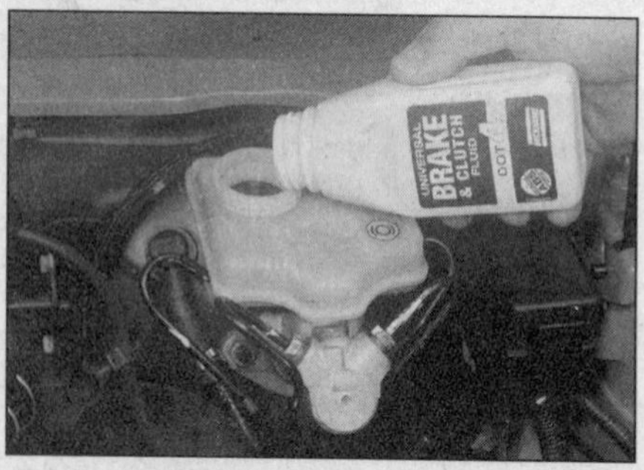

3 Carefully add fluid, taking care not to spill it onto the surrounding components. Use only the specified fluid; mixing different types can cause damage to the system. After topping-up to the correct level, securely refit the cap and wipe off any spilt fluid.

Power steering fluid level

Before you start:

✔ Park the vehicle on level ground.

✔ Set the steering wheel straight-ahead.

✔ The engine should be turned off.

HAYNES HiNT ***For the check to be accurate, the steering must not be turned once the engine has been stopped.***

Safety First!

● The need for frequent topping-up indicates a leak, which should be investigated immediately.

1 The reservoir is located in the front left-hand side of the engine compartment, behind the lock carrier panel.

2 When the system is cold, the level should be above the "MIN" mark. With the system at operating temperature (after a run), the level should be between the "MAX" and "MIN" marks. If topping-up is required, wipe clean the area around the reservoir filler neck and unscrew the filler cap from the reservoir.

3 When topping-up, use the specified type of fluid, and do not overfill the reservoir. When the level is correct, securely refit the cap.

Screen washer fluid level *

**** On models with a headlight washer system, the screen wash is also used to clean the headlights. The underbonnet reservoir also serves the tailgate washer.***

Screenwash additives not only keep the winscreen clean during foul weather, they also prevent the washer system freezing in cold weather - which is when you are likely to need it most. Don't top up using plain water as the screenwash will become too diluted, and will freeze during cold weather. ***On no account use coolant antifreeze in the washer system - this could discolour or damage paintwork.***

1 The screen washer fluid reservoir filler neck is located in the right-hand side of the engine compartment, behind the headlight.

2 The screen washer level cannot easily be seen. Remove the filler cap, and look down the filler neck - if fluid is not visible, topping-up may be required.

3 When topping-up the reservoir, add a screenwash additive in the quantities recommended on the additive bottle. The exact level is not critical - add fluid slowly until the level reaches the base of the filler neck.

Tyre condition and pressure

It is very important that tyres are in good condition, and at the correct pressure - having a tyre failure at any speed is highly dangerous. Tyre wear is influenced by driving style - harsh braking and acceleration, or fast cornering, will all produce more rapid tyre wear. As a general rule, the front tyres wear out faster than the rears. Interchanging the tyres from front to rear ("rotating" the tyres) may result in more even wear. However, if this is completely effective, you may have the expense of replacing all four tyres at once!

Remove any nails or stones embedded in the tread before they penetrate the tyre to cause deflation. If removal of a nail does reveal that the tyre has been punctured, refit the nail so that its point of penetration is marked. Then immediately change the wheel, and have the tyre repaired by a tyre dealer.

Regularly check the tyres for damage in the form of cuts or bulges, especially in the sidewalls. Periodically remove the wheels, and clean any dirt or mud from the inside and outside surfaces. Examine the wheel rims for signs of rusting, corrosion or other damage. Light alloy wheels are easily damaged by "kerbing" whilst parking; steel wheels may also become dented or buckled. A new wheel is very often the only way to overcome severe damage.

New tyres should be balanced when they are fitted, but it may become necessary to re-balance them as they wear, or if the balance weights fitted to the wheel rim should fall off. Unbalanced tyres will wear more quickly, as will the steering and suspension components. Wheel imbalance is normally signified by vibration, particularly at a certain speed (typically around 50 mph). If this vibration is felt only through the steering, then it is likely that just the front wheels need balancing. If, however, the vibration is felt through the whole car, the rear wheels could be out of balance. Wheel balancing should be carried out by a tyre dealer or garage.

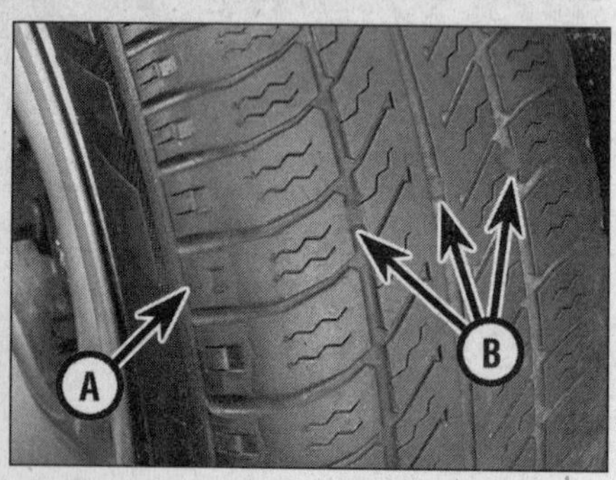

1 ***Tread Depth - visual check***

The original tyres have tread wear safety bands (B), which will appear when the tread depth reaches approximately 1.6 mm. The band positions are indicated by a triangular mark on the tyre sidewall (A).

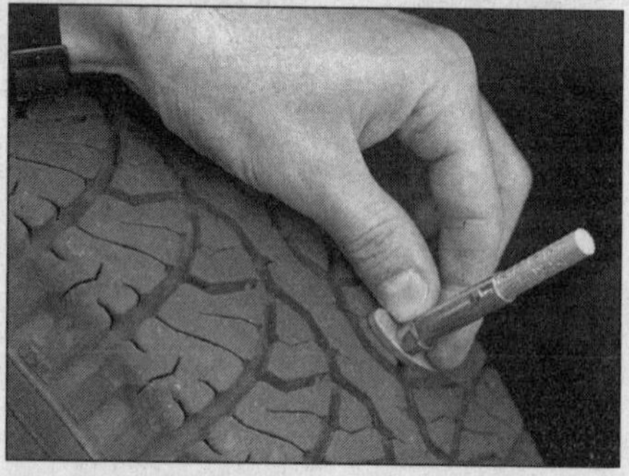

2 ***Tread Depth - manual check***

Alternatively, tread wear can be monitored with a simple, inexpensive device known as a tread depth indicator gauge.

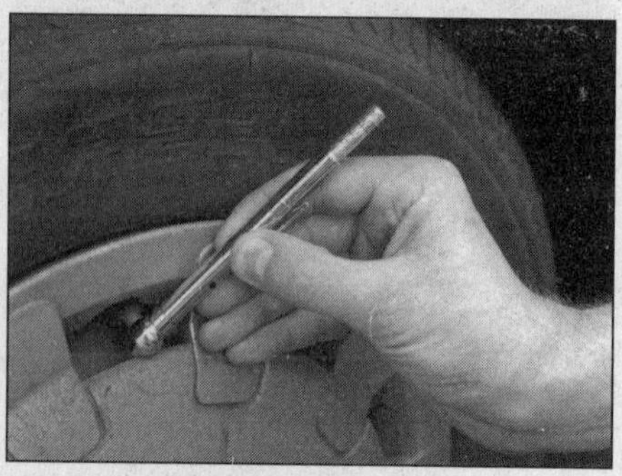

3 ***Tyre Pressure Check***

Check the tyre pressures regularly with the tyres cold. Do not adjust the tyre pressures immediately after the vehicle has been used, or an inaccurate setting will result.

Tyre tread wear patterns

Shoulder Wear

Underinflation (wear on both sides)

Under-inflation will cause overheating of the tyre, because the tyre will flex too much, and the tread will not sit correctly on the road surface. This will cause a loss of grip and excessive wear, not to mention the danger of sudden tyre failure due to heat build-up.

Check and adjust pressures

Incorrect wheel camber (wear on one side)

Repair or renew suspension parts

Hard cornering

Reduce speed!

Centre Wear

Overinflation

Over-inflation will cause rapid wear of the centre part of the tyre tread, coupled with reduced grip, harsher ride, and the danger of shock damage occurring in the tyre casing.

Check and adjust pressures

If you sometimes have to inflate your car's tyres to the higher pressures specified for maximum load or sustained high speed, don't forget to reduce the pressures to normal afterwards.

Uneven Wear

Front tyres may wear unevenly as a result of wheel misalignment. Most tyre dealers and garages can check and adjust the wheel alignment (or "tracking") for a modest charge.

Incorrect camber or castor

Repair or renew suspension parts

Malfunctioning suspension

Repair or renew suspension parts

Unbalanced wheel

Balance tyres

Incorrect toe setting

Adjust front wheel alignment

Note: *The feathered edge of the tread which typifies toe wear is best checked by feel.*

Wiper blades

Note: *Fitting details for wiper blades vary according to model, and according to whether genuine Citroën wiper blades have been fitted. Use the procedures and illustrations shown as a guide for your car.*

> HAYNES HiNT
>
> ***If smearing is still a problem despite fitting new wiper blades, try cleaning the windscreen with neat screen-wash additive or methylated spirit.***

• Wiper blades should be renewed annually, regardless of their apparent condition.

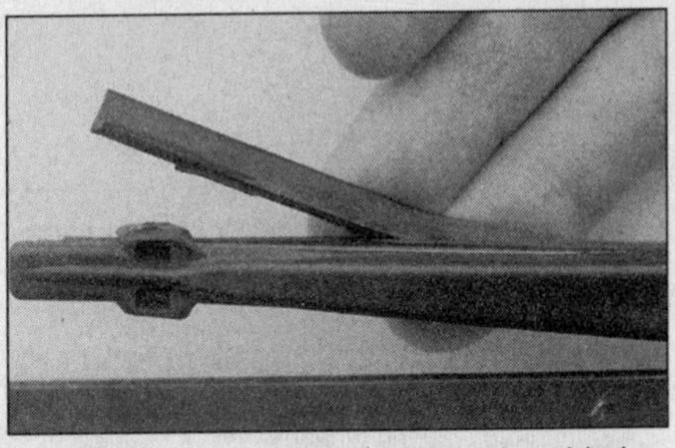

1 Check the condition of the wiper blades; if they are cracked or show any signs of deterioration, or if the glass swept area is smeared, renew them.

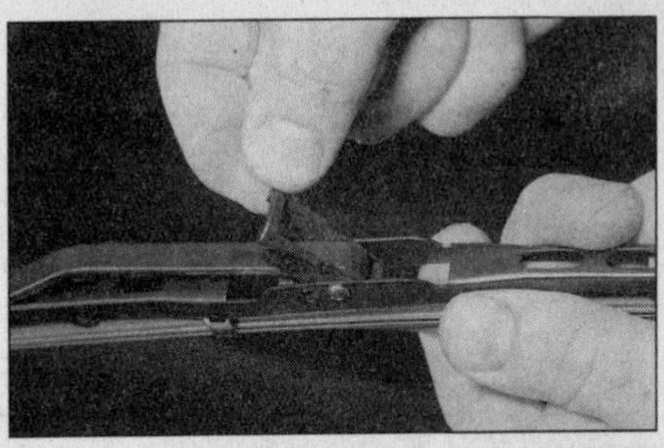

2 To remove a windscreen wiper blade, lift the arm away from the screen, and pull up the locking handle.

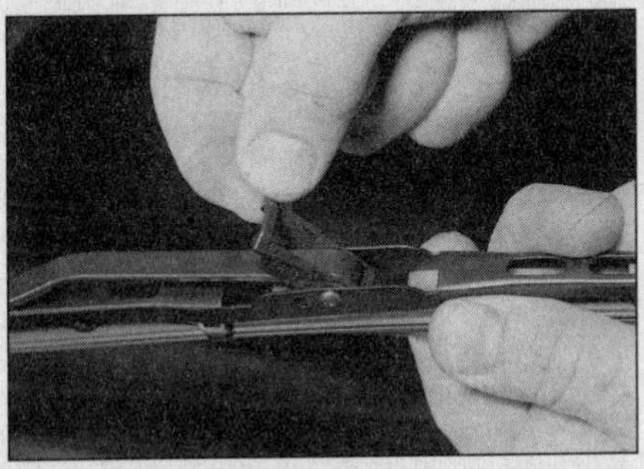

3 Pull the arm away from the screen until it locks. Noting how it fits, swivel the blade to slide it out of the arm's hooked end.

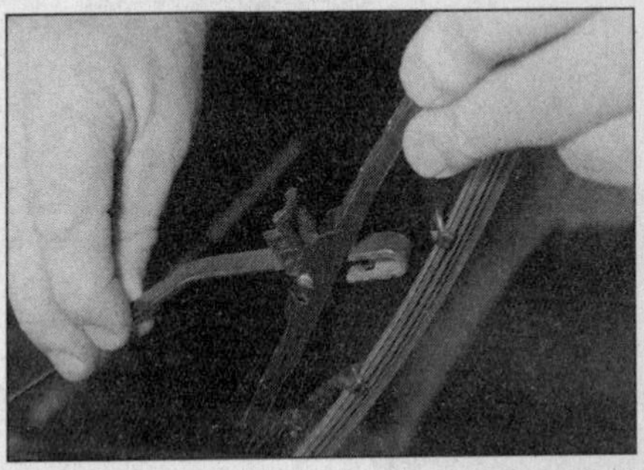

4 Don't forget to check the tailgate wiper blade as well. To remove the blade, turn the blade 90° to the arm, and slide the blade out of the hooked end of the arm.

Battery

Caution: *Before carrying out any work on the vehicle battery, read the precautions given in "Safety first" at the start of this manual.*

✔ Make sure that the battery tray is in good condition, and that the clamp is tight. Corrosion on the tray, retaining clamp and the battery itself can be removed with a solution of water and baking soda. Thoroughly rinse all cleaned areas with water. Any metal parts damaged by corrosion should be covered with a zinc-based primer, then painted.

✔ Periodically (approximately every three months), check the charge condition of the battery as described in Chapter 5A.

✔ If the battery is flat, and you need to jump start your vehicle, see ***Roadside Repairs***.

> HAYNES HiNT
>
> 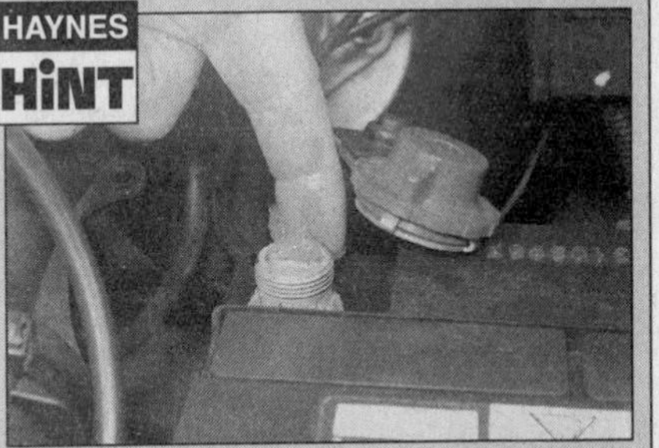
>
> ***Battery corrosion can be kept to a minimum by applying a layer of petroleum jelly to the clamps and terminals after they are reconnected.***

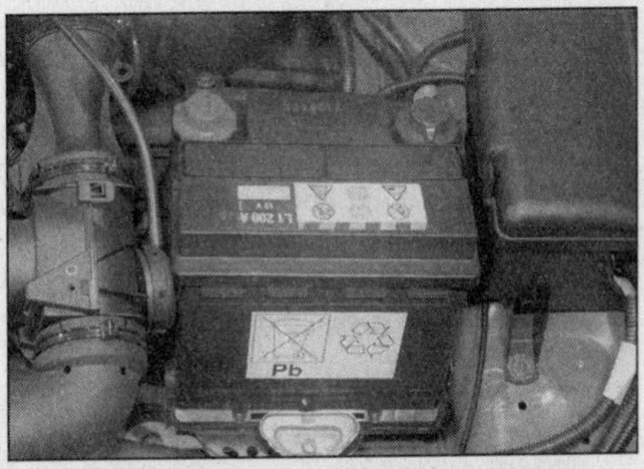

1 The battery is located on the left-hand side of the engine compartment. The exterior of the battery should be inspected periodically for damage such as a cracked case or cover.

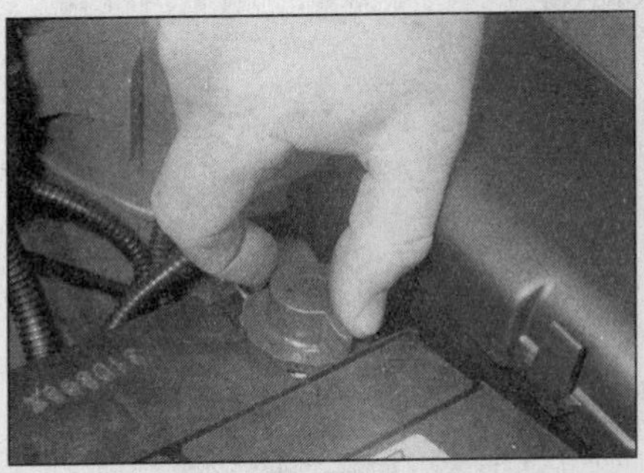

2 Check the tightness of the screw-on battery clamps to ensure good electrical connections. You should not be able to move them. Also check each cable for cracks and frayed conductors.

3 If corrosion (white, fluffy deposits) is evident, remove the cables from the battery terminals, clean them with a small wire brush, then refit them. Automotive stores sell a useful tool for cleaning the battery post . . .

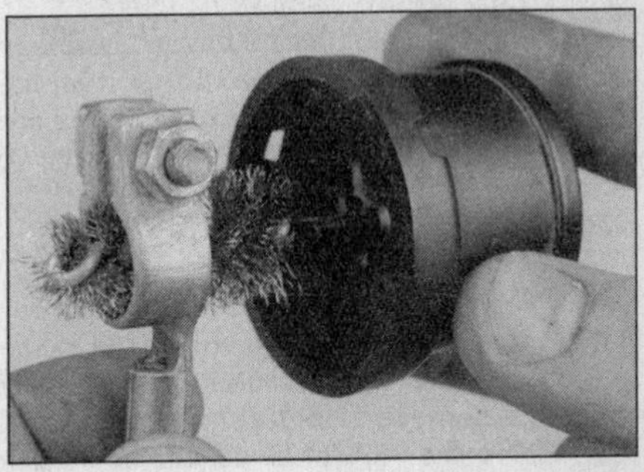

4 . . . as well as the battery cable clamps

Bulbs and fuses

✔ Check all external lights and the horn. Refer to the appropriate Sections of Chapter 12 for details if any of the circuits are found to be inoperative.

✔ Visually check all accessible wiring connectors, harnesses and retaining clips for security, and for signs of chafing or damage.

HAYNES HiNT *If you need to check your brake lights and indicators unaided, back up to a wall or garage door and operate the lights. The reflected light should show if they are working properly.*

1 If a single indicator light, stop-light or headlight has failed, it is likely that a bulb has blown and will need to be replaced. Refer to Chapter 12 for details. If both stop-lights have failed, it is possible that the switch on the brake pedal has failed (see Chapter 9).

2 If more than one indicator light or tail light has failed, it is likely that either a fuse has blown or that there is a fault in the circuit (see Chapter 12). The main fuses are located behind a panel on the bottom of the passenger's side of the facia panel. Certain fuses are located in a fusebox next to the battery.

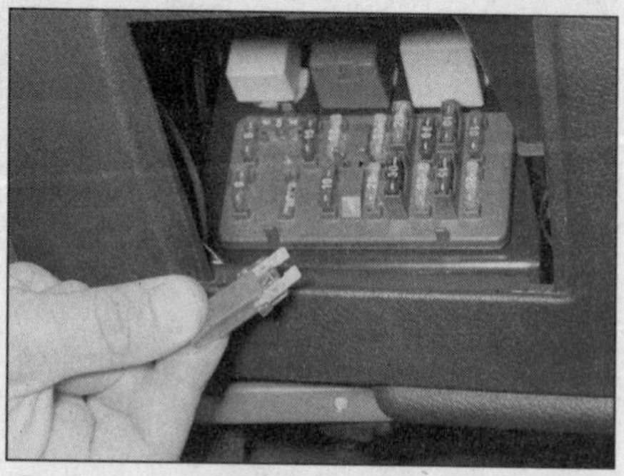

3 To replace a blown fuse, simply pull it out using the tweezer tool provided, and fit a new fuse of the correct rating (see Chapter 12). If the fuse blows again, it is important that you find out why - a complete checking procedure is given in Chapter 12.

Advanced driving

Many people see the words 'advanced driving' and believe that it won't interest them or that it is a style of driving beyond their own abilities. Nothing could be further from the truth. Advanced driving is straightforward safe, sensible driving - the sort of driving we should all do every time we get behind the wheel.

An average of 10 people are killed every day on UK roads and 870 more are injured, some seriously. Lives are ruined daily, usually because somebody did something stupid. Something like 95% of all accidents are due to human error, mostly driver failure. Sometimes we make genuine mistakes - everyone does. Sometimes we have lapses of concentration. Sometimes we deliberately take risks.

For many people, the process of 'learning to drive' doesn't go much further than learning how to pass the driving test because of a common belief that good drivers are made by 'experience'.

Learning to drive by 'experience' teaches three driving skills:

- ☐ Quick reactions. (Whoops, that was close!)
- ☐ Good handling skills. (Horn, swerve, brake, horn).
- ☐ Reliance on vehicle technology. (Great stuff this ABS, stop in no distance even in the wet...)

Drivers whose skills are 'experience based' generally have a lot of near misses and the odd accident. The results can be seen every day in our courts and our hospital casualty departments.

Advanced drivers have learnt to control the risks by controlling the position and speed of their vehicle. They avoid accidents and near misses, even if the drivers around them make mistakes.

The key skills of advanced driving are **concentration,** effective all-round **observation, anticipation** and **planning.** When **good vehicle handling** is added to these skills, all driving situations can be approached and negotiated in a safe, methodical way, leaving nothing to chance.

Concentration means applying your mind to safe driving, completely excluding anything that's not relevant. Driving is usually the most dangerous activity that most of us undertake in our daily routines. It deserves our full attention.

Observation means not just looking, but seeing and seeking out the information found in the driving environment.

Anticipation means asking yourself what is happening, what you can reasonably expect to happen and what could happen unexpectedly. (One of the commonest words used in compiling accident reports is 'suddenly'.)

Planning is the link between seeing something and taking the appropriate action. For many drivers, planning is the missing link.

If you want to become a safer and more skilful driver and you want to enjoy your driving more, contact the Institute of Advanced Motorists at www.iam.org.uk, phone 0208 996 9600, or write to IAM House, 510 Chiswick High Road, London W4 5RG for an information pack.

Lubricants and fluids

Engine (petrol)	Multigrade engine oil, viscosity SAE 10W/40 or 15W/40
Engine (diesel)	Multigrade engine oil, viscosity SAE 15W/40
Cooling system	Ethylene glycol-based antifreeze with corrosion inhibitor
Manual transmission and final drive	Gear oil, viscosity SAE 75W/80
Automatic transmission and final drive	Dexron type ATF
Brake hydraulic system	Hydraulic fluid to FMVSS 116 DOT 4
Power steering	Dexron type ATF

Choosing your engine oil

Engines need oil, not only to lubricate moving parts and minimise wear, but also to maximise power output and to improve fuel economy.

HOW ENGINE OIL WORKS

• *Beating friction*

Without oil, the moving surfaces inside your engine will rub together, heat up and melt, quickly causing the engine to seize. Engine oil creates a film which separates these moving parts, preventing wear and heat build-up.

• *Cooling hot-spots*

Temperatures inside the engine can exceed 1000° C. The engine oil circulates and acts as a coolant, transferring heat from the hot-spots to the sump.

• *Cleaning the engine internally*

Good quality engine oils clean the inside of your engine, collecting and dispersing combustion deposits and controlling them until they are trapped by the oil filter or flushed out at oil change.

OIL CARE - FOLLOW THE CODE

To handle and dispose of used engine oil safely, always:

OIL BANK LINE
0800 66 33 66
www.oilbankline.org.uk

- ***Avoid skin contact with used engine oil. Repeated or prolonged contact can be harmful.***
- ***Dispose of used oil and empty packs in a responsible manner in an authorised disposal site. Call 0800 663366 to find the one nearest to you. Never tip oil down drains or onto the ground.***

Tyre pressures (cold)

	Front	Rear
1.0 and 1.1 litre models:		
155/70 R 13 tyres:		
Normal load	2.3 bar (33 psi)	2.0 bar (29 psi)
Full load	2.3 bar (33 psi)	2.2 bar (32 psi)
165/70 R 13 tyres	2.2 bar (32 psi)	2.0 bar (29 psi)
1.4 and 1.6 litre models:		
165/65 R 14 tyres	2.2 bar (32 psi)	2.2 bar (32 psi)
185/55 R 14 tyres	2.1 bar (30 psi)	2.1 bar (30 psi)
1.5 litre diesel models	2.2 bar (32 psi)	2.0 bar (29 psi)
Entreprise models:		
165/70 R 13 tyres	2.3 bar (33 psi)	2.3 bar (33 psi)
165/65 R 14 tyres	2.2 bar (32 psi)	2.0 bar (29 psi)
Spare wheel:		
155/70 R 13 tyre	2.5 bar (36 psi)	
165/70 R 13 and 165/65 R 14 tyres	2.4 bar (35 psi)	
185/55 R 14 tyre	2.7 bar (39 psi)	

Note: *Pressures apply to original-equipment tyres, and may vary if any other make of tyre is fitted; check with the tyre manufacturer or supplier for the correct pressures if necessary.*

Chapter 1 Part A:
Routine maintenance & servicing - petrol models

Contents

Degrees of difficulty

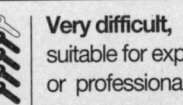

Easy, suitable for novice with little experience	**Fairly easy,** suitable for beginner with some experience	**Fairly difficult,** suitable for competent DIY mechanic	**Difficult,** suitable for experienced DIY mechanic	**Very difficult,** suitable for expert DIY or professional

Lubricants and fluids

Lubricants and fluids	Refer to end of "Weekly checks"

Capacities

Engine oil (with filter change)	
All engines	3.5 litres
Between dipstick 'MAX' and 'MIN' markings	1.5 litres
Cooling system	
1.0 and 1.1 litre engines	5.7 litres
1.4 litre engines	5.5 litres
1.6 litre engines	5.8 litres
1.6 litre 16v engines	6.1 litres
Transmission	
Manual	2.0 litres
Automatic:	
After draining	2.5 litres
From dry	4.5 litres
Braking system	
Without ABS	0.45 litres
With ABS	0.36 litres
Fuel tank	
All models	45 litres
Screen wash	
All models	2.8 litres

Engine

Auxiliary drivebelt tension:	
Without air conditioning	52 to 58 SEEM units
With air conditioning	117 to 123 SEEM units

Cooling system

Antifreeze mixture:*	
50% antifreeze	Protection down to -37°C
55% antifreeze	Protection down to -45°C

***Note:** *Refer to antifreeze manufacturer for latest recommendations.*

Fuel system

Idle speed:	
Models without air conditioning	850 ± 50 rpm (not adjustable, controlled by ECU)
Models with air conditioning	900 ± 50 rpm (not adjustable, controlled by ECU)
Exhaust gas CO content at idle	< 0.5 % (not adjustable, controlled by ECU)

Ignition system

	Type	**Electrode gap**
Spark plugs:		
All engines	Bosch FR 7 DE	0.9 mm

Brakes

Front/rear brake pad friction material minimum thickness	2.0 mm
Rear brake shoe friction material minimum thickness	1.0 mm

Tyre pressures

Tyre pressures	Refer to the end of "Weekly checks"

Torque wrench settings

	Nm	**lbf ft**
Auxiliary drivebelt tensioner assembly retaining bolts	25	18
Manual transmission filler/level and drain plugs	25	18
Roadwheel bolts	85	63
Spark plugs	25	18
Sump drain plug	30	22

The maintenance intervals in this manual are provided with the assumption that you, not the dealer, will be carrying out the work. These are the minimum maintenance intervals recommended for vehicles driven on a daily basis. If you wish to keep your vehicle in peak condition at all times, you may wish to perform some of these procedures more often. We encourage frequent maintenance, because it enhances the efficiency, performance and resale value of your vehicle.

When the vehicle is new, it should be serviced by a factory-authorised dealer service department, in order to preserve the factory warranty.

Weekly, or every 250 miles (400 km)

- ☐ Refer to "*Weekly checks*"

Every 9000 miles (15 000 km) or 12 months - whichever comes first

- ☐ Engine oil and filter renewal (Section 3)*
- ☐ Automatic transmission fluid level check (Section 4)
- ☐ Pollen filter renewal (Section 5)
- ☐ Clutch pedal height check and adjustment (Section 6)
- ☐ Underbonnet/underbody component/hose fluid leak check (Section 7)
- ☐ Suspension and steering check (Section 8)
- ☐ Driveshaft rubber gaiter check (Section 9)
- ☐ Front brake wear check (Section 10)
- ☐ Retrieve fault codes from engine management system memory (Section 11)
- ☐ Road test (Section 12)
- ☐ Handbrake operation check and adjustment (Section 13)

***Note:** *Citroën state that from 1998 model-year onwards, the engine oil renewal interval can be extended, provided that either semi-synthetic or fully synthetic engine oil is used. No more information was available at the time of writing - refer to your Citroën dealer for further details.*

Every 18 000 miles (30 000 km)

In addition to all the items listed above, carry out the following:

- ☐ Automatic transmission fluid and filter renewal (Section 14)
- ☐ Rear brake pad wear check - models with rear disc brakes (Section 15)

Every 36 000 miles (60 000 km)

In addition to all the items listed above, carry out the following:

- ☐ Manual transmission oil level check (Section 16)
- ☐ Spark plug renewal (Section 17)
- ☐ Fuel filter renewal (Section 18)
- ☐ Air filter renewal (Section 19)
- ☐ Brake fluid renewal (Section 20)
- ☐ Rear brake shoe wear check - models with rear drum brakes (Section 21)
- ☐ Braking system condition check (Section 22)
- ☐ Auxiliary drivebelt check and renewal (Section 23)

Every 72 000 miles (120 000 km)

In addition to all the items listed above, carry out the following:

- ☐ Timing belt renewal (Section 24)

Note: *It is strongly recommended that the timing belt renewal interval is halved to 36 000 miles (60 000 km) on vehicles which are subjected to intensive use, ie. mainly short journeys or a lot of stop-start driving. The actual belt renewal interval is therefore very much up to the individual owner, but bear in mind that severe engine damage will result if the belt breaks.*

Every 72 000 miles (120 000 km) or 2 years, whichever comes first

- ☐ Engine coolant renewal (Section 25)

Every year, regardless of mileage

- ☐ Exhaust gas emission check (Section 26)

Every 10 years, regardless of mileage

- ☐ Renew the air bag and seat belt tensioners (Section 27)

Underbonnet view of a 1.1 litre model

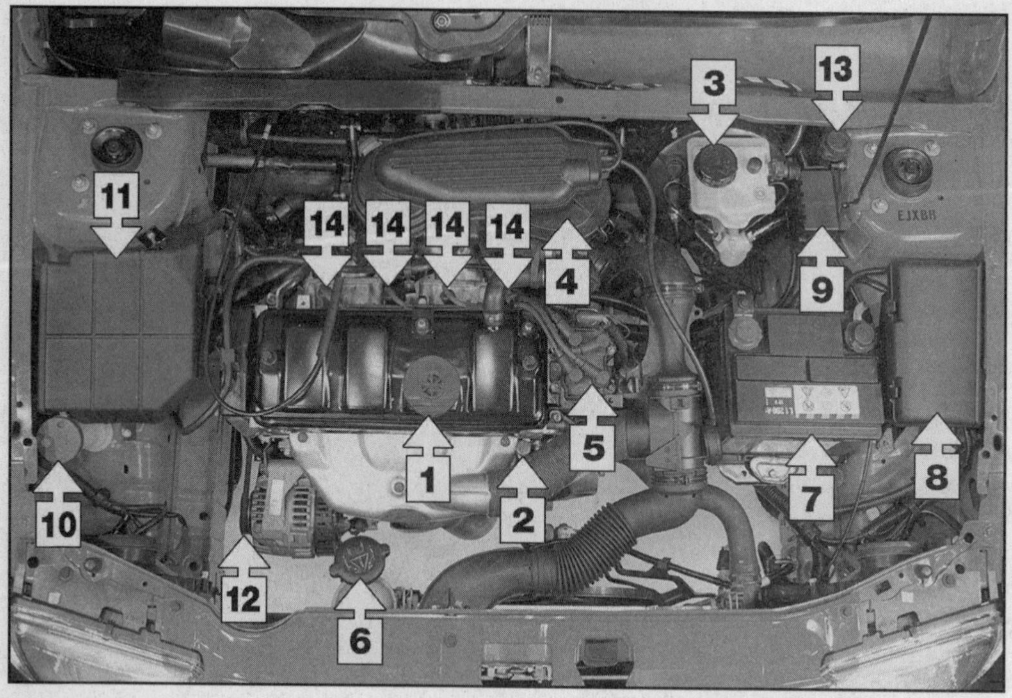

1. *Engine oil filler cap*
2. *Engine oil dipstick*
3. *Brake fluid reservoir*
4. *Air cleaner housing*
5. *Ignition coil*
6. *Coolant filler cap*
7. *Battery*
8. *Main fuse/relay box*
9. *Fusible link box*
10. *Windscreen washer fluid reservoir filler cap*
11. *Engine management system ECU*
12. *Auxiliary drivebelt*
13. *Inertia (fuel cut-off) switch*
14. *Spark plugs*

Underbonnet view of a 1.6 litre 8-valve model

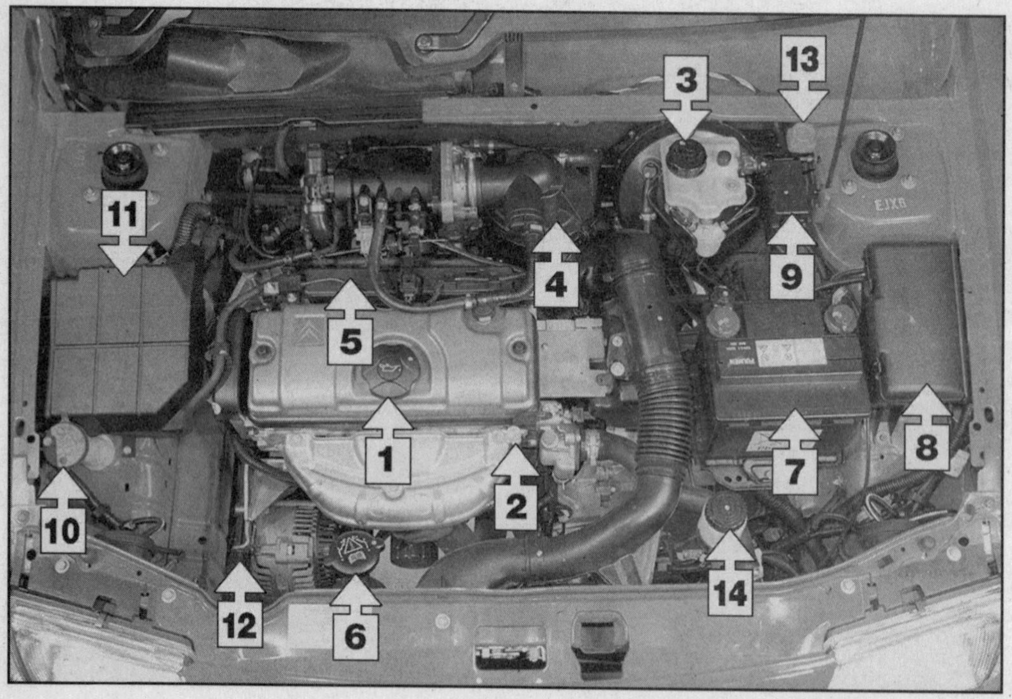

1. *Engine oil filler cap*
2. *Engine oil dipstick*
3. *Brake fluid reservoir*
4. *Air cleaner housing*
5. *Ignition coil module/spark plugs*
6. *Coolant filler cap*
7. *Battery*
8. *Main fuse/relay box*
9. *Fusible link box*
10. *Windscreen washer fluid reservoir filler cap*
11. *Engine management system ECU*
12. *Auxiliary drivebelt*
13. *Inertia (fuel cut-off) switch*
14. *Power steering fluid reservoir*

Front underbody view (1.1 litre model shown, others similar)

1 Engine oil drain plug
2 Engine oil filter
3 Alternator
4 Exhaust front pipe
5 Radiator cooling fan
6 Radiator
7 Manual transmission
8 Driveshaft
9 Suspension lower arm
10 Brake caliper
11 Gearchange selector rod
12 Anti-roll bar

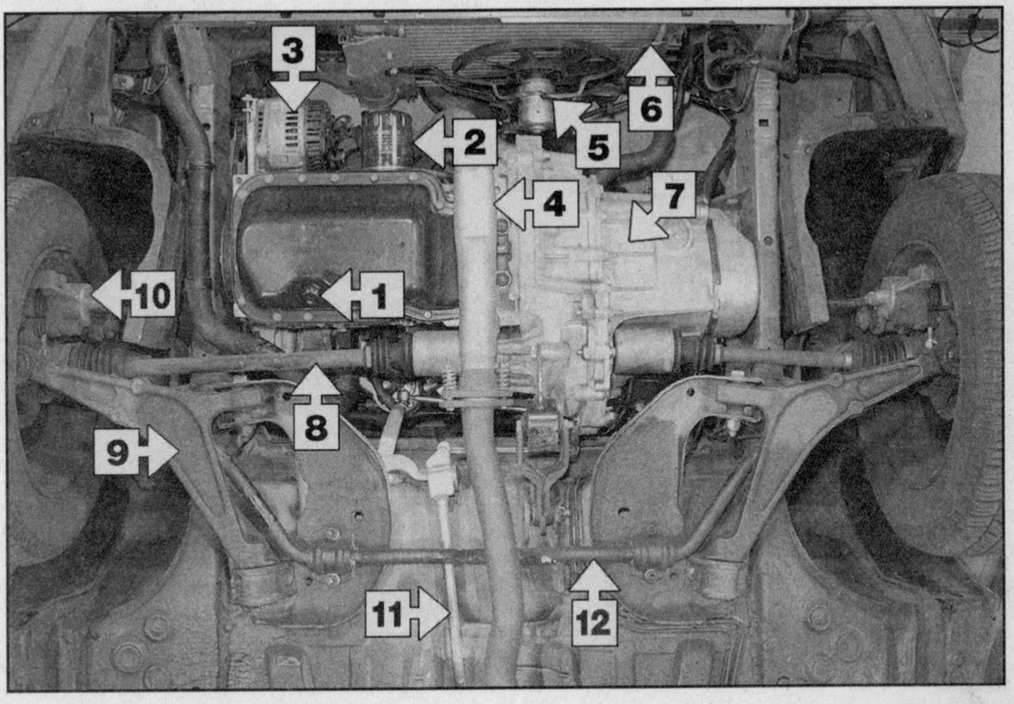

Rear underbody view (1.1 litre model shown, others similar)

1 Handbrake cable
2 Heat shield
3 Fuel filter
4 Exhaust tailbox
5 Suspension shock absorber
6 Rear drum brake backplate
7 Fuel tank filler pipe
8 Fuel tank
9 Rear suspension beam axle
10 Rear torsion bar
11 Front torsion bar
12 Rear suspension arm

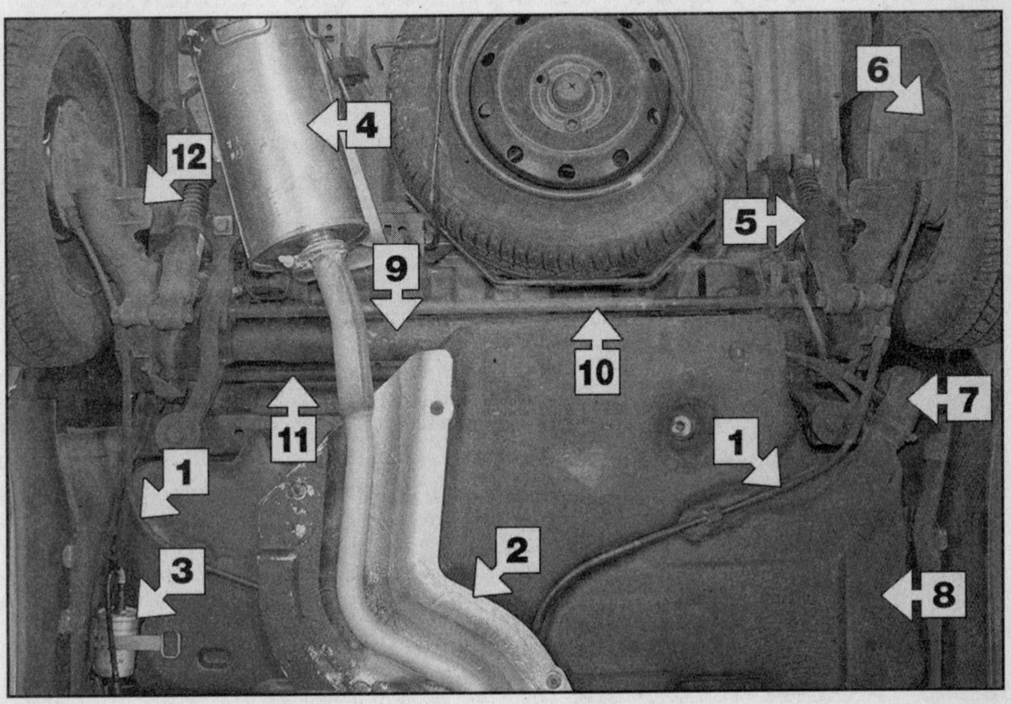

1 General information

This Chapter is designed to help the home mechanic maintain his/her vehicle for safety, economy, long life and peak performance.

The Chapter contains a master maintenance schedule, followed by Sections dealing specifically with each task in the schedule. Visual checks, adjustments, component renewal and other helpful items are included. Refer to the accompanying illustrations of the engine compartment and the underside of the vehicle for the locations of the various components.

Servicing your vehicle in accordance with the mileage/time maintenance schedule and the following Sections will provide a planned maintenance programme, which should result in a long and reliable service life. This is a comprehensive plan, so maintaining some items but not others at the specified service intervals, will not produce the same results.

As you service your vehicle, you will discover that many of the procedures can - and should - be grouped together, because of the particular procedure being performed, or because of the proximity of two otherwise-unrelated components to one another. For example, if the vehicle is raised for any reason, the exhaust can be inspected at the same time as the suspension and steering components.

The first step in this maintenance programme is to prepare yourself before the actual work begins. Read through all the Sections relevant to the work to be carried out, then make a list and gather all the parts and tools required. If a problem is encountered, seek advice from a parts specialist, or a dealer service department.

2 Intensive maintenance

1 If, from the time the vehicle is new, the routine maintenance schedule is followed closely, and frequent checks are made of fluid levels and high-wear items, as suggested throughout this manual, the engine will be kept in relatively good running condition, and the need for additional work will be minimised.

2 It is possible that there will be times when the engine is running poorly due to the lack of regular maintenance. This is even more likely if a used vehicle, which has not received regular and frequent maintenance checks, is purchased. In such cases, additional work may need to be carried out, outside of the regular maintenance intervals.

3 If engine wear is suspected, a compression test (refer to Chapter 2A) will provide valuable information regarding the overall performance of the main internal components. Such a test can be used as a basis to decide on the extent of the work to be carried out. If, for example, a compression test indicates serious internal engine wear, conventional maintenance as described in this Chapter will not greatly improve the performance of the engine, and may prove a waste of time and money, unless extensive overhaul work is carried out first.

4 The following series of operations are those often required to improve the performance of a generally poor-running engine:

Primary operations

a) Clean, inspect and test the battery (refer to "Weekly checks").
b) Check all the engine-related fluids (refer to "Weekly checks").
c) Check the condition and tension of the auxiliary drivebelt.
d) Renew the engine oil and filter.
e) Renew the spark plugs.
f) Check the condition of the air filter, and renew if necessary.
g) Renew the fuel filter.
h) Check the condition of all hoses, and check for fluid leaks.

5 If these operations do not prove effective, carry out the following secondary operations:

Secondary operations

All items listed under "*Primary operations*", plus the following:

a) Check the charging system (refer to Chapter 5A).
b) Check the ignition system (refer to Chapter 5B).
c) Check the fuel system (refer to Chapter 4Aor 4B).
d) Renew the ignition HT leads - where fitted.

Every 9000 miles (15 000 km) or 12 months

3 Engine oil and filter renewal

Note 1: *Frequent oil and filter changes are good for the engine. We recommend changing the oil at the mileage specified here, or at least twice a year if the mileage covered is less.*

Note 2: *A suitable square-section wrench may be required to undo the sump drain plug on some models. These wrenches can be obtained from most motor factors or your Citroën dealer.*

3.3a Slacken the drain plug using a square-section wrench . . .

Note 3: *Citroën state that from 1998 model-year onwards, the engine oil renewal interval can be extended, provided that either semi-synthetic or fully synthetic engine oil is used. No more information was available at the time of writing - refer to your Citroën dealer for further details.*

> **HAYNES HiNT** ***Frequent oil and filter changes are the most important preventative maintenance procedures which can be undertaken by the DIY owner. As engine oil ages, it becomes diluted and contaminated, which can lead to premature engine wear.***

1 Before starting this procedure, gather together all the necessary tools and materials. Also make sure that you have plenty of clean rags and newspapers handy, to mop up any spills. Ideally, the engine oil should be warm, as it will drain better, and more built-up sludge will be removed with it. Take care, however, not to touch the exhaust or any other hot parts of the engine when working under the vehicle. To avoid any possibility of scalding, and to protect yourself from possible skin irritants and other harmful contaminants in used engine oils, it is advisable to wear gloves, or at least apply a good quality barrier hand cream, when carrying out this work.

2 Access to the underside of the vehicle will be greatly improved if it can be raised on a lift, driven onto ramps, or jacked up and supported on axle stands (see "*Jacking and vehicle support*"). Whichever method is chosen, make sure that the vehicle remains level, or if it is at an angle, that the drain plug is at the lowest point.

3 Slacken the drain plug about half a turn; on some models, a square-section wrench may be needed to slacken the plug. Position the draining container under the drain plug, then unscrew and remove the plug completely. If possible, try to keep the plug pressed into the sump while unscrewing it by hand the last couple of turns. As the plug releases from the threads, move it away sharply so the stream of oil issuing from the sump runs into the container, not up your sleeve! Recover the sealing ring from the drain plug **(see illustrations)**.

4 Allow some time for the old oil to drain, noting that it may be necessary to reposition the container as the oil flow slows to a trickle.

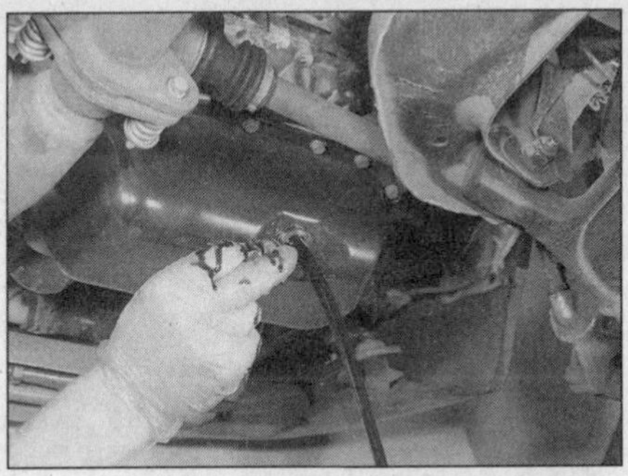

3.3b . . . then remove the plug and allow the oil to run into the draining container

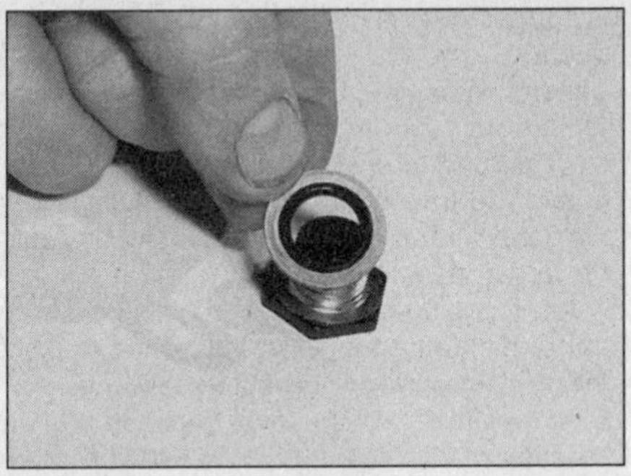

3.5 Fit a new sealing washer to the drain plug

3.7a Slacken the oil filter using a removal tool . . .

3.7b . . . then unscrew it from the engine by hand

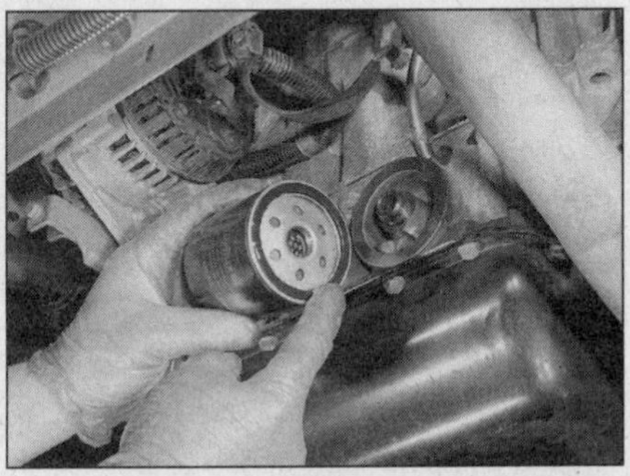

3.9 Apply a light coating of clean engine oil to the sealing ring on the new filter

3.11a Remove the dipstick . . .

5 After all the oil has drained, wipe off the drain plug with a clean rag, and fit a new sealing washer **(see illustration)**. Clean the area around the drain plug opening, and refit the plug. Tighten the plug securely.

3.11b . . . and wipe it clean . . .

6 If the filter is also to be renewed, move the container into position under the oil filter, which is located on the front side of the cylinder block, below the inlet manifold.

7 Using an oil filter removal tool if necessary, slacken the filter initially, then unscrew it by hand the rest of the way **(see illustrations)**. Empty any oil that remains inside the old filter into the container.

8 Use a clean rag to remove all oil, dirt and sludge from the filter sealing area on the engine. Check the old filter to make sure that the rubber sealing ring hasn't stuck to the engine. If it has, carefully remove it.

9 Apply a light coating of clean engine oil to the sealing ring on the new filter, then screw it into position on the engine **(see illustration)**. Tighten the filter firmly by hand only - **do not** use any tools.

10 Remove the old oil and all tools from under the car then lower the car to the ground.

11 Remove the dipstick, then unscrew the oil filler cap from the cylinder head cover. Fill the engine, using the correct grade and type of oil (see *"Lubricants and fluids"*). An oil can spout or funnel may help to reduce spillage. Pour in half the specified quantity of oil first, then wait a few minutes for the oil to fall to the sump. Continue adding oil a small quantity at a time until the level is up to (but **not** above) the upper mark on the dipstick. Refit the filler cap **(see illustrations)**.

12 Start the engine and allow it to idle for a few minutes - do not 'rev' the engine. Check for leaks around the oil filter seal and the sump drain plug. Note that there may be a delay of a few seconds before the oil pressure warning light goes out when the engine is first started, as the oil circulates through the engine oil galleries and the new oil filter (where fitted) before the pressure builds up.

13 Switch off the engine, and wait a few

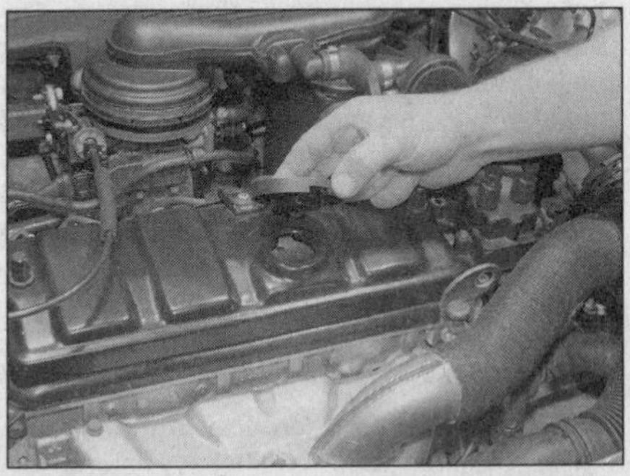

3.11c . . . then unscrew the oil filler cap from the cylinder head cover

3.11d Fill the engine, using the correct grade and type of oil

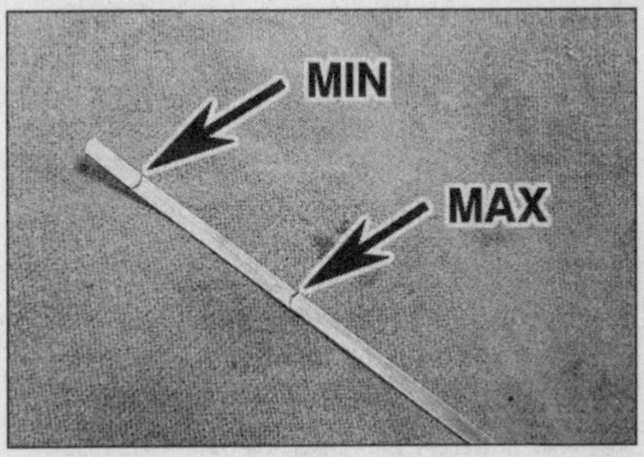

3.11e Continue adding oil until the level is up to (but *not* above) the 'MAX' mark on the dipstick

1A

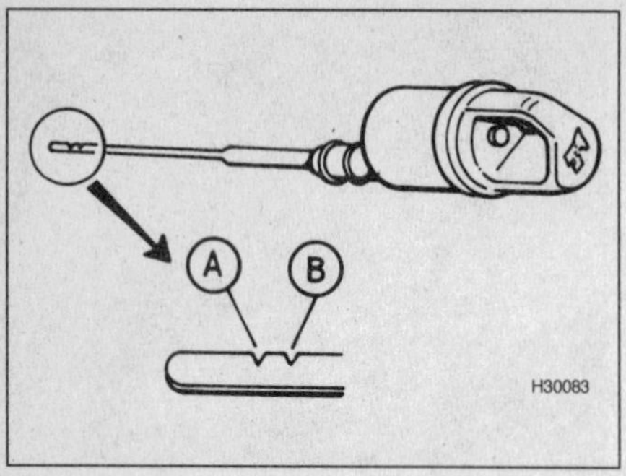

4.2 Automatic transmission fluid dipstick: the fluid level should be between the upper (B) and lower (A) marks

minutes for the oil to settle in the sump once more. With the new oil circulated and the filter completely full, recheck the level on the dipstick, and add more oil as necessary.

14 Dispose of the used engine oil safely, with reference to *"General repair procedures"* in the Reference Section of this manual.

4 Automatic transmission fluid level check

1 Take the vehicle on a short journey, to warm the transmission up to normal operating temperature, then park the vehicle on level ground. The fluid level is checked using the dipstick located at the front of the engine compartment, directly in front of the engine/transmission. The dipstick top is brightly-coloured for easy identification.

2 With the engine idling and the handbrake and footbrake firmly applied, move the selector lever through all the gear positions then return it to the "P" (Park) position. With the selector lever in the "P" (Park) position, withdraw the dipstick from the tube, and wipe all the fluid from its end with a clean rag or paper towel. Insert the clean dipstick back into the tube as far as it will go, then withdraw it once more. Note the fluid level on the end of the dipstick; it should be between the upper and lower marks **(see illustration)**.

HAYNES HiNT

A leak in the cooling system will usually manifest itself as white or rust-coloured, crusty deposits on the area adjacent to the leak

3 If topping-up is necessary, add the required quantity of the specified fluid to the transmission via the dipstick tube. Use a funnel with a fine-mesh gauze, to avoid spillage, and to ensure that no foreign matter enters the transmission. **Note:** *Never overfill the transmission so that the fluid level is above the upper mark.*

4 After topping-up, take the vehicle on a short run to distribute the fresh fluid, then recheck the level again, topping-up if necessary.

5 Always maintain the level between the two dipstick marks. If the level is allowed to fall below the lower mark, fluid starvation may result, which could lead to severe transmission damage.

6 Frequent need for topping-up indicates that there is a leak, which should be found and corrected before it becomes serious.

5 Pollen filter renewal

1 Remove the windscreen wiper arms as described in Chapter 12.

2 Access to the pollen filter is gained via the engine compartment; open the bonnet and support it in the upright position.

3 Remove the securing screw and the two nuts, and withdraw the windscreen cowl panel from the scuttle. Note the panel clips around the edge of the windscreen and the front wings.

4 Remove the securing nuts, and unclip the plastic cover panel from the right-hand end of the scuttle to expose the heater blower motor securing nuts.

5 Release the securing clips and detach the pollen filter housing from its mountings.

6 Fit a new filter element then refit all components removed for access using a reversal of the removal procedure.

6 Clutch pedal height check and adjustment

Refer to the information given in Chapter 6.

7 Underbonnet/underbody component/hose fluid leak check

Warning: Refer to the safety information given in "Safety First" and Chapter 3 before disturbing any of the cooling system components.

1 Carefully check the radiator and heater coolant hoses along their entire length. Renew any hose which is cracked, swollen or which shows signs of deterioration. Cracks will show up better if the hose is squeezed. Pay close attention to the clips that secure the hoses to the cooling system components. Hose clips that have been over-tightened can pinch and puncture hoses, resulting in cooling system leaks.

2 Inspect all the cooling system components (hoses, joint faces etc.) for leaks. Where any problems of this nature are found on system components, renew the component or gasket with reference to Chapter 3 **(see Haynes Hint)**.

Fuel

Warning: Refer to the safety information given in "Safety First" and the relevant Part of Chapter 4 before disturbing any of the fuel system components.

3 Petrol leaks are difficult to pinpoint, unless the leakage is significant and hence easily visible. Fuel tends to evaporate quickly once it comes into contact with air, especially in a hot engine bay. Small drips can disappear before you get a chance to identify the point of leakage. If you suspect that there is a fuel leak from the area of the engine bay, leave the vehicle overnight then start the engine from cold, with the bonnet open. Metal components tend to shrink when they are cold, and rubber seals and hoses tend to harden, so any leaks will be more apparent whilst the engine is warming up from a cold start.

4 Check all fuel lines at their connections to the fuel rail, fuel pressure regulator and fuel filter. Examine each rubber fuel hose along its length for splits or cracks. Check for leakage from the crimped joints between rubber and metal fuel lines. Examine the unions between the metal fuel lines and the fuel filter housing. Also check the area around the fuel injectors for signs of O-ring leakage.

5 To identify fuel leaks between the fuel tank and the engine bay, the vehicle should be raised and securely supported on axle stands (see *"Jacking and vehicle support"*). Inspect the petrol tank and filler neck for punctures, cracks and other damage. The connection between the filler neck and tank is especially critical. Sometimes a rubber filler neck or connecting hose will leak due to loose retaining clamps or deteriorated rubber.

6 Carefully check all rubber hoses and metal fuel lines leading away from the petrol tank. Check for loose connections, deteriorated hoses, kinked lines, and other damage. Pay particular attention to the vent pipes and hoses, which often loop up around the filler neck and can become blocked or kinked, making tank filling difficult. Follow the fuel supply and return lines to the front of the vehicle, carefully inspecting them all the way for signs of damage or corrosion. Renew damaged sections as necessary.

Engine oil

7 Inspect the area around the camshaft cover, cylinder head, oil filter and sump joint faces. Bear in mind that, over a period of time, some very slight seepage from these areas is to be expected - what you are really looking for is any indication of a serious leak caused by gasket failure. Engine oil seeping from the base of the timing belt cover or the transmission bellhousing may be an indication of crankshaft or transmission input shaft oil seal failure. Should a leak be found, renew the failed gasket or oil seal by referring to the appropriate Chapters in this manual.

Automatic transmission fluid

8 Where applicable, check the hoses leading to the transmission fluid cooler at the front of the engine bay for leakage. Look for deterioration caused by corrosion and damage from grounding, or debris thrown up from the road surface. Automatic transmission fluid is a thin oil and is usually red in colour.

Power assisted steering (PAS) fluid

9 Examine the hose running between the fluid reservoir and the power steering pump, and the return hose running from the steering rack to the fluid reservoir. Also examine the high pressure supply hose between the pump and the steering rack.

10 Check the condition of each hose carefully. Look for deterioration caused by corrosion and damage from grounding, or debris thrown up from the road surface.

11 Pay particular attention to crimped unions, and the area surrounding the hoses that are secured with adjustable worm drive clips. Like automatic transmission fluid, PAS fluid is a thin oil, and is usually red in colour.

Air conditioning refrigerant

Warning: Refer to the safety information given in "Safety First" and Chapter 3, regarding the dangers of disturbing any of the air conditioning system components.

12 The air conditioning system is filled with a liquid refrigerant, which is retained under high pressure. If the air conditioning system is opened and depressurised without the aid of specialised equipment, the refrigerant will immediately turn into gas and escape into the atmosphere. If the liquid comes into contact with your skin, it can cause severe frostbite. In addition, the refrigerant contains substances which are environmentally damaging; for this reason, it should not be allowed to escape into the atmosphere.

13 Any suspected air conditioning system leaks should be immediately referred to a Citroën dealer or air conditioning specialist. Leakage will be shown up as a steady drop in the level of refrigerant in the system.

14 Note that water may drip from the condenser drain pipe, underneath the car, immediately after the air conditioning system has been in use. This is normal, and should not be cause for concern.

Brake fluid

Warning: Refer to the safety information given in "Safety First" and Chapter 9, regarding the dangers of handling brake fluid.

15 With reference to Chapter 9, examine the area surrounding the brake pipe unions at the master cylinder for signs of leakage. Check the area around the base of fluid reservoir, for signs of leakage caused by seal failure. Also examine the brake pipe unions at the ABS hydraulic unit.

16 If fluid loss is evident, but the leak cannot be pinpointed in the engine bay, the brake calipers and underbody brake lines should be carefully checked with the vehicle raised and supported on axle stands. Leakage of fluid from the braking system is a serious fault that must be rectified immediately.

17 Brake/clutch hydraulic fluid is a toxic substance with a watery consistency. New fluid is almost colourless, but it becomes darker with age and use.

Unidentified fluid leaks

18 If there are signs that a fluid of some description is leaking from the vehicle, but you cannot identify the type of fluid or its exact origin, park the vehicle overnight and slide a large piece of card underneath it. Providing that the card is positioned in roughly the right location, even the smallest leak will show up on the card. Not only will this help you to pinpoint the exact location of the leak, it should be easier to identify the fluid from its colour. Bear in mind, though, that the leak may only be occurring when the engine is running!

Vacuum hoses

19 Although the braking system is hydraulically-operated, the brake servo unit amplifies the effort applied at the brake pedal, by making use of the vacuum in the inlet manifold, generated by the engine. Vacuum is ported to the servo by means of a large-bore hose. Any leaks that develop in this hose will reduce the effectiveness of the braking system, and may affect the running of the engine.

20 In addition, a number of the underbonnet components, particularly the emission control components, are driven by vacuum supplied from the inlet manifold via narrow-bore hoses. A leak in a vacuum hose means that air is being drawn into the hose (rather than escaping from it) and this makes leakage very difficult to detect. One method is to use an old length of vacuum hose as a kind of stethoscope - hold one end close to (but not in!) your ear and use the other end to probe the area around the suspected leak. When the end of the hose is directly over a vacuum leak, a hissing sound will be heard clearly through the hose. Care must be taken to avoid contacting hot or moving components, as the engine must be running, when testing in this manner. Renew any vacuum hoses that are found to be defective.

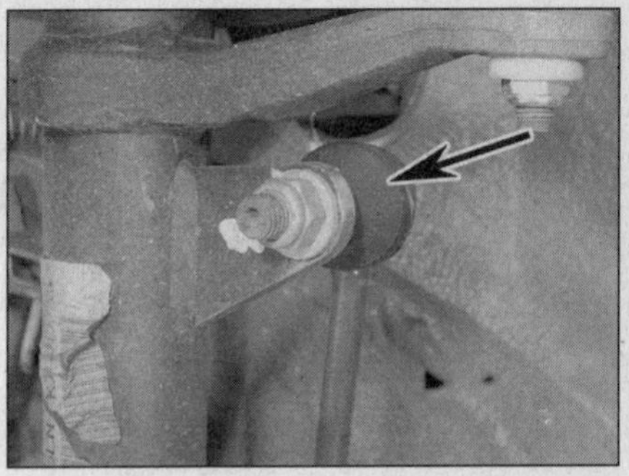

8.2 Visually inspect all balljoint dust covers for signs of deterioration

8 Suspension and steering check

Front suspension and steering check

1 Raise the front of the vehicle, and securely support it on axle stands (see "*Jacking and vehicle support*").

2 Visually inspect the balljoint dust covers and the steering rack-and-pinion gaiters for splits, chafing or deterioration **(see illustration)**. Any wear of these components will cause loss of lubricant, together with dirt and water entry, resulting in rapid deterioration of the balljoints or steering gear.

3 Check the power steering fluid hoses for chafing or deterioration, and the pipe and hose unions for fluid leaks. Also check for signs of fluid leakage under pressure from the steering gear rubber gaiters, which would indicate failed fluid seals within the steering gear.

4 Grasp the roadwheel at the 12 o'clock and 6 o'clock positions, and try to rock it **(see illustration)**. Very slight free play may be felt, but if the movement is appreciable, further investigation is necessary to determine the source. Continue rocking the wheel while an assistant depresses the footbrake. If the movement is now eliminated or significantly reduced, it is likely that the hub bearings are at fault. If the free play is still evident with the footbrake depressed, then there is wear in the suspension joints or mountings.

8.4 Check for wear in the hub bearings by trying to 'rock' the wheel

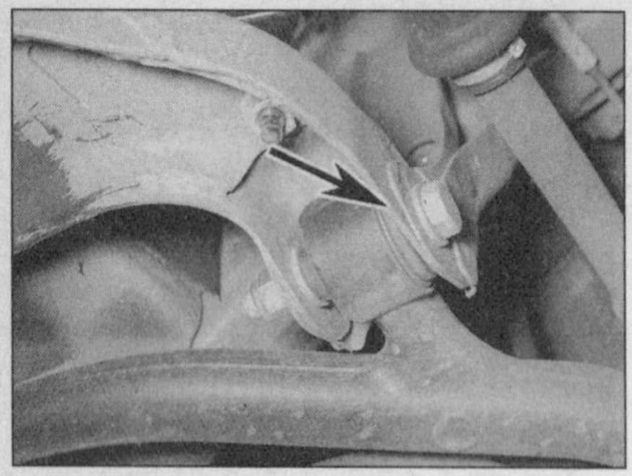

8.6 Check the condition of all visible rubber bushes

5 Now grasp the wheel at the 9 o'clock and 3 o'clock positions, and try to rock it as before. Any movement felt now may again be caused by wear in the hub bearings or the steering track-rod balljoints. If the inner or outer balljoint is worn, the visual movement will be obvious.

6 Using a large screwdriver or flat bar, check for wear in the suspension mounting bushes by levering between the relevant suspension component and its attachment point. Some movement is to be expected as the mountings are made of rubber, but excessive wear should be obvious. Also check the condition of any visible rubber bushes, looking for splits, cracks or contamination of the rubber **(see illustration)**.

7 With the car standing on its wheels, have an assistant turn the steering wheel back and forth about an eighth of a turn each way. There should be very little, if any, lost movement between the steering wheel and roadwheels. If this is not the case, closely observe the joints and mountings previously described, but in addition, check the steering column universal joints for wear, and the rack-and-pinion steering gear itself.

Suspension strut/shock absorber check

8 Check for any signs of fluid leakage around the suspension strut/shock absorber body, or from the rubber gaiter around the piston rod. Should any fluid be noticed, the suspension strut/shock absorber is defective internally, and should be renewed. **Note:** *Suspension struts/shock absorbers should always be renewed in pairs on the same axle, or the handling of the vehicle will be impaired.*

10.2 The thickness of the friction material is visible through the inspection aperture at the front of the brake caliper

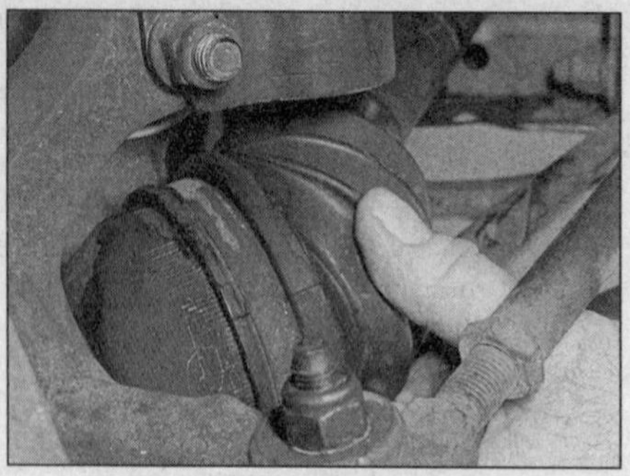

9.1 Inspecting a CV joint rubber gaiter

9 The efficiency of the suspension strut/shock absorber may be checked by bouncing the vehicle at each corner. Generally speaking, the body will return to its normal position and stop after being depressed. If it rises and returns on a rebound, the suspension strut/shock absorber is probably suspect. Examine also the suspension strut/shock absorber upper and lower mountings for any signs of wear.

9 Driveshaft rubber gaiter check

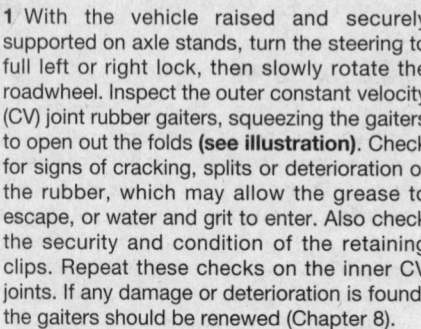

1 With the vehicle raised and securely supported on axle stands, turn the steering to full left or right lock, then slowly rotate the roadwheel. Inspect the outer constant velocity (CV) joint rubber gaiters, squeezing the gaiters to open out the folds **(see illustration)**. Check for signs of cracking, splits or deterioration of the rubber, which may allow the grease to escape, or water and grit to enter. Also check the security and condition of the retaining clips. Repeat these checks on the inner CV joints. If any damage or deterioration is found, the gaiters should be renewed (Chapter 8).

2 At the same time, check the general condition of the CV joints themselves by first holding the driveshaft and attempting to rotate the wheel. Repeat this check whilst holding the inner joint and attempting to rotate the driveshaft. Any appreciable movement indicates wear in the CV joints, wear in the driveshaft splines, or a loose driveshaft retaining nut.

10 Front brake wear check

1 Apply the handbrake, then jack up the front of the car and support it securely on axle stands (see "*Jacking and vehicle support*"). Remove the front roadwheels.

2 Clean the brake calipers with proprietary brake cleaning fluid and a stiff brush. Working through the inspection aperture in the front of the caliper, remove all traces of brake dust from the front edge of the brake pads, so that the friction material is visible. The brake pad wear can be assessed by observing the thickness of the friction material remaining on each brake pad. If the thickness of the friction material remaining is less than the specified limit, then the brake pads must be renewed **(see illustration)**.

3 For a comprehensive check, the brake pads should be removed and cleaned. The operation of the caliper can then also be checked, and the condition of the brake disc itself can be fully examined on both sides. Refer to Chapter 9 for further information.

4 If any pad's friction material is worn to the specified thickness or less, all four pads must be renewed as a set - do not change individual brake pads, as uneven braking may result.

5 On completion, refit the roadwheels and lower the car to the ground. Tighten the roadwheel bolts to the specified torque.

11 Retrieve fault codes from engine management system memory

1 The vehicle's engine management system ECU has a built-in self-diagnostic capability. It can monitor the system's sensors and actuators and is able to detect when they fail, even if the failure is temporary or intermittent. These faults are allocated a 'code' by the ECU and are stored in its memory.

2 Periodically, the ECU fault memory must be analysed and checked for stored fault codes. These can be used to identify components that have failed without the driver noticing, or may help to pinpoint problems that occur intermittently under conditions that are difficult to simulate in a workshop.

3 On some models, an engine management system warning lamp, mounted on the instrument panel is fitted. The ECU illuminates this lamp when it detects certain types of fault. After the fault has been rectified, the ECU fault code memory must be 'cleared', before the lamp will extinguish.

4 These operations must be carried out by a Citroën dealer, or fuel injection system specialist, as access to specialist diagnostic equipment is required.

12 Road test

Instruments and electrical equipment

1 Check the operation of all instruments and electrical equipment.

2 Make sure all instruments read correctly, and switch on all electrical equipment in turn, to check that it functions properly.

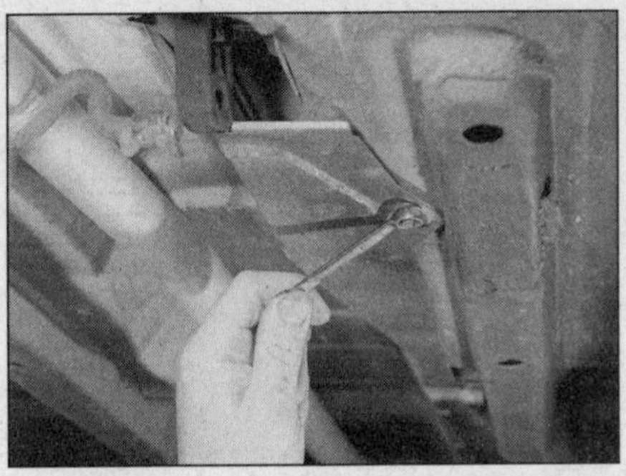

13.7a Slacken and withdraw the securing screws and nuts . . .

Steering and suspension

3 Check for any abnormalities in the steering, suspension, handling or road "feel".

4 Drive the vehicle, and check that there are no unusual vibrations or noises.

5 Check that the steering feels positive, with no excessive "sloppiness", or roughness, and check for any suspension noises when cornering and driving over bumps.

Drivetrain

6 Check the performance of the engine, clutch (where applicable), gearbox/transmission and driveshafts.

7 Listen for any unusual noises from the engine, clutch and gearbox/transmission.

8 Make sure that the engine runs smoothly when idling, and that there is no hesitation when accelerating.

9 Check that, where applicable, the clutch action is smooth and progressive, that the drive is taken up smoothly, and that the pedal travel is not excessive. Also listen for any noises when the clutch pedal is depressed.

10 On manual gearbox models, check that all gears can be engaged smoothly without noise, and that the gear lever action is not abnormally vague or "notchy".

11 On automatic transmission models, make sure that all gearchanges occur smoothly, without snatching, and without an increase in engine speed between changes. Check that all the gear positions can be selected with the vehicle at rest. If any problems are found, they should be referred to a Citroën dealer.

Check the operation and performance of the braking system

12 Make sure that the vehicle does not pull to one side when braking, and that the wheels do not lock prematurely when braking hard.

13 Check that there is no vibration through the steering when braking.

14 Check that the handbrake operates correctly without excessive movement of the lever, and that it holds the vehicle stationary on a slope.

15 Test the operation of the brake servo unit as follows. With the engine off, depress the footbrake four or five times to exhaust the vacuum. Hold the brake pedal depressed, then start the engine. As the engine starts, there should be a noticeable "give" in the brake pedal as vacuum builds up. Allow the engine to run for at least two minutes, and then switch it off. If the brake pedal is depressed now, it should be possible to detect a hiss from the servo as the pedal is depressed. After about four or five applications, no further hissing should be heard, and the pedal should feel much harder.

13 Handbrake operation check and adjustment

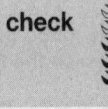

1 Park the vehicle on level ground and apply the handbrake, counting the number of notches the lever passes through. If the number is less than four or greater than seven, then the handbrake requires adjustment.

2 Chock the front wheels, release the handbrake, select first gear (or 'P' on models with automatic transmission) then jack up the rear of the vehicle, and support it securely on axle stands (see "*Jacking and vehicle support*").

3 Apply the footbrake firmly several times to establish correct shoe-to-drum clearance, then apply and release the handbrake several times to ensure that the self-adjust mechanism has compensated fully for any wear in the linings.

4 Fully release the handbrake, and check that the rear wheels rotate freely, without binding. If not, check that all cables are routed correctly, and check that the cable components and levers move freely.

> **HAYNES HiNT** *If the handbrake mechanism fails to operate, or appears to be seized on one side of the vehicle only, remove the relevant brake drum (see Chapter 9) and check the handbrake lever pivot on the trailing brake shoe - it is possible for the lever to seize due to corrosion. If necessary, remove the lever, and clean the contact faces of the lever, brake shoe, and pivot.*

5 If all components are free to move, but the wheels still bind when rotated, then adjustment is required as follows.

6 Again, apply the footbrake several times to settle the shoes. Ensure that the handbrake is fully released.

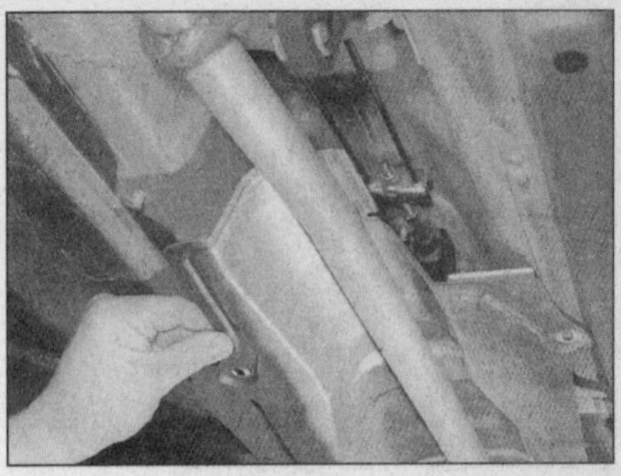

13.7b . . . and slide the exhaust heat shielding towards the front of the vehicle

7 Working under the vehicle, slacken and withdraw the securing screws and slide the exhaust heat shielding towards the front of the vehicle - there is no need to remove it completely **(see illustrations)**. Note that on models with a centre silencer, it will be necessary to unbolt and remove the section of the exhaust system containing the centre silencer, to gain access to the heatshield screws.

8 Slacken the adjuster nut on the handbrake cable equaliser assembly until the rear wheels are free to rotate **(see illustration)**.

9 Inside the vehicle, apply the handbrake so that the lever is on its 4th notch up from the "off" position.

10 Tighten the adjuster nut until there is slight resistance, as the rear wheels are rotated.

11 Check that there is a total handbrake lever travel of between 4 and 7 notches (the wheels should lock fully after a maximum 7 notches of handbrake lever movement).

12 Check that both the left- and right-hand rear cables move together when the handbrake is operated.

13 Fully release the handbrake, and check that both rear wheels turn freely by hand.

14 Check that the handbrake warning light illuminates from the 4th notch of handbrake lever travel.

15 On completion, lower the vehicle to the ground.

13.8 Slacken the adjuster nut (arrowed) on the handbrake cable equaliser assembly

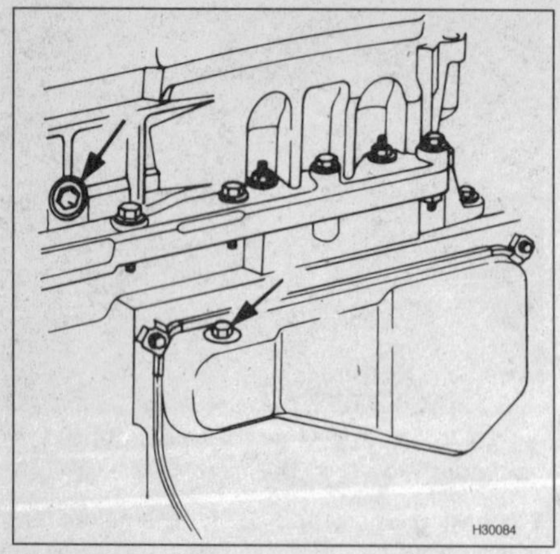

14.3 Automatic transmission drain plugs (arrowed)

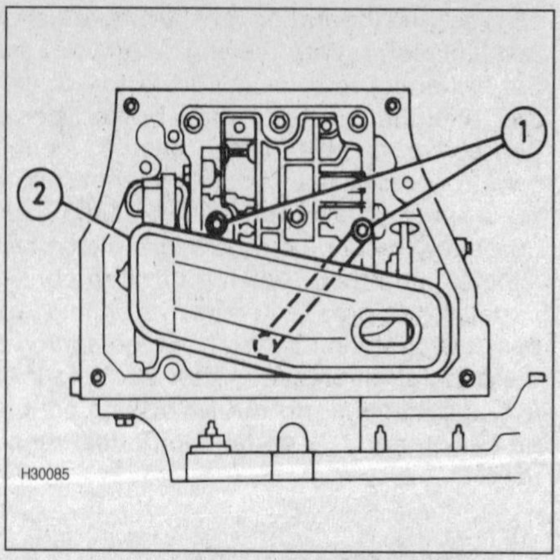

14.8 Undo the two securing screws (1) and detach the filter (2) from the underside of the transmission

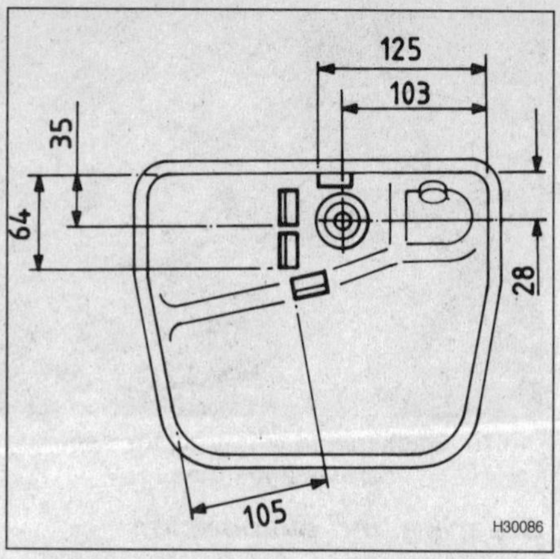

14.9 If the magnets are removed for cleaning, they *must* be refitted in their original positions

Every 18 000 miles (30 000 km)

14 Automatic transmission fluid and filter renewal

1 Take the vehicle on a short run, to warm the transmission up to normal operating temperature.

2 Park the vehicle on level ground, switch off the ignition and apply the handbrake firmly. For improved access, jack up the front of the vehicle and support it securely on axle stands (see "*Jacking and vehicle support*"). Note that the vehicle must be lowered to the ground and be level, to ensure accuracy when refilling and checking the fluid level.

3 Remove the dipstick, then position a suitable container under the transmission drain plugs. There are two plugs; one is located under the side of the lower cover, the other is located underneath the differential casing **(see illustration)**.

4 Unscrew the drain plugs and allow the fluid to drain completely into the container. Note that only approximately 2.5 litres will drain out as it is not possible to completely drain the torque converter. The fluid will be hot, so take precautions against scalding. Clean the drain plugs, being especially careful to wipe any metallic particles off the magnetic inserts. Discard the original sealing washers, which should be renewed whenever they are disturbed.

5 When the fluid has finished draining, clean the drain plug threads and those of the transmission casing, fit new sealing washers to the drain plugs and refit them to the transmission, tightening securely.

6 To renew the fluid filter proceed as follows. Ensure that the work surface below the transmission is clean, to prevent the ingress of dirt during the filter renewal procedure. Line the ground with a dust sheet if necessary.

7 Progressively slacken and remove the securing screws, noting the orientation of the support brackets, then withdraw the lower cover from the underside of the transmission. Discard the gasket - a new item must be used on refitting.

8 Undo the two securing screws and detach the filter from the underside of the transmission **(see illustration)**.

9 Clean the inside of the lower cover, paying particular attention to the sealing surface. Also remove any traces of swarf from the magnets attached to the inside of the lower cover. The magnets can be removed for cleaning, but they **must** be refitted in their original positions **(see illustration)**.

10 Fit the new filter into position, using the new seal provided. Insert and tighten the securing bolts, ensuring that the support lug locates underneath the washer of the bolt nearest the front of the filter .

11 Refit the lower cover together with the new gasket, then insert the securing screws and tighten them securely. Ensure that the orientation of the support brackets is as noted during removal. On completion, lower the vehicle to the ground.

12 Refilling the transmission is an extremely awkward operation, adding the specified type of fluid to the transmission a little at a time via the dipstick tube. Use a funnel with a fine mesh gauze, to avoid spillage and to ensure that no foreign matter enters the transmission. Allow plenty of time for the fluid level to settle properly before checking. Note that the vehicle must be parked on flat level ground when checking the fluid level.

13 Add approximately 2.5 litres and check the level on the dipstick continuously as the last half-litre is added. Once the level is up to the MAX mark on the dipstick, refit the dipstick then start the engine and allow it to idle for a few minutes. Switch the engine off and recheck the level, topping-up if necessary. Take the vehicle on a short run to fully distribute the new fluid around the transmission, then recheck the fluid level.

15 Rear brake pad wear check - models with rear disc brakes

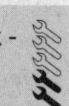

1 Chock the front wheels, then jack up the rear of the vehicle and support it on axle stands (see "*Jacking and vehicle support*"). Remove the rear roadwheels.

2 For a quick check, the thickness of friction material remaining on each brake pad can be measured through the top of the caliper body **(see illustration)**. If any pad's friction material is worn to the specified thickness or less, all four pads must be renewed as a set.

3 For a comprehensive check, the brake pads should be removed and cleaned. This will permit the operation of the caliper to be checked, and the condition of the brake disc itself to be fully examined on both sides. Refer to Chapter 9 for further information.

4 If any pad's friction material is worn to the specified thickness or less, *all four pads must be renewed as a set.*

5 On completion, refit the roadwheels and lower the car to the ground. Tighten the roadwheel bolts to the specified torque.

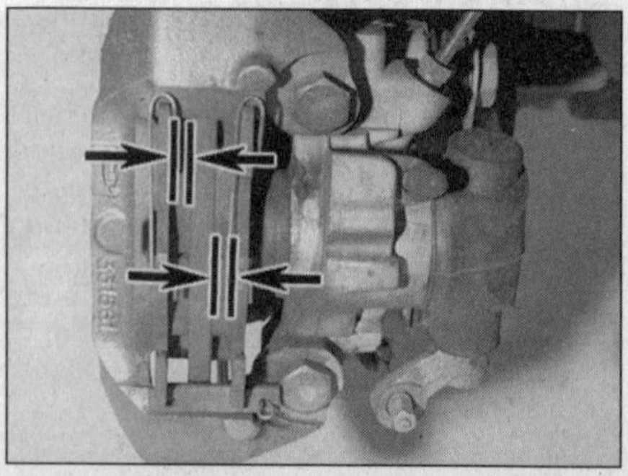

15.2 The thickness of the friction material is visible through the inspection aperture at the front of the rear brake caliper

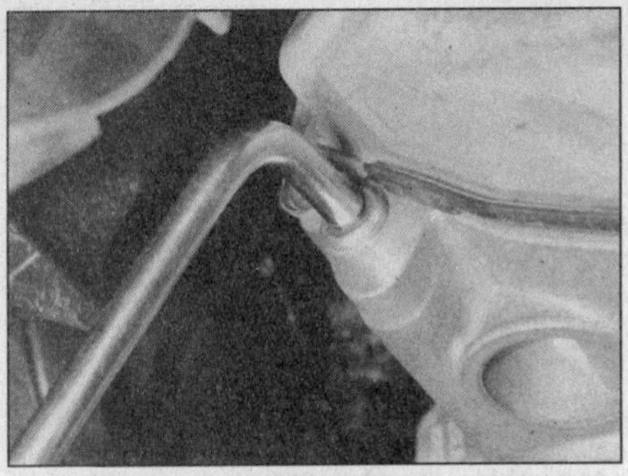

16.3 Unscrew the filler/level plug from the transmission using a square-section wrench

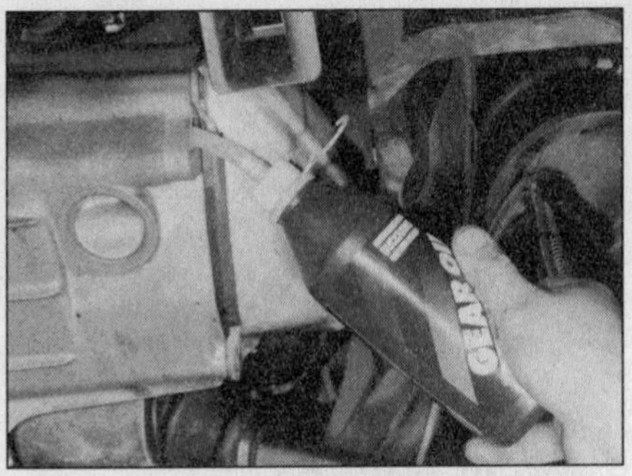

16.4 Topping-up the manual transmission oil level

17.3 Disconnect the HT leads from the spark plugs (1.1 litre model shown)

Every 36 000 miles (60 000 km)

16 Manual transmission oil level check

Note: *A suitable square-section wrench may be required to undo the transmission filler/level plug on some models. These wrenches can be obtained from most motor factors or your Citroën dealer. A new sealing washer will also be required when refitting the transmission filler/level plug.*

1 The manual transmission oil does not need to be renewed as part of the regular maintenance schedule, but the oil level must be checked and if necessary topped-up at the interval specified here. To drain the transmission as part of a repair procedure, refer to the information given in Chapter 7A.

2 Park the car on a level surface. The oil level must be checked before the car is driven, or at least 5 minutes after the engine has been switched off.

Caution: If the oil is checked immediately after driving the car, some of the oil will remain distributed around the transmission components, resulting in an inaccurate level reading.

3 Wipe clean the area around the filler/level plug, which is situated on the left-hand end of the transmission. Unscrew the plug and clean it; discard the sealing washer **(see illustration)**.

4 The oil level should reach the lower edge of the filler/level hole. A certain amount of oil will have gathered behind the filler/level plug, and will trickle out when it is removed; this does **not** necessarily indicate that the level is correct. To ensure that a true level is established, wait until the initial trickle has stopped, then add oil as necessary until a trickle of new oil can be seen emerging. The level will be correct when the flow ceases; use only good-quality oil of the specified type **(see illustration)**.

5 Filling the transmission with oil is an extremely awkward operation; above all, allow plenty of time for the oil level to settle properly before checking it. If a large amount is added to the transmission, and a large amount flows out on checking the level, refit the filler/level plug and take the vehicle on a short journey so that the new oil is distributed fully around the transmission components, then recheck the level when it has settled again.

6 If the transmission has been overfilled so that oil flows out as soon as the filler/level plug is removed, check that the car is completely level (front-to-rear and side-to-side), and allow the surplus to drain off into a suitable container.

7 When the level is correct, fit a new sealing washer to the filler/level plug. Refit the plug, tightening it to the specified torque wrench setting. Wash off any spilt oil.

17 Spark plug renewal

General information

1 The correct functioning of the spark plugs is vital for the correct running and efficiency of the engine. It is essential that the plugs fitted are appropriate for the engine (a suitable type is specified at the beginning of this Chapter). If the correct type is used and the engine is in good condition, the spark plugs should not need attention between scheduled replacement intervals. Spark plug cleaning is rarely necessary, and should not be attempted unless specialised equipment is available, as damage can easily be caused to the firing ends.

2 On VTS models, the spark plugs are threaded into the top of the cylinder head; access is gained by removing the engine cover and the ignition coil module - see Chapter 5B for details. On all other models, the spark plugs are threaded into the rear of the cylinder head, and can be accessed after removing the air intake ducting and the ignition coil module on later 1.4 and 1.6 litre models.

3 On all except VTS 16-valve models (and later 1.4 and 1.6 models with plug-top ignition coil modules), if the marks on the original-equipment spark plug (HT) leads cannot be seen, mark the leads "1" to "4", to correspond to the cylinder the lead serves. No 1 cylinder is at the left hand (flywheel) end of the engine. Disconnect the HT leads from the spark plugs by gripping the end fitting, not the lead itself, otherwise the lead's internal connection may be fractured **(see illustration)**.

4 On VTS 16-valve models only, slacken and remove the securing screws, then lift off the engine cover panel. With reference to Chapter 5B, undo the securing screws and withdraw the ignition coil module from the top of the cylinder head. On later 1.4 and 1.6 litre models fitted with plug-top ignition coil modules, undo the securing screws and carefully pull the ignition coil module away from the tops of the spark plugs.

5 It is advisable to remove the dirt from the spark plug recesses using a clean brush, vacuum cleaner or compressed air before removing the plugs, to prevent dirt dropping into the cylinders.

6 Unscrew the plugs using a spark plug spanner, suitable box spanner or a deep socket and extension bar **(see illustrations)**. Keep the socket aligned with the spark plug - if force is applied with the socket fitted at a slight angle, the ceramic insulator may be cracked or broken off. As each plug is removed, examine it as described in the following paragraphs.

7 Examination of the spark plugs will give a good indication of the condition of the engine. If

17.6a Unscrew the spark plug . . .

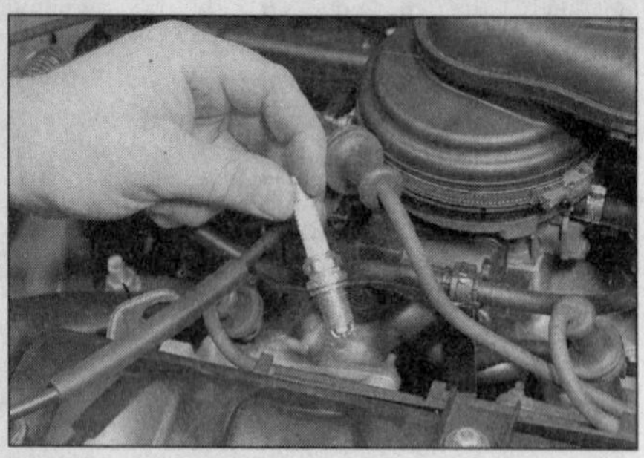

17.6b . . . and remove it from the cylinder head

the insulator nose of the spark plug is clean and white with no deposits, or has a 'glazed' appearance, this is indicative of a weak mixture.

8 If the tip and insulator nose are covered with powdered, black-looking deposits, then this is indicative that the mixture is too rich. Should the plug be black and oily, or have a thick coating of white crusty deposits, then it is possible that either the valve guides or piston rings are worn.

9 If the insulator nose is covered with light tan to greyish-brown deposits, then the mixture is correct and it is likely that the engine is in good condition.

10 The spark plug electrode gap is of considerable importance as, if it is too large or too small, the size of the spark and its efficiency will be seriously impaired. **Note:** *Spark plugs with multiple earth electrodes are becoming an increasingly common fitment, especially to vehicles equipped with catalytic converters. Unless there is clear information to the contrary, no attempt should be made to adjust the plug gap on a spark plug with more than one earth electrode.*

11 To set the gap, measure it with a feeler blade, and then bend the outer plug electrode until the correct gap is achieved. The centre electrode should never be bent, as this may crack the insulator and cause plug failure, if nothing worse. If using feeler blades, the gap is correct when the appropriate-size blade is a firm sliding fit.

12 Special spark plug electrode gap adjusting tools are available from most motor accessory shops, or from some spark plug manufacturers. Read the manufacturers information before gapping a new set of plugs; some types of plugs have specially shaped electrodes which cannot be adjusted.

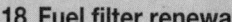

HAYNES HiNT

It is very often difficult to insert spark plugs into their holes without cross-threading them. To avoid this possibility, fit a short length of 5/16 inch internal diameter rubber hose over the end of the spark plug. The flexible hose acts as a universal joint to help align the plug with the plug hole. Should the plug begin to cross-thread, the hose will slip on the spark plug, preventing thread damage to the aluminium cylinder head. Remove the rubber hose, and tighten the plug to the specified torque using the spark plug socket and a torque wrench.

13 Before fitting the spark plugs, check that the threaded connector sleeves are tight, and that the plug exterior surfaces and threads are clean. It is very often difficult to insert spark plugs into their holes without cross-threading them. To avoid this possibility, fit a short length of hose over the end of the spark plug **(see Haynes Hint)**.

14 Remove the rubber hose (if used), and tighten the plug to the specified torque (see *"Specifications"*) using the spark plug socket and a torque wrench. Refit the remaining plugs in the same way.

15 Where applicable, reconnect the HT leads in the correct firing order (1-3-4-2, No 1 cylinder at the flywheel end of the engine) and refit any components removed for access. On VTS models, and later 1.4 and 1.6 litre models, refit the ignition coil module with reference to Chapter 5B. On VTS models, refit the engine cover panel.

18 Fuel filter renewal

Warning: Before carrying out the following operation, refer to the precautions given in "Safety first!" at the beginning of this manual, and follow them implicitly. Petrol is a highly-dangerous and volatile liquid, and the precautions necessary when handling it cannot be overstressed.

1 The fuel filter is situated underneath the rear of the vehicle, on the left-hand side of the fuel tank. To gain access to the filter, chock the front wheels, then jack up the rear of the vehicle and support it on axle stands (see "*Jacking and vehicle support*").

2 Seal off the fuel hoses leading to and from the filter, using proprietary hose clamps, with rounded jaws - do not use G-clamps, Mole Grips or similar with flat or square jaws as these could damage the hose internally, causing leakage later.

3 Unclip the filter retaining strap from the left-hand side of the fuel tank **(see illustration)**.

4 Noting the direction of the arrow marked on the filter body, release the retaining clips and disconnect the fuel hoses from the filter. Where the original Citroën crimped-type clips are still fitted, cut and discard them; replace them with standard worm-drive hose clips on installation **(see illustrations)**.

5 Remove the filter from the vehicle. Dispose safely of the old filter; it will be highly inflammable, and may explode if thrown on a fire.

6 Slide the new filter into position, ensuring that the arrow on the filter body is pointing in the direction of the fuel flow, as noted when removing the old filter **(see illustration)**. The flow direction can otherwise be determined by tracing the fuel hoses back along their length.

7 Connect the fuel hoses to the filter, securing them in position with their retaining clips (where applicable). Where quick-release hose unions are fitted, press each hose onto its respective filter port until it 'snaps' into position.

8 Clip the filter strap back onto the fuel tank **(see illustration)**. Remove the hose clamps.

18.3 Unclip the filter retaining strap from the left-hand side of the fuel tank

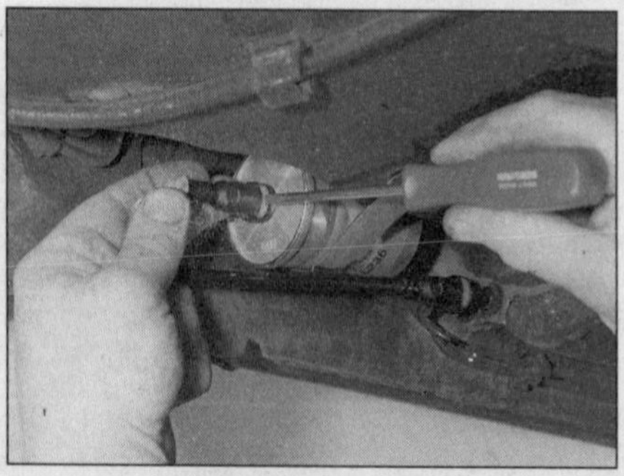

18.4a Depress the locking tabs . . .

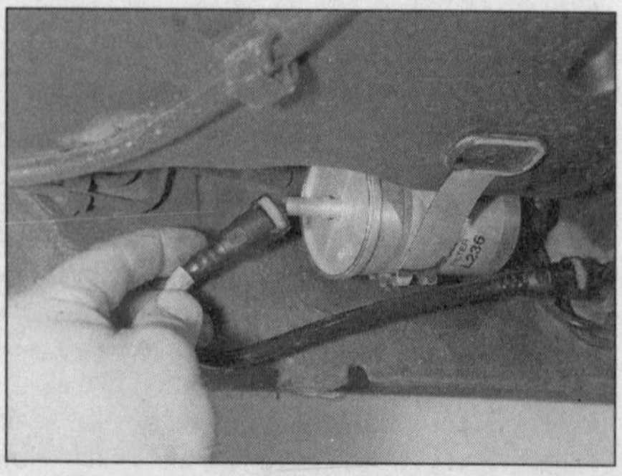

18.4b . . . to release the fuel hose unions

9 Start the engine, check the filter hose connections for leaks, then lower the vehicle to the ground

19 Air filter renewal

1.0 and 1.1 litre models

1 Slacken the retaining clips (where fitted) and disconnect the vacuum and breather hoses from the front of the air cleaner housing-to-throttle body duct. Where crimped-type hose clips or ties are fitted, cut and discard them; replace them with standard worm-drive hose clips or new cable ties on refitting.

2 Slacken the retaining clips, then lift the duct off the top of the throttle body and air cleaner housing **(see illustrations)**. Disconnect the air temperature control valve hose from the end of the duct, and remove the duct from the engine compartment. Recover the rubber sealing ring(s) from the top of the throttle body and/or air cleaner housing (as applicable).

19.2a Slacken the retaining clips . . .

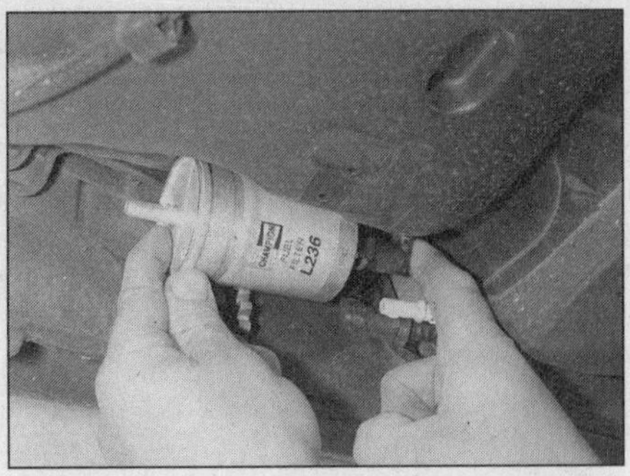

18.6 Slide the new filter into position, ensuring that the arrow on the filter body is pointing in the direction of the fuel flow

3 Release the retaining clips securing the lid to the top of the air cleaner housing. Lift the lid away from the housing, and recover the sealing ring **(see illustrations)**. On some models, it will be necessary to twist the lid to release it. Inspect the sealing ring for signs of damage or deterioration, and renew if necessary.

4 Where the air filter element is not an integral part of the lid, lift the element out of the housing **(see illustration)**.

5 Remove all traces of dirt and debris from the inside of the air cleaner housing, then fit the new element, making sure it is correctly seated in the housing.

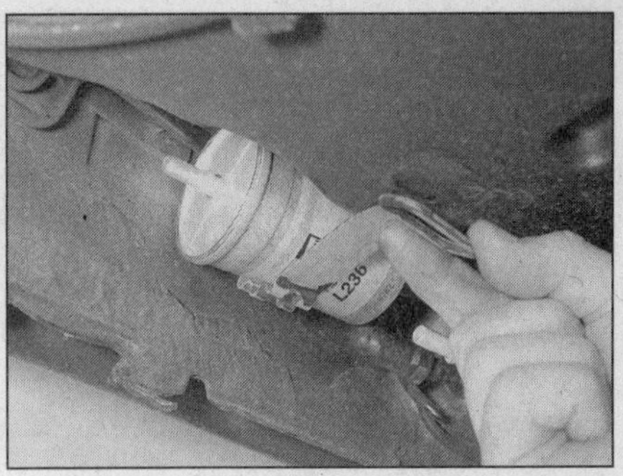

18.8 Secure the filter in position by fastening the strap to the fuel tank

6 Fit the sealing ring to the housing, then refit the lid (noting the locking lugs) and secure it in position with the retaining clips **(see illustration)**.

7 Refit the air cleaner-to-throttle body duct. Ensure that the duct is correctly seated on its sealing rings, and securely tighten its retaining clips.

8 Reconnect the vacuum and breather hoses to the duct, and secure them in position with the retaining clips (where fitted).

1.4 and 1.6 litre models (excluding VTS)

9 Depress the retaining tabs and disconnect the breather hose from the air cleaner housing-to-throttle body duct **(see illustration)**.

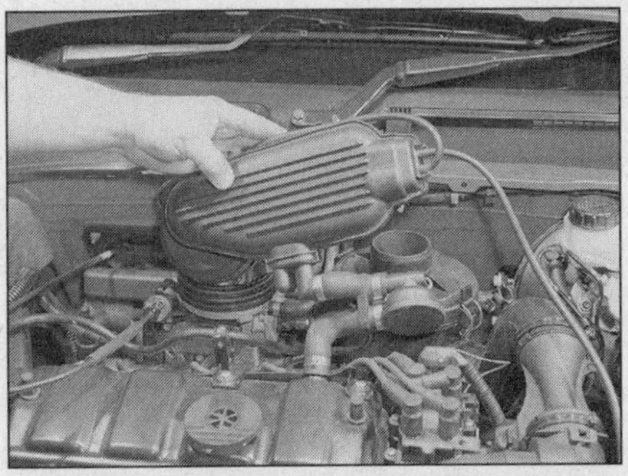

19.2b . . . then lift the duct off the top of the throttle body and air cleaner housing

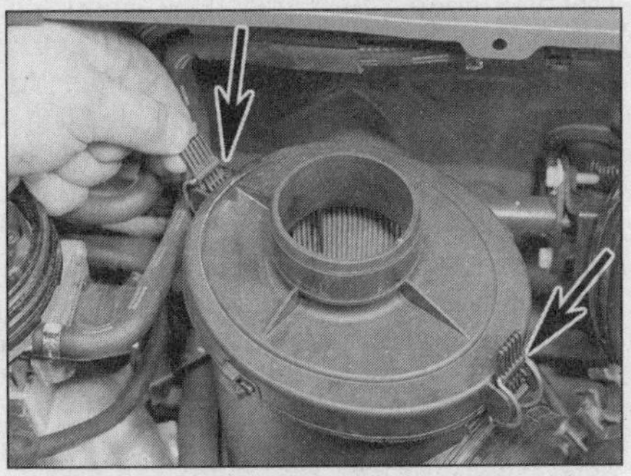

19.3a Release the retaining clips . . .

19.3b . . . then lift the cover from the air cleaner housing . . .

19.3c . . . and recover the sealing ring

19.4 Lift the air filter element from its housing

19.6 Ensure that the locking lugs (arrowed) on the air filter housing lid engage with those on the lower half of the housing

19.9 Depress the retaining tabs and disconnect the breather hose from the air cleaner housing-to-throttle body duct

19.10 Release the retaining clips securing the duct to the top of the air cleaner housing

19.11a Slacken the retaining clips . . .

10 Release the retaining clips securing the duct to the top of the air cleaner housing **(see illustration)**.

11 Slacken the retaining clips, then lift the duct off the top of the throttle body and air cleaner housing. On some models, it will be necessary to twist the duct to release it **(see illustrations)**.

12 Lift the air filter element out of its housing **(see illustration)**.

13 Remove all traces of dirt and debris from the inside of the air cleaner housing, then fit the new element, making sure it is correctly seated in the housing.

14 Fit the sealing ring to the housing, then refit the air cleaner-to-throttle body duct (noting the locking lugs) and secure it in position with the retaining clips **(see illustration)**.

15 Ensure that the duct is correctly seated on the throttle body, then securely tighten the retaining clip.

16 Reconnect the breather hose to the duct, and secure them in position with the retaining clips (where fitted).

VTS models

17 Release the retaining clips, then remove the cover from the air cleaner housing. Withdraw the filter element, noting its orientation.

18 Remove all traces of dirt and debris from the inside of the air cleaner housing, using a cloth.

19 Fit the new element, ensuring that it is fitted the correct way around and is correctly seated in the housing. Install the cover, and secure it in position with the retaining clips.

20 Brake fluid renewal

Warning: Brake hydraulic fluid can harm your eyes and damage painted surfaces, so use extreme caution when handling and pouring it. Do not use fluid that has been standing open for some time, as it absorbs moisture from the air. Excess moisture can cause a dangerous loss of braking effectiveness.

1 The procedure is similar to that for the bleeding of the hydraulic system as described in Chapter 9, except that the brake fluid reservoir should be emptied by siphoning, using a clean poultry baster or similar before starting, and allowance should be made for the old fluid to be expelled when bleeding a section of the circuit.

2 Working as described in Chapter 9, open the first bleed screw in the sequence, and pump the brake pedal gently until nearly all the old fluid has been emptied from the master cylinder reservoir. Top-up to the "MAX" level with new fluid, and continue pumping until only the new fluid remains in the reservoir, and new fluid can be seen emerging from the bleed screw. Tighten the screw, and top the reservoir level up to the "MAX" level line.

3 The age of hydraulic fluid can be judged by its colour; old fluid tends to be much darker in colour than new fluid. This makes it easy to judge when a section of the braking system has been sufficiently bled - when the colour of the fluid flowing from the bleed screw turns from dark to light, this means that the new fluid has ejected all the old fluid from that section.

4 Work through all the remaining bleed screws in the sequence until new fluid can be seen at all of them. Be careful to keep the master cylinder reservoir topped-up to above the "MIN" level at all times, or air may enter the system and greatly increase the length of the task.

5 When the operation is complete, check that all bleed screws are securely tightened, and that their dust caps are refitted. Wash off all traces of spilt fluid, and recheck the master cylinder reservoir fluid level.

6 Check the operation of the brakes before taking the car on the road.

21 Rear brake shoe wear check - models with rear drum brakes

1 Chock the front wheels then jack up the rear of the vehicle and support it on axle stands (see "*Jacking and vehicle support*").

2 For a quick check, the thickness of friction material remaining on one of the brake shoes can be measured through the slot in the brake

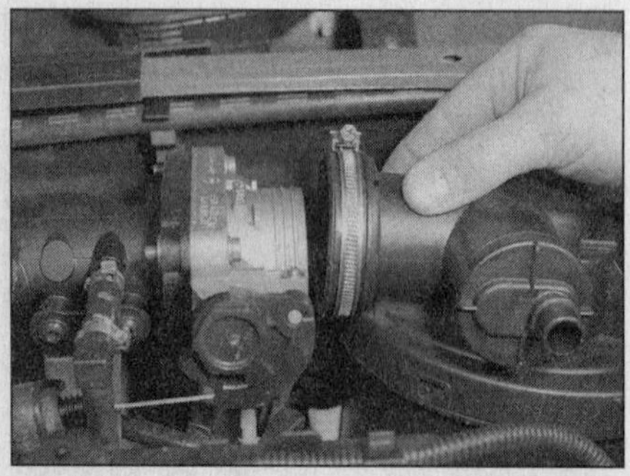

19.11b . . . then lift the duct off the top of the throttle body and air cleaner housing

19.12 Lift the air filter element out of its housing

19.14 Refit the air cleaner-to-throttle body duct, noting the locking lugs (arrowed)

backplate that is exposed by prising out its sealing grommet **(see illustrations)**. If a rod of the same diameter as the specified minimum thickness is placed against the shoe friction material, the amount of wear can quickly be assessed - a small mirror may help observation. If any shoe's friction material is worn to the specified thickness or less, all four shoes must be renewed as a set.

3 For a comprehensive check, the brake drums should be removed and cleaned. This will permit the wheel cylinders to be checked and the condition of the brake drum itself to be fully examined. Refer to Chapter 9 for further information.

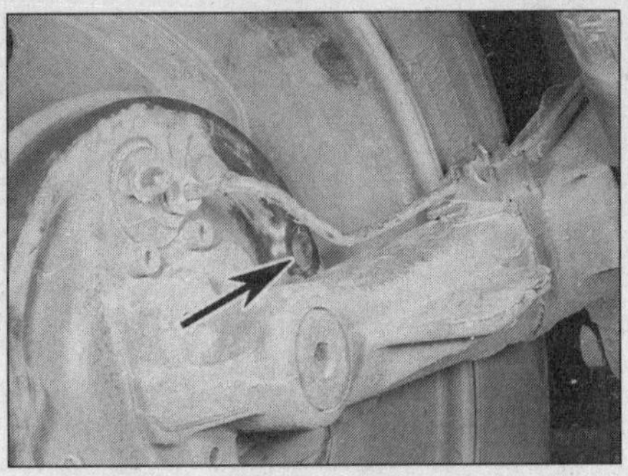

21.2a Prise the grommet (arrowed) from the rear drum brake back plate

21.2b Viewing the thickness of the brake shoe lining using a small mirror

22 Braking system condition check

1 Raise the front of the vehicle, support securely on axle stands (see "*Jacking and vehicle support*") and remove the front roadwheels.

2 Inspect the area around both brake calipers for signs of brake fluid leakage, either from the piston seals, the brake pipe union or the bleed screw.

3 Examine the brake hoses leading to each caliper and check for signs of cracking, chaffing or damage. Renew a hose which shows signs of deterioration without delay.

4 Using proprietary brake cleaning fluid and a stiff brush, wash all traces of dirt and brake dust from the brake calipers - take care to avoid inhaling any of the airborne brake dust. Examine the piston dust seal for signs of damage or deterioration and check that it is securely seated in its retaining groove.

5 Ensure that the transmission is in neutral, then grasp each brake disc and turn it by hand. Slight resistance is normal, but if the brake disc is difficult to turn smoothly, this indicates that the brake caliper is binding; refer to Chapter 9 for details of caliper removal and overhaul.

6 Check the condition of the brake disc with reference to the information given in Chapter 9.

7 Refit the front roadwheels, then lower the front of the car to the ground. Check the front wheels and select first gear (or 'P' on models with automatic transmission) then release the handbrake, raise the rear of the car and support it on axle stands.

8 Ensure that the handbrake is released, then grasp each roadwheel and turn it by hand. Slight resistance is normal, but if the wheel is difficult to turn smoothly, this could be due to poor handbrake adjustment; refer to Chapter 9 for a description of the adjustment procedure.

9 Remove the rear roadwheels, then with reference to Chapter 9, remove the brake drums and check them for wear and/or damage.

10 Check the area around the wheel cylinder piston seals for signs of fluid leakage. Check at the rear of the brake backplate for evidence of fluid leakage from the brake pipe union or bleed screw. Renew the wheel cylinder without delay if it shows signs of leakage; see Chapter 9 for details.

11 Using proprietary brake cleaning fluid and a stiff brush, wash all traces of dirt and brake dust from the brake shoes and associated components - take care to avoid inhaling any of the airborne brake dust. Examine the brake shoes and measure the depth of the remaining friction material. Renew all four brake shoes, with reference to Chapter 9, if any are worn below their minimum limit.

12 On completion refit the brake drums and roadwheels, then lower the car to the ground. Tighten the roadwheel bolts to the specified torque.

23 Auxiliary drivebelt check and renewal

1 On all models, only one auxiliary drivebelt is fitted. The belt drives the alternator and (where fitted) the air conditioning compressor.

Condition check

2 Apply the handbrake, jack up the front of the car and support it on axle stands (see "*Jacking and vehicle support*"), then remove the right-hand front roadwheel.

3 Undo the securing screws and remove the plastic liner from the wheel arch. Where necessary, undo the retaining nut, and free the coolant hoses from the retaining clip to improve access to the crankshaft sprocket bolt

4 Using a suitable socket and extension bar fitted to the crankshaft sprocket bolt, rotate the crankshaft so that the entire length of the drivebelt can be examined. Examine the drivebelt for cracks, splitting, fraying, or other damage. Check also for signs of glazing (shiny patches) and for separation of the belt plies. Renew the belt if worn or damaged.

5 If the condition of the belt is satisfactory, check the drivebelt tension as described below under the relevant sub-heading.

Removal, refitting and tensioning - models without air conditioning (excluding 16-valve models)

1A

Removal

6 If not already done, carry out the operations described in paragraphs 2 and 3. Disconnect the battery negative cable and position it away from the terminal.

7 Slacken both the alternator upper and lower mounting bolts. On models where the adjustment strut is located underneath the alternator, also slacken the bolt securing the strut to its mounting bracket **(see illustrations)**.

8 Turn the adjuster bolt to relieve the tension in the drivebelt, then slip the drivebelt from the pulleys **(see illustrations)**.

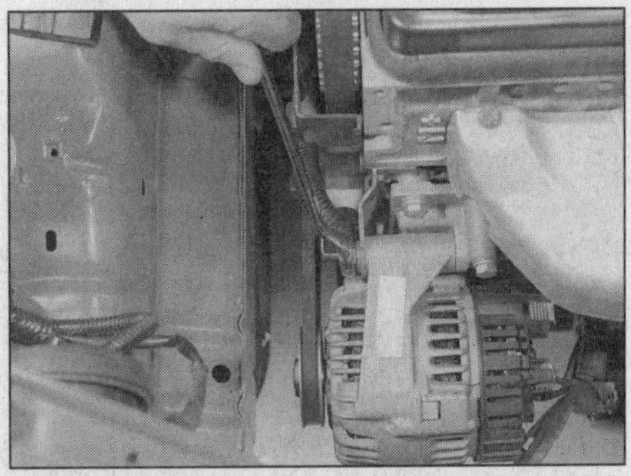

23.7a Slacken the alternator upper mounting bolt (1.1 litre models shown) . . .

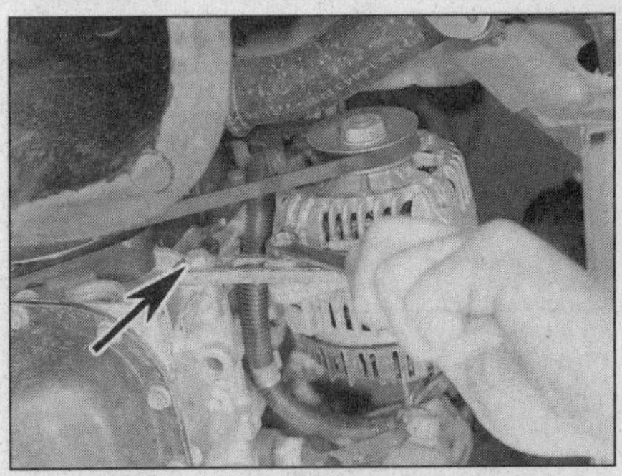

23.7b . . . and the alternator lower mounting bolt. On models where the adjustment strut is located underneath the alternator, also slacken the bolt (arrowed) securing the strut to its mounting bracket

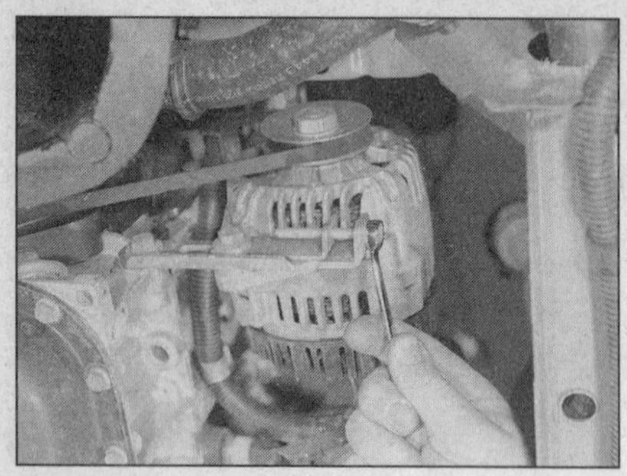

23.8a Turn the adjuster bolt to relieve the tension in the drivebelt . . .

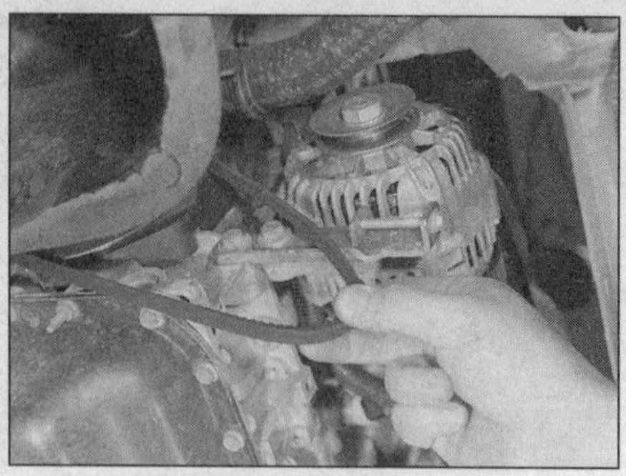

23.8b . . .then slip the drivebelt from the pulleys (1.1 litre model shown)

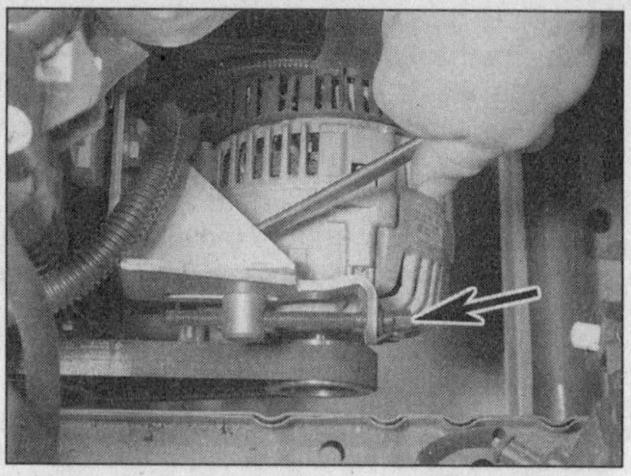

23.8c Auxiliary drivebelt adjuster bolt (arrowed, 1.6 litre 8-valve model shown)

Refitting

9 Fit the belt around the pulleys, ensuring that the belt is of the correct type if it is being renewed, and take up the slack in the belt by tightening the adjuster bolt.
10 Tension the drivebelt as described in the following paragraphs.

Tensioning

11 If not already done, carry out the operations described in paragraphs 2 and 3.
12 Correct tensioning of the drivebelt will ensure that it has a long life. Beware, however, of overtightening, as this can cause wear in the alternator bearings.
13 The belt should be tensioned so that, under firm thumb pressure, there is approximately 5.0 mm of free movement at the mid-point between the pulleys, on the longest belt run.
14 To adjust, with the upper mounting bolt just holding the alternator firm, and the lower mounting bolt loosened, turn the adjuster bolt until the correct tension is achieved. Rotate the crankshaft through two complete turns, then recheck the tension. When the tension is correct, tighten the alternator mounting bolts and where necessary, tighten securely the bolt securing the adjuster strap to its mounting bracket.
15 Reconnect the battery negative lead.
16 Clip the coolant hoses in position and secure them with the retaining nut (where removed). Refit the wheel arch liner, then refit the roadwheel, and lower the vehicle to the ground. Tighten the roadwheel bolts to the specified torque.

Removal, refitting and tensioning - models with air conditioning and all 16-valve models

Removal

17 If not already done, carry out the operations described in paragraphs 2 and 3.
18 Disconnect the battery negative lead.
19 Slacken the two bolts securing the tensioner pulley assembly to the engine.
20 Rotate the adjuster bolt to move the tensioner pulley away from the drivebelt, until there is sufficient slack for the drivebelt to be removed from the pulleys.

Refitting

21 Fit the belt around the pulleys, ensuring that the belt is of the correct type if it is being renewed, and take up the slack in the belt by tightening the adjuster bolt.
22 Tension the drivebelt as described in the following paragraphs.

Tensioning

23 If not already done, carry out the operations described in paragraphs 2 and 3.
24 Correct tensioning of the drivebelt will ensure that it has a long life. Beware, however, of overtightening, as this can cause wear in the alternator bearings.
25 The belt should be tensioned so that, under firm thumb pressure, there is approximately 5.0 mm of free movement at the mid-point of the longest belt run between two pulleys.
26 To adjust the tension, with the two tensioner pulley assembly retaining bolts slackened, rotate the adjuster bolt until the correct tension is achieved. Once the belt is correctly tensioned, rotate the crankshaft through two complete turns, and recheck the tension.
27 When the belt is correctly tensioned, tighten the tensioner pulley assembly retaining bolts to the specified torque.
28 Reconnect the battery negative lead.
29 Clip the coolant hoses back in position, and secure with the retaining nut (where removed). Refit the wheel arch liner and roadwheel, then lower the vehicle to the ground. Tighten the roadwheel bolts to the specified torque.

Every 72 000 miles (120 000 km)

24 Timing belt renewal

Refer to the information given in Chapter 2A.

Every 72 000 miles (120 000 km) or 2 years

25 Engine coolant renewal

Cooling system draining

Warning: Wait until the engine is cold before starting this procedure. Do not allow antifreeze to come in contact with your skin, or with the painted surfaces of the vehicle. Rinse off spills immediately with plenty of water. Never leave antifreeze lying around in an open container, or in a puddle in the driveway or on the garage floor. Children and pets are attracted by its sweet smell, but antifreeze can be fatal if ingested.

1 With the engine completely cold, remove the expansion tank filler cap. Turn the cap anti-clockwise until it reaches the first stop. Wait until any pressure remaining in the system is released, then push the cap down, turn it anti-clockwise to the second stop, and lift it off.
2 Position a suitable container beneath the coolant drain outlet at the lower left-hand side of the radiator **(see illustration)**.

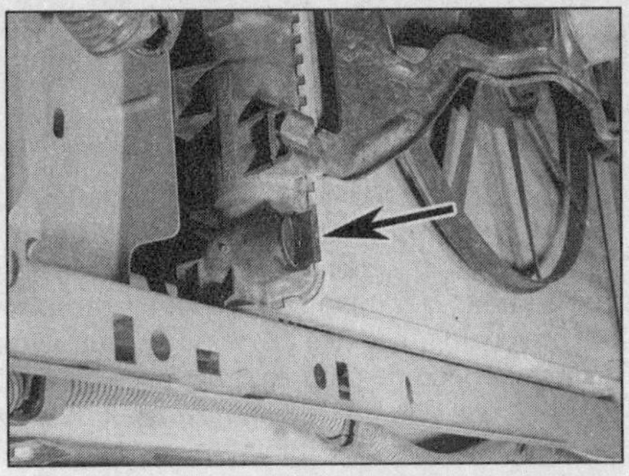

25.2 Radiator drain plug (arrowed)

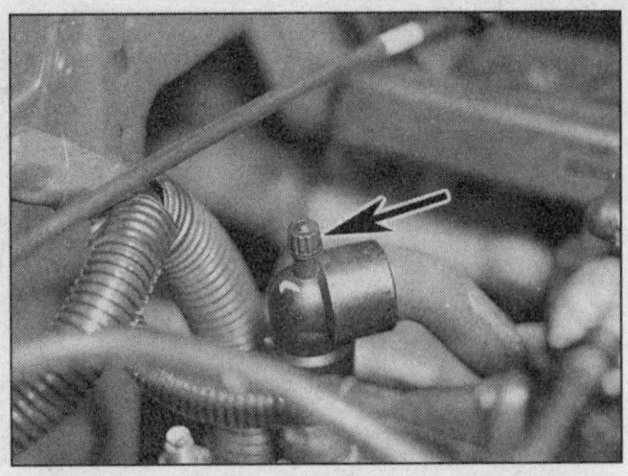

25.4a Cooling system bleed screws located in the heater hose at the right-hand side of the engine compartment . . .

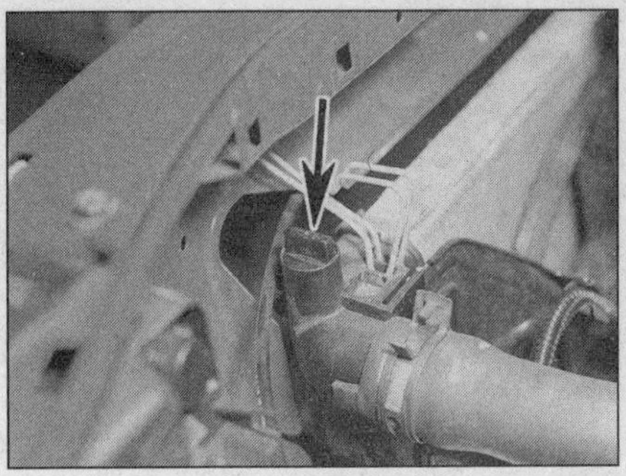

25.4b . . . the radiator . . .

3 Loosen the drain plug (there is no need to remove it completely) and allow the coolant to drain into the container.

4 To assist draining, open the cooling system bleed screws. These are located in the coolant gallery/heater hose (as applicable) at the right-hand side of the engine compartment, in the thermostat housing, and in the top left-hand side of the radiator **(see illustrations)**.

Caution: When refilling the engine with coolant, it's important to make sure that all the trapped air is allowed to escape, by 'bleeding' , as described in the text. Air trapped in the cooling system could cause overheating problems later, which will quickly lead to expensive engine damage.

5 When the flow of coolant stops, reposition the container below the cylinder block drain plug, located at the front left-hand corner of the cylinder block **(see illustration)**.

6 Remove the drain plug, and allow the coolant to drain into the container.

7 If the coolant has been drained for a reason other than renewal, then provided it is clean and less than two years old, it can be re-used, though this is not recommended.

8 Refit the radiator and cylinder block drain plugs on completion of draining.

Cooling system flushing

9 If coolant renewal has been neglected, or if the antifreeze mixture has become diluted, then in time, the cooling system may gradually lose efficiency, as the coolant passages become restricted due to rust, scale deposits, and other sediment. The cooling system efficiency can be restored by flushing the system clean.

10 The radiator should be flushed independently of the engine, to avoid unnecessary contamination.

Radiator flushing

11 To flush the radiator, first tighten the radiator drain plug, and the radiator bleed screw, where applicable.

12 Disconnect the top and bottom hoses from the radiator, with reference to Chapter 3.

13 Insert a garden hose into the radiator top inlet. Direct a flow of clean water through the radiator, and continue flushing until clean water emerges from the radiator bottom outlet.

14 If after a reasonable period, the water still does not run clear, the radiator can be flushed with a good proprietary cleaning agent. It is important that their manufacturer's instructions are followed carefully. If the contamination is particularly bad, insert the hose in the radiator bottom outlet, and reverse-flush the radiator.

Engine flushing

15 To flush the engine, first refit the cylinder block drain plug, and tighten the cooling system bleed screws.

16 Remove the thermostat as described in Chapter 3, then temporarily refit the thermostat cover.

17 With the top and bottom hoses disconnected from the radiator, insert a garden hose into the radiator top hose. Direct a clean flow of water through the engine, and continue flushing until clean water emerges from the radiator bottom hose.

18 On completion of flushing, refit the thermostat and reconnect the hoses with reference to Chapter 3.

Cooling system filling

19 Before attempting to fill the cooling system, make sure that all hoses and clips are in good condition, and that the clips are tight. Note that an antifreeze mixture must be used all year round, to prevent corrosion of the engine components (see following sub-Section). Also check that the radiator and cylinder block drain plugs are in place and tight.

20 Remove the expansion tank filler cap.

21 Open all the cooling system bleed screws (see paragraph 4) **(see illustration)**.

22 Some of the cooling system hoses are positioned at a higher level than the top of the radiator expansion tank. It is therefore necessary to use a "header tank" when refilling the cooling system, to reduce the possibility of air being trapped in the system.

TOOL TiP ***Although Citroën dealers use a special header tank, the same effect can be achieved by using a suitable bottle, with a rubber water-tight seal between the bottle and the expansion tank neck.***

1A

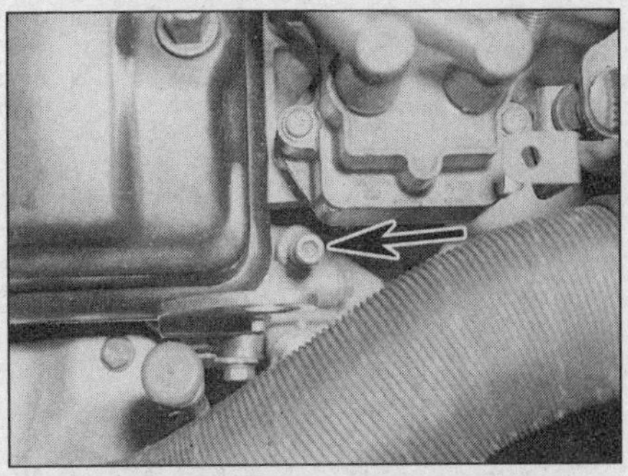

25.4c . . . and the thermostat housing

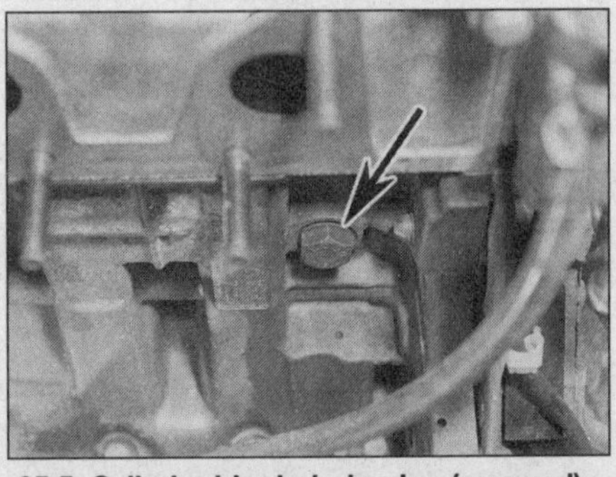

25.5 Cylinder block drain plug (arrowed) - 1.1 litre model shown with inlet manifold removed for clarity

25.21 Opening the thermostat housing bleed screw

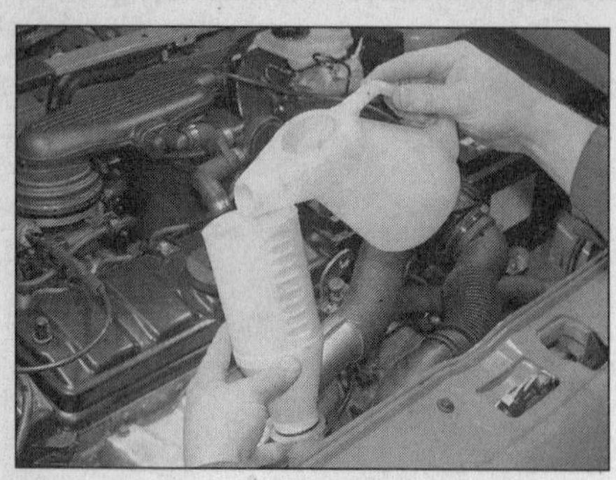

25.23 Fill the cooling system using a home made header tank (see text)

25.25 Refit the cooling system filler cap securely

23 Fit the "header tank" to the expansion tank, then slowly fill the cooling system **(see illustration)**. Coolant will emerge from each of the bleed screws in turn, starting with the lowest screw. As soon as coolant free from air bubbles emerges from the lowest screw, tighten that screw, and watch the next bleed screw in the system. Repeat the procedure until the coolant is emerging from the highest bleed screw in the cooling system and all bleed screws are securely tightened. Note that the bleed screws should be tightened in the following order:

a) Radiator bleed screw..
b) Thermostat housing bleed screw.
c) Coolant gallery or heater hose bleed screw.

24 Ensure that the "header tank" is full (at least 0.5 litres of coolant). Start the engine, and run it at a fast idle speed (do not exceed 2000 rpm) until the cooling fan cuts in and out again three times. Stop the engine.

25 Remove the "header tank", taking great care not to scald yourself with the hot coolant, then fit the expansion tank cap **(see illustration)**.

26 Allow the engine to cool, then check the coolant level with reference to "*Weekly checks*". Top-up the level if necessary.

Antifreeze mixture

27 The antifreeze should always be renewed at the specified intervals. This is necessary not only to maintain the antifreezing properties, but also to prevent corrosion which would otherwise occur as the corrosion inhibitors become progressively less effective.

28 Always use an ethylene-glycol based antifreeze which is suitable for use in mixed-metal cooling systems. The quantity of antifreeze and levels of protection are indicated in the Specifications.

29 Before adding antifreeze, the cooling system should be completely drained, preferably flushed, and all hoses checked for condition and security.

30 After filling with antifreeze, a label should be attached to the expansion tank, stating the type and concentration of antifreeze used, and the date installed. Any subsequent topping-up should be made with the same type and concentration of antifreeze.

31 Do not use engine antifreeze in the windscreen/tailgate washer system, as it will cause damage to the vehicle's paintwork and washer system components.

Every year, regardless of mileage

26 Exhaust gas emissions check

1 The air:fuel mixture is controlled directly by the engine management system (refer to the relevant Part of Chapter 4 for greater detail). As a result, the idle exhaust gas CO content is not manually adjustable, without the aid of special test equipment.

2 However, experienced home mechanics equipped with an accurate tachometer and a calibrated exhaust gas analyser should be able to check the exhaust gas CO content, as described in the following sub-Section.

3 If the results of the test show that the CO content is different to that quoted in the Specifications, this indicates a fault within the fuel delivery, engine management or emission control systems (assuming the vehicle is otherwise in good mechanical order).

4 The engine management system wiring harness incorporates a diagnostic socket, which can only be used in conjunction with Citroën dedicated test equipment. The socket allows the engine management system to be electronically 'interrogated' to establish the presence of faults detected by the ECU.

5 Testing the engine management system components individually, with standard workshop equipment, in an attempt to locate the fault by elimination is a time consuming operation that is unlikely to be fruitful (particularly if the fault occurs dynamically). It also carries a high risk of damage to the electronic control unit's internal components.

Exhaust gas CO content check

6 Take the vehicle on a short run to allow it to warm up to normal operating temperature. Allow it to idle and wait until the auxiliary cooling fan has cut in and out again, at least twice, before proceeding.

7 Switch on the CO meter and allow it to warm up and stabilise, in accordance with the manufacturers instructions.

8 Insert the CO meter probe into the exhaust tailpipe. Connect a calibrated tachometer to the engine, again in accordance with the manufacturers instructions.

9 Check (and if necessary, adjust) the engine idle speed, with reference to Chapter 4A.

10 Ensure that all electrical and mechanical loads (such as headlights, heater blower motor, air conditioning) are switched off.

11 Raise the engine speed and maintain it at 2500-3000 rpm for at least two minutes. If the auxiliary cooling fan cuts in, wait until it cuts out again.

12 Check the reading on the CO meter, when the display has stabilised.

13 Repeat the test procedure to obtain an average figure, then compare your result with the figure given in the Specifications.

Every 10 years, regardless of mileage

27 Air bag and seat belt tensioners renewal

Due to safety critical nature of the air bag and seat belt tensioner components, these operations must be carried out by a Citroën dealer.

Chapter 1 Part B:
Routine maintenance & servicing - diesel models

Contents

Degrees of difficulty

Easy, suitable for novice with little experience	**Fairly easy,** suitable for beginner with some experience	**Fairly difficult,** suitable for competent DIY mechanic	**Difficult,** suitable for experienced DIY mechanic	**Very difficult,** suitable for expert DIY or professional

Lubricants and fluids

Refer to end *"Weekly checks"*

Capacities

Engine oil (with filter change)	
All models	4.75 litres
Between dipstick 'MAX' and 'MIN' markings	2.0 litres
Cooling system	
All models	7.1 litres
Manual transmission	
All models	2.0 litres
Braking system	
Without ABS	0.45 litres
With ABS	0.36 litres
Fuel tank	
All models	45 litres
Screen wash	
All models	2.8 litres

Engine

Auxiliary drivebelt tension:	
Without air conditioning	117 to 123 SEEM units
With air conditioning	117 to 123 SEEM units

Cooling system

Antifreeze mixture:*	
50% antifreeze	Protection down to -37°C
55% antifreeze	Protection down to -45°C

***Note:** *Refer to antifreeze manufacturer for latest recommendations.*

Fuel system

Idle speed	800 ± 25 rpm

Brakes

Front/rear brake pad friction material minimum thickness	2.0 mm
Brake shoe friction material minimum thickness	1.0 mm

Tyre pressures

Refer to the end of *"Weekly checks"*

Torque wrench settings

	Nm	lbf ft
Auxiliary drivebelt tensioner assembly retaining bolts	25	18
Glow plugs	25	18
Manual transmission filler/level and drain plugs	25	18
Roadwheel bolts	85	63
Sump drain plug	30	22

The maintenance intervals in this manual are provided with the assumption that you, not the dealer, will be carrying out the work. These are the minimum maintenance intervals recommended by us for vehicles driven daily. If you wish to keep your vehicle in peak condition at all times, you may wish to perform some of these procedures more often. We encourage frequent maintenance, because it enhances the efficiency, performance and resale value of your vehicle.

When the vehicle is new, it should be serviced by a factory-authorised dealer service department, in order to preserve the factory warranty.

Weekly, or every 250 miles (400 km)

☐ Refer to "*Weekly checks*"

Every 6000 miles (10 000 km) or 12 months - whichever comes first

In addition to all the items listed above, carry out the following:

☐ Engine oil and filter renewal (Section 3)*
☐ Clutch pedal operation check (Section 4)
☐ Underbonnet and underbody component/hose fluid leak check (Section 5)
☐ Steering and suspension condition and security check (Section 6)
☐ Driveshaft rubber gaiter condition check (Section 7)
☐ Hinges and locks lubrication (Section 8)
☐ Front brake pad wear check (Section 9)
☐ Road test (Section 10)

***Note:** Citroën state that from 1998 model-year onwards, the engine oil renewal interval can be extended, provided that either semi-synthetic or fully synthetic engine oil is used. No more information was available at the time of writing - refer to your Citroën dealer for further details.*

Every 12 000 miles (20 000 km)

In addition to all the items listed above, carry out the following:

☐ Drain water from the fuel filter (Section 11)
☐ Renew the pollen filter (where fitted) (Section 12)
☐ Carry out an exhaust smoke test (Section 13)
☐ Handbrake operation check (Section 14)

Every 18 000 miles (30 000 km)

In addition to all the items listed above, carry out the following:

☐ Fuel filter renewal (Section 15)

Every 36 000 miles (60 000 km)

In addition to all the items listed above, carry out the following:

☐ Manual transmission oil level check (Section 16)
☐ Renew the air filter (Section 17)
☐ Rear brake shoe wear check (Section 18)
☐ Braking system condition check (Section 19)
☐ Auxiliary drivebelt condition check and renewal (Section 20)

Every 36 000 miles (60 000 km) or 2 years, whichever comes sooner

In addition to all the items listed above, carry out the following:

☐ Brake fluid renewal (Section 21)

Every 72 000 miles (120 000 km)

In addition to all the items listed above, carry out the following:

☐ Timing belt renewal (Section 22)

Note: *It is strongly recommended that the timing belt renewal interval is halved to 36 000 miles (60 000 km) on vehicles which are subjected to intensive use, i.e. mainly short journeys or a lot of stop-start driving. The actual belt renewal interval is therefore very much up to the individual owner, but bear in mind that severe engine damage will result if the belt breaks.*

Every 72 000 miles (120 000 km) or 2 years, whichever comes sooner

In addition to all the items listed above, carry out the following:

☐ Coolant renewal (Section 23)

Every 10 years, regardless of mileage

☐ Renew air bag and seat belt tensioners (Section 24)

Underbonnet view

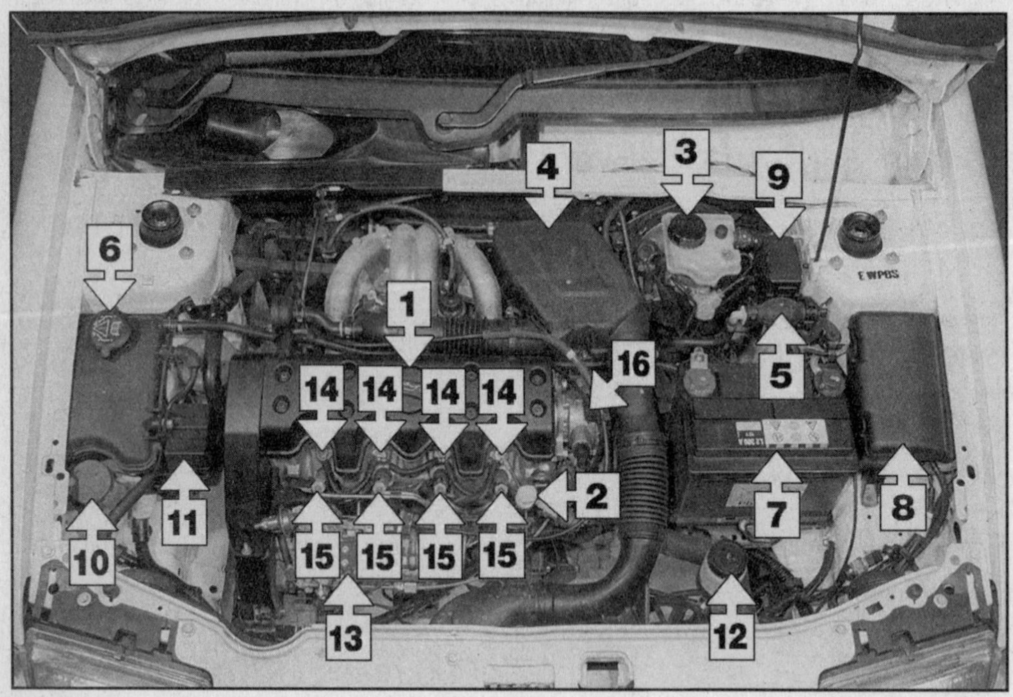

1. *Engine oil filler cap*
2. *Engine oil dipstick*
3. *Brake fluid reservoir*
4. *Air filter housing*
5. *Fuel system priming bulb*
6. *Coolant expansion tank filler cap*
7. *Battery*
8. *Main fuse/relay box*
9. *Fusible link box*
10. *Windscreen washer fluid reservoir filler cap*
11. *Glow plug control module*
12. *Power steering fluid reservoir*
13. *Fuel injection pump*
14. *Glow plugs*
15. *Fuel injectors*
16. *Vacuum pump*

Front underbody view

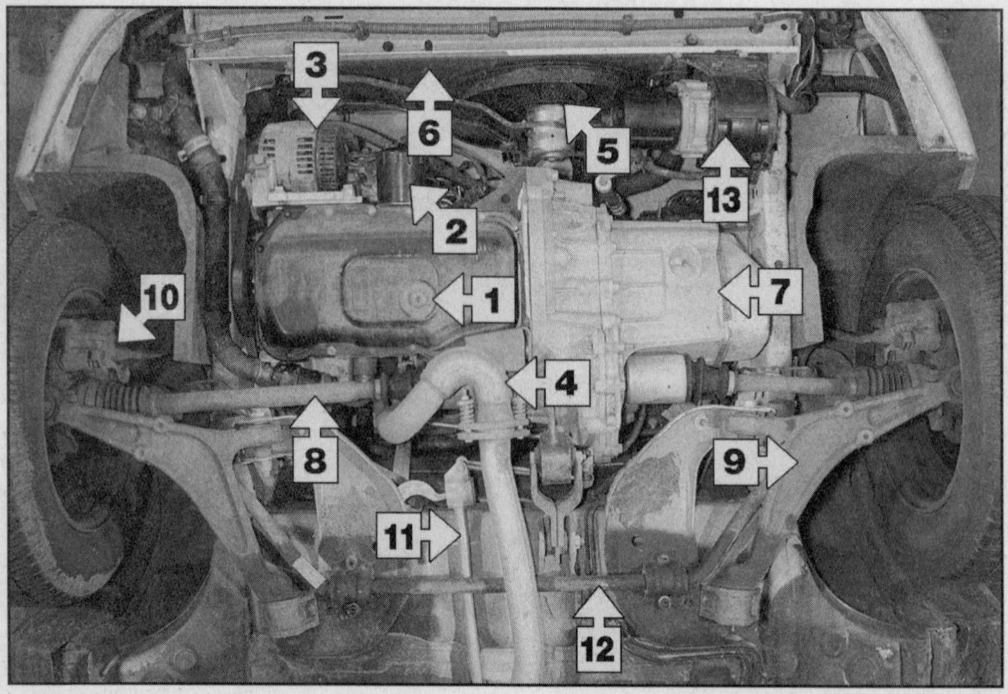

1. *Engine oil drain plug*
2. *Engine oil filter*
3. *Alternator*
4. *Exhaust front pipe*
5. *Radiator cooling fan*
6. *Radiator*
7. *Manual transmission*
8. *Driveshaft*
9. *Suspension lower arm*
10. *Brake caliper*
11. *Gearchange selector rod*
12. *Anti-roll bar*
13. *Power steering pump*

Rear underbody view (petrol model shown, diesel model similar)

1 *Handbrake cable*
2 *Heat shield*
3 *Fuel filter**
4 *Exhaust tailbox*
5 *Suspension shock absorber*
6 *Rear drum brake backplate*
7 *Fuel tank filler pipe*
8 *Fuel tank*
9 *Rear suspension beam axle*
10 *Rear torsion bar*
11 *Front torsion bar*
12 *Rear suspension arm*

** Not in this location on diesel models*

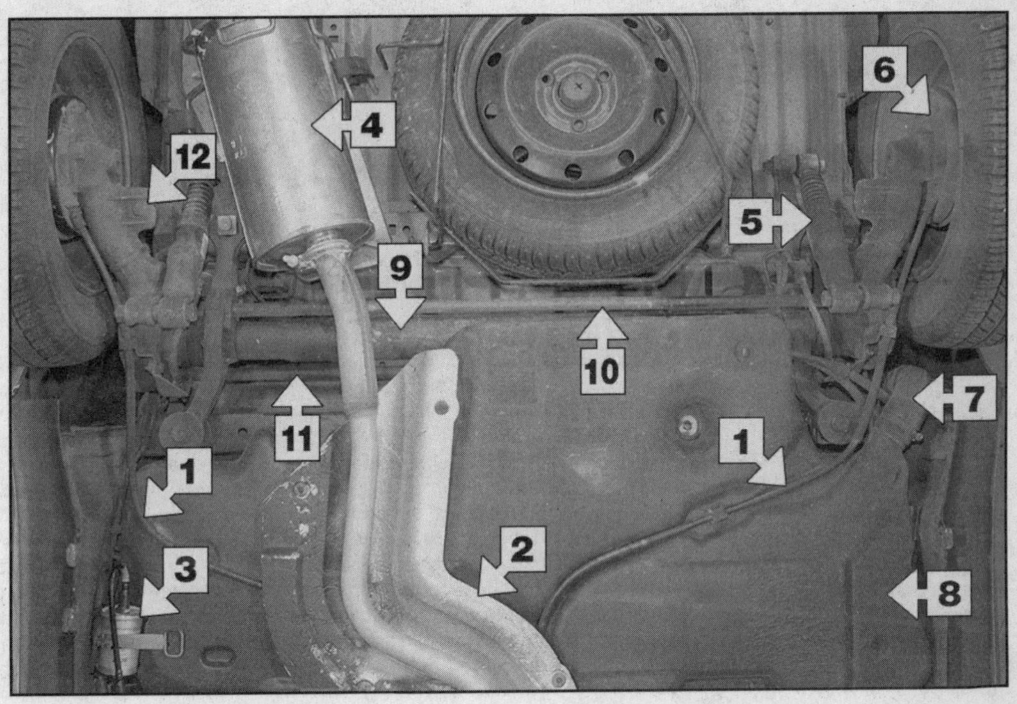

1 General information

This Chapter is designed to help the home mechanic maintain his/her vehicle for safety, economy, long life and peak performance.

The Chapter contains a master maintenance schedule, followed by Sections dealing specifically with each task in the schedule. Visual checks, adjustments, component renewal and other helpful items are included. Refer to the accompanying illustrations of the engine compartment and the underside of the vehicle for the locations of the various components.

Servicing your vehicle in accordance with the mileage/time maintenance schedule and the following Sections will provide a planned maintenance programme, which should result in a long and reliable service life. This is a comprehensive plan, so maintaining some items but not others at the specified service intervals, will not produce the same results.

As you service your vehicle, you will discover that many of the procedures can - and should - be grouped together, because of the particular procedure being performed, or because of the proximity of two otherwise-unrelated components to one another. For example, if the vehicle is raised for any reason, the exhaust can be inspected at the same time as the suspension and steering components.

The first step in this maintenance programme is to prepare yourself before the actual work begins. Read through all the Sections relevant to the work to be carried out, then make a list and gather all the parts and tools required. If a problem is encountered, seek advice from a parts specialist, or a dealer service department.

2 Intensive maintenance

1 If, from the time the vehicle is new, the routine maintenance schedule is followed closely, and frequent checks are made of fluid levels and high-wear items, as suggested throughout this manual, the engine will be kept in relatively good running condition, and the need for additional work will be minimised.

2 It is possible that there will be times when the engine is running poorly due to the lack of regular maintenance. This is even more likely if a used vehicle, which has not received regular and frequent maintenance checks, is purchased. In such cases, additional work may need to be carried out, outside of the regular maintenance intervals.

3 If engine wear is suspected, a compression test (refer to Chapter 2B) will provide valuable information regarding the overall performance of the main internal components. Such a test can be used as a basis to decide on the extent of the work to be carried out. If, for example, a compression test indicates serious internal engine wear, conventional maintenance as described in this Chapter will not greatly improve the performance of the engine, and may prove a waste of time and money, unless extensive overhaul work is carried out first.

4 The following series of operations are those most often required to improve the performance of a generally poor-running engine:

Primary operations

a) Clean, inspect and test the battery (refer to "Weekly checks").
b) Check all the engine-related fluids (refer to "Weekly checks").
c) Check the condition and tension of the auxiliary drivebelt (Section 20).
d) Check the condition of the air filter, and renew if necessary (Section 17).
e) Check the condition of all hoses, and check for fluid leaks (Section 5).
f) Renew the fuel filter (Section 15).

5 If the above operations do not prove fully effective, carry out the following secondary operations:

Secondary operations

All items listed under "Primary operations", plus the following:

a) Check the charging system (refer to Chapter 5A).
b) Check the preheating system (refer to Chapter 5C).
c) Check the fuel system (refer to Chapter 4C).

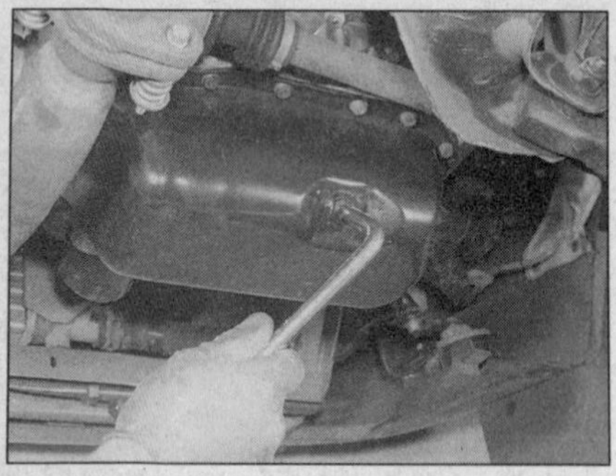

3.3a Slacken the drain plug using a square-section wrench . . .

3.3b . . . then remove the plug and allow the oil to run into the draining container

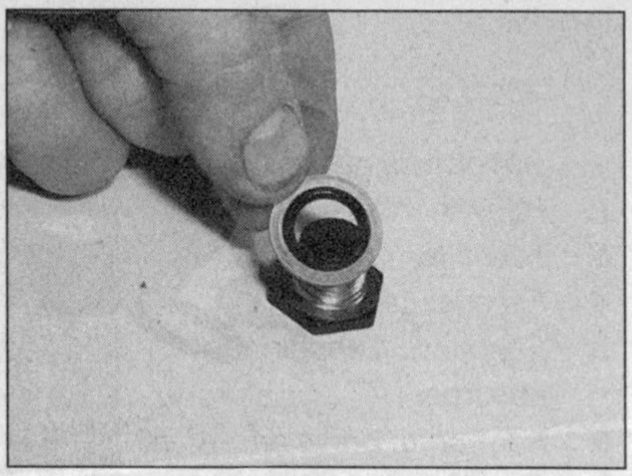

3.5 Fit a new sealing washer to the drain plug

Every 6000 miles (10 000 km) or 12 months

3 Engine oil and filter renewal

Note: *Frequent oil and filter changes are good for the engine. We recommend changing the oil at the mileage specified here, or at least twice a year if the mileage covered is less.*

Note: *A suitable square-section wrench may be required to undo the sump drain plug on some models. These wrenches can be obtained from most motor factors or your Citroën dealer.*

HAYNES HiNT ***Frequent oil and filter changes are the most important preventative maintenance procedures which can be undertaken by the DIY owner. As engine oil ages, it becomes diluted and contaminated, which leads to premature engine wear.***

1 Before starting this procedure, gather together all the necessary tools and materials. Also make sure that you have plenty of clean rags and newspapers handy, to mop up any spills. Ideally, the engine oil should be warm, as it will drain better, and more built-up sludge will be removed with it. Take care, however, not to touch the exhaust or any other hot parts of the engine when working under the vehicle. To avoid any possibility of scalding, and to protect yourself from possible skin irritants and other harmful contaminants in used engine oils, it is advisable to wear gloves, or at least apply a good quality barrier hand cream, when carrying out this work.

2 Access to the underside of the vehicle will be greatly improved if it can be raised on a lift, driven onto ramps, or jacked up and supported on axle stands (see "*Jacking and vehicle support*"). Whichever method is chosen, make sure that the vehicle remains level, or if it is at an angle, that the drain plug is at the lowest point.

3 Slacken the drain plug about half a turn; on some models, a square-section wrench may be needed to slacken the plug **(see illustrations)**. Position the draining container under the drain plug, then remove the plug completely. If possible, try to keep the plug pressed into the sump while unscrewing it by hand the last couple of turns. As the plug releases from the threads, move it away sharply so the stream of oil issuing from the sump runs into the container, not up your sleeve! Recover the sealing ring from the drain plug.

4 Allow some time for the old oil to drain, noting that it may be necessary to reposition the container as the oil flow slows to a trickle.

5 After all the oil has drained, wipe off the drain plug with a clean rag, and fit a new sealing washer **(see illustration)**. Clean the area around the drain plug opening, and refit the plug. Tighten the plug securely.

6 If the filter is also to be renewed, move the container into position under the oil filter, which is located on the front side of the cylinder block, below the inlet manifold.

7 Using an oil filter removal tool if necessary, slacken the filter initially, then unscrew it by hand the rest of the way **(see illustrations)**. Empty any oil that remains inside the old filter into the container.

8 Use a clean rag to remove all oil, dirt and sludge from the filter sealing area on the engine. Check the old filter to make sure that the rubber sealing ring hasn't stuck to the engine. If it has, carefully remove it.

9 Apply a light coating of clean engine oil to the sealing ring on the new filter, then screw it into position on the engine **(see illustration)**. Tighten the filter firmly by hand only - **do not** use any tools.

10 Remove the old oil and all tools from under the car then lower the car to the ground (if applicable).

11 Remove the dipstick, then unscrew the oil filler cap from the cylinder head cover. Fill the engine, using the correct grade and type of oil (see *"Lubricants and fluids"*). An oil can spout or funnel may help to reduce spillage. Pour in half the specified quantity of oil first, then wait a few minutes for the oil to fall to the sump.

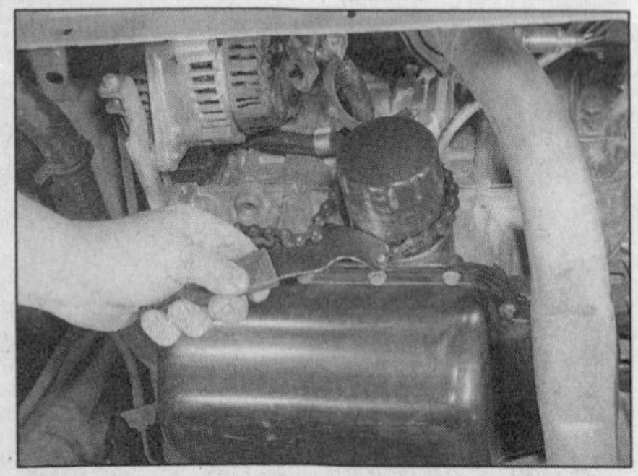

3.7a Slacken the oil filter using a removal tool . . .

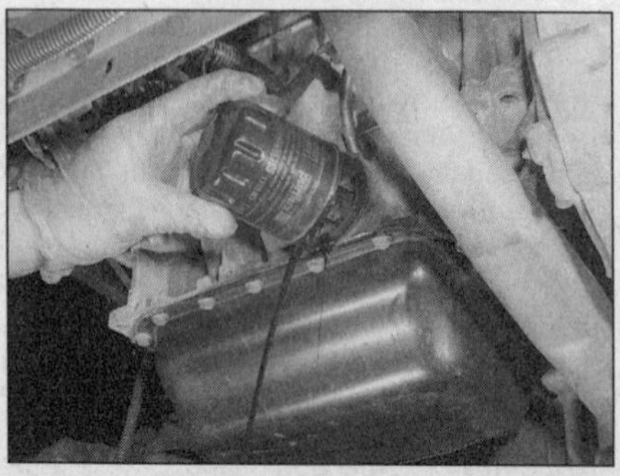

3.7b . . . then unscrew it from the engine by hand

3.9 Apply a light coating of clean engine oil to the sealing ring on the new filter

3.11a Remove the dipstick . . .

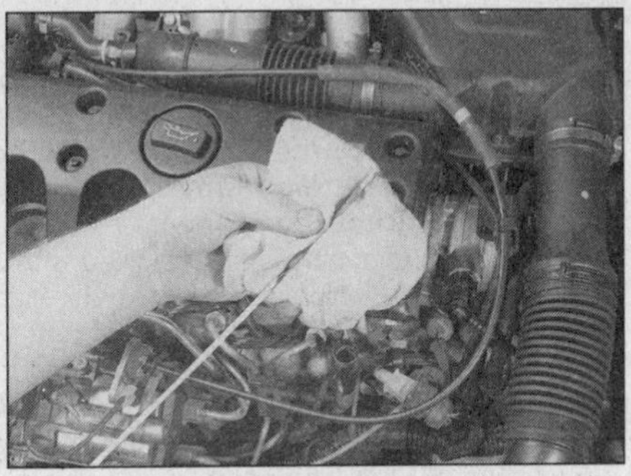

3.11b . . . and wipe it clean . . .

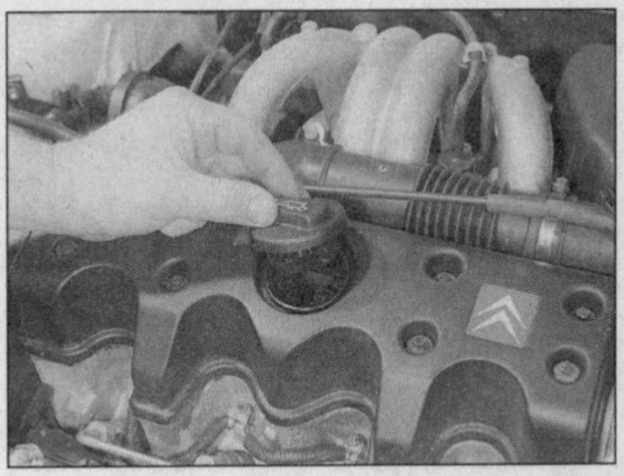

3.11c . . . then unscrew the oil filler cap from the cylinder head cover

Continue adding oil a small quantity at a time until the level is up to (but **not** above) the upper mark on the dipstick. Refit the filler cap **(see illustrations)**.

12 Start the engine and allow it to idle for a few minutes - do not 'rev' the engine. Check for leaks around the oil filter seal and the sump drain plug. Note that there may be a delay of a few seconds before the oil pressure warning light goes out when the engine is first started, as the oil circulates through the engine oil galleries and the new oil filter (where fitted) before the pressure builds up.

13 Switch off the engine, and wait a few minutes for the oil to settle in the sump once more. With the new oil circulated and the filter completely full, recheck the level on the dipstick, and add more oil as necessary.

14 Dispose of the used engine oil safely, with reference to *"General repair procedures"* in the Reference Section of this manual.

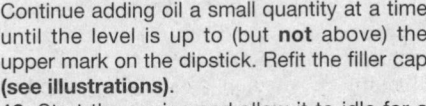

4 Clutch pedal operation check

Refer to the information given in Chapter 6.

5 Underbonnet/underbody component/hose fluid leak check

Warning: Refer to the safety information given in "Safety First" and Chapter 3 before disturbing any of the cooling system components.

1 Carefully check the radiator and heater coolant hoses along their entire length. Renew any hose which is cracked, swollen or which shows signs of deterioration. Cracks will show up better if the hose is squeezed. Pay close attention to the clips that secure the hoses to the cooling system components. Hose clips that have been over-tightened can pinch and puncture hoses, resulting in cooling system leaks.

2 Inspect all the cooling system components (hoses, joint faces etc.) for leaks. Where any problems of this nature are found on system components, renew the component or gasket with reference to Chapter 3 **(see Haynes Hint)**.

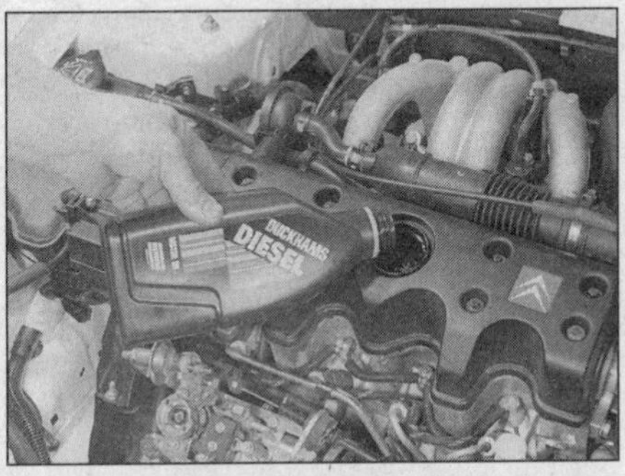

3.11d Fill the engine, using the correct grade and type of oil

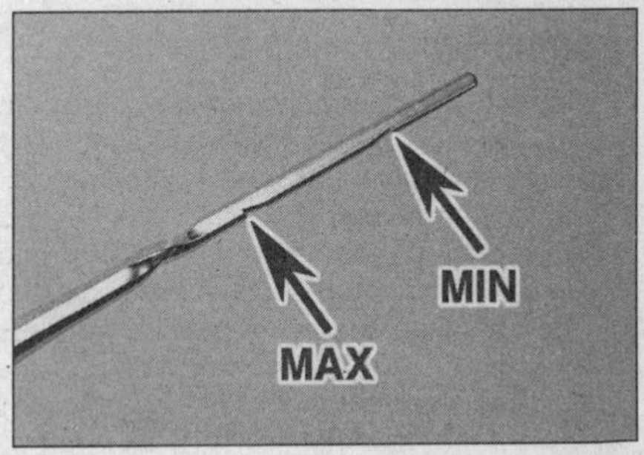

3.11e Continue adding oil until the level is up to (but *not* above) the 'MAX' mark on the dipstick

Fuel

Warning: Refer to the safety information given in "Safety First" and Chapter 4 before disturbing any of the fuel system components.

3 Unlike petrol leaks, diesel leaks are fairly easy to pinpoint; diesel fuel tends to settle on the surface around the point of leakage collecting dirt, rather than evaporate. If you suspect that there is a fuel leak from the area of the engine bay, leave the vehicle overnight then start the engine from cold, and allow it to idle with the bonnet open. Metal components tend to shrink when they are cold, and rubber seals and hoses tend to harden, so any leaks may be more apparent whilst the engine is warming up from a cold start.

4 Check all fuel lines at their connections to the fuel injection pump and fuel filter. Examine each rubber fuel hose along its length for splits or cracks. Check for leakage from the crimped joints between rubber and metal fuel lines. Examine the unions between the metal fuel lines and the fuel filter housing. Also check the area around the fuel injectors for signs of leakage.

5 To identify fuel leaks between the fuel tank and the engine bay, the vehicle should be raised and securely supported on axle stands (see "*Jacking and vehicle support*"). Inspect the fuel tank and filler neck for punctures, cracks and other damage. The connection between the filler neck and tank is especially critical. Sometimes a rubber filler neck or connecting hose will leak due to loose retaining clamps or deteriorated rubber.

6 Carefully check all rubber hoses and metal fuel lines leading away from the fuel tank. Check for loose connections, deteriorated hoses, kinked lines, and other damage. Pay particular attention to the vent pipes and hoses, which often loop up around the filler neck and can become blocked or kinked, making tank filling difficult. Follow the fuel supply and return lines to the front of the vehicle, carefully inspecting them all the way for signs of damage or corrosion. Renew damaged sections as necessary.

1B

HAYNES HiNT

A leak in the cooling system will usually manifest itself as white or rust-coloured, crusty deposits on the area adjacent to the leak

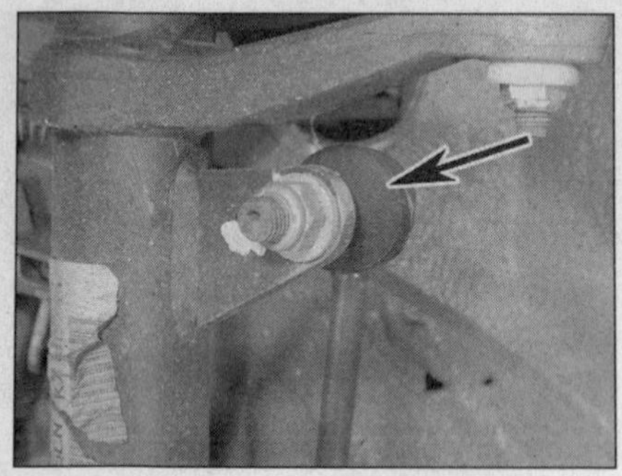

6.2 Visually inspect all balljoint dust covers for signs of deterioration

Engine oil

7 Inspect the area around the camshaft cover, cylinder head, oil filter and sump joint faces. Bear in mind that, over a period of time, some very slight seepage from these areas is to be expected - what you are really looking for is any indication of a serious leak caused by gasket failure. Engine oil seeping from the base of the timing belt cover or the transmission bellhousing may be an indication of crankshaft or transmission input shaft oil seal failure. Should a leak be found, renew the failed gasket or oil seal by referring to the appropriate Chapters in this manual.

Power assisted steering (PAS) fluid

8 Examine the hose running between the fluid reservoir and the power steering pump, and the return hose running from the steering rack to the fluid reservoir. Also examine the high pressure supply hose between the pump and the steering rack.
9 Where applicable, check the hoses leading to the PAS fluid cooler at the front of the engine bay. Look for deterioration caused by corrosion and damage from grounding, or debris thrown up from the road surface.
10 Pay particular attention to crimped unions, and the area surrounding the hoses that are secured with adjustable worm drive clips. Like automatic transmission fluid, PAS fluid is a thin oil, and is usually red in colour.

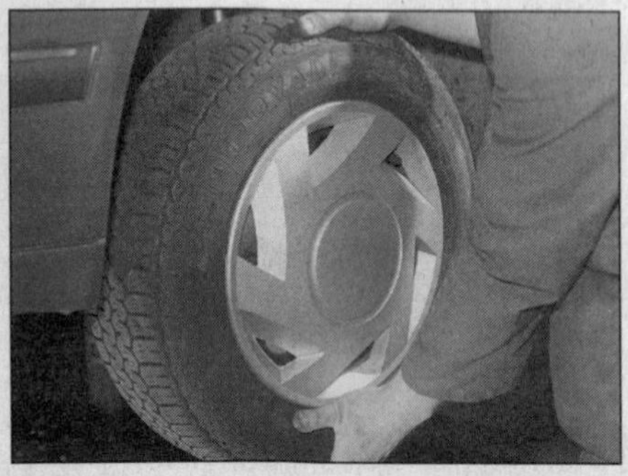

6.4 Check for wear in the hub bearings by trying to 'rock' the wheel

Air conditioning refrigerant

Warning: Refer to the safety information given in "Safety First" and Chapter 3, regarding the dangers of disturbing any of the air conditioning system components.

11 The air conditioning system is filled with a liquid refrigerant, which is retained under high pressure. If the air conditioning system is opened and depressurised without the aid of specialised equipment, the refrigerant will immediately turn into gas and escape into the atmosphere. If the liquid comes into contact with your skin, it can cause severe frostbite. In addition, the refrigerant contains substances which are environmentally damaging; for this reason, it should not be allowed to escape into the atmosphere.
12 Any suspected air conditioning system leaks should be immediately referred to a Citroën dealer or air conditioning specialist. Leakage will be shown up as a steady drop in the level of refrigerant in the system.
13 Note that water may drip from the condenser drain pipe, underneath the car, immediately after the air conditioning system has been in use. This is normal, and should not be cause for concern.

Brake fluid

Warning: Refer to the safety information given in "Safety First" and Chapter 9, regarding the dangers of handling brake fluid.

14 With reference to Chapter 9, examine the area surrounding the brake pipe unions at the master cylinder for signs of leakage. Check the area around the base of fluid reservoir, for signs of leakage caused by seal failure. Also examine the brake pipe unions at the ABS hydraulic unit.
15 If fluid loss is evident, but the leak cannot be pinpointed in the engine bay, the brake calipers and underbody brake lines should be carefully checked with the vehicle raised and supported on axle stands (see "*Jacking and vehicle support*"). Leakage of fluid from the braking system is a serious fault that must be rectified immediately.
16 Brake/clutch hydraulic fluid is a toxic substance with a watery consistency. New fluid is almost colourless, but it becomes darker with age and use.

Unidentified fluid leaks

17 If there are signs that a fluid of some description is leaking from the vehicle, but you cannot identify the type of fluid or its exact origin, park the vehicle overnight and slide a large piece of card underneath it. Providing that the card is positioned in roughly the right location, even the smallest leak will show up on the card. Not only will this help you to pinpoint the exact location of the leak, it should be easier to identify the fluid from its colour. Bear in mind, though, that the leak may only be occurring when the engine is running!

Vacuum hoses

18 Although the braking system is hydraulically-operated, the brake servo unit amplifies the effort applied at the brake pedal, by making use of the vacuum generated by the engine-driven vacuum pump. Vacuum is ported to the servo by means of a large-bore hose. Any leaks that develop in this hose will seriously reduce the effectiveness of the braking system.
19 In addition, a number of the underbonnet components, particularly the emission control components, are driven by vacuum supplied from the inlet manifold via narrow-bore hoses. A leak in a vacuum hose means that air is being drawn into the hose (rather than escaping from it) and this makes leakage very difficult to detect. One method is to use an old length of vacuum hose as a kind of stethoscope - hold one end close to (but not in!) your ear and use the other end to probe the area around the suspected leak. When the end of the hose is directly over a vacuum leak, a hissing sound will be heard clearly through the hose. Care must be taken to avoid contacting hot or moving components, as the engine must be running, when testing in this manner. Renew any vacuum hoses that are found to be defective.

6 Steering and suspension condition and security check

Front suspension and steering check

1 Raise the front of the vehicle, and securely support it on axle stands (see "*Jacking and vehicle support*").
2 Visually inspect the balljoint dust covers and the steering rack-and-pinion gaiters for splits, chafing or deterioration **(see illustration)**. Any wear of these components will cause loss of lubricant, together with dirt and water entry, resulting in rapid deterioration of the balljoints or steering gear.
3 Check the power steering fluid hoses for chafing or deterioration, and the pipe and hose unions for fluid leaks. Also check for signs of fluid leakage under pressure from the steering gear rubber gaiters, which would indicate failed fluid seals within the steering gear.
4 Grasp the roadwheel at the 12 o'clock and 6 o'clock positions, and try to rock it **(see illustration)**. Very slight free play may be felt, but if the movement is appreciable, further investigation will be necessary to determine the source. Continue rocking the wheel while an assistant depresses the footbrake. If the movement is now eliminated or significantly reduced, it is likely that the hub bearings are at fault. If the free play is still evident with the footbrake depressed, then there is wear in the suspension joints or mountings.

5 Now grasp the wheel at the 9 o'clock and 3 o'clock positions, and try to rock it as before. Any movement felt now may again be caused by wear in the hub bearings or the steering track-rod balljoints. If the inner or outer balljoint is worn, the visual movement will be obvious.

6 Using a large screwdriver or flat bar, check for wear in the suspension mounting bushes by levering between the relevant suspension component and its attachment point. Some movement is to be expected as the mountings are made of rubber, but excessive wear should be obvious. Also check the condition of any visible rubber bushes, looking for splits, cracks or contamination of the rubber **(see illustration)**.

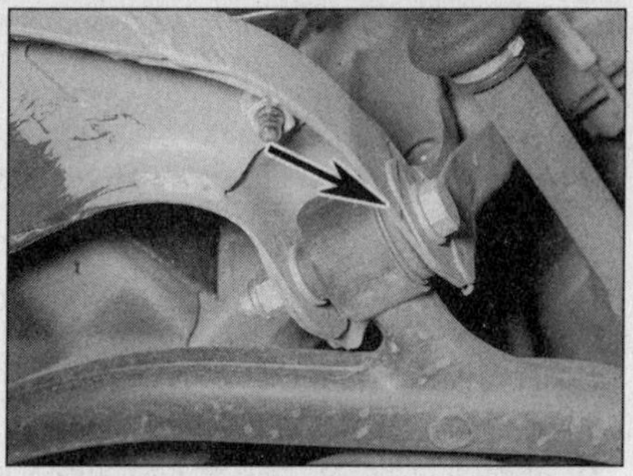

6.6 Check the condition of all visible rubber bushes

7 With the car standing on its wheels, have an assistant turn the steering wheel back and forth about an eighth of a turn each way. There should be very little, if any, lost movement between the steering wheel and roadwheels. If this is not the case, closely observe the joints and mountings previously described, but in addition, check the steering column universal joints for wear, and the rack-and-pinion steering gear itself.

Suspension strut/shock absorber check

8 Check for any signs of fluid leakage around the suspension strut/shock absorber body, or from the rubber gaiter around the piston rod. Should any fluid be noticed, the suspension strut/shock absorber is defective internally, and should be renewed. **Note:** *Suspension struts/shock absorbers should always be renewed in pairs on the same axle, or the handling of the vehicle will be impaired.*

9 The efficiency of the suspension strut/shock absorber may be checked by bouncing the vehicle at each corner. Generally speaking, the body will return to its normal position and stop after being depressed. If it rises and returns on a rebound, the suspension strut/shock absorber is probably suspect. Examine also the suspension strut/shock absorber upper and lower mountings for any signs of wear.

7 Driveshaft rubber gaiter condition check

1 With the vehicle raised and securely supported on axle stands (see "*Jacking and vehicle support*"), turn the steering to full left or right lock, then slowly rotate the roadwheel. Inspect the outer constant velocity (CV) joint rubber gaiters, squeezing the gaiters to open out the folds **(see illustration)**. Check for signs of cracking, splits or deterioration of the rubber, which may allow the grease to escape, or water and grit to enter. Also check the security and condition of the retaining clips. Repeat these checks on the inner CV joints. If any damage or deterioration is found, the gaiters should be renewed (Chapter 8).

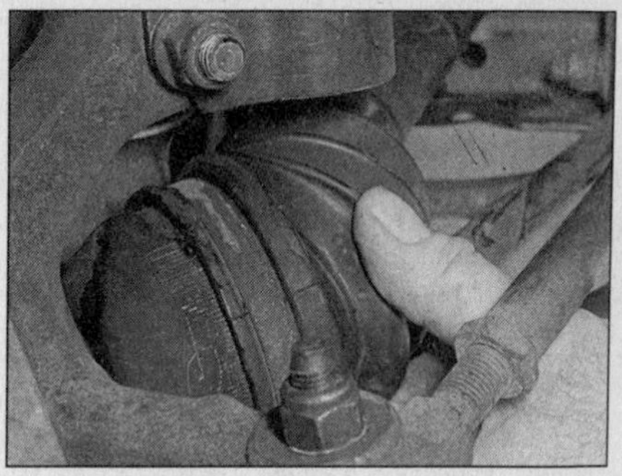

7.1 Inspecting a CV joint rubber gaiter

2 At the same time, check the general condition of the CV joints themselves by first holding the driveshaft and attempting to rotate the wheel. Repeat this check whilst holding the inner joint and attempting to rotate the driveshaft. Any appreciable movement indicates wear in the CV joints, wear in the driveshaft splines, or a loose driveshaft retaining nut.

8 Hinges and locks lubrication

1 Work around the vehicle, and lubricate the hinges of the bonnet, doors and tailgate with a light machine oil.

2 Lightly lubricate the bonnet release mechanism and exposed section of inner cable with a smear of grease.

3 Check carefully the security and operation of all hinges, latches and locks, adjusting them where required. Check the operation of the central locking system (if fitted).

4 Check the condition and operation of the tailgate struts, renewing them if either is leaking or no longer able to support the tailgate securely when raised.

9 Front brake pad wear check

1 Apply the handbrake, then jack up the front of the car and support it securely on axle stands (see "*Jacking and vehicle support*"). Remove the front roadwheels.

2 Clean the brake calipers with proprietary brake cleaning fluid and a stiff brush. Working through the inspection aperture in the front of the caliper, remove all traces of brake dust from the front edge of the brake pads, so that the friction material is visible. The brake pad wear can be assessed by observing the thickness of the friction material remaining on each brake pad. If the thickness of the friction material remaining is less than the specified limit, then the brake pads must be renewed **(see illustration)**.

9.2 The thickness of the friction material is visible through the inspection aperture at the front of the brake caliper

3 For a comprehensive check, the brake pads should be removed and cleaned. The operation of the caliper can then also be checked, and the condition of the brake disc itself can be fully examined on both sides. Refer to Chapter 9 for further information.

4 If any pad's friction material is worn to the specified thickness or less, all four pads must be renewed as a set - do not change individual brake pads, as uneven braking may result.

5 On completion, refit the roadwheels, lower the car to the ground and tighten the roadwheel bolts to the specified torque.

10 Road test

Instruments and electrical equipment

1 Check the operation of all instruments and electrical equipment.

2 Make sure all instruments read correctly, and switch on all electrical equipment in turn, to check that it functions properly.

Steering and suspension

3 Check for any abnormalities in the steering, suspension, handling or road "feel".

4 Drive the vehicle, and check that there are no unusual vibrations or noises.

5 Check that the steering feels positive, with no excessive "sloppiness", or roughness, and check for any suspension noises when cornering and driving over bumps.

Drivetrain

6 Check the performance of the engine, clutch (where applicable), gearbox/transmission and driveshafts.

7 Listen for any unusual noises from the engine, clutch and gearbox/transmission.

8 Make sure that the engine runs smoothly when idling, and that there is no hesitation when accelerating.

9 Check that, where applicable, the clutch action is smooth and progressive, that the drive is taken up smoothly, and that the pedal travel is not excessive. Also listen for any noises when the clutch pedal is depressed.

10 On manual gearbox models, check that all gears can be engaged smoothly without noise, and that the gear lever action is not abnormally vague or "notchy".

11 On automatic transmission models, make sure that all gearchanges occur smoothly, without snatching, and without an increase in engine speed between changes. Check that all the gear positions can be selected with the vehicle at rest. If any problems are found, they should be referred to a Citroën dealer.

Check the operation and performance of the braking system

12 Make sure that the vehicle does not pull to one side when braking, and that the wheels do not lock prematurely when braking hard.

13 Check that there is no vibration through the steering when braking.

14 Check that the handbrake operates correctly without excessive movement of the lever, and that it holds the vehicle stationary on a slope.

15 Test the operation of the brake servo unit as follows. With the engine off, depress the footbrake four or five times to exhaust the vacuum. Hold the brake pedal depressed, then start the engine. As the engine starts, there should be a noticeable "give" in the brake pedal as vacuum builds up. Allow the engine to run for at least two minutes, and then switch it off. If the brake pedal is depressed now, it should be possible to detect a hiss from the servo as the pedal is depressed. After about four or five applications, no further hissing should be heard, and the pedal should feel much harder.

Every 12 000 miles (20 000 km)

11 Drain water from the fuel filter

1 A water drain screw and tube are provided at the base of the fuel filter **(see illustration)**.

2 Place a suitable container beneath the drain tube, and cover the clutch bellhousing.

3 Open the drain screw by turning it anti-clockwise, and allow fuel and water to drain until fuel, free from water, emerges from the end of the tube. Close the drain screw and tighten it securely.

4 Dispose of the drained fuel safely.

5 Start the engine. If difficulty is experienced, bleed the fuel system as described in Chapter 4C.

12 Pollen filter renewal (where fitted)

1 Remove the windscreen wiper arms as described in Chapter 12.

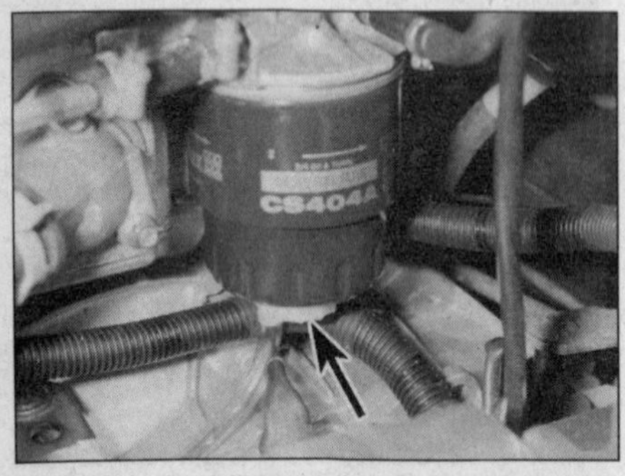

11.1 Fuel filter water drain screw (arrowed) - battery and intake air ducting removed for clarity

2 Access to the pollen filter is gained via the engine compartment; open the bonnet and support it in the upright position.

3 Remove the securing screw and the two nuts, and withdraw the windscreen cowl panel from the scuttle. Note that the panel clips around the edge of the windscreen and the front wings.

4 Remove the securing nuts, and unclip the plastic cover panel from the right-hand end of the scuttle to expose the heater blower motor securing nuts.

5 Release the securing clips and detach the pollen filter housing from its mountings.

6 Fit a new filter element then refit all components removed for access using a reversal of the removal procedure.

13 Exhaust smoke test

Refer to the information given in the *MOT Test Checks* Section, in the *Reference* Chapter. The exhaust smoke test involves measuring the density of the soot particles leaving the exhaust pipe whilst the engine is under free acceleration. It involves the use of special test equipment and hence should be entrusted to a Citroën dealer or diesel fuel injection specialist.

14 Handbrake operation check

1 Park the vehicle on level ground and apply the handbrake, counting the number of notches the lever passes through. If the number is less than four or greater than seven, then the handbrake requires adjustment.

2 Chock the front wheels, release the handbrake, select first gear (or 'P' on models with automatic transmission) then jack up the rear of the vehicle, and support it securely on axle stands (see "*Jacking and vehicle support*").

3 Apply the footbrake firmly several times to establish correct shoe-to-drum clearance, then apply and release the handbrake several times to ensure that the self-adjust mechanism has compensated fully for any wear in the linings.

4 Fully release the handbrake, and check that the rear wheels rotate freely, without binding. If not, check that all cables are routed correctly, and check that the cable components and levers move freely.

HAYNES HiNT ***If the handbrake mechanism fails to operate, or appears to be seized on one side of the vehicle only, remove the relevant brake drum (see Chapter 9) and check the handbrake lever pivot on the trailing brake shoe - it is possible for the lever to seize due to corrosion. If necessary, remove the lever, and clean the contact faces of the lever, brake shoe, and pivot.***

5 If all components are free to move, but the wheels still bind when rotated, then adjustment is required as follows.

6 Again, apply the footbrake several times to settle the shoes. Ensure that the handbrake is fully released.

7 Working under the vehicle, slacken and withdraw the securing screws and slide the exhaust heat shielding towards the front of the vehicle - there is no need to remove it completely. Note that on models with a centre silencer, it will be necessary to unbolt and remove the section of the exhaust system

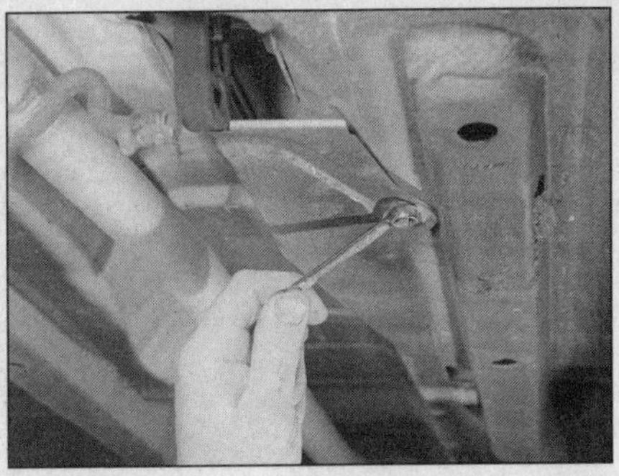

14.7a Slacken and withdraw the securing screws and nuts . . .

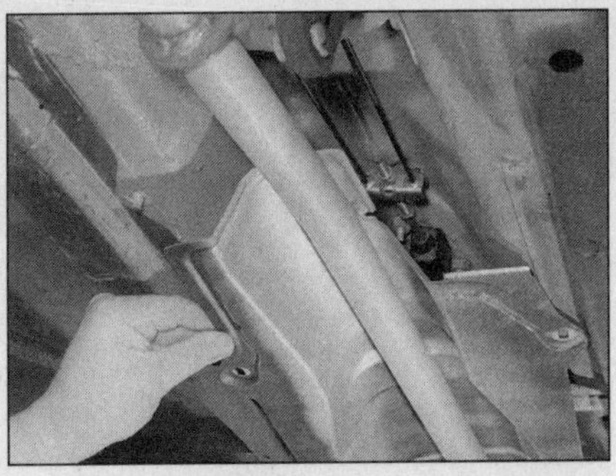

14.7b . . . and slide the exhaust heat shielding towards the front of the vehicle

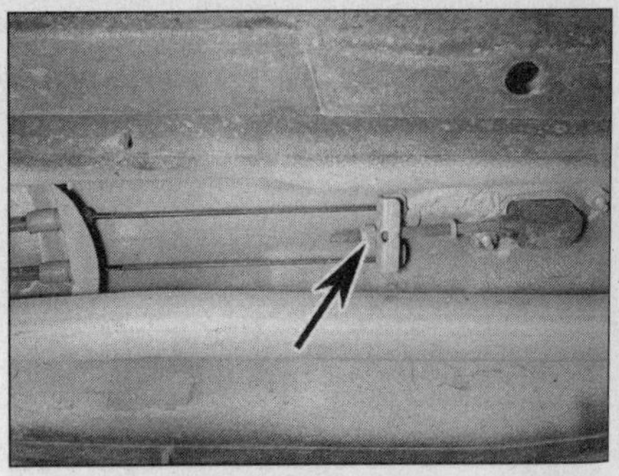

14.8 Slacken the adjuster nut (arrowed) on the handbrake cable equaliser assembly

containing the centre silencer, to gain access to the heatshield screws **(see illustrations)**.

8 Slacken the adjuster nut on the handbrake cable equaliser assembly until the rear wheels are free to rotate **(see illustration)**.

9 Inside the vehicle, apply the handbrake so that the lever is on its 4th notch up from the "off" position.

10 Tighten the adjuster nut until there is slight resistance, as the rear wheels are rotated.

11 Check that there is a total handbrake lever travel of between 4 and 7 notches (the wheels should lock fully after a maximum 7 notches of handbrake lever movement).

12 Check that both the left- and right-hand rear cables move together when the handbrake is operated.

13 Fully release the handbrake, and check that both rear wheels turn freely by hand.

14 Check that the handbrake warning light illuminates from the 4th notch of the handbrake lever travel.

15 On completion, lower the vehicle to the ground.

Every 18 000 miles (30 000 km)

15 Fuel filter renewal

1 The fuel filter is screwed onto the underside of the filter/thermostat housing on the left-hand end of the cylinder head. To improve access to the filter, remove the battery as described in Chapter 5A , and the intake air ducting as described in Chapter 4C.

2 Cover the clutch bellhousing with a piece of plastic sheeting, to protect the clutch from fuel spillage.

3 Position a suitable container under the end of the fuel filter drain hose. Open the drain screw on the base of the filter, and allow the fuel to drain completely.

4 When the filter has drained, close the bleed screw and unscrew the filter using a suitable strap or chain wrench **(see illustration)**.

5 Remove the filter, and dispose of it safely. Ensure that the sealing ring comes away with the filter, and does not stick to the filter/thermostat housing mating surface.

6 Apply a smear of clean diesel to the filter sealing ring, and wipe clean the housing mating surface. Screw the filter on until its sealing ring lightly contacts the housing mating surface, then tighten it through a further three-quarters of a turn.

7 Prime the fuel system as described in Chapter 4C.

8 Open the drain screw until clean fuel flows from the hose, then close the drain screw and withdraw the container from under the hose.

9 Refit the battery, and start the engine. If difficulty is encountered, bleed the fuel system as described in Chapter 4C.

15.4 Using a chain wrench to unscrew the fuel filter

1B

Every 36 000 miles (60 000 km)

16 Manual transmission oil level check

Note: *A suitable square-section wrench, or socket adapter may be required to undo the transmission filler/level plug on some models. These tools can be obtained from most motor factors or your Citroën dealer. A new sealing washer will also be required when refitting the transmission filler/level plug.*

1 The manual transmission oil does not need to be renewed as part of the regular maintenance schedule, but the oil level must be checked and if necessary topped-up at the interval specified here. To drain the transmission as part of a repair procedure, refer to the information given in Chapter 7A.

2 Park the car on a level surface. The oil level must be checked before the car is driven, or at least 5 minutes after the engine has been switched off.

Caution: If the oil is checked immediately after driving the car, some of the oil will remain distributed around the transmission components, resulting in an inaccurate level reading.

3 Wipe clean the area around the filler/level plug, which is situated on the left-hand end of the transmission **(see illustration)**. Unscrew the plug and clean it; discard the sealing washer.

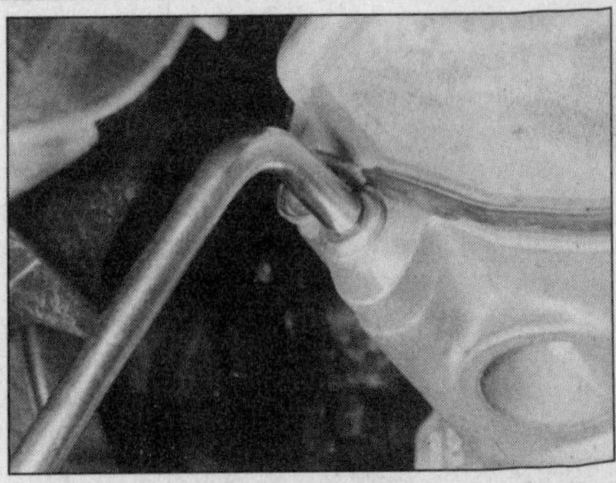

16.3 Unscrew the filler/level plug from the transmission using a square-section wrench

16.4 Topping-up the manual transmission oil level

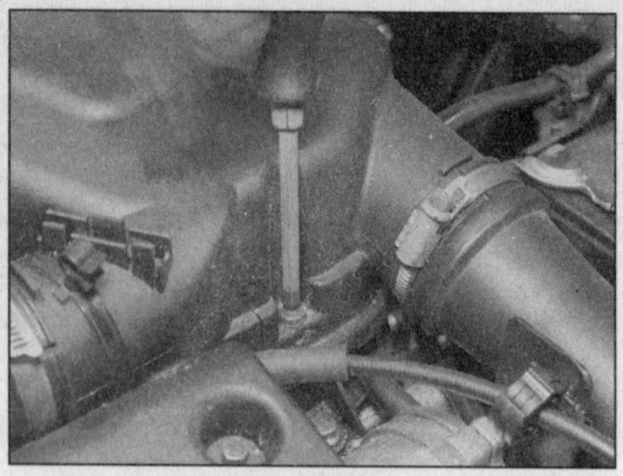

17.2a Slacken and withdraw the retaining screws . . .

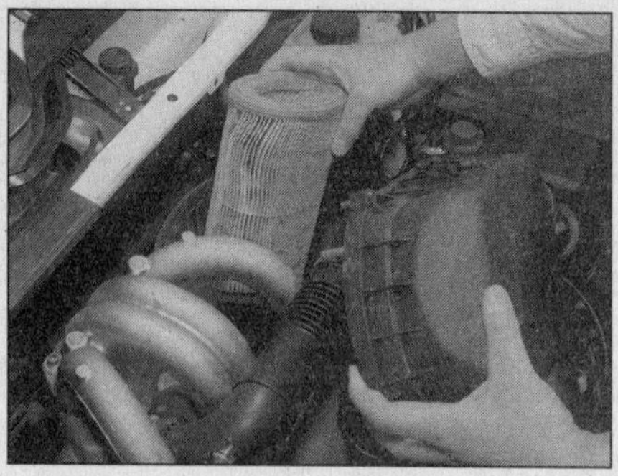

17.2b . . . then remove the cover from the air cleaner housing and withdraw the filter element

4 The oil level should reach the lower edge of the filler/level hole. A certain amount of oil will have gathered behind the filler/level plug, and will trickle out when it is removed; this does **not** necessarily indicate that the level is correct. To ensure that a true level is established, wait until the initial trickle has stopped, then add oil as necessary until a trickle of new oil can be seen emerging. The level will be correct when the flow ceases; use only good-quality oil of the specified type **(see illustration)**.

5 Filling the transmission with oil is an extremely awkward operation; above all, allow plenty of time for the oil level to settle properly before checking it. If a large amount is added to the transmission, and a large amount flows out on checking the level, refit the filler/level plug and take the vehicle on a short journey so that the new oil is distributed fully around the transmission components, then recheck the level when it has settled again.

6 If the transmission has been overfilled so that oil flows out as soon as the filler/level plug is removed, check that the car is completely level (front-to-rear and side-to-side), and allow the surplus to drain off into a suitable container.

7 When the level is correct, fit a new sealing washer to the filler/level plug. Refit the plug, tightening it to the specified torque wrench setting. Wash off any spilt oil.

17 Air filter renewal

1 Slacken the clips and detach the intake air ducts from the air cleaner housing cover.

2 Slacken and withdraw the retaining screws, then remove the cover from the air cleaner housing. Withdraw the filter element, noting its orientation **(see illustrations)**.

3 Remove all traces of dirt and debris from the inside of the air cleaner housing, using a cloth.

4 Fit the new element, ensuring that it is fitted the correct way around and is correctly seated in the housing.

5 Install the cover, and secure it in position with the retaining screws. Reconnect the intake air ducts and tighten the retaining clips securely.

18 Rear brake shoe wear check

1 Chock the front wheels then jack up the rear of the vehicle and support it on axle stands (see "*Jacking and vehicle support*").

2 For a quick check, the thickness of friction material remaining on one of the brake shoes can be measured through the slot in the brake backplate that is exposed by prising out its sealing grommet **(see illustrations)**. If a rod of the same diameter as the specified minimum thickness is placed against the shoe friction material, the amount of wear can quickly be assessed. If any shoe's friction material is worn to the specified thickness or less, all four shoes must be renewed as a set.

3 For a comprehensive check, the brake drums should be removed and cleaned. This will permit the wheel cylinders to be checked and the condition of the brake drum itself to be fully examined. Refer to Chapter 9 for further information.

19 Braking system condition check

1 Raise the front of the vehicle, support securely on axle stands (see "*Jacking and vehicle support*") and remove the front roadwheels.

2 Inspect the area around both brake calipers for signs of brake fluid leakage, either from the piston seals, the brake pipe union or the bleed screw.

3 Examine the brake hoses leading to each caliper and check for signs of cracking, chaffing or damage. Renew a hose which shows signs of deterioration without delay.

4 Using proprietary brake cleaning fluid and a stiff brush, wash all traces of dirt and brake dust from the brake calipers - take care to avoid inhaling any of the airborne brake dust. Examine the piston dust seal for signs of damage or deterioration and check that it is securely seated in its retaining groove.

5 Ensure that the transmission is in neutral, then grasp each brake disc and turn it by hand. Slight resistance is normal, but if the brake disc is difficult to turn smoothly, this indicates that the brake caliper is binding; refer to Chapter 9 for details of caliper removal and overhaul.

6 Check the condition of the brake disc with reference to the information given in Chapter 9.

7 Refit the front roadwheels, then lower the front of the car to the ground. Check the front wheels and select first gear (or 'P' on models with automatic transmission) then release the handbrake, raise the rear of the car and support it on axle stands (see "*Jacking and vehicle support*").

8 Ensure that the handbrake is released, then grasp each roadwheel and turn it by hand. Slight resistance is normal, but if the wheel is difficult to turn smoothly, this could be due to poor handbrake adjustment; refer to Chapter 9 for a description of the adjustment procedure.

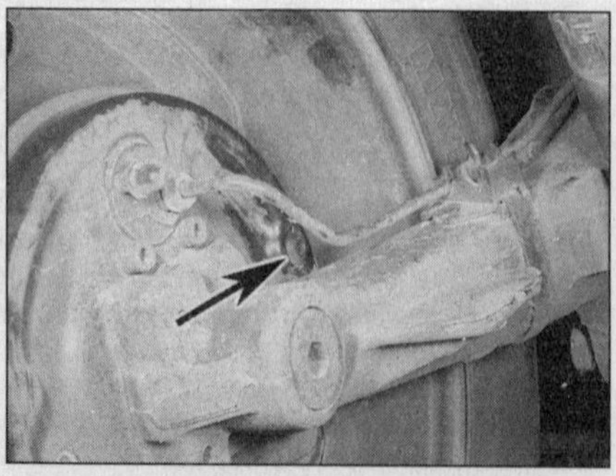

18.2a Prise the grommet (arrowed) from the rear drum brake backplate

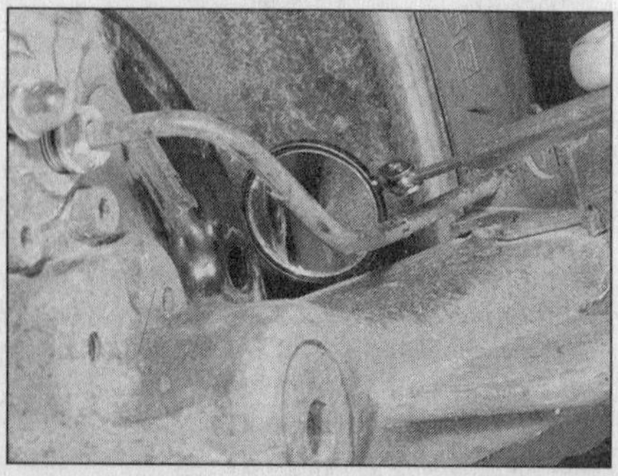

18.2b Viewing the thickness of the brake shoe lining using a small mirror

9 Remove the rear roadwheels, then with reference to Chapter 9, remove the brake drums and check them for wear and/or damage.
10 Check the area around the wheel cylinder piston seals for signs of fluid leakage. Check at the rear of the brake backplate for evidence of fluid leakage from the brake pipe union or bleed screw. Renew the wheel cylinder without delay if it shows signs of leakage; see Chapter 9 for details.
11 Using proprietary brake cleaning fluid and a stiff brush, wash all traces of dirt and brake dust from the brake shoes and associated components - take care to avoid inhaling any of the airborne brake dust. Examine the brake shoes and measure the depth of the remaining friction material. Renew all four brake shoes, with reference to Chapter 9, if any are worn below their minimum limit.
12 On completion, refit the brake drums and roadwheels, then lower the car to the ground and tighten the roadwheel bolts to the specified torque.

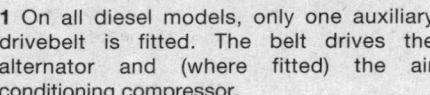

20 Auxiliary drivebelt check and renewal

1 On all diesel models, only one auxiliary drivebelt is fitted. The belt drives the alternator and (where fitted) the air conditioning compressor.

Condition check

2 Apply the handbrake, jack up the front of the car and support it on axle stands (see "*Jacking and vehicle support*"), then remove the right-hand front roadwheel.
3 Undo the securing screws and remove the plastic liner from the wheel arch. Where necessary, undo the retaining nut, and free the coolant hoses from the retaining clip to improve access to the crankshaft sprocket bolt.
4 Using a suitable socket and extension bar fitted to the crankshaft sprocket bolt, rotate the crankshaft so that the entire length of the drivebelt can be examined. Examine the drivebelt for cracks, splitting, fraying, or other damage. Check also for signs of glazing (shiny patches) and for separation of the belt plies. Renew the belt if worn or damaged.
5 If the condition of the belt is satisfactory, check the drivebelt tension as described below under the relevant sub-heading.

Removal

6 If not already done, carry out the operations described in paragraph 2 and 3.
7 Disconnect the battery negative lead.
8 Slacken the two bolts securing the tensioner pulley assembly to the engine **(see illustration)**.
9 Rotate the (vertical) adjuster bolt on the underside of the tensioner pulley assembly to move the pulley away from the drivebelt. When there is sufficient slack, remove the drivebelt from the pulleys.

Refitting

10 Fit the belt around the pulleys, ensuring that the belt is of the correct type if it is being renewed, and take up the slack in the belt by tightening the adjuster bolt.
11 Tension the drivebelt as described in the following paragraphs.

Tensioning

12 If not already done, carry out the operations described in paragraph 2 and 3.
13 Correct tensioning of the drivebelt will ensure that it has a long life. Beware, however, of over-tightening, as this can cause wear in the alternator bearings.
14 The belt should be tensioned so that, under firm thumb pressure, the belt can be displaced by approximately 5.0 mm, at the mid-point of the longest belt run between two pulleys.

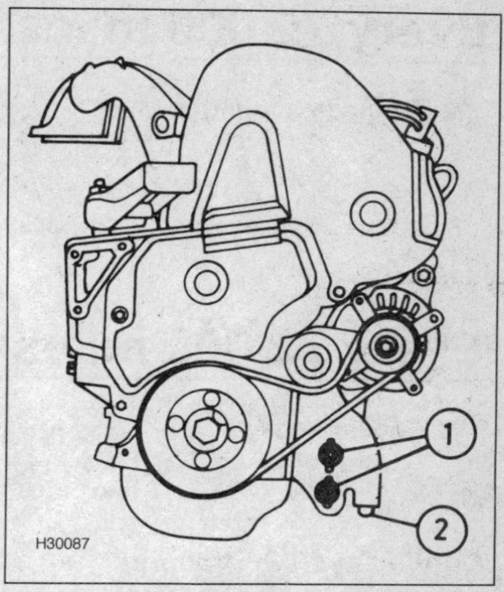

20.8 Auxiliary drivebelt tensioner securing bolts (1) and adjustment bolt (2)

15 To adjust the tension, with the two tensioner pulley assembly retaining bolts slackened, rotate the adjuster bolt until the correct belt tension is achieved. Once the belt is correctly tensioned, rotate the crankshaft through two complete turns, and recheck the tension.
16 When the belt is correctly tensioned, securely tighten the tensioner pulley assembly retaining bolts.
17 Reconnect the battery negative lead.
18 Clip the coolant hoses back in position, and secure with the retaining nut (where removed). Refit the wheel arch liner and roadwheel, then lower the vehicle to the ground and tighten the roadwheel bolts to the specified torque.

Every 36 000 miles (60 000 km) or 2 years

21 Brake fluid renewal

Warning: Brake hydraulic fluid can harm your eyes and damage painted surfaces; certain types of brake fluid are also flammable, so use extreme caution when handling and pouring it. Do not use fluid that has been standing open for some time, as it absorbs moisture from the air. Excess moisture can cause a dangerous loss of braking effectiveness.

1 The procedure is similar to that for the bleeding of the braking system as described in Chapter 9, except that the brake fluid reservoir should be emptied by siphoning, using a clean poultry baster or similar before starting, and allowance should be made for the old fluid to be expelled when bleeding a section of the circuit.
2 Working as described in Chapter 9, open the first bleed screw in the sequence, and pump the brake pedal gently until nearly all the old fluid has been emptied from the master cylinder reservoir. Top-up to the "MAX" level with new fluid, and continue pumping until only the new fluid remains in the reservoir, and new fluid can be seen emerging from the bleed screw. Tighten the screw, and top the reservoir level up to the "MAX" level line.
3 The age of hydraulic fluid can be judged by its colour; old fluid tends to be much darker in colour than new fluid. This makes it easy to judge when a section of the braking system has been sufficiently bled - when the colour of the fluid flowing from the bleed screw turns from dark to light, this means that the new fluid has ejected all the old fluid from that section.
4 Work through all the remaining bleed screws in the sequence until new fluid can be seen at all of them. Be careful to keep the master cylinder reservoir topped-up to above the "MIN" level at all times, or air may enter the system and greatly increase the length of the task.
5 When the operation is complete, check that all bleed screws are securely tightened, and that their dust caps are refitted. Wash off all traces of spilt fluid, and recheck the master cylinder reservoir fluid level.
6 Check the operation of the brakes before taking the car on the road.

Every 72 000 miles (120 000 km)

22 Timing belt renewal

Refer to the information given in Chapter 2B.

Every 72 000 miles (120 000 km) or every 2 years

23 Coolant renewal

Cooling system draining

Warning: Wait until the engine is cold before starting this procedure. Do not allow antifreeze to come in contact with your skin, or with the painted surfaces of the vehicle. Rinse off spills immediately with plenty of water. Never leave antifreeze lying around in an open container, or in a puddle in the driveway or on the garage floor. Children and pets are attracted by its sweet smell, but antifreeze can be fatal if ingested.

1 With the engine completely cold, remove the expansion tank filler cap. Turn the cap anti-clockwise until it reaches the first stop. Wait until any pressure remaining in the system is released, then push the cap down, turn it anti-clockwise to the second stop, and lift it off.

2 Position a suitable container beneath the radiator bottom hose. Slacken the clip and carefully release the hose from the radiator stub, allowing the coolant to drain into the container.

3 To assist draining, open the cooling system bleed screw. This is located in the heater hose at the right-hand side of the engine compartment **(see illustration)**.

4 When the flow of coolant stops, reposition the container below the cylinder block drain plug, located at the front left-hand corner of the cylinder block.

23.3 *Cooling system bleed screw (arrowed)*

5 Remove the drain plug, and allow the coolant to drain into the container.

6 If the coolant has been drained for a reason other than renewal, then provided it is clean and less than two years old, it can be re-used, though this is not recommended.

7 On completion of draining, refit the radiator bottom hose tighten the bottom hose clip securely. Refit the cylinder block drain plug using a new sealing washer and tighten it to the specified torque.

Cooling system flushing

8 If coolant renewal has been neglected, or if the antifreeze mixture has become diluted, then in time, the cooling system may gradually lose efficiency, as the coolant passages become restricted due to rust, scale deposits, and other sediment. The cooling system efficiency can be restored by flushing the system clean.

9 The radiator should be flushed independently of the engine, to avoid unnecessary contamination.

Radiator flushing

10 To flush the radiator, first tighten the radiator drain plug, and the radiator bleed screw, where applicable.

11 Disconnect the top and bottom hoses from the radiator, with reference to Chapter 3.

12 Insert a garden hose into the radiator top inlet. Direct a flow of clean water through the radiator, and continue flushing until clean water emerges from the radiator bottom outlet.

13 If after a reasonable period, the water still does not run clear, the radiator can be flushed with a good proprietary cleaning agent. It is important that their manufacturer's instructions are followed carefully. If the contamination is particularly bad, insert the hose in the radiator bottom outlet, and reverse-flush the radiator.

23.19 *Removing the coolant expansion tank filler cap*

Engine flushing

14 To flush the engine, first refit the cylinder block drain plug, and tighten the cooling system bleed screws.

15 Remove the thermostat as described in Chapter 3, then temporarily refit the thermostat cover.

16 With the top and bottom hoses disconnected from the radiator, insert a garden hose into the radiator top hose. Direct a clean flow of water through the engine, and continue flushing until clean water emerges from the radiator bottom hose.

17 On completion of flushing, refit the thermostat and reconnect the hoses with reference to Chapter 3.

Cooling system filling

18 Before attempting to fill the cooling system, make sure that all hoses and clips are in good condition, and that the clips and drain plugs are tight. Note that an antifreeze mixture must be used all year round, to prevent corrosion of the engine components (see following sub-Section). Check that the radiator bottom hose and cylinder block drain plug are secure.

19 Remove the expansion tank filler cap **(see illustration)**.

20 Open the cooling system bleed screw (see paragraph 3).

Caution: When refilling the engine with coolant, it's important to make sure that all the trapped air is allowed to escape, by 'bleeding', as described here. Air trapped in the cooling system could cause overheating problems later, which will quickly lead to expensive engine damage.

21 Some of the cooling system hoses are positioned at a higher level than the top of the radiator expansion tank. It is therefore necessary to use a "header tank" when refilling the cooling system, to reduce the possibility of air being trapped in the system. Although Citroën dealers use a special header tank, the same effect can be achieved by using a suitable bottle, with a rubber seal between the bottle and the expansion tank neck.

22 Fit the "header tank" to the expansion tank, then slowly fill the cooling system. Coolant will eventually begin to seep from the bleed screw hole; as soon as coolant free from air bubbles emerges from the hole, tighten the bleed screw securely. As the bleed screw is at the highest point in the cooling system, the system should now be full.

23 Ensure that the "header tank" is at least half-full (at least 0.5 litres of coolant). Start the engine, and run it at a fast idle speed (do not exceed 2000 rpm) until the cooling fan cuts in and out again three times. Stop the engine.

24 Remove the "header tank", taking great care not to scald yourself with the hot coolant, then fit the expansion tank cap.

25 Allow the engine to cool, then check the coolant level with reference to "*Weekly checks*". Top-up the level if necessary.

Antifreeze mixture

26 The antifreeze should always be renewed at the specified intervals. This is necessary not only to maintain the antifreeze properties, but also to prevent corrosion which would otherwise occur as the corrosion inhibitors become progressively less effective.

27 Always use an ethylene-glycol based antifreeze which is suitable for use in mixed-metal cooling systems. The quantity of antifreeze and levels of protection are indicated in the Specifications.

28 Before adding antifreeze, the cooling system should be completely drained, preferably flushed, and all hoses checked for condition and security.

29 After filling with antifreeze, a label should be attached to the expansion tank, stating the type and concentration of antifreeze used, and the date installed. Any subsequent topping-up should be made with the same type and concentration of antifreeze.

Caution: Do not use engine antifreeze in the windscreen/tailgate washer system, as it will cause damage to the vehicle paintwork. A screenwash additive should be added to the washer system in the quantities stated on the bottle.

Every 10 years

24 Air bag and seat belt tensioners renewal

Due to the safety critical nature of the air bag and seat belt tensioner components, these operations must be carried out by a Citroën dealer.

Chapter 2 Part A:
Petrol engine in-car repair procedures

Contents

Degrees of difficulty

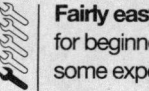

Easy, suitable for novice with little experience	**Fairly easy,** suitable for beginner with some experience	**Fairly difficult,** suitable for competent DIY mechanic	**Difficult,** suitable for experienced DIY mechanic	**Very difficult,** suitable for expert DIY or professional

Specifications

General

Designation:	
954 cc engine	TU9
1124 cc engine	TU1M+
1360 cc engine	TU3JP
1587 cc engine	TU5JP
1587 cc 16-valve engine	TU5JP4
Engine codes*:	
954 cc single-point fuel-injected engine	CDZ
1124 cc single-point fuel-injected engine	HDZ
1360 cc multi-point fuel-injected engine	KFX
1587 cc multi-point fuel-injected engine	NZF
1587 cc 16-valve multi-point fuel-injected engine	NFX
Bore:	
954 cc engine	70.00 mm
1124 cc engine	72.00 mm
1360 cc engine	75.00 mm
1587 cc engine	78.50 mm
1587 cc 16-valve engine	78.50 mm
Stroke:	
954 cc engine	62.00 mm
1124 cc engine	69.00 mm
1360 cc engine	77.00 mm
1587 cc engine	82.00 mm
1587 cc 16-valve engine	82.00 mm
Direction of crankshaft rotation	Clockwise (viewed from right-hand side of vehicle)
No 1 cylinder location	At transmission end of block
Compression ratio (typical):	
954 cc engine	9.4:1
1124 cc engine	9.7:1
1360 cc engine	10.2:1
1587 cc engine	9.6:1
1587 cc 16-valve engine	10.8:1

General (continued)

Maximum power (typical):	
954 cc engine	50 bhp (37 kW) @ 6000 rpm
1124 cc engine	60 bhp (44.1 kW) @ 6200 rpm
1360 cc engine	75 bhp (55 kW) @ 5500 rpm
1587 cc engine	90 bhp (65 kW) @ 5600 rpm
1587 cc 16-valve engine	120 bhp (87 kW) @ 6600 rpm
Maximum torque (typical):	
954 cc engine	73.5 Nm @ 3700 rpm
1124 cc engine	88 Nm @ 3800 rpm
1360 cc engine	111 Nm @ 3400 rpm
1587 cc engine	135 Nm @ 3000 rpm
1587 cc 16-valve engine	145 Nm @ 5200 rpm

Camshaft

Drive	Toothed belt and sprocket(s)
Number of bearings	5

Valve clearances (engine cold)

954 cc, 1124 cc, 1360 and 1587 cc engines:	
Inlet	0.20 mm
Exhaust	0.40 mm
1587 cc 16-valve engines	Automatic by hydraulic tappets

Lubrication system

Oil pump type	Gear-type, chain-driven off the crankshaft
Minimum oil pressure at 90°C	4 bars at 4000 rpm
Oil pressure warning switch operating pressure	0.8 bars

Torque wrench settings

Torque wrench settings	Nm	lbf ft
Cylinder head cover nuts (8-valve engines)	5	4
Cylinder head cover bolts (16-valve engines)	8	6
Timing belt cover bolts	5	4
Crankshaft pulley retaining bolts	10	7
Timing belt tensioner pulley nut	20	15
Timing belt idler pulley nut (16-valve engines)	20	15
Camshaft sprocket retaining bolt (8-valve engines)	80	60
Camshaft sprocket-to-hub bolts (16-valve engines)	10	7
Camshaft sprocket hub-to-camshaft bolt (16-valve engines)	80	60
Crankshaft sprocket retaining bolt	100	74
Camshaft thrust fork retaining bolt	15	11
Camshaft bearing ladder bolts (16-valve engine):		
Stage 1	2	1.5
Stage 2	8	6
Cylinder head bolts (aluminium block engine):		
Stage 1	20	15
Stage 2	Angle-tighten a further 240°	
Cylinder head bolts (cast-iron block 8-valve engine):		
Stage 1	20	15
Stage 2	Angle-tighten a further 120°	
Stage 3	Angle-tighten a further 120°	
Cylinder head bolts (16-valve engine):		
Stage 1	20	15
Stage 2	Angle-tighten a further 260°	
Sump drain plug	30	22
Sump retaining nuts and bolts	10	7
Oil pump retaining bolts	10	7
Oil cooler centre bolt	8	6
Crankshaft oil seal housing bolts	8	6
Flywheel retaining nuts and bolts	65	48
Piston oil jet spray tube bolts (16-valve models)	10	7
Big-end bearing cap nuts	38	28
Main bearing ladder casting (aluminium block engine):		
M11 bolts:		
Stage 1	20	15
Stage 2	Angle-tighten a further 45°	
M6 bolts	10	7

Torque wrench settings (continued)

	Nm	lbf ft
Main bearing cap bolts (cast-iron block engine):		
Stage 1	20	15
Stage 2	Angle-tighten a further 50°	
Engine/transmission right-hand mounting:		
Mounting bracket-to-engine nuts	45	33
Mounting bracket-to-body nut(s)	30	22
Engine/transmission left-hand mounting:		
Mounting bracket-to-body bolts	30	22
Centre nut	65	48
Mounting bracket-to-transmission nuts	25	18
Engine/transmission rear mounting:		
Mounting link-to-body bolt:		
(8-valve engine)	70	51
(16-valve engine)	55	40
Mounting link-to-transmission bracket bolt	50	37
Transmission bracket-to-transmission casing bolts	85	63
Engine-to-transmission bolts	35	26

1 General information

How to use this Chapter

1 This Part of Chapter 2 describes those petrol-engine repair procedures that can reasonably be carried out with the engine still in the car. If the engine has been removed from the car and is being dismantled as described in Part C, any preliminary dismantling procedures can be ignored.

2 Note that, while it may be possible physically to remove items such as the piston/connecting rod assemblies while the engine is in the car, such tasks are normally carried out as part of a complete overhaul, not as separate operations. Usually, several additional procedures (not to mention the cleaning of components and of oilways) have to be carried out. For this reason, all such tasks are classed as major overhaul procedures, and are described in Part C of this Chapter.

3 Part C describes the removal of the engine/transmission from the vehicle, and the full overhaul procedures that can then be carried out.

Engine description

4 All petrol engines in the Citroën Saxo model range come from the TU series of engines. The TU engine is a well-proven unit which has been used in several other Citroën and Peugeot vehicles. The engine is of the in-line four-cylinder, overhead camshaft (OHC) type, mounted transversely at the front of the car. The clutch and transmission are attached to its left-hand end. The Saxo range is fitted with 954 cc, 1124 cc, 1360 cc, 1587 cc 8-valve and 1587 cc 16-valve versions of the engine, with either single-point or multi-point fuel-injection. The engine is manufactured with either an aluminium or cast-iron cylinder block, depending on capacity.

5 The crankshaft runs in five main bearings. Thrustwashers are fitted to No 2 main bearing (upper half) to control crankshaft endfloat.

6 The connecting rods rotate on horizontally-split bearing shells at their big-ends. The pistons are attached to the connecting rods by gudgeon pins, which are an interference fit in the connecting rod small-end eyes. The aluminium-alloy pistons are fitted with three piston rings - two compression rings and an oil control ring.

7 On aluminium block engines, the cylinder bores have replaceable wet liners. Sealing O-rings are fitted at the base of each liner, to prevent the escape of coolant into the sump.

8 On cast-iron block engines, the cylinder bores are an integral part of the cylinder block. On this type of engine, the cylinder bores are sometimes referred to as having dry liners.

9 The inlet and exhaust valves are each closed by coil springs, and operate in guides pressed into the cylinder head; the valve seat inserts are also pressed into the cylinder head, and can be renewed separately if worn.

10 On SOHC engines, the camshaft rotates directly in the cylinder head, is driven by a toothed timing belt, and operates the eight valves via rocker arms. Valve clearances are adjusted by a screw-and-locknut arrangement. The timing belt also drives the coolant pump.

11 On 16-valve engines, the cylinder head houses double overhead camshafts (DOHC) which run directly in the cylinder head and are driven by a single toothed belt. Each camshaft has five bearings, eight lobes and operates either the inlet or exhaust valves via hydraulic tappets. The timing belt also drives the coolant pump, as on SOHC TU engines.

12 Lubrication is by means of an oil pump, which is driven (via a chain and sprocket) off the right-hand end of the crankshaft. It draws oil through a strainer located in the sump, and then forces it through an externally-mounted filter into galleries in the cylinder block/crankcase. From there, the oil is distributed to the crankshaft (main bearings) and camshaft. The big-end bearings are supplied with oil via internal drillings in the crankshaft, while the camshaft bearings also receive a pressurised supply. The camshaft lobes and valves are lubricated by splash, as are all other engine components. On 1587 cc 16-valve models, an oil-to-water engine oil cooler is fitted, to control the oil temperature under arduous operating conditions.

13 Throughout this manual, it is often necessary to identify the engines not only by their capacity, but also by their engine code, which can be found on the front face of the cylinder block, at the transmission end. On models with an aluminium cylinder block, the code is stamped on a plate which is riveted to the block; on models with a cast-iron cylinder block, the number is stamped on a machined surface on the cylinder block itself. The first part of the engine number gives the engine code - eg "NFX" **(see illustration)**.

Repair operations possible with the engine in the car

14 The following work can be carried out with the engine in the car:

a) *Compression pressure - testing.*
b) *Cylinder head cover - removal and refitting.*
c) *Timing belt covers - removal and refitting.*
d) *Timing belt - removal, refitting and adjustment.*
e) *Timing belt tensioner and sprockets - removal and refitting.*

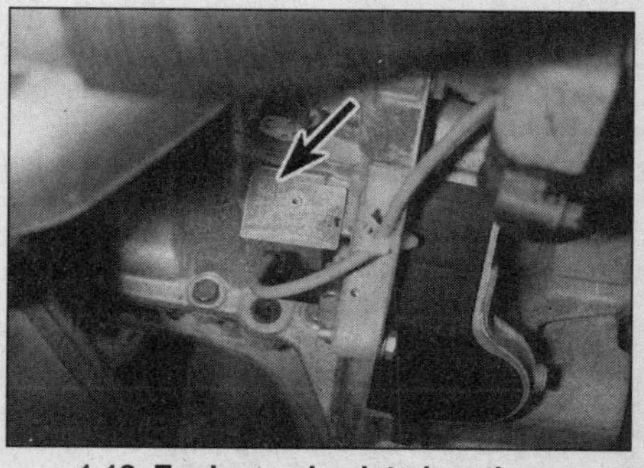

1.13 Engine code plate location - models with aluminium cylinder blocks

f) Camshaft oil seal - renewal.
*g) Camshaft and rocker arms (8-valve engines) - removal, inspection and refitting.**
h) Camshaft(s) and hydraulic tappets (16-valve engines) - removal, inspection and refitting.
i) Cylinder head - removal and refitting.
j) Cylinder head and pistons - decarbonising (refer to Part C of this Chapter).
k) Sump - removal and refitting.
l) Oil pump - removal, overhaul and refitting.
m) Oil cooler (where fitted) - removal and refitting.
n) Crankshaft oil seals - renewal.
o) Engine/transmission mountings - inspection and renewal.
p) Flywheel - removal, inspection and refitting.

**The cylinder head must be removed for the successful completion of this work. Refer to Section 10 for details.*

2 Compression test - description and interpretation

1 When engine performance is down, or if misfiring occurs which cannot be attributed to the ignition or fuel systems, a compression test can provide diagnostic clues as to the engine's condition. If the test is performed regularly, it can give warning of trouble before any other symptoms become apparent.

2 The engine must be fully warmed-up to normal operating temperature, the battery must be fully charged, and all four spark plugs must be removed (see Chapter 1A). The aid of an assistant will also be required.

3 Disable the ignition system by disconnecting the LT wiring connector from the ignition HT coil, referring to Chapter 5B for further information.

4 Fit a compression tester to the No 1 cylinder spark plug hole. The type of tester which screws into the plug hole thread will produce more reliable results than one which is simply pressed against the top of the spark plug hole.

5 Have the assistant hold the throttle wide open, and crank the engine on the starter motor; after one or two revolutions, the compression pressure should build up to a maximum figure, and then stabilise. Record the highest reading obtained.

6 Repeat the test on the remaining cylinders, recording the pressure in each.

7 All cylinders should produce very similar pressures; a difference of more than 2 bars between any two cylinders indicates a fault. Note that the compression should build up quickly in a healthy engine; low compression on the first stroke, followed by gradually-increasing pressure on successive strokes, indicates worn piston rings. A low compression reading on the first stroke, which does not build up during successive strokes, indicates leaking valves or a blown head gasket (a cracked head could also be the cause). Deposits on the undersides of the valve heads can also cause low compression.

8 Although Citroën do not specify exact compression pressures, as a guide, any cylinder pressure of below 10 bars can be considered as less than healthy. Refer to a Citroën dealer or other specialist if in doubt as to whether a particular pressure reading is acceptable.

9 If the pressure in any cylinder is low, carry out the following test to isolate the cause. Introduce a teaspoonful of clean oil into that cylinder through its spark plug hole, and repeat the test.

10 If the addition of oil temporarily improves the compression pressure, this indicates that bore or piston wear is responsible for the pressure loss. No improvement suggests that leaking or burnt valves, or a blown head gasket, may be to blame.

11 A low reading from two adjacent cylinders is almost certainly due to the head gasket having blown between them; the presence of coolant in the engine oil will confirm this.

12 If one cylinder is about 20 percent lower than the others and the engine has a slightly rough idle, a worn camshaft lobe could be the cause.

13 If the compression reading is unusually high, the combustion chambers are probably coated with carbon deposits. If this is the case, the cylinder head should be removed and decarbonised.

14 On completion of the test, refit the spark plugs and reconnect the ignition system.

3 Engine assembly/ valve timing holes - general information and usage

Caution: Do not attempt to rotate the engine whilst the crankshaft/camshaft are locked in position. If the engine is to be left in this state for a long period of time, it is a good idea to place warning notices inside the vehicle, and in the engine compartment. This will reduce the possibility of the engine being accidentally cranked on the starter motor, which is likely to cause damage with the locking tools in place.

3.5 Crankshaft locking tool in position

1 On all models, timing holes are drilled in the camshaft sprocket(s) and in the flywheel. The holes are used to ensure that the crankshaft and camshaft(s) are correctly positioned when assembling the engine (to prevent the possibility of the valves contacting the pistons when refitting the cylinder head). They also ensure that the correct valve timing is preserved, when removing/refitting the timing belt. When the timing holes are aligned with access holes in the cylinder head and the front of the cylinder block, suitable-diameter pins or bolts can be inserted to lock the camshaft(s) and crankshaft in position, preventing them from rotating. Proceed as follows. **Note:** *With the timing holes aligned, No 1 cylinder is at TDC on its compression stroke.*

2 On DOHC engines, raise the front of the vehicle and rest it securely on axle stands with the front roadwheels clear of the ground (see "*Jacking and vehicle support*"). Unbolt and remove the engine management system ECU splash shield, then remove the ECU together with its support bracket, with reference to the relevant part of Chapter 4. Slacken and withdraw the securing bolts, then remove the exhaust manifold heat shield.

3 Remove the timing belt cover as described in Section 5. Note that on SOHC engines, only the upper section of the cover need be removed.

4 The crankshaft must now be turned until the timing hole in the camshaft sprocket(s) is aligned with the corresponding hole in the cylinder head. On SOHC engines, the holes are aligned when the camshaft sprocket hole is in the 2 o'clock position, when viewed from the right-hand end of the engine. On DOHC engines, the holes are aligned when the inlet camshaft sprocket is in the 5 o'clock position, and the exhaust camshaft is in the 7 o'clock position. The crankshaft can be turned by using a spanner on the crankshaft sprocket bolt, noting that it should always be rotated in a clockwise direction (viewed from the right-hand end of the engine). Turning the engine will be much easier if the spark plugs are removed first (see Chapter 1A).

5 With the camshaft sprocket hole(s) correctly positioned, insert a 6 mm diameter bolt or drill bit through the hole in the front left-hand flange of the cylinder block, and locate it in the timing hole in the flywheel **(see illustration)**. Note that it may be necessary to rotate the crankshaft slightly, to get the holes to align.

6 With the flywheel locked in position, insert a10 mm diameter bolt or drill bit through the timing hole in the camshaft sprocket (one for each sprocket on DOHC engines), and locate it in the hole in the cylinder head **(see illustrations)**.

7 The crankshaft and camshaft(s) are now locked in the TDC on cylinder No 1 position, preventing unwanted rotation.

3.6a Camshaft locking tool in position - SOHC engine

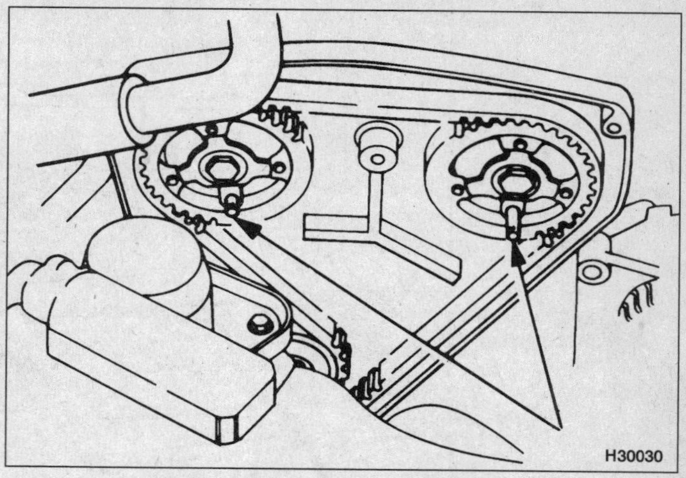

3.6b Camshaft locking tools in position - DOHC engine

4 Cylinder head cover - removal and refitting

SOHC engines

Removal

1 Disconnect the battery negative lead.

2 Where necessary, undo the bolts securing the HT lead retaining clips to the rear of the cylinder head cover, and position the clips clear of the cover.

3 Slacken the retaining clip, and disconnect the breather hose from the left-hand end of the cylinder head cover **(see illustration)**. Where the original crimped-type hose clip is still fitted, cut it off and discard it - use a standard worm-drive clip on refitting.

4 Undo the two retaining nuts, and remove the washer from each of the cylinder head cover studs **(see illustration)**.

5 Lift off the cylinder head cover, and remove it along with its rubber seal **(see illustration)**. Examine the seal for signs of damage and deterioration, and if necessary, renew it.

6 Remove the spacer from each stud, and lift off the oil baffle plate **(see illustrations)**.

Refitting

7 Carefully clean the cylinder head and cover mating surfaces, and remove all traces of oil.

8 Fit the rubber seal over the edge of the cylinder head cover, ensuring that it is correctly located along its entire length **(see illustration)**.

9 Refit the oil baffle plate to the engine, and locate the spacers in their recesses in the baffle plate.

10 Carefully refit the cylinder head cover to the engine, taking great care not to displace the rubber seal.

11 Check that the seal is correctly located,

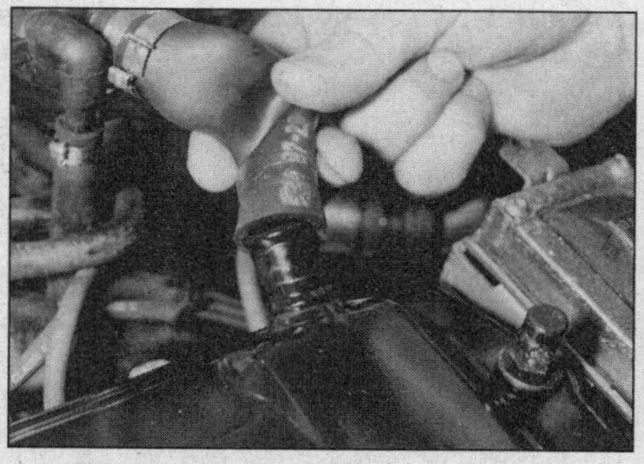

4.3 Disconnect the breather hose from the left-hand end of the cylinder head cover

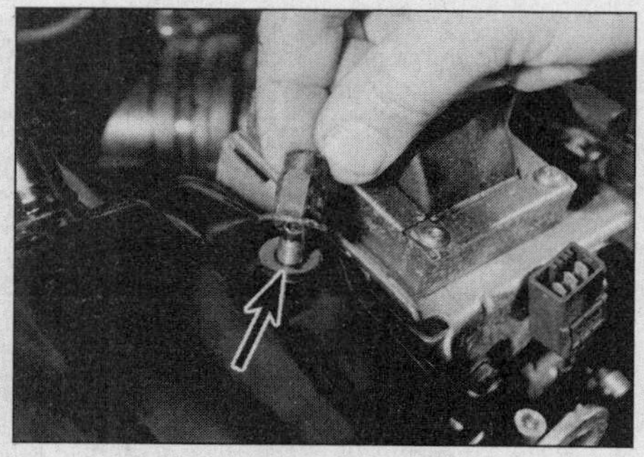

4.4 Remove the retaining nut and washer (arrowed) from each stud

4.5 Lift off the cylinder head cover

4.6a Remove the spacer (arrowed) from each stud . . .

4.6b . . . and lift off the oil baffle plate

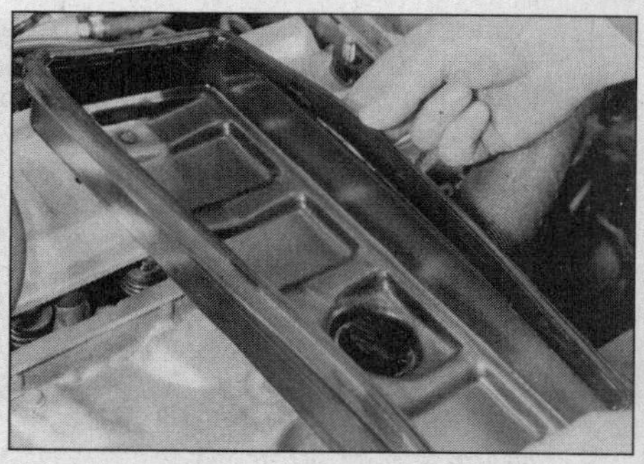

4.8 Fit the rubber seal over the edge of the cylinder head cover

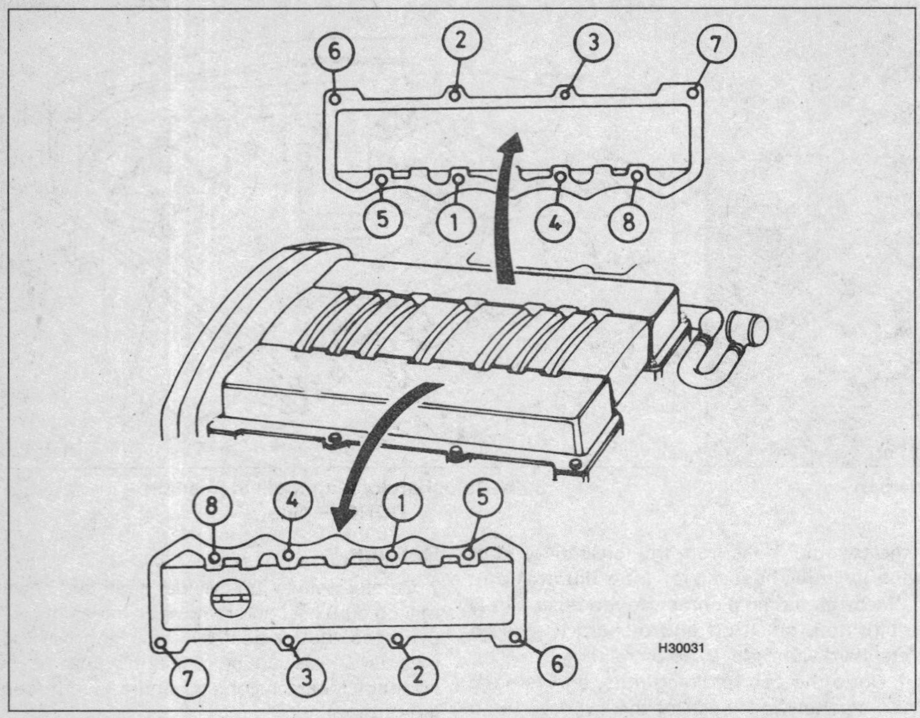

4.19 Tighten the cylinder head cover securing screws in the sequence shown

then refit the washers and cover retaining nuts, and tighten them to the specified torque.

12 Where necessary, refit the HT lead clips to the rear of the head cover, and securely tighten their retaining bolts.

13 Reconnect the breather hose to the cylinder head cover, securely tightening its retaining clip, and reconnect the battery negative lead.

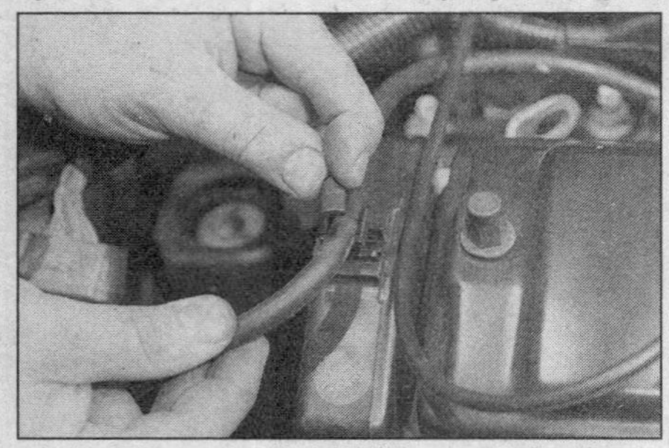

5.1a Unclip the hose from the top of the upper cover

DOHC engines

Removal

14 Refer to Chapter 5B and remove the HT coil module from the top of the cylinder head.

15 Working around the edge of the relevant cylinder head cover in a spiral sequence, progressively slacken and withdraw the securing screws.

16 Carefully lift the cover away from the cylinder head and recover the gasket. If required, the remaining cylinder head cover can be removed in a similar manner.

Refitting

17 Carefully clean the mating surfaces of the cylinder head and the cover. The gasket can be re-used providing that it is undamaged; clean it thoroughly to ensure that a good seal is achieved on refitting.

18 Fit the gasket to the cover then lay the gasket and cover in position on the cylinder head. Ensure that the screw holes in the gasket, cover and cylinder head are aligned.

19 Insert the securing screws and tighten them by hand initially. Work around the cylinder head cover in the sequence shown **(see illustration)** and tighten the screws to the specified torque.

20 Refit the HT coil module with reference to Chapter 5B.

5 Timing belt covers - removal and refitting

Removal - SOHC models

Upper cover

1 Unclip the hose from the top of the upper cover. Slacken and remove the two retaining bolts (one at the front and one at the rear), and remove the timing belt upper cover from the cylinder head **(see illustrations)**.

Centre cover

2 Remove the upper cover as described in paragraph 1, then free the wiring from its retaining clips on the centre cover **(see illustration)**.

3 On some models, the centre timing belt cover cannot be withdrawn from the engine without first removing the left hand engine mounting bracket; see Section 18 for engine mounting removal and refitting details.

4 Slacken and remove the retaining bolts, and manoeuvre the centre cover out from the engine compartment **(see illustration)**.

Lower cover

Note: *On some later models, the lower and centre covers are combined.*

5 Remove the auxiliary drivebelt as described in Chapter 1A.

6 Remove the upper and centre covers as described in paragraphs 1 to 3.

7 Undo the three crankshaft pulley retaining bolts and remove the pulley, noting which way round it is fitted **(see illustrations)**.

8 Slacken and remove the retaining bolt(s), and slide the lower cover off the end of the crankshaft **(see illustrations)**.

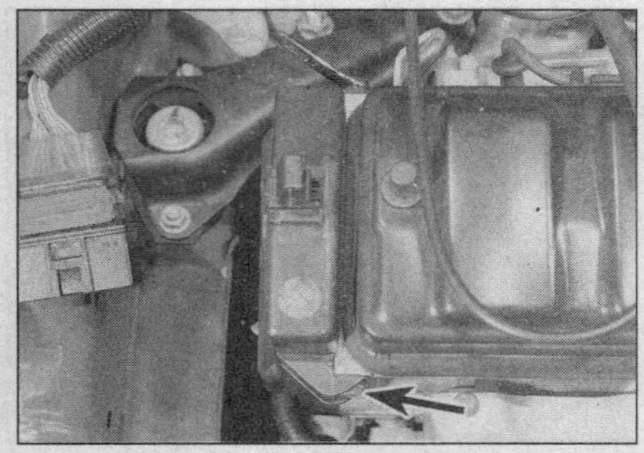

5.1b Slacken and remove the two retaining bolts (second bolt arrowed) . . .

5.1c . . . and remove the timing belt upper cover from the cylinder head

5.2 Free the wiring from its retaining clips on the centre cover

5.4 Remove the retaining bolts and withdraw the centre cover

5.7a Undo the three retaining bolts . . .

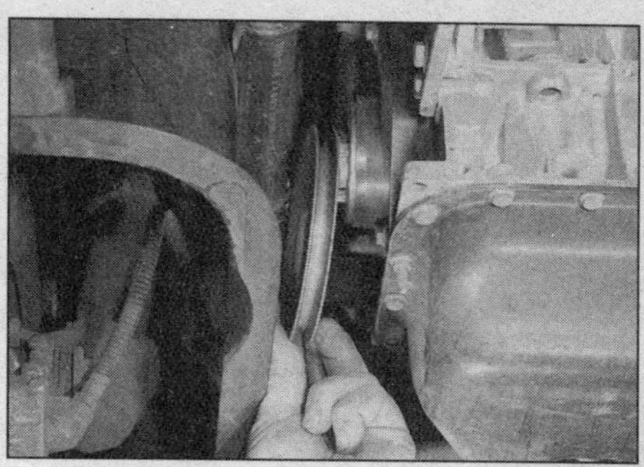

5.7b . . . and remove the crankshaft pulley

Refitting - SOHC models

Upper cover

9 Refit the cover, ensuring that it is correctly located with the centre cover, and tighten its retaining bolts.

Centre cover

10 Manoeuvre the centre cover back into position, ensuring that it is correctly located with the lower cover, and tighten its retaining bolts.

11 Clip the wiring loom into its retaining clips on the front of the centre cover, then refit the upper cover as described in paragraph 9.

Lower cover

12 Locate the lower cover over the timing belt sprocket, and tighten its retaining bolt(s).

13 Fit the pulley to the end of the crankshaft, ensuring that it is fitted the correct way round, and tighten its retaining bolts to the specified torque.

14 Refit the centre and upper covers as described above, then refit and tension the auxiliary drivebelt as described in Chapter 1A.

Removal - DOHC models

Upper cover

15 Disconnect the battery negative cable and position it away from the terminal.

16 Remove the screws and lift the cover away from the engine management system ECU. Unscrew the bolts and remove the ECU, together with its mounting bracket, from the inner wing.

17 Work around the edge of the upper timing cover, slackening and withdrawing the retaining bolts, then manoeuvre the cover out from the engine compartment **(see illustration)**.

Lower cover

18 Remove the auxiliary drivebelt as described in Chapter 1A.

19 Remove the upper cover as described in the previous sub-Section.

20 Undo the crankshaft pulley retaining bolt(s) and remove the pulley, noting which way round it is fitted.

21 Slacken and remove the remaining retaining bolt(s), and slide the lower cover off the end of the crankshaft.

5.8a Slacken and remove the retaining bolts . . .

5.8b . . . and slide the lower cover off the end of the crankshaft

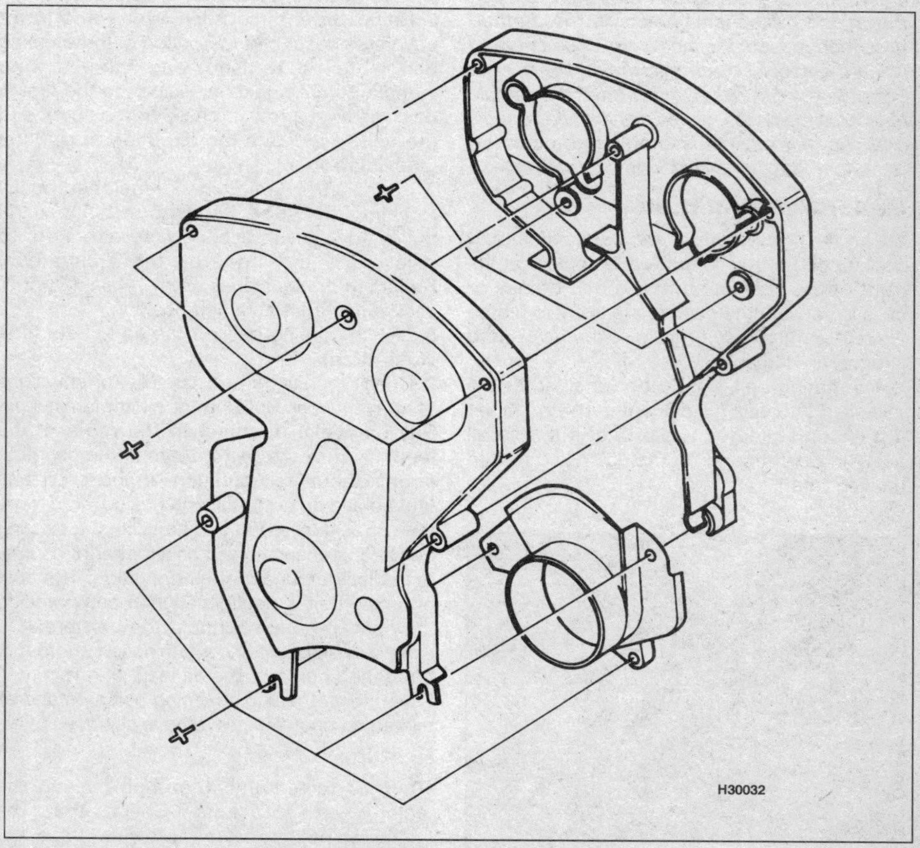

5.17 Timing belt cover components - DOHC engine

2A

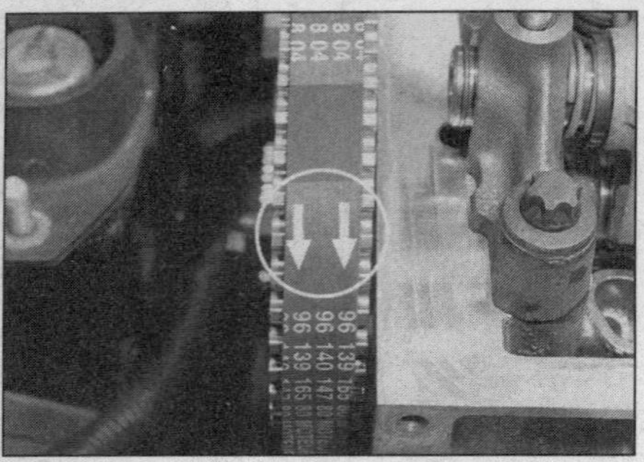

6.6 Manufacturers markings indicating direction of rotation

Refitting - DOHC models

22 Refitting is a reversal of removal. Ensure that the groove at the base of the upper cover engages correctly with the upper edge of the lower cover.

6 Timing belt - removal, refitting and tensioning

Note: *Citroën specify the use of a special electronic tool (SEEM belt tensioning measuring tool) to correctly set the timing belt tension. If access to this equipment cannot be obtained, an approximate setting can be achieved using the method described below. If the method described is used, the tension must be checked using the special electronic tool at the earliest possible opportunity. Do not drive the vehicle over large distances, or use high engine speeds, until the belt tension is known to be correct. Refer to a Citroën dealer for advice.*

General information

1 The timing belt drives the camshaft(s) and coolant pump from a toothed sprocket on the front of the crankshaft. If the belt breaks or slips in service, the pistons are likely to hit the valve heads, resulting in extensive (and expensive) damage.

2 The timing belt should be renewed at the specified intervals (see Chapter 1A), or earlier if it is contaminated with oil, or if it is at all noisy in operation (a "scraping" noise due to uneven wear).

6.8 Slip the timing belt off the sprockets

6.7 Loosen the timing belt tensioner pulley retaining nut

3 If the timing belt is being removed, it is a wise precaution to check the condition of the coolant pump at the same time (check for signs of coolant leakage). This may avoid the need to remove the timing belt again at a later stage, should the coolant pump fail.

SOHC models

Removal

4 Disconnect the battery negative cable and position it away from the terminal.

5 Align the engine assembly/valve timing holes as described in Section 3, and lock the camshaft sprocket and the flywheel in position. *Do not* attempt to rotate the engine whilst the locking tools are in position.

6 Remove the timing belt centre and lower covers as described in Section 5. If the timing belt is to be re-used, and there are no manufacturers markings visible on the timing belt, mark an arrow in chalk on the surface of the belt to indicate the direction of rotation **(see illustration)**.

7 Loosen the timing belt tensioner pulley retaining nut **(see illustration)**. Allow the pulley to pivot in a clockwise direction, to relieve the tension from the timing belt. Retighten the tensioner pulley retaining nut to secure it in the slackened position.

8 Slip the timing belt off the sprockets **(see illustration)**.

9 Check the timing belt carefully for any signs of uneven wear, splitting, or oil contamination. Pay particular attention to the roots of the teeth. Renew the belt if there is the slightest doubt about its condition. If the engine is undergoing an overhaul, and has covered more than 36 000 miles (60 000 km) with the existing belt fitted, renew the belt as a matter of course, regardless of its apparent condition. The cost of a new belt is negligible when compared to the cost of repairs, should the belt break in service. If signs of oil contamination are found, trace the source of the oil leak, and rectify it. Wash down the engine timing belt area and all related components, to remove all traces of oil.

Refitting

10 Prior to refitting, thoroughly clean the timing belt sprockets. Check that the tensioner pulley rotates freely, without any sign of roughness. If necessary, renew the tensioner pulley as described in Section 7. Make sure that the locking tools are still in place, as described in Section 3.

11 Manoeuvre the timing belt into position, ensuring that the arrows indicating the belt's direction of rotation are pointing in the right direction (clockwise, when viewed from the right-hand end of the engine).

12 Do not twist or kink the timing belt while refitting it. Fit the belt over the crankshaft and camshaft sprockets. Make sure that the "front run" of the belt is taut - ie, ensure that any slack is on the tensioner pulley side of the belt. Fit the belt over the coolant pump sprocket and tensioner pulley. Ensure that the belt teeth are seated centrally in the sprockets.

13 Loosen the tensioner pulley retaining nut. Pivot the pulley anti-clockwise to remove all freeplay from the timing belt, then retighten the nut. Tension the timing belt as described under the relevant sub-heading.

Tensioning without the special electronic measuring tool

Note: *If this method is used, ensure that the belt tension is checked by a Citroën dealer at the earliest possible opportunity.*

14 Citroën dealers use a special tool to tension the timing belt. A similar tool may be fabricated using a length of 8mm square-section bar attached to an arm made from a metal strip; a hole should be drilled in the strip at a distance of 80 mm from the centre of the square-section bar. Fit the tool to the square hole on the front face of the tensioner pulley, keeping the tool arm as close to the horizontal as possible, and hang a 1.5 kg (3.3 lb) weight (aluminium block engine) or 2.0 kg (4.4 lb) weight (cast-iron block engine) from the hole in the tool **(see illustration)**. In the absence of an object of the specified weight, a spring balance can be used to exert the required force, ensuring that the spring balance is held at 90° to the tool arm. Slacken the pulley retaining nut, allowing the force exerted to rotate the tensioner pulley against the belt, then retighten the pulley nut.

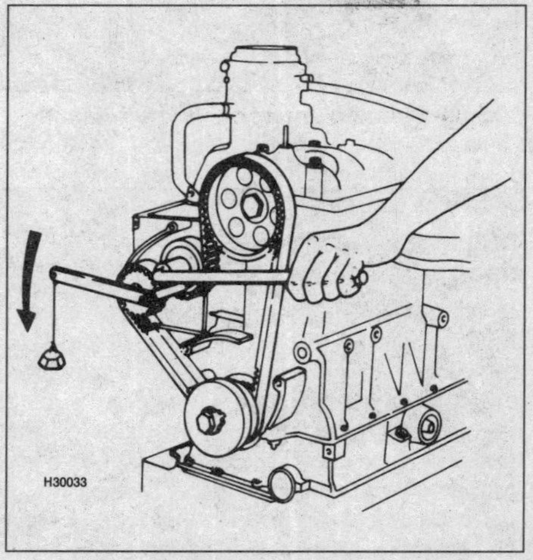

6.14 Using a fabricated tool to set the timing belt tension

TOOL TiP

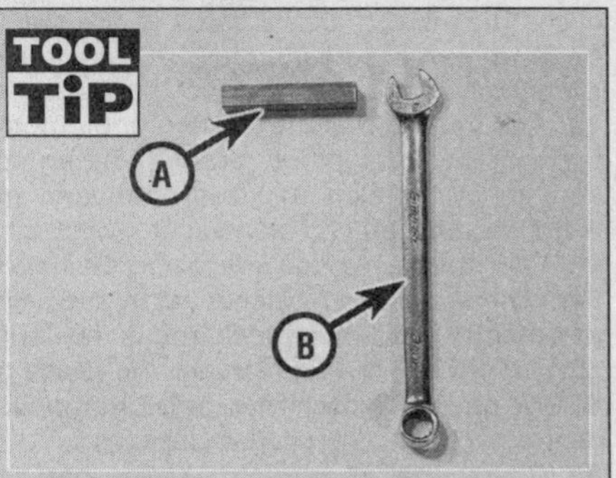

If you're having difficulty finding a square section tool that will fit the tensioner pulley, obtain a length of standard 8mm door handle rod from a DIY shop and cut it down to size (A). Once the rod has been fitted to the tensioner, the timing belt can be tensioned by turning the rod with an 8mm spanner (B).

15 If the materials needed to fabricate this special tool are not available, an approximate setting may be achieved by pivoting the tensioner pulley anti-clockwise, using a length of 8mm square bar and a spanner, until it is just possible to twist the timing belt through 90° by finger and thumb, midway between the crankshaft and camshaft sprockets. The deflection of the belt at the mid-point between the sprockets should be approximately 6.0 mm **(see Tool Tip and illustrations)**.

16 Remove the locking tools from the camshaft sprocket and flywheel.

17 Using a suitable socket and extension bar on the crankshaft sprocket bolt, rotate the crankshaft through four complete rotations in a clockwise direction (viewed from the right-hand end of the engine). *Do not* at any time rotate the crankshaft anti-clockwise.

18 Slacken the tensioner pulley nut, re-tension the belt as described in paragraph 14 or 15, then tighten the tensioner pulley nut to the specified torque.

19 Rotate the crankshaft through a further two turns clockwise, and check that both the camshaft sprocket and flywheel timing holes are still correctly aligned.

20 If all is well, refit the timing belt covers as described in Section 5, and reconnect the battery negative terminal.

Tensioning using the special electronic measuring tool

21 Fit the special belt tensioning measuring equipment to the "front run" of the timing belt, approximately midway between the camshaft and crankshaft sprockets. Fit an 8mm square key to the hole in the front face of the tensioner pulley. Turn the tensioner so that the timing belt is tensioned to a setting of 45 units, then retighten its retaining nut.

22 Remove the locking tools from the camshaft sprocket and flywheel, and remove the measuring tool from the belt.

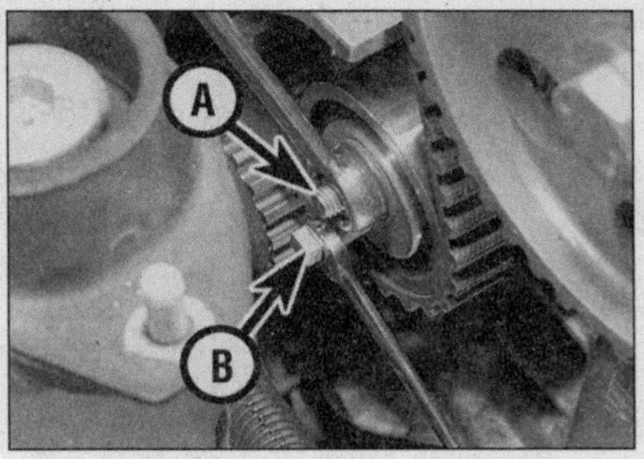

6.15a Slacken the tensioner centre nut, then pivot the tensioner pulley anti-clockwise using the 8mm bar and spanner

A 8mm bar
B Tensioner centre nut

23 Using a suitable socket and extension bar on the crankshaft sprocket bolt, rotate the crankshaft through four complete rotations in a clockwise direction (viewed from the right-hand end of the engine). *Do not* at any time rotate the crankshaft anti-clockwise.

24 Slacken the tensioner pulley retaining nut, and refit the measuring tool to the belt. If a "new" belt is being fitted, tension it to a setting of 40 units. If an "old" belt is being re-used, tighten it to a setting of 36 units. **Note:** *Citroën state that a belt becomes "old" after 1 hour's use.* With the belt correctly tensioned, tighten the pulley retaining nut to the specified torque.

25 Remove the measuring tool from the belt, then rotate the crankshaft through another two complete rotations in a clockwise direction, so that both the camshaft sprocket and flywheel timing holes are realigned. *Do not* at any time rotate the crankshaft anti-clockwise. Fit the measuring tool to the belt, and check the belt tension. A "new" belt should give a reading of 51 ± 3 units; an "old" belt should be 45 ± 3 units.

26 If the belt tension is incorrect, repeat the procedures in paragraphs 24 and 25.

27 With the belt tension correctly set, refit the timing belt covers as described in Section 5, and reconnect the battery negative terminal.

DOHC models

Caution: It is recommended that the special Citroën belt tensioning tool is hired or borrowed for this operation; attempting to set the belt tension by approximation is unlikely to be successful and could lead to belt slippage or failure, resulting in extensive and engine damage.

Removal

28 Refer to the relevant part of Chapter 4 and remove the air cleaner housing and resonator.

29 Remove the cover panel from the engine management system ECU, then refer to the relevant part of Chapter 4 and remove the ECU together with its mounting bracket.

30 Remove the relay casing from the bodywork and position it to one side, away from the timing belt cover.

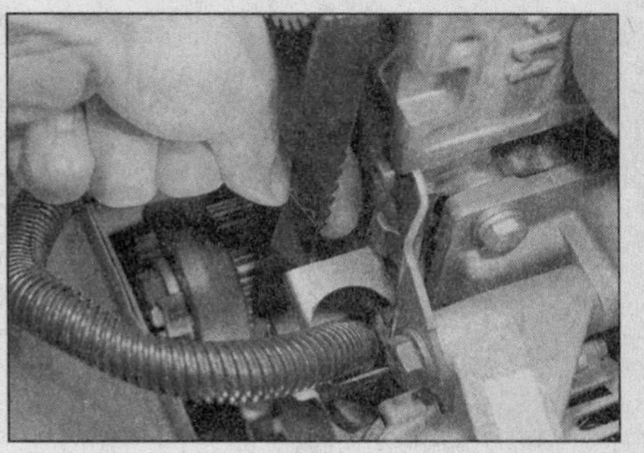

6.15b When the timing belt tension is correct, it should be just possible to twist the belt through 90° by finger and thumb, midway between the crankshaft and camshaft sprockets

31 Refer to Chapter 1A and drain the cooling system.

32 Slacken the clip and disconnect the radiator top hose from the engine. Slacken and withdraw the securing screws, then remove the air inlet ducting from behind the radiator.

33 Refer to Chapter 1A and remove the auxiliary drivebelt, then unbolt and remove the crankshaft pulley.

34 Where applicable, release the air conditioning refrigerant pipe from its securing clips and move it to one side, to give greater access to the timing belt cover.

35 Refer to Section 5 and remove the timing belt upper cover.

36 Unbolt the heat shield from the exhaust manifold, then refer to Section 3 and lock the crankshaft and camshafts in the TDC position using bolts or rods of suitable diameter.

37 Remove the securing screws and lift off the lower timing belt cover.

38 If the timing belt is to be re-used, mark an arrow, in chalk, on the surface of the belt to indicate the direction of rotation.

39 Loosen the timing belt tensioner pulley retaining nut **(see illustration)**. Pivot the pulley in a clockwise direction, using a square-section key fitted to the hole in the pulley hub, then retighten the retaining nut to secure the pulley in the slackened position.

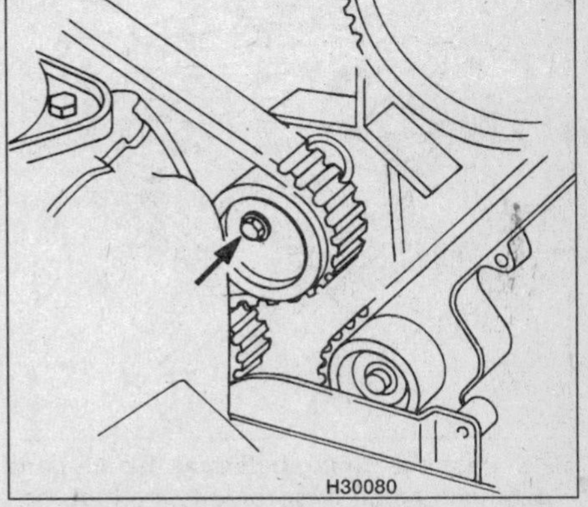

6.39 Loosen the timing belt tensioner pulley retaining nut (arrowed)

2A

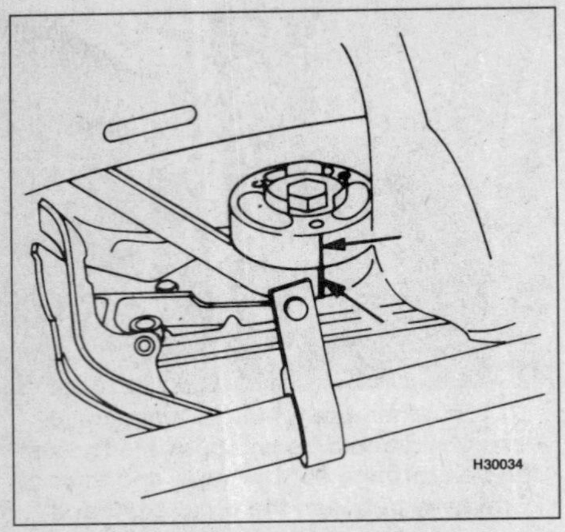

6.44a Ensure that the timing belt mark lines up with the marking on the lower edge of the crankshaft pulley hub

40 Slip the timing belt off the sprockets.

41 Check the timing belt carefully for any signs of uneven wear, splitting, or oil contamination. Pay particular attention to the 'roots' of the teeth. Renew the belt if there is the slightest doubt about its condition. If the engine is undergoing an overhaul, and has covered more than 36 000 miles (60 000 km) with the existing belt fitted, renew the belt as a matter of course, regardless of its apparent condition. The cost of a new belt is negligible when compared to the cost of repairs, should the belt break in service. If signs of oil contamination are found, trace the source of the oil leak, and rectify it. Wash down the engine timing belt area and all related components, to remove all traces of oil.

Refitting

42 Prior to refitting, thoroughly clean the timing belt sprockets. Check that the tensioner and idler pulleys rotate freely, without any sign of roughness. If necessary, renew the tensioner pulley as described in Section 7. Make sure that the locking tools are still in place, as described in Section 3.

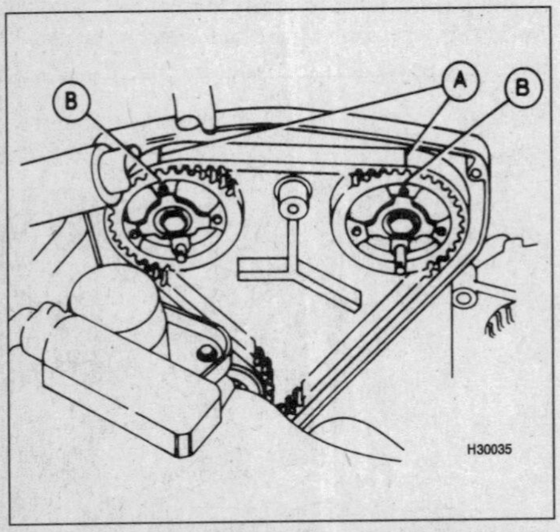

6.46 Pass the timing belt over the inlet and exhaust camshaft sprockets, so that the two marks on the belt (A) line up with the marks on the edges of the sprockets (B)

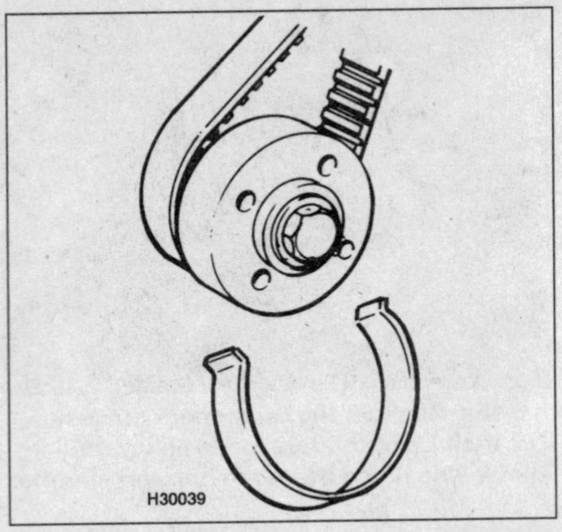

6.44b Secure the belt in position over the sprocket using a 'Ω'-shaped tool board clip or similar

43 The timing belt has three line markings on its flat outer surface. When the belt is correctly fitted, these markings must line up with corresponding markings on the crankshaft sprocket hub and camshaft sprockets. Note that the markings are not evenly spaced around the belt; the first marking must line up with the bottom of the crankshaft sprocket hub, the second and third markings line up with the top of the inlet camshaft and exhaust camshaft sprockets respectively. Identify the markings and then hold the belt up the sprockets, to be sure of its correct orientation, before attempting to refit it.

44 Fit the belt underneath the crankshaft sprocket, ensuring that the first belt mark lines up with the marking on the lower edge of the crankshaft sprocket hub. Secure the belt in position over the sprocket using a 'Ω'-shaped tool board clip or similar, to ensure that the belt cannot disengage from the sprocket teeth **(see illustrations)**.

45 Ensure that both camshaft sprockets are still locked in the TDC position, then with reference to Section 7, slacken the bolts securing both camshaft sprockets to their respective hubs (three bolts on each sprocket). *Do not* remove the bolts completely, but slacken them just enough to allow the sprockets to be rotated by hand. Do not slacken the centre bolts that secure the sprocket hubs to the ends of the camshafts. Turn both sprockets fully clockwise, so that the sprocket securing bolts are positioned at the ends of their slots.

46 Pass the timing belt over the inlet and exhaust camshaft sprockets, so that the two remaining marks on the timing belt line up with the marks on the edges of the sprockets **(see illustration)**. Ensure that the section of the belt that runs between the exhaust camshaft and crankshaft sprockets passes over the idler pulley and remains taught at all times.

47 Keep the belt engaged with the camshaft sprockets, then pass it over the coolant pump sprocket and the tensioner pulley. It may be necessary to remove the crankshaft sprocket clip at this point, as the slack in the belt is taken up, but ensure that the belt-to-sprocket alignment is not lost.

48 Attach the belt tensioning tool to the timing belt, at a point mid-way along the section of the belt that runs between the exhaust camshaft and crankshaft sprockets.

49 Fit a square-section adapter to the hole in the front face of the tensioner pulley and using a wrench, pivot the tensioner pulley anti-clockwise until the tensioning tool reads 63 SEEM units. Tighten the tensioner pulley centre nut to secure it in this position.

50 Check that the belt markings are still aligned with those on the camshaft and crankshaft sprockets. Also check that the camshaft sprocket securing bolts are now positioned part-way along their slots **(see illustration)**. If the belt and sprocket marks are not aligned, or if the sprocket securing bolts are positioned hard against the end of their slots, the belt may be positioned one tooth out - remove the belt and start again from paragraph 42.

51 Remove the belt tensioning tool, then tighten the inlet and exhaust camshaft sprocket securing bolts to the specified torque.

52 Remove the flywheel and camshaft locking tools. Using a ring spanner on the pulley hub bolt, turn the crankshaft in its normal direction of rotation through four revolutions. Bring the engine to TDC as before, then re-insert the flywheel locking tool.

53 Slacken the six exhaust and inlet camshaft sprocket securing bolts slightly, and allow the sprockets to rotate slightly to equalise the belt tension. Insert the sprocket locking tools - if they cannot be inserted, it may be necessary to turn the camshaft(s) slightly, by means of a spanner on the sprocket hub securing bolt(s).

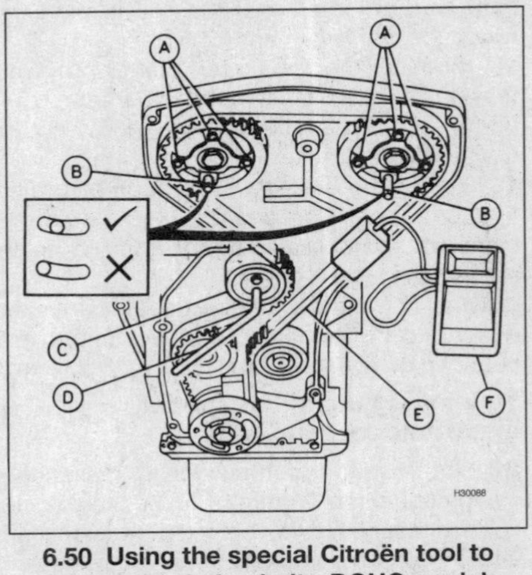

6.50 Using the special Citroën tool to tension the timing belt - DOHC models

A Camshaft sprocket securing bolts
B Sprocket locking tools
C Tensioner
D Square section adapter and wrench
E Timing belt
F Citroën belt tensioning tool

54 Attach the belt tensioning tool to the timing belt as described in paragraph 48.
55 Loosen the tensioner pulley centre nut, then fit a square-section adapter to the hole in the front face of the tensioner pulley and using a wrench, pivot the tensioner pulley anti-clockwise until the tensioning tool now reads 37 SEEM units. Tighten the tensioner pulley centre nut to the specified torque, to secure it in this position.
56 Tighten the inlet and exhaust camshaft sprocket securing bolts to the specified torque, then remove the sprocket locking tools.
57 Remove the flywheel locking tool, then remove the belt tensioning tool. Refit both sections of the timing belt cover, then refit all components removed for access, in the reverse order of removal.
58 On completion, refill and bleed the cooling system as described in Chapter 1A and reconnect the battery.

7 Timing belt tensioner and sprockets - removal, inspection and refitting

Removal

1 Disconnect the battery negative terminal.
2 Remove the timing belt covers as described Section 5.
3 Refer to Section 6 and remove the timing belt.

Camshaft sprocket

4 Temporarily remove the locking pin from the camshaft sprocket.
5 On SOHC models, slacken the camshaft sprocket retaining bolt and remove it, along with its washer **(see illustrations)**. *Do not* attempt to use the sprocket TDC locking pin to prevent the sprocket from rotating whilst the bolt is slackened (refer to the ***Tool Tip*** in the *'Refitting'* sub-section).
6 On DOHC models, the sprockets are of two-piece construction. Slacken and withdraw the centre sprocket hub-to-camshaft bolt, but *do not* attempt to use the sprocket hub locking pin to prevent the sprocket from rotating whilst the bolt is slackened.

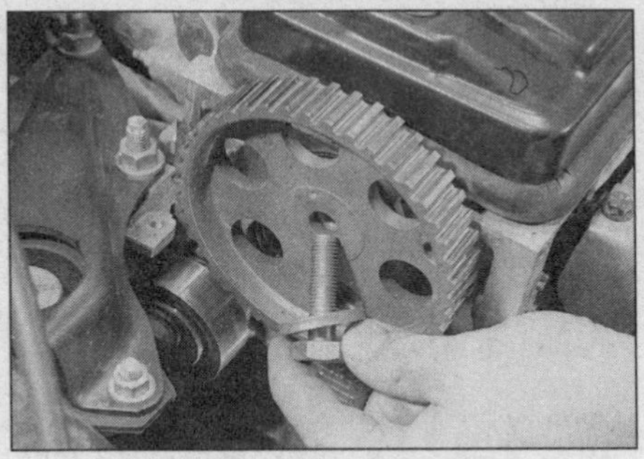

7.5a Slacken the retaining bolt and washer . . .

7 With the retaining bolt removed, slide the sprocket off the end of the camshaft. If the locating peg is a loose fit in the rear of the sprocket, remove it for safe-keeping. Examine the camshaft oil seal for signs of oil leakage and, if necessary, renew it as described in Section 8.

Crankshaft sprocket

8 To prevent crankshaft rotation whilst the crankshaft sprocket bolt is slackened, select top gear, and have an assistant apply the brakes firmly. *Do not* be tempted to use the flywheel locking pin to prevent the crankshaft from rotating; temporarily remove the locking pin from the rear of the flywheel prior to slackening the sprocket bolt, then refit it once the bolt has been slackened.
9 Unscrew the retaining bolt and washer, then slide the sprocket off the end of the crankshaft **(see illustrations)**. Refit the locating pin through the timing hole into the rear of the flywheel.
10 If the Woodruff key is a loose fit in the crankshaft, remove it and store it with the sprocket for safe-keeping. If necessary, also slide the flanged spacer off the end of the crankshaft **(see illustration)**. Examine the crankshaft oil seal for signs of oil leakage and, if necessary, renew as described in Section 15.

Tensioner/idler pulley

11 Slacken and remove the timing belt tensioner pulley retaining nut, and slide the

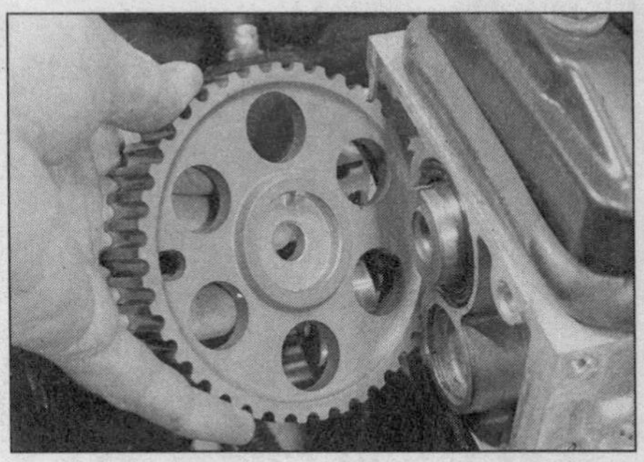

7.5b . . . then remove the camshaft sprocket

pulley off its mounting stud. Examine the mounting stud for signs of damage and, if necessary, renew it.
12 On DOHC models, an idler pulley is also fitted; its removal is as described for the tensioner pulley.

Inspection

13 Clean the sprockets thoroughly, and renew any that show signs of wear, damage or cracks.
14 Clean the tensioner assembly, but do not use any strong solvent which may enter the pulley bearing. Check that the pulley rotates freely about its hub, with no sign of stiffness or of free play. Renew the tensioner pulley if there is any doubt about its condition, or if there are any obvious signs of wear or damage.

Refitting

Camshaft sprocket

15 On SOHC models, refit the locating peg (where applicable) to the rear of the sprocket, then locate the sprocket on the end of the camshaft. Ensure that the locating peg is correctly engaged with the cut-out in the end of the camshaft.
16 On DOHC models, ensure that the peg on the rear surface of the sprocket hub locates correctly in the cut-out in the end of the camshaft.
17 Refit the sprocket retaining bolt and

7.9a Unscrew the retaining bolt and washer . . .

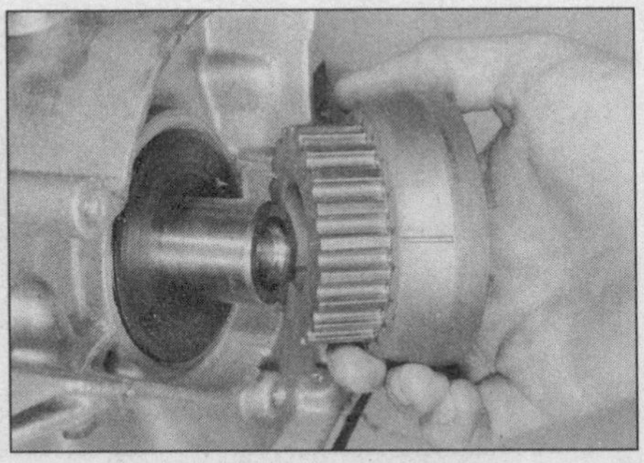

7.9b . . . then slide the sprocket off the end of the crankshaft

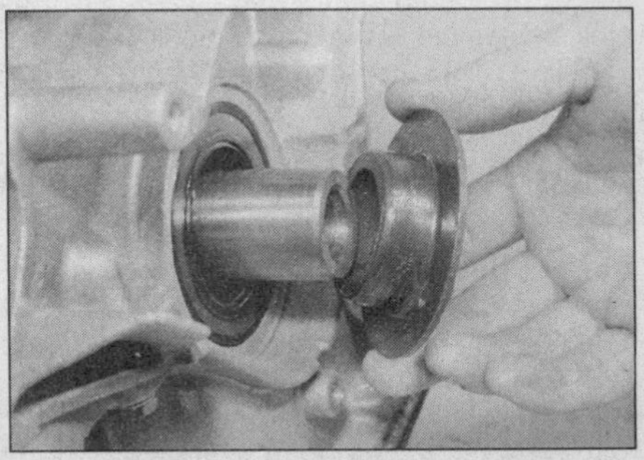

7.10 Recover the flanged spacer (where fitted)

TOOL TiP

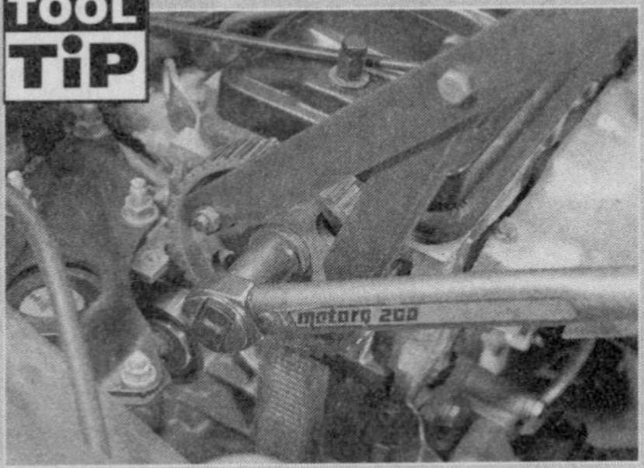

To make a camshaft sprocket holding tool, obtain two lengths of steel strip about 6 mm thick by 30 mm wide or similar, one 600 mm long, the other 200 mm long (all dimensions approximate). Bolt the two strips together to form a forked end, leaving the bolt slack so that the shorter strip can pivot freely. At the end of each 'prong' of the fork, secure a bolt with a nut and a locknut, to act as the fulcrums; these will engage with the cut-outs in the sprocket, and should protrude by about 30 mm

washer. Tighten the bolt to the specified torque, whilst retaining the sprocket with the tool used on removal **(see Tool Tip)**.

18 Realign the timing hole in the camshaft sprocket (see Section 3) with the corresponding hole in the cylinder head, and refit the locking pin.

19 Refit and tension the timing belt as described in Section 6.

20 Refit the timing belt covers (followed by the crankshaft pulley and auxiliary drivebelt, where applicable) as described in Section 5.

Crankshaft sprocket

21 Where removed, locate the Woodruff key in the crankshaft end, then slide on the flanged spacer, aligning its slot with the Woodruff key.

22 Align the crankshaft sprocket slot with the Woodruff key, and slide it onto the end of the crankshaft.

23 Temporarily remove the locking pin from the rear of the flywheel, then refit the crankshaft sprocket retaining bolt and washer. Tighten the bolt to the specified torque, whilst preventing crankshaft rotation using the method employed on removal. Refit the locking pin to the rear of the flywheel.

24 Refit and tension the timing belt as described in Section 6.

25 Refit the timing belt covers (followed by the crankshaft pulley and auxiliary drivebelt, where applicable) as described in Section 5.

Tensioner/idler pulley

26 Refit the tensioner pulley to its mounting stud, and fit the retaining nut.

27 Refit and tension the timing belt as described in Section 6.

28 Refit the timing belt covers (followed by the crankshaft pulley and auxiliary drivebelt, where applicable) as described in Section 5.

8 Camshaft oil seal - renewal

1 Remove the camshaft sprocket as described in Section 7.

2 Punch or drill two small holes opposite each other in the oil seal. Screw a self-tapping screw into each, and pull on the screws with pliers to extract the seal. Alternatively, carefully prise the seal from its housing with a flat bladed screwdriver **(see illustration)**. Take great care to avoid scoring the cylinder head and camshaft sealing surfaces.

3 Clean the seal housing, and polish off any burrs or raised edges, which may have caused the seal to fail in the first place.

4 Lubricate the lips of the new seal with clean engine oil, and drive it into position until it seats on its locating shoulder. Use a suitable tubular drift, such as a socket, which bears only on the hard outer edge of the seal. Take care not to damage the seal lips during fitting. Note that the seal lips should face inwards.

5 Refit the camshaft sprocket as described in Section 7.

8.2 Carefully prise the camshaft oil seal from its housing with a flat bladed screwdriver

9 Valve clearances (SOHC models) - checking and adjustment

Note: *The valve clearances must be checked and adjusted only when the engine is cold.*

1 This procedure only applies to SOHC models. DOHC models employ hydraulic tappets which automatically adjust the valve clearances.

2 The importance of having the valve clearances correctly adjusted cannot be overstressed, as they vitally affect the performance of the engine. If the clearances are too big, the engine will be noisy (characteristic rattling or tapping noises) and engine efficiency will be reduced, as the valves open too late and close too early. A more serious problem arises if the clearances are too small, however. If this is the case, the valves may not close fully when the engine is hot, resulting in serious damage to the engine (eg. burnt valve seats and/or cylinder head warping/cracking). The clearances are checked and adjusted as follows.

9.6 Adjusting a valve clearance

3 Remove the cylinder head cover as described in Section 4.

4 The engine can now be turned using a suitable socket and extension bar fitted to the crankshaft sprocket/pulley bolt.

HAYNES HiNT *Turning the engine will be easier if the spark plugs are removed first - see Chapter 1A.*

5 It is important that the clearance of each valve is checked and adjusted only when the valve is fully closed, with the rocker arm resting on the heel of the cam (directly opposite the peak). This can be ensured by carrying out the adjustments in the following sequence, noting that No 1 cylinder is at the transmission end of the engine. The correct valve clearances are given in the Specifications at the start of this Chapter. The valve locations can be determined from the position of the manifolds.

Valve fully open	Adjust valves
No 1 exhaust	*No 3 inlet and No 4 exhaust*
No 3 exhaust	*No 4 inlet and No 2 exhaust*
No 4 exhaust	*No 2 inlet and No 1 exhaust*
No 2 exhaust	*No 1 inlet and No 3 exhaust*

6 With the relevant valve fully open, check the clearances of the two valves specified. Clearances are checked by inserting a feeler blade of the correct thickness between the valve stem and the rocker arm adjusting screw. The feeler blade should be a light, sliding fit. If adjustment is necessary, slacken the adjusting screw locknut, and turn the screw as necessary **(see illustration)**. Once the correct clearance is obtained, hold the adjusting screw and securely tighten the locknut. Recheck the valve clearance, and adjust again if necessary.

7 Rotate the crankshaft until the next valve in the sequence is fully open, and check the clearances of the next two specified valves.

8 Repeat the procedure until all eight valve clearances have been checked (and if necessary, adjusted), then refit the cylinder head cover as described in Section 4.

10.4 Remove the circlip and slide the rocker components off the end of the rocker shaft

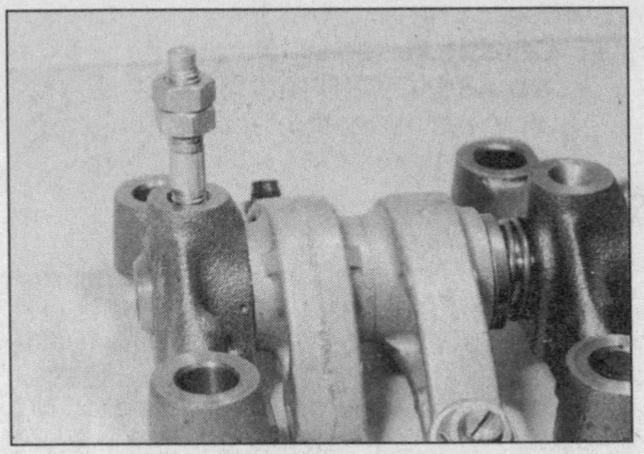

10.5a Use two locknuts to unscrew the left hand pedestal . . .

10.5b . . . then remove the grub screw beneath

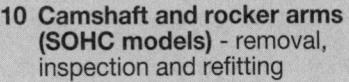

10 Camshaft and rocker arms (SOHC models) - removal, inspection and refitting

1 The rocker arm assembly is secured to the top of the cylinder head by the cylinder head bolts. Although in theory it is possible to undo the head bolts and remove the rocker arm assembly without removing the head, in practice, this is not recommended. Once the bolts have been removed, the head gasket will be disturbed, and the gasket will almost certainly leak or blow after refitting. For this reason, removal of the rocker arm assembly cannot be done without removing the cylinder head and renewing the head gasket.

2 The camshaft is slid out of the right-hand end of the cylinder head, and it therefore cannot be removed without first removing the cylinder head, due to a lack of clearance.

Removal

Rocker arm assembly

3 Remove the cylinder head as described in Section 12.

4 To dismantle the rocker arm assembly, carefully prise off the circlip from the right-hand end of the rocker shaft; retain the rocker pedestal, to prevent it being sprung off the end of the shaft. Slide the rocker components off the end of the shaft, keeping all components in their correct fitted order **(see illustration)**. Make a careful note of each component's correct fitted position and orientation as it is removed, to ensure it is refitted correctly on reassembly.

5 To separate the left-hand pedestal and shaft, first unscrew the cylinder head cover retaining stud from the top of the pedestal; this can be achieved using a stud extractor, or two nuts locked together. With the stud removed, unscrew the grub screw from the top of the pedestal, and withdraw the rocker shaft **(see illustrations)**.

Camshaft

6 Remove the cylinder head as described in Section 12.

7 With the head on a bench, remove the TDC locking pin, then remove the camshaft sprocket as described in Section 7.

8 Where applicable, unbolt the ignition coil module (see Chap-ter 5B) and its mounting bracket from the left-hand end of the cylinder head, then undo the retaining bolt, and remove the camshaft thrust fork from the cylinder head **(see illustration)**.

9 Using a large flat-bladed screwdriver, carefully prise the oil seal out of the right-hand end of the cylinder head (see Section 8), then slide out the camshaft **(see illustration)**. Discard the seal - a new one must be used on refitting.

Inspection

Rocker arm assembly

10 Examine the rocker arm bearing surfaces which contact the camshaft lobes for wear ridges and scoring; renew any rocker arm which displays signs of wear. If a rocker arm bearing surface is badly scored, also examine the corresponding lobe on the camshaft for wear, as it is likely to be worn also. Renew worn components as necessary. The rocker arm assembly can be dismantled as described in paragraphs 4 and 5.

11 Inspect the ends of the (valve clearance) adjusting screws for signs of wear or damage, and renew as required.

12 If the rocker arm assembly has been dismantled, examine the rocker arm and shaft bearing surfaces for wear ridges and scoring. If there are obvious signs of wear, the relevant rocker arm(s) and/or the shaft must be renewed.

10.8 Undo the retaining bolt then remove the camshaft thrust fork (arrowed) from the cylinder head

Camshaft

13 Examine the camshaft bearing surfaces and cam lobes for signs of wear ridges and scoring. Renew the camshaft if any of these conditions are apparent. Examine the condition of the bearing surfaces, both on the camshaft journals and in the cylinder head. If the head bearing surfaces are worn excessively, the cylinder head will need to be renewed.

14 Examine the thrust fork for signs of excessive wear or scoring, and renew as necessary.

Refitting

Rocker arm assembly

15 If the rocker arm assembly was dismantled, refit the rocker shaft to the left-hand pedestal, aligning its locating hole with the pedestal threaded hole. Refit the grub screw, and tighten it securely. With the grub screw in position, refit the cylinder head cover mounting stud to the pedestal, and tighten it securely. Apply a smear of clean engine oil to the shaft, then slide on all removed components, ensuring each is correctly fitted in its original position. Once all components are in position on the shaft, compress the right-hand pedestal and refit the circlip. Ensure that the circlip is correctly located in its groove on the shaft.

16 Refit the cylinder head and rocker arm assembly as described in Section 12.

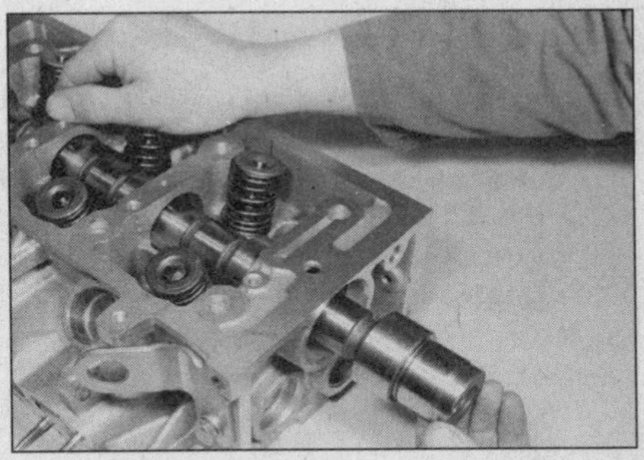

10.9 Carefully slide the camshaft from the cylinder head

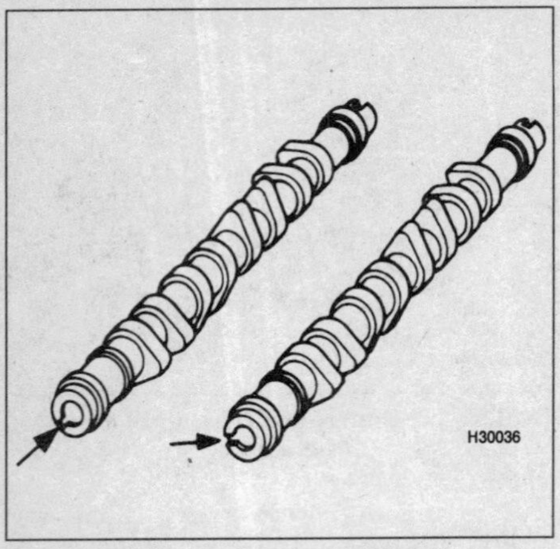

11.17 When refitting the camshafts, position them using the slots (arrowed) at the sprocket end of each camshaft as a guide

Camshaft

17 Ensure that the cylinder head and camshaft bearing surfaces are clean, then liberally oil the camshaft bearings and lobes. Slide the camshaft back into position in the cylinder head.

18 Locate the thrust fork with the left-hand end of the camshaft. Refit the fork retaining bolt, tightening it to the specified torque setting.

19 Ensure that the housing and cylinder head mating surfaces are clean and dry, then apply a smear of sealant to the housing mating surface. Refit the ignition coil module to the left-hand end of the head with reference to Chapter 5B, and securely tighten its retaining bolts.

20 Lubricate the lips of the new seal with clean engine oil, then drive it into position until it seats on its locating shoulder. Use a suitable tubular drift, such as a socket, which bears only on the hard outer edge of the seal. Take care not to damage the seal lip during fitting. Note that the seal lip should face inwards.

21 Refit the camshaft sprocket as described in Section 7.

22 Refit the cylinder head as described in Section 12.

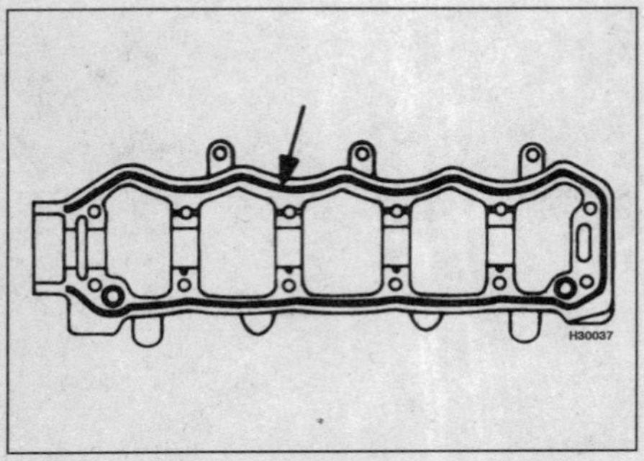

11.18 Apply a bead of suitable sealant (arrowed) to the camshaft bearing ladder mating surface

11 Camshaft and hydraulic tappets (DOHC models) - removal inspection and refitting

Removal

Note: *The removal, inspection and refitting procedures described in this Section are applicable to both the exhaust and inlet camshaft.*

1 Refer to Section 3 and set the engine to TDC on cylinder No 1. Check that the flywheel and camshaft locking tools can be inserted, then remove them and turn the engine anticlockwise (against its normal direction of rotation) by one quarter of a crankshaft revolution.

2 Refer to Section 4 and remove the cylinder head covers. Ensure that the securing screws are removed in a spiral sequence to avoid distorting the cover.

3 Refer to Section 6 and remove the timing belt.

4 Refer to Section 7 and remove the camshaft sprocket centre bolts. Prevent the camshafts from rotating as the bolts are slackened, by fitting an open ended spanner over the flats at the right hand end of the camshaft. Lift the sprockets from the end of the camshafts.

5 Unbolt and remove the inner section of the timing belt cover.

6 Slacken the relevant camshaft bearing ladder bolts progressively and in a spiral sequence to avoid distorting the ladder. Withdraw the bolts as they become free, then carefully release the bearing ladder from the cylinder head. Recover the locating dowels if they are loose.

7 Remove the oil seal from the end of the camshaft, then gently tap the right hand end of the camshaft to release it from its bearings.

8 Lift the camshaft away from the cylinder head and place it on a clean work surface.

9 If the hydraulic tappets are to be removed proceed as follows. Obtain eight small containers, or a large container divided into eight compartments to store the tappets (sixteen if both camshafts are to be removed).

10 Withdraw the tappets from their cylinder head bores - a tool fitted with a rubber suction cup (such as valve grinding tool) will aid in this operation. Store the tappets in the order that they are removed from the cylinder head, to ensure that they are refitted in the same locations. Failure to do this could lead to accelerated tappet and camshaft wear after reassembly, resulting in early failure.

11 After removing all the tappets, ensure that any excess oil accidentally spilled into the camshaft bearing ladder securing bolt holes is removed, using compressed air or an absorbent rag. This will prevent damage to the ladder by hydraulic action during reassembly.

Inspection

12 Examine the camshaft bearing surfaces and cam lobes for signs of wear ridges and scoring. Renew the camshaft if any of these conditions are apparent. Examine the condition of the bearing surfaces, both on the bearing ladder journals and in the cylinder head.

13 Inspect the tappet upper surfaces for signs of wear. If evident, examine the corresponding camshaft lobe as is likely to be worn in a similar manner. Check the sides of each tappet for signs of excessive scoring.

Refitting

14 Carefully clean the mating surfaces of the cylinder head and the bearing ladder, removing all traces of the old sealant.

15 Lubricate the hydraulic tappets with clean engine oil, the slide them carefully into their respective bores in the cylinder head. Ensure that each tappet is refitted to the same bore that it was originally removed from. Make sure that once fitted, the tappets are free to rotate in their bores.

16 Lubricate the cylinder head camshaft bearings using clean engine oil. Take care to avoid oiling the cylinder head-to-bearing ladder mating surface.

17 Lubricate the bearings on the camshaft itself using clean engine oil, then lower the camshaft onto the cylinder head. Position the camshaft using the slot at the sprocket end of the camshaft as a guide: on the exhaust camshaft, the slot must be in 8 o'clock position; on the inlet camshaft, the slot must be in 7 o'clock position **(see illustration)**. This is only a rough guide to allow reassembly to proceed - exact camshaft orientation will be set when the sprocket is refitted.

18 Ensure that the mating surface is clean and dry, then apply a bead of suitable sealant to the camshaft bearing ladder **(see illustration)**.

19 Ensure that the locating dowels are in place, then refit the bearing ladder to the cylinder head. Coat the threads of the securing bolts with locking compound, insert them into the holes in the bearing ladder and turn them by hand until the bolt heads contact the surface of the bearing ladder. Tighten the bolts progressively, and in the sequence shown, to the specified first stage torque wrench setting **(see illustration)**. On completion, tighten the bolts (again in the sequence shown) to the second stage torque wrench setting.

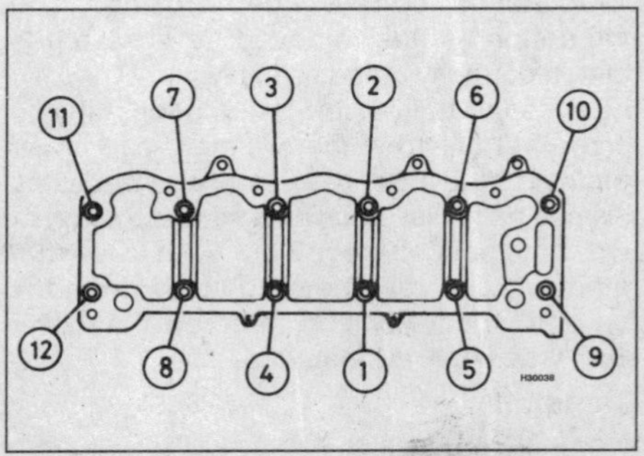

11.19 Tightening sequence for the camshaft bearing ladder securing bolts

20 Refer to Section 8 and fit a new camshaft oil seal.

21 Refit the inner section of the timing belt cover and tighten its securing bolts. Ensure that the cupped lower edge of the cover engages correctly with the lip at the top of the crankshaft oil seal housing **(see illustration)**.

22 Refer to Section 7 and refit the camshaft sprocket.

23 The engine will now have to be rotated clockwise to bring it back up to TDC on cylinder No 1, before the timing belt can be refitted. To avoid valve-to-piston contact, rotate the camshaft sprockets through one eighth of a turn to their TDC positions first, then turn the crankshaft sprocket through one quarter of a turn to its TDC position. Check that the engine is correctly set by inserting the TDC sprocket locking tools (see Section 3) then refit and tension the timing belt as described in Section 6.

24 Refit the timing belt outer covers as described in Section 9.

25 Refit the cylinder head cover with reference to Section 4. Note that the gasket can be reused providing that it is good condition.

26 Refit the remainder of the components removed for access, by following the removal procedure in reverse.

12 Cylinder head - removal and refitting

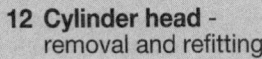

SOHC models

Removal

1 Disconnect the battery negative lead.

2 Drain the cooling system as described in Chapter 1A.

3 Remove the cylinder head cover as described in Section 4.

4 Align the engine assembly/valve timing holes as described in Section 3, and lock both the camshaft sprocket and flywheel in position. *Do not* attempt to rotate the engine whilst the tools are in position.

5 The cylinder head may be removed with both inlet and exhaust manifolds attached.

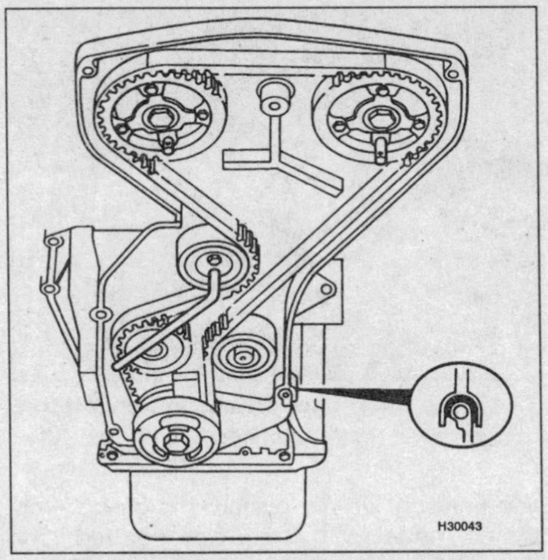

11.21 The cupped lower edge of the timing belt cover must engage correctly with the lip at the top of the crankshaft oil seal housing

This involves less dismantling work, but makes the cylinder head assembly bulky and heavy to handle. If you want to remove the manifolds first, proceed as described in the relevant Part(s) of Chapter 4. The illustrations here show the removal of the head without the manifolds.

6 Working as described in the relevant Part of Chapter 4, disconnect the exhaust system front pipe from the manifold. Disconnect or release the lambda sensor wiring, so that it is not strained by the weight of the exhaust.

7 Remove the entire air cleaner housing and inlet duct assembly as described in the relevant Part of Chapter 4.

8 Carry out the following operations as described in the relevant Part of Chapter 4:

a) Depressurise the fuel system, and disconnect the fuel feed and return hoses from the throttle body/fuel rail (plug all ports, to prevent loss of fuel and entry of dirt into the fuel system).

b) Disconnect the accelerator cable.

c) On single-point injection models, disconnect the relevant electrical connectors from the throttle body.

d) On multi-point injection models, disconnect the relevant electrical connectors from the throttle housing, fuel injectors and (where necessary) the idle speed auxiliary air valve.

e) Disconnect the vacuum servo unit hose, coolant hose(s) and all the other relevant/breather hoses from the manifold.

9 Remove the centre and upper timing belt covers as described in Section 5.

10 Loosen the timing belt tensioner pulley retaining nut. Pivot the pulley in a clockwise direction, using a suitable square-section key fitted to the hole in the pulley hub, then retighten the retaining nut.

11 Disengage the timing belt from the camshaft sprocket, and position the belt clear of the sprocket. Ensure that the belt is not bent or twisted sharply (see Section 6 for details).

12 Slacken the retaining clips, and disconnect the coolant hoses from the thermostat housing (on the left-hand end of the cylinder head) - refer to Chapter 3 **(see illustration)**.

13 Depress the retaining clip(s), and disconnect the wiring connector(s) from the electrical switch and/or sensor(s) which are screwed into the thermostat housing/cylinder head (as appropriate).

14 Disconnect the wiring connector from the ignition HT coil. If the cylinder head is to be dismantled for overhaul, remove the ignition HT coil as described in Chapter 5B. If the cylinder numbers are not already marked on the HT leads, number each lead, to avoid the possibility of the leads being incorrectly connected on refitting. Note that the HT leads should be disconnected from the spark plugs instead of the coil, and the coil and leads removed as an assembly.

15 Slacken and remove the bolt securing the engine oil dipstick tube to the cylinder head **(see illustration)**.

16 Progressively slacken the ten cylinder head bolts by half a turn at a time, in the *reverse* of the tightening sequence shown **(refer to illustration 12.34b)** until all bolts can be unscrewed by hand **(see illustrations)**.

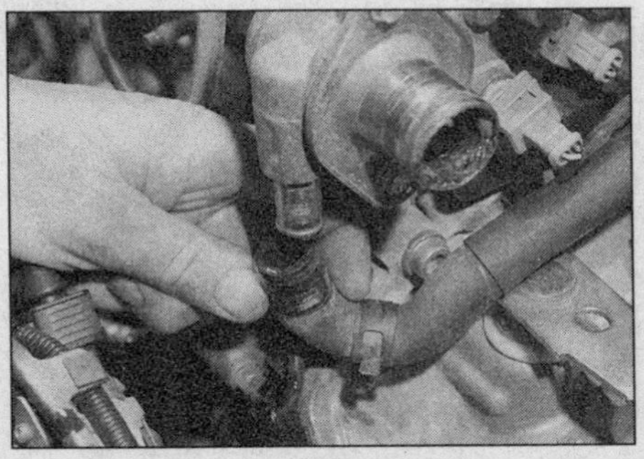

12.12 Disconnect the coolant hoses from the thermostat housing

12.15 Remove the bolt securing the engine oil dipstick tube to the cylinder head

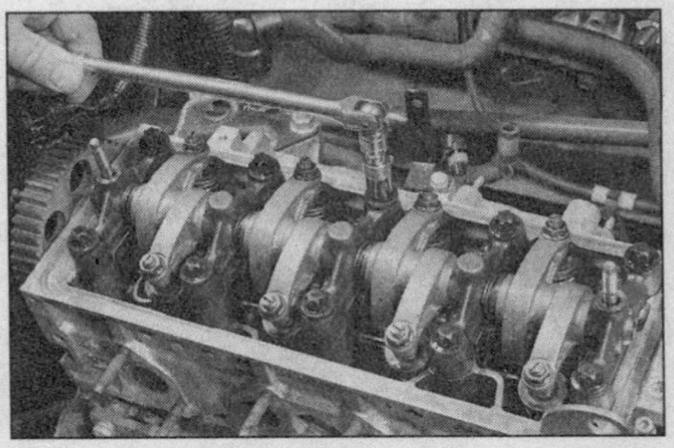

12.16a Progressively slacken the cylinder head bolts by half a turn at a time, in the *reverse* of the tightening sequence . . .

12.16b . . . until all bolts can be unscrewed by hand

12.17 Lift the rocker arm assembly off the cylinder head

12.19a Fit two stout screwdrivers into the cylinder head bolt holes and gently rock the head to release it from the cylinder block

17 With all the cylinder head bolts removed, lift the rocker arm assembly off the cylinder head **(see illustration)**. Note the locating pins which are fitted to the base of each rocker arm pedestal. If any pin is a loose fit in the head or pedestal, remove it for safe-keeping.

18 On engines with a cast-iron cylinder block, lift the cylinder head away; seek assistance if possible, as it is a heavy assembly, especially if it is being removed complete with the manifolds.

19 On engines with an aluminium cylinder block, the joint between the cylinder head and gasket and the cylinder block/crankcase must now be broken without disturbing the wet liners. To break the joint, obtain two L-shaped metal bars (or two stout screwdrivers) which fit into the cylinder head bolt holes. Gently "rock" the cylinder head free towards the front of the car. Do not try to swivel the head on the cylinder block/crankcase; it is located by dowels, as well as by the tops of the liners. **Note:** *If care is not taken and the liners are moved, there is also a possibility of the bottom seals being disturbed, causing leakage after refitting the head.* When the joint is broken, lift the cylinder head away; seek assistance if possible, as it is a heavy assembly, especially if it is being removed complete with the manifolds **(see illustrations)**.

20 On all models, remove the gasket from the top of the block, noting the two locating dowels **(see illustration)**.

21 If the locating dowels are a loose fit, remove them and store them with the head for safe-keeping. Do not discard the gasket - on some models it will be needed for identification purposes (see paragraph 26).

Caution: On aluminium block engines, do not attempt to rotate the crankshaft with the cylinder head removed, otherwise the wet liners may be displaced. Operations that require the rotation of the crankshaft (eg cleaning the piston crowns), should only be carried out once the cylinder liners are firmly clamped in position (see illustration). In the absence of the special Citroën liner clamps, the liners can be clamped in position using large flat washers positioned underneath suitable-length bolts. Alternatively, the original head bolts could be temporarily refitted, with suitable spacers fitted to their shanks.

22 If the cylinder head is to be dismantled for overhaul, remove the camshaft as described in Section 10, then refer to Part C of this Chapter.

Preparation for refitting

23 The mating faces of the cylinder head and cylinder block/crankcase must be perfectly clean before refitting the head. Citroën recommend the use of a scouring agent for this purpose, but acceptable results can be achieved by using a hard plastic or wood scraper to remove all traces of gasket and carbon. The same method can be used to clean the piston crowns, but refer to the *Caution* above before turning the crankshaft on aluminium block engines. Take particular care to avoid scoring or gouging the cylinder head/cylinder block mating surfaces during the cleaning operations, as aluminium alloy is easily damaged. Also, make sure that the carbon debris is not allowed to enter the oil and water passages - this is particularly important for the lubrication system, as carbon could block the oil supply to the engine's components. Using adhesive tape and paper, seal the water, oil and bolt holes in the cylinder block/crankcase. Clean all the pistons in the same way.

HAYNES HiNT ***To prevent carbon debris entering the gap between the pistons and bores, smear a little grease in the gap. After cleaning each piston, use a small brush to remove all traces of grease and carbon from the gap, then wipe away the remainder with a clean rag.***

24 Check the mating surfaces of the cylinder block/crankcase and the cylinder head for nicks, deep scratches and other damage. If slight, they may be removed carefully with a file. More extensive damage may cause head gasket leakage, and machining may be the only alternative to renewal.

25 If warpage of the cylinder head gasket surface is suspected, use a straight-edge to check it for distortion. Refer to Part C of this Chapter if necessary.

12.19b Lift the cylinder head away from the block

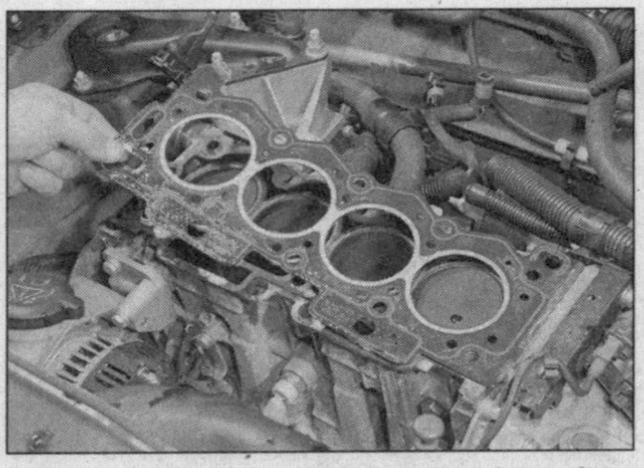

12.20 Remove the head gasket from the top of the cylinder block

12.21 The cylinder liners MUST be clamped in position before the crankshaft is rotated (clamps arrowed)

12.28 The two locating dowels (arrowed) must be in position at each end of the cylinder block surface (aluminium block engine shown)

12.29a Position a new gasket on the cylinder block/crankcase surface . . .

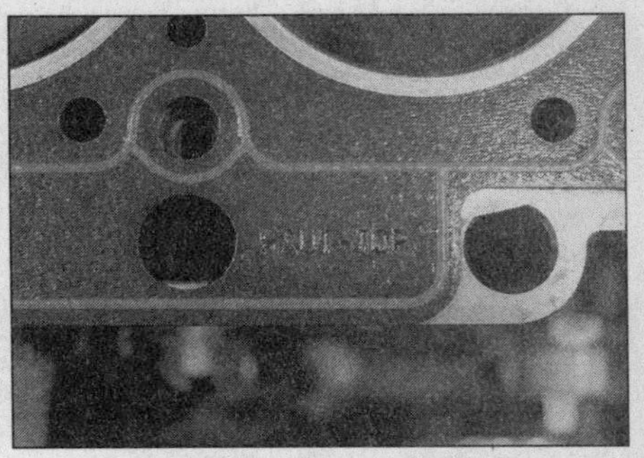

12.29b . . . ensuring that the manufacturers identification markings ("HAUT - TOP") face upwards

26 When purchasing a new cylinder head gasket, it is essential that a gasket of the correct thickness is obtained. At the time of writing, only one thickness of gasket was available, but confirm that this is still the case with your dealer or parts supplier. If you have any doubts, take the old gasket along to your dealer or parts supplier, and have him confirm the type of replacement gasket required.

27 Check the condition of the cylinder head bolts, and particularly their threads, whenever they are removed. Wash the bolts in suitable solvent, and wipe them dry. Check each for any sign of visible wear or damage, renewing any bolt if necessary. Measure the length of each bolt, to check for stretching (although this is not a conclusive test, in the event that all ten bolts have stretched by the same amount).

Caution: Although Citroën do not actually specify that the cylinder head bolts must be renewed, it is strongly recommended that the bolts should be renewed as a complete set whenever they are disturbed.

Refitting

28 Wipe clean the mating surfaces of the cylinder head and cylinder block/crankcase. Check that the two locating dowels are in position at each end of the cylinder block/crankcase surface **(see illustration)** and, where necessary, remove the cylinder liner clamps.

29 Position a new gasket on the cylinder block/crankcase surface, ensuring that the manufacturers identification markings face upwards **(see illustrations)**.

30 Check that the flywheel and camshaft sprocket are still correctly locked in position with their respective tools then, with the aid of an assistant, carefully refit the cylinder head assembly to the block, aligning it with the locating dowels.

31 Ensure that the locating pins are in position in the base of each rocker pedestal, then refit the rocker arm assembly to the cylinder head **(see illustration)**.

32 Apply a smear of grease to the threads, and to the underside of the heads of the cylinder head bolts **(see illustration)**. Citroën recommend the use of Molykote G Rapid Plus grease (available from your Citroën dealer - a sachet is supplied with the top-end gasket set); in the absence of the specified grease, a good-quality high-melting-point grease may be used.

33 Carefully enter each bolt into its relevant hole (*do not drop them in*) and screw in, by hand only, until finger-tight.

34 Working progressively and in the sequence shown, tighten the cylinder head bolts to their Stage 1 torque setting, using a torque wrench and suitable socket **(see illustrations)**.

35 Once all the bolts have been tightened to their Stage 1 setting, working again in the given sequence, angle-tighten the bolts through the specified Stage 2 angle, using a socket and extension bar. It is recommended that an angle-measuring gauge is used during this stage of the tightening, to ensure accuracy **(see illustration)**.

12.31 Refit the rocker arm assembly to the cylinder head

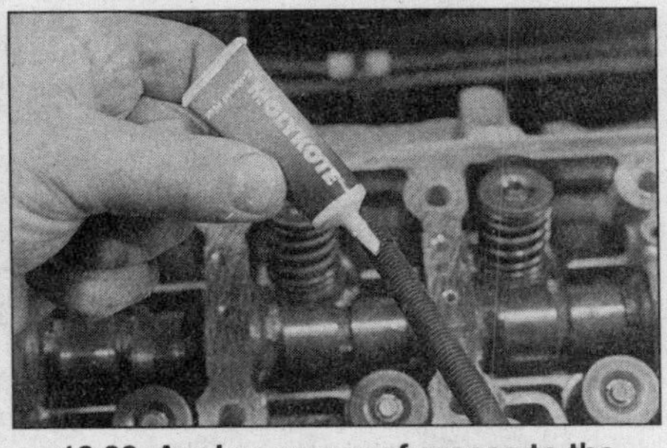

12.32 Apply a smear of grease to the threads, and to the underside of the heads of the cylinder head bolts

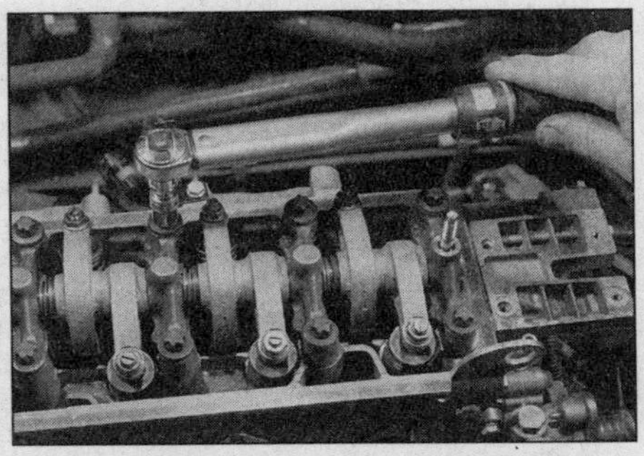

12.34a Tighten the cylinder head bolts, in the correct sequence, to the Stage 1 torque setting

12.34b Cylinder head bolt tightening sequence

12.35 Angle-tighten the bolts, in the correct sequence, through the specified Stage 2 angle

> **HAYNES HiNT** ***If an angle-measuring gauge is not available, use white paint to make alignment marks between the bolt head and cylinder head prior to tightening; the marks can then be used to check that the bolt has been rotated through the correct angle during tightening.***

36 On cast-iron block engines, it will then be necessary to tighten the bolts through the specified Stage 3 angle setting. Again, use an angle-measuring gauge to ensure accuracy.
37 With the cylinder head bolts correctly tightened, refit the dipstick tube retaining bolt and tighten it securely.
38 Refit and tension the timing belt as described in Section 6.
39 Refit the timing belt covers as described in Section 5.
40 If the head was stripped for overhaul, refit the ignition HT coil and leads as described in Chapter 5B.
41 Reconnect the wiring connector(s) to the coolant switch/sensor(s) on the left-hand end of the head.
42 Reconnect the coolant hoses to the thermostat housing, securely tightening their retaining clips.
43 Working as described in the relevant Part of Chapter 4, carry out the following tasks:

a) Refit all disturbed wiring, hoses and control cable(s) to the inlet manifold and fuel system components.
b) Reconnect and adjust the accelerator cable.
c) Reconnect the exhaust system front pipe to the manifold. Reconnect the lambda sensor wiring connector.
d) Refit the air cleaner housing and inlet ducts.

44 Check (and if necessary, adjust) the valve clearances as described in Section 9, then refit the cylinder head cover as described in Section 4.
45 On completion, reconnect the battery negative cable, then refill the cooling system as described in Chapter 1A.

DOHC models

Removal

46 Disconnect the battery negative lead.
47 Drain the cooling system as described in Chapter 1A.
48 Remove the cylinder head covers as described in Section 4.
49 Remove the air cleaner, resonator and its associated ducting as described in of Chapter 4B.
50 Refer to Section 5 and remove the timing belt upper and lower covers.
51 Align the engine assembly/valve timing holes as described in Section 3, and lock the camshaft sprockets and flywheel in position in the TDC position. *Do not* attempt to rotate the engine whilst the tools are in position.
52 With reference to Section 6, release the tension from the timing belt and disengage it from the camshaft sprockets. Keep the belt taught so that the lower end remains engaged with the crankshaft sprocket.
53 Remove the exhaust and inlet manifolds from the cylinder head, with reference to the relevant part of Chapter 4.
54 Working at the left hand side of the engine, slacken the clip and disconnect the heater matrix supply hose from the coolant housing at the side of the cylinder head.
55 Depress the retaining clip(s), and disconnect the wiring connector(s) from the electrical switch and/or sensor(s) which are screwed into the thermostat housing/cylinder head (as appropriate).
56 Slacken and remove the bolt securing the engine oil dipstick tube to the cylinder head.
57 Remove the securing screw and disconnect the earth lead from the cylinder head.
Note: *The cylinder head is removed with the inner section of the timing belt still attached. If required, the camshaft sprockets can be removed (as described in Section 7) allowing the inner cover to be unbolted and removed.*
58 Using a size STX 14 TORX socket, progressively slacken the ten cylinder head bolts by half a turn at a time, in the *reverse* order of the tightening sequence **(refer to illustration 12.34b)** until all bolts can be unscrewed by hand.
59 Break the joint between the cylinder head and gasket and the cylinder block/crankcase using two L-shaped metal bars fitted into the cylinder head bolt holes. Gently "rock" the cylinder head free towards the front of the car. Do not try to swivel the head on the cylinder block/crankcase as it is located by dowels.
60 Lift the cylinder head away from the cylinder block; seek assistance if possible, as it is a heavy assembly.
61 Remove the gasket from the top of the cylinder block, noting the two locating dowels.
62 If the cylinder head is to be dismantled for overhaul, remove the camshaft as described in Section 10, then refer to Part C of this Chapter.

Preparation for refitting

63 Refer to the information given in paragraphs 23 to 26.
64 Check the condition of the cylinder head bolts, and particularly their threads, whenever they are removed. Wash the bolts in suitable solvent, and wipe them dry. Check each for any sign of visible wear or damage, renewing any bolt if necessary. Measure the length of each bolt, to check for stretching. Citroën state that the bolts may be re-used, provided that their lengths do not exceed 122.6 mm; if any of the bolts are stretched beyond this limit, the cylinder head bolts must be renewed as a complete set of 10.
Caution: We recommended that the cylinder head bolts are renewed as a complete set whenever they are disturbed, as a precautionary measure.

Refitting

65 Wipe clean the mating surfaces of the cylinder head and cylinder block/crankcase. Check that the two locating dowels are in position at each end of the cylinder block/crankcase surface.
66 Position a new gasket on the cylinder block/crankcase surface, ensuring that the manufacturers identification markings face upwards.
67 Check that the flywheel and camshaft sprockets are still correctly locked in position with their respective tools then, with the aid of an assistant, carefully refit the cylinder head assembly to the block, aligning it with the locating dowels. Ensure that the lower edge of the inner section of the timing belt cover engages correctly with the lug on the crankshaft oil seal housing.
68 Apply a smear of grease to the threads, and to the underside of the heads, of the cylinder head bolts. Citroën recommend the use of Molykote G Rapid Plus grease (available from your Citroën dealer - a sachet is supplied with the top-end gasket set); in the absence of the specified grease, a good-quality high-melting-point grease may be used.
69 Carefully enter each bolt into its relevant hole (*do not drop them in*) and screw in, by hand only, until finger-tight.
70 Working progressively and in the sequence shown, tighten the cylinder head bolts to their Stage 1 torque setting, using a torque wrench and suitable socket **(see illustration 12.34b).**
71 Once all the bolts have been tightened to their Stage 1 setting, working again in the given sequence, angle-tighten the bolts through the specified Stage 2 angle, using a socket and extension bar. It is recommended that an angle-measuring gauge is used during this stage of the tightening, to ensure accuracy.

> **HAYNES HiNT** ***If an angle-measuring gauge is not available, use white paint to make alignment marks between the bolt head and cylinder head prior to tightening; the marks can then be used to check that the bolt has been rotated through the correct angle during tightening.***

72 Pour a small quantity of clean engine oil into the cavities above each of the hydraulic tappet bores.
73 Refit the cylinder head covers as described in Section 4.
74 Refit the dipstick tube retaining bolt and tighten it securely.
75 With reference to Section 6, refit and tension the timing belt.
76 Refit the timing belt covers as described in Section 5.

77 Reconnect the earth lead to the cylinder head and tighten the securing bolt.
78 Reconnect the wiring connector(s) to the coolant switch/sensor(s) and secure the TDC sensor wiring in its clip.
79 Reconnect the coolant hoses to the coolant housing, securely tightening their retaining clips.
80 Refit the exhaust and inlet manifolds to the cylinder head, with reference to the relevant part of Chapter 4.
81 Refit the air cleaner, resonator and ducting with reference to the relevant part of Chapter 4.
82 Reconnect the battery negative cable, then refill the cooling system as described in Chapter 1A.

13 Sump - removal and refitting

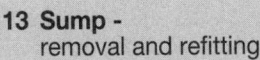

Removal

1 Firmly apply the handbrake, then jack up the front of the vehicle and support it on axle stands (see "*Jacking and vehicle support*"). Disconnect the battery negative lead.
2 Drain the engine oil, then clean and refit the engine oil drain plug, tightening it to the specified torque. If the engine is nearing its service interval when the oil and filter are due for renewal, it is recommended that the filter is also removed, and a new one fitted. After reassembly, the engine can then be refilled with fresh oil. Refer to Chapter 1A for further information.
3 Remove the exhaust system front pipe as described in Chapter 4D.
4 Progressively slacken and remove all the sump retaining nuts and bolts **(see illustration)**. On cast-iron block engines, it may be necessary to unbolt the flywheel cover plate from the transmission to gain access to the left-hand sump fasteners.
5 Break the joint by striking the sump with the palm of your hand, then lower the sump and withdraw it from underneath the vehicle **(see illustration)**.
6 While the sump is removed, take the opportunity to check the oil pump pick-up/strainer for signs of clogging or splitting. If necessary, remove the pump as described in Section 14, and clean or renew the strainer.

Refitting

7 Clean all traces of sealant from the mating surfaces of the cylinder block/crankcase and sump, then use a clean rag to wipe out the sump and the engine's interior.
8 Ensure that the sump and cylinder block/crankcase mating surfaces are clean and dry, then apply a coating of

13.4 Progressively slacken and remove all the sump retaining nuts and bolts

suitable sealant to the sump mating surface.
9 Offer up the sump, locating it on its retaining studs, and refit its retaining nuts and bolts. Tighten the nuts and bolts evenly and progressively to the specified torque.
10 Refit the exhaust front pipe as described in the relevant Part of Chapter 4.
11 Replenish the engine oil as described in Chapter 1A.

14 Oil pump - removal, inspection and refitting

Removal

1 Remove the sump as described in Section 13.
2 Slacken and remove the three bolts securing the oil pump to the crankcase **(see illustration)**. Disengage the pump sprocket from the chain, and remove the oil pump. If the pump locating dowel is a loose fit, remove and store it with the retaining bolts for safe-keeping.

Inspection

3 Examine the oil pump sprocket for signs of damage and wear such as chipped or missing teeth. If the sprocket is worn, the pump assembly must be renewed, as the sprocket is not available separately. It is also recommended that the chain and drive sprocket, fitted to the crankshaft, is renewed at the same time. On aluminium block engines, renewal of the chain and drive sprocket is an involved operation requiring the removal of the main bearing ladder and crankshaft, and therefore cannot be carried out with the engine still fitted to the vehicle. On cast-iron block engines, the oil pump drive sprocket and chain can be removed with the engine in situ, once the crankshaft sprocket has been removed and the crankshaft oil seal housing has been unbolted. Refer to Part C for further information.
4 Slacken and remove the bolts securing the

13.5 Remove the sump from the crankcase

strainer cover to the pump body, then lift off the strainer cover. Remove the relief valve piston and spring (and guide pin - cast-iron block engines only), noting which way round they are fitted.
5 Examine the pump rotors and body for signs of wear ridges and scoring. If worn, the complete pump assembly must be renewed.
6 Examine the relief valve piston for signs of wear or damage, and renew if necessary. The condition of the relief valve spring can only be measured by comparing it with a new one; if there is any doubt about its condition, it should also be renewed. Both the piston and spring are available individually.
7 Thoroughly clean the oil pump strainer with a suitable solvent, and check it for signs of clogging or splitting. If the strainer is damaged, the strainer and cover assembly must be renewed.
8 Locate the relief valve spring, piston and (where fitted) the guide pin in the strainer cover, then refit the cover to the pump body. Align the relief valve piston with its bore in the pump. Refit the cover retaining bolts, tightening them securely.

Refitting

9 Ensure that the locating dowel is in position, then engage the pump sprocket with its drive chain. Locate the pump on its dowel and refit the pump retaining bolts, tightening them to the specified torque setting.
10 Refit the sump as described in Section 13.

14.2 Remove the three bolts securing the oil pump to the crankcase

15 Crankshaft oil seals - renewal

Right-hand oil seal

1 Remove the crankshaft sprocket and flanged spacer as described in Section 7. Secure the timing belt clear of the working area, so that it cannot be contaminated with oil. Make a note of the correct fitted depth of the seal in its housing.

> **HAYNES HiNT** *Punch or drill two small holes opposite each other in the seal. Screw a self-tapping screw into each, and pull on the screws with pliers to extract the seal.*

2 Alternatively, the seal can be levered out of position using a suitable flat-bladed screwdriver, taking **great care** not to damage the crankshaft shoulder or seal housing **(see illustration)**.

3 Clean the seal housing, and polish off any burrs or raised edges, which may have caused the seal to fail in the first place.

4 Lubricate the lip of the new seal with clean engine oil, and carefully locate the seal on the end of crankshaft. Note that its sealing lip must face inwards. Take care not to damage the seal lip during fitting.

5 Using a suitable tubular drift (such as a socket) which bears only on the hard outer edge of the seal, tap the seal into position, to the same depth in the housing as the original was prior to removal. The inner face of the seal must end up flush with the inner wall of the crankcase.

6 Wash off any traces of oil, then refit the crankshaft sprocket as described in Section 7.

Left-hand oil seal

7 Remove the flywheel as described in Section 17.

8 Make a note of the correct fitted depth of the seal in its housing. Punch or drill two small holes opposite each other in the seal. Screw a self-tapping screw into each, and pull on the screws with pliers to extract the seal.

15.2 The right-hand crankshaft oil seal can be levered out of position using a flat-bladed screwdriver

9 Clean the seal housing, and polish off any burrs or raised edges, which may have caused the seal to fail in the first place.

10 Lubricate the lip of the new seal with clean engine oil, and carefully locate the seal on the end of the crankshaft.

11 Using a suitable tubular drift, which bears only on the hard outer edge of the seal, drive the seal into position, to the same depth in the housing as the original was prior to removal.

12 Wash off any traces of oil, then refit the flywheel as described in Section 17.

16 Oil cooler (1587 cc 16-valve models) - removal and refitting

Removal

1 Firmly apply the handbrake, then jack up the front of the vehicle and support it on axle stands (see "*Jacking and vehicle support*").

2 Drain the cooling system as described in Chapter 1A. Alternatively, clamp the oil cooler coolant hoses directly above the cooler pipes, and be prepared for some coolant loss as the hoses are disconnected.

3 With reference to Chapter 1A, drain the engine oil and remove the oil filter.

4 Release the hose clips, and disconnect the coolant hoses from the oil cooler.

5 Undo the bolt securing the oil cooler pipes to the front of the crankcase, then unscrew the oil cooler/oil filter mounting bolt from the cylinder block, and withdraw the cooler. Note that the mounting bolt may be stiff as the threads will be coated wit locking compound. Discard the oil cooler sealing ring; a new one must be used on refitting.

Refitting

6 Fit a new sealing ring to the recess in the rear of the cooler, then offer up the cooler to the cylinder block. Coat the threads of the mounting bolt with locking compound, then refit it and tighten to the specified torque. Fit the bolt securing the cooler pipes to the front of the crankcase, and tighten it securely.

7 Fit the oil filter, then lower the vehicle to the ground. Refill the engine with oil, as described in Chapter 1A.

8 Refill or top-up the cooling system (as applicable) as described in Chapter 1A or "*Weekly checks*", then start the engine and check the oil cooler for signs of oil or coolant leakage.

17 Flywheel - removal, inspection and refitting

Removal

1 Remove the transmission as described in Chapter 7A, then remove the clutch assembly as described in Chapter 6.

2 Prevent the flywheel from turning by locking the ring gear teeth with a similar arrangement to that described in Section 7. Alternatively, bolt a strap between the flywheel and the cylinder block/crankcase. *Do not* attempt to lock the flywheel in position using the TDC locking pin described in Section 3.

3 Slacken and remove the flywheel retaining bolts, and discard them; they must be renewed whenever they are disturbed.

4 Remove the flywheel. Do not drop it, as it is very heavy. If the locating dowel is a loose fit in the crankshaft end, remove and store it with the flywheel for safe-keeping.

Inspection

5 If the flywheel's clutch mating surface is deeply scored, cracked or otherwise damaged, the flywheel must be renewed. However, it may be possible to have it surface-ground; seek the advice of a Citroën dealer or engine reconditioning specialist.

6 If the ring gear is badly worn or has missing teeth, it must be renewed. This job is best left to a Citroën dealer or engine reconditioning specialist. The temperature to which the new ring gear must be heated for installation is critical and, if not done accurately, the hardness of the teeth will be destroyed.

Refitting

7 Clean the mating surfaces of the flywheel and crankshaft. Remove any remaining locking compound from the threads of the crankshaft holes, using the correct-size tap, if available.

> **HAYNES HiNT** *If a suitable tap is not available, cut two slots into the threads of one of the old flywheel bolts and use the bolt to remove the locking compound from the threads.*

8 If the new flywheel retaining bolts are not supplied with their threads already pre-coated, apply a suitable thread-locking compound to the threads of each bolt.

9 Ensure that the locating dowel is in position. Offer up the flywheel, locating it on the dowel, and fit the new retaining bolts.

10 Lock the flywheel using the method employed during dismantling, and tighten the retaining bolts to the specified torque.

11 Refit the clutch as described in Chapter 6. Remove the locking tool, and refit the transmission as described in Chapter 7A.

18 Engine/transmission mountings - inspection and renewal

Inspection

1 If improved access is required, raise the front of the car and support it securely on axle stands (see "*Jacking and vehicle support*").

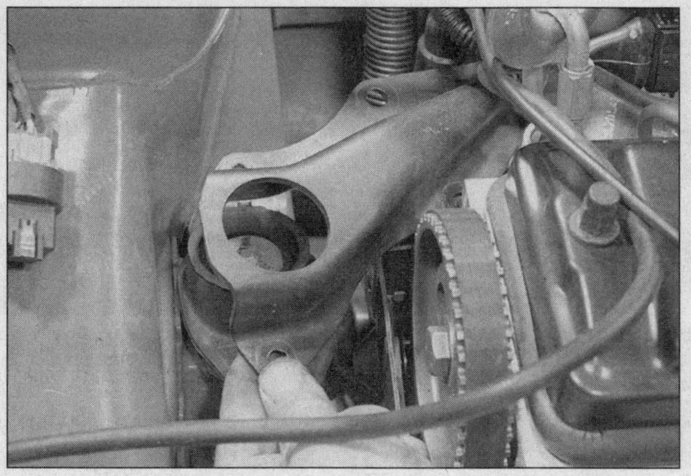

18.7 Removing the right-hand engine mounting bracket

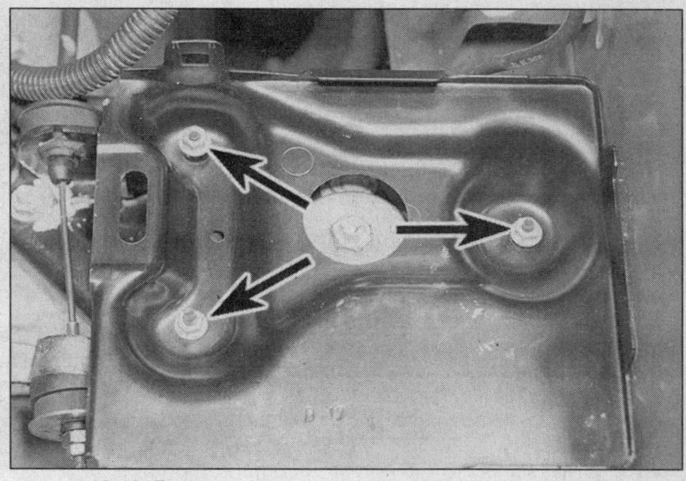

18.13 Battery support tray securing nuts (arrowed)

2 Check the mounting rubber to see if it is cracked, hardened or separated from the metal at any point; renew the mounting if any such damage or deterioration is evident.

3 Check that all the mounting's fasteners are securely tightened; use a torque wrench to check if possible.

4 Using a large screwdriver or a crowbar, check for wear in the mounting by carefully levering against it to check for freeplay. Where this is not possible, enlist the aid of an assistant to move the engine/transmission back and forth, or from side to side, while you watch the mounting. While some free play is to be expected even from new components, excessive wear should be obvious. If excessive free play is found, check first that the fasteners are correctly secured, then renew any worn components as described below.

18.15a Slacken and remove the mounting rubber centre nut and washer . . .

Renewal

Right-hand mounting

5 Disconnect the battery negative lead.

6 Place a jack beneath the engine, with a block of wood on the jack head. Raise the jack until it is supporting the weight of the engine (see "*Jacking and vehicle support*").

7 Slacken and remove the nuts securing the right-hand engine mounting upper bracket to the engine bracket (four nuts on cast iron block engines, three or four nuts on alloy block engines) **(see illustration)**.

8 Slacken and remove the two bolts securing the rubber mounting to the vehicle body, and then remove the mounting, together with the upper bracket, from the vehicle.

9 Check carefully for signs of wear or damage on all components, and renew them where necessary.

10 On reassembly, securely tighten the bolts securing the mounting rubber to the body.

11 Tighten the mounting bracket retaining nuts to the specified torque setting.

12 Remove the jack from underneath the engine, and reconnect the battery negative lead.

Left-hand mounting

13 Remove the battery as described in Chapter 5A, then unbolt and remove the battery support tray **(see illustration)**.

14 Place a jack beneath the transmission, with a block of wood on the jack head. Raise the jack until it is supporting the weight of the transmission (see "*Jacking and vehicle support*").

15 Slacken and remove the mounting rubber centre nut and washer, then unscrew the two bolts securing the bracket to the body. Remove the mounting rubber, and slide the spacer off the mounting bracket stud **(see illustrations)**.

16 Where necessary, unscrew the nuts and remove the bracket from the transmission.

17 Check carefully for signs of wear or damage on all components, and renew them where necessary.

18 Refit the bracket to the transmission, tightening its mounting nuts to the specified torque.

19 Refit the spacer, then fit the mounting to the body, and tighten its retaining bolts to the specified torque.

20 Refit the mounting centre nut, and tighten it to the specified torque.

18.15b . . . then unscrew the two securing bolts . . .

18.15c . . . and remove the mounting rubber from the body

18.15d Slide the spacer off the mounting bracket stud

21 Remove the jack from underneath the transmission, then refit the battery as described in Chapter 5A.

Rear mounting

22 If not already done, firmly apply the handbrake, then jack up the front of the vehicle and support it securely on axle stands (see "*Jacking and vehicle support*").

23 Unscrew and remove the bolts securing the rear mounting link to the rear of the transmission **(see illustration)**.

24 Remove the bolt securing the rear mounting link to the bracket on the underbody. Withdraw the link **(see illustration)**.

25 Check carefully for signs of wear or damage on all components, and renew them where necessary.

26 On reassembly, fit the rear mounting assembly to the rear of the transmission, and tighten its retaining bolts to the specified torque.

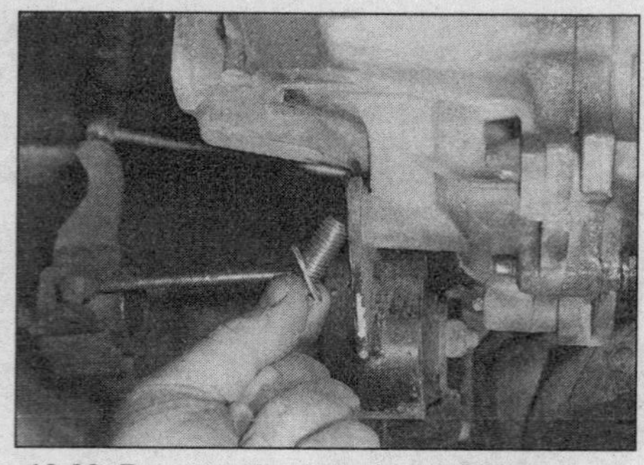

18.23 Remove the bolts securing the rear mounting link to the rear of the transmission

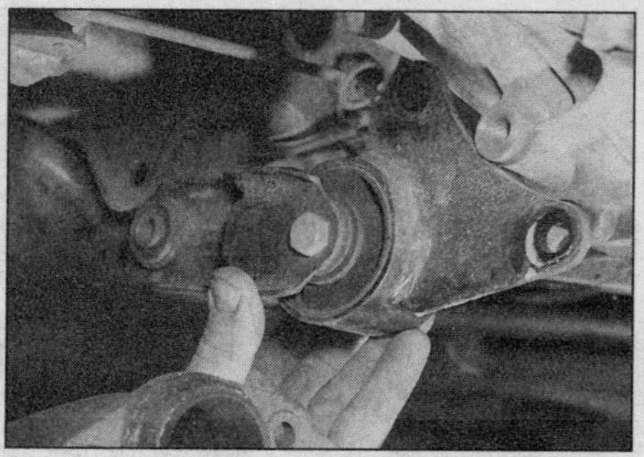

18.24 Unbolt the rear mounting link from the bracket on the underbody

27 Refit the rear mounting link, and tighten both its bolts to the specified torque.

28 Lower the vehicle to the ground.

Chapter 2 Part B:
Diesel engine in-car repair procedures

Contents

Degrees of difficulty

Easy, suitable for novice with little experience	**Fairly easy,** suitable for beginner with some experience	**Fairly difficult,** suitable for competent DIY mechanic	**Difficult,** suitable for experienced DIY mechanic	**Very difficult,** suitable for expert DIY or professional

Specifications

General

Engine code	TUD 5
Legislation type code*	VJZ or VJY
Capacity	1527 cc
Bore	77.0 mm
Stroke	82.0 mm
Direction of crankshaft rotation	Clockwise (viewed from right-hand side of vehicle)
No 1 cylinder location	At transmission end of block
Compression ratio	23 : 1
Maximum power (DIN)	55/58 bhp (40/42 kW) at 5000 rpm
Maximum torque (DIN)	95 Nm (70 lbf ft) at 2250 rpm

**The legislation type code is stamped on a plate, attached to the front left-hand end of the cylinder block.*

Camshaft

Drive	Toothed belt
Number of bearings	3
Cylinder head bearing journal internal diameters:	
No 1 (vacuum pump end)	27.533 to 27.538 mm
No 2 (centre)	28.033 to 28.038 mm
No 3 (timing belt end)	28.533 to 28.538 mm

Valve clearances (engine cold)

Inlet	0.15 ± 0.08 mm
Exhaust	0.30 ± 0.08 mm

Timing belt tension

(Using special Citroën electronic belt tension measuring equipment)	
Stage 1	100 SEEM units
Final stage	55 ± 5 SEEM units

Cylinder

Cylinder head bolt maximum overall length	
Hex head bolts	197.1 mm
TORX head bolts	197.5 mm
Nominal cylinder head height	136.4 ± 0.1 mm
Maximum gasket face distortion	0.05 mm

Lubrication system

Oil pump type	Gear-type, chain-driven from crankshaft
Minimum oil pressure at 90°C:	
At 4000 rpm	4 bar
At 2000 rpm	3 bar
Oil pressure warning switch operating pressure	0.8 bars

Torque wrench settings

Torque wrench settings Nm lbf ft

Torque wrench settings	Nm	lbf ft
Timing belt cover bolts	7	5
Crankshaft pulley bolts	15	11
Sump retaining nuts and bolts	10	7
Sump drain plug	30	22
Oil pump retaining bolts	10	7
Flywheel retaining bolts	65	48
Big-end bearing cap nuts	40	30
Main bearing cap bolts		
Stage 1	20	15
Stage 2	Angle-tighten a further 50°	
Timing belt tensioner pulley nut	25	18
Timing belt idler pulley bolt	20	15
Fuel injection pump sprocket hub bolts	23	17
Camshaft bearing cap	20	15
Camshaft sprocket hub-to-camshaft bolt:		
Models up to December 1998	80	59
Models from January 1999 onwards:		
Stage 1	40	30
Stage 2	Angle-tighten a further 20°	
Camshaft sprocket-to-hub bolts	23	17
Crankshaft sprocket retaining bolt:		
Models up to December 1998	110	81
Models from January 1999 onwards:		
Stage 1	70	52
Stage 2	Angle-tighten a further 45°	
Cylinder head bolts:		
Stage 1	40	30
Stage 2 (up to December 1998)	Angle-tighten a further 260 ± 5°	
Stage 2 (January 1999 onwards)	Angle-tighten a further 300 ± 5°	
Cylinder head cover bolts:		
Pre-tighten by	5	4
Then to	10	7
Engine/transmission right-hand mounting:		
Mounting bracket-to-engine nuts	45	33
Mounting bracket-to-body nut(s)	30	22
Engine/transmission left-hand mounting:		
Mounting bracket-to-body bolts	30	22
Centre nut	65	48
Mounting bracket-to-transmission nuts	25	18
Engine/transmission rear mounting:		
Mounting link-to-body bolt	70	51
Mounting link-to-transmission bracket bolt	50	37
Transmission bracket-to- casing bolts	85	63

1 General information

How to use this Chapter

1 This Part of Chapter 2 describes the repair procedures that can reasonably be carried out on the diesel engine while it remains in the vehicle. If the engine has been removed from the vehicle and is being dismantled as described in Part C, any preliminary dismantling procedures can be ignored.

2 Note that, while it may be physically possible to remove items such as the piston/connecting rod assemblies while the engine is in the car, such tasks are normally carried out as part of a complete overhaul, not as separate operations. Usually, several additional procedures are required (not to mention the cleaning of components and of oilways); for this reason, all such tasks are classed as major overhaul procedures, and are described in Part C of this Chapter.

3 Part C describes the removal of the engine/transmission from the vehicle, and the full overhaul procedures that can then be carried out.

Engine description

4 The diesel engine fitted to the Citroën Saxo is derived from the TU series of engines. The TUD is a well-proven engine which has been fitted to several other Citroën and Peugeot vehicles. The bottom end of the engine is very similar to that of the cast iron block TU petrol engine, covered in Part A of this Chapter. The Saxo range is fitted with a 1527 cc (TUD5) version of the engine. The engine is of the in-line four-cylinder, overhead camshaft (OHC) type, mounted transversely at the front of the car. The flywheel, clutch and transmission are attached to its left-hand end.

5 The crankshaft runs in five main bearings. Thrustwashers are fitted to No 2 main bearing (upper half) to control crankshaft endfloat.

6 The connecting rods rotate on horizontally-split bearing shells at their big-ends. The pistons are attached to the connecting rods by gudgeon pins, which are secured in position with circlips. The aluminium-alloy pistons are fitted with three piston rings - two compression rings and an oil control ring.

7 The inlet and exhaust valves are each closed by coil springs, and operate in guides pressed into the cylinder head. The valve seat inserts are also pressed into the cylinder head, and can be renewed separately if worn.

8 The camshaft is driven by a toothed timing belt, and operates the eight valves via bucket-type followers which are positioned directly below the camshaft. Valve clearance adjustment is by means of shims. The camshaft is supported by three bearings machined directly in the cylinder head and is retained by bearing caps.

9 Lubrication is by means of an oil pump, which is driven (via a chain and sprocket) off the right-hand end of the crankshaft. It draws oil through a strainer located in the sump, and then forces it through an externally-mounted filter into galleries in the cylinder block/crankcase. From there, the oil is distributed to the crankshaft (main bearings) and camshaft. The big-end bearings are supplied with oil via internal drillings in the crankshaft, while the camshaft bearings also receive a pressurised supply. The camshaft lobes and valves are lubricated by splash, as are all other engine components.

10 Throughout this manual, it is often necessary to identify the engines not only by their capacity, but also by their engine code which can be found on the left-hand end of the front face of the cylinder block. The code is stamped on a metal plate which is riveted to the front face of the cylinder block. The first part of the engine number gives the legislation type code - eg "VJZ"

Repair operations possible with the engine in the car

11 The following work can be carried out with the engine in the car:

a) Compression pressure and leakdown - testing.
b) Cylinder head cover - removal and refitting.
c) Timing belt covers - removal and refitting.
d) Timing belt - removal, refitting and adjustment.
e) Timing belt tensioner and sprockets - removal and refitting.
f) Camshaft oil seal - renewal.
g) Camshaft and followers - removal, inspection and refitting.
h) Cylinder head - removal and refitting.
i) Cylinder head and pistons - decarbonising (refer to Part C of this Chapter).
j) Sump - removal and refitting.
k) Oil pump - removal, overhaul and refitting.
l) Crankshaft oil seals - renewal.
m) Engine/transmission mountings - inspection and renewal.
n) Flywheel - removal, inspection and refitting.

2 Compression and leakdown tests - description and interpretation

Compression test

Note: *A compression tester specifically designed for diesel engines must be used for this test.*

1 When engine performance is down, or if misfiring occurs which cannot be attributed to the fuel system, a compression test can provide diagnostic clues as to the engine's condition. If the test is performed regularly, it can give warning of trouble before any other symptoms become apparent.

2 A compression tester specifically intended for diesel engines must be used, because of the higher pressures involved. The tester is connected to an adapter which screws into the glow plug or injector hole. It is unlikely to be worthwhile buying such a tester for occasional use, but it may be possible to borrow or hire one - if not, have the test performed by a garage.

3 Unless specific instructions to the contrary are supplied with the tester, observe the following points:

a) The battery must be in a good state of charge, the air filter must be clean, and the engine should be at normal operating temperature.
b) All the injectors or glow plugs should be removed before starting the test. If removing the injectors, also remove the flame shield washers, otherwise they may be blown out.
c) The stop solenoid must be disconnected, to prevent the engine from running or fuel from being discharged.

4 There is no need to hold the accelerator pedal down during the test, because unlike a petrol engine, the inlet air passing into a diesel engine is not throttled.

5 Although Citroën do not specify exact compression pressures, as a guide, a cylinder pressure of less than 20 bars should be considered unhealthy. Refer to a Citroën dealer or other diesel specialist if in doubt as to whether a particular pressure reading is acceptable.

6 The cause of poor compression is harder to establish on a diesel engine, in comparison with a petrol engine. The effect of introducing oil into the cylinders ("wet" testing) is not conclusive, because there is a risk that the oil will collect in the swirl chamber, or in the recess on the piston crown, instead of passing to the piston rings. However, the following can be used as a rough guide to diagnosis.

7 All cylinders should produce very similar pressures; a difference of more than 4 bars between any two cylinders indicates the existence of a fault. Note that the compression should build up quickly in a healthy engine. Low compression on the first stroke, followed by gradually-increasing pressure on several successive strokes, indicates worn piston rings. A low compression reading on the first stroke, which does not build up during successive strokes, indicates leaking valves or a blown head gasket (a cracked head could also be the cause).

8 A low reading from two adjacent cylinders is almost certainly due to the head gasket having blown between them; the presence of coolant in the engine oil will confirm this.

9 If the compression reading is unusually high, the cylinder head surfaces, valves and pistons are probably coated with carbon deposits. If this is the case, the cylinder head should be removed and decarbonised (refer to Part C of this Chapter).

Leakdown test

10 A leakdown test measures the rate at which compressed air fed into the cylinder is lost. It is an alternative to a compression test, and in many ways it is better, since the escaping air provides easy identification of where pressure loss is occurring (piston rings, valves or head gasket).

11 The equipment needed for leakdown testing is unlikely to be available to the home mechanic. If poor compression is suspected, have the test performed by a suitably-equipped garage.

3 Engine assembly/valve timing holes - general information and usage

Caution: Do not attempt to rotate the engine whilst the crankshaft, camshaft or injection pump are locked in position. If the engine is to be left in this state for a long period of time, it is a good idea to place warning notices inside the vehicle, and in the engine compartment. This will reduce the possibility of the engine being accidentally cranked on the starter motor, which is likely to cause damage with the locking tools in place.

1 Timing holes are drilled in the camshaft sprocket, fuel injection pump sprocket and in the flywheel. The holes are used to ensure that the crankshaft, camshaft and injection pump are correctly positioned when assembling the engine (to prevent the possibility of the valves contacting the pistons when refitting the cylinder head), or refitting the timing belt. When the timing holes are aligned with access holes, suitable-diameter pins or bolts can be inserted to lock the camshaft, injection pump sprocket and crankshaft in position, preventing them from

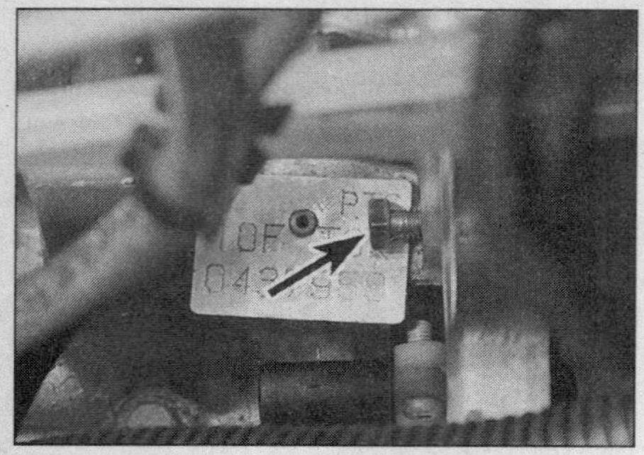

3.4 Insert a 6 mm bolt through the hole in the cylinder block flange and into the timing hole in the flywheel

rotating. Proceed as follows. **Note:** *With the timing holes aligned, No 4 cylinder is at TDC on its compression stroke.*

2 Remove the upper and centre timing belt covers as described in Section 5.

3 The crankshaft must now be turned until the timing holes in the camshaft sprocket and injection pump sprocket are aligned with the corresponding holes in the cylinder head and pump mounting bracket. The holes are aligned when the camshaft sprocket hole is in the 4 o'clock position, when viewed from the right-hand end of the engine. The crankshaft can be turned by using a spanner on the crankshaft sprocket bolt, noting that it should always be rotated in a clockwise direction (viewed from the right-hand end of the engine). If necessary, firmly apply the handbrake then jack up the front of the car, support it on axle stands and remove the right-hand roadwheel and wheel arch liner (see Chapter 11, section 23) to improve access to the crankshaft pulley. Turning the engine will be much easier if the glow plugs are removed first.

4.3 Unscrew the eight retaining bolts and remove them along with their washers

4.4 Lift the cover away from the engine, and recover the seal

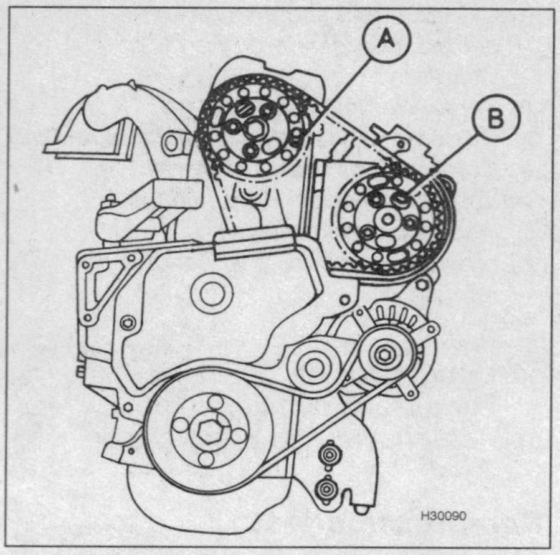

3.5 Insert 8 mm bolts through the elongated timing holes in the camshaft sprocket (A) and the injection pump sprocket (B)

4 With the camshaft sprocket hole correctly positioned, insert a 6 mm diameter bolt or drill bit through the hole in the front left-hand flange of the cylinder block, and locate it in the timing hole in the flywheel **(see illustration)**. Note that it may be necessary to rotate the crankshaft slightly, to get the holes to align.

5 With the flywheel correctly positioned, insert an 8 mm diameter bolt through the elongated timing hole in the camshaft sprocket, and screw it into the cylinder head. Also insert an 8 mm diameter bolt through the elongated timing hole on the injection pump sprocket, and screw it into the hole in the mounting bracket **(see illustration)**.

6 The crankshaft, camshaft and injection pump are now locked in position, preventing unwanted rotation.

4 Cylinder head cover - removal and refitting

Removal

1 Disconnect the breather hose from the right-hand end of the cylinder head cover **(see illustration)**.

4.6 Ensure that the rubber seal is correctly located in the cover groove prior to refitting

4.1 Disconnect the breather hose from the right-hand end of the cylinder head cover

2 Remove the upper timing belt cover as described in Section 5.

3 Unscrew the eight retaining bolts in a spiral sequence starting from the outside. Note their correct fitted locations, as they are of two different lengths. Recover the washers from the bolts/cover **(see illustration)**.

4 Lift the cover away from the engine **(see illustration)**, and recover the rubber seal. Examine the seal for signs of damage and deterioration, and if necessary, renew it.

Refitting

5 Carefully clean the cylinder head and cover mating surfaces, and remove all traces of oil.

6 Fit the rubber seal to the cylinder head cover groove, ensuring that it is correctly located along its entire length **(see illustration)**.

7 Carefully refit the cylinder head cover to the engine, taking great care not to displace the rubber seal.

8 Install the retaining bolts and washers, and tighten them to the specified torque setting. Initially, screw the bolts hand-tight through to the head in the following sequence: 8-5-7-6-4-1-3-2 **(see illustration)**. Pre-tighten the screws (to the specified torque), in numerical sequence (1 through to 8) and then finally complete by tightening to the specified torque, again in numerical sequence.

9 Refit the upper timing belt cover as described in Section 5.

10 Reconnect the breather hose to the cylinder head cover, and securely tighten its retaining clip.

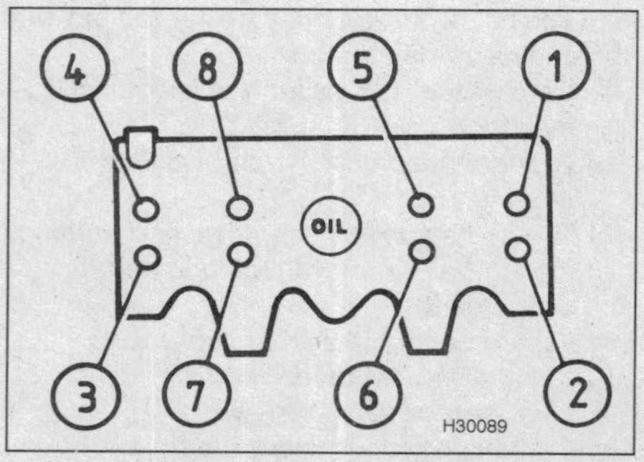

4.8 Cylinder head cover tightening sequence

5.5 Removing the timing belt upper cover

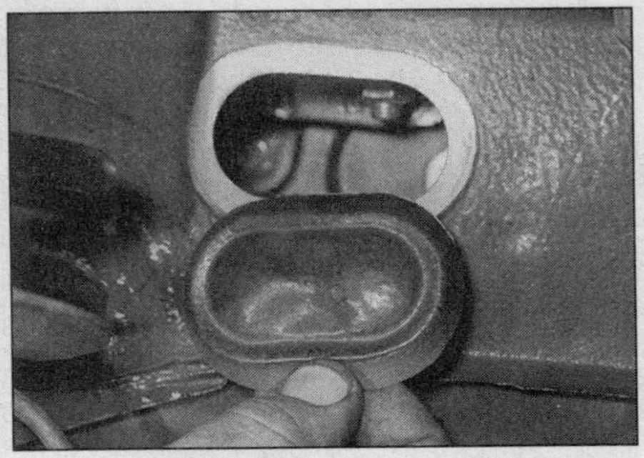

5.7a Remove the rubber plug from the right-hand wing valance . . .

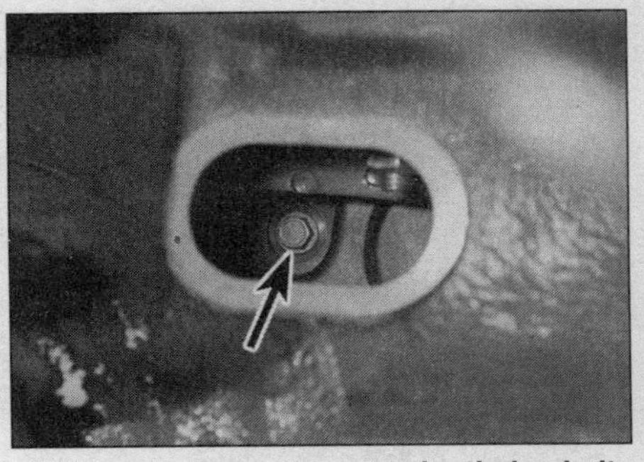

5.7b . . . to gain access to the timing belt centre cover bolt (arrowed)

5 Timing belt covers - removal and refitting

Removal

Upper cover

1 Disconnect the battery negative cable and position it away from the terminal.
2 Disconnect the wiring from the underside of the pre-heating system control unit, with reference to Chapter 5C.
3 Remove the securing screw and detach the glow plug controller from the side of the cooling system expansion tank.
4 Remove the expansion tank securing screws. Move the expansion tank to one side to gain greater access to the timing belt cover; there is no need to disconnect the cooling hoses.
5 Slacken and remove the three upper cover retaining screws; two are located at the front of the cover - above and below the injection pump sprocket - and the third is located at the rear of the cover. Disengage the upper timing cover from the lower cover and then remove it from the cylinder head **(see illustration)**.

Lower cover

6 Remove the upper cover as described in paragraph 1.
7 Turn the wheels onto full right-hand lock, then prise out the rubber plug from underneath the right-hand front wheel arch. Unscrew the timing belt cover bolt which is accessible through the hole in the wheel arch liner **(see illustrations)**.
8 Remove the auxiliary drivebelt as described in Chapter 1B.
9 Undo the crankshaft pulley retaining bolts and remove the pulley, noting which way round it is fitted **(see illustrations)**.
10 Slacken and remove the three remaining retaining bolts, and withdraw the lower cover over the crankshaft sprocket outer flange and manoeuvre it out of the engine compartment.

Refitting

11 Refitting is a reversal of removal. When refitting the upper cover ensure that the inner edge engages with the lug on the side of the cylinder head cover **(see illustration)**.

6 Timing belt - general information, removal and refitting

Caution: It is recommended that the special Citroën belt tensioning tool is hired or borrowed for this operation; attempting to set the belt tension by approximation is unlikely to be successful and could lead to belt slippage or failure, resulting in extensive engine damage.

General information

1 The timing belt drives the camshaft, injection pump, and coolant pump from a toothed sprocket on the front of the crankshaft. If the belt breaks or slips in service, the pistons are likely to hit the valve heads, resulting in extensive (and expensive) damage.
2 The timing belt should be renewed at the specified intervals, or earlier if it is contaminated with oil, or at all noisy in operation (a "scraping" noise due to uneven wear).
3 If the timing belt is being removed, it is a wise precaution to check the condition of the coolant pump at the same time (check for signs of coolant leakage). This may avoid the need to remove the timing belt again at a later stage, should the coolant pump fail.

Removal

4 Disconnect the battery negative cable and position it away from the terminal.
5 Align the engine assembly/valve timing holes, and lock the crankshaft, camshaft and fuel injection pump sprockets in the TDC position as described in Section 3. *Do not attempt to rotate the engine whilst the locking tools are in position.*
6 Unbolt the glow plug control module from the side of the coolant expansion tank and position it to one side.
7 Remove the upper and lower timing belt covers as described in Section 5. If the belt is to be re-used and there are no manufacturer's direction of rotation markings on the belt's surface, make your own using chalk or similar **(see Haynes Hint)**. The crankshaft rotates clockwise, as viewed from the right hand end of the engine.

5.9a Undo the retaining bolts (arrowed) . . .

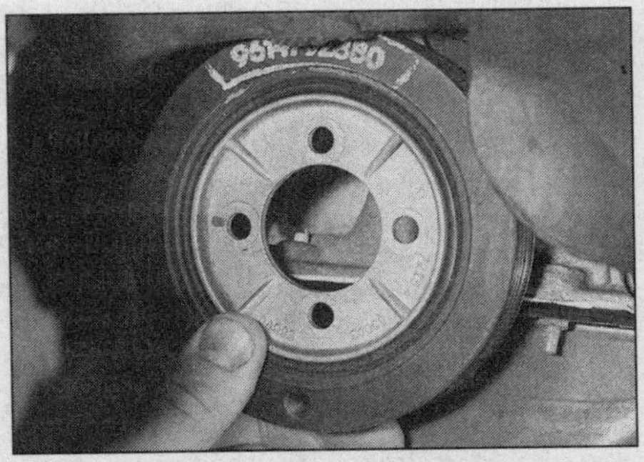

5.9b . . . and remove the crankshaft pulley from the engine

5.11 Ensure that the inner edge engages with the lug (arrowed) on the side of the cylinder head cover

If the timing belt is to be re-used, use white paint or similar to mark the direction of rotation on the belt (if markings do not already exist)

8 Loosen the timing belt tensioner pulley retaining nut. Pivot the pulley in a clockwise direction, using wrench and square-section adapter fitted to the hole in the front face pulley hub. Retighten the retaining nut, with the pulley in the slackened position.

9 Slip the timing belt off the sprockets, idler and tensioner pulleys, and remove it from the engine.

10 Check the timing belt carefully for any signs of uneven wear, splitting, or oil contamination. Pay particular attention to the roots of the teeth. Renew the belt if there is the slightest doubt about its condition. If the engine is undergoing an overhaul, and has covered more than 36 000 miles (60 000 km) with the existing belt fitted, renew the belt as a matter of course, regardless of its apparent condition. The cost of a new belt is negligible when compared to the cost of repairs, should the belt break in service. If signs of oil contamination are found, trace the source of the oil leak, and rectify it. Wash down the engine timing belt area and all related components, to remove all traces of oil.

Refitting

11 Prior to refitting, thoroughly clean the timing belt sprockets. Check that both the tensioner and idler pulleys rotate freely, without any sign of roughness. If necessary, renew damaged pulley(s) as described in Section 7. Make sure that the sprocket and flywheel TDC locking tools are still in place, as described in Section 3.

6.15 Engage the timing belt with the camshaft sprocket as described in text

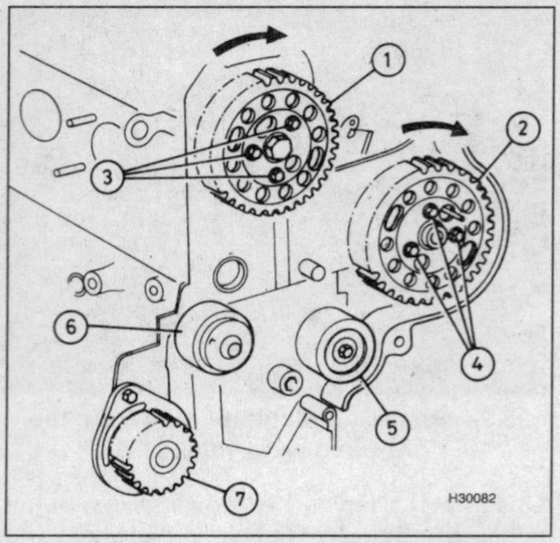

6.12 Camshaft and injection pump sprocket hub bolts

1 *Camshaft sprocket*
2 *Injection pump sprocket*
3 *Camshaft sprocket hub bolts*
4 *Injection pump sprocket hub bolts*
5 *Tensioner*
6 *Idler roller*
7 *Coolant pump sprocket*

12 Slacken the three camshaft sprocket hub bolts. Similarly, slacken the three injection pump sprocket hub bolts **(see illustration)**. Do not be tempted to use the TDC locking tools as a means of bracing the sprockets, whilst the bolts are being slackened **(see Tool Tip)**. Ensure that both sprockets move freely on their hubs (as far as the sprockets' slotted bolt holes will allow). Now finger-tighten all the sprocket hub bolts, so that it is just possible to turn the sprockets by hand.

13 Turn the camshaft and injection pump sprockets fully clockwise, so that the sprocket mounting bolts are positioned against the end of their slotted holes.

14 Pass the timing belt under the crankshaft sprocket, then over the idler pulley (nearest to the injection pump), paying attention to the direction of rotation markings on the belt where applicable. Pass the belt around the injection pump sprocket, ensuring that the belt does not 'jump' on the crankshaft sprocket. If necessary, move the injection pump sprocket anti-clockwise - by no more than *one* tooth - to enable the belt to seat properly. Ensure that the belt remains taught at all times.

15 Fit the belt on the camshaft sprocket in the same way. If necessary, move the camshaft sprocket anti-clockwise (again, by no more than *one* tooth) to enable the belt to seat properly **(see illustration)**. Ensure that the belt remains taught at all times.

16 Feed the belt around the tensioner pulley and finally around the coolant pump sprocket.

17 Ensure that the camshaft and injection sprocket hub bolts are positioned in the centre of their slotted holes **(see illustration)**. If they are hard against either end of their slotted holes, the belt has been probably been incorrectly fitted - remove the belt and start the refitting procedure again.

To make a camshaft sprocket holding tool, obtain two lengths of steel strip about 6 mm thick by 30 mm wide, or similar, one 600 mm long, the other 200 mm long (all dimensions approximate). Bolt the two strips together to form a forked end, leaving the bolt slack so that the shorter strip can pivot freely. At the end of each 'prong' of the fork, secure a bolt with a nut and locknut, protruding about 30 mm; these will engage with the cut-outs in the sprocket.

18 Ensure that the fuel injection pump and camshaft sprocket hub bolts are still only hand-tight, then fit the special belt tension measuring tool to the 'front run' of the timing belt, midway between the camshaft and injection pump sprockets.

19 Fit a square-section adapter to the hole in the front face of the tensioner pulley and using a wrench, pivot the tensioner pulley anti-clockwise until the tensioning tool displays the specified 'Stage 1' tension setting. Tighten the tensioner pulley centre nut to secure it in this position **(see illustration)**.

20 Fully tighten the injection pump and camshaft sprocket hub bolts to their specified torque settings. Do not use the TDC tools as a means of bracing the sprockets whilst the bolts are being tightened.

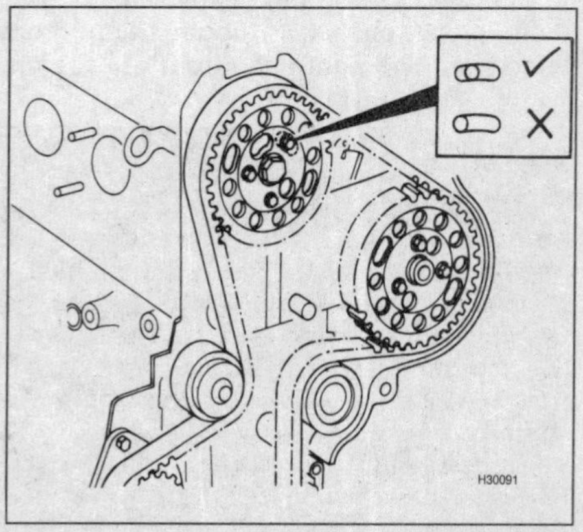

6.17 Correct location of camshaft and injection pump sprocket hub bolts

21 Remove the locking tools from the camshaft sprocket, injection pump sprocket and flywheel, and remove the measuring tool from the belt.

22 Using a socket and extension bar on the crankshaft sprocket bolt, rotate the crankshaft through ten complete rotations in a clockwise direction (viewed from the right-hand end of the engine). *Do not* at any time rotate the crankshaft anti-clockwise.

23 Refit the TDC locking tools as described in Section 3. Allow the belt to stand for approximately one minute then slacken the tensioner pulley retaining nut. Fully slacken the camshaft and injection pump sprocket hub bolts, then finger-tighten them, so that the sprockets can just be turned by hand.

24 Refit the measuring tool to the timing belt, as described earlier in this Section. Again using a square-section adapter and wrench, pivot the tensioner pulley anti-clockwise until the tensioning tool now displays the specified 'Final stage' tension setting. Tighten the tensioner pulley centre nut to its specified torque setting to secure it in this position.

25 Tighten the camshaft and injection pump hub sprocket bolts to their specified torque settings. Do not use the TDC tools as a means of bracing the sprockets whilst the bolts are being tightened.

26 Remove the measuring tool from the belt. Rotate the crankshaft through another two complete rotations in a clockwise direction, and check that the belt sits squarely on the injection pump and camshaft sprockets. Bring the engine up to TDC as described in Section 3 and check that the locking tools can still be inserted through the camshaft sprocket, injection pump sprocket and flywheel alignment holes. If this is not the case, the timing belt has been fitted incorrectly and it will be necessary to remove the belt and start the refitting procedure again **(see illustration)**.

27 With the belt tension correctly set, remove locking tools, and refit the timing belt covers as described in Section 5.

7 Timing belt tensioner and sprockets - removal, inspection and refitting

Removal

Note: *This Section describes the removal and refitting of the components concerned as individual operations. If more than one of them is to be removed at the same time, start by removing the timing belt as described in Section 6; remove the actual component as described below, ignoring the preliminary dismantling steps.*

1 Disconnect the battery negative terminal.

2 Remove the timing belt upper cover, then align the engine assembly/valve timing holes as described in Section 3, and lock the camshaft sprocket, injection pump sprocket and flywheel in position. *Do not* attempt to rotate the engine whilst the locking tools are in position.

6.19 Tightening the tensioner pulley retaining nut

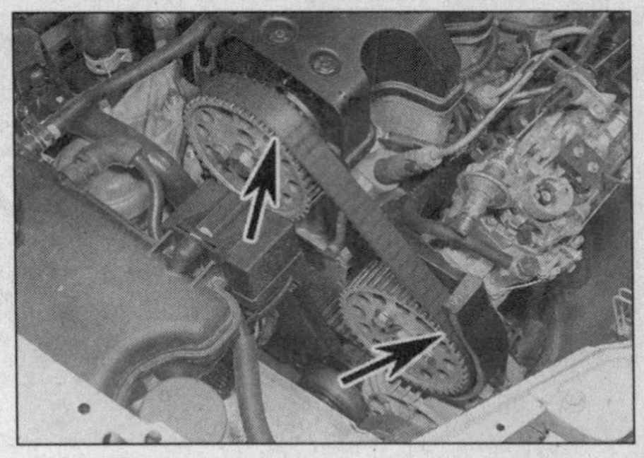

6.26 Check that the timing belt sits squarely on the injection pump and camshaft sprockets (arrowed)

Camshaft sprocket

3 Loosen the timing belt tensioner pulley retaining nut. Rotate the pulley in a clockwise direction, using a suitable square-section key fitted to the hole in the front face of the pulley hub, then retighten the retaining nut.

4 Disengage the timing belt from the sprocket, and move the belt clear, taking care not to bend or twist it sharply. Remove the locking tool from the camshaft sprocket.

5 Slacken the camshaft sprocket hub retaining bolt and remove it, along with its washer **(see illustration)**.

Caution: Do not attempt to use the sprocket locking tool to prevent the sprocket from rotating whilst the retaining bolt is slackened (see Tool Tip on previous page).

6 With the retaining bolt removed, slide the sprocket off the end of the camshaft. Note the key on the rear of the sprocket hub, which engages with a cut-out on the end of the camshaft. Examine the camshaft oil seal for signs of oil leakage and, if necessary, renew it as described in Section 8.

Crankshaft sprocket

7 Remove the lower timing belt cover as described in Section 5.

8 Loosen the timing belt tensioner pulley retaining nut. Rotate the pulley in a clockwise direction, using a suitable square-section adapter and wrench fitted to the hole in the front face of the pulley hub, then retighten the retaining nut.

9 Disengage the timing belt from the crankshaft sprocket, and move the belt clear, taking care not to bend or twist it sharply.

10 To prevent crankshaft rotation whilst the sprocket retaining bolt is slackened, select top gear, and have an assistant apply the brakes firmly. If the engine has been removed from the vehicle, lock the flywheel ring gear, using an arrangement similar to that shown in Section 7 of Chapter 2A. *Do not* be tempted to use the flywheel TDC locking pin to prevent the crankshaft from rotating; temporarily remove the pin from the rear of the flywheel prior to slackening the pulley bolt, then refit it once the bolt has been slackened.

11 Unscrew the retaining bolt and washer, then slide the sprocket off the end of the crankshaft. Refit the locking pin/bolt through the timing hole into the rear of the flywheel.

12 If the Woodruff key is a loose fit in the crankshaft, remove it and store it with the sprocket for safe-keeping. If necessary, also slide the flanged spacer off the end of the crankshaft. Examine the crankshaft oil seal for signs of oil leakage and, if necessary, renew as described in Section 14 in Part A of this Chapter.

Fuel injection pump sprocket

13 Loosen the timing belt tensioner pulley retaining nut. Rotate the pulley in a clockwise direction, using a suitable square-section key fitted to the hole in the pulley hub, then retighten the retaining nut.

14 Disengage the timing belt from the injection pump sprocket, and move the belt clear, taking care not to bend or twist it sharply. If necessary, remove the right-hand headlight unit as described in Chapter 12 to improve access to the sprocket.

15 Unscrew the locking bolt from the pump sprocket.

16 Slacken the injection pump sprocket-to-hub retaining bolts, whilst holding the sprocket stationary with a suitable tool **(see illustration)**. Undo and remove the screws.

Caution: Do not attempt to use the sprocket locking tool to prevent the sprocket from rotating whilst the retaining bolt is slackened (see Tool Tip on previous page).

7.5 Remove the retaining bolt and washer, then remove the camshaft sprocket

7.16 Fuel injection pump sprocket-to-hub retaining screws (arrowed)

17 Remove the sprocket from the injection pump shaft hub.

Tensioner pulley

18 Slacken and remove the timing belt tensioner pulley retaining nut, and slide the pulley off its mounting stud **(see illustration)**. Examine the mounting stud for signs of damage and, if necessary, renew it - it is removed by unscrewing it from the cylinder block. Carefully tie the timing belt up so that it is kept in full engagement with all of the sprockets.

Idler pulley

19 Loosen the timing belt tensioner pulley retaining nut. Rotate the pulley in a clockwise direction, using a suitable square-section key fitted to the hole in the pulley hub, then retighten the retaining nut. In order to provide some slack in the timing belt between the crankshaft and injection pump sprockets, it will be necessary to remove the locking tool from the flywheel and rotate the crankshaft slightly anti-clockwise.

20 Unscrew the bolt retaining the idler to the cylinder block **(see illustration)**, and withdraw the idler pulley. Carefully tie the timing belt up so that it is kept in full engagement with all of the sprockets.

Inspection

21 Clean the sprockets thoroughly, and renew any that show signs of wear, damage or cracks.

22 Clean the tensioner pulley and idler, but do not use any strong solvent which may enter the bearings. Check that each roller rotates freely about its hub, with no sign of stiffness or free play. Renew the tensioner pulley or idler if there is any doubt about its condition, or if there are any obvious signs of wear or damage.

7.18 Timing belt tensioner pulley retaining nut (arrowed)

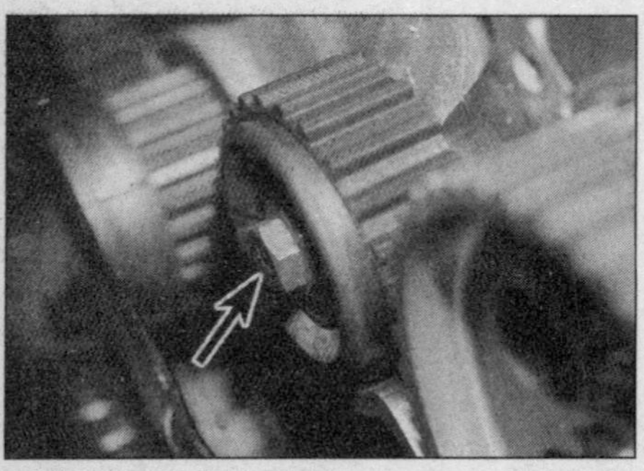

7.20 Timing belt idler pulley retaining bolt (arrowed)

Refitting

Camshaft sprocket

23 Locate the sprocket and hub on the end of the camshaft. Ensure that the locating key at the rear of the sprocket hub is correctly engaged with the cut-out at the end of the camshaft.

24 Coat the threads of the sprocket hub bolt with locking compound. Refit the sprocket and hub then insert the bolt, together with the washer (where applicable). Tighten the bolt to the specified torque, whilst retaining the sprocket with the tool used during removal.

25 Realign the timing hole in the camshaft sprocket (see Section 3) with the corresponding hole in the cylinder head, and refit the locking tool.

26 With the crankshaft, injection pump and camshaft locked in position, refit the timing belt to the camshaft sprocket, as described in Section 6. Do not twist the belt sharply while refitting it, and ensure that the belt teeth are seated centrally in the sprockets.

27 Ensure that the belt is taut around the crankshaft sprocket, idler pulley and injection pump sprocket, so that any slack is on the tensioner pulley side of the belt. Tension the timing belt as described at the end of Section 6.

28 Remove the TDC locking tools, then verify that the timing belt has been refitted correctly by rotating the engine through two revolutions, then checking that the TDC locking tools can be reinserted.

29 Refit the timing belt covers as described in Section 5.

30 Reconnect the battery negative terminal.

Crankshaft sprocket

31 Coat the rear surface of the spacer and the Woodruff key with a suitable sealant. Locate the Woodruff key in the crankshaft end, then slide on the flanged spacer, aligning its slot with the Woodruff key.

32 Align the crankshaft sprocket slot with the Woodruff key, and slide it onto the end of the crankshaft.

33 Temporarily remove the locking tool from the rear of the flywheel, then refit the crankshaft sprocket retaining bolt and washer. Tighten the bolt to the specified torque, whilst preventing crankshaft rotation using the method employed on removal. Refit the locking tool to the rear of the flywheel.

Caution: Ensure that there are no traces of adhesive on the crankshaft sprocket teeth.

34 With the crankshaft, injection pump and camshaft locked in position, refit the timing belt to the crankshaft sprocket. Ensure that the belt is taut between the crankshaft, idler pulley, injection pump and camshaft sprockets, so that any slack is on the tensioner pulley side of the belt. Do not twist the belt sharply while refitting it, and ensure that the belt teeth are seated centrally in the sprockets.

35 Loosen the tensioner pulley retaining nut. Rotate the pulley anti-clockwise to remove all free play from the timing belt, then retighten the nut.

36 Tension the belt as described in Section 6.

37 Refit the timing belt covers as described in Section 5.

Fuel injection pump sprocket

38 Thoroughly clean the mating surfaces of the fuel injection pump shaft hub and the rear of the sprocket.

39 Locate the sprocket on the injection pump shaft hub.

40 Tighten the sprocket retaining screws to the specified torque, preventing the pump shaft from turning using the method employed during removal. Align the sprocket timing hole, and refit the locking tool.

41 With the crankshaft, injection pump and camshaft locked in position, refit the timing belt to the injection pump sprocket, as described in Section 6. Do not twist the belt excessively while refitting it, and ensure that the belt teeth are seated centrally in the sprockets.

42 Ensure that the belt is taut around the crankshaft sprocket, idler pulley and camshaft sprocket, so that any slack is on the tensioner pulley side of the belt. Tension the timing belt as described at the end of Section 6.

43 Remove the TDC locking tools, then verify that the timing belt has been refitted correctly by rotating the engine through two revolutions, then checking that the TDC locking tools can be reinserted.

44 Refit the timing belt covers as described in Section 5.

Tensioner pulley

45 Check that the mounting stud is tightened in the cylinder block.

46 Locate the tensioner pulley on the stud, and lightly tighten its retaining nut.

47 With the crankshaft, injection pump and camshaft locked in position, ensure that the belt is taut between the crankshaft, idler pulley, injection pump and camshaft sprockets, so that any slack is on the tensioner pulley side of the belt.

48 Loosen the tensioner pulley retaining nut. Rotate the pulley anti-clockwise to remove all free play from the timing belt, then retighten the nut.
49 Tension the belt as described in Section 6.
50 Refit the timing belt covers as described in Section 5.

Idler pulley

51 Refit the idler pulley to the cylinder block, and tighten its retaining bolt to the specified torque.
52 Carefully turn the crankshaft clockwise until the locking tool can be inserted into the flywheel.
53 With the crankshaft, injection pump and camshaft locked in position, ensure that the belt is taut between the crankshaft, idler pulley, injection pump and camshaft sprockets, so that any slack is on the tensioner pulley side of the belt.
54 Loosen the tensioner pulley retaining nut. Rotate the pulley anti-clockwise to remove all free play from the belt, then retighten the nut.
55 Tension the belt as described in Section 6.
56 Refit the timing belt covers as described in Section 5.

8 Camshaft oil seal - renewal

Note: *If the camshaft oil seal is to be renewed with the timing belt still in place, check first that the belt is free from oil contamination. (Renew the belt as a matter of course if signs of oil contamination are found; see Section 6.) Cover the belt to protect it from oil contamination while work is in progress. Ensure that all traces of oil are removed from the area before the belt is refitted.*
1 Remove the camshaft sprocket as described in Section 7.
2 Punch or drill two small holes opposite each other in the oil seal. Screw a self-tapping screw into each, and pull on the screws with pliers to extract the seal **(see illustration)**.
3 Clean the seal housing, and polish off any burrs or raised edges, which may have caused the seal to fail in the first place.
4 Drive or lever the new seal into position until it seats on its locating shoulder. Use a suitable tubular drift, such as a socket, which bears only on the hard outer edge of the seal **(see illustration)**. Take care not to damage the seal lip during fitting. Note that the seal lips should face inwards. Do not apply oil or any other lubricant to the seal, to aid fitting.
5 Refit the camshaft sprocket as described in Section 7.

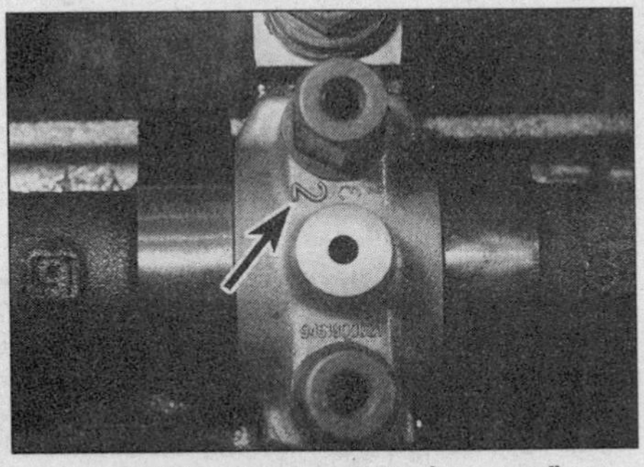

9.4 Identification numbers (arrowed) are cast onto the camshaft bearing caps

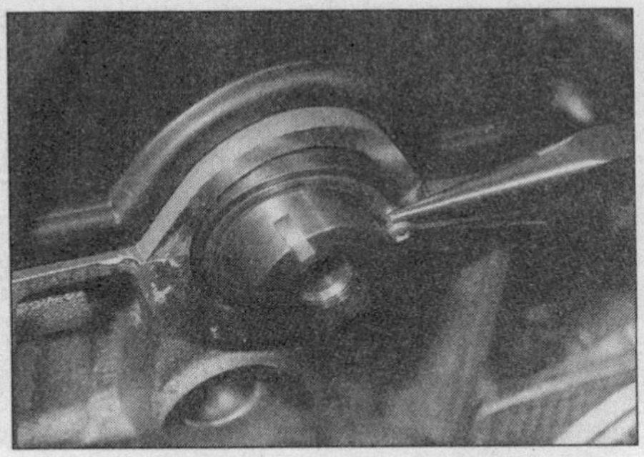

8.2 Removing the camshaft oil seal

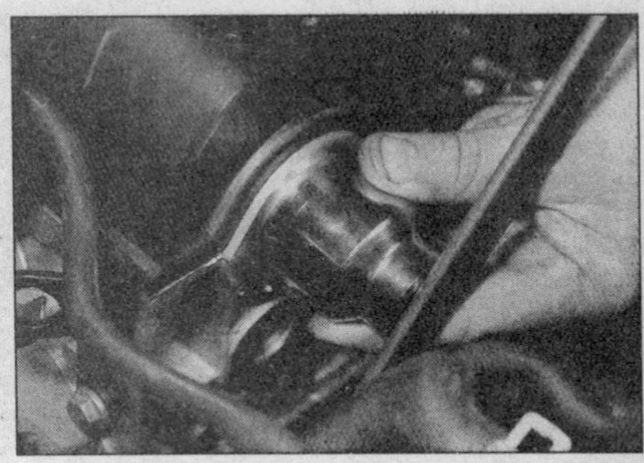

8.4 Levering the camshaft oil seal into position with a suitable socket

9 Camshaft and followers - removal, inspection and refitting

Removal

1 Remove the cylinder head cover as described in Section 4. Remove the air cleaner assembly and inlet ducting, as described in Chapter 4C.
2 Set the engine to TDC as described in Section 3, then remove the camshaft sprocket, complete with hub, as described in Section 7.
3 Unclip the wiring harness from the support rail at the left-hand end of the cylinder head, then unbolt and remove the support bracket. Remove the braking system vacuum pump, as described in Chapter 9.
4 The camshaft bearing caps should be numbered 1 to 3, No 1 being at the transmission end of the engine **(see illustration)**. If not, make identification marks on the caps using white paint or a suitable marker pen. Also mark each cap in some way to indicate its correct fitted orientation. This will avoid the possibility of installing the caps the wrong way around on refitting.
5 Evenly and progressively slacken the camshaft bearing cap retaining nuts by one turn at a time, in a spiral pattern starting from the outside. This will relieve the pressure of the valve springs on the bearing caps gradually and evenly. Once the valve spring pressure has been relieved, the nuts can be fully unscrewed and removed.
6 Note the correct fitted orientation of the bearing caps, then remove them from cylinder head.
7 Lift the camshaft away from the cylinder head, and slide the oil seal off the camshaft end.
8 Obtain eight small, clean plastic containers, and number them 1 to 8. Alternatively, divide a larger container into eight compartments. Using a rubber sucker (such as that found at the end of a valve grinding tool) withdraw each shim and follower in turn, and place it in its respective container. Do not interchange the cam followers, or the rate of wear will be much increased.

Inspection

9 Examine the camshaft bearing surfaces and cam lobes for signs of wear ridges and scoring. Renew the camshaft if any of these conditions are apparent. Examine the condition of the bearing surfaces both on the camshaft journals and in the cylinder head/bearing caps. If the head bearing surfaces are worn excessively, the cylinder head will need to be renewed. No camshaft journal dimensions are listed by the manufacturer, but refer to the Specifications for details of the cylinder head camshaft bearing diameters. Seek the advice of a Citroën dealer or engine overhaul specialist before condemning the camshaft or cylinder head. If either the camshaft or the tappets are replacements, fit 3.20 mm shims to allow basic valve clearance measurements to be made. The clearances can then be adjusted as required, using the information given in Section 10.

Refitting

10 Liberally oil the cylinder head cam follower bores and the followers. Carefully refit the followers to the cylinder head, ensuring that each follower is refitted to its original bore **(see illustration)**. Some care will

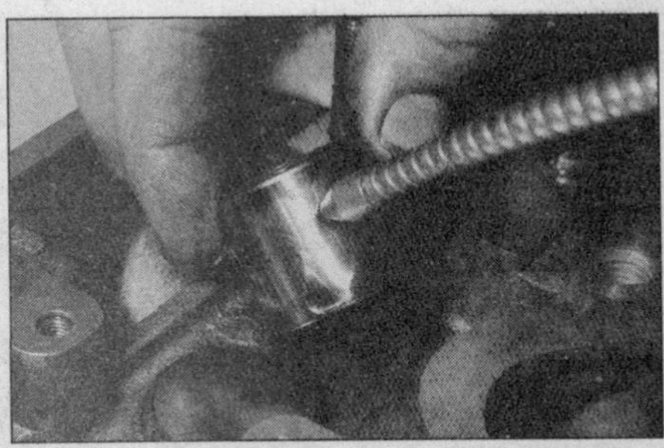

9.10 Oil the camshaft followers, and refit them to their original locations in the cylinder head

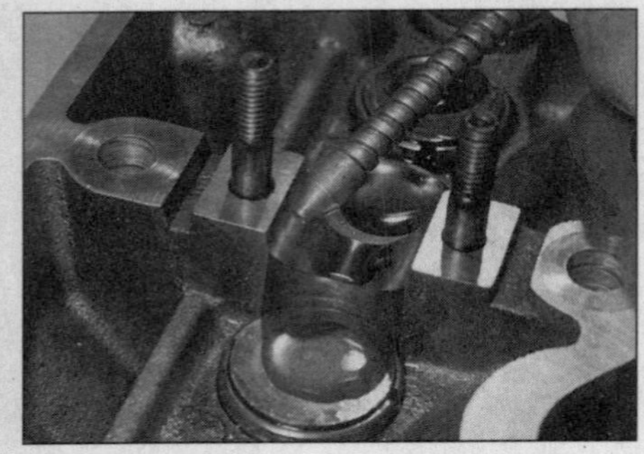

9.12 Thoroughly oil the camshaft bearing surfaces prior to installing the camshaft

be required to enter the followers squarely into their bores.

11 Ensure that all the shims are correctly seated in the top of each follower.

12 Lubricate the camshaft bearing and lobe contact surfaces with clean engine oil, then refit the camshaft to the cylinder head **(see illustration)**. Temporarily refit the sprocket to the end of the shaft, and position it so that the sprocket hub timing hole is aligned with the threaded hole in the cylinder head (tips of No 4 cylinder cam lobes should be facing away from their followers). Also ensure that the flywheel is still locked in position (see Section 3).

13 Ensure that the bearing cap and cylinder head mating surfaces are completely clean, unmarked, and free from oil. Apply a smear of suitable sealant to the mating surfaces of bearing caps Nos 1 and 3 as shown **(see illustration)**.

14 Refit the bearing caps, using the identification marks noted on removal to ensure that each is installed the correct way round and in its original location **(see illustration)**.

15 Evenly and progressively tighten the camshaft bearing cap nuts by one turn at a time in a spiral pattern, starting from the inside until the caps touch the cylinder head. On completion, work around the bearing cap nuts again in the same sequence, this time tightening them to the specified torque setting **(see illustrations)**. Work only in the sequence described, to impose the pressure of the valve springs gradually and evenly on the bearing caps and camshaft.

9.15a . . . and refit the retaining nuts . . .

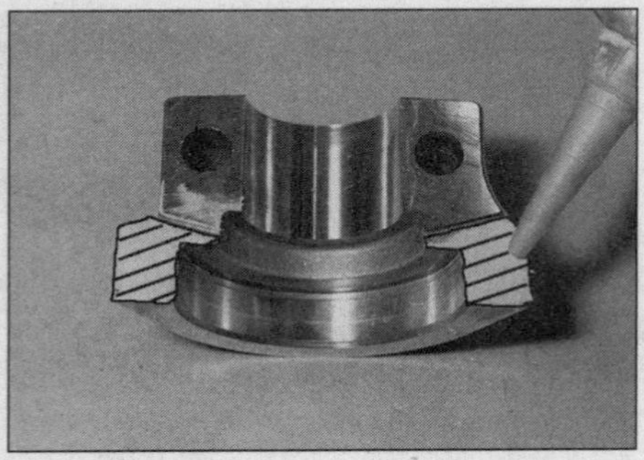

9.13 Apply sealant to the shaded areas of Nos 1 and 3 bearing caps

16 Fit a new camshaft oil seal, using the information given in Section 8. Refit the camshaft sprocket as described in Section 7 and timing belt described in Section 6.

17 Check and, if necessary, adjust the valve clearances as described in Section 10.

18 Refit the braking system vacuum pump as described in Chapter 9.

19 Refit the cylinder head cover as described in Section 4. Refit the air cleaner assembly and inlet pipe, followed by the remainder of the components removed for access. On completion, reconnect the battery negative cable.

10 Valve clearances - checking and adjustment

Note: *This is not a routine operation. It should only be necessary at high mileage, after overhaul, or when investigating noise or power loss which may be attributable to the valve gear. Shims are available in thicknesses between 3.20 mm and 4.90 mm, in steps of 0.025 mm. If work that is likely to have altered the valve clearances has been carried out (such as camshaft and/or follower renewal, or valve grinding, for example) 3.20 mm shims should be fitted initially, to allow basic valve clearance measurements to be carried out. The clearances can then be adjusted as required.*

1 The importance of having the valve clearances correctly adjusted cannot be

9.15b . . . tightening them evenly and progressively to the specified torque setting

9.14 Install the bearings caps, using the identification markings to ensure they are correctly positioned . . .

overstressed, as they vitally affect the performance of the engine. However, the check should not be regarded as routine maintenance, and should only be carried out when the valve gear has become noisy, after engine overhaul, or when trying to trace the cause of power loss which may be attributed to the valve gear. The clearances are checked as follows, noting that the engine must be **cold** for the check to be accurate.

2 Apply the handbrake, then jack up the front of the car and support it on axle stands (see "*Jacking and vehicle support*"). Remove the right-hand front roadwheel and wheel arch liner (see Chapter 11, section 23).

3 The engine can then be turned over using a suitable socket and extension bar fitted to the crankshaft sprocket bolt. Where necessary, undo the retaining nut and free the coolant hoses from the bracket to improve access further.

HAYNES HiNT ***Turning the engine will be much easier if the glow plugs are removed first.***

4 Remove the cylinder head cover as described in Section 4.

5 To obtain accurate valve clearance measurements, it is important to check that the camshaft bearing cap nuts are tightened to the correct torque. This is particularly relevant if the camshaft and followers have been removed during overhaul. Working in the sequence detailed in Section 9, check that each of the camshaft bearing cap nuts are tightened to the specified torque, using a torque wrench.

6 Draw the outline of the engine on a piece of paper, numbering the cylinders 1 to 4 (with No 1 cylinder at the transmission end of the engine). Show the position of each valve, together with the specified valve clearance (see paragraph 9). Above each valve, draw two lines; these will be used for noting the actual clearance and the amount of adjustment required.

7 Turn the crankshaft until the inlet valve of No 1 cylinder (nearest the transmission) is fully closed, with the tip of the cam facing directly away from the cam follower.

10.8 Checking a valve clearance

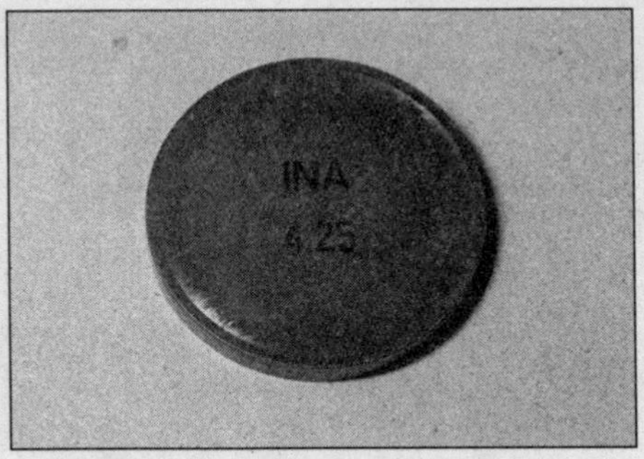

10.15a Shim thickness is stamped on the bottom face of the shim . . .

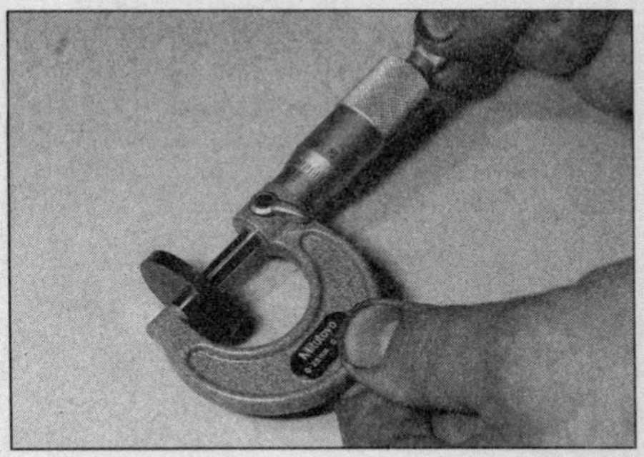

10.15b . . . however, shims should be measured to determine their true thickness

8 Using feeler blades, measure the clearance between the base of the cam and the follower **(see illustration)**. Record the clearance on the paper above the appropriate valve.

9 Repeat the measurement for the other seven valves, turning the crankshaft as necessary so that the cam lobe in question is always facing directly away from the relevant follower.

10 Calculate the difference between each measured clearance and the desired value, and record it on the piece of paper. Since the clearance is different for inlet and exhaust valves, make sure that you are aware which valve you are dealing with. The valve sequence from either end of the engine is:

Inlet - Exhaust - Inlet - Exhaust - Exhaust - Inlet - Exhaust - Inlet

11 Where a valve clearance differs from the specified value, then the shim for that valve must be replaced with a thinner or thicker shim accordingly.

12 To remove the shim, the follower has to be pressed down against valve spring pressure just far enough to allow the shim to be slid out. To do this, first make sure that the cam lobe above the shim to be removed is pointing away from the shim. Then, rotate the follower so that the notch on its edge is facing the front of the cylinder head, (i.e. the side into which the fuel injectors are threaded).

13 Using a suitable C-spanner or stout screwdriver, carefully lever down between the camshaft and the edge of the follower, until the follower is depressed as far as it will go into the cylinder head. Keep the follower in this position, then insert a thin, flat bladed screwdriver into the slot on the upper edge of the follower and prise out the shim.

14 With the shim removed, slowly release the follower. If difficulty is experienced in removing the shims, it will be necessary to remove the camshaft as described in Section 9.

15 The shim size is stamped on the bottom face of the shim, but it is advisable to use a micrometer to measure the true thickness of any shim removed, as it may have been reduced by wear **(see illustrations)**. The size of shim required is calculated as follows.

16 If the measured clearance is less than specified, subtract the measured clearance from the specified clearance, and subtract the result from the thickness of the existing shim. For example:

Sample calculation - inlet valve clearance too small

Specified clearance = 0.15 mm
Clearance measured = 0.10 mm
Difference = 0.05 mm
Shim thickness fitted = 3.70 mm
Thickness required = ***3.70 - 0.05***
New shim thickness = 3.65 mm

17 If the measured clearance is greater than specified, subtract the specified clearance from the measured clearance, and add the result to the thickness of the existing shim. For example:

Sample calculation - exhaust valve clearance too large

Specified clearance = 0.30 mm
Clearance measured = 0.40 mm
Difference = 0.10 mm
Shim thickness fitted = 3.45 mm
Thickness required = ***3.45 + 0.10***
New shim thickness = 3.55 mm

18 Depress the follower, then slide the required size shim into position, with its marked face facing downwards. Ensure that the shim is correctly seated, then repeat the procedure (as required) for the remaining valve(s) which require adjustment.

19 Once all valves have been adjusted, rotate the crankshaft through at least four complete turns in the correct direction of rotation, to settle all disturbed shims in position, then recheck the clearances as described above.

20 With all valve clearances correctly adjusted, refit the cylinder head cover as described in Section 4.

21 Refit the wheel arch liner and the roadwheel, then lower the vehicle to the ground and tighten the wheel bolts to the specified torque setting (see Chapter 10 Specifications). Refit the glow plugs, where applicable. Where necessary, clip the coolant hoses into position, and securely tighten the bracket retaining nut.

HAYNES HiNT ***It is worthwhile noting down all the valve shim thicknesses to save time when the engine is next overhauled; provided they are not worn or damaged, the shims can be moved to other locations.***

11 Cylinder head - removal and refitting

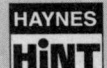

HAYNES HiNT ***To aid refitting, make notes on the locations of all relevant brackets, and the routing of hoses and cables, before removal.***

Removal

1 Disconnect the battery negative cable and position it away from the terminal.

2 Drain the cooling system as described in Chapter 1B.

3 Align the engine assembly/valve timing holes as described in Section 3, and lock the camshaft sprocket, injection pump sprocket and flywheel in position. *Do not* attempt to rotate the engine whilst the locking tools are in position.

4 Loosen the timing belt tensioner pulley retaining nut. Rotate the pulley in a clockwise direction, using a suitable square-section key fitted to the hole in the pulley hub, then retighten the retaining nut.

5 Disengage the timing belt from the camshaft sprocket, and move the belt clear, taking care not to bend or twist it sharply.

6 Working as described in the relevant Section of Chapter 4C, carry out the following operations:

a) Remove the air cleaner and inlet ducting.
b) Disconnect the accelerator cable from the fuel injection pump.
c) Disconnect the fast idle cable from the injection pump (so that the thermostatic valve is free to be removed with the cylinder head).
d) Disconnect the injector pipes from the rear of the injection pump and the fuel injectors, then remove them from the engine compartment.
e) Remove the inlet manifold. This operation is not essential, but gives improved working clearance when removing the head from the cylinder block.

7 Disconnect the exhaust system down pipe from the exhaust manifold as described in Chapter 4D.

2B

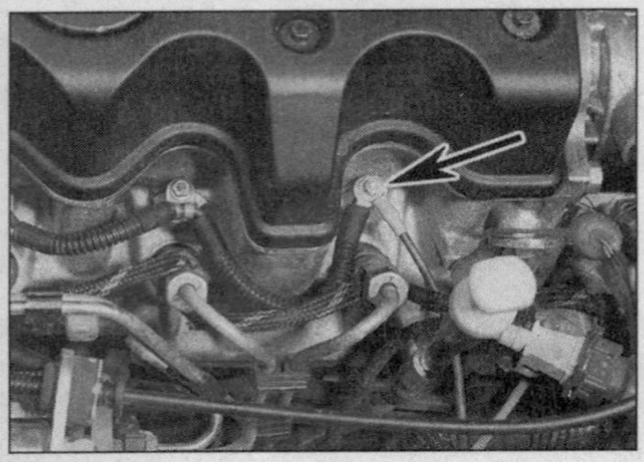

11.8 Disconnect the main supply wiring from No 1 glow plug (arrowed)

11.9a Disconnect the coolant hoses from the front . . .

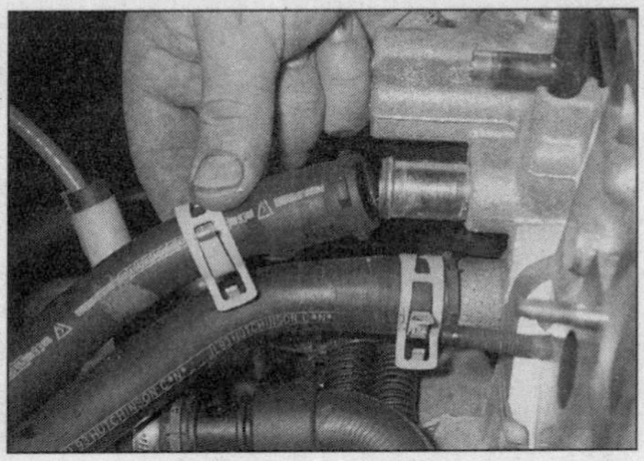

11.9b . . . and rear of the fuel filter/thermostat housing

8 Refer to Chapter 5C and disconnect the main supply wiring from No 1 glow plug (at the transmission end of the engine) **(see illustration)**. Screw the nut back onto the plug, for safe-keeping.

9 Release the retaining clips, and disconnect the coolant hoses from the fuel filter/thermostat housing, noting their fitted positions **(see illustrations)**.

10 Slacken the retaining clips, and disconnect the fuel supply hose and pump feed hose from the fuel filter/thermostat housing, which is mounted onto the left-hand end of the cylinder head **(see illustration)**. Where the original crimped-type Citroën hose clips are still fitted, cut and discard them. Use standard worm-drive clips on refitting.

11 Disconnect the fuel return pipe from No 1 cylinder injector, and position the pipe clear of the head so that it will not hinder removal.

12 Disconnect the wiring from the temperature sensor(s) located on the front left-hand end of the cylinder head **(see illustration)**.

13 Loosen the retaining clip, and disconnect the vacuum pipe from the braking system vacuum pump located on the left-hand end of the cylinder head **(see illustration)**. Later models may be fitted with quick-release hose unions, rather than worm-drive hose clips.

14 Unscrew the bolt securing the engine oil dipstick tube to the front of the cylinder head.

15 Remove the cylinder head cover as described in Section 4.

16 Starting on the outside and working inwards in a spiral sequence, progressively loosen the cylinder head bolts, a half a turn at a time. Use the reverse sequence shown in paragraph 34, of this Section.

17 Lift out the cylinder head bolts, and recover the washers.

18 The joint between the cylinder head and gasket and the cylinder block/crankcase must now be broken. To break the joint, obtain two L-shaped metal bars which fit into the cylinder head bolt holes. Gently "rock" the cylinder head free towards the front of the car (refer to the information given for petrol engined models, in Part A of this Chapter). Do not try to swivel the head on the cylinder block/crankcase; it is located by dowels.

19 When the joint is broken, lift the cylinder head away; seek assistance if possible, as it is a heavy assembly. Remove the gasket from the top of the block, noting the two locating dowels. If the locating dowels are a loose fit, remove them and store them with the head for safe-keeping. Do not discard the gasket - it will be needed for identification purposes.

20 If the cylinder head is to be dismantled for overhaul, remove the camshaft and followers as described in Section 9, then refer to Part C of this Chapter.

Preparation for refitting

21 The mating faces of the cylinder head and cylinder block/crankcase must be perfectly clean before refitting the head. Use a hard plastic or wood scraper to remove all traces of gasket and carbon; also clean the piston crowns. Take particular care during the cleaning operations, as the soft aluminium alloy cylinder head is damaged easily. Also, make sure that the carbon is not allowed to enter the oil and water passages - this is particularly important for the lubrication system, as carbon could block the oil supply to the engine's components. Using adhesive tape, seal the water, oil and bolt holes in the cylinder block/crankcase. Clean all the pistons in the same way.

HAYNES HiNT ***To prevent carbon entering the gap between the pistons and bores, smear a little grease in the gap. After cleaning each piston, use a small brush to remove all traces of grease and carbon from the gap, then wipe away the remainder with a clean rag.***

22 Check the mating surfaces of the cylinder block/crankcase and the cylinder head for nicks, deep scratches and other damage. If slight, they may be removed carefully with a file, but if excessive, machining may be the only alternative to renewal.

23 If warpage of the cylinder head gasket surface is suspected, use a straight-edge to check it for distortion. Refer to Part C of this Chapter if necessary.

24 Only one thickness of cylinder head gasket is available for the diesel engine covered in this Chapter. The correct gasket has three cut-outs at the rear of its left-hand side, and identify the type of engine (i.e. TUD 1527cc) to which the gasket should be fitted

11.10 Disconnect the fuel supply and pump feed hoses (arrowed) from the fuel filter/thermostat housing

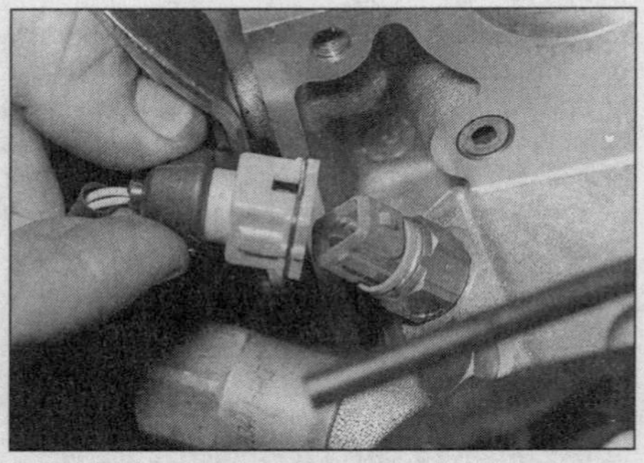

11.12 Disconnect the wiring connector from the temperature sensor

11.13 Disconnect the hose from the braking system vacuum pump

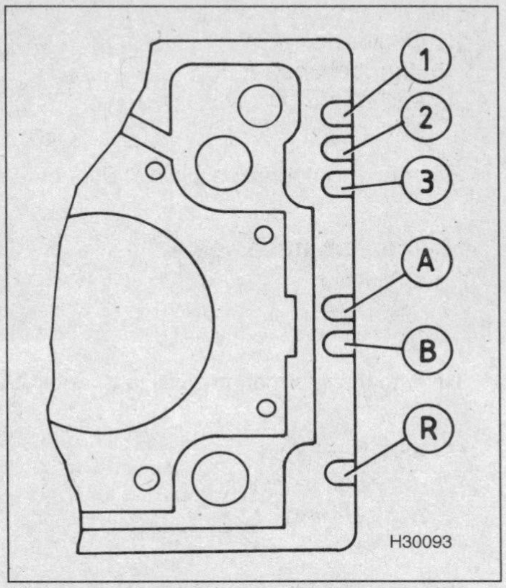

11.24 Cylinder head gasket identification markings

1, 2, 3	*Engine type (3 notches = TUD5)*
A, B	*Gasket manufacturer*
R	*Denotes repair gasket*

(see illustration). The remaining cut-outs at the centre of the left hand side of the gasket indicate the manufacturer of the gasket and whether or not it contains asbestos and are of no relevance to this procedure. If there is any doubt as to which gasket is fitted, take the old gasket along to your Citroën dealer or parts supplier, and have him confirm the gasket type.

11.31 Screw the head bolts into position

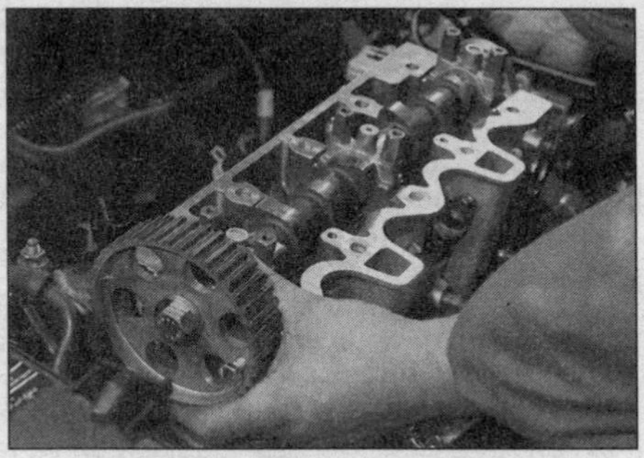

11.29 Carefully refit the cylinder head assembly to the block, aligning it with the locating dowels

25 The manufacturer recommends that the cylinder head bolts are measured, to assess the amount of stretch and hence to determine whether renewal is necessary. Measure the overall length of each bolt in turn; if any one bolt is greater than specified length (refer to the Specifications), *all* of the bolts should be renewed as a complete set. Considering the mechanical stress that the cylinder head bolts work under, it is highly recommended that they are renewed, regardless of their apparent condition.

26 Prior to refitting the cylinder head, check the cylinder liner protrusion as described in Part C of this Chapter.

Refitting

27 Wipe clean the mating surfaces of the cylinder head and cylinder block/crankcase. Check that the two locating dowels are in position at each end of the cylinder block/crankcase surface. Clean out the head bolt threads in the cylinder block with a suitable size of tap. **Note:** *Ensure that the exhaust manifold is in position, as this can not be refitted with the head in position without disturbing the right-hand engine mounting.*

28 Position a new gasket on the cylinder block/crankcase surface (manufacturers name facing upwards), ensuring that its identification cut-outs are at the left-hand end of the gasket (see illustration 11.24).

29 Check that the flywheel, injection pump sprocket and camshaft sprocket are still correctly locked in position then, with the aid of an assistant, carefully refit the cylinder head assembly to the block, aligning it with the locating dowels **(see illustration)**.

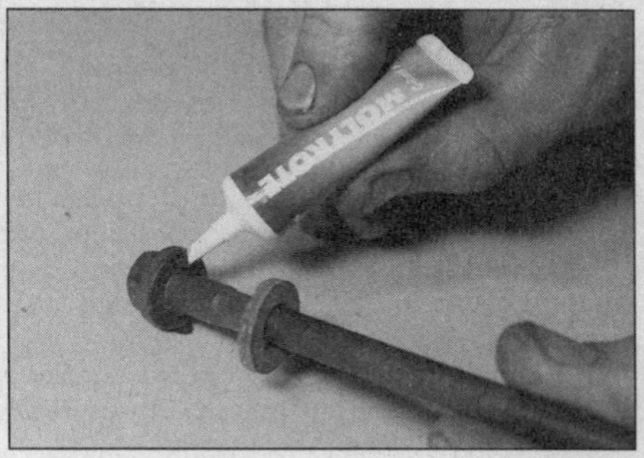

11.30 Apply a smear of the specified grease to the underside of the heads and to the threads of all cylinder head bolts

30 Apply a smear of grease to the threads, and to the underside of the heads, of the cylinder head bolts. Citroën recommend the use of Molykote G Rapid Plus grease (available from your Citroën dealer - a sachet is supplied with the top-end gasket set); in the absence of the specified grease, a good-quality high-melting-point grease may be used **(see illustration)**.

31 Carefully enter each bolt and washer into its relevant hole (*do not drop them in*) and screw in, by hand only, until finger-tight **(see illustration)**.

32 Working progressively and in the sequence shown, tighten the cylinder head bolts to their Stage 1 torque setting, using a torque wrench and suitable socket **(see illustrations)**.

33 Using a angle gauge, tighten the bolts in the same sequence to the specified Stage 2 angle setting, then continue on to paragraph 38 **(see illustration)**.

HAYNES HiNT ***If an angle-tightening gauge is not available, use white paint to make alignment marks between the bolt head and cylinder head prior to tightening; the marks can then be used to check that the bolt has been rotated through the correct angle during tightening.***

34 Refit the dipstick tube retaining bolt, and tighten it securely.

2B

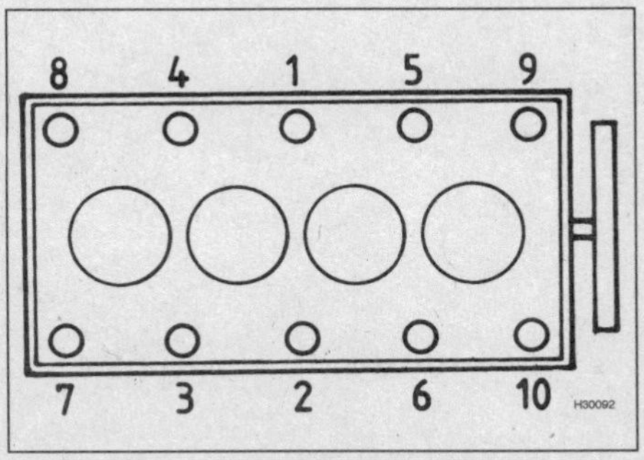

11.32a Head bolt tightening sequence for TUD 5 engine

11.32b Tighten the head bolts to the Stage 1 torque setting . . .

11.33 . . . and angle settings as described in text

35 Connect the wiring connector to the cylinder head temperature sensors.
36 Connect the supply wire to No 1 cylinder glow plug, and securely tighten its retaining nut.
37 Ensure that all pipes and hoses are correctly routed, reconnect the fuel and coolant hoses to the filter/thermostat housing, and secure them in position with their retaining clips.
38 Connect the return pipe to No 1 cylinder injector, ensuring that the pipe is correctly routed with no kinks or restrictions.
39 Connect the vacuum pipe to the braking system pump (see Chapter 9)
40 Carry out the following operations as described in Chapter 4C:

a) Refit the injector pipes, and tighten the union nuts to the specified torque.
b) Reconnect and adjust the fast idle cable.
c) Reconnect and adjust the accelerator cable.
d) Refit the inlet manifold (where applicable).
e) Refit the air cleaner and inlet ducting.

41 Reconnect the exhaust system downpipe to the exhaust manifold with reference to Chapter 4D.
42 With the crankshaft, injection pump and camshaft locked in position, refit the timing belt to the camshaft sprocket. Ensure that the belt is taut around the crankshaft sprocket, idler pulley and injection pump sprocket, so that any slack is on the tensioner pulley side of the belt. Do not twist the belt sharply while refitting it, and ensure that the belt teeth are seated centrally in the sprockets.
43 Loosen the tensioner pulley retaining nut. Rotate the pulley anti-clockwise to remove all free play from the timing belt, then retighten the nut.
44 Tension the belt as described in Section 6.
45 Check and, if necessary, adjust the valve clearances as described in Section 10.
46 Refit the cylinder head cover as described in Section 4.
47 Refill the cooling system as described in Chapter 1B.
48 Reconnect the battery negative cable, then prime and bleed the fuel system as described in Chapter 4C.

12 Sump - removal and refitting

Refer to Chapter 2A, noting that it is not necessary to remove the exhaust system front pipe.

13 Oil pump - removal, inspection and refitting

Refer to the information given in Chapter 2A.

14 Crankshaft oil seals - renewal

Refer to the information given in Chapter 2A.

15 Flywheel - removal, inspection and refitting

Refer to the information given in Chapter 2A.

16 Engine/transmission mountings - inspection and renewal

Refer to the information given in Chapter 2A.

Chapter 2 Part C:
Engine removal and general overhaul procedures

Contents

Degrees of difficulty

Easy, suitable for novice with little experience	**Fairly easy,** suitable for beginner with some experience	**Fairly difficult,** suitable for competent DIY mechanic	**Difficult,** suitable for experienced DIY mechanic	**Very difficult,** suitable for expert DIY or professional

Specifications

Cylinder head

Maximum gasket face distortion	0.05 mm
Cylinder head height:	
954,1124, 1360 and 1587 cc SOHC petrol engines	111.2 ± 0.8 mm
1587 cc DOHC petrol engine	135.0 ± 0.1 mm
1527 cc diesel engine	136.4 ± 0.1 mm
Swirl chamber protrusion (diesel engine)	0 to 0.03 mm

Cylinder block

Cylinder bore diameter:	
Cast-iron block engine:	
1360 cc petrol engine:	
Nominal	75.000 to 75.018 mm
Oversize	75.400 to 75.418 mm
1587 cc petrol engine:	
Nominal	78.500 to 78.518 mm
Oversize	78.900 to 78.918 mm
1527 cc diesel engine:	
Nominal	77.0 mm
Oversize	n/a
Aluminium block engine:	
954 cc engine:	
Size group A	70.000 to 70.010 mm
Size group B	70.010 to 70.020 mm
Size group C	70.020 to 70.030 mm
1124 cc engine:	
Size group A	72.000 to 72.010 mm
Size group B	72.010 to 72.020 mm
Size group C	72.020 to 72.030 mm
1360 cc engine:	
Size group A	75.000 to 75.010 mm
Size group B	75.010 to 75.020 mm
Size group C	75.020 to 75.030 mm
Liner protrusion (aluminium block engine)	0.03 to 0.10 mm
Maximum difference in protrusion between any two liners (aluminium block engine)	0.05 mm

Valves

	Inlet	Exhaust
Valve head diameter (typical):		
954 cc engine	34.8 mm	27.9 mm
1124 cc engine	36.8 mm	29.4 mm
1360 cc engine	36.8 mm	29.4 mm
1587 cc SOHC engine	39.5 mm	31.4 mm
1587 cc DOHC engine	28.75 mm	24.5 mm
1527 cc diesel engine	37.5 mm	31.55 mm
Valve stem diameter:		
954 cc engine	6.980 to 6.965 mm	6.960 to 6.945 mm
1124 cc engine	6.980 to 6.965 mm	6.960 to 6.945 mm
1360 cc engine	6.980 to 6.965 mm	6.960 to 6.945 mm
1587 cc SOHC engine	6.970 to 6.955 mm	6.970 to 6.955 mm
1587 cc DOHC engine	5.965 to 5.950 mm	5.965 to 5.950 mm
1527 cc diesel engine	6.995 to 6.980 mm	6.995 to 6.980 mm
Overall length:		
954 cc engine	112.76 mm	112.56 mm
1124 cc engine	112.76 mm	112.56 mm
1360 cc engine	112.76 mm	112.56 mm
1587 cc SOHC engine	111.50 mm	111.50 mm
1587 cc DOHC engine	104.35 mm	104.40 mm
1527 cc diesel engine	108.60 - 108.26 mm	108.34 - 108.00 mm

Pistons

Piston diameter:	
954 cc petrol engine:	
Size group A	69.940 to 69.950 mm
Size group B	69.950 to 69.960 mm
Size group C	69.960 to 69.970 mm
1124 cc petrol engine:	
Size group A	71.940 to 71.950 mm
Size group B	71.950 to 71.960 mm
Size group C	71.960 to 71.970 mm
1360 cc petrol engine:	
Aluminium block engine:	
Size group A	74.940 to 74.950 mm
Size group B	74.950 to 74.960 mm
Size group C	74.960 to 74.970 mm
Cast-iron block engine:	
Standard	74.960 to 74.975 mm
Oversize	75.360 to 75.375 mm
1527 cc diesel engine	76.93 mm
1587 cc SOHC and DOHC petrol engine:	
Standard	78.455 to 78.470 mm
Oversize	78.855 to 78.870 mm
Piston ring end gaps	At the time of writing, no exact values were available from the manufacturer - refer to your dealer or parts supplier for details.
Piston protrusion above cylinder head (diesel engine)	1.09 ± 0.05 mm

Crankshaft

Endfloat	0.07 to 0.27 mm
Main bearing journal diameter - all engines:	
Standard	49.965 to 49.981 mm
Undersize	49.665 to 49.681 mm
Big-end bearing journal diameter:	
954 cc petrol engine:	
Standard	37.992 to 38.008 mm
Undersize	36.692 to 37.708 mm
1124 cc petrol engines:	
Standard	44.992 to 45.008 mm
Undersize	44.692 to 44.708 mm
1360 cc petrol engine (with aluminium block):	
Standard	44.992 to 45.008 mm
Undersize	44.692 to 44.708 mm
1360cc petrol engine (with steel block):	
Standard	44.991 to 44.975 mm
Undersize	44.691 to 44.675 mm
1587 cc SOHC and DOHC petrol engines:	
Standard	44.991 to 44.975 mm
Undersize	44.691 to 44.675 mm

Crankshaft (continued)

Big-end bearing journal diameter (continued):	
1527 cc diesel engine:	
Standard	44.991 to 44.975 mm
Undersize	44.691 to 44.675 mm
Maximum bearing journal out-of-round	
All engines	0.007 mm
Main bearing running clearance - all engines	0.01 to 0.036 mm
Big-end bearing running clearance	0.025 to 0.050 mm*

**This is a suggested figure, typical for this type of engine; At the time of writing, no exact values were available from the manufacturer - refer to your dealer or parts supplier for details.*

Torque wrench settings

Petrol engines

Refer to Chapter 2A Specifications.

Diesel engines

Refer to Chapter 2B Specifications.

1 General information

Included in this Part of Chapter 2 are details of removing the engine from the vehicle, and general overhaul procedures for the cylinder head, cylinder block/crankcase, and all other engine internal components.

The information given ranges from advice concerning preparation for an overhaul and the purchase of replacement parts, to detailed step-by-step procedures covering removal, inspection, renovation and refitting of engine internal components.

After Section 6, all instructions are based on the assumption that the engine has been removed from the vehicle. For information concerning in-car engine repair, as well as the removal and refitting of those external components necessary for full overhaul, refer to Part A or B of this Chapter (as applicable) and to Section 6. Ignore any preliminary dismantling operations described in Part A (petrol engine) or Part B (diesel engine) that are no longer relevant once the engine has been removed from the vehicle.

Apart from torque wrench settings, which are given at the beginning of Part A or Part B, all specifications relating to engine overhaul are at the beginning of this Part of Chapter 2.

2 Engine overhaul - general information

It is not always easy to determine when, or if, an engine should be completely overhauled, as a number of factors must be considered.

High mileage is not necessarily an indication that an overhaul is needed, while low mileage does not preclude the need for an overhaul. Frequency of servicing is probably the most important consideration. An engine which has had regular and frequent oil and filter changes, as well as other required maintenance, should perform reliably for many tens of thousands of miles. Conversely, a neglected engine may require an overhaul very early in its life.

Excessive oil consumption is an indication that piston rings, valve seals and/or valve guides are in need of attention. Make sure that oil leaks are not responsible before deciding that the rings and/or guides are worn. Perform a compression test, as described in Part A or B of this Chapter (as applicable), to determine the likely cause of the problem.

Check the oil pressure with a gauge fitted in place of the oil pressure switch, and compare it with that specified in Chapters 2A or 2B. If it is extremely low, the main and big-end bearings, and/or the oil pump, are probably worn out.

Loss of power, rough running, knocking or metallic engine noises, excessive valve gear noise, and high fuel consumption may also point to the need for an overhaul, especially if they are all present at the same time. If a complete service does not remedy the situation, major mechanical work is the only solution.

An engine overhaul involves restoring all internal parts to the specification of a new engine. During an overhaul, the cylinder liners (where applicable), the pistons and the piston rings are renewed. New main and big-end bearings are generally fitted; if necessary, the crankshaft may be reground, to restore the journals. The valves are also serviced as well, since they are usually in less-than-perfect condition at this point. While the engine is being overhauled, other components, such as the distributor, starter and alternator, can be overhauled as well. The end result should be an as-new engine that will give many trouble-free miles.

Note: *Critical cooling system components such as the hoses, thermostat and water pump should be renewed when an engine is overhauled. The radiator should be checked carefully, to ensure that it is not clogged or leaking. Also, it is a good idea to renew the oil pump whenever the engine is overhauled.*

Before beginning the engine overhaul, read through the entire procedure, to familiarise yourself with the scope and requirements of the job. Overhauling an engine is not difficult if you follow all of the instructions carefully, have the necessary tools and equipment, and pay close attention to all specifications. It can, however, be time-consuming. Plan on the car being off the road for a minimum of two weeks, especially if parts must be taken to an engineering works for repair or reconditioning. Check on the availability of parts, and make sure that any necessary special tools and equipment are obtained in advance. Most work can be done with typical hand tools, although a number of precision measuring tools are required for inspecting parts to determine if they must be renewed. Often, the engineering works will handle the inspection of parts, and offer advice concerning reconditioning and renewal.

Always wait until the engine has been completely dismantled, and until all components (especially the cylinder block/crankcase and the crankshaft) have been inspected, before deciding what service and repair operations must be performed by an engineering works. The condition of these components will be the major factor to consider when determining whether to overhaul the original engine, or to buy a reconditioned unit. Do not, therefore, purchase parts or have overhaul work done on other components until they have been thoroughly inspected. As a general rule, time is the primary cost of an overhaul, so it does not pay to fit worn or sub-standard parts.

As a final note, to ensure maximum life and minimum trouble from a reconditioned engine, everything must be assembled with care, in a spotlessly-clean environment.

3 Engine removal - methods and precautions

If you have decided that the engine must be removed for overhaul or major repair work, several preliminary steps should be taken.

Locating a suitable place to work is extremely important. Adequate work space, along with storage space for the vehicle, will be needed. If a workshop or garage is not available, at the very least, a flat, level, clean work surface is required.

Cleaning the engine compartment and engine/transmission before beginning the removal procedure will help keep tools clean and organised.

An engine hoist or A-frame will also be necessary. Make sure that the equipment is rated in excess of the combined weight of the engine and transmission. Safety is of primary importance, considering the potential hazards involved in lifting the engine/transmission out of the vehicle.

If this is the first time you have removed an engine, an assistant should ideally be available. Advice and aid from someone more experienced would also be helpful. There are many instances when one person cannot simultaneously perform all of the operations required when lifting the engine out of the vehicle.

Plan the operation ahead of time. Before starting work, arrange for the hire of (or obtain) all of the tools and equipment you will need. Some of the equipment necessary to perform engine/transmission removal and installation safely and with relative ease (in addition to an engine hoist) is as follows: a heavy-duty trolley jack, complete sets of spanners and sockets as described in the front of this manual, wooden blocks, and plenty of rags and cleaning solvent for mopping up spilled oil, coolant and fuel. If the hoist must be hired, make sure that you arrange for it in advance, and perform all of the operations possible without it beforehand. This will save you money and time.

Plan for the vehicle to be out of use for quite a while. An engineering works will be required to perform some of the work which the do-it-yourselfer cannot accomplish without special equipment. These places often have a busy schedule, so it would be a good idea to consult them before removing the engine, in order to accurately estimate the amount of time required to rebuild or repair components that may need work.

Always be extremely careful when removing and refitting the engine/transmission. Serious injury can result from careless actions. Plan ahead and take your time, and a job of this nature, although major, can be accomplished successfully.

The engine and transmission unit is removed from under the vehicle on all models described in this manual.

4 Engine and transmission - removal, separation and refitting

Removal

Note: *The engine and transmission can be removed from the car as a complete unit; the two are then separated for overhaul. The text in this Section describes the removal of the engine/transmission unit via the underside of the engine compartment (but note that on the smaller capacity petrol models, the removal of the bonnet, radiator and left-hand engine mounting bracket should permit withdrawal of the unit via the top of the engine compartment). To allow adequate clearance underneath the vehicle, there should be at least 65cm between the lower edge of the front bumper and the ground when the vehicle is raised and supported; this figure does not include the height of any jacks or support cradles positioned underneath the engine/transmission unit. Note that this measurement was obtained from work carried out on a 1.1 litre petrol model; extra clearance may be necessary when working on diesel or 16-valve petrol models, to take into account the increased height of the engine/transmission.*

1 Park the vehicle on firm, level ground. Chock the rear wheels, then firmly apply the handbrake. Jack up the front of the vehicle, and securely support it on axle stands (see "*Jacking and vehicle support*"), bearing in mind the note at the start of this Section.

4.12a Release the spring clip . . .

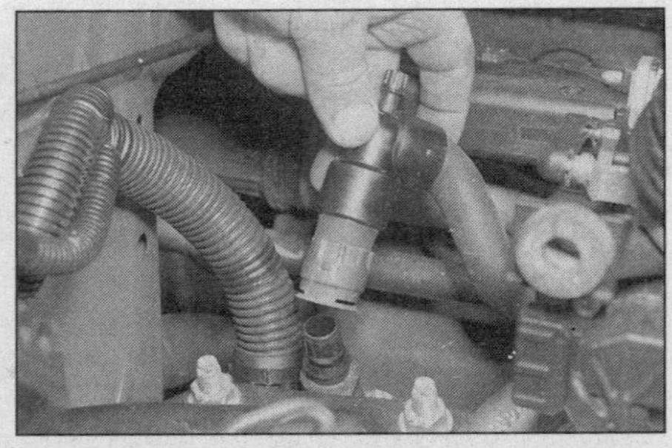

4.12b . . . and disconnect the heater return hose from the coolant pump housing (1.1 litre model shown)

2 Remove both front roadwheels.

3 Set the bonnet in the upright position, and remove the battery as described in Chapter 5A.

4 Drain the cooling system (see Chapter 1A or 1B, as applicable), saving the coolant if it is fit for re-use. On vehicles with power steering, protect the electric power steering pump with plastic sheeting, to prevent it from being splashed with coolant.

5 Drain the transmission oil as described in Chapter 7A or 7B, as applicable. Refit the drain and filler plugs, and tighten them securely or to the specified torque setting, where applicable (see Chapter 1A or 1B).

6 If the engine is to be dismantled, drain the oil and (if required) remove the oil filter as described in Chapter 1A or 1B, as applicable. Clean and refit the drain plug, tightening it securely.

7 Remove the auxiliary drivebelt as described in Chapter 1A or 1B (as applicable) then remove the alternator as described in Chapter 5A.

8 Where applicable on models equipped with power steering, refer to Chapter 10 carry out the following:

a) *Drain the hydraulic fluid from the power steering fluid reservoir.*
b) *Disconnect the hydraulic fluid hoses from the steering rack and position them away from the underside of the transmission casing.*
c) *Unbolt the power steering pump from its mounting bracket and position it to one side.*

9 On models with air conditioning, unbolt the compressor, and position it clear of the engine unit. Support the weight of the compressor by tying it to the vehicle body, to prevent any excess strain being placed on the compressor lines whilst the engine is removed. **Do not** disconnect the refrigerant lines from the compressor (see the warnings given in Chapter 3).

10 Proceed as described under the relevant sub-heading.

Petrol models

11 Refer to Chapter 4A, 4B or 4D, as applicable, and carry out the following operations:

a) *Remove the air cleaner housing and intake duct.*
b) *Depressurise the fuel system, and disconnect the fuel feed and return hoses from the throttle body.*
c) *Disconnect the accelerator cable from the throttle body.*
d) *Disconnect the purge valve and braking system servo vacuum hoses from the manifold.*
e) *Remove the complete exhaust system.*
f) *Unbolt the engine management system ECU and its support bracket from the inner wing to allow them to be removed with the engine.*

12 Disconnect the heater matrix supply and return coolant hoses at the quick release bulkhead and coolant pump housing/cylinder block connections **(see illustrations)**.

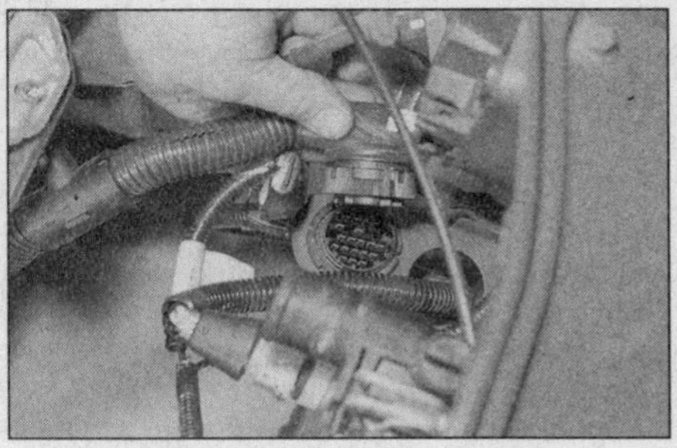

4.21a Unplug the main engine wiring harness back at the connector in the front, left-hand corner of the engine compartment

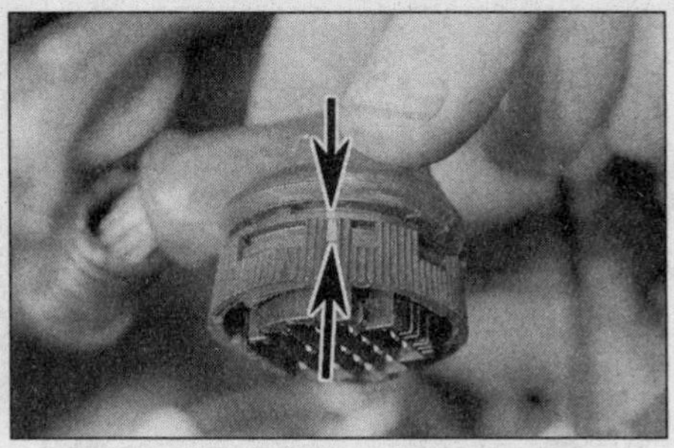

4.21b Release the wiring connector by twisting its locking ring anti-clockwise until the markings (arrowed) are aligned

4.21c On petrol models, remove the cover from the fusible link box . . .

Diesel models

13 On diesel models, carry out the following operations using the information in Chapter 4C and 4D:

a) *Remove the intake duct.*
b) *Disconnect the fuel supply hose from the fuel filter/thermostat housing and the return hose.*
c) *Disconnect the accelerator cable from the injection pump.*
d) *Disconnect the vacuum hose from the braking system vacuum pump.*
e) *Remove the complete exhaust system.*

14 Remove the preheating system control unit, with reference to Chapter 5C. Free the wiring harness from any relevant retaining clips, so that it is free to be removed with the engine/transmission.

15 Noting each hose's correct routing, slacken the retaining clips and disconnect the coolant hoses from the front and rear of the thermostat/fuel filter housing on the left-hand end of the cylinder head. Some later models have quick-release hose fittings, which are separated by depressing the tab at the side of the fitting.

All models

16 Remove the radiator cooling fan and radiator as described in Chapter 3.

17 Remove both driveshafts as described in Chapter 8.

18 On models with manual transmission, disconnect the clutch cable from the transmission (see Chapter 6), then refer to Chapter 7A and disconnect the gearchange linkage link rods from the transmission control levers.

19 On models with automatic transmission, disconnect the gear selector cable from the transmission as described in Chapter 7B.

20 Disconnect the wiring from the speedometer transducer, at the rear of the differential casing (see Chapter 7A or 7B as applicable). On models with automatic transmission, remove the speed sensor and the multifunction switch from the transmission casing and move them to one side. Note that these components are hard-wired to the transmission ECU and cannot be disconnected; see Chapter 7B for details.

21 Trace the main engine wiring harness back to the connector in the front, left-hand corner of the engine compartment. Release the wiring connector by twisting its locking ring anti-clockwise until the markings on the surface of the rings are aligned, and then disconnect it. On petrol models, also trace the harness lead(s) back to the auxiliary fuse/relay box and fusible link box, situated directly behind the battery; disconnect the connectors and/or undo the nut(s) and release the lead(s) **(see illustrations)**. Check that all the relevant

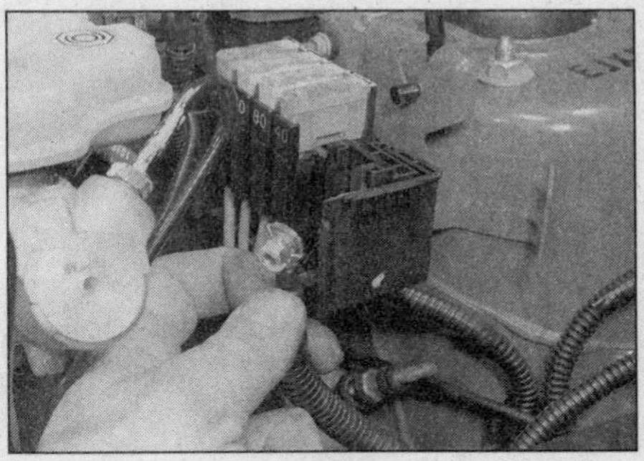

4.21d . . . then unscrew the retaining nuts and disconnect the harness leads

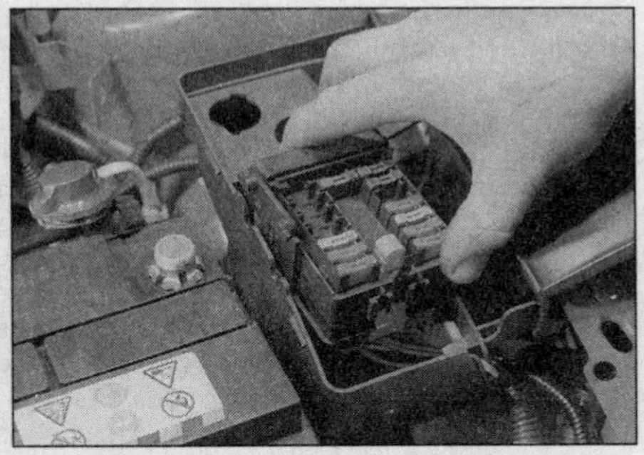

4.21e At the auxiliary fuse/relay box, withdraw the base from the fusebox . . .

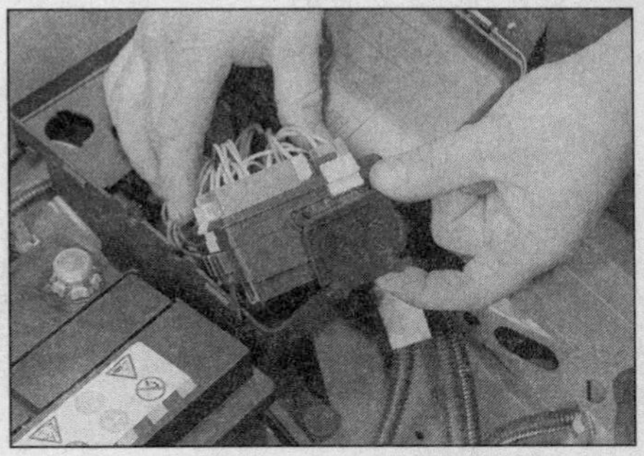

4.21f . . . remove the retaining clip . . .

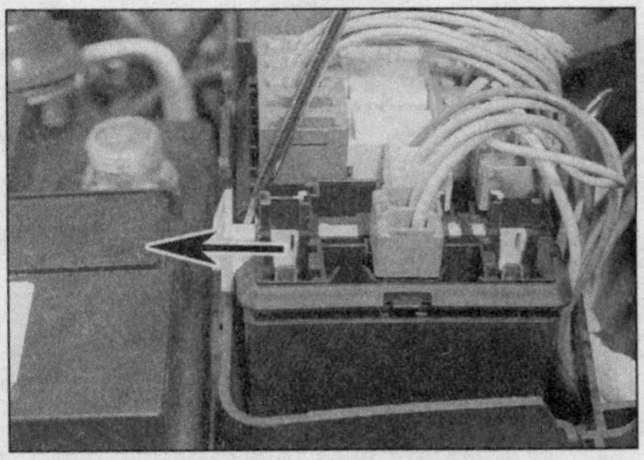

4.21g . . . then release the locking bar . . .

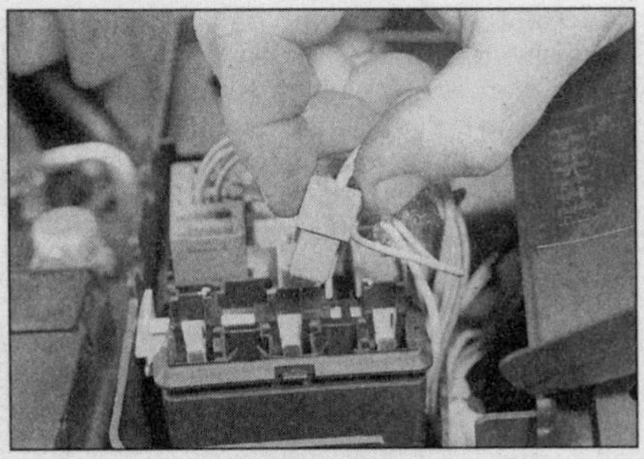

4.21h . . . and unplug the wiring harness connector(s)

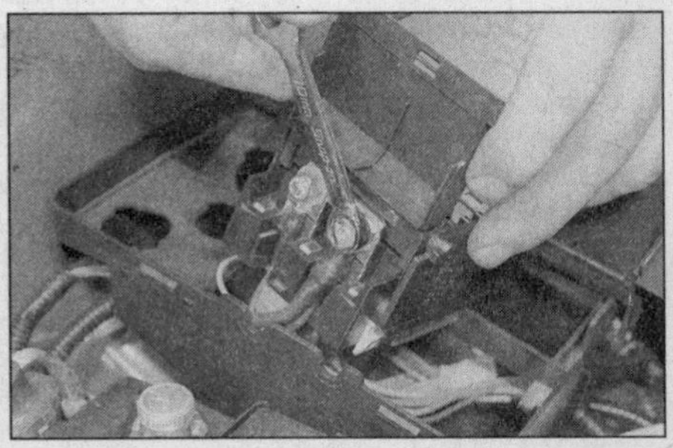

4.21i Unscrew the securing nuts and release the power lead(s) from the side of the fusebox base

connectors have been disconnected, and that the wiring is released from any relevant clips or ties, so that it is free to be removed with the engine/transmission.

22 Unscrew the securing nut and disconnect the engine/transmission earth cable from the bodywork, at the left hand side of the engine compartment (see Chapter 7A or 7B as applicable).

23 Manoeuvre the engine hoist into position, and attach it to the lifting brackets bolted onto the cylinder head. Raise the hoist until it is just supporting the weight of the engine.

24 Slacken and remove the bolt securing the rear engine mounting link to the mounting on the transmission, then loosen the bolt securing the link to the body. Pivot the link away from the transmission, so that it will not hinder removal (see Chapter 2A or 2B as applicable).

25 Slacken and remove the left-hand mounting rubber centre nut, and the two bolts securing the bracket to the body. Remove the mounting rubber, and slide the spacer off the mounting bracket stud (see Chapter 2A or 2B as applicable).

26 Slacken and remove the nuts securing the right-hand engine mounting upper bracket to the mounting rubber and bracket on the cylinder block. Withdraw the bracket, and lift off the rubber buffer plate (where fitted) from the mounting stud. On diesel models, recover the reinforcement plate from the engine (see Chapter 2A or 2B as applicable).

27 Make a final check that any components which would prevent the removal of the engine/transmission from the car have been removed or disconnected. Ensure that components such as the gearchange link rods are secured so that they cannot be damaged on removal.

28 If available, a low trolley should be placed under the engine/transmission assembly, to facilitate its easy removal from under the vehicle. Lower the engine/transmission assembly, making sure that nothing is trapped or damaged. Enlist the help of an assistant during this procedure, as it may be necessary to tilt the assembly slightly to clear the body panels **(see illustration)**.

29 Withdraw the engine/transmission assembly from under the vehicle.

Separation

30 With the engine/transmission assembly removed, support the assembly on suitable blocks of wood, on a workbench (or failing that, on a clean area of the workshop floor).

31 Unscrew the retaining bolts and remove the starter motor from the transmission.

32 Disconnect the wiring from the reversing light switch.

33 Ensure that both engine and transmission are adequately supported, then slacken and remove the bolts securing the transmission housing to the engine. Note the correct fitted positions of each bolt (and where fitted, the relevant brackets) as they are removed, to use as a reference on refitting. On cast-iron block engines, it will also be necessary to unbolt the flywheel cover plate from the transmission.

4.28 Lower the engine/transmission assembly away from the underside of the engine compartment

34 Carefully withdraw the transmission from the engine, ensuring that the weight of the transmission is not allowed to hang on the input shaft while it is engaged with the clutch friction disc.

35 If they are loose, remove the locating dowels from the engine or transmission, and keep them in a safe place.

Refitting

36 If the engine and transmission have been separated, perform the operations described below in paragraphs 37 to 42. If not, proceed as described from paragraph 43 onwards.

37 Apply a smear of high-melting-point grease to the splines of the transmission input shaft. Do not apply too much, otherwise there is a possibility of the grease contaminating the clutch friction plate.

38 Ensure that the locating dowels are correctly positioned in the engine or transmission, and that the release bearing is correctly engaged with the fork.

39 Carefully offer the transmission to the engine, until the locating dowels are engaged. Ensure that the weight of the transmission is not allowed to hang on the input shaft as it is engaged with the clutch friction plate.

40 Refit the transmission housing-to-engine bolts, ensuring that all the necessary brackets are correctly positioned, and tighten them to the specified torque setting. On cast-iron block engines, refit the flywheel cover plate and securely tighten its retaining bolts.

41 Reconnect the wire to the reversing light switch.

42 Refit the starter motor, and tighten the retaining bolts.

43 Locate the engine/transmission assembly under the vehicle, then reconnect the hoist and lifting tackle to the engine lifting brackets.

44 With the aid of an assistant, lift the assembly up into the engine compartment. Make sure that it clears the surrounding components, and the radiator in particular.

45 Refit the rubber buffer plate (where fitted) and the right-hand engine mounting upper bracket to the body mounting and bracket, and lightly tighten its fasteners. On diesel models, do not omit the reinforcement plate from underneath the mounting bracket.

46 Refit the spacer, then install mounting to the body, and lightly tighten its retaining bolts. Refit the mounting centre nut again, tightening it lightly.

47 Reconnect the rear mounting link to the transmission mounting, and refit its centre bolt.

48 With engine/transmission mounting nuts and bolts lightly tightened, rock the engine/transmission unit to settle it in position, then go around and tighten all the mounting nuts and bolts to their specified torque settings. The hoist can then be detached from the engine unit and removed.

49 The remainder of the refitting procedure is a direct reversal of the removal sequence, noting the following points:

a) Ensure that the wiring harness is correctly routed and retained by all the relevant retaining clips, and that all connectors are correctly and securely reconnected.
b) Prior to refitting the driveshafts to the transmission, renew the driveshaft oil seals as described in Chapter 7A or 7B, as applicable.
c) Ensure that all coolant hoses are correctly reconnected, and securely retained by their retaining clips.
d) Adjust the accelerator cable as described in the relevant Part of Chapter 4.
e) On models with manual transmission, connect and adjust the clutch cable as described in Chapter 6.
f) Refit and adjust the auxiliary drivebelt as described in the relevant Part of Chapter 1.
g) Refill the engine and transmission with correct quantity and type of lubricant, as described in the relevant Part of Chapter 1.
h) Refill the cooling system as described in the relevant Part of Chapter 1.
i) On completion, start the engine and check for leaks. If the engine has been dismantled and overhauled, refer to Section 19 for further information.

5 Engine overhaul - dismantling sequence

1 It is much easier to dismantle and work on the engine if it is mounted on a portable engine stand. These stands can often be hired from a tool hire shop. Before the engine is mounted on a stand, the flywheel should be removed, so that the stand bolts can be tightened into the end of the cylinder block/crankcase.

2 If a stand is not available, it is possible to dismantle the engine with it blocked up on a sturdy workbench, or on the floor. Be extra-careful not to tip or drop the engine when working without a stand.

3 If you are going to obtain a reconditioned engine, all the external components must be removed first, to be transferred to the replacement engine (just as they will if you are doing a complete engine overhaul yourself).

These components include the following:

a) Alternator mounting bracket (Chapter 5A).
b) On petrol engines, HT leads and spark plugs (Chapters 1A and 5B).
c) On diesel engines, the fuel injection pump and mounting bracket, the fuel injectors and glow plugs (Chapter 4C and 5C).
d) Thermostat housing, and coolant outlet chamber/elbow (Chapter 3). On diesel engines, the housing also includes the fuel filter housing.
e) Where applicable, the dipstick tube.
f) On petrol engines, fuel injection system components (Chapter 4A or 4B).
g) All electrical switches and sensors, and the engine wiring harness.
h) Inlet and exhaust manifolds (see relevant Part of Chapter 4).
i) Oil filter (Chapter 1A or 1B).
j) Engine mountings (Chapter 2A or 2B).
k) Flywheel (Chapter 2A or 2B).

Note: *When removing the external components from the engine, pay close attention to details that may be helpful or important during refitting. Note the fitted position of gaskets, seals, spacers, pins, washers, bolts, and other small items.*

4 If you are obtaining a "short" engine (which consists of the engine cylinder block/crankcase, crankshaft, pistons and connecting rods all assembled), then the cylinder head, sump, oil pump, and timing belt will have to be removed also.

5 If you are planning a complete overhaul, the engine can be dismantled, and the internal components removed, in the order given below, referring to Part A or B of this Chapter unless otherwise stated:

a) Inlet and exhaust manifolds (see relevant Part of Chapter 4).
b) Timing belt, sprockets and tensioner.
c) Cylinder head.
d) Flywheel.
e) Sump.
f) Oil pump.
g) Piston/connecting rod assemblies.
h) Crankshaft.

6 Before beginning the dismantling and overhaul procedures, make sure that you have all of the correct tools necessary. Refer to *"Tools and working facilities"* at the end of this manual for further information.

6 Cylinder head - dismantling

Note: *New and reconditioned cylinder heads are available from the manufacturer, and from engine overhaul specialists. Be aware that some specialist tools are required for the dismantling and inspection procedures, and new components may not be readily available. It may therefore be more practical and economical for the home mechanic to purchase a reconditioned head, rather than to dismantle, inspect and recondition the original head.*

6.3 Valve components - DOHC 16-valve engine

1 Inlet valve
2 Exhaust valve
3 Hydraulic tappet
4 Collet
5 Spring retainer
6 Valve spring
7 Spring seat
8 Valve stem oil seal

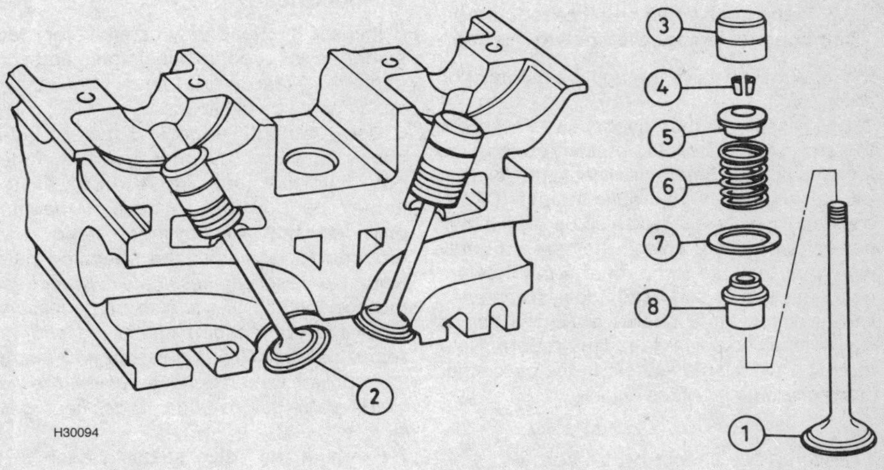

1 Remove the cylinder head from the cylinder block as described in Part A or B of this Chapter (as applicable).

2 If not already done, remove the inlet and exhaust manifolds with reference to the relevant Part of Chapter 4.

3 Remove the camshaft(s) (and followers on diesel engines, or hydraulic tappets on DOHC engines) as described in Part A or B of this Chapter **(see illustration)**.

4 Using a valve spring compressor, compress each valve spring in turn until the split collets can be removed. Release the compressor, and lift off the spring retainer, spring and spring seat **(see illustration)**.

5 Using a pair of pliers, carefully extract the valve stem seal from the top of the guide **(see illustration)**.

> **HAYNES HiNT** ***If, when the valve spring compressor is screwed down, the spring retainer refuses to free and expose the split collets, gently tap the top of the tool, directly over the retainer, with a light hammer. This should free the retainer.***

6.4 Using a valve spring compressor to compress the valve spring

6.5 Remove the valve stem oil seal using a pair of pliers

2C

6.7 Place each valve and its associated components in a labelled polythene bag

6 Withdraw the valve through the combustion chamber.

7 It is essential that each valve is stored together with its collets, retainer, spring, and spring seat, and where applicable, its follower (diesel engine) or hydraulic tappet (DOHC engine). The valves should also be kept in their correct sequence, unless they are so badly worn that they are to be renewed. If they are going to be kept and used again, place each valve assembly in a labelled polythene bag or similar small container **(see illustration)**. Note that No 1 cylinder is nearest to the passenger (transmission) end of the engine.

7 Cylinder head and valves - cleaning and inspection

1 Thorough cleaning of the cylinder head and valve components, followed by a detailed inspection, will enable you to decide how much valve service work must be carried out during the engine overhaul. **Note:** *If the engine has been severely overheated, it is best to assume that the cylinder head is warped - check carefully for signs of this.*

Cleaning

2 Scrape away all traces of old gasket material from the cylinder head, taking care to avoid gouging or scoring the mating surface.

3 Scrape away the carbon from the combustion chambers and ports, then wash the cylinder head thoroughly with paraffin or a suitable solvent.

4 Scrape off any heavy carbon deposits that may have formed on the valves, then use a power-operated wire brush to remove deposits from the valve heads and stems.

Inspection

Note: *Be sure to perform all the following inspection procedures before concluding that the services of a machine shop or engine overhaul specialist are required. Make a list of all items that require attention.*

Cylinder head

5 Inspect the head very carefully for cracks, evidence of coolant leakage, and other damage. If cracks are found, a new cylinder head should be obtained.

6 Use a straight-edge and feeler blade to check that the cylinder head surface is not distorted **(see illustration)**. If it is, it may be possible to have it machined, provided that the cylinder head is not reduced to less than the specified height. **Note:** *On diesel engines, if the cylinder head is to be machined, it will also be necessary to recut the combustion chambers and valve seat recesses. This is necessary to maintain the correct dimensions between the valve heads, valve guides and cylinder head gasket face.*

7 Examine the valve seats in each of the combustion chambers. If they are severely pitted, cracked, or burned, they will need to be renewed or re-cut by an engine overhaul specialist. If they are only slightly pitted, this can be removed by grinding-in the valve heads and seats with fine valve-grinding compound, as described below.

8 Check the valve guides for wear by inserting the relevant valve, and checking for side-to-side motion of the valve. A very small amount of movement is acceptable. If the movement seems excessive, remove the valve. Measure the valve stem diameter (see below), and renew the valve if it is worn. If the valve stem is not worn, the wear must be in the valve guide, and the guide must be renewed. The renewal of valve guides is best carried out by a Citroën dealer or engine overhaul specialist, who will have the necessary tools available.

9 If renewing the valve guides, the valve seats should be re-cut or re-ground only *after* the guides have been fitted.

10 On diesel models, inspect the swirl chambers for burning or damage such as cracking. Small cracks in the chambers are acceptable; renewal of the chambers will only be required if chamber tracts are badly burned and disfigured, if they are no longer a tight fit in the cylinder head, or if the cylinder head is to be machined. If there is any doubt as to the swirl chamber condition, seek the advice of a Citroën dealer or a suitable repairer who specialises in diesel engines. Swirl chamber renewal should be entrusted to a specialist. Using a dial test indicator, check that the swirl chamber protrusion is within the limits given in the Specifications **(see illustration)**. Zero the dial test indicator on the gasket surface of the cylinder head, then measure the protrusion of the surface of the chamber. If the protrusion is not within the specified limits, the advice of a Citroën dealer or suitable repairer who specialises in diesel engines should be sought.

Valves

11 Examine the head of each valve for pitting, burning, cracks and general wear. Check the valve stem for scoring and wear ridges. Rotate the valve, and check for any obvious indication that it is bent. Look for pits or excessive wear on the tip of each valve stem. Renew any valve that shows any such signs of wear or damage.

12 If the valve appears satisfactory at this stage, measure the valve stem diameter at several points using a micrometer **(see illustration)**. Any significant difference in the readings obtained indicates wear of the valve stem. Should any of these conditions be apparent, the valve(s) must be renewed.

13 If the valves are in satisfactory condition, they should be ground (lapped) into their respective seats, to ensure a smooth, gas-tight seal. If the seat is only lightly pitted, or if it has been re-cut, fine grinding compound *only* should be used to produce the required finish. Coarse valve-grinding compound should *not* be used, unless a seat is badly burned or deeply pitted. If this is the case, the cylinder head and valves should be inspected

7.6 Checking the cylinder head gasket surface for distortion

7.10 Checking swirl chamber protrusion - diesel engine

7.12 Measuring a valve stem diameter

by an expert, to decide whether seat re-cutting, or even the renewal of the valve or seat insert (where possible) is required.

14 Valve grinding is carried out as follows. Place the cylinder head upside-down on a bench.

15 Smear a trace of (the appropriate grade of) valve-grinding compound on the seat face, and press a suction grinding tool onto the valve head **(see illustration)**. With a semi-rotary action, grind the valve head to its seat, lifting the valve occasionally to redistribute the grinding compound.

HAYNES HiNT *A light spring placed under the valve head will help to lift the valve and will greatly ease the valve grinding operation.*

16 If coarse grinding compound is being used, work only until a dull, matt even surface is produced on both the valve seat and the valve, then wipe off the used compound, and repeat the process with fine compound. When a smooth unbroken ring of light grey matt finish is produced on both the valve and seat, the grinding operation is complete. Do not grind-in the valves any further than absolutely necessary, or the seat will be prematurely sunk into the cylinder head.

17 When all the valves have been ground-in, carefully wash off all traces of grinding compound using paraffin or a suitable solvent, before reassembling the cylinder head.

Valve components

18 Examine the valve springs for signs of damage and discoloration. No minimum free length is specified by Citroën, so the only way of judging valve spring wear is by comparison with a new component.

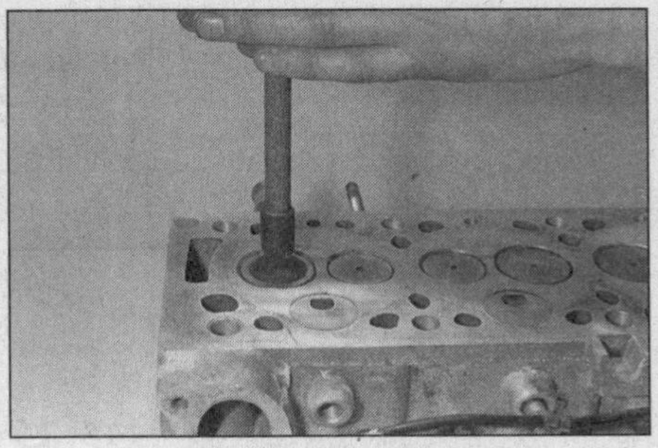

7.15 Grinding-in a valve

19 Stand each spring on a flat surface, and check it for squareness. If any of the springs are damaged, distorted or have lost their tension, obtain a complete new set of springs. It is normal to renew the valve springs as a matter of course if a major overhaul is being carried out.

20 Renew the valve stem oil seals regardless of their apparent condition.

8 Cylinder head - reassembly

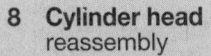

1 Lubricate the stems of the valves, and insert the valves into their original locations **(see illustration)**. If new valves are being fitted, insert them into the locations to which they have been ground.

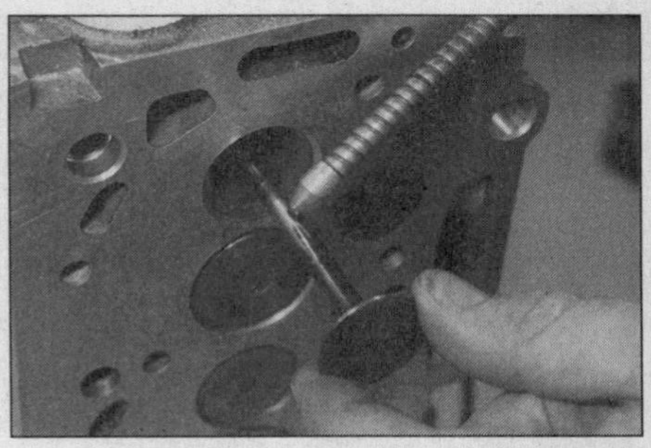

8.1 Lubricate the valve stems prior to refitting

2 Refit the spring seat then, working on the first valve, dip the new valve stem seal in fresh engine oil. Carefully locate it over the valve and onto the guide. Take care not to damage the seal as it is passed over the valve stem. Use a suitable socket or metal tube to press the seal firmly onto the guide **(see illustrations)**.

3 Locate the valve spring on top of its seat, then refit the spring retainer **(see illustrations)**.

4 Compress the valve spring, and locate the split collets in the recess in the valve stem. Release the compressor, then repeat the procedure on the remaining valves **(see illustrations)**.

HAYNES HiNT *Use a little dab of grease to hold the collets in position on the valve stem while the spring compressor is released.*

2C

8.2a Refit the spring seat . . .

8.2b . . . then fit a new valve stem oil seal using a socket

8.3a Refit the valve spring . . .

8.3b . . . and the spring retainer . . .

8.4a . . . and compress the spring with a spring compressor

8.4b Locate the collets on the valve, using a dab of grease to hold them in position

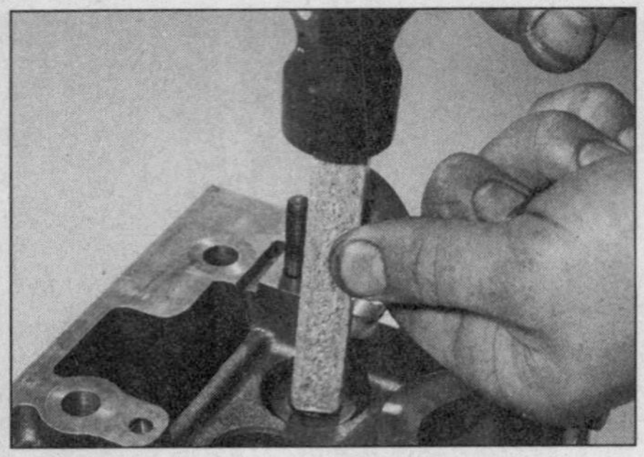

8.5 Remove the spring compressor, and tap the end of the valve to seat the collets in position

5 With all the valves installed, place the cylinder head flat on the bench and, using a hammer and interposed block of wood, tap the end of each valve stem to settle the components **(see illustration)**.

6 On DOHC engines, refit the hydraulic tappets and camshafts as described in Chapter 2A. On diesel engines, refit the followers and fit basic 3.20 mm shims initially, to allow the valve clearances to be measured as described in Chapter 2B.

7 The cylinder head may now be refitted as described in Part A or B of this Chapter (as applicable).

9 Piston/connecting rod assembly - removal

1 Remove the cylinder head, sump and oil pump as described in Part A or B of this Chapter (as applicable).

2 If there is a pronounced wear ridge at the top of any bore, it may be necessary to remove it with a scraper or ridge reamer, to avoid piston damage during removal. Such a ridge indicates excessive wear of the cylinder bore.

3 Using a hammer and centre-punch, paint or similar, mark each connecting rod big-end bearing cap with its respective cylinder number on the flat machined surface provided; if the engine has been dismantled before, note carefully any identifying marks made previously **(see illustration)**. Note that No 1 cylinder is at the transmission (flywheel) end of the engine.

9.6 To protect the crankshaft journals and cylinder bores, tape over the connecting rod stud threads prior to removal

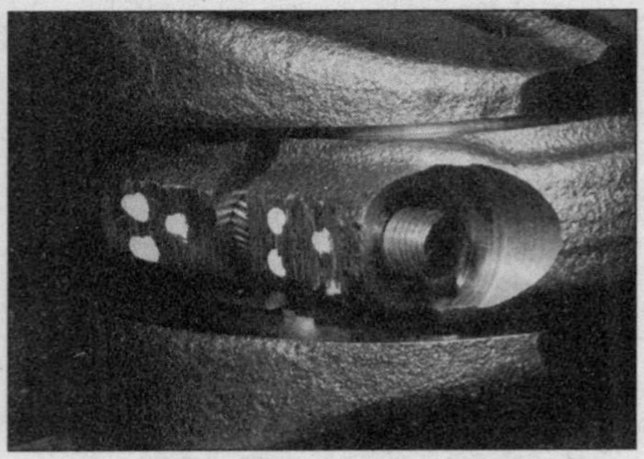

9.3 Connecting rod and big-end bearing cap marked for identification

4 Turn the crankshaft to bring pistons 1 and 4 to BDC (bottom dead centre).

5 Unscrew the nuts from No 1 piston big-end bearing cap. Take off the cap, and recover the bottom half bearing shell **(see illustration)**. If the bearing shells are to be re-used, tape the cap and the shell together.

6 To prevent the possibility of damage to the crankshaft bearing journals, tape over the connecting rod stud threads **(see illustration)**.

7 Using a hammer handle, push the piston up through the bore, and remove it from the top of the cylinder block. Recover the bearing shell, and tape it to the connecting rod for safe-keeping.

8 Loosely refit the big-end cap to the connecting rod, and secure with the nuts - this will help to keep the components in their correct order.

9 Remove No 4 piston assembly in the same way.

10 Turn the crankshaft through 180° to bring pistons 2 and 3 to BDC (bottom dead centre), and remove them in the same way.

10 Crankshaft - removal

1 Remove the crankshaft timing sprocket, the oil pump and the flywheel as described in Part A or B of this Chapter (as applicable).

2 Remove the pistons and connecting rods, as described in Section 9. **Note:** *If no work is to be done on the pistons and connecting rods, there is no need to remove the cylinder head, or to push the pistons out of the cylinder bores. The pistons should just be pushed far enough up the bores that they are positioned clear of the crankshaft journals.*

3 Check the crankshaft endfloat as described in Section 13, then proceed as follows.

Aluminium block engines

4 Work around the outside of the cylinder block, and unscrew all the small (6 mm) bolts securing the main bearing ladder to the base of the cylinder block. Note the correct fitted depth of both the right and left crankshaft oil seals in the cylinder block/main bearing ladder.

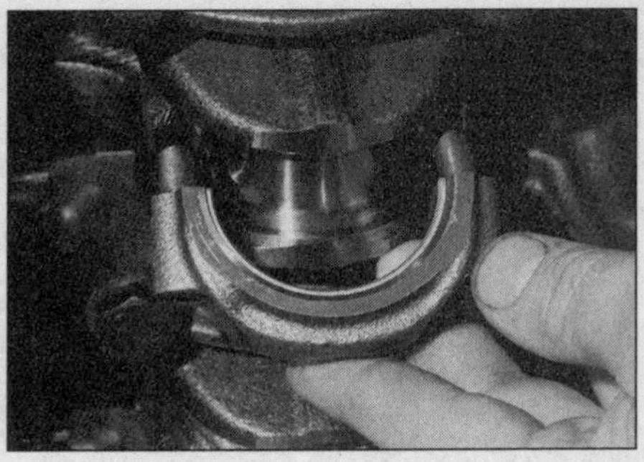

9.5 Removing a big-end bearing cap and shell

5 Working in a diagonal sequence, evenly and progressively slacken the ten large (11 mm) main bearing ladder retaining bolts by a turn at a time. Once all the bolts are loose, remove them from the ladder.

6 With all the retaining bolts removed, carefully lift the main bearing ladder casting away from the base of the cylinder block. Recover the lower main bearing shells, and tape them to their respective locations in the casting. If the two locating dowels are a loose fit, remove them and store them with the casting for safe-keeping.

7 Lift out the crankshaft, and discard both the oil seals. Remove the oil pump drive chain from the end of the crankshaft, then slide off the drive sprocket and recover the Woodruff key.

8 Recover the upper main bearing shells, and store them along with the relevant lower bearing shells. Also recover the two thrustwashers (one fitted either side of No 2 main bearing) from the cylinder block.

Cast-iron block engines

9 Unbolt and remove the crankshaft right and left oil seal housings from each end of the cylinder block, noting the correct fitted locations of the locating dowels **(see illustration)**. If the locating dowels are a loose fit, remove them and store them with the housings for safe-keeping.

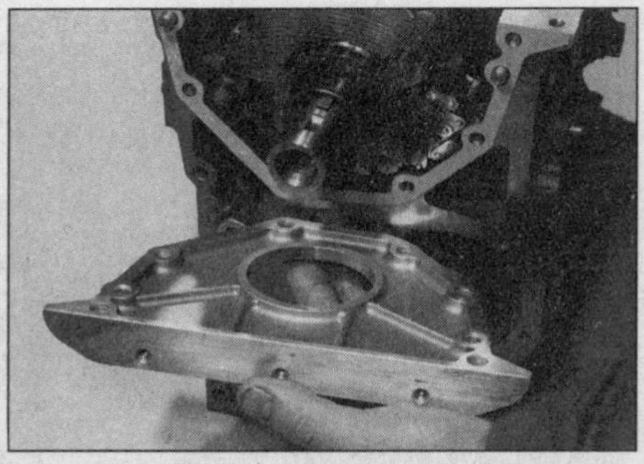

10.9 On cast-iron block engines, remove the oil seal carrier from the right of the cylinder block . . .

10.10a . . . then remove the oil pump drive chain . . .

10.10b . . . and drive sprocket . . .

10.10c . . . then remove the Woodruff key from the crankshaft

10 Remove the oil pump drive chain, and slide the drive sprocket off the end of the crankshaft. Remove the Woodruff key, and store it with the sprocket for safe-keeping **(see illustrations)**.

11 The main bearing caps should be numbered 1 to 5 from the transmission (flywheel) end of the engine **(see illustration)**. If not, mark them accordingly using a centre-punch or paint.

12 Unscrew and remove the main bearing cap retaining bolts, and withdraw the caps. Recover the lower main bearing shells, and tape them to their respective caps for safe-keeping.

10.11 Main bearing cap identification markings (arrowed)

13 Carefully lift out the crankshaft, taking care not to displace the upper main bearing shells as you do this **(see illustration)**.

14 With the crankshaft removed, recover the upper main bearing shells from the cylinder block, and tape them to their respective caps for safe-keeping. Remove the thrustwasher halves from the side of No 2 main bearing, and store them with the No 2 main bearing cap **(see illustration)**.

11 Cylinder block/crankcase - cleaning and inspection

Cleaning

1 Remove all external components and electrical switches/sensors from the block. For complete cleaning, the core plugs should ideally be removed. Drill a small hole in the plugs, then insert a self-tapping screw into the hole. Pull out the plugs by pulling on the screw with a pair of grips, or by using a short-stroke slide hammer.

2 On aluminium block engines, remove the liners as described in paragraph 16.

3 On diesel and DOHC petrol models, undo the retaining bolts and remove the piston oil jet spray tubes (there are four - one for each cylinder) from inside the cylinder block.

4 Scrape all traces of sealant from the cylinder block/crankcase, and from the main bearing ladder (where fitted), taking care not to damage the gasket/sealing surfaces.

5 Remove all oil gallery plugs (where fitted). The plugs are usually very tight - they may have to be drilled out, and the holes re-tapped. Use new plugs when the engine is reassembled.

6 If any of the castings are extremely dirty, all should be steam-cleaned.

7 After the castings are returned, clean all oil holes and oil galleries one more time. Flush all internal passages with warm water until the water runs clear. Dry thoroughly, and apply a light film of oil to all mating surfaces, to prevent rusting. On cast-iron block engines, also oil the cylinder bores. If you have access to compressed air, use it to speed up the drying process, and to blow out all the oil holes and galleries.

Warning: Wear eye protection when using compressed air!

8 If the castings are not very dirty, you can do an adequate cleaning job with hot, soapy water and a stiff brush. Take plenty of time, and do a thorough job. Regardless of the cleaning method used, be sure to clean all oil

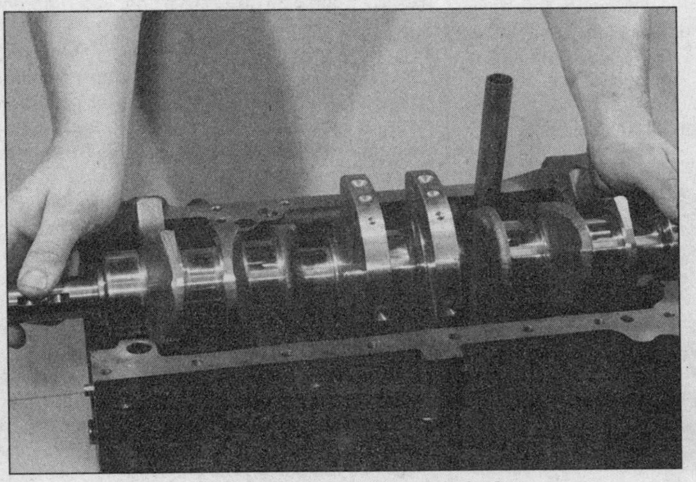

10.13 Lifting out the crankshaft

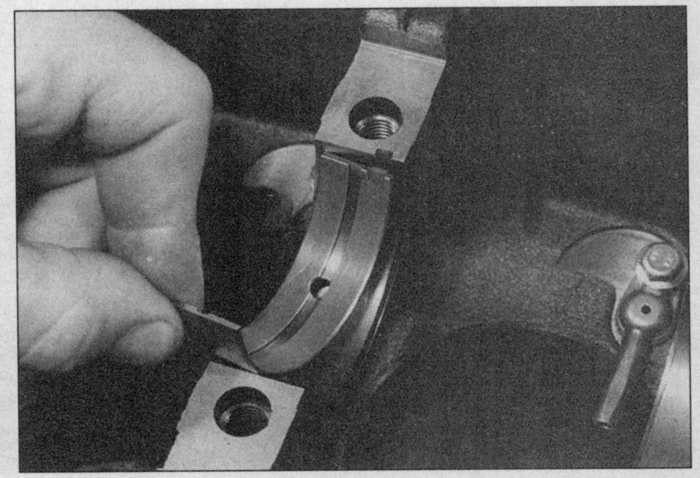

10.14 Remove the upper main bearing shells from the cylinder block/crankcase, and store them with their lower shells

11.9 Cleaning a cylinder block threaded hole using a suitable tap

holes and galleries very thoroughly, and to dry all components well. On cast-iron block engines, protect the cylinder bores as described above, to prevent rusting.

9 All threaded holes must be clean, to ensure accurate torque readings during reassembly. To clean the threads, run the correct-size tap into each of the holes to remove rust, corrosion, thread sealant or sludge, and to restore damaged threads **(see illustration)**. If possible, use compressed air to clear the holes of debris produced by this operation.

HAYNES HiNT *A good alternative to compressed air is to inject an aerosol water-dispersant lubricant into each hole, using the long, thin tube usually supplied. However, be sure to remove the excess lubricant from blind tapped holes, to prevent damage through hydraulic action during reassembly.*

Warning: Wear eye protection when cleaning out these holes in this way!

10 Apply suitable sealant to the new oil gallery plugs, and insert them into the holes in the block. Tighten them securely.

11 On diesel and DOHC petrol engines, clean the threads of the piston oil jet retaining bolts, and apply a drop of suitable thread-locking compound to the bolt threads. Refit the piston oil jet spray tubes to the cylinder block, and tighten their retaining bolts to the specified torque setting.

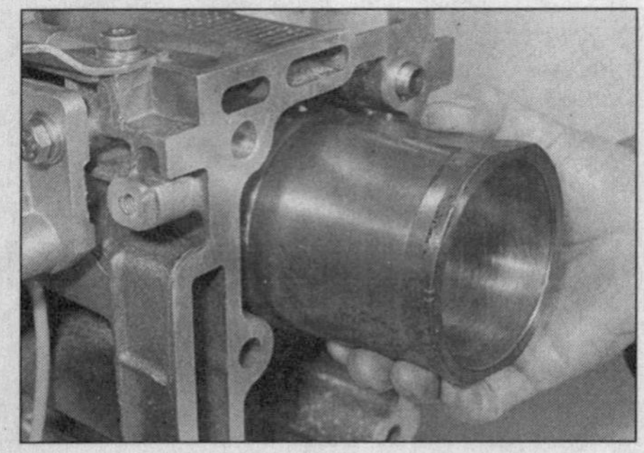

11.16a On aluminium block engines, remove each liner . . .

12 If the engine is not going to be reassembled right away, cover it with a large plastic bag to keep it clean; protect all mating surfaces and the cylinder bores as described above, to prevent rusting.

Inspection

Cast-iron block engines

13 Visually check the casting for cracks and corrosion. Look for stripped threads in the threaded holes. If there has been any history of internal water leakage, it may be worthwhile having an engine overhaul specialist check the cylinder block/crankcase with special equipment. If defects are found, have them repaired if possible, or renew the assembly.

14 Check each cylinder bore for scuffing and scoring. Check for signs of a wear ridge at the top of the cylinder, indicating that the bore is excessively worn.

15 Since Citroën do not state any specific wear limits for the cylinder bores or pistons, it is not possible to assess the amount of wear by direct measurement. If there is any doubt about the condition of the cylinder bores, seek the advice of a Citroën dealer or engine reconditioning specialist. At the time of writing, it was not clear whether oversize pistons are available from Citroën. Consult your Citroën dealer for piston availability; if oversize pistons are available, the cylinders can be rebored, but if not, and the bores are worn, renewal of the block seems to be the only option. Seek the advice of an engine overhaul specialist as to the best course of action.

Aluminium cylinder block (with wet liners)

16 Remove the liner clamps (where used), then use a hardwood drift to tap out each liner from inside the cylinder block. When all the liners are released, tip the cylinder block/crankcase on its side and remove each liner from the top of the block. As each liner is removed, stick masking tape on its left-hand (transmission side) face, and write the cylinder number on the tape. No 1 cylinder is at the passenger (transmission) end of the engine. Remove the O-ring from the base of each liner, and discard it **(see illustrations)**.

11.16b . . . and recover the bottom O-ring seal (arrowed)

17 Check each cylinder liner for scuffing and scoring. Check for signs of a wear ridge at the top of the liner, indicating that its bore is excessively worn.

18 If the necessary measuring equipment is available, measure the bore diameter of each cylinder liner at the top (just under the wear ridge), centre, and bottom of the cylinder bore, parallel to the crankshaft axis.

19 Next, measure the bore diameter at the same three locations, but this time at right-angles to the crankshaft axis. Compare the results with the figures given in the Specifications.

20 Repeat the procedure for the remaining cylinder liners.

21 If the liner wear exceeds the permitted tolerances at any point, if the cylinder liner walls are badly scored or scuffed, or if they exhibit signs of severe corrosion, then renewal of the relevant liner assembly will be necessary. If there is any doubt about the condition of the cylinder bores, seek the advice of a Citroën dealer or engine reconditioning specialist.

22 If renewal is necessary, new liners, complete with pistons and piston rings, can be purchased from a Citroën dealer. Note that it is not possible to buy liners individually - they are supplied only as a matched assembly complete with piston and rings.

23 To allow for manufacturing tolerances, on most engines, pistons and liners are separated into three size groups. The size group of each piston is indicated by a letter (A, B or C) stamped onto its crown, and the size group of each liner is indicated by a series of 1 to 3 notches on the upper lip of the liner; a single notch for group A, two notches for group B, and three notches for group C. Ensure that each piston and its respective liner are both of the same size group. It is permissible to have different size group piston and liner assemblies fitted to the same engine, but never fit a piston of one size group to a liner in a different group.

24 Prior to installing the liners, thoroughly clean the liner mating surfaces in the cylinder block, and use fine abrasive paper to polish away any burrs or sharp edges which might damage the liner O-rings. Clean the liners and wipe dry, then fit a new O-ring to the base of each liner. To aid installation, apply a smear of oil to each O-ring and to the base of the liner.

25 If the original liners are being refitted, use the marks made on removal to ensure that each is refitted the correct way round, and is inserted into its original position. Insert each liner into the cylinder block, taking care not to damage the O-ring, and press it home as far as possible by hand. Using a hammer and a block of wood, tap each liner lightly but fully onto its locating shoulder. Wipe clean, then lightly oil, all exposed liner surfaces, to prevent rusting.

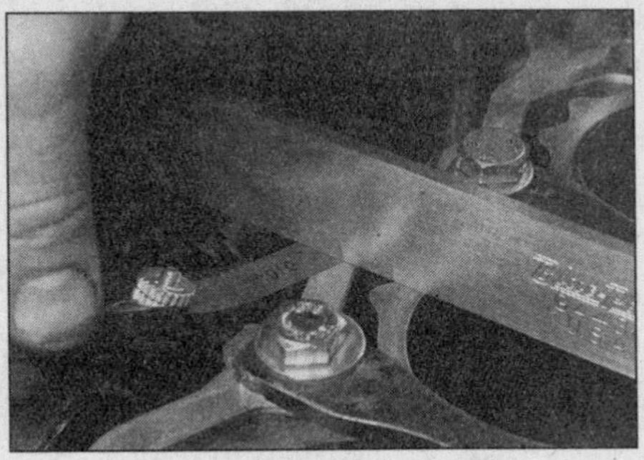

11.26 Checking cylinder liner protrusion - aluminium block engine

26 With all four liners correctly installed, use a dial gauge (or a straight-edge and feeler blade) to check that the protrusion of each liner above the upper surface of the cylinder block is within the limits given in the Specifications at three points on the upper surface of the liner **(see illustration)**. In addition, the maximum difference in protrusion between any two liners must not exceed the specified limit.

27 If new liners are being fitted, it is permissible to interchange them to bring the difference in protrusion within limits, but remember that each piston **must** be kept with its respective liner.

28 If liner protrusion cannot be brought within limits, seek the advice of a Citroën dealer or engine reconditioning specialist before proceeding with the engine rebuild.

12 Piston/connecting rod assembly - inspection

1 Before the inspection process can begin, the piston/connecting rod assemblies must be cleaned, and the original piston rings removed from the pistons.

2 Carefully expand the old rings over the top of the pistons. Be careful not to scratch the piston with the ends of the ring. The rings are brittle, and will snap if they are spread too far. They're also very sharp - protect your hands and fingers. Note that the third ring incorporates an expander. Always remove the rings from the top of the piston. Keep each set of rings with its piston if the old rings are to be re-used **(see Tool Tip)**.

3 Scrape away all traces of carbon from the top of the piston. A hand-held wire brush (or a piece of fine emery cloth) can be used, once the majority of the deposits have been scraped away.

4 Remove the carbon from the ring grooves in the piston, using an old ring. Break the ring in half to do this (be careful not to cut your fingers - piston rings are sharp). Be careful to remove only the carbon deposits - do not remove any metal, and do not nick or scratch the sides of the ring grooves.

5 Once the deposits have been removed, clean the piston/connecting rod assembly with paraffin or a suitable solvent, and dry thoroughly. Make sure that the oil return holes in the ring grooves are clear.

6 If the pistons and cylinder bores are not damaged or worn excessively, and if the cylinder block does not need to be rebored (as applicable), the original pistons can be refitted. Normal piston wear shows up as even vertical wear on the piston thrust surfaces, and slight looseness of the top ring in its groove. New piston rings should always be used when the engine is reassembled.

7 Carefully inspect each piston for cracks around the skirt, around the gudgeon pin holes, and at the piston ring "lands" (between the ring grooves).

8 Look for scoring and scuffing on the piston skirt, holes in the piston crown, or burned areas at the edge of the crown. If the skirt is scored or scuffed, the engine may have been suffering from overheating, and/or abnormal combustion which caused excessively high operating temperatures. The cooling and lubrication systems should be checked thoroughly. Scorch marks on the sides of the pistons show that blow-by has occurred. A hole in the piston crown, or burned areas at the edge of the piston crown, indicates that abnormal combustion (pre-ignition, knocking, or detonation) has been occurring. If any of the above problems exist, the causes must be investigated and corrected, or the damage will occur again. The causes may include incorrect ignition/injection pump timing, or a faulty injector (as applicable).

9 Corrosion of the piston, in the form of pitting, indicates that coolant has been leaking into the combustion chamber and/or the crankcase. Again, the cause must be corrected, or the problem may persist in the rebuilt engine.

10 On aluminium-block engines with wet liners, it is not possible to renew the pistons separately; pistons are only supplied with piston rings and a liner, as a part of a matched assembly (see Section 11). On cast-iron block engines, pistons can be purchased from a Citroën dealer, but note that on diesel engines, pistons of the correct height class must be selected, to ensure that the piston crown protrusion above the surface of the cylinder block at TDC is within the specified tolerance for each cylinder; refer to your Citroën dealer for advice.

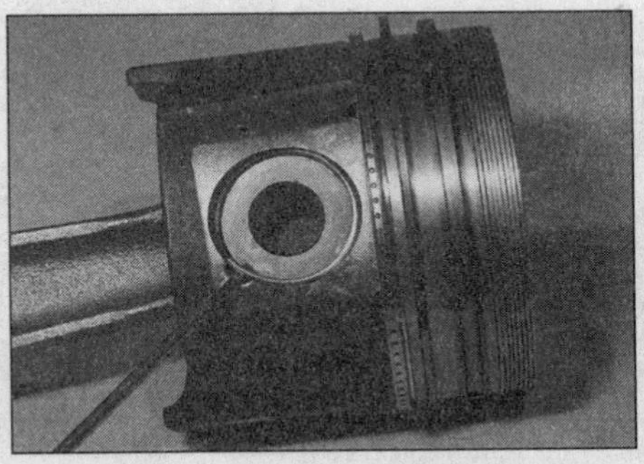

12.14a On diesel and DOHC 16-valve petrol engines, prise out the circlip . . .

TOOL TIP

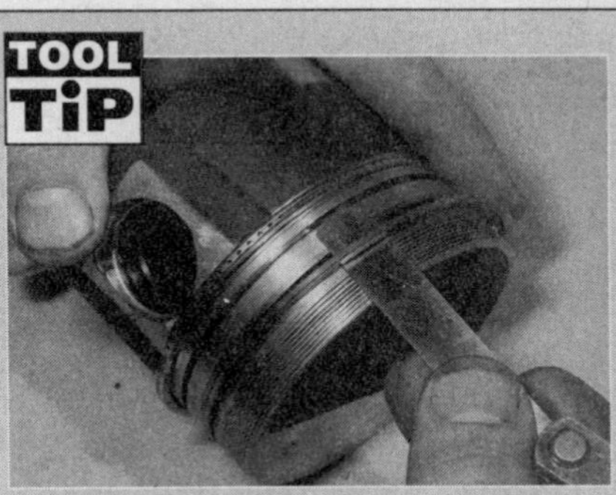

The use of two or three old feeler blades will be helpful in preventing the rings dropping into empty grooves.

11 Examine each connecting rod carefully for signs of damage, such as cracks around the big-end and small-end bearings. Check that the rod is not bent or distorted. Damage is highly unlikely, unless the engine has been seized or badly overheated. Detailed checking of the connecting rod assembly can only be carried out by a Citroën dealer or engine repair specialist with the necessary equipment.

12 On all single overhead camshaft (SOHC) petrol engines (aluminium and cast-iron block), the gudgeon pins are an interference fit in the connecting rod small-end bearing. Therefore, piston and/or connecting rod renewal should be entrusted to a Citroën dealer or engine repair specialist, who will have the necessary tooling to remove and install the gudgeon pins.

13 On diesel and double overhead camshaft (DOHC) petrol engines, the gudgeon pins are of the floating type, secured in position by two circlips. On these engines, the pistons and connecting rods can be separated and reassembled as follows.

Caution: Pistons and gudgeon pins are supplied as matched pairs and must not be interchanged.

14 Using a small flat-bladed screwdriver, prise out the circlips, and push out the gudgeon pin. Hand pressure should be sufficient to remove the pin. Identify the piston, gudgeon pin and rod to ensure correct reassembly **(see illustrations)**. Discard the circlips - new ones *must* be used on refitting.

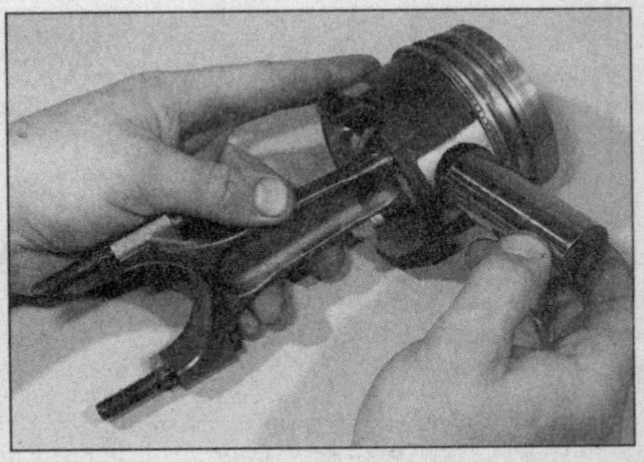

12.14b . . . withdraw the gudgeon pin . . .

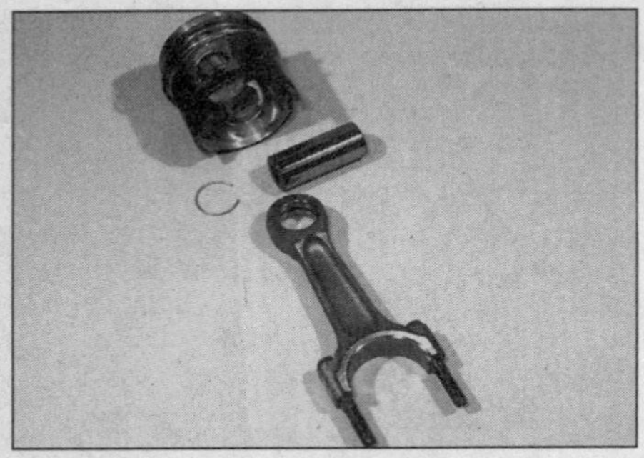

12.14c . . . and separate the piston from the connecting rod

15 Examine the gudgeon pin and connecting rod small-end bearing for signs of wear or damage. Wear can be cured by renewing both the pin and bush. Bush renewal, however, is a specialist job - hydraulic press facilities are required, and the new bush must be reamed accurately.

16 The connecting rods themselves should not need renewal, unless seizure or some other major mechanical failure has occurred. Check the alignment of the connecting rods visually, and if the rods are not straight, take them to an engine overhaul specialist for a more detailed check.

17 Examine all components, and obtain any new parts from your Citroën dealer. If new pistons are purchased, they will be supplied complete with gudgeon pins and circlips. Circlips can also be purchased individually.

18 Position the piston so that the marking/recess(es) on the piston crown is positioned correctly in relation to the connecting rod big-end bearing shell cut-outs - note that the markings and orientation are different for each type of engine **(see illustrations)**. Apply a smear of clean engine oil to the gudgeon pin. Slide it into the piston and through the connecting rod small-end. Check that the piston pivots freely on the rod, then secure the gudgeon pin in position with two new circlips. Ensure that each circlip is correctly located in its groove in the piston.

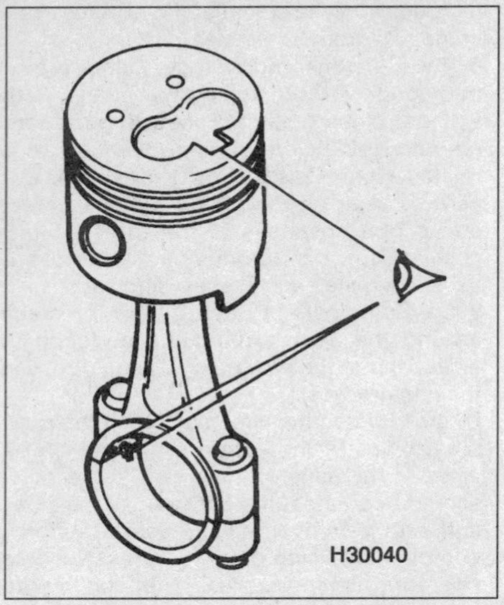

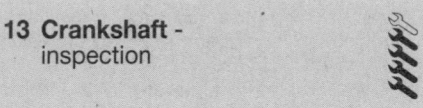

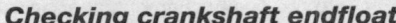

12.18a The piston combustion recess must be positioned as shown, in relation to the connecting rod bearing shell cut-outs (arrowed) (diesel engines)

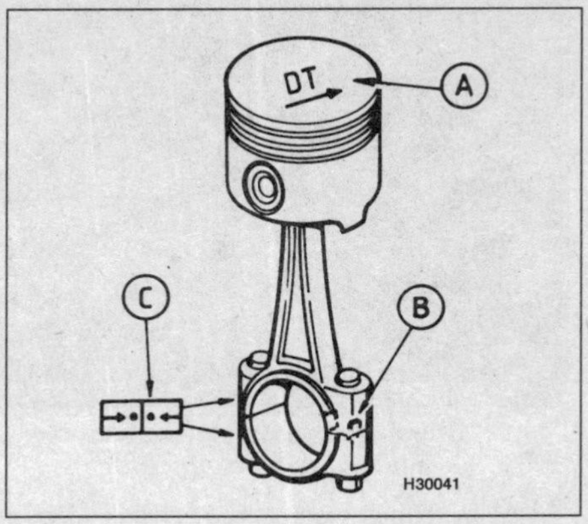

12.18b The arrow on the piston crown (A) must be positioned as shown, in relation to the connecting rod bearing shell cut-outs (B) and cylinder number markings (C) (SOHC 8-valve petrol engines)

13 Crankshaft - inspection

Checking crankshaft endfloat

1 If the crankshaft endfloat is to be checked, this must be done when the crankshaft is still installed in the cylinder block/crankcase, but is free to move (see Section 10).

2 Check the endfloat using a dial gauge in contact with the end of the crankshaft. Push the crankshaft fully one way, and then zero the gauge **(see illustration)**. Push the crankshaft fully the other way, and check the endfloat. The result can be compared with the specified amount, and will give an indication as to whether new thrustwashers are required.

3 If a dial gauge is not available, feeler gauges can be used. First push the crankshaft fully towards the flywheel end of the engine, then use feeler blades to measure the gap between the No 1 crankpin web and No 2 main bearing thrustwasher **(see illustration)**.

Inspection

4 Clean the crankshaft using paraffin or a suitable solvent, and dry it, preferably with compressed air if available. Be sure to clean the oil holes with a pipe cleaner or similar probe, to ensure that they are not obstructed.

Warning: Wear eye protection when using compressed air!

5 Check the main and big-end bearing journals for uneven wear, scoring, pitting and cracking.

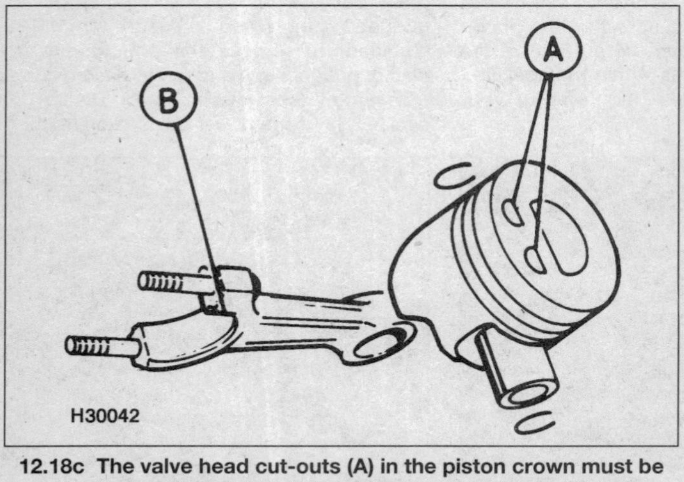

12.18c The valve head cut-outs (A) in the piston crown must be positioned as shown, in relation to the connecting rod bearing shell cut-outs (B) (DOHC 16-valve petrol engines)

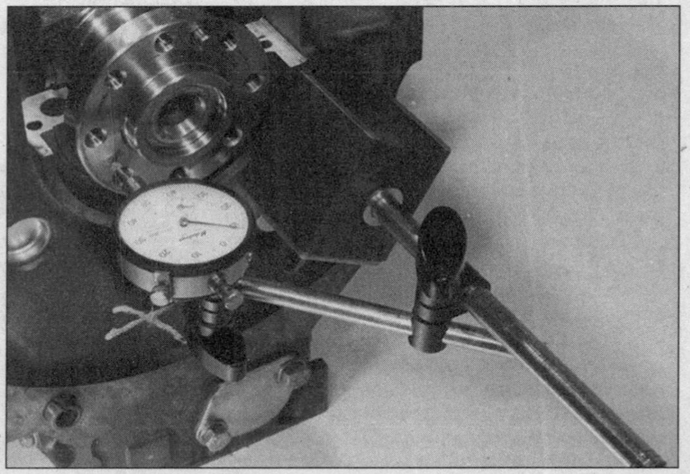

13.2 Checking crankshaft endfloat using a dial gauge

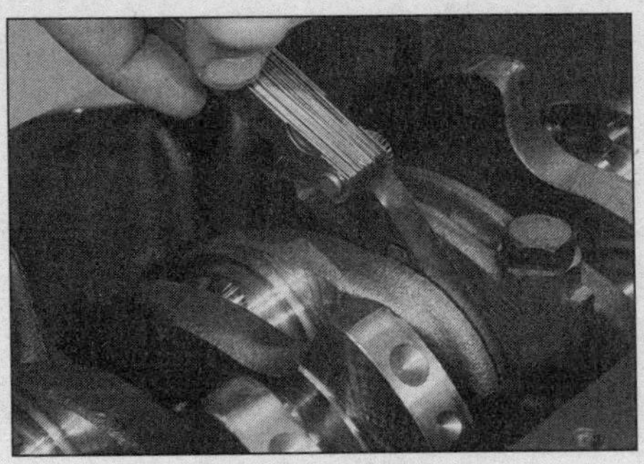

13.3 Checking crankshaft endfloat using feeler blades

6 Big-end bearing wear is accompanied by distinct metallic knocking when the engine is running (particularly noticeable when the engine is pulling from low speed) and some loss of oil pressure.

7 Main bearing wear is accompanied by severe engine vibration and rumble - getting progressively worse as engine speed increases - and again by loss of oil pressure.

8 Check the bearing journal for roughness by running a finger lightly over the bearing surface. Any roughness (which will be accompanied by obvious bearing wear) indicates that the crankshaft requires regrinding (where possible) or renewal.

9 If the crankshaft has been reground, check for burrs around the crankshaft oil holes (the holes are usually chamfered, so burrs should not be a problem unless regrinding has been carried out carelessly). Remove any burrs with a fine file or scraper, and thoroughly clean the oil holes as described previously.

10 Using a micrometer, measure the diameter of the main and big-end bearing journals, and compare the results with the Specifications **(see illustration)**. By measuring the diameter at a number of points around each journal's circumference, you will be able to determine whether or not the journal is out-of-round. Take the measurement at each end of the journal, near the webs, to determine if the journal is tapered. Compare the results obtained with those given in the Specifications. Where no specified journal diameters are quoted, seek the advice of a Citroën dealer.

11 Check the oil seal contact surfaces at each end of the crankshaft for wear and damage. If the seal has worn a deep groove in the surface of the crankshaft, consult an engine overhaul specialist. Repair may be possible, but otherwise a new crankshaft will be required.

12 Citroën produce a set of undersize bearing shells for both the main bearings and big-end bearings for most engines; refer to your Citroën dealer for further information on parts availability. If undersize bearing shells are available, and the crankshaft has worn beyond the specified limits, providing that the crankshaft journals have not already been reground, it may be possible to have the

13.10 Measuring a crankshaft big-end journal diameter

crankshaft reconditioned, and to fit the undersize shells. Seek the advice of your Citroën dealer or engine specialist on the best course of action.

14 Main and big-end bearings - inspection

1 Even though the main and big-end bearings should be renewed during the engine overhaul, the old bearings should be retained for close examination, as they may reveal valuable information about the condition of the engine. The bearing shells are graded by thickness, the grade of each shell being indicated by the colour code marked on it. Repair (undersize) bearing shells have the letter 'R' stamped on their side faces.

2 Bearing failure can occur due to lack of lubrication, the presence of dirt or other foreign particles, overloading the engine, corrosion or incorrect assembly/repair **(see illustration)**. Regardless of the cause of bearing failure, the cause must be corrected (where applicable) before the engine is reassembled, to prevent it from happening again.

3 When examining the bearing shells, remove them from the cylinder block/crankcase, the main bearing ladder/caps (as appropriate), the connecting rods and the connecting rod big-end bearing caps. Lay them out on a clean surface in the same general position as their location in the engine. This will enable you to match any bearing problems with the corresponding crankshaft journal. *Do not touch any shell's bearing surface with your fingers while checking it, or the delicate surface may be scratched.*

4 Dirt and other foreign matter gets into the engine in a variety of ways. It may be left in the engine during assembly, or it may pass through filters or the crankcase ventilation system. It may get into the oil, and from there into the bearings. Metal chips from machining operations and normal engine wear are often present. Abrasives are sometimes left in engine components after reconditioning, especially when parts are not thoroughly cleaned using the proper cleaning methods. Whatever the source, these foreign objects often end up embedded in the soft bearing material, and are easily recognised. Large particles will not embed in the bearing, and will score or gouge the bearing and journal. The best prevention for this cause of bearing failure is to clean all parts thoroughly, and keep everything spotlessly-clean during engine assembly. Frequent and regular engine oil and filter changes are also recommended.

5 Lack of lubrication (or lubrication breakdown) has a number of interrelated causes. Excessive heat (which thins the oil), overloading (which squeezes the oil from the bearing face) and oil leakage (from excessive bearing clearances, worn oil pump or high engine speeds) all contribute to lubrication breakdown. Blocked oil passages, which usually are the result of misaligned oil holes in a bearing shell, will also oil-starve a bearing, and destroy it. When lack of lubrication is the cause of bearing failure, the bearing material is wiped or extruded from the steel backing of the bearing. Temperatures may increase to the point where the steel backing turns blue from overheating.

6 Driving habits can have a definite effect on bearing life. Full-throttle, low-speed operation (labouring the engine) puts very high loads on bearings, tending to squeeze out the oil film. These loads cause the bearings to flex, which produces fine cracks in the bearing face (fatigue failure). Eventually, the bearing material will loosen in pieces, and tear away from the steel backing.

7 Short-distance driving leads to corrosion of bearings, because insufficient engine heat is produced to drive off the condensed water and corrosive gases. These products collect in the engine oil, forming acid and sludge. As the oil is carried to the engine bearings, the acid attacks and corrodes the bearing material.

2C

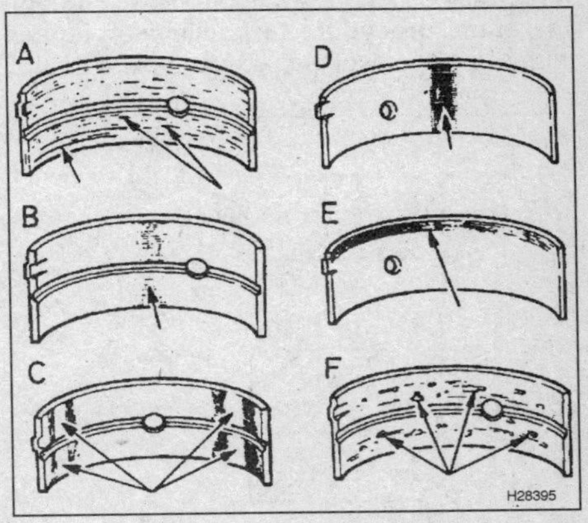

14.2 Typical bearing failures

A Scratched by dirt; dirt embedded in bearing material
B Lack of oil; overlay wiped out
C Improper seating; bright (polished) sections
D Tapered journal; overlay gone from entire surface
E Radius ride
F Fatigue failure; craters or pockets

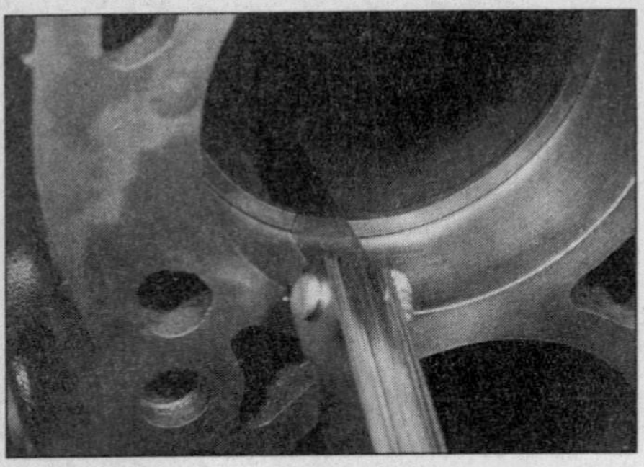

16.5 Measuring a piston ring end gap

8 Incorrect bearing installation during engine assembly will lead to bearing failure as well. Tight-fitting bearings leave insufficient bearing running clearance, and will result in oil starvation. Dirt or foreign particles trapped behind a bearing shell result in high spots on the bearing, which lead to failure.

9 *Do not* touch any shell's bearing surface with your fingers during reassembly; there is a risk of scratching the delicate surface, or of depositing particles of dirt on it.

10 As mentioned at the beginning of this Section, the bearing shells should be renewed as a matter of course during engine overhaul; to do otherwise is false economy. Refer to Section 17 for details of bearing shell selection.

15 Engine overhaul - reassembly sequence

1 Before reassembly begins, ensure that all new parts have been obtained, and that all necessary tools are available. Read through the entire procedure to familiarise yourself with the work involved, and to ensure that all items necessary for reassembly of the engine are at hand. In addition to all normal tools and materials, thread-locking compound will be needed. A suitable tube of liquid sealant will also be required for the joint faces that are fitted without gaskets. It is recommended that Citroën's own product(s) are used.

2 In order to save time and avoid problems, engine reassembly can be carried out in the following order:

a) Crankshaft (Section 17).
b) Piston/connecting rod assemblies (Section 18).
c) Oil pump.
d) Sump (See Part A or B - as applicable).
e) Flywheel (See Part A or B - as applicable).
f) Cylinder head (See Part A or B - as applicable).
g) Timing belt tensioner and sprockets, and timing belt (See Part A or B - as applicable).
h) Engine external components.

3 At this stage, all engine components should be absolutely clean and dry, with all faults repaired. The components should be laid out (or in individual containers) on a completely clean work surface.

16 Piston rings - refitting

1 Before fitting new piston rings, the ring end gaps must be checked as follows.

2 Lay out the piston/connecting rod assemblies and the new piston ring sets, so that the ring sets will be matched with the same piston and cylinder/liner during the end gap measurement and subsequent engine reassembly.

3 Insert the top ring into the first cylinder/liner, and push it down the bore using the top of the piston. This will ensure that the ring remains square with the cylinder walls. Position the ring near the bottom of the cylinder bore, at the lower limit of ring travel. Note that the top and second compression rings are different.

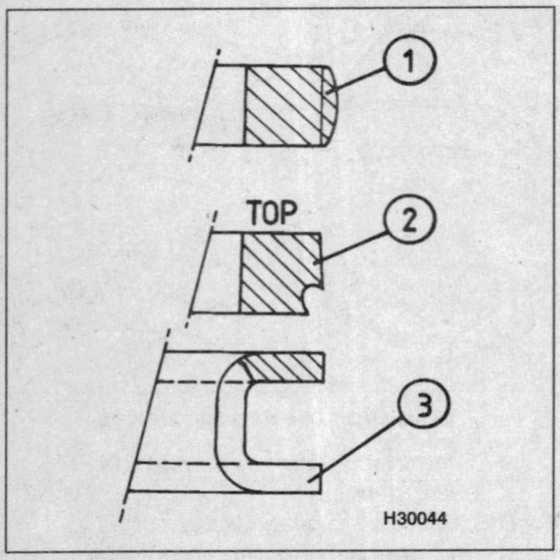

16.10a Piston ring fitting diagram - SOHC 8-valve petrol engines

1 Top compression ring
2 Second compression ring
3 Oil control ring

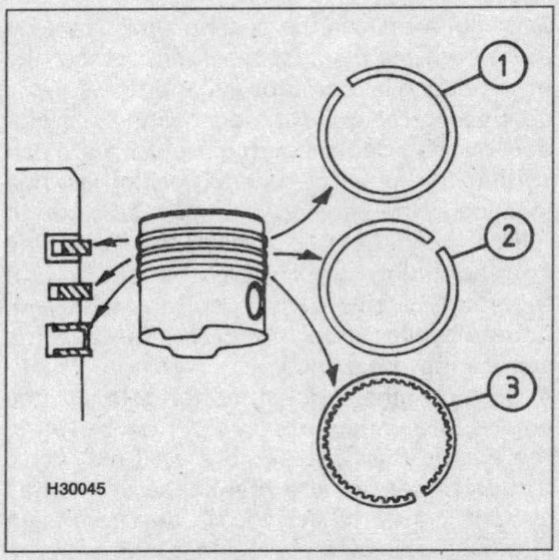

16.10b Piston ring fitting diagram - diesel and DOHC 16-valve petrol engines

1 Top compression ring
2 Second compression ring
3 Oil control ring

4 Measure the end gap using feeler gauges.

5 Repeat the procedure with the ring at the top of the cylinder bore, at the upper limit of its travel, and compare the measurements with the figures given in the Specifications **(see illustration)**.

6 If the gap is too small (unlikely if genuine Citroën parts are used), it must be enlarged, or the ring ends may contact each other during engine operation, causing serious damage. Ideally, new piston rings providing the correct end gap should be fitted. As a last resort, the end gap can be increased by filing the ring ends very carefully with a fine file. Mount the file in a vice equipped with soft jaws, slip the ring over the file with the ends contacting either side of the file face, and slowly move the ring back and forth to remove material from the ends. Take care, as piston rings are sharp, and are easily broken.

7 With new piston rings, it is unlikely that the end gap will be too large. If the gaps are too large, check that you have the correct rings for your engine and for the particular cylinder bore size.

8 Repeat the checking procedure for each ring in the first cylinder, and then for the rings in the remaining cylinders. Remember to keep rings, pistons and cylinders matched up.

9 Once the ring end gaps have been checked and if necessary corrected, the rings can be fitted to the pistons.

10 Fit the piston rings using the same technique as for removal. Fit the bottom (oil control) ring first, and work up. When fitting the oil control ring, where applicable first insert the expander, then fit the ring with its gap positioned 180° from the expander gap. Ensure that the second compression ring is fitted the correct way up **(see illustrations)**. Arrange the gaps of the top and second compression rings 120° either side of the oil control ring gap. **Note:** *Always follow any instructions supplied with the new piston ring sets - different manufacturers may specify different procedures. Do not mix up the top and second compression rings, as they have different cross-sections.*

17 Crankshaft - refitting and main bearing running clearance check

Selection of new bearing shells

1 To allow for manufacturing and repair machining tolerances, three different grades of main bearing shell are available, in both standard sizes and undersizes. The grades are indicated by a colour-coding marked on the edge of each shell, which denotes the shell's thickness, as listed in the following tables. Repair (undersize) shells have the letter 'R' stamped into their side faces.

2 The upper shell on all bearings is of the same size (class B, colour code black), and the running clearance is controlled by fitting a lower bearing shell of the required thickness. Note, however, that although the upper bearings on both aluminium and cast-iron block engines have the same colour code, they are in fact of different thickness for each engine, and have different part numbers. Ensure that the correct grade of bearings is obtained for the correct type of engine.

Bearing classes - aluminium block petrol engines:

	Colour code	Thickness (mm)
Standard sizes:		
	Blue (class A)	1.823
	Black (class B)	1.835
	Green (class C)	1.849
Undersizes:		
	Blue (class Z)	1.973
	Black (class Y)	1.985
	Green (class X)	1.998

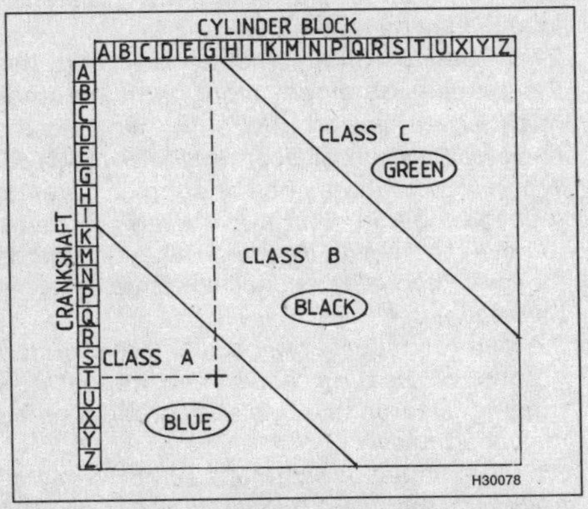

17.6a Main bearing shell selection chart: 8-valve petrol engines with alloy cylinder blocks (1.0 l up to engine no. 1328021, 1.1 l up to engine no. 1735572, 1.4 l up to engine no. 1400220)

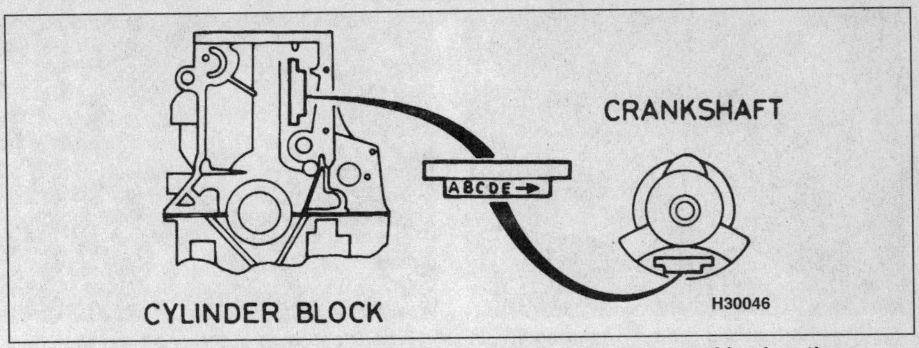

17.4 Cylinder block and crankshaft main bearing reference marking locations

Bearing classes - cast-iron block petrol and diesel engines:

	Colour code	Thickness (mm)
Standard sizes:		
	Blue (class A)	1.844
	Black (class B)	1.858
	Green (class C)	1.869
Undersizes:		
	Blue (class Z)	1.994
	Black (class Y)	2.008
	Green (class X)	2.019

3 The crankshaft and cylinder block/crankcase have reference marks on them, to identify the size of the journals and bearing bores.

4 The cylinder block reference marks are on the right-hand (timing belt) end of the block, and the crankshaft reference marks are on the right-hand (timing belt) end of the crankshaft, on the right-hand web of No 4 crankpin. These marks can be used to select bearing shells of the required thickness as follows **(see illustration)**.

5 On both the crankshaft and block, there are two lines of identification: a bar code, which is used by Citroën during production, and a row of five letters. The first letter in the sequence refers to the size of No 1 bearing (at the flywheel end). The last letter in the sequence (which is followed by an arrow) refers to the size of No 5 main bearing. These marks can be used to select the required bearing shell grade as follows.

6 Obtain the identification letter of both the relevant crankshaft journal and the cylinder block bearing bore. Noting that the cylinder block letters are listed across the top of the chart, and the crankshaft letters down the side, trace a vertical line down from the relevant cylinder block letter, and a horizontal line across from the relevant crankshaft letter, and find the point at which both lines cross. This crossover point will indicate the grade of lower bearing shell required to give the correct main bearing running clearance. **For example**, illustration 17.6a shows cylinder block reference G, and crankshaft reference T, crossing at a point within the area of Class A, indicating that a blue-coded (Class A) lower bearing shell is required to give the correct main bearing running clearance **(see illustrations)**. Note that 'VE' = Green, 'BE'/'BL' = Blue and 'NR' = Black.

2C

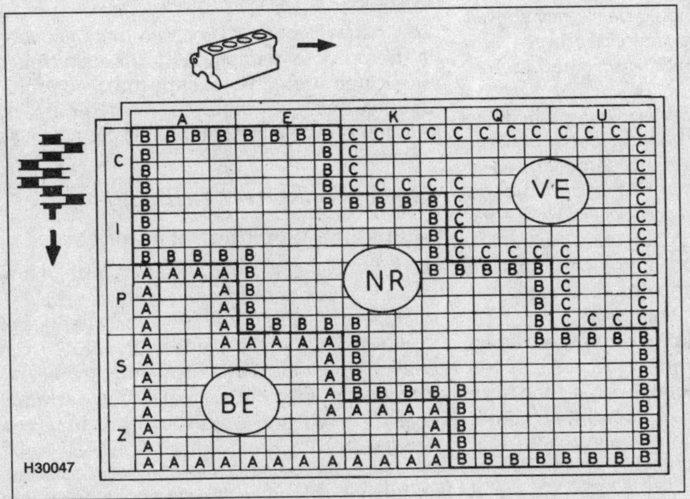

17.6b Main bearing shell selection chart: diesel engines, 8-valve petrol engines with cast-iron cylinder blocks, 8-valve petrol engines with alloy cylinder blocks (1.0 l from engine no. 1328022, 1.1 l from engine no. 1735573, 1.4 l from engine no. 1400221)

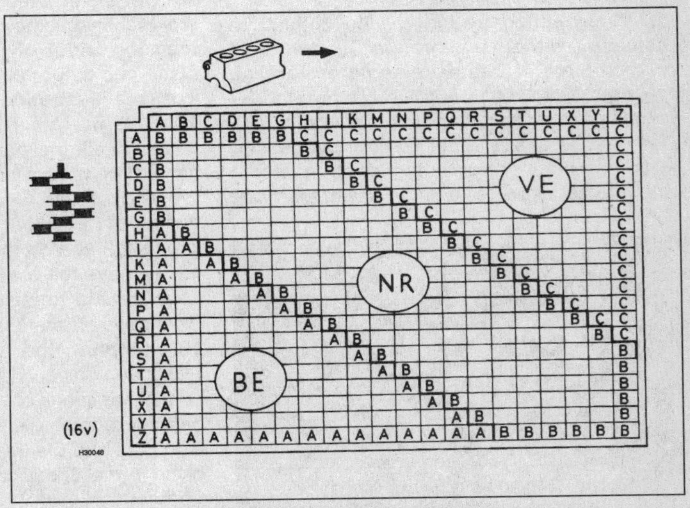

17.6c Main bearing shell selection chart: 16-valve petrol engines

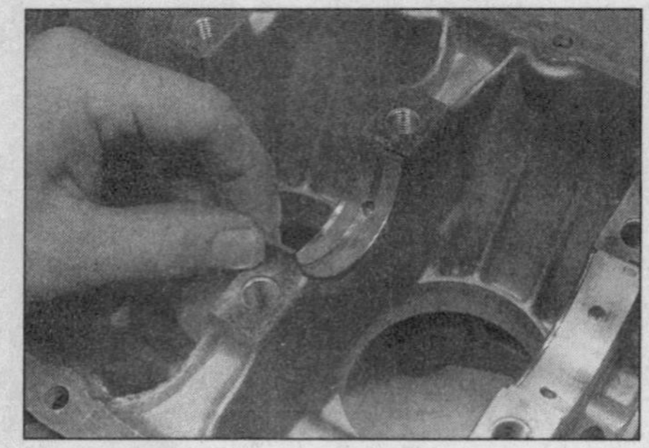

17.11 Note that the grooved bearing shells are fitted to Nos 2 and 4 main bearing journals

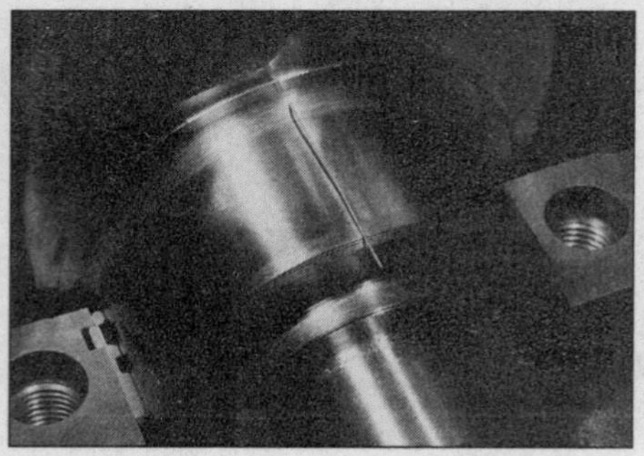

17.16 Plastigage in place on a crankshaft main bearing journal

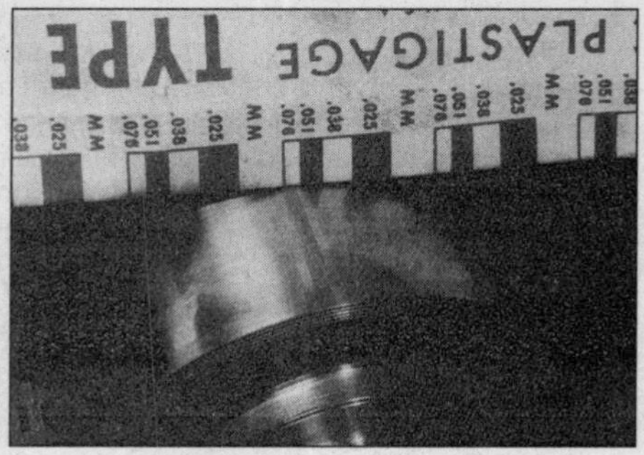

17.19 Measuring the width of the deformed Plastigage using the scale on the card provided

7 Repeat this procedure so that the required bearing shell grade is obtained for each of the five main bearing journals.

Main bearing running clearance check

Aluminium block petrol engines

8 The running clearance check can be carried out using the original bearing shells. However, it is preferable to use a new set, since the results obtained will be more conclusive.

9 Clean the backs of the bearing shells, and the bearing locations in both the cylinder block/crankcase and the main bearing ladder.

10 Press the bearing shells into their locations, ensuring that the tab on each shell engages in the notch in the cylinder block/crankcase or main bearing ladder location. Take care not to touch any shell's bearing surface with your fingers.

11 If the original bearing shells are being used for the check, ensure that they are refitted in their original locations. The clearance can be checked in either of two ways. **Note:** *The grooved bearing shells, both upper and lower, are fitted to Nos 2 and 4 main bearings* ***(see illustration)***.

12 One method (which will be difficult to achieve without a range of internal micrometers or internal/external expanding calipers) is to refit the main bearing ladder casting to the cylinder block/crankcase, with the bearing shells in place. With the casting retaining bolts correctly tightened, measure the internal diameter of each assembled pair of bearing shells. If the diameter of each corresponding crankshaft journal is measured and then subtracted from the bearing internal diameter, the result will be the main bearing running clearance.

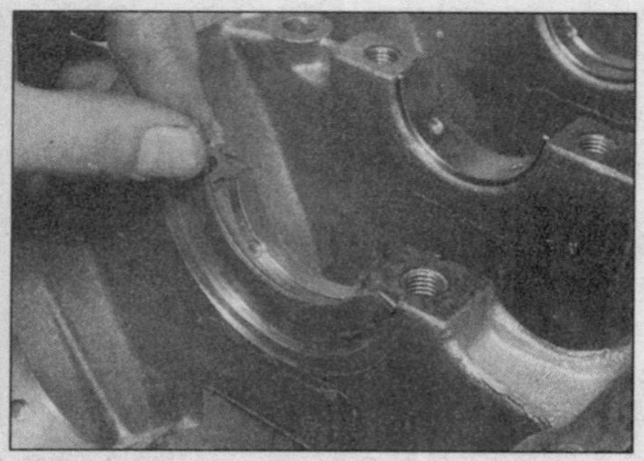

17.26 Refitting a crankshaft thrustwasher

13 The second (and more accurate) method is to use an American product known as "Plastigage". This consists of a fine thread of perfectly-round plastic, which is compressed between the bearing shell and the journal. When the shell is removed, the plastic is deformed, and its width can be measured with a special card gauge supplied with the kit. The running clearance is determined from this gauge.

14 Plastigage should be available from your Citroën dealer; otherwise, enquiries at one of the larger specialist motor factors should produce the name of a stockist in your area. The procedure for using Plastigage is as follows.

15 With the main bearing upper shells in place, carefully lay the crankshaft in position. Do not use any lubricant; the crankshaft journals and bearing shells must be perfectly clean and dry.

16 Cut several lengths of the appropriate-size Plastigage (they should be slightly shorter than the width of the main bearings), and place one length on each crankshaft journal axis **(see illustration)**.

17 With the main bearing lower shells in position, refit the main bearing ladder casting, tightening its retaining bolts as described at the end of this Section. Take care not to disturb the Plastigage, and *do not* rotate the crankshaft at any time during this operation.

18 Remove the main bearing ladder casting, again taking great care not to disturb the Plastigage or rotate the crankshaft.

19 Compare the width of the crushed Plastigage on each journal to the scale printed on the Plastigage envelope, to obtain the main bearing running clearance **(see illustration)**. Compare the clearance measured with that given in the Specifications at the start of this Chapter.

20 If the clearance is significantly different from that expected, the bearing shells may be the wrong size (or excessively worn, if the original shells are being re-used). Before deciding that different-size shells are required, make sure that no dirt or oil was trapped between the bearing shells and the main bearing ladder or block when the clearance was measured. If the Plastigage was wider at one end than at the other, the crankshaft journal may be tapered.

21 If the clearance is not as specified, use the reading obtained, along with the shell thicknesses quoted above, to calculate the necessary grade of bearing shells required. When calculating the bearing clearance required, bear in mind that it is always better to have the running clearance slightly towards the lower end of the specified range, to allow for wear in use.

22 Where necessary, obtain the required grades of bearing shell, and repeat the running clearance checking procedure as described above.

23 On completion, carefully scrape away all traces of the Plastigage material from the crankshaft and bearing shells. Use your fingernail, or a wooden or plastic scraper which is unlikely to score the bearing surfaces.

Cast-iron block petrol and diesel engines

24 The procedure is similar to that described in the previous paragraphs for the aluminium block petrol engine, except that each main bearing has a separate cap, which must be fitted and the bolts tightened to the specified torques.

Final crankshaft refitting

Aluminium block petrol engines

25 Carefully lift the crankshaft out of the cylinder block once more.

26 Using a little grease, stick the upper thrustwashers to each side of the No 2 main bearing upper location; ensure that the oilway grooves on each thrustwasher face outwards (away from the cylinder block) **(see illustration)**.

27 Place the bearing shells in their locations as described earlier. If new shells are being fitted, ensure that all traces of protective grease are cleaned off using paraffin. Wipe dry the shells and connecting rods with a lint-free cloth. Liberally lubricate each bearing

17.27 Ensure each bearing shell tab (arrowed) is correctly located, and lubricate the shell with clean engine oil

17.28 Refitting the oil pump drive chain and sprocket

17.29 On aluminium block engines, apply a thin film of sealant to the cylinder block/crankcase mating surface . . .

shell in the cylinder block/crankcase with clean engine oil **(see illustration)**.

28 Refit the Woodruff key, then slide on the oil pump drive sprocket, and locate the drive chain on the sprocket **(see illustration)**. Lower the crankshaft into position so that Nos 2 and 3 cylinder crankpins are at TDC; Nos 1 and 4 cylinder crankpins will be at BDC, ready for fitting No 1 piston. Check the crankshaft endfloat as described in Section 13.

29 Thoroughly degrease the mating surfaces of the cylinder block/crankcase and the main bearing ladder. Apply a thin bead of suitable sealant to the cylinder block/crankcase mating surface of the main bearing ladder casting, then spread to an even film **(see illustration)**.

30 Lubricate the lower bearing shells with clean engine oil, then refit the main bearing ladder, ensuring that the shells are not displaced, and that the locating dowels engage correctly **(see illustration)**.

31 Install all the 11 mm main bearing ladder retaining bolts, and tighten them all by hand only. Working progressively outwards from the centre bolts, tighten all the bolts, by a turn at a time, to the specified Stage 1 torque wrench setting. Once all the bolts have been tightened to the Stage 1 setting, angle-tighten the bolts through the specified Stage 2 angle using a socket and extension bar. It is recommended that an angle-measuring gauge is used during this stage of the tightening, to ensure accuracy **(see illustrations)**. If a gauge is not available, use a dab of white paint to make alignment marks between the bolt head and casting prior to tightening; the marks can then be used to check that the bolt has been rotated sufficiently during tightening.

32 Refit all the 6 mm bolts securing the main bearing ladder to the base of the cylinder block, and tighten them to the specified torque. Check that the crankshaft rotates freely.

33 Refit the piston/connecting rod assemblies to the crankshaft as described in Section 18.

34 Ensuring that the drive chain is correctly located on the sprocket, refit the oil pump and sump as described in Chapter 2A.

35 Fit two new crankshaft oil seals as described in Chapter 2A.

36 Refit the flywheel as described in Chapter 2A.

37 Refit the cylinder head (where removed), crankshaft sprocket and timing belt as described in Chapter 2A.

Cast-iron block petrol and diesel engines

38 Carefully lift the crankshaft out of the cylinder block once more.

39 Using a little grease, stick the upper thrustwashers to each side of the No 2 main bearing upper location. Ensure that the oilway grooves on each thrustwasher face outwards (away from the cylinder block)

40 Place the bearing shells in their locations as described earlier. If new shells are being fitted, ensure that all traces of protective grease are cleaned off using paraffin. Wipe dry the shells and connecting rods with a lint-free cloth. Liberally lubricate each bearing shell in the cylinder block/crankcase and cap with clean engine oil.

41 Lower the crankshaft into position so that Nos 2 and 3 cylinder crankpins are at TDC; Nos 1 and 4 cylinder crankpins will be at BDC, ready for fitting No 1 piston. Check the crankshaft endfloat as described in Section 13.

42 Lubricate the lower bearing shells in the main bearing caps with clean engine oil. Make sure that the locating lugs on the shells engage with the corresponding recesses in the caps. Check that the grooved upper and lower bearing shells are fitted to main bearings Nos 2 and 4.

43 Fit the main bearing caps to their correct locations, ensuring that they are fitted the correct way round (the bearing shell lug recesses in the block and caps must be on the same side). Insert the bolts loosely.

44 Tighten the main bearing cap bolts to the specified Stage 1 torque wrench setting **(see illustration)**. Once all the bolts have been tightened to the Stage 1 setting, angle-tighten the bolts through the specified Stage 2 angle, using a socket and extension bar. It is recommended that an angle-measuring gauge is used during this stage of the tightening, to ensure accuracy. If a gauge is not available, use a dab of white paint to make alignment marks between the bolt head and casting prior to tightening; the marks can then

17.30 . . . then lower the main bearing ladder into position

17.31a Tighten the ten 11 mm main bearing bolts to the Stage 1 torque setting . . .

17.31b . . . then angle-tighten them through the specified Stage 2 angle

17.44 On cast-iron block engines, tighten the main bearing cap retaining bolts to the specified Stage 1 torque

be used to check that the bolt has been rotated sufficiently during tightening.

45 Check that the crankshaft rotates freely.

46 Refit the piston/connecting rod assemblies to the crankshaft as described in Section 18.

47 Refit the Woodruff key to the crankshaft groove, and slide on the oil pump drive sprocket. Locate the drive chain on the sprocket.

48 Ensure that the mating surfaces of front oil seal housing and cylinder block are clean and dry. Note the correct fitted depth of the front oil seal then, using a large flat-bladed screwdriver, lever the seal out of the housing.

49 Apply a smear of suitable sealant to the oil seal housing mating surface, and make sure that the locating dowels are in position. Slide the housing over the end of the crankshaft, and into position on the cylinder block. Tighten the housing retaining bolts securely.

50 Repeat the operations in paragraphs 48 and 49, and fit the rear oil seal housing.

51 Fit a new front and rear crankshaft oil seal as described in Part A or B of this Chapter (as applicable).

52 Ensuring that the chain is correctly located on the drive sprocket, refit the oil pump and sump as described in Part A or B of this Chapter (as applicable).

53 Refit the flywheel as described in Part A or B of this Chapter (as applicable).

54 Where removed, refit the cylinder head and install the crankshaft sprocket and timing belt as described in the relevant Sections of Part A or B (as applicable).

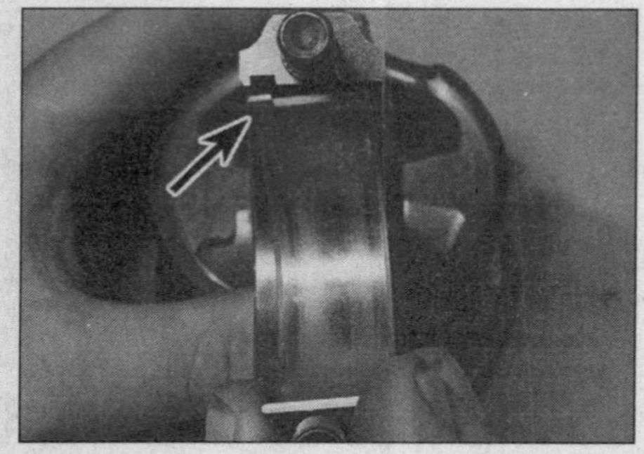

18.4 Fitting a bearing shell to a connecting rod - ensure that the tab (arrowed) engages with the recess in the connecting rod

18 Piston/connecting rod assembly - refitting and big-end bearing running clearance check

Selection of bearing shells

1 There are two sizes of big-end bearing shell produced by Citroën; a standard size for use with the standard crankshaft, and an undersize for use once the crankshaft journals have been reground. When ordering shells, quote the diameter of the crankshaft big-end crankpins, to ensure that the correct set of shells are purchased.

2 Prior to refitting the piston/connecting rod assemblies, it is recommended that the big-end bearing running clearance is checked as follows.

Big-end bearing running clearance check

3 Clean the backs of the bearing shells, and the bearing locations in both the connecting rod and bearing cap.

4 Press the bearing shells into their locations, ensuring that the tab on each shell engages in the recess in the connecting rod and cap **(see illustration)**. Take care not to touch any shell's bearing surface with your fingers. If the original bearing shells are being used for the check, ensure that they are refitted in their original locations. The clearance can be checked in either of two ways.

5 One method is to refit the big-end bearing cap to the connecting rod, ensuring that they are fitted the correct way round (see paragraph 19), with the bearing shells in place. With the cap retaining nuts correctly tightened, use an internal micrometer or vernier caliper to measure the internal diameter of each assembled pair of bearing shells. If the diameter of each corresponding crankshaft journal is measured and then subtracted from the bearing internal diameter, the result will be the big-end bearing running clearance.

6 The second, and more accurate, method is to use Plastigage (see Section 17).

7 Ensure that the bearing shells are correctly fitted. Place a strand of Plastigage on each (cleaned) crankpin journal.

8 Refit the (clean) piston/connecting rod assemblies to the crankshaft, and refit the big-end bearing caps, using the marks made or noted on removal to ensure that they are fitted the correct way round.

9 Tighten the bearing cap nuts as described below in paragraph 20. Take care not to disturb the Plastigage, nor to rotate the connecting rod during the tightening sequence.

10 Dismantle the assemblies without rotating the connecting rods. Use the scale printed on the Plastigage envelope to obtain the big-end bearing running clearance.

11 If the clearance is significantly different from that expected, the bearing shells may be the wrong size (or excessively worn, if the original shells are being re-used). Make sure that no dirt or oil was trapped between the bearing shells and the caps or connecting rods when the clearance was measured. If the Plastigage was wider at one end than at the other, the crankpins may be tapered.

12 Note that Citroën do not specify a recommended big-end bearing running clearance. The figure given in the Specifications is a guide figure, which is typical for this type of engine. Before condemning the components concerned, refer to your Citroën dealer or engine reconditioning specialist for further information on the specified running clearance. Their advice on the best course of action to be taken can then also be obtained.

13 On completion, carefully scrape away all traces of the Plastigage material from the crankshaft and bearing shells. Use your fingernail, or some other object which is unlikely to score the bearing surfaces.

Final piston/connecting rod refitting

14 Note that the following procedure assumes that the cylinder liners (where fitted) are in position in the cylinder block/crankcase as described in Section 11, and that the crankshaft and main bearing ladder/caps are in place (see Section 17). It is possible to fit the pistons to the liners before fitting the liners to the cylinder block; the advantage of using this method is that the pistons enter the liner from the bottom end, which is tapered to allow easy entry of the piston rings (a piston ring compressor will still be required, though).

15 Ensure that the bearing shells are correctly fitted as described in paragraphs 3 and 4. If new shells are being fitted, ensure that all traces of the protective grease are cleaned off using paraffin. Wipe dry the shells and connecting rods with a lint-free cloth.

16 Lubricate the cylinder bores/liners, the pistons, and piston rings, then lay out each piston/connecting rod assembly in its respective position.

17 Start with assembly No 1. Make sure that the piston rings are still spaced as described in Section 16, then clamp them in position with a piston ring compressor.

18 Insert the piston/connecting rod assembly into the top of cylinder/liner No 1. Orientate the piston in the cylinder bore as follows:

a) *On diesel engines, ensure that the 'cloverleaf' cutout on the piston crown faces the oil filter side of the cylinder block.*

b) *On DOHC 16-valve petrol engines, ensure that the valve head cutouts on the piston crown face the side of the cylinder block* ***opposite*** *the oil filter.*

c) *On SOHC 8-valve petrol engines, with either alloy or cast-iron cylinder blocks, ensure that the arrow on the piston crown is pointing towards the timing belt end of the engine.*

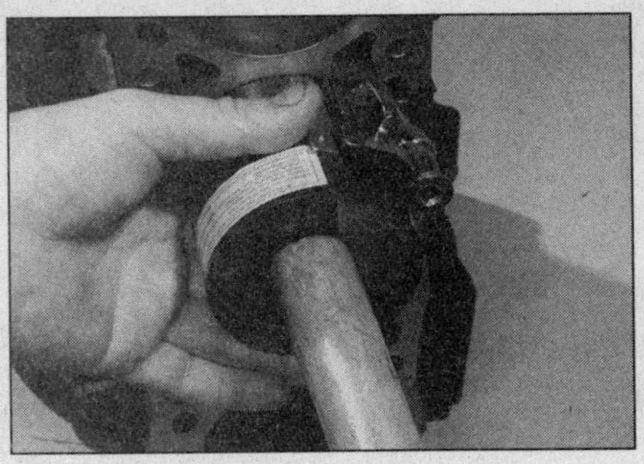

18.18 Tap the piston into the bore using a hammer handle

18.20 Tighten the big-end bearing cap nuts to the specified torque setting

Using a block of wood or hammer handle against the piston crown, tap the assembly into the cylinder/liner until the piston crown is flush with the top of the cylinder/liner **(see illustration)**.

19 Ensure that the bearing shell is still correctly installed. Liberally lubricate the crankpin and both bearing shells. Taking care not to mark the cylinder/liner bores, tap the piston/connecting rod assembly down the bore/liner and onto the crankpin. Refit the big-end bearing cap, tightening its retaining nuts finger-tight at first. Note that the faces with the identification marks must match (which means that the bearing shell locating tabs abut each other).

20 Tighten the bearing cap retaining nuts evenly and progressively to the specified torque setting **(see illustration)**.

21 Rotate the crankshaft. Check that it turns freely; some stiffness is to be expected if new components have been fitted, but there should be no signs of binding or tight spots.

22 Refit the remaining three piston/ connecting rod assemblies in the same way.

Diesel engines

23 Before refitting the cylinder head, the protrusion of each piston crown above the surface of the cylinder block at TDC must be checked for each cylinder, as follows.

24 Stand the cylinder block upright on a workbench or stand, so that that the crankshaft is free to turn. Rotate the crankshaft so that No1 piston is approximately at TDC.

25 Mount a DTI gauge, with a magnetic base or similar, on the cylinder block head gasket mating surface. Bring the end of the DTI gauge probe into contact with the centre of the crown of No 1 piston.

26 Turn the crankshaft slowly back and forth by a few degrees at a time, until the gauge indicates that the piston is at TDC, then zero the gauge.

27 Turn the DTI gauge and its base horizontally, so that the tip of the gauge probe now rests against the cylinder block head gasket mating surface and record the measurement indicated on the gauge dial.

28 Check that the piston protrusion for each cylinder is within the tolerance given in the Specifications. If the original pistons have been refitted and excessive or insufficient protrusion is recorded, this is indication that either the piston and connecting rods from different cylinders have been interchanged, or that the piston and connecting rods have been incorrectly reassembled. If new pistons have been fitted, incorrect protrusion indicates that a piston of the wrong height class has been fitted. Identify the cause and rectify before proceeding.

All engines

29 Refit the cylinder head, oil pump and sump as described in Part A or B of this Chapter (as applicable).

19 Engine - initial start-up after overhaul

1 With the engine refitted in the vehicle, double-check the engine oil and coolant levels (see "*Weekly checks*"). Make a final check that everything has been reconnected, and that there are no tools or rags left in the engine compartment.

Petrol engine models

2 Remove the spark plugs (see Chapter 1A), then remove the fuel injection pump fuse, with reference to Chapter 12.

3 Turn the engine on the starter until the oil pressure warning light goes out. Refit the spark plugs, and reconnect the spark plug (HT) leads, referring to Chapter 1A for further information. Refit the fuel injection pump fuse.

Diesel engine models

4 Disconnect the wiring from the stop solenoid on the injection pump (see Chapter 4C), then turn the engine on the starter motor until the oil pressure warning light goes out. Reconnect the wire to the stop solenoid.

5 Prime the fuel system as described in Chapter 4C.

6 Fully depress the accelerator pedal, turn the ignition key to position "M", and wait for the preheating warning light to go out.

All models

7 Start the engine, noting that this may take a little longer than usual, due to the fuel system components having been disturbed.

8 While the engine is idling, check for fuel, water and oil leaks. Don't be alarmed if there are some odd smells and smoke from parts getting hot and burning off oil deposits.

9 Assuming all is well, keep the engine idling until hot water is felt circulating through the top hose, then switch off the engine.

10 After a few minutes, recheck the oil and coolant levels as described in "*Weekly checks*", and top-up as necessary.

11 There is no requirement to re-tighten the cylinder head bolts once the engine has first run after reassembly, provided that they were tightened as described during reassembly.

12 If new pistons, rings or crankshaft bearings have been fitted, the engine must be treated as new, and run-in for the first 500 miles (800 km). *Do not* operate the engine at full-throttle, or above 3000 rpm, or allow it to labour at low engine speeds in any gear. It is recommended that the oil and filter be changed at the end of this period (see Chapter 1A or 1B).

Chapter 3
Cooling, heating and ventilation systems

Contents

Degrees of difficulty

Easy, suitable for novice with little experience	**Fairly easy,** suitable for beginner with some experience	**Fairly difficult,** suitable for competent DIY mechanic	**Difficult,** suitable for experienced DIY mechanic	**Very difficult,** suitable for expert DIY or professional

Specifications

General

Expansion tank cap opening pressure (all models)	1.4 bars
Thermostat opening temperature (all models)	88°C
Air conditioning cut-out temperature	112°C
Temperature warning light illuminates at	118°C

Electric cooling fan

Cut-in temperature:	
Petrol models:	
Fan No 1:	
Low speed	96°C
High speed	101°C
Fan No 2 (where fitted)	
Low speed	97°C
High speed (1.6 litre 16v models only)	101°C
Diesel models:	
Fan No 1	96°C
Fan No 2 (where fitted):	
Low speed	97°C
High speed	101°C
Maximum post-ignition cooling fan operation	6 minutes

Air conditioning system

Refrigerant fluid type	R134a
Refrigerant fluid quantity:	
Models up to 02/96	600 ± 25g
Models from 04/96	775 ± 25g

Torque wrench settings

Torque wrench settings	Nm	lbf ft
Cooling fan thermostatic switch	45	33
Coolant pump impeller housing - cylinder block bolts (cast-iron block engine)	18	13
Larger coolant pump housing securing bolts (alloy block engine)	65	48
Smaller coolant pump housing securing bolts (alloy block engine)	30	22
Temperature gauge/temperature warning light sender	18	13

1 General information and precautions

General information

1 The cooling system is of pressurised type, comprising a coolant pump driven by the timing belt, an aluminium crossflow radiator, with integral expansion tank on petrol models, electric cooling fan, a thermostat, heater matrix, and all associated hoses and switches. A separate remotely-mounted coolant expansion tank is fitted to diesel models **(see illustrations)**.

2 The system functions as follows. Cold coolant in the bottom of the radiator passes through the bottom hose to the coolant pump, where it is pumped around the cylinder block and head passages, and through the oil cooler (where fitted). After cooling the cylinder bores, combustion surfaces and valve seats, the coolant reaches the underside of the thermostat, which is initially closed. The coolant passes through the heater, and is returned via the cylinder block to the coolant pump.

3 When the engine is cold, the coolant circulates only through the cylinder block, cylinder head, and heater. When the coolant reaches a predetermined temperature, the thermostat opens, and the coolant passes through the top hose to the radiator. As the coolant circulates through the radiator, it is cooled by the inrush of air when the car is in forward motion. The airflow is supplemented by the action of the electric cooling fan when necessary. Upon reaching the bottom of the radiator, the coolant has now cooled, and the cycle is repeated.

4 When the engine is at normal operating temperature, the coolant expands, and some of it is displaced into the expansion tank. Coolant collects in the tank, and is returned to the radiator when the system cools.

5 On some models, the coolant is also passed through the engine oil cooler.

6 The electric cooling fan(s) mounted in front of the radiator are controlled by a thermostatic switch. At a predetermined coolant temperature, the switch/sensor actuates the fan.

Precautions

Cooling system

7 When the engine is hot, the coolant in the cooling system is under high pressure. The increased pressure raises the boiling point of the coolant and this allows the coolant to circulate at temperatures close to 100°C without actually boiling. If the pressure is reduced suddenly, e.g. by removing the expansion tank filler cap, the coolant will boil very rapidly, resulting in boiling water and steam being ejected through the expansion tank filler neck. This can happen very quickly and the risk of scalding is high.

8 For this reason, **do not** attempt to remove the expansion tank filler cap or to disturb any part of the cooling system whilst the engine is hot. Allow the engine to cool for several hours after switching off. When removing the expansion tank filler cap, as a precaution cover the cap with a thick layer of cloth, to avoid scalding, and slowly unscrew the filler cap until a hissing sound can be heard. When the hissing has stopped, showing that pressure has been released, slowly unscrew the filler cap until it can be removed. If more hissing sounds are heard, wait until they have stopped before unscrewing the cap completely. At all times keep well away from the filler opening.

9 Do not allow antifreeze to come in contact with your skin or painted surfaces of the vehicle. Rinse off spills immediately with plenty of water. Never leave antifreeze lying around; it is fatal if ingested.

10 If the engine is hot, the electric cooling fan may start rotating even if the engine is not running, so be careful to keep hands, hair and loose clothing well clear when working in the engine compartment.

Air conditioning system

11 On models equipped with an air conditioning system, it is necessary to observe special precautions whenever dealing with any part of the system, its associated components and any items which necessitate disconnection of the system. If for any reason the system must be disconnected, entrust this task to your Citroën dealer or a refrigeration engineer.

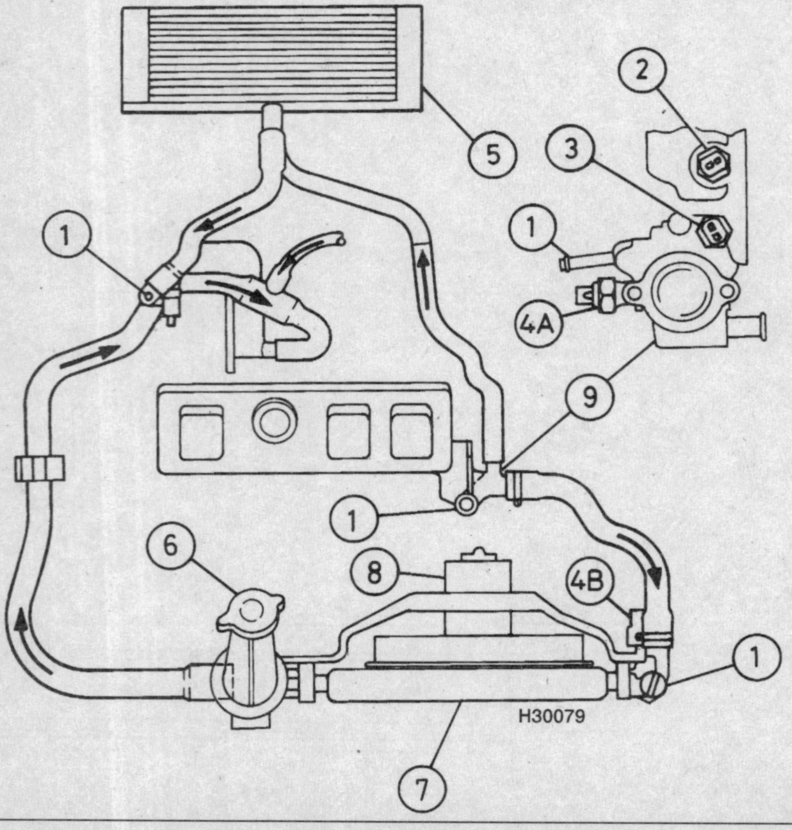

1.1a Typical cooling system layout (8-valve petrol engine)

1 *Bleed screws*
2 *Temperature gauge/warning light sensor/switch*
3 *Fuel injection system coolant temperature sensor*
4A *Cooling fan switch - models with air conditioning*
4B *Cooling fan switch- models without air conditioning*
5 *Heater matrix*
6 *Expansion tank filler cap*
7 *Radiator*
8 *Cooling fan*
9 *Thermostat housing*

1.1b Typical cooling system layout (16-valve petrol engine)

1 Bleed screws
2 Fuel injection system coolant temperature sensor
3 Temperature gauge sensor/warning light switch
4 Cooling fan switch/air conditioning control unit temperature sensor
5 Expansion tank filler cap
6 Radiator
7 Cooling fans
8 To heater matrix
9 Oil cooler

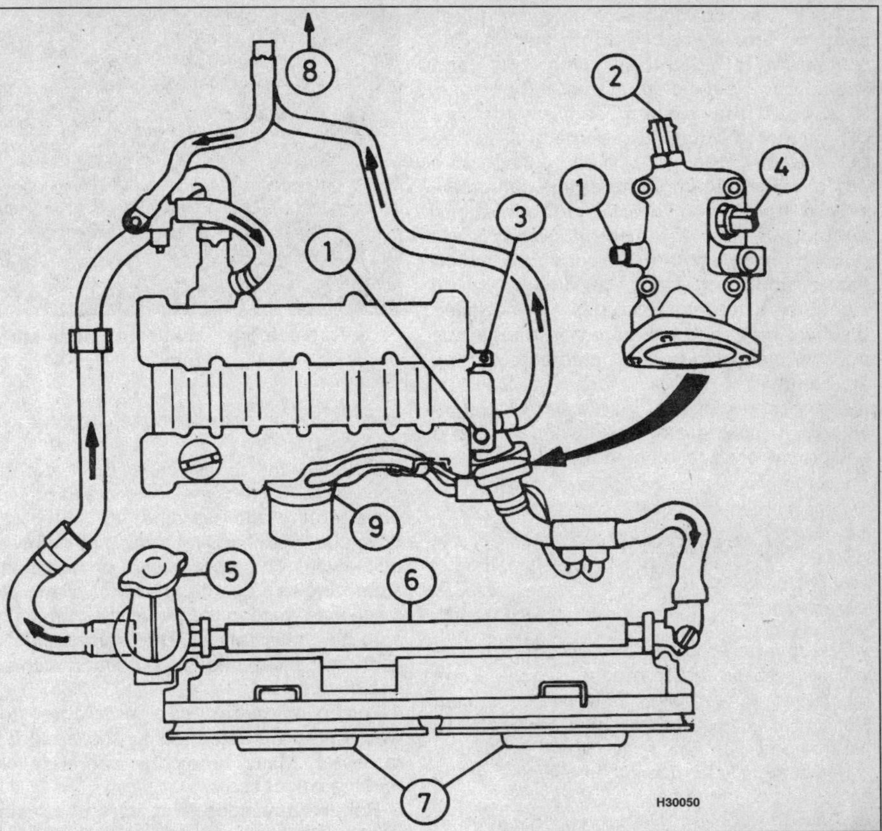

1.1c Typical cooling system layout (diesel engine)

1 Bleed screw
2 Temperature gauge sensor - models with air conditioning
3A Warning light switch/temperature gauge sensor - models without air conditioning
3B Cooling fan sensor/warning light switch - models with air conditioning
4 Glow plug control unit temperature coolant sensor
5 Cooling fan switch - models without air conditioning
6 Supply to/return from heater matrix
7 Expansion tank filler cap
8 Radiator
9 Oil cooler
10 Thermostat housing
11 Cooling fans

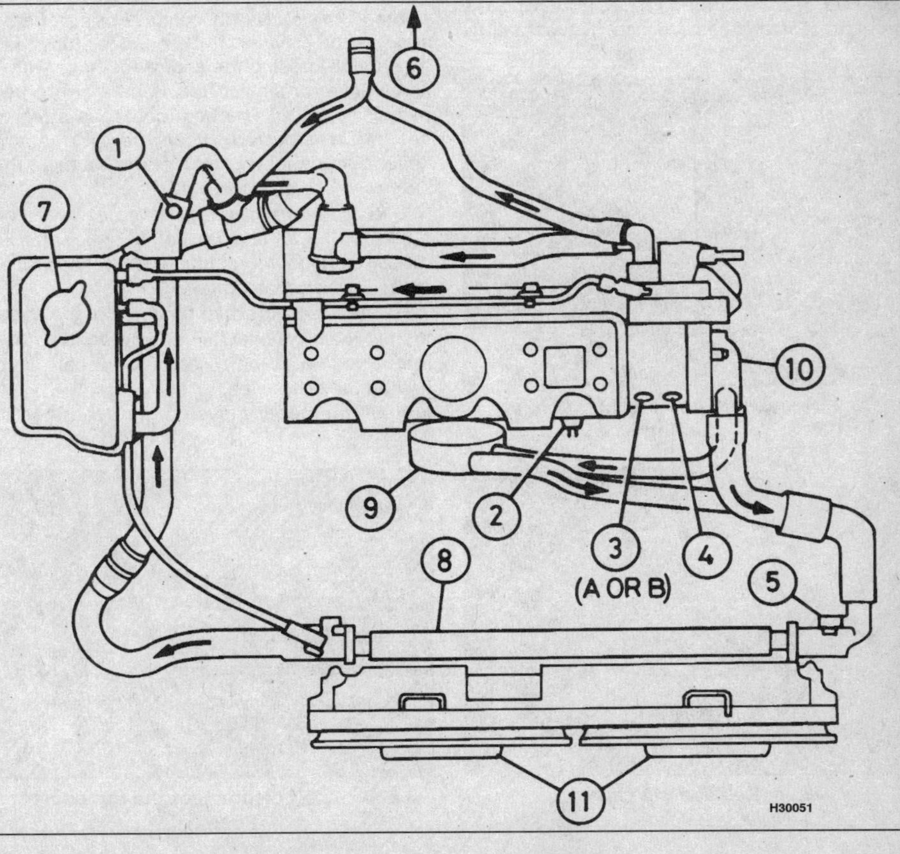

12 The air conditioning system pipes contains pressurised liquid refrigerant. The refrigerant is potentially dangerous, and should only be handled by qualified persons. If any of the system components are disconnected before discharging is carried out, the refrigerant will boil and escape as a gas at very low temperature; this can cause severe frostbite if allowed to come into contact with the skin. The refrigerant is not poisonous, but in the presence of a naked flame (including that produced by a cigarette), it forms a toxic gas. Uncontrolled discharging of the refrigerant is dangerous and is also extremely damaging to the environment. For these reasons, disconnection of any part of the system without specialised knowledge and equipment is not recommended.

2 Cooling system hoses - disconnection and renewal

1 The number, routing and pattern of hoses will vary according to model, but the same basic procedure applies. Before commencing work, make sure that the new hoses are to hand, along with new hose clips if needed. It is good practice to renew the hose clips at the same time as the hoses.

2 Drain the cooling system, as described in Chapter 1A or 1B (as applicable), saving the coolant if it is fit for re-use. Squirt a little penetrating oil onto the hose clips if they are corroded.

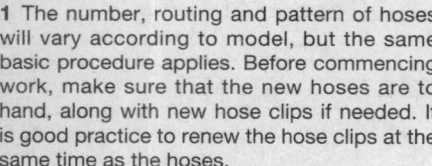

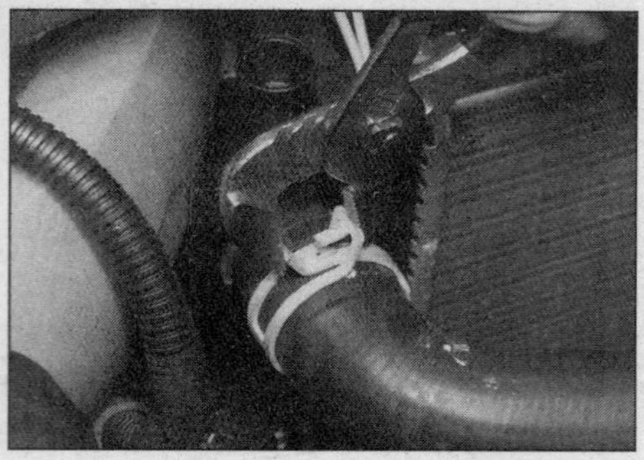

2.3 Releasing a radiator top hose spring clip

3 Release the hose clips from the hose concerned. Three types of clip are used; worm-drive, spring and "sardine-can". The worm-drive clip is released by turning its screw anti-clockwise. The spring clip is released by squeezing its tags together with pliers, at the same time working the clip away from the hose stub **(see illustration)**. The "sardine-can" clip is not re-usable, and is best cut off with snips or side cutters.

4 Unclip any wires, cables or other hoses which may be attached to the hose being removed. Make notes for reference when refitting if necessary.

5 Release the hose from its stubs, using a gentle twisting motion. Be careful not to damage the stubs on delicate components such as the radiator. If the hose is stuck fast, try carefully prising the end of the hose with a screwdriver or similar, taking care not to use excessive force. The best course is often to cut off a stubborn hose using a sharp knife, but again be careful not to damage the stubs.

6 Before fitting the new hose, smear the stubs with washing-up liquid or a suitable rubber lubricant to aid fitting. Do not use oil or grease, which may attack the rubber.

7 Fit the hose clips over the ends of the hose, then fit the hose over its stubs. Work the hose into position. When satisfied, locate and tighten the hose clips.

8 Refill the cooling system as described in Chapter 1A or 1B. Run the engine, and check that there are no leaks.

9 Recheck the tightness of the hose clips on any new hoses after a few hundred miles.

10 Top-up the coolant level if necessary (see "*Weekly checks*").

3 Radiator - removal, inspection and refitting

Note: *If the reason for removing the radiator is to cure a leak, it is worth trying the effect of a radiator sealing compound - this is added to the coolant, and will often cure minor leaks with the radiator in situ.*

Removal

1 Disconnect the battery negative cable and position it away from the terminal.

2 Drain the cooling system as described in Chapter 1A or 1B as applicable.

3 Where applicable, to improve access, remove the exhaust manifold heat shield.

4 Remove the air cleaner air inlet ducting as described in the relevant Part of Chapter 4 **(see illustration)**.

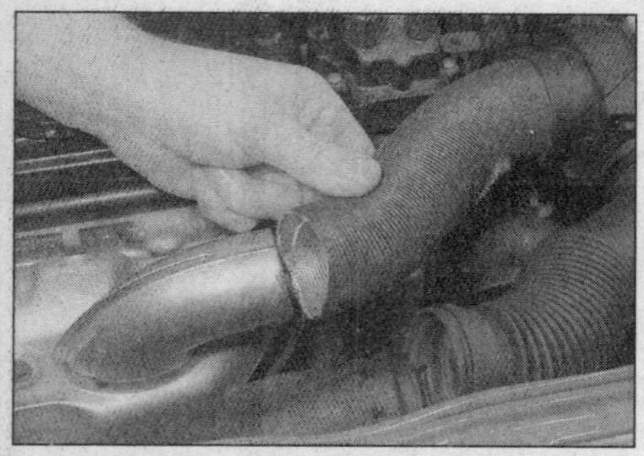

3.4 Remove the air cleaner air inlet ducting

5 Disconnect all coolant hoses from the radiator, with reference to Section 2 if necessary **(see illustrations)**.

6 Remove the cooling fan shroud securing bolts, then disengage the shroud lugs from the brackets on the end of the radiator, and lift the cooling fan and shroud assembly from the radiator (see Section 5). Note that on certain models, due to limited clearance, the fan/shroud assembly must be withdrawn from underneath the vehicle.

7 Where applicable, disconnect the wiring plugs from the cooling fan, and from the cooling fan switch, which is mounted in the top left-hand corner of the radiator **(see illustration)**. Where applicable, release the wiring harness from the clips on the fan shroud, and move the harness to one side.

8 Refer to Chapter 11 and remove the radiator grille. Slacken and withdraw the screws, then

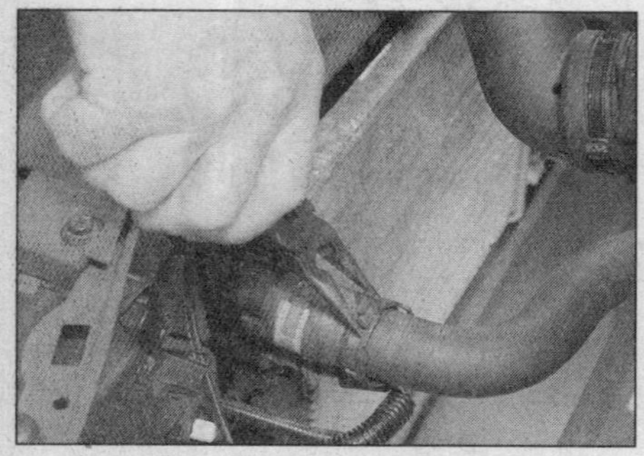

3.5a Release the clips . . . .

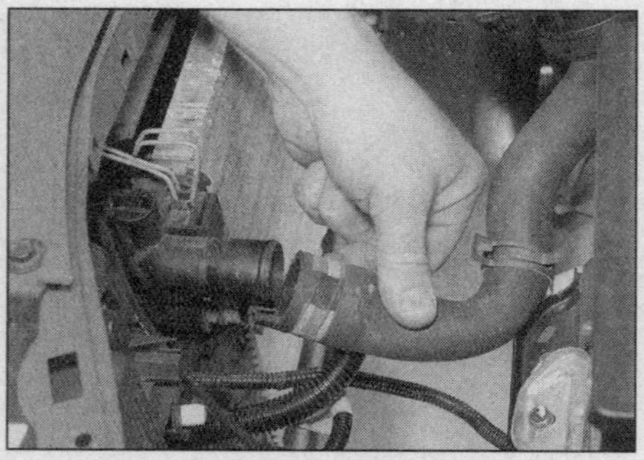

3.5b . . . and disconnect the top coolant hose . . .

3.5c . . . and bottom coolant hose from the radiator stubs

3.7 Disconnect the wiring from the cooling fan switch

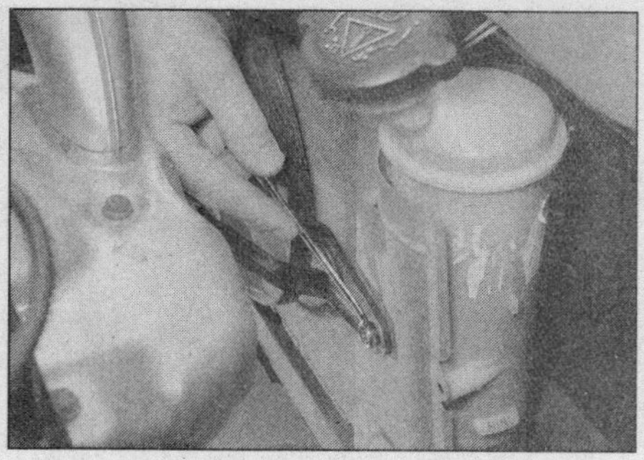

3.8a Slacken and withdraw the securing screws . . .

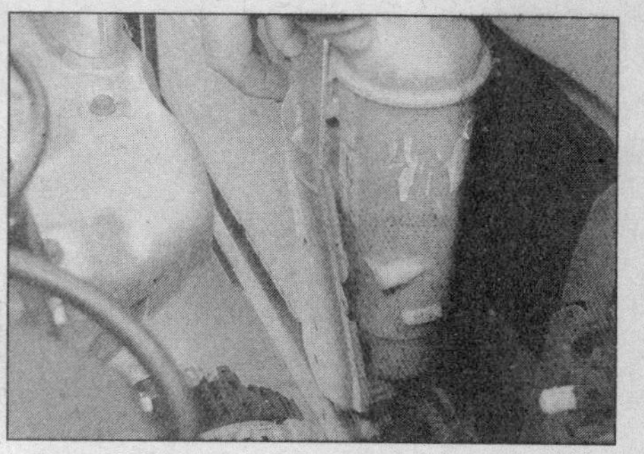

3.8b . . . and remove the expansion tank heat shield

detach the heat shield from the rear of the expansion tank (where applicable) **(see illustrations)**.

9 Using a suitable pair of pliers, release the two securing spring clips from the top of the radiator and the body front panel, and withdraw the clips **(see illustration)**.

10 The radiator can now be withdrawn from the engine compartment. On diesel and larger capacity petrol models, the radiator is most easily withdrawn from underneath the vehicle. On other models, the radiator can be withdrawn through the top of the engine compartment, in which case, it may be necessary to remove the nuts/screws and detach the air inlet tube from the front body panel **(see illustrations)**. Take care not to damage the radiator fins during removal.

Warning: Wear protective gloves when handling the radiator - the cooling fins are very sharp and can cause injury.

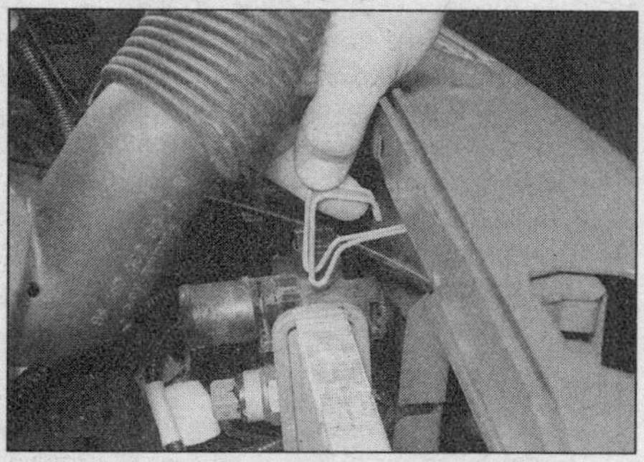

3.9 Release the upper radiator securing spring clips

11 Where applicable, recover the lower mounting rubbers, and lift out the radiator shield **(see illustration)**.

Inspection

12 If the radiator has been removed due to suspected blockage, reverse-flush it as described in Chapter 1A or 1B (as applicable). Clean dirt and debris from the radiator fins, using an air line (in which case, wear eye protection) or a soft brush. Be careful, as the fins are sharp, and easily damaged.

13 If necessary, a radiator specialist can perform a "flow test" on the radiator, to establish whether an internal blockage exists.

14 A leaking radiator must be referred to a specialist for permanent repair. Do not attempt to weld or solder a leaking radiator, as damage to the plastic components may result.

15 In an emergency, minor leaks from the radiator can be cured by using a suitable radiator sealant, in accordance with its manufacturer's instructions, with the radiator *in situ*.

16 If the radiator is to be sent for repair or renewed, remove all hoses, and the cooling fan switch.

17 Inspect the condition of the radiator mounting rubbers, and renew them if necessary.

Refitting

18 Refitting is a reversal of removal, bearing in mind the following points:

a) Ensure that the lower lugs on the radiator are correctly engaged with the mounting rubbers in the body panel.

b) Ensure that the upper radiator securing spring clips are correctly engaged.

c) Refit the radiator grille, with reference to Chapter 11.

d) Reconnect the hoses with reference to Section 2.

e) Where applicable, refit the air inlet tube using new pop-rivets.

f) On completion, refill the cooling system as described in Chapter 1A or 1B (as applicable).

4 Thermostat - removal, testing and refitting

Removal

1 Drain the cooling system as described in Chapter 1A or 1B (as applicable).

2 If desired for improved access, remove the air cleaner and/or the air inlet ducting as described in the relevant Part of Chapter 4. Similarly, remove the battery as described in Chapter 5A.

3 Release the clips and disconnect all coolant hoses from the thermostat housing ports **(see illustrations)**.

4 Unscrew the retaining bolts, and carefully withdraw the thermostat housing cover to expose the thermostat **(see illustrations)**. Note that the design of the thermostat housing varies between engine types, but the thermostat removal procedure for each type is similar.

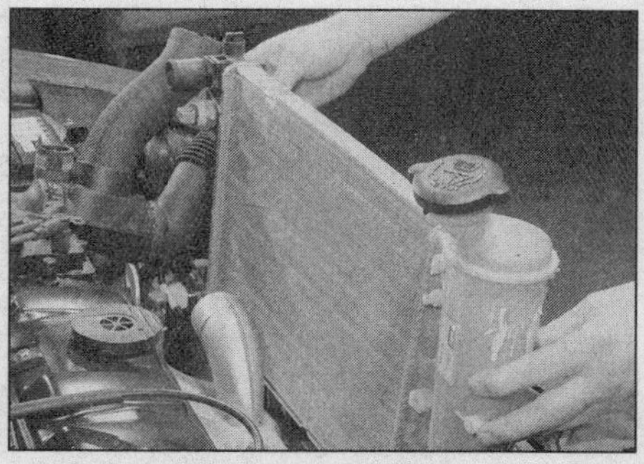

3.10a Withdraw the radiator from the engine compartment

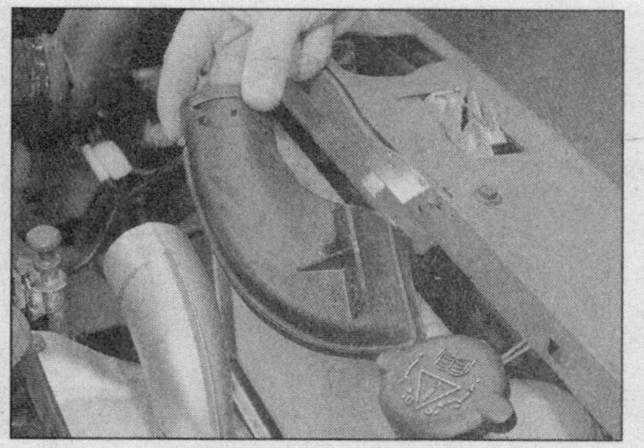

3.10b It may be necessary to remove the air inlet tube from the front body panel

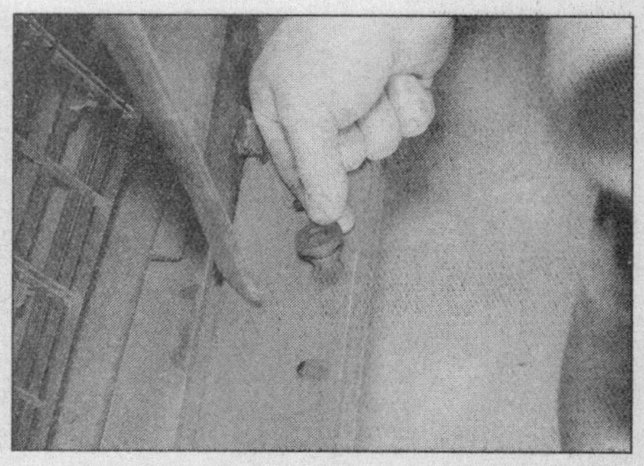

3.11 Recover the lower mounting rubbers

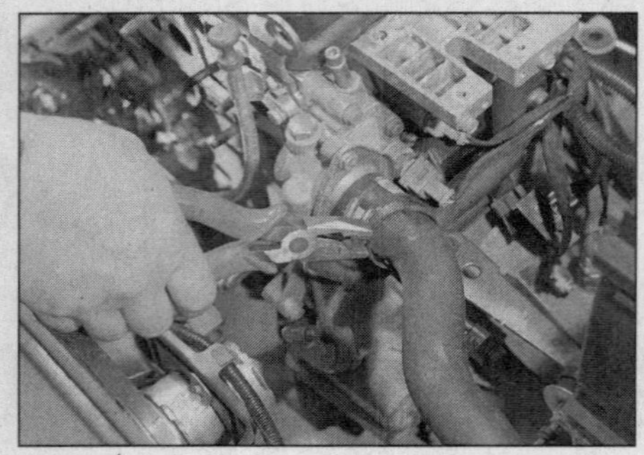

4.3a Release the clips . . .

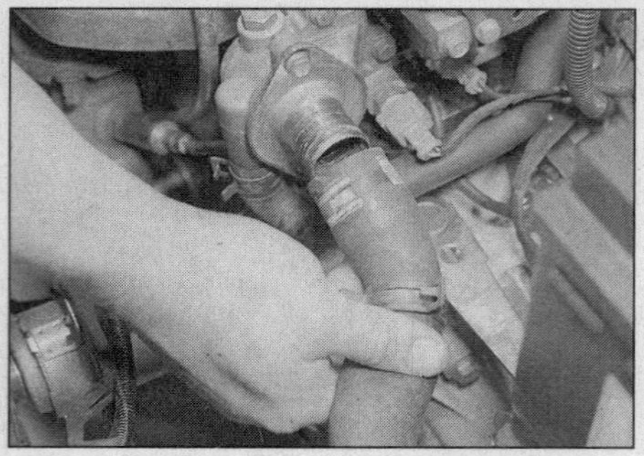

4.3b . . . and disconnect all coolant hoses from the thermostat housing ports

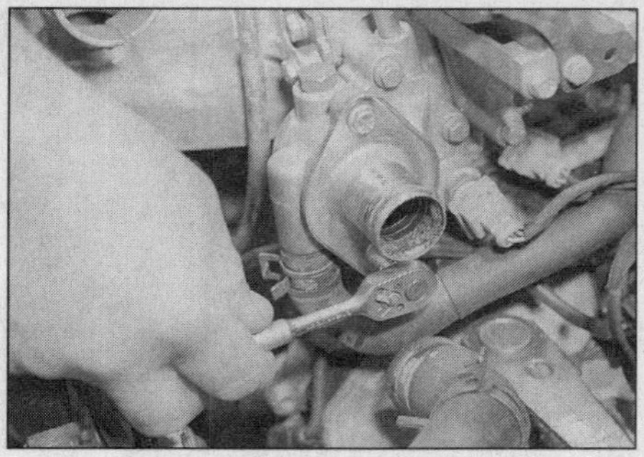

4.4a Unscrew the thermostat housing cover retaining bolts . . .

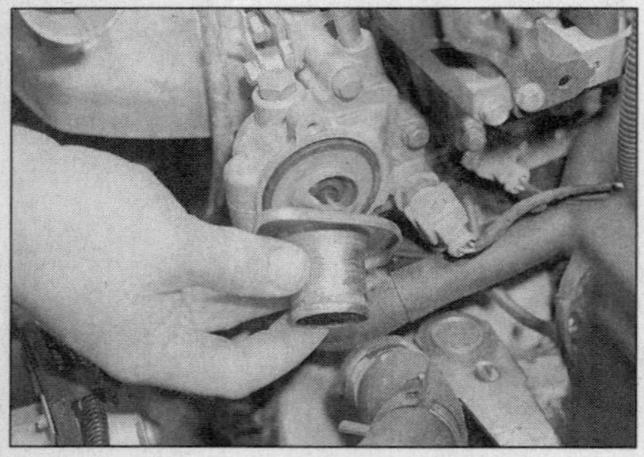

4.4b . . . then carefully withdraw the cover to expose the thermostat

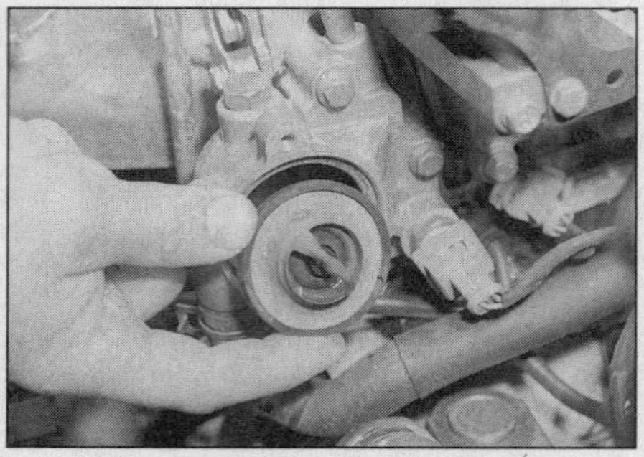

4.5a Lift the thermostat from the housing . . .

4.5b . . . and recover the sealing ring

5 Lift the thermostat from the housing, noting which way round the thermostat is fitted, and recover the sealing ring **(see illustrations)**.

Testing

6 A rough test of the thermostat may be made by suspending it with a piece of string in a container full of water. Heat the water to bring it to the boil - the thermostat must open by the time the water boils. If not, renew it.

7 If a thermometer is available, the precise opening temperature of the thermostat may be determined; compare with the figures given in the Specifications. The opening temperature is also marked on the thermostat.

8 A thermostat which fails to close as the water cools must also be renewed.

Refitting

9 Refitting is a reversal of removal, bearing in mind the following points:

a) Examine the sealing ring for signs of damage or deterioration, and if necessary, renew.

b) Ensure that the thermostat is fitted the correct way round, as noted before removal.

c) Where applicable, refit the air cleaner and/or the air inlet ducting, with reference to the relevant Part of Chapter 4.

d) On completion, refill the cooling system as described in Chapter 1A or 1B (as applicable).

5 Electric cooling fan - removal and refitting

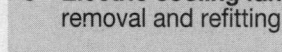

General information

1 On models without air conditioning, the current supply to the cooling fan is via the ignition switch (see Chapter 5A) and a fuse (see Chapter 12). The circuit is completed by the cooling fan thermostatic switch, which is mounted in the upper left-hand corner of the radiator. On 1.6 litre 16-valve petrol models, and all models with air conditioning, the twin cooling fans are controlled by a two-stage temperature switch and the coolant temperature sensor (via the air conditioning control unit) - refer to Section 6 for details. At the time of writing, very little information was available for models fitted with twin cooling fans; the scope of this Section is therefore limited to models fitted with a single cooling fan.

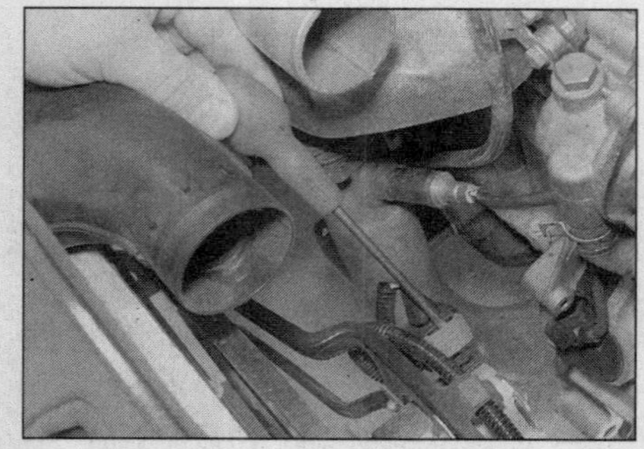

5.5a Release the locking bar . . .

5.5b . . . and unplug the wiring connector from the cooling fan

Removal

2 Disconnect the battery negative lead.

3 Remove the air cleaner air inlet ducting as described in the relevant Part of Chapter 4. If necessary for improved access, unscrew the nuts and bolts and remove the air inlet tube from the front body panel.

4 Where applicable, remove the heat shield from the exhaust manifold.

5 Disconnect the wiring plug from the cooling fan, then release the wiring harness from the retaining clip **(see illustrations)**.

6 Remove the cooling fan shroud securing bolt(s) on the right hand side, then disengage the shroud legs from the brackets on the left hand end of the radiator, and lift the cooling fan and shroud assembly from the radiator **(see illustration)**.

7 If desired, the fan blades can be removed from the end of the motor shaft after removing

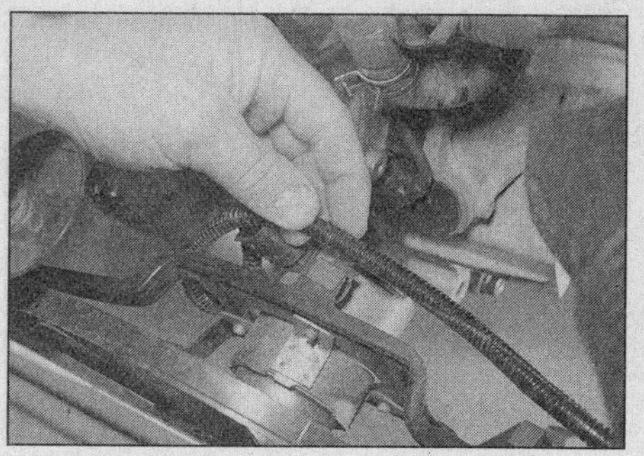

5.5c Release the wiring harness from the retaining clip

the securing circlip. The motor can be removed from the shroud assembly after drilling out the securing rivets **(see illustration)**.

Refitting

8 Refitting is a reversal of removal. Where applicable, use new rivets to secure the fan motor. Ensure that the shroud legs engage with the brackets on the left-hand end of the radiator **(see illustration)**.

6 Cooling system electrical switches and sensors - removal and refitting

Switch/sensor location and description - diesel engine models

Cooling fan switch

1 On models without air conditioning, the cooling fan switch has a blue body with a yellow ring and is mounted on the left-hand side of the radiator.

2 On models with air conditioning, the cooling fan switch has a brown body with a grey ring and is located in the front of the thermostat housing.

Temperature warning light switch

3 On models with no temperature gauge and without air conditioning, the warning light switch has a blue body with a grey or yellow ring and is located in the front of the thermostat housing **(see illustration)**.

6.3 Temperature warning light switch (arrowed)

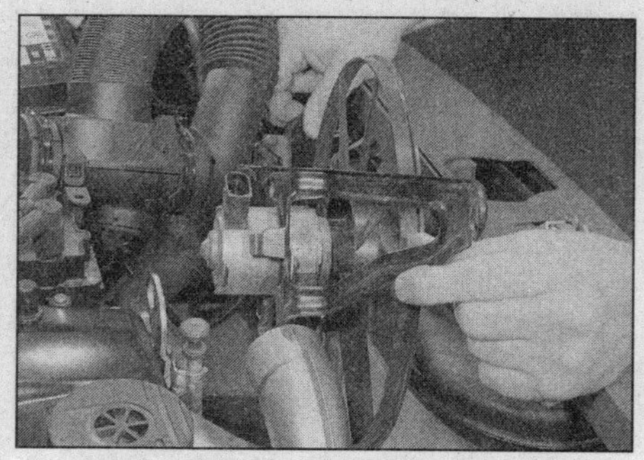

5.6 Lift the cooling fan and shroud assembly from the radiator

4 On models with no temperature gauge and with air conditioning, the warning light switch has a brown body with a yellow ring and is located in the front of the thermostat housing.

Temperature gauge sensor

5 On models without air conditioning, the gauge sensor has a blue body and is mounted on the front face of the cylinder head.

6 On models with air conditioning, the gauge sensor has a blue body with a grey ring and is located in the front of the thermostat housing.

Glow plug control unit coolant temperature sensor

7 On all diesel models, the glow plug control unit coolant temperature sensor has a green body with either a white or grey sleeve and is mounted in the front of the thermostat housing.

Switch/sensor location and description - petrol engine models

Cooling fan switch

8 On without air conditioning, the cooling fan switch has a blue body with a red ring (16-valve models) or a yellow ring (8-valve models) and is located in the top left-hand corner of the radiator.

9 On models with air conditioning, the cooling fan control unit temperature sensor has a brown body (with a grey ring on 16-valve models) and is located in the top of the thermostat housing.

Temperature warning light switch/temperature gauge sensor

10 The coolant temperature warning light switch/temperature gauge sensor has a blue body with a grey ring and is located at the left hand end of the cylinder head **(see illustration)**.

Fuel injection system coolant temperature sensor

11 The fuel injection system coolant temperature sensor has a green body (with a yellow sleeve on 8-valve models) and is mounted in the left hand side of the thermostat housing.

5.7 The motor can be removed from the shroud assembly after drilling out the securing rivets (arrowed)

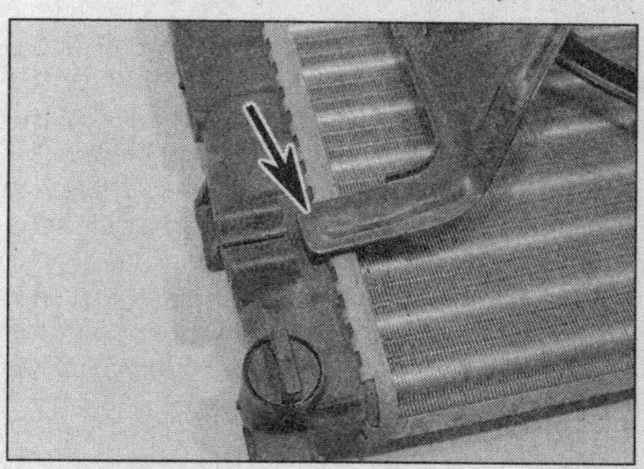

5.8 On refitting, ensure that the shroud legs (arrowed) engage with the brackets on the left-hand end of the radiator

Removal

Warning: The engine and radiator should be cold before removing a cooling system switch or sensor.

12 Disconnect the battery negative cable and position it away from the terminal.

13 Partially drain the cooling system to just below the level of the switch/sensor (as described in Chapter 1A or 1B).

14 Alternatively, have ready a suitable bung to plug the switch aperture in the radiator when the switch is removed. If this method is used, take great care not to damage the radiator, and do not use anything which will allow foreign matter to enter the radiator.

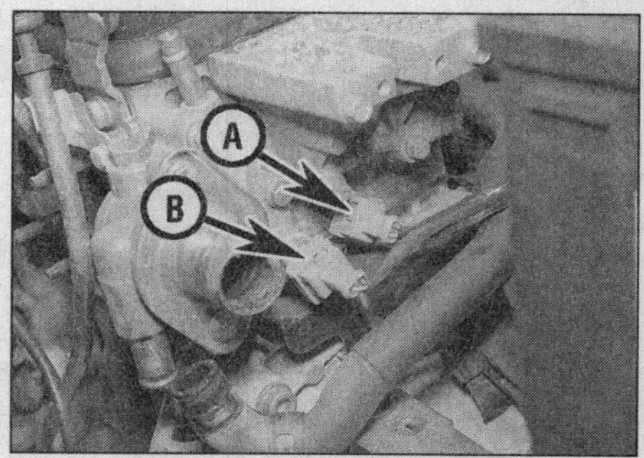

6.10 Cooling system switch/sensor locations - 1.1 litre petrol model without air conditioning shown

A Temperature warning light switch/temperature gauge sensor
B Fuel injection system coolant temperature sensor

15 Unplug the wiring connector from the switch/sensor **(see illustration)**.

16 Carefully unscrew the switch/sensor from its mounting **(see illustration)** and recover the sealing ring (where applicable). If the system has not been drained, plug the switch/sensor aperture to prevent further coolant loss.

17 If the switch was originally fitted using sealing compound, clean the switch threads thoroughly, and coat them with fresh sealing compound.

18 If the switch was originally fitted using a sealing ring, use a new sealing ring on refitting.

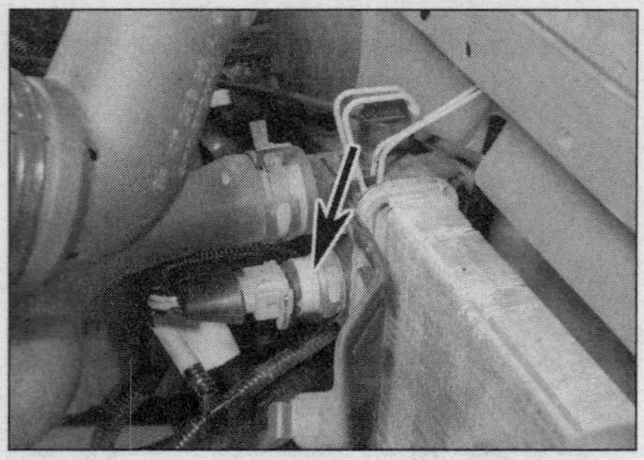

6.15 Disconnect the wiring plug from the switch (arrowed)

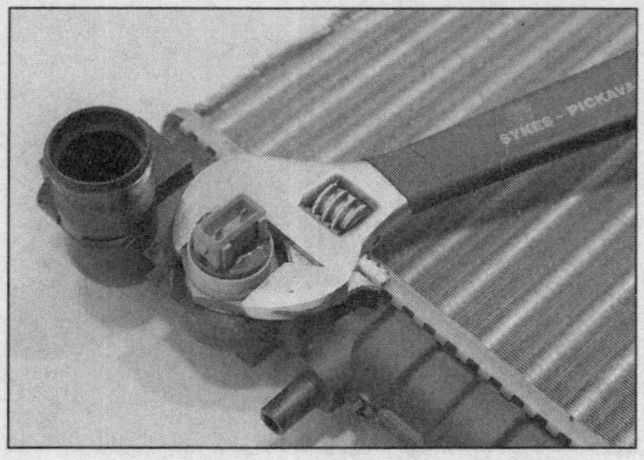

6.16 Carefully unscrew the switch (radiator removed for clarity)

Refitting

19 Refitting is a reversal of removal. Tighten the switch/sensor to the specified torque (where applicable), then refill and bleed the cooling system, as described in Chapter 1A or 1B applicable. Follow the bleeding instructions carefully, to ensure that all air is expelled from the cooling system.

20 On completion, start the engine and run it until it reaches normal operating temperature. Continue to run the engine, and check that the cooling fan cuts in and out correctly.

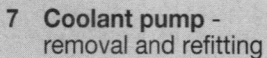

7 Coolant pump - removal and refitting

Models with aluminium cylinder block

Note: *A new impeller assembly O-ring, and where applicable, a new impeller housing O-ring, will be required on refitting.*

Removal

1 The coolant pump is driven by the timing belt, and is located in a housing at the timing belt end of the cylinder block, below the right hand engine mounting bracket.

2 Drain the cooling system as described in Chapter 1A.

3 Remove the timing belt as described in the relevant part of Chapter 2.

4 Remove the securing bolts, and withdraw the pump impeller assembly from the housing. Manipulate the pump past the engine mounting, and withdraw it from the top of the engine compartment. Recover the O-ring **(see illustrations)**.

5 If desired, the pump impeller housing can be removed from the rear of the coolant pump housing. Access is most easily obtained from underneath the vehicle (it may be necessary to remove the exhaust heat shield). Disconnect the coolant hoses from the impeller housing (be prepared for coolant spillage), then remove the securing bolts and withdraw the impeller housing. Again, recover the O-ring.

Refitting

6 Ensure that all mating faces are clean.

7 Where applicable, refit the impeller housing to the rear of the coolant pump housing, using a new O-ring. Reconnect the coolant hoses.

8 Refit the impeller assembly to the pump housing, using a new O-ring. Tighten the retaining bolts securely.

9 Refit the timing belt as described in Chapter 2A.

10 Refill and bleed the cooling system as described in Chapter 1A.

Models with cast-iron cylinder block

Note: *A new pump O-ring must be used on refitting.*

11 The pump is driven by the timing belt, and is located in a recess in the cylinder block housing, at the timing belt end of the engine, below the right hand engine mounting bracket. Note that there is no separate coolant pump impeller housing.

12 Proceed as described previously for models with an aluminium cylinder block, but ignoring all references to the separate impeller housing.

8 Heating/ventilation system - general information

The heating/ventilation system consists of a multi-speed blower motor (housed behind the facia), face level vents in the centre and at each end of the facia, windscreen demister ducts and air ducts to the front footwells.

The control unit is located in the facia, and the controls operate flap valves to deflect and mix the air flowing through the various parts of the heating/ventilation system. The flap valves are contained in the air distribution housing, which acts as a central distribution unit, passing air to the various ducts and vents.

Cold air enters the system through the grille at the rear of the engine compartment. If required, the airflow is boosted by the blower, and then flows through the various ducts, according to the settings of the controls. Stale air is expelled through ducts at the rear of the vehicle. If warm air is required, the cold air is passed over the heater matrix, which is heated by the engine coolant.

On models fitted with air conditioning, a recirculation switch enables the outside air supply to be closed off, while the air inside the vehicle is recirculated. This can be useful to prevent unpleasant odours entering from

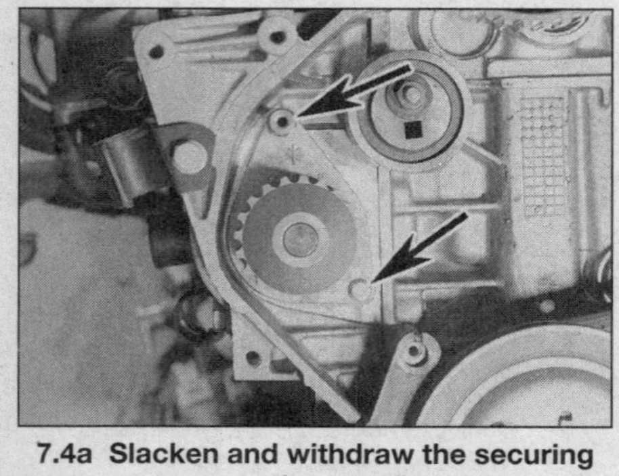

7.4a Slacken and withdraw the securing screws (arrowed) . . .

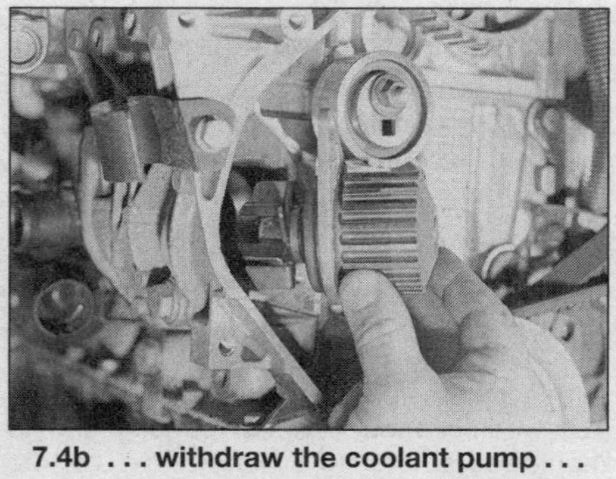

7.4b . . . withdraw the coolant pump . . .

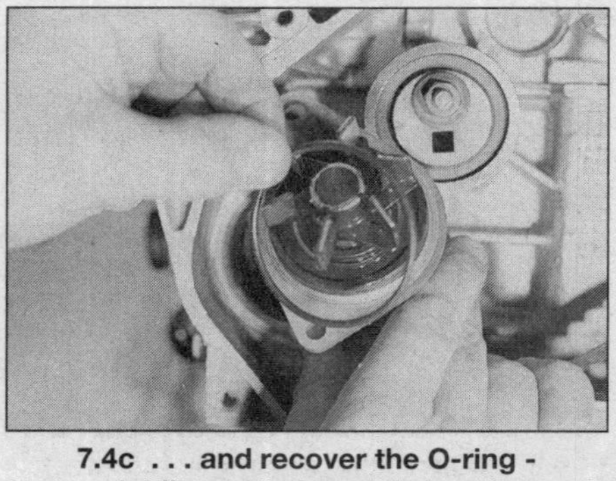

7.4c . . . and recover the O-ring - 1.1 litre petrol model shown

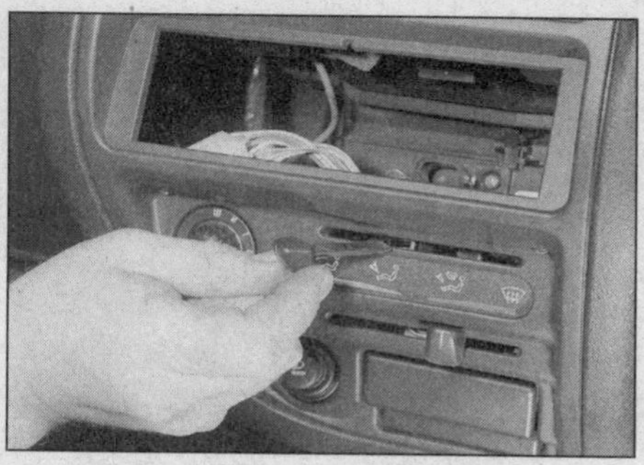

9.3 Carefully prise the two plastic knobs from the sliding heater controls

outside the vehicle, or to aid rapid demisting, but should only be used briefly, as the recirculated air inside the vehicle will soon become stale.

9 Heating/ventilation system components - removal and refitting

Heating/ventilation control unit

1 With the exception of the heater blower motor switch, the heater controls are integral with the heater assembly. The controls are operated by levers pushed through the heater control panel, which engage with the control levers on the heater assembly. Removal of the blower motor switch, and the heater illumination bulb, is described in Chapter 12.

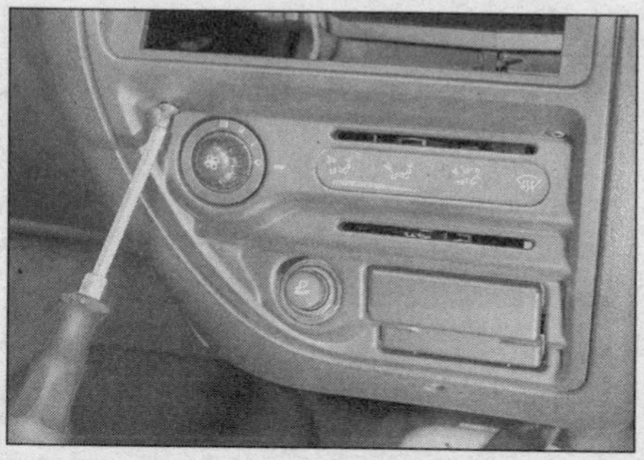

9.5 Slacken and withdraw the two screws located above the heater slide controls

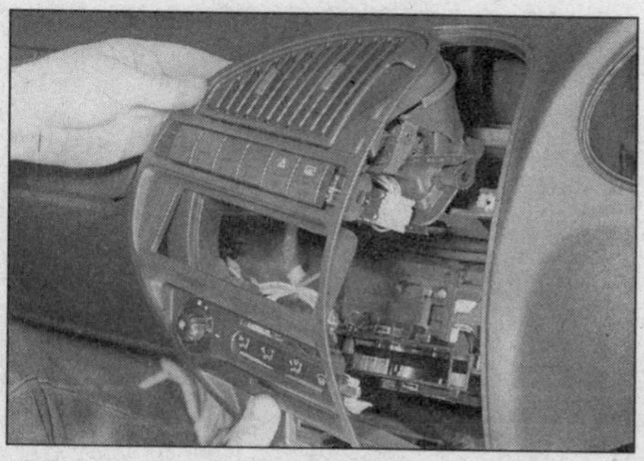

9.7b Withdraw the control panel from the facia

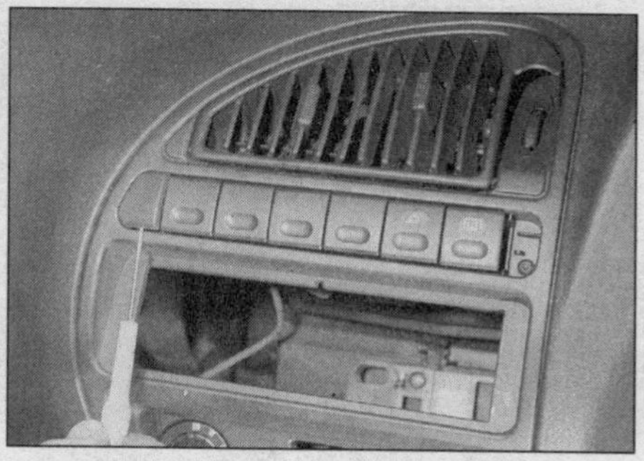

9.4a Release the cover panels from either side of the centre switch panel . . .

Heater control panel

Removal

2 Disconnect the battery negative cable and position it away from the terminal.

3 Carefully prise the two plastic knobs from the sliding heater controls **(see illustration)**.

4 Release the cover panels from either side of the centre switch panel, then slacken and withdraw the screws **(see illustrations)**.

5 Slacken and withdraw the two screws located above the heater slide controls **(see illustration)**.

6 Undo the screw securing the lower edge of the heater control panel to the facia.

7 Withdraw the control panel from the facia, then at the rear of the panel, unplug all electrical wiring from the illumination bulb holders, blower motor switch and cigar lighter (as applicable). Label each wiring connector to ensure correct refitting **(see illustrations)**.

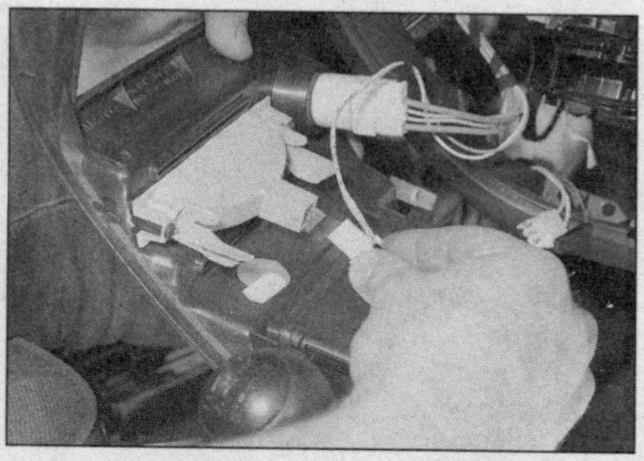

9.7a Unplug all electrical wiring from the rear of the heater control panel

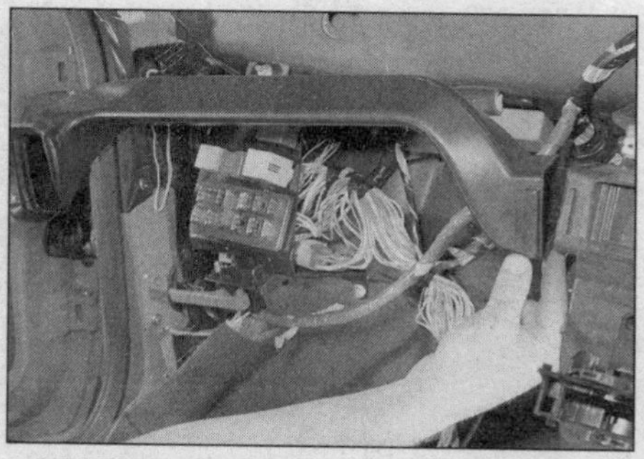

9.11 Disconnect the air ducts from each side of the heater assembly

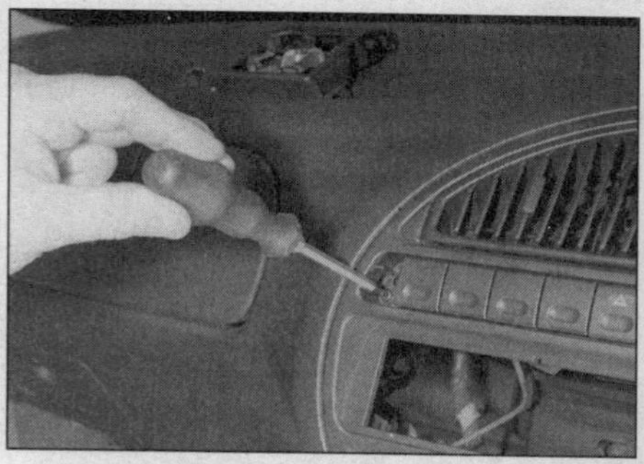

9.4b . . . then slacken and withdraw the securing screws

Refitting

8 Refitting is a reversal of removal.

Complete heater assembly

Removal

9 Drain the cooling system as described in Chapter 1A or 1B as applicable.

10 Remove the heater control panel as described earlier in this Section, then remove the complete facia assembly as described in Chapter 11.

11 Disconnect the air ducts from each side of the heater assembly **(see illustration)**.

12 Where applicable, release the electrical wiring from the clips on the rear of the heater assembly. Note the routing of the wiring to aid refitting.

13 Working in the engine compartment, disconnect the heater coolant hoses from the heater matrix pipes at the bulkhead. On larger capacity petrol models and diesel models, access to these connections is limited. One solution is to trace the heater hoses back along their lengths, disconnecting them at the relevant ports on the inlet manifold and thermostat housing. The hoses can then be drawn through the bulkhead aperture as the heater unit is removed **(see illustrations)**.

14 Working inside the vehicle, remove the lower heater assembly securing nut **(see illustration)**.

15 Carefully pull the heater assembly rearwards from its location, until the heater pipe grommet is free from the bulkhead **(see illustrations)**. Withdraw the assembly from

9.13a Disconnect the heater coolant hoses from the heater matrix pipes at the bulkhead

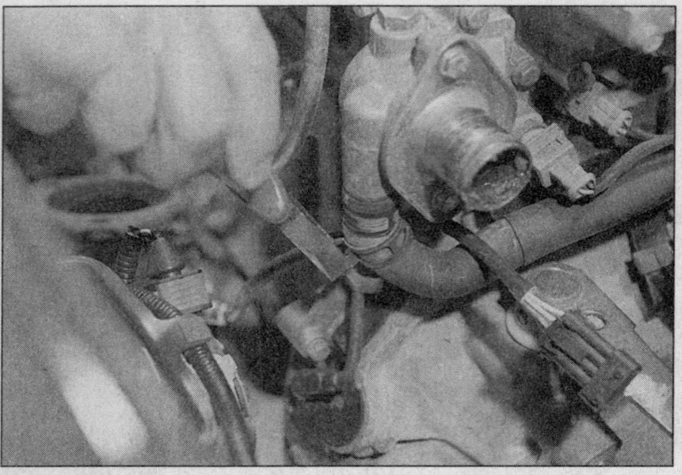

9.13b On models where access to the bulkhead connections is limited, disconnect the coolant hoses at the inlet manifold and thermostat housing . . .

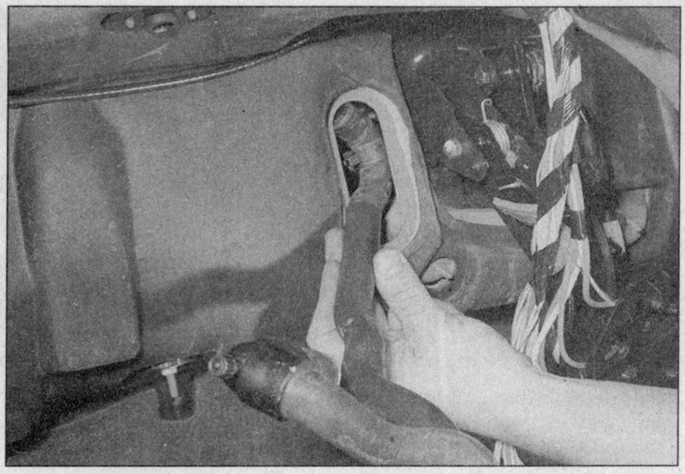

9.13c . . . and draw the hoses through the bulkhead aperture when the heater unit is removed

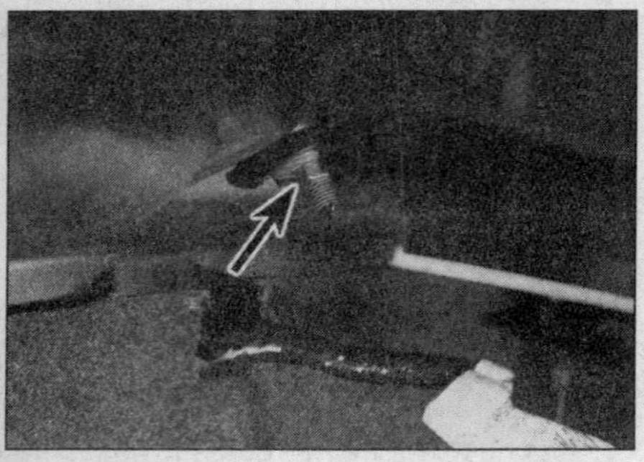

9.14 Remove the lower heater assembly securing nut (arrowed)

9.15a Carefully lift the heater assembly from its mountings (arrowed) . . .

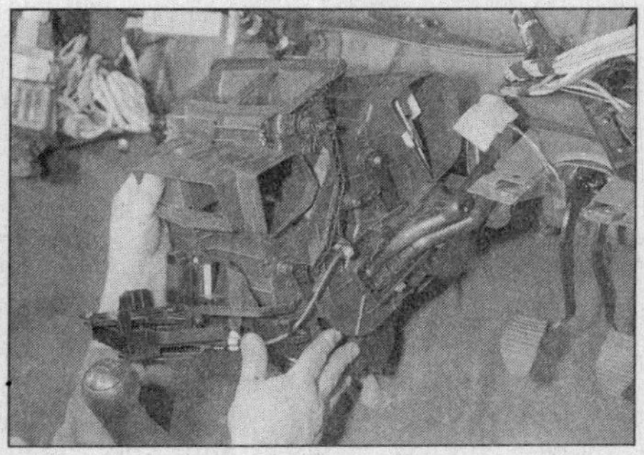

9.15b . . . until the heater pipe grommet is free from the bulkhead

the vehicle. Be prepared for coolant spillage from the heater matrix; try to keep the heater unit level as it is removed.

Refitting

16 Refitting is a reversal of removal, bearing in mind the following points:

a) When refitting the heater hose grommet to the bulkhead, lubricate the grommet with washing-up liquid to ease fitting.

b) Ensure that the wiring harness is correctly routed behind the heater assembly.

c) Refit the facia assembly with reference to Chapter 11.

d) On completion, refill the cooling system as described in Chapter 1A or 1B as applicable.

Heater matrix

Removal

17 Remove the complete heater assembly, as described previously in this Section.

18 Remove the three screws securing the heater matrix to the heater assembly **(see illustration)**.

19 Release the securing clips, and withdraw the heater matrix from the heater assembly. Be prepared for coolant spillage **(see illustrations)**.

Refitting

20 Refitting is a reversal of removal. Refit the heater assembly as described previously, and refit the facia assembly as described in Chapter 11. On completion, refill the cooling system as described in Chapter 1A or 1B.

Heater blower motor

Removal

21 Remove the complete facia assembly as described in Chapter 11.

22 Detach the air ducting from the side of the blower motor casing **(see illustration)**.

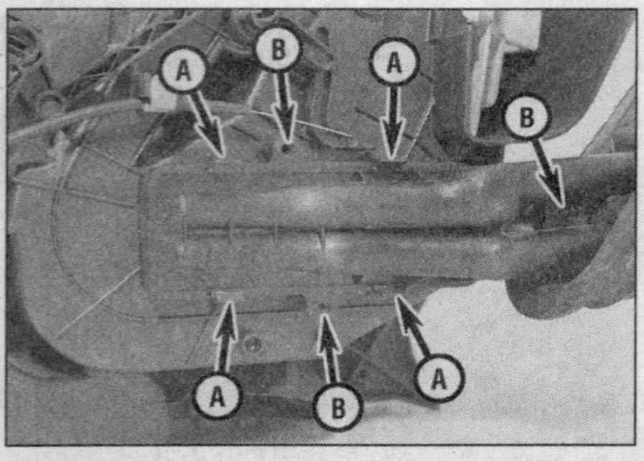

9.18 Remove the securing screws (B) and release the clips (A) . . .

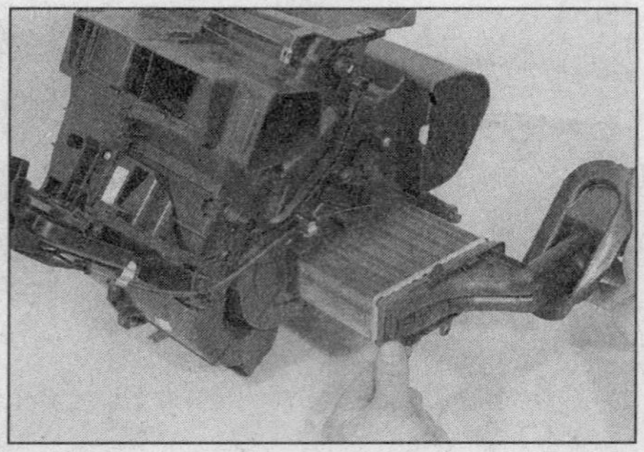

9.19 . . . and withdraw the heater matrix from its housing

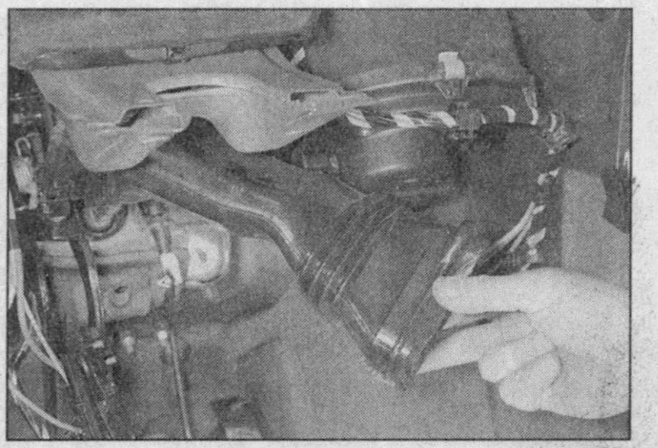

9.22 Detach the air ducting from the side of the blower motor casing . . .

23 Release the wiring harness from the clips on the underside of the blower casing, then disconnect the wiring plug from the blower motor **(see illustrations)**.
24 Remove the windscreen wiper arms as described in Chapter 12.
25 Open the bonnet and secure it in the upright position.
26 Remove the securing screw and the two nuts, and withdraw the windscreen cowl panel from the scuttle. Note that the panel clips around the edge of the windscreen and the front wings.
27 Remove the securing nuts, and unclip the plastic cover panel from the right-hand end of the scuttle to expose the heater blower motor securing nuts.
28 Unscrew the securing nuts, and lower the heater blower assembly into the vehicle interior **(see illustrations)**.

Refitting

29 Refitting is a reversal of removal. Refit the windscreen wiper arms and the facia assembly as described in Chapters 12 and 11 respectively.

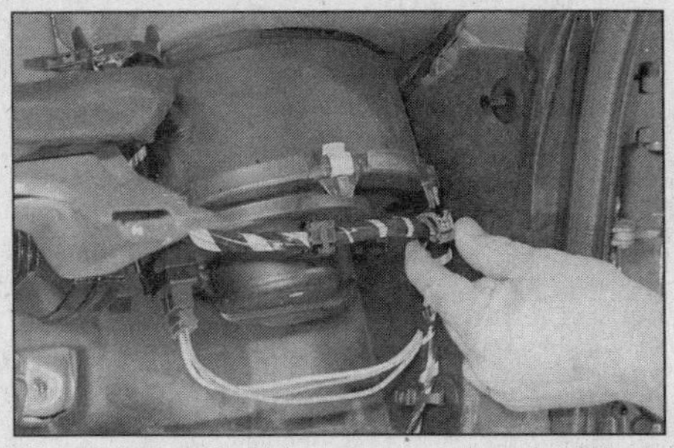

9.23a Release the wiring harness from the clips on the underside of the blower casing . . .

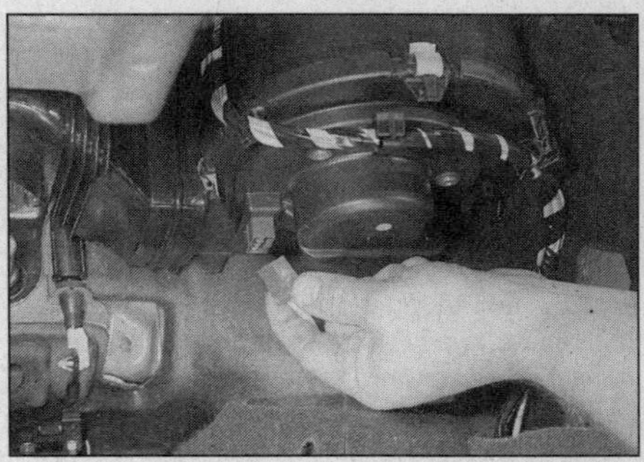

9.23b . . . then disconnect the wiring plug from the blower motor

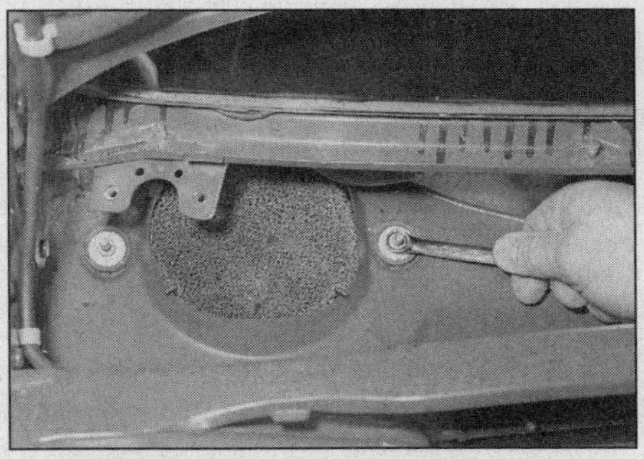

9.28a Unscrew the securing nuts . . .

9.28b . . . and lower the heater blower assembly into the vehicle interior

10 Air conditioning system - general information and precautions

General information

1 An air conditioning system is available on certain models **(see illustration)**. When activated, the air conditioning system allows air entering the passenger to be cooled giving greater control over the temperature inside the car and leading to increased comfort. The cooled air is also dehumidified, enabling faster windscreen demisting.
2 The cooling side of the system works in the same way as a domestic refrigerator. Refrigerant gas, contained in a sealed network of alloy pipes, is drawn into a belt-driven compressor, and is forced through a condenser mounted on the front of the radiator. On entering the condenser, the refrigerant changes state from gas to liquid and releases heat,

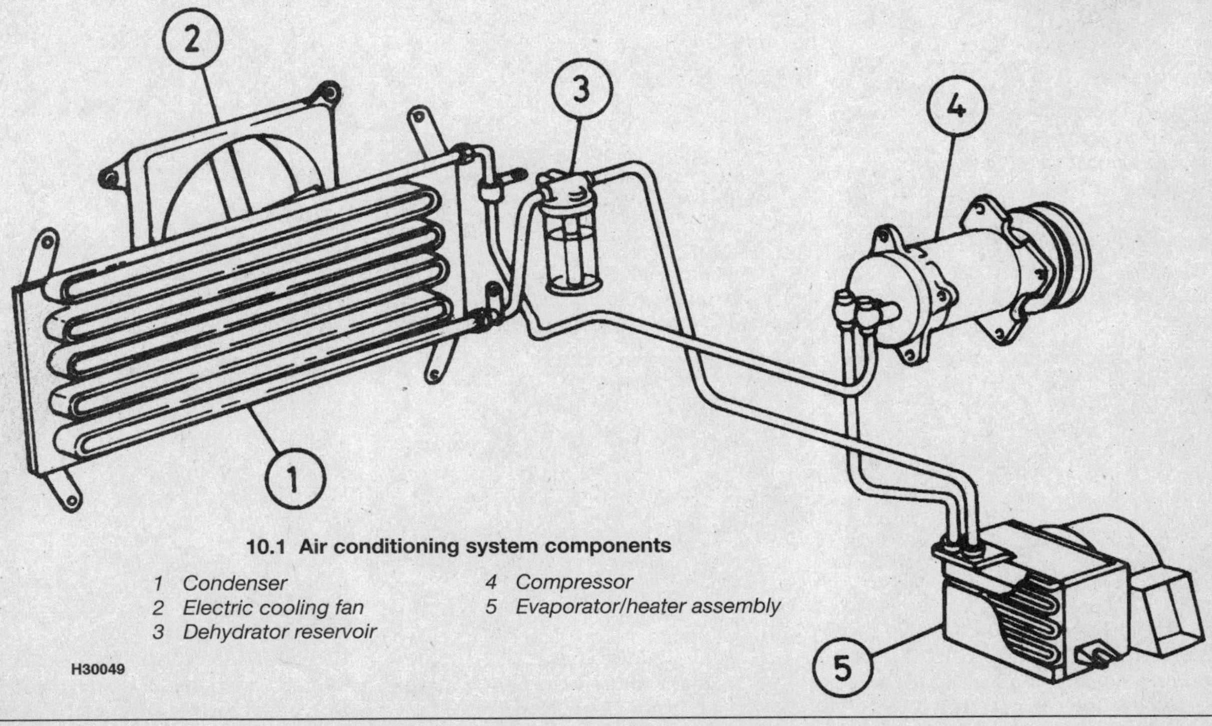

10.1 Air conditioning system components

1 Condenser
2 Electric cooling fan
3 Dehydrator reservoir
4 Compressor
5 Evaporator/heater assembly

which is absorbed by the air flowing into the engine compartment through the condenser. The liquid refrigerant passes through an expansion valve to an evaporator, where it changes from liquid under high pressure to gas under low pressure. This change in state accompanied by a drop in temperature, which cools the evaporator. Air passing through the evaporator is cooled before flowing into the air distribution unit. The refrigerant then returns to the compressor, and the cycle begins again.

3 Cool air passes to the air distribution unit, where it is mixed with hot air blown through the heater matrix, to achieve the desired temperature in the passenger compartment.

4 The heating side of the system works in the same way as on models without air conditioning (see Section 8).

5 The operation of the system is controlled by an electronic control unit, which controls the electric cooling fan, the compressor, and the facia-mounted warning light. Any problems with the system should be referred to a Citroën dealer.

Precautions

6 When an air conditioning system is fitted, it is necessary to observe special precautions whenever dealing with any part of the system, or its associated components. If for any reason the system must be disconnected, entrust this task to your Citroën dealer or a refrigeration engineer.

Warning: The air conditioning system contains a liquid refrigerant, and it is therefore dangerous to disconnect any part of the system without specialised knowledge and equipment.

7 The refrigerant is potentially dangerous, and should only be handled by qualified persons. If it is splashed onto the skin, it can cause frostbite. It is not itself poisonous, but in the presence of a naked flame (including a cigarette) it forms a poisonous gas. Uncontrolled discharging of the refrigerant is dangerous, and potentially damaging to the environment.

8 Do not operate the air conditioning system if it is known to be short of refrigerant, as this may damage the compressor.

11 Air conditioning system components - removal and refitting

Warning: Do not attempt to open the refrigerant circuit. Refer to the precautions given in Section 10.

1 The only operation which can be carried out easily without discharging the refrigerant is renewal of the compressor drivebelt. This is described in Chapter 1A or 1B (as applicable). All other operations must be referred to a Citroën dealer or an air conditioning specialist.

2 If necessary for access to other components, the compressor can be unbolted and moved aside, without disconnecting its flexible hoses, after removing the drivebelt.

Chapter 4 Part A:
Fuel system - single-point petrol injection models

Contents

Degrees of difficulty

Easy, suitable for novice with little experience	**Fairly easy,** suitable for beginner with some experience	**Fairly difficult,** suitable for competent DIY mechanic	**Difficult,** suitable for experienced DIY mechanic	**Very difficult,** suitable for expert DIY or professional

Specifications

System type

954 cc and 1124 cc models	Bosch Monopoint MA3.1

Fuel system data

Fuel pump type	Electric, immersed in tank
Fuel pump delivery rate	80 litres per hour
Fuel pump delivery pressure at full load	1.1 bar
Regulated fuel pressure	0.7 to 0.9 bar
Specified idle speed	850 ± 50 rpm (controlled by ECU, non-adjustable)
Idle mixture CO content	Less than 0.5 % (controlled by ECU, non-adjustable)

Recommended fuel

Minimum octane rating	95 RON unleaded (ie unleaded Premium) only

Torque wrench settings

	Nm	lbf ft
Inlet manifold retaining nuts	10	7
Exhaust manifold retaining nuts	15	11
Exhaust system fasteners:		
Front pipe-to-manifold nut	35	26
Front pipe-to-intermediate pipe/catalytic converter nuts	10	7
Clamping ring nuts	15	11

1 General information and precautions

The fuel system consists of a fuel tank mounted under the rear of the car (with an electric fuel pump immersed in it), a fuel filter, fuel feed and return lines, the throttle body assembly (which incorporates the single fuel injector and the fuel pressure regulator), as well as the Electronic Control Unit (ECU) and the various sensors, electrical components and related wiring. The air cleaner contains a disposable paper filter element, and incorporates a flap valve air temperature control system, which allows cold air from the outside of the car, and air warmed by the exhaust manifold, to enter the air cleaner in the correct proportions.

Refer to Section 7 for further information on the operation of the fuel injection system, and to Chapter 4D for information on the exhaust system.

Warning: Many of the procedures in this Chapter require the removal of fuel lines and connections, which may result in some fuel spillage. Before carrying out any operation on the fuel system, refer to the precautions given in "Safety first!" at the beginning of this manual, and follow them implicitly. Petrol is a highly-dangerous and volatile liquid, and the precautions necessary when handling it cannot be overstressed.

Note: *Residual pressure will remain in the fuel lines long after the vehicle was last used. Before disconnecting any fuel line, depressurise the fuel system as described in Section 8.*

4A

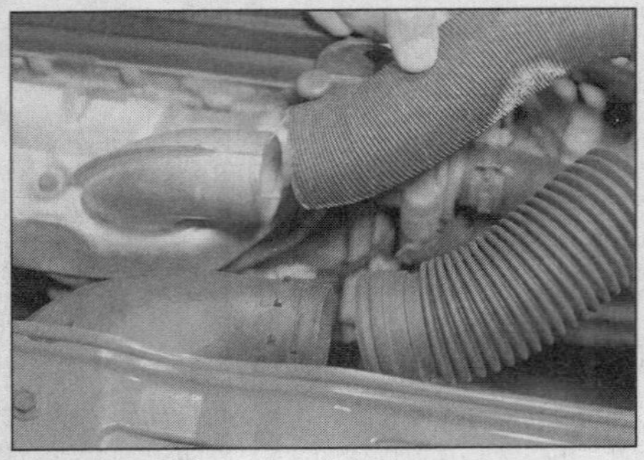
2.1 Disconnect the hot air and cold air inlet hoses from the exhaust manifold shroud and intake scoop

2.2 Disconnect the vacuum and breather hoses from the front of the air cleaner housing-to-throttle body duct

2.3 Slacken the retaining clips, then lift the moulded duct from the top of the throttle body and air cleaner housing

2 Air cleaner assembly - removal and refitting

Removal

1 Disconnect the hot air and cold air inlet hoses from the exhaust manifold shroud and intake scoop **(see illustration)**.

2 Slacken the retaining clips (where fitted) and disconnect the vacuum and breather hoses from the front of the air cleaner housing-to-throttle body duct **(see illustration)**. Where crimped-type hose clips or ties are fitted, cut and discard them; replace them with standard worm-drive hose clips or new cable ties when refitting.

2.4 Disconnect the vacuum hoses from the air temperature control valve housing

3 Slacken the retaining clips, then lift the moulded duct from the top of the throttle body and air cleaner housing **(see illustration)**. Recover the rubber sealing ring from the top of the throttle body and air cleaner housing.

4 Disconnect the air temperature control valve vacuum hoses from the end of the valve housing **(see illustration)**.

5 Rotate the quick-release fixing, to free the intake ducting from its support bracket, adjacent to the ignition coil module **(see illustration)**.

6 Lift the air cleaner intake ducting and air temperature control valve assembly from the engine compartment **(see illustration)**.

Refitting

7 Refitting is a reversal of the removal procedure, noting the following points:

a) *Examine the rubber sealing ring(s) for signs of damage or deterioration, and if necessary renew. Note that on some models, the throttle body seal is fitted with an O-ring; this should also be renewed if it is damaged.*
b) *Ensure that the air cleaner housing locating peg is correctly engaged with its mounting on the top of the transmission **(see illustration)**.*
c) *Prior to tightening the air cleaner-to-throttle body duct retaining clips, ensure that the duct is correctly seated on both the air cleaner housing and throttle body flanges.*

3 Air cleaner air temperature control system - information and component renewal

Information

1 The system is controlled by a heat-sensitive vacuum switch mounted in the end of the air cleaner housing-to-throttle body duct. When the engine is started from cold, the switch is open, and allows inlet manifold depression to act on the air temperature control valve diaphragm in the intake duct. This vacuum causes the diaphragm to rise, and draws a flap valve across the cold-air intake, thus allowing only (warmed) air from the exhaust manifold to enter the air cleaner.

2 As the temperature of the exhaust-warmed air in the air cleaner to throttle body duct rises, the wax capsule in the vacuum switch deforms and closes the switch to shut off vacuum supply to the air temperature control valve assembly. As the vacuum supply is cut, the flap is gradually lowered across the hot-air intake until, when the engine is fully warmed-up to normal operating temperature, only cold air from the front of the car is entering the air cleaner.

3 To check the system, allow the engine to cool down completely, then disconnect the intake duct from the front of the control valve assembly; the flap valve in the duct should be securely seated across the hot-air intake.

2.5 Rotate the quick-release fixing, to free the intake ducting from its support bracket, adjacent to the ignition coil module

2.6 Lift the air cleaner and intake ducting from the engine compartment

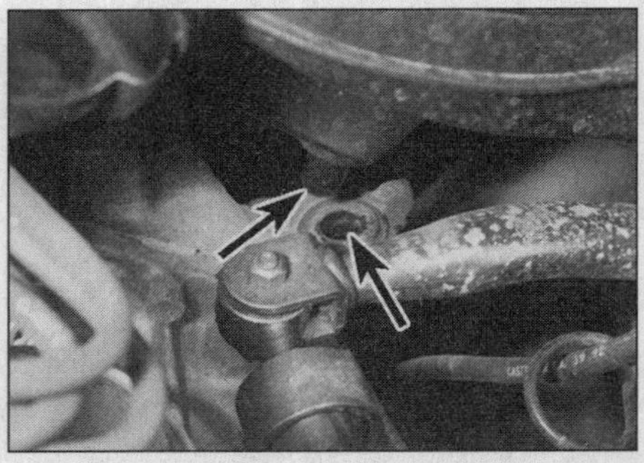
2.7 Ensure that the air cleaner housing locating peg is correctly engaged with its mounting on the top of the transmission

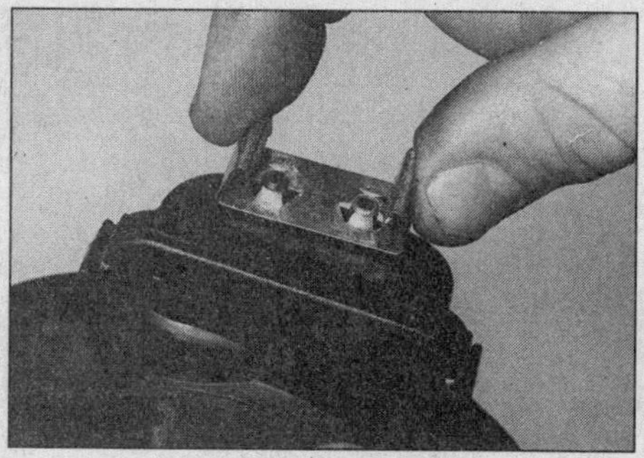

3.8a Remove the retaining clip . . .

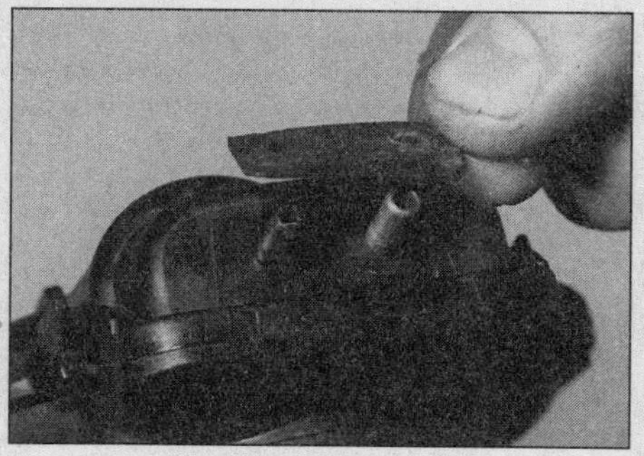

3.8b . . . and seal . . .

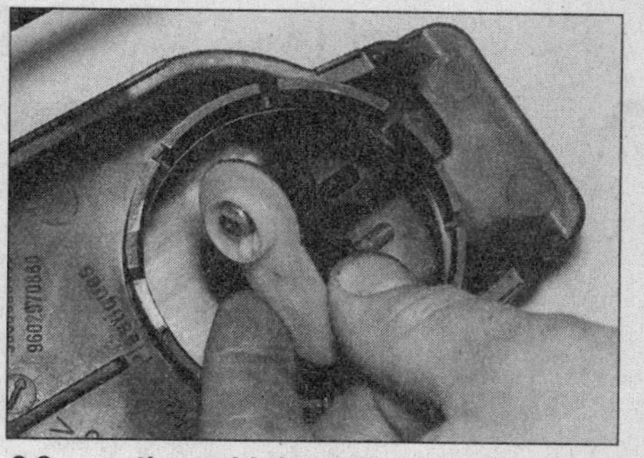

3.8c . . . then withdraw the vacuum switch from inside the duct

Start the engine; the flap should immediately rise to close off the cold-air intake, and should then lower steadily as the engine warms up until it is eventually seated across the hot-air intake again.

4 To check the vacuum switch, disconnect the vacuum pipe from the control valve when the engine is running, and place a finger over the pipe end. When the engine is cold, full inlet manifold vacuum should be present in the pipe; at normal operating temperature, there should be no vacuum in the pipe.

5 To check the air temperature control valve assembly, disconnect the intake duct from the front of the valve assembly; the flap valve should be securely seated across the hot-air intake. Disconnect the vacuum pipe, and apply vacuum to the control valve stub; the flap should rise to shut off the cold-air intake.

6 If either component is faulty, it must be renewed.

Vacuum switch - renewal

7 Remove the air cleaner housing-to-throttle body duct as described in Section 2.

8 Bend up the tangs on the switch retaining clip, then remove the clip, along with its seal, and withdraw the switch from inside the duct **(see illustrations)**. Examine the seal for signs of damage or deterioration, and renew if necessary.

9 When refitting, ensure that the switch and duct mating surfaces are clean and dry, and position the switch inside the duct.

10 Fit the seal over the switch unions, and refit the retaining clip. Ensure that the switch is pressed firmly against the duct, and secure it in position by bending down the retaining clip tangs.

11 Refit the duct as described in Section 2.

Air temperature control valve - renewal

12 Disconnect the vacuum pipe from the air temperature control valve, then slacken the retaining clips securing the intake ducts to the valve.

13 Disconnect both intake ducts and the hot-air intake hose from the control valve assembly.

14 Turn the quick release fixing anticlockwise to release the control valve mounting bracket from the left hand side of the ignition coil assembly. Remove the control valve and mounting bracket from the engine compartment.

15 Refitting is the reverse of the removal procedure, noting that the air temperature control valve assembly can only be renewed as a complete unit.

4 Accelerator cable - removal, refitting and adjustment

Removal

1 Free the accelerator inner cable from the throttle body throttle cam **(see illustration)**.

2 Pull the cable outer out from its mounting bracket rubber grommet **(see illustration)**. Ensure that the plain washer and spring clip remain in position.

3 Working back along the length of the cable, free it from any relevant retaining clips or ties, whilst noting its correct routing.

4 Working inside the vehicle, undo the push-in clips and remove the undercover panel from the driver's side of the facia.

5 Reach up behind the facia, then depress the retaining clips with a pair of pliers and detach the inner cable from the top of the accelerator pedal **(see illustration)**.

6 Release the rubber grommet from the bulkhead-mounted bracket, and tie a length of string to the end of the inner cable.

7 Return to the engine compartment, and release the cable outer retainer from the engine compartment bulkhead. Withdraw the cable through the bulkhead aperture, until the end of the cable appears, then untie the string and leave it in position. The string can then be used to draw the cable back into position when refitting.

Refitting

8 Tie the string to the end of the cable, then use the string to draw the cable into position through the bulkhead. Once the cable end is visible, untie the string.

9 Align the cable outer retainer lug with the cut-out in the bulkhead, then securely clip the retainer into position.

10 Working inside the car under the facia, press the rubber grommet into the bulkhead-

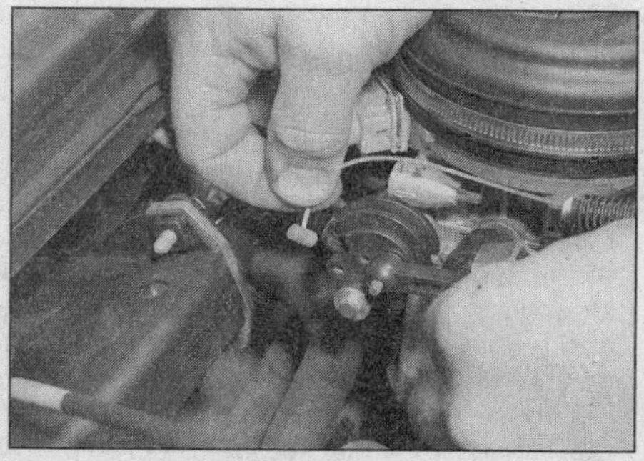

4.1 Free the accelerator inner cable from the throttle body throttle cam

4.2 Withdraw the accelerator cable outer from its mounting bracket rubber grommet

4.5 Detach the inner cable from the top of the accelerator pedal by depressing the retaining clips with a pair of pliers (facia removed for clarity)

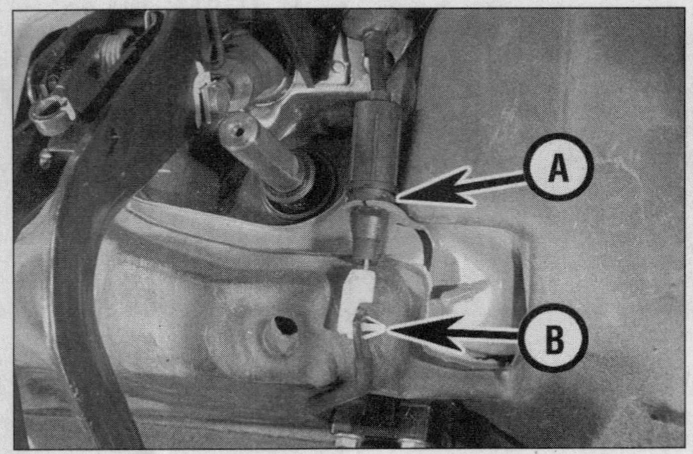

4.10 Press the rubber grommet (A) into the bulkhead-mounted bracket, then clip the cable inner into the lug (B) at the top of the accelerator pedal (facia removed for clarity)

4.14 Adjust the accelerator cable by repositioning the spring clip (see text)

mounted bracket, then clip the cable inner into the lug at the top of the accelerator pedal **(see illustration)**.

11 Make sure that the cable is securely retained, then refit the facia undercover panel.

12 From within the engine compartment, ensure that the cable outer is correctly seated in the bulkhead grommet. Work along the cable, securing it in position with all the relevant retaining clips and ties, whilst ensuring that it is correctly routed.

13 Pass the cable outer through its throttle body mounting bracket, so that the plain washer and spring clip rest against the rubber grommet. Reconnect the cable inner to the throttle cam. Adjust the cable as described in the following sub-section.

Adjustment

14 Remove the spring clip from the accelerator outer cable then, ensuring that the throttle cam is fully against its stop, gently pull the cable out of its grommet until all free play is removed from the inner cable. With the cable held in this position, ensure that the flat washer is pressed securely against the grommet, then fit the spring clip to the third outer cable groove visible in front of the rubber grommet and washer **(see illustration)**. This will leave an amount of freeplay in the cable inner, which is necessary to ensure correct operation of the idle control stepper motor.

15 Have an assistant depress the accelerator pedal fully and check that the throttle cam opens to its full throttle stop peg. Release the pedal and check that the cam then returns smoothly to its idle stop peg.

Note: *On models with automatic transmission it will now be necessary to 'initialise' the transmission control system ECU after adjusting the accelerator cable; refer to Chapter 7B for details.*

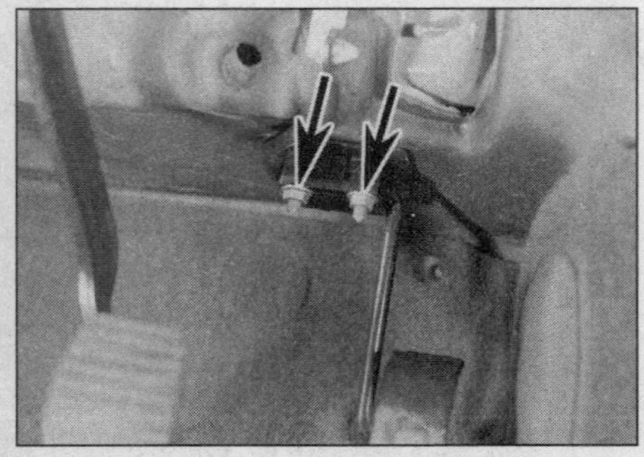

5.3 Slacken and remove the two nuts (arrowed) securing the pedal bearing to the bulkhead

5 Accelerator pedal - removal and refitting

Removal

1 Undo the retaining nuts, and remove the undercover panel from the driver's side of the facia.

2 Depress the retaining clips, and detach the inner cable from the top of the accelerator pedal.

3 Slacken and remove the two nuts securing the pedal bearing to the bulkhead **(see illustration)**. Slide off the outer part of the bearing, then withdraw the pedal from behind the facia, and slide off the inner part of the bearing.

4 Examine the bearing and pedal pivot points for signs of wear, and renew as necessary.

Refitting

5 Refitting is a reversal of the removal procedure, applying a little multi-purpose grease to the pedal pivot point. On completion, adjust the accelerator cable as described in Section 4.

6 Unleaded petrol - general information and usage

Note: *The information given in this Chapter is correct at the time of writing, and applies only to fuels currently available in the UK. If updated information is thought to be required, check with a Citroën dealer. If travelling abroad, consult one of the motoring organisations (or a similar authority) for advice on the fuels available, and their suitability for your vehicle.*

All Citroën Saxo single-point injection models are designed to run on fuel with a minimum octane rating of 95 (RON). All models are equipped with catalytic converters, and therefore must be run on unleaded fuel **only - under no circumstances** should leaded fuel be used.

RON and MON are different testing standards; RON stands for Research Octane Number (also written as RM), while MON stands for Motor Octane Number (also written as MM).

7 Fuel injection system - general information

1 The Bosch Monopoint MA3.1 engine management (fuel injection/ignition) system is fitted to all 954 and 1124 cc models **(see illustration)**. The system is a full engine management system, controlling both the fuel injection and ignition functions (refer to Chapter 5B for information on the ignition side of the system). The system employs closed-loop fuelling by means of a catalytic converter and a Lambda sensor, to minimise exhaust gas emissions. An evaporative loss emission control system is also integrated, to minimise the escape of unburned hydrocarbons into the atmosphere from the fuel tank. The overall operation of the system is as follows.

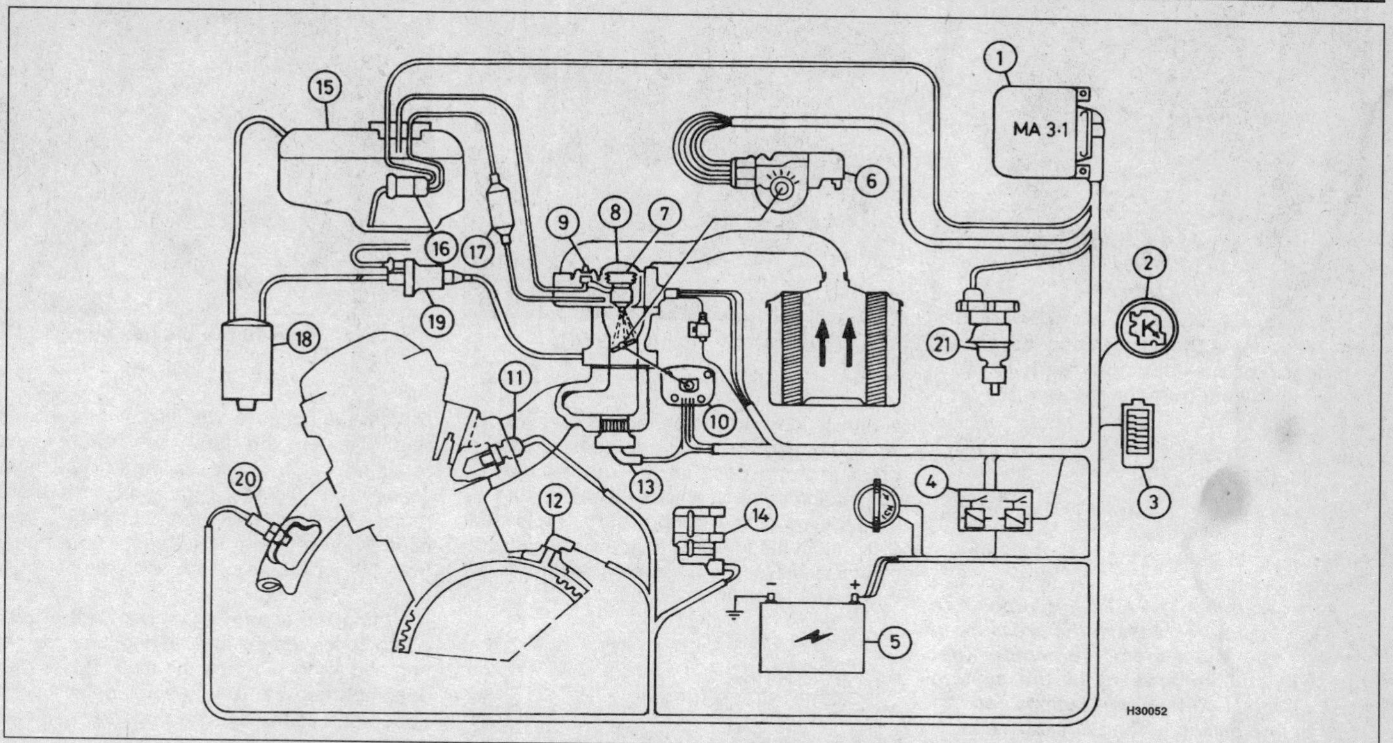

7.1 Bosch Monopoint MA3.1 engine management system schematic

1 *ECU*
2 *Warning lamp*
3 *Diagnostic connector*
4 *Relay*
5 *Battery*
6 *Idle control stepper motor*
7 *Injector*
8 *Inlet air temperature sensor*
9 *Fuel pressure regulator*
10 *Throttle potentiometer*
11 *Coolant temperature sensor*
12 *Crankshaft speed/TDC sensor*
13 *Manifold heater*
14 *Ignition coil module*
15 *Fuel tank*
16 *Fuel pump*
17 *Fuel filter*
18 *Charcoal canister*
19 *Purge valve*
20 *Lambda sensor*
21 *Vehicle speed sensor*

2 The fuel pump, which is immersed in the fuel tank, pumps fuel from the fuel tank to the fuel injector, via a filter mounted underneath the rear of the vehicle. Fuel supply pressure is controlled by the pressure regulator in the throttle body assembly, which lifts to allow excess fuel to return to the tank when the optimum operating pressure of the fuel system is exceeded.

3 The electrical control system consists of the ECU, along with the following sensors and actuators:

a) Throttle potentiometer - informs the ECU of the throttle valve position, and the rate of throttle opening/closing.

b) Coolant temperature sensor - informs the ECU of engine temperature.

c) Intake air temperature sensor - informs the ECU of the temperature of the air passing through the throttle body.

d) Lambda sensor - informs the ECU of the oxygen content of the exhaust gases.

e) Throttle position switch (built into the idle speed stepper motor) - informs the ECU when the throttle valve is closed (ie. if the accelerator pedal is fully released).

f) Crankshaft sensor to inform the ECU of engine speed and crankshaft angular position.

g) Vehicle speed sensor - (1124cc models only) informs the ECU of the vehicle's road speed, allowing manual gear selection to be monitored.

h) Idle control stepper motor - controls the position of the throttle during idling to maintain a constant engine idle speed.

i) Inlet manifold heater - raises the temperature of the inlet manifold to minimise fuel condensation.

j) Instrument panel-mounted warning indicator - illuminated by the ECU when a malfunction is detected.

k) Relay pack - two separate relays mounted in one housing provide separate current supplies to the fuel pump and ECU, sensors and actuators.

4 Signals from each of the sensors are compared by the ECU and, based on this information, the ECU selects the response appropriate to those values, and controls the fuel injector (varying its pulse width - the length of time the injector is held open - to provide a richer or weaker mixture, as appropriate). The mixture and idle speed are constantly varied by the ECU, to provide the best settings for cranking, starting (with either a hot or cold engine) and engine warm-up, idle, cruising and acceleration.

5 The ECU also has full control over the engine idle speed via a stepper motor which is fitted to the throttle body. The motor pushrod rests against a cam on the throttle valve spindle. When the throttle valve is closed (accelerator pedal released), the ECU uses the motor to vary the opening of the throttle valve, and so control the idle speed.

6 The exhaust and evaporative loss emission control systems are described in more detail in Chapter 4D.

7 If there is any abnormality in any of the readings obtained from either the coolant temperature sensor, the intake air temperature sensor or the Lambda sensor, the ECU enters its back-up mode. If this happens, the sensor signal is overridden, and the ECU assumes a pre-programmed 'back-up' value which will allow the engine to continue running, albeit at reduced efficiency. If the ECU enters this back-up mode, the warning lamp on the instrument panel will be illuminated, and the relevant fault code will be stored in the ECU memory.

8 If the warning light illuminates, the vehicle should be taken to a Citroën dealer at the earliest opportunity. Once there, a complete test of the engine management system can be carried out, using a special electronic diagnostic test unit which is simply plugged into the system's diagnostic connector.

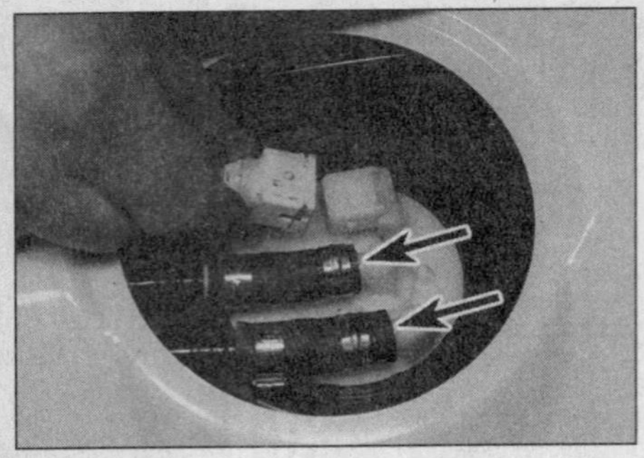

9.4 **Disconnect the wiring connector, then release the fuel feed and return hoses (arrowed) from the fuel pump**

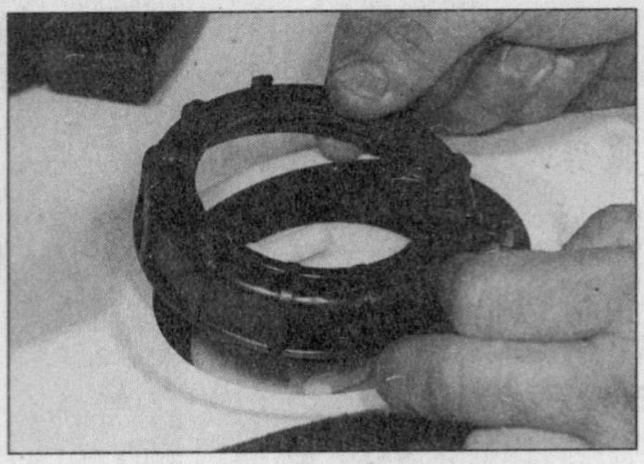

9.6 **Unscrew the locking ring . . .**

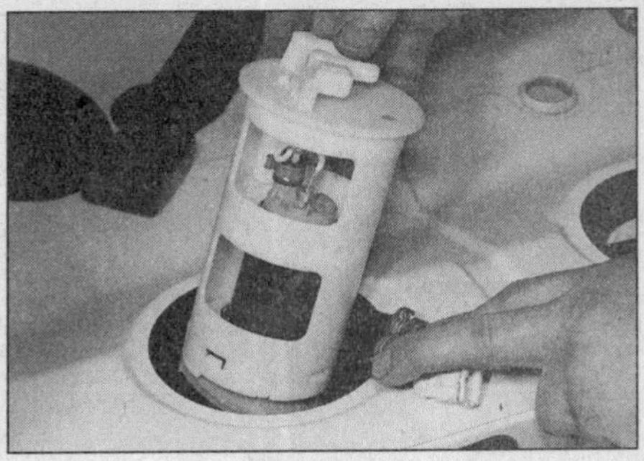

9.7a **. . . then lift out the fuel pump . . .**

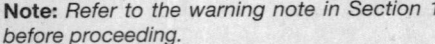

8 Fuel system - depressurisation

Note: *Refer to the warning note in Section 1 before proceeding.*

Warning: The following procedure will merely relieve the pressure in the fuel system - remember that fuel will still be present in the system components, and take precautions accordingly before disconnecting any of them.

1 The fuel system referred to in this Section is defined as the tank-mounted fuel pump, the fuel filter, the fuel injector and the pressure regulator in the injector housing, and the metal pipes and flexible hoses of the fuel lines between these components. All these contain fuel, which will be under pressure while the engine is running and/or while the ignition is switched on. The pressure will remain for some time after the ignition has been switched off, and must be relieved before any of these components are disturbed for servicing work.

2 Ensure that the engine has cooled completely before starting work. Disconnect the battery negative cable and position it away from the terminal.

3 Place a suitable container beneath the relevant connection/union to be disconnected, and have a large rag ready to soak up any escaping fuel not being caught by the container.

4 Slowly loosen the connection or union nut (as applicable) to avoid a sudden release of pressure, and position the rag around the connection to catch any fuel spray which may be expelled. Once the pressure is released, disconnect the fuel line. Plug the openings, to minimise fuel loss and prevent the entry of dirt into the fuel system.

9 Fuel pump - removal and refitting

Note: *Refer to the warning note in Section 1 before proceeding.*

Removal

1 Disconnect the battery negative lead.

2 For access to the fuel pump, fold the rear seat cushion forwards.

3 Using a screwdriver, carefully prise the plastic access cover from the floor to expose the fuel pump (the pump is located under the access hatch on the right hand side of the fuel tank, viewed facing the front of the vehicle).

Note: *On later models, the fuel gauge sender unit is integral with the fuel pump. On early models, the fuel gauge sender is a separate unit and is located underneath the left hand access hatch.*

4 Disconnect the wiring connector(s) from the fuel pump **(see illustration)**. Tape the connector to the vehicle body, to prevent it falling down behind the tank.

5 Mark the hoses for identification purposes, then slacken the feed and return hose retaining clips. Where crimped-type hose clips are fitted, cut the clips and discard them; replace them with standard worm-drive hose clips when refitting. Disconnect both hoses from the top of the pump, and plug the hose ends.

6 Noting the alignment marks on the tank, pump cover and the locking ring, unscrew the ring and remove it from the tank. This is best accomplished by using a screwdriver on the raised ribs of the locking ring. Carefully tap the screwdriver to turn the ring anti-clockwise until it can be unscrewed by hand **(see illustration)**.

7 Carefully lift the fuel pump assembly out of the fuel tank, taking great care not to damage the filter, or to spill fuel onto the interior of the vehicle. On earlier models, guide the sender unit float through the fuel tank aperture, taking care to avoid damaging it. Recover the rubber sealing ring and discard it; a new one must be used on refitting **(see illustrations)**.

8 Note that the fuel pump assembly is only available as a complete assembly; no individual components are available separately.

Refitting

9 Ensure that the fuel pump pick-up filter is clean and free of debris.

10 Fit a new sealing ring to the top of the fuel tank. Carefully manoeuvre the pump assembly into the fuel tank, aligning the mark noted on removal.

11 Refit the locking ring, tightening it so that its mark is correctly aligned with the line on the fuel tank, as noted prior to removal **(see illustration)**.

12 Reconnect the feed and return hoses to the top of the fuel pump, using the marks made on removal to ensure that they are correctly reconnected, and securely tighten their retaining clips.

13 Reconnect the pump wiring connector.

14 Reconnect the battery negative terminal, and start the engine. Check the fuel pump feed and return hose unions for signs of leakage.

15 If all is well, refit the plastic access cover and fold back the rear seat cushion.

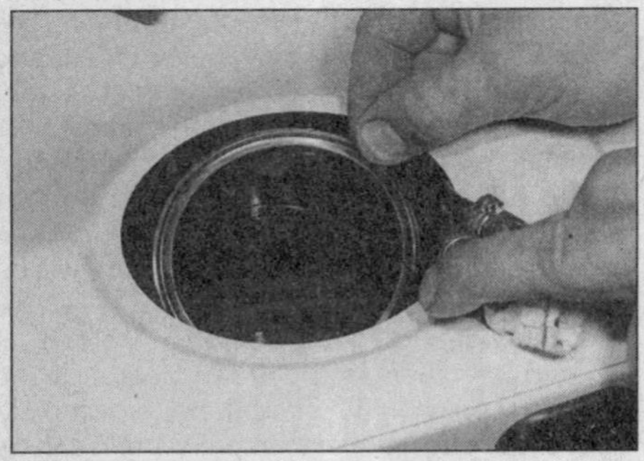

9.7b **. . . and recover the rubber sealing ring**

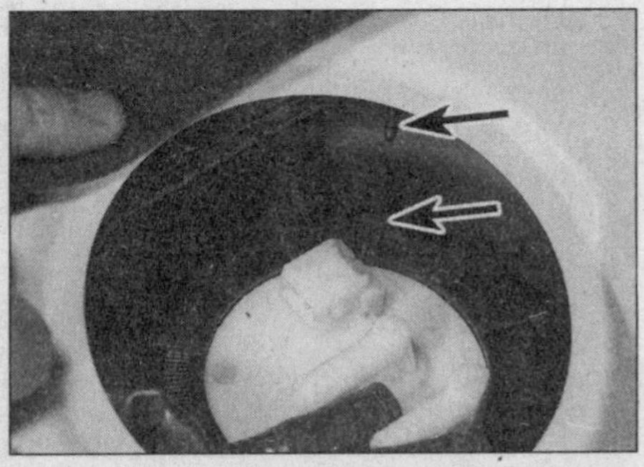

9.11 **When refitting, tighten the locking ring until it is correctly aligned with the fuel tank mark (arrowed)**

10 Fuel gauge sender unit - removal and refitting

1 On later models, the fuel gauge sender unit is integral with the fuel pump; refer to the information given in Section 9. On early models, the fuel gauge sender is a separate unit - proceed as described in the next sub-Section.

Removal

Note: *Refer to the warning note in Section 1 before proceeding.*

2 Disconnect the battery negative cable and position it away from the terminal.

3 For access to the sender unit, fold the rear seat cushion forwards.

4 Using a screwdriver, carefully prise the plastic access cover from the floor to expose the sender unit **(see illustration)**; the sender unit is located under the left-hand cover, viewed facing towards the front of the vehicle.

5 Disconnect the wiring connector from the sender unit. Tape the connector to the vehicle body, to prevent it disappearing behind the tank. Noting the alignment marks on the tank, sender unit and the locking ring, unscrew the ring and remove it from the tank. This is best accomplished by using a screwdriver on the raised ribs of the locking ring. Carefully tap the screwdriver to turn the ring anti-clockwise until it can be unscrewed by hand

6 Carefully lift the sender unit from the top of the fuel tank, taking great care not to bend the sender unit float arm, or to spill fuel onto the interior of the vehicle. Recover the rubber sealing ring and discard it; a new one must be used when refitting **(see illustration)**.

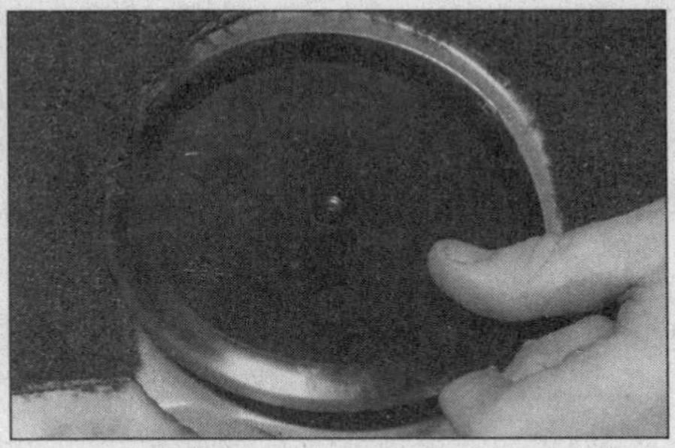

10.4 Carefully prise the plastic access cover from the floor to expose the sender unit

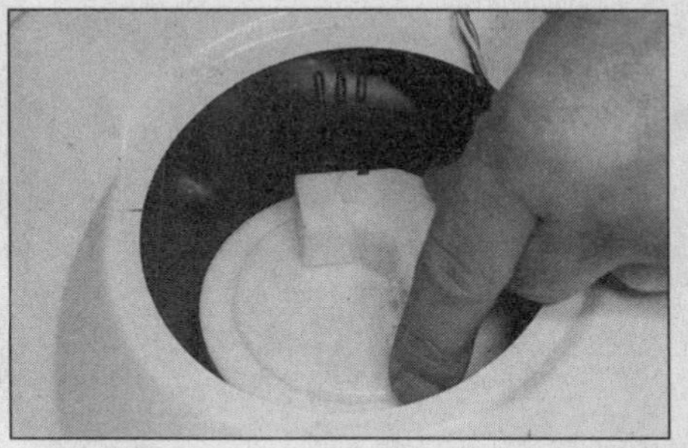

10.6 Removing the fuel gauge sender unit

Refitting

7 Refitting is a reversal of the removal procedure noting the following points:

a) *Prior to refitting, fit a new rubber sealing ring to the fuel tank.*

b) *Refit the sender unit to the tank, aligning its arrow with the centre of the three alignment marks on the fuel tank. Hold the sender in position, then refit the locking ring and tighten it until its mark is correctly aligned with the centre of the three fuel tank marks. All three marks should now be in alignment as noted prior to removal; misalignment will result in inaccurate fuel gauge readings.*

11 Fuel tank - removal and refitting

Note: *Refer to the warning note in Section 1 before proceeding.*

Removal

1 Before removing the fuel tank, all fuel must be drained from the tank. Since a fuel tank drain plug is not provided, it is therefore preferable to carry out the removal operation when the tank is nearly empty. Before proceeding, disconnect the battery negative cable, and syphon or hand-pump the remaining fuel from the tank.

2 Remove the exhaust system as described in Chapter 4D. Where applicable, undo the fixings and remove the heat shield panelling.

3 Free both handbrake cables from their retaining clips on the base of the fuel tank.

4 Disconnect the wiring connector and fuel hoses from the fuel gauge sender unit and/or fuel pump unit, as described in Section 9 and/or Section 10.

5 Unclip the fuel filter retaining strap, and free the filter from the left-hand side of the fuel tank.

6 Working at the right-hand side of the fuel tank, release the retaining clips, then disconnect the filler neck vent pipe and main filler neck hose from the fuel tank/filler neck. Where necessary, also disconnect the breather hose(s). Some breather hoses are joined to the tank with quick-release fittings; to disconnect these fittings, slide the cover along the hose, then depress the centre ring and pull the hose out of its fitting.

7 Place a trolley jack with an interposed block of wood beneath the tank, then raise the jack until it is just supporting the weight of the tank.

8 Slacken and remove the two retaining nuts and washers, then incline the fuel tank towards the rear of the car and slowly lower it out of position, disconnecting any other relevant vent pipes as they become accessible (where necessary). Remove the tank from underneath the vehicle, and recover the tank mounting rubbers, noting their correct fitted positions.

9 If the tank is contaminated with sediment or water, remove the sender unit and/or fuel pump unit (as applicable) as described in Section 9 and/or Section 10 and swill the tank out with clean fuel. The tank is injection-moulded from a synthetic material, and if damaged, it should be renewed. However, in certain cases, it may be possible to have small leaks or minor damage repaired. Seek the advice of a suitable specialist.

Refitting

10 Refitting is the reverse of the removal procedure, noting the following points:

a) *When lifting the tank back into position, make sure that the mounting rubbers are correctly positioned, and take great care to ensure that none of the hoses become trapped between the tank and vehicle body.*

b) *Ensure that all pipes and hoses are correctly routed, and securely held in position with their retaining clips.*

c) *On completion, refill the tank with fuel, and check for signs of leakage prior to taking the vehicle out on the road.*

12 Throttle body - removal and refitting

Note: *Refer to the warning note in Section 1 before proceeding.*

Removal

1 Disconnect the battery negative cable and position it away from the terminal.

2 Remove the air cleaner housing-to-throttle body duct, using the information given in Section 2. Slacken and withdraw the securing screws, then remove the plastic adapter ring and recover the O-ring seal **(see illustrations)**.

12.2a Slacken and withdraw the securing screws . . .

12.2b . . . then remove the plastic adapter ring and recover the O-ring seal

4A

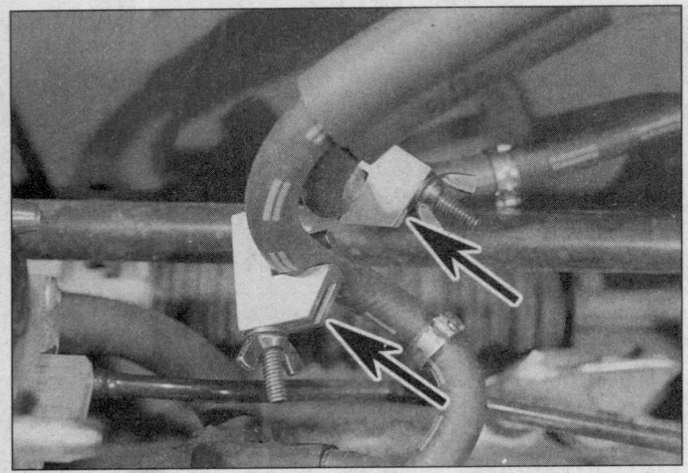

12.4a Clamp off the fuel supply and return hoses; use proprietary clamps (arrowed) to avoid pinching the hoses

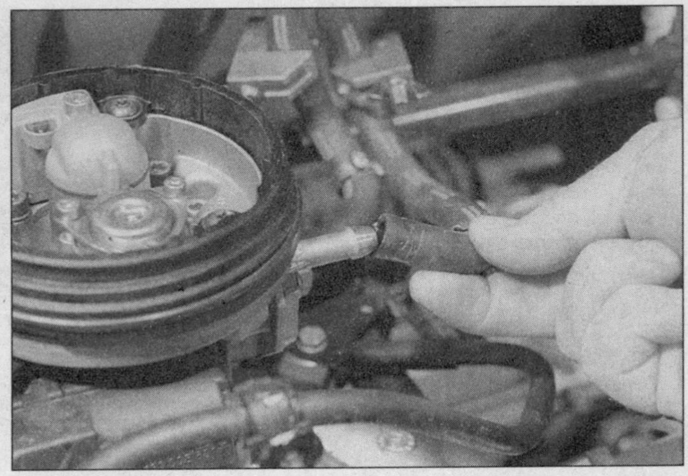

12.4b Release the retaining clips and disconnect the fuel hoses from the throttle body assembly

3 Depress the retaining clips, and uncouple the wiring connectors from the throttle potentiometer, the idle control stepper motor, and the injector wiring loom connector; refer to Section 14 for details.

4 Bearing in mind the information given in Section 8 about depressurising the fuel system, clamp off the fuel supply and return hoses, then release the retaining clips and disconnect the fuel hoses from the throttle body assembly **(see illustrations)**. If the original crimped-type clips are still fitted, cut the clips and discard them; replace them with standard worm-drive hose clips on refitting.

12.7a Slacken and remove the securing bolts . . .

5 Disconnect the accelerator inner cable from the throttle cam, then withdraw the outer cable from the mounting bracket, along with its flat washer and spring clip; refer to Section 4 for details.

6 Where necessary, disconnect the air temperature control vacuum hose and purge valve vacuum hose from the throttle body (as applicable).

7 Slacken and remove the bolts securing the throttle body assembly to the inlet manifold, then remove the assembly along with its gasket **(see illustrations)**.

8 If necessary, with the throttle body removed, undo the retaining screws and separate the upper and lower sections, noting the insulating spacer and gaskets, or the single gasket (as applicable) fitted between the two.

Refitting

9 Refitting is a reverse of the removal procedure, bearing in mind the following points:

a) Where applicable, ensure that the mating surfaces of the upper and lower throttle body sections are clean and dry, then fit the insulating spacer and new gaskets, or a new gasket (as applicable) and reassemble the two, tightening the retaining screws securely.

b) Ensure that the mating surfaces of the manifold and throttle body are clean and dry, then fit a new gasket. Securely tighten the throttle body retaining bolts.

c) Ensure that all hoses are correctly reconnected and, where necessary, that their retaining clips are securely tightened.

*d) Fit a new air cleaner duct O-ring seal if the existing one is in poor condition **(see illustration)**.*

e) On completion, adjust the accelerator cable using the information given in Section 4.

13 Fuel injection system - testing and adjustment

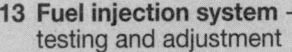

Testing

1 If a fault appears in the fuel injection system, first ensure that all the system wiring connectors are securely connected and free of corrosion. Then ensure that the fault is not due to poor maintenance; ie, check that the air cleaner filter element is clean, the spark plugs are in good condition and correctly gapped, the valve clearances are correctly adjusted, the cylinder compression pressures are correct,

12.7b . . . then remove the throttle body assembly from the inlet manifold . . .

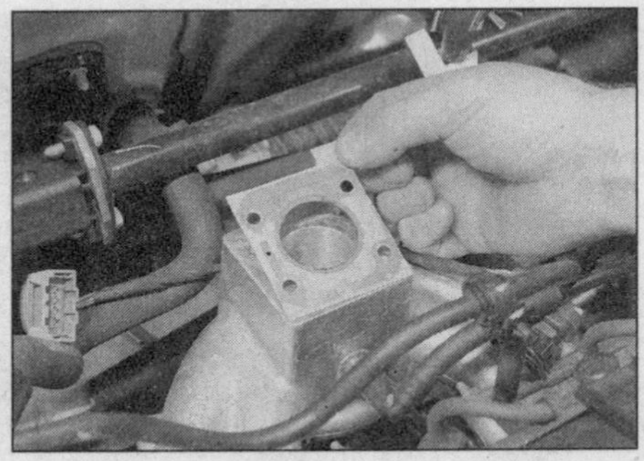

12.7c . . . and recover the gasket

12.9 Fit a new air cleaner duct O-ring seal, if necessary

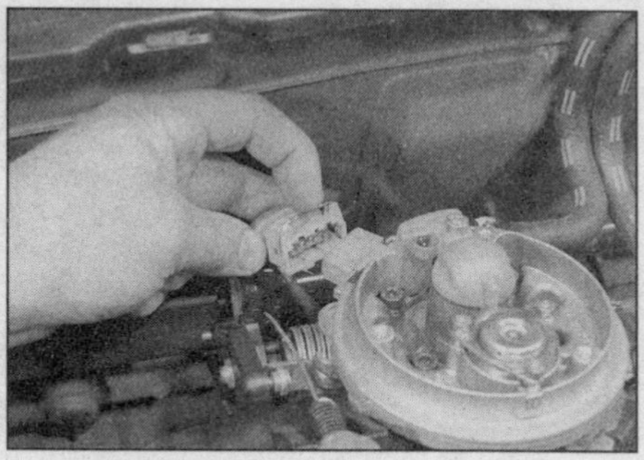
14.3 Unplug the wiring harness from the fuel injector at the multiway connector

14.4a Slacken and withdraw the securing screw . . .

14.4b . . . then remove the injector cap . . .

14.4c . . . recover the gasket . . .

14.4d . . . and lift out the injector

and that the engine breather hoses are clear and un-damaged, referring to Chapters 1A and 2A for further information.

2 If these checks fail to reveal the cause of the problem, the vehicle should be taken to a suitably equipped Citroën dealer for testing. A wiring block connector is incorporated in the engine management circuit, into which a special electronic diagnostic tester can be plugged; the connector is clipped onto the side of the ECU mounting bracket. The tester will locate the fault quickly and simply, alleviating the need to test all the system components individually, which is a time-consuming operation that carries a high risk of damaging the ECU.

Adjustment

3 Experienced home mechanics with a considerable amount of skill and equipment (including a good-quality tachometer and a good-quality, carefully-calibrated exhaust gas analyser) may be able to *check* the exhaust CO level and the idle speed. However, if these are found to be in need of *adjustment*, the car **must** be taken to a suitably-equipped Citroën dealer.

4 On the Bosch Monopoint system, no adjustment is possible without the aid of dedicated test equipment. Should the idle speed or exhaust gas CO level be incorrect, then a fault may be present in the fuel injection system.

14 Bosch Monopoint system components - removal and refitting

Fuel injector

Note: *Refer to the warning note in Section 1 before proceeding. If a faulty injector is suspected, before condemning the injector, it is worth trying the effect of one of the proprietary injector-cleaning treatments.*

1 Disconnect the battery negative cable and position it away from the terminal.

2 Remove the air cleaner-to-throttle body duct using the information given in Section 2, then remove the plastic adapter ring as described in Section 12.

3 Unplug the wiring harness from the fuel injector at the multiway connector **(see illustration)**.

4 Pad the area around and above the injector cap with absorbent rag, to prevent fuel spray. Slacken and withdraw the securing screw, then remove the injector cap, recover the gasket and lift out the injector **(see illustrations)**.

5 Refitting is a reversal of the removal procedure, ensuring that the injector sealing ring(s) and injector cap O-ring are in good condition. When refitting the injector cap, ensure that the injector pins are correctly aligned with the cap terminals **(see illustration)**; the cap is shaped so that it can only be refitted the correct way around.

Fuel pressure regulator

Note 1: *Refer to the warning note in Section 1 before proceeding.*

Note 2: *At the time of writing, the fuel pressure regulator assembly is not available separately. If the fuel pressure regulator assembly is faulty, the complete throttle body assembly must be renewed. Refer to a Citroën dealer for further information on parts availability. Although the unit can be dismantled for cleaning, if required, it should not be disturbed unless absolutely necessary.*

6 Disconnect the battery negative cable and position it away from the terminal.

7 Remove the air cleaner-to-throttle body duct, referring to the information given in Section 2.

8 Using a marker pen, make alignment marks between the regulator cover and throttle body. Slacken and remove the cover retaining screws **(see illustration)**.

9 As the screws are slackened, place an absorbent rag over the cover, to catch any fuel spray which may be released.

10 Lift off the cover, then remove the spring

14.5 When refitting the injector cap, ensure that the injector pins (arrowed) are correctly aligned with the cap terminals

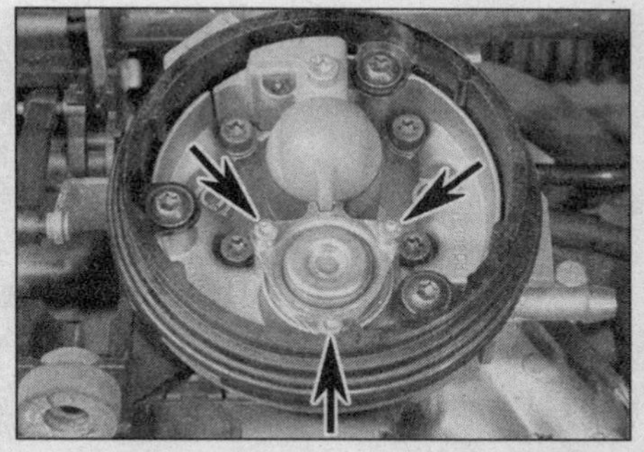
14.8 Slacken and remove the fuel pressure regulator cover retaining screws (arrowed)

14.14 Unplug the wiring connector from the idle control stepper motor

14.17 Unplug the wiring from the throttle potentiometer

14.21 Remove the injector cap securing screw; the inlet air temperature sensor (arrowed) is an integral part of the cap

and withdraw the diaphragm, noting its correct fitted orientation.

11 Remove all traces of dirt, and examine the diaphragm for signs of splitting; renew if necessary.

12 Refitting is a reverse of the removal procedure, ensuring that the diaphragm and cover are fitted the correct way around and the retaining screws are securely tightened.

Idle control stepper motor

13 Disconnect the battery negative able and position it away from the terminal.

14 Depress the retaining clip, and disconnect the wiring connector from the idle control stepper motor **(see illustration)**.

15 Undo the retaining screws, and remove the motor from the throttle body. There are three securing screws; two on the lower edge of the motor casing and one on the upper edge at the right hand side (as viewed from the front of the engine compartment).

16 Refitting is a reverse of the removal procedure, ensuring that the motor retaining screws are securely tightened.

Throttle potentiometer

17 The throttle potentiometer is a sealed unit, and under **no** circumstances should it be disturbed. For this reason, on some models, it is secured to the throttle body assembly by tamperproof screws. If the throttle potentiometer is faulty, the complete throttle body assembly must be renewed. Refer to your Citroën dealer for further information. The illustration shows the wiring connector being unplugged for the purposes of the throttle body removal **(see illustration)**.

Intake air temperature sensor

Note 1: *Refer to the warning note in Section 1 before proceeding.*

Note 2: *On some later models, at the time of writing, the intake air temperature sensor is not available separately. If the sensor is faulty, the complete throttle body assembly must be renewed. Refer to your Citroën dealer for further information on parts availability.*

18 The intake air temperature sensor is an integral part of the throttle body injector cap. To remove the cap, first disconnect the battery negative terminal, then remove the air cleaner-to-throttle body duct using the information given in Section 2.

19 Undo the three retaining screws, and remove the circular plastic ring from the top of the throttle body. Recover its sealing ring.

20 Depress the retaining clip, and unplug the wiring connector from the injector wiring connector.

21 Undo the injector cap retaining screw, then lift off the cap and recover the gasket **(see illustration)**. As the cap screw is slackened, place a rag over the injector, to catch any fuel spray which may be released.

22 Refitting is a reversal of the removal procedure, ensuring that the injector cap gasket and/or O-ring is in good condition. Take care to ensure that the cap terminals are correctly aligned with the injector pin, and securely tighten the cap retaining screw.

Coolant temperature sensor

23 Refer to the information given in Chapter 3.

Electronic control unit (ECU)

24 The ECU is located on the right-hand side of the engine compartment, underneath a large plastic cover.

25 To remove the ECU, first disconnect the battery negative cable and position it away from the terminal.

26 Unfasten the securing clips and release the purge valve vacuum hose from the side of the ECU plastic cover. Unclip the cover from the mounting plate, then lift the retaining clip and disconnect the wiring connector from the ECU. Slacken and remove the ECU retaining bolts, and remove it from the vehicle. Alternatively, unbolt the mounting bracket from the bodywork and remove it complete with the ECU **(see illustrations)**.

27 Refitting is a reverse of the removal procedure, ensuring that the wiring connector is securely reconnected.

Fuel injection system relay unit

28 The relay unit is clipped onto the underside of the ECU mounting plate, on the right-hand side of the engine compartment **(see illustration)**.

29 To remove the relay unit, first disconnect the battery negative cable and position it away from the terminal.

30 Remove the ECU mounting bracket as

14.26a Release the purge valve vacuum hose from the side of the ECU plastic cover

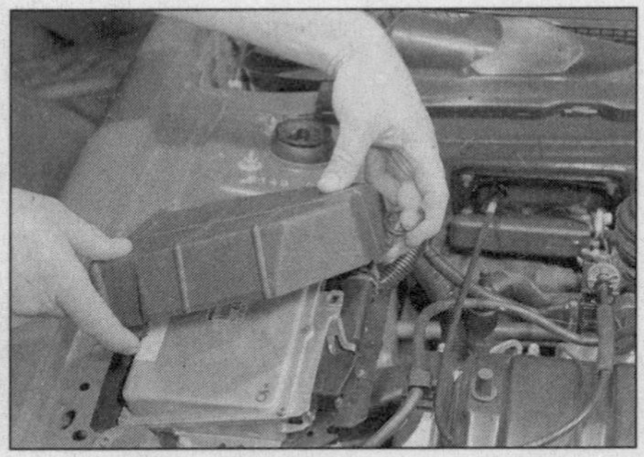

14.26b Unclip the cover from the mounting plate

14.26c Unbolt the mounting bracket from the bodywork and remove it complete with the ECU

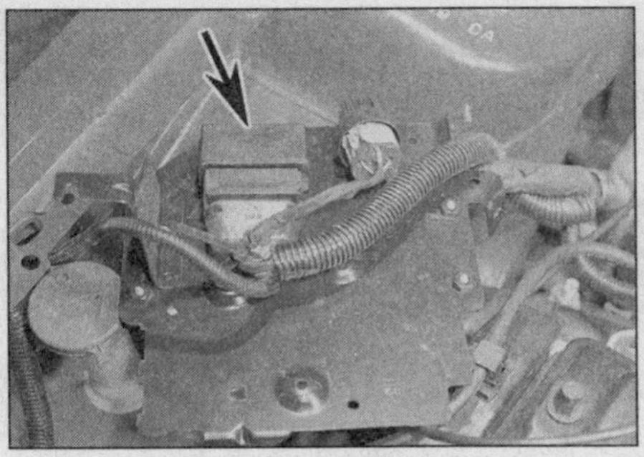

14.28 Fuel injection system relay location (arrowed)

described in the previous sub-Section. Unclip the relay unit from the mounting plate, disconnect the wiring connector and remove the unit from the vehicle.

31 Refitting is the reverse of removal, ensuring that the relay unit is securely held in position by its retaining clip.

Crankshaft/TDC sensor

32 The crankshaft sensor is situated on the front face of the transmission clutch housing.

33 To remove the sensor, first disconnect the battery negative cable and position it away from the terminal.

34 Trace the wiring back from the sensor to the wiring connector, and disconnect it from the main harness **(see illustration)**.

35 Prise out the plastic cover plate, then undo the retaining bolt and withdraw the sensor from the transmission **(see illustration)**.

36 Refitting is the reverse of the removal procedure. Ensure that the sensor retaining bolt is securely tightened, and that the grommet is correctly seated in the transmission housing.

Vehicle speed sensor - 1124 cc models

37 The vehicle speed sensor is an integral part of the speedometer drive housing. Refer to Chapter 7A or 7B as applicable for removal and refitting details.

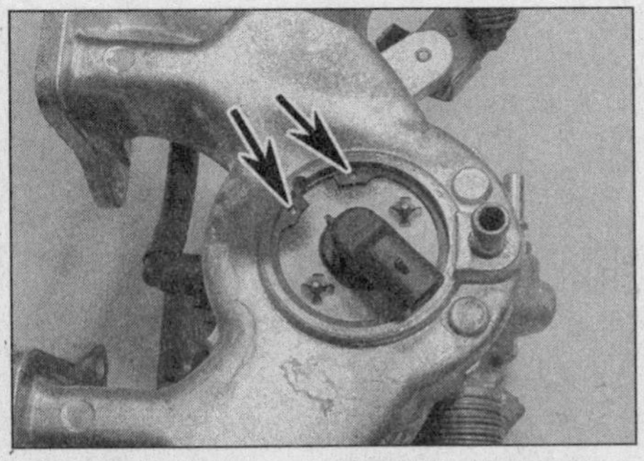

14.39 Release the circlip and withdraw the heater from the underside of the manifold casting

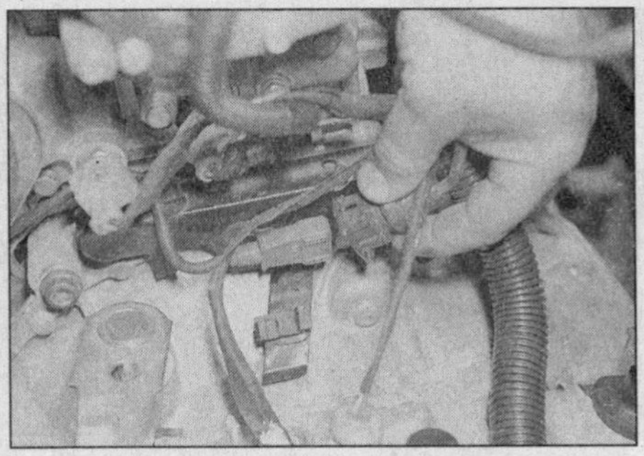

14.34 Unplug the crankshaft/TDC sensor wiring from the main harness at the connector

Inlet manifold heater

38 Remove the inlet manifold as described in Section 15.

39 Release the circlip and withdraw the heater from the underside of the manifold casting **(see illustration)**.

40 Refitting is a reversal of removal.

Lambda sensor

Removal

41 The Lambda sensor is threaded into the exhaust downpipe, and is easily accessible from the front of the engine bay **(see illustration)**. Access may be further improved by removing the radiator and cooling fan(s) as described in Chapter 3.

42 Unplug the wiring harness from the oxygen sensor at the connector, which is mounted on the bracket at the top of the transmission casing.

43 Note that a flying lead remains connected to the sensor after it has been disconnected; if the appropriate size of an open-ended spanner is not available, a slotted socket will be required to remove the sensor. Slacken and withdraw the sensor, taking care to avoid damaging the sensor probe as it is removed.

Refitting

44 Apply a little anti-seize grease to the sensor threads - avoid contaminating the probe tip.

45 Refit the sensor to its housing, tightening it securely. Restore the harness connection.

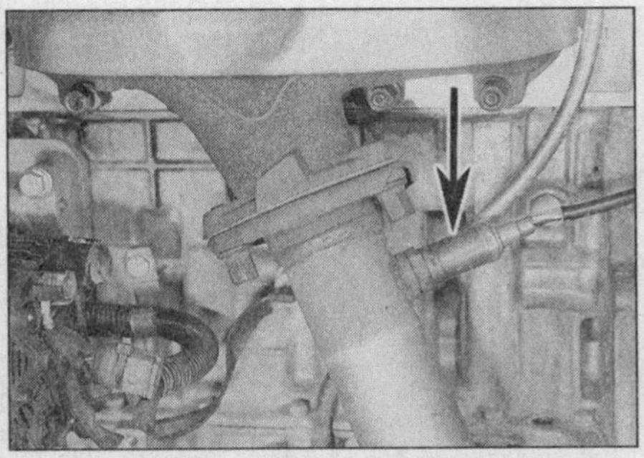

14.41 Lambda sensor location (arrowed) in the exhaust system downpipe

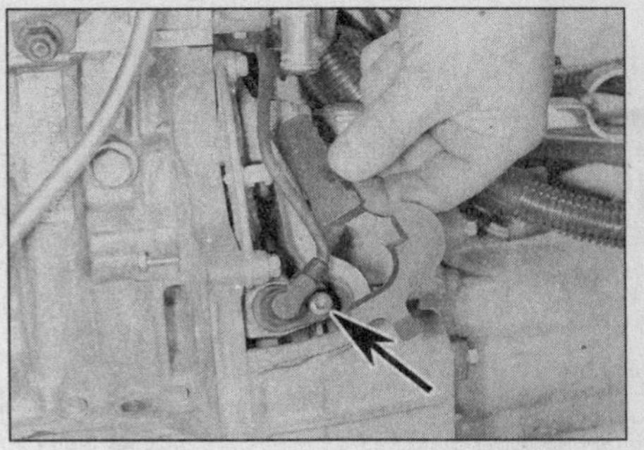

14.35 Prise out the plastic cover plate, then undo the retaining bolt (arrowed) and withdraw the sensor

15 Inlet manifold - removal and refitting

Removal

1 If required, remove the throttle body as described in Section 12, however note that the manifold may be removed with the throttle body in place. If this is the case, carry out the operations described in Section 12, paragraphs 1 to 6 inclusive.

2 Drain the cooling system as described in Chapter 1A.

3 Slacken the retaining clip and disconnect the coolant hose(s) from the underside of the manifold.

4 Disconnect the vacuum servo unit hose from the port at the rear of the manifold **(see illustration)**. To do this, depress the tangs at either side of the quick release hose fitting.

5 Unplug the purge valve vacuum hose from the rear of the manifold.

6 Disconnect the vacuum hose that runs from the front of the manifold to the crankcase breather valve, at the quick release connector on the underside the valve. Leave the hose connected to the manifold.

7 Make a final check that all the necessary vacuum/breather hoses have been disconnected from the manifold.

8 Unscrew the retaining nuts, then manoeuvre the manifold assembly away from

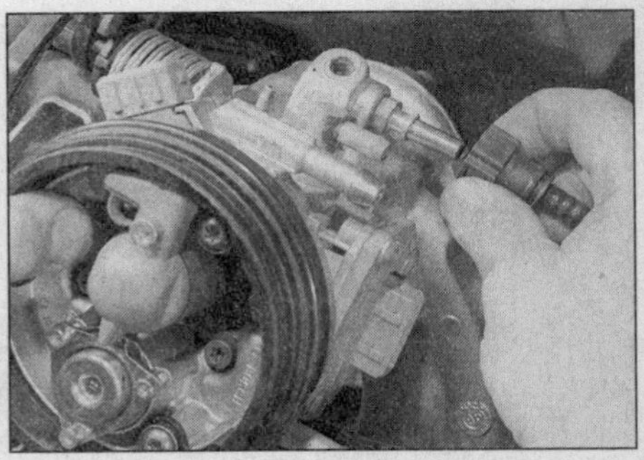

15.4 Disconnect the vacuum servo unit hose from the port at the rear of the manifold

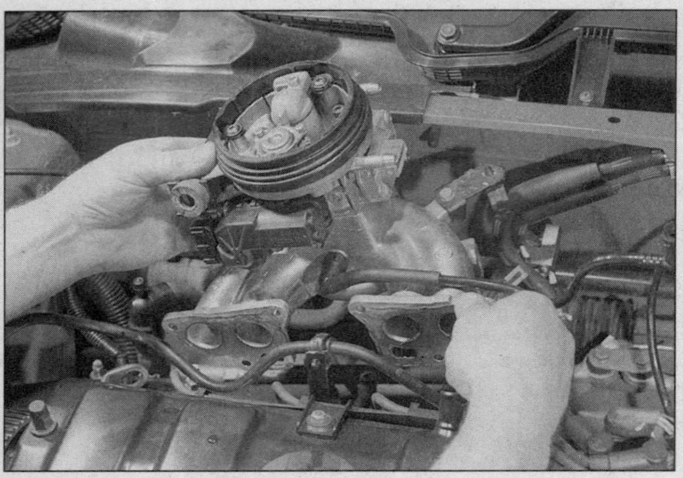

15.8 Unscrew the retaining nuts, then manoeuvre the manifold assembly away from the cylinder head

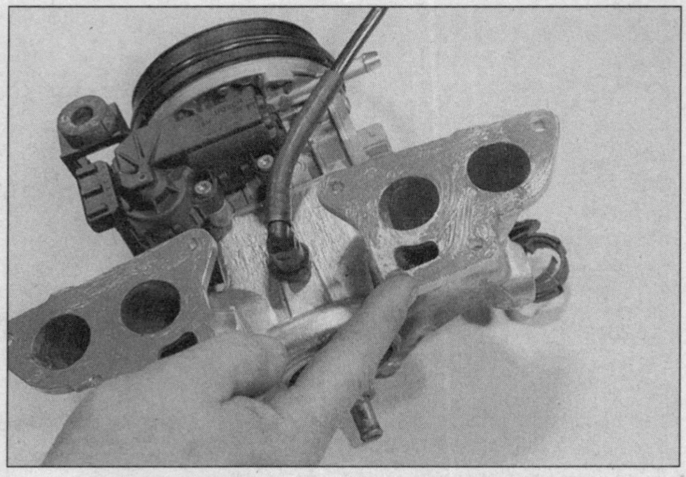

15.9 Before refitting, apply a thin coating of suitable sealing compound to the inlet manifold mating surface

the head and out of the engine compartment **(see illustration)**. Note that there is no manifold gasket, but the remains of the sealant should be carefully cleaned away before the manifold is refitted.

Refitting

9 Refitting is the reverse of the removal procedure, noting the following points:

*a) Ensure that the manifold and cylinder head mating surfaces are clean and dry, and apply a thin coating of suitable sealing compound to the manifold mating surface **(see illustration)**. Install the manifold, and tighten its retaining nuts to the specified torque setting.*

b) Ensure that all relevant hoses are reconnected to their original positions, and are securely held (where necessary) by their retaining clips.

c) Refit the throttle body as described in Section 12.

d) On completion, refill the cooling system as described in Chapter 1A.

Chapter 4 Part B: Fuel system - multi-point petrol injection models

Contents

Degrees of difficulty

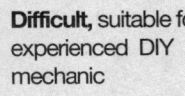

Easy, suitable for novice with little experience	**Fairly easy,** suitable for beginner with some experience	**Fairly difficult,** suitable for competent DIY mechanic	**Difficult,** suitable for experienced DIY mechanic	**Very difficult,** suitable for expert DIY or professional

Specifications

System type

1360 cc models	Magneti Marelli 1 AP
1587 cc models:	
Up to 97 model year	Bosch Motronic MP5.1
97 model year onwards	Bosch Motronic MP5.2
1587 cc 16-valve models	Magneti Marelli 1 AP 41

Fuel system data

Fuel pump type	Electric, immersed in tank
Fuel pump delivery rate	115 to 120 litres per hour
Fuel pump delivery pressure at full load	3.0 bar
Regulated fuel pressure:	
1360 cc models	2.5 to 3.0 bar
1587 cc (including 16-valve) models	2.0 to 2.5 bar
Specified idle speed:	
Models without air conditioning	850 ± 50 rpm (not adjustable, controlled by ECU)
Models with air conditioning	900 ± 50 rpm (not adjustable, controlled by ECU)
Exhaust gas CO content at idle	< 0.5 % (not adjustable, controlled by ECU)

Recommended fuel

Octane rating	Unleaded premium 95 RON and 98 RON

Torque wrench settings	Nm	lbf ft
Inlet manifold retaining nuts:		
1587 cc 16-valve models	9	7
All other models	10	7
Exhaust manifold retaining nuts:		
1587 cc 16-valve models:		
Stage 1	10	7
Stage 2	18	13
All other models	15	11
Exhaust manifold heat shield	8	6
Exhaust system fasteners:		
Front pipe-to-manifold nut:		
1587 cc 16-valve models	8	6
All other models	35	26
Front pipe-to-intermediate pipe/catalytic converter nuts	10	7
Clamping ring nuts	15	11
Knock sensor	20	15

1 General information and precautions

The fuel supply system consists of a fuel tank mounted under the rear of the car, a fuel pump (mounted inside the fuel tank), a fuel filter, fuel feed and return lines. The fuel pump supplies fuel to the fuel rail, which acts as a reservoir for the four fuel injectors which inject fuel into the inlet tracts. A fuel filter is incorporated in the feed line from the pump, to ensure that the fuel supplied to the injectors is clean. A mechanical fuel pressure regulator with an integral vacuum diaphragm maintains the pressure of the fuel in the fuel rail at a level which ensures that the volume of fuel-injected is not affected by engine speed or inlet manifold vacuum.

Refer to Section 6 for further information on the operation of the relevant fuel injection system.

Warning: Many of the procedures in this Chapter require the removal of fuel lines and connections, which may result in some fuel spillage. Before carrying out any operation on the fuel system, refer to the precautions given in "Safety first!" at the beginning of this manual, and follow them implicitly. Petrol is a highly-dangerous and volatile liquid, and the precautions necessary when handling it cannot be overstressed.

Note: *Residual pressure will remain in the fuel lines long after the engine has been switched off. Before disconnecting a fuel line, depressurise the fuel system as described in Section 7.*

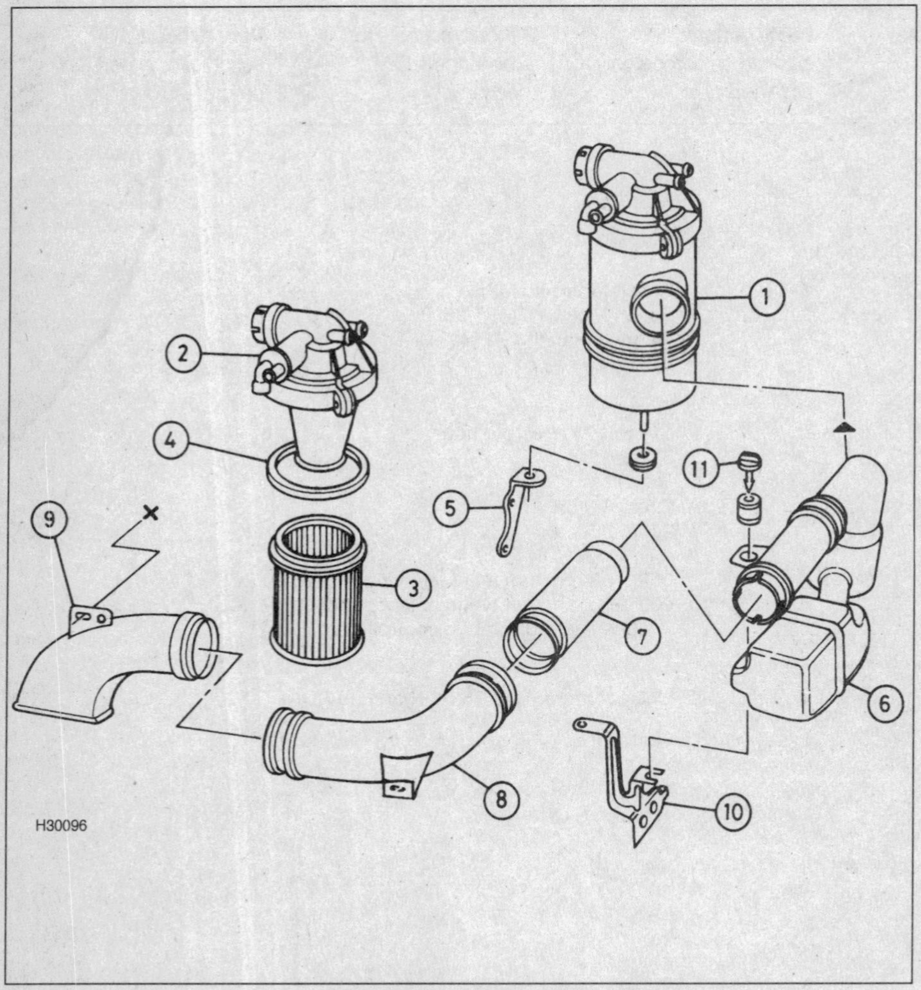

2.4 Inlet air trunking and air cleaner assembly (1.6 litre 8-valve model shown)

1 Air cleaner housing
2 Air cleaner cover
3 Air filter element
4 Sealing ring
5 Mounting bracket
6 Resonator
7 Flexible duct
8 Inlet duct
9 Inlet scoop
10 Mounting bracket
11 Quick release fastener

2 Air cleaner assembly - removal and refitting

Removal

1360 and 1587 cc models

1 Slacken the retaining clips (where fitted) and disconnect the vacuum and breather hoses from the top of the air cleaner housing. Where crimped-type hose clips or ties are fitted, cut and discard them; replace them with standard worm-drive hose clips or new cable-ties when refitting.

2 Slacken the retaining clips or ties, and free the throttle housing duct from the top of the air cleaner housing. Also remove the inlet duct from the side of the housing. If necessary, free the duct from the throttle housing and remove it, along with its sealing ring.

3 Lift the air cleaner housing assembly out of the engine compartment.

4 To remove the inlet duct assembly, drill out the rivets securing the duct to the crossmember, then release the fastener securing the rear of the duct to the cylinder head, and remove the duct and hose assembly from the engine compartment **(see illustration)**.

1587 cc 16-valve models

5 Release the securing screws and lift off the air cleaner cover. Slacken the hose clips and detach the air ducting from the air cleaner cover and throttle body. Release the clips and disconnect the breather hose from the side of the air cleaner cover.

6 Lift out the air filter element, then slacken and withdraw screws securing the air cleaner housing to its mounting bracket.

7 Slacken the hose clip and detach the inlet air hose from the underside of the air cleaner housing. Lift the housing from the engine compartment - recover the mounting rubbers if they are loose.

8 Release the hose clip and disconnect the inlet duct assembly from the air inlet scoop. Undo the securing screws and lift the duct assembly, together with the resonator, from the engine compartment.

Refitting

1360 cc and 1587 cc models

9 Refitting is a reversal of the removal procedure. Also note the following:

a) Where applicable, ensure that the air cleaner housing locating peg is correctly engaged with its mounting on the top of the transmission.
b) Make sure all the ducts are correctly seated and securely held in position.
c) If the inlet duct was removed, secure it to the crossmember with new pop-rivets.

1587 cc 16-valve models

10 Refitting is a reversal of removal. Ensure that the cylinder head breather hose is correctly reconnected and that all hose clips are securely tightened

3 Accelerator cable - removal, refitting and adjustment

Refer to the information given in Chapter 4A.

Note: *On models with automatic transmission it will be necessary to 'initialise' the transmission control system ECU after adjusting the accelerator cable; refer to Chapter 7B for details.*

4 Accelerator pedal - removal and refitting

Refer to the information given in Chapter 4A.

5 Unleaded petrol - general information and usage

Note: *The information given in this Chapter is correct at the time of writing, and applies only to petrol fuel currently available in the UK. For up-to-date information, check with a Citroën dealer. If travelling abroad, consult one of the motoring organisations for advice on the fuels available, and their suitability for your vehicle.*

1 All Citroën Saxo multi-point injection models are designed to run on fuel with a minimum octane rating of 95 (RON). All models have catalytic converters, and must therefore be run on unleaded fuel **only**. Under no circumstances should leaded fuel be used on a catalytic converter-equipped vehicle.

2 RON and MON are different testing standards; RON stands for Research Octane Number (also written as RM), while MON stands for Motor Octane Number (also written as MM).

6 Fuel injection system - general information

1 All versions of the Magneti Marelli and Bosch Motronic systems covered in this Chapter are full engine management systems, controlling both the fuel injection and ignition functions; refer to the Specifications for system application data. As the layout and overall operation of each of the systems is very similar, a general description is given in the following paragraphs. Sections 13 and 14 contain fuel injection component removal and refitting information specific to each individual system. Refer to Chapter 5B for information relating to the ignition system.

2 The systems all employ closed-loop fuelling by means of a catalytic converter and a Lambda sensor, to minimise exhaust gas emissions. An evaporative loss emission control system is also integrated, to minimise the escape of unburned hydrocarbons into the atmosphere from the fuel tank.

3 The fuel pump supplies fuel from the tank to the fuel rail, via a replaceable cartridge filter mounted underneath the rear of the vehicle. The pump itself is mounted inside the fuel tank, the pump motor is permanently immersed in fuel, to keep it cool. The fuel rail is mounted directly above the fuel injectors and acts as a fuel reservoir.

4 The fuel injectors are electromagnetic pintle valves, which spray atomised fuel into the combustion chambers under the control of the engine management system ECU. There are four injectors, one per cylinder, mounted on the fuel rail close to the cylinder head. Each injector is mounted at an angle that allows it to spray fuel directly onto the back of the inlet valve(s). The ECU controls the volume of fuel-injected by varying the length of time for which each injector is held open (the 'duty ratio').

5 The Bosch Motronic systems employ 'banked' fuel injection, where all four injectors are activated simultaneously. Fuel is injected into each cylinder's inlet tract on every engine stroke and is then drawn into the combustion chamber during the induction stroke.

6 The Magneti Marelli systems employ semi-sequential fuel injection, where fuel is injected into each cylinder's inlet tract twice per engine cycle; once during the power stroke and once during the induction stroke.

7 Fuel rail supply pressure is controlled by the pressure regulator, mounted at the end of the fuel rail. The regulator contains a spring-loaded valve, which lifts to allow excess fuel to return to the tank when the optimum operating pressure of the fuel system is exceeded (eg during low speed, light load cruising). The regulator also contains a diaphragm which is supplied with vacuum from the inlet manifold. This allows the regulator to reduce the fuel supply pressure during light load, high manifold depression conditions (e.g. during idling or deceleration) to prevent excess fuel being 'sucked' through the open injectors. Note that on later models, a fuel pressure regulator is not fitted; a fuel pressure monitoring point is provided at the left hand end of the fuel rails **(see illustration)**.

8 The electrical control system consists of the ECU, along with the following sensors and actuators:

a) Throttle potentiometer - informs the ECU of the throttle valve position, and the rate of throttle opening/closing.

b) Coolant temperature sensor - informs the ECU of engine temperature.

c) Inlet air temperature sensor - informs the ECU of the temperature of the air passing through the throttle body.

d) Lambda sensor - informs the ECU of the oxygen content of the exhaust gases.

e) Inlet manifold pressure sensor - informs the ECU of the engine load.

f) Crankshaft sensor to inform the ECU of engine speed and crankshaft angular position.

g) Vehicle speed sensor - informs the ECU of the vehicle's road speed, allowing manual gear selection to be monitored.

h) Throttle body heater - raises the temperature of the throttle body to minimise fuel condensation and prevent throttle valve icing.

i) Instrument panel-mounted warning indicator - illuminated by the ECU when a malfunction is detected.

j) Relay pack - two separate relays mounted in one housing, providing separate current supplies to the fuel pump and ECU, sensors and actuators.

9 Signals from each of the sensors are compared by the ECU and, based on this information, the ECU selects the response appropriate to those values, and controls the fuel injector duty ratio to provide a richer or weaker air/fuel mixture, as appropriate. The air/fuel mixture is constantly varied by the ECU, to provide the best settings for cranking, starting (with either a hot or cold engine) and engine warm-up, idle, cruising and acceleration.

10 All systems are equipped with a knock sensor, mounted on the front of the cylinder block. The knock sensor is part of the ignition control system and is described in Chapter 5B.

11 The ECU also has full control over the engine idle speed, via a stepper motor fitted to the throttle body (Magneti Marelli systems), or an idle actuator valve (Bosch Motronic systems). On models with Magneti Marelli systems, the stepper motor pushrod controls the amount of air passing through a by-pass drilling at the side of the throttle. When the throttle valve is closed (accelerator pedal released), the ECU uses the motor to alter the position of the pushrod, controlling the amount of air bypassing the throttle valve and so controlling the idle speed. On models with Bosch Motronic systems, the same principle is applied, but the flow of air bypassing the throttle valve is controlled by an idle actuator

6.7 Fuel pressure monitoring point (arrowed) - later 1.6 litre 8-valve model shown

valve, which is separate from the throttle body. The ECU also carries out 'fine tuning' of the idle speed by varying the ignition timing to increase or reduce the torque of the engine as it is idling. This helps to stabilise the idle speed when electrical or mechanical loads (such as headlights, air conditioning etc) are switched on and off.

12 The throttle body is fitted with an electric heating element. The heater is supplied with current by the ECU, warming the throttle body on cold starts to help prevent icing of the throttle valve.

13 The exhaust and evaporative loss emission control systems are described in more detail in Chapter 4D.

14 If there is any abnormality in any of the readings obtained from either the coolant temperature sensor, the inlet air temperature sensor or the Lambda sensor, the ECU enters its 'back-up' mode. If this happens, the erroneous sensor signal is overridden, and the ECU assumes a pre-programmed 'back-up' value, which will allow the engine to continue running, albeit at reduced efficiency. If the ECU enters this mode, the warning lamp on the instrument panel will be illuminated, and the relevant fault code will be stored in the ECU memory.

15 If the warning light illuminates, the vehicle should be taken to a Citroën dealer at the earliest opportunity. Once there, a complete test of the engine management system can be carried out, using a special electronic diagnostic test unit, which is plugged into the system's diagnostic connector.

7 Fuel system - depressurisation

Note: *Refer to the warning note in Section 1 before proceeding.*

Warning: The following procedure will merely relieve the pressure in the fuel system - remember that fuel will still be present in the system components, and take precautions accordingly before disconnecting any of them.

1 The fuel system referred to in this Section is defined as the tank-mounted fuel pump, the fuel filter, the fuel injectors, the fuel rail and the pressure regulator, and the metal pipes and flexible hoses of the fuel lines between these components. All these contain fuel, which will be under pressure while the engine is running and/or while the ignition is switched on. The pressure will remain for some time *after the ignition has been switched off*, and must be relieved before any of these components are disturbed for servicing work.

2 Disconnect the battery negative cable and position it away from the terminal.

3 If a hand operated vacuum pump is available, disconnect the manifold vacuum pipe from the port at the top of the fuel pressure regulator, then connect the pump in its place. Operate the pump, to apply vacuum to the regulator - this will cause any residual pressure in the fuel supply line to be relieved via the fuel return line. Note that on later models, a fuel pressure regulator is not fitted.

4 Place a suitable container beneath the relevant connection/union to be disconnected, and have a large rag ready to soak up any escaping fuel not being caught by the container.

5 Slowly loosen the connection or union nut (as applicable) to avoid a sudden release of pressure, and position the rag around the connection to catch any fuel spray which may be expelled. Once the pressure is released, disconnect the fuel line. Plug the openings, to minimise fuel loss and prevent the entry of dirt into the fuel system.

8 Fuel pump - removal and refitting

Refer to the information given in Chapter 4A.

9 Fuel gauge sender unit - removal and refitting

Refer to the information given in Chapter 4A.

10 Fuel tank - removal and refitting

Refer to the information given in Chapter 4A.

11 Fuel injection system - testing and adjustment

Testing

1 If a fault appears in the fuel injection system, first ensure that all the system wiring connectors are securely connected and free of corrosion. Then ensure that the fault is not due to poor maintenance; ie, check that the air cleaner filter element is clean, the spark plugs are in good condition and correctly gapped, the fuel filter is in good condition, the cylinder compression pressures are correct and that the engine breather hoses are clear and undamaged, referring to Chapter 1A, Chapter 2A and Chapter 2C as appropriate.

2 If these checks fail to reveal the cause of the problem, the vehicle should be taken to a suitably-equipped Citroën dealer for testing. A wiring block connector is incorporated in the engine management circuit, into which a special electronic diagnostic tester can be plugged; the connector is clipped onto the side of the ECU mounting bracket. The tester will locate the fault quickly and simply, alleviating the need to test all the system components individually, which is a time-consuming operation that carries a high risk of damaging the ECU.

Adjustment

3 Experienced home mechanics with a considerable amount of skill and equipment (including a good-quality tachometer and a good-quality, carefully-calibrated exhaust gas analyser) may be able to *check* the exhaust CO level and the idle speed. However, if these are found to be in need of *adjustment*, the car **must** be taken to a suitably-equipped Citroën dealer. Neither the mixture (exhaust gas CO level) nor the idle speed are adjustable, and should either be incorrect, a fault may be present in the fuel injection system.

12 Throttle housing - removal and refitting

Removal

1 Disconnect the battery negative terminal.

2 Slacken the retaining clip, then disconnect the inlet duct from the throttle housing and recover the sealing ring. Where a crimped-type hose clip or tie fitted, cut and discard it; replace it with a standard worm-drive hose clip or new cable-tie on refitting.

3 Disconnect the accelerator inner cable from the throttle cam, then withdraw the outer cable from the mounting bracket, along with its rubber washer and spring clip **(see illustration)**.

12.3 Disconnect the accelerator inner cable from the throttle cam (A), withdraw the outer cable from the mounting bracket with its rubber washer (B) and spring clip (C)

4 Depress the retaining clip and disconnect the wiring connector(s) from the throttle potentiometer, and, where necessary, from the electric heating element, the air temperature sensor, and/or the stepper motor (as applicable).

5 Slacken and remove the retaining screws, and remove the throttle housing from the inlet manifold. Recover the O-ring from manifold (where fitted) and discard it; a new one must be used when refitting **(see illustration)**.

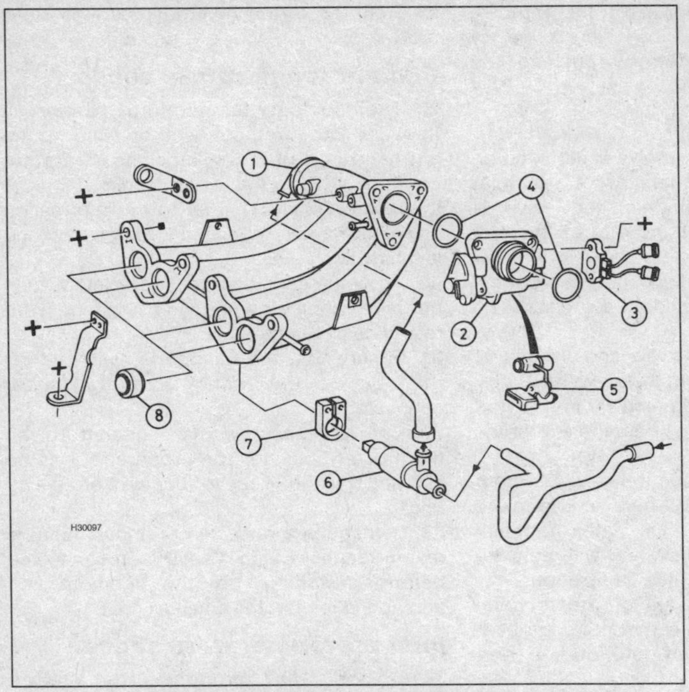

12.5 Inlet manifold and throttle body assembly (1.6 litre 8-valve model shown)

1 *Inlet manifold*
2 *Throttle body*
3 *Throttle potentiometer*
4 *O-ring seals*
5 *Throttle heating element*
6 *Idle actuator valve*
7 *Mounting bracket*
8 *Sealing rings*

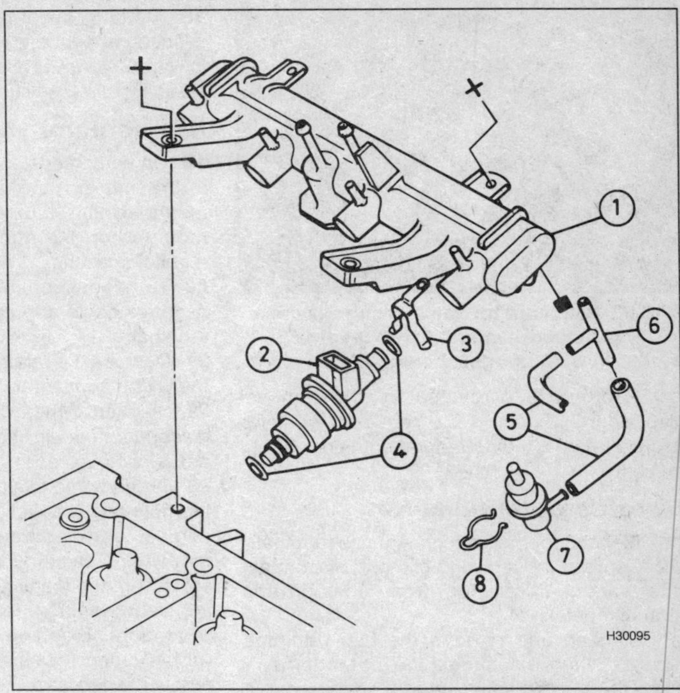

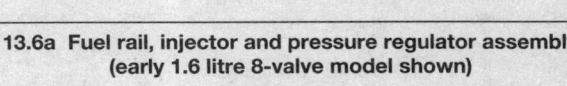

13.6a Fuel rail, injector and pressure regulator assembly (early 1.6 litre 8-valve model shown)

1 *Fuel rail*
2 *Injector*
3 *Retaining clip*
4 *O-ring seals*
5 *Fuel hoses*
6 *T-piece*
7 *Fuel pressure regulator*
8 *Retaining clip*

Refitting

6 Refitting is a reversal of the relevant removal procedure, noting the following points:

a) *Fit a new O-ring to the manifold, then refit the throttle housing and securely tighten its screws.*
b) *Ensure that all hoses are correctly reconnected and, where necessary, are securely held in position by the retaining clips.*
c) *Ensure that all wiring is correctly routed and the connectors are securely reconnected.*
d) *On completion, adjust the accelerator cable with reference to Chapter 4A.*

13 Bosch Motronic system components - removal and refitting

Fuel rail and injectors

Note: *Refer to the warning note in Section 1 before proceeding.*

Note: *If a faulty injector is suspected, before condemning the injector, it is worth trying the effect of one of the proprietary injector-cleaning treatments.*

1 Disconnect the battery negative cable and position it away from the terminal, then depressurise the fuel system, with reference to Section 7.

2 Disconnect the vacuum pipe from the port at the top of the fuel pressure regulator.

3 Bearing in mind the information given in Section 7, slacken the retaining clips and disconnect the fuel feed and return hoses from the fuel rail. Where the original crimped-type Citroën hose clips are still fitted, cut them off and discard; replace them with standard worm-drive hose clips on refitting.

4 Depress the retaining tangs and disconnect the wiring connectors from the four injectors.

5 Slacken and remove the fuel rail retaining bolts nuts, then carefully ease the fuel rail and injector assembly out from the inlet manifold and remove it from the vehicle. Remove the O-rings from the lower end of each injector, and discard them; they must be renewed whenever they are disturbed.

6 Slide out the retaining clip(s) and remove the relevant injector(s) from the fuel rail. Remove the upper O-ring from each disturbed injector and discard; any O-rings which are disturbed during removal must be renewed **(see illustrations)**.

7 Refitting is a reversal of the removal procedure, noting the following points:

a) *Fit new O-rings to all injector unions disturbed on removal.*
b) *Apply a smear of engine oil to the O-rings to aid installation, then ease the injectors and fuel rail into position, ensuring that none of the O-rings are displaced.*
c) *On completion, start the engine and check for fuel leaks.*

Fuel pressure regulator

Note: *Later models are not fitted with a fuel pressure regulator.*

Caution: Refer to the warning note in Section 1 before proceeding.

8 Disconnect the vacuum pipe from the regulator.

9 Place a wad of rag under and around the regulator, to catch any fuel spray which may be released, then remove the retaining clip and ease the regulator out from the fuel rail.

13.6b Fuel rail securing screws (arrowed) - later 1.6 litre 8-valve model shown

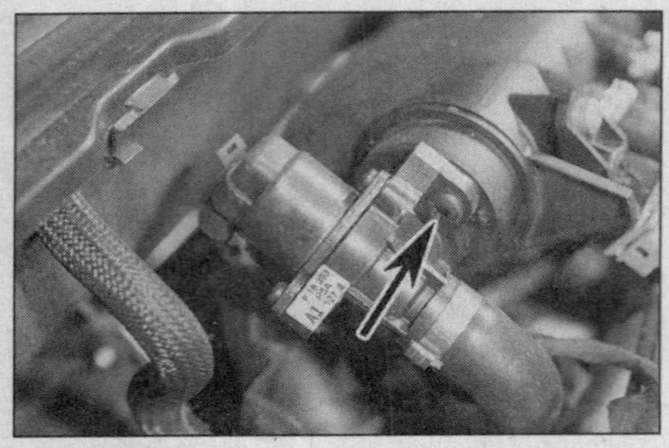

13.23 Idle actuator valve securing screw (arrowed) - later 1.6 litre 8-valve model shown

10 Refitting is a reversal of the removal procedure. Examine the regulator seal for signs of damage or deterioration, and renew if necessary.

Throttle potentiometer

11 Disconnect the battery negative terminal.
12 Depress the retaining clip and disconnect the wiring connector from the throttle potentiometer.
13 Slacken and remove the two retaining screws, then disengage the potentiometer from the throttle valve spindle and remove it from the vehicle.
14 Refitting is a reverse of the removal procedure, ensuring that the potentiometer is correctly engaged with the throttle valve spindle.

Electronic Control Unit (ECU)

15 The ECU is located on the right-hand side of the engine compartment. On some models, a large plastic cover is mounted over the ECU.
16 To remove the ECU, first disconnect the battery negative lead.
17 Unclip the cover from the mounting plate, then lift the retaining clip and disconnect the wiring connector from the ECU. Slacken and remove the ECU retaining bolts, and remove it from the vehicle (refer to the illustrations in Chapter 4A for greater detail).
18 Refitting is a reverse of the removal procedure, ensuring that the wiring connector is securely reconnected by pushing the retaining clip firmly home.

Idle actuator valve

19 On early models, the valve is mounted on a bracket on the underside of the inlet manifold. On later models, the valve is mounted on the right hand end of the inlet manifold casting.
20 To remove it, first disconnect the battery negative cable and position it away from the terminal.
21 Depress the retaining clip, and disconnect the wiring connector from the air valve.
22 Slacken the retaining clips, and disconnect the air hose(s) from the end of the auxiliary air valve.
23 On early models, slide the valve out from its mounting bracket, and remove it from the engine compartment. On later models, remove the securing screw and withdraw the valve from the manifold **(see illustration)**.
24 Refitting is a reversal of the removal procedure. Examine the mounting bracket rubber lining for signs of deterioration, and renew it if necessary.

Manifold pressure sensor

25 On early models, the manifold pressure sensor is mounted remotely on the right-hand side of the engine compartment bulkhead. On later models, the sensor is mounted directly on the front of the inlet manifold casting. To remove the sensor, first disconnect the battery negative cable and position it away from the terminal.
26 On early models, undo the retaining nut, and free the sensor from its mounting bracket. On later models, remove the securing screw and withdraw the sensor from the manifold **(see illustration)**.
27 Disconnect the wiring connector and vacuum hose, and remove the sensor from the engine compartment.
28 Refitting is the reverse of the removal procedure.

Coolant temperature sensor

29 The coolant temperature sensor is threaded into the thermostat housing, at the left hand end of the cylinder head. Do not confuse it with the other sensors in the thermostat housing - refer to the information given in Chapter 3, Section 6 for location and identification details.
30 Allow the engine to cool completely, then partially drain the cooling system with reference to Chapter 1A.
31 Ensure that the ignition is switched off then unplug the wiring from the sensor connector.
32 Carefully unscrew the sensor from the thermostat housing - be prepared for some coolant spillage. Recover the sensor sealing ring.
33 Refitting is a reversal of removal. Ensure that the sensor wiring is securely reconnected before switching on the ignition and attempting to start the engine.

Inlet air temperature sensor

34 On early 1587 cc models, the inlet air temperature sensor is screwed into the top of the air cleaner housing. On later models, the sensor is threaded into the underside of the throttle body. Before removing the sensor, first ensure that the ignition is switched off **(see illustration)**.
35 Unplug the wiring from the sensor connector, then unscrew the sensor and remove it from the vehicle. Recover the sealing ring, where applicable.
36 Refitting is the reverse of removal.

Crankshaft/TDC sensor

37 The crankshaft/TDC sensor is situated on the front face of the transmission clutch housing.
38 To remove the sensor, first ensure that the ignition is switched off.

13.26 Remove the securing screw (arrowed) and withdraw the sensor from the manifold - later 1.6 litre 8-valve model shown

13.34 Inlet air temperature sensor (air cleaner ducting removed for clarity) - later 1.6 litre 8-valve model shown

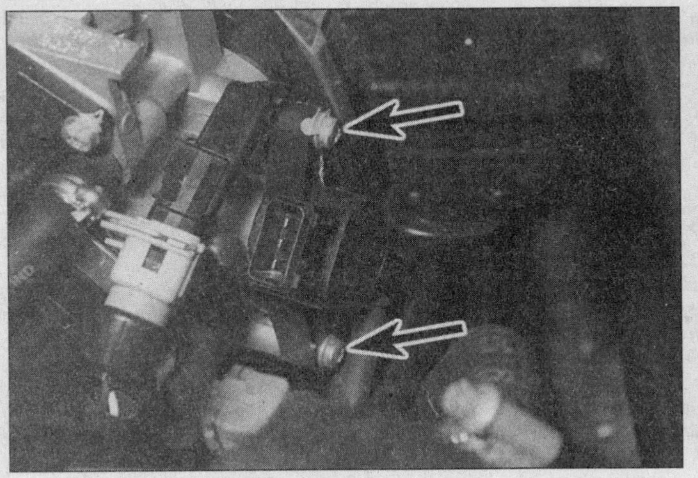

14.3 Throttle potentiometer securing screws (arrowed)

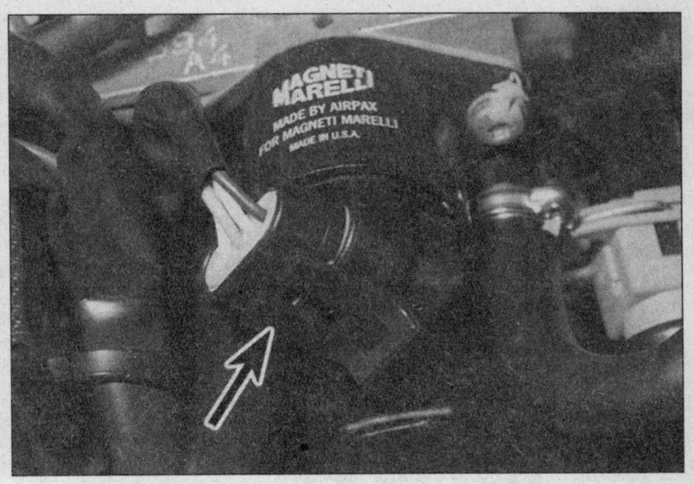

14.6 Unplug the wiring connector from the idle speed control stepper motor. . .

39 Trace the wiring back from the sensor to the wiring connector, and disconnect it from the main harness.

40 Prise out the rubber grommet, then undo the retaining bolt and withdraw the sensor from the transmission. Refer to the illustrations in Chapter 4A for greater detail.

41 Refitting is reverse of the removal procedure, ensuring that the sensor retaining bolt is securely tightened and the grommet is correctly seated in the transmission housing.

Fuel injection system relay unit

42 The relay unit is clipped onto the underside of the ECU mounting plate, on the right-hand side of the engine compartment.

43 To remove the relay unit, first disconnect the battery negative lead.

44 Unclip the relay unit from the mounting plate, disconnect the wiring connector and remove the unit from the vehicle.

45 Refitting is the reverse of removal, ensuring that the relay unit is securely held in position by its retaining clip.

Lambda sensor

46 Refer to the information given in Chapter 4A.

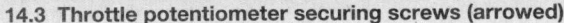

14 Magneti Marelli system components - removal and refitting

Fuel rail and injectors

1 Refer to the information given in Section 13.

Fuel pressure regulator

2 Refer to the information given in Section 13.

Throttle potentiometer

3 Refer to the information given in Section 13 **(see illustration)**.

Electronic Control Unit (ECU)

4 Refer to the information given in Section 13.

Idle speed control stepper motor

5 The idle speed control stepper motor is located on the side of the throttle housing assembly. To remove the motor, first disconnect the battery negative terminal.

6 Release the retaining clip, and disconnect the wiring connector from the motor **(see illustration)**.

7 Slacken and remove the two retaining screws, and withdraw the motor from the throttle housing **(see illustration)**.

8 Refitting is a reversal of the removal procedure.

Manifold pressure sensor

9 On early models, the sensor is mounted on a bracket on the bulkhead at the rear of the engine compartment bulkhead **(see illustration)**. On later models, the manifold pressure sensor is mounted directly on the inlet manifold casting. To remove it, first ensure that the ignition is switched off.

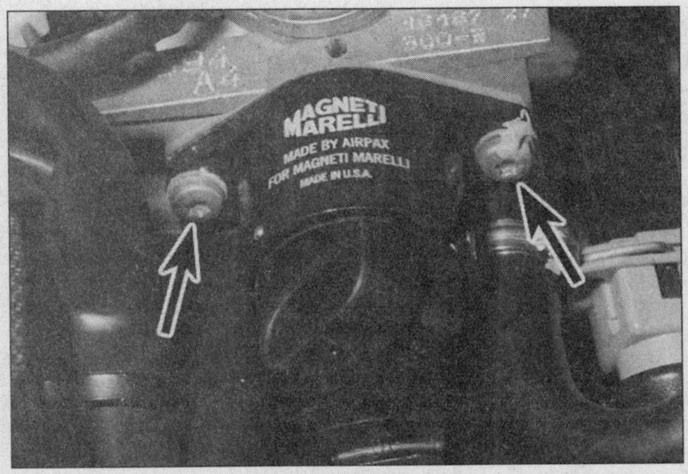

14.7 . . . then undo the two screws and withdraw the motor from the throttle housing

14.9 Manifold pressure sensor - early 1.6 litre 8-valve model shown

10 Release the locking tab and unplug the wiring from the sensor connector.
11 On early models, disconnect the vacuum hose, then remove the screws and withdraw the sensor from the mounting bracket. On later models, remove the securing screws and withdraw the sensor from the manifold, recovering the sealing ring.
12 Refitting is a reversal of removal.

Coolant temperature sensor

13 Refer to the information given in Section 13 and in Chapter 3, Section 6.

Inlet air temperature sensor

14 The sensor is threaded into the underside of the throttle body. Before removing the sensor, first ensure that the ignition is switched off.
15 Unplug the wiring from the sensor connector, then unscrew the sensor and remove it from the vehicle. Recover the sealing ring, where applicable.
16 Refitting is the reverse of removal.

Crankshaft /TDC sensor

17 Refer to the information given in Section 13.

Fuel injection system relay unit

18 Refer to the information given in Section 13.

Knock sensor

19 The knock sensor is screwed onto the rear face of the cylinder block.
20 To gain access to the sensor, firmly apply the handbrake, then jack up the front of the vehicle and support it on axle stands (see "*Jacking and vehicle support*"). Access to the sensor can then be gained from underneath the vehicle.
21 Trace the wiring back from the sensor to its wiring connector, and disconnect it from the main loom.
22 Slacken and remove the bolt securing the sensor to the cylinder block, and remove it from underneath the vehicle.
23 Refitting is a reversal of the removal procedure, ensuring that the sensor wiring is correctly routed and its retaining bolt is tightened to the correct torque.
Note: *The knock sensor will only operate correctly if its securing bolt is tightened accurately to the specified torque setting.*

Throttle housing heating element

24 The throttle housing heating element is fitted to the side of the throttle housing. To remove the element, first disconnect the battery negative cable and position it away from the terminal.
25 To improve access, disconnect the accelerator inner cable from the throttle cam, then withdraw the outer cable from the mounting bracket, along with its flat washer and spring clip.
26 Disconnect the element wiring connector, then undo the retaining screw, and free the wiring connector from the throttle housing.
27 Undo the screws securing the accelerator cable bracket to the side of the throttle housing. Carefully remove the bracket, and recover the spring from the top of the heating element.
28 Ease the heating element out from the throttle housing. Examine the O-ring for signs of damage or deterioration, and renew if necessary.
29 Refitting is a reversal of the removal procedure; where necessary, use a new O-ring.

Vehicle speed sensor

30 The vehicle speed sensor is an integral part of the speedometer drive housing. Refer to Chapter 7A or B, as applicable, for removal and refitting details.

Lambda sensor

31 Refer to the information given in Chapter 4A. Note that in some markets, 1360 cc Saxo models conforming to CEE 2000 emissions standards are fitted with two Lambda sensors; one upstream of the catalytic converter, and one downstream.

15 Inlet manifold - removal and refitting

Removal

1 Disconnect the battery negative terminal.
2 Refer to Section 2 and remove the air cleaner.
3 Remove the throttle housing as described in Section 13 or 14 as applicable.
4 On 1360 cc and 1587 cc 16-valve models, unplug the wiring from the manifold pressure sensor, with reference to Section 14.
5 On 1587 cc 16-valve models, progressively slacken and withdraw the plenum chamber to inlet manifold screws. Lift the chamber away from the manifold and recover the gasket.
6 On 1587 cc 8-valve models, depress the retaining clip and disconnect the wiring connector from the idle actuator valve with reference to Section 13. Slacken the retaining clip, and disconnect the vacuum hose connecting the valve to the inlet duct, leaving the valve free to be removed with the manifold. On early models, the valve is located underneath the inlet manifold. On later models, it is located at the right hand end of the manifold.
7 Release the retaining clips (where fitted), and disconnect all the relevant vacuum and breather hoses from the manifold. Make identification marks on the hoses, to ensure that they are connected correctly on refitting.
8 Bearing in mind the information given in Section 7, slacken the retaining clips and disconnect the fuel feed and return hoses from the fuel rail. Where the original crimped-type Citroën hose clips are still fitted, cut them off and discard; replace them with standard worm-drive hose clips on refitting.
9 Depress the retaining tangs, and disconnect the wiring connectors from the four injectors. Free the wiring from any relevant retaining clips, and position it clear of the manifold.
10 Where applicable, undo the retaining bolts and remove the support bracket from the underside of the manifold.
11 Undo the manifold retaining nuts, and withdraw the manifold from the engine compartment. Recover the four manifold seals, and discard them; new ones must be used on refitting.

Refitting

12 Refitting is a reverse of the relevant removal procedure, noting the following points:

a) Ensure that the manifold and cylinder head mating surfaces are clean and dry.
b) Locate the new seals in their recesses in the manifold. Refit the manifold and tighten its retaining nuts to the specified torque.
c) On 1587 cc 16-valve models, fit a new manifold to plenum chamber gasket.
d) Ensure that all relevant hoses are reconnected to their original positions, and are securely held (where necessary) by the retaining clips.

Chapter 4 Part C: Fuel system - diesel

Contents

Degrees of difficulty

Easy, suitable for novice with little experience	**Fairly easy,** suitable for beginner with some experience	**Fairly difficult,** suitable for competent DIY mechanic	**Difficult,** suitable for experienced DIY mechanic	**Very difficult,** suitable for expert DIY or professional

Specifications

General

System type	Rear-mounted fuel tank, distributor fuel injection pump with integral transfer pump, indirect injection. Fuel injection pump immobiliser in some markets.
Firing order	1-3-4-2 (No 1 at transmission end)

Fuel

Type	Commercial diesel fuel for road vehicles (DERV)
Fuel tank capacity	45 litres

Injection pump

Direction of rotation	Clockwise, viewed from timing belt end
Idle speed	800 ± 25 rpm
Anti-stall speed:	
Bosch injection pump	835 ± 40 rpm
Lucas injection pump	1600 ± 100 rpm
Fast idle speed	1000 ± 100 rpm
Maximum speed	5450 rpm ± 125 rpm
Fast idle lever travel (between 'cold' and 'hot' positions)	6.0 mm
Anti-stall speed adjustment shim thickness:	
Bosch fuel injection pump	1.0 mm
Lucas fuel injection pump	1.5 mm

Injectors

Type	Pintle, single-stage
Opening pressure:	
Bosch	115 to 125 bar
Lucas	135 to 140 bar

Torque wrench settings

Torque wrench settings	Nm	lbf ft
Injector pipe union nuts	20	15
Injection pump fixings	20	15
Injection pump fuel feed/return union bolts	25	18
Injectors	55	41
Inlet manifold nuts and bolts	20	15
Fast idle thermostatic valve	25	18

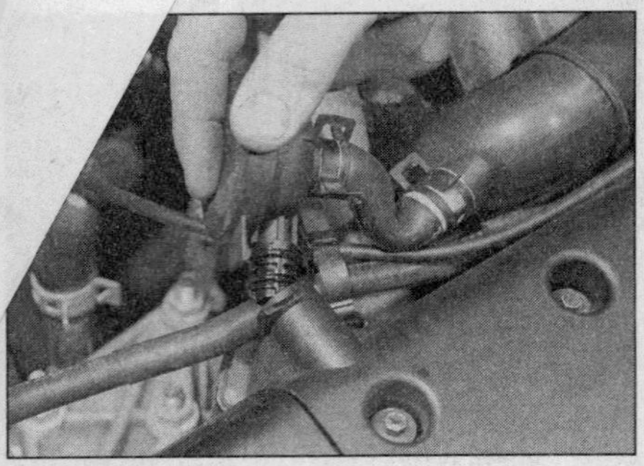

2.1 Release the breather valve from the rear of the cylinder head cover

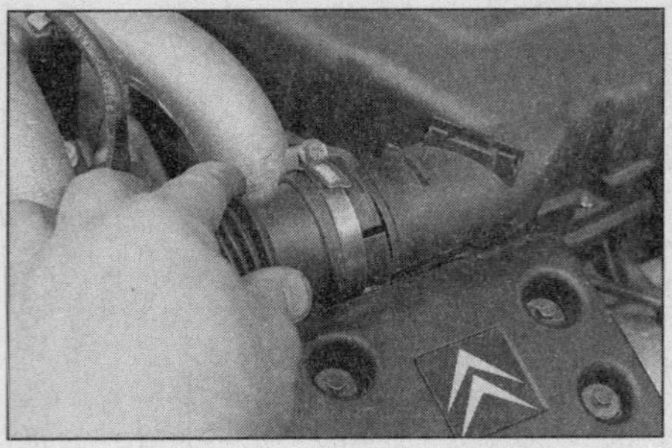

2.2 Slacken the hose clip and detach the intake ducting from the side of the air cleaner housing

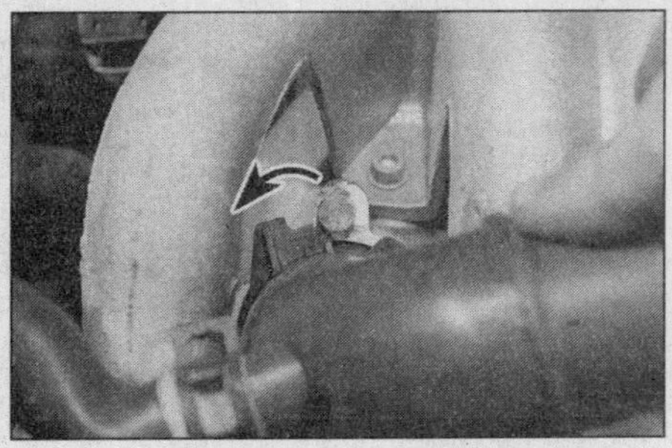

2.3 Release the intake ducting from the inlet manifold by turning it anticlockwise, to disengage the retaining lugs

1 General information and precautions

The fuel system consists of a rear-mounted fuel tank, a fuel filter with integral water separator, a fuel injection pump, injectors and associated components. As the fuel passes through the filter, the fuel is heated by coolant flowing through the filter housing.

The exhaust system is conventional, but on certain models, an unregulated catalytic converter may be fitted to reduce exhaust gas emissions.

Fuel is drawn from the fuel tank to the fuel injection pump by a vane-type transfer pump incorporated in the fuel injection pump. Before reaching the pump, the fuel passes through a fuel filter, where foreign matter and water are removed. Excess fuel lubricates the moving components of the pump, and is then returned to the tank.

The fuel injection pump is driven at half-crankshaft speed by the timing belt. The high pressure required to inject the fuel into the compressed air in the swirl chambers is achieved by two opposed pistons forced together by rollers running in a cam ring on the pump. The fuel passes through a central rotor with a single outlet drilling which aligns with ports leading to the injector pipes.

Fuel metering is controlled by a centrifugal governor, which reacts to accelerator pedal position and engine speed. The governor is linked to a metering valve which increases or decreases the amount of fuel delivered at each pumping stroke.

Basic injection timing is pre-determined and cannot be adjusted by altering the position of the injection pump in relation to its mounting bracket, as with previous derivatives of the TUD engine. When the engine is running, the injection timing is varied automatically to suit the prevailing engine speed by a mechanism which turns the cam plate or ring.

The four fuel injectors produce a homogeneous spray of fuel into the swirl chambers located in the cylinder head. The injectors are calibrated to open and close at critical pressures to provide efficient and even combustion. Each injector needle is lubricated by fuel, which accumulates in the spring chamber and is channelled to the injection pump return hose by leak-off pipes.

Cold starting and running is assisted by preheater (or 'glow') plugs fitted to each swirl chamber (see Chapter 5C for further details).

The fast idle system is operated by a thermostatic valve which is screwed into the fuel filter/thermostat housing. The valve operates a fast idle lever on the injection pump, via a cable, to increase the idle speed when the engine is cold.

A stop solenoid cuts the fuel supply to the injection pump rotor when the ignition is switched off. There is also a hand-operated stop lever mounted on the fuel injection pump for use in an emergency.

Provided that the specified maintenance is carried out, the fuel injection equipment will give long and trouble-free service; the injection pump itself may well outlast the engine. The main potential cause of damage to the injection pump and injectors is dirt, water or air in the fuel.

Servicing of the injection pump and injectors is very limited for the home mechanic, and any dismantling or adjustment other than that described in this Chapter must be entrusted to a Citroën dealer or fuel injection specialist.

Warning: It is necessary to take certain precautions when working on the fuel system components, particularly the fuel injectors. Before carrying out any operations on the fuel system, refer to the precautions given in "Safety first!" at the beginning of this manual, and to any additional warning notes at the start of the relevant Sections.

2 Air cleaner housing - removal and refitting

Removal

1 Release the breather valve from the rear of the cylinder head cover **(see illustration)**.

2 Slacken the hose clip and detach the intake ducting from the side of the air cleaner housing **(see illustration)**.

3 Release the intake ducting from the inlet manifold by turning it anticlockwise, to disengage the retaining lugs **(see illustration)**.

4 Slacken the hose clip and detach the cold air ducting from the front of the air cleaner housing **(see illustration)**.

2.4 Slacken the hose clip and detach the cold air ducting from the front of the air cleaner housing

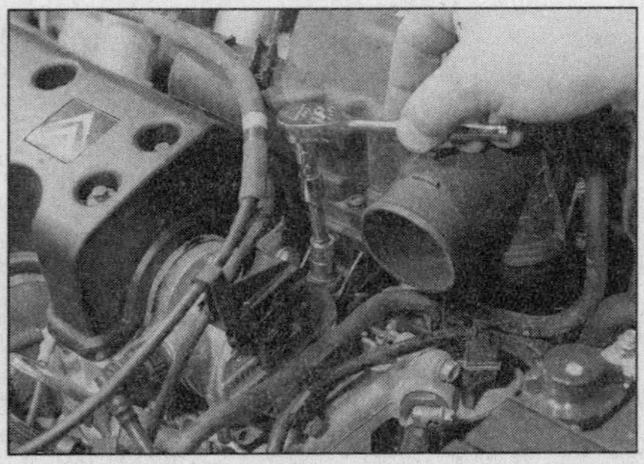

2.5a Slacken and withdraw the securing screw . . .

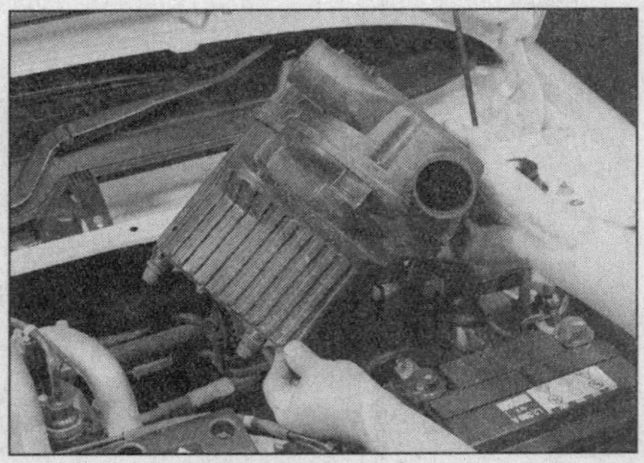

2.5b . . . then lift the air cleaner away from its lower mounting bracket

5 Slacken and withdraw the securing screw, then lift the air cleaner away from its lower mounting bracket. Recover the rubber supports, if they are loose **(see illustrations)**.

Refitting

6 Refitting is a reversal of removal.

3 Accelerator cable - removal, refitting and adjustment

Removal and refitting

1 Refer to Chapter 4A, Section 4, substituting "injection pump" for all references to the throttle body. Adjust the cable as described below.

Adjustment

2 Remove the spring clip from the accelerator outer cable then, ensuring that the pump accelerator lever is fully against the anti-stall screw, gently pull the cable out of its grommet until all free play is removed from the inner cable.
3 With the cable held in this position, fit the spring clip to the first outer cable groove visible in front of the rubber grommet **(see illustration)**.
4 Have an assistant depress the accelerator pedal, and check that the accelerator lever opens fully, so that it contacts the maximum speed screw, and returns smoothly to its stop against the anti-stall screw.

4 Accelerator pedal - removal and refitting

Refer to the information given in Chapter 4A.

5 Fuel gauge sender unit - removal and refitting

1 On later models, the fuel gauge sender unit is integral with the fuel pick-up unit; refer to the information given in Section 6. On early models, the fuel gauge sender is a separate unit - proceed as described in the following paragraphs.

Removal

Note: *Refer to the warning note in Section 1 before proceeding.*
2 Disconnect the battery negative cable and position it away from the terminal.
3 For access to the sender unit, fold the rear seat cushion forwards.
4 Using a screwdriver, carefully prise the plastic access cover from the floor to expose the sender unit (the sender unit is located under the left-hand cover, viewed facing towards the front of the vehicle).
5 Disconnect the wiring connector from the sender unit. Tape the connector to the vehicle body, to prevent it disappearing behind the tank.
6 Noting the alignment marks on the tank, sender unit and the locking ring, unscrew the ring and remove it from the tank. This is best accomplished by using a screwdriver on the raised ribs of the locking ring. Carefully tap the screwdriver to turn the ring anti-clockwise until it can be unscrewed by hand.
7 Carefully lift the sender unit from the top of the fuel tank, taking great care not to bend the sender unit float arm, or to spill fuel onto the interior of the vehicle. Recover the rubber sealing ring and discard it; a new one must be used when refitting.

Refitting

8 Refitting is a reversal of the removal procedure noting the following points:
a) Prior to refitting, fit a new rubber sealing ring to the fuel tank.
b) Refit the sender unit to the tank, aligning its arrow with the centre of the three alignment marks on the fuel tank. Hold the sender in position, then refit the locking ring and tighten it until its mark is correctly aligned with the centre of the three fuel tank marks. All three marks should now be in alignment as noted prior to removal; misalignment will result in inaccurate fuel gauge readings.

3.3 Fit the spring clip (arrowed) to the first outer cable groove visible in front of the rubber grommet (see text)

6 Fuel pick-up unit - removal and refitting

1 On early models, the fuel pick-up and fuel gauge sender are separate units; Section 5 describes the removal and refitting of the fuel gauge sender unit. On later models, the fuel pick-up unit is integral with the fuel gauge sender unit; removal/refitting is as described in the following sub-sections.

Removal

2 Disconnect the battery negative lead.
3 For access to the fuel pick-up unit, fold the rear seat cushion forwards.
4 Using a screwdriver, carefully prise the plastic access cover from the floor to expose the fuel pick-up. On early models, where separate fuel pick-up and gauge sender units are fitted, the pick-up is located under the right-hand cover, viewed facing towards the front of the vehicle. On later models, where a combined fuel pick-up/gauge sender unit is fitted, the unit is located under the cover on the left-hand side **(see illustration)**.
5 Mark the hoses for identification purposes, then slacken the feed and return hose retaining clips. Where crimped-type hose clips are fitted, cut the clips and discard them, replace them with standard worm-drive hose clips on refitting. On later models, quick-release fittings may be fitted to the fuel hoses; these are released by depressing their metal collars with a small, flat-bladed screwdriver **(see illustrations)**.

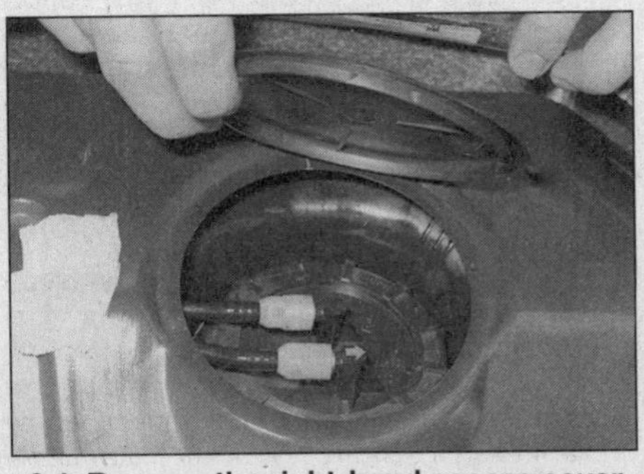

6.4 Remove the right-hand access cover to reveal the fuel pick-up unit

6.5a Where quick-release type fittings are used, depress their metal centre collars to release them . . .

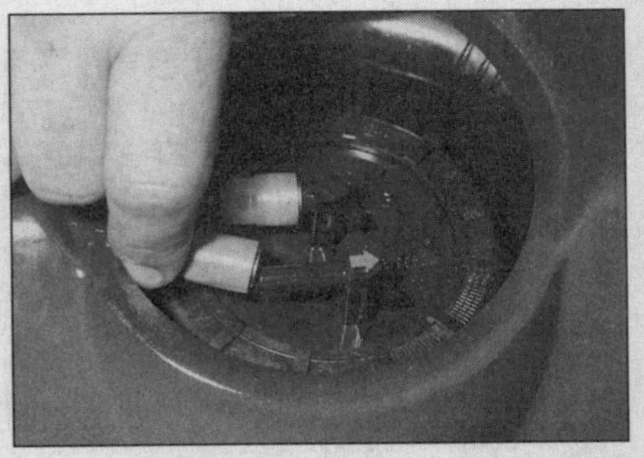

6.5b . . . then pull the hoses away from the pick-up unit

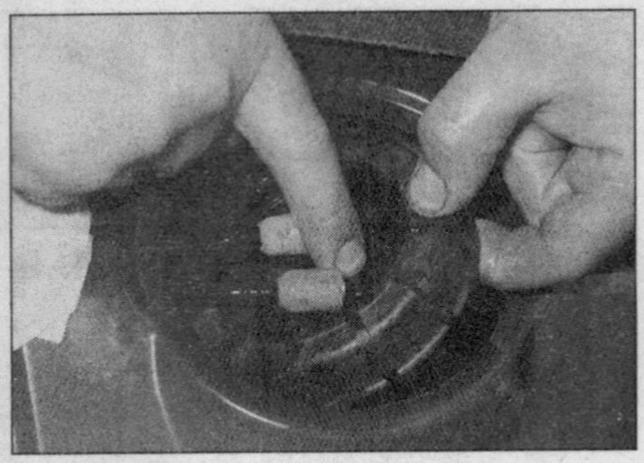

6.7 Unscrew the locking ring . . .

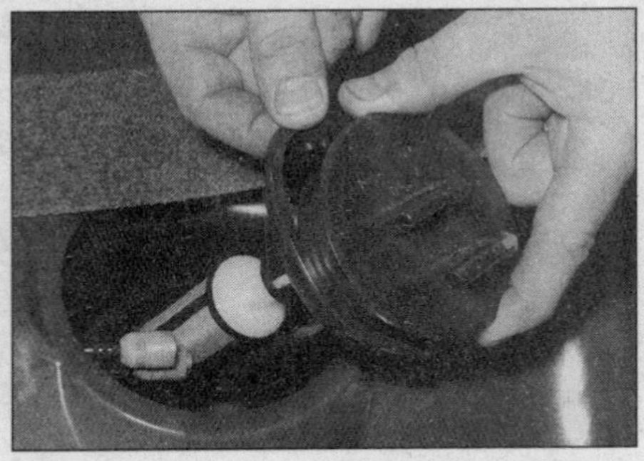

6.8 . . . then lift out the pick-up unit and recover the rubber sealing ring

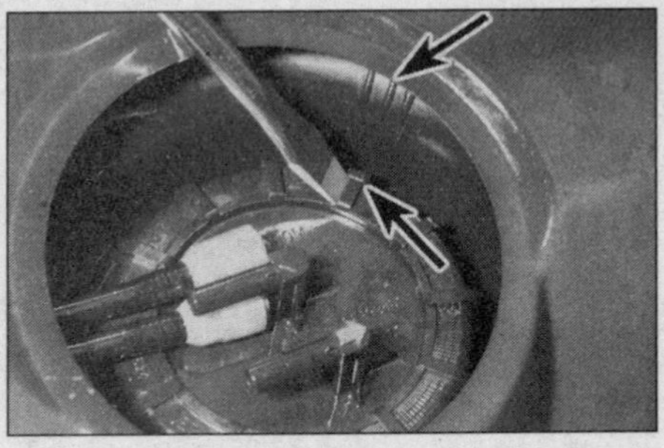

6.12 Tighten the locking ring until its mark is aligned with the centre of the three ribs on the fuel tank (arrowed)

6 Disconnect both hoses from the top of the pick-up, and plug the hose ends. Where applicable, unplug the sender unit wiring connector. Tape the connector to the vehicle body, to prevent it disappearing behind the tank

7 Noting the alignment marks on the tank, pick-up unit and the locking ring, unscrew the ring and remove it from the tank **(see illustration)**. This is best accomplished by using a screwdriver on the raised ribs of the locking ring. Carefully tap the screwdriver to turn the ring anti-clockwise until it can be unscrewed by hand.

8 Carefully lift the fuel pick-up assembly out of the fuel tank, taking great care not to damage the filter, or to spill fuel onto the interior of the vehicle. Where applicable, take care not to bend the sender unit float arm, as the unit is withdraw. Recover the rubber sealing ring and discard it; a new one must be used on refitting **(see illustration)**.

9 Note that the fuel pick-up assembly is only available as a complete assembly, no individual components are available separately.

Refitting

10 Ensure that the fuel pick-up filter is clean and free of debris. Fit the new sealing ring to the top of the fuel tank.

11 Carefully manoeuvre the pick-up into the fuel tank, guiding the float arm into position (where applicable) and aligning the mark noted on removal.

12 Refit the locking ring, tightening it until its mark is correctly aligned with the centre of the three lines on the fuel tank, as noted prior to removal **(see illustration)**.

8.3 Fuel system bleed screw (arrowed)

13 Reconnect the feed and return hoses, using the marks made on removal to ensure that they correctly reconnected, and (where necessary) securely tighten their retaining clips.

14 Where applicable, reconnect the sender unit wiring.

15 Reconnect the battery negative terminal, and start the engine. Check the fuel feed and return hose unions for signs of leakage.

16 If all is well, refit the plastic access cover, and fold back the rear seat cushion.

7 Fuel tank - removal, repair and refitting

Removal

1 Before removing the fuel tank, all fuel must be drained from the tank. Since a fuel tank drain plug is not provided, it is therefore preferable to carry out the removal operation when the tank is nearly empty. Before proceeding, disconnect the battery negative cable, and syphon or hand-pump the remaining fuel from the tank.

2 Remove the exhaust system as described in Chapter 4D. Where applicable, undo the fixings and remove the heat shield panelling.

3 Free both handbrake cables from their retaining clips on the base of the fuel tank.

4 Disconnect the wiring connector and fuel hoses from the fuel gauge sender unit and/or fuel pick-up unit, as described in Sections 5 and 6 (as applicable).

5 Working at the right-hand side of the fuel tank, release the retaining clips, then disconnect the filler neck vent pipe and main filler neck hose from the fuel tank/filler neck. Where necessary, also disconnect the breather hose(s). Some breather hoses are joined to the tank with quick-release fittings; to disconnect these fittings, slide the cover along the hose, then depress the centre ring and pull the hose out of its fitting.

6 Place a trolley jack with an interposed block of wood beneath the tank, then raise the jack until it is supporting the weight of the tank.

7 Slacken and remove the two retaining nuts and washers, then incline the fuel tank towards the rear of the car and slowly lower it out of position, disconnecting any other relevant vent pipes as they become accessible (where necessary). Remove the tank from underneath the vehicle, and recover the tank mounting rubbers, noting their correct fitted positions.

Repair

8 If the tank is contaminated with sediment or water, remove the sender unit and/or fuel pump unit (as applicable) as described in Section 5 and swill the tank out with clean fuel. The tank is injection-moulded from a synthetic material, and if damaged, it should be renewed. However, in certain cases, it may be possible to have small leaks or minor damage repaired. Seek the advice of a suitable specialist.

Refitting

9 Refitting is the reverse of the removal procedure, noting the following points:

a) *When lifting the tank back into position, make sure that the mounting rubbers are correctly positioned, and take great care to ensure that none of the hoses become trapped between the tank and vehicle body.*
b) *Ensure that all pipes and hoses are correctly routed, and securely held in position with their retaining clips.*
c) *On completion, refill the tank with fuel, and check for signs of leakage before and after taking the vehicle out on the road.*

8 Fuel system - priming and bleeding

1 After disconnecting part of the fuel supply system or running out of fuel, it will be necessary to prime the system and bleed off any air which may have been admitted.

2 All models are fitted with a hand-operated priming bulb, which is located close to the main fuse box, on the left-hand side of the engine compartment.

3 To prime the system, first loosen the bleed screw located on the top of the fuel filter/thermostat housing, mounted on the left-hand end of the cylinder head **(see illustration)**. On models where a bleed screw is not fitted, loosen the fuel outlet union at the filter/thermostat housing, or if this is difficult to reach, at the injection pump.

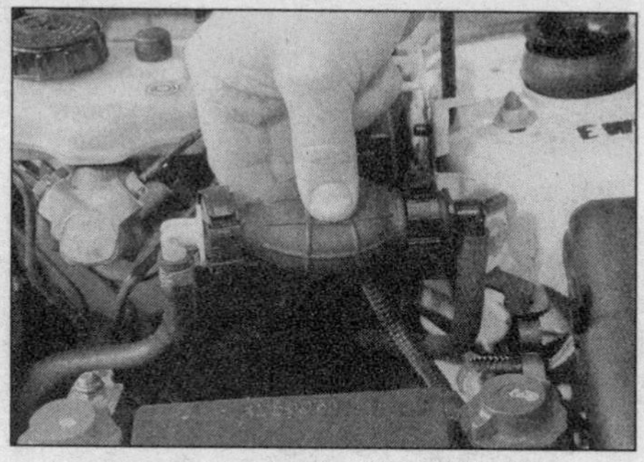

8.4 Fuel system priming bulb

4 Squeeze the priming bulb repeatedly, until fuel free from air bubbles emerges from the outlet union or bleed screw (as applicable) **(see illustration)**. Retighten the bleed screw or outlet union.

5 Switch on the ignition (to activate the injection pump stop solenoid) and continue squeezing the priming bulb until firm resistance is felt, then pump a few more times.

6 If a large amount of air has entered the pump, place a wad of rag around the fuel return union on the pump (to absorb spilt fuel), then slacken the union slightly. Operate the priming plunger (with the ignition switched on to activate the stop solenoid), until fuel free from air bubbles emerges from the fuel union. Tighten the union, and mop up split fuel.

7 If air has entered the injector pipes, place wads of rag around the injector pipe unions at the injectors to absorb spilt fuel, then slacken the unions slightly - **do not** unscrew them completely. Crank the engine on the starter motor until fuel emerges from the unions, then stop cranking the engine and retighten the unions. Mop up spilt fuel.

Warning: Be prepared to stop the engine immediately if it starts, to avoid excessive fuel spray and spillage . The injector supply pipes carry fuel at very high pressure- do not allow the spray to come into contact with bare skin as blood poisoning could result.

8 Start the engine with the accelerator pedal fully depressed. Additional cranking may be necessary to finally bleed the system before the engine starts. Keep the engine speed at a fast idle for a few minutes, to help bleed any remaining air bubbles from the fuel system.

9 Maximum engine speed - checking and adjustment

Caution: The maximum speed adjustment screw is sealed by the manufacturers at the factory using locking wire and a lead seal, and should not be disturbed

1 Run the engine to normal operating temperature. If the vehicle is not equipped with a tachometer (rev counter), connect a suitable instrument in accordance with its manufacturer's instructions.

2 Have an assistant fully depress the accelerator pedal, and check that the maximum engine speed is as given in the Specifications. Do not keep the engine at maximum speed for more than two or three seconds.

3 If adjustment is necessary, the vehicle should be taken to Citroën dealer or suitable diesel specialist. Adjustment should not be attempted by the home mechanic.

10 Fast idle thermostatic valve - removal and refitting

Removal

1 Disconnect the battery negative terminal.

2 Partially drain the cooling system as described in Chapter 1B.

3 Loosen the clamp nut, and slide the fast idle cable end fitting off the injection pump end of the inner cable **(see illustration)**.

4 Free the fast idle cable from the bracket on the fuel injection pump.

5 Using a suitable close fitting spanner, unscrew the thermostatic valve from the thermostat housing, at the left hand end of the cylinder head. Remove the valve and cable assembly from the engine compartment and recover the sealing washer **(see illustrations)**.

Refitting

6 Fit a new sealing washer to the valve, and screw the valve into position in the thermostat housing and tighten it to the specified torque.

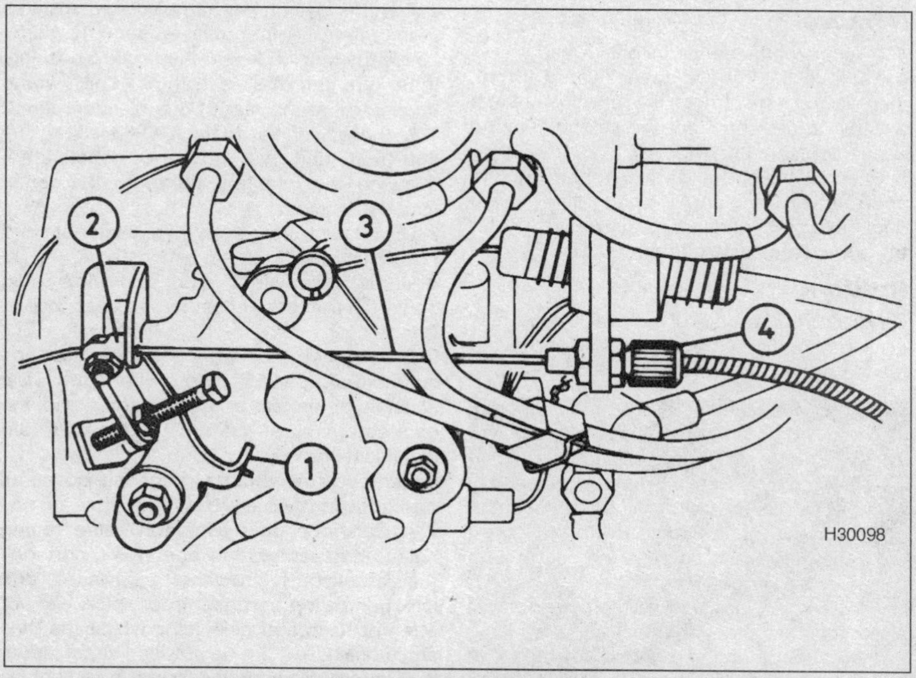

10.3 Slacken the clamp nut, and slide the end fitting off the fast idle cable (Lucas fuel injection pump shown)

1 Fast idle lever *2 Clamp nut* *3 Fast idle cable* *4 Adjustment collar*

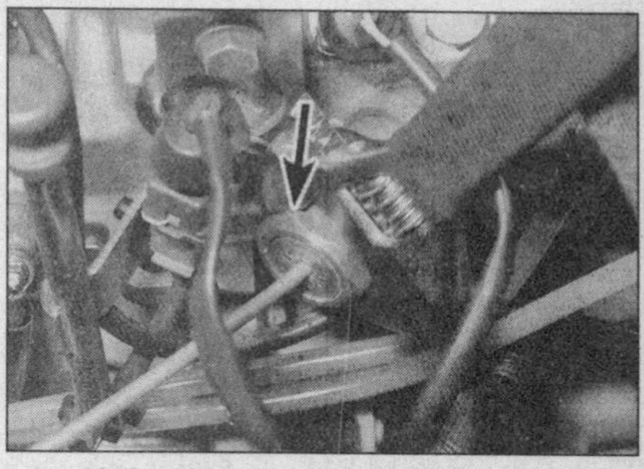

10.5a Unscrew the fast idle valve (arrowed) from the cylinder head . . .

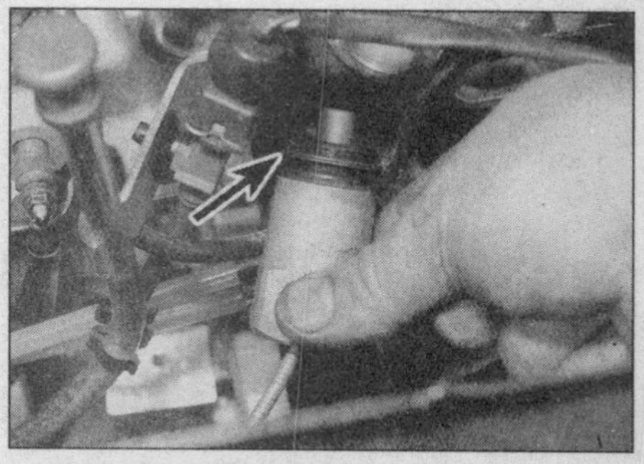

10.5b . . . and remove it along with its sealing washer (arrowed)

4C

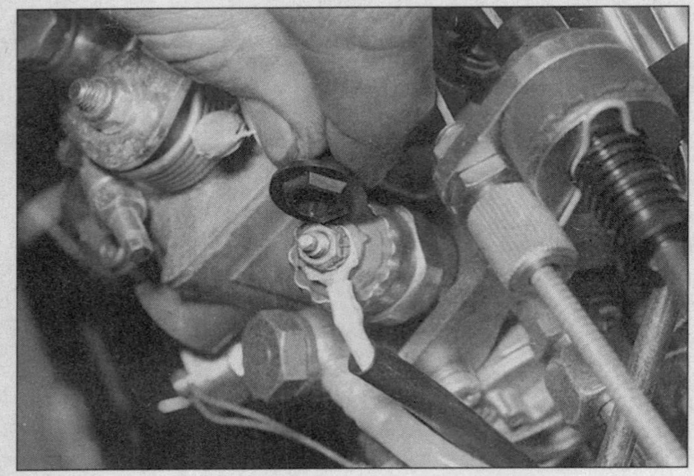

11.5a Remove the rubber cover . . .

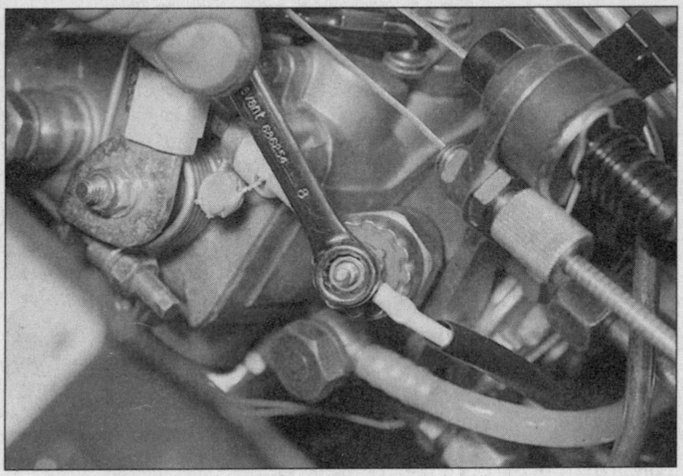

11.5b . . . then unscrew the retaining nut and disconnect the stop solenoid wiring connector

7 Insert the cable through the pump bracket, and pass the inner cable through the fast idle lever. Slide the end fitting onto the inner, and lightly tighten its clamp nut.
8 Refill the cooling system as described in Chapter 1B.
9 Adjust the fast idle cable as described in Section 14.

11 Stop solenoid - description, removal and refitting

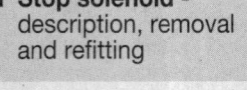

Note: *This procedure does not apply to models fitted with Citroën's keypad-operated engine immobiliser system. On these models, (with either Lucas or Bosch fuel injection pumps) the stop solenoid cannot be removed as an individual component, as it is integral with the anti-theft module, which is mounted on the rear of the fuel injection pump.*

Description

1 The stop solenoid is located on the rear upper surface of the fuel injection pump. Its purpose is to cut the fuel supply when the ignition is switched off. If an open-circuit occurs in the solenoid or its electrical supply, it will be impossible to start the engine, as the fuel will not be allowed to pass through the injection pump. The same applies if the solenoid jams shut. If the solenoid jams open, the engine will not stop when the ignition is switched off.
2 If the solenoid has failed and the engine will not run, a temporary repair may be made be removing the solenoid as described in the following paragraphs.
3 Refit the solenoid body without the plunger and spring, and tape up its feed wire so that it cannot touch earth. The engine can then be started as usual, but it will be necessary to use the manual stop lever on the injection pump (see Section 14), or to stall the engine in gear, to stop it.

Removal

4 Disconnect the battery negative lead.
5 Remove the rubber cover (where fitted), then slacken and remove the retaining nut and washer, and disconnect the solenoid wiring connector **(see illustrations)**.
6 Unscrew the solenoid valve from the pump, and recover the plunger, spring and sealing ring. Take great care not to allow dirt to enter the pump **(see illustrations)**.

Refitting

7 Refitting is a reversal of removal, using a new sealing ring. On completion, prime and bleed the fuel system as described in Section 8.

11.6a Unscrew the stop solenoid from the pump, and recover the O-ring (arrowed)

11.6b Remove the solenoid, and withdraw the plunger and spring

12 Fuel injection pump - removal and refitting

Removal

1 On models fitted with Citroën's keypad-operated engine immobiliser system, the anti-theft module must be deactivated before the injection pump is removed. To do this, carry out the operations described in paragraph 2. If a standard Citroën engine immobiliser is not fitted, proceed from paragraph 3 onwards.
2 Turn the ignition key to the second position, then enter the immobiliser security code. Leave the ignition key in the second position, then unplug the anti-theft unit wiring connector, at the rear of the injection pump. Turn the ignition key to the 'OFF' position. The anti-theft unit will now be deactivated, allowing the injection pump to be bench tested if required.
3 Disconnect the battery negative cable and position it away from the terminal.
4 Unplug the wiring from the glow plug control unit at the connector, as described in Chapter 5C.
5 Disconnect the wiring for the advance solenoid/air conditioning switch and stop solenoid at the rear of the injection pump; the connectors are colour coded to aid identification.
6 Remove the upper timing belt cover as described in Chapter 2B.
7 Align the engine assembly/valve timing holes as described in Chapter 2B, and lock the crankshaft, camshaft sprocket and injection pump sprocket in position. *Do not attempt to rotate the engine whilst the pins are in position.*
8 Remove the injection pump sprocket as described in Chapter 2B.
9 Loosen the clamp nut, and slide the fast idle cable end fitting off the injection pump

end of the inner cable. Free the fast idle cable from the bracket on the fuel injection pump.
10 Free the accelerator inner cable from the pump lever, then pull the outer cable out from its mounting bracket rubber grommet. Slide the flat washer off the end of the cable (where fitted), and remove the spring clip.
11 Wipe clean the fuel feed and return unions on the injection pump. Cover the alternator with a clean cloth or plastic bag, to guard against fuel being spilt onto it during the following operations.
12 Slacken and remove the fuel feed hose union bolt from the pump. Recover the sealing washer from each side of the hose union, and position the hose clear of the pump. Screw the union bolt back into position on the pump for safe-keeping, and cover both the hose end and union bolt to prevent the ingress of dirt into the fuel system.
13 Detach the fuel return hose from the pump as described in the previous paragraph. **Note:** *The injection pump feed and return hose union bolts are not interchangeable.*
14 Wipe clean the pipe unions, then slacken the union nut securing the injector pipes to the top of each injector, and the four union nuts securing the pipes to the rear of the injection pump; as each pump union nut is slackened, retain the adapter with a suitable open-ended spanner to prevent it being unscrewed from the pump. With all the union nuts undone, remove the injector pipes from the engine (the pipes are removed in pairs).
15 On models not fitted with a Citroën engine immobiliser, remove the rubber cover, then undo the retaining nut and disconnect the wiring from the injection pump stop solenoid.
16 Unscrew the nut and washer securing the injection pump rear mounting bracket to the cylinder block.
17 Slacken and remove the three bolts securing the pump to its front mounting bracket, then manoeuvre the pump out of the engine compartment. Ensure that the sprocket hub locking tool remains in position - tape it to the hub if necessary.

Refitting

18 Manoeuvre the pump into position, and refit its three front mounting bolts, and the rear mounting nut, tightening them to the specified torque.
19 Refit the injection pump sprocket as described in Chapter 2B. Ensure that the sprocket locking tool remains engaged with the sprocket hub.
20 Check the crankshaft, camshaft and injection pump sprockets are all correctly positioned, then engage the timing belt and tension it as described in Chapter 2B. With the timing belt correctly fitted, remove the locking pins/bolts from the camshaft and injection pump sprockets and flywheel.
21 With the pump timing correctly set, reconnect the wiring to the advance solenoid/air conditioning switch and stop solenoid (as applicable) at the rear of the injection pump.
22 Reconnect the fuel feed and return hose unions to the pump, not forgetting to fit the filter to the feed hose union (where applicable). Position a new sealing washer on each side of both unions, and tighten the union bolts to the specified torque setting.
23 Refit the injector pipes, and tighten their union nuts to the specified torque setting.
24 Mop up any spilt fuel, then remove the cover from the alternator.
25 Reconnect the accelerator cable, and adjust as described in Section 3.
26 Reconnect the fast idle valve cable, as described in Section 10, then adjust the fast idle speed as described in Section 14.
27 Reconnect the wiring to the glow plug control unit, as described in Chapter 5C.
28 Reconnect the battery negative lead.
29 Prime and bleed the fuel system as described in Section 8.
30 On models with a Citroën engine immobiliser, reconnect the wiring to the anti-theft unit, at the rear of the injection pump.
31 On completion, start the engine, and adjust the idle speed and anti-stall speed as described in Section 14.

13 Injection timing - general information

Both types of fuel injection pump (Bosch and Lucas) are fitted to the TUD5 engine by means of non-adjustable mountings. This means that the static injection timing is fixed and cannot be adjusted by rotating the pump body with respect to the engine. The only way of checking that the timing is correct is to set the engine to TDC, as described in Chapter 2B. In this position, the timing hole in the injection pump sprocket hub should line up with a corresponding hole in the injection pump body, allowing the fitment of a sprocket locking tool. Misalignment of the timing holes means that the timing belt has been incorrectly fitted.

If you suspect that the injection timing is incorrect (because of excessive smoke, noisy combustion, poor performance or heavy fuel consumption for example) there may be a fault with the injection pump. Have the car inspected by a Citroën dealer or diesel injection specialist, who will have the equipment needed to check the injection pump timing dynamically (ie whilst the engine is running).

14 Fuel injection pump - adjustment

General information

1 The usual type of tachometer (rev counter), which works from ignition system pulses, cannot be used on diesel engines. A diagnostic socket is provided for the use of Citroën test equipment, but this will not normally be available to the home mechanic. If it is not felt that adjusting the idle speed "by ear" is satisfactory, it will be necessary to purchase or hire an appropriate tachometer, or else leave the task to a Citroën dealer or other suitably equipped specialist.
2 Before making adjustments, warm up the engine to normal operating temperature. Make sure that the accelerator cable is correctly adjusted (see Section 3).

Engine idle speed

3 Check that the engine idles at the specified speed. If necessary, adjustments can be made using the idle speed adjustment screw on the top of the fuel injection pump **(see illustrations)**.
4 On models with a Bosch fuel injection pump, first slacken the anti-stall screw until its tip is just clear of the throttle lever.
5 Loosen the locknut (where applicable), then adjust the idle speed screw (as necessary) until the position is found where the engine is idling at the specified speed. Once the screw is correctly positioned, securely tighten the locknut.

4C

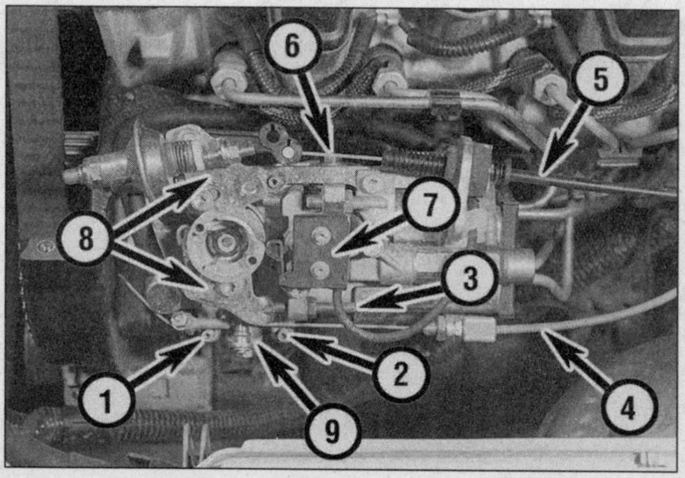

14.3a Bosch fuel injection pump adjustment points
1 Fast idle screw
2 Idle screw
3 Anti-stall screw
4 Fast idle cable
5 Accelerator cable
6 Manual stop lever
7 EGR system throttle position microswitch
8 Throttle lever
9 Fast idle lever

6 Check (and if necessary, adjust) the anti-stall speed as described in the next sub-Section.

Anti stall speed

7 Adjust the idle speed as described in the previous sub-Section, then switch off the engine.
8 Insert a shim or feeler blade, of the correct thickness (see Specifications), between the pump throttle lever and the anti-stall adjustment screw.
9 Start the engine and allow it to idle. The engine should now run at the specified anti-stall speed (see Specifications).
10 If adjustment is necessary, loosen the locknut, and turn the anti-stall adjustment screw as required, until the anti-stall speed is correct. Hold the screw in this position, and securely tighten the locknut.
11 Remove the shim or feeler blade, then recheck the idle speed.
12 Move the accelerator lever to increase the engine speed to approximately 3000 rpm, then quickly release the lever. The deceleration period should be between 2.5 and 3.5 seconds, and the engine speed should drop to approximately 50 rpm below the specified idle speed, before stabilising.
13 If the deceleration is too fast and the engine stalls, screw the anti-stall adjustment screw in a quarter of a turn towards the accelerator lever. If the deceleration is too slow, resulting in high idle speed and poor engine braking, unscrew it a quarter of a turn away from the lever. Adjust as necessary, then securely retighten the locknut.
14 Recheck the idle speed and, if necessary, adjust as described above.
15 With the engine idling, check the operation of the manual stop control by turning the stop lever anti-clockwise (refer to the relevant sub-Section). The engine must stop instantly.
16 Where applicable, disconnect the tachometer on completion.

Fast idle speed

Bosch fuel injection pump

17 Start the engine and allow it to idle. Operate the fast idle lever by hand until it contacts the fast idle screw. Hold the lever in this position, and adjust the fast idle screw until the specified fast idle speed is obtained. Release the lever.
18 Slacken the fast idle cable end fitting clamp nut. With the engine cold, operate the fast idle lever until it contacts the fast idle screw. Hold the lever in this position, and slide the cable end fitting along the cable until its abuts the fast idle lever. Securely tighten the end fitting clamp nut.
19 Start the engine, and warm it up to its normal operating temperature. As the engine warms up, the fast idle cable should extend so that the fast idle lever moves away from the fast idle screw.
20 Wait until the cooling fan has cut in and cut out, then switch off the engine. Measure the total travel of the fast idle lever between the cold and hot positions and compare it with the figure give in the Specifications. If the measured travel is incorrect, slacken the clamp nut, move the end fitting to achieve the correct travel, then securely retighten the screw or nut. Fine adjustment of the cable can be carried out by turning the knurled adjustment collar, at the end of the fast idle cable outer sleeve.
21 With the cable correctly adjusted, allow the engine to cool. As it cools, the fast idle cable should be drawn back into the valve, pulling the fast idle lever back against its stop.

Lucas fuel injection pump

22 With the engine cold, check that the fast idle lever rests against the stop on the top of the fuel injection pump. If this is not the case, slacken the fast idle cable end fitting clamp nut, move the end fitting to achieve the correct lever travel, then securely retighten the screw or nut.
23 Start the engine, and warm it up to its normal operating temperature. As the engine warms up, the fast idle cable should extend so that the fast idle lever moves away from its stop.
24 Wait until the cooling fan has cut in and cut out, then switch off the engine. Measure the total travel of the fast idle lever between the cold and hot positions and compare it with the figure given in the Specifications. If the measured travel is incorrect, slacken the clamp nut, move the end fitting to achieve the correct travel, then securely retighten the screw or nut. Fine adjustment of the cable can be carried out by turning the knurled collar, at the end of the fast idle cable outer sleeve.

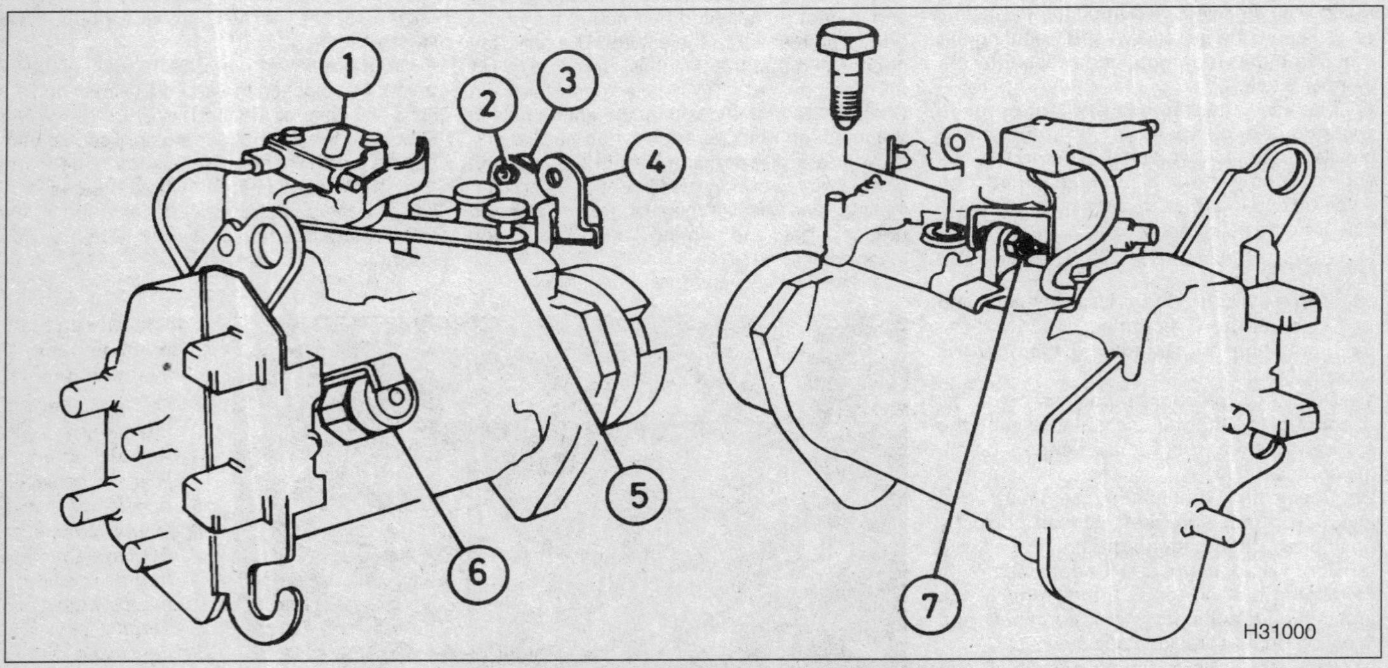

14.3b Lucas fuel injection pump adjustment points

1 *EGR system throttle position switch*
2 *Idle screw*
3 *Manual stop lever*
4 *Fast idle lever*
5 *Throttle lever*
6 *Electromagnetic advance mechanism*
7 *Anti-stall screw*

Manual stop lever

25 Both types of fuel injection pump (Bosch and Lucas) fitted to the TUD5 engine are equipped with a manual stop lever. This device cuts off the fuel supply from the injection pump, allowing the engine to be stopped in an emergency if required. The operation of the manual stop lever should be checked regularly.

26 On Bosch injection pumps, the manual stop lever is located on the rear of the pump body, between the pump and the engine. On Lucas injection pumps, the manual stop lever is located on the front of the pump body below the fast idle lever. To check the operation of the manual stop lever, start the engine and allow it to idle. Rotate the manual stop lever fully to the end of its travel; the engine should stop immediately. If the engine continues to run, adjust the anti-stall speed as described earlier in this Section. If the problem persists, then a fault may exist within the fuel injection pump - refer to a Citroën dealer, or diesel fuel injection specialist for further advice.

15 Fuel injectors - testing, removal and refitting

Warning: Exercise extreme caution when working on the fuel injectors. Never expose the hands (or any part of the body) to injector spray, as the high working pressure can cause the fuel to penetrate the skin, with possibly fatal results. You are strongly advised to have any work which involves testing the injectors under pressure carried out by a dealer or fuel injection specialist. Refer to the precautions given in Section 1 of this Chapter before proceeding.

Testing

1 Injectors do deteriorate with prolonged use, and it is reasonable to expect them to need reconditioning or renewal after 60 000 miles (100 000 km) or so. Accurate testing, overhaul and calibration of the injectors must be left to a specialist. A defective injector which is causing knocking or smoking can be located without dismantling, as follows.

2 Run the engine at fast idle. Slacken each injector union in turn, placing rag around the union to catch spilt fuel, and *being careful not to expose the skin to any spray*. When the union on the defective injector is slackened, the knocking or smoking will stop.

Removal

Note: *Take great care not to allow dirt into the injectors or fuel pipes during this procedure. Do not drop the injectors, or allow the needles at their tips to become damaged. The injectors are precision-made to fine limits, and must not be handled roughly. In particular, do not mount them in a bench vice.*

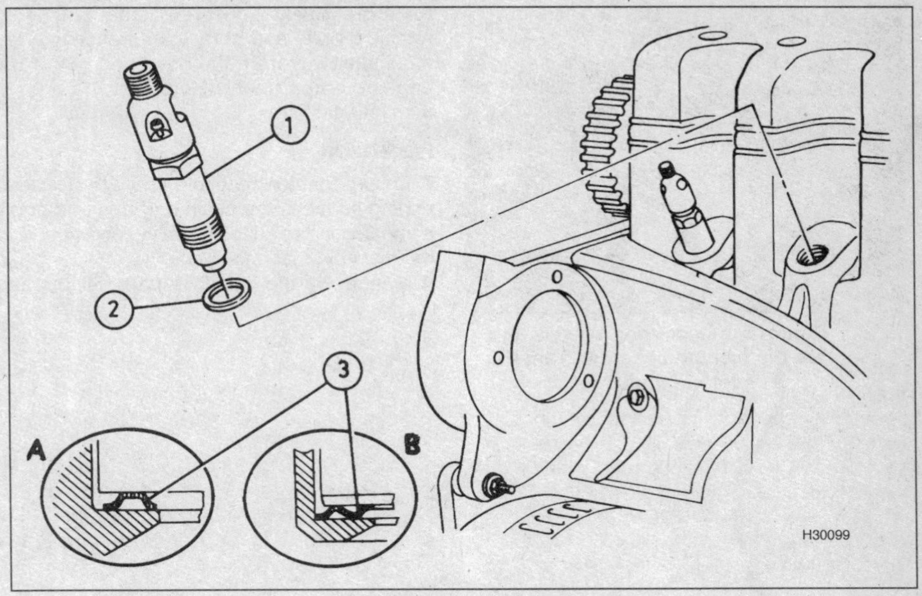

15.7 Fuel injector assembly

1 Injector and holder assembly
2 Sealing washer
3 Flame shield washer
A Lucas injector
B Bosch injector

3 Disconnect the battery negative lead. Cover the alternator with a clean cloth or plastic bag, to guard against fuel being spilt onto it.

4 Carefully clean around the injectors and pipe union nuts, and disconnect the return pipe from the injector.

5 Wipe clean the pipe unions, then slacken the union nut securing the relevant injector pipes to each injector. Slacken the relevant union nuts securing the pipes to the rear of the injection pump (the pipes are removed in pairs). As each pump union nut is slackened, retain the adapter with a suitable open-ended spanner, to prevent it being unscrewed from the pump. With the union nuts undone, remove the relevant injector pipes from the engine. Note the position of any clips attached to the pipes, for use when refitting. Cover the injector and pipe unions, to prevent the entry of dirt into the system.

6 Unscrew the injector, using a deep socket or box spanner, and remove it from the cylinder head.

15.9 Refit the injector and tighten it to the specified torque setting

7 Recover the sealing washers. Note that the flame shield washer is fitted between the base of the injector and the injector holder/sleeve **(see illustration)**.

Refitting

8 Obtain a new sealing washer and fit it squarely to the base of the injector port in the cylinder head.

9 Screw the injector into position, and tighten it to the specified torque **(see illustration)**.

10 Refit the injector pipes, and tighten the union nuts to the specified torque setting. Position any clips attached to the pipes as noted before removal.

11 Reconnect the return pipe securely to the injector.

12 Prime and bleed the fuel system as described in Section 8.

16 Inlet manifold - removal and refitting

Removal

1 Disconnect the battery negative terminal.

2 Remove the air cleaner housing and intake ducting as described in Section 2.

3 Where applicable, remove the EGR valve as described in Chapter 4D.

4 Remove the securing screws and detach the support bracket from the plenum chamber, on the underside of the manifold.

5 Remove the securing screws and separate the plenum chamber from the inlet manifold **(see illustration)**.

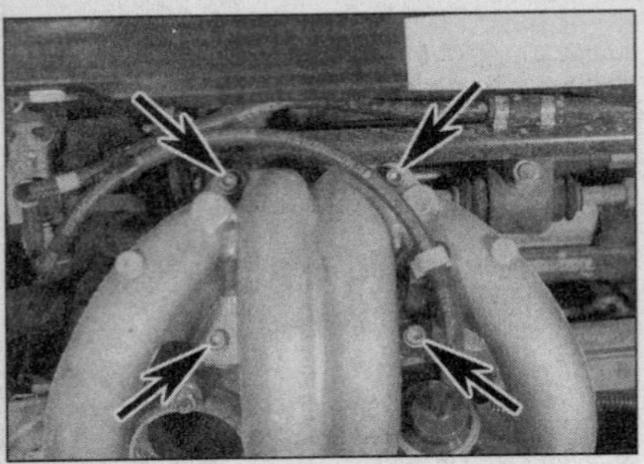

16.5 Remove the securing screws and separate the plenum chamber from the inlet manifold

6 Progressively unscrew the manifold retaining bolts and nuts, then manoeuvre the manifold away from the head and out of the engine compartment. Note that there is no manifold gasket.

Refitting

7 Ensure that the manifold and cylinder head mating surfaces are clean and dry, and apply a thin coating of suitable sealing compound to the manifold mating surface.

8 Manoeuvre the manifold into position, and refit its retaining nuts and bolts. Tighten them evenly and progressively to the specified torque setting.

9 Apply a thin coating of suitable sealing compound to the mating surface, then refit the plenum chamber to the inlet manifold, tightening the retaining screws securing.

10 Insert the manifold support bracket bolts and tighten them securely.

11 Refit the air cleaner housing and intake ducting as described in Section 2.

Chapter 4 Part D:
Emission control and exhaust systems

Contents

Degrees of difficulty

Easy, suitable for novice with little experience	**Fairly easy,** suitable for beginner with some experience	**Fairly difficult,** suitable for competent DIY mechanic	**Difficult,** suitable for experienced DIY mechanic	**Very difficult,** suitable for expert DIY or professional

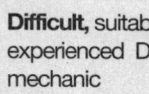

Specifications

Torque wrench settings	**Nm**	**lbft**
Exhaust manifold retaining nuts (petrol models):		
1587 cc 16-valve models:		
Stage 1	10	7
Stage 2	18	13
All other models	15	11
Exhaust manifold (diesel models)	18	13
Exhaust manifold heat shield	8	6
Exhaust system fasteners:		
Front pipe-to-manifold nut:		
1587 cc 16-valve models	8	6
All other models	35	26
Front pipe to intermediate pipe/catalytic converter	10	7
Clamping ring nuts	15	11

1 General information

Emission control systems

All petrol engined models covered in this manual are controlled by fuel injection or engine management systems that are "tuned" to give the best compromise between driveability, fuel consumption and exhaust emission production. In addition, a number of systems are fitted that help to minimise other harmful emissions: a crankcase emission-control system that reduces the release of pollutants from the engines lubrication system is fitted to all models, catalytic converters that reduce exhaust gas pollutants are fitted to all models and an evaporative loss emission control system that reduces the release of gaseous hydrocarbons from the fuel tank is fitted to all models.

All diesel engined models are also equipped with a crankcase emission control system. In addition, all models are fitted with an Exhaust Gas Recirculation (EGR) system to reduce exhaust emissions.

Crankcase emission control

To reduce the emission of unburned hydrocarbons from the crankcase into the atmosphere, the engine is sealed and the blow-by gases and oil vapour are drawn from inside the crankcase, through a wire mesh oil separator, into the inlet tract to be burned by the engine during normal combustion.

Under conditions of high manifold depression (idling, deceleration) the gases will be sucked positively out of the crankcase. Under conditions of low manifold depression (acceleration, full-throttle running) the gases are forced out of the crankcase by the (relatively) higher crankcase pressure; if the engine is worn, the raised crankcase pressure (due to increased blow-by) will cause some of the flow to return under all manifold conditions. On certain engines, a pressure regulating valve (mounted on the camshaft cover) controls the flow of gases from the crankcase.

Exhaust emission control - petrol models

To minimise the amount of pollutants which escape into the atmosphere, all models are fitted with a catalytic converter in the exhaust system. The fuelling system is of the closed-loop type, in which a Lambda sensor in the exhaust system provides the engine management system ECU with constant feedback, enabling the ECU to adjust the air/fuel mixture to optimise combustion. Certain 1360 cc models are fitted with two Lambda sensors, one upstream of the catalytic converter and one downstream, to give greater control over the engines fuelling and exhaust emissions. In addition, models supplied to some markets are fitted with a catalyst temperature monitoring system, consisting of a exhaust pipe-mounted temperature sensor, an electronic control unit and an associated wiring harness. At the time of writing, very little information was available regarding this particular system.

The Lambda sensor has a heating element built-in that is controlled by the ECU through the Lambda sensor relay to quickly bring the sensor's tip to its optimum operating temperature. The sensor's tip is sensitive to oxygen and relays a voltage signal to the ECU that varies according on the amount of oxygen in the exhaust gas. If the intake air/fuel mixture is too rich, the exhaust gases are low in oxygen

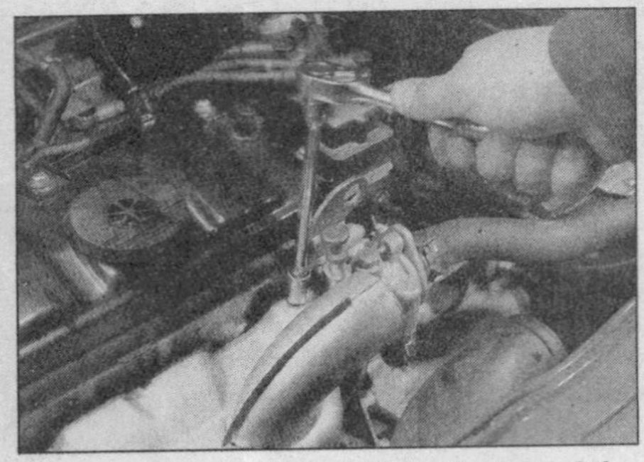

2.2 Remove the shroud from the top of the exhaust manifold

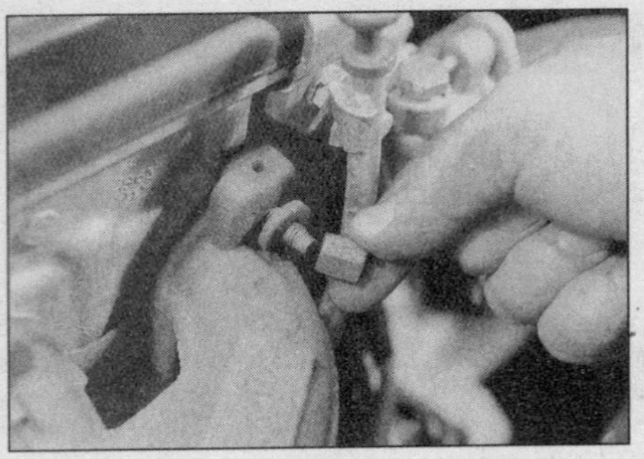

2.5a Undo the nuts . . .

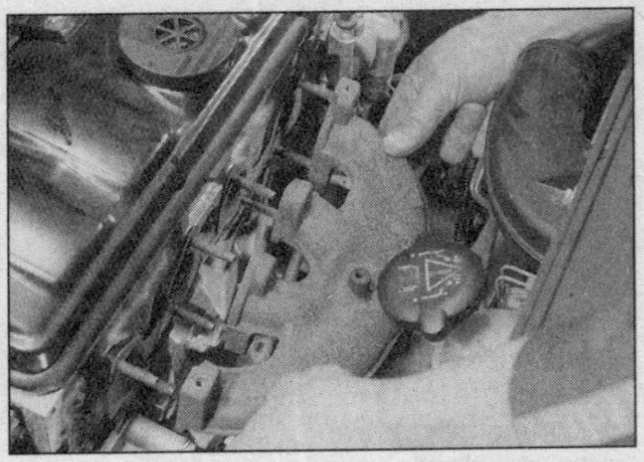

2.5b . . . and remove the manifold from the cylinder head

so the sensor sends a low-voltage signal, the voltage rising as the mixture weakens and the amount of oxygen rises in the exhaust gases. Peak conversion efficiency of all major pollutants occurs if the intake air/fuel mixture is maintained at the chemically-correct ratio for the complete combustion of petrol of 14.7 parts (by weight) of air to 1 part of fuel (the 'stoichiometric' ratio). The sensor output voltage alters in a large step at this point, the ECU using the signal change as a reference point and correcting the intake air/fuel mixture accordingly by altering the fuel injector pulse width.

Exhaust emission control - diesel models

An Exhaust Gas Recirculation (EGR) system is fitted to certain diesel models. This reduces the level of nitrogen oxides produced during combustion by flowing a proportion of the exhaust gases back into the inlet manifold, via a plunger valve, under certain engine operating conditions.

Evaporative loss emission control - petrol models

To minimise the escape of unburned hydrocarbons into the atmosphere, an evaporative loss emission control system is fitted to certain petrol models. The fuel tank filler cap is sealed and a charcoal-filled canister, mounted in the engine compartment, collects the petrol vapours released from the fuel contained in the fuel tank. It stores them until they can be drawn from the canister (under the control of the fuel-injection/ignition system ECU) via the purge valve(s) into the inlet tract, where they are then burned by the engine during normal combustion.

To ensure that the engine runs correctly when it is cold and/or idling and to protect the catalytic converter from the effects of an over-rich mixture, the purge control valve is not opened by the ECU until the engine has warmed up, and the engine is under load. The purge valve is then modulated (i.e. switched on and off) to allow the stored vapour to pass into the inlet tract.

Exhaust systems

Refer to the information given in Section 4.

2 Exhaust manifold (petrol models) - removal and refitting

Removal

1 Disconnect the hot-air intake hose from the manifold shroud, and remove it from the vehicle (see Chapter 4A or 4B, as applicable).

2 Slacken and remove the retaining screws, and remove the shroud from the top of the exhaust manifold **(see illustration)**.

3 Firmly apply the handbrake, then jack up the front of the vehicle and support it on axle stands (see "*Jacking and vehicle support*").

4 Undo the nuts securing the exhaust front pipe to the manifold, then free the front pipe and recover the gasket. Support the front pipe on a block of wood, to avoid straining the Lambda sensor wiring. Alternatively, unplug the Lambda sensor wiring at the multiway connector.

5 Undo the nuts securing the manifold to the head **(see illustrations)**. Manoeuvre the manifold out of the engine compartment, and discard the manifold gaskets.

Refitting

6 Refitting is the reverse of the removal procedure, noting the following points **(see illustrations)**:

a) *Examine all the exhaust manifold studs for signs of damage and corrosion. Remove all traces of corrosion, and repair or renew any damaged studs.*

b) *Ensure that the manifold and cylinder head sealing faces are clean and flat, and fit new manifold gaskets. Tighten the manifold retaining nuts to the specified torque.*

c) *Reconnect the front pipe to the manifold using the information given in Section 4.*

3 Exhaust manifold (diesel models) - removal and refitting

Removal

1 Firmly apply the handbrake, then jack up the front of the vehicle and support it on axle stands (see "*Jacking and vehicle support*").

2 Remove the inlet manifold as described in Chapter 4C. On models with EGR, it will be necessary to remove the bolts and detach the recirculation pipe from the exhaust manifold flange.

3 Place a jack beneath the engine, with a block of wood on the jack head. Raise the jack until it is supporting the weight of the engine.

4 Slacken and remove the four nuts securing the right-hand engine mounting upper bracket to the cylinder block and body, and lift off the bracket. Lift the buffer plate off the mounting stud. Note that this is necessary to allow access to the far right-hand exhaust manifold stud **(see illustrations)**.

5 Unscrew the bolt securing the front pipe to its mounting, then undo the nuts securing the exhaust front pipe to the manifold. Free the

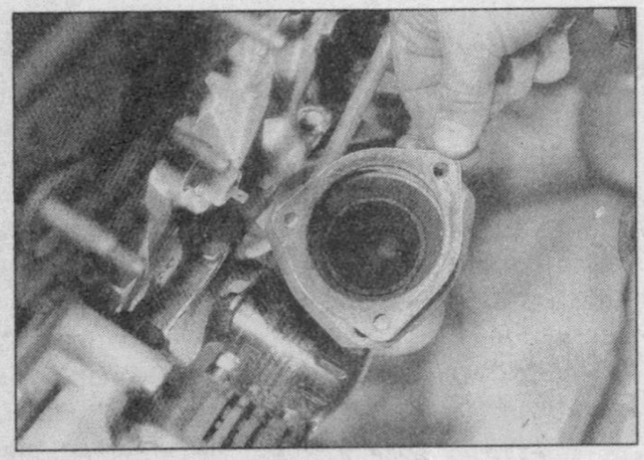

2.6a When refitting the manifold, fit new gaskets to the exhaust front pipe . . .

2.6b . . . and cylinder head

3.4a Slacken and remove the four nuts (arrowed) . . .

3.4b . . . then lift off the engine mounting bracket . . .

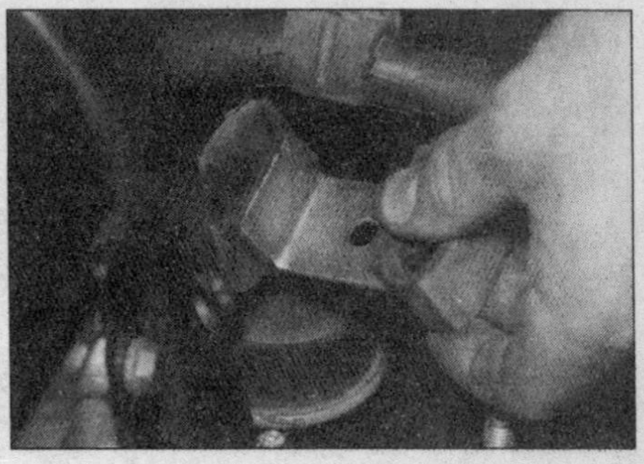

3.4c . . . and recover the buffer plate

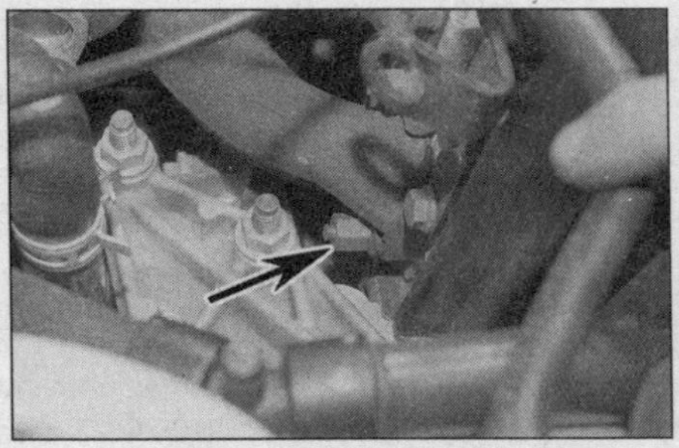

3.4d Removal of the engine mounting allows access to the far right-hand manifold stud (arrowed)

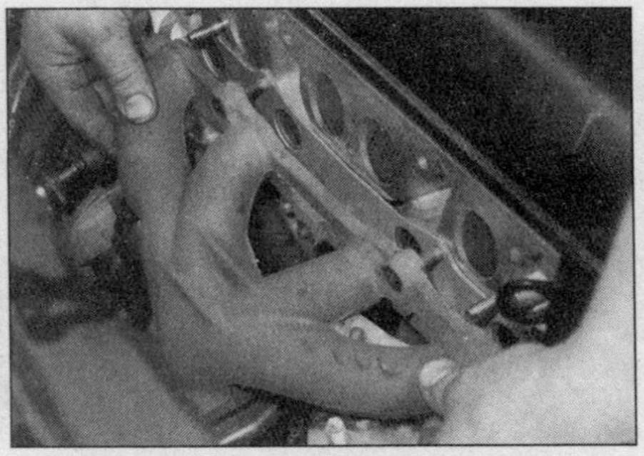

3.6 Undo the retaining nuts and remove the manifold from the cylinder head

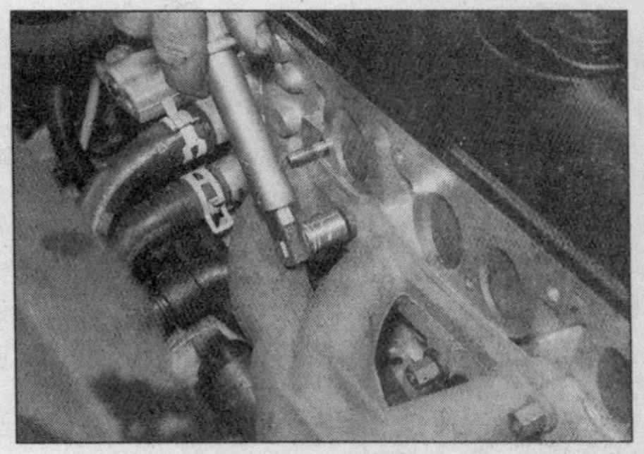

3.7 On refitting, tighten the manifold retaining nuts to the specified torque

front pipe from the manifold, and recover the gasket.

6 Undo the eight retaining nuts securing the manifold to the head. Manoeuvre the manifold out of the engine compartment, and discard the manifold gasket(s) **(see illustration)**.

Refitting

7 Refitting is the reverse of the removal procedure, noting the following points:

a) *Examine all the exhaust manifold studs for signs of damage and corrosion. Remove all traces of corrosion, and repair or renew any damaged studs.*

b) *Ensure that the manifold and cylinder head sealing faces are clean and flat, and fit the new manifold gaskets. Tighten the manifold retaining nuts to the specified torque* ***(see illustration)****.*

c) *Refit the right-hand engine mounting bracket, and tighten its retaining nuts to the specified torque (see Chapter 2B).*

d) *Reconnect the front pipe to the manifold using the information given in Section 4.*

4 Exhaust system - general information and component renewal

General information

1 On all petrol models, the exhaust system consists of four sections: the front pipe, the catalytic converter, the intermediate pipe, and the tailpipe silencer box. The joint between the front pipe and the catalytic converter is secured by nuts and bolts and is of the spring-loaded, flanged balljoint type, to allow for movement in the exhaust system. All remaining sections are connected by slip-joints and secured by clamping rings **(see illustration)**.

2 On diesel models, the exhaust system consists of three sections: the front pipe, the intermediate section (which contains an oxidation catalyst on some models) and the tailpipe silencer box **(see illustration)**.

3 The system is suspended throughout its entire length by rubber mountings. On certain models, the front pipe is bolted to a mounting bracket, to provide additional support. In some markets, early 1587 cc models were fitted with a catalyst overheat detection system, consisting of a temperature sensor mounted downstream of the catalyst, an electronic control unit and an associated

4.1 Typical exhaust system layout - petrol models

1 Front pipe
2 Catalytic converter
3 Intermediate pipe
4 Tailpipe/silencer box

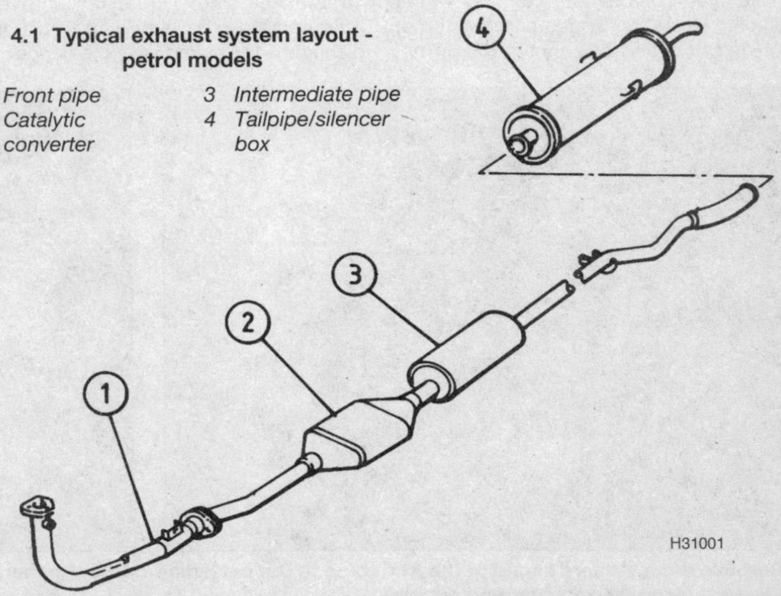

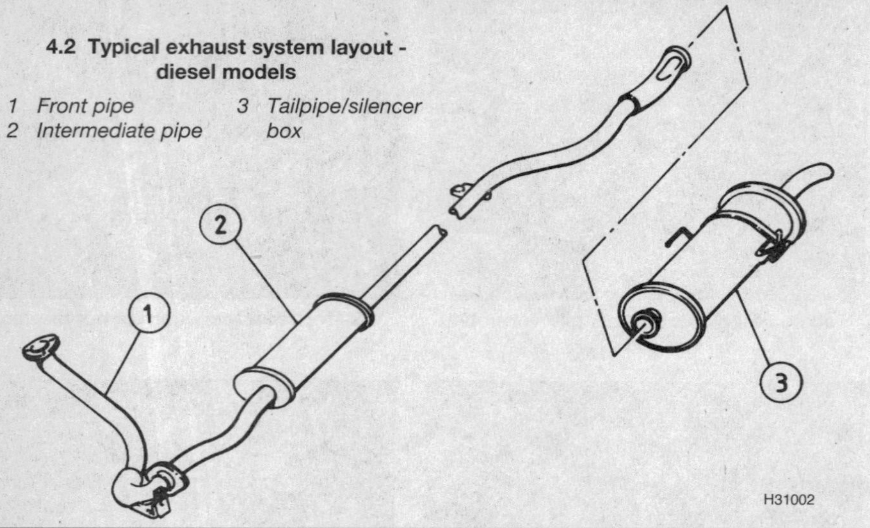

4.2 Typical exhaust system layout - diesel models

1 *Front pipe*
2 *Intermediate pipe*
3 *Tailpipe/silencer box*

wiring harness. In addition, certain 1360 cc models are fitted with two Lambda sensors - one mounted upstream, and another mounted downstream, of the catalytic converter. These points should be borne in mind when disconnecting the section of the exhaust that contains the catalytic converter.

Removal

4 Each exhaust section can be removed individually or, alternatively, the complete system can be removed as a unit.

5 To remove the system or part of the system, first jack up the front or rear of the car, and support it on axle stands (see "*Jacking and vehicle support*"). Alternatively, position the car over an inspection pit, or on car ramps.

Front pipe

6 On petrol models, trace the wiring back from the Lambda sensor to its wiring connectors, which are clipped onto the top of the transmission, and disconnect them from the main wiring harness.

7 Undo the nuts securing the front pipe flange joint to the manifold and, where necessary, the single bolt securing the front pipe to its mounting bracket, on the underside of the transmission. Separate the flange joint and collect the gasket.

8 Remove the fasteners securing the front pipe to the catalytic converter/intermediate pipe (as applicable), and recover the spring cups and springs **(see illustrations)**. Remove the bolts, then withdraw the front pipe from underneath the vehicle, taking great care not to damage the Lambda sensor. Recover the wire-mesh gasket from the joint.

Catalytic converter - petrol models

9 Undo the two nuts securing the front pipe flange joint to the catalytic converter. Recover the springs and spring cups, and withdraw the bolts.

10 Slacken the catalytic converter-to-intermediate pipe clamping ring bolts, and disengage the clamp from the flange joint.

11 Free the catalytic converter from the intermediate pipe, then withdraw it from underneath the vehicle. Do not drop the catalytic converter, as it contains a fragile ceramic element. Recover the wire-mesh gasket from the front pipe joint.

Intermediate pipe/catalytic converter - diesel models

12 Undo the two nuts securing the front pipe flange joint to the intermediate pipe. Recover the springs and spring cups, and withdraw the bolts.

13 Slacken the clamping ring bolts, and disengage the clamp from the intermediate pipe-to-tailpipe joint.

14 Free the intermediate pipe from its mounting rubbers, then disengage it from the tailpipe and the front pipe, and remove it from underneath the vehicle. Recover the wire-mesh gasket from the front pipe joint.

Intermediate pipe - petrol models

15 Slacken the clamping ring bolts, and disengage the clamps from both the intermediate pipe joints.

16 Free the intermediate pipe from its mounting rubbers, then disengage it first from the tailpipe then the catalytic converter, and remove it from underneath the vehicle.

Tailpipe

17 Slacken the intermediate pipe-to-tailpipe clamping ring bolts, and disengage the clamp from the joint.

18 Unhook the tailpipe from its mounting rubbers, and remove it from the vehicle.

Complete system

19 Disconnect the front pipe from the manifold as described in paragraphs 6 and 7.

20 With the aid of an assistant, free the system from its mounting rubbers, and manoeuvre it out from underneath the vehicle. Where applicable, take care to avoid straining the catalyst overheat sensor and Lambda sensor wiring.

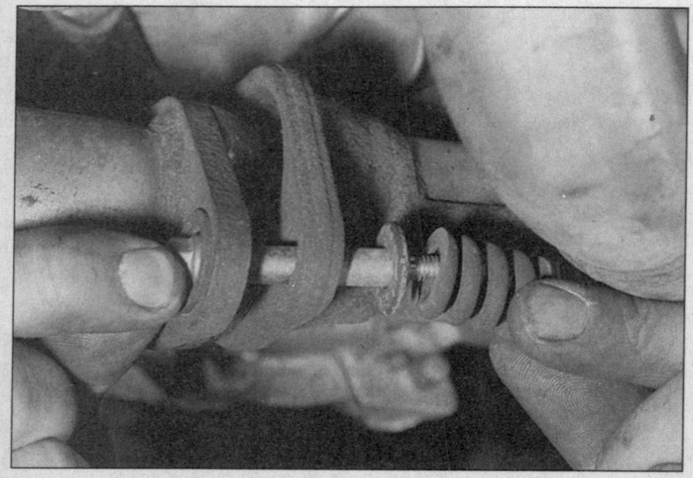

4.8a Remove the fasteners securing the front pipe to the catalytic converter/intermediate pipe . . .

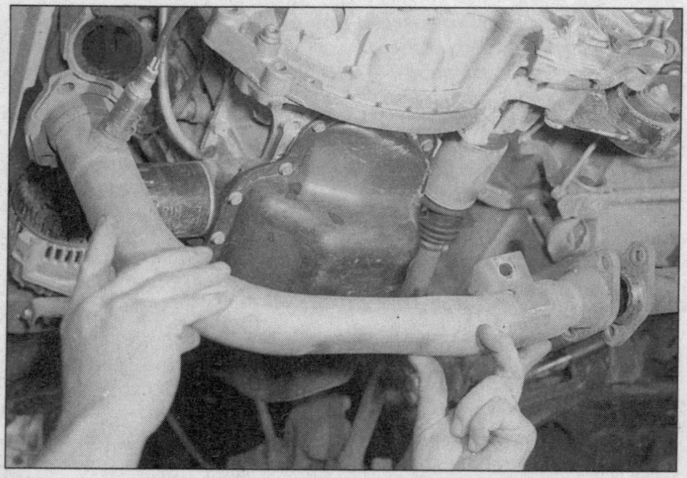

4.8b . . . then withdraw the front pipe from underneath the vehicle (petrol model shown)

Heat shield(s)

21 The heat shields are secured to the underside of the body by a mixture of nuts and bolts. Each shield can be removed once the relevant exhaust section has been removed. If the shield is being removed to gain access to a component located behind it, in some cases it may prove sufficient to remove the retaining nuts and/or bolts and simply lower the shield, without disturbing the exhaust system.

Refitting

22 Each section is refitted by a reverse of the removal sequence, noting the following points:

a) Ensure that all traces of corrosion have been removed from the flanges, and renew all necessary gaskets.

b) Inspect the rubber mountings for signs of damage or deterioration, and renew as necessary.

c) Prior to assembling the spring-loaded ball type joint, a smear of high-temperature grease should be applied to the joint mating surfaces.

d) On joints which are secured by clamping rings, apply a smear of exhaust system jointing paste to the joint mating surfaces, to ensure an air-tight seal. Tighten the clamping ring nuts evenly and progressively to the specified torque, so that the clearance between the clamp halves is equal on either side.

e) Prior to tightening the exhaust system fasteners, ensure that all rubber mountings are correctly located, and that there is adequate clearance between the exhaust system and vehicle underbody.

5 Catalytic converters - general information and precautions

1 The catalytic converter is a reliable and simple device, with no moving parts and as such requires no maintenance. There are, however, some facts of which an owner should be aware if the converter is to function properly for its full service life.

Petrol models

a) DO NOT use leaded petrol in a car equipped with a catalytic converter - the lead will coat the precious metals reagents, reducing their converting efficiency and eventually destroying the converter.

b) Always keep the ignition and fuel systems well-maintained in accordance with the manufacturer's schedule.

c) If the engine develops a misfire, do not drive the car at all (or at least as little as possible) until the fault is cured. Under these condition, unburned fuel can be passed from the engine through the exhaust to the catalytic converter, where it can ignite causing damage to the ceramic interior.

d) DO NOT push- or tow-start the car - this can soak the catalytic converter in unburned fuel, causing it to overheat when the engine does eventually start.

e) DO NOT switch off the ignition at high engine speeds.

f) In some cases a sulphurous smell (like that of rotten eggs) may be noticed from the exhaust. This is common to many catalytic converter-equipped cars. Low quality fuel with a high sulphur content will exacerbate this effect.

g) The catalytic converter, used on a well-maintained and well-driven car, should last for between 50 000 and 100 000 miles - if the converter is no longer effective it must be renewed.

Petrol and diesel models

h) DO NOT use fuel or engine oil additives - these may contain substances harmful to the catalytic converter.

i) DO NOT continue to use the car if the engine burns oil to the extent of leaving a visible trail of blue smoke.

j) Remember that the catalytic converter operates at very high temperatures and its external casing can take a while to cool down. DO NOT, therefore, park the car in dry undergrowth, over long grass, or piles of dead leaves after a long run.

k) Remember that the catalytic converter is FRAGILE - do not strike it with tools during servicing work.

6 Crankcase emission system - general information

The crankcase emission control system consists of a series of hoses that connect the camshaft cover vent to the air intake, a pressure regulating valve (where applicable) and an oil separator unit.

The components of this system require no attention, other than to check at regular intervals that the hose(s) are free of blockages and undamaged.

7 Evaporative loss emission control system (petrol models) - component renewal

General information

1 The evaporative loss emission control system consists of the control solenoid (or purge valve), the activated charcoal filter canister and a series of connecting vacuum hoses.

2 The purge valve and charcoal canister are mounted inside the right-hand wheel arch, behind the plastic wheel arch liner **(see illustrations)**.

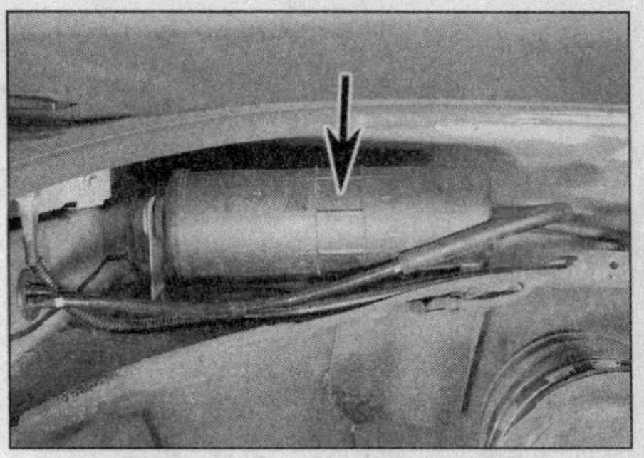

7.2a The charcoal canister (arrowed) . . .

Component renewal

Purge valve

3 Raise the front of the vehicle and support it securely on axle stands (see "*Jacking and vehicle support*"). Remove the right-hand roadwheel.

4 Remove the securing screws and withdraw the plastic liner from the wheel arch.

5 Detach the vapour hoses from the purge valve ports.

6 Unplug the wiring connector, then release the purge valve from its rubber mountings and remove it from the wheel arch.

7 Refitting is a reversal of removal.

Charcoal canister

8 Disconnect the vapour hoses from the canister.

9 Remove the securing screw and release the canister from its mounting bracket.

10 Refitting is a reversal of removal.

8 Exhaust gas recirculation system (diesel models) - component renewal

General information

1 The EGR system consists of a plunger-type recirculation valve, mounted on the inlet manifold, a vacuum solenoid valve, mounted on the rear of the engine compartment bulkhead, a throttle position switch mounted on the fuel injection pump, and a number of interconnecting vacuum hoses.

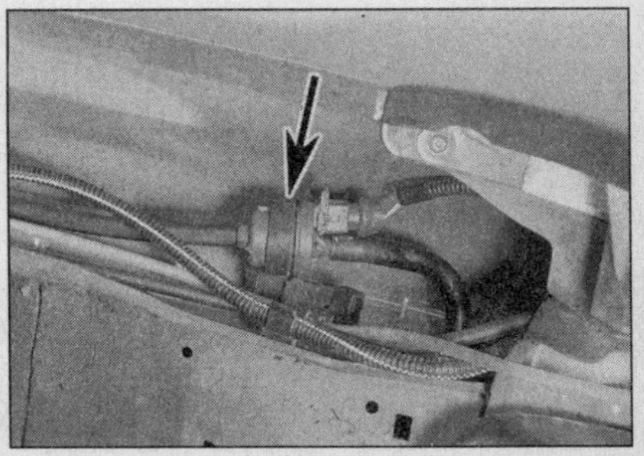

7.2b . . . and purge valve (arrowed) are located inside the right-hand wheel arch

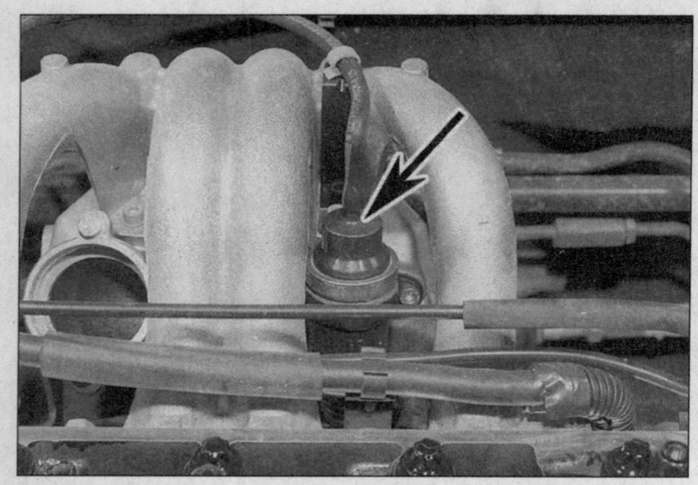

8.4 Disconnect the vacuum hose (arrowed) from the port on the top of the EGR valve

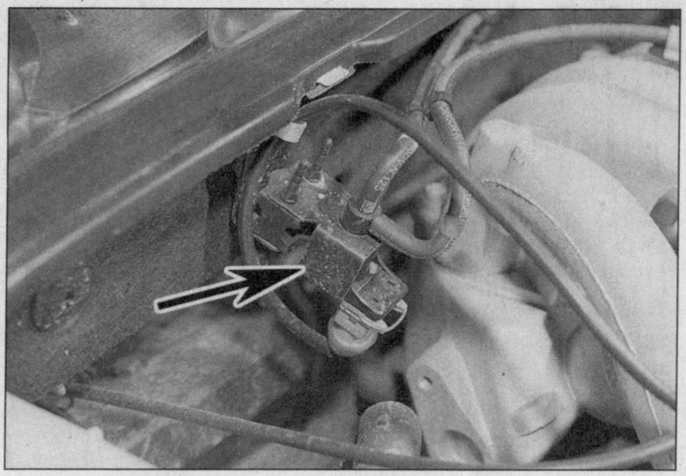

8.8 The EGR solenoid valve (arrowed) is mounted on the rear of the engine compartment bulkhead

2 The throttle position switch switches the solenoid valve on and off according to the position of the throttle lever (and hence the load being placed on the engine). The solenoid valve allows vacuum (supplied by the braking system vacuum pump) to be applied to the recirculation valve. The recirculation valve then opens and allows a small percentage of the exhaust gases to flow into the inlet manifold.

EGR valve

Removal

3 Ensure that the engine has cooled completely before starting work. Jack up the front of the car and rest it securely on axle stands (see "*Jacking and vehicle support*").

4 Disconnect the vacuum hose from the port on the top of the EGR valve **(see illustration)**.

5 Slacken the clamp ring screw and release the recirculation pipe from the base of the EGR valve.

6 Slacken and remove the nuts or screws and lift the EGR valve from the inlet manifold.

Refitting

7 Refitting is a reversal of removal. Use a new gasket and ensure that the securing nuts or screws are tightened securely.

Vacuum solenoid valve

Removal

8 The solenoid valve is mounted on the rear of the engine compartment bulkhead **(see illustration)**.

9 Disconnect the hoses from the valve, noting their order of connection to aid refitting.

10 Release the valve from its rubber mounting block and remove it from the engine bay.

Refitting

11 Refitting is a reversal of removal.

Chapter 5 Part A: Starting and charging systems

Contents

Degrees of difficulty

Easy, suitable for novice with little experience	**Fairly easy,** suitable for beginner with some experience	**Fairly difficult,** suitable for competent DIY mechanic	**Difficult,** suitable for experienced DIY mechanic	**Very difficult,** suitable for expert DIY or professional

Specifications

System type	12-volt, negative earth
Battery	
Type	Fulmen or Delco
Capacity	42 Ah
Charge condition:	
Poor	12.5 volts
Normal	12.6 volts
Good	12.7 volts
Alternator	
Type	Valeo or Bosch (depending on model)
Starter motor	
Type	Valeo or Bosch (depending on model)

1 General information and precautions

General information

Because of their engine-related functions, the components of the starting and charging systems are covered separately from the body electrical devices, such as the lights, instruments, etc; these are covered in Chapter 12. On petrol models, refer to Chapter 5B for information relating to the ignition system. On diesel models, refer to Chapter 5C for information on the preheating (glow-plug) system.

The electrical system is of the 12-volt negative earth type.

The battery is of the low-maintenance or "maintenance-free" (sealed for life) type, and is charged by the alternator, which is driven from the crankshaft pulley by a V-belt or a multi-ribbed auxiliary drivebelt.

The starter motor is of the pre-engaged type, incorporating an integral solenoid. On starting, the solenoid moves the drive pinion into engagement with the flywheel ring gear before the starter motor is energised. Once the engine has started, a one-way clutch prevents the motor armature being driven by the engine until the pinion disengages from the flywheel under the pressure of a return spring.

Precautions

Further details of the various systems are given in the relevant Sections of this Chapter. While some repair procedures are given, the usual course of action is to renew the component concerned. The owner whose interest extends beyond mere component renewal should obtain a copy of the *"Automobile Electrical & Electronic Systems Manual"*, available from the publishers of this manual.

It is necessary to take extra care when working on the electrical system, to avoid damage to semi-conductor devices (diodes, transistors, integrated circuits and microprocessors), and to avoid the risk of personal injury. In addition to the precautions given in *"Safety first!"* at the beginning of this manual, observe the following when working on the system:

Always remove rings, watches, etc before working on the electrical system. Even with the battery disconnected, capacitive discharge could occur if a component's live terminal is earthed through a metal object. This could cause a shock or nasty burn.

Do not reverse the battery connections. Components such as the alternator, electronic control units, or any other components having semi-conductor circuitry could be irreparably damaged.

If the engine is being started using jump leads and a slave battery, connect the batteries *positive-to-positive* and *negative-to-negative* (see *"Jump starting"*). This also applies when connecting a battery charger.

Never disconnect the battery terminals, the alternator, any electrical wiring or any test instruments, when the engine is running.

Do not allow the engine to turn the alternator when the alternator wiring is not connected.

Never "test" for alternator output by "flashing" the output lead to earth.

Never use an ohmmeter of the type incorporating a hand-cranked generator for circuit or continuity testing.

Always ensure that the battery negative lead is disconnected when working on the electrical system.

Before using electric-arc welding equipment on the car, disconnect the battery, alternator and components such as the fuel injection/ignition electronic control unit, to protect them from the risk of damage.

The radio/cassette unit fitted as standard equipment by Citroën has a built-in security code, to deter thieves. If the power source to the unit is cut, the anti-theft system will activate. Even if the power source is immediately reconnected, the radio/cassette unit will not function until the correct security code has been entered. Therefore, if you do not know the correct security code for the radio/cassette unit, **do not** disconnect the battery negative terminal or remove the radio/cassette unit from the vehicle. Refer to *"Radio/cassette unit anti-theft system - precaution"* Section at the end of this manual for further information.

2 Electrical fault-finding - general information

Refer to the information given in Chapter 12.

3 Battery - testing and charging

Standard and low-maintenance battery - testing

1 If the vehicle covers a small annual mileage, it is worthwhile checking the specific gravity of the electrolyte every three months, to determine the state of charge of the battery. Use a hydrometer to make the check, and compare the results with the following table. Note that the specific gravity readings assume an electrolyte temperature of 15°C (59°F); for every 10°C (18°F) below 15°C (59°F), subtract 0.007. For every 10°C (18°F) above 15°C (59°F), add 0.007.

	Temp. above 25°C (77°F)	Temp. below 25°C (77°F)
Fully-charged	1.210 to 1.230	1.270 to 1.290
70% charged	1.170 to 1.190	1.230 to 1.250
Fully-discharged	1.050 to 1.070	1.110 to 1.130

2 If the battery condition is suspect, first check the specific gravity of electrolyte in each cell. A variation of 0.040 or more between any cells indicates loss of electrolyte or deterioration of the internal plates.

3 If the specific gravity variation is 0.040 or more, the battery should be renewed. If the cell variation is satisfactory but the battery is discharged, it should be charged as described later in this Section.

Maintenance-free battery - testing

4 In cases where a "sealed for life" maintenance-free battery is fitted, topping-up and testing of the electrolyte in each cell is not possible. The condition of the battery can therefore only be tested using a battery condition indicator or a voltmeter.

5 Certain models may be fitted with a 'maintenance-free' battery, with a built-in charge condition indicator. The indicator is located in the top of the battery casing, and indicates the condition of the battery from its colour. If the indicator shows green, then the battery is in a good state of charge. If the indicator turns darker, eventually to black, then the battery requires charging, as described later in this Section. If the indicator shows clear/yellow, then the electrolyte level in the battery is too low to allow further use, and the battery should be renewed.

Caution: Do not attempt to charge, load or jump start a battery when the indicator shows clear/yellow.

6 If testing the battery using a voltmeter, connect the voltmeter across the battery, and compare the results with those given in the Specifications under "charge condition". The test is only accurate if the battery has not been subjected to any kind of charge for the previous six hours, including charging by the alternator. If this is not the case, switch on the headlights for 30 seconds, then wait four to five minutes after switching off the headlights before testing the battery. All other electrical circuits must be switched off, so check (for instance) that the doors and tailgate are fully shut when making the test.

7 If the voltage reading is less than 12.2 volts, then the battery is discharged, whilst a reading of 12.2 to 12.4 volts indicates a partially-discharged condition.

8 If the battery is to be charged, remove it from the vehicle (Section 4) and charge it as described later in this Section.

Standard and low-maintenance battery - charging

Caution: The following is intended as a guide only. Always refer to the manufacturer's recommendations (often printed on a label attached to the battery) before charging a battery.

9 Charge the battery at a rate of 3.5 to 4 amps, and continue to charge the battery at this rate until no further rise in specific gravity is noted over a four-hour period.

10 Alternatively, a trickle charger charging at the rate of 1.5 amps can safely be used overnight.

11 Specially rapid "boost" charges, which are claimed to restore the power of the battery in 1 to 2 hours, are not recommended, as they can cause serious damage to the battery plates through overheating.

12 While charging the battery, note that the temperature of the electrolyte should never exceed 37°C (100°F).

Maintenance-free battery - charging

Note: *The following is intended as a guide only. Always refer to the manufacturer's recommendations (often printed on a label attached to the battery) before charging a battery.*

13 This battery type takes considerably longer to fully recharge than the standard type, the time taken being dependent on the extent of discharge, but it can take anything up to three days.

14 A constant-voltage type charger is required, to be set, when connected, to 13.9 to 14.9 volts with a charger current below 25 amps. Using this method, the battery should be usable within three hours, giving a voltage reading of 12.5 volts, but this is for a partially-discharged battery and, as mentioned, full charging can take considerably longer.

15 If the battery is to be charged from a fully-discharged state (condition reading less than 12.2 volts), have it recharged by your Citroën dealer or local automotive electrician, as the charge rate is higher, and constant supervision during charging is necessary.

4 Battery - removal and refitting

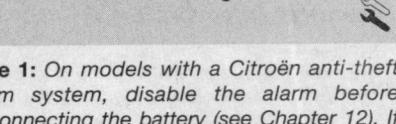

Note 1: *On models with a Citroën anti-theft alarm system, disable the alarm before disconnecting the battery (see Chapter 12). If a Citroën radio/cassette unit is fitted, refer to "Radio/cassette unit anti-theft system - precaution" at the end of this manual.*

Note 2: *After reconnecting the battery on 1.6 litre petrol-engined models with Bosch Motronic multi-point fuel injection, the sequence described in the last paragraph of this Section must be observed, to ensure that the idle speed actuator valve is correctly reset.*

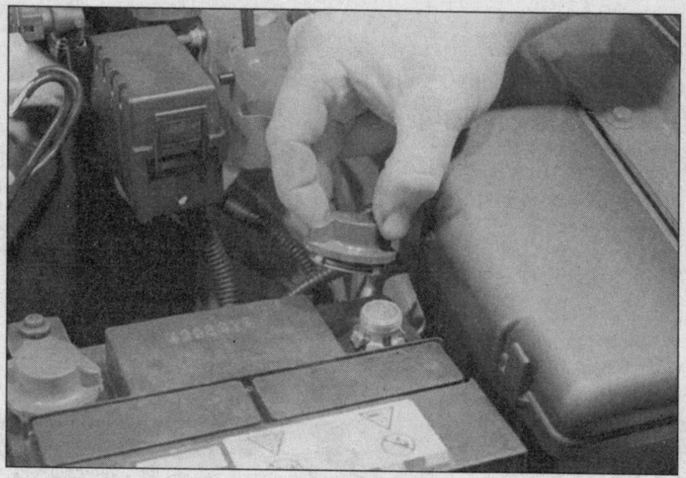

4.2 **Unscrew the plastic-capped nut and disconnect the cable from the battery negative terminal**

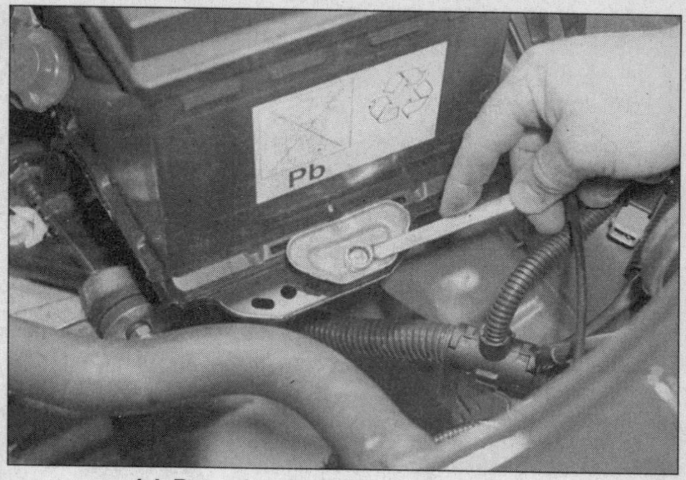

4.4 **Removing the battery retaining clamp**

Removal

1 The battery is located on the left-hand side of the engine compartment.
2 Disconnect the lead(s) at the negative (earth) terminal. There are two possible types of battery terminal fixings fitted on these models. With the first type, the leads are secured to a stud on the top of the terminal by means of a plastic-capped nut **(see illustration)**, on the second, a conventional fitting is used, secured in position by a clamp bolt and nut.
3 Remove the insulation cover (where fitted) and disconnect the positive terminal lead(s) in the same way.
4 Unscrew the nut/bolt (as applicable) and remove the battery retaining clamp **(see illustration)**.
5 Lift the battery out of the engine compartment and, where necessary, remove the insulation plate(s).
6 If required for access, the battery support tray may be unbolted and removed from the bodywork **(see illustration)**.

Refitting

7 Refitting is a reversal of removal, but smear petroleum jelly on the terminals when reconnecting the leads, and always reconnect the positive lead first, and the negative lead last.
8 On 1.6 litre petrol models with Bosch Motronic multi-point fuel injection, carry out the following steps, to reset the position of the idle speed actuator valve:

1. *Switch off the ignition.*
2. *Wait at least 10 seconds.*
3. *Switch on the ignition.*
4. *Wait at least 10 seconds.*
5. *Start the engine and allow it to idle; check that the idle speed stabilises at the figure specified in the relevant part of Chapter 4. Introduce loads by switching on the headlights and/or air conditioning, and turn the steering from lock to lock (models with PAS only) - check that the idle speed remains stable.*

5 Charging system - testing

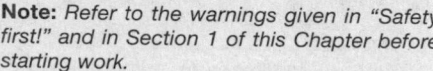

Note: *Refer to the warnings given in "Safety first!" and in Section 1 of this Chapter before starting work.*

1 If the ignition/no-charge warning light does not come on when the ignition is switched on, first check the alternator wiring connections for security. If satisfactory, check that the warning light bulb has not blown, and that the bulbholder is secure in its location in the instrument panel. If the light still does not come on, check the continuity of the warning light feed wire from the alternator to the bulbholder. If all is satisfactory, the alternator is at fault, and should be renewed or taken to an auto-electrician for testing and repair.
2 If the ignition warning light comes on when the engine is running, stop the engine and check that the drivebelt is correctly tensioned (see Chapter 1A or 1B) and that the alternator connections are secure. If all is so far satisfactory, check the alternator brushes and slip rings as described later in this Chapter. If the fault persists, the alternator should be renewed, or taken to an auto-electrician for testing and repair.
3 If the alternator output is suspect even though the warning light functions correctly, the regulated voltage may be checked as follows.
4 Connect a voltmeter across the battery terminals, and start the engine.
5 Increase the engine speed until the voltmeter reading remains steady; the reading should be approximately 12 to 13 volts, and no more than 14 volts.
6 Switch on as many electrical accessories (eg, the headlights, heated rear window and heater blower) as possible, and check that the alternator maintains the regulated voltage at around 13 to 14 volts.
7 If the regulated voltage is not as stated, the fault may be due to worn brushes, weak brush springs, a faulty voltage regulator, a faulty diode, a severed phase winding, or worn or damaged slip rings. The brushes and slip rings may be checked (see Section 8), but if the fault persists, the alternator should be renewed, or taken to an auto-electrician for testing and repair.

6 Alternator drivebelt - removal, refitting and tensioning

Refer to the auxiliary drivebelt checking and renewal procedure, given in Chapter 1A or 1B (as applicable).

7 Alternator - removal and refitting

Removal

1 Disconnect the battery negative lead.
2 Slacken the auxiliary drivebelt as described in the relevant part of Chapter 1, and disengage it from the alternator pulley.

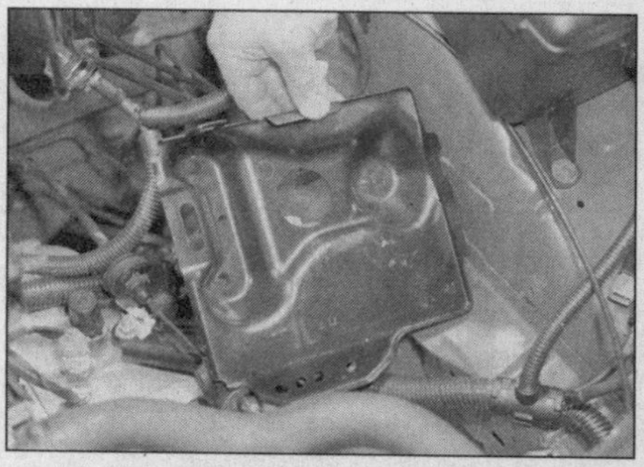

4.6 **If required for access, the battery support tray may be unbolted and removed from the bodywork**

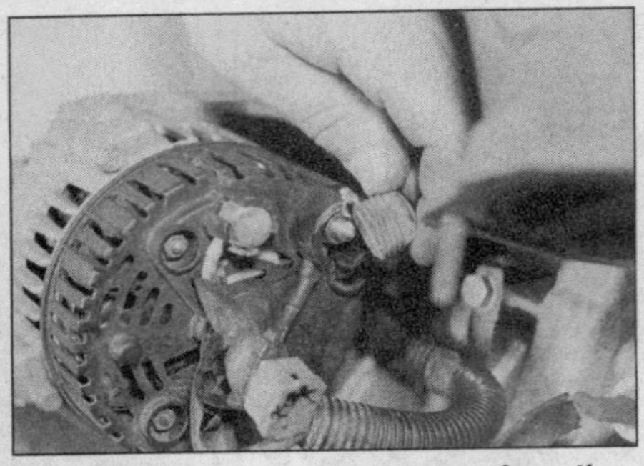

7.3a Remove the rubber covers from the alternator terminals . . .

3 Remove the rubber covers (where fitted) from the alternator terminals, then unscrew the retaining nuts and disconnect the wiring from the rear of the alternator **(see illustrations)**.

4 Unscrew the alternator upper and lower mounting bolts, then manoeuvre the alternator away from its mounting brackets and out of position. On diesel models, prise out the cover shield fastener to allow the cover to be lifted slightly to improve access to the upper bolt **(see illustrations)**.

Refitting

5 Refitting is a reversal of removal, ensuring that the alternator mountings are securely tightened, and tensioning the auxiliary drivebelt as described in the relevant part of Chapter 1.

8.3a On the Valeo alternator, undo the retaining nuts (arrowed) . . .

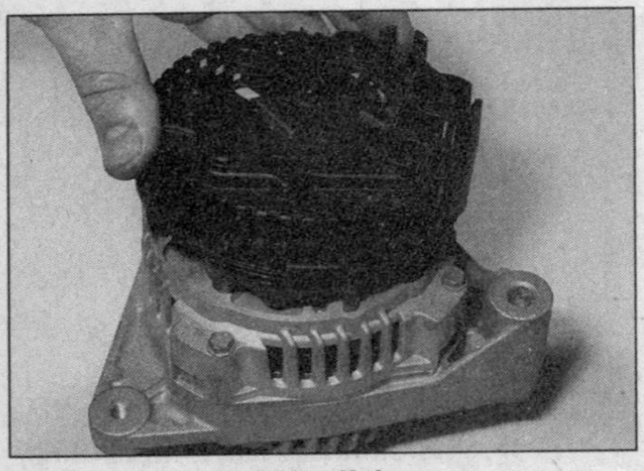

8.3b . . . and lift off the rear cover

7.3b . . . then unscrew the retaining nuts (arrowed) and disconnect the wiring from the rear of the alternator

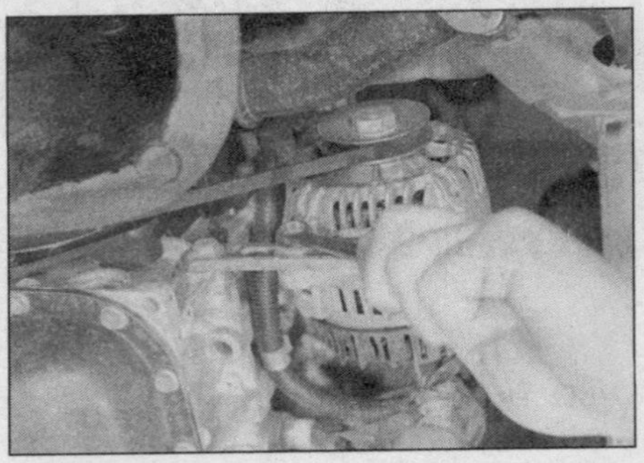

7.4b . . . and lower mounting bolts . . .

8 Alternator brushes and regulator - inspection and renewal

1 Remove the alternator as described in Section 7. Proceed as described below the relevant sub-heading.

Valeo alternator

2 Where applicable, scrape the sealing compound from the rear plastic cover to expose the three rear cover retaining nuts.

3 Undo the retaining nuts and remove the rear cover **(see illustrations)**.

4 If necessary, scrape the sealing compound from the rear of the alternator to expose the regulator/brush holder assembly fixings. The assembly is retained by two nuts and a single screw.

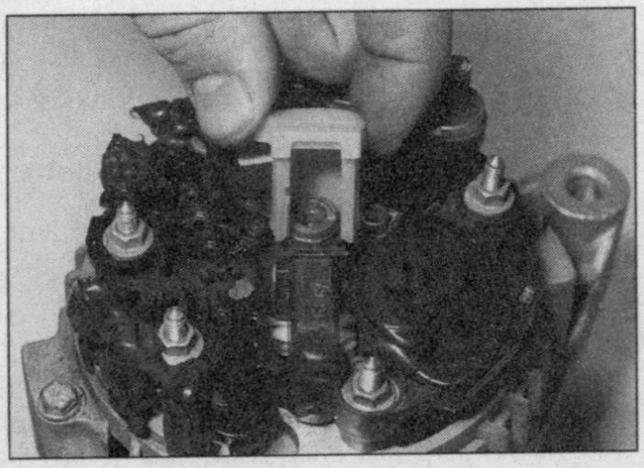

8.5 Pull the plastic cover to reveal the armature shaft

7.4a Unscrew the alternator upper . . .

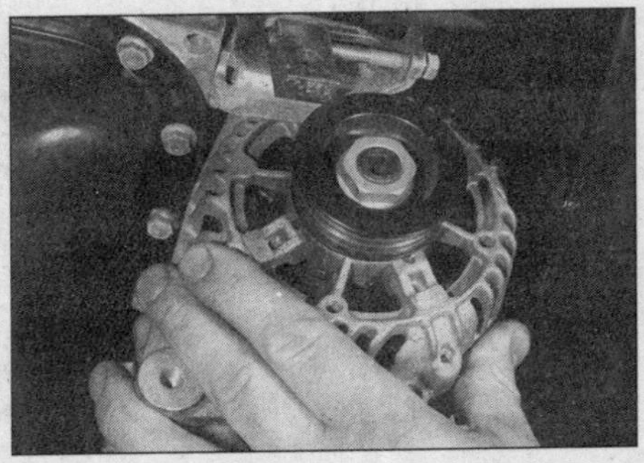

7.4c . . . then manoeuvre the alternator away from its mounting brackets and out of the engine compartment

5 Pull the plastic cover from the rear of the armature shaft **(see illustration)**.

6 Undo the retaining nuts and the screw, and withdraw the regulator/brush holder assembly from the rear of the alternator **(see illustration)**.

7 Measure the protrusion of each brush from its holder. No minimum dimension is specified by the manufacturers, but excessive wear should be self-evident. If either brush requires renewal, the complete regulator/brush holder assembly must be renewed. It is not possible to renew the brushes separately.

8 If the brushes are still serviceable, clean them with a petrol-moistened cloth. Check that the brush spring tension is equal for both brushes, and provides a reasonable pressure. The brushes must move freely in their holders.

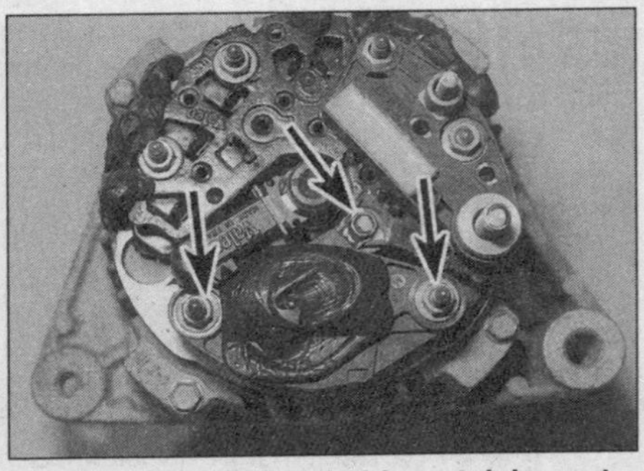

8.6 Regulator/brush holder retaining nuts and screw (arrowed)

9 Clean the alternator slip rings with a petrol-moistened cloth. Check for signs of scoring, burning or severe pitting on the surface of the slip rings. It may be possible to have the slip rings renovated by an electrical specialist.
10 Refit the regulator/brush holder assembly using a reverse of the removal procedure.
11 Refit the alternator as described in Section 7.

Bosch alternator

12 Unclip the cover from the rear of the alternator.
13 If necessary, scrape the sealing compound from the rear of the alternator to expose the regulator/brush holder assembly retaining screws. Slacken and remove the two retaining screws, and remove the regulator/brush holder from the rear of the alternator.
14 Examine the alternator components as described above in paragraphs 7 to 9.
15 Refit the regulator/brush holder assembly, and securely tighten its retaining screws.
16 Clip the rear cover onto the alternator, and refit the alternator as described in Section 7.

9 Starting system - testing

Note: *Refer to the precautions given in "Safety first!" and in Section 1 of this Chapter before starting work.*
1 If the starter motor fails to operate when the ignition key is turned to the appropriate position, the following possible causes may be to blame:

a) *The battery is faulty.*
b) *The electrical connections between the switch, solenoid, battery and starter motor are somewhere failing to pass the necessary current from the battery through the starter to earth.*
c) *The solenoid is faulty.*
d) *The starter motor is mechanically or electrically defective.*

2 To check the battery, switch on the headlights. If they dim after a few seconds, this indicates that the battery is discharged - recharge (see Section 3) or renew the battery. If the headlights glow brightly, operate the ignition switch and observe the lights. If they dim, then this indicates that current is reaching the starter motor, therefore the fault must lie in the starter motor. If the lights continue to glow brightly (and no clicking sound can be heard from the starter motor solenoid), this indicates that there is a fault in the circuit or solenoid - see following paragraphs. If the starter motor turns slowly when operated, but the battery is in good condition, then this indicates that either the starter motor is faulty, or there is considerable resistance somewhere in the circuit.
3 If a fault in the circuit is suspected, disconnect the battery leads (including the earth connection to the body), the starter/solenoid wiring and the engine/ transmission earth strap. Thoroughly clean the connections, and reconnect the leads and wiring, then use a voltmeter or test light to check that full battery voltage is available at the battery positive lead connection to the solenoid, and that the earth is sound. Smear petroleum jelly around the battery terminals to prevent corrosion - corroded connections are amongst the most frequent causes of electrical system faults.
4 If the battery and all connections are in good condition, check the circuit by disconnecting the wire from the solenoid blade terminal. Connect a voltmeter or test light between the wire end and a good earth (such as the battery negative terminal), and check that the wire is live when the ignition switch is turned to the "start" position. If it is, then the circuit is sound - if not, the circuit wiring can be checked as described in Chapter 12.
5 The solenoid contacts can be checked by connecting a voltmeter or test light between the battery positive feed connection on the starter side of the solenoid, and earth. When the ignition switch is turned to the "start" position, there should be a reading or lighted bulb, as applicable. If there is no reading or lighted bulb, the solenoid is faulty, and should be renewed.
6 If the circuit and solenoid are proved sound, the fault must lie in the starter motor. In this event, it may be possible to have the starter motor overhauled by a specialist and fitted with new brushes, but check on the availability and cost of spares before proceeding, as it may prove more economical to obtain a new or exchange motor.

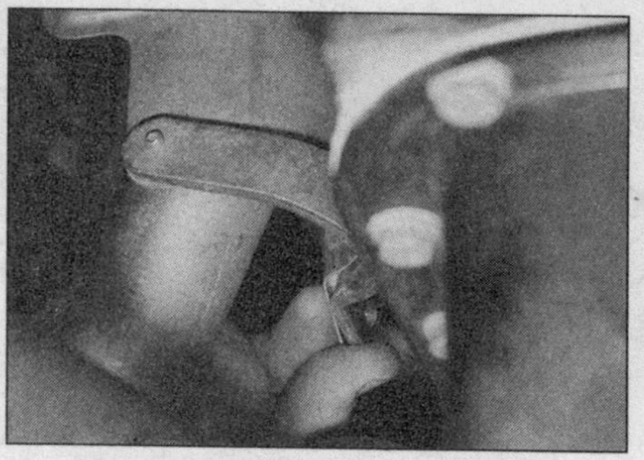

10.3a On diesel models, remove the exhaust system heat shield . . .

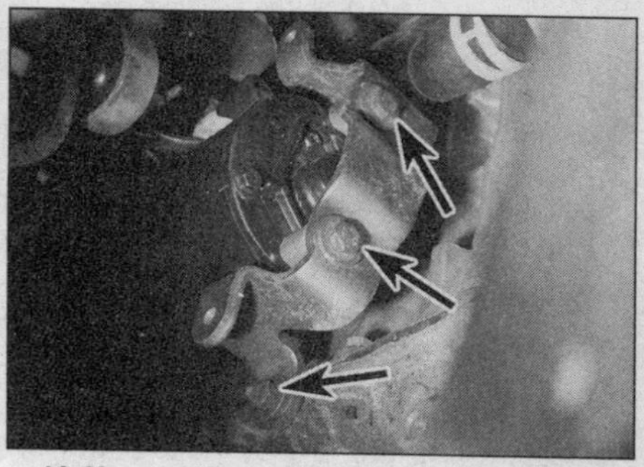

10.3b . . . then undo the retaining bolts (three arrowed) and remove the rear mounting bracket from the starter

10 Starter motor - removal and refitting

Removal

1 Disconnect the battery negative lead.
2 So that access to the motor can be gained both from above and below, firmly apply the handbrake, then jack up the front of the vehicle and support it on axle stands (see "*Jacking and vehicle support*").
3 On diesel models, although not strictly necessary, access to the starter motor is considerably improved if the exhaust system front pipe is first removed as described in Chapter 4D. Undo the retaining bolts and remove the heat shield from the rear of the starter motor. Slacken and remove the retaining bolts, and remove the rear mounting bracket **(see illustrations)**.
4 On all models, slacken and remove the two retaining nuts and disconnect the wiring from the starter motor solenoid. Recover the washers under the nuts **(see illustration)**.
5 Undo the three mounting bolts (two at the rear of the motor, and one which comes through from the top of the transmission housing), supporting the motor as the bolts are withdrawn **(see illustration)**.. Recover the

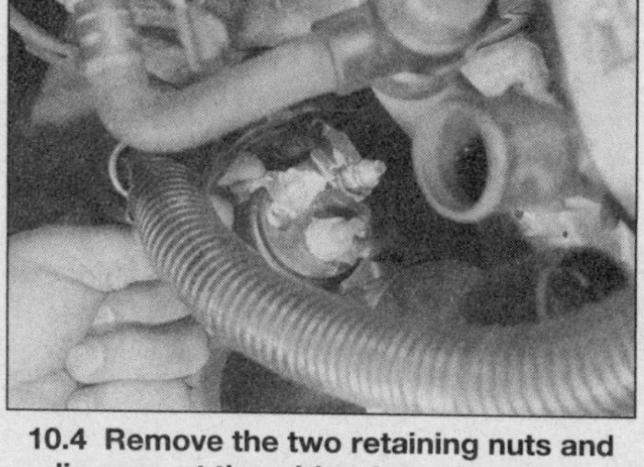

10.4 Remove the two retaining nuts and disconnect the wiring from the starter motor solenoid

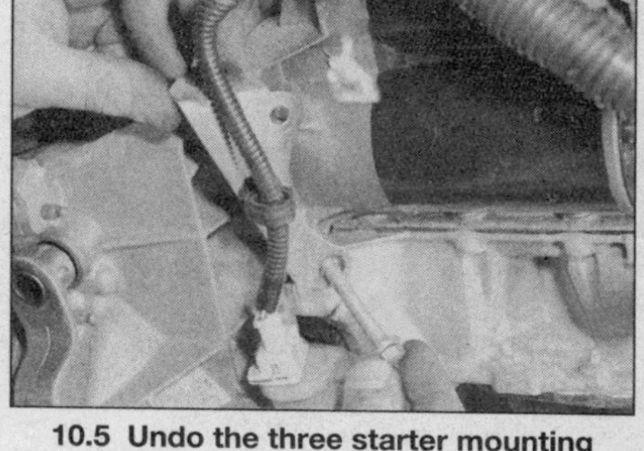

10.5 Undo the three starter mounting bolts, and withdraw the inlet air ducting support bracket (petrol models)

washers from under the bolt heads, and note the locations of any wiring or hose brackets secured by the bolts.

6 Manoeuvre the starter motor out from underneath the engine, and recover the locating dowel(s) from the motor/transmission bellhousing (as applicable) **(see illustration)**.

Refitting

7 Refitting is a reversal of removal, ensuring that the locating dowel(s) are correctly positioned. Also make sure that any wiring or hose brackets are in place under the bolt heads, as noted prior to removal.

11 Starter motor - testing and overhaul

If the starter motor is thought to be suspect, it should be removed from the vehicle and taken to an auto-electrician for testing. Most auto-electricians will be able to supply and fit brushes at a reasonable cost. However, check on the cost of repairs before proceeding as it may prove more economical to obtain a new or exchange motor.

12 Ignition switch - removal and refitting

The ignition switch is integral with the steering column lock, and can be removed as described in Chapter 10.

13 Oil pressure warning light switch - removal and refitting

Removal

1 The switch is located at the front of the cylinder block, above the oil filter mounting **(see illustration)**. On some models, access to the switch may be improved if the vehicle is jacked up and supported on axle stands (see "*Jacking and vehicle support*"), so that the switch can be reached from underneath.

2 Disconnect the battery negative lead.

3 Remove the protective sleeve from the wiring plug (where applicable), then disconnect the wiring from the switch.

4 Unscrew the switch from the cylinder block, and recover the sealing washer. Be prepared for oil spillage; if the switch is to be left removed from the engine for any length of time, plug the hole in the cylinder block.

10.6 Withdraw the starter motor away from the transmission bellhousing

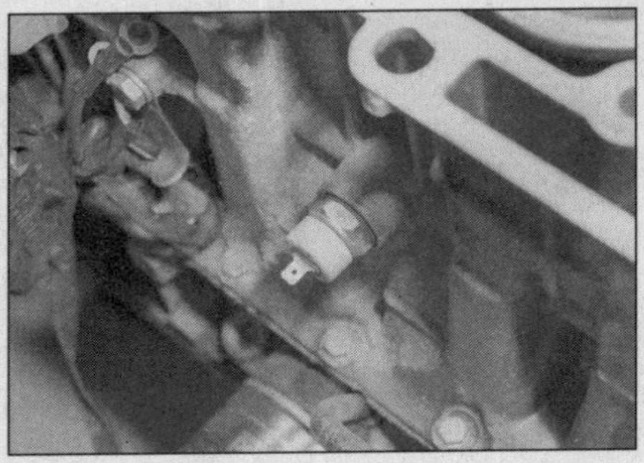

13.1 Oil pressure switch location - petrol model with alloy cylinder block shown

Refitting

5 Examine the sealing washer for signs of damage or deterioration, and if necessary renew it.

6 Refit the switch, complete with washer, and tighten it securely. Reconnect the wiring connector.

7 Lower the vehicle to the ground. Check and, if necessary, top-up the engine oil as described in "*Weekly checks*".

14 Oil level sensor - removal and refitting

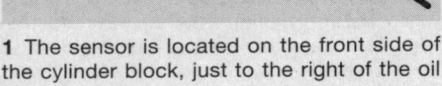

1 The sensor is located on the front side of the cylinder block, just to the right of the oil filter.

2 The removal and refitting procedure is as described for the oil pressure switch in Section 13. Access is most easily obtained from underneath the vehicle.

15 Oil temperature sensor - removal and refitting

Removal

1 The oil temperature sensor is screwed into the rear of the sump.

2 To gain access to the sensor, firmly apply the handbrake, then jack up the front of the vehicle and support it on axle stands (see "*Jacking and vehicle support*").

3 Drain the engine oil into a clean container, then refit the drain plug and tighten it to the specified torque setting (see Chapter 1A or 1B as applicable).

4 Unplug the wiring connector, then unscrew the sensor from the sump, and remove it from underneath the vehicle along with its sealing washer.

Refitting

5 Examine the sealing washer for signs of damage or deterioration, and if necessary renew it.

6 Refit the sensor, tightening it securely, and reconnect the wiring connector.

7 Lower the vehicle to the ground. Refill the engine with oil as described in the relevant part of Chapter 1.

Chapter 5 Part B:
Ignition system - petrol models

Contents

Degrees of difficulty

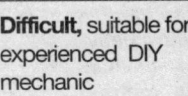

Easy, suitable for novice with little experience	**Fairly easy,** suitable for beginner with some experience	**Fairly difficult,** suitable for competent DIY mechanic	**Difficult,** suitable for experienced DIY mechanic	**Very difficult,** suitable for expert DIY or professional

Specifications

General

System type	Static (distributorless) ignition system controlled by engine management ECU
Firing order	1-3-4-2 (No 1 cylinder at transmission end)
Ignition timing	Controlled by the engine management system
Ignition HT coil resistances:*	
Primary windings	0.6 to 0.8 Ω
Secondary windings	19.0 kΩ

**The above results are approximate values, and are accurate only when the coil is at 20°C.*

Torque wrench setting

	Nm	lbf ft
Knock sensor	20	15

1 General information

The ignition system is integrated with the fuel injection system to form a combined engine management system under the control of one ECU (see the relevant Part of Chapter 4 for further information).

On all models, the ignition system is of the static (distributorless) type, consisting only of two twin-output ignition coils. On all early 954 cc, 1124 cc, 1360 cc and 1587 cc SOHC models, the ignition coils are housed in a single unit, mounted on the left hand end of the cylinder head; four HT leads connect the coil output terminals to the spark plugs. On later 1360 cc and 1587 cc SOHC models and all 1587 cc DOHC models, the ignition coils are housed in a single unit, which is mounted directly above the spark plugs - no HT leads are fitted.

Each ignition coil serves two cylinders (one coil supplies cylinders 1 and 4, and the other cylinders 2 and 3).

Under the control of the ECU, the ignition coils operate on the "wasted spark" principle, ie. each spark plug sparks twice for every cycle of the engine, once during the compression stroke and once during the exhaust stroke. The spark voltage is greatest in the cylinder which is under compression; in the cylinder on its exhaust stroke, the compression is low and this produces a very weak spark which has no effect on the exhaust gases. This arrangement means that direct ignition can be employed without the need for a separate ignition coil for each cylinder.

The ECU uses its inputs from the various sensors to calculate the required ignition advance setting and coil charging time, depending on engine temperature, load and speed. At idle speeds, the ECU varies the ignition timing to alter the torque characteristic of the engine, enabling the idle speed to be controlled. This system operates in conjunction with the idle speed stepper motor/idle actuator valve - see Chapter 4A or 4B (as applicable) for details.

On multi-point fuel injection models, a knock sensor is incorporated into the ignition system. Mounted onto the cylinder block, the sensor detects the high frequency vibrations caused when the engine starts to pre-ignite, or "pink". Under these conditions, the knock sensor sends an electrical signal to the ECU, which in turn retards the ignition advance setting in small steps until the "pinking" ceases.

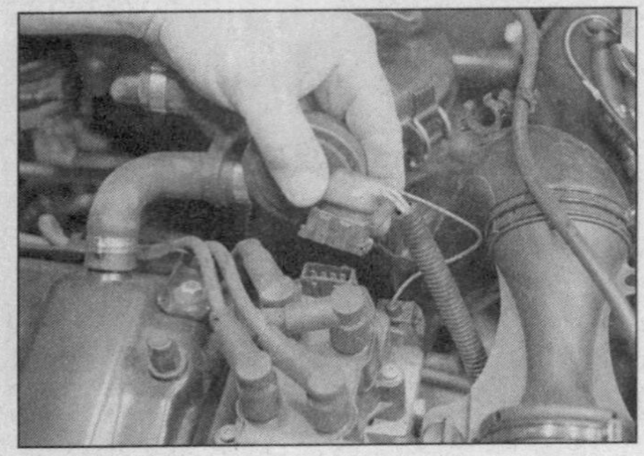

3.2 Unplug the wiring connector from the HT ignition coil

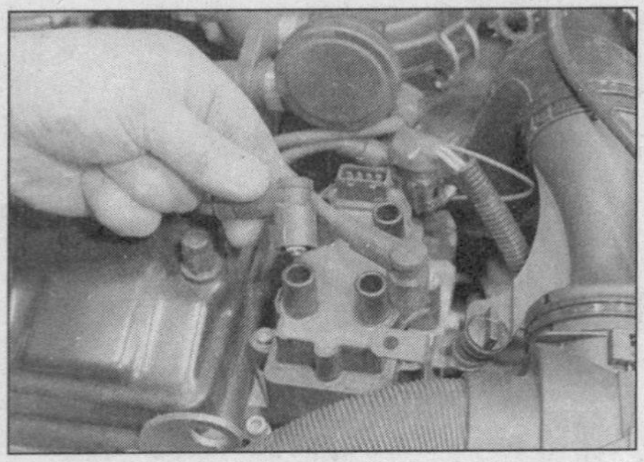

3.3 Disconnect the HT leads from the coil terminals

3.4 Undo the four retaining screws and remove the HT ignition coil from its mounting bracket

2 Ignition system - testing

Warning: Voltages produced by an electronic ignition system are considerably higher than those produced by conventional ignition systems. Extreme care must be taken when working on the system if the ignition is switched on. Persons with surgically-implanted cardiac pacemaker devices should keep well clear of the ignition circuits, components and test equipment

If a fault appears in the engine management (fuel injection/ignition) system, first ensure that the fault is not due to a poor electrical connection or poor maintenance; ie, check that the air cleaner filter element is clean, the spark plugs are in good condition and correctly gapped, and that the engine breather hoses are clear and undamaged, referring to Chapter 1A for further information. Also check that the accelerator cable is correctly adjusted, as described in the relevant Part of Chapter 4. If the engine is running very roughly, check the compression pressures and the valve clearances as described in Chapter 2A.

If these checks fail to reveal the cause of the problem, the vehicle should be taken to a suitably-equipped Citroën dealer for testing. A wiring block connector is incorporated in the engine management circuit, into which a special electronic diagnostic tester can be plugged. The tester will locate the fault quickly and simply, alleviating the need to test all the system components individually, which is a time-consuming operation that carries a high risk of damaging the ECU.

The only ignition system checks which can be carried out by the home mechanic are those described in Chapter 1A, relating to the spark plugs, and the ignition coil test described in this Chapter. If necessary, the system wiring and wiring connectors can be checked as described in Chapter 12, ensuring that the ECU wiring connector(s) have first been disconnected.

3 Ignition HT coil module - removal, testing and refitting

Removal

954 cc, 1124 cc, 1360 cc and 1587 cc models with cylinder head-mounted ignition coil

1 Disconnect the battery negative cable and position it away from the terminal. The ignition HT coil is mounted on the left-hand end of the cylinder head.

2 Release the retaining clip, and disconnect the wiring connector from the HT coil **(see illustration)**.

3 Make a note of the correct fitted positions of the HT leads, then disconnect them from the coil terminals **(see illustration)**. Alternatively, disconnect the HT leads from the spark plugs (see Chapter 1A) and allow them to be removed with the coil module.

3.6 Unplug the wiring connector from the top of the ignition coil module

4 Undo the four retaining screws securing the coil to its mounting bracket, and remove it from the engine compartment **(see illustration)**.

1360 cc and 1587 cc 8-valve models with spark plug-mounted ignition coil module

5 Disconnect the battery negative cable and position it away from the terminal.

6 Unplug the wiring connector from the top of the ignition coil module **(see illustration)**.

7 Where applicable, unscrew the securing nut and remove the radio suppresser from the right hand end of the coil module, together with its mounting bracket **(see illustrations)**.

8 Undo the securing nut and remove the hose clip support bracket from the left hand end of the coil module **(see illustration)**.

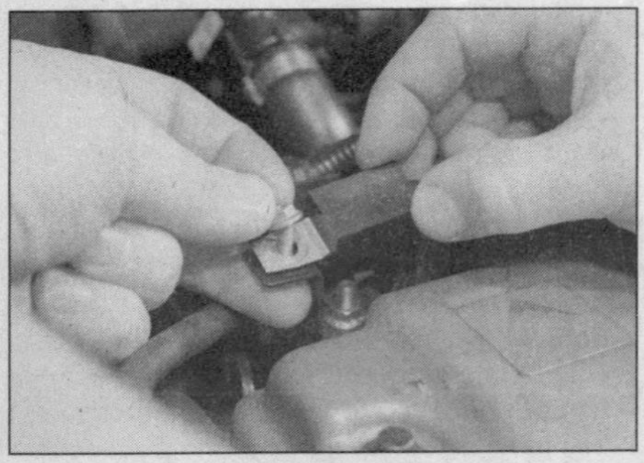

3.7a Remove the radio suppresser from the right hand end of the coil module . . .

3.7b . . . together with its mounting bracket

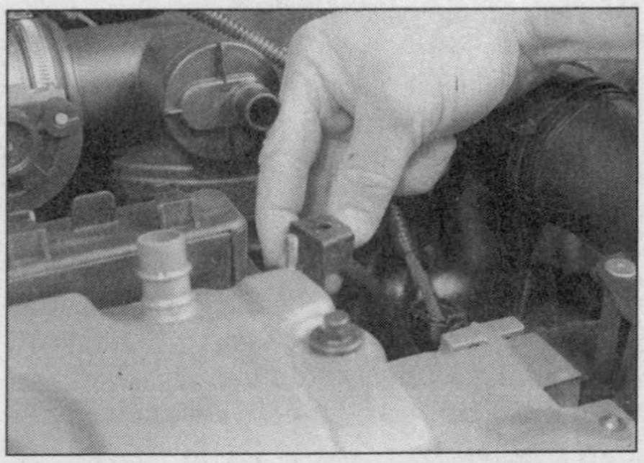

3.8 Remove the hose clip support bracket from the left hand end of the coil module

9 Remove the securing nuts and free the ignition coil module from its mounting studs. Carefully ease the HT extension pillars away from the tops of the spark plugs and remove the module from the engine compartment **(see illustrations)**.

1587 cc 16v models

10 Disconnect the battery negative cable and position it away from the terminal.
11 Remove the securing screws and lift the trim panel away from the top of the ignition coil unit, located between the cylinder head covers.
12 Slacken and withdraw the ignition coil module securing screws, then lift the module away from the cylinder head. Remove the HT extension pillars if they remain connected to the tops of the spark plugs **(see illustration)**.

Testing

13 Testing of the coil is carried out using a multi-meter set to its resistance function, to check the primary (LT "+" to "-" terminals) and secondary (LT "+" to HT lead terminal) windings for continuity. Bear in mind that on the four-output, direct ignition HT coil module , there are two sets of each windings("double-ended" coil). Compare the results obtained to those given in the Specifications at the start of this Chapter. The resistance of the coil windings will vary slightly according to the coil temperature - the results in the Specifications are approximate values for when the coil is at 20°C.
14 Where applicable, check that there is no continuity between the HT lead terminal and the coil body/mounting bracket.
15 If the coil is thought to be faulty, have your findings confirmed by a Citroën dealer before renewing the coil.

Refitting

16 Refitting is a reversal of the relevant removal procedure. Ensure that the wiring connectors and the HT lead(s) are securely reconnected.

4 Ignition timing - checking and adjustment

1 When the engine is running, the ignition timing is constantly being monitored and adjusted by the engine management system. When the engine is idling, small changes are made to the ignition timing, to help maintain a constant idle speed.
2 Although it is possible to observe the base ignition timing using a standard timing light, it is not possible to adjust it. The reading obtained will only be approximate, due to the constantly changing ignition timing.
3 For those wishing to observe the ignition timing, a stroboscopic timing lamp will be required. The lamp will need to be the type which incorporates a variable delay, so that the advance angle can be determined from a single TDC marking on the flywheel. It is recommended that the timing mark is highlighted as follows.
4 Remove the plug from the top of the transmission casing (above the crankshaft speed/TDC sensor - see Chapter 4B) then turn the engine slowly (using a spanner on the

3.9a Remove the securing nuts . . .

3.9b . . . and lift the ignition coil module from its mounting studs

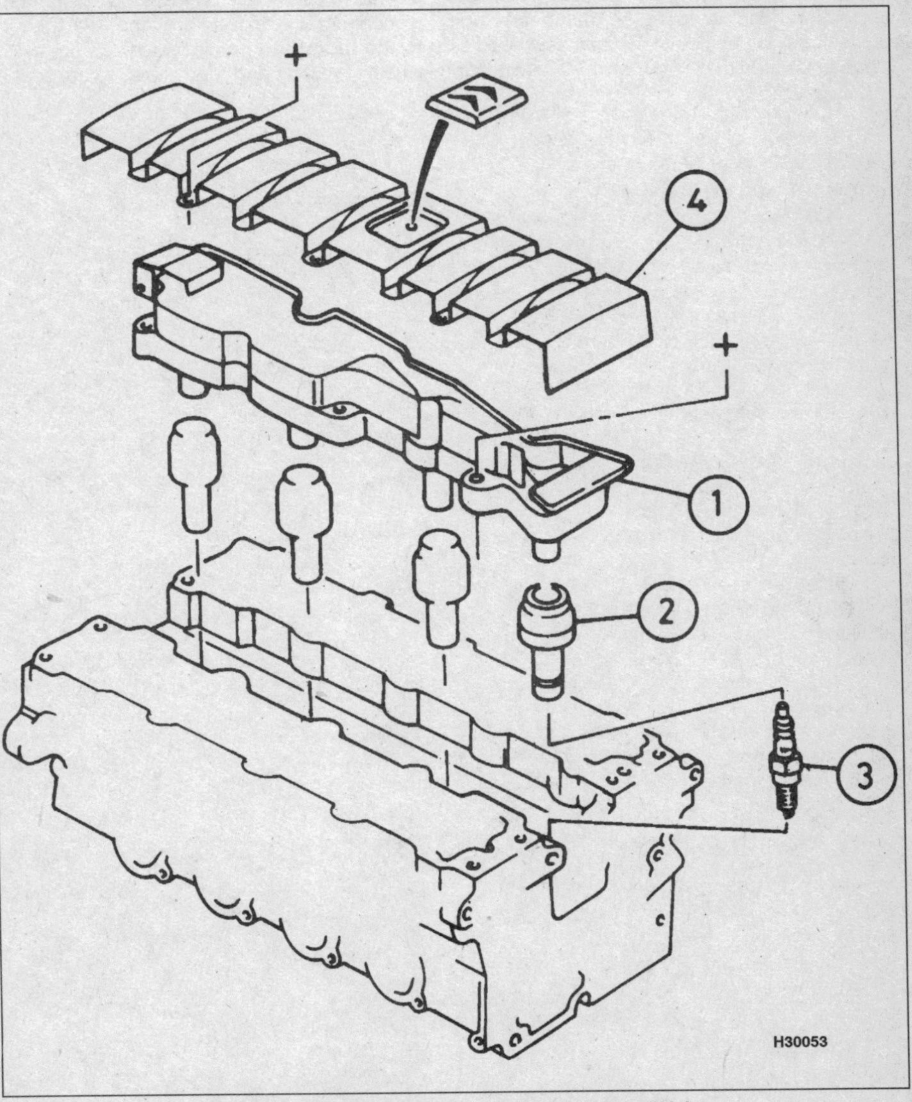

3.12 HT ignition coil module (16-valve models)

1 HT ignition coil module
2 Extension pillars
3 Spark plugs
4 Trim panel

5B

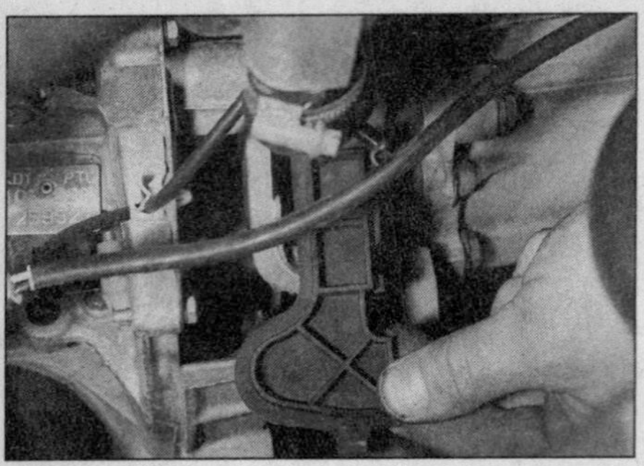

4.4 Removing the timing inspection hole plug

crankshaft pulley bolt) until the timing mark scribed on the edge of the flywheel appears in the aperture **(see illustration)**. Highlight the line with quick-drying white paint; typist's correction fluid is ideal. If marks are not present, set the engine to TDC as described in Chapter 2A, and make your own TDC markings on the flywheel and transmission casing.

5 Start the engine and run it to normal operating temperature, then stop it.

6 Connect the timing light to No 1 cylinder spark plug lead (No 1 cylinder is at the transmission end of the engine) as described in the timing light manufacturer's instructions.

7 Start the engine, allowing it to idle at the specified speed (see Chapter 4A or 4B), and point the timing light at the transmission housing aperture/crankshaft pulley. Adjust the timing lamp firing point, using the variable delay function, until the TDC marks are aligned with each other and read off the corresponding ignition advance figure.

8 If the ignition timing is incorrect, the car should be taken to a Citroën dealer who will be able to check the system quickly using special diagnostic equipment.

9 After making the check stop the engine, disconnect the timing light, and refit the plug to the top of the transmission casing, or the wheel arch liner and roadwheel, as applicable.

5 Knock sensor - removal and refitting

Removal

1 The knock sensor is located on the front face of the cylinder block.

2 Ensure that the ignition is switched off. Unplug the wiring harness from the knock sensor at the connector.

3 Slacken and withdraw the retaining bolt, then remove the knock sensor from the cylinder block.

Refitting

4 Refitting is a reversal of removal. Note that the tightness of the retaining bolt is critical to the operation of the knock sensor - ensure that it is tightened to the specified torque.

Chapter 5 Part C: Pre-heating system (diesel models)

Contents

Degrees of difficulty

Easy, suitable for novice with little experience	**Fairly easy,** suitable for beginner with some experience	**Fairly difficult,** suitable for competent DIY mechanic	**Difficult,** suitable for experienced DIY mechanic	**Very difficult,** suitable for expert DIY or professional

Specifications

Glow plugs

Type	Bosch 0 250 202 020
Nominal supply voltage	11.0 V
Steady state current consumption (after 20 seconds operation)	9.0 A
Time taken to reach 850°C	4.0 ± 1.5 seconds

Torque wrench setting

	Nm	lbf ft
Glow plugs	25	18

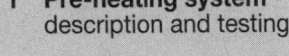

1 Pre-heating system - description and testing

Description

1 To assist cold starting, diesel engined models are fitted with a pre-heating system, which comprises a number of glow plugs (one per cylinder), a glow plug control unit, a facia mounted warning lamp, a coolant temperature sensor mounted on the thermostat housing, an ambient air temperature sensor mounted inside the glow plug control unit, and the associated electrical wiring.

2 The glow plugs are miniature electric heating elements, encapsulated in a metal case with a probe at one end and electrical connection at the other. Each combustion chamber has one glow plug threaded into it, with the tip of the glow plug probe positioned directly in line with incoming spray of fuel from the injectors. When the glow plug is energised, it heats up to rapidly, causing the fuel passing over the glow plug probe to be heated to its optimum combustion temperature, ready for combustion. In addition, some of the fuel passing over the glow plugs is actually ignited and this helps to trigger the combustion process.

3 The pre-heating system begins to operate as soon as the ignition key is switched to the second position, but only if the engine coolant temperature is below 60°C. A facia mounted warning lamp informs the driver that pre-heating is taking place. The lamp extinguishes when sufficient pre-heating has taken place to allow the engine to be started, but power will still be supplied to the glow plugs for a further period until the engine is started. If no attempt is made to start the engine, the power supply to the glow plugs is switched off after a period of time, to prevent battery drain and glow plug burn-out.

4 The duration of the pre-heating period is governed by the glow plug control unit. This device monitors the temperature of the air in the engine bay via a built-in ambient air temperature sensor then alters the pre-heating time (the length for which the glow plugs are supplied with current) to suit the conditions.

5 Post-glowing takes place after the ignition key has been released from the 'Start' position; the glow plugs continue to operate for at least a further 15 seconds, helping to improve fuel combustion whilst the engine is warming up, resulting in quieter, smoother running and reduced exhaust emissions. The overall duration of the post-glowing period is dependant on the coolant temperature, which is measured by a sensor mounted in the thermostat housing.

Testing

6 If the system malfunctions, testing is ultimately by substitution of known good units, but some preliminary checks may be made as follows.

7 Connect a voltmeter or 12-volt test light across (not between) the glow plug supply cable and earth (engine or vehicle metal). Make sure that the live connection is kept clear of the engine and bodywork.

8 Have an assistant switch on the ignition, and check that voltage is supplied to the glow plugs. Note the time for which the warning light is lit, and the total time for which voltage is supplied before the system cuts out. Switch off the ignition.

9 If all is well, voltage will be supplied, and the warning light will stay on for approximately 5 to 6 seconds.

10 If there is no supply at all, the control unit or associated wiring is at fault.

11 To locate a defective glow plug, disconnect the main supply cable and interconnecting wire from the top of the glow plugs.

Caution: Be careful not to drop the nuts and washers.

12 Use a continuity tester, or a 12-volt test light connected to the battery positive terminal, to check for continuity between each glow plug terminal and earth. The resistance of a glow plug in good condition is very low (less than 1 ohm), so if the test light does not come on, or if the continuity tester shows a high resistance, the glow plug is certainly defective.

13 If an ammeter is available, the current consumption of each glow plug can be measured. After an initial surge of around 15 to 20 amps, each plug should draw around 9 amps. Any plug which draws appreciably more or less than this is probably defective.

14 As a final check, the glow plugs can be removed and inspected as described in Section 2.

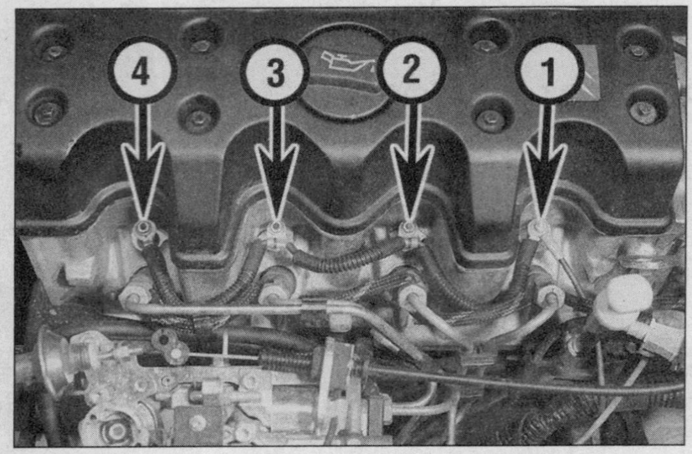

2.2 Glow plug locations; note that the main supply cable is connected to No 1 glow plug and an interconnecting wire is fitted between the four plugs

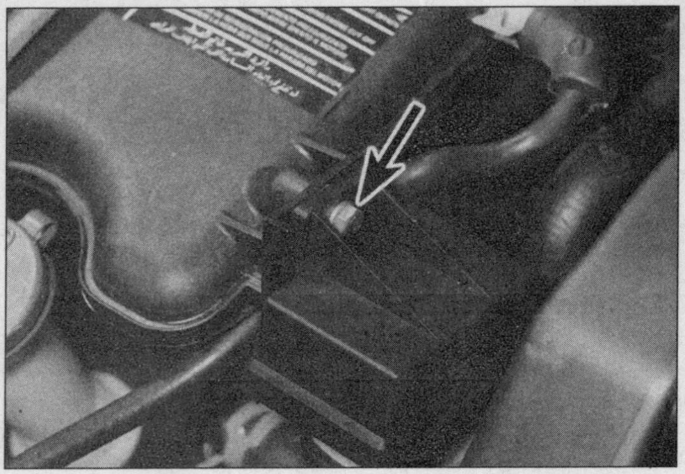

3.3 Unscrew the retaining bolt securing the control unit to the coolant expansion tank

2 Glow plugs - removal, inspection and refitting

Removal

Caution: If the pre-heating system has just been energised, or if the engine has been running, the glow plugs will be very hot.

1 Disconnect the battery negative lead.

2 Unscrew the nut from the relevant glow plug terminal(s), and recover the washer(s). Note that the main supply cable is connected to No 1 cylinder glow plug (at the transmission end) and an interconnecting wire is fitted between the four plugs **(see illustration)**.

3 Where applicable, carefully move any obstructing pipes or wires to one side, to gain access to the relevant glow plug(s).

4 Unscrew the glow plug(s) and remove from the cylinder head.

Inspection

5 Inspect each glow plug for physical damage. Burnt or eroded glow plug tips can be caused by a bad injector spray pattern. Have the injectors checked if this sort of damage is found.

6 If the glow plugs are in good physical condition, check them electrically using a 12-volt test light or continuity tester as described in the previous Section.

7 The glow plugs can be energised by applying 12 volts to them, to verify that they heat up evenly and in the required time. Observe the following precautions:

a) Support the glow plug by clamping it carefully in a vice or self-locking pliers. ***Remember - it will become red-hot.***

b) Make sure that the power supply or test lead incorporates a fuse or overload trip, to protect against damage from a short-circuit.

c) After testing, allow the glow plug to cool for several minutes before attempting to handle it.

3.4a Unplug the wiring connector from the base of the unit . . .

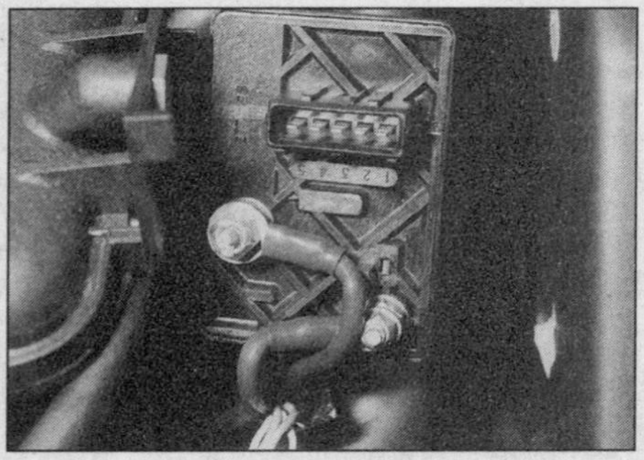

3.4b . . . then unscrew the two retaining nuts, and free the main feed and supply wires from the unit

8 A glow plug in good condition will start to glow red at the tip after drawing current for 5 seconds or so. Any plug which takes much longer to start glowing, or which starts glowing in the middle instead of at the tip, is defective.

Refitting

9 Refit by reversing the removal operations. Apply a smear of copper-based anti-seize compound to the plug threads, and tighten the glow plugs to the specified torque. Do not overtighten, as this can damage the glow plug element.

3 Pre-heating system control unit - removal and refitting

Removal

1 The unit is located on the right-hand side of the engine compartment, on the coolant expansion tank.

2 Disconnect the battery negative lead.

3 Unscrew the retaining bolt securing the unit to the coolant expansion tank **(see illustration)**.

4 Disconnect the wiring connector from the base of the unit. Unscrew the two retaining nuts, and free the main feed and supply wires from the unit - note their locations for use when refitting **(see illustrations)**. Remove the unit from the engine compartment.

Refitting

5 Refitting is a reversal of removal, ensuring that all wiring is securely connected to its original location, as noted on removal.

Chapter 6
Clutch

Contents

Degrees of difficulty

Easy, suitable for novice with little experience	**Fairly easy,** suitable for beginner with some experience	**Fairly difficult,** suitable for competent DIY mechanic	**Difficult,** suitable for experienced DIY mechanic	**Very difficult,** suitable for expert DIY or professional

Specifications

Type	Single dry plate with diaphragm spring. Cable-operated release mechanism	
Clutch pedal travel	130 ± 5 mm	
Friction plate diameter		
954 cc, 1124 cc and 1360 cc petrol models	180 mm	
1587 cc 8-valve and 16-valve petrol models	200 mm	
1527 cc Diesel models	180 mm	
Torque wrench setting	**Nm**	**lbf ft**
Pressure plate retaining bolts	20	15

6

1 General information

1 The clutch consists of a friction plate, a pressure plate assembly, a release bearing, and the release mechanism; all of these components are contained in the large cast aluminium alloy bellhousing, sandwiched between the engine and the transmission. The release mechanism is mechanical, being operated by a cable.

2 The friction plate is fitted between the engine flywheel and the clutch pressure plate, and is allowed to slide on the transmission input shaft splines. It consists of two circular facings of friction material riveted in position to provide the clutch bearing surface, and a spring-cushioned hub to damp out transmission shocks.

3 The pressure plate assembly is bolted to the engine flywheel, and is located by three dowel pins. When the engine is running, drive is transmitted from the crankshaft via the flywheel to the friction plate (these components being clamped securely together by the pressure plate assembly) and from the friction plate to the transmission input shaft.

4 To interrupt the drive, the spring pressure must be relaxed. This is achieved by means of a sealed release bearing, fitted concentrically around the transmission input shaft. When the driver depresses the clutch pedal, the release bearing is pressed against the fingers at the centre of the diaphragm spring. Since the spring is held by rivets between two annular fulcrum rings, the pressure at its centre causes it to deform so that it flattens and thus releases the clamping force it exerts, at its periphery, on the pressure plate.

5 Depressing the clutch pedal pulls the control cable inner wire, and this in turn rotates the release fork by acting on the lever at the fork's upper end, above the bellhousing. The fork itself is clipped to the left of the release bearing.

6 As the friction plate facings wear, the pressure plate moves towards the flywheel; this causes the diaphragm spring fingers to push against the release bearing, thus reducing the clearance which must be present in the mechanism. To ensure correct operation, the clutch cable must be regularly adjusted.

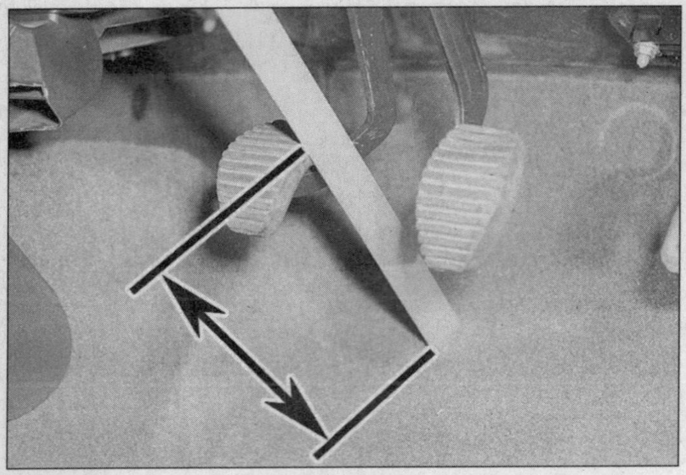

2.2 Measure the distance between the top surface of the clutch pedal footpad and the floor

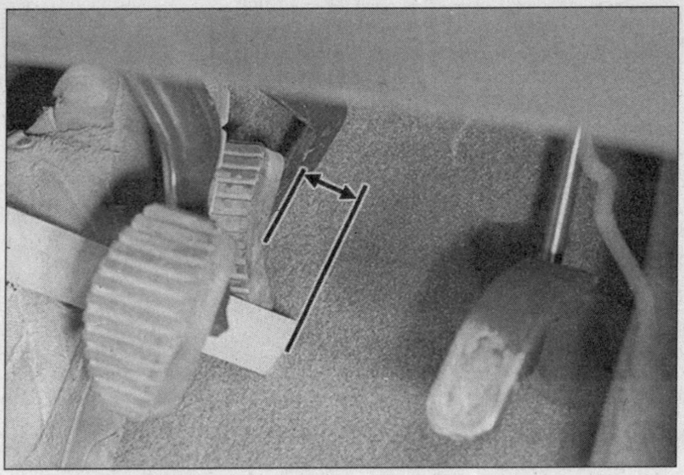

2.3 Depress the clutch pedal fully, then measure the new distance between the top surface of the clutch pedal footpad and the floor

2 Clutch - adjustment

1 The clutch adjustment is checked by measuring the total travel of the clutch.
2 Using a tape measure or similar, measure the distance between the top surface of the clutch pedal footpad and the floor (call this measurement No 1) **(see illustration)**.
3 Depress the clutch pedal fully, ensuring that there are no obstructions between it and the floor. Measure the new distance between the top surface of the clutch pedal footpad and the floor (call this measurement No 2) **(see illustration)**.
4 Subtract measurement No 2 from measurement No 1 to give the total clutch pedal travel, and compare this figure with that given in the Specifications. If the pedal travel is incorrect, adjust the clutch as follows.
5 The clutch cable is adjusted by means of the adjuster nut on the transmission end of the cable. Access to the locknut is limited and, if required, the battery can be removed to improve access - refer to Chapter 5A for further information. Alternatively, easier access to the adjuster nut can be gained from underneath the engine compartment. Apply the handbrake, then raise the front of the vehicle and support on axle stands (see "*Jacking and vehicle support*").
6 Slacken the locknut from the end of the clutch cable. Adjust the position of the adjuster nut **(see illustration)**, then re-measure the clutch pedal travel. Repeat this procedure until the clutch pedal travel is as specified.
7 Once the adjuster nut is correctly positioned and the pedal travel is correctly set, securely tighten the cable locknut. Where necessary, refit the battery as described in Chapter 5A.

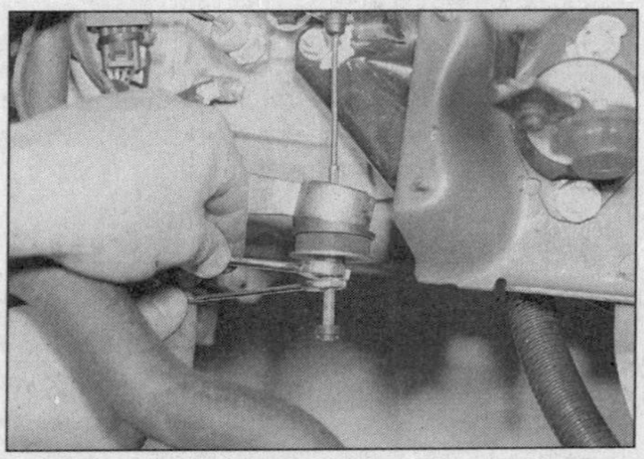

2.6 The clutch pedal travel is adjusted by means of the adjuster nut on the transmission end of the cable (battery and air cleaner ducting removed for clarity)

3 Clutch cable - removal and refitting

Removal

1 Working in the engine compartment, fully slacken the locknut and adjuster nut from the end of the clutch cable, with reference to Section 2. On some models, access to the nuts is limited and, if required, the battery and its support tray can be removed to improve access. Refer to Chapter 5A for further information. Alternatively, easier access to the adjuster nut can be gained from underneath. Apply the handbrake, then raise and support the vehicle on axle stands.
2 Release the inner cable and outer cable fittings from the clutch release lever and mounting bracket, and free the cable from the transmission housing **(see illustrations)**.
3 Slacken and remove the nut (where fitted) securing the cable guide to the engine compartment bulkhead. Unclip the two-piece cable guide from the bulkhead, together with its sealing grommet.
4 Working inside the vehicle, undo the retaining nuts and remove the under-facia trim panel from the driver's side of the facia.
5 Raise the clutch pedal to the extent of its travel, then unhook the clutch inner cable from the top of the clutch pedal **(see illustration)**. Note that access to the top of the pedal is very restricted.
6 Withdraw the cable from the bulkhead into the engine compartment, releasing it from any relevant retaining clips and guides **(see illustrations)**. Make a note of the cable's correct routing, then remove it from the vehicle.
7 Examine the cable, looking for worn end fittings or a damaged outer casing, and for signs of fraying of the inner wire. Check the

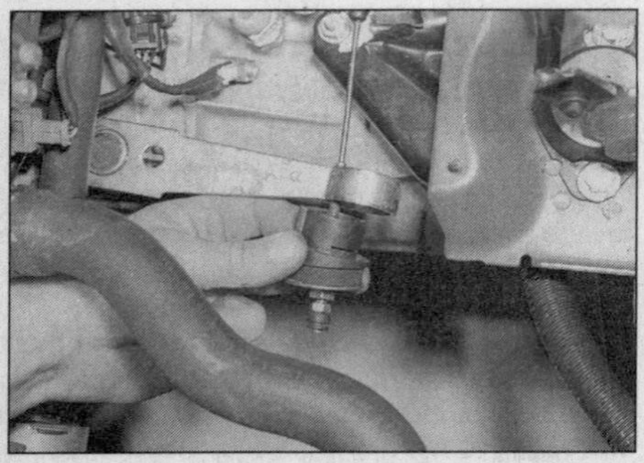

3.2a Release the inner cable from the clutch release lever . . .

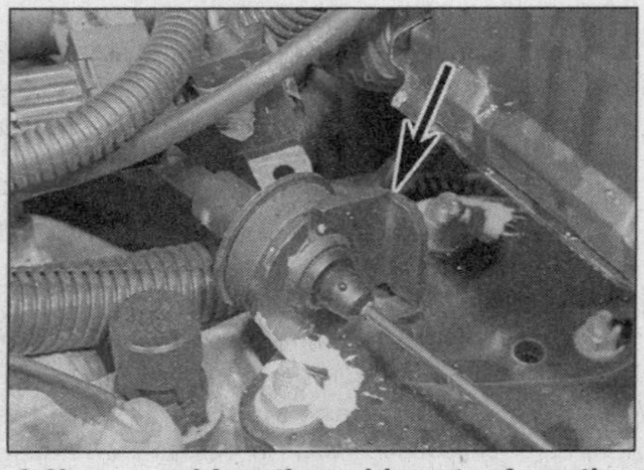

3.2b . . . and free the cable outer from the transmission bracket (arrowed)

3.5 Raise the clutch pedal to the extent of its travel, then unhook the clutch cable inner from the top of the clutch pedal (arrowed) - facia removed for clarity

cable's operation - the inner wire should move smoothly and easily through the outer casing. Remember, however, that a cable that appears serviceable when tested off the car may well be much 'heavier' in operation, when compressed into its working position. Renew the cable if it shows any signs of excessive wear or damage.

Refitting

8 Apply a thin smear of multi-purpose grease to the cable end fittings, then lay the cable in position in the engine compartment. Secure it in position with the retaining clips.

9 Separate the two halves of the cable guide, then press the outer section of the cable guide into bulkhead aperture so that it clicks into position, with rubber grommet compressed between the guide and the bulkhead.

10 Pass the hooked cable end through the engine compartment bulkhead into the space above the clutch pedal.

11 Raise the clutch pedal to the end of its travel, then engage the hook at the end of the clutch cable inner with the top of the clutch pedal end **(see illustration)**. Depress the clutch pedal bay hand and check that the cable is securely retained

12 Press the inner section of the cable guide into the outer section at the engine compartment bulkhead.

13 Working inside the car, under the driver's side of the facia, refit the under-facia trim panel, and securely tighten its retaining nuts.

14 At the transmission, refit the plastic locating collar to the clutch release lever, and ensure that the rubber spacer is correctly located on the transmission end of the outer cable.

15 Ensuring that the cable is correctly routed and retained by all the relevant retaining clips and guides, pass the lower end through the release lever/mounting bracket at the transmission, and engage the inner cable with the clutch release lever/mounting bracket (as applicable). Refit the rubber spacer and flat washer to the end of the inner cable, and screw on the adjuster nut and locknut.

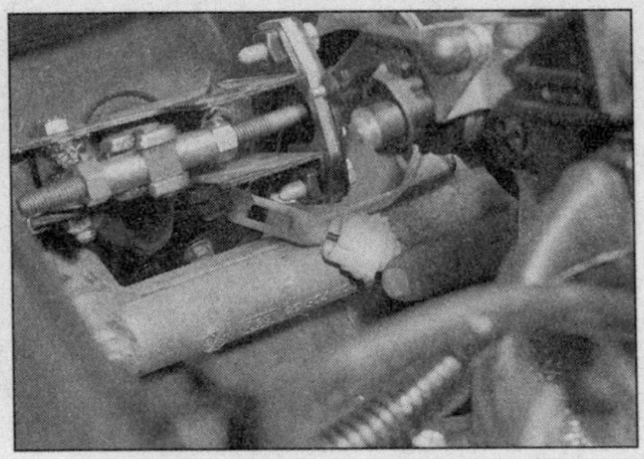

3.6a Withdraw the cable from the bulkhead . . .

16 Fully depress the clutch pedal at least twenty times, to bed the new cable in. On completion, adjust the clutch cable as described in Section 2.

4 Clutch pedal - removal and refitting

Note: *Access to the pedal pivot bolt is very poor, and can only be significantly improved by removing the facia as described in Chapter 11.*

Removal

Right-hand drive models

1 With the use of an assistant, unscrew a couple of brake caliper bleeding nipples to enable the brake pedal to be pressed to the floor. Make sure that you catch any leaking brake fluid, as it attacks plastics.

2 While the brake pedal is pressed out of the way, unhook the cable from the upper end of the clutch pedal (see Section 3 for details). Tighten the caliper bleed nipples.

3 Slacken and remove the nut and pivot bolt, then withdraw the clutch pedal from the vehicle, along with its assister spring.

4 Carefully clean all components, renewing any that are worn or damaged; check the bearing surfaces of the pivot bushes and bolt with particular care; the bushes can be renewed separately if worn.

Left-hand drive models

5 Working as described in Section 2, slacken the clutch cable locknut and adjuster nut to obtain maximum freeplay in the cable.

6 Working inside the vehicle, undo the retaining nuts and remove the under-facia trim panel from the driver's side of the facia.

7 Unhook the clutch inner cable from the top of the clutch pedal.

8 Unscrew the nut from the pedal pivot bolt.

9 Noting the correct fitted position of the clutch pedal assister spring, withdraw the pivot bolt sufficiently to allow the pedal, spring and spacer to be removed.

10 Carefully clean all components, renewing any that are worn or damaged; check the bearing surfaces of the pivot bush and bolt with particular care; the bushes can be renewed separately if worn.

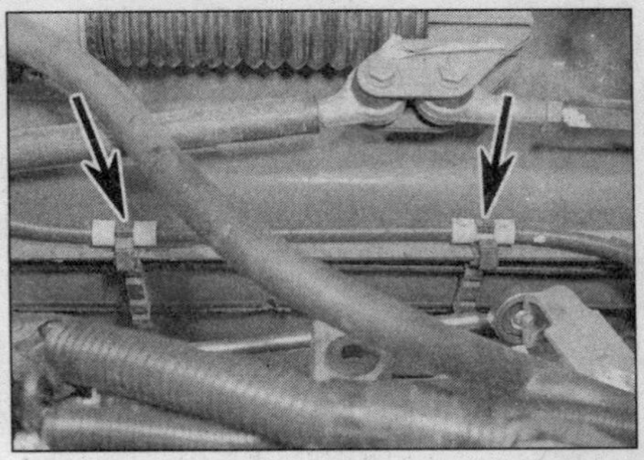

3.6b . . . and release it from the retaining clips (arrowed)

3.11 Raise the clutch pedal to the end of its travel, then engage the hook at the end of the clutch cable inner with the top of the clutch pedal end

Refitting

Right-hand drive models

11 Press the pivot bushes into the pedal bore, then apply a smear of multi-purpose grease to their bearing surfaces.

12 Refit the pedal and spring to the vehicle, and install the pivot bolt. Refit the pivot bolt nut, and tighten it securely. Slacken the brake caliper bleeding nipples, press the brake pedal to the floor and refit the clutch cable to the pedal. Tighten the caliper bleed nipples.

13 Check that the pedal pivots smoothly. Top up the brake fluid and, if necessary, bleed the brake system (see Chapter 9)

14 On completion check and, if necessary, adjust the clutch cable as described in Section 2.

Left-hand drive models

15 Press the pivot bush into the pedal bore, then apply a smear of multi-purpose grease to its bearing surface.

16 Refit the pedal, spring and spacer to the vehicle, and install the pivot bolt. Ensure that the bolt is correctly engaged with the brake pedal, then refit the pivot bolt nut and tighten it securely.

17 Hook the clutch cable onto the end of the pedal, then adjust the clutch cable as described in Section 2.

18 With the clutch cable correctly adjusted, refit the under-facia trim panel to the driver's side of the facia.

5.4a Prise the pressure plate assembly off its locating dowels . . .

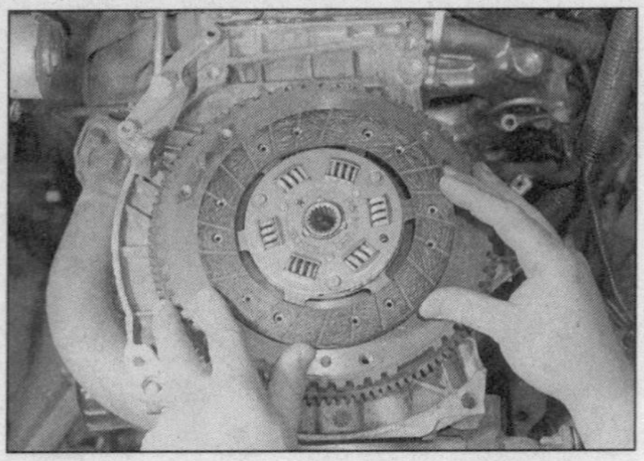

5.4b . . . and collect the friction plate as it falls out

5 Clutch assembly - removal, inspection and refitting

Warning: Dust created by clutch wear and deposited on the clutch components may contain asbestos, which is a health hazard. DO NOT blow it out with compressed air or inhale any of it. DO NOT use petrol or petroleum-based solvents to clean off the dust. Brake system cleaner or methylated spirit should be used to flush the dust into a suitable receptacle. After the clutch components are wiped clean with rags, dispose of the contaminated rags and cleaner in a sealed, marked container. Although some friction materials may no longer contain asbestos, it is safest to assume that they DO, and to take precautions accordingly.

Removal

1 Unless the engine/transmission is to be removed from the car and separated for major overhaul (Chapter 2C), the clutch can be reached by removing the transmission alone, as described in Chapter 7A.

2 Before disturbing the clutch, use chalk or a marker pen to mark the relationship of the pressure plate assembly to the flywheel. These marks can then be used during refitting, to ensure that the clutch is secured to the flywheel in the same position.

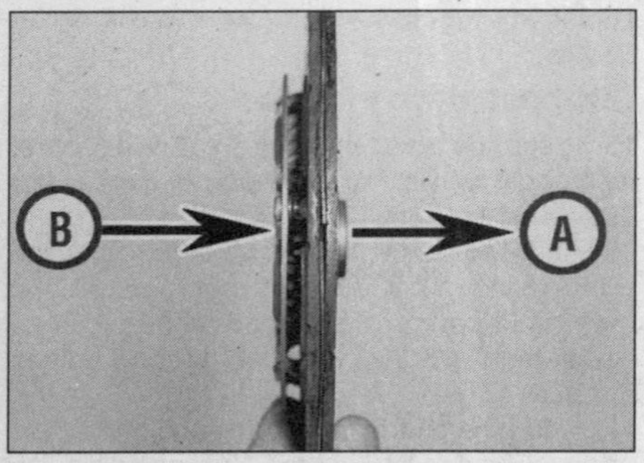

5.14 Orientate the friction plate so that its spring hub assembly faces away from the flywheel

A Towards flywheel *B Spring hub*

3 Working in a diagonal sequence, slacken the pressure plate bolts by half a turn at a time, until spring pressure is released and the bolts can be unscrewed by hand.

4 Prise the pressure plate assembly off its locating dowels, and collect the friction plate as it falls out, noting which way round the friction plate is fitted **(see illustrations)**.

Inspection

Note: *Due to the amount of work necessary to gain access to the clutch components, it is usually considered good practice to renew the clutch friction plate, pressure plate assembly and release bearing as a matched set, even if only one of these is actually worn enough to require renewal.*

5 Remove the clutch assembly.

6 When cleaning clutch components, read first the warning at the beginning of this Section; remove any dust using a clean, dry cloth, and working in a well-ventilated atmosphere.

7 Check the friction plate facings for signs of wear, damage or oil contamination. If the friction material is cracked, burnt, scored or damaged, or if it is contaminated with oil or grease (shown by shiny black patches), the friction plate must be renewed.

8 If the friction material is still serviceable, check that the centre boss splines are unworn, that the torsion springs are in good condition and securely fastened, and that all the rivets are tightly fastened. If any wear or damage is found, the friction plate must be renewed.

9 If the friction material is fouled with oil, this must be due to an oil leak from the crankshaft left-hand oil seal, from the sump-to-cylinder block joint, or from the transmission input shaft. If a leak is evident, renew the seal or repair the joint (as appropriate) as described in Chapter 2A or 2B (as applicable) or Chapter 7A, before installing the new friction plate.

10 Check the pressure plate assembly for obvious signs of wear or damage. Shake it to check for loose rivets or damaged fulcrum rings; check that the drive straps securing the pressure plate to the cover do not show signs (such as a deep yellow or blue discoloration) of overheating. If the diaphragm spring is worn or damaged, or if its pressure is in any way suspect, the pressure plate assembly should be renewed.

11 Examine the machined bearing surfaces of the pressure plate and of the flywheel; they should be clean, completely flat and free from scratches or scoring (minor damage of this nature can sometimes be polished away using emery paper). If either is discoloured from excessive heat, or shows signs of cracking, it should be renewed.

12 Check that the release bearing contact surface rotates smoothly and easily, with no sign of noise or roughness, and that the surface itself is smooth and unworn, with no signs of cracks, pitting or scoring. If there is any doubt about its condition, the bearing must be renewed.

Refitting

Using conventional tools

13 On reassembly, ensure that the bearing surfaces of the flywheel and pressure plate are completely clean, smooth, and free from oil or grease. Use solvent to remove any protective grease from new components.

14 Orientate the friction plate so that when it is refitted, its spring hub faces away from the flywheel **(see illustration)**. There may also be a manufacturer's marking stamped on the hub, showing which way round the plate should be refitted.

15 Hold the clutch friction plate centrally against the flywheel, then place the pressure plate assembly in position over it, aligning the marks made on dismantling (if the original pressure plate is re-used). Ensure that the pressure plate is located correctly on its three dowels.

16 Insert the pressure plate securing bolts, but do them up finger-tight only at this stage, so that the friction plate is held in position, but can still be moved without excessive effort.

17 The friction plate must now be centralised, so that when the transmission is refitted, its input shaft will be aligned with the splines at the centre of the friction plate. Centralisation can be achieved by passing a length of steel bar or a wooden dowel through the friction plate and into the recess machined into the end face of the crankshaft. The friction plate can then be moved around until it is centred inside the pressure plate **(see illustration)**.

5.17 Align the friction plate centrally inside the pressure plate

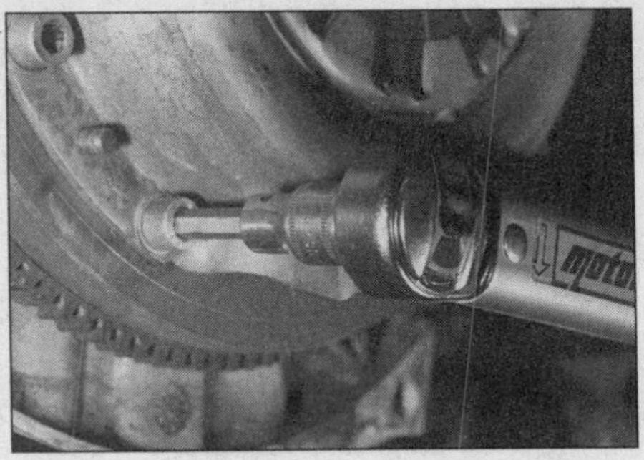

5.18 Tighten the pressure plate bolts evenly and in a diagonal sequence to the specified torque setting

18 When the friction plate is centralised, tighten the pressure plate bolts evenly and in a diagonal sequence to the specified torque setting **(see illustration)**.

Using a clutch assembly/alignment tool

19 When the clutch is refitted, care must be taken to ensure that the friction plate is centred between the pressure plate and flywheel, before the transmission is refitted. If this is not the case, the transmission input shaft will not pass through the friction plate hub and it will be impossible to refit the transmission. In practice, aligning the clutch accurately can be a rather tricky operation, but the process can be simplified considerably by using a clutch assembly/alignment tool - these can be obtained for a reasonable cost from motor accessory shops. The tool aligns the friction plate and pressure plate radially and clamps them together as an assembly, allowing the clutch to be refitted and aligned in one easy operation.

20 Place the friction plate on a clean workbench, with the spring hub facing upwards. Position the pressure plate centrally over the friction plate, then fit the assembly/alignment tool, so that the friction plate and pressure plate are clamped together **(see illustration)**.

21 Fit the pressure plate and friction plate assembly to the flywheel, ensuring the flywheel dowels pass through the corresponding holes in the pressure plate **(see illustration)**. If the original pressure plate is being re-used, observe the alignment markings made during removal.

5.20 Fit the clutch assembly/alignment tool, so that the friction plate and pressure plate are clamped together

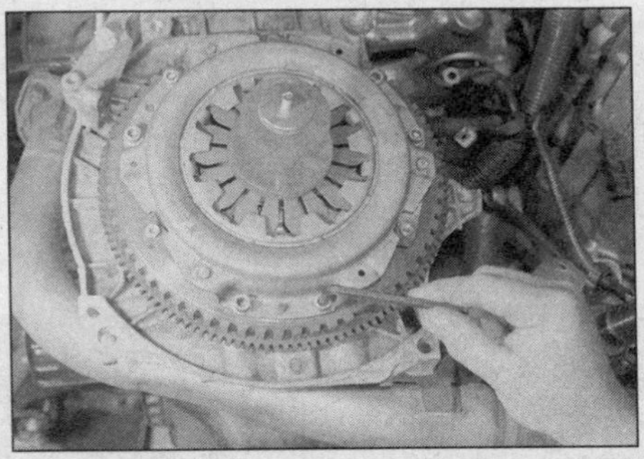

5.22a Insert all the pressure plate securing bolts and partially tighten them. . .

22 Insert all the pressure plate securing bolts and partially tighten them, so that the fiction plate is held firmly against the flywheel. Remove the clutch assembly/alignment tool, then tighten the pressure plate securing bolts progressively in a diagonal sequence to the specified torque wrench setting **(see illustrations)**.

All methods

23 Apply a thin smear of high-melting point grease to the splines of the friction plate and the transmission input shaft, also to the release bearing bore and release fork shaft.

24 Refit the transmission as described in Chapter 7A.

25 On completion, check and if necessary adjust the clutch pedal travel, as described in Section 2.

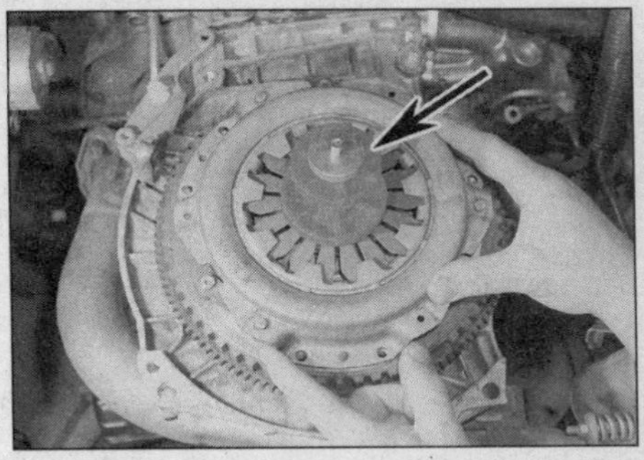

5.21 Fitting the pressure plate and friction plate to the flywheel, with the aid of a clutch assembly/alignment tool (arrowed)

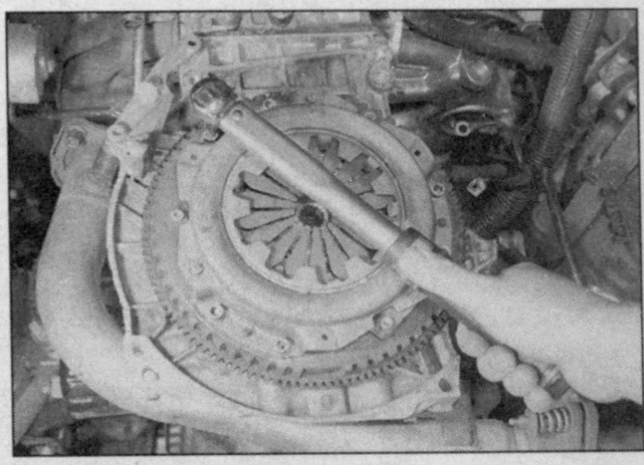

5.22b . . . then remove the clutch assembly/alignment tool and tighten the pressure plate securing bolts to the specified torque

6 Clutch release mechanism - removal, inspection and refitting

Note: *Refer to the warning concerning the dangers of asbestos dust at the beginning of Section 5.*

Removal

1 Unless the engine/transmission is to be removed from the car and separated for major overhaul (Chapter 2C), the clutch release mechanism can be reached by removing the transmission alone (Chapter 7A).

2 Unhook the release bearing from the fork, and slide it off the input shaft. Drive out the retaining pin or unscrew the retaining bolt (as applicable). Remove the release lever from the top of the release fork shaft **(see illustrations)**.

6.2a Using a hammer and suitable punch . . .

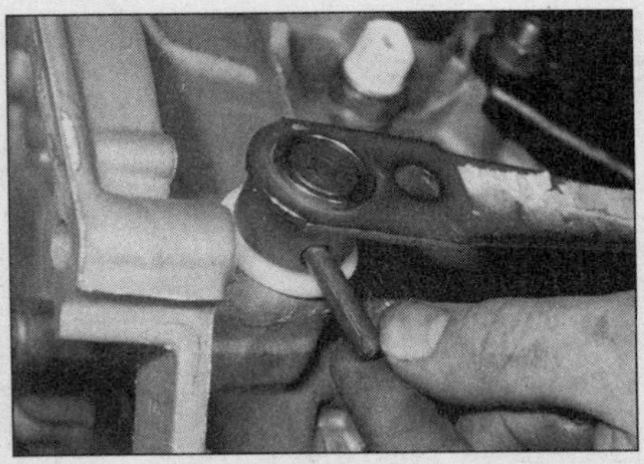

6.2b . . . tap out the retaining pin . . .

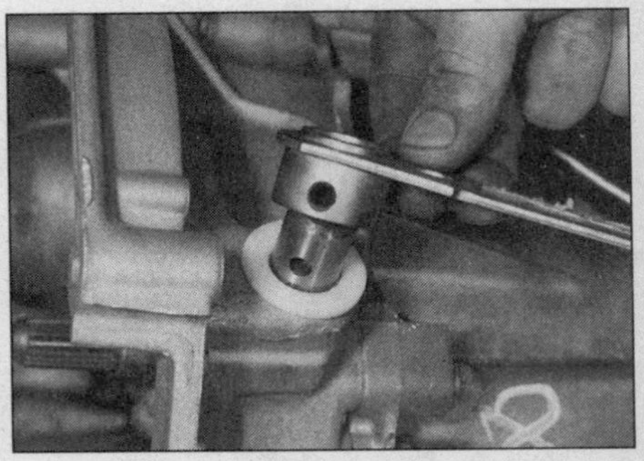

6.2c . . . then remove the release lever from the top of the release fork shaft

3 Depress the retaining tabs, then slide the upper bush off the end of the release fork shaft, then disengage the shaft from its lower bush and manoeuvre it out from the transmission **(see illustrations)**. Depress the retaining tabs, and remove the lower pivot bush from the transmission housing.

Inspection

4 Check the release mechanism, renewing any component which is worn or damaged. Carefully check all bearing surfaces and points of contact.

5 Check the release bearing itself, noting that it is often considered worthwhile to renew it as a matter of course. Check that the contact surface rotates smoothly and easily, with no sign of noise or roughness, and that the surface itself is smooth and unworn, with no signs of cracks, pitting or scoring. If there is any doubt about its condition, the bearing must be renewed.

Refitting

6 Apply a smear of high-melting point grease to the shaft pivot bushes and the contact surfaces of the release fork.

7 Locate the lower pivot bush in the transmission, ensuring that it is securely retained by its locating tangs, and refit the release fork **(see illustration)**. Slide the upper bush down the shaft, and clip it into position in the transmission housing.

8 Refit the release lever to the shaft. Align the lever with the shaft hole, and secure it in position by tapping in the retaining pin or securely tightening its retaining bolt (as applicable). Slide the release bearing onto the input shaft, and engage it with the release fork **(see illustration)**.

9 Refit the transmission (Chapter 7A).

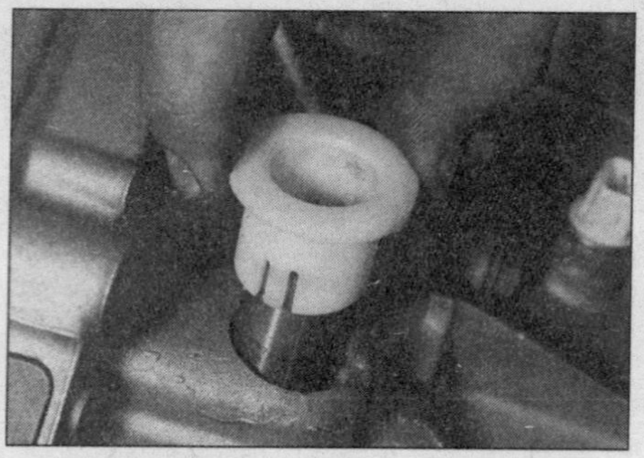

6.3a Release the upper pivot bush, and slide it off the shaft . . .

6.3b . . . then withdraw the release fork shaft and remove the lower bush (arrowed)

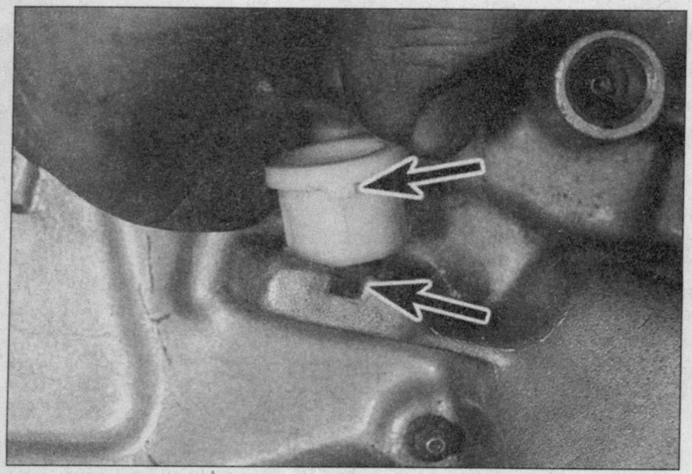

6.7 On refitting, ensure that the bush lug and housing recess (arrowed) are correctly aligned

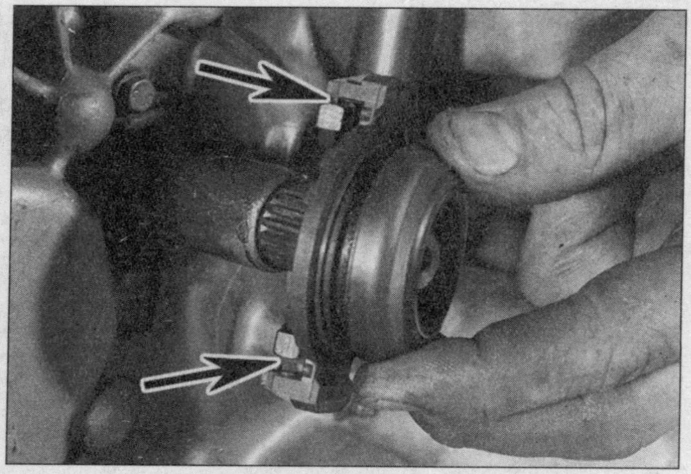

6.8 Install the release bearing, ensuring that its hooks (arrowed) are correctly engaged with the release fork

Chapter 7 Part A:
Manual transmission

Contents

Degrees of difficulty

Easy, suitable for novice with little experience	**Fairly easy,** suitable for beginner with some experience	**Fairly difficult,** suitable for competent DIY mechanic	**Difficult,** suitable for experienced DIY mechanic	**Very difficult,** suitable for expert DIY or professional

Specifications

General

Type	Five forward speeds and reverse. Synchromesh on all forward speeds
Designation	MA5

Gear ratios

954 cc and 1124 cc petrol models:	
1st	3.417 : 1 (12/41 teeth)
2nd	1.810 : 1 (21/38 teeth)
3rd	1.276 : 1 (29/37 teeth)
4th	1.026 : 1 (40/39 teeth)
5th	0.767 : 1 (43/33 teeth)
Reverse	2.500 : 1 (12/30 teeth)
Final drive	4.286 : 1 (14/60 teeth)
1360 cc petrol models:	
1st	3.636 : 1 (11/40 teeth)
2nd	1.950 : 1 (20/39 teeth)
3rd	1.276 : 1 (29/37 teeth)
4th	1.026 : 1 (40/39 teeth)
5th	0.767 : 1 (43/33 teeth)
Reverse	2.500 : 1 (12/30 teeth)
Final drive	3.765 : 1 (17/64 teeth)
1587 cc petrol models:	
1st	3.417 : 1 (12/41 teeth)
2nd	1.810 : 1 (21/38 teeth)
3rd	1.276 : 1 (29/37 teeth)
4th	1.026 : 1 (40/39 teeth)
5th	0.767 : 1 (43/33 teeth)
Reverse	2.500 : 1 (12/30 teeth)
Final drive	3.765 : 1 (17/64 teeth)
1587 cc 16v petrol models:	
1st	3.417 : 1 (12/41 teeth)
2nd	1.950 : 1 (20/39 teeth)
3rd	1.360 : 1 (28/38 teeth)
4th	1.050 : 1 (37/39 teeth)
5th	0.850 : 1 (41/35 teeth)
Reverse	2.500 : 1 (12/30 teeth)
Final drive	3.938 : 1 (16/63 teeth)
1527 cc diesel models:	
1st	3.636 : 1 (11/40 teeth)
2nd	1.950 : 1 (20/39 teeth)
3rd	1.276 : 1 (29/37 teeth)
4th	1.026 : 1 (40/39 teeth)
5th	0.767 : 1 (43/33 teeth)
Reverse	2.500 : 1 (12/30 teeth)
Final drive	3.765 : 1 (17/64 teeth) or 3.588 : 1 (17/61 teeth, depending on model)

Lubrication

Recommended oil	See "*Lubricants and Fluids*"
Capacity	2.0 litres

Torque wrench settings

	Nm	lbf ft
Oil filler/level plug	25	18
Oil drain plug	25	18
Clutch release bearing guide sleeve bolts	6	4
Reversing light switch	25	18
Engine-to-transmission fixing bolts	35	26

1 General information

The transmission is contained in a cast aluminium alloy casing bolted to the engine's left-hand end, and consists of the gearbox and final drive differential.

Drive is transmitted from the crankshaft via the clutch to the input shaft, which has a splined extension to accept the clutch friction plate, and rotates in sealed ball-bearings. From the input shaft, drive is transmitted to the output shaft, which rotates in a roller bearing at its right-hand end, and a sealed ball-bearing at its left-hand end. From the output shaft, the drive is transmitted to the differential crownwheel, which rotates with the differential case and planetary gears, thus driving the sun gears and driveshafts. The rotation of the planetary gears on their shaft allows the inner roadwheel to rotate at a slower speed than the outer roadwheel when the car is cornering.

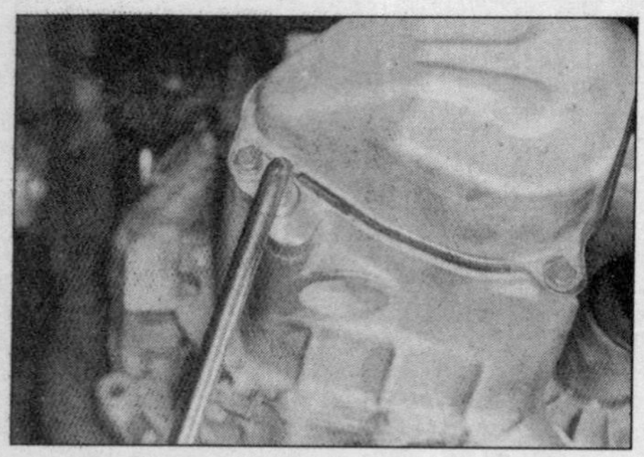

2.3a Unscrew the filler/level plug . . .

The input and output shafts are arranged side by side, parallel to the crankshaft and driveshafts, so that their gear pinion teeth are in constant mesh. In the neutral position, the output shaft gear pinions rotate freely, so that drive cannot be transmitted to the crownwheel.

Gear selection is via a floor-mounted lever and selector rod mechanism. The selector rod causes the appropriate selector fork to move its respective synchro-sleeve along the shaft, to lock the gear pinion to the synchro-hub. Since the synchro-hubs are splined to the output shaft, this locks the pinion to the shaft so that drive can be transmitted. To ensure that gear-changing can be made quickly and quietly, a synchromesh system is fitted to all forward gears, consisting of baulk rings and spring-loaded fingers as well as the gear pinions and synchro-hubs; the synchromesh cones are formed on the mating faces of the baulk rings and gear pinions.

2 Manual transmission - draining and refilling

Note: *A suitable square-section wrench may be required to undo the transmission filler/level and drain plugs on some models. These wrenches can be obtained from most motor factors, or from your Citroën dealer.*

1 This operation is much quicker and more effective if the car is first taken on a journey of sufficient length to warm the engine/transmission up to normal operating temperature.

2 Park the car on level ground, switch off the ignition, and apply the handbrake firmly. For improved access, jack up the front of the car and support it securely on axle stands (see "*Jacking and vehicle support*"). Note that the car must be lowered to the ground, and level, to ensure accuracy when refilling and checking the oil level.

3 Wipe clean the area around the filler/level plug, which is situated on the left-hand end of the transmission, next to the end cover. Unscrew the filler/level plug from the transmission, and recover the sealing washer **(see illustrations)**.

4 Position a suitable container under the drain plug, situated on the left-hand side of the differential housing, and unscrew the plug from the transmission **(see illustrations)**.

5 Allow the oil to drain completely into the container. If the oil is hot, take precautions against scalding. Clean both the filler/level and the drain plugs, being especially careful to wipe any metallic particles off the magnetic inserts. Discard the original sealing washers; they should be renewed whenever they are disturbed.

6 When the oil has finished draining, clean the drain plug threads and those of the transmission casing. Fit a new sealing washer and refit the drain plug, tightening it to the specified torque wrench setting. If the car was raised for the draining operation, lower it to the ground.

7 Refilling the transmission is an extremely awkward operation. Above all, allow plenty of time for the oil level to settle properly before checking the level. Note that the car must be parked on flat level ground when checking the oil level.

8 Refill the transmission with the exact amount of the specified type of oil, then check the oil level as described in Chapter 1A or 1B as applicable **(see illustration)**. If the correct amount was poured into the transmission, and a large amount flows out on checking the

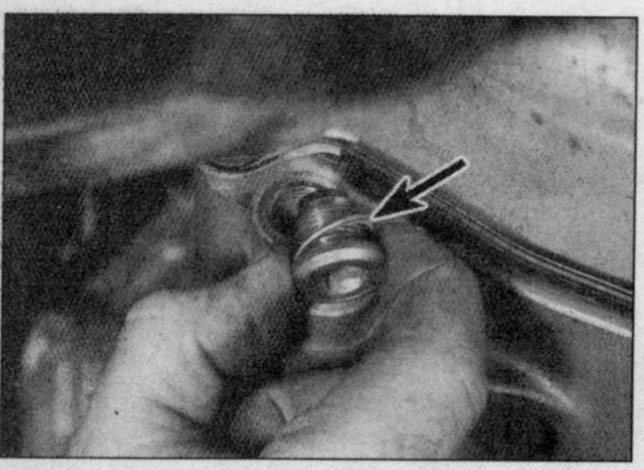

2.3b . . . and recover the sealing washer (arrowed)

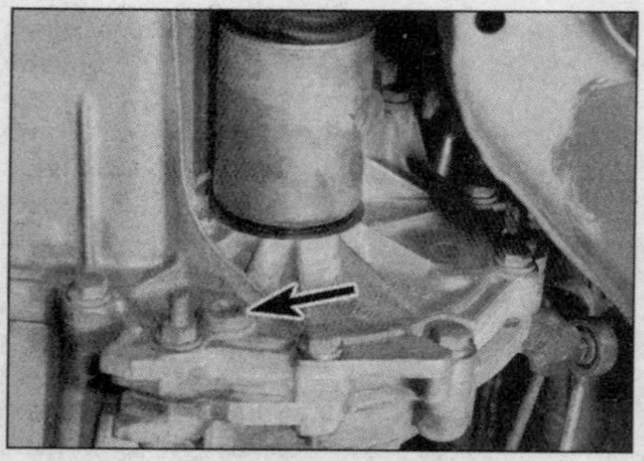

2.4a Drain plug location (arrowed)

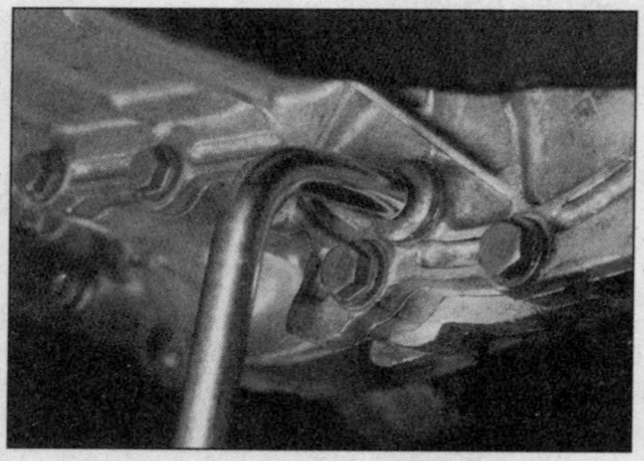

2.4b Unscrew the drain plug from the transmission

2.8 **Refill the transmission with the specified grade and quantity of oil**

level, refit the filler/level plug and take the car on a short journey. When the new oil is distributed fully around the transmission components, check the level again on your return, and top-up if necessary.

3 Gearchange linkage - general information

If a stiff, sloppy or imprecise gearchange leads you to suspect that a fault exists within the linkage, dismantle it completely and check it for wear or damage as described in Section 4. Reassemble the linkage, applying a smear of multi-purpose grease to all bearing surfaces.

If this does not cure the fault, the car should be examined by an expert, as the fault must lie within the transmission itself. There is no adjustment as such in the linkage; the balljoint fittings at either end of the linkage are not threaded, and so cannot be turned to alter its overall length.

4 Gearchange linkage - removal and refitting

Removal

1 Firmly apply the handbrake, then jack up the front of the vehicle and support it on axle stands (see "*Jacking and vehicle support*").

2 Slacken and remove the nut, and withdraw the pivot bolt securing the selector rod to the base of the gearchange lever.

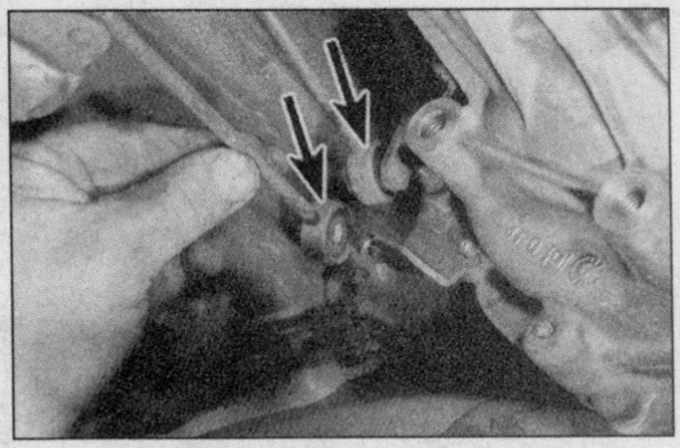

4.3 **Carefully lever the two selector rod link rods (arrowed) off their balljoints on the transmission**

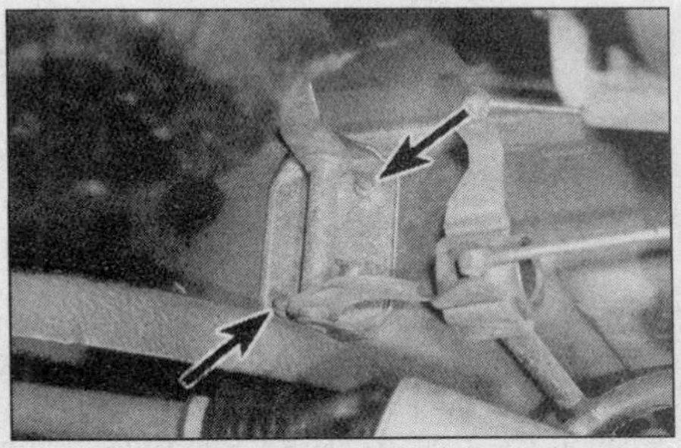

4.4b **. . . then undo the two retaining nuts (arrowed) and remove the bellcrank assembly from the bulkhead**

3 Using a flat-bladed screwdriver, carefully lever the two selector rod link rods off their balljoints on the transmission **(see illustration)**. Disengage the selector rod from the bellcrank pivot and remove it, complete with link rods, from underneath the vehicle.

4 Carefully lever the bellcrank link rod balljoint off the transmission lever, then undo the two retaining nuts and remove the bellcrank assembly from the bulkhead **(see illustrations)**.

5 Inspect all the linkage components for signs of wear or damage, paying particular attention to the pivot bushes and link rod balljoints, and renew worn components as necessary. If necessary, the gearchange lever can also be removed as follows.

6 Remove the centre console as described in Chapter 11, then undo the four retaining nuts and remove the gearchange lever, complete with rubber mounting plate, from the vehicle. The lever can be separated from its baseplate after the retaining ring has been unclipped **(see illustrations)**.

4.4a **Carefully lever the bellcrank link rod balljoint off the transmission lever . . .**

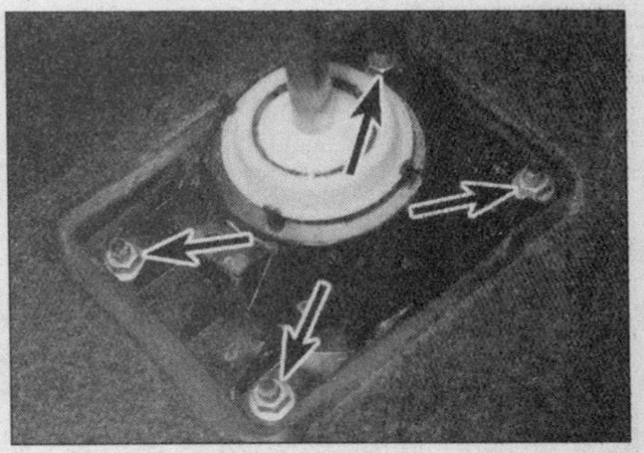

4.6a **Gearchange lever securing nuts (arrowed)**

7 Examine the lever components for signs of wear or damage, paying particular attention to the rubber gaiters, and renew components as necessary.

Refitting

8 Refitting is a reversal of the removal procedure, noting the following points:

a) Prior to refitting the linkage, place the gearchange lever in the neutral position.

b) Apply a smear of multi-purpose grease to the gearchange lever pivot ball. Do not grease the link rod balljoints, the bellcrank ball or the pivot bushes.

c) Ensure that all link rods are securely pressed onto their balljoints ***(see illustration)****.*

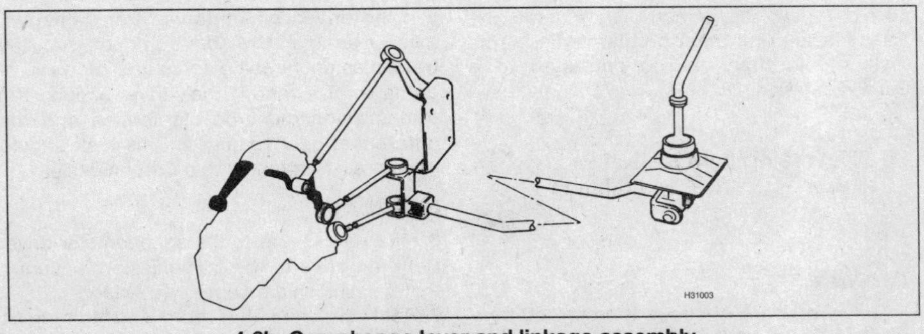

4.6b **Gearchange lever and linkage assembly**

4.8 **Ensure that all link rods are securely pressed onto their balljoints**

5.4 Carefully prise the oil seal out of the transmission, using a large flat-bladed screwdriver

5 Oil seals - renewal

Driveshaft oil seal

1 Chock the rear wheels of the car, firmly apply the handbrake, then jack up the front of the car and support it on axle stands (see "*Jacking and vehicle support*"). Remove the appropriate front roadwheel.

2 Drain the transmission oil as described in Section 2.

3 Working as described in Chapter 8, free the inner end of the driveshaft (or intermediate shaft, as applicable) from the transmission, placing it clear of the seal. There is no need to unscrew the driveshaft-to-hub retaining nut; the driveshaft can be left secured to the hub. Support the driveshaft, to avoid placing any strain on the driveshaft joints or gaiters.

4 Carefully prise the oil seal out of the transmission, using a large flat-bladed screwdriver **(see illustration)**. Do not score the inner surface of the seal housing with the screwdriver.

5 Remove all traces of dirt from the area around the oil seal aperture, then apply a smear of grease to the outer lip of the new oil seal. Fit the new seal into its aperture, and drive it squarely into position until it abuts its locating shoulder. Use a suitable tubular drift (such as a socket) which bears only on the hard outer edge of the seal **(see illustration)**.

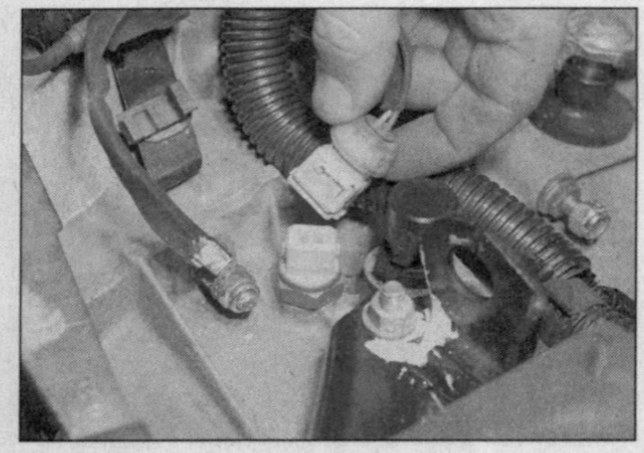

6.4 Disconnect the wiring connector from the reversing light switch

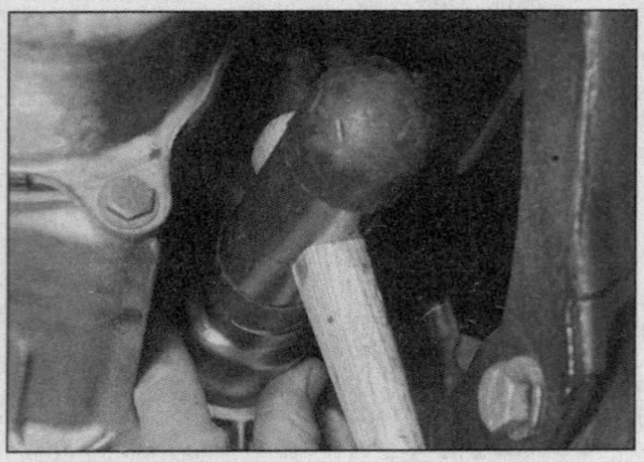

5.5 Fit the new seal into its aperture, and drive it squarely into position using a suitable tubular drift

If the seal was supplied with a plastic protector sleeve, leave this in position until the driveshaft has been refitted.

6 Refit the driveshaft as described in Chapter 8.

7 Refill the transmission with the specified type and amount of oil.

Input shaft oil seal

8 Remove the transmission from the car as described in Section 8.

9 Undo the three bolts securing the clutch release bearing guide sleeve in position, and slide the guide off the input shaft along with its O-ring or gasket (as applicable). Recover any relevant thrustwashers which have stuck to the rear of the guide sleeve, and refit them to the input shaft.

10 Before fitting a new seal, check the input shaft's seal rubbing surface for signs of burrs, scratches or other damage which may have caused the seal to fail in the first place. It may be possible to polish away minor defects of this sort using fine abrasive paper; however, more serious defects will require the renewal of the input shaft. Ensure that the input shaft is clean and greased, to protect the seal lip on refitting.

11 Fit a new O-ring or gasket (as applicable) to the rear of the guide sleeve, then carefully slide the sleeve into position over the input shaft. Refit the retaining bolts, and tighten them to the specified torque setting.

12 Refit the transmission to the car as described in Section 8.

Selector shaft oil seal

13 To renew the selector shaft seal, the transmission unit must be dismantled. This task should therefore be entrusted to a Citroën dealer.

6 Reversing light switch - testing, removal and refitting

Testing

1 The reversing light circuit is controlled by a plunger-type switch screwed into the top of the transmission casing. If a fault develops in the circuit, first ensure that the circuit fuse has not blown.

2 To test the switch, disconnect the wiring connector, and use a multi-meter (set to the resistance function) or a battery-and-bulb test circuit to check that there is continuity between the switch terminals only when reverse gear is selected. If this is not the case, and there are no obvious breaks or other damage to the wires, the switch is faulty and must be renewed.

Removal

3 To improve access to the switch, remove the battery as described in Chapter 5A.

4 Disconnect the wiring connector from the switch **(see illustration)**. Unscrew it from the transmission casing, and remove it along with its sealing washer.

Refitting

5 Fit a new sealing washer to the switch, then screw it back into position in the top of the transmission housing, tightening it to the specified torque setting. Reconnect the wiring connector, then refit the battery and test the operation of the circuit.

7 Speedometer drive - removal and refitting

Removal

1 Chock the rear wheels of the car, and firmly apply the handbrake. Jack up the front of the car, and support it securely on axle stands (see "*Jacking and vehicle support*"). The speedometer drive is situated on the rear of the transmission housing, next to the inner end of the right-hand driveshaft.

2 Unplug the wiring connector from the speedometer sensor.

3 Slacken and remove the retaining bolt, and withdraw the speedometer sensor from the transmission housing, along with its O-ring.

4 Examine the drive pinion for signs of wear, and renew if necessary. Renew the housing O-ring as a matter of course. The drive assembly is a sealed unit and cannot be dismantled.

5 If the driven pinion is worn or damaged, also examine the drive pinion in the transmission housing for signs of wear or damage. To renew the drive pinion, the transmission must be dismantled and the differential gear removed. This task should therefore be entrusted to a Citroën dealer.

Refitting

6 Fit a new O-ring to the speedometer drive. Refit the drive to the transmission, ensuring that the pinions are correctly engaged.

7 Refit the retaining bolt and tighten it securely. Reconnect the wiring connector to the speedometer transducer.

8 Manual transmission - removal and refitting

Removal

1 Chock the rear wheels, then firmly apply the handbrake. Jack up the front of the vehicle, and support it securely on axle stands (see "*Jacking and vehicle support*"). Remove both front roadwheels.

2 Drain the transmission oil as described in Section 2, then refit the drain and filler/level plugs and tighten them to their specified torque settings.

3 Remove the battery as described in Chapter 5A.

4 With reference to Chapter 4D, unbolt the exhaust system downpipe mounting bracket from the underside of the transmission casing bellhousing.

5 Remove the securing screws and detach the plastic liner from the left hand wheel arch.

6 Unbolt and remove the battery support tray, as described in Chapter 5A, section 4.

7 To improve access to the top of the transmission, remove the air cleaner housing and/or intake duct (as applicable), as described in the relevant Part of Chapter 4.

8 Remove the starter motor as described in Chapter 5A.

9 Fully slacken the clutch cable locknut and adjuster nut, then free the inner and outer cable end fittings from the mounting bracket and release lever (see Chapter 6 for details). Release the cable from any relevant retaining clips, and place it clear of the transmission.

10 Disconnect the wiring connectors from the reversing light switch, TDC sensor and speedometer drive housing (as applicable). Undo the retaining nut, and disconnect the earth strap from the top of the transmission housing **(see illustration)**. Free the wiring from any relevant retaining clips, and place it clear of the transmission.

11 Using a flat-bladed screwdriver, carefully lever the three gearchange mechanism link rods off their respective balljoints on the transmission (see Section 4). Position the rods clear of the transmission unit **(see illustration)**.

12 On cast-iron block engines, unbolt the flywheel cover plate from the base of the transmission, and remove it from the vehicle.

13 Working as described in Chapter 8, free the inner end of each driveshaft from the transmission, and position them clear of the transmission. Note that there is no need to unscrew the driveshaft retaining nuts; each driveshaft can be left secured to the hub. Support the driveshafts, however, to avoid placing any strain on the driveshaft joints or gaiters.

14 Place a jack with interposed block of wood beneath the engine, to take the weight of the engine. Alternatively, attach a hoist or support bar to the engine lifting eyes, and take the weight of the engine.

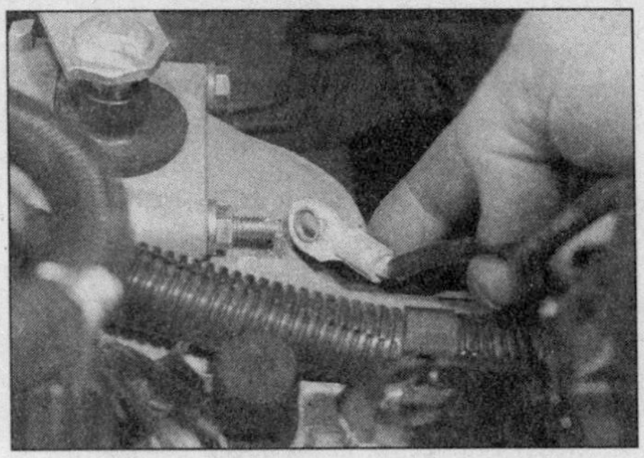

8.10 Undo the retaining nut, and disconnect the earth strap from the top of the transmission housing

15 Place a trolley jack and block of wood beneath the transmission, and raise the jack to take the weight of the transmission. Alternatively, attach a lifting hoist to the transmission and raise it to take the weight of the transmission.

16 Slacken and remove the centre nut and washer from the left-hand engine/ transmission mounting. Undo the two bolts securing the mounting bracket assembly to the vehicle body, then remove the mounting bracket assembly (see Chapter 2A or 2B, as applicable, for details). Recover the spacer from the stud.

17 Slacken and remove the two bolts securing the rear engine mounting to the transmission (see Chapter 2A or 2B as applicable). Unscrew the nut and bolt securing the mounting link to the vehicle body, and remove the mounting assembly from the vehicle.

18 On diesel models, refer to Chapter 1B and remove the fuel filter, to gain access to the upper transmission-to-engine unit bolts. If the filter is damaged on removal, a new one must be used on refitting.

19 With the jack beneath the transmission taking its weight, slacken and remove the bolts securing the transmission housing to the engine **(see illustration)**. Note the correct fitted positions of each bolt, and the necessary brackets, as they are removed, to use as a reference on refitting. Note that the transmission retaining bolt adjacent to the starter motor is accessed from the right hand side of the engine

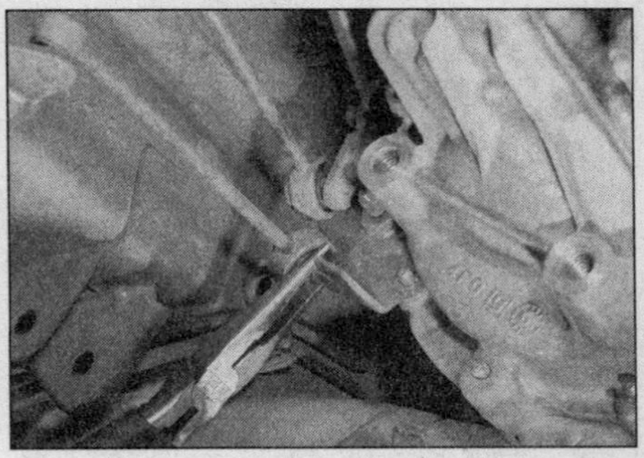

8.11 Lever the gearchange mechanism link rods off their respective balljoints on the transmission

20 Make a final check that all necessary components have been disconnected, and are positioned clear of the transmission so that they will not hinder the removal procedure.

21 With the bolts removed, move the trolley jack and transmission/hoist to the left to free it from its locating dowels **(see illustration)**.

22 Once the transmission is free, lower the jack/hoist and manoeuvre the unit out from under the car. If they are loose, remove the locating dowels from the transmission or engine, and keep them in a safe place.

Refitting

23 The transmission is refitted using a reversal of the removal procedure, bearing in mind the following points:

a) Apply a little high-melting point grease to the splines of the transmission input shaft. Do not apply too much, otherwise there is a possibility of the grease contaminating the clutch friction plate.

b) Ensure that the locating dowels are correctly positioned prior to installation.

c) Tighten all nuts and bolts to the specified torque (where given).

d) Renew the driveshaft oil seals using the information given in Section 5.

e) On completion, refill the transmission with the specified type and quantity of oil as described in Section 2.

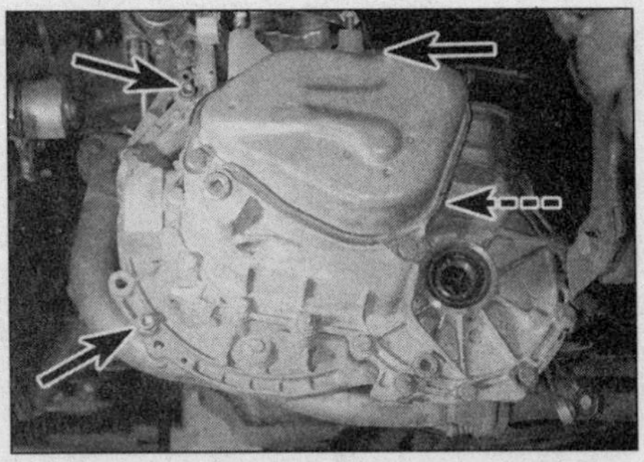

8.19 Remove the bolts (arrowed) securing the transmission housing to the engine

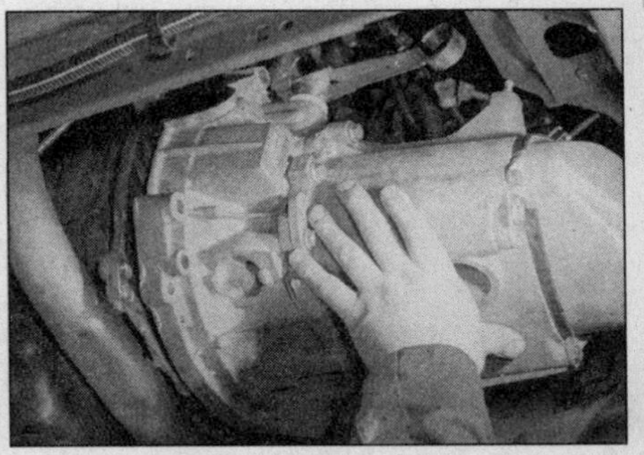

8.21 Withdraw the transmission from the engine

9 Manual transmission overhaul - general information

Overhauling a manual transmission unit is a difficult and involved job for the DIY home mechanic. In addition to dismantling and reassembling many small parts, clearances must be precisely measured and, if necessary, changed by selecting shims and spacers. Internal transmission components are also often difficult to obtain and, in many instances, extremely expensive. Because of this, if the transmission develops a fault or becomes noisy, the best course of action is to have the unit overhauled by a specialist repairer, or to obtain an exchange reconditioned unit.

Nevertheless, it is not impossible for the more experienced mechanic to overhaul the transmission, provided the special tools are available, and the job is done in a deliberate step-by-step manner so that nothing is overlooked.

The tools necessary for an overhaul include internal and external circlip pliers, bearing pullers, a slide hammer, a set of pin punches, a dial test indicator, and (possibly) a hydraulic press. In addition, a large, sturdy workbench and a vice will be required.

During dismantling of the transmission, make careful notes of how each component is fitted, to make reassembly easier and more accurate.

Before dismantling the transmission, it will help if you have some idea of which area is malfunctioning. Certain problems can be closely related to specific areas in the transmission, which can reduce the amount of dismantling and component examination required. Refer to the "Fault finding" Section at the end of this manual for more information.

Chapter 7 Part B: Automatic transmission

Contents

Degrees of difficulty

Easy, suitable for novice with little experience	**Fairly easy,** suitable for beginner with some experience	**Fairly difficult,** suitable for competent DIY mechanic	**Difficult,** suitable for experienced DIY mechanic	**Very difficult,** suitable for expert DIY or professional

Specifications

General

Type	Automatic with hydraulic torque converter, three forward speeds and one reverse, electronically-controlled gear shift strategy.
Designation	MB3
Overall weight	45 kg (approx.)

Lubrication

Recommended fluid	Refer to "*Lubricants and Fluids*"
Capacity:	
Total	4.5 litres
Drain and refill	2.5 litres*

**2 litres will remain in the torque converter after the transmission has been drained.*

Torque wrench settings	Nm	lbft
Fluid cooler securing bolts	15	11
Rear engine transmission mounting:		
Mounting to transmission casing	85	63
Flexible mounting to bodwork	65	48
Engine/transmission left-hand mounting:		
Mounting bracket-to-body bolts	30	22
Centre nut	65	48
Mounting bracket-to-transmission nuts	25	18
Engine-to-transmission securing bolts	35	26
Torque converter-to-driveplate bolts	25	18
Speedometer drive housing bolt	10	7

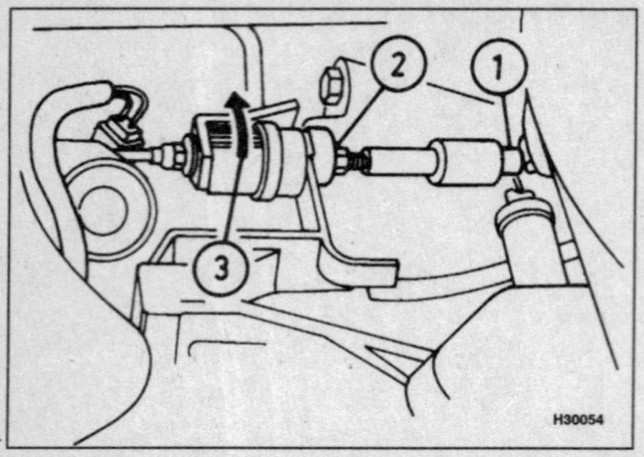

2.5 Gearchange cable and linkrod details

1 Balljoint
2 Retaining clip
3 Locking collar

1 General information and precautions

General information

1 1.4 and 1.6 litre petrol models may be fitted with an optional three-speed fully-automatic transmission, consisting of a torque converter, an epicyclic geartrain, hydraulically-operated clutches and brakes and a dedicated electronic control system.

2 The torque converter provides a fluid coupling between the engine and transmission, and acts as an automatic clutch, also providing a degree of torque multiplication when accelerating.

3 The epicyclic geartrain provides either of the three forward or one reverse gear ratios, according to which of its component parts are held stationary or allowed to turn. The components of the geartrain are held or released by brakes and clutches which are activated by a hydraulic control unit. An internal fluid pump provides the necessary hydraulic pressure to operate the brakes and clutches within the transmission.

4 Driver control of the transmission is by a six-position selector lever. The transmission has a "drive" position, and a "hold" facility on the first three gear ratios. The "drive" position "D" provides automatic changing throughout the range of all four gear ratios, and is the one to select for normal driving. An automatic kickdown facility shifts the transmission down a gear if the accelerator pedal is fully depressed. The "hold" facility is very similar, but limits the number of gear ratios available - ie in the "2" position, only the first two gears will be selected, and so on. The these low ratio 'hold' positions are useful for providing engine braking when towing and travelling down steep gradients, or for preventing unwanted selection of top gear on twisty roads. Note, however, that the transmission should *never* be shifted down a position if the engine speed exceeds 4000 rpm.

5 Due to the complexity of the automatic transmission, any repair or overhaul work must be left to a Citroën dealer with the necessary special equipment for fault diagnosis and repair. The contents of the following Sections are therefore confined to supplying general information, and any service information and instructions that can be used by the owner.

Precautions

6 The automatic transmission is controlled by an electronic system which monitors the position of the throttle and the road speed of the vehicle via sensors mounted on the engine and transmission. The operation of the system relies on accurate synchronisation between the throttle valve (see the relevant part of Chapter 4, as applicable) and the transmission control system's throttle position sensor. If the accelerator cable is removed and/or adjusted, or if the transmission control system ECU or throttle position sensor are renewed, the ECU must be 'initialised'. The initialisation procedure requires access to specialised electronic test equipment and so it is recommended that this operation is entrusted to a suitably-equipped Citroën dealer.

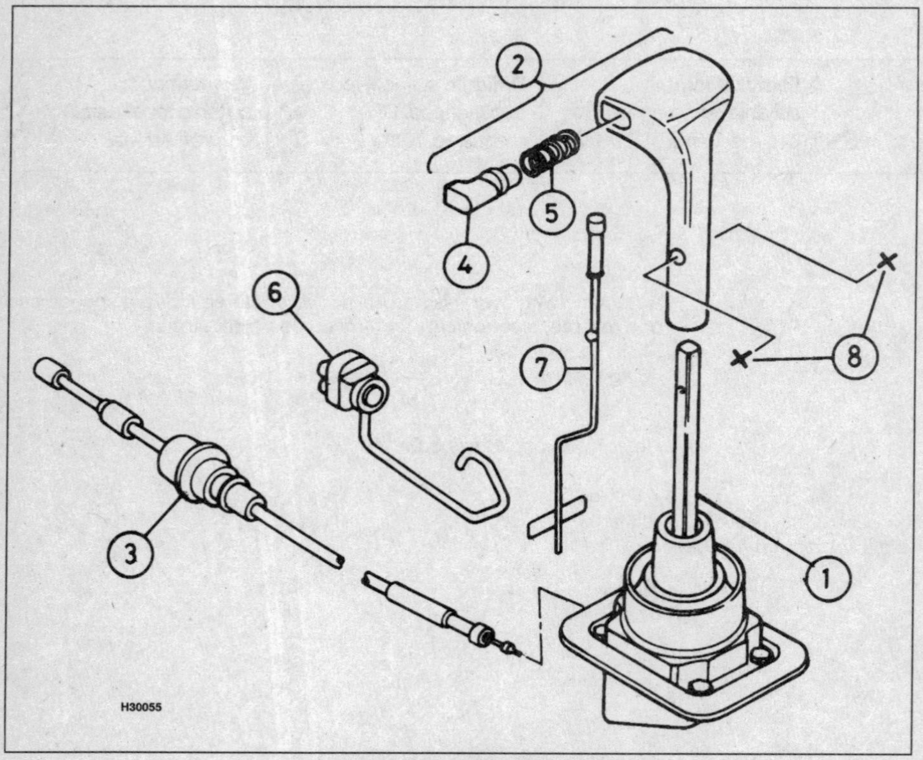

2.8 Gear selector lever assembly

1 Selector lever shaft
2 Handle
3 Gearchange cable
4 Locking button
5 Spring
6 Cable clamp
7 Link rod
8 Screws

2 Gearchange linkage - removal, refitting and adjusting

Removal

1 Raise the front of the car and rest it securely on axle stands (see "*Jacking and vehicle support*").

2 Disconnect the battery negative cable and position it away from the terminal.

3 Refer to the relevant part of Chapter 4 and remove the air cleaner together with its associated inlet air ducting.

4 Working in the engine compartment, carefully prise the balljoint at the end of the gearchange cable off the linkrod pivot lever.

5 Release the gearchange cable outer sheath from its support bracket by turning the locking collar anticlockwise through one quarter of a turn. Once free, extract the retaining clip and then pull the cable upwards and away from the bracket **(see illustration)**.

6 Working underneath the front of the car, refer to Chapter 4D, unbolt and remove the exhaust system intermediate pipe and catalytic converter. Undo the retaining nuts and bolts and remove the exhaust system heat shielding.

7 Undo the securing screw and release the gearchange cable from the support bracket on the floorpan.

8 Working inside the vehicle, remove the centre console as described in chapter 11 **(see illustration)**.

9 Slacken and withdraw the selector lever housing securing nuts and screws **(see**

illustration). Lift the housing and lever away from the floorpan, guiding the gearchange cable through the aperture into the car.

Refitting and adjusting

10 Working inside the vehicle, lower the selector lever housing into position whilst feeding the gear change cable through the floorpan aperture. Insert the housing retaining screws and tighten them securely.
11 Refit the centre console as described in Chapter 11, then refit the selector lever indicator panel.
12 Move the selector lever to the '1' position and ensure that it stays in this position during the remainder of the refitting procedure.
13 Working underneath the vehicle, fit the gearchange cable into its support bracket, then refit the exhaust system heat shields, intermediate pipe and catalytic converter with reference to Chapter 4D.
14 Feed the gearchange cable through into the engine compartment and lay it in position on the mounting bracket at the rear of the transmission. Place the gear selector lever on the transmission in the first gear position; to do this, rotate the lever until the markings on the selector lever and shaft are in alignment **(see illustration)**.
15 Press the balljoint at the end of the gearchange cable onto the stud at the end of the transmission linkrod. Ensure that the gearchange cable outer sheath is correctly located in its recess in the mounting bracket, then fit the retaining clip to secure it in position. Turn the gearchange cable locking collar through one quarter turn clockwise until the markings on the collar's outer surface line up **(see illustration)**.
16 Refer to the relevant part of Chapter 4 and refit the air cleaner together with its associated inlet air ducting.
17 Reconnect the battery and lower the car to the ground.

3 Oil seals - renewal

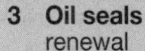

Driveshaft oil seal

1 Chock the rear wheels of the car, firmly apply the handbrake, then jack up the front of the car and support it on axle stands (see "*Jacking and vehicle support*"). Remove the appropriate front roadwheel.
2 Drain the transmission oil as described in Chapter 1A.
3 Working as described in Chapter 8, unscrew the retaining nuts and bolts, and then free the inner end of the driveshaft (or intermediate shaft, as applicable) from the transmission, placing it clear of the seal. There is no need to unscrew the driveshaft-to-hub retaining nut; the driveshaft can be left secured to the hub. Support the driveshaft, to avoid placing any strain on the driveshaft joints or gaiters.
4 Carefully prise the oil seal out of the transmission, using a large flat-bladed screwdriver. Do not score the inner surface of the seal housing with the screwdriver.
5 Remove all traces of dirt from the area around the oil seal aperture, then apply a smear of grease to the outer lip of the new oil seal. Fit the new seal into its aperture, and drive it squarely into position until it abuts its locating shoulder. Use a suitable tubular drift (such as a socket) which bears only on the hard outer edge of the seal. If the seal was supplied with a plastic protector sleeve, leave this in position until the driveshaft has been refitted.
6 Refit the driveshaft as described in Chapter 8.
7 Refill the transmission with the specified type and amount of oil as described in Chapter 1A.

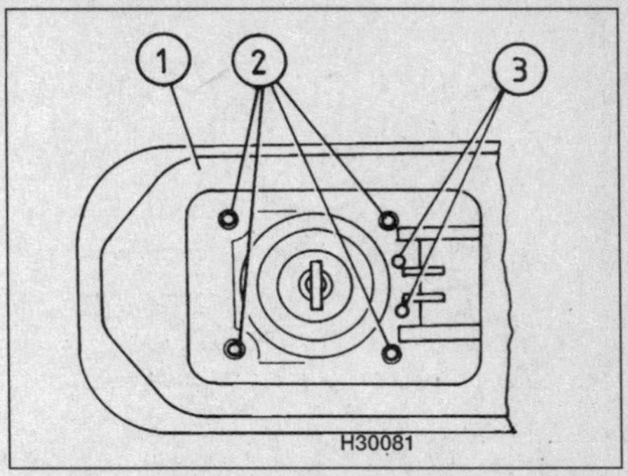

2.9 Slacken and withdraw the selector lever housing securing nuts and screws

1 Selector lever housing   *2 Nuts*   *3 Screws*

Selector lever oil seal

8 To renew the selector shaft seal, the transmission must be dismantled. This task should therefore be entrusted to a Citroën dealer.

Torque converter oil seal

9 Remove the transmission from the engine, as described in Section 7.
10 Withdraw the torque converter from the transmission. Be prepared for a significant amount of transmission fluid leakage - the torque converter will still contain up to 2.0 litres of fluid, even after the transmission has been drained.
11 Withdraw the pump and turbine shafts from the transmission, noting their orientation.
12 Carefully prise the seal from the transmission using a flat bladed screwdriver - take great care to avoid scoring the seal housing. Alternatively, drill two small holes in the surface of the seal and thread self-tapping screws into them. Grip the screws with pliers and use them to pull the seal from the housing.

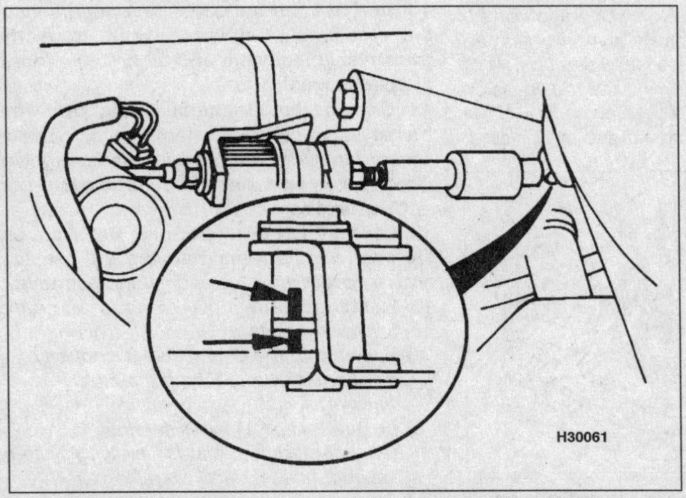

2.14 Rotate the transmission gear selector lever until the markings on the selector lever and shaft are in alignment (arrowed)

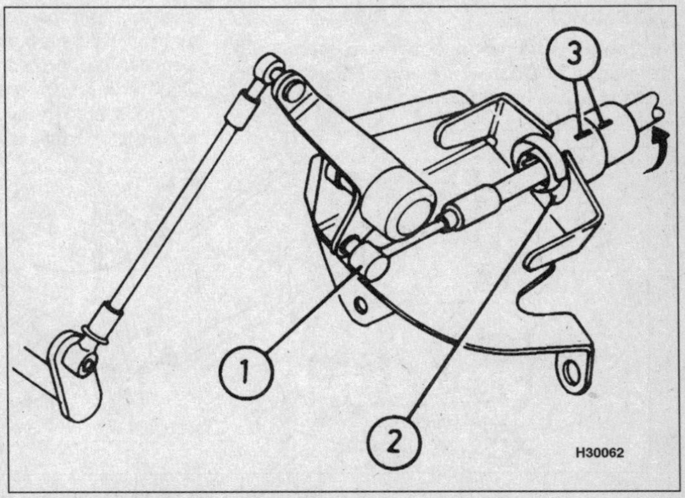

2.15 Gearchange cable, linkrod and mounting bracket details

1 Gearchange cable balljoint   *2 Retaining clip*   *3 Locking collar alignment markings*

7B

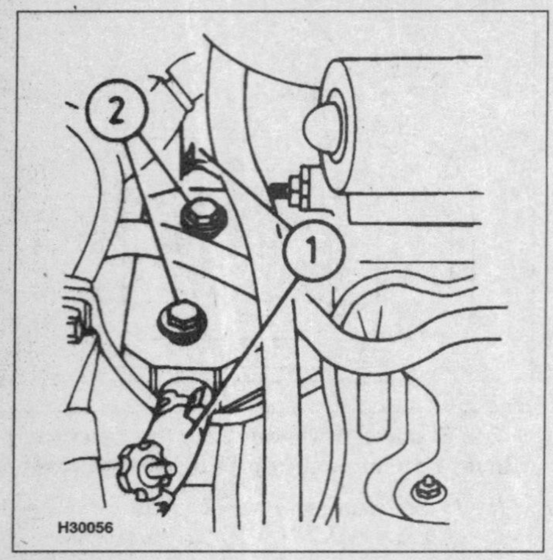

4.6 Disconnect the coolant hoses (1) from either side of the transmission cooler, then withdraw the two union bolts (2)

13 Ensure that the seal housing us clean, then drive a new seal into position using a tubular drift of suitable diameter. Lubricate the inner edge of the seal with clean transmission fluid.

14 Refit the turbine shaft to the transmission, observing its correct orientation.

15 Fit the oil pump shaft to the torque converter, then fill the torque converter with new transmission fluid.

16 Fit the torque converter to the transmission. Rotate the torque converter from left to right to ease its engagement with the turbine shaft splines.

17 Refit the transmission to the engine as described in Section 7.

4 Fluid cooler - removal and refitting

Removal

1 Partially drain the cooling system, with reference to Chapter 1A. Alternatively, carry out the operations in paragraphs 2 to 4 below, then clamp the coolant hoses leading to and from the transmission fluid cooler, to minimise coolant loss.

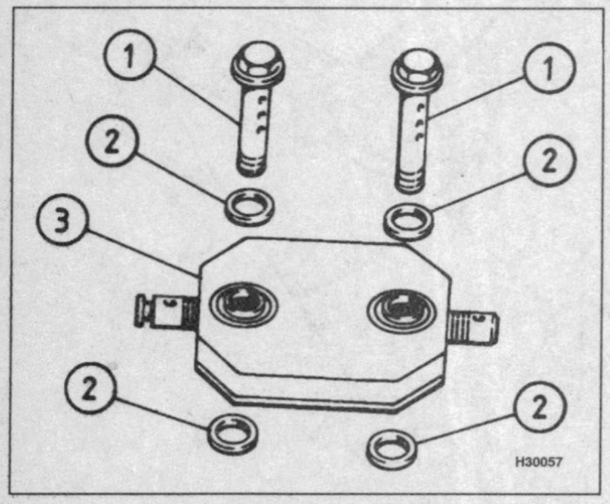

4.8 Fluid cooler components

1 Union bolts
2 Seals
3 Fluid cooler

2 Remove the battery as described in Chapter 5A.

3 Refer to Chapter 9 and disconnect the vacuum hose from the braking system servo.

4 Remove the air filter and its associated air inlet ducting with reference to the relevant part of Chapter 4.

5 Slacken the clips, then disconnect the coolant hoses from either side of the transmission cooler **(see illustration 4.6)**.

6 Slacken and withdraw the two union bolts securing the transmission cooler and recover the seals **(see illustration)**.

7 Lift the cooler away from the transmission.

Refitting

8 Refitting is a reversal of removal noting the following points:

a) Fit new seals to the transmission cooler union bolts and lubricate them with clean transmission fluid ***(see illustration).***

b) Tighten the union bolts to the specified torque.

c) Refit the battery with reference to Chapter 5A.

d) On completion, refill/top-up the cooling system as described in "Weekly checks" and Chapter 1A.

5 Electronic control system - information, component removal and refitting

Information

1 The automatic transmission is controlled by an electronic system, which selects an appropriate gear shift point by monitoring throttle position and transmission speed information, via sensors mounted on the engine and transmission. The operation of the system relies on accurate synchronisation between the throttle valve (see relevant part of Chapter 4, as applicable) and the transmission control system's throttle position sensor. If the accelerator cable is removed and/or adjusted, or if the transmission control system ECU or throttle position sensor are renewed, the ECU must be 'initialised'. The initialisation procedure requires access to specialised electronic test equipment and so it is recommended that this operation is entrusted to a suitably-equipped Citroën dealer.

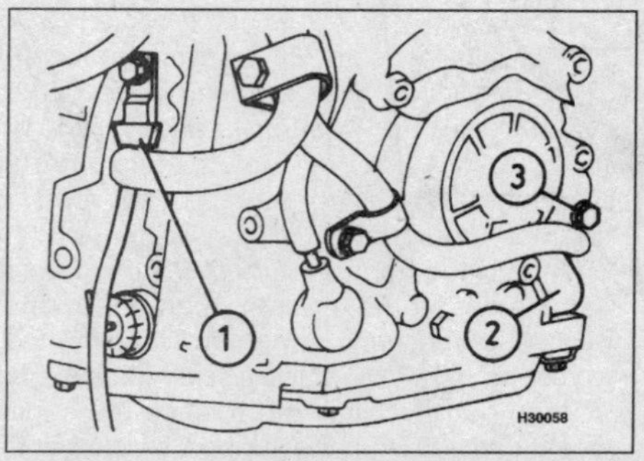

5.13 Remove the transmission speed sensor (1) and the multi-function switch (2) from the transmission casing and unbolt the earth strap (3)

Note: *Some of the transmission electronic control system components are 'hard-wired' to the ECU - that is they cannot be simply disconnected. In these cases, the component removal/refitting information given is limited to that which is necessary to allow the removal of the transmission.*

Component removal and refitting

Electronic control unit

2 Disconnect the batter negative cable and position it away from the terminal.

3 Raise the front of the vehicle and rest it securely on axle stands (see "*Jacking and vehicle support*").

4 Refer to Chapter 1A and drain the transmission fluid.

5 Remove the battery with reference to Chapter 5A.

6 Refer to Chapter 9 and disconnect the vacuum hose from the braking system servo.

7 Remove the air filter and its associated air inlet ducting with reference to the relevant part of Chapter 4.

8 Unbolt and remove the battery mounting tray.

9 Release the ECU securing strap, then unplug the electrical harness from the ECU at the multiway connectors.

10 Refer to Chapter 1A and remove the transmission fluid level dipstick.

11 Remove the left hand front roadwheel, then undo the securing screws and remove the plastic wheel arch liner.

12 Undo the securing screws and release the wiring harness from the clamps at the left hand end of the transmission casing.

13 Remove the transmission speed sensor and the multi-function switch from the transmission casing and unbolt the earth strap **(see illustration)**.

14 Unplug the electrical wiring from the transmission control system throttle position sensor (do not confuse it with the fuel system throttle potentiometer - see the relevant part of Chapter 4 for details).

15 Lift the ECU away from the transmission, together with its wiring harness and sensors, and remove it from the engine compartment.

16 Refitting is a reversal of removal, noting the following points:

a) Ensure that the O-ring seal is correctly positioned when refitting the multi-function switch.

b) Ensure that all wiring is securely reconnected, and that the braking system vacuum hose is securely refitted.

c) On completion, refill the transmission with the specified grade and quantity of automatic transmission fluid; see Chapter 1A for details.

Throttle position sensor

17 Disconnect the battery negative cable and position it away from the terminal.

18 Unplug the two wiring harness connectors, then undo the securing screws and withdraw the throttle position sensor from the throttle body **(see illustration)**. Note that on refitting, the transmission control ECU must be 'initialised'; refer to the note at the beginning of this Section for details.

Transmission speed sensor

19 Disconnect the battery negative cable and position it away from the terminal.

20 Refer to Chapter 1A and drain the fluid from the transmission.

21 Remove the securing screw and withdraw the sensor from the transmission casing.

22 Note that the sensor is hard-wired to the ECU harness and cannot be unplugged separately. Renewal involves cutting off the old sensor and splicing the new sensor wiring onto the harness; it is recommended that this procedure is entrusted to a Citroën dealer.

23 On completion, tighten the sensor retaining screw securely, then refill the transmission with the specified grade and quantity of automatic transmission fluid; see Chapter 1A for details.

Multi-function switch

24 Disconnect the battery negative cable and position it away from the terminal.

25 Refer to Chapter 1A and drain the fluid from the transmission.

26 Remove the securing screw and withdraw the switch from the transmission casing. Recover the O-ring seal.

27 Note that the switch is hard-wired to the ECU harness and cannot be unplugged separately. Renewal involves cutting off the old switch and splicing the new switch wiring onto the harness; it is recommended that this procedure is entrusted to a Citroën dealer.

28 On completion, fit a new O-ring seal to the switch, then insert the switch into the transmission casing and tighten the switch retaining screw securely. Refill the transmission with the specified grade and quantity of automatic transmission fluid; see Chapter 1A for details.

6 Speedometer drive - removal and refitting

Removal

1 Chock the rear wheels of the car, and firmly apply the handbrake. Jack up the front of the car, and support it securely on axle stands (see "*Jacking and vehicle support*"). The speedometer drive is situated on the rear of the transmission housing, next to the inner end of the right-hand driveshaft.

2 Unplug the wiring connector from the speedometer drive.

3 Slacken and remove the retaining bolt, and withdraw the speedometer drive and driven pinion assembly from the transmission housing, along with its O-ring.

4 Examine the pinion for signs of damage, and renew if necessary. Renew the housing O-ring as a matter of course. On later models the assembly is a sealed unit, but on earlier models, the driven pinion and oil seal can be renewed individually if required.

5 If the driven pinion is worn or damaged, also examine the drive pinion in the transmission housing for signs of wear or damage. To renew the drive pinion, the transmission must be dismantled and the differential gear removed. This task should therefore be entrusted to a Citroën dealer.

Refitting

6 Fit a new O-ring to the speedometer drive. Refit the drive to the transmission, ensuring that the pinions are correctly engaged.

7 Refit the retaining bolt and tighten it to the specified torque. Reconnect the electrical wiring to the speedometer drive.

8 Lower the vehicle to the ground.

7 Automatic transmission - removal and refitting

Removal

1 Chock the rear wheels and place the selector lever in the "N" (neutral) position. Jack up the front of the vehicle, and securely support it on axle stands (see *"Jacking and vehicle support"*). Remove both front roadwheels.

2 Drain the transmission fluid as described in Chapter 1A.

3 Refit the drain plugs, tightening them securely.

4 Remove the air cleaner housing and/or inlet duct as described in the relevant part of Chapter 4.

5 Remove the battery, battery tray and mounting plate as described in Chapter 5A.

6 With reference to Section 4, clamp the coolant hoses leading to the transmission fluid cooler, then slacken the clips and disconnect the hoses from either side of the cooler.

7 With reference to Section 5, unplug the electrical wiring from the transmission control system throttle position sensor (do not confuse it with the fuel system throttle potentiometer - see the relevant part of Chapter 4 for details).

8 Unplug the wiring connector from the left hand side of the transmission ECU, then release the securing strap and allow the ECU to rest on top of the transmission casing.

9 Prise out the clips and release the engine wiring harness from the support bracket at the top of the transmission casing. Unbolt and remove the support bracket.

10 Refer to Section 2 and disconnect the gearchange linkage from the transmission.

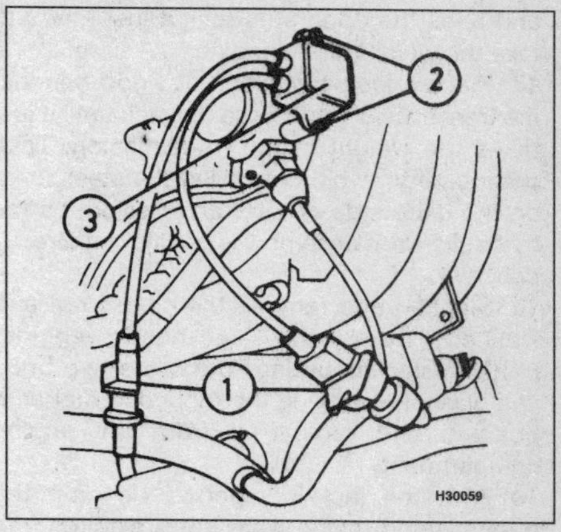

5.18 Unplug the two wiring harness connectors (1), undo the screws (2) and withdraw the throttle position sensor (3) from the throttle body

11 Remove the starter motor as described in Chapter 5A.

12 Working underneath the vehicle, remove the screws and withdraw the cover plate from the underside of the transmission bellhousing, to expose the surface of the torque converter. Using a socket and extension bar to rotate the crankshaft pulley, undo the three nuts securing the torque converter to the drive-plate using a ring spanner **(see illustration)**. As each nut is removed, turn the crankshaft to expose the next nut.

13 To ensure that the torque converter does not fall out as the transmission is removed, secure it in position using a length of metal strip bolted to one of the starter motor bolt holes.

14 Disconnect the wiring from the speedometer drive, as described in Section 6.

15 Remove the driveshafts with reference to Chapter 8.

16 Fit a lifting beam across the top of the engine compartment, in line with the cylinder head. Alternatively, position a hoist over the engine. Attach the beam/hoist to the lifting eye at the left hand end of the cylinder head

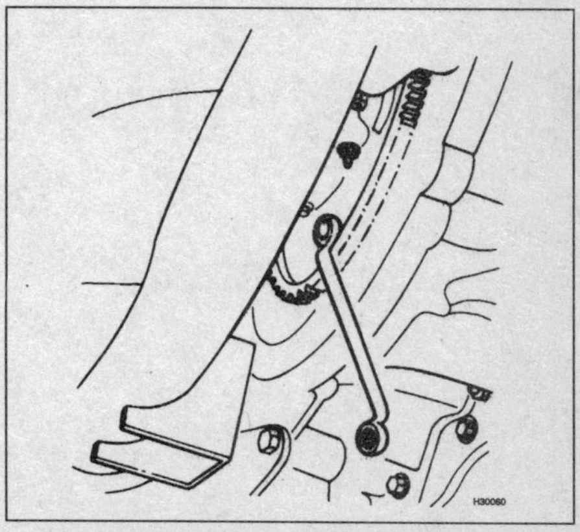

7.12 Remove the cover plate, then undo the three nuts securing the torque converter to the driveplate

and raise the apparatus until it just starts to take the weight of the engine.

17 Place a jack and block of wood beneath the transmission, and raise the jack until it just takes the weight of the transmission. Take great care to avoid deforming the steel sump on the underside of the transmission, as the hydraulic valve assembly is positioned directly behind it.

18 Slacken and remove the centre nut and washer from the left-hand engine/ transmission mounting. Undo the two bolts and washers securing the mounting rubber in position and remove it from the engine compartment.

19 With the jack positioned beneath the transmission taking its weight, slacken and remove the remaining bolts securing the transmission housing to the engine. Note the correct fitted position of each bolt as it is removed, to use as a reference on refitting. Make a final check that all necessary components have been disconnected, and positioned clear of the transmission so that they will not hinder the removal procedure.

20 With the bolts removed, move the trolley jack and transmission to the left, to free the locating dowels from the engine block.

21 Once the transmission is free, lower the jack and manoeuvre the unit out from under the car. If they are loose, remove the locating dowels from the transmission or engine, and keep them in a safe place.

Refitting

22 The transmission is refitted by a reversal of the removal procedure, bearing in mind the following points:

a) Ensure that the bush fitted to the centre of the crankshaft is in good condition, and apply a little Molykote G1 grease to the torque converter centring pin. Do not apply too much, otherwise there is a possibility of the grease contaminating the torque converter.

b) Ensure that the engine/transmission locating dowels are correctly positioned prior to installation.

c) Once the transmission and engine are correctly joined, refit the securing bolts, tightening them to the specified torque setting, then remove the metal strip used to retain the torque converter.

d) Apply thread-locking fluid to the left-hand engine/transmission mounting stud threads prior to refitting it to the transmission. Tighten the stud to the specified torque.

e) Tighten all nuts and bolts to the specified torque (where given).

f) Renew the driveshaft oil seals and refit the driveshafts to the transmission, using the information given in Section 3 and Chapter 8.

g) Refit the gearchange linkage with reference to the information given in Section 2.

h) On completion, top-up the cooling system (see "Weekly checks"), then refill the transmission with the specified type and quantity of fluid as described in Chapter 1A.

8 Automatic transmission overhaul - general information

In the event of a fault occurring with the transmission, it is first necessary to determine whether it is of an electrical, mechanical or hydraulic nature, and to do this, special test equipment is required. It is therefore essential to have the work carried out by a Citroën dealer or transmission specialist if a transmission fault is suspected.

Do not be hasty in removing the transmission from the vehicle for possible repair before professional fault diagnosis has been carried out, since most of the testing is carried out with the transmission still in the car.

Chapter 8
Driveshafts

Contents

Degrees of difficulty

Easy, suitable for novice with little experience	**Fairly easy,** suitable for beginner with some experience	**Fairly difficult,** suitable for competent DIY mechanic	**Difficult,** suitable for experienced DIY mechanic	**Very difficult,** suitable for expert DIY or professional

Specifications

General

Lubrication (overhaul only)	Use only special grease supplied in sachets with gaiter kits - joints are otherwise pre-packed with grease and sealed

Torque wrench settings	Nm	lbf ft
Driveshaft intermediate bearing bracket securing bolts	45	33
Driveshaft intermediate bearing securing nuts	10	7
Driveshaft nut	250	184
Driveshaft to transmission bolts/nuts (automatic transmission models)	25	18

1 General information

1 Drive is transmitted from the differential to the front wheels by means of two solid-steel driveshafts of unequal length **(see illustration).**

2 Both driveshafts are splined at their outer ends, to accept the wheel hubs, and are threaded so that each hub can be fastened to the driveshaft by a large nut. The inner end of each driveshaft is also splined, to accept the differential sun gear.

3 Constant velocity (CV) joints are fitted to each end of the driveshafts, to ensure that the smooth and efficient transmission of power at all suspension and steering angles. The inner and outer constant velocity joints are of the spider-and-yoke type.

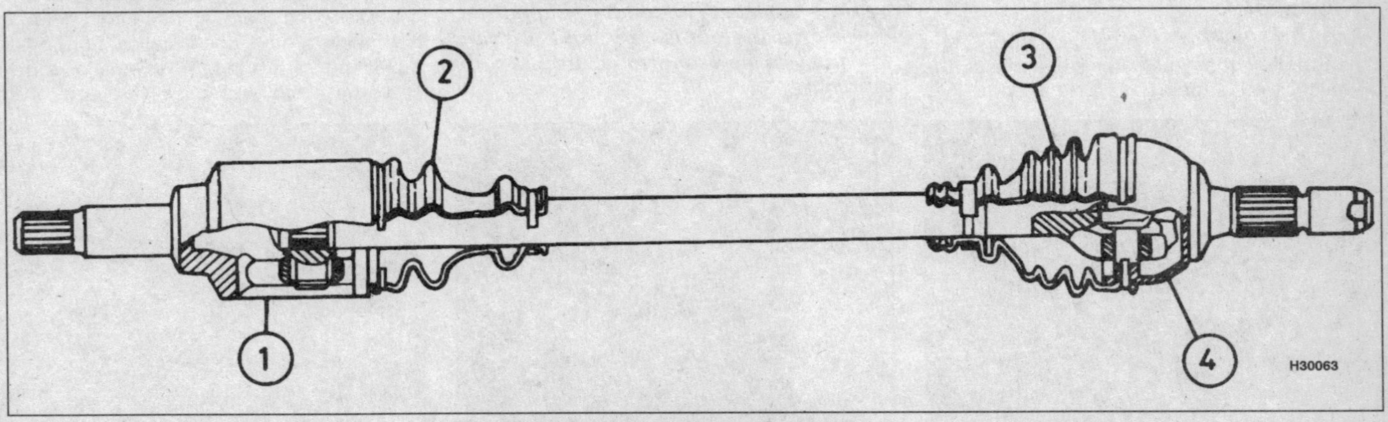

1.1 Typical driveshaft assembly

1 Inner constant velocity joint *2 Inner joint gaiter* *3 Outer joint gaiter* *4 Outer constant velocity joint*

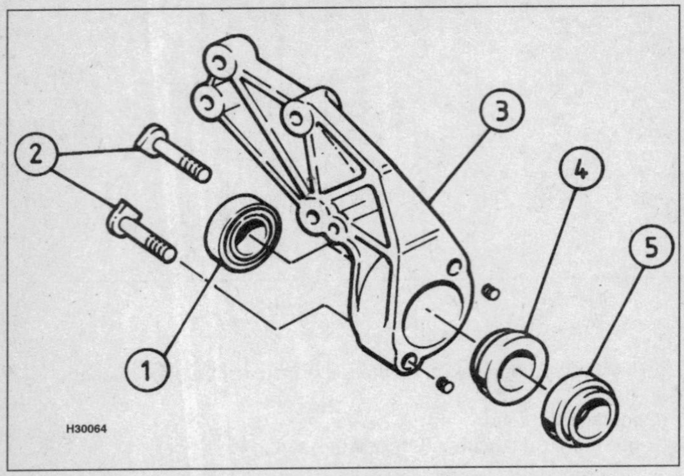

1.4 Right-hand driveshaft intermediate bearing components - 1587 cc petrol models

1 Bearing
2 Offset head bolts
3 Support bracket
4 Bush
5 Dust shield

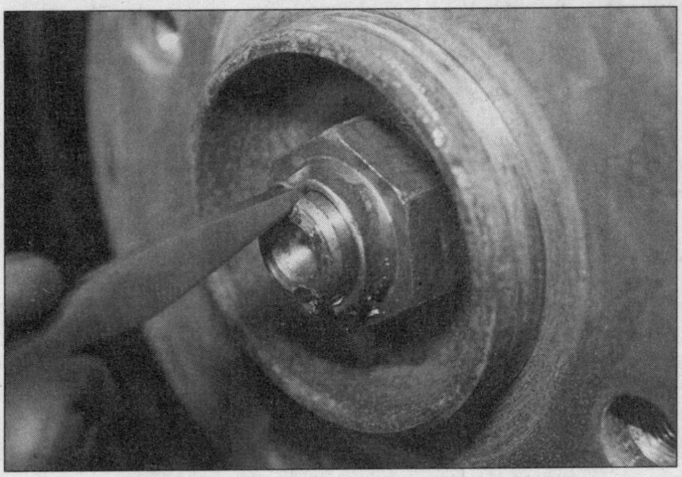

2.4 Relieving the staking on the driveshaft nut

4 On 1587 cc petrol engine models, the right-hand driveshaft is supported by an intermediate bearing, which is mounted in a bracket and bolted to the rear of the cylinder block **(see illustration)**. The inner section of the driveshaft passes through the centre of the bearing; this arrangement prevents lateral flexing of the driveshaft and helps to reduce the effects of torque steer. Smaller capacity models are not fitted with an intermediate bearing; the driveshaft removal sections are divided into appropriate sub-sections to reflect this.

2 Driveshafts (models with manual transmission) - removal and refitting

Note: *A balljoint separator tool will be required for this operation. A new driveshaft nut and a new hub carrier-to-lower arm balljoint clamp nut and, where applicable, a new anti-roll bar hub lock nut (see Chapter 10) must be used on refitting.*

Removal

1 Chock the rear wheels, apply the handbrake, then jack up the front of the vehicle and support on axle stands (see *"Jacking and vehicle support"*). Remove the appropriate roadwheel.

2 Drain the transmission oil as described in Chapter 7A.

3 Where applicable, to avoid any possibility of damage during the following procedure, remove the ABS wheel sensor from the hub carrier as described in Chapter 9.

4 Using a hammer and a suitable cold chisel or punch, relieve the staking on the driveshaft nut **(see illustration)**.

Warning: Wear suitable eye protection during this operation.

5 The front hub must now be held stationary in order to loosen the driveshaft nut. Ideally, the hub should be held by a suitable tool bolted into place using two of the wheel bolts. Alternatively, refit at least two wheel bolts, tighten them securely, then have an assistant firmly apply the brake pedal to prevent the hub from rotating. Using a socket and extension bar, slacken and remove the driveshaft nut.

Warning: Take care that the vehicle is adequately supported, as the nut is very tight! Discard the nut - a new one must be used on refitting.

6 On models where the anti-roll bar is connected to the suspension strut body, undo the nut and washer securing the drop link to the strut, and position the link clear of the strut.

7 On models where the anti-roll bar is connected directly to the lower arm, remove the two screws and washers securing the anti-roll bar end clamp to the lower arm. Remove the clamp and the rubber bush.

8 Undo the nut (while counterholding the bolt) and withdraw the hub carrier-to-lower arm clamp bolt, noting which way round it is fitted **(see illustrations)**.

9 Using a suitable metal bar, lever the lower arm downwards just enough to release the balljoint taper from the lower arm. If the taper is a tight fit in the hub carrier, use a large flat-bladed screwdriver to carefully open up the clamp a little. Recover the balljoint rubber gaiter protector if it is loose.

10 Release the hub from the driveshaft splines by pulling the strut/hub carrier assembly outwards **(see illustration)**. If necessary, the shaft can be tapped out of the hub using a soft-faced mallet. Support the driveshaft with a length of wire, or a nylon cable-tie - do not allow the end of the

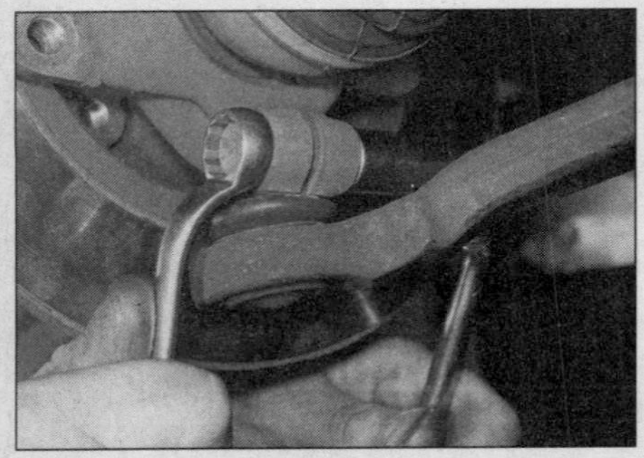

2.8a Undo the nut, while counterholding the bolt . . .

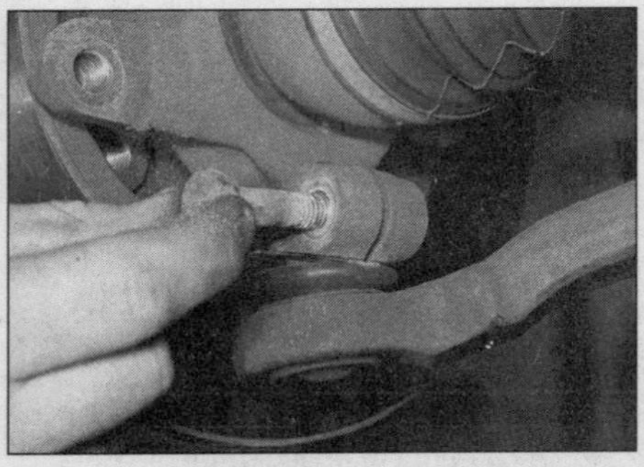

2.8b . . . and withdraw the bolt. Note that the bolt fits from the front of the strut

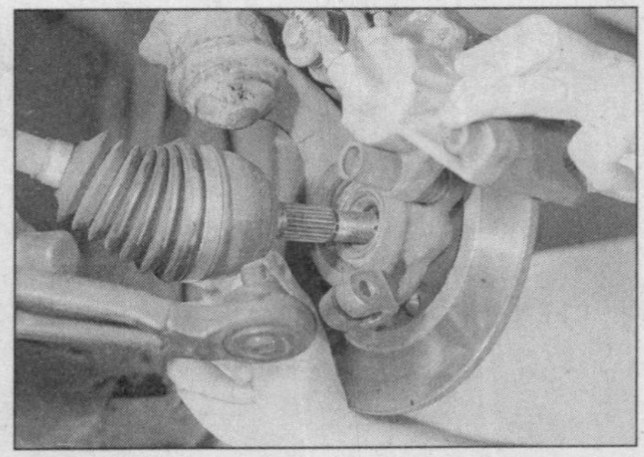

2.10 Releasing the driveshaft from the hub

driveshaft to hang down unsupported, or the joint may be damaged.

Left-hand and right-hand driveshafts without intermediate bearing

11 Support the driveshaft, then withdraw the inner constant velocity joint from the transmission, taking care not to damage the driveshaft oil seal **(see illustration)**. Note that a circlip is not fitted to the inner end of the driveshaft, and removal of the shaft should only require slight effort. Remove the driveshaft from the vehicle.

Right-hand driveshaft with intermediate bearing

12 Loosen the two intermediate bearing retaining bolt nuts, then rotate the bolts through 90°, so that their offset heads are clear of the bearing outer race.

13 Support the outer end of the driveshaft, then pull on the inner end of the shaft to free the intermediate bearing from its mounting bracket, and the driveshaft from the transmission. Note that a circlip is not fitted to the inner end of the driveshaft, and removal of the shaft should only require slight effort.

14 Once the driveshaft end is free from the transmission, slide the dust seal (where fitted) off the inner end of the shaft, noting which way around it is fitted, and remove the driveshaft from the vehicle.

Refitting

15 Before installing the driveshaft, examine the driveshaft oil seal in the transmission for signs of damage or deterioration and, if necessary, renew it, referring to Chapter 7A for further information (it is advisable to renew the seal as a matter of course).

16 Thoroughly clean the driveshaft splines, and the apertures in the transmission and hub assembly. Apply a thin film of grease to the oil seal lips, and to the driveshaft splines and shoulders. Check that all driveshaft gaiter clips are securely fastened.

Left-hand and right-hand driveshafts with intermediate bearing

17 Offer up the driveshaft to the transmission, and engage the joint splines with those of the differential sun gear, taking great care not to damage the oil seal. Push the joint fully into position. Support the driveshaft until both ends have been refitted.

18 Ensure that the driveshaft splines and the corresponding splines in the hub are clean, then engage the driveshaft with the hub. Fit a new driveshaft nut, tightening it by hand only at this stage.

19 Ensure that the protector plate is in place over the lower arm balljoint, then engage the balljoint taper with the hub carrier **(see illustration)**.

20 If necessary, lever the arm downwards just enough to engage the balljoint, as during removal. Similarly, use a screwdriver to open up the clamp a little if necessary.

21 Fit the hub carrier-to-lower arm clamp bolt (inserting the bolt from the front of the strut) and a new nut, and tighten to the specified torque.

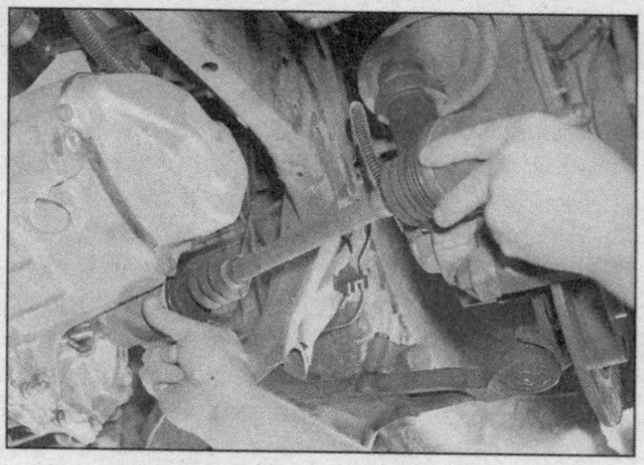

2.11 Withdraw the driveshaft from the transmission (left-hand driveshaft shown)

22 Reconnect the anti-roll bar to the lower arm, or the anti-roll bar drop link to the strut, as applicable. Ensure that the washers are in place, then tighten the fixings to the specified torque.

23 Grease the driveshaft nut contact face on the hub bearing, and the threads of the driveshaft nut, then hold the hub stationary as during removal, and tighten the new driveshaft nut to the specified torque **(see illustration)**. On completion, stake the nut into position using a hammer and punch.

24 Where applicable, refit the ABS wheel sensor.

25 Refit the roadwheel, and lower the vehicle to the ground.

26 Refill the transmission with oil as described in Chapter 7A.

Right-hand driveshaft with intermediate bearing

27 Check that the intermediate bearing rotates smoothly, without any sign of roughness or undue free play between its inner and outer races. If necessary, renew the bearing as described in Section 6. Examine the dust seal (where fitted) for signs of damage or deterioration, and renew if necessary.

28 Apply a smear of grease to the outer race of the intermediate bearing, and to the inner lip of the dust seal.

29 Pass the inner end of the shaft through the bearing mounting bracket, then carefully slide the dust seal into position on the driveshaft, ensuring that its flat surface is facing the transmission.

2.23 Tighten the new driveshaft nut to the specified torque

2.19 Ensure that the balljoint protector plate is in place

30 Carefully engage the inner driveshaft splines with those of the differential sun gear, taking care not to damage the oil seal. Align the intermediate bearing with its mounting bracket, and push the driveshaft fully into position. If necessary, use a soft-faced mallet to tap the outer race of the bearing into position in the mounting bracket. Support the driveshaft until it is completely refitted.

31 Ensure that the driveshaft splines and the corresponding splines in the hub are clean, then engage the driveshaft with the hub. Fit a new driveshaft nut, tightening it by hand only at this stage.

32 Ensure that the intermediate bearing is correctly seated, then rotate its retaining bolts back through 90°, so that their offset heads are resting against the bearing outer race. Tighten the retaining nuts to the specified torque. Ensure that the dust seal (where fitted) is tight against the driveshaft oil seal.

33 Carry out the operations described previously in paragraphs 19 to 26.

3 Driveshafts (models with automatic transmission) - removal and refitting

Removal

1 Chock the rear wheels, apply the handbrake, then jack up the front of the vehicle and support on axle stands (see *"Jacking and vehicle support"*). Remove the appropriate roadwheel.

2 Drain the transmission fluid as described in Chapter 1A.

3 Proceed as described in Section 2, paragraphs 3 to 10 inclusive.

Left-hand driveshaft

4 With the driveshaft now detached from the hub and supported, slacken and withdraw the nut and the two screws that secure the inner gaiter flange to the transmission housing **(see illustration)**. Carefully withdraw the driveshaft from the transmission.

Caution: Keep the driveshaft horizontal as it is withdrawn, to avoid dislodging the CV joint needle bearings.

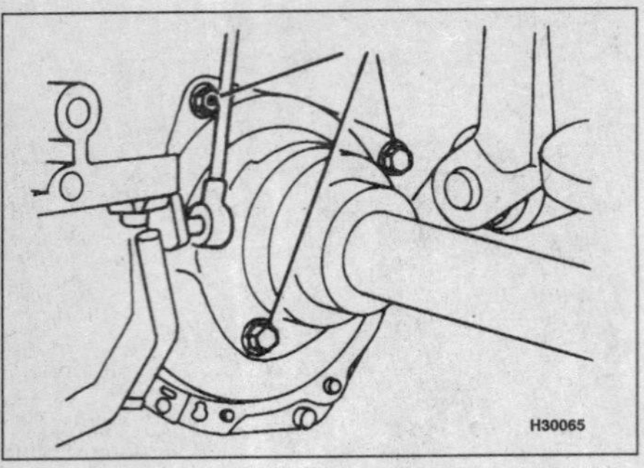

3.4 Withdraw the nut and two screws (arrowed) that secure the inner gaiter flange to the transmission housing

Right-hand driveshaft without intermediate bearing

5 Support the driveshaft, then withdraw the inner constant velocity joint from the transmission, taking care not to damage the driveshaft oil seal. Note that a circlip is not fitted to the inner end of the driveshaft, and removal of the shaft should only require slight effort. Remove the driveshaft from the vehicle.

Right-hand driveshaft with intermediate bearing

6 Loosen the two intermediate bearing retaining bolt nuts, then rotate the bolts through 90°, so that their offset heads are clear of the bearing outer race.
7 Support the outer end of the driveshaft, then pull on the inner end of the shaft to free the intermediate bearing from its mounting bracket, and the driveshaft from the transmission. Note that a circlip is not fitted to the inner end of the driveshaft, and removal of the shaft should only require slight effort.
8 Once the driveshaft end is free from the transmission, slide the dust seal (where fitted) off the inner end of the shaft, noting which way around it is fitted, and remove the driveshaft from the vehicle.

Refitting

9 Before installing the driveshaft, examine the driveshaft oil seal in the transmission for signs of damage or deterioration and, if necessary, renew it, referring to Chapter 7B for further information (it is advisable to renew the seal as a matter of course).
10 Thoroughly clean the driveshaft splines, and the apertures in the transmission and hub assembly. Apply a thin film of grease to the oil seal lips, and to the driveshaft splines and shoulders. Check that all driveshaft gaiter clips are securely fastened.

Left-hand driveshaft

11 Offer up the driveshaft to the transmission and engage the inner CV joint tripod with the differential. Ensure that the shaft is kept horizontal as it is inserted into the transmission, to avoid dislodging the CV joint needle bearings. Insert the inner gaiter flange-to-transmission housing nut and screws, then tighten them to the specified torque. Continue to support the driveshaft until both ends have been refitted.
12 Ensure that the driveshaft splines and the corresponding splines in the hub are clean, then engage the driveshaft with the hub. Fit a new driveshaft nut, tightening it by hand only at this stage.
13 Ensure that the protector plate is in place over the lower arm balljoint, then engage the balljoint taper with the hub carrier. If necessary, lever the arm downwards just enough to engage the balljoint, as during removal. Similarly, use a screwdriver to open up the clamp a little if necessary.
14 Fit the hub carrier-to-lower arm clamp bolt (inserting the bolt from the front of the strut) and a new nut, and tighten to the specified torque.
15 Reconnect the anti-roll bar to the lower arm, or the anti-roll bar drop link to the strut, as applicable. Ensure that the washers are in place, then tighten the fixings to the specified torque.
16 Grease the driveshaft nut contact face on the hub bearing, and the threads of the driveshaft nut, then hold the hub stationary as during removal, and tighten the new driveshaft nut to the specified torque. On completion, stake the nut into position using a hammer and punch.
17 Where applicable, refit the ABS wheel sensor.
18 Refit the roadwheel, and lower the vehicle to the ground.
19 Refill the transmission with fluid as described in Chapter 1A.

Right-hand driveshaft without intermediate bearing

20 Offer up the driveshaft to the transmission, and engage the joint splines with those of the differential sun gear, taking great care not to damage the oil seal. Push the joint fully into position. Support the driveshaft until both ends have been refitted.
21 Proceed as described in paragraphs 12 to 19 inclusive.

Right-hand driveshaft with intermediate bearing

22 Check that the intermediate bearing rotates smoothly, without any sign of roughness or undue free play between its inner and outer races. If necessary, renew the bearing as described in Section 6. Examine the dust seal (where fitted) for signs of damage or deterioration, and renew if necessary.
23 Apply a smear of grease to the outer race of the intermediate bearing, and to the inner lip of the dust seal.
24 Pass the inner end of the shaft through the bearing mounting bracket, then carefully slide the dust seal into position on the driveshaft, ensuring that its flat surface is facing the transmission.
25 Carefully engage the inner driveshaft splines with those of the differential sun gear, taking care not to damage the oil seal. Align the intermediate bearing with its mounting bracket, and push the driveshaft fully into position. If necessary, use a soft-faced mallet to tap the outer race of the bearing into position in the mounting bracket. Support the driveshaft until it is completely refitted.
26 Ensure that the driveshaft splines and the corresponding splines in the hub are clean, then engage the driveshaft with the hub. Fit a new driveshaft nut, tightening it by hand only at this stage.
27 Ensure that the intermediate bearing is correctly seated, then rotate its retaining bolts back through 90°, so that their offset heads are resting against the bearing outer race. Tighten the retaining nuts to the specified torque. Ensure that the dust seal (where fitted) is tight against the driveshaft oil seal.
28 Proceed as described in paragraphs 12 to 19 inclusive.

4 Driveshaft rubber gaiters - renewal

Models with manual transmission

Outer joint

1 Remove the driveshaft as described in Section 2.
2 Remove the inner constant velocity joint and gaiter as described in paragraphs 13 to 20. It is recommended that the inner gaiter is also renewed, regardless of its apparent condition.
3 Release the two outer gaiter retaining clips, then slide the gaiter off the inner end of the driveshaft.
4 Thoroughly clean the outer constant velocity joint using paraffin, or a suitable solvent, and dry it thoroughly. Carry out a visual inspection of the joint.
5 Check the driveshaft spider and outer member yoke for signs of wear, pitting or scuffing on their bearing surfaces. Also check that the outer member pivots smoothly and easily, with no traces of roughness.
6 If on inspection, the spider or outer member reveal signs of wear or damage, it will be necessary to renew the complete driveshaft as an assembly, since no components are available separately. If the joint components are in satisfactory condition, obtain a repair kit from your Citroën dealer, consisting of a new gaiter, retaining clips, and the correct type and quantity of grease **(see illustration)**.
7 Tape over the splines on the inner end of the driveshaft, then carefully slide the outer gaiter onto the shaft **(see illustration)**.
8 Pack the joint with the grease supplied in the repair kit **(see illustration)**. Work the grease well into the bearing tracks whilst twisting the joint, and fill the rubber gaiter with any excess.
9 Ease the gaiter over the joint, and ensure

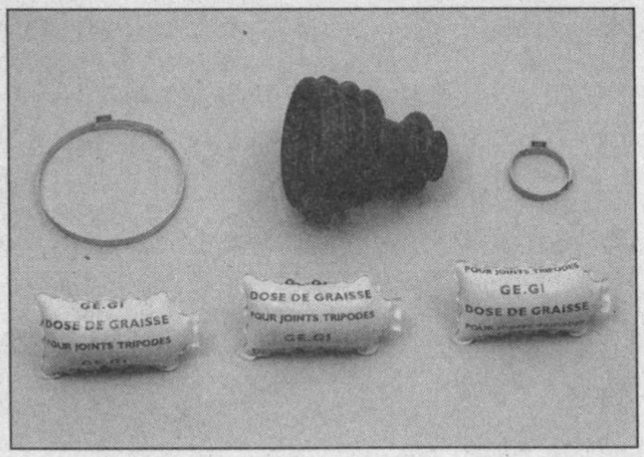

4.6 Driveshaft outer joint gaiter repair kit components

4.7 Sliding the outer joint gaiter onto the driveshaft

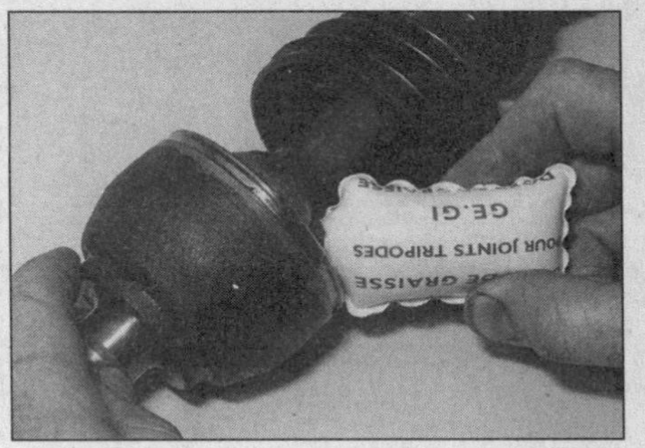

4.8 Pack the joint with the grease supplied in the repair kit

that the gaiter lips are correctly located in the grooves on both the driveshaft and constant velocity joint. Lift the outer sealing lip of the gaiter, to equalise air pressure within the gaiter.

10 Fit the large metal retaining clip to the gaiter. Remove any slack in the gaiter retaining clip by carefully compressing the raised section of the clip. In the absence of the special tool, a pair of side cutters may be used. Secure the small retaining clip using the same procedure **(see illustration)**. Check that the constant velocity joint moves freely in all directions before proceeding further.

11 Refit the inner constant velocity joint as described in paragraphs 21 to 28.

Inner joint

12 Remove the driveshaft as described in Section 2.

13 Secure the driveshaft in a vice equipped with soft jaws then, using a suitable pair of pliers, carefully bend back the lip around the circumference of the constant velocity joint outer member cover **(see illustration)**.

14 Once the lip of the cover is fully released, pull the joint outer member out from the cover, and recover the spring and thrust cap from the end of the shaft. Remove the O-ring from the outside of the outer member, and discard it.

15 Fold the gaiter back, and wipe away the excess grease from the tripod joint. If the rollers are not secured to the joint with circlips, wrap adhesive tape around the joint to hold them in position.

16 Using a dab of paint, or a hammer and punch, mark the relative position of the tripod joint in relation to the driveshaft. Using circlip pliers, extract the circlip securing the joint to the driveshaft **(see illustration)**.

17 The tripod joint can now be removed. If it is tight, draw the joint off the driveshaft end, using a two- or three-legged bearing puller. Ensure that the legs of the puller are located behind the joint inner member, and do not contact the joint rollers **(see illustrations)**. Alternatively, support the inner member of the tripod joint, and press the shaft out of the joint using a hydraulic press, ensuring that no load is applied to the joint rollers.

18 With the tripod joint removed, slide the gaiter and inner retaining collar off the end of the driveshaft.

19 Thoroughly clean the constant velocity joint components using paraffin, or a suitable solvent, and dry them thoroughly - take great care not to remove the alignment marks made on dismantling, especially if paint was used. Carry out a visual inspection of the joint.

20 Examine the tripod joint, rollers and outer member for any signs of scoring or wear, and for smoothness of movement of the rollers on the tripod stems. If any component is worn, the complete driveshaft assembly must be renewed; no joint components are available separately. If the joint components are in good condition, obtain a repair kit from your Citroën dealer, consisting of a new rubber gaiter and outer cover assembly, circlip, thrust cap, spring, O-ring, and the correct quantity of the special grease **(see illustration)**.

21 Tape over the splines on the end of the driveshaft, and carefully slide the inner retaining collar and gaiter/cover assembly onto the shaft **(see illustrations)**.

22 Remove the tape, then aligning the marks

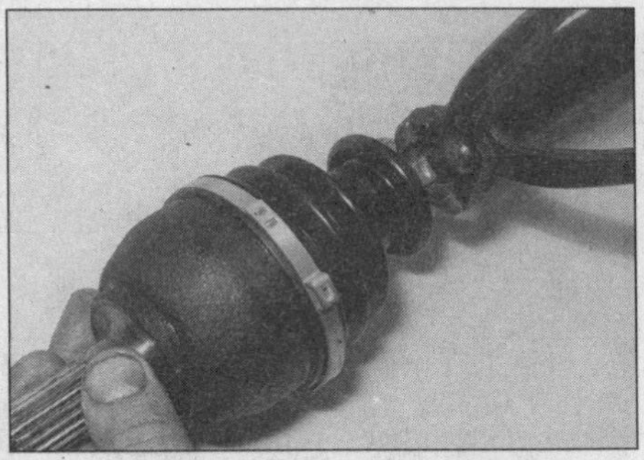

4.10 Securing a gaiter securing clip using side cutters

4.13 Peeling back the lip of the joint outer member cover

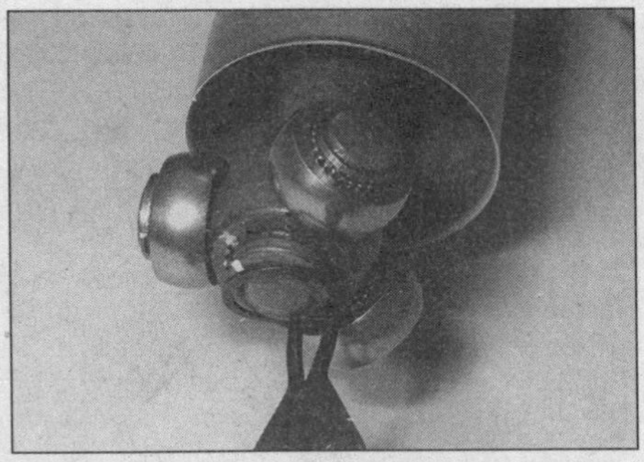

4.16 Removing the inner tripod joint securing circlip

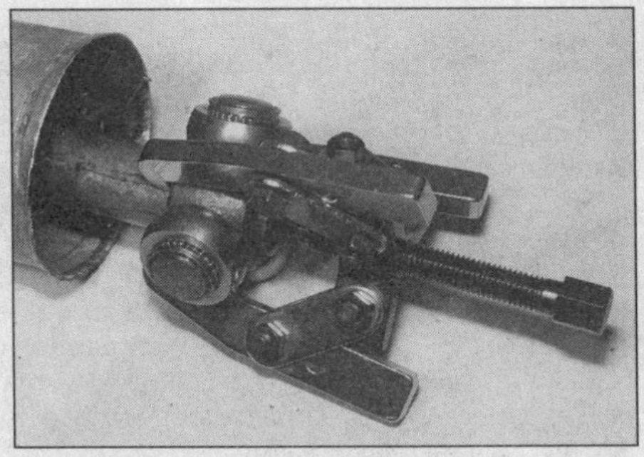

4.17a Using a three-legged puller to remove the inner tripod joint

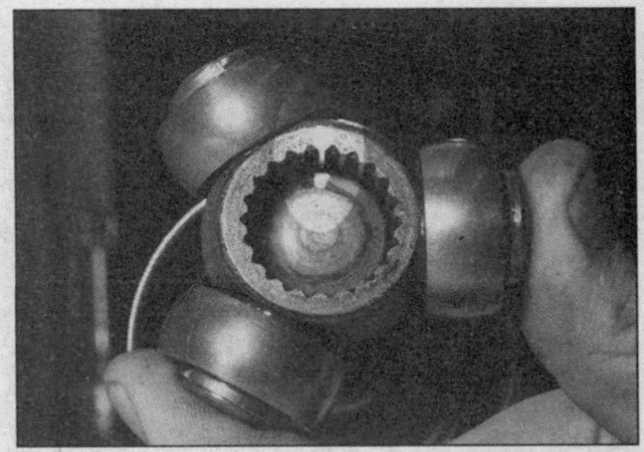

4.17b Withdrawing the inner tripod joint. Note the alignment marks (made in the previous paragraph)

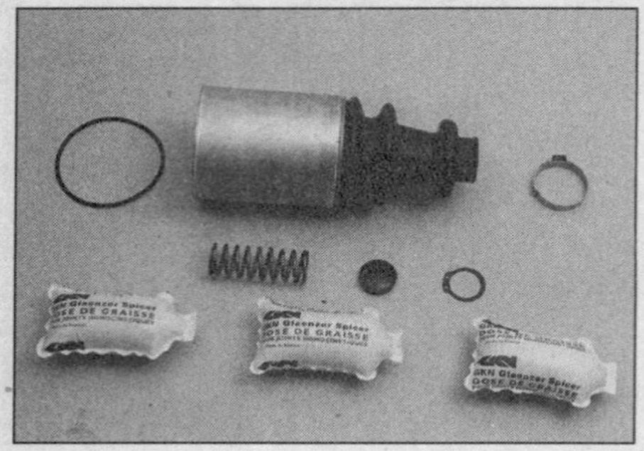

4.20 Driveshaft inner joint gaiter repair kit components

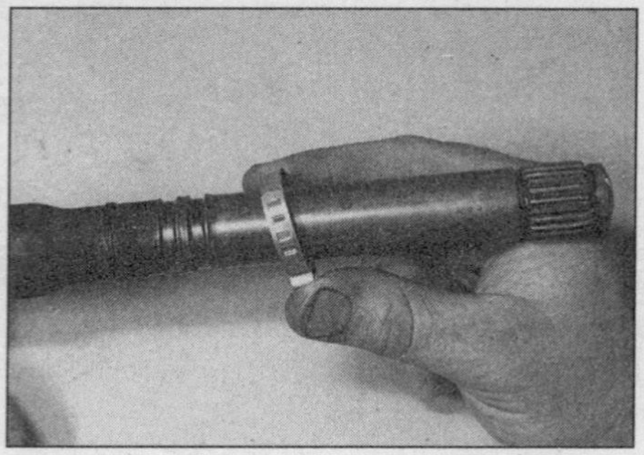

4.21a Slide on the inner retaining collar . . .

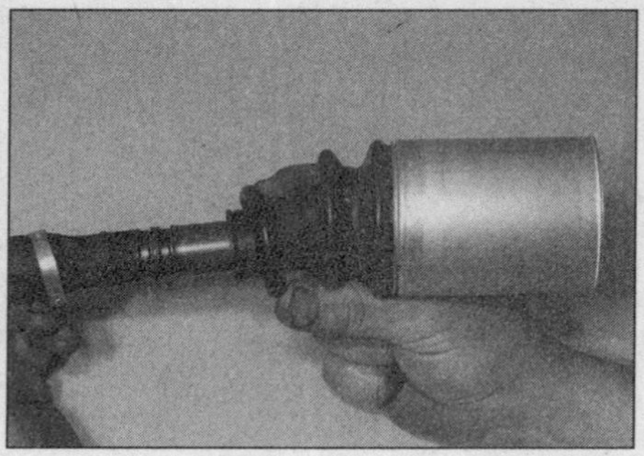

4.21b . . . and the gaiter/cover assembly

made on dismantling, engage the tripod joint with the driveshaft splines. Use a hammer and soft metal drift (or a suitable tube or socket) to tap the joint onto the shaft, taking great care not to damage the driveshaft splines or joint rollers **(see illustration)**.

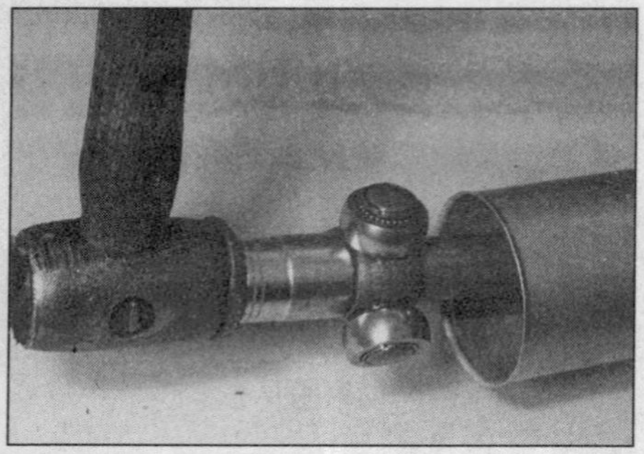

4.22 Using a hammer and a socket to tap the joint onto the driveshaft

23 Secure the tripod joint in position with the new circlip, ensuring that it is correctly located in the driveshaft groove.

24 Remove the tape, and evenly distribute the special grease contained in the repair kit around the tripod joint and outer member **(see illustration)**. Pack the gaiter/cover with more grease, then draw the cover over the tripod joint. Leave one sachet of grease to lubricate the outer member as the joint is fitted.

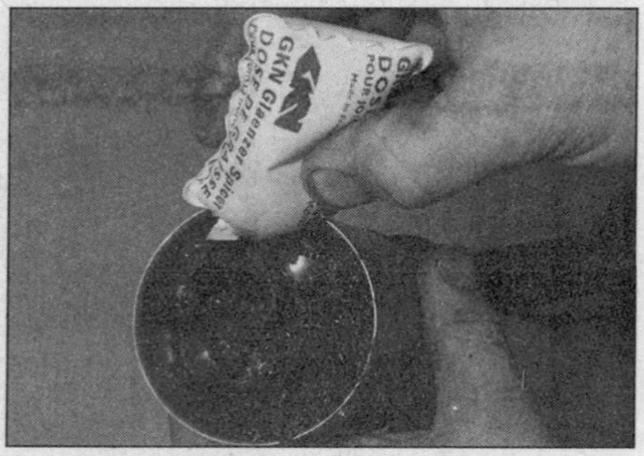

4.24 Pack the joint and gaiter/cover with grease

25 Fit the new spring, thrust cap and O-ring to the joint outer member **(see illustrations)**.

26 Position the outer member assembly over the tripod joint, and locate the thrust cap against the end of the driveshaft. Apply the remainder of the grease to the joint, then push the outer member onto the shaft, compressing the spring, and locate it inside the outer cover. Secure the outer member in position by peening the end of the cover evenly over the joint outer edge **(see illustrations)**.

27 Briefly lift the inner gaiter clip, using a blunt instrument such as a knitting needle, to equalise the air pressure within the gaiter.

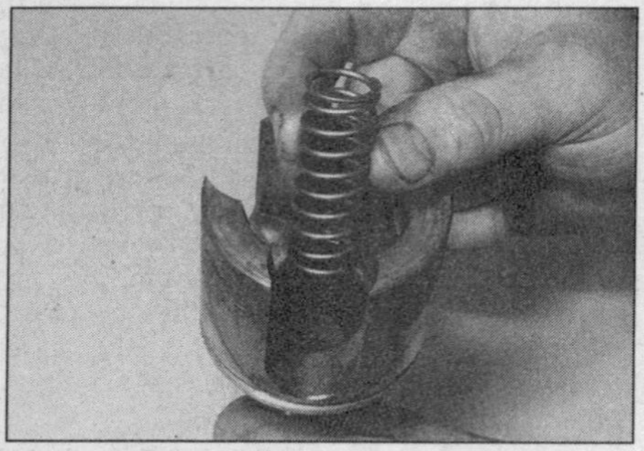

4.25a Fit the new spring . . .

4.25b . . . thrust cap . . .

4.25c . . . and O-ring

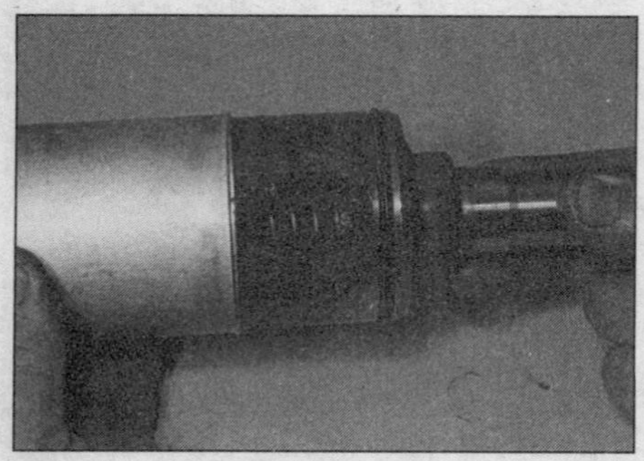

4.26a Position the outer member over the tripod joint . . .

4.26b . . . then apply the remainder of the grease . . .

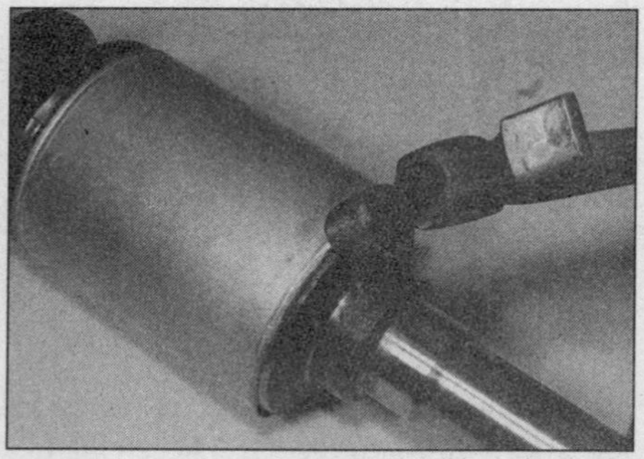

4.26c . . . and peen over the end of the cover

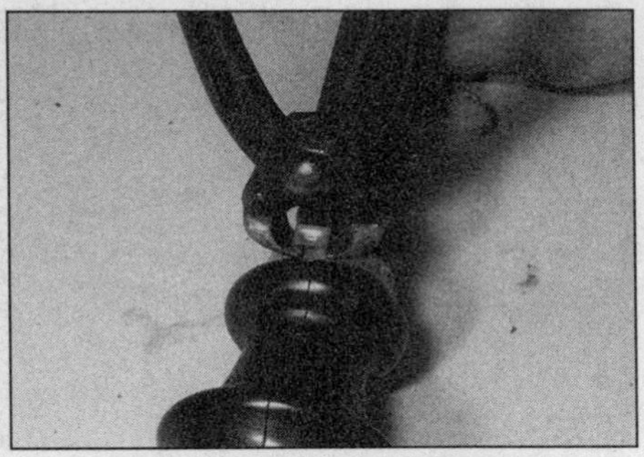

4.27 Securing the inner gaiter clip in position

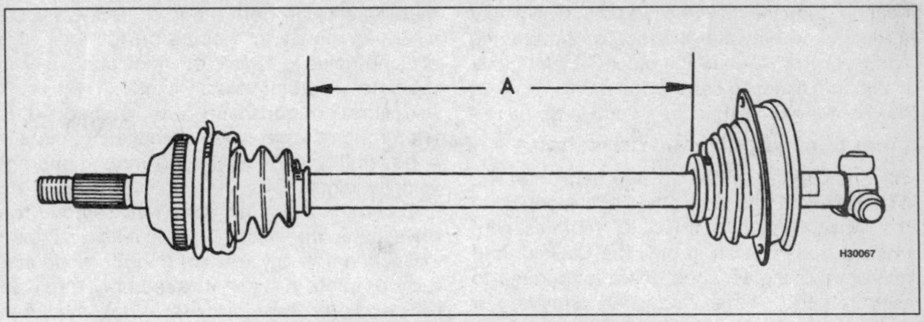

4.38 Outer CV joint gaiter refitting details - models with automatic transmission

A = 256 mm

Secure the inner clip in position **(see illustration)**.

28 Check that the constant velocity joint moves freely in all directions, then refit the driveshaft to the vehicle as described in Section 2.

Models with automatic transmission

Outer joint

29 Remove the driveshaft as described in Section 3.

30 Release the two outer gaiter retaining clips, then slide the gaiter along the driveshaft away from the joint. Position a small container underneath the gaiter, to catch any grease that may leak from the joint as it is dismantled.

31 Mount the driveshaft in a bench vice, using strips of aluminium or wood to prevent the jaws of the vice damaging the surface of the driveshaft. Attach a slide hammer or similar tool to the driveshaft nut threads and draw the outer CV joint off the end of the driveshaft. Note that you will have to exert enough force to overcome the internal circlip that secures the joint to the driveshaft.

32 With the joint removed, extract the circlip from groove in the end of the driveshaft, then slide the outer gaiter off the outer end of the driveshaft.

33 Thoroughly clean the outer constant velocity joint using paraffin, or a suitable solvent, and then dry it thoroughly. Carry out a visual inspection of the joint.

34 If on inspection, the joint reveals signs of wear or damage, it will be necessary to renew the complete driveshaft as an assembly, since no components are available separately. If the joint components are in satisfactory condition, obtain a repair kit from your Citroën dealer, consisting of a new gaiter, retaining clips, and the correct type and quantity of grease.

35 Slide the smaller of the two new gaiter retaining clips onto the driveshaft. Tape over the splines on the outer end of the driveshaft, then carefully slide the outer gaiter onto the shaft.

36 Fit a new circlip into the groove at the outer end of the driveshaft. The circlip must now be compressed to allow the outer CV joint to be refitted; this can be done by fitting a small diameter worm drive hose over the circlip and tightening it.

37 Fit the CV joint to the end of the driveshaft and push it firmly into position. The hose clip will be pushed along the shaft, allowing the circlip to expand inside the CV joint. Pull firmly on the joint to ensure that it is securely retained. Fully slacken the hose clip and remove it from the driveshaft.

38 Pack the joint and gaiter with the grease supplied with the repair kit, then slide the gaiter over the joint. Position the gaiter so that there is a distance of 256mm between the inside edge of the gaiter and the surface of the bearing, at the opposite end of the driveshaft **(see illustration)**.

39 Fit the large metal retaining clip to the gaiter. Remove any slack in the gaiter retaining clip by carefully compressing the raised section of the clip. In the absence of the special tool, a pair of side cutters may be used. Secure the small retaining clip using the same procedure. Check that the constant velocity joint moves freely in all directions before refitting the driveshaft.

Inner joint - left-hand driveshaft

40 Remove the driveshaft as described in Section 3.

41 Mount the driveshaft in a bench vice; protect the surface of the shaft by lining the jaws of the vice with strips of aluminium or wood.

42 Wipe away the excess grease from the tripod joint. If the rollers are not secured to the joint with circlips, wrap adhesive tape around the joint to hold them in position.

43 Using a dab of paint, or a hammer and punch, mark the position of the tripod joint in relation to the driveshaft. Using circlip pliers, extract the circlip securing the joint to the driveshaft.

44 The tripod joint can now be removed. If it is tight, draw the joint off the driveshaft end, using a long-reach universal bearing puller. Ensure that the legs of the puller are located behind the joint inner member, and do not contact the joint rollers. Alternatively, support the inner member of the tripod joint, and press the shaft out of the joint using a hydraulic press, ensuring that no load is applied to the joint rollers.

45 Release the clip securing the gaiter to the bearing, then slide the gaiter along the shaft. Mark the position of the bearing in relation to the shaft. Use a two or three legged bearing puller to draw the gaiter bearing off the shaft. Alternatively, support the bearing, and press the shaft out of the bearing using a hydraulic press.

46 Slide the gaiter, together with its flange, off the inboard end of the driveshaft.

47 Thoroughly clean the constant velocity joint components using paraffin, or a suitable solvent, and dry them thoroughly - take great care not to remove the alignment marks made on dismantling, especially if paint was used. Carry out a visual inspection of the joint.

48 Examine the tripod joint and rollers for any signs of scoring or wear, and for smoothness of movement of the rollers on the tripod stems. If any component is worn, the complete driveshaft assembly must be renewed; no joint components are available separately. If the joint components are in good condition, obtain a repair kit from your Citroën dealer, consisting of a new rubber gaiter, retaining collars, circlip and the correct quantity of the special grease.

49 Tape over the splines on the end of the driveshaft, and carefully slide the inner retaining collar and new gaiter onto the shaft.

50 Drive the gaiter bearing into position on the driveshaft, using a length of tubing and a mallet. Use the markings made during disassembly to position the bearing correctly on the driveshaft.

51 Remove the tape, then aligning the marks made on dismantling, engage the tripod joint with the driveshaft splines. Use a hammer and soft metal drift (or a suitable tube or socket) to tap the joint onto the shaft, taking great care not to damage the driveshaft splines or joint rollers.

52 Secure the tripod joint in position with the new circlip, ensuring that it is correctly located in the driveshaft groove.

53 Remove the tape, then draw the gaiter over the tripod joint. Evenly distribute the special grease contained in the repair kit around the tripod joint, inside the gaiter.

54 Secure the gaiter to the outer edge of the

bearing using the new retaining clip. Check that the distance between the face of the bearing and the inside edge of the outer CV joint gaiter is 256 mm **(refer to illustration 4.38)**.

55 Refit the driveshaft (see Section 3).

Inner joint - right-hand driveshaft

56 Remove the driveshaft (see Section 3).

57 The right hand inner CV joint is identical to the inner CV joints fitted to vehicles with manual transmission. If only the CV joint and gaiter are being serviced, there is no need to remove the inner adapter sleeve or intermediate bearing (where applicable) from the inner end of the driveshaft. Refer to the dismantling and reassembly information given earlier in this Section (paragraphs 13 to 28 inclusive).

58 On completion, refit the driveshaft as described in Section 3.

5 Driveshaft overhaul - general information

If any of the checks described in Chapter 1A or 1B reveal wear in any driveshaft joint, first remove the roadwheel trim or centre cap (as appropriate).

If the staking is still effective, the driveshaft nut should be correctly tightened; if in doubt, relieve the staking, then tighten the nut to the specified torque and restake it into the driveshaft grooves. Refit the roadwheel trim or centre cap (as applicable), and repeat the check on the remaining driveshaft nut.

Road test the vehicle, and listen for a metallic clicking from the front as the vehicle is driven slowly in a circle on full-lock. If a clicking noise is heard, this indicates wear in the outer constant velocity joint.

If vibration, consistent with road speed, is felt through the car when accelerating, there is a possibility of wear in the inner constant velocity joints.

To check the joints for wear, remove the driveshafts, then dismantle them as described in Section 4. If any wear or free play is found, the complete driveshaft assembly must be renewed, as the joints are not available separately. Refer to a Citroën dealer for information on the availability of driveshaft components.

6 Right-hand driveshaft intermediate bearing - renewal

Note: *A suitable bearing puller will be required, to draw the bearing and collar off the driveshaft end.*

1 Remove the right-hand driveshaft as described in Section 2 or 3 as applicable.

2 On models with automatic transmission, mount the adapter sleeve at the inboard end of the driveshaft in a bench vice, and then tap the driveshaft out through the sleeve using a mallet and punch.

3 Check that the bearing outer race rotates smoothly and easily, without any signs of roughness or undue free play between the inner and outer races. If necessary, renew the bearing as follows.

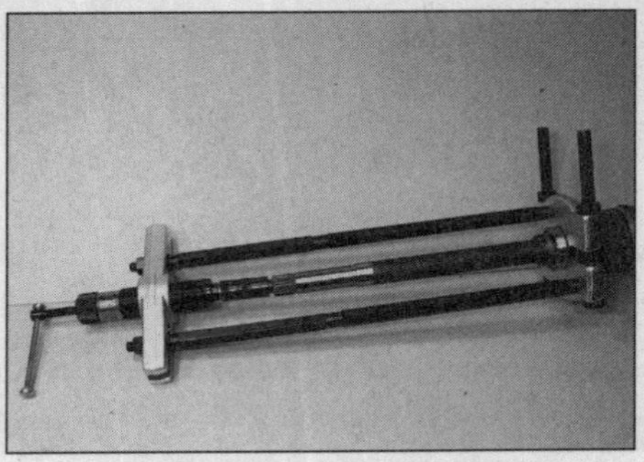

6.4 Use a long-reach bearing puller to remove the intermediate bearing from the right-hand driveshaft

4 Using a long-reach universal bearing puller, carefully draw the collar and intermediate bearing off the driveshaft inner end **(see illustration)**. Apply a smear of grease to the inner race of the new bearing, then fit the bearing over the end of the driveshaft. Using a hammer and a suitable long piece of tubing which bears only on the bearing inner race, tap the new bearing into position on the driveshaft, until it abuts the constant velocity joint outer member. Once the bearing is correctly positioned, tap the bearing collar onto the shaft until it contacts the bearing inner race.

5 On models with automatic transmission, mount the driveshaft in a bench vice and drive the adapter sleeve onto the inboard end of the driveshaft.

6 Check that the bearing rotates freely, then refit the driveshaft as described in Section 2 or 3 as applicable.

Chapter 9
Braking system

Contents

Degrees of difficulty

Easy, suitable for novice with little experience	**Fairly easy,** suitable for beginner with some experience	**Fairly difficult,** suitable for competent DIY mechanic	**Difficult,** suitable for experienced DIY mechanic	**Very difficult,** suitable for expert DIY or professional

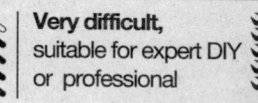

Specifications

General

System type	Dual hydraulic circuit, split diagonally. Anti-lock braking system (ABS) available as an option. Front disc brakes (ventilated on 1.6 litre engine models), and rear drum brakes fitted on all except VTR and VTS models. Rear disc brakes on 1.6 litre VTR and VTS models. Vacuum servo-assistance on all models, vacuum provided by camshaft-driven pump on diesel models. Cable-operated handbrake acting on rear wheels.

Front brakes

Type	Disc, with single-piston sliding caliper
Caliper type:	
All except 1587 cc engine models (solid discs):	
Without power steering	ATE/Teves FR 12
With power steering	Bendix Series 4
1587 cc engine models (ventilated discs)	ATE/Teves FN 48
Disc diameter:	
954 cc and 1124 cc engine models:	
Non-ABS models without power steering	238.0 mm
Models with ABS and/or power steering	247.0 mm
1360 cc, 1527 cc and 1587 cc engine models	247.0 mm
Disc thickness:	
New:	
238.0 mm diameter disc	8.0 mm
247.0 mm diameter disc:	
Solid discs	10.0 mm
Ventilated discs	20.4 mm
Minimum thickness (1.0 mm maximum variation between sides):	
238.0 mm diameter disc	6.0 mm
247.0 mm diameter disc:	
Solid discs	8.0 mm
Ventilated discs	18.4 mm
Maximum disc run-out	0.07 mm
Minimum pad friction material thickness	2.0 mm

Rear drum brakes

Type	Drum with leading and trailing shoes
Drum diameter:	
New:	
Non-ABS models without power steering	165.0 mm
Non-ABS models with power steering	180.0 mm
Models with ABS	203.0 mm
Maximum diameter after machining:	
165.0 mm drums	167.0 mm
180.0 mm drums	182.0 mm
203.0 mm drums	205.0 mm
Minimum shoe lining thickness	1.0 mm

Rear disc brakes

Type	Solid (non-ventilated) disc, with single-piston sliding caliper
Disc diameter	247.0 mm
Disc thickness:	
New	8.0 mm
Minimum (1.0 mm maximum variation between sides)	6.0 mm
Maximum disc run-out	0.07 mm
Minimum pad friction material thickness	2.0 mm

Torque wrench settings

Torque wrench settings	Nm	lbf ft
ABS wheel sensor securing stud/bolt*	8	6
Brake fluid pipe union nuts	15	11
Brake pad bracket bolts:		
Bendix calipers	120	88
ATE/Teves calipers:		
FR 12	32	24
FN 48	120	88
Brake pedal bracket-to-bulkhead nuts	5	4
Brake vacuum pump	20	15
Front brake caliper guide pin bolts	27	20
Front brake caliper-to-hub carrier bolts*:		
Bendix Series 4 caliper (M12)	120	88
ATE/Teves FR 12:		
M8 bolts	35	26
M12 bolts	105	77
Handbrake lever securing bolts	15	11
Hydraulic system bleed screws	3	2
Master cylinder-to-servo nuts	10	7
Rear brake caliper mounting bolts (M12)	120	88
Rear hub nut**	140	103
Roadwheel bolts	85	63
Vacuum servo securing nuts	20	15

**Use suitable thread-locking compound.*
***Use a new nut.*

1 General information

The braking system is of the servo-assisted, dual-circuit hydraulic type. The arrangement of the hydraulic system is such that each circuit operates one front and one rear brake from a tandem master cylinder. Under normal circumstances, both circuits operate in unison. However, in the event of hydraulic failure in one circuit, full braking force will still be available at two diagonally-opposite wheels.

All models are fitted with front disc brakes and rear drum brakes, apart from the 1587cc 16v models which have rear disc brakes. An anti-lock braking system (ABS) is available as an option on certain models (refer to Section 23 for further information on ABS operation).

The front disc brakes are actuated by single-piston sliding type calipers, which ensure that equal pressure is applied to each disc pad.

The rear drum brakes incorporate leading and trailing shoes, which are actuated by twin-piston wheel cylinders. On models without ABS, the wheel cylinders incorporate integral pressure-regulating valves, which control the hydraulic pressure applied to the rear brakes. The regulating valves help to prevent rear wheel lock-up during emergency braking. On models with ABS, a load-sensitive rear pressure-regulating valve is fitted, linked to the rear axle. A self-adjusting mechanism is incorporated, to automatically compensate for brake shoe wear. As the brake shoe linings wear, the footbrake operation automatically operates the adjuster mechanism, which effectively lengthens the shoe strut and repositions the brake shoes, to remove the lining-to-drum clearance.

On models with rear disc brakes, the brakes are actuated by single-piston sliding calipers which incorporate mechanical handbrake mechanisms. A pressure-regulating valve is situated in the brake line to each rear caliper. The regulating valve is similar to that fitted to the rear wheel cylinders on drum brake models, and helps to prevent rear wheel lock-up during emergency braking. On models with ABS, a load-sensitive rear pressure-regulating valve is fitted, linked to the rear axle.

On all models, the handbrake provides an independent mechanical means of rear brake application.

On diesel models, there is insufficient vacuum in the inlet manifold to operate the braking system servo effectively. To overcome this problem, a vacuum pump is fitted to the engine, to provide vacuum to the servo unit. The vacuum pump is mounted on the end of the cylinder head, and is driven directly from the camshaft.

When servicing any part of the system, work carefully and methodically; also observe scrupulous cleanliness when overhauling any part of the hydraulic system. Always renew components (in axle sets, where applicable) if in doubt about their condition, and use only genuine Citroën replacement parts, or at least those of known good quality. Note the warnings given in "*Safety first*" and at relevant points in this Chapter concerning the dangers of asbestos dust and hydraulic fluid.

Note: *Early Saxos without ABS or power steering had three wheel bolts per wheel; later models, or those with ABS or power steering, had four bolts per wheel. At the time of writing, no information was available to clearly indicate the changeover date from three to four bolts. This change does not affect any of the procedures in the Manual, however.*

2 Hydraulic system - bleeding

Warning: Hydraulic fluid is poisonous; wash off immediately and thoroughly in the case of skin contact, and seek immediate medical advice if any fluid is swallowed or gets into the eyes. Certain types of hydraulic fluid are inflammable, and may ignite when allowed into contact with hot components; when servicing any hydraulic system, it is safest to assume that the fluid IS inflammable, and to take precautions against the risk of fire as though it is petrol that is being handled. Finally, it is hygroscopic (it absorbs moisture from the air). The more moisture is absorbed by the fluid, the lower its boiling point becomes, leading to a dangerous loss of braking under hard use. Old fluid may be contaminated and unfit for further use. When topping-up or renewing the fluid, always use the recommended type, and ensure that it comes from a freshly-opened sealed container. Hydraulic fluid is an effective paint stripper, and will attack plastics; if any is spilt, it should be washed off immediately, using copious quantities of fresh water.

Non-ABS models

General

1 The correct operation of any hydraulic system is only possible after removing all air from the components and circuit; and this is achieved by bleeding the system.

2 During the bleeding procedure, add only clean, fresh hydraulic fluid of the recommended type; never re-use fluid that has already been bled from the system. Ensure that sufficient fluid is available before starting work.

3 If there is any possibility of incorrect fluid being already in the system, the brake components and circuit must be flushed completely with uncontaminated, correct fluid, and new seals should be fitted throughout the system.

4 If hydraulic fluid has been lost from the system, or air has entered because of a leak, ensure that the fault is cured before proceeding further.

5 Park the vehicle on level ground, and switch off the engine.

6 Check that all pipes and hoses are secure, unions tight and bleed screws closed. Remove the dust caps (where applicable), and clean any dirt from around the bleed screws.

7 Unscrew the master cylinder reservoir cap, and top the master cylinder reservoir up to the "MAX" level line. Refit the cap loosely, and remember to maintain the fluid level at least above the "MIN" level line throughout the procedure, otherwise there is a risk of further air entering the system.

8 There are a number of one-man, do-it-yourself brake bleeding kits currently available from motor accessory shops. It is recommended that one of these kits is used whenever possible, as they greatly simplify the bleeding operation, and also reduce the risk of expelled air and fluid being drawn back into the system. If such a kit is not available, the basic (two-man) method must be used, which is described in detail below.

9 If a kit is to be used, prepare the vehicle as described previously, and follow the kit manufacturer's instructions, as the procedure may vary slightly according to the type being used; generally, they are as outlined below in the relevant sub-section.

10 Whichever method is used, the same sequence must be followed (paragraphs 11 and 12) to ensure the removal of all air from the system.

Bleeding sequence

11 If the system has been only partially disconnected, and suitable precautions were taken to minimise fluid loss, it should be necessary to bleed only that part of the system (ie the primary or secondary circuit).

12 If the complete system is to be bled, then it should be done working in the following sequence:

a) Left-hand rear wheel.
b) Right-hand front wheel.
c) Right-hand rear wheel.
d) Left-hand front wheel.

Bleeding - basic (two-man) method

13 Collect a clean glass jar, a suitable length of plastic or rubber tubing which is a tight fit over the bleed screw, and a ring spanner to fit the screw. The help of an assistant will also be required.

14 Remove the dust cap from the first screw in the sequence (if not already done) **(see illustration)**. Fit a suitable spanner and tube to the screw. Place the other end of the tube in the jar, and pour in sufficient fluid to cover the end of the tube.

2.14 Rear brake bleed screw dust cap (arrowed)

15 Ensure that the master cylinder reservoir fluid level is maintained at least above the "MIN" level line throughout the procedure.

16 Have the assistant fully depress the brake pedal several times to build up pressure, then maintain it on the final downstroke.

17 While pedal pressure is maintained, unscrew the bleed screw (approximately one turn) and allow the compressed fluid and air to flow into the jar. The assistant should maintain pedal pressure, following the pedal down to the floor if necessary, and should not release the pedal until instructed to do so. When the flow stops, tighten the bleed screw again, have the assistant release the pedal slowly, and recheck the reservoir fluid level.

18 Repeat the steps given in paragraphs 16 and 17 until the fluid emerging from the bleed screw is free from air bubbles. If the master cylinder has been drained and refilled, and air is being bled from the first screw in the sequence, allow approximately five seconds between cycles for the master cylinder passages to refill.

19 When no more air bubbles appear, tighten the bleed screw securely, remove the tube and spanner, and refit the dust cap (where applicable). Do not overtighten the bleed screw.

20 Repeat the procedure on the remaining screws in the sequence, until all air is removed from the system and the brake pedal feels firm again.

Bleeding - using a one-way valve kit

21 As their name implies, these kits consist of a length of tubing with a one-way valve fitted, to prevent expelled air and fluid being drawn back into the system; some kits include a translucent container, which can be positioned so that the air bubbles can be more easily seen flowing from the end of the tube.

22 The kit is connected to the bleed screw, which is then opened **(see illustration)**. The user returns to the driver's seat, depresses the brake pedal with a smooth, steady stroke, and slowly releases it; this is repeated until the expelled fluid is clear of air bubbles.

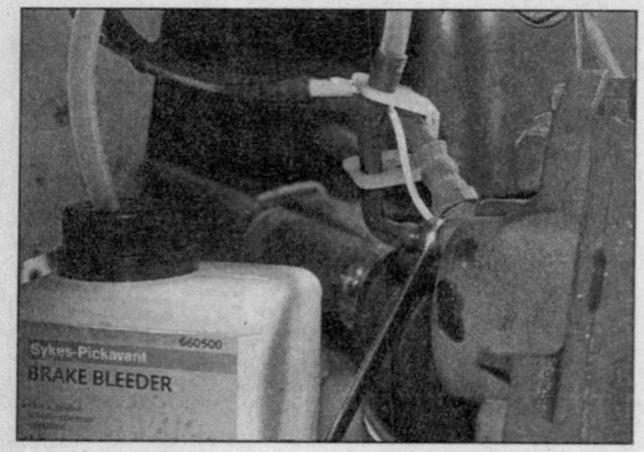

2.22 Bleeding a front brake caliper using a one-way valve kit

23 Note that these kits simplify work so much that it is easy to forget the master cylinder reservoir fluid level; ensure that this is maintained at least above the "MIN" level line at all times.

Bleeding - using a pressure-bleeding kit

24 These kits are usually operated by the reservoir of pressurised air contained in the spare tyre. However, note that it will probably be necessary to reduce the pressure to a lower level than normal; refer to the instructions supplied with the kit.

25 By connecting a pressurised, fluid-filled container to the master cylinder reservoir, bleeding can be carried out simply by opening each screw in turn (in the specified sequence), and allowing the fluid to flow out until no more air bubbles can be seen in the expelled fluid.

26 This method has the advantage that the large reservoir of fluid provides an additional safeguard against air being drawn into the system during bleeding.

27 Pressure-bleeding is particularly effective when bleeding "difficult" systems, or when bleeding the complete system at the time of routine fluid renewal.

All methods

28 When bleeding is complete, and firm pedal feel is restored, wash off any spilt fluid, tighten the bleed screws securely, and refit their dust caps (where applicable).

29 Check the hydraulic fluid level in the master cylinder reservoir, and top-up if necessary (see "*Weekly checks*").

30 Discard any hydraulic fluid that has been bled from the system; it will not be fit for re-use.

31 Check the feel of the brake pedal. If it feels at all spongy, air must still be present in the system, and further bleeding is required. Failure to bleed satisfactorily after a reasonable repetition of the bleeding procedure may be due to worn master cylinder seals.

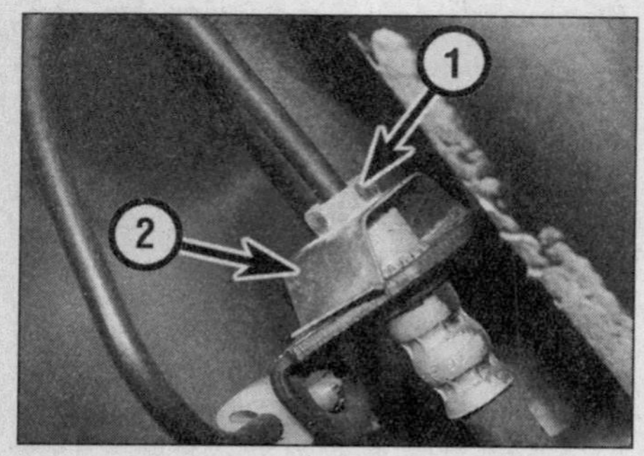

3.2 Brake pipe union nut (1) and hose spring clip (2)

Anti-lock braking system (ABS)

Warning: On ABS models, ensure that the ignition is switched off before starting the bleeding procedure, to avoid any possibility of voltage being applied to the modulator before the bleeding procedure is completed. Ideally, the battery should be disconnected. If voltage is applied to the modulator before the bleeding procedure is complete, this will effectively drain the hydraulic fluid in the modulator, rendering the unit unserviceable. Do not, therefore, attempt to "run" the modulator in order to bleed the brakes.

32 A pressure-bleeding kit must be used for bleeding the hydraulic system on ABS models - see paragraphs 24 to 27.

33 Following the sequence given in paragraph 12, bleed each brake in turn until clean fluid, free of air bubbles, is seen to emerge. Pause between bleeding each brake to ensure that the fluid level in the reservoir is above the "MIN" or "DANGER" level.

34 On completion of bleeding, proceed as described in paragraphs 28 to 31 inclusive.

3 Hydraulic pipes and hoses - renewal

Note: *Before starting work, refer to the warning at the beginning of Section 2 concerning the dangers of hydraulic fluid.*

1 If any pipe or hose is to be renewed, minimise fluid loss by first removing the master cylinder reservoir cap, then tightening it down onto a piece of polythene to obtain an airtight seal. Alternatively, flexible hoses can be sealed, if required, using a proprietary brake hose clamp; metal brake pipe unions can be plugged (if care is taken not to allow dirt into the system) or capped immediately they are disconnected. Place a wad of rag under any union that is to be disconnected, to catch any spilt fluid.

2 If a flexible hose is to be disconnected, unscrew the brake pipe union nut before removing the spring clip which secures the hose to its mounting bracket **(see illustration)**.

3 To unscrew the union nuts, it is preferable to obtain a brake pipe spanner of the correct size; these are available from most large motor accessory shops. Failing this, a close-fitting open-ended spanner will be required, though if the nuts are tight or corroded, their flats may be rounded-off if the spanner slips. In such a case, a self-locking wrench is often the only way to unscrew a stubborn union, but it follows that the pipe and the damaged nuts must be renewed on reassembly. Always clean a union and surrounding area before disconnecting it. If disconnecting a component with more than one union, make a careful note of the connections before disturbing any of them.

4 If a brake pipe is to be renewed, it can be obtained, cut to length and with the union nuts and end flares in place, from Citroën dealers. All that is then necessary is to bend it to shape, following the line of the original, before fitting it to the vehicle. Alternatively, most motor accessory shops can make up brake pipes from kits, but this requires very careful measurement of the original, to ensure that the replacement is of the correct length. The safest answer is usually to take the original to the shop as a pattern.

5 On refitting, do not overtighten the union nuts. It is not necessary to exercise brute force to obtain a sound joint.

6 Ensure that the pipes and hoses are correctly routed, with no kinks, and that they are secured in the clips or brackets provided. After fitting, remove the polythene from the reservoir, and bleed the hydraulic system as described in Section 2. Wash off any spilt fluid, and check carefully for fluid leaks.

4 Front brake pads - renewal

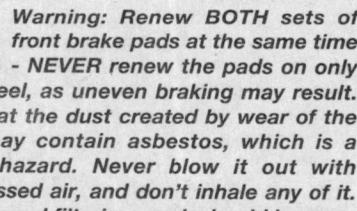

Warning: Renew BOTH sets of front brake pads at the same time - NEVER renew the pads on only one wheel, as uneven braking may result. Note that the dust created by wear of the pads may contain asbestos, which is a health hazard. Never blow it out with compressed air, and don't inhale any of it. An approved filtering mask should be worn when working on the brakes. DO NOT use petrol or petroleum-based solvents to clean brake parts; use brake cleaner or methylated spirit only.

Caution: New pads will not give full braking efficiency until they have bedded-in. Be prepared for this, and avoid hard braking as far as possible for the first hundred miles or so after pad renewal.

1 Apply the handbrake, then jack up the front of the vehicle and support it on axle stands (see *"Jacking and vehicle support"*). Remove the front roadwheels.

2 Push the piston into its bore by pulling the caliper outwards.

3 There are three different types of front brake caliper fitted to the models covered in this Manual. Identify the relevant caliper by reference to the Specifications at the start of this Chapter, and to the accompanying illustrations (the manufacturer's name is usually stamped on part of the caliper, in any case), then proceed as described under the relevant sub-heading.

4.4a Extract the spring clip (arrowed) . . .

4.4b . . . and slide out the pad retaining plate - Bendix caliper

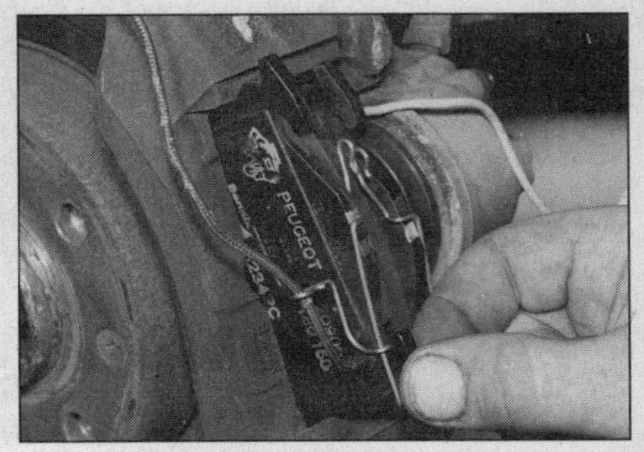

4.5a Withdraw the outer . . .

Bendix caliper

4 Using pliers, extract the small spring clip from the pad retaining plate, and then slide the plate out of the caliper (it will probably be necessary to tap the plate from the caliper) **(see illustrations)**.

5 Withdraw the pads from the caliper, then make a note of the correct fitted position of each anti-rattle spring, and remove the spring from each pad **(see illustrations)**. It may be necessary to push the inboard pad back against the piston, to retract the piston into its bore, before the pad can be removed.

6 First measure the thickness of each brake pad's friction material. If either pad is worn at any point to the specified minimum thickness or less, *all four* pads must be renewed. Also, the pads should be renewed if any are fouled with oil or grease; there is no satisfactory way of degreasing friction material, once contaminated. If any of the brake pads are worn unevenly, or are fouled with oil or grease, trace and rectify the cause before reassembly. New brake pads and spring kits are available from Citroën dealers.

7 If the brake pads are still serviceable, carefully clean them using a clean, fine wire brush or similar, paying particular attention to the sides and back of the metal backing. Clean out the grooves in the friction material, and pick out any large embedded particles of dirt or debris. Carefully clean the pad locations in the caliper body/mounting bracket.

8 Prior to fitting the pads, check that the guide pins are free to slide easily in the caliper body/mounting bracket, and check that the rubber guide pin gaiters are undamaged. Brush the dust and dirt from the caliper and piston, but *do not* inhale it, as it is injurious to health.

9 Inspect the dust seal around the piston for damage, and the piston for evidence of fluid leaks, corrosion or damage. If attention to any of these components is necessary, refer to Section 10.

10 If new brake pads are to be fitted, the caliper piston must be pushed back into the cylinder to make room for them. Either use a G-clamp or similar tool, or use suitable pieces of wood as levers.

11 Provided that the master cylinder reservoir has not been overfilled with hydraulic fluid, there should be no spillage, but keep a careful watch on the fluid level while retracting the piston. If the fluid level rises above the "MAX" level line at any time, the surplus should be syphoned off or ejected via a plastic tube connected to the bleed screw (see Section 2).

Warning: Do not syphon the fluid by mouth, as it is poisonous; use a syringe or an old poultry baster.

12 Apply a little copper-based brake grease to the pad backing plates, but take great care not to allow any grease onto the pad friction linings.

13 Fit the anti-rattle springs to the pads, so that when the pads are installed in the caliper, the spring end will be located at the opposite end of the pad in relation to the pad retaining plate.

14 Locate the pads in the caliper, ensuring that the friction material of each pad is against the brake disc, and check that the anti-rattle spring ends are at the opposite end of the pad to which the retaining plate is to be inserted.

15 Slide the retaining plate into place, and install the new small spring clip at its inner end. It may be necessary to file an entry chamfer on the edge of the retaining plate, to enable it to be fitted without difficulty.

16 Depress the brake pedal repeatedly, until the pads are pressed into firm contact with the brake disc, and normal (non-assisted) pedal pressure is restored.

17 Repeat the above procedure on the remaining front brake caliper.

4.20 Note the orientation of the pad anti-rattle spring (arrowed) - ATE caliper (solid discs)

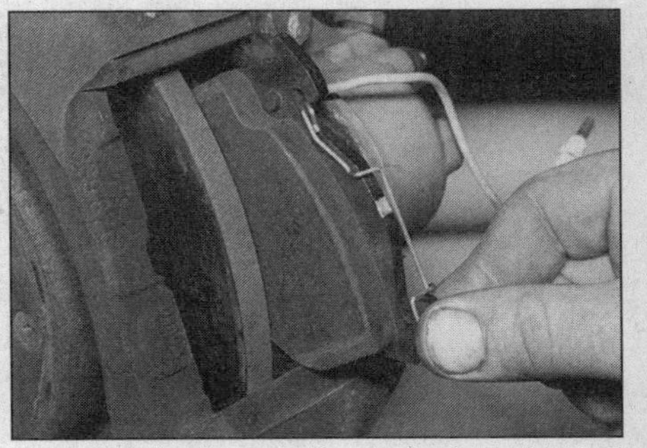

4.5b . . . and inner pads - Bendix caliper

18 Refit the roadwheels, then lower the vehicle to the ground and tighten the roadwheel bolts to the specified torque.

19 Check the hydraulic fluid level as described in *"Weekly checks"*.

ATE/Teves FR 12 caliper (models with solid discs)

20 Note the location and orientation of the pad anti-rattle spring **(see illustration)**.

21 Remove the pad retaining pins by tapping them from the caliper using a suitable pin-punch **(see illustrations)**. Note that the pad anti-rattle spring will be released as the pins are removed.

22 Withdraw the pad retaining spring **(see illustration)**.

23 Withdraw the pads from the caliper **(see illustrations)**. It may be necessary to push the inboard pad back against the piston, to retract

4.21a Free the pad retaining pins from the caliper using a pin-punch . . .

4.21b . . . then withdraw the pins from the caliper

4.22 Remove the pad anti-rattle spring

4.23a Withdraw the inner . . .

4.23b . . . and outer brake pads - ATE caliper (solid discs)

4.28a Refit the lower pad retaining pin, ensuring that it passes through the retaining spring . . .

4.28b . . . then tap the pin into position in the caliper

the piston into its bore, before the pad can be removed. Retrieve the anti-squeal shims from the backs of the pads.

24 Proceed as described in paragraphs 6 to 12 inclusive.

4.30 Prising out the pad retaining spring from the caliper - ATE caliper (ventilated discs)

25 Slide the anti-squeak shims and pads into position in the caliper, ensuring that the friction material of each pad is against the brake disc.

26 Locate the anti-rattle spring on the pads, as noted before removal.

27 Fit the upper pad retaining pin, ensuring that the top arms of the pad retaining spring locate behind the pin, then tap the pin into position in the caliper.

28 Refit the lower pad retaining pin, ensuring that it passes through the retaining spring, then tap the pin into position in the caliper **(see illustrations)**.

29 Proceed as described in paragraphs 16 to 19 inclusive.

ATE/Teves FN 48 caliper (models with ventilated discs)

30 Using a screwdriver, prise the pad retaining spring from the outer edge of the caliper, noting its correct fitted position **(see illustration)**.

31 Prise out the two guide bolt dust caps from the inner edge of the caliper **(see illustration)**.

32 Unscrew the guide bolts from the caliper, and lift the caliper and inner pad away from the mounting bracket. Tie the caliper to the suspension strut using a suitable piece of wire **(see illustrations)**. Do not allow the caliper to hang unsupported on the flexible brake hose. If the pads are likely to be removed for some time, insert a piece of wood into the caliper body, to prevent the piston being ejected if the brake pedal is accidentally pressed.

33 Remove the inner pad from the caliper piston, noting that it is retained by a clip attached to the pad backing plate, and recover the outer pad from the mounting bracket.

34 Proceed as described in paragraphs 6 to 12.

35 Fit the inner pad to the caliper, ensuring

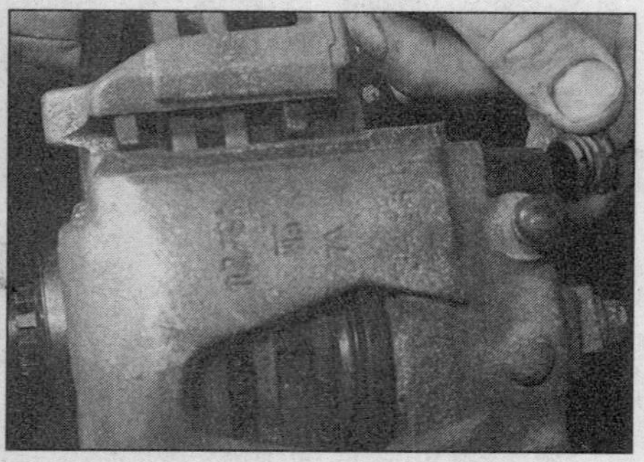

4.31 Remove the guide bolt dust caps . . .

4.32a . . . then unscrew the guide bolts . . .

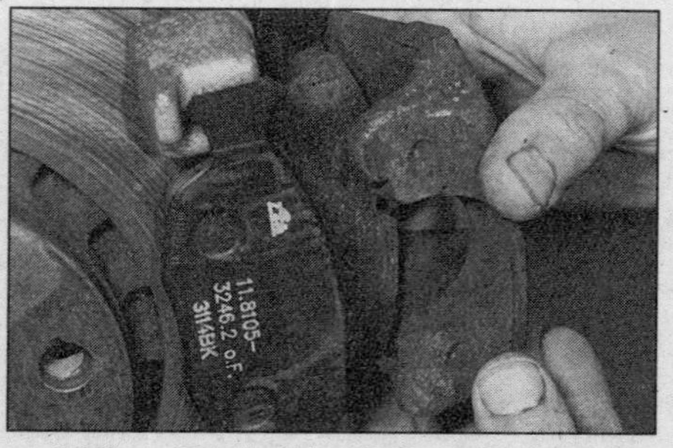

4.32b . . . and slide off the caliper and inner pad assembly - ATE caliper (ventilated discs)

that its clip is correctly located in the caliper piston **(see illustration)**.

36 Fit the outer pad to the caliper mounting bracket, ensuring that its friction material is facing the brake disc **(see illustration)**.

37 Slide the caliper and inner pad into position over the outer pad, and locate it in the mounting bracket.

38 Install the caliper guide bolts, and tighten them to the specified torque **(see illustration)**.

39 Refit the guide bolt dust caps to the caliper.

40 Refit the pad retaining spring to the caliper, ensuring that its ends are correctly located in the caliper holes **(see illustration)**.

41 Depress the brake pedal repeatedly, until normal (non-assisted) pedal pressure is restored, and the pads are pressed into firm contact with the brake disc.

42 Repeat the above procedure on the remaining front brake caliper.

43 Refit the roadwheels, then lower the vehicle to the ground and tighten the roadwheel bolts to the specified torque setting.

44 Check the hydraulic fluid level as described in *"Weekly checks"*.

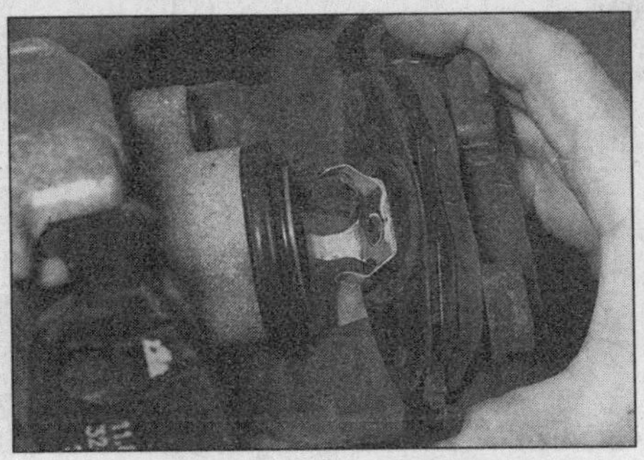

4.35 Clip the inner pad securely into the caliper piston . . .

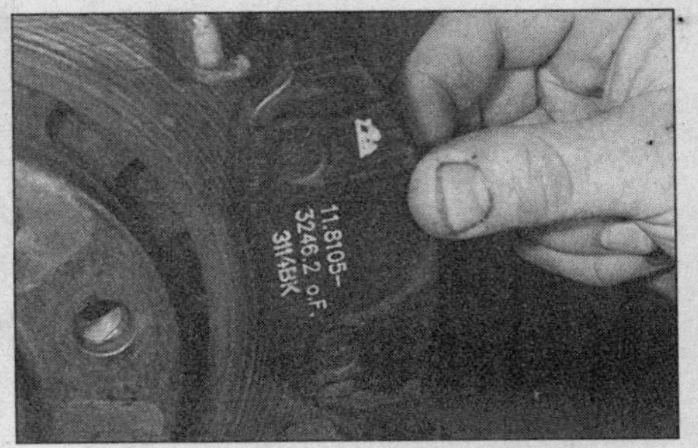

4.36 . . . and fit the outer pad to the caliper mounting bracket - ATE caliper (ventilated discs)

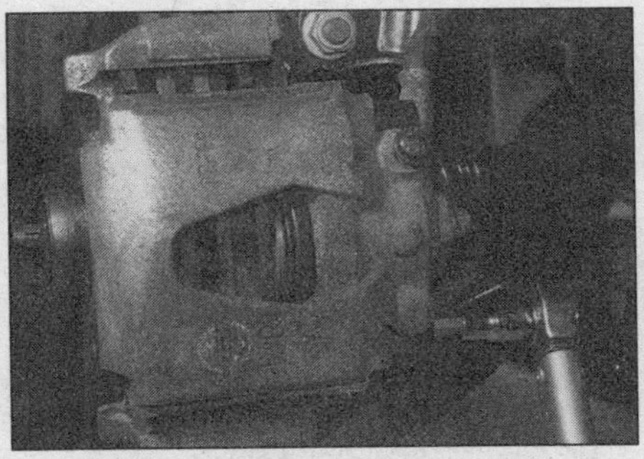

4.38 Slide the caliper into position and install the guide bolts, tightening them to the specified torque

4.40 Ensure that the pad retaining spring ends are correctly located in the caliper holes (arrowed)

5 Rear brake shoes - renewal

Warning: Renew BOTH sets of rear brake shoes at the same time - NEVER renew the shoes on only one wheel, as uneven braking may result. Note that the dust created by wear of the shoes may contain asbestos, which is a health hazard. Never blow it out with compressed air, and don't inhale any of it. An approved filtering mask should be worn when working on the brakes. DO NOT use petrol or petroleum-based solvents to clean brake parts; use brake cleaner or methylated spirit only.

Caution: New pads will not give full braking efficiency until they have bedded-in. Be prepared for this, and avoid hard braking as far as possible for the first hundred miles or so after pad renewal.

5.3 Rear brake shoes and associated components - Bendix brake shoes. Note the locations of the springs

Bendix brake shoes - models without ABS

1 Remove the rear brake drums, as described in Section 8.

2 Working on one side of the vehicle, brush the dirt and dust from the brake backplate and drum. **Do not** inhale the dust, as it may be a health hazard.

3 Note the position of each shoe, and the location of the return and steady springs **(see illustration)**.

4 Remove the shoe hold-down springs. Use pliers to depress the outer spring cups, and turn them through 90° **(see illustrations)**.

5 Recover the springs and cups, and remove the spring retainer pins from the backplate.

6 Carefully pull the leading brake shoe forwards from the backplate, and using a suitable pair of pliers, unhook and remove the lower return spring **(see illustrations)**.

HAYNES HiNT ***Complete all work on one rear drum at a time - in other words, renew the shoes on one side, before starting work on the other side. In this way, you will always have an assembled set of shoes to use as a reference.***

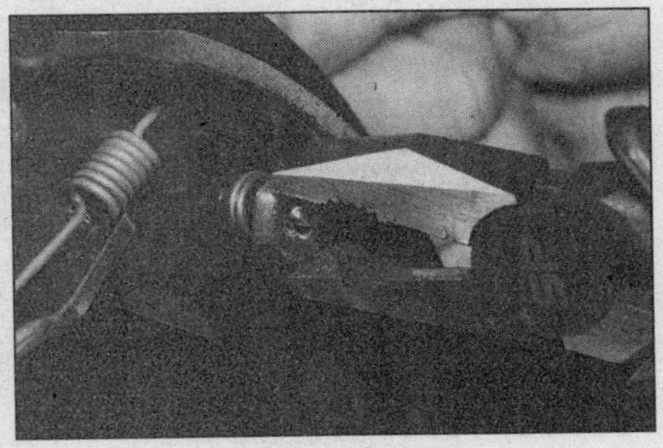

5.4a Use pliers . . .

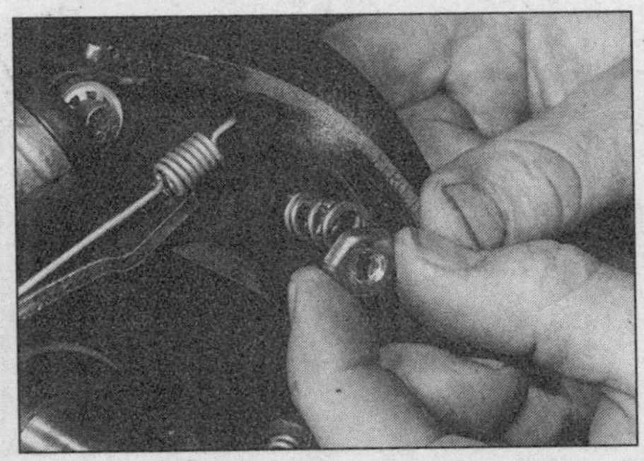

5.4b . . . to remove the outer hold-down spring cups

5.6a Pull the leading brake shoe forwards . . .

5.6b . . . and remove the lower return spring

7 Disengage the lower ends of the shoes from the bottom anchor, and pull the upper ends of the shoes from the wheel cylinder, then withdraw the shoe assembly, and unhook the handbrake cable from the lever on the trailing brake shoe **(see illustration)**.

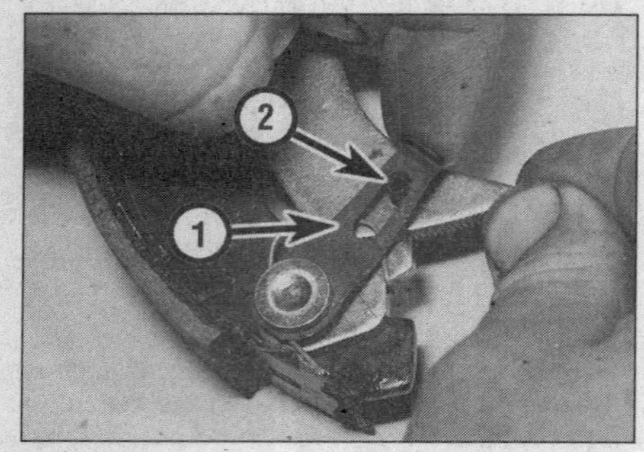

5.10a Prise the retaining plate (1) over the pivot pin (2) . . .

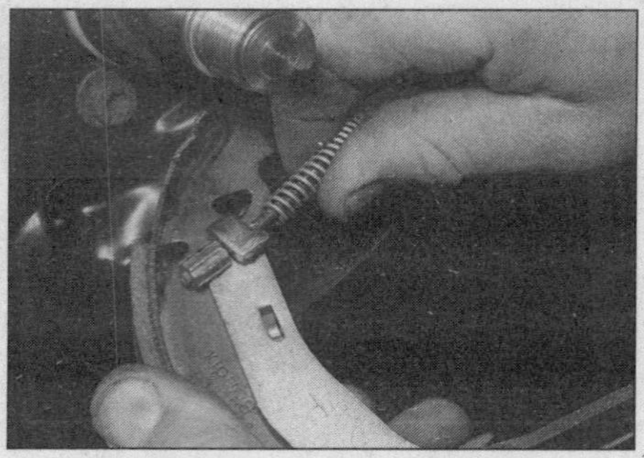

5.7 Unhooking the handbrake cable from the lever on the trailing shoe

8 If necessary, position a rubber band or a cable-tie over the wheel cylinder, to prevent the pistons from being ejected **(see illustration)**. If there is any evidence of fluid leakage from the wheel cylinder, renew it or overhaul it as described in Section 11.

9 Unhook the upper return spring from the shoes, and unhook the adjuster strut spring.

10 Working on the leading brake shoe, prise the adjuster lever retaining plate over the pivot pin on the adjuster lever, then pull the adjuster lever forwards to allow the adjuster strut to be removed **(see illustrations)**.

11 Transfer the handbrake and automatic adjuster levers to the new shoes, as required (prise off the spring clips to remove the levers) **(see illustration)**. Note that the levers and strut on each rear wheel are different, and that the leading and trailing shoes are fitted with different grade linings. New shoes will be supplied complete with the adjuster retaining plate riveted to the leading shoe.

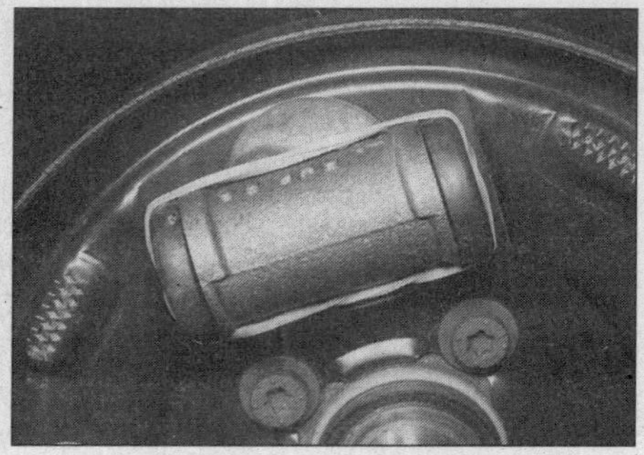

5.8 Rubber band positioned over wheel cylinder to retain pistons

12 Place the shoes on the bench in their correct positions, and lay the adjuster strut in position.

13 With the adjuster strut engaged with the leading shoe, push the adjuster lever back towards the shoe, and clip the adjuster lever retaining plate over the pivot pin on the adjuster lever.

14 Fit the adjuster strut spring between the trailing shoe and the adjuster strut **(see illustration)**, but do not fully engage the adjuster strut with the trailing shoe at this stage.

15 Fit the upper return spring to the shoes, then carefully manipulate the adjuster strut into position to engage it with the slot in the trailing shoe **(see illustrations)**.

16 Apply copper-based brake grease sparingly to the shoe contact areas of the brake backplate **(see illustration)**. Where

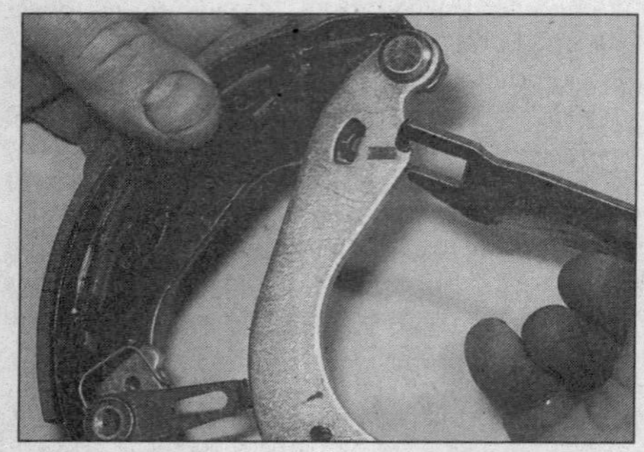

5.10b . . . and remove the adjuster strut

5.11 Prising off the spring clip to remove the adjuster lever from the trailing shoe

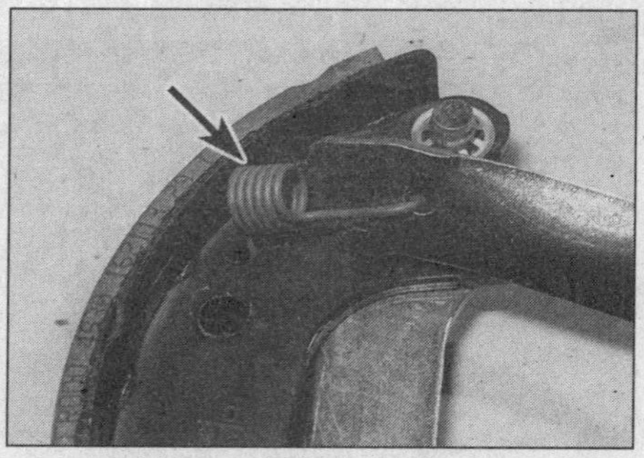

5.14 Fit the adjuster strut spring (arrowed) between the shoe and the adjuster strut

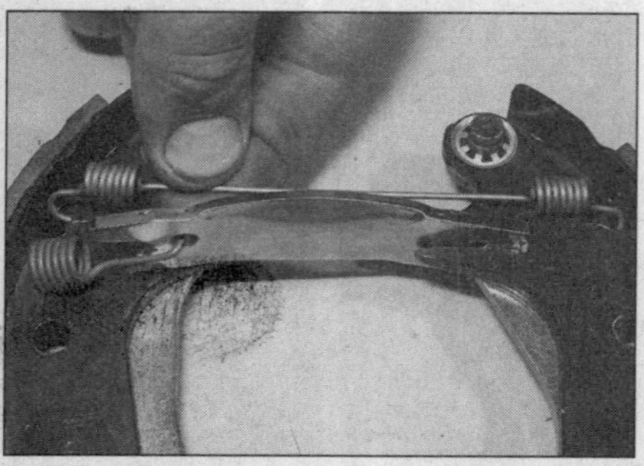

5.15a Fit the upper return spring to the shoes . . .

5.15b . . . then engage the adjuster strut

5.16 Apply copper-based brake grease to the shoe contact areas

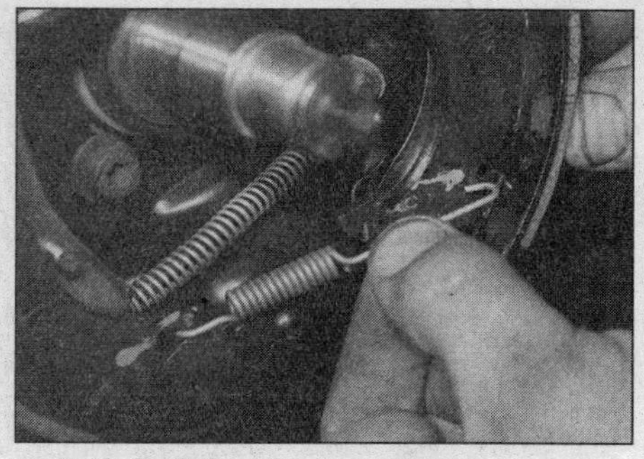

5.19 Refitting the lower return spring

applicable, remove the rubber band or cable tie from the wheel cylinder.

17 Offer the shoes into position, and reconnect the handbrake cable to the handbrake lever on the trailing shoe.

18 Position the shoes on the backplate, and lever the upper ends of the shoes apart to engage them with the wheel cylinder.

19 Carefully refit the lower return spring to the shoes **(see illustration)**, then lever the lower ends of the shoes apart to engage them with the lower anchor.

20 Insert the steady spring retainer pins in the backplate and through the holes in the shoes, then fit the hold-down springs and the cups.

21 Move the serrated automatic adjuster lever quadrant against the spring tension, to set the shoes at their minimum diameter.

22 Check that the handbrake lever on the trailing brake shoe is positioned with the lug on the edge of the shoe web, and not behind the shoe.

23 Repeat the procedure on the remaining side of the vehicle, then refit the brake drums as described in Section 8.

24 On completion, check the handbrake adjustment as described in Chapter 1A or 1B.

Lucas/Girling brake shoes - models with ABS

25 Make a note of the correct fitted positions of the springs and adjuster strut, to use as a guide on reassembly **(see illustration)**.

26 Carefully unhook both the upper and lower return springs, and remove them from the brake shoes.

27 Using a pair of pliers, remove the leading shoe retainer spring cup by depressing it and turning through 90°. With the cup removed, lift off the spring, then withdraw the retainer pin and remove the shoe from the backplate. Unhook the adjusting lever spring, and remove it from the leading shoe.

28 Detach the adjuster strut, and remove it from the trailing shoe.

29 Remove the trailing shoe retainer spring cup, spring and pin as described above, then detach the handbrake cable and remove the shoe from the vehicle. Do not depress the brake pedal until the brakes are reassembled; wrap a strong elastic band around the wheel cylinder pistons to retain them.

30 If genuine Citroën brake shoes are being installed, it will be necessary to remove the adjusting lever from the original leading shoe, and install it on the new shoe. All return springs should be renewed, regardless of their apparent condition; spring kits are also available from Citroën dealers.

31 Withdraw the forked end from the strut, and carefully examine the assembly for signs of wear or damage. Pay particular attention to the threads and the knurled adjuster wheel, and renew if necessary. Note that left-hand and right-hand struts are not interchangeable; the left-hand fork has a right-handed thread, and the right-hand fork a left-handed thread.

32 Peel back the rubber protective caps, and check the wheel cylinder for fluid leaks or other damage; check that both cylinder pistons are free to move easily. Refer to Section 11, if necessary, for information on wheel cylinder renewal.

33 Prior to installation, clean the backplate, and apply a thin smear of high-temperature brake grease or anti-seize compound (eg Duckhams Copper 10) to all those surfaces of the backplate which bear on the shoes, particularly the wheel cylinder pistons and lower pivot point. Do not allow the lubricant to foul the friction material.

34 Ensure that the handbrake lever stop-peg is correctly located against the edge of the trailing shoe, and remove the elastic band fitted to the wheel cylinder.

35 Locate the upper end of the trailing shoe in the wheel cylinder piston, then refit the retainer pin and spring, and secure it in position with the spring cup. Connect the handbrake cable to the lever.

36 Screw in the adjuster wheel until the minimum strut length is obtained, then hook the strut into position on the trailing shoe. Rotate the adjuster strut forked end, so that the cut-out of the fork will engage with the leading shoe adjusting lever once the shoe is installed **(see illustration)**.

37 Fit the spring to the leading shoe adjusting lever, so that the shorter hook of the spring engages with the lever.

38 Slide the leading shoe assembly into position, ensuring that it is correctly engaged with the adjuster strut fork, and that the fork cut-out is engaged with the adjusting lever. Ensure that the upper end of the shoe is located in the wheel cylinder piston, then secure the shoe in position with the retainer pin, spring and spring cup.

39 Install the upper and lower return springs, then tap the shoes to centralise them with the backplate.

40 Using a screwdriver, turn the strut adjuster wheel to expand the shoes until the brake drum just slides over the shoes.

41 Refit the brake drum as described in Section 8.

42 Repeat the above procedure on the remaining rear brake.

43 Once both sets of rear shoes have been renewed, adjust the lining-to-drum clearance by repeatedly depressing the brake pedal. Whilst depressing the pedal, have an assistant listen to the rear drums, to check that the adjuster strut is functioning correctly; if so, a clicking sound will be emitted by the strut as the pedal is depressed.

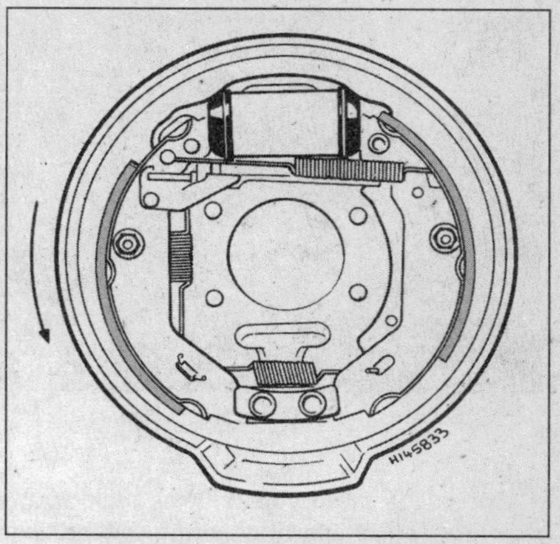

5.25 Correct fitted positions of Lucas/Girling rear brake components

Arrow indicates direction of wheel rotation

44 Check and, if necessary, adjust the handbrake as described in Chapter 1A or 1B.

45 On completion, check the hydraulic fluid level as described in *"Weekly checks"*.

6 Rear brake pads - renewal

Warning: Renew BOTH sets of rear brake pads at the same time - NEVER renew the pads on only one wheel, as uneven braking may result. Dust created by wear of the pads may contain asbestos, which is a health hazard. Never blow it out with compressed air, and don't inhale any of it. An approved filtering mask should be worn when working on the brakes. DO NOT use petrol or petroleum-based solvents to clean brake parts; use brake cleaner or methylated spirit only.

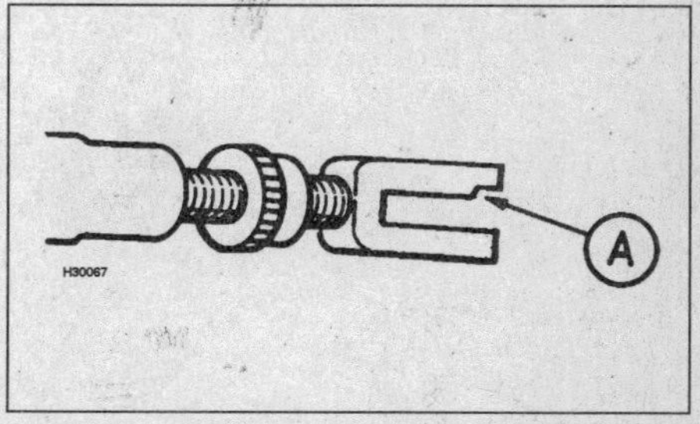

5.36 On Lucas/Girling rear brake shoes, adjuster strut fork cut-out (A) must engage with leading shoe adjusting lever on refitting

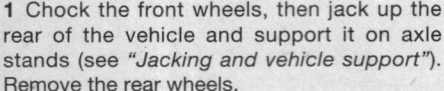

6.2a Extract the spring clip . . .

6.2b . . . then slide out the pad retaining plate . . .

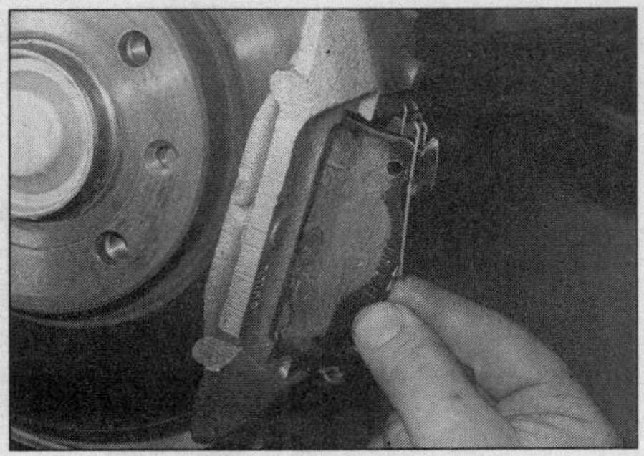

6.3 . . . and withdraw the brake pads from the caliper

1 Chock the front wheels, then jack up the rear of the vehicle and support it on axle stands (see *"Jacking and vehicle support"*). Remove the rear wheels.

2 Extract the small spring clip from the pad retaining plate, and then slide the plate out of the caliper **(see illustrations)**. Discard the spring clip - a new one must be used on refitting.

3 Using pliers if necessary, withdraw both the inner and outer pads from the caliper **(see illustration)**. Make a note of the correct fitted position of the anti-rattle springs, and remove the springs from each pad.

4 First measure the thickness of the friction material of each brake pad. If either pad is worn at any point to the specified minimum thickness or less, all four pads must be renewed. Also, the pads should be renewed if any are fouled with oil or grease; there is no satisfactory way of degreasing friction material, once contaminated. If any of the brake pads are worn unevenly, or fouled with oil or grease, trace and rectify the cause before reassembly. New brake pads and spring kits are available from Citroën dealers.

5 If the brake pads are still serviceable, carefully clean them using a clean, fine wire brush or similar, paying particular attention to the sides and back of the metal backing. Clean out the grooves in the friction material, and pick out any large embedded particles of dirt or debris. Carefully clean the pad locations in the caliper body/mounting bracket.

6 Prior to fitting the pads, check that the guide sleeves are free to slide easily in the caliper body, and check that the rubber guide sleeve gaiters are undamaged. Brush the dust and dirt from the caliper and piston, but **do not** inhale it, as it is injurious to health. Inspect the dust seal around the piston for damage, and the piston for evidence of fluid leaks, corrosion or damage. If attention to any of these components is necessary, refer to Section 12.

7 If new brake pads are to be fitted, it will be necessary to retract the piston fully into the caliper bore, by rotating it in a clockwise direction. This can be achieved using a suitable square-section bar, such as the shaft of a screwdriver, which locates snugly in the caliper piston slots **(see illustration)**. Provided that the master cylinder reservoir has not been overfilled with hydraulic fluid, there should be no spillage, but keep a careful watch on the fluid level while retracting the piston. If the fluid level rises above the "MAX" level line at any time, the surplus should be siphoned off, or ejected via a plastic tube connected to the bleed screw (see Section 2).

6.7 Retract the piston using a square-section bar . . .

Warning: Do not syphon the fluid by mouth, as it is poisonous; use a syringe or an old poultry baster.

8 Position the caliper piston so that its piston reference slot (A) is positioned horizontally, above or below the piston groove (B); this is necessary to ensure that the lug on the inner pad will locate with the caliper piston slot on installation **(see illustration)**.

9 The brake pad with the lug on its backing plate is the inner pad. Refit the anti-rattle springs to the pads, so that when the pads are fitted in the caliper, the spring end will be located at the opposite end of the pad, in relation to the pad retaining plate **(see illustration)**.

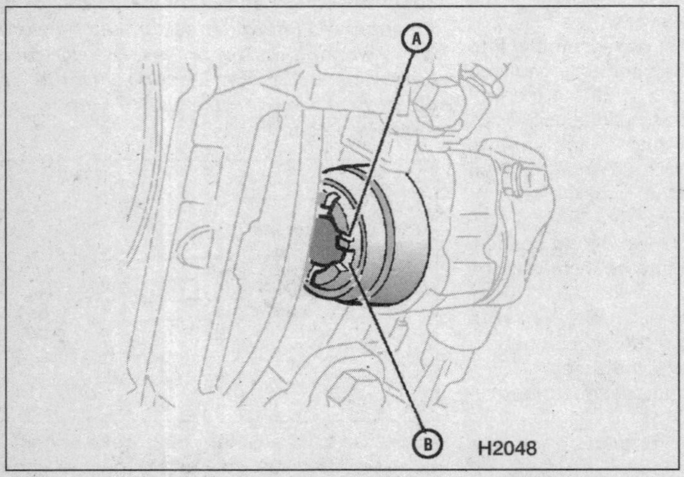

6.8 . . . and position the piston so that the reference slot (A) is positioned horizontally above or below the piston groove (B)

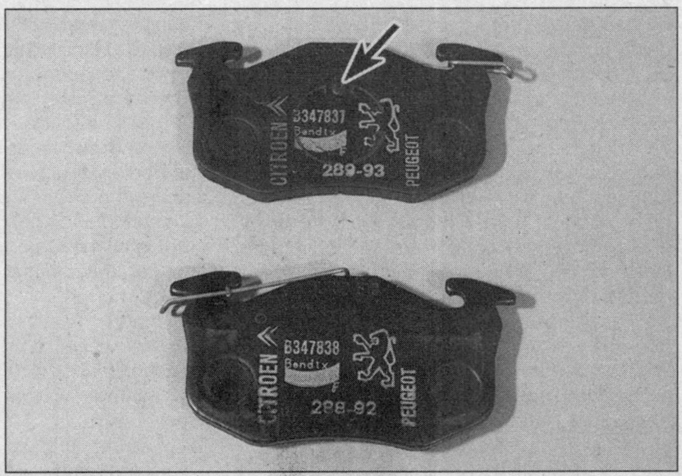

6.9 Inner brake pad can be identified by its locating lug (arrowed). Note the correct fitted positions of the anti-rattle springs

10 Locate the outer brake pad in the caliper body, ensuring that its friction material is against the brake disc. Slide the inner pad into position in the caliper, ensuring that the lug on its backing plate is aligned with the slot in the caliper piston **(see illustration)**.

11 Ensure that the anti-rattle spring ends on both pads are correctly positioned, then slide the retaining plate into place, and secure it in position with a new spring clip. It may be necessary to file an entry chamfer on the edge of the retaining plate, to enable it to be fitted without difficulty.

12 Depress the brake pedal repeatedly until the pads are pressed into firm contact with the brake disc, and normal (non-assisted) pedal pressure is restored. Check that the inner pad lug is correctly engaged with one of the caliper piston slots.

13 Repeat the above procedure on the remaining rear brake caliper.

14 Check the handbrake cable adjustment as described in Chapter 1A or 1B, then refit the roadwheels and lower the vehicle to the ground. Tighten the roadwheel bolts to the specified torque setting.

15 Check the hydraulic fluid level as described in *"Weekly checks"*.

16 New pads will not give full braking efficiency until they have bedded-in. Be prepared for this, and avoid hard braking as far as possible for the first hundred miles or so after pad renewal.

7 Front brake disc - inspection, removal and refitting

Note: *Before starting work, refer to the warning at the beginning of Section 4 concerning the dangers of asbestos dust.*

Inspection

Note: *If either disc requires renewal, BOTH should be renewed at the same time, to ensure even and consistent braking. New brake pads should also be fitted.*

1 Apply the handbrake, then jack up the front of the vehicle and support it on axle stands (see *"Jacking and vehicle support"*). Remove the appropriate front roadwheel.

6.10 Install the inner pad, ensuring its locating lug is correctly engaged in the piston slot

2 Slowly rotate the brake disc so that the full area of both sides can be checked; remove the brake pads (see Section 4) if better access is required to the inboard surface. Light scoring is normal in the area swept by the brake pads, but if heavy scoring or cracks are found, the disc must be renewed.

3 It is normal to find a lip of rust and brake dust around the disc's perimeter; this can be scraped off if required. If, however, a lip has formed due to excessive wear of the brake pad swept area, then the disc's thickness must be measured using a micrometer **(see illustration)**. Take measurements at several places around the disc, at the inside and outside of the pad swept area; if the disc has worn at any point to the specified minimum thickness or less, the disc must be renewed.

4 If the disc is thought to be warped, it can be checked for run-out. Either use a dial gauge mounted on any convenient fixed point, while the disc is slowly rotated **(see illustration)**, or use feeler blades to measure (at several points all around the disc) the clearance between the disc and a fixed point, such as the caliper mounting bracket. If the measurements obtained are at the specified maximum or beyond, the disc is excessively warped, and must be renewed; however, it is worth checking first that the hub bearing is in good condition (Chapters 1A or 1B and/or 10). Also try the effect of removing the disc and turning it through 180°, to reposition it on the hub; if the run-out is still excessive, the disc must be renewed.

5 Check the disc for cracks, especially

7.3 Using a micrometer to measure disc thickness

around the wheel bolt holes, and any other wear or damage, and renew if necessary.

Removal

6 Remove the brake pads as described in Section 4.

7 On models with ventilated discs, the brake caliper must be removed as described in Section 10 in order to allow sufficient clearance to remove the disc. There is no need to disconnect the brake fluid hose from the caliper; as long as the caliper is supported with wire or string, so that the hose is not strained.

8 Use chalk or paint to mark the relationship of the disc to the hub, then remove the screw(s) securing the brake disc to the hub, and withdraw the disc **(see illustrations)**. Note that it may be necessary to use an impact screwdriver to free the disc securing screw(s). If the disc is tight, lightly tap its rear face with a hide or plastic mallet. Where applicable (if the brake caliper is still fitted), tilt the disc as necessary to clear the hub and caliper.

Refitting

9 Ensure that the mating faces of the disc and the hub are clean and flat. If necessary, wipe the mating surfaces clean.

10 Refit the disc, then refit and securely tighten the disc retaining screw(s).

11 If a new disc has been fitted, use a suitable solvent to wipe any preservative coating from the disc.

12 Where applicable, refit the caliper as described in Section 10.

13 Refit the brake pads (see Section 4).

7.4 Checking disc run-out using a dial gauge

7.8a Using an impact screwdriver to free a brake disc securing screw

7.8b Removing a brake disc - model with three-bolt hub

8.2 Tapping off the dust cap

8.4a Remove the hub nut . . .

8.4b . . . and withdraw the thrustwasher

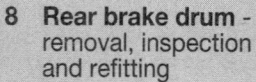

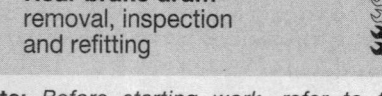

8 Rear brake drum - removal, inspection and refitting

Note: *Before starting work, refer to the warning at the beginning of Section 5 concerning the dangers of asbestos dust.*
Note: *A new rear hub nut and dust cap must be used on refitting.*

Removal

1 Chock the front wheels, then jack up the rear of the vehicle and support it on axle stands (see *"Jacking and vehicle support"*). Remove the appropriate rear wheel.

2 Using a hammer and a large flat-bladed screwdriver, carefully tap and prise the dust cap out of the centre of the brake drum **(see illustration)**. Discard the cap - a new one must be used on refitting.

3 Using a hammer and a suitable cold chisel or punch, relieve the staking on the driveshaft nut.

> ***Warning: Wear suitable eye protection.***

4 Using a socket and long bar, slacken and remove the rear hub nut, and withdraw the thrustwasher **(see illustrations)**. Discard the hub nut - a new nut must used on refitting.

5 It should now be possible to withdraw the brake drum assembly from the stub axle by hand **(see illustration)**. It may be difficult to remove the drum, due to the tightness of the hub bearing on the stub axle, or due to the brake shoes binding on the inner circumference of the drum. If the bearing is tight, tap the periphery of the drum using a hide or plastic mallet, or use a universal puller, secured to the drum with the wheel bolts, to pull it off. If the brake shoes are binding, first check that the handbrake is fully released, then proceed as follows.

6 Insert a screwdriver through one of the wheel bolt holes in the brake drum, so that it contacts the handbrake shoe adjuster lever on the leading brake shoe. Push the lever to release the ratchet until the brake shoes are fully retracted **(see illustration)**. The brake drum can now be withdrawn.

Inspection

Note: *If either drum requires renewal, BOTH should be renewed at the same time, to ensure even and consistent braking. New brake shoes should also be fitted.*

7 Working carefully, remove all traces of brake dust from the drum, but *avoid inhaling the dust, as it is a health hazard.*

8 Clean the outside of the drum, and check it for obvious signs of wear or damage, such as cracks around the roadwheel bolt holes; renew the drum if necessary.

9 Carefully examine the inside of the drum. Light scoring of the friction surface is normal, but if heavy scoring is found, the drum must be renewed. It is usual to find a lip on the drum's inboard edge which consists of a mixture of rust and brake dust; this should be scraped away, to leave a smooth surface which can be polished with fine (120- to 150-grade) emery paper. If, however, the lip is due to the friction surface being recessed by excessive wear, then the drum must be renewed.

10 If the drum is thought to be excessively worn, or oval, its internal diameter must be measured at several points using an internal micrometer. Take measurements in pairs, the second at right-angles to the first, and compare the two, to check for signs of ovality. Provided that it does not enlarge the drum to beyond the specified maximum diameter, it may be possible to have the drum refinished by skimming or grinding; if this is not possible, the drums on both sides must be renewed. Note that if the drum is to be skimmed, BOTH drums must be refinished, to maintain a consistent internal diameter on both sides.

11 Check the condition of the oil seal on the stub axle, and renew if necessary. To renew the oil seal, simply prise the old seal from the stub axle, then push the new seal into position until it is seated on the spacer. At the same time, check the condition of the oil seal seating ring in the rear of the drum, and if any signs of wear or damage are present, renew the ring (if the surface of the ring is damaged, this is likely to quickly result in damage to the oil seal).

Refitting

12 If a new brake drum is to be installed, use a suitable solvent to remove any preservative coating that may have been applied to its internal friction surfaces. Note that it may also be necessary to shorten the adjuster strut length, by rotating the strut wheel, to allow the drum to pass over the brake shoes.

13 Ensure that the handbrake lever stop-peg is correctly repositioned against the edge of the brake shoe web **(see illustration)**, then apply a smear of clean engine oil to the stub axle, and slide on the drum assembly.

8.5 Withdrawing the brake drum

8.6 Using a screwdriver to release the shoe adjuster mechanism and retract the shoes - four-bolt model shown

8.13 Ensure that the handbrake lever stop-peg (arrowed) is positioned against the edge of the shoe web

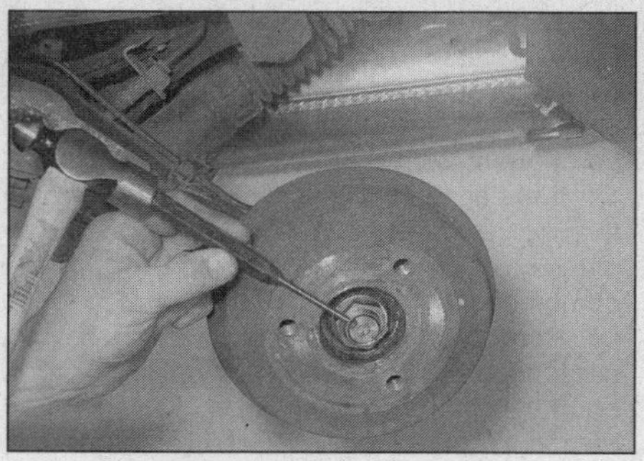

8.14 Stake the nut in position

14 Fit the thrustwasher and new hub nut, and tighten the hub nut to the specified torque. Stake the nut firmly into the groove on the stub axle, to secure it in position **(see illustration)**.

15 Tap the new dust cover into place in the centre of the brake drum **(see illustration)**.

16 Depress the footbrake several times to operate the self-adjusting mechanism.

17 Repeat the above procedure on the remaining rear brake assembly (where necessary), then check and, if necessary, adjust the handbrake cable as described in Chapter 1A or 1B.

18 On completion, refit the roadwheel(s), then lower the vehicle to the ground and tighten the roadwheel bolts to the specified torque.

9.4 Removing a rear brake disc

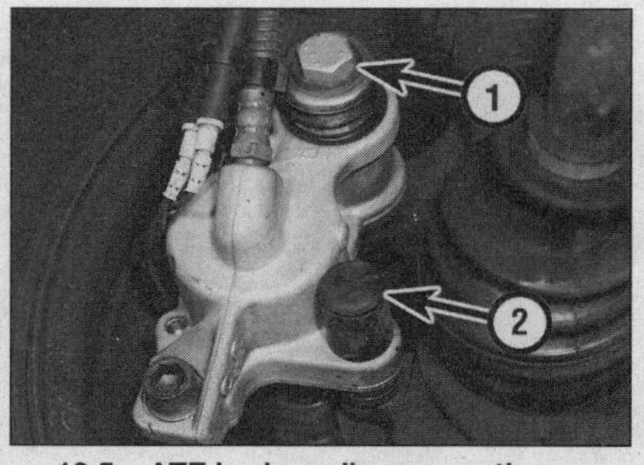

10.5a ATE brake caliper mountings - models with solid discs

1 Upper (M12) mounting bolt
2 Lower (M8) mounting bolt dust cover

8.15 Tap on the new dust cap

9 Rear brake disc - inspection, removal and refitting

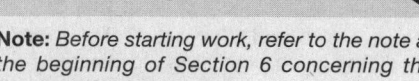

Note: *Before starting work, refer to the note at the beginning of Section 6 concerning the dangers of asbestos dust.*

Inspection

Note: *If either disc requires renewal, BOTH should be renewed at the same time, to ensure even and consistent braking. New brake pads should also be fitted.*

1 Firmly chock the front wheels, then jack up the rear of the car and support it on axle stands (see *"Jacking and vehicle support"*). Remove the appropriate rear roadwheel.

2 Inspect the disc as described in Section 7.

Removal

3 Remove the brake pads as described in Section 6.

4 Use chalk or paint to mark the relationship of the disc to the hub, then remove the screw(s) securing the brake disc to the hub, and remove the disc **(see illustration)**. If it is tight, lightly tap its rear face with a hide or plastic mallet.

Refitting

5 Refitting is the reverse of the removal procedure, noting the following points:

a) Ensure that the mating surfaces of the disc and hub are clean and flat.

b) Align (if applicable) the marks made on removal, and securely tighten the disc retaining screw(s).

c) If a new disc has been fitted, use a suitable solvent to wipe any preservative coating from the disc, before refitting the caliper.

d) Refit the brake pads as described in Section 6.

e) Refit the roadwheel, then lower the vehicle to the ground and tighten the roadwheel bolts to the specified torque.

10 Front brake caliper - removal, overhaul and refitting

Note: *Before starting work, refer to the warning at the beginning of Section 2 concerning the dangers of hydraulic fluid, and to the warning at the beginning of Section 4 concerning the dangers of asbestos dust. If the caliper is merely being unbolted for other servicing work, insert a piece of wood into the caliper body, to prevent the piston being accidentally ejected.*

Removal

1 Apply the handbrake, then jack up the front of the vehicle and support it on axle stands (see *"Jacking and vehicle support"*). Remove the appropriate roadwheel.

2 Minimise fluid loss by first removing the master cylinder reservoir cap, then tightening it down onto a piece of polythene, to obtain an airtight seal. Alternatively, use a brake hose clamp, a G-clamp or a similar tool to clamp the flexible hose running to the caliper.

3 Remove the brake pads as described in Section 4.

4 Clean the area around the union, then loosen the brake hose union nut.

5 Where applicable, remove the dust cover(s) from the caliper securing bolts, then slacken the two bolts securing the caliper assembly to the hub carrier, and remove them. On models with Bendix calipers, recover the mounting plate from the bolts, noting which way around the plate is fitted **(see illustrations)**.

6 Lift the caliper assembly away from the brake disc **(see illustration)**, and unscrew it from the end of the brake hose.

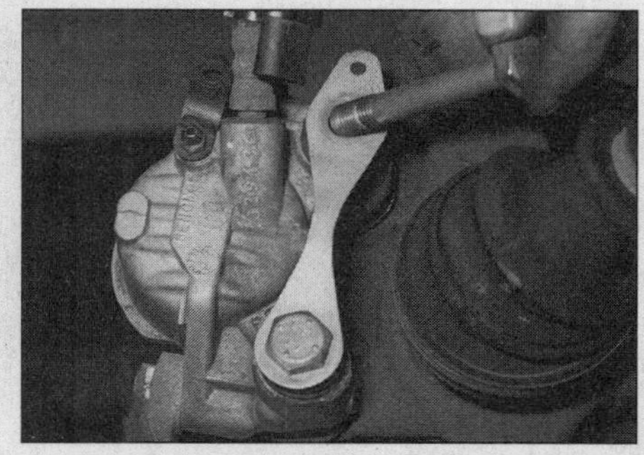

10.5b Removing a brake caliper mounting bolt - Bendix caliper

10.6 Withdrawing a brake caliper

Overhaul

7 With the caliper on the bench, wipe away all traces of dust and dirt, but *avoid inhaling the dust, as it is a health hazard.*

8 Where necessary, use a small flat-bladed screwdriver to carefully prise the dust seal retaining clip out of the caliper bore **(see illustration)**.

9 Withdraw the partially-ejected piston from the caliper body, and remove the dust seal. The piston can be withdrawn by hand, or if necessary pushed out by applying compressed air to the brake hose union hole. Only low pressure should be required, such as is generated by a foot pump.

Caution: Be careful! The piston may be ejected with some force.

10 Using a small screwdriver, extract the piston hydraulic seal, taking great care not to damage the caliper bore.

11 Where applicable, prise off the retaining clips, then withdraw the guide sleeves/pins from the caliper body/mounting bracket (as applicable), and remove the rubber gaiters.

12 Thoroughly clean all components, using only methylated spirit, isopropyl alcohol or clean hydraulic fluid as a cleaning medium. Never use mineral-based solvents such as petrol or paraffin, as they will attack the hydraulic system's rubber components. Dry the components immediately, using compressed air or a clean, lint-free cloth. Use compressed air to blow clear the fluid passages.

Warning: Wear eye protection when using compressed air!

13 Check all components, and renew any that are worn or damaged. Check particularly the cylinder bore and piston; these should be renewed (note that this means the renewal of the complete body assembly) if they are scratched, worn or corroded in any way. Similarly check the condition of the guide sleeves/pins and their bores in the caliper body/mounting bracket (as applicable); both sleeves/pins should be undamaged and (when cleaned) a reasonably tight sliding fit in the body/mounting bracket bores. If there is any doubt about the condition of any component, renew it.

14 If the assembly is fit for further use, obtain the appropriate repair kit; the components are available from Citroën dealers in various combinations.

15 Renew all rubber seals, dust covers and caps disturbed on dismantling as a matter of course; these should never be re-used.

16 On reassembly, ensure that all components are absolutely clean and dry.

17 Soak the piston and the new piston (fluid) seal in clean hydraulic fluid. Smear clean fluid on the cylinder bore surface.

18 Fit the new piston (fluid) seal, using only your fingers (no tools) to manipulate it into the cylinder bore groove. Fit the new dust seal to the piston, and refit the piston to the cylinder bore using a twisting motion; ensure that the piston enters squarely into the bore. Press the piston fully into the bore, then press the dust seal into the caliper body.

19 Where fitted, install the dust seal retaining clip, ensuring that it is correctly seated in the caliper groove.

20 Apply the grease supplied in the repair kit, or a copper-based high-temperature brake grease or anti-seize compound (eg Duckhams Copper 10), to the guide sleeves/pins. Fit the guide sleeves/pins to the caliper body/mounting bracket, and fit the new rubber gaiters, ensuring that they are correctly located in the grooves on both the sleeve/pin and body/mounting bracket (as applicable).

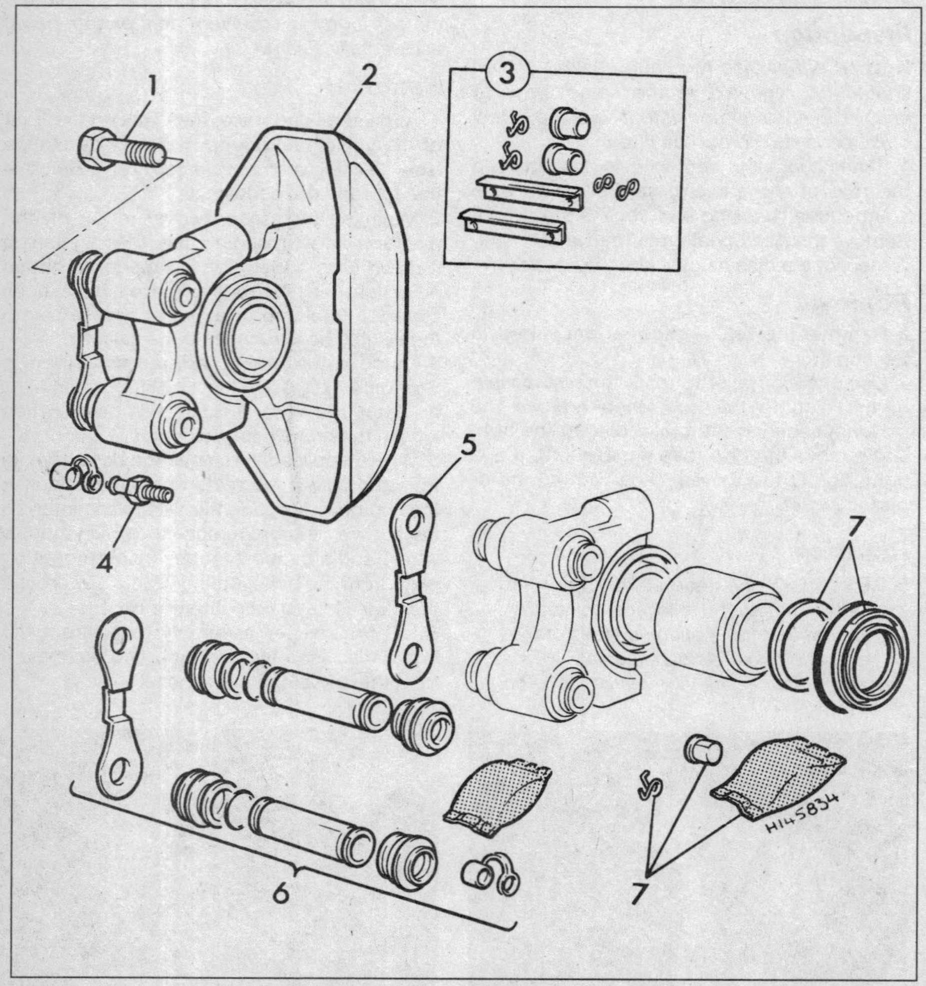

10.8 Bendix brake caliper components

1 *Mounting bolt*
2 *Caliper assembly*
3 *Pad retaining plate*
4 *Bleed screw*
5 *Mounting plate*
6 *Guide pin kit with grease*
7 *Caliper repair kit with grease*

Refitting

21 Screw the caliper fully onto the flexible hose union, then position the caliper over the brake disc.

22 If the threads of the new caliper mounting bolts are not already pre-coated with locking compound, apply a suitable locking compound to them. Refit the bolts, along with the mounting plate on models with Bendix calipers, ensuring that the plate is fitted so that its bend curves away from the caliper body **(see illustration)**. Tighten the caliper bolts to the specified torque. Where applicable, refit the dust cover(s) to the bolt(s).

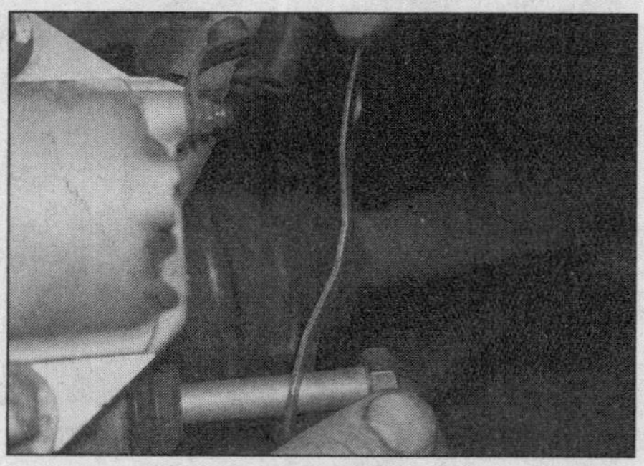

10.22 The mounting plate fits with the bend curving away from the caliper body - Bendix caliper

23 Securely tighten the brake hose union nut, then refit the brake pads as described in Section 4.

24 Remove the brake hose clamp, or remove the polythene from the fluid reservoir, as applicable, and bleed the hydraulic system as described in Section 2. Note that, providing the precautions described were taken to minimise brake fluid loss, it should only be necessary to bleed the relevant front brake circuit.

25 Refit the roadwheel, then lower the vehicle to the ground and tighten the roadwheel bolts to the specified torque.

11 Rear wheel cylinder - removal, overhaul and refitting

Removal

1 Remove the brake drum as described in Section 8.

2 Using pliers, carefully unhook the brake shoe upper return spring, and remove it from both brake shoes (note the orientation of the spring, to ensure correct refitting). Pull the upper ends of the shoes away from the wheel cylinder, to disengage them from the pistons.

HAYNES HiNT ***Pull the handbrake lever on the trailing shoe fully forwards, so that the upper ends of the shoes are clear of the wheel cylinder. Wedge the lever in this position using a block of wood.***

3 Minimise fluid loss by first removing the master cylinder reservoir cap, then tightening it down onto a piece of polythene, to obtain an airtight seal. Alternatively, use a brake hose clamp, a G-clamp or a similar tool to clamp the flexible hose (connected between the metal pipe sections on the rear axle and trailing arm) at the nearest convenient point to the wheel cylinder **(see illustration)**.

4 Wipe away all traces of dirt around the brake pipe union at the rear of the wheel cylinder, and unscrew the union nut **(see illustration)**. Carefully ease the pipe out of the wheel cylinder, and plug or tape over its end to prevent dirt entry. Wipe off any spilt fluid immediately.

5 Unscrew the two wheel cylinder retaining bolts from the rear of the backplate, and remove the cylinder, taking great care not to allow surplus hydraulic fluid to contaminate the brake shoe linings.

Overhaul

Non-ABS models

6 On non-ABS models, the rear brake pressure-regulating valves are integral with the rear wheel cylinders, and the cylinders **must not** be dismantled. No spare parts are available, and if a cylinder is faulty or damaged, the complete assembly must be renewed.

ABS models

7 Clean the exterior of the cylinder to remove all traces of dirt and brake dust.

8 Pull the dust seals from the ends of the cylinder **(see illustration)**.

9 Extract the pistons, seals spring seats, and return spring, noting the locations of all components to ensure correct refitting.

10 Examine the surfaces of the cylinder bore and pistons for signs of scoring and corrosion, and if evident, renew the complete wheel cylinder. If the components are in good condition, discard the seals and obtain a repair kit, which will contain all the necessary renewable components.

11 Clean the pistons and the cylinder with methylated spirit or clean brake fluid, and reassemble in the reverse order to dismantling, making sure that the components are fitted in the correct sequence and orientated correctly, as noted before removal. Ensure that the lips of the seals face into the cylinder.

11.3 To minimise fluid loss, fit a brake hose clamp to the flexible hose

12 On completion, wipe the outer surfaces of the dust seals to remove any excess brake fluid.

Refitting

13 Clean the backplate, then place the wheel cylinder in position, and refit the securing bolts.

14 Reconnect the brake pipe to the rear of the wheel cylinder, taking care not to allow dirt into the system.

15 Where applicable, release the handbrake lever on the trailing shoe, and reposition the upper ends of the shoes to engage them with the wheel cylinder pistons.

16 Refit the brake shoe upper return spring, ensuring that it is orientated as noted before removal.

17 Refit the brake drum as described in Section 8.

18 On completion, remove the brake hose clamp, or remove the polythene from the fluid reservoir, as applicable, and bleed the hydraulic system as described in Section 2. Note that, providing the precautions described were taken to minimise brake fluid loss, it should only be necessary to bleed the relevant rear brake circuit.

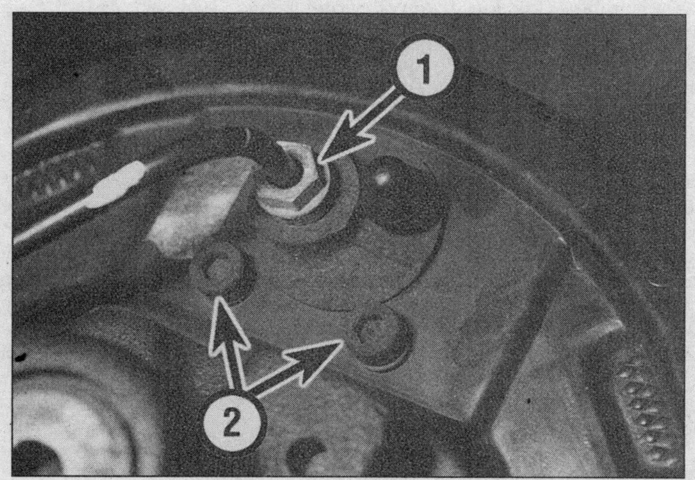

11.4 Wheel cylinder brake pipe union nut (1) and wheel cylinder retaining bolts (2)

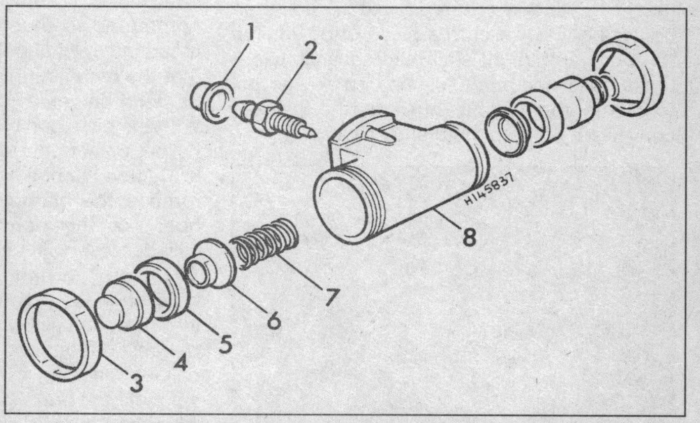

11.8 Exploded view of rear wheel cylinder - ABS model

1 Bleed screw dust cover
2 Bleed screw
3 Dust seal
4 Piston
5 Seal
6 Spring seat
7 Return spring
8 Cylinder body

9

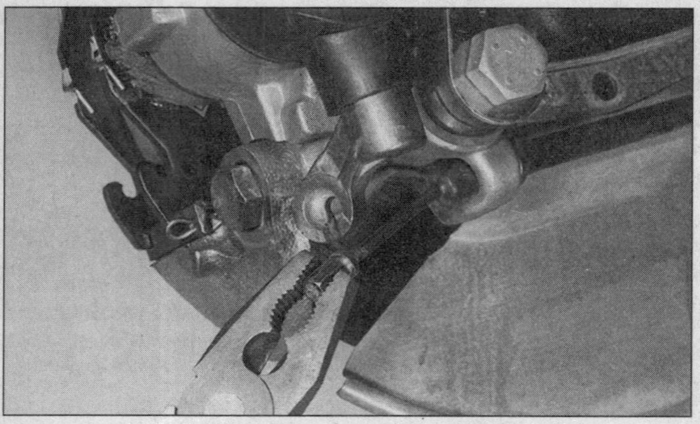

12.3a Disconnect the handbrake inner cable from the caliper lever . . .

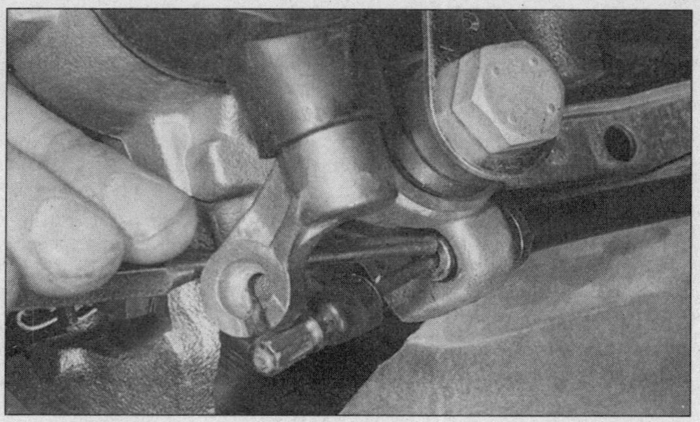

12.3b . . . then tap the outer cable out from the caliper body

12 Rear brake caliper - removal, overhaul and refitting

Note: *Before starting work, refer to the note at the beginning of Section 2 concerning the dangers of hydraulic fluid, and to the warning at the beginning of Section 6 concerning the dangers of asbestos dust. If the caliper is merely being unbolted for other servicing work, insert a piece of wood into the caliper body, to prevent the piston being accidentally ejected.*

Removal

1 Chock the front wheels, then jack up the rear of the vehicle and support on axle stands (see *"Jacking and vehicle support"*). Remove the relevant rear wheel.
2 Remove the brake pads (see Section 6).
3 Ensure that the handbrake is fully released, then free the handbrake inner cable from the caliper handbrake operating lever. Tap the outer cable out of its bracket on the caliper body **(see illustrations)**.
4 Minimise fluid loss by first removing the master cylinder reservoir cap, and then tightening it down onto a piece of polythene, to obtain an airtight seal. Alternatively, use a brake hose clamp, a G-clamp or a similar tool to clamp the flexible hose at the nearest convenient point to the brake caliper.

13.1 Disconnect the wiring plug from the brake fluid reservoir

5 Wipe away all traces of dirt around the brake pipe union on the caliper, and slacken the union nut.
6 Slacken the two bolts securing the caliper assembly to the trailing arm, and remove them along with the mounting plate, noting which way around the plate is fitted. Lift the caliper assembly away from the brake disc, and unscrew it from the end of the brake hose.

Overhaul

7 The caliper can be overhauled after obtaining the relevant repair kit from a Citroën dealer. Ensure that the correct repair kit is obtained for the caliper being worked on. Note the locations of all components (this applies particularly if the handbrake mechanism is dismantled) to ensure correct refitting, and lubricate the new seals using brake fluid. Follow the assembly instructions supplied with the repair kit.

Refitting

8 Screw the caliper fully onto the brake hose, then position the caliper over the brake disc. If the threads of the new caliper mounting bolts are not already pre-coated with locking compound, apply a suitable locking compound to them. Install the new caliper mounting bolts and the mounting plate, noting that the mounting plate must be fitted so that its bend curves away from the caliper body. With the plate correctly positioned, tighten the caliper bolts to the specified torque.
9 Tighten the brake hose union securely, then remove the clamp from the flexible brake hose, or the polythene from the master cylinder reservoir (as applicable).
10 Insert the handbrake cable through its bracket on the caliper, and tap the outer cable into position using a hammer and suitable pin punch. Reconnect the inner cable to the caliper operating lever.
11 Refit the brake pads (see Section 6).
12 Bleed the hydraulic system as described in Section 2. Note that, providing the precautions described were taken to minimise brake fluid loss, it should only be necessary to bleed the relevant rear brake.
13 Repeatedly apply the brake pedal until normal (non-assisted) pedal pressure returns. Check and if necessary adjust the handbrake cable as described in Chapter 1A or 1B.
14 Refit the roadwheel, then lower the vehicle to the ground and tighten the wheel bolts to the specified torque. Finally, check the fluid level as described in *"Weekly checks"*.

13 Master cylinder - removal, overhaul and refitting

Note: *Before starting work, refer to the warning at the beginning of Section 2 concerning the dangers of hydraulic fluid.*

Removal

1 Remove the master cylinder fluid reservoir cap, and syphon the hydraulic fluid from the reservoir. Alternatively, open any convenient bleed screw in the system, and gently pump the brake pedal to expel the fluid through a plastic tube connected to the screw (see Section 2). Disconnect the wiring connector from the brake fluid level sender unit **(see illustration)**.

Warning: Do not syphon the fluid by mouth, as it is poisonous; use a syringe or an old poultry baster.

2 Wipe clean the area around the brake pipe unions on the side of the master cylinder, and place absorbent rags beneath the pipe unions to catch any surplus fluid. Make a note of the correct fitted positions of the unions, then unscrew the union nuts and carefully withdraw the pipes. Plug or tape over the pipe ends and master cylinder orifices, to minimise the loss of brake fluid, and to prevent the entry of dirt into the system. Wash off any spilt fluid immediately with cold water.
3 Slacken and remove the two nuts securing the master cylinder to the vacuum servo unit, then withdraw the unit from the engine compartment.
4 Where applicable, recover the seal from the rear of the master cylinder, and discard it.

Overhaul

5 Pull the fluid reservoir from the top of the master cylinder. Prise the reservoir seals from the reservoir or the master cylinder, as applicable **(see illustration)**.

6 Using a wooden dowel, press the piston assembly into the master cylinder body, then extract the circlip from the end of the master cylinder bore.

7 Noting the order of removal, and the direction of fitting of each component, withdraw the washer and the piston assemblies with their springs and seals, tapping the body on to a clean wooden surface to dislodge them. If necessary, clamp the master cylinder body in a vice (fitted with soft jaw covers) and use compressed air (applied through the secondary circuit fluid port) to assist the removal of the secondary piston assembly.

⚠ ***Warning: Wear eye protection when using compressed air!***

8 Thoroughly clean all components, using only methylated spirit, isopropyl alcohol or clean hydraulic fluid as a cleaning medium. Never use mineral-based solvents such as petrol or paraffin, as they will attack the hydraulic system's rubber components. Dry the components immediately, using compressed air or a clean, lint-free cloth.

9 Check all components, and renew any that are worn or damaged. Check particularly the cylinder bores and pistons; the complete assembly should be renewed if these are scratched, worn or corroded. If there is any doubt about the condition of the assembly or of any of its components, renew it. Check that the cylinder body fluid passages are clear.

10 If the assembly is fit for further use, obtain a repair kit from your Citroën dealer; the kit consists of both piston assemblies and springs, complete with all seals and washers. Never re-use the old components.

11 Before reassembly, soak the pistons and the new seals in clean hydraulic fluid. Smear clean fluid into the cylinder bore.

12 Insert the piston assemblies into the cylinder bore, using a twisting motion to avoid trapping the seal lips. Ensure that all components are refitted in the correct order and the right way round, then fit the washer to the end of the primary piston. Where applicable, follow the assembly instructions supplied with the repair kit.

13 Press the piston assemblies fully into the bore using a clean wooden dowel, and secure them in position with the new circlip. Ensure that the circlip is correctly located in the groove in the cylinder bore.

14 Examine the fluid reservoir seals, and if necessary renew them. Fit the reservoir seals to the master cylinder body, then refit the reservoir.

Refitting

15 Remove all traces of dirt from the master cylinder and servo unit mating surfaces, and where applicable, fit a new seal between the master cylinder body and the servo.

16 Fit the master cylinder to the servo unit, ensuring that the servo unit pushrod enters the master cylinder bore centrally. Refit the master cylinder mounting nuts, and tighten them to the specified torque.

17 Wipe clean the brake pipe unions, then refit them to the correct master cylinder ports, as noted before removal, and tighten the union nuts securely.

18 Refill the master cylinder reservoir with new fluid, and bleed the complete hydraulic system as described in Section 2.

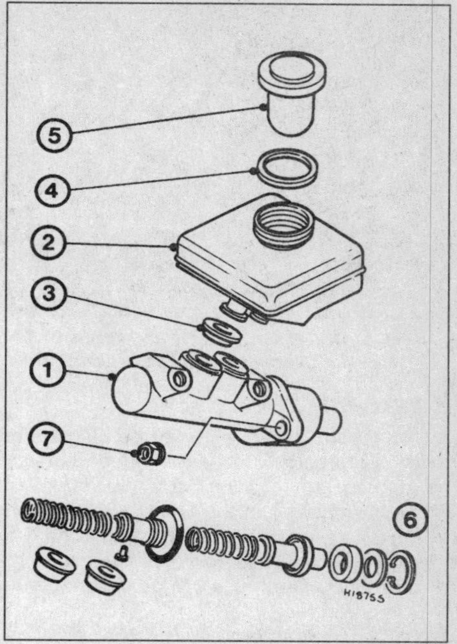

13.5 Exploded view of a typical master cylinder assembly

1 Master cylinder body
2 Fluid reservoir
3 Seal
4 Seal
5 Filler cap
6 Seal/piston kit (primary and secondary)
7 Securing nut

14 Brake pedal - removal and refitting

Removal

1 Remove retaining clips from the fabric panel at the bottom of the dashboard and remove the panel.

2 Remove the pivot bolt which secures the pedal to its mounting bracket and recover the return spring.

3 Withdraw the brake pedal-to-pushrod clevis pin before the brake pedal is removed.

Refitting

4 Refitting is the reverse of removal, but make sure that the return spring is fitted correctly.

15 Brake pedal-to-servo linkage (right-hand-drive models) - removal, overhaul and refitting

Removal

1 Removal of the servo-end linkage, and the main crossover linkage, is described in Section 16 as part of the vacuum servo unit removal and refitting procedure.

2 To remove the brake pedal bracket and linkage, proceed as follows.

3 Remove the brake and clutch pedals, with reference to Section 14 of this Chapter, and Chapter 6.

4 Where necessary for improved access, remove the inlet manifold as described in the relevant Part of Chapter 4.

5 Remove the linkage crosstube securing bolts (two at each end of the tube) **(see illustrations)**.

6 Unclip the plastic cover from the pedal end of the linkage, then slacken the link rod end nut sufficiently to disconnect the link rod end fitting from the pedal relay lever **(see illustrations)**. **Do not** move the inner nut on the link rod (this should be left in position to preserve the link rod adjustment).

7 Working in the engine compartment, unscrew the four nuts securing the pedal bracket to the bulkhead, and withdraw the bracket and linkage into the engine compartment.

15.5a Brake pedal linkage crosstube securing bolts at the pedal end . . .

15.5b . . . and at the servo end (arrowed) - right-hand-drive models

9

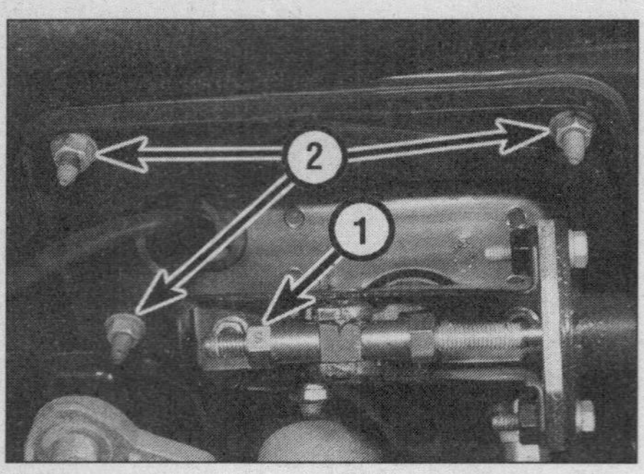

15.6a Link rod end nut (1) and three of the pedal bracket securing nuts (2)

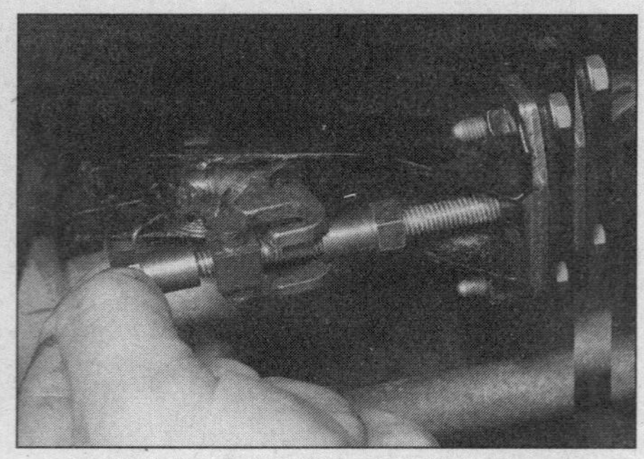

15.6b Disconnecting the link rod end fitting

Overhaul

8 If desired, the linkage can be dismantled with reference to the accompanying illustration, but if the link rod is to be removed, mark the position of the adjuster nuts before removal, to ensure that the adjustment is maintained on reassembly **(see illustration)**.

9 Individual spare parts can be obtained from a Citroën dealer.

10 When reassembling the linkage, grease all moving parts sparingly, and ensure that the adjustment nuts are refitted to the link rod in the positions noted before removal.

Refitting

11 Refitting is a reversal of removal, bearing in mind the following points:

a) Where removed, refit the inlet manifold as described in the relevant Part of Chapter 4.

b) Where applicable, refit the brake and clutch pedals with reference to Section 14 and Chapter 6.

c) Where applicable, refit the servo-end linkage, and the main crossover linkage, as described in Section 16.

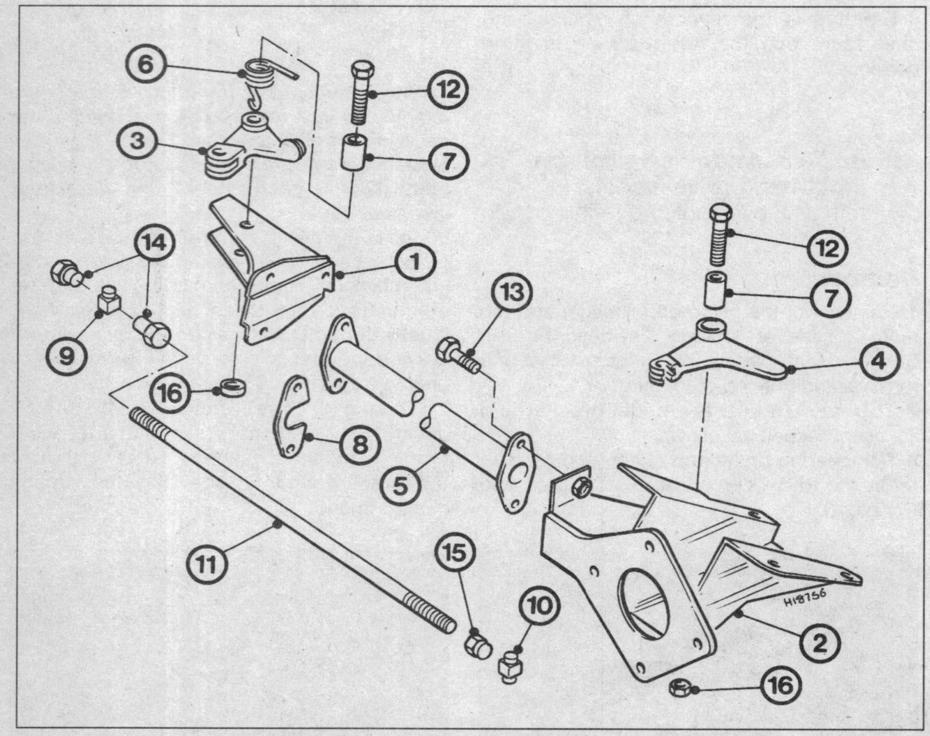

15.8 Exploded view of brake pedal-to-servo linkage - right-hand-drive models

1 Bracket
2 Servo mounting bracket
3 Pedal relay lever
4 Servo relay lever
5 Cross-shaft housing
6 Return spring
7 Spacer
8 Shim
9 Cross-shaft barrel
10 Cross-shaft barrel
11 Link rod
12 Bolt
13 Bolt
14 Adjuster nuts
15 Adjuster nut
16 Nut

16 Vacuum servo unit - testing, removal and refitting

Right-hand-drive models

Testing

1 To test the operation of the servo unit, with the engine switched off, depress the footbrake several times to exhaust the vacuum. Keep the pedal firmly depressed, and start the engine. As the engine starts, there should be a noticeable "give" in the brake pedal as the vacuum builds up. Allow the engine to run for at least two minutes, then switch it off. If the brake pedal is now depressed, it should feel normal, but further applications should result in the pedal feeling firmer, with the pedal stroke decreasing on each application.

2 If the servo does not operate as described, first inspect the servo unit check valve as described in Section 17. On diesel models, also check the operation of the vacuum pump, as described in Section 26.

3 If the servo unit still fails to operate satisfactorily, the fault lies within the unit itself. Repairs to the unit are not possible - if faulty, the servo unit must be renewed.

Removal

Note: *A new spring clip must be fitted to the servo pushrod clevis pin on refitting.*

4 If wished, to improve access, remove the battery as described in Chapter 5A. On diesel models, unclip the hand-priming bulb from its mountings, and move it out of the way **(see illustration)**.

5 Unclip any relevant hoses and/or wiring from the fusebox next to the servo, then unclip the fusebox, and move it clear of the working area **(see illustrations)**.

6 Where applicable, unscrew the two securing nuts **(see illustration)**, then disconnect the wiring plug and remove the inertia switch.

7 Where necessary for improved access, remove the inlet manifold as described in the relevant Part of Chapter 4.

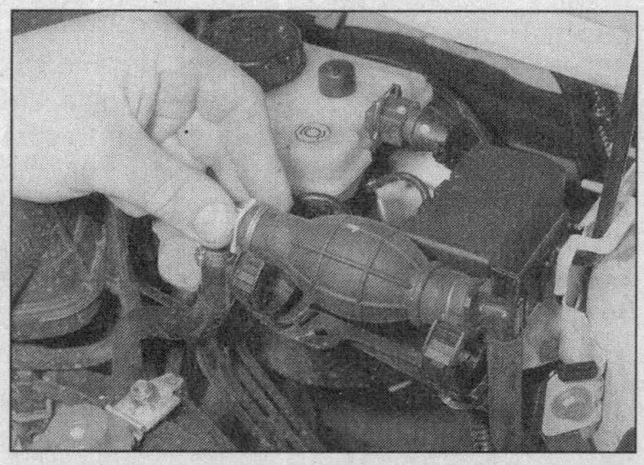

16.4 On diesel models, unclip the hand-priming bulb and move it out of the way

16.5a Using a screwdriver, release the clips . . .

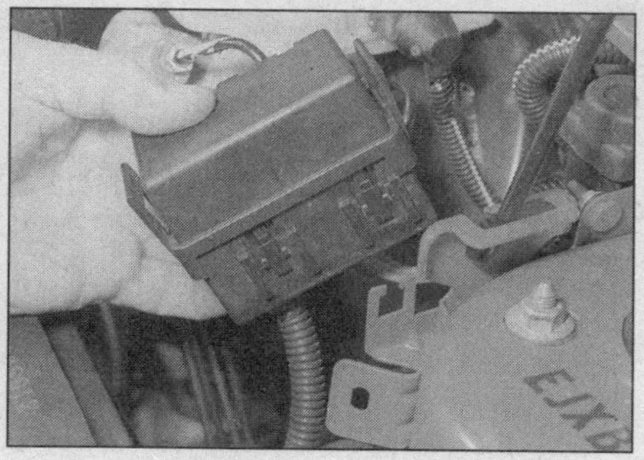

16.5b . . . and remove the fusebox next to the servo

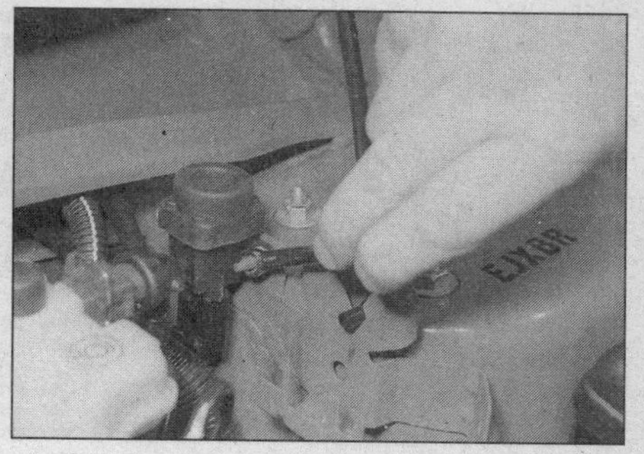

16.6 Unscrew the two securing nuts, and remove the inertia switch

8 Carefully pull the non-return valve from the front of the servo, leaving the vacuum hose connected.

9 Working under the servo, unclip the master cylinder brake fluid pipes from the supporting brackets, as applicable. On models with ABS, remove the module assembly (see section 24).

10 Unscrew the two master cylinder securing nuts, and detach the master cylinder from the servo **(see illustrations)**. Where applicable, recover the seal.

11 Carefully pull the master cylinder forwards from the servo, taking care not to strain the fluid pipes.

12 Unclip the plastic cover from the pedal end of the linkage, then slacken the link rod end nut sufficiently to disconnect the link rod end fitting from the pedal relay lever. **Do not** move the inner nut on the link rod (this should be left in position, to preserve the link rod adjustment).

13 Remove the linkage crosstube securing bolts (two at each end of the tube) **(see illustration)**.

14 Slide the link rod end fitting from the pedal relay lever.

15 Unscrew the four nuts securing the servo mounting bracket to the bulkhead, then carefully manipulate the servo and crossover linkage assembly from the engine compartment, taking care not to strain the master cylinder brake pipes.

16 Prise off the spring clip, and withdraw the clevis pin securing the servo pushrod to the crossover linkage.

17 Unscrew the four securing nuts, and withdraw the servo from the mounting bracket.

Refitting

18 Refitting is a reversal of removal, bearing in mind the following points:

a) Tighten all fixings to the specified torque (where given).

b) Where removed, refit the inlet manifold as described in the relevant Part of Chapter 4.

c) Where applicable, refit the servo-end linkage, and the main crossover linkage.

Left-hand-drive models

Testing

19 Proceed as described in paragraphs 1 to 3 inclusive.

Removal

Note: *A new spring clip must be fitted to the servo pushrod clevis pin on refitting.*

20 Proceed as described in paragraphs 4 to 10 inclusive, then proceed as follows.

21 Working inside the vehicle, remove the two push-in clips securing the front edge of the under-facia trim panel from the facia, and lower the panel.

22 Working in the footwell, unscrew the securing nut from the lower column pinch-bolt, then carefully tap the pinch-bolt from the universal joint.

23 Make alignment marks on the universal joint and the steering gear pinion, then push the universal joint upwards to separate it from the pinion. Manipulate the lower steering column as necessary for access to the brake pedal assembly.

24 Remove the spring clip from the end of the brake servo pushrod-to-brake pedal clevis pin, then withdraw the clevis pin.

25 Working in the engine compartment, remove the four securing nuts from the studs at the rear of the servo, then remove the servo from its mounting bracket.

Refitting

26 Refit the servo to its mounting bracket, and tighten the securing nuts.

27 Reconnect the servo pushrod to the pedal, and fit the clevis pin. Secure the clevis pin with a new spring clip.

28 Slide the column universal joint over steering gear pinion, ensuring that the marks made before removal are still aligned.

29 Fit a new lower column pinch-bolt and nut, ensuring that the lugs on the bolt engage with the cut-outs in the universal joint, and tighten the nut to the specified torque (see Chapter 10 Specifications).

30 Refit the under-facia trim panel.

31 Further refitting is a reversal of removal, but tighten all fixings to the specified torque. On diesel models, refit the inlet manifold as described in the relevant Part of Chapter 4.

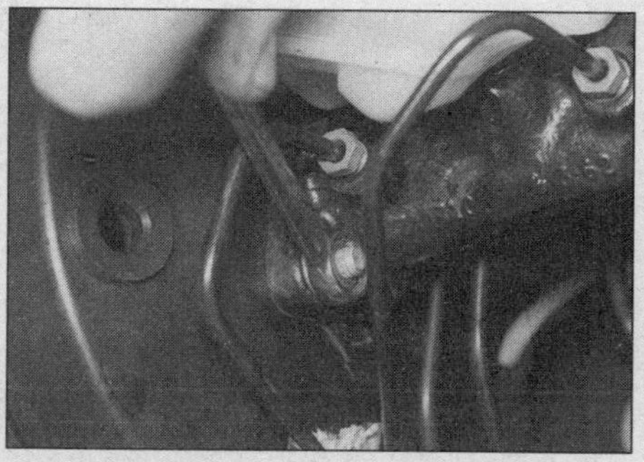

16.10a Unscrew the securing nuts . . .

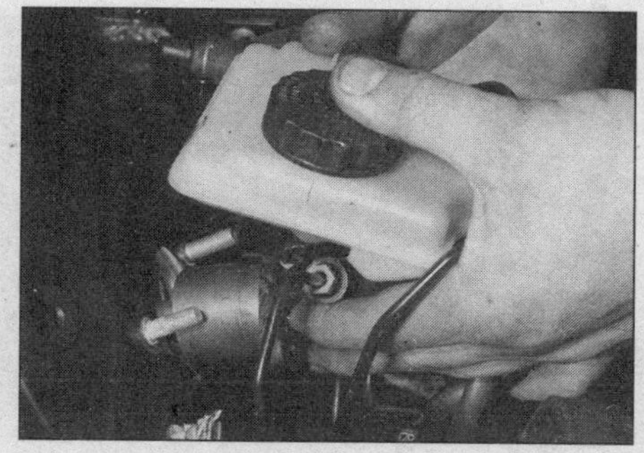

16.10b . . . and detach the master cylinder from the servo

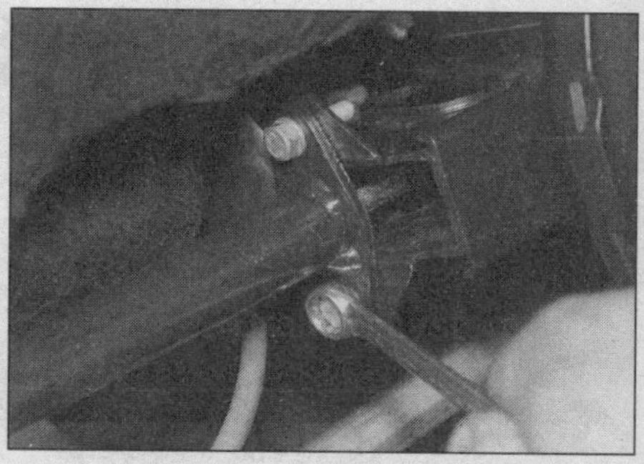

16.13 Unscrewing a linkage crosstube securing bolt

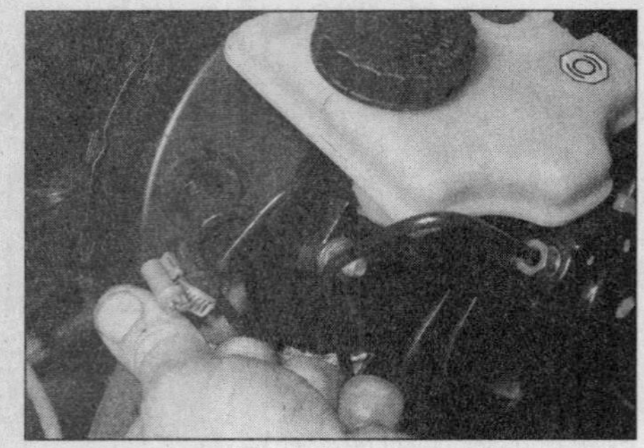

17.1 Pulling the check valve from the brake servo

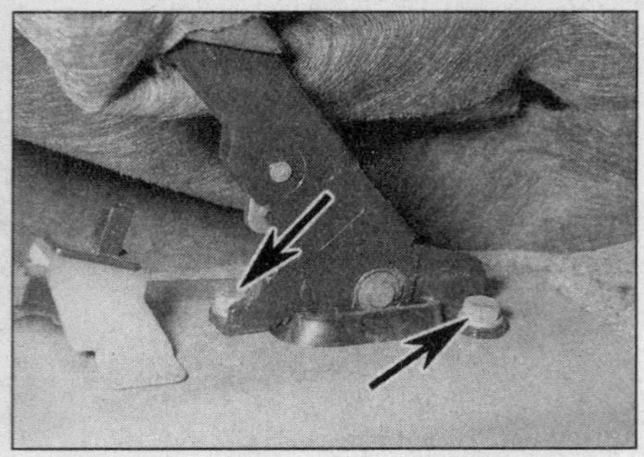

18.3 Handbrake lever securing bolts (arrowed)

17 Vacuum servo unit check valve - removal, testing and refitting

Removal

1 Withdraw the valve from its rubber sealing grommet, using a pulling and twisting motion. Remove the grommet from the servo **(see illustration)**.

2 Slacken or release the retaining clip (where fitted), and disconnect the vacuum hose from the valve.

Testing

3 Examine the check valve for signs of damage, and renew if necessary. The valve may be tested by blowing through it in both directions. Air should flow through the valve in one direction only - when blown through from the servo unit end of the valve. Renew the valve if this is not the case.

4 Examine the rubber sealing grommet and flexible vacuum hose for signs of damage or deterioration, and renew as necessary.

Refitting

5 Fit the sealing grommet into position in the servo unit.

6 Carefully ease the check valve into position, taking great care not to displace or damage the grommet. Reconnect the vacuum hose to the valve and, where necessary, securely tighten its retaining clip.

7 On completion, start the engine and check the check valve-to-servo unit connection for signs of air leaks. Test the servo operation as described at the start of Section 16.

18 Handbrake lever - removal and refitting

Removal

1 Working under the vehicle, slacken the adjuster nut on the cable equaliser assembly until the rear handbrake cables can be disengaged from the equaliser plate.

2 The handbrake lever securing bolts are well hidden under the carpet, and no access flaps are provided. To gain access to the bolts, it will be necessary to remove at least one of the front seats as described in Chapter 11. The carpet is secured by various clips, and by large plastic plate nuts which can be unscrewed.

3 Unscrew the securing bolts **(see illustration)**, then lift the lever assembly from the floor. Disengage the cable grommet from the floor, then feed the front section of the cable through into the passenger compartment, and withdraw the assembly from the vehicle.

Refitting

4 Refitting is a reversal of removal. Ensure that the cable grommet is correctly located in the aperture in the floor, and on completion, adjust the handbrake mechanism as described in Chapter 1A or 1B.

19.3 Handbrake cables seen with exhaust heat shields removed - adjuster nut arrowed

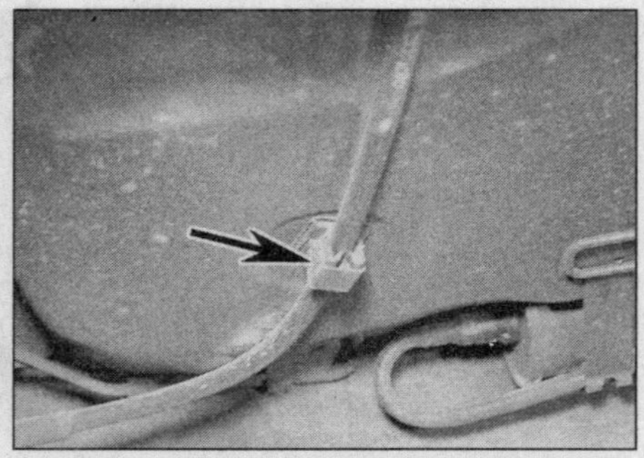

19.7 Typical handbrake cable securing clip (arrowed)

19 Handbrake cables - removal and refitting

Front cable

1 The front cable is integral with the handbrake lever assembly, and must be removed complete with the lever assembly, as described in Section 18. The cable cannot be renewed individually, and if faulty, the complete lever assembly must be renewed.

Rear cables

Removal - drum brake models

2 Chock the front wheels, then jack up the rear of the vehicle and support securely on axle stands (see *"Jacking and vehicle support"*). Remove the relevant rear roadwheel(s).

3 Working under the vehicle, remove the heat shields above the exhaust pipe as necessary for access. Slacken the adjuster nut on the cable equaliser assembly until the handbrake rear cables can be disengaged from the equaliser plate **(see illustration)**.

4 Remove the brake drum as described in Section 8.

5 Remove the trailing brake shoe, and unhook the end of the handbrake cable from the shoe, as described in Section 5.

6 Feed the cable through the rear brake backplate. If necessary, prise the cable outer from the backplate.

7 Unhook the cable from the clips and brackets under the vehicle **(see illustration)**, noting the cable routing, then withdraw the cable from the vehicle. Note that it may be necessary to completely remove the exhaust heat shield to allow the cable to be removed.

Removal - disc brake models

8 Chock the front wheels, then jack up the rear of the vehicle and support securely on axle stands (see *"Jacking and vehicle support"*). Remove the relevant rear roadwheel(s).

9 Working under the vehicle, slacken the adjuster nut on the cable equaliser assembly (see Chapter 1A or 1B) until the handbrake rear cables can be disengaged from the equaliser plate.

10 Unhook the inner cable from the caliper handbrake lever.

11 Using a hammer and pin punch, tap the outer cable out of its mounting bracket on the caliper.

12 Unhook the cable from the clips and brackets under the vehicle, noting the cable routing, then withdraw the cable from the vehicle. Note that it may be necessary to completely remove the exhaust heat shield to allow the cable to be removed.

Refitting

13 Refitting is a reversal of removal, noting the following points:

a) *Attach the cable to the brackets and clips under the rear of the vehicle, ensuring that it is routed as noted before removal.*

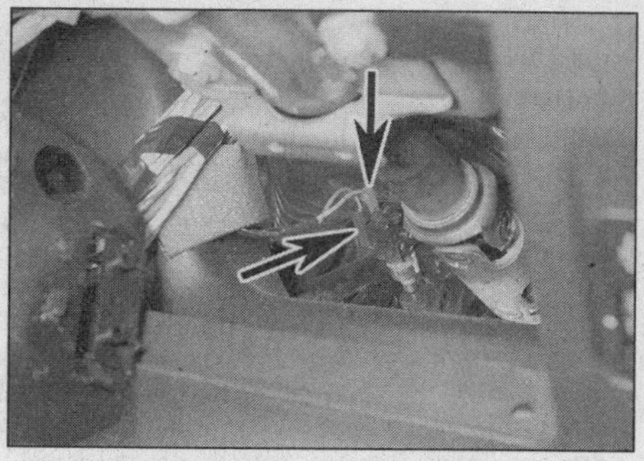

21.6 Brake stop-light switch wiring (arrowed)

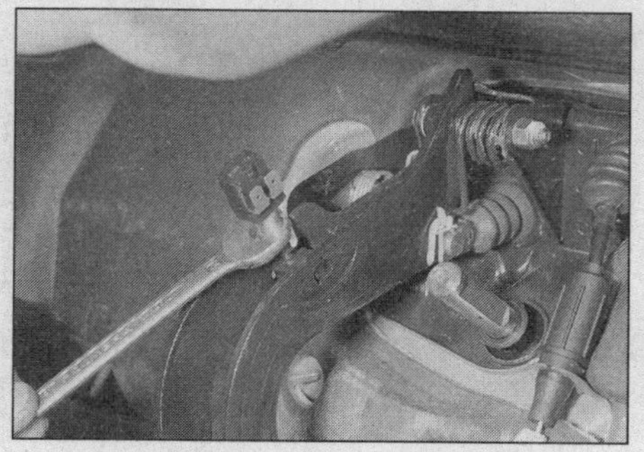

21.7a Loosen the stop-light switch locknut . . .

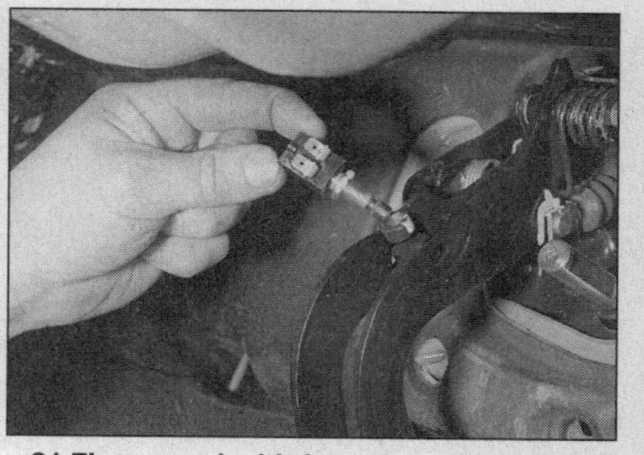

21.7b . . . and withdraw the switch from the top of the brake pedal

b) Ensure that the inner cable is securely hooked onto the brake shoe or handbrake lever on the brake caliper, as applicable. Also make sure that the outer cable is fully entered into its location in the backplate or caliper.

c) On completion, adjust the handbrake as described in Chapter 1A or 1B.

20 Rear brake pressure-regulating valves - adjustment, removal and refitting

Conventional braking system - rear drum brakes

1 On models with a conventional braking system, the pressure-regulating valves are integral with the rear wheel cylinders. The cylinders must not be dismantled, and if a fault is suspected, the complete wheel cylinder must be renewed as described in Section 11.

Conventional braking system - rear disc brakes

Removal

Note: *Before starting work, refer to the warning at the beginning of Section 2 concerning the dangers of hydraulic fluid.*

2 The pressure-regulating valves are located just in front of the rear axle assembly; there are two valves, one for each rear brake caliper.

3 Firmly chock the front wheels, then jack up the rear of the vehicle and support it on axle stands (see *"Jacking and vehicle support"*).

4 Minimise fluid loss by first removing the master cylinder reservoir cap, and then tightening it down onto a piece of polythene, to obtain an airtight seal.

5 Wipe clean the area around the brake pipe unions on the relevant valve, and place absorbent rags beneath the pipe unions to catch any surplus fluid. Retain the relevant pressure-regulating valve with a suitable open-ended spanner, then slacken the union nuts, disconnect both brake pipes, and remove the valve from underneath the vehicle. Plug or tape over the pipe ends and valve orifices, to minimise the loss of brake fluid, and to prevent the entry of dirt into the system. Wash off any spilt fluid immediately with cold water.

Refitting

6 Refitting is a reverse of the removal procedure, ensuring that the pipe union nuts are securely tightened. On completion, bleed the complete braking system (see Section 2).

Anti-lock braking system (ABS)

Adjustment

7 On models with ABS, a load-sensitive pressure-regulating valve is fitted, which is connected to the rear axle assembly to sense the load on the rear of the vehicle.

8 To carry out a complete check on the valve, pressure-testing equipment must be used. This work must therefore be entrusted to a Citroën dealer.

Removal

9 To remove the valve, first disconnect the four fluid pipes (noting their locations). Unhook the spring, then remove the two mounting bolts securing the assembly to the rear suspension.

Refitting

10 Refitting is a reversal of removal, but on completion, the valve adjustment must be checked by a Citroën dealer on completion.

21 Stop-light switch - adjustment, removal and refitting

Adjustment

1 The switch is screwed into the mounting bracket, and a locknut must be loosened before the switch can be moved (it will also be necessary to disconnect the wiring before the switch is rotated).

2 The switch must operate the stop-lights when the pedal has travelled a maximum of 5.0 mm.

Removal

3 Disconnect the battery negative lead.

4 Working in the driver's footwell, remove the two push-in fasteners from the front edge of the under-facia trim panel from the facia, and lower the panel.

5 To improve access further, remove the steering column lower shroud as described in Chapter 10, Section 12.

6 Reach up and disconnect the wiring from the switch **(see illustration)**.

7 Loosen the locknut, and unscrew the switch from the bracket **(see illustrations)**.

Refitting

8 Refitting is a reversal of removal. On completion, check the adjustment of the switch as described previously in this Section.

22 Handbrake "on" warning light switch - removal and refitting

Removal

1 Disconnect the battery negative lead.

2 Although not essential, removing the centre console as described in Chapter 11 will make access easier.

3 Lift the carpet panel for access to the switch **(see illustration)**; it may be necessary to make a small cut in the carpet to gain access.

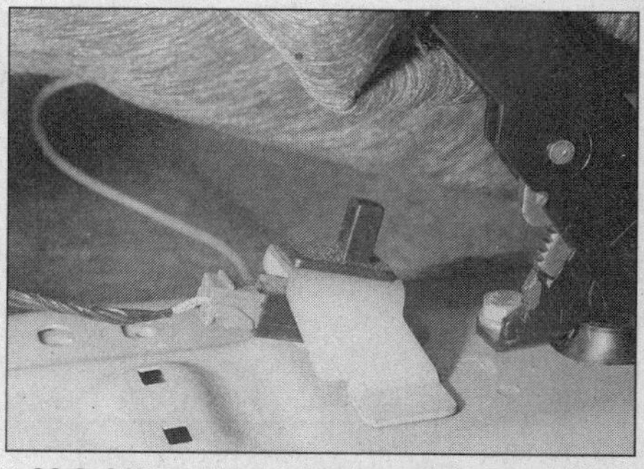

22.3 Lift up the carpet for access to the handbrake switch

9

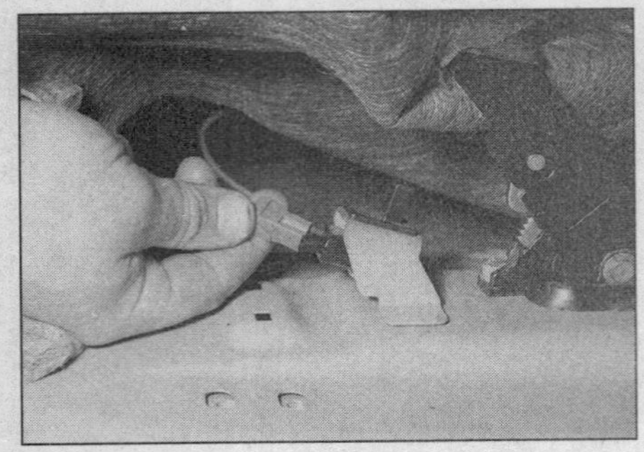

22.4a Disconnect the wiring plug . . .

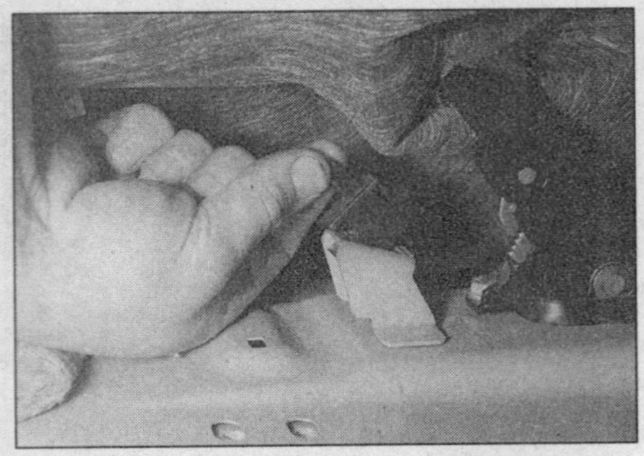

22.4b . . . then prise out and remove the handbrake switch as shown

4 Disconnect the wiring plug, then carefully prise out the switch **(see illustrations)**.

Refitting

5 Refitting is a reversal of removal. Where removed, refit the centre console as described in Chapter 11.

23 Anti-lock Braking System (ABS) - general information

An ATE/Teves Anti-lock Braking System is available as an option on certain models.

The system is fail-safe, and is fitted in addition to the conventional braking system, which allows the vehicle to retain conventional braking in the event of ABS failure.

To prevent wheel locking, the system provides pressure modulation in the braking circuits. To achieve this, sensors mounted at each wheel monitor the rotational speeds of the wheels, and are this able to detect when there is a risk of wheel locking (low rotational speed). Solenoid valves are positioned in the brake circuits to each wheel, and the solenoid valves are incorporated in a modulator assembly, which is controlled by an electronic control unit (ECU). The ECU controls modulation of the braking effort applied to each wheel, according to the information supplied by the wheel sensors.

When a wheel is about to lock, the hydraulic pressure to that wheel is released by the modulator, to allow the wheel to start turning. When the danger of wheel locking has passed, the hydraulic pressure is re-applied. This cycle can be performed several times a second. When the system is operational, it may be felt as a series of pulses through the brake pedal.

Should a fault develop in the system, a self-diagnostic facility is incorporated in the ECU, which can be used in conjunction with special diagnostic equipment available to a Citroën dealer, to determine the nature of the fault.

The braking system components used on models fitted with ABS are similar to those used on models with a conventional braking system.

Note that when bleeding the brake hydraulic system, the modulator assembly must also be bled, as described in Section 2.

24 Anti-lock Braking System (ABS) components - removal and refitting

Modulator assembly

Note: *Before starting work, refer to the warning at the beginning of Section 2 concerning the dangers of hydraulic fluid.*

Removal

1 Disconnect the battery negative lead.

2 Remove the battery and battery tray as described in Chapter 5A.

3 Remove the air cleaner as described in the relevant Part of Chapter 4.

4 Unclip the engine compartment fuse holder from its location, and move it aside, disconnecting as little wiring as possible.

5 Mark the locations of the hydraulic fluid pipes to ensure correct refitting, then unscrew the union nuts, and disconnect the pipes from the modulator assembly. Start with the two unions from the master cylinder, then remove the four unions which feed the wheels. Be prepared for fluid spillage, and plug the open ends of the pipes and the modulator, to prevent dirt ingress and further fluid loss.

6 Disconnect the wiring connector from the modulator assembly.

7 Remove the three securing nuts from the modulator mounting bracket, then withdraw the assembly from its mounting bracket.

Refitting

Warning: Do not reconnect the wiring connectors to the modulator until the hydraulic circuits have been bled as described in Section 2.

8 Commence refitting by positioning the assembly in the engine compartment, and refitting the securing nuts.

9 Reconnect the fluid pipes to the assembly, as noted before removal, ensuring that no dirt enters the system.

10 Bleed the complete hydraulic system as described in Section 2.

11 Reconnect the modulator assembly wiring plugs.

12 Refit the air cleaner as described in the relevant Part of Chapter 4.

13 Refit the battery and battery tray as described in Chapter 5A.

14 Reconnect the battery negative lead.

Electronic control unit

15 The unit is removed with the modulator assembly, as described above. On later models, the control unit is integral with the modulator, and cannot be renewed separately.

Wheel sensor

Note: *Suitable thread-locking compound must be applied to the sensor securing stud/bolt on refitting.*

Removal - front

16 Disconnect the battery negative lead.

17 Apply the handbrake, then jack up the front of the vehicle, and support securely on axle stands (see *"Jacking and vehicle support"*). If desired, remove the appropriate roadwheel to improve access.

18 Unscrew the nut and remove the plastic guard over the sensor **(see illustration)**.

19 Trace the wiring back from the sensor, and detach it from the retaining clips around the base of the suspension strut.

20 Open the hinged trim cover and disconnect the wiring connector from the sensor **(see illustration)**.

21 Unscrew the stud and remove the sensor from the hub.

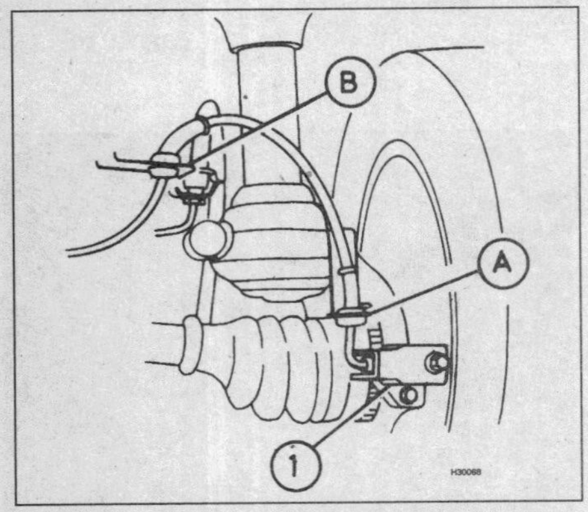

24.18 ABS front wheel sensor plastic guard (1) and wiring harness mountings (a and b)

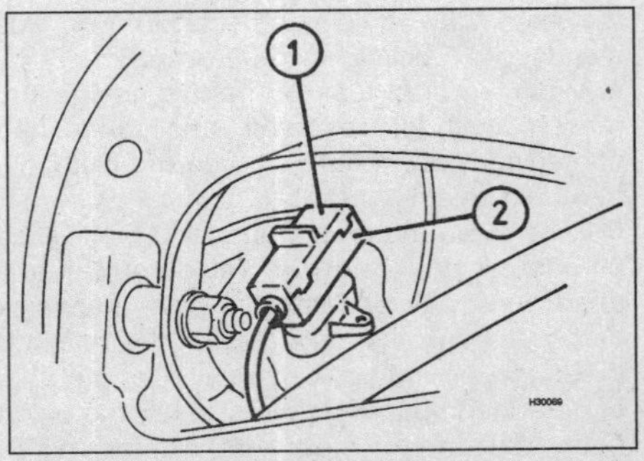

24.20 ABS front wheel sensor hinged cover (1) and wiring connector (2)

Removal - rear

22 Disconnect the battery negative lead.
23 Chock the front wheels, then jack up the rear of the vehicle, and support securely on axle stands (see *"Jacking and vehicle support"*). If desired, remove the appropriate roadwheel to improve access.
24 Trace the wiring back from the sensor, and detach it from the retaining clips on the trailing arm and the rear of the brake assembly. Separate the in-line wiring connector.
25 Unscrew the retaining bolt, and remove the sensor from the brake backplate/rear hub **(see illustrations).**

Refitting

26 Refitting is a reversal of removal, bearing in mind the following points:
a) *Ensure that the mating faces of the sensor and the mounting bracket are clean, and apply a little grease to the mounting bracket bore before refitting.*
b) *Ensure that the end face of the sensor is clean.*
c) *Apply thread-locking compound to the threads of the sensor securing stud/bolt, and tighten to the specified torque.*
d) *Ensure that the sensor wiring is routed and secured as noted before removal.*

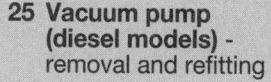

25 Vacuum pump (diesel models) - removal and refitting

Removal

Note: *A new O-ring should be used on refitting.*
1 The pump is located at the transmission end of the cylinder head.
2 Remove the air cleaner as described in the relevant Part of Chapter 4, and move the air ducting aside for access to the vacuum pump.
3 Unclip the accelerator cable and hoses from the bracket attached to the vacuum pump, then unbolt and remove the bracket, and move it aside **(see illustrations)**.
4 Disconnect the vacuum hose from the front of the pump, squeezing either side of the click-fit connection to release it **(see illustration)**.

25.3c . . . and remove the bracket from the vacuum pump

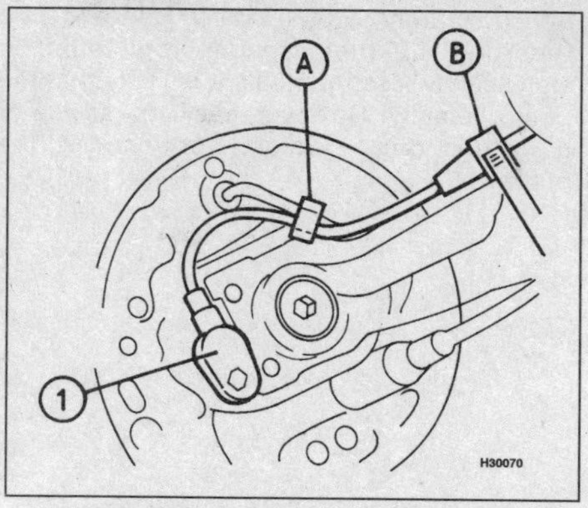

24.25a ABS rear wheel sensor (1) and wiring harness mountings (a and b) - drum brake models

5 Slacken and remove the two securing bolts and washers **(see illustration)**, then withdraw the pump from the cylinder head. Recover the O-ring.

Refitting

6 Refitting is a reversal of removal, noting the following points:
a) *Fit a new O-ring to the pump, then align the pump drive dogs with the slots in the end of the camshaft, and refit the pump to the cylinder head.*
b) *Refit the securing bolts and washers, and tighten them to the specified torque.*
c) *Reconnect the vacuum hose to the pump, ensuring that the connection is securely made.*

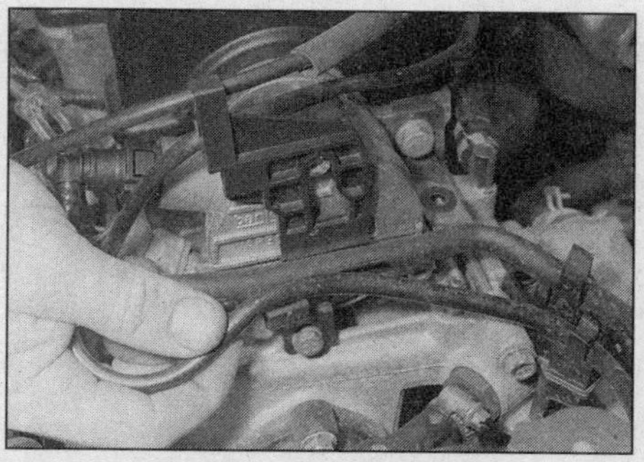

25.3a Unclip the hoses from the vacuum pump bracket . . .

25.4 Disconnect the vacuum hose by releasing the click-fit connection

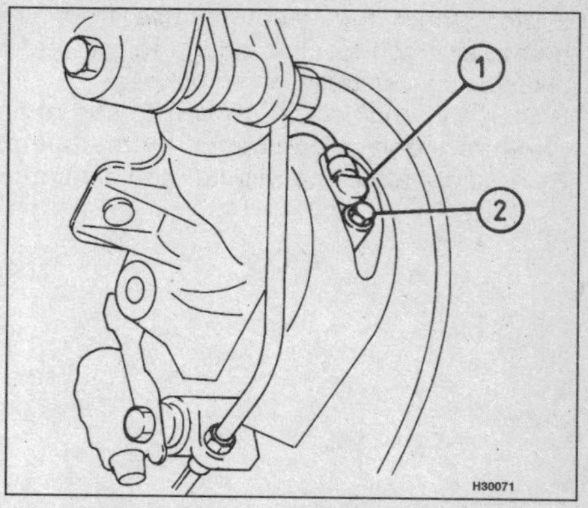

24.25b ABS rear wheel sensor (1) and mounting bolt (2) - disc brake models

d) *Refit all components removed or disturbed for access.*
e) *On completion, test the operation of the brake vacuum servo as described in Section 16 before bringing the car back into service.*

26 Vacuum pump (diesel models) - testing and overhaul

Testing

1 The operation of the braking system vacuum pump can be checked using a suitable vacuum gauge.

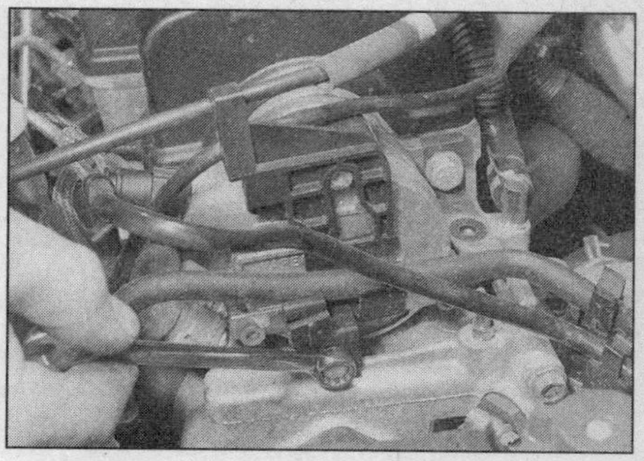

25.3b . . . then remove the bracket mounting bolt . . .

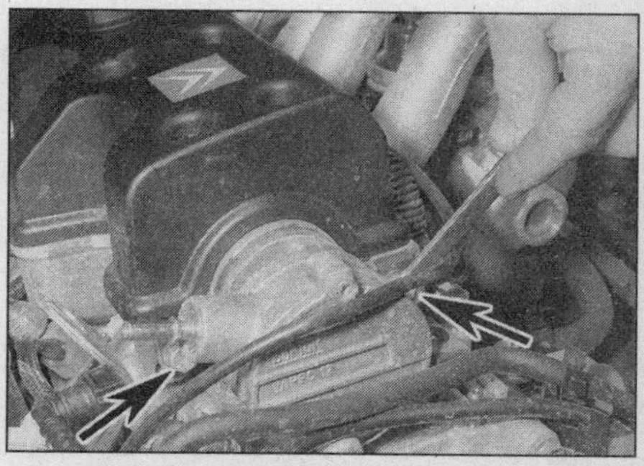

25.5 Remove the two mounting bolts (arrowed) to remove the pump

2 Disconnect the vacuum hose from the pump, and connect the gauge to the pump union using a suitable length of hose.

3 Start the engine and allow it to idle, then measure the vacuum created by the pump. As a guide, after one minute, a minimum of approximately 500 mmHg should be recorded. If the vacuum registered is significantly less than this, it is likely that the pump is faulty. However, seek the advice of a Citroën dealer before condemning the pump.

Overhaul

4 Overhaul of the vacuum pump is not possible, since no components are available separately for it. If faulty, the pump must be renewed complete.

Chapter 10
Suspension and steering

Contents

Degrees of difficulty

Easy, suitable for novice with little experience	**Fairly easy,** suitable for beginner with some experience	**Fairly difficult,** suitable for competent DIY mechanic	**Difficult,** suitable for experienced DIY mechanic	**Very difficult,** suitable for expert DIY or professional

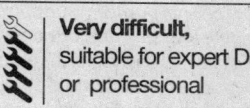

Specifications

Front suspension

Type	Independent by MacPherson struts, with inclined coil springs and integral shock absorbers. Certain models have anti-roll bar linked to the lower arms or struts (depending on model)

Rear suspension

Type	Trailing arms with transverse torsion bars and telescopic shock absorbers. Certain models have rear anti-roll bar running through axle tube, linking both trailing arms

Vehicle ride height (see text)

Front ride height (H1) = R1 minus L1:	
L1 dimension	71 ± 10 mm
Rear ride height (H2) = R2 plus L2:	
L2 dimension	49 ± 6 mm
Maximum side-to-side difference	7.5 mm

Steering

Type	Rack-and-pinion, power-assisted on certain models

Wheel alignment and steering angles

Front wheel camber angle:	
954 cc and 1124 cc models without power steering or ABS	0°9' ± 30' negative
All other models	0°40' ± 30' negative
Front wheel castor angle:	
Without power steering	2°13' ± 30'
With power steering	3°14' ± 30'
Steering axis/king pin inclination:	
Without power steering	12°41' ± 40'
With power steering	12°42' ± 40'
Front wheel toe setting:	
Without power steering	1 to 3 mm (0°10' to 0°31') toe-out
With power steering	1 to 3 mm (0°10' to 0°31') toe-in
Rear wheel camber setting (all models)	0°59' ± 20' negative
Rear wheel toe setting (all models)	1.49 to 6.39 mm (0°16' to 1°6') toe-in

Tyre pressures	See end of *"Weekly checks"*

Torque wrench settings	Nm	lbf ft
Front suspension		
Driveshaft nut*	250	184
Front anti-roll bar drop-link nuts*	70	52
Front anti-roll bar end clamp-to-lower arm screws	25	18
Front anti-roll bar mounting clamp-to-body bolts	55	41
Front suspension strut damper rod nut*	70	52
Front suspension strut upper mounting-to-body nuts	20	15
Lower arm balljoint-to-hub carrier nut and clamp bolt*	38	28
Lower arm rear mounting bracket-to-body nuts	40	30
Lower arm-to-body front mounting nut and through-bolt	85	63
Rear suspension		
Rear hub nut*	140	103
Rear shock absorber lower mounting bolt and nut	110	81
Rear shock absorber upper mounting bolt and nut	90	66
Rear suspension assembly-to-body mounting bolts	90	66
Rear torsion bar retaining bolts	20	15
Steering		
Lower steering column pinch-bolt and nut**	23	17
Power steering fluid unions:		
High-pressure hose to pump	20	15
All other hoses (as applicable)	25	18
Power steering pump mounting collar clamp screws	8	6
Power steering pump mountings	20	15
Power steering ram mountings	80	59
Steering column securing bolts	23	17
Steering gear-to-bulkhead bolts	22	16
Steering wheel bolt	30	22
Steering yoke-to-steering gear bolts and nuts	24	18
Track-rod balljoint locknuts	35	26
Track-rod end locknut*:		
M14 nut	45	33
M16 nut	50	37
Track-rod-to-steering gear bolts and nuts	21	15
Roadwheels		
Roadwheel bolts	85	63

**Use a new nut.*

***Use a new nut and bolt.*

1 General information

The independent front suspension is of the MacPherson strut type, incorporating coil springs and integral telescopic shock absorbers. The MacPherson struts are located by transverse lower suspension arms, which utilise rubber inner mounting bushes, and incorporate a balljoint at the outer ends. The front hub carriers, which carry the wheel bearings, brake calipers and the hub/disc assemblies, are integral with the MacPherson struts, and are connected to the lower arms via the balljoints. A front anti-roll bar is fitted to all models. The anti-roll bar is rubber-mounted onto the subframe, and is either connected to both lower suspension arms or directly to the front suspension struts, depending on the model.

The rear suspension is of the independent trailing arm type, which consists of two trailing arms, linked by a tubular crossmember. Torsion bars linking the trailing arms are situated in front of and behind the crossmember, and on certain models, an anti-roll bar linking the arms passes through the centre of the crossmember.

The complete rear axle assembly is mounted onto the vehicle underbody by four rubber mountings.

The steering column has a universal joint fitted at its lower end, which is clamped to the steering gear pinion by means of a clamp bolt and nut.

The steering gear is mounted on the engine compartment bulkhead. It is connected by two track-rods (with balljoints at their inner and outer ends) to the steering arms projecting rearwards from the suspension struts. The track-rod ends are threaded, to facilitate steering angle adjustment.

Power-assisted steering is fitted as standard on some models, and is available as an option on most others. The hydraulic steering system is unusual in that it is fed by an electric pump, rather than one driven from the crankshaft pulley.

Note: *Early Saxos without ABS or power steering had three wheel bolts per wheel; later models, or those with ABS or power steering, had four bolts per wheel. At the time of writing, no information was available to clearly indicate the changeover date from three to four bolts. This change does not affect any of the procedures in the Manual, however.*

2 Front hub bearings - renewal

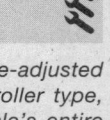

Note: *The bearing is a sealed, pre-adjusted and pre-lubricated, double-row roller type, and is intended to last the vehicle's entire service life without maintenance or attention. Never overtighten the driveshaft nut beyond the specified torque wrench setting in an attempt to "adjust" the bearing.*

Note: *Citroën special tools are available to carry out this operation, in which case the task can be carried out without removing the suspension strut. The procedure described in this Section assumes that the special tools are not available, in which case the task can be accomplished using improvised tools, once the suspension strut assembly has been removed.*

Note: *A press will be required to dismantle and rebuild the assembly; if such a tool is not available, a large bench vice and spacers (such as large sockets) will serve as an adequate substitute. The bearing's inner races are an interference fit on the hub; if the inner race remains on the hub when it is pressed out of the hub carrier, a knife-edged bearing puller will be required to remove it.*

1 Remove the relevant front suspension strut assembly, as described in Section 3.

2 If not already done, remove the securing screw(s) and withdraw the brake disc from the hub.

3 Support the strut assembly securely on blocks or in a vice. Using a tubular spacer which bears only on the inner end of the hub flange, press or drive the hub flange out of the bearing **(see illustration)**. If the bearing outboard inner race remains on the hub, remove it using a bearing puller (see note above).

4 Extract the bearing retaining circlip from the inner end of the hub carrier **(see illustration)**.

5 Where necessary, refit the bearing inner race back in position over the ball cage, and securely support the inner face of the hub carrier. Using a tubular spacer which bears only on the bearing inner race, press or drive the complete bearing assembly out of the hub carrier.

6 Thoroughly clean the hub and hub carrier, removing all traces of dirt and grease, and polish away any burrs or raised edges which might hinder reassembly. Check the components for cracks or any other signs of wear or damage, and renew them if necessary. Renew the bearing retaining circlip, regardless of its apparent condition.

7 Commence reassembly by applying a light film of oil to the bearing outer race and the contact faces of the hub, to aid installation of the bearing.

8 Securely support the hub carrier, and locate the bearing in the hub. Press the bearing fully into position, ensuring that it enters the hub squarely, using a tubular spacer which bears only on the bearing outer race.

9 Once the bearing is correctly seated, fit a new bearing retaining circlip, ensuring that it

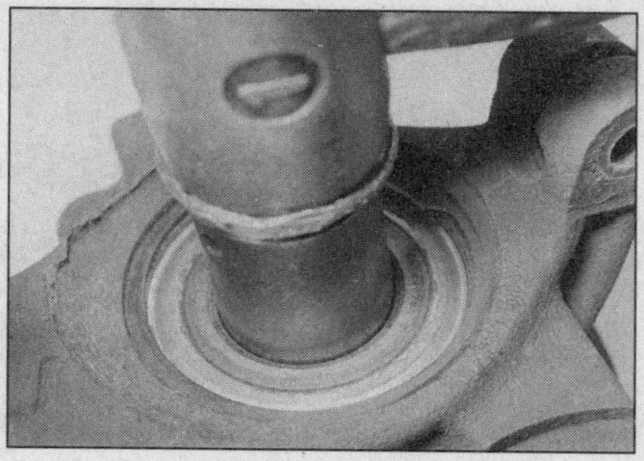

2.3 Driving the hub flange from the front hub bearing

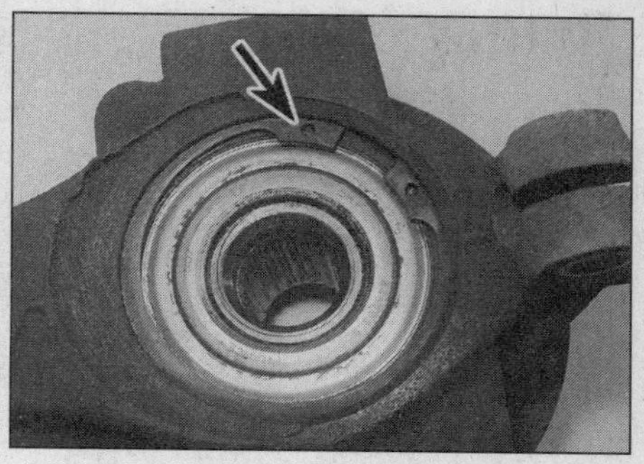

2.4 Front hub bearing retaining circlip (arrowed)

is correctly located in the groove in the hub carrier.

10 Securely support the outer face of the hub, and the suspension strut, and locate the hub carrier bearing inner race over the end of the hub. Press the bearing onto the hub, using a tubular spacer which bears only on the inner race of the bearing, until the bearing seats against the hub shoulder. Check that the hub rotates freely, and wipe off any excess oil or grease.

11 Refit the suspension strut assembly as described in Section 3.

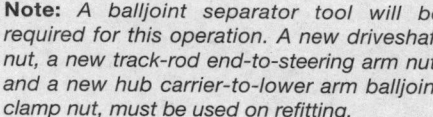

3 Front suspension strut - removal, overhaul and refitting

Note: *A balljoint separator tool will be required for this operation. A new driveshaft nut, a new track-rod end-to-steering arm nut, and a new hub carrier-to-lower arm balljoint clamp nut, must be used on refitting.*

Removal

1 Chock the rear wheels, apply the handbrake, then jack up the front of the vehicle and support on axle stands (see *"Jacking and vehicle support"*). Remove the appropriate roadwheel.

2 Disconnect the driveshaft from the hub, as described in Chapter 8. Note that there is no need to remove the driveshaft completely - the inner end can be left engaged with the gearbox. Support the driveshaft by suspending it from the vehicle body using wire or string - do not allow the end of the driveshaft to hang down.

3 Unbolt and remove the brake caliper (and, where applicable, the ABS wheel sensor), with reference to Chapter 9. Using a piece of wire or string, suspend the caliper from the body, to avoid placing any strain on the hydraulic brake hose **(see illustration)**. If the brake pads are removed, it is a wise precaution to insert a block of wood into the caliper body, to prevent the piston being ejected if the brake pedal is accidentally pressed.

4 Ensure that any wires or hoses attached to the strut are released from the clips or brackets, and moved to one side to facilitate strut removal. Note the locations of any clips or brackets.

5 Have an assistant support the strut from under the wheel arch, then slacken and remove the suspension strut upper mounting nuts **(see illustration)**. **Do not** attempt to slacken the large central nut at this stage.

6 Note the positions of the strut upper mounting nuts to ensure correct refitting (there are four holes in the body, only three of which are used), as the positions differ for models with or without power steering **(see illustration)**.

7 Carefully lower the suspension strut, and withdraw it from under the wheel arch **(see illustration)**.

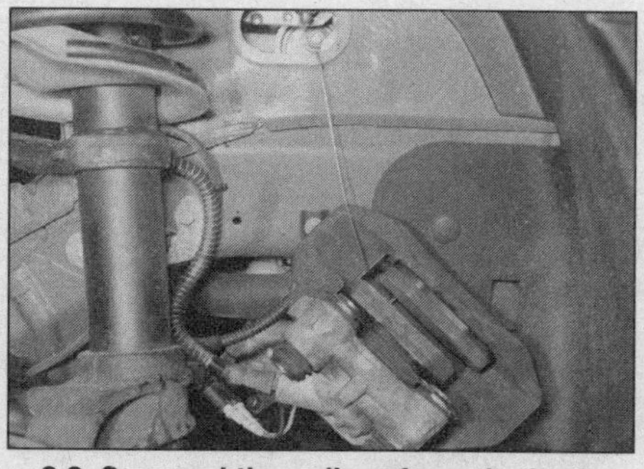

3.3 Suspend the caliper from the body

3.5 Remove the suspension strut upper mounting nuts (model without power steering shown)

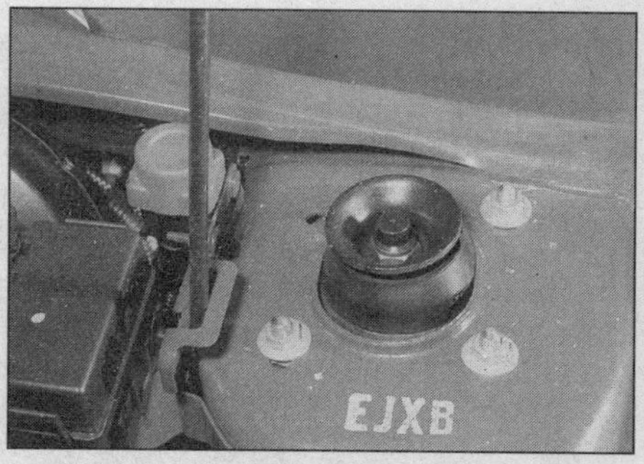

3.6 Suspension strut mounting nuts (model with power steering)

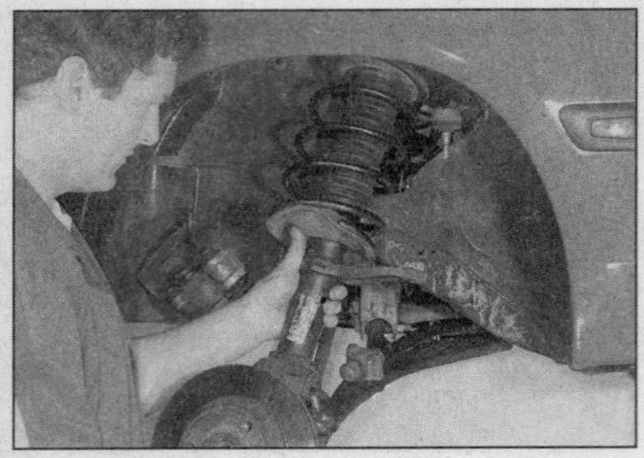

3.7 Withdrawing the suspension strut

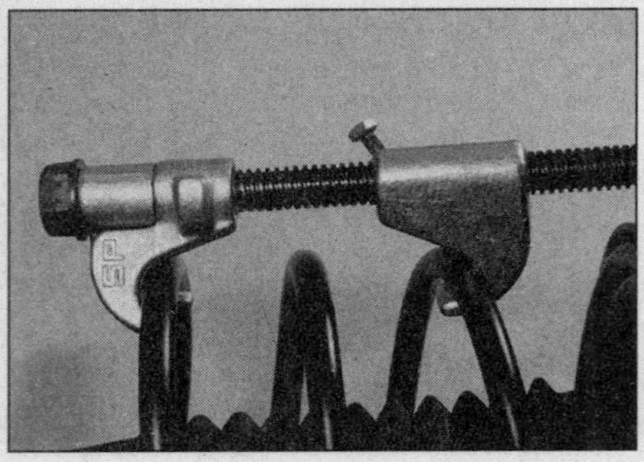

3.9 Coil spring compressor fitted to suspension strut coil spring

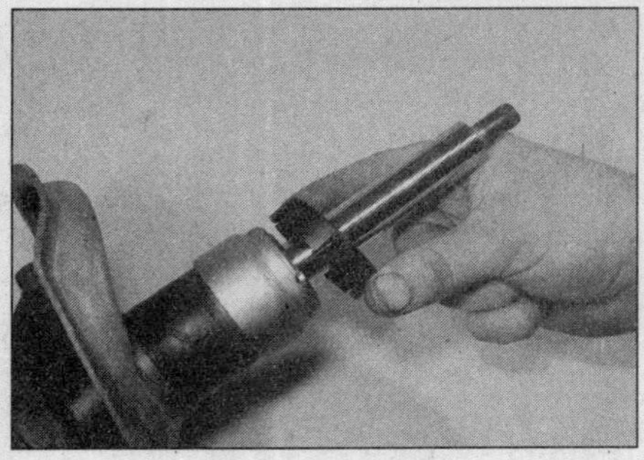

3.16a Fit the bump rubber collar . . .

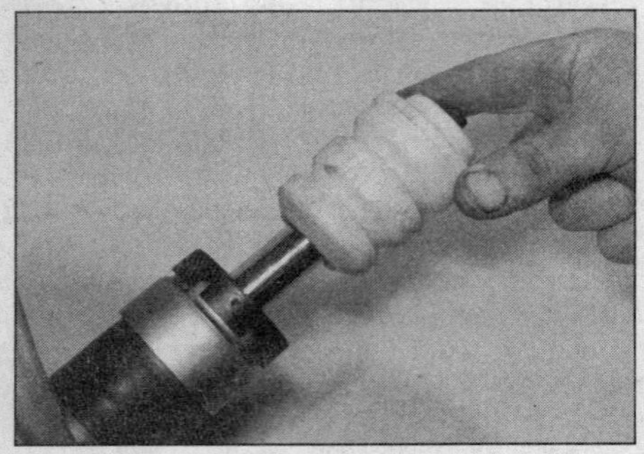

3.16b . . . the bump rubber . . .

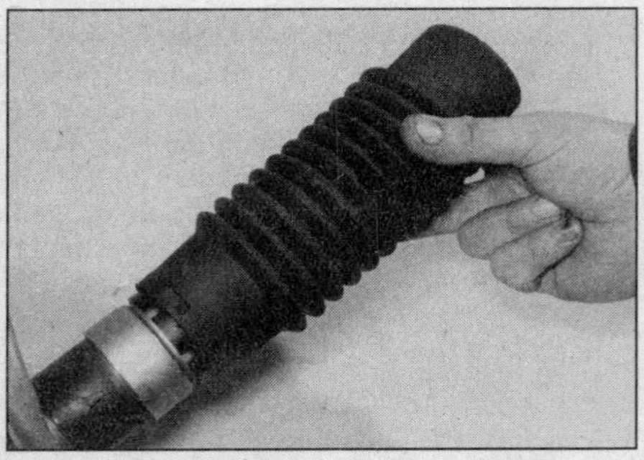

3.16c . . . and the rubber gaiter

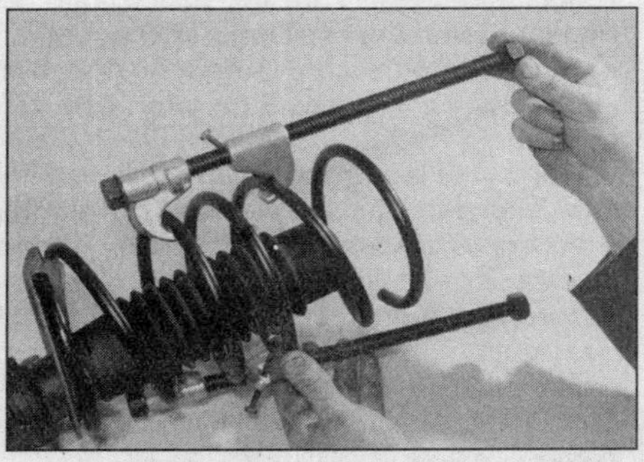

3.16d Slide the spring, complete with compressors, onto the strut . . .

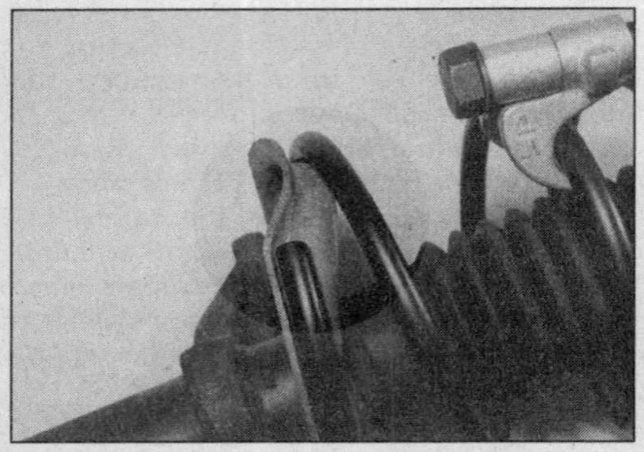

3.16e . . . ensuring that the end of the spring locates against the stop on the lower seat

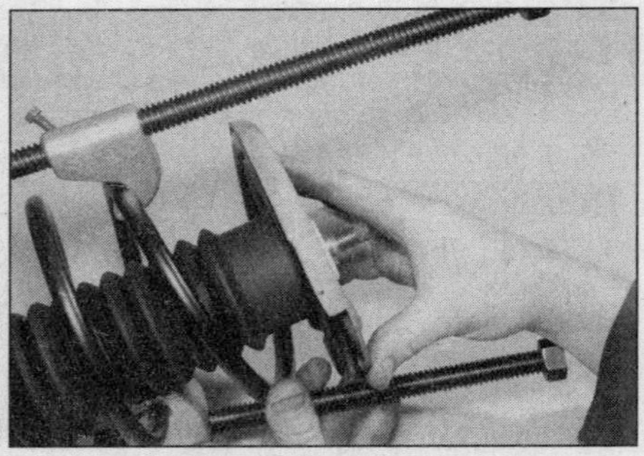

3.16f Fit the upper spring seat . . .

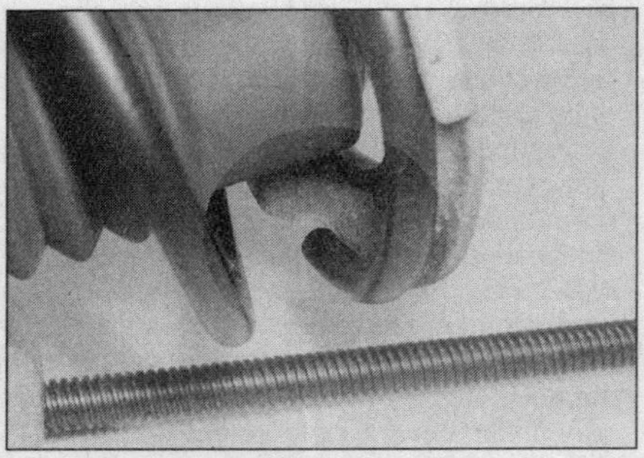

3.16g . . . again ensuring that the end of the spring locates against the stop

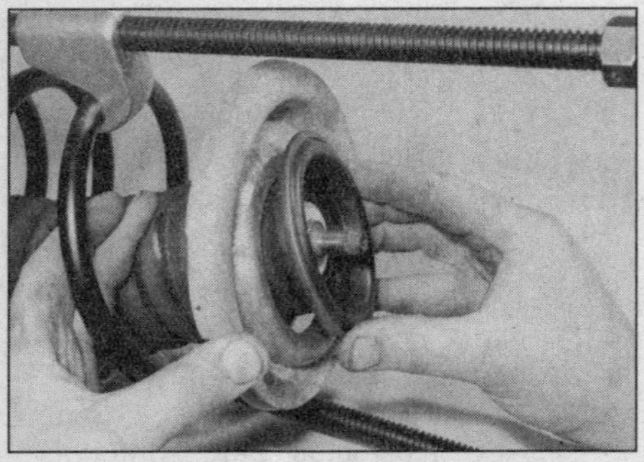

3.16h Fit the spring seat collar . . .

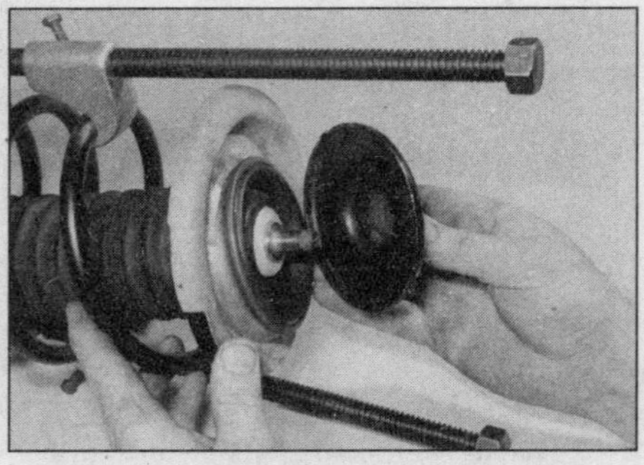

3.16i . . . the top mounting lower seat . . .

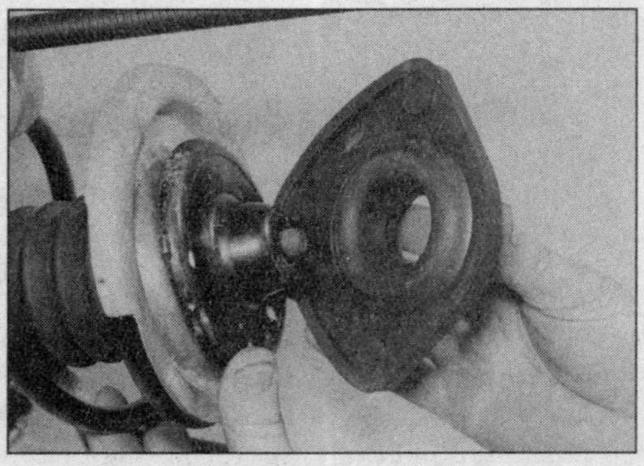

3.16j . . . the top mounting plate . . .

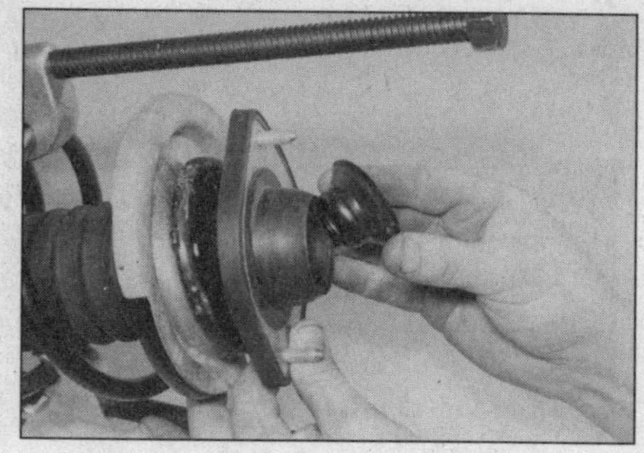

3.16k . . . and the top mounting upper seat . . .

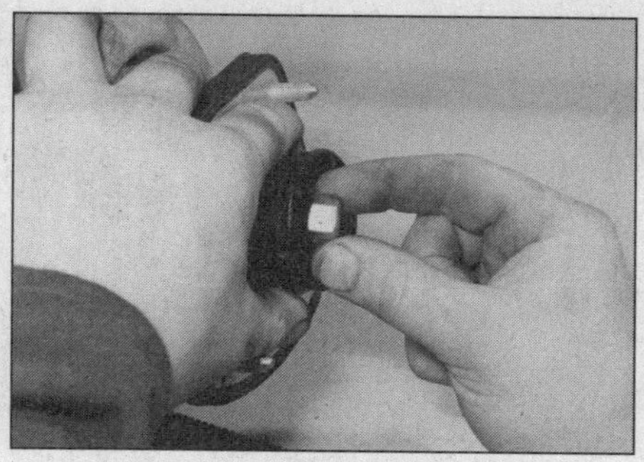

3.16l . . . then refit the top nut . . .

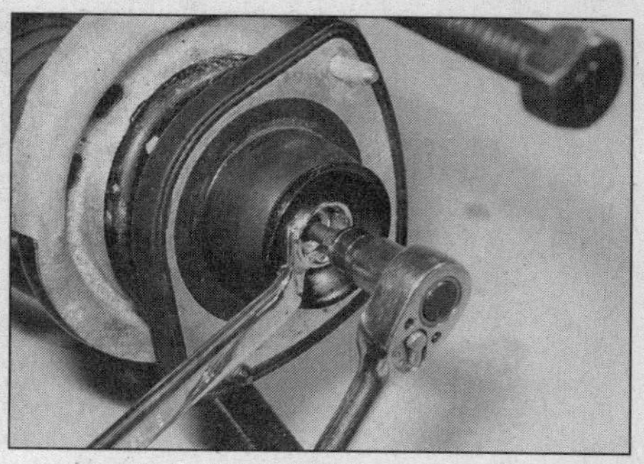

3.16m . . . and tighten using a spanner, whilst counterholding the piston rod

Overhaul

Warning: Before attempting to dismantle the front suspension strut, suitable tools to hold the coil spring in compression must be obtained. Adjustable coil spring compressors are readily available, and are recommended for this operation. Any attempt to dismantle the strut without such a tool is likely to result in damage or personal injury.

Note: *A new damper rod nut must be used on reassembly.*

8 With the strut removed from the vehicle as described previously in this Section, clean away all external dirt, then mount the strut upright in a vice.

9 Fit the spring compressors, and compress the coil spring until all tension is relieved from the upper spring seat **(see illustration)**.

10 Hold the strut damper rod using a T40 Torx bit, and unscrew the strut top nut. Discard the nut - a new nut must be used when refitting.

11 Withdraw the upper spring seat and associated components, the spring, complete with the compressors, then the rubber gaiter, thrustwasher (where applicable), bump rubber and bump rubber collar. Remove the compressors from the spring.

12 With the strut now dismantled, examine all the components for wear, damage or deformation, and check the upper bearing for smoothness of operation. Renew any of the components as necessary.

13 Examine the strut for signs of fluid leakage. Check the strut piston for signs of pitting along its entire length, and check the strut body for signs of damage. While holding it in an upright position, test the operation of the strut by moving the piston through a full stroke, and then through short strokes of 50 to 100 mm. In both cases, the resistance felt should be smooth and continuous. If the resistance is jerky, or uneven, or if there is any visible sign of wear or damage to the strut, renewal is necessary. The strut damper cartridge can be renewed independently of the strut, but a special peg spanner tool is required to unscrew the damper nut. This nut is very tight, and it is not possible to safely improvise a suitable tool. Unless the Citroën special tool is available (tool no 4605-T.K), the strut should be taken to a Citroën dealer for renewal of the damper cartridge.

14 If any doubt exists about the condition of the coil spring, carefully remove the spring compressors, and check the spring for distortion and signs of cracking. Renew the spring if it is damaged or distorted, or if there is any doubt as to its condition.

15 Inspect all other components for signs of damage or deterioration, and renew any that are suspect.

16 To reassemble the strut, follow the accompanying photo sequence, beginning with illustration 3.16a. Be sure to follow each step in sequence, and carefully read the caption underneath each photo **(see illustrations)**. Compress the spring sufficiently to allow the top mounting components to be refitted, and if necessary pull on the end of the piston rod to extend the damper.

Refitting

17 Manoeuvre the strut assembly into position under the wheel arch, passing the mounting studs through the holes in the body turret, then refit the upper mounting nuts, and tighten them to the specified torque.

Warning: It is essential to ensure that the upper mounting nuts are fitted in their correct positions, as noted before removal (if necessary, turn the upper mounting on the strut until the studs line up with the relevant holes) - if the strut is fitted incorrectly, the castor angle will be incorrect, and there is a risk of contact between the track-rods and the wheel arches.

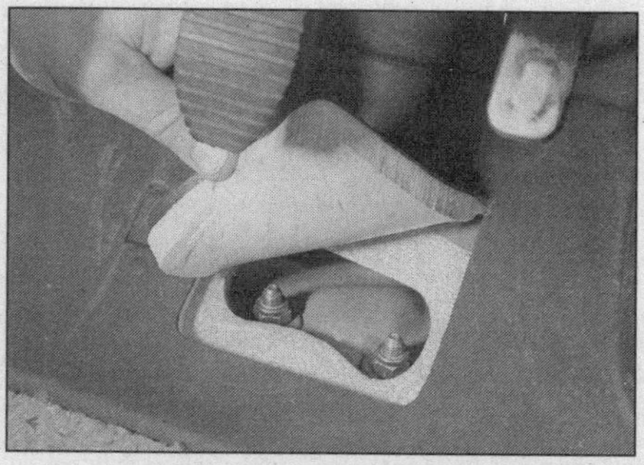

4.5 Lower arm rear nuts are accessed by lifting up a flap in the sound insulation

18 Ensure that the driveshaft splines and the corresponding splines in the hub are clean, then reconnect the driveshaft to the hub as described in Chapter 8.

19 Refit the brake caliper, brake pads and ABS wheel sensor (as applicable), as described in Chapter 9.

20 Clip any relevant wires or hoses back into position on the strut.

21 Refit the roadwheel, then lower the vehicle to the ground and tighten the roadwheel bolts to the specified torque.

4 Front suspension lower arm - removal, overhaul and refitting

Note: *A new hub carrier-to-lower arm balljoint clamp nut must be used on refitting.*

Removal

1 Chock the rear wheels, firmly apply the handbrake, then jack up the front of the vehicle and support on axle stands (see *"Jacking and vehicle support"*). Remove the appropriate front roadwheel.

2 On models where the anti-roll bar is mounted onto the suspension lower arm, remove the two screws and washers securing the anti-roll bar end clamp to the lower arm. Remove the clamp and the rubber bush.

3 Undo the nut and withdraw the hub carrier-to-lower arm clamp bolt, noting which way round it is fitted.

4 Using a suitable metal bar, lever the lower arm downwards just enough to release the balljoint taper from the lower arm. If the taper is a tight fit in the hub carrier, use a large flat-bladed screwdriver to carefully open up the clamp a little.

5 Working inside the passenger compartment, lift and fold back the carpet for access to the two lower arm rear bracket securing nuts. The carpet is secured by various clips and plastic plate nuts, which can be unscrewed. With the carpet folded back, locate the flap in the sound-deadening foam, and lift it up. There may be a further foam membrane which must be cut through for access to the nuts **(see illustration)**. Unscrew the securing nuts.

10

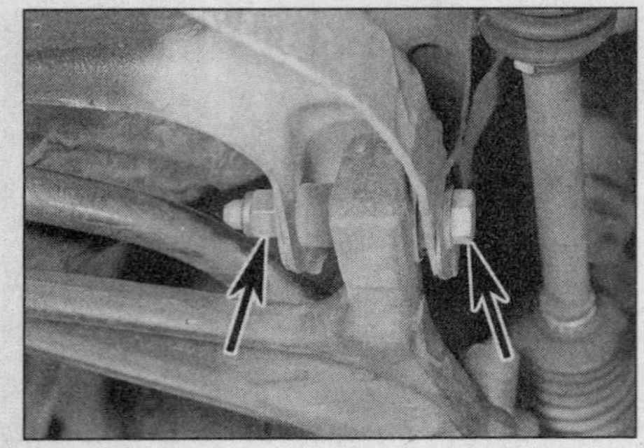

4.6 Lower arm front securing bolt and nut (arrowed)

6 Working under the vehicle, unscrew the nut, and remove the through-bolt securing the front of the lower arm to the bracket on the body **(see illustration)**.

7 Pull the lower arm down to disengage the front mounting studs from the holes in the body, and withdraw the lower arm from under the vehicle.

Overhaul

8 It is possible to renew the lower arm pivot bushes, but due to the requirement for Citroën special tools (a suitable press, positioning jig and socket adapter will be required), it is recommended that the job is entrusted to a Citroën dealer. Similarly, it is also possible to renew the lower arm balljoint, which is a press-fit in the end of the lower arm.

Refitting

9 Commence refitting by ensuring that the bushes, the bush contact faces on the body, and the lower arm securing bolt and studs, are clean.

10 Place the lower arm in position under the vehicle, then refit the front through-bolt and nut, and tighten to the specified torque.

11 Working inside the passenger compartment, refit the rear bracket securing nuts, and tighten them to the specified torque.

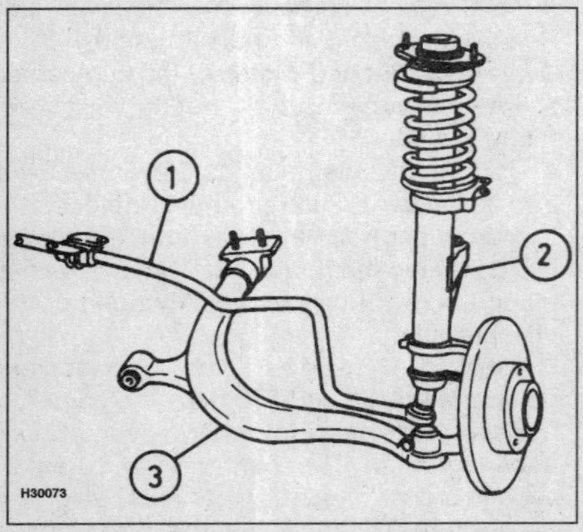

5.3 Front suspension layout for models with anti-roll bar incorporating drop-links

1 *Anti-roll bar*
2 *Drop link (to rear of suspension strut)*
3 *Lower arm*

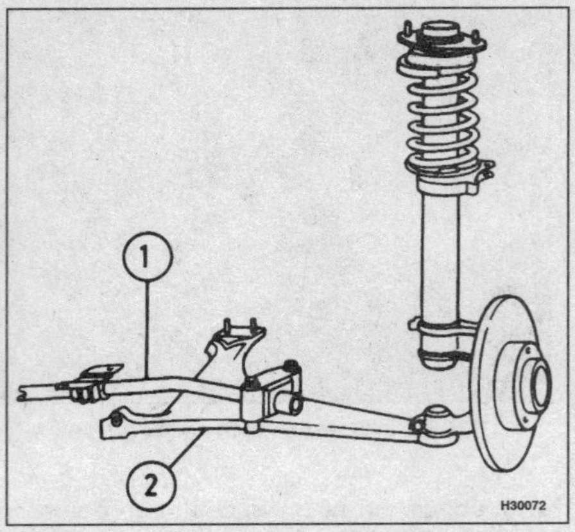

5.2a Front suspension layout for models with anti-roll bar mounted directly on lower arms

1 *Anti-roll bar* 2 *Lower arm*

Fit the carpet and sound insulation panels back in to position.

12 Ensure that the protector plate is in place over the lower arm balljoint, then engage the balljoint taper with the hub carrier. If necessary, lever the arm downwards just enough to engage the balljoint, as during removal. Similarly, use a screwdriver to open up the clamp a little if necessary.

13 Fit the hub carrier-to-lower arm clamp bolt (insert the bolt from the front of the strut) and a new nut, and tighten to the specified torque.

14 Where applicable, refit the anti-roll bar end clamp and bush. Position the end of the anti-roll bar on the lower arm, and refit the securing screws and washers. Tighten the screws to the specified torque.

15 Refit the roadwheel, then lower the vehicle to the ground and tighten the roadwheel bolts to the specified torque.

16 If the driver's side lower arm has been removed, ensure that the sound insulation and carpet panels have been correctly refitted. Check the operation of the throttle pedal, and check that the pedal can be depressed smoothly to the full-throttle position (check that full-throttle is available at the engine with the pedal fully depressed - see the relevant Part of Chapter 4).

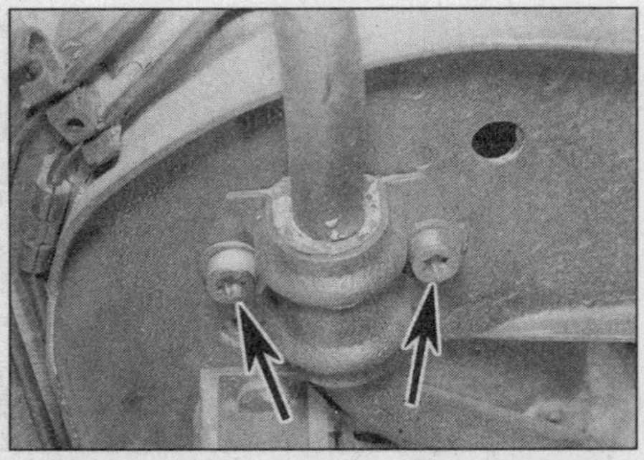

5.4a Anti-roll bar clamp bolts (arrowed) - model without drop-links

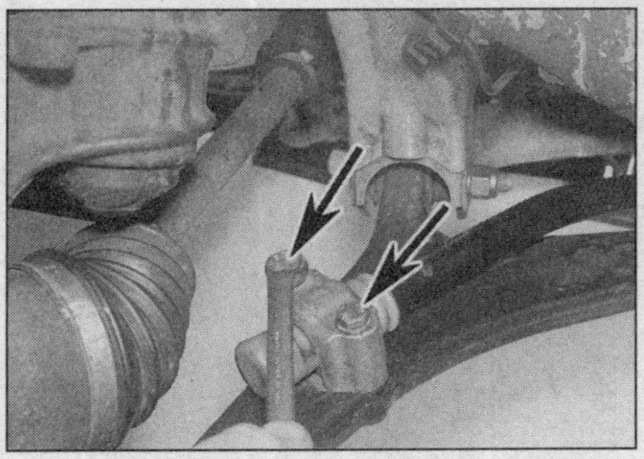

5.2b Removing the anti-roll bar clamp screws (arrowed)

5 Front suspension anti-roll bar - removal and refitting

Anti-roll bar

Note: *On models where the anti-roll bar is connected to the suspension struts by drop-links, new drop-link-to-anti-roll bar nuts must be used on refitting.*

Removal

1 Chock the rear wheels, firmly apply the handbrake, then jack up the front of the vehicle and support on axle stands (see *"Jacking and vehicle support"*). Remove both front roadwheels.

2 On models where the anti-roll bar is mounted onto the lower arms, working at each end of the anti-roll bar, remove the screws and washers securing the anti-roll bar end clamps to the lower arms. Remove the clamps and the rubber bushes **(see illustrations)**.

3 On models where the anti-roll bar has drop-links connecting the ends of the bar to the suspension struts, remove the nuts securing the lower ends of the drop-links to the anti-roll bar **(see illustration)**.

4 Remove the Torx bolts securing the anti-roll bar mounting clamps to the body **(see illustrations)**. Withdraw the clamps.

5 Manipulate the anti-roll bar out from under the vehicle.

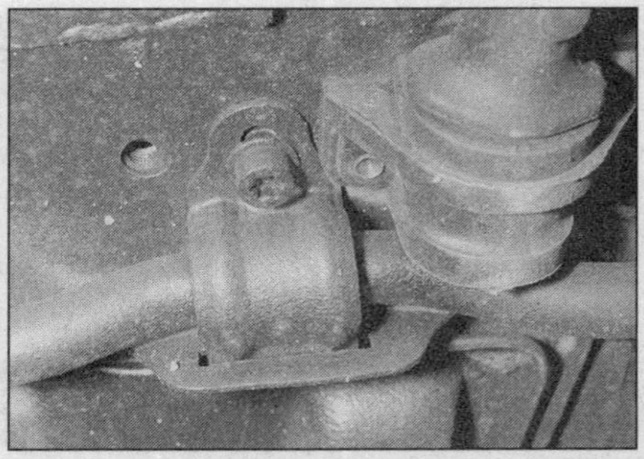

5.4b On models with the drop-link anti-roll bar, only one clamp bolt is fitted

Refitting

6 Examine the condition of the anti-roll bar mounting bushes, and renew if necessary. The anti-roll bar-to-body clamp bushes can be renewed by sliding the old bushes from the bar, and sliding the new bushes into position. Before removing the old bushes, mark their fitted positions on the bar, so that the new bushes can be fitted in the same position. Citroën state that the bushes should be lubricated on models with the anti-roll bar mounted on the lower arms, but advise against lubricating the bushes on models with the drop-link type anti-roll bar.
7 Manipulate the bar into position under the vehicle, then refit the mounting clamps. Fit the mounting clamp securing bolts, but do not fully tighten them at this stage.
8 On models where the anti-roll bar is connected to the suspension struts by drop-links, reconnect the drop-links to the ends of the bar, and fit new securing nuts. Tighten the nuts to the specified torque.
9 On models where the anti-roll bar is mounted onto the lower arms, refit the rubber bushes and the clamps, then refit the washers and the screws. Tighten the screws to the specified torque.
10 Finally tighten the anti-roll bar clamp-to-body bolts to the specified torque.
11 Refit the roadwheels, then lower the vehicle to the ground and tighten the roadwheel bolts to the specified torque.

Drop-link (models with strut-mounted anti-roll bar)

Note: *New drop-link securing nuts must be used on refitting.*

Removal

12 Chock the rear wheels, firmly apply the handbrake, then jack up the front of the vehicle and support on axle stands (see *"Jacking and vehicle support"*). Remove the relevant front roadwheel.
13 Unscrew the nut securing the lower end of the drop-link to the end of the anti-roll bar **(see illustration)**.
14 If necessary, using a suitable metal bar, carefully lever the end of the anti-roll bar down, to separate it from the end of the drop-link.

5.13 Anti-roll bar drop-link securing nuts (arrowed)

15 Unscrew the nut securing the drop-link to the suspension strut, and remove the drop-link from the vehicle.

Refitting

16 Check the drop-link balljoints for excessive wear, and check the condition of the balljoint rubber gaiters **(see illustration)**. If the balljoints or gaiters are worn or damaged, the complete drop-link must be renewed, as the components cannot be renewed individually. Note that wear in the drop-links is often indicated by a "clonking" noise produced when driving over bumps or cornering.
17 Refitting is a reversal of removal, but use new securing nuts and tighten them to the specified torque.

6 Rear hub assembly - removal and refitting

Rear drum brakes

1 The rear hub is integral with the brake drum. Refer to Chapter 9 for details of brake drum removal and refitting.

Rear disc brakes

Removal

Note: *Do not remove the hub assembly unless it is absolutely necessary. A puller will be required to draw the hub assembly off the stub axle, and the hub bearing will almost certainly be damaged by the removal procedure. A new hub nut and hub cap will be required on refitting.*

5.16 Check the condition of the drop-link balljoint rubber gaiters

2 Remove the rear brake disc as described in Chapter 9.
3 Using a hammer and a large flat-bladed screwdriver, carefully tap and prise the cap out of the centre of the hub. Discard the cap - a new one must be used on refitting. Using a hammer and a chisel-nosed tool, tap up the staking securing the hub retaining nut to the groove in the stub axle **(see illustrations)**.
4 Using a socket and long bar, slacken and remove the rear hub nut, and withdraw the thrustwasher. Discard the hub nut - a new nut must be used on refitting.
5 Using a puller, draw the hub assembly off the stub axle, along with the outer bearing race **(see illustration)**. With the hub removed, use the puller to draw the inner bearing race off the stub axle, then remove the hub spacer, noting which way round it is fitted.
6 Refit the races to the hub bearing, and check the hub bearing for signs of roughness. It is recommended that the bearing should be renewed as a matter of course, as it is likely to have been damaged during removal. This means that the complete hub assembly must be renewed, since it is not possible to obtain the bearing separately.
7 With the hub removed, examine the stub axle shaft for signs of wear or damage. The shaft is an integral part of the trailing arm, and if worn or damaged, the complete trailing arm must be renewed (see Section 10).

Refitting

8 Lubricate the stub axle shaft with clean engine oil, then slide on the spacer, ensuring it is fitted the correct way round.

6.3a Tap off the hub centre cap . . .

6.3b . . . then tap up the rear hub staking using a hammer and suitable punch

6.5 Use a suitable legged puller to draw the hub assembly off the stub axle

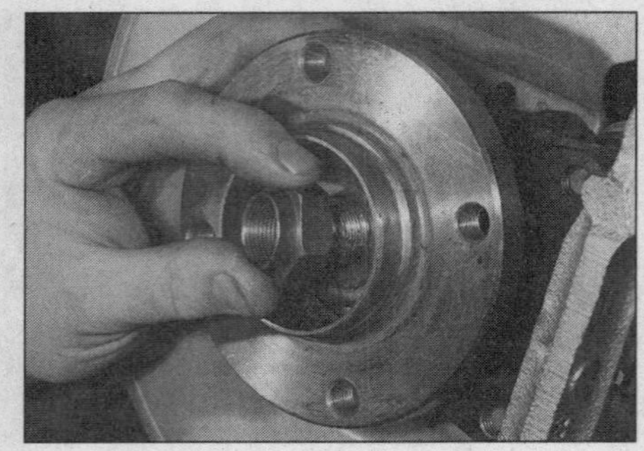

6.11a Fit the thrustwasher and new hub nut, and tighten to the specified torque

6.11b Using a hammer and suitable punch . . .

6.11c . . . stake the hub nut firmly into the stub axle groove . . .

6.11d . . . then fit the new hub cap

7.2 Extracting the rear wheel bearing circlip

7.3 Prising the oil seal seating ring from the rear hub

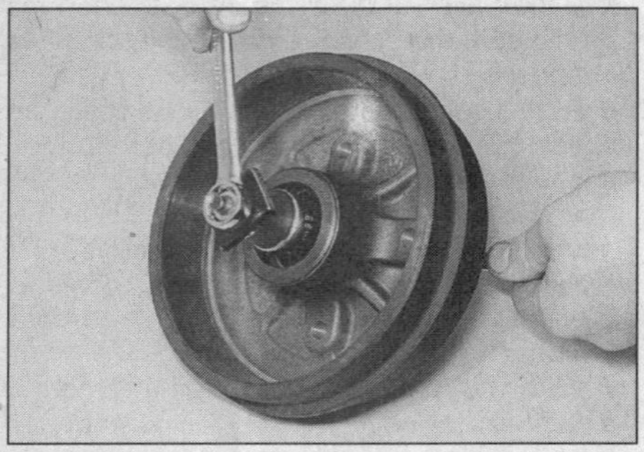

7.4 Drawing the hub bearing from the hub using improvised tools

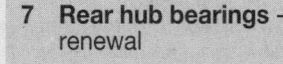

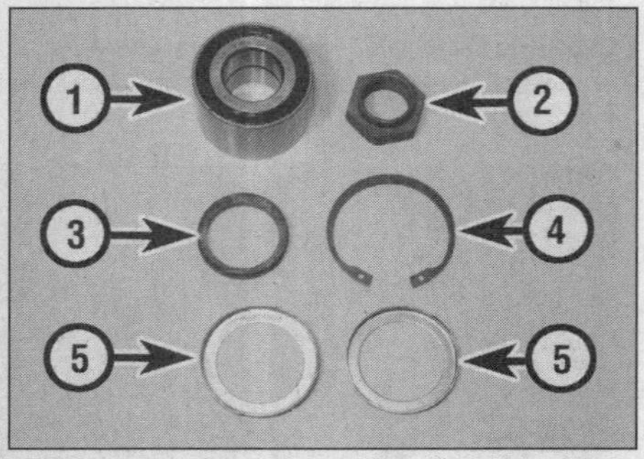

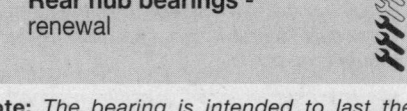

7.5 Rear hub bearing kit (details may differ according to model)

1 Bearing
2 Hub nut
3 Oil seal
4 Circlip
5 Oil seal seating rings (alternative sizes)

9 Fit the new bearing inner race, and tap it fully onto the stub axle using a hammer and a tubular drift which bears only on the flat inside edge of the race.

10 Ensure that the bearing is packed with grease, then slide the hub assembly onto the stub axle. Fit the new outer bearing race, and tap it into position using the tubular drift.

11 Fit the thrustwasher and a new hub nut, and tighten the hub nut to the specified torque. Stake the nut firmly into the groove on the stub axle to secure it in position, then tap the new hub cap into place in the centre of the hub **(see illustrations)**.

12 Refit the rear brake disc as described in Chapter 9.

7 Rear hub bearings - renewal

Note: *The bearing is intended to last the vehicle's entire service life without maintenance or attention. Never overtighten the hub nut beyond the specified torque wrench setting, in an attempt to "adjust" the bearings.*

Rear drum brakes

1 Remove the rear brake drum as described in Chapter 9.

2 Using circlip pliers, extract the bearing retaining circlip from the centre of the brake drum **(see illustration)**.

3 Prise the oil seal seating ring from the rear of the hub **(see illustration)**.

4 Securely support the drum hub, then press or drive the bearing out of position, using a tubular drift which bears on the bearing inner race. Alternatively, the bearing can be removed using an improvised tool made up from a suitable socket or tube, washers, nut, and a suitable long bolt or threaded rod **(see illustration)**.

5 Thoroughly clean the hub, removing all traces of dirt and grease, and polish away any burrs or raised edges which might hinder reassembly. Check the hub for cracks or any other signs of wear or damage, and renew them if necessary. The bearing and its circlip must be renewed whenever they are disturbed. Obtain a new bearing kit from a Citroën dealer **(see illustration)**.

6 Carefully prise the oil seal from the stub axle, and fit the new seal supplied in the bearing kit. Note the spacer fitted behind the oil seal **(see illustration)**.

7.6 Fitting a new oil seal to the stub axle. Note spacer (arrowed)

7.9a Locate the bearing in the hub . . .

7.9b . . . then draw the bearing into position

7.11a Fit the new oil seal seating ring . . .

7 Examine the stub axle shaft for signs of wear or damage. The shaft is an integral part of the trailing arm, and if worn or damaged, the complete trailing arm must be renewed (see Section 10).

8 On reassembly, apply a light film of clean engine oil to the bearing outer race, to aid installation of the bearing.

9 Securely support the drum, and locate the bearing in the hub. Press the bearing fully into position, ensuring that it enters the hub squarely, using a tubular spacer which bears only on the bearing outer race. Alternatively, the bearing can be drawn into position with the improvised tool used previously, but note that a different socket or tube will be required, to bear on the bearing outer race **(see illustrations)**.

10 Ensure that the bearing is correctly seated against the hub shoulder, and secure it in position with the new circlip. Ensure that the circlip is correctly seated in its hub groove.

11 Tap the new oil seal seating ring into position in the rear of the hub, taking care not to damage the oil seal seating surface **(see illustrations)**. Note that two different-size oil seal seating rings may be supplied in the bearing kit - ensure that the correct ring is used.

12 Refit the brake drum as described in Chapter 9.

Rear disc brakes

13 On models with rear disc brakes, it is not possible to renew the rear hub bearing separately. If the bearing is worn, the complete rear hub assembly must be renewed. Refer to Section 6 for hub removal and refitting procedures.

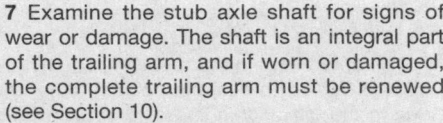

8 Rear shock absorber - removal, testing and refitting

Note: *Shock absorbers should always be renewed in pairs, to preserve safe handling.*

Removal

1 Chock the front wheels, then jack up the rear of the vehicle and support it on axle stands (see *"Jacking and vehicle support"*). Remove the relevant rear roadwheel.

2 Using a trolley jack, raise the trailing arm until the shock absorber is slightly compressed.

3 Slacken and remove the nuts from both the upper and lower shock absorber mounting bolts. Note that it will be necessary to counterhold the bolts **(see illustration)**.

4 Withdraw the mounting bolts, noting which way around they are fitted, and manoeuvre the shock absorber out from underneath the vehicle **(see illustrations)**.

Testing

5 Examine the shock absorber for signs of fluid leakage or damage. Test the operation of the shock absorber, while holding it in an upright position, by moving the piston through a full stroke, and then through short strokes of 50 to 100 mm. In both cases, the resistance felt should be smooth and continuous. If the resistance is jerky, or uneven, or if there is any visible sign of wear or damage, renewal is necessary. Also check the rubber mounting bushes for damage and deterioration. Renew the complete unit if any damage or excessive wear is evident; the mounting bushes are not available separately. Inspect the shanks of the mounting bolts for signs of wear or damage, and renew as necessary. If one shock absorber is found to be defective, both should be renewed, or the handling may become unpredictable.

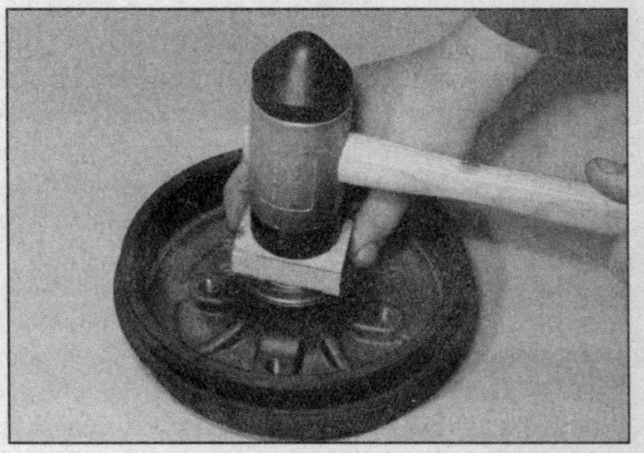

7.11b . . . and tap it into position

Refitting

6 Prior to refitting the shock absorber, mount it upright in the vice, and operate it fully through several strokes in order to prime it. Apply a smear of multi-purpose grease to both the shock absorber mounting bolts.

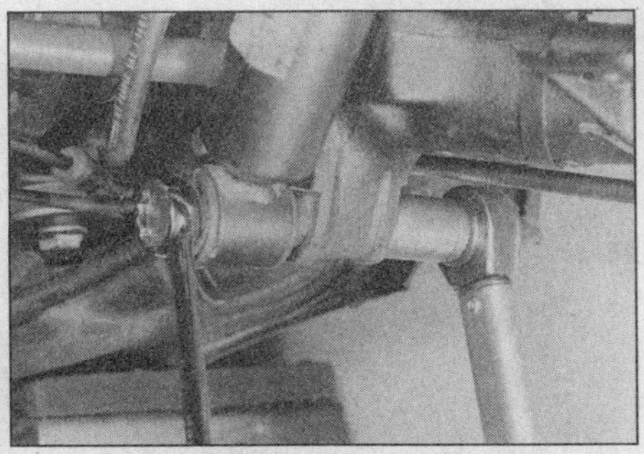

8.3 Counterhold the bolts when unscrewing the rear shock absorber mounting nuts

8.4a Remove the upper . . .

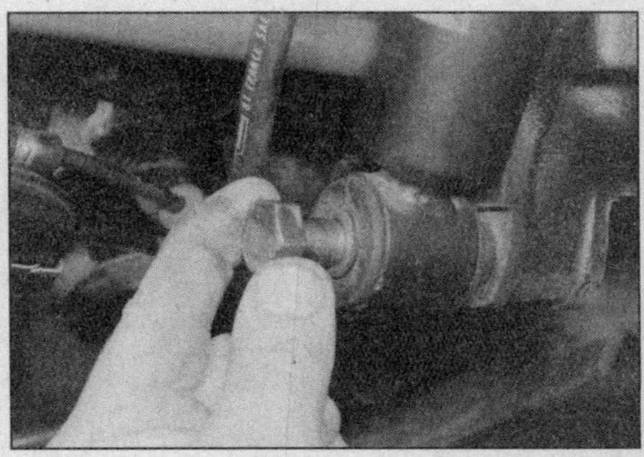

8.4b . . . and lower rear shock absorber mounting bolts

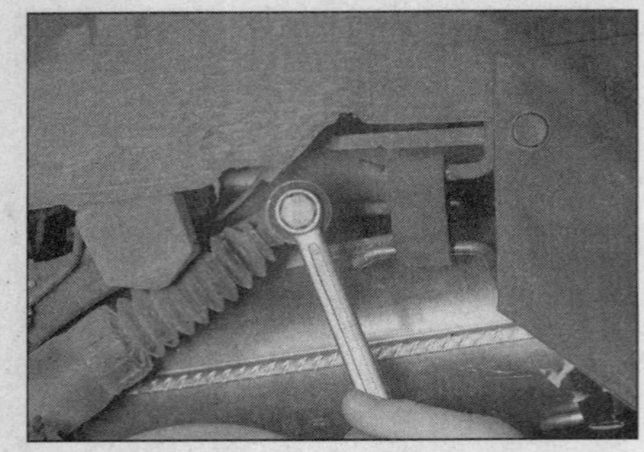
8.8 On refitting, don't fully tighten the mounting bolts until the car is resting on its wheels

7 Manoeuvre the shock absorber into position, and insert the mounting bolts. Ensure that the upper bolt is inserted from the outside of the trailing arm, and the lower bolt from the inside, as noted on removal.
8 Refit the nuts, tightening them lightly only at this stage **(see illustration)**.
9 Refit the roadwheel, then lower the vehicle to the ground and tighten the roadwheel bolts to the specified torque.
10 With the vehicle standing on its wheels, rock the vehicle to settle the shock absorber in position, then tighten both the upper and lower mountings to the specified torque setting.

9 Ride height - checking and adjustment

Checking

Note: *After each movement of the bodyshell, and each measurement during the following procedure, the manufacturers recommend rolling the car backwards and forwards slightly; this will relieve any stress in the suspension components. This will, however, only be possible if the car is on the ground, or raised on a four-post lift. If moving the car in this way is not possible, bear it in mind if the ride heights measured are slightly out of specification. The ride height should only be measured when the vehicle has no load and the fuel tank is full.*
1 Check the tyre pressures (see end of "*Weekly checks*"), and adjust if necessary.
2 Park the car on a level surface, and chock the wheels. Release the handbrake.
3 To make measuring the ride height easier, the car should now be raised to provide working room underneath, but the weight of the car must rest on the wheels for the check to be relevant. In the absence of a four-post lift, a set of four wheel ramps could be used, if available - drive the front of the car up onto the ramps for the front wheels, then jack up the rear of the car and lower the rear wheels onto the ramps. Do not use makeshift means to raise the car - checking the heights is possible with the car on the ground.
4 Measure the front ride height at each side, by measuring the distance between the ground (or the surface on which the roadwheels are resting), and the lower surface of the suspension lower arm mounting bracket **(see illustration)**. Take the average of the measurements on each side of the vehicle to give the front ride height, and call this "H1".
5 Similarly, measure the rear ride height by measuring the distance between the ground (or the surface on which the roadwheels are resting), and the base of the rear crossmember **(see illustration)**. Again, take the average of the measurements on each side of the vehicle to give the rear ride height, and call this "H2".
6 On completion of the measurements, lower the car to the ground (where applicable).
7 Now measure the radius of the front roadwheel and tyre - the distance from the wheel centre to the ground - and call this "R1". Also measure the radius of the rear roadwheel and tyre (in most cases, this will be identical to the front wheel), and call this "R2".
8 The front ride height, "H1", should be equal to "R1" minus dimension "L1", given in the Specifications at the start of this Chapter. Provided the "H1" dimension is within the tolerance quoted, the ride height is correct.

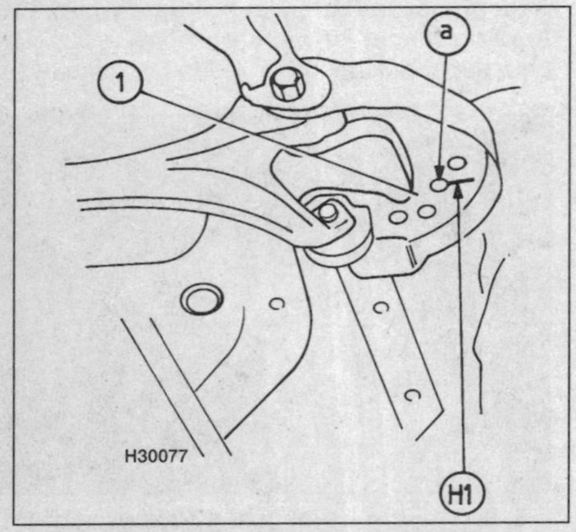

9.4 Front ride height (H1) is measured from point (a) on the suspension arm mounting (1)

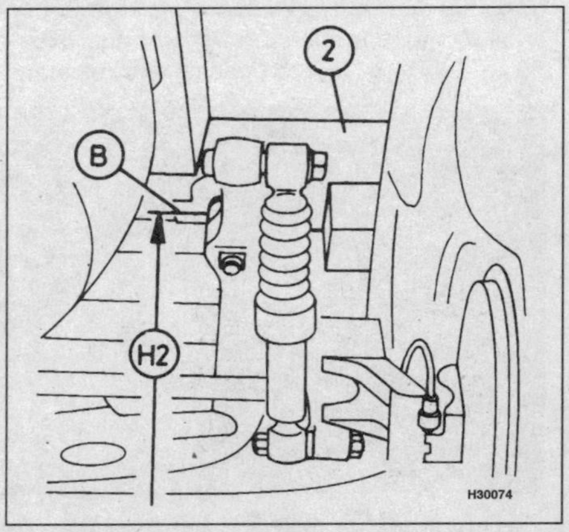

9.5 Rear ride height (H2) is measured from point (b) on the rear crossmember (2)

9 The rear ride height, "H2", should equal "R2" plus dimension "L2", specified at the start of this Chapter. As long as the rear ride height falls within the quoted tolerance, all is well.

Adjustment

10 The ride height can only be adjusted by dismantling the rear suspension and turning the torsion bars in relation to the trailing arms. If the ride height proves to be incorrect, and adjustment is required, the task should be referred to a Citroën dealer.

10 Rear suspension assembly - general

The operations in the following list can be carried out using suitable special tools, but due to the difficulty in improvising such tools easily, these procedures are considered to be beyond the scope of the home mechanic, and should be referred to a Citroën dealer:

a) *Removal and refitting of torsion bars.*
b) *Removal and refitting of rear anti-roll bar (where applicable).*
c) *Removal and refitting of trailing arms.*
d) *Renewal of suspension bushes and bearings.*
e) *Adjustment of rear suspension ride height.*

11 Steering wheel - removal and refitting

Note: *A new steering wheel securing nut must be used on refitting.*

Removal

1 Set the front wheels in the straight-ahead position, and release the steering lock by inserting the ignition key. Check that the direction indicator switch is in the central, cancelled position.
2 On models with a driver's airbag, remove the airbag unit as described in Chapter 12.
3 On models without a driver's airbag, carefully prise out the steering wheel centre pad.
4 Slacken the steering wheel Torx retaining bolt (T50) by a few turns, but do not remove it yet **(see illustration)**.

11.4 Slacken the steering wheel Torx bolt

11.5a Once the wheel is free, remove the bolt . . .

5 Mark the steering wheel and steering column shaft in relation to each other, then pull the steering wheel towards you. If it is tight, tap it up near the centre, using the palm of your hand, or twist it from side to side, whilst pulling upwards to release it from the shaft splines. If the wheel is particularly tight, a suitable puller should be used. When the wheel has been released from the splines, remove the securing bolt and the wheel **(see illustrations)**.

Refitting

6 Refitting is a reversal of removal, bearing in mind the following points:

a) Ensure that the indicator switch is in the central, cancelled position, and make sure the lug on the steering wheel engages with the switch lever.

11.5b . . . and lift off the steering wheel

b) Align the marks made on the wheel and the column shaft before removal.

c) If necessary, the position of the steering wheel on the column shaft can be altered in order to centralise the wheel, by moving the wheel the required number of splines on the shaft. Ensure that the front roadwheels are pointing in the straight-ahead position. If the wheel cannot be centralised this way, it is likely that the problem arose due to the front wheel alignment having been inexpertly set up. Have the alignment checked by a qualified specialist.

*d) Tighten the retaining bolt to the specified torque **(see illustration)**.*

e) Where applicable, refit the driver's airbag as described in Chapter 12.

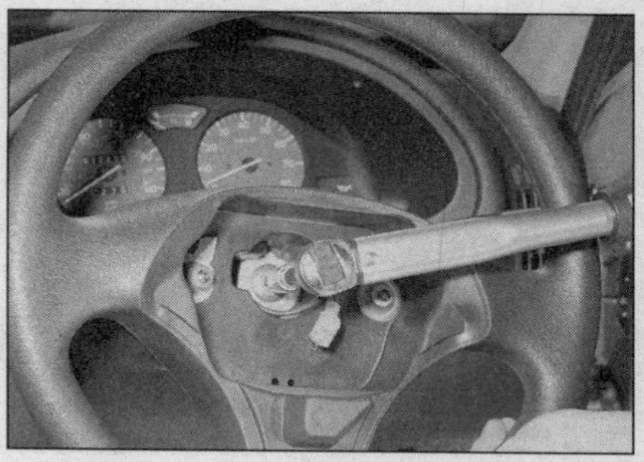

11.6 Tighten the steering wheel bolt to the specified torque

12 Ignition switch/steering column lock - removal and refitting

Removal

1 Disconnect the battery negative lead.

2 Working under the steering column, remove the two steering column shroud Torx screws (T20). Unclip and withdraw the lower shroud, then lift off the upper shroud **(see illustrations)**. Disconnect the wiring plug from the instrument lighting rheostat. On certain models, it may be necessary to remove the steering wheel in order to facilitate removal of the steering column shrouds (see Section 11).

3 Unscrew the lock retaining screw, and recover the washer from behind the lock **(see illustration)**.

4 Insert the ignition key, and rotate it so that it is aligned with the mark positioned between the "A" and "S" marks on the barrel.

5 Using a small flat-bladed screwdriver or a suitable pin-punch through the small hole, depress the lock retaining lug at the top of the barrel, then partially withdraw the ignition switch/lock assembly from the steering column **(see illustrations)**.

6 On models with a driver's airbag, disconnect the airbag wiring connector (the wiring is typically orange in colour). Unclip the plastic retaining brackets, then disconnect the three ignition switch wiring connectors under the

12.2a Remove the two shroud securing screws (arrowed) . . .

12.2b . . . then unclip the lower shroud . . .

12.2c . . . and lift off the upper shroud

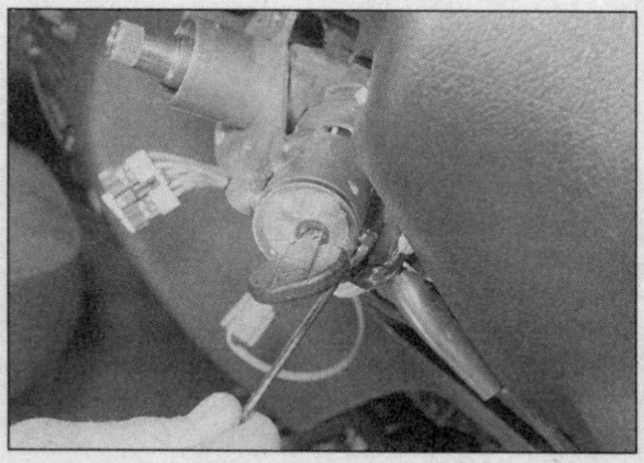

12.3 Remove the lock securing screw

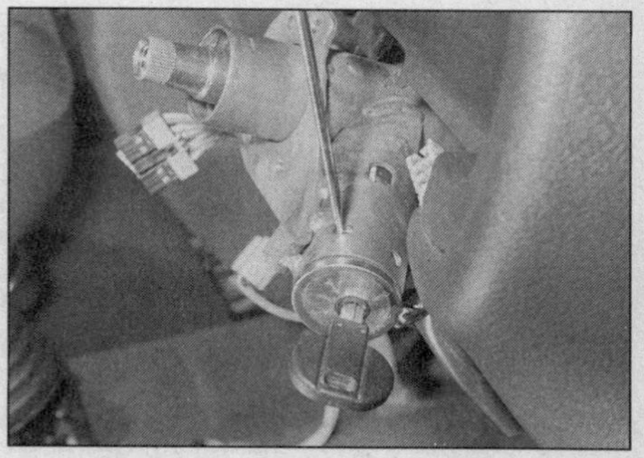

12.5a Depress the lock retaining lug . . .

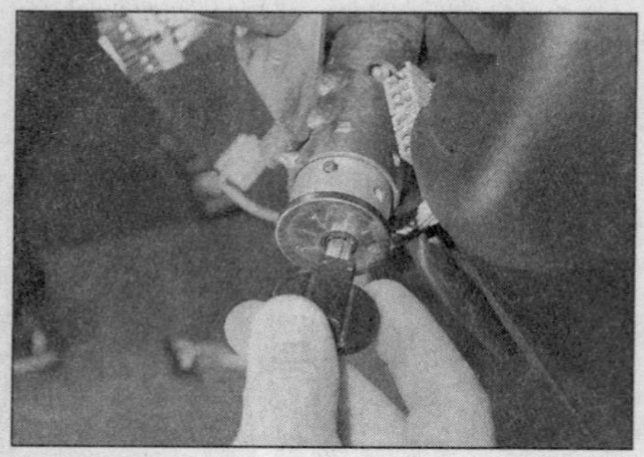

12.5b . . . and partially withdraw the ignition switch

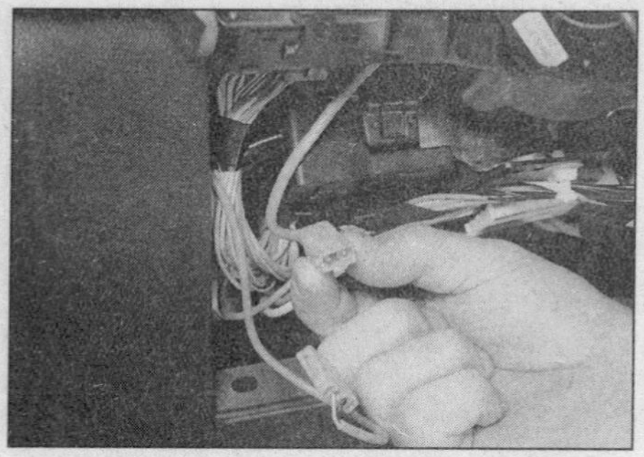

12.6a Disconnect the airbag wiring connector . . .

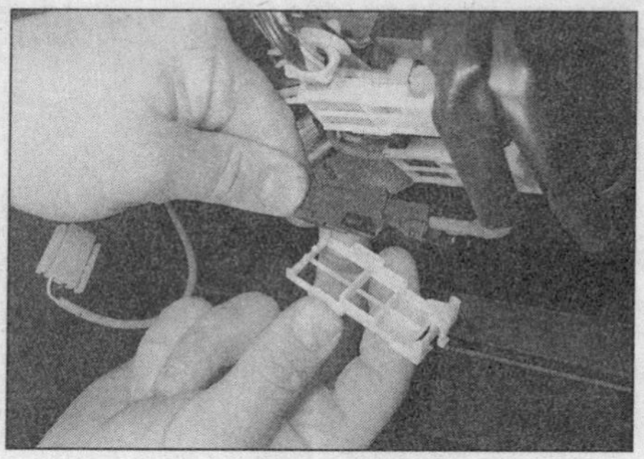

12.6b . . . then unclip the plastic brackets . . .

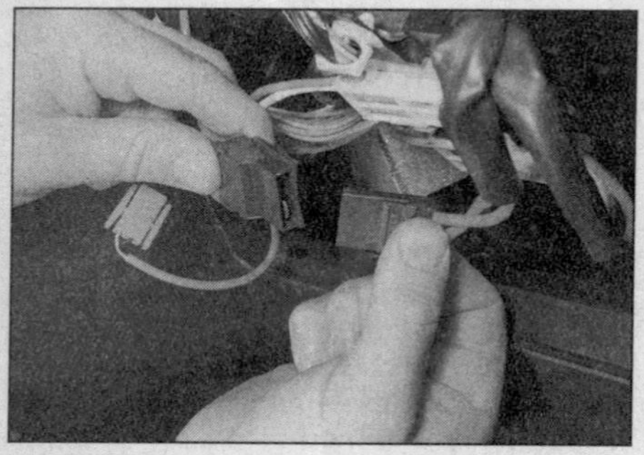

12.6c . . . and disconnect the ignition switch wiring connectors

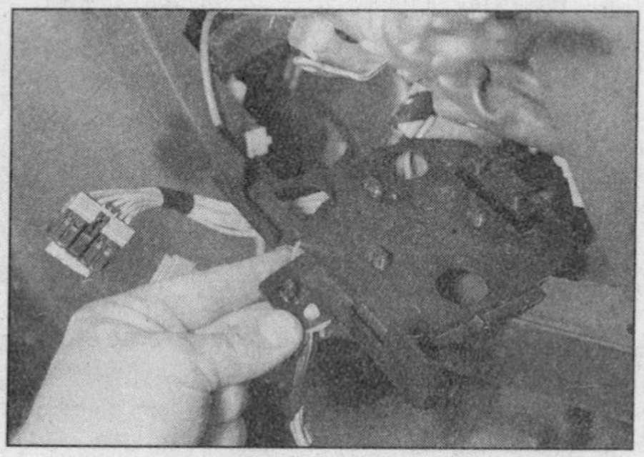

12.7 Unclip the wiring harness support plate

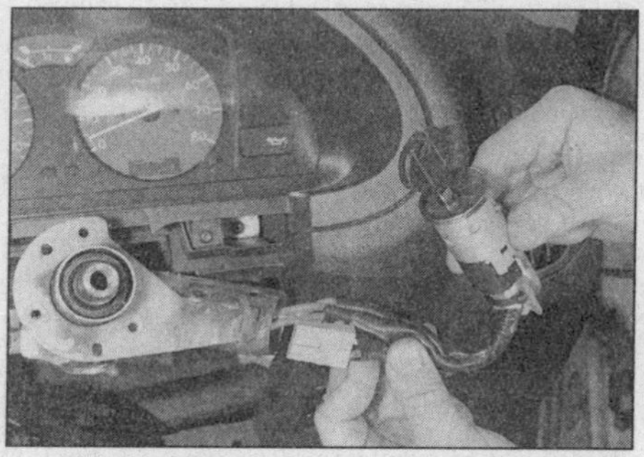

12.8 Withdraw the ignition switch and wiring through the lock barrel tube

steering column bracket **(see illustrations)**. Note the location of all connectors, so that they can be refitted in their original positions.

7 Unclip the wiring harness plastic support plate from the underside of the steering column mounting bracket, and lower it out of the way **(see illustration)**.

8 Feed the wiring through the lock barrel tube, and remove the ignition switch from the car **(see illustration)**.

Refitting

9 Refitting is a reversal of the removal procedure, ensuring that the lock assembly is securely held in position by its retaining lugs. Before refitting the steering column shrouds, remove the ignition key, and check that the steering lock functions correctly.

13 Steering column - removal, inspection and refitting

Note: *A new lower column pinch-bolt and nut must be used on refitting.*

Removal

1 Disconnect the battery negative lead.

2 Remove the steering wheel as described in Section 11.

3 Remove the ignition switch, referring to Section 12. If preferred, the switch can remain in place, but all the wiring under the steering column must be detached and disconnected as described.

4 Remove the steering column switches as described in Chapter 12.

5 Remove the two push-in clips from the front edge of the under-facia trim panel, and lower the panel **(see illustration)**.

6 If necessary, temporarily refit the steering wheel and turn the steering so that access can be gained to the securing nut on the lower column pinch-bolt **(see illustration)**. Unscrew the nut, then carefully tap the pinch-bolt from the universal joint.

7 Working in the footwell, pull off the metal clip securing the column to the steering gear pinion **(see illustration)**.

8 Make alignment marks on the universal joint and the steering gear pinion, then push the universal joint upwards to separate it from the pinion.

9 Ensure that all wiring has been moved clear of the column to facilitate removal.

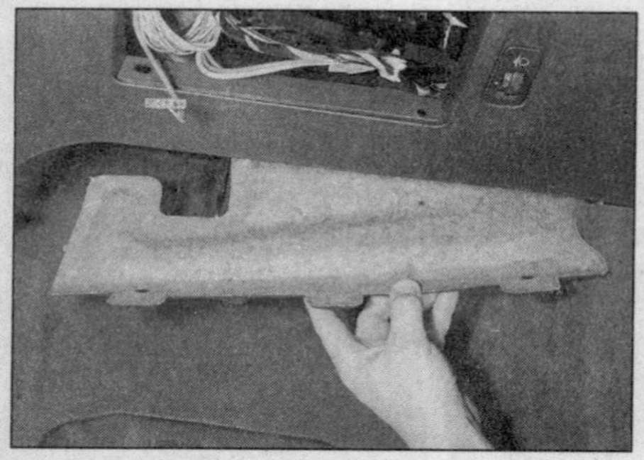

13.5 Removing the under-facia trim panel

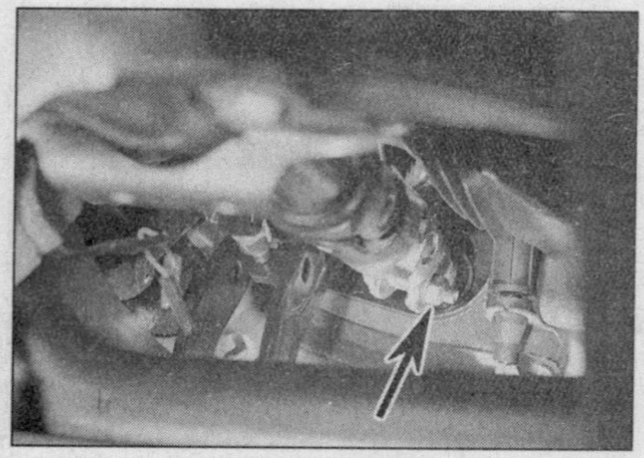

13.6 Lower column pinch-bolt nut (arrowed)

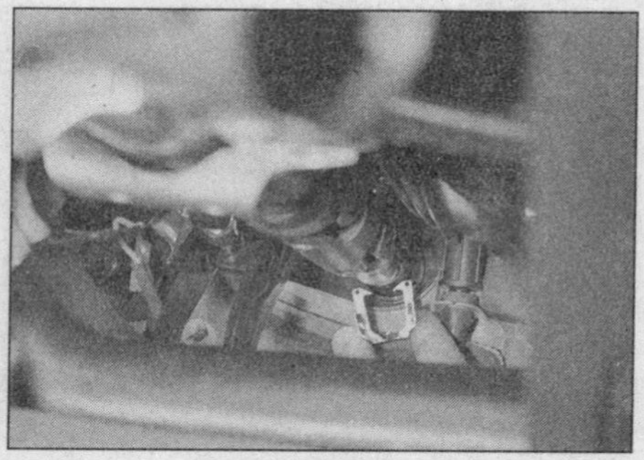

13.7 Removing the column-to-pinion metal clip

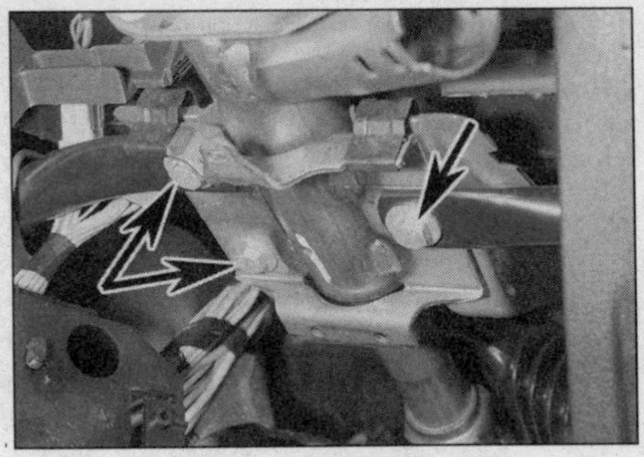

13.10a Remove the three mounting bolts (arrowed) . . .

10 Working under the steering column, unscrew the three steering column securing bolts, then lift the steering column from the facia, and withdraw it from the car **(see illustrations)**.

Inspection

11 The steering column incorporates a telescopic safety feature. In the event of a front-end crash, the shaft collapses, reducing the chance of the steering wheel injuring the driver. Before refitting the steering column, examine the column assembly for signs of damage and deformation, and renew as necessary.

12 Check the steering shaft for signs of free play in the column bushes, and check the universal joints for signs of damage or roughness in the joint bearings. If any damage or wear is found on the steering column universal joints or shaft bushes, the column must be renewed as an assembly.

Refitting

13 Offer the steering column into position, and refit the securing bolts. Tighten the bolts to the specified torque.

14 Reconnect the ignition switch wiring connectors and the combination switch wiring plugs. Fasten the ignition switch wiring connectors in position as noted before removal.

15 Slide the column universal joint over the steering gear pinion, ensuring that the marks made before removal are still aligned.

16 Refit the metal clip securing the column to the steering gear pinion.

17 Fit a new lower column pinch-bolt and nut, ensuring that the lugs on the bolt engage with the cut-outs in the universal joint. Tighten the nut to the specified torque.

18 Refit the steering column shrouds and the under-facia trim panel.

19 Refit the steering wheel as described in Section 11.

20 Reconnect the battery negative lead.

14 Steering gear assembly - removal, overhaul and refitting

Note: *New track-rod end balljoint nuts and a new lower steering column pinch-bolt and nut must be used on refitting.*

Manual steering gear

Removal

1 Ensure that the steering lock is engaged.

2 Remove the two push-in clips from the front edge of the under-facia trim panel, and lower the panel.

3 Working in the footwell, pull off the metal clip securing the column to the steering gear pinion.

4 If necessary, temporarily refit the steering wheel and turn the steering so that access can be gained to the securing nut on the lower column pinch-bolt. Unscrew the nut, then carefully tap the pinch-bolt from the universal joint. Make alignment marks on the universal joint and the steering gear pinion, then push the universal joint upwards to separate it from the pinion.

5 On diesel models, and petrol models with multi-point fuel injection, the inlet manifold may have to be removed, as described in the relevant Part of Chapter 4.

6 To improve access, chock the rear wheels, firmly apply the handbrake, then jack up the front of the vehicle and support on axle stands (see *"Jacking and vehicle support"*). Remove both front roadwheels.

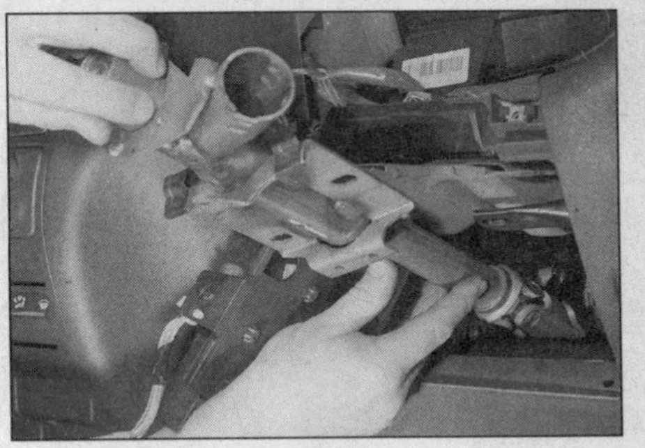

13.10b . . . and withdraw the steering column from the car

7 Working on each side of the vehicle in turn, unscrew the nut securing the track-rod end to the steering arm on the suspension strut, and recover the washer. Using a balljoint separator tool, separate the track-rod end from the steering arm.

8 Working through the right-hand wheel arch, unscrew the three Torx bolts securing the steering gear to the engine compartment bulkhead, and recover the washers **(see illustration)**.

9 Withdraw the steering gear, complete with the track-rods, through the right-hand wheel arch. If the pinion shaft seal comes away with the steering gear, make sure it is refitted to the bulkhead before refitting the steering gear **(see illustration)**.

Overhaul

10 Examine the steering gear assembly for signs of wear or damage. Check that the rack moves freely throughout the full length of its travel, with no signs of roughness or excessive free play between the steering gear pinion and rack. It is possible to overhaul the steering gear assembly housing components, but this task should be entrusted to a Citroën

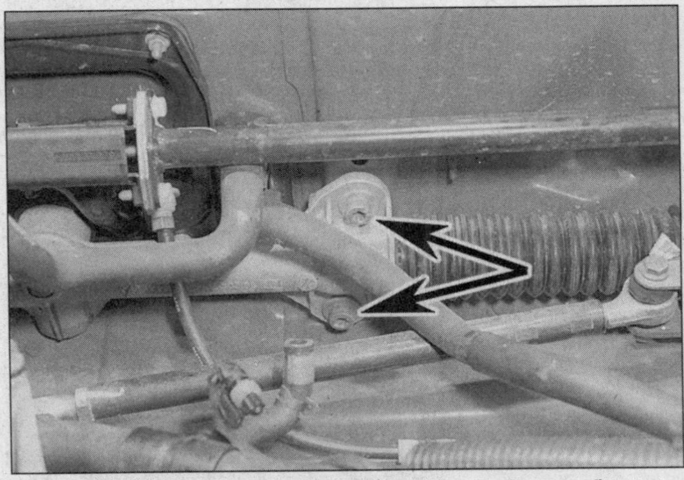

14.8 Two of the steering gear Torx bolts (arrowed)

14.9 Withdrawing the steering gear - note the pinion shaft seal (arrowed)

10

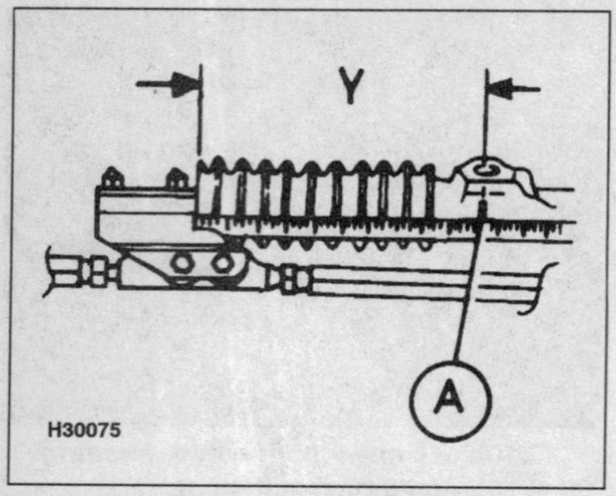

14.13 Steering rack centralisation - rack at maximum-travel position (left-hand-drive steering gear shown)

A Mark on rack housing
Y Maximum movement of rack - gaiter fully extended

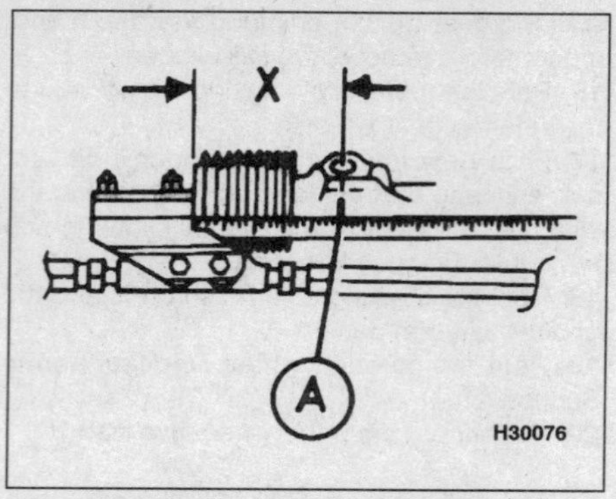

14.14 Steering rack centralisation - rack at minimum-travel position (left-hand-drive steering gear shown)

A Mark on rack housing
X Minimum movement of rack - gaiter fully compressed

dealer. The only components which can be renewed easily by the home mechanic are the steering gear rubber gaiter, the track-rod balljoints and the track-rods. Steering gear rubber gaiter, track-rod balljoint, and track-rod renewal procedures, are covered in Sections 15, 18 and 19 respectively.

Refitting

11 Before refitting the steering gear, the rack must be centralised as follows.

12 Make a mark on the rack housing, corresponding with the centre-line of the steering gear securing bolt hole nearest the steering gear rubber gaiter.

13 Move the rack to its full extent of movement, so that the steering gear rubber gaiter is fully extended. Measure the distance from the mark made on the rack housing to the end of the steering gear rubber gaiter nearest the track-rod sleeve. Call this dimension "Y" **(see illustration)**.

14 Move the rack to its full extent of movement in the opposite direction, until the rubber gaiter is fully compressed. Again, measure the distance from the mark made on the rack housing to the end of the steering gear rubber gaiter nearest the track-rod sleeve. Call this dimension "X" **(see illustration)**.

15 Calculate the dimension between the mark on the rack housing and the end of the steering gear rubber gaiter, which corresponds to the mid-position of the rack. Call this dimension "Z". Dimension "Z" can be calculated as follows:

a) Subtract "X" from "Y", and divide the result by 2.
b) Add "X" to the result of the previous calculation, to give dimension "Z". ie: $Z = (Y - X)/2 + X$

16 Set the steering gear to dimension "Z", then proceed with the refitting procedure as follows, ensuring that the rack position is not altered during the refitting procedure.

17 Check the condition of the pinion shaft seal located in the engine compartment bulkhead. Ensure that the seal is correctly located, and renew the seal if there are any signs of damage or wear.

18 Offer the steering gear into position through the right-hand wheel arch.

19 Check the routing of the clutch cable, making sure that the cable is not trapped between the steering gear and the track-rod.

20 Locate the steering gear on the bulkhead, ensuring that the pegs on the rear of the steering gear engage with the corresponding holes in the bulkhead.

21 Fit the steering gear securing bolts, and tighten them to the specified torque.

22 Reconnect the track-rods to the steering arms, then fit the washers and new nuts, and tighten the nuts to the specified torque.

23 Slide the column universal joint over the steering gear pinion, ensuring that the marks made before removal are still aligned. Refit the metal clip securing the column to the steering gear pinion.

24 Fit a new lower column pinch-bolt and nut, ensuring that the lugs on the bolt engage with the cut-outs in the universal joint. Tighten the nut to the specified torque.

25 Refit the under-facia trim panel.

26 Refit the roadwheels, then lower the vehicle to the ground and tighten the roadwheel bolts to the specified torque. Where removed, refit the inlet manifold as described in the relevant Part of Chapter 4.

27 Have the front wheel alignment checked at the earliest opportunity (refer to Section 20 for details), and check that the steering wheel is centralised (if necessary, the steering wheel position can be altered by removing the wheel and moving it the required number of splines on the column shaft before refitting - see Section 11).

Power steering gear

Removal

28 Using suitable clamps, clamp both the fluid supply and return hoses near the power steering fluid reservoir. This will minimise fluid loss during subsequent operations.

29 Mark the unions to ensure that they are correctly positioned on reassembly, then unscrew the feed and return pipe union nuts from the steering gear assembly; be prepared for fluid spillage, and position a suitable container beneath the pipes whilst unscrewing the union nuts. Disconnect both pipes, and plug the pipe ends and steering gear orifices, to prevent fluid leakage and to keep dirt out of the hydraulic system.

30 Free the power steering pipes from any retaining clips, and position them clear of the steering gear so that they will not hinder the removal procedure.

31 Remove the steering gear as described in paragraphs 1 to 9 inclusive.

Overhaul

32 Refer to paragraph 10, but additionally, inspect all the steering gear fluid unions for signs of leakage, and check that all union nuts are securely tightened. Also examine the steering gear hydraulic ram for signs of fluid leakage or damage, and if necessary renew it.

Refitting

33 Refitting is as described in paragraphs 11 to 27 inclusive, but additionally, note the following:

a) Reconnect the fluid pipes to the steering gear, ensuring that they are correctly reconnected as noted before removal.
b) Ensure that the pipes are repositioned correctly in any relevant clips, and correctly routed to avoid straining the pipes.
c) On completion, bleed the power steering hydraulic system as described in Section 16, and if necessary top-up the fluid level (see "Weekly checks").

15 Steering gear rubber gaiter - renewal

1 Where necessary to improve access, remove the inlet manifold as described in the relevant Part of Chapter 4.

2 Unscrew the securing bolts (while counterholding the nuts), and disconnect the inner ends of the track-rods from the steering gear **(see illustration)**.

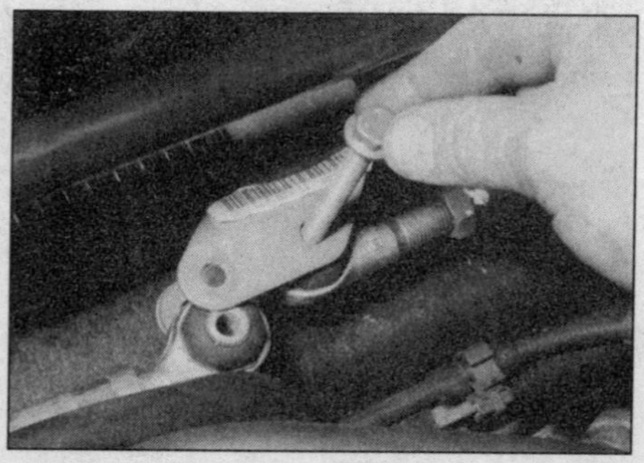

15.2 Remove the track-rod securing bolts

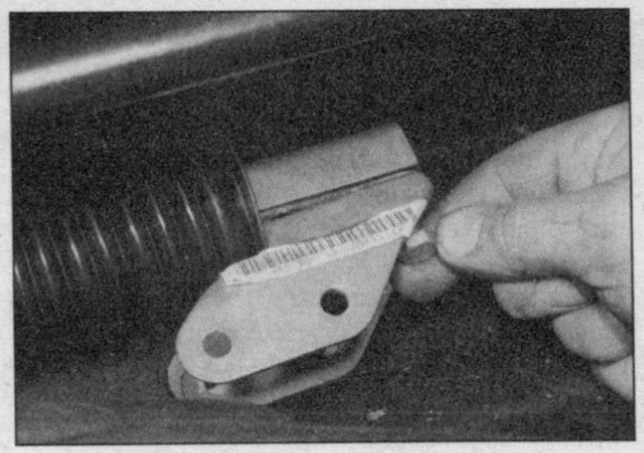

15.3a Unscrew the securing bolts . . .

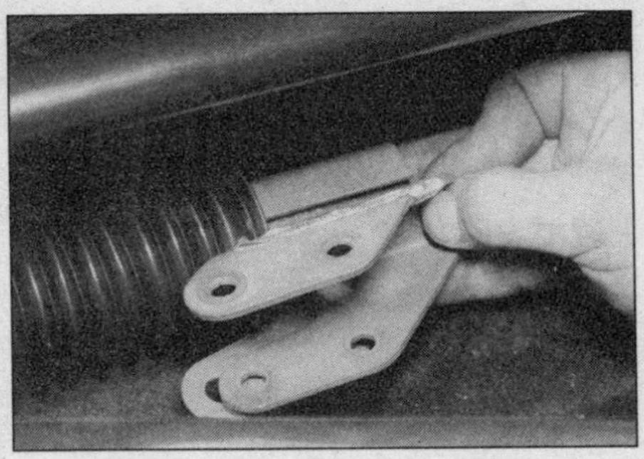

15.3b . . . and remove the upper . . .

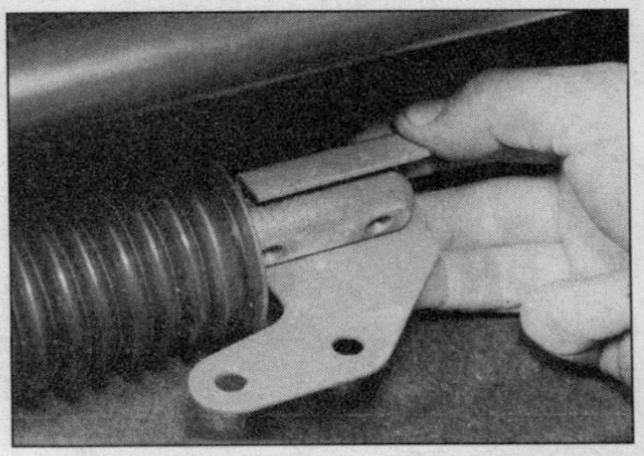

15.3c . . . and lower sections of the track-rod bracket

3 Unscrew the two securing bolts, and remove the upper and lower sections of the track-rod bracket **(see illustrations)**.

4 Release the securing clip from the pinion end of the gaiter, then slide the gaiter from the steering gear **(see illustration)**.

5 Fit the new gaiter using a reversal of the removal procedure. Tighten all fixings to the specified torque, and (where applicable) refit the inlet manifold as described in the relevant Part of Chapter 4.

16 Power steering hydraulic system - bleeding

1 This procedure will only be necessary when any part of the hydraulic system has been disconnected.

2 Referring to "*Weekly checks*", remove the fluid reservoir filler cap, and top-up with the specified fluid to the maximum level mark.

3 With the engine stopped (ignition key removed), slowly move the steering from lock-to-lock several times to purge out any trapped air, then top-up the level in the fluid reservoir. Repeat this procedure until the fluid level in the reservoir does not drop any further.

4 Start the engine, then slowly move the steering from lock-to-lock several times, to purge out any remaining air in the system. Repeat this procedure until bubbles cease to appear in the fluid reservoir.

5 If, when turning the steering, an abnormal noise is heard from the fluid lines, it indicates that there is still air in the system. Check this by turning the wheels to the straight-ahead position and switching off the engine. If the fluid level in the reservoir rises, then air is present in the system, and further bleeding is necessary.

6 Once all traces of air have been removed from the power steering hydraulic system, stop the engine and allow the system to cool. Once cool, check that the fluid level is up to the maximum mark on the reservoir. Top-up if necessary.

17 Power steering pump - removal and refitting

1 All models with power steering are equipped with a remote-mounted electrically-operated pump, rather than one which is driven by the auxiliary drivebelt.

Removal

2 The power steering pump may be mounted inside its own plastic housing - where necessary, to gain access to the top of the pump, remove the screws and clips, and lift off the top cover.

3 Disconnect the battery negative lead.

4 Using suitable clamps, clamp both the fluid supply and return hoses near the power steering fluid reservoir. This will minimise fluid loss during subsequent operations.

5 Apply the handbrake, then raise and support the front of the car on axle stands (see *"Jacking and vehicle support"*).

U-shaped mounting bracket pump

6 Disconnect the wiring from the pump body - some models have a multi-plug connector, on others, the wiring is secured to the pump body by two nuts. Note the location of the wires, for use when refitting.

7 Disconnect the low-pressure fluid return hose, and place the end in a clean container. Turn the steering from lock to lock a few times, to purge the fluid from the pump and further minimise spillage.

8 Disconnect the high-pressure supply hose leading to the rack, and plug the pump hole to minimise fluid loss and prevent dirt entry.

9 Support the mounting bracket from below, then loosen (do not remove) the mounting bracket-to-body bolts.

10 Loosen and remove the three pump mounting bolts. It may be necessary to move the steering pump fusebox upwards and to one side for access to one of the bolts.

11 Unclip the steering fluid reservoir from its mounting, and remove the pump and reservoir from the engine compartment.

Collar-mounted pump

12 On models with automatic transmission, remove the transmission ECU support bracket

15.4 Slide the gaiter from the steering gear

to improve access to the pump.

13 Disconnect the low-pressure fluid return hose, and place the end in a clean container. Turn the steering from lock to lock a few times, to purge the fluid from the pump and further minimise spillage.

14 Disconnect the high-pressure supply hose leading to the rack, and plug the pump hole to minimise fluid loss and prevent dirt entry.

15 Unclip the relay and the wiring harness from the pump mounting.

16 Support the pump from below, then unscrew and remove the four pump mounting-to-body bolts **(see illustration)**.

17 Disconnect the wiring connector located below the pump fuse. Unclip the pipework around the pump, noting its routing **(see illustration)**.

18 Unclip the steering fluid reservoir from its mounting, and remove the pump and reservoir from the engine compartment.

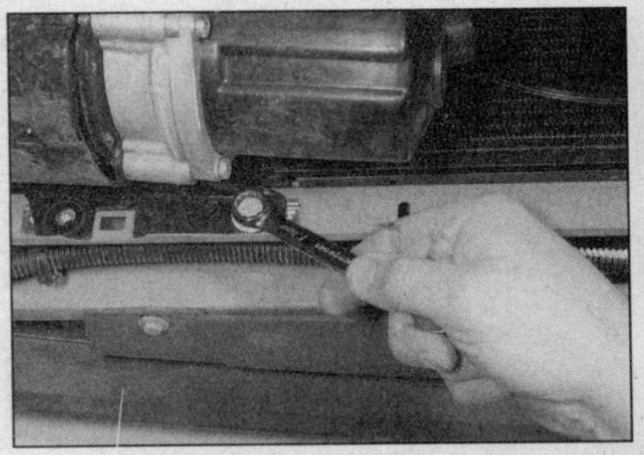

17.16 Removing the power steering pump mounting bolts

17.17 Unclip the pump pipework above the pump

19 Loosen the clamp bolts, and release the pump from its mounting clamp.

Refitting

U-shaped mounting bracket pump

20 Refitting is a reversal of removal, noting the following points:
- a) *Before refitting the pump, check the condition of the mounting bracket rubber bushes, and replace if necessary.*
- b) *Tighten all fixings and fluid unions to the specified torque, and ensure that the wiring connections are securely re-made.*
- c) *Fill and bleed the power steering system, taking care to ensure that as much air as possible is bled out before the engine is started. If preferred, pre-fill the steering pump with fluid before finally connecting and tightening the unions.*

Collar-mounted pump

21 Refitting is a reversal of removal, noting the following points:
- a) *Fit the pump into its collar, and tighten the clamp screws to the specified torque.*
- b) *Tighten all fixings and fluid unions to the specified torque, and ensure that the wiring connections are securely re-made.*
- c) *Fill and bleed the power steering system, taking care to ensure that as much air as possible is bled out before the engine is started. If preferred, pre-fill the steering pump with fluid before finally connecting and tightening the unions.*

18 Track-rod balljoint - removal and refitting

Inner balljoint

Removal

1 Remove the track-rod as described in Section 19.

2 Note the number of exposed threads on the balljoint shank, then loosen the locknut, and unscrew the balljoint from the end of the track-rod.

Refitting

3 Screw the balljoint onto the end of the track-rod to leave the same number of threads exposed as noted during removal, then tighten the locknut. Ensure that the bolt hole in the balljoint is vertical - ie parallel to the outer track-rod balljoint pin.

4 Refit the track-rod as described in Section 19.

Outer balljoint

Note: *A new track-rod end balljoint nut must be used on refitting.*

Removal

5 Chock the rear wheels, firmly apply the handbrake, then jack up the front of the vehicle and support on axle stands (see *"Jacking and vehicle support"*). Remove the relevant front roadwheel.

6 Loosen the nut securing the track-rod end to the steering arm on the suspension strut, leaving it on the shank by a few threads. Using a balljoint separator tool, separate the track-rod end from the steering arm. Remove the nut and recover the washer.

7 Note the number of exposed threads on the balljoint shank, then loosen the locknut, and unscrew the balljoint from the end of the track-rod.

Refitting

8 Screw the balljoint onto the end of the track-rod, to leave the same number of threads exposed as noted during removal, then tighten the locknut. Ensure that the balljoint pin is pointing vertically downwards.

9 Reconnect the track-rod to the steering arms, then fit the washer and new nut, and tighten the nut to the specified torque.

10 Refit the roadwheel, then lower the vehicle to the ground and tighten the roadwheel bolts to the specified torque.

11 Have the front wheel alignment checked at the earliest opportunity (refer to Section 20 for details). Check also that the steering wheel is centralised (if necessary, the steering wheel position can be altered, albeit roughly, by removing the wheel and moving it the required number of splines on the column shaft before refitting - see Section 11).

19 Track-rod - removal and refitting

Note: *A new track-rod outer end balljoint nut, and a new track-rod-to-steering gear nut, must be used on refitting.*

Removal

1 Chock the rear wheels, firmly apply the handbrake, then jack up the front of the vehicle and support on axle stands (see *"Jacking and vehicle support"*). Remove the relevant front roadwheel.

2 Loosen the nut securing the track-rod end to the steering arm on the suspension strut, leaving it on the shank by a few threads. Using a balljoint separator tool, separate the track-rod end from the steering arm **(see illustrations)**. Remove the nut and recover the washer.

3 Working in the engine compartment, unscrew the bolt securing the inner end of the track-rod to the steering gear **(see illustration)**. It will be necessary to counterhold the nut as the bolt is unscrewed. Recover the washer from under the nut.

4 Withdraw the track-rod through the wheel arch.

Refitting

5 Refitting is a reversal of removal, bearing in mind the following points:
- a) *Use a new track-rod outer end balljoint nut.*
- b) *Use a new track-rod-to-steering gear nut.*
- c) *Tighten all fixings to the specified torques.*

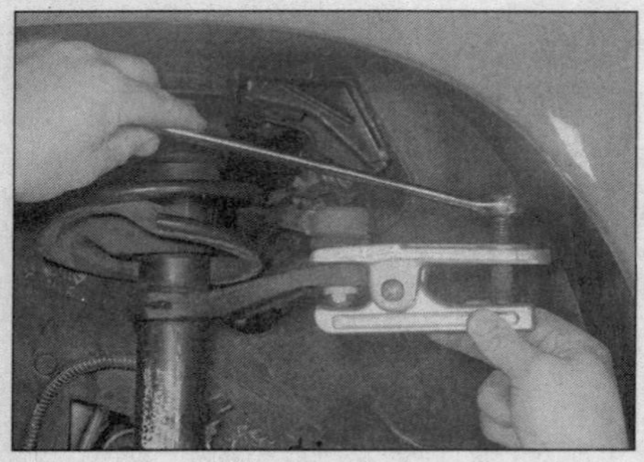

19.2a Using a balljoint separator tool . . .

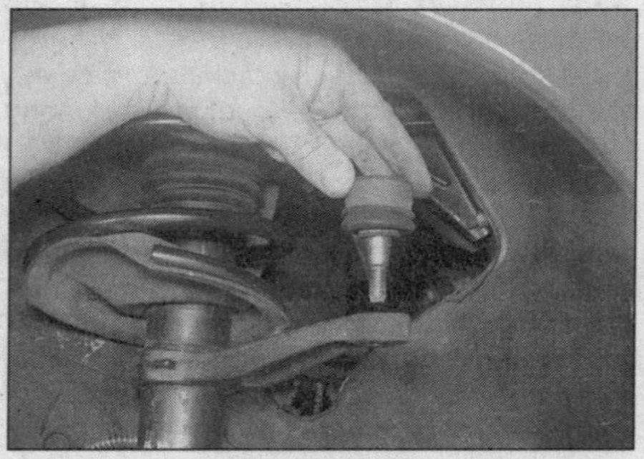

19.2b . . . separate the track-rod end from the steering arm on the suspension strut

19.3 Track-rod-to-steering gear bolts (arrowed)

d) On completion, have the front wheel alignment checked at the earliest opportunity (refer to Section 20 for details), and check that the steering wheel is centralised (if necessary, the steering wheel position can be altered, albeit roughly, by removing the wheel and moving it the required number of splines on the column shaft before refitting - see Section 11).

20 Wheel alignment and steering angles - general information

Definitions

1 A vehicle's steering and suspension geometry is defined in four basic settings - all angles are expressed in degrees (toe settings are also expressed as a measurement); the steering axis is defined as an imaginary line drawn through the axis of the suspension strut, extended where necessary to contact the ground.

2 **Camber** is the angle between each roadwheel and a vertical line drawn through its centre and tyre contact patch, when viewed from the front or rear of the car. "Positive" camber is when the roadwheels are tilted outwards from the vertical at the top; "negative" camber is when they are tilted inwards.

3 Camber is not adjustable, and is given for reference only; while it can be checked using a camber checking gauge, if the figure obtained is significantly different from that specified, the vehicle must be taken for careful checking by a professional, as the fault can only be caused by wear or damage to the body or suspension components.

4 **Castor** is the angle between the steering axis and a vertical line drawn through each roadwheel centre and tyre contact patch, when viewed from the side of the car. "Positive" castor is when the steering axis is tilted so that it contacts the ground ahead of the vertical; "negative" castor is when it contacts the ground behind the vertical.

5 Castor is not adjustable, and is given for reference only; while it can be checked using a castor checking gauge, if the figure obtained is significantly different from that specified, the vehicle must be taken for careful checking by a professional, as the fault can only be caused by wear or damage to the body or suspension components.

6 **Steering axis inclination/SAI** - also known as **kingpin inclination/KPI** - is the angle between the steering axis and a vertical line drawn through each roadwheel centre and tyre contact patch, when viewed from the front or rear of the car.

7 SAI/KPI is not adjustable, and is given for reference only.

8 **Toe** is the difference, viewed from above, between lines drawn through the roadwheel centres and the car's centre-line. "Toe-in" is when the roadwheels point inwards, towards each other at the front, while "toe-out" is when they splay outwards from each other at the front.

9 The front wheel toe setting is adjusted by screwing the balljoints in or out of their track-rods, to alter the effective length of the track-rod assemblies.

10 Rear wheel toe setting is not adjustable, and is given for reference only. While it can be checked, if the figure obtained is significantly different from that specified, the vehicle must be taken for careful checking by a professional, as the fault can only be caused by wear or damage to the body or suspension components.

Checking - general

11 Due to the special measuring equipment necessary to check the wheel alignment, and the skill required to use it properly, the checking and adjustment of these settings is best left to a Citroën dealer or similar expert. Note that most tyre-fitting centres now possess sophisticated checking equipment.

12 For **accurate** checking, the vehicle **must** be at the kerb weight, ie unladen and with a full tank of fuel, and the ride height must be correct (see Section 9).

13 Before starting work, check first that the tyre sizes and types are as specified, then check the tyre pressures and tread wear, the roadwheel run-out, the condition of the hub bearings, the steering wheel free play, and the condition of the front suspension components (see "*Weekly checks*" and Chapter 1A or 1B). Correct any faults found.

14 Park the vehicle on level ground, check that the front roadwheels are in the straight-ahead position, then rock the rear and front ends to settle the suspension. Release the handbrake, and roll the vehicle backwards approximately 1 metre, then forwards again, to relieve any stresses in the steering and suspension components.

Toe setting - checking and adjusting

Front wheel toe setting

15 The front wheel toe setting is checked by measuring the distance between the front and rear inside edges of the roadwheel rims. Proprietary toe measurement gauges are available from motor accessory shops.

16 Prepare the vehicle as described in paragraphs 12 to 14 above.

17 A tracking gauge must now be obtained. Two types of gauge are available, and can be obtained from motor accessory shops. The first type measures the distance between the front and rear inside edges of the roadwheels, as described previously, with the car stationary. The second type, known as a scuff plate, measures the actual position of the contact surface of the tyre in relation to the road surface, with the vehicle in motion. This is achieved by pushing or driving the front tyre over a plate, which then moves slightly according to the scuff of the tyre, and shows this movement on a scale. Both types have their advantages and disadvantages, but either can give satisfactory results if used correctly and carefully. Alternatively, a tracking gauge can be fabricated from a length of steel tubing, suitably cranked to clear the engine and gearbox assembly, with a setscrew and a locknut at one end.

18 Many tyre specialists will also check toe settings free, or for a small charge.

19 Make sure that the steering is in the straight-ahead position when taking measurements.

20 If adjustment is found to be necessary, clean the ends of the track-rods in the areas of the adjustment pin locknuts.

21 Slacken the locknuts (one at the inner and outer end of each adjustment pin), and turn the adjustment pin on each track-rod by equal amounts in the same direction **(see illustration)**. Only turn each pin by a quarter of a turn at a time before rechecking.

22 Check that the track-rod end balljoints are centralised, and not forced to the limit of movement in any direction.

23 When adjustment is correct, tighten the locknuts.

24 Check that the track-rod lengths are equal, and that the steering wheel spokes are in the straight-ahead position.

Rear wheel toe setting

25 The procedure for checking the rear toe setting is same as described for the front wheel setting in paragraph 17. The setting is not adjustable - see paragraph 10.

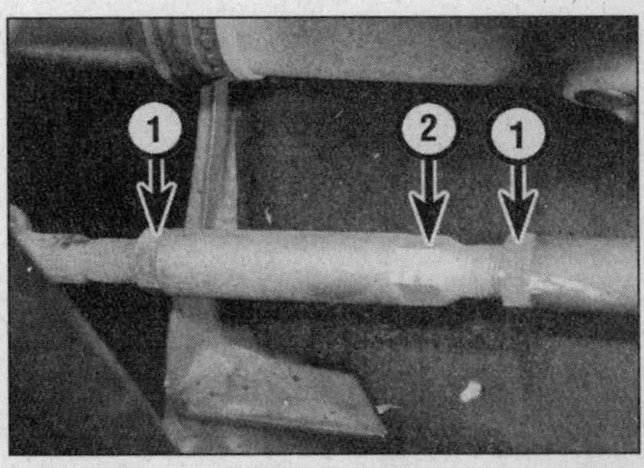

20.21 Track-rod adjuster pin locknuts (1) and adjuster pin flats (2)

Chapter 11
Bodywork and fittings

Contents

Degrees of difficulty

Easy, suitable for novice with little experience	**Fairly easy,** suitable for beginner with some experience	**Fairly difficult,** suitable for competent DIY mechanic	**Difficult,** suitable for experienced DIY mechanic	**Very difficult,** suitable for expert DIY or professional

Specifications

Torque wrench settings

	Nm	lbf ft
Seat rail-to-floor securing bolts	25	18
Seat belt mounting bolts	20	15

1 General information

The bodyshell is made of pressed-steel sections, and is available in both three- and five-door Hatchback versions. Most components are welded together, but some use is made of structural adhesives; the front wings are bolted on.

The bonnet, door, and some other vulnerable panels are made of zinc-coated metal, and are further protected by being coated with an anti-chip primer, prior to being sprayed.

Extensive use is made of plastic materials, mainly in the interior, but also in exterior components. The front and rear bumpers are injection-moulded from a synthetic material which is very strong and yet light. Plastic components such as wheel arch liners are fitted to the underside of the vehicle, to improve the body's resistance to corrosion.

2 Maintenance - bodywork and underframe

The general condition of a vehicle's bodywork is the one thing that significantly affects its value. Maintenance is easy, but needs to be regular. Neglect, particularly after minor damage, can lead quickly to further deterioration and costly repair bills. It is important also to keep watch on those parts of the vehicle not immediately visible, for instance the underside, inside all the wheel arches, and the lower part of the engine compartment.

The basic maintenance routine for the bodywork is washing - preferably with a lot of water, from a hose. This will remove all the loose solids which may have stuck to the vehicle. It is important to flush these off in such a way as to prevent grit from scratching the finish. The wheel arches and underframe need washing in the same way, to remove any accumulated mud, which will retain moisture and tend to encourage rust. Paradoxically enough, the best time to clean the underframe and wheel arches is in wet weather, when the mud is thoroughly wet and soft. In very wet weather, the underframe is usually cleaned of large accumulations automatically, and this is a good time for inspection.

Periodically, except on vehicles with a wax-based underbody protective coating, it is a good idea to have the whole of the underframe of the vehicle steam-cleaned, engine compartment included, so that a thorough inspection can be carried out to see what minor repairs and renovations are necessary. Steam-cleaning is available at many garages, and is necessary for the removal of the accumulation of oily grime, which sometimes is allowed to become thick in certain areas. If steam-cleaning facilities are not available, there are some excellent grease solvents available which can be brush-applied; the dirt can then be simply hosed off. Note that these methods should not be used on vehicles with wax-based underbody protective coating, or the coating will be removed. Such vehicles should be inspected annually, preferably just prior to Winter, when the underbody should be washed down, and any damage to the wax coating repaired. Ideally, a completely fresh coat should be applied. It would also be worth considering the use of such wax-based protection for injection into door panels, sills, box sections, etc, as an additional safeguard against rust damage, where such protection is not provided by the vehicle manufacturer.

After washing paintwork, wipe off with a chamois leather to give an unspotted clear finish. A coat of clear protective wax polish will give added protection against chemical pollutants in the air. If the paintwork sheen has dulled or oxidised, use a cleaner/polisher combination to restore the brilliance of the shine. This requires a little effort, but such dulling is usually caused because regular washing has been neglected. Care needs to be taken with metallic paintwork, as special non-abrasive cleaner/polisher is required to avoid damage to the finish. Always check that the door and ventilator opening drain holes and pipes are completely clear, so that water can be drained out **(see illustration).** Brightwork should be treated in the same way as paintwork. Windscreens and windows can be kept clear of the smeary film which often appears, by the use of proprietary glass cleaner. Never use any form of wax or other body or chromium polish on glass.

3 Maintenance - upholstery and carpets

Mats and carpets should be brushed or vacuum-cleaned regularly, to keep them free of grit. If they are badly stained, remove them from the vehicle for scrubbing or sponging, and make quite sure they are dry before refitting. Seats and interior trim panels can be kept clean by wiping with a damp cloth. If they do become stained (which can be more apparent on light-coloured upholstery), use a little liquid detergent and a soft nail brush to scour the grime out of the grain of the material. Do not forget to keep the headlining clean in the same way as the upholstery. When using liquid cleaners inside the vehicle, do not over-wet the surfaces being cleaned. Excessive damp could get into the seams and padded interior, causing stains, offensive odours or even rot.

HAYNES HiNT *If the inside of the vehicle gets wet accidentally, it is worthwhile taking some trouble to dry it out properly, particularly where carpets are involved. Do not leave oil or electric heaters inside the vehicle for this purpose.*

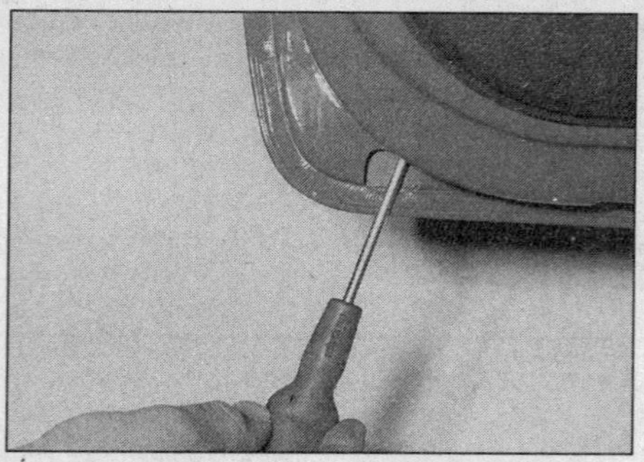

2.4 Probe the door drain holes with a suitable tool to keep them clear

4 Minor body damage - repair

Repairs of minor scratches in bodywork

If the scratch is very superficial, and does not penetrate to the metal of the bodywork, repair is very simple. Lightly rub the area of the scratch with a paintwork renovator, or a very fine cutting paste, to remove loose paint from the scratch, and to clear the surrounding bodywork of wax polish. Rinse the area with clean water.

Apply touch-up paint to the scratch using a fine paint brush; continue to apply fine layers of paint until the surface of the paint in the scratch is level with the surrounding paintwork. Allow the new paint at least two weeks to harden, then blend it into the surrounding paintwork by rubbing the scratch area with a paintwork renovator or a very fine cutting paste. Finally, apply wax polish.

Where the scratch has penetrated right through to the metal of the bodywork, causing the metal to rust, a different repair technique is required. Remove any loose rust from the bottom of the scratch with a penknife, then apply rust-inhibiting paint to prevent the formation of rust in the future. Using a rubber or nylon applicator, fill the scratch with bodystopper paste. If required, this paste can be mixed with cellulose thinners to provide a very thin paste which is ideal for filling narrow scratches. Before the stopper-paste in the scratch hardens, wrap a piece of smooth cotton rag around the top of a finger. Dip the finger in cellulose thinners, and quickly sweep it across the surface of the stopper-paste in the scratch; this will ensure that the surface of the stopper-paste is slightly hollowed. The scratch can now be painted over as described earlier in this Section.

Repairs of dents in bodywork

When deep denting of the vehicle's bodywork has taken place, the first task is to pull the dent out, until the affected bodywork almost attains its original shape. There is little point in trying to restore the original shape completely, as the metal in the damaged area will have stretched on impact, and cannot be reshaped fully to its original contour. It is better to bring the level of the dent up to a point which is about 3 mm below the level of the surrounding bodywork. In cases where the dent is very shallow anyway, it is not worth trying to pull it out at all. If the underside of the dent is accessible, it can be hammered out gently from behind, using a mallet with a wooden or plastic head. Whilst doing this, hold a suitable block of wood firmly against the outside of the panel, to absorb the impact from the hammer blows and thus prevent a large area of the bodywork from being "belled-out".

Should the dent be in a section of the bodywork which has a double skin, or some other factor making it inaccessible from behind, a different technique is called for. Drill several small holes through the metal inside the area - particularly in the deeper section. Then screw long self-tapping screws into the holes, just sufficiently for them to gain a good purchase in the metal. Now the dent can be pulled out by pulling on the protruding heads of the screws with a pair of pliers.

The next stage of the repair is the removal of the paint from the damaged area, and from an inch or so of the surrounding "sound" bodywork. This is accomplished most easily by using a wire brush or abrasive pad on a power drill, although it can be done just as effectively by hand, using sheets of abrasive paper. To complete the preparation for filling, score the surface of the bare metal with a screwdriver or the tang of a file, or alternatively, drill small holes in the affected area. This will provide a really good "key" for the filler paste.

To complete the repair, see the Section on filling and respraying.

Repairs of rust holes or gashes in bodywork

Remove all paint from the affected area, and from an inch or so of the surrounding "sound" bodywork, using an abrasive pad or a wire brush on a power drill. If these are not available, a few sheets of abrasive paper will do the job most effectively. With the paint removed, you will be able to judge the severity of the corrosion, and therefore decide whether to renew the whole panel (if this is possible) or to repair the affected area. New body panels are not as expensive as most people think, and it is often quicker and more satisfactory to fit a new panel than to attempt to repair large areas of corrosion.

Remove all fittings from the affected area, except those which will act as a guide to the original shape of the damaged bodywork (eg headlight shells etc). Then, using tin snips or a hacksaw blade, remove all loose metal and any other metal badly affected by corrosion. Hammer the edges of the hole inwards, in order to create a slight depression for the filler paste.

Wire-brush the affected area to remove the powdery rust from the surface of the remaining metal. Paint the affected area with rust-inhibiting paint, if the back of the rusted area is accessible, treat this also.

Before filling can take place, it will be necessary to block the hole in some way. This can be achieved by the use of aluminium or plastic mesh, or aluminium tape.

Aluminium or plastic mesh, or glass-fibre matting, is probably the best material to use for a large hole. Cut a piece to the approximate size and shape of the hole to be filled, then position it in the hole so that its edges are below the level of the surrounding bodywork. It can be retained in position by several blobs of filler paste around its periphery.

Aluminium tape should be used for small or very narrow holes. Pull a piece off the roll, trim it to the approximate size and shape required, then pull off the backing paper (if used) and stick the tape over the hole; it can be overlapped if the thickness of one piece is insufficient. Burnish down the edges of the tape with the handle of a screwdriver or similar, to ensure that the tape is securely attached to the metal underneath.

Bodywork repairs - filling and respraying

Before using this Section, see the Sections on dent, deep scratch, rust holes and gash repairs.

Many types of bodyfiller are available, but generally speaking, those proprietary kits which contain a tin of filler paste and a tube of resin hardener are best for this type of repair. A wide, flexible plastic or nylon applicator will be found invaluable for imparting a smooth and well-contoured finish to the surface of the filler.

Mix up a little filler on a clean piece of card or board - measure the hardener carefully (follow the maker's instructions on the pack), otherwise the filler will set too rapidly or too slowly. Using the applicator, apply the filler paste to the prepared area; draw the applicator across the surface of the filler to achieve the correct contour and to level the surface. As soon as a contour that approximates to the correct one is achieved, stop working the paste - if you carry on too long, the paste will become sticky and begin to "pick-up" on the applicator. Continue to add thin layers of filler paste at 20-minute intervals, until the level of the filler is just proud of the surrounding bodywork.

Once the filler has hardened, the excess can be removed using a metal plane or file. From then on, progressively-finer grades of abrasive paper should be used, starting with a 40-grade production paper, and finishing with a 400-grade wet-and-dry paper. Always wrap the abrasive paper around a flat rubber, cork, or wooden block - otherwise the surface of the filler will not be completely flat. During the smoothing of the filler surface, the wet-and-dry paper should be periodically rinsed in water. This will ensure that a very smooth finish is imparted to the filler at the final stage.

At this stage, the "dent" should be surrounded by a ring of bare metal, which in turn should be encircled by the finely "feathered" edge of the good paintwork. Rinse the repair area with clean water, until all of the dust produced by the rubbing-down operation has gone.

Spray the whole area with a light coat of primer - this will show up any imperfections in the surface of the filler. Repair these imperfections with fresh filler paste or bodystopper, and once more smooth the surface with abrasive paper. Repeat this spray-and-repair procedure until you are satisfied that the surface of the filler, and the feathered edge of the paintwork, are perfect. Clean the repair area with clean water, and allow to dry fully.

HAYNES HiNT ***If bodystopper is used, it can be mixed with cellulose thinners to form a really thin paste which is ideal for filling small holes.***

The repair area is now ready for final spraying. Paint spraying must be carried out in a warm, dry, windless and dust-free atmosphere. This condition can be created artificially if you have access to a large indoor working area, but if you are forced to work in the open, you will have to pick your day very carefully. If you are working indoors, dousing the floor in the work area with water will help to settle the dust which would otherwise be in the atmosphere. If the repair area is confined to one body panel, mask off the surrounding panels; this will help to minimise the effects of a slight mis-match in paint colours. Bodywork fittings (eg chrome strips, door handles etc) will also need to be masked off. Use genuine masking tape, and several thicknesses of newspaper, for the masking operations.

Before commencing to spray, agitate the aerosol can thoroughly, then spray a test area (an old tin, or similar) until the technique is mastered. Cover the repair area with a thick coat of primer; the thickness should be built up using several thin layers of paint, rather than one thick one. Using 400-grade wet-and-dry paper, rub down the surface of the primer until it is really smooth. While doing this, the work area should be thoroughly doused with water, and the wet-and-dry paper periodically rinsed in water. Allow to dry before spraying on more paint.

Spray on the top coat, again building up the thickness by using several thin layers of paint. Start spraying at one edge of the repair area, and then, using a side-to-side motion, work until the whole repair area and about 2 inches of the surrounding original paintwork is covered. Remove all masking material 10 to 15 minutes after spraying on the final coat of paint.

Allow the new paint at least two weeks to harden, then, using a paintwork renovator, or a very fine cutting paste, blend the edges of the paint into the existing paintwork. Finally, apply wax polish.

Plastic components

With the use of more and more plastic body components by the vehicle manufacturers (eg bumpers. spoilers, and in some cases major body panels), rectification of more serious damage to such items has become a matter of either entrusting repair work to a specialist in this field, or renewing complete components. Repair of such damage by the DIY owner is not really feasible, owing to the cost of the equipment and materials required for effecting such repairs. The basic technique involves making a groove along the line of the crack in the plastic, using a rotary burr in a power drill. The damaged part is then welded back together, using a hot-air gun to heat up and fuse a plastic filler rod into the groove. Any excess plastic is then removed, and the area rubbed down to a smooth finish. It is important that a filler rod of the correct plastic is used, as body components can be made of a variety of different types (eg polycarbonate, ABS, polypropylene).

Damage of a less serious nature (abrasions, minor cracks etc) can be repaired by the DIY owner using a two-part epoxy filler repair material. Once mixed in equal proportions, this is used in similar fashion to the bodywork filler used on metal panels. The filler is usually cured in twenty to thirty minutes, ready for sanding and painting.

If the owner is renewing a complete component himself, or if he has repaired it with epoxy filler, he will be left with the problem of finding a suitable paint for finishing which is compatible with the type of plastic used. At one time, the use of a universal paint was not possible, owing to the complex range of plastics encountered in body component applications. Standard paints, generally speaking, will not bond to plastic or rubber satisfactorily. However, it is now possible to obtain a plastic body parts finishing kit which consists of a pre-primer treatment, a primer and coloured top coat. Full instructions are normally supplied with a kit, but basically, the method of use is to first apply the pre-primer to the component concerned, and allow it to dry for up to 30 minutes. Then the primer is applied, and left to dry for about an hour before finally applying the special-coloured top coat. The result is a correctly-coloured component, where the paint will flex with the plastic or rubber, a property that standard paint does not normally possess.

5 Major body damage - repair

Where serious damage has occurred, or large areas need renewal due to neglect, it means that complete new panels will need welding-in, and this is best left to professionals. If the damage is due to impact, it will also be necessary to check completely

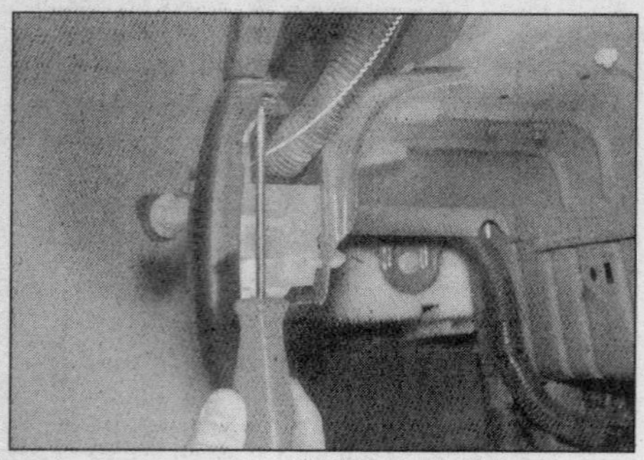

6.5 Removing a bumper end securing screw

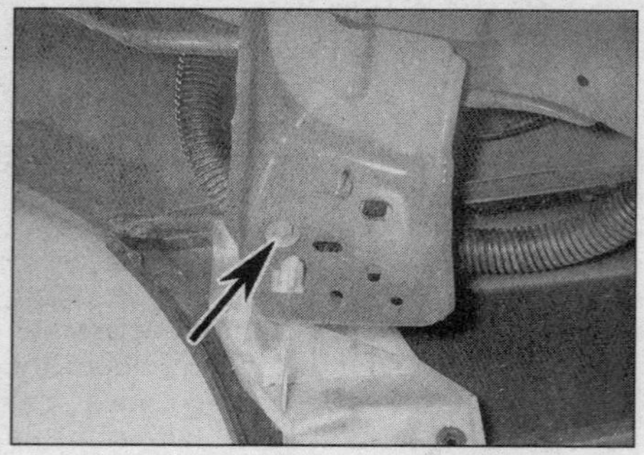

6.6a Under the wheel arch, remove the bumper securing bolt at the side . . .

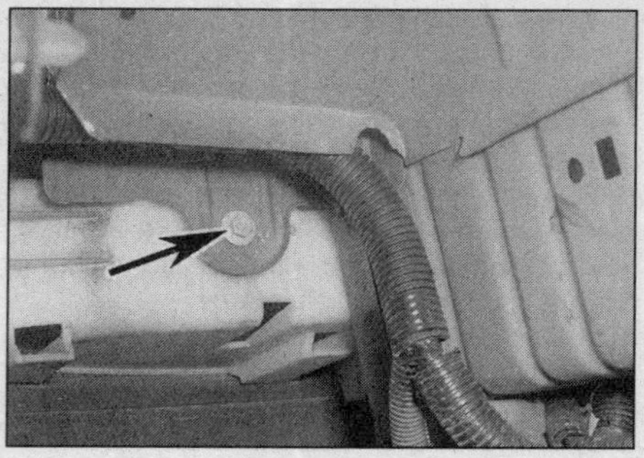

6.6b . . . and at the front (arrowed)

the alignment of the bodyshell, and this can only be carried out accurately by a Citroën dealer, using special jigs. If the body is left misalighed, it is primarily dangerous, as the car will not handle properly; secondly, uneven stresses will be imposed on the steering, suspension and possibly transmission, causing abnormal wear, or complete failure, particularly to such items as the tyres.

6 Front bumper - removal and refitting

Removal

1 Disconnect the battery negative lead.
2 Remove the radiator grille/headlight surround as described in Section 23.
3 Apply the handbrake, then jack up the front of the vehicle and support securely on axle stands (see *"Jacking and vehicle support"*). Remove both front roadwheels.
4 Remove the wheel arch liners as described in Section 23.
5 Remove the screw each side securing the bumper end to the bodywork **(see illustration)**.
6 Working under each wheel arch, unscrew the bumper securing bolt at the side, and the one at the front **(see illustrations)**.
7 Unscrew the two securing bolts from the bottom edge of the bumper **(see illustration)**.
8 Where applicable, noting its routing, disconnect the wiring from the front foglights, and the washer tubes from the headlight washers.

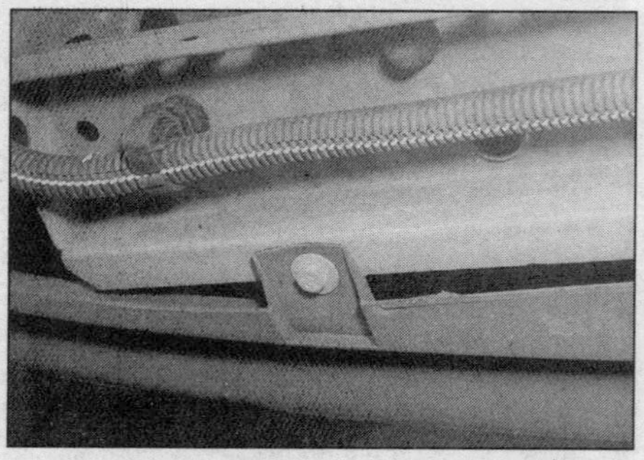

6.7 One of the securing bolts at the bottom edge of the bumper

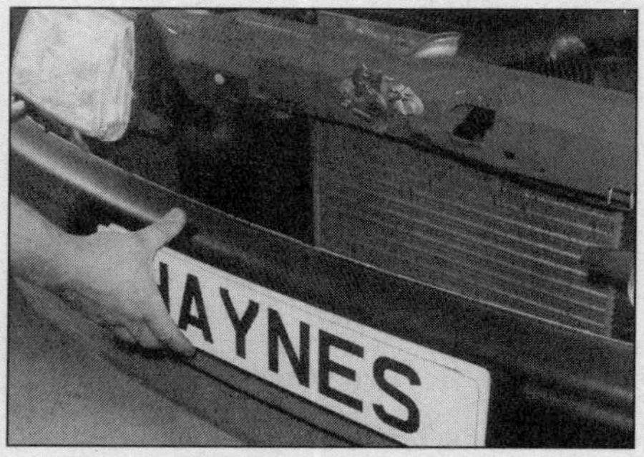

6.9 Withdrawing the front bumper

9 Unclip the bumper end at each side, then pull the bumper forwards to disengage the two locating clips from the front panel, and remove it from the front of the car **(see illustration)**.

Refitting

10 Refitting is a reversal of removal, bearing in mind the following points:

a) Engage the two locating clips into the front panel first, then engage the bumper end clips.
b) Ensure that all the fixings are securely tightened.
c) Where applicable, the fog/driving light wiring and headlight washer tubing should be routed as noted on removal.
d) Refit the wheel arch liners as described in Section 23.

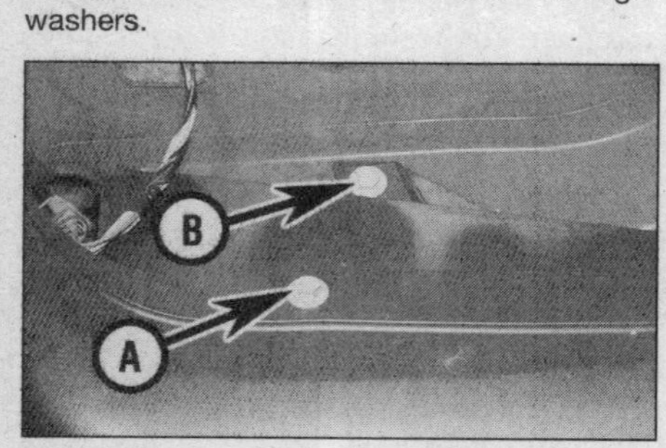

7.6 Rear bumper securing bolts - bolt (A) secures the bumper cover, while (B) secures the bumper inner section to the rear bodywork

7.7 Removing a rear bumper end securing bolt

7 Rear bumper - removal and refitting

Removal

1 Disconnect the battery negative lead.
2 Open the tailgate.
3 Remove both rear light units as described in Chapter 12.
4 To improve access, chock the front wheels, then jack up the rear of the car and support it on axle stands (see *"Jacking and vehicle support"*). Remove both rear wheels.
5 Remove the wheel arch liners as described in Section 23.
6 Unscrew the bumper securing bolt from below each rear light aperture; remove the bolt furthest to the rear - the innermost bolt secures the bumper inner section to the rear bodywork **(see illustration)**.
7 Working under the rear of the car, remove the bumper end securing bolt from each front edge of the bumper **(see illustration)**.
8 Also under the rear of the car, remove the two bolts under the rear edge of the bumper **(see illustration)**.
9 Gently pull the end of the bumper outwards from the wheel arch, to release the securing pegs from the vehicle bodywork **(see illustration)**.
10 Pull the bumper rearwards and remove it from the car.

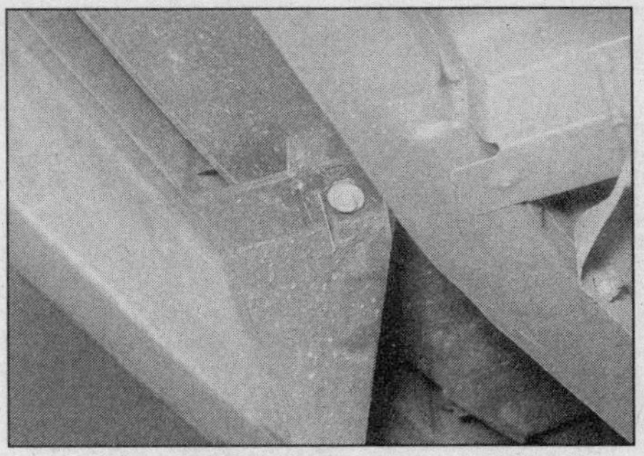

7.8 One of the securing bolts under the rear bumper

Refitting

11 Refitting is a reversal of removal, but make sure that all fixings are securely refitted. Refit the wheel arch liners as described in Section 23, and the rear light units as described in Chapter 12.

8 Bonnet - removal, refitting and adjustment

Removal

1 Open the bonnet, and have an assistant support it. Using a pencil or felt tip pen, mark the outline of each bonnet hinge relative to the bonnet, to use as a guide on refitting.

2 Noting its routing, unclip the windscreen washer supply hose from the clip at the side

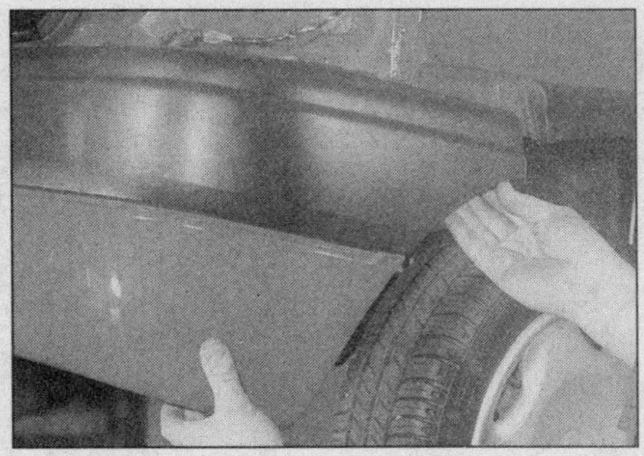

7.9 Pull the bumper end outwards to disengage its peg from the bodywork

of the bonnet, and from the rubber seal which runs across its width. Disconnect the washer hose from the first windscreen jet, and tuck it down out of the way **(see illustrations)**.

3 Unscrew the bonnet hinge retaining bolts **(see illustration)**, and recover the washers. With the help of an assistant, carefully lift the bonnet clear. Store the bonnet out of the way in a safe place.

4 Inspect the bonnet hinges for signs of wear and free play at the pivots, and if necessary, renew them. Each hinge is secured to the body by two bolts.

Refitting

5 With the aid of an assistant, offer up the bonnet, and loosely fit the retaining bolts and washers. Align the hinges with the marks made on removal, then tighten the retaining bolts securely. Reconnect the windscreen washer supply hose, and clip it back into position, ensuring that it is routed as noted before removal.

6 Adjust the alignment of the bonnet as follows.

Adjustment

7 Close the bonnet, and check for alignment with the adjacent panels. If necessary, slacken the hinge bolts and re-align the bonnet to suit. Once the bonnet is correctly aligned, tighten the hinge bolts securely.

8 If the lock striker has been removed from the bonnet, ensure that the washer is in place between the bonnet and the striker when refitting.

9 Once the bonnet is correctly aligned, check that the bonnet fastens and releases in a satisfactory manner. If adjustment is necessary, slacken the bonnet lock retaining bolts, and adjust the position of the lock to suit. Once the lock is operating correctly, securely tighten its retaining bolts.

9 Bonnet release cable - removal and refitting

Removal

1 Working in the engine compartment, unhook the end of the bonnet release cable from the lock lever. If necessary, unbolt the lock and move it to one side to facilitate this.

2 Unclip the cable outer from the securing clip from the front body panel **(see illustration)**.

8.2a The washer fluid hose is clipped to the bonnet . . .

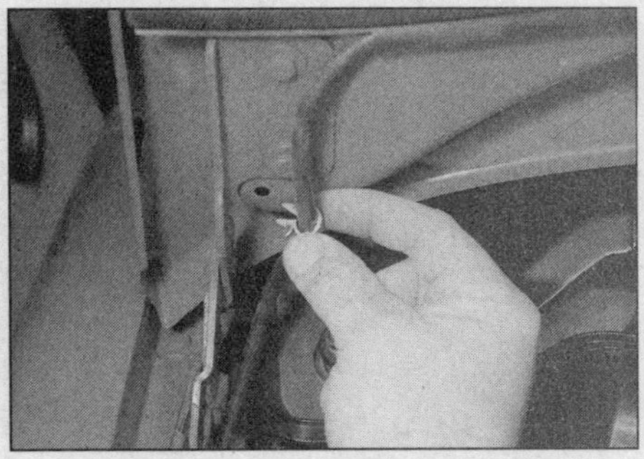

8.2b . . . prise out the clip . . .

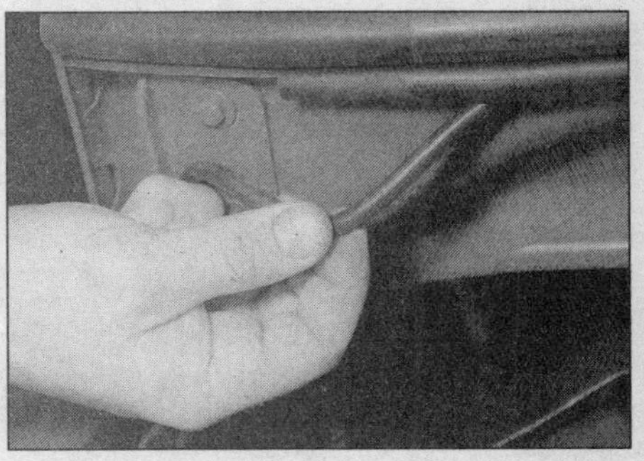

8.2c . . . detach the hose from the rubber seal . . .

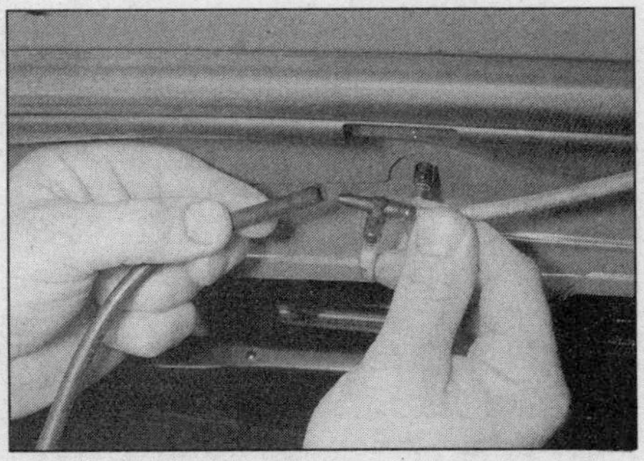

8.2d . . . and disconnect it from the first washer jet

8.3 Unscrewing one of the bonnet hinge bolts

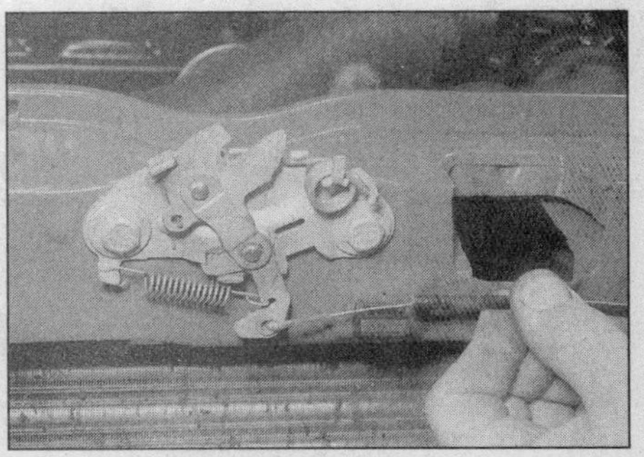

9.2 Unhook the bonnet release cable outer from the clip

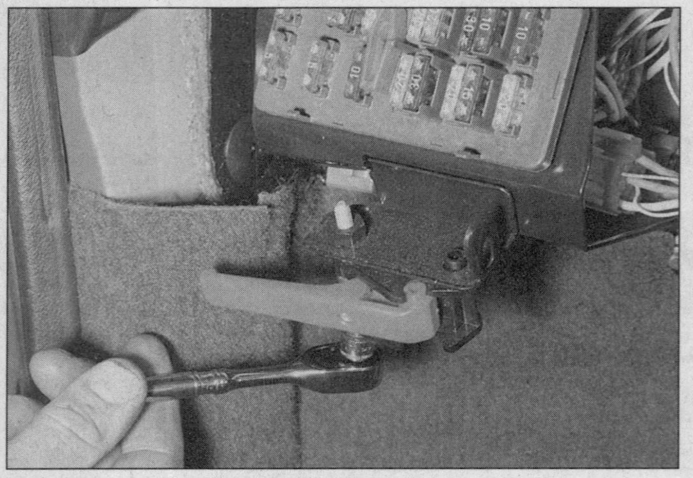

9.3a Unscrew and remove the pivot bolt . . .

9.3b . . . then withdraw the bonnet release lever from under the facia

3 Working inside the vehicle, remove the pivot bolt, and withdraw the bonnet release lever from under the facia **(see illustrations)**.

4 Note the routing of the cable, and release it from any clips in the engine compartment, then feed the cable through the bulkhead grommet into the vehicle interior. Note that the cable is integral with the release lever, and cannot be renewed separately.

Refitting

5 Refitting is a reversal of removal, but ensure that the bulkhead grommet is securely located, and make sure that the cable is routed as noted before removal.

10.2 Unscrewing the bonnet lock securing bolts

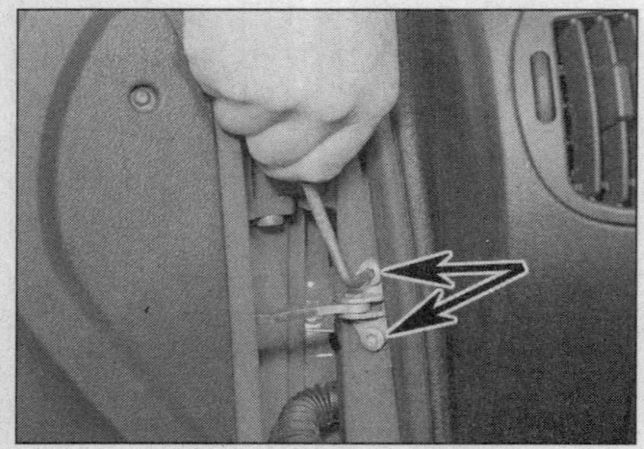

11.2 Unscrew the two door check strap bolts (arrowed)

10 Bonnet lock - removal and refitting

Removal

1 Open the bonnet.

2 Unscrew the two securing bolts, and remove the lock assembly from the body panel **(see illustration)**.

3 Unhook the end of the bonnet release cable from the lock lever, and withdraw the assembly from the vehicle.

11.1 Disconnect the door wiring plug by twisting its locking collar

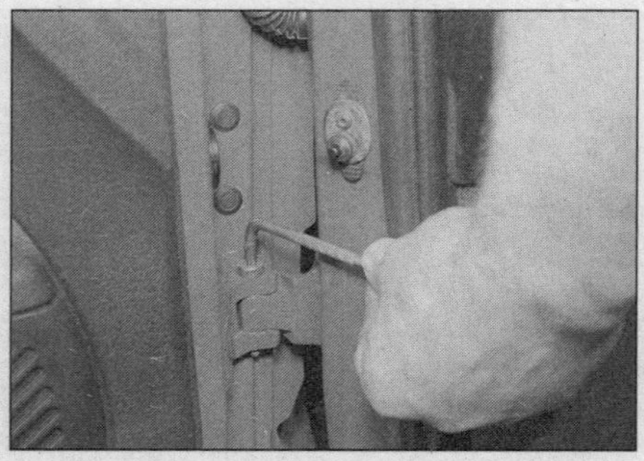

11.4 Removing the door lower hinge pin

Refitting

4 Refitting is a reversal of removal. If necessary, adjust the position of the striker on the bonnet, as described in Section 8.

11 Door - removal, refitting and adjustment

Front door

Removal

1 Open the door and, where applicable, disconnect the battery negative lead before disconnecting the door wiring plug. Twist the locking collar to release the wiring plug **(see illustration)**.

2 Unscrew the two bolts securing the door check strap to the body pillar **(see illustration)**.

3 Support the door either with the aid of an assistant, or using a trolley jack and a block of wood.

4 Using a suitable Torx key or bit, unscrew the door lower hinge pin, then the upper hinge pin **(see illustration)**. Lift the door from the vehicle.

Refitting

5 Refitting is a reversal of removal, noting the following points:

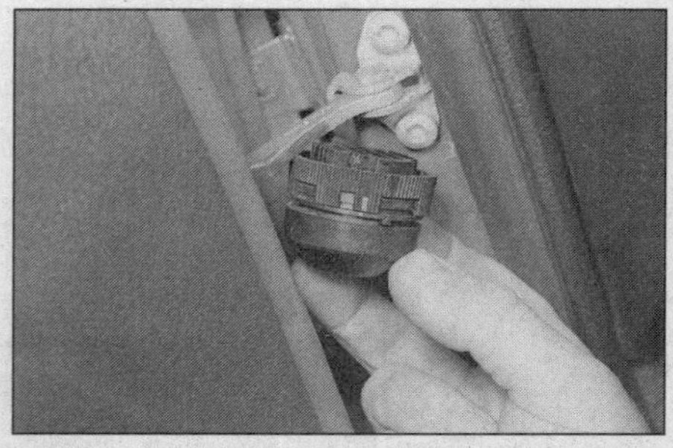

11.5 Ensure the orange markings on the locking collar are aligned when reconnecting the door wiring plug

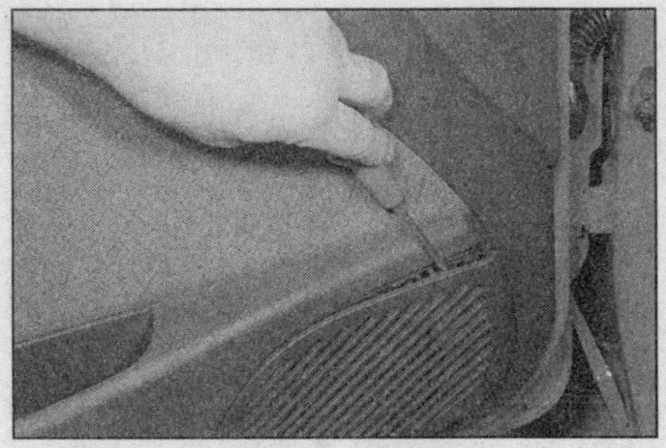

12.2 Prise off the door speaker grille panel

a) *Lightly grease the hinge pins before refitting.*
b) *When reconnecting the door wiring plug, align the orange markings on the locking collar* **(see illustration)** *before offering it into position and twisting to secure.*

Adjustment

6 No adjustment of the door is possible.

Rear door

7 The procedure is as described previously for the front door, but note that on certain models, it will be necessary to remove the door inner trim panel (see Section 12) in order to disconnect the wiring from the components inside the door (no door wiring connector is used). Note the routing of the wiring, release it from any clips inside the door, then feed the wiring harness through the grommet in the front edge of the door.

12 Door inner trim panels - removal and refitting

Front door trim panel

Note: *If the sealing sheet is removed from the inside of the door, a new sealing sheet may be required on refitting.*

Removal

1 Where applicable, pull the window regulator handle from its spindle. Recover the trim disc.

2 Carefully prise off the speaker grille panel **(see illustration)**.

3 Prise off the trim panel from the door mirror adjuster.

12.7a Remove the door trim mounting bracket . . .

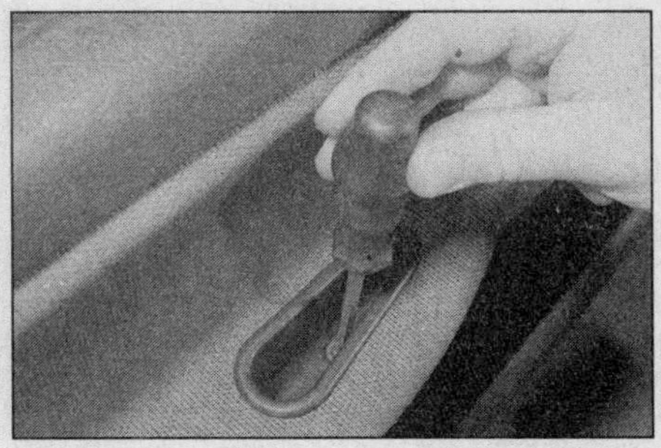

12.5a Remove the screw from inside the door pull . . .

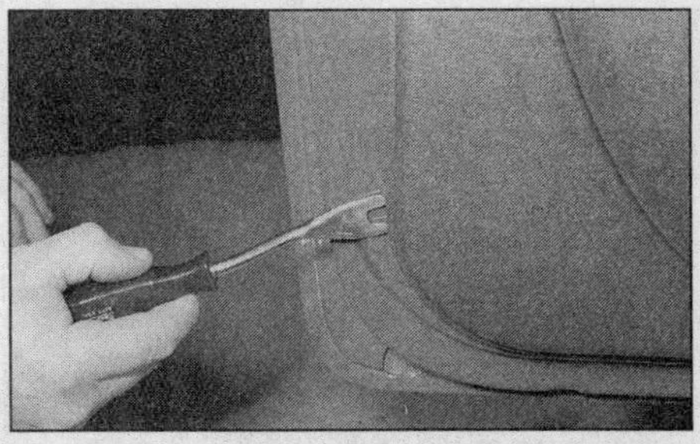

12.6a Use a suitable forked or flat-bladed tool to release the securing clips around the panel . . .

4 On models with electric mirrors, prise out the switch from the armrest and disconnect the wiring plug.

5 Remove the screw under the electric mirror switch location (or from inside the door pull, as applicable) and the screw from the front upper corner of the trim panel **(see illustrations)**.

6 Release the securing clips, and pull the trim panel from the door, lifting it over the door lock knob **(see illustrations)**.

7 If desired (if the door internal components are to be worked on), remove the door trim bracket from the centre of the door. The sealing sheet must now be removed from the door. Note that the sheet will probably be destroyed during removal, but if great care is taken, the sheet may be removed intact if the bead of adhesive is cut through with a sharp knife **(see illustrations)**.

Refitting

8 Refitting is a reversal of removal. Where necessary, use a new sealing sheet; noting that it may be necessary to cut suitable holes in the sealing sheet for the door trim bracket, etc.

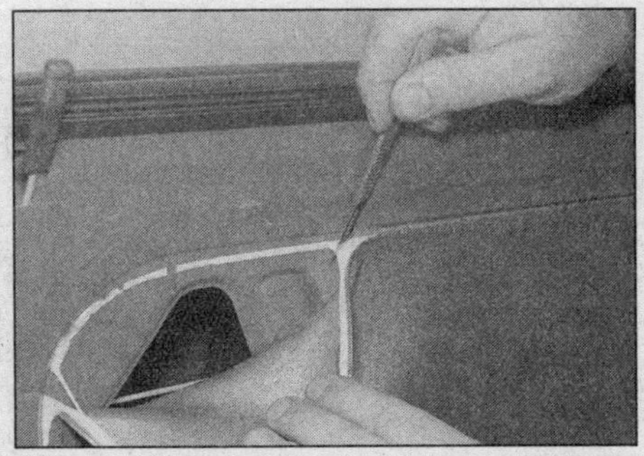

12.7b . . . then remove the sealing sheet by cutting the adhesive with a sharp knife

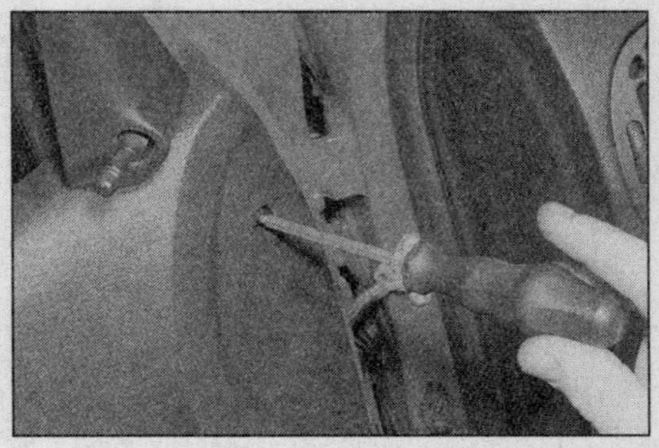

12.5b . . . and from the front corner of the trim panel

12.6b . . . then remove the trim panel from the door

Rear door trim panel

Removal

9 Pull the window regulator handle from its spindle. Recover the trim discs, noting their fitted order and orientation **(see illustration)**.

10 Remove the screw from inside the door pull, and the screw from the front lower corner of the trim panel.

11 Release the securing clips, and pull the trim panel from the door, lifting it over the door lock knob.

12 If desired (if the door internal components are to be worked on), remove the door trim bracket from the centre of the door. The sealing sheet must now be removed from the door (refer to paragraph 7).

Refitting

13 Refer to paragraph 8.

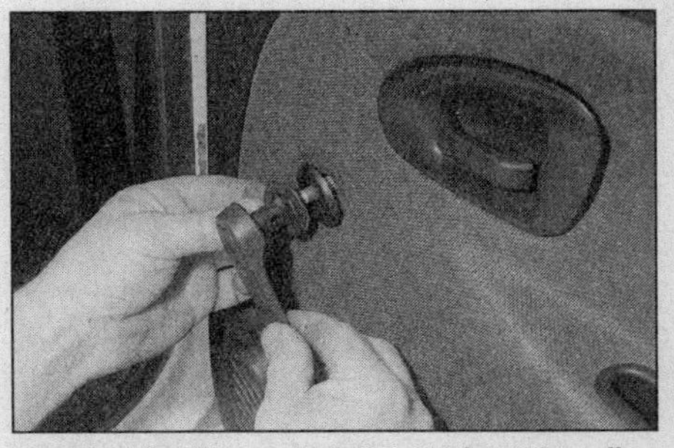

12.9 Pull off the window regulator handle, noting the fitted order of the trim discs behind

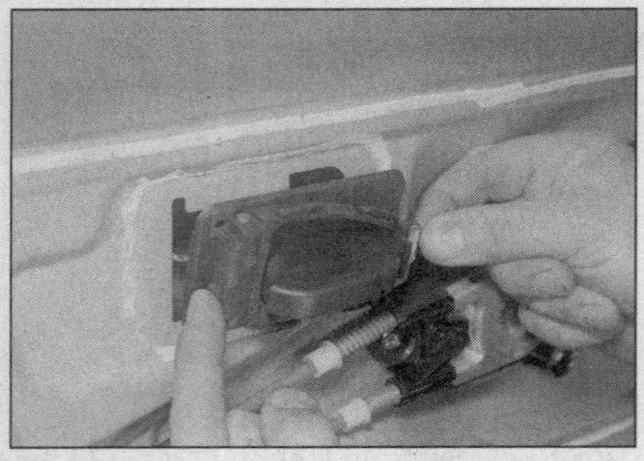

13.2a Push the handle forwards to release it . . .

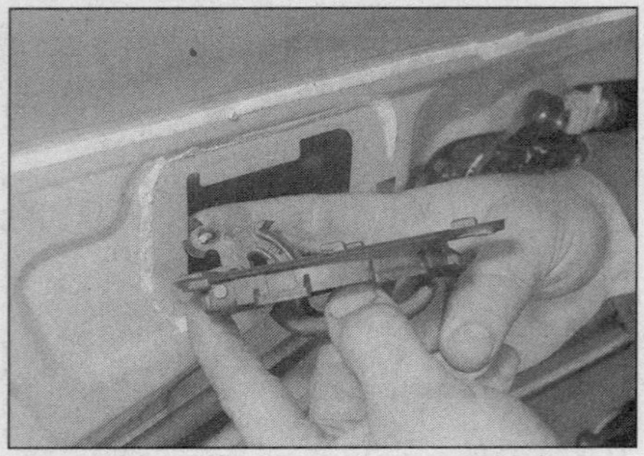

13.2b . . . then detach the link rod and remove

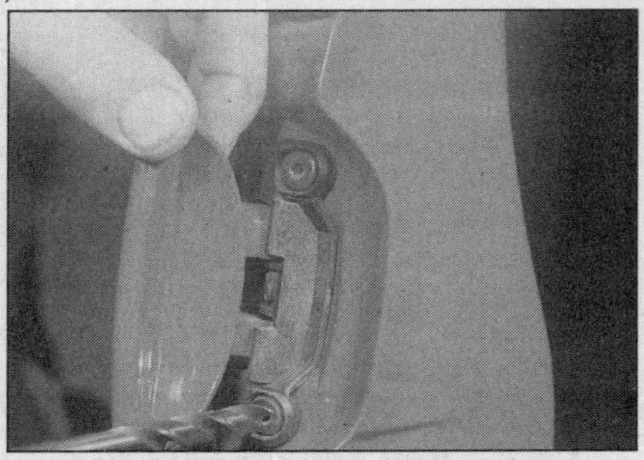

13.6 Drilling out the door handle securing rivets

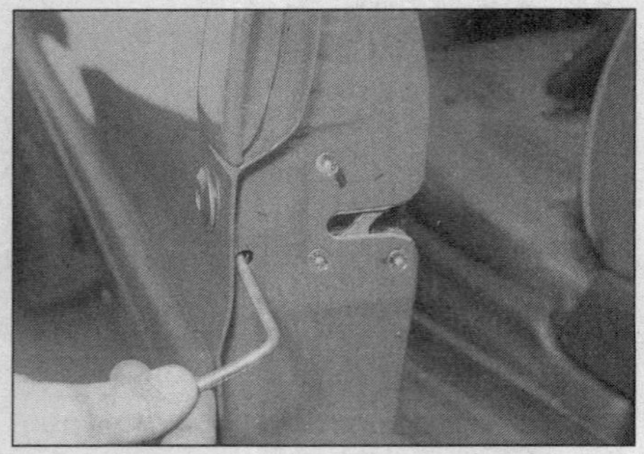

13.8a Screwing the home-made tool into the lock cylinder retaining clip

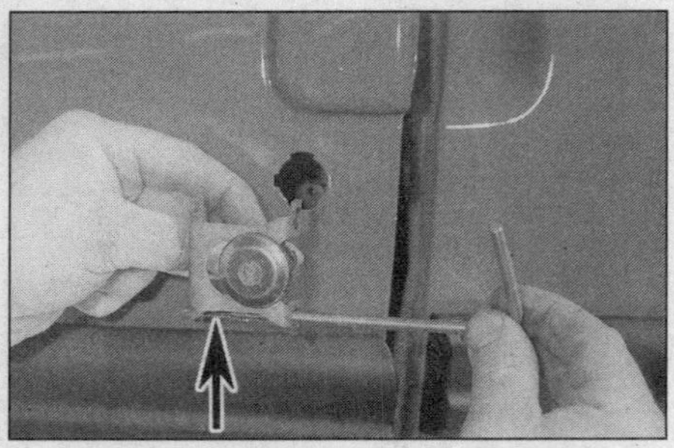

13.8b Lock cylinder and clip removed to show home-made tool in use - screw arrowed

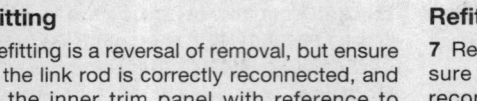

13 Door handle and lock components - removal and refitting

Interior door handle

Removal

1 Remove the door inner trim panel, as described in Section 12.

2 Slide the handle assembly towards the front of the door, then pull the assembly from the door aperture, and disconnect the link rod (if necessary, release the link rod from the clips on the door) **(see illustrations)**.

Refitting

3 Refitting is a reversal of removal, but ensure that the link rod is correctly reconnected, and refit the inner trim panel with reference to Section 12.

Exterior door handle

Note: *New rivets will be required when refitting the handle.*

Removal

4 Working outside the door, stick masking tape around the area surrounding the handle, to protect the paintwork.

5 Lift the handle for access to the securing rivets. Have an assistant hold the handle in the raised position, or wedge the handle in position.

6 Using a 4.0 mm drill bit, drill out the two securing rivets **(see illustration)**, then pull the handle assembly from the door, and disconnect the link rods.

Refitting

7 Refitting is a reversal of removal, but make sure that the link rods are correctly reconnected to the handle, and secure the assembly using new rivets.

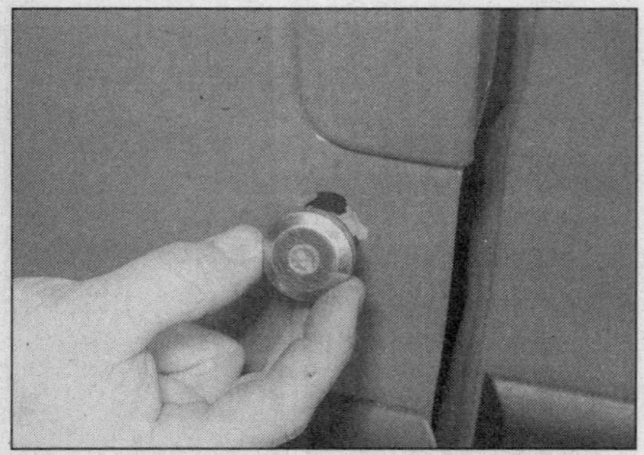

13.11a With the retaining clip released, pull out the lock cylinder . . .

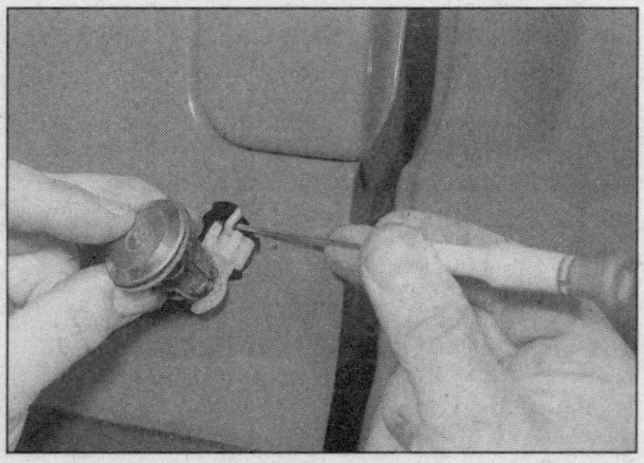

13.11b . . . and prise off the link rod

Front door lock cylinder

8 The lock cylinder can be removed as follows, without the need to remove the door inner trim panel:

a) Make up a suitable tool as shown in the accompanying illustrations, using a medium-size self-tapping screw brazed to a length of rod, bent at a right-angle.
b) Open the door, and prise the grommet from the rear edge of the door.
*c) Insert the tool through the aperture in the edge of the door, and screw the self-tapping screw into the lock securing clip to the end of the thread on the screw **(see illustrations)**.*
d) Push the tool to release the securing clip, and withdraw the lock cylinder from outside the door. Leave the tool engaged with the clip.
e) Refit the lock, and use the tool to pull the securing clip into position.
f) Ensure that the clip is securely engaged with the lock cylinder, then unscrew the tool from the clip, and refit the grommet.

Removal

9 Remove the door inner trim panel and the sealing sheet, as described in Section 12.

10 Reach in through the aperture in the door, and unclip the plastic shield from the rear of the door lock.

11 Working inside the door, pull the securing clip from the rear of the lock cylinder. Remove the lock cylinder from the outside of the door, and disconnect the link rod **(see illustrations)**.

Refitting

12 Refitting is a reversal of removal, but ensure that the lock cylinder securing clip is securely refitted, and use a new sealing sheet if necessary. Refit the door inner trim panel with reference to Section 12.

Front door lock

Removal

13 Remove the door inner trim panel and the sealing sheet, as described in Section 12.

14 Remove the interior handle by pulling it towards the front of the door to release it, and unclip the link rod from the handle.

15 Unclip the link rod from the door panel, and recover the clips **(see illustrations)**.

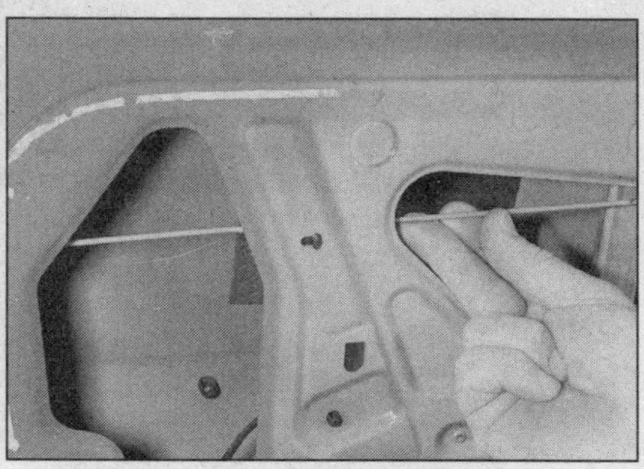

13.15a Release the link rod from the door panel . . .

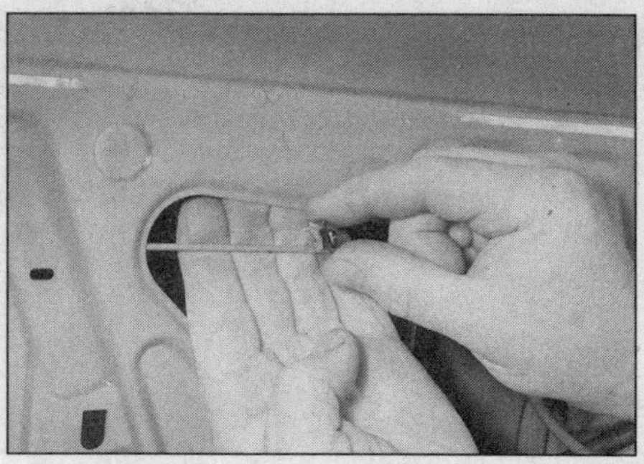

13.15b . . . and recover the clips

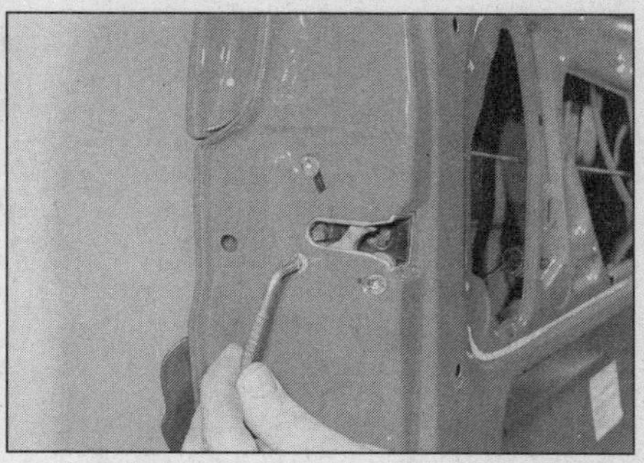

13.17a Remove the three lock assembly securing screws . . .

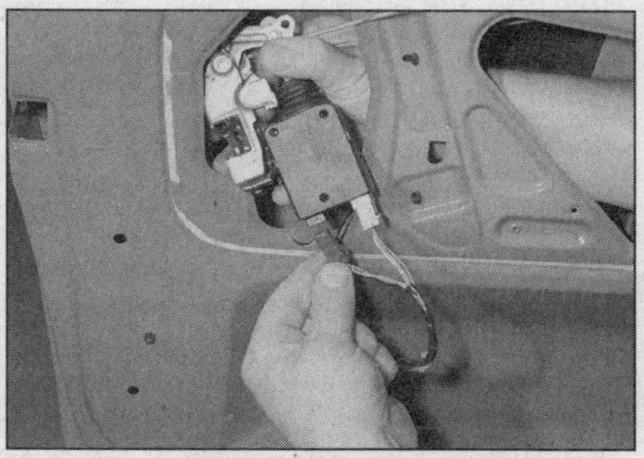

13.17b . . . disconnect the central locking motor wiring plugs . . .

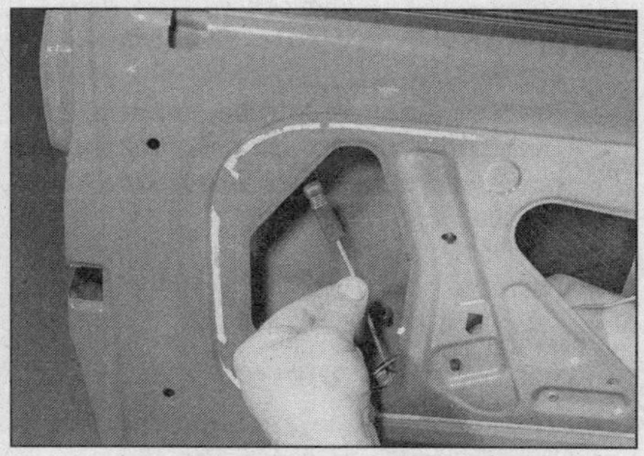

13.17c . . . lower the assembly to manoeuvre out the locking knob . . .

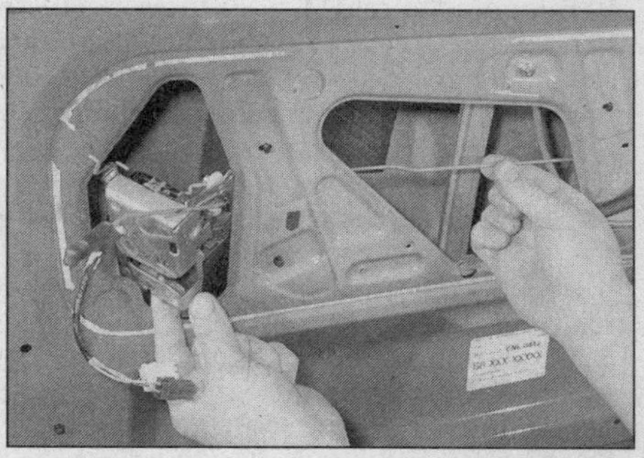

13.17d . . . then withdraw the assembly, complete with link rods, from the door

16 Reach in through the door aperture behind the lock, and unclip the plastic shield from the rear of the lock. Where applicable, also disconnect the wiring from the central locking motor (disconnect the battery negative lead first).

17 Remove the three securing screws from the rear edge of the door, then withdraw the lock assembly, complete with the rods, through the aperture in the inner door skin. Where applicable, disconnect the wiring plug from the lock assembly as it is withdrawn. As the lock is withdrawn, feed the lock button operating rod down through the hole in the top of the door **(see illustrations)**. Note the routing of the lock rods to ensure correct refitting.

Refitting

18 Refitting is a reversal of removal, bearing in mind the following points:

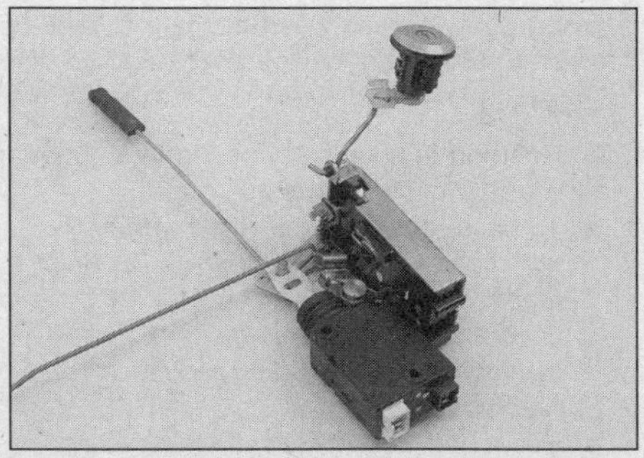

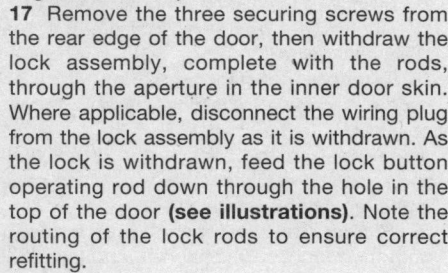

13.18 Showing the arrangement of the door lock components and link rods

a) Ensure that the lock rods are correctly reconnected and routed ***(see illustration)****. Note that the link rod must pass in front of the window regulator operating cable.*

b) Check the operation of the lock before fitting the sealing sheet.

c) Use a new sealing sheet if necessary, and refit the door inner trim panel with reference to Section 12.

Rear door lock

Removal

19 Remove the door inner trim panel and the sealing sheet, as described in Section 12.

20 Remove the door exterior handle as described previously in this Section.

21 Slide the door interior handle assembly towards the rear of the door, then pull the assembly from the door aperture, and disconnect the link rod. Release the link rod from the clips on the door.

22 Reach in through the door aperture, then release the securing clip and disconnect the lock button operating rod from the rear of the lock. Where applicable, also disconnect the wiring plug from the central locking motor (disconnect the battery negative lead first).

23 Unscrew the three lock securing screws, then withdraw the lock, complete with the operating rod, through the aperture.

Refitting

24 Refitting is a reversal of removal, bearing in mind the following points:

a) Ensure that the lock rods are correctly reconnected and routed.

b) Refit the door exterior handle, using new rivets.

c) Check the operation of the lock before fitting the sealing sheet.

d) Use a new sealing sheet if necessary, and refit the door inner trim panel with reference to Section 12.

14 Door window glass and regulator - removal and refitting

Front door window glass

Removal

1 Remove the door inner trim panel and the sealing sheet, as described in Section 12.

2 Prise the weatherstrip from the inside top of the window aperture **(see illustration)**.

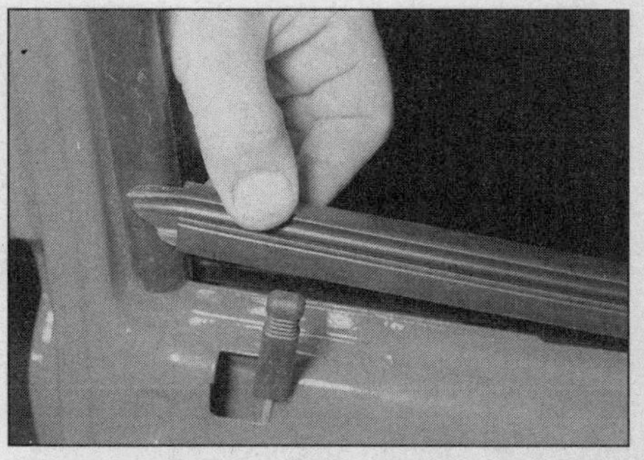

14.2 Pull up the weatherstrip from the top of the window aperture

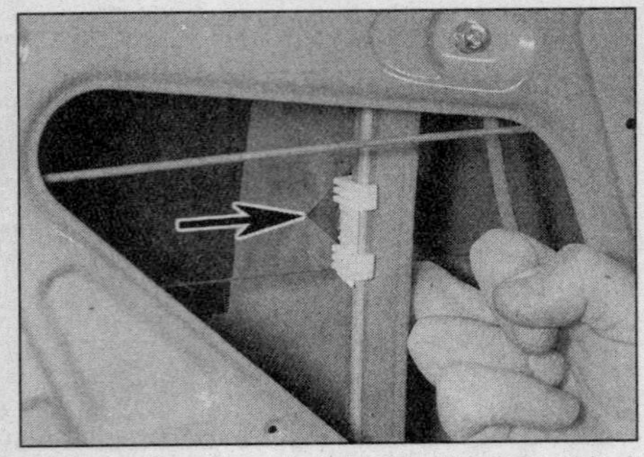

14.4a Twist the clip (arrowed) from behind the glass . . .

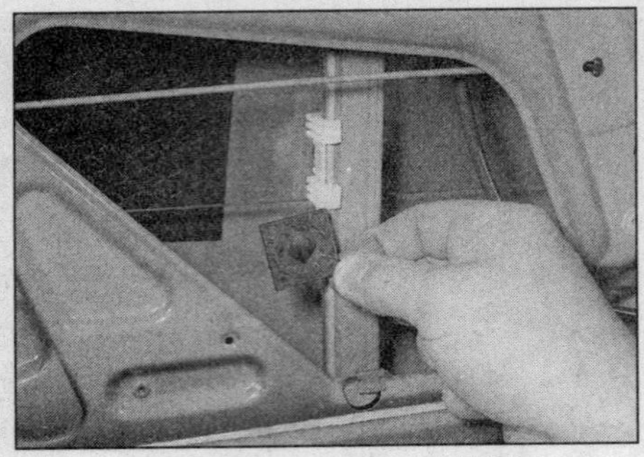

14.4b . . . and remove it

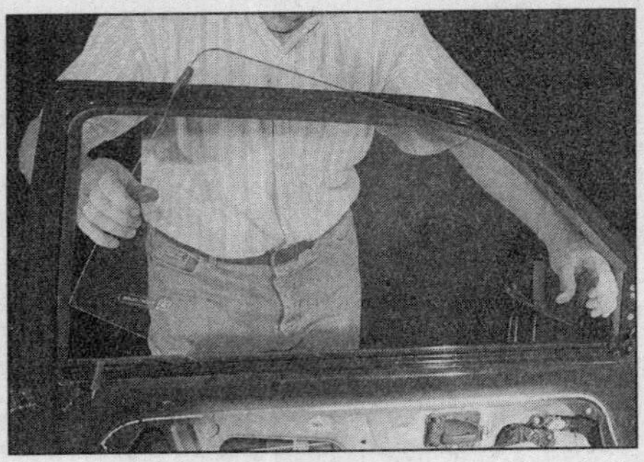

14.6 Tilt the glass forwards and remove it from the door

3 Temporarily refit the window regulator handle, or reconnect the switch (and reconnect the battery), as applicable, and lower the window to around the three-quarters closed position.

4 Working at the back of the glass, twist and remove the clip securing the glass panel to the regulator mechanism **(see illustrations)**.

5 Support the glass, then detach it from the regulator mechanism.

6 Tilt the glass forwards, and release the plastic guide from its groove in the rear edge of the door-to-glass seal. Manipulate the glass out through the window aperture, taking care not to scratch the paint on the door edge **(see illustration)**.

Refitting

7 Refitting is a reversal of removal, bearing in mind the following points:

a) *To ease refitting, coat the weatherstrips with soapy water (washing-up liquid is ideal).*

b) *Ensure that the plastic guide at the rear edge of the glass is located properly in the door-to-glass seal* ***(see illustration)****.*

c) *Before fitting the sealing sheet, check the operation of the window regulator mechanism.*

d) *Use a new sealing sheet if necessary.*

e) *Refit the door inner trim panel with reference to Section 12.*

Front door regulator

Note: *New rivets will be required when refitting the regulator mechanism.*

Removal

8 Remove the window glass as described previously.

9 Where applicable, disconnect the wiring plug(s) from the window lift motor **(see illustration)**.

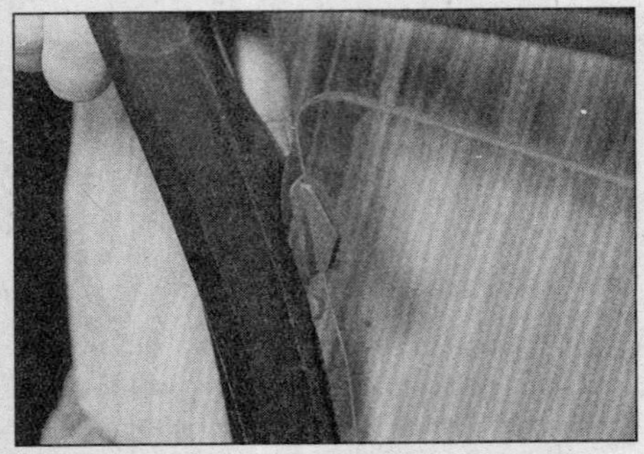

14.7 Plastic guide locates into the door-to-glass seal

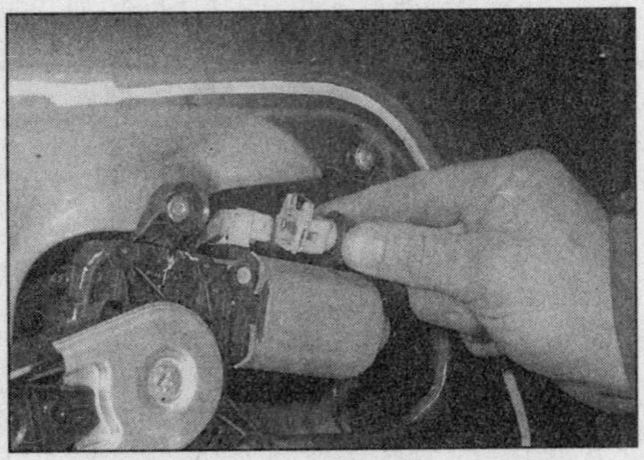

14.9 Disconnect the window motor wiring plug

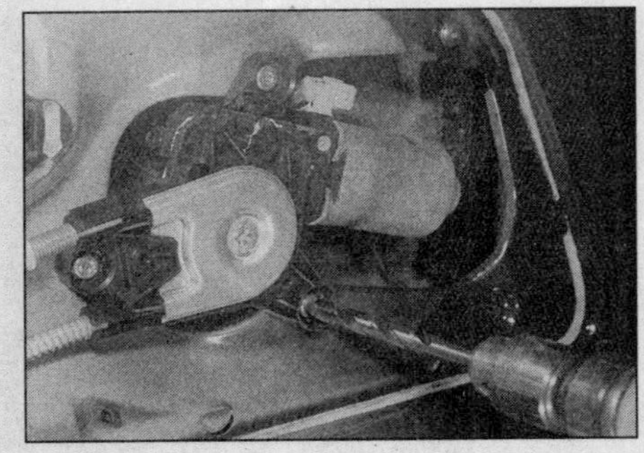

14.10 Drilling out the window motor securing rivets

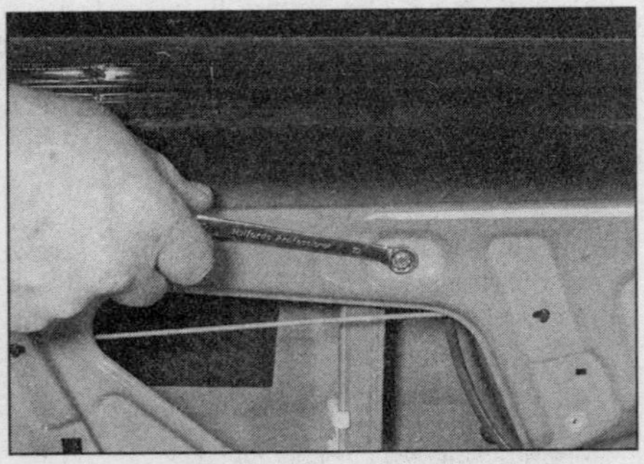

14.11 Remove the window lift rail securing nuts

10 Using a 6.0 mm drill, drill out the rivets securing the regulator mechanism (and, where applicable, the window lift motor) to the door **(see illustration)**.

11 Where applicable, remove the two nuts securing the window lift rail **(see illustration)**.

12 Carefully tilt the assembly, and lift it out through the aperture in the door.

Refitting

13 Refitting is a reversal of removal, but refit the regulator mechanism using new rivets, and refit the window glass as described previously in this Section.

Rear door sliding window glass

Removal

14 Fully lower the sliding window glass.

15 Remove the door inner trim panel and the sealing sheet, as described in Section 12.

16 Carefully pull the weatherstrips from the lower edge of the sliding window aperture.

17 Unclip the weatherstrip from the rear glass channel.

18 Temporarily refit the window regulator handle, and raise the sliding glass to its mid-position.

19 Working at the back of the glass, twist and remove the clip securing the glass panel to the regulator mechanism.

20 Support the glass panel, then detach it from the regulator mechanism, and lower the panel to the bottom of the door.

21 Remove the upper and lower screws securing the rear glass channel to the door, and withdraw the channel.

22 Lift the glass panel, and manipulate it out through the window aperture, taking care not to scratch the paint on the door edge.

Refitting

23 Refitting is a reversal of removal, bearing in mind the following points:

a) *To ease refitting, coat the weatherstrips with soapy water (washing-up liquid is ideal).*

b) *Before fitting the sealing sheet, check the operation of the window regulator mechanism.*

c) *Use a new sealing sheet if necessary.*

d) *Refit the door inner trim panel with reference to Section 12.*

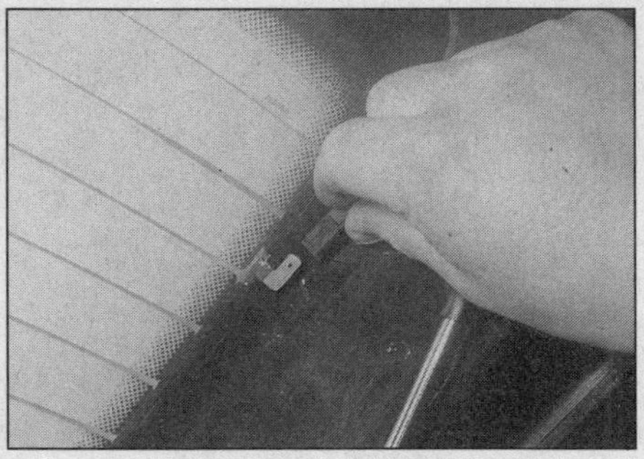

15.3 Disconnecting a heated rear window wiring plug

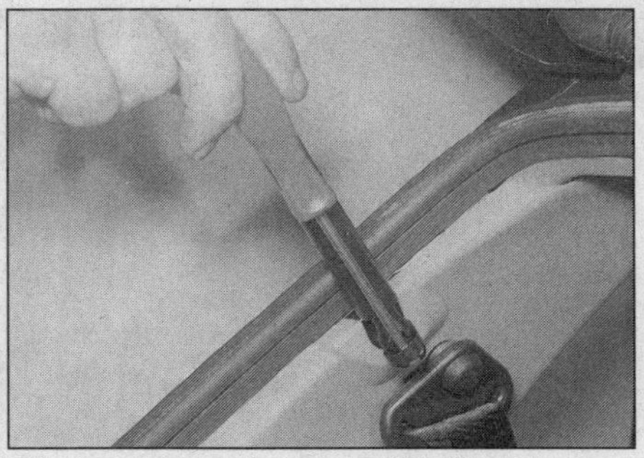

15.9 Prising out a tailgate support strut lower spring clip

15.10 Removing the tailgate hinge bolts (arrowed)

Rear door fixed window glass

Removal

24 Proceed as described in paragraphs 14 to 22 inclusive.

25 Carefully pull the fixed glass panel towards the front of the door, and withdraw it.

Refitting

26 Refer to paragraph 23.

Rear door regulator

27 The procedure is as described previously in this Section for the front door regulator. Note that there is no need to remove the fixed window glass.

15 Tailgate and support struts - removal, refitting and adjustment

Tailgate

Removal

1 Disconnect the battery negative lead.

2 Remove the three screws (one at each side, one in the pull handle) securing the tailgate trim panel, then release the securing clips and withdraw the panel from the tailgate.

3 Disconnect the heated rear window wiring plugs from either side of the window **(see illustration)**.

4 As applicable, working through the aperture in the tailgate, disconnect the tailgate wiper motor, central locking motor and number plate light wiring plugs.

5 Remove the high-level stop-light as described in Chapter 12.

6 Pull the wiring grommets from the corners of the tailgate.

7 If the original tailgate is to be refitted, tie string to the ends of all the relevant wiring, then feed the wiring through the top of the tailgate. Untie the string, leaving it in position in the tailgate to assist refitting.

8 Where applicable, prise the washer nozzle from the tailgate, and disconnect the fluid hose from the nozzle. Tie a length of string to the hose, then pull the hose through the tailgate. Leave the string in position to aid refitting, as for the wiring.

9 Support the tailgate, then prise out the support strut spring clips **(see illustration)**, and pull the struts from the balljoints on the tailgate or on the body.

10 Unscrew the hinge securing bolts **(see illustration)**, and carefully lift the tailgate from the vehicle.

Refitting

11 If a new tailgate is to be fitted, transfer all serviceable components (rubber buffers, lock mechanism, etc) to it.

12 Refitting is a reversal of removal, bearing in mind the following points:

- *a) If the original tailgate is being refitted, draw the wiring and washer fluid hose (where applicable) through the tailgate using the string.*
- *b) If necessary, adjust the rubber buffers to obtain a good fit when the tailgate is shut.*
- *c) If necessary, adjust the operation of the lock striker on the body, to achieve satisfactory lock operation.*

Adjustment

13 It is not possible to adjust the position of the tailgate on the hinges. If necessary, the rubber buffers at the lower corners of the tailgate can be adjusted to obtain a good fit when the tailgate is shut. The tailgate lock operation can be adjusted as described in Section 16.

Support struts

Removal

14 Support the tailgate in the open position, with the help of an assistant, or using a stout piece of wood.

15 Using a suitable flat-bladed screwdriver, release the spring clip, and pull the support strut from its balljoint on the tailgate **(see illustration)**.

16 Similarly, release the strut from the balljoint on the body, and withdraw the strut from the vehicle.

Refitting

17 Refitting is a reversal of removal, but ensure that the spring clips are correctly engaged.

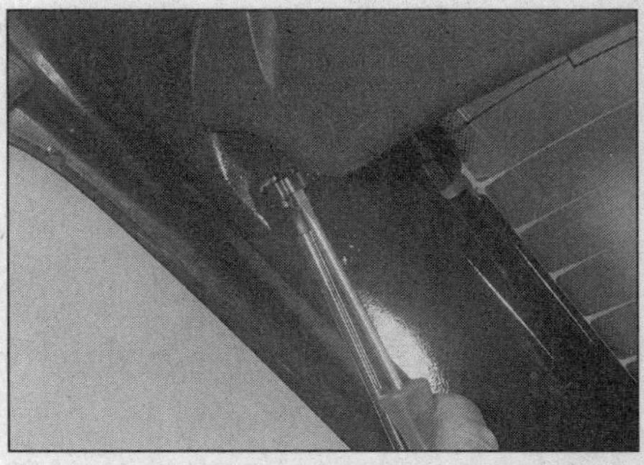

15.15 Prising out a tailgate support strut upper spring clip

16 Tailgate lock components - removal and refitting

Tailgate lock

Removal

1 Open the tailgate.

2 Remove the three screws (one at each side, one in the pull handle) securing the tailgate trim panel, then release the securing clips and withdraw the panel from the tailgate **(see illustrations)**.

3 Remove the two lock retaining bolts, then disconnect the link rod and remove the lock from the tailgate **(see illustrations)**.

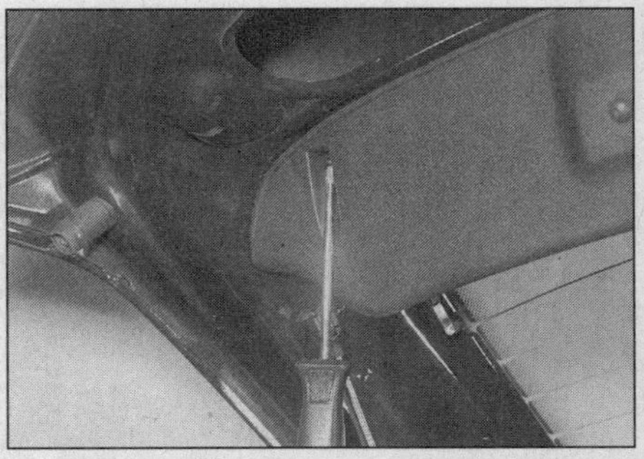

16.2a Remove the tailgate trim panel screw at each side . . .

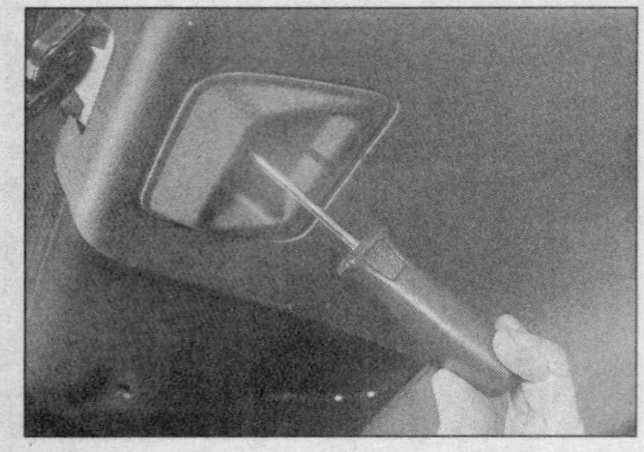

16.2b . . . and the one in the pull handle . . .

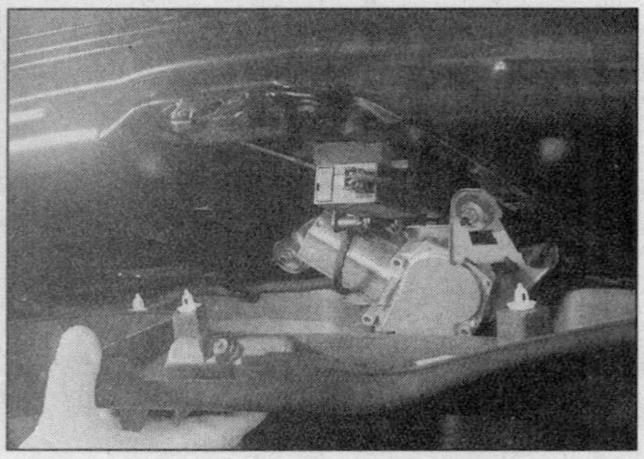

16.2c . . . then release the trim panel clips and lower the panel

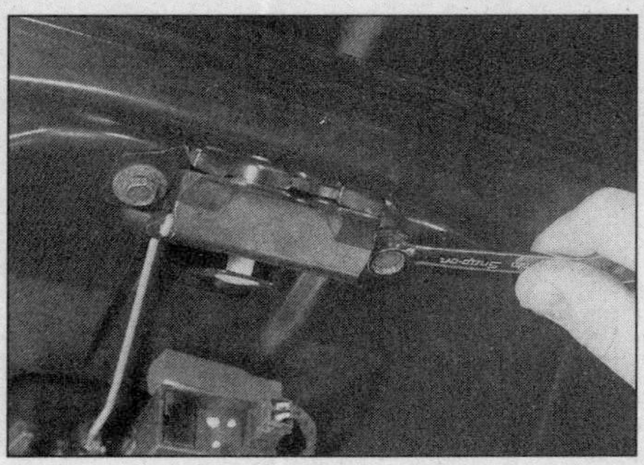

16.3a Remove the tailgate lock retaining bolts . . .

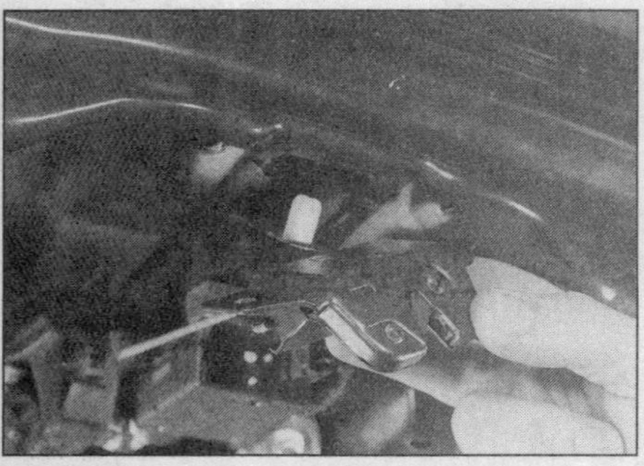

16.3b . . . then remove the lock and unhook the link rod

16.7 Unclip the operating rod and disconnect the wiring plug (arrowed) from the tailgate lock actuator

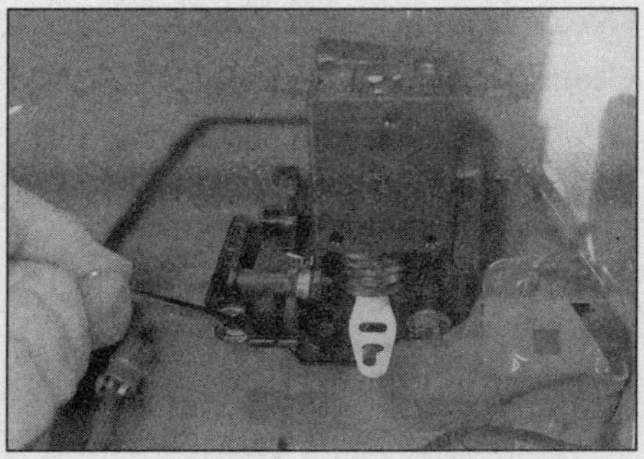

16.9 Removing the lock cylinder mounting bracket bolts

Refitting

4 Refitting is a reversal of removal, but ensure that the lock lever engages correctly as the lock is positioned in the tailgate.

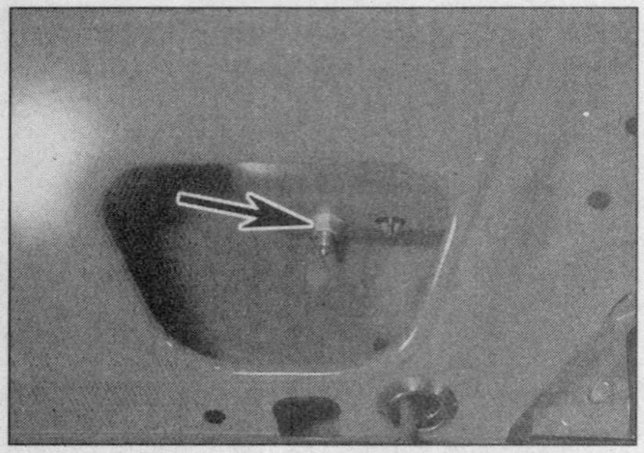

16.10a Remove the retaining nuts (one arrowed) . . .

Tailgate lock cylinder

Removal

5 Open the tailgate.

6 Remove the three screws (one at each side, one in the pull handle) securing the tailgate trim panel, then release the securing clips and withdraw the panel from the tailgate.

7 On models with central locking, unclip the operating rod from the tailgate lock actuator, and disconnect the actuator wiring plug **(see illustration)**.

8 Remove the tailgate wiper motor as described in Chapter 12.

9 Remove the two bolts securing the lock cylinder mounting bracket to the tailgate **(see illustration)**.

10 Working inside the tailgate, remove the nuts securing the number plate light shroud, and lift the shroud off the outside of the tailgate **(see illustrations)**.

11 Support the lock cylinder assembly inside the tailgate, then depress the two lock cylinder securing tabs using a suitable screwdriver **(see illustration)**.

12 Withdraw the lock cylinder assembly from the tailgate, disengaging the operating rod from the lock (if not already done) as it is removed **(see illustration)**.

13 On models with central locking, the tailgate lock actuator can be separated from the lock cylinder mounting bracket by twisting it to release the retaining lugs at either side, and to release the top of the actuator from the lock cylinder.

Refitting

14 Refitting is a reversal of removal. Refit the wiper motor with reference to Chapter 12.

16.10b . . . and lift the number plate light shroud from the tailgate

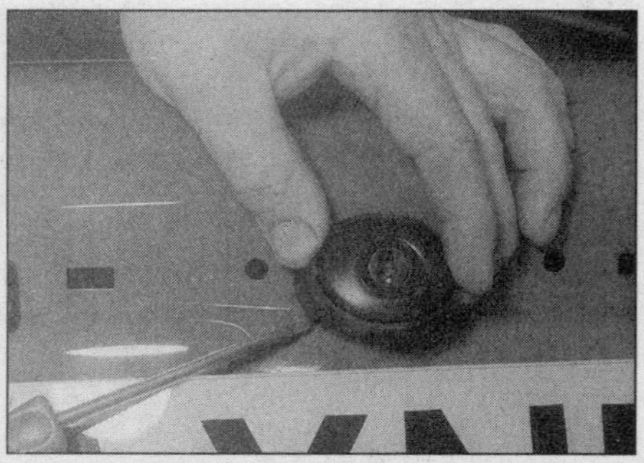

16.11 Depress the lock cylinder tabs . . .

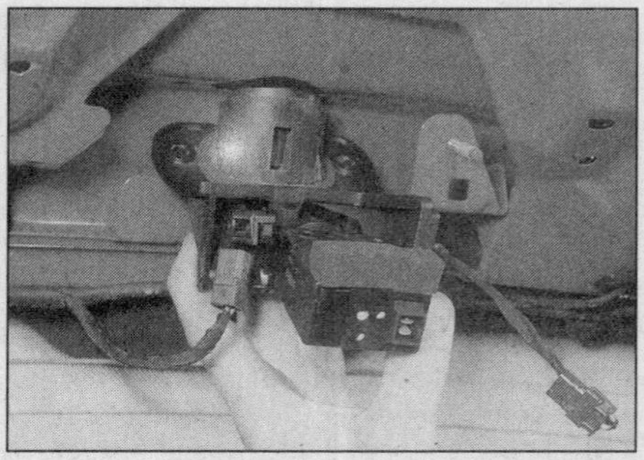

16.12 . . . then withdraw the lock cylinder assembly from the tailgate

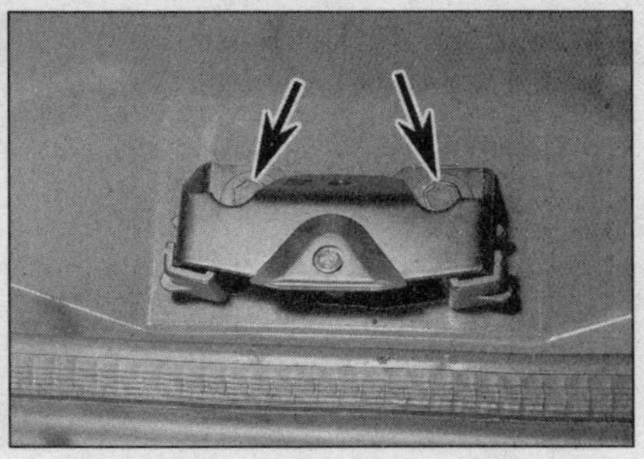
16.15 Tailgate lock striker securing bolts (arrowed)

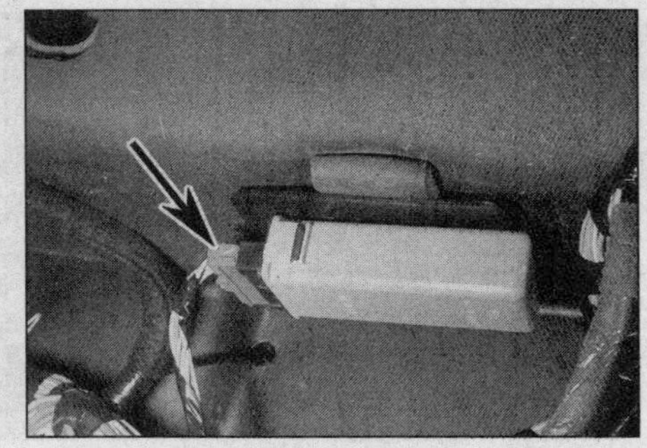
17.2 Central locking control unit located behind the glovebox - wiring plug arrowed

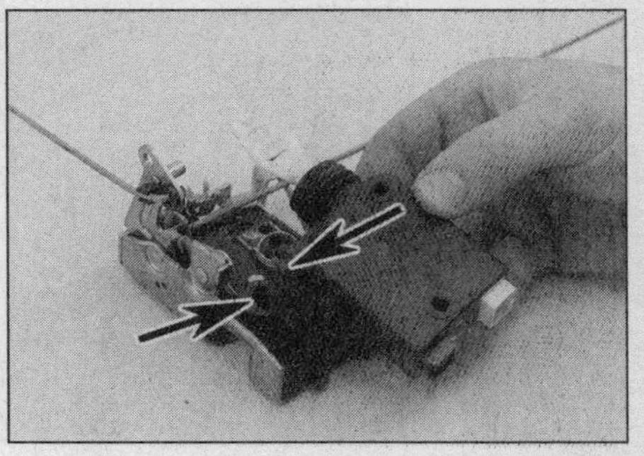
17.5 The door lock actuator peg locates in a hole in the door lock (arrowed)

Tailgate lock striker

Removal

15 Mark the position of the striker on the body, for use when refitting. Unscrew the two securing bolts **(see illustration)**, and remove the striker from the body.

Refitting

16 Refitting is a reversal of removal. Before tightening the securing bolts, the position of the striker should be altered (the securing bolt holes are elongated) until satisfactory lock operation is obtained. Use the marks made prior to removal, if appropriate.

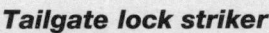

17 Central locking components - removal and refitting

Note: *Before attempting work on any of the central locking system components, disconnect the battery negative lead. Reconnect the lead on completion of work.*

Electronic control unit

1 The electronic control unit is located behind the glovebox, on all models except 5-door versions with remote-controlled "plip" locking. On these models, the control unit is located above the foot pedals in the driver's footwell.

Removal - all models except 5-door with remote locking

2 Reach up behind the facia, and disconnect the wiring plug from the control unit **(see illustration)**. On models with the upper glovebox, access may be easier with the upper glovebox removed (see Section 26). Unclip the unit from its mounting bracket, and remove it from behind the facia.

Removal - 5-door with remote locking

3 Working in the driver's footwell, remove the under-dash trim for access to the control unit. Disconnect the wiring plug and release the unit from its fixings.

Refitting

4 Refitting is a reversal of removal. Ensure that the wiring plug is securely reconnected, and check the system for correct operation before refitting any trim removed for access.

Door lock actuator

5 The actuator is attached to the door lock assembly, and can be detached from the lock after removing the lock assembly as described in Section 13 **(see illustration)**.

Tailgate lock actuator

Removal

6 Open the tailgate.

7 Remove the three screws (one at each side, one in the pull handle) securing the tailgate trim panel, then release the securing clips and withdraw the panel from the tailgate.

8 Disconnect the actuator wiring connector **(see illustration)**, and unclip the operating rod from the lock.

9 Tilt the bottom of the actuator body towards the tailgate, to release the securing lugs at either side from the lock cylinder mounting bracket, and to release the top of the actuator from the lock cylinder **(see illustrations)**.

10 Withdraw the actuator from the lock cylinder mounting bracket, and remove it from the tailgate.

Refitting

11 Refitting is a reversal of removal.

Remote control receiver unit

Removal

12 Remove the roof console as described in Section 26.

13 Release the securing clips, and remove the receiver unit from the top of the console.

Refitting

14 Refitting is a reversal of removal.

Remote control transmitter batteries - renewal

15 Using a small screwdriver, remove the screw from the remote control. Carefully prise the two halves of the transmitter apart, and remove the two batteries, noting which way round they are fitted.

16 Fit the two new batteries, ensuring that they are fitted the correct way round; the battery and transmitter terminals are marked "+" and "-" to avoid confusion. Clip the transmitter back together, and tighten the securing screw.

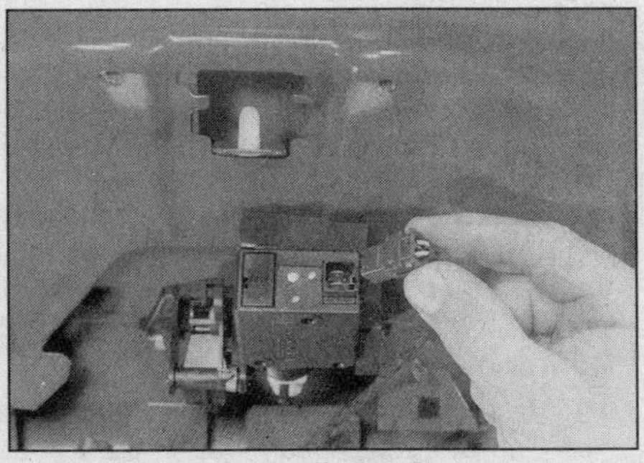
17.8 Disconnect the wiring connector from the tailgate actuator

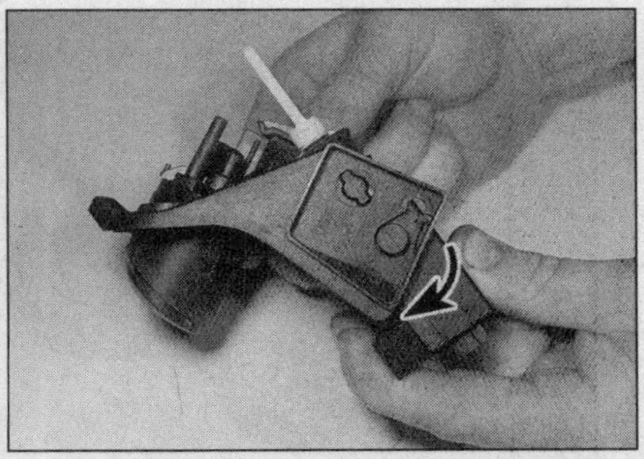
17.9a Tilt the bottom of the actuator inwards . . .

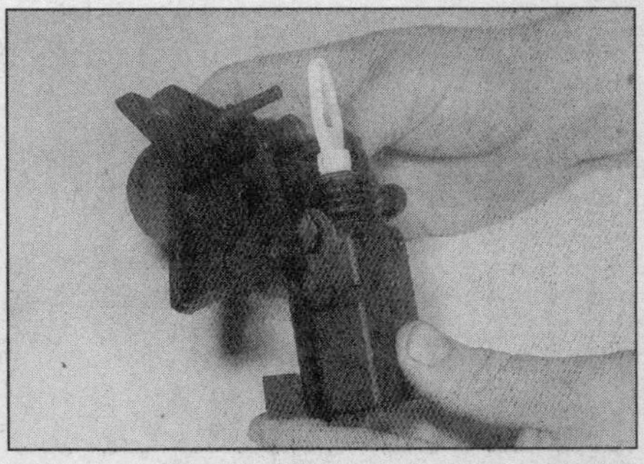
17.9b . . . to release it from the lock cylinder mounting bracket (removed for clarity)

19.2a Prise off the mirror trim plate . . .

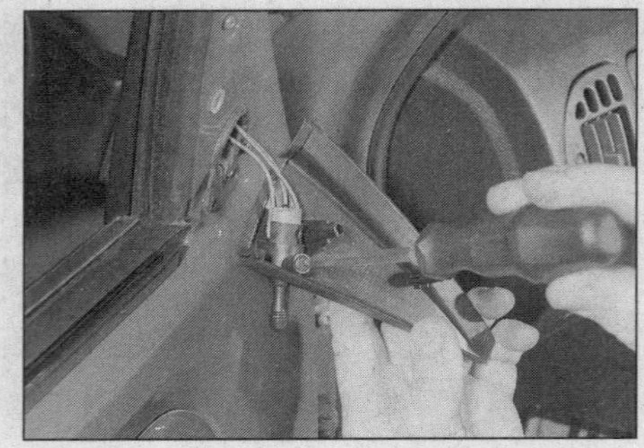

19.2b . . . remove the adjuster knob clamp screw (manual mirror shown) . . .

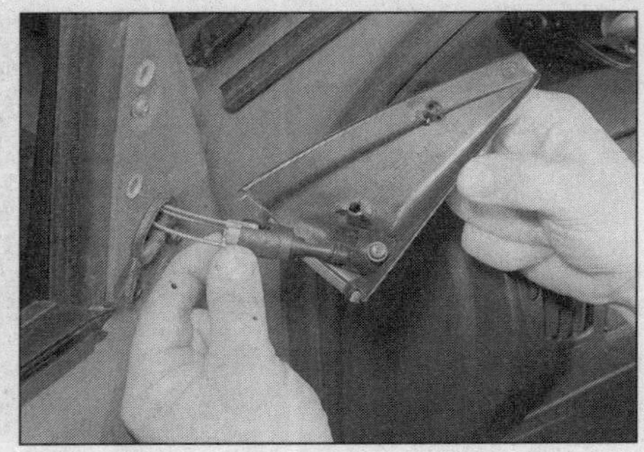

19.2c . . . withdraw the mirror trim plate . . .

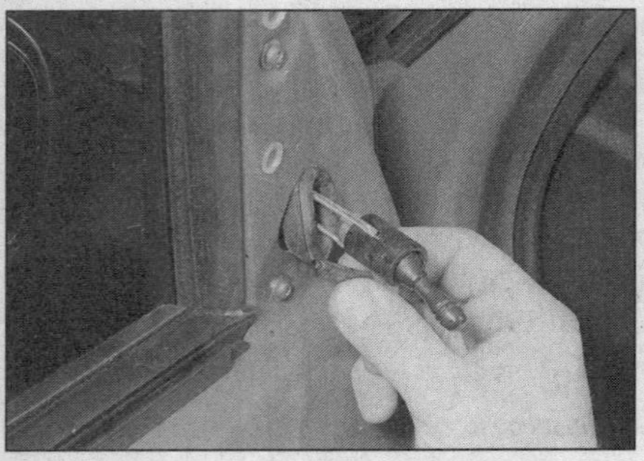

19.2d . . . and pull out the adjuster grommet

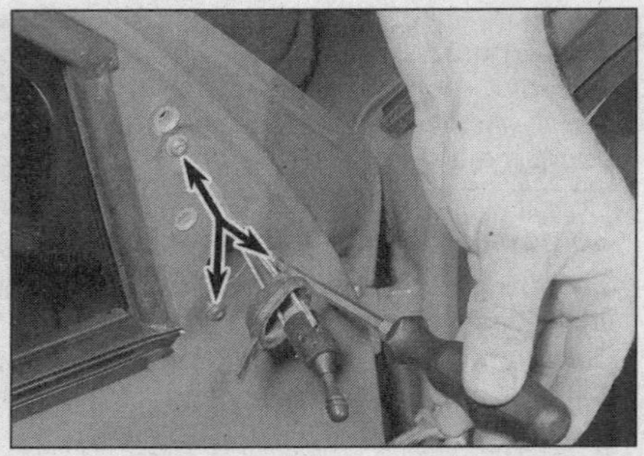

19.4a Remove the three mirror mounting screws (arrowed) . . .

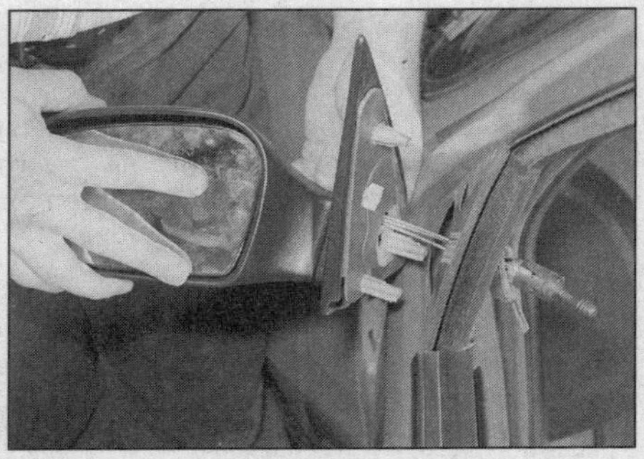

19.4b . . . and withdraw the mirror from the door

18 Electric window components - removal and refitting

Window switches

1 Refer to Chapter 12.

Window regulator motors

2 The regulator motors are integral with the regulator assemblies, and cannot be obtained separately.
3 Removal and refitting details for the regulator assemblies are given in Section 14.

19 Exterior mirror and associated components - removal and refitting

Mirror assembly

Removal

1 On models with electric mirrors, disconnect the battery negative lead.
2 Prise the mirror trim plate from the inner edge of the door. On manually-operated mirrors, remove the clamp screw securing the adjuster knob to the trim plate, and withdraw the trim plate; pull the adjuster grommet from the door **(see illustrations)**.
3 For access to the mirror screws, the door trim panel must be removed as described in Section 12.
4 Remove the three mirror securing screws. On electric mirrors, disconnect the wiring plug(s). Withdraw the mirror assembly from the door, complete with the adjuster mechanism and grommet (where applicable) **(see illustrations)**.

Refitting

5 Refitting is a reversal of removal.

Mirror glass

Removal

Warning: If the mirror glass is broken, wear thick gloves to protect your hands.

6 Working at the inside edge (the side nearest the car) of the mirror glass, locate the ends of the spring clip which secures the glass.
7 Using a suitable screwdriver, carefully unhook one end of the spring clip from the lugs on the rear of the glass **(see illustration)**. Lift the lower end of the spring upwards, or push the upper end of the spring downwards. If the glass is to be refitted, do not use excessive force, or the lugs will be broken.
8 Withdraw the glass, and recover the spring clip if it is loose **(see illustration)**. Disconnect the wiring plug from the glass heating element, where applicable.

Refitting

9 Fit the spring clip to the rear of the mirror glass, ensuring that both ends of the clip are correctly located in the lugs in the rear of the mirror glass **(see illustration)**.

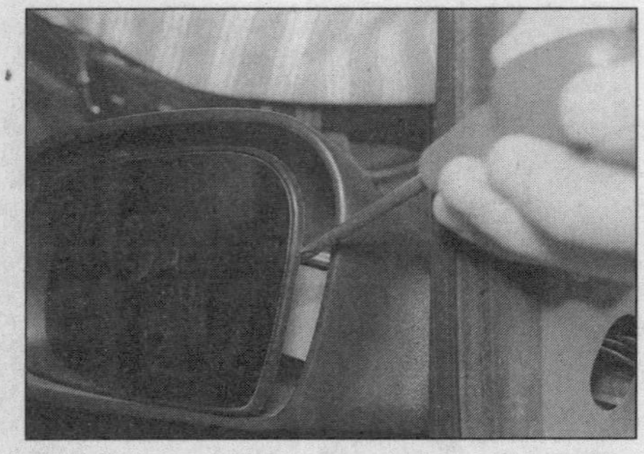

19.7 Using a slim screwdriver, unhook the mirror retaining clip

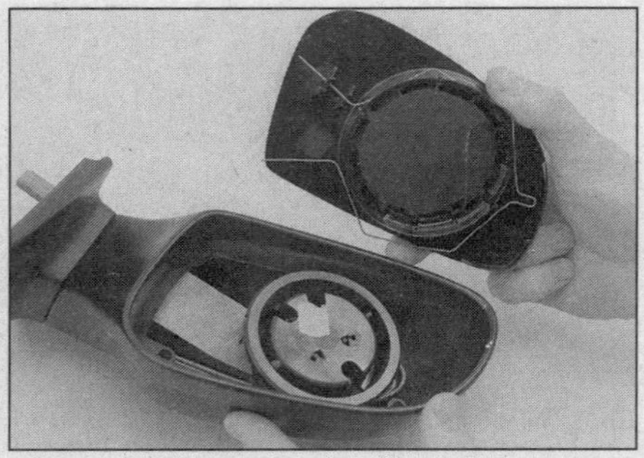

19.8 Mirror glass removed, showing retaining clip unhooked

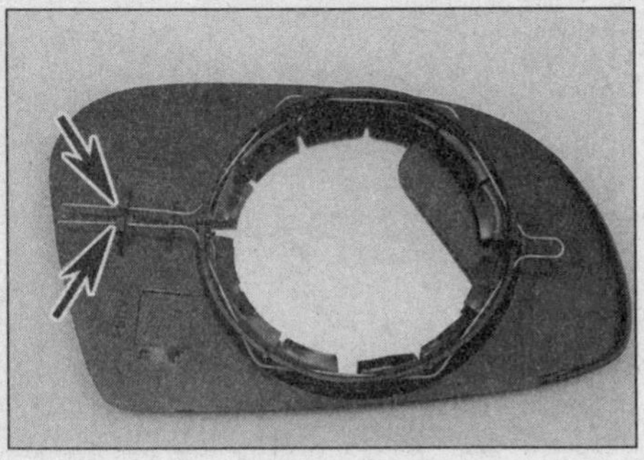

19.9 Before fitting the mirror glass, ensure that the retaining clip legs are engaged as shown (arrowed)

10 Push the mirror glass into the mirror until the spring clip locks into position in the mirror adjuster groove.

> **HAYNES HiNT** *Lightly grease the plastic ring on the adjuster to aid refitting of the spring clip.*

Manual adjustment mechanism

Removal

11 Prise the mirror trim plate from the inner edge of the door. Remove the clamp screw securing the adjuster knob to the trim plate, and withdraw the trim plate.

12 Remove the mirror glass as described previously in this Section.

13 Working inside the mirror housing, remove the three adjuster mechanism securing screws.

14 Pull the mechanism from the mirror housing, and feed the adjuster cables and grommet through the door.

Refitting

15 Refitting is a reversal of removal. Make sure that the adjuster cables are free to move, and not twisted. Refit the mirror glass as described previously in this Section.

Electric mirrors - general

16 No spare parts are available for the electric adjustment mechanism, and if faulty, the complete mirror assembly must be renewed. The mirror glass can be renewed as described previously in this Section. Removal and refitting of the switch is described in Chapter 12.

20 Windscreen, tailgate and fixed windows - general information

These areas of glass are secured by the tight fit of the weatherstrip in the body aperture, and are bonded in position with a special adhesive. Renewal of such fixed glass is a difficult, messy and time-consuming task, which is considered beyond the scope of the home mechanic. It is difficult, unless one has plenty of practice, to obtain a secure, waterproof fit. Furthermore, the task carries a high risk of breakage; this applies especially to the laminated glass windscreen. In view of this, owners are strongly advised to have this sort of work carried out by one of the many specialist windscreen fitters.

21 Opening rear quarter windows - removal and refitting

Removal

1 Open the window.

2 Support the glass, then working inside the vehicle, remove the screws securing the glass panel to the hinges and the handle. Withdraw the panel, taking care not to damage the surrounding paintwork. Where applicable, recover the plastic nuts and the trim from the panel.

3 To remove the handle, drill out the rivets securing the assembly to the body.

Refitting

4 Refitting is a reversal of removal. Where applicable, use new rivets to secure the handle to the body. Take care not to overtighten the glass panel securing screws (it is easy to strip the threads of the plastic nuts).

22 Sunroof - general information

Two different types of sunroof may be fitted, depending on model. A simple tilt sunroof is fitted to some models, whilst a more complicated tilt/slide sunroof is fitted to higher-specification models.

Removal of the sunroof glass on models with a tilt roof is straightforward. Remove the trim from the securing screws, then remove the screws securing the glass panel to the hinges and the handle. Refitting is a reversal of removal, ensuring that the trim plates are correctly refitted to the panel and the securing screws.

On models with a tilt/slide sunroof, due to the complexity of the sunroof mechanism, considerable expertise is required to repair, replace or adjust the sunroof components successfully. Removal of the roof first requires the headlining to be removed, which is a tedious operation, and not a task to be undertaken lightly (see Section 26). Therefore, any problems with this type of sunroof should be referred to a Citroën dealer.

23 Body exterior fittings - removal and refitting

Radiator grille/headlight surround - models up to September 1999

Removal

1 Remove both front direction indicator light units as described in Chapter 12.

2 Using a small flat-bladed screwdriver, prise up and remove the U-shaped plastic retaining clips at the base of each direction indicator light aperture **(see illustration)**.

3 Again using a screwdriver, gently prise each end of the headlight surround forwards to release the peg from the hole in the body **(see illustration)**.

4 Remove the three retaining bolts along the top of the radiator grille **(see illustrations)**.

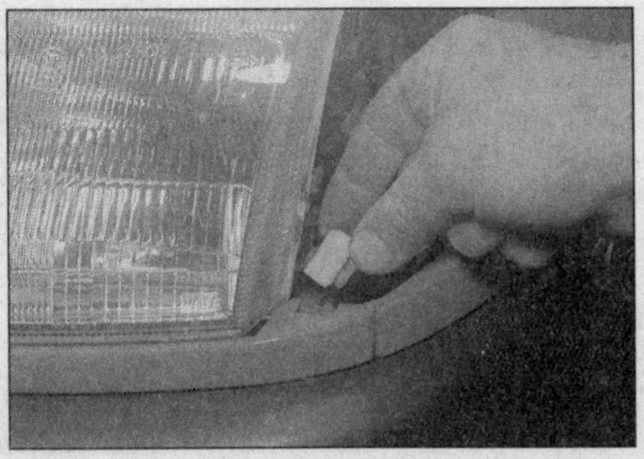

23.2 Remove the U-shaped clip from the direction indicator aperture

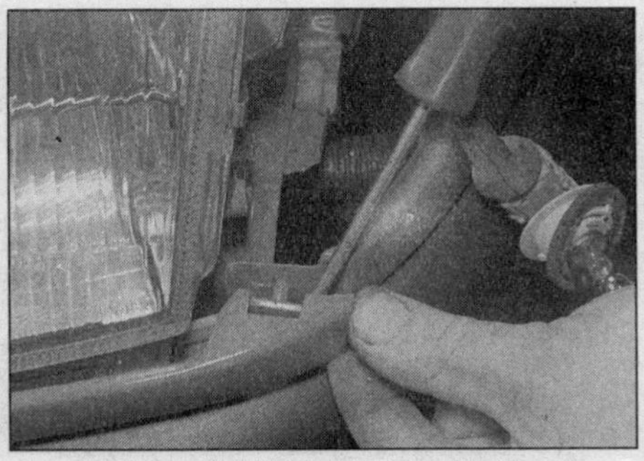

23.3 Prise the end of the surround forwards to disengage the locating peg

23.4a Radiator grille/headlight surround retaining bolts (arrowed)

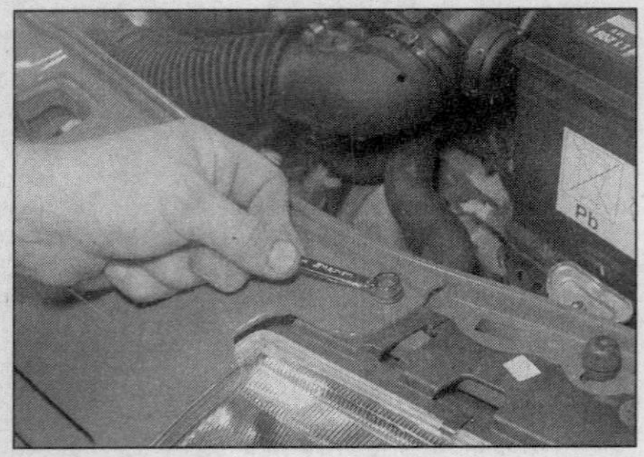

23.4b Removing one of the grille/surround bolts

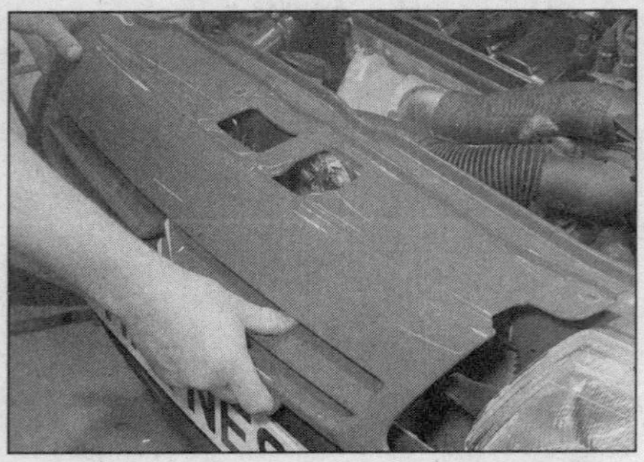

23.5 Pull the grille/surround forwards, releasing the two clips each side

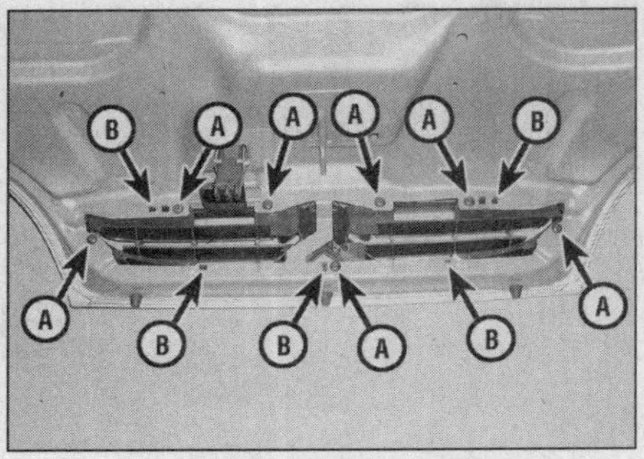

23.8a Remove the Torx screws and release the retaining clips . . .
A Torx screws B Retaining clips

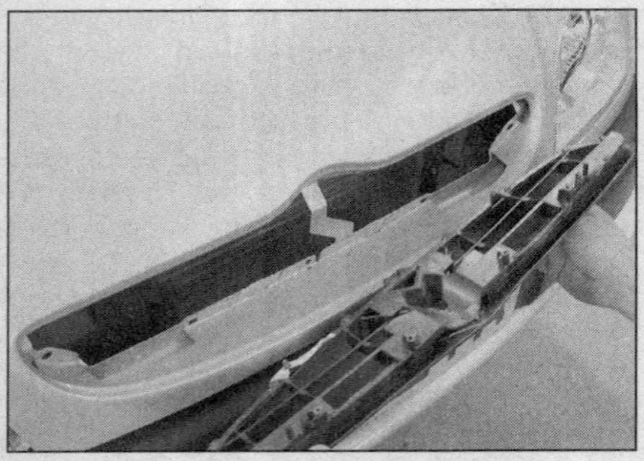

23.8b . . . and remove the grille

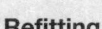

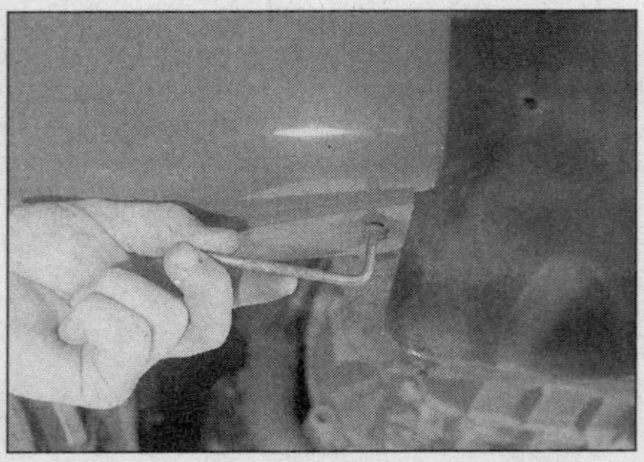

23.10a Removing the bumper-to-liner screw on a front wheel arch liner . . .

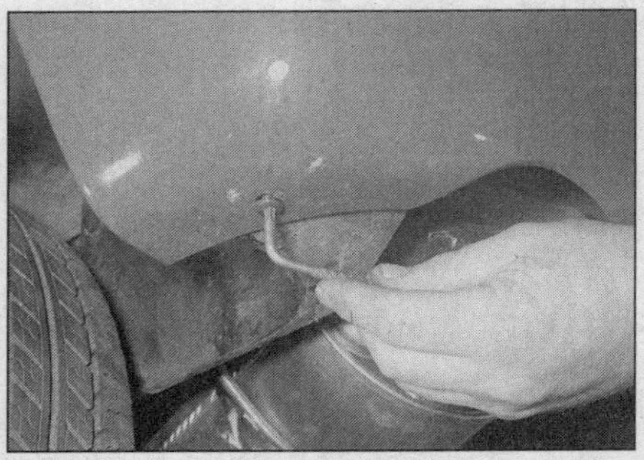

23.10b . . . and on the rear wheel arch liner

5 Pull the grille/headlight surround gently forwards to release the two slotted clips under each headlight unit, and remove it from the car **(see illustration)**. Care must be taken, as the clips (and the section of the panel under each headlight) are rather fragile.

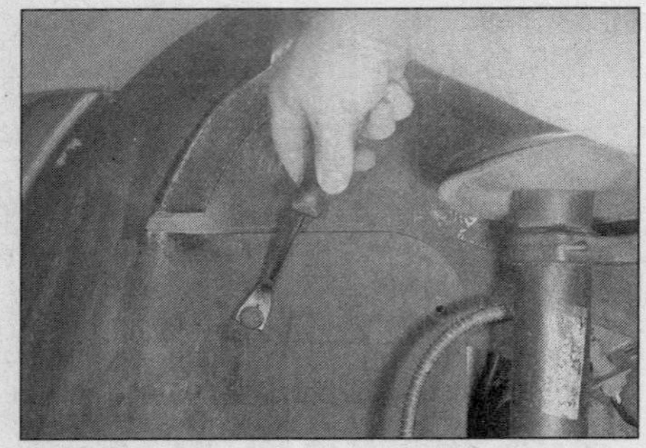

23.11a Prising out a securing clip from the front . . .

Refitting

6 Refitting is a reversal of removal. Make sure that the clips under each headlight are lined up with their respective slots before pushing the panel back into place. Refit the direction indicator light units as described in Chapter 12.

Radiator grille - models from October 1999

Removal

7 Lift the bonnet and place it on its stand.
8 Remove the seven Torx screws (size 20) and unclip the grille from the bonnet **(see illustrations)**.

Refitting

9 Refitting is the reverse of removal.

Wheel arch liners

Removal

10 Remove the screws securing the wheel arch liners to the ends of the bumper **(see illustrations)**.
11 Using a suitable forked tool (if available), prise out and remove the push-in securing clips **(see illustrations)**.
12 Ensure that nothing else in the wheel arch is preventing removal, then manipulate the liner out from under the wheel arch **(see illustrations)**.

Refitting

13 Refitting is a reversal of removal.

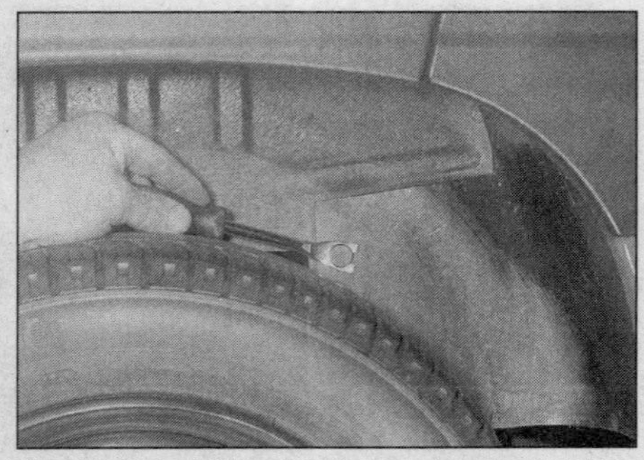

23.11b . . . and from a rear wheel arch liner

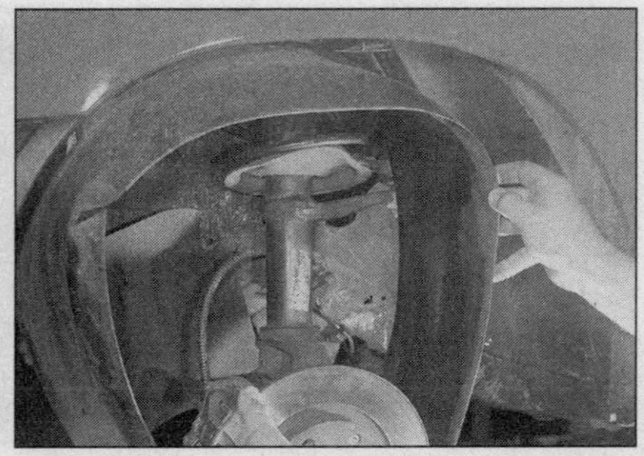

23.12a The front wheel arch liner must be removed past the suspension strut

23.12b Removing a rear wheel arch liner

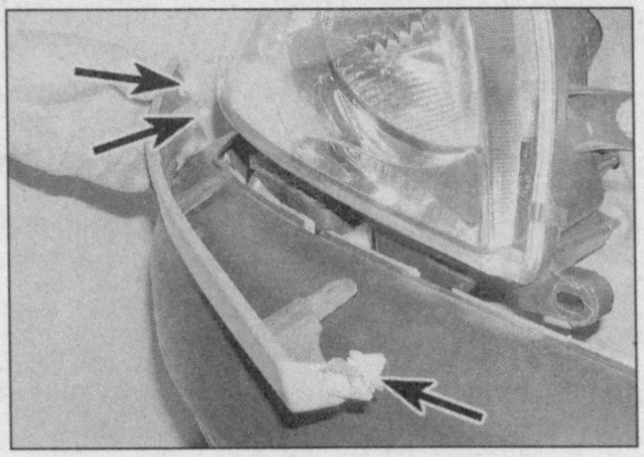

23.16 The headlight surround retaining clips

Body trim strips and badges

14 The various body trim strips and badges are held in position with a special adhesive tape. Removal requires the trim/badge to be heated, to soften the adhesive, and then cut away from the surface. Due to the high risk of damage to the vehicle paintwork during this operation, it is recommended that this task should be entrusted to a Citroën dealer.

Rear spoiler - later VTR and VTS models

15 At the time of writing, no removal details were available for the rear spoiler.

Headlight surround - models from October 1999

Removal

16 With the use of a screw driver, carefully prise the three retaining clips to release the plastic trim **(see illustration)**

Refitting

17 Put the plastic trim in place, but make sure that the location lugs slide into the slots underneath the headlight and clip the trim in to position.

24 Seats - removal and refitting

Front seat

Removal

Warning: The front seats are fitted with seat belt tensioners which are triggered by the airbag control system. Before removing the front seats, disconnect the battery and wait at least 10 minutes to allow the system capacitors to discharge.

1 Disconnect the battery negative lead, and wait for at least 10 minutes before proceeding.

2 Move the seat fully forwards, and tilt the seat backrest forwards.

3 Remove the bolts (one bolt on each side) securing the rear of the seat rails to the floor, noting that the inner bolt is longer than the outer; recover the washer **(see illustrations)**.

4 Disconnect the wiring connector for the seat belt tensioner - this is located on the underside of the seat cushion **(see illustration)**. Noting its routing for refitting, unclip the wiring harness from under the seat cushion.

5 Move the seat fully rearwards.

6 Remove the bolts (one bolt on each side) securing the front of the seat rails to the floor **(see illustration)**, noting again that the inner bolt is longer than the outer; recover the washer.

7 Lift the seat from the vehicle.

Refitting

8 Refitting is a reversal of removal, but it is essential to tighten the outer seat rail securing bolts (nearest the door) **before** tightening the inner seat rail securing bolts (nearest the handbrake lever).

Rear seat back

Removal

9 Tilt the seat cushion forwards against the front seats, and fold the seat back(s) forwards.

10 Remove the two hinge nuts at each bottom corner of the seat back **(see illustration)**. On models with a split folding rear seat, a further hinge bolt is located between the two halves of the rear seat.

11 Pull the seat back(s) upwards to release the hinge pins, and withdraw from the vehicle.

Refitting

12 Refitting is a reversal of removal.

Rear seat cushion

Removal

13 Tilt the cushion forwards against the front seats.

14 Remove the hinge nuts (two on models with a single-piece cushion, or four nuts if a split folding rear seat is fitted) **(see illustration)**

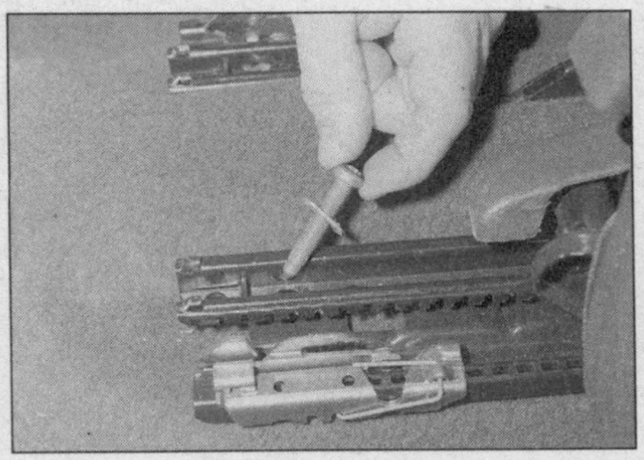

24.3a Removing a seat rail rear inner bolt and washer . . .

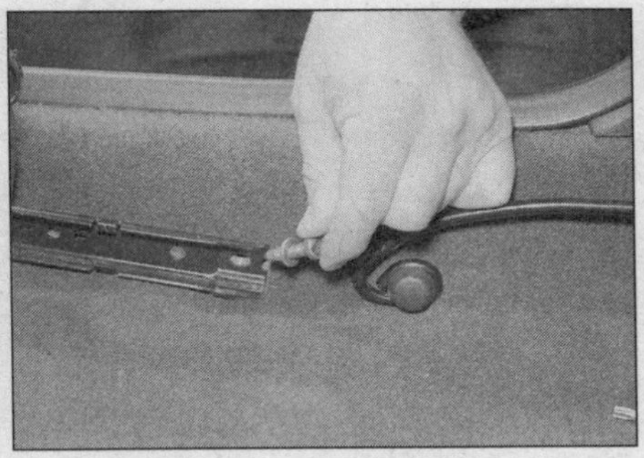

24.3b . . . and outer bolt and washer

24.4 Disconnect the seat belt tensioner wiring connector under the seat

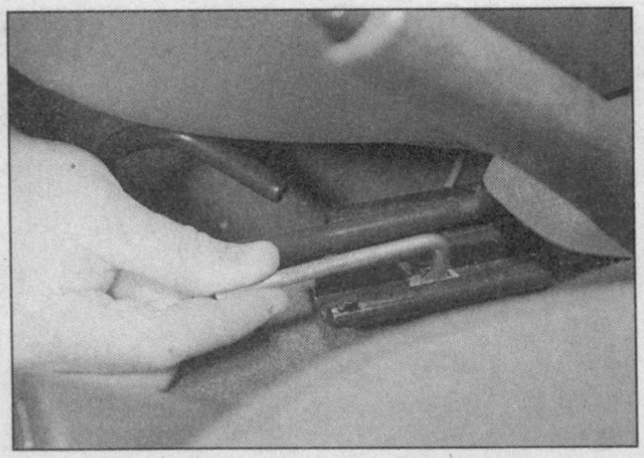

24.6 Removing a seat rail front inner bolt

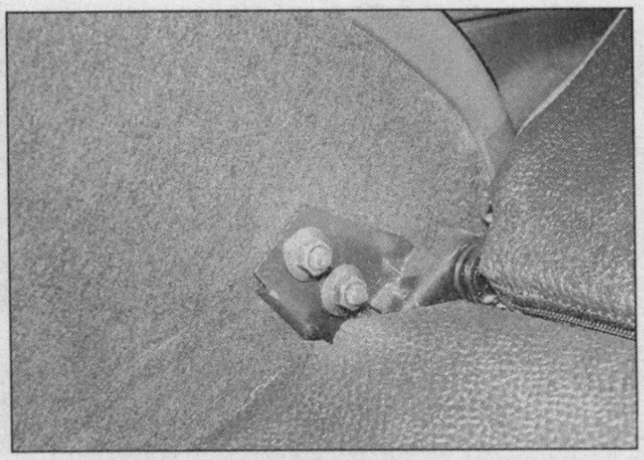

24.10 Rear seat back hinge nuts

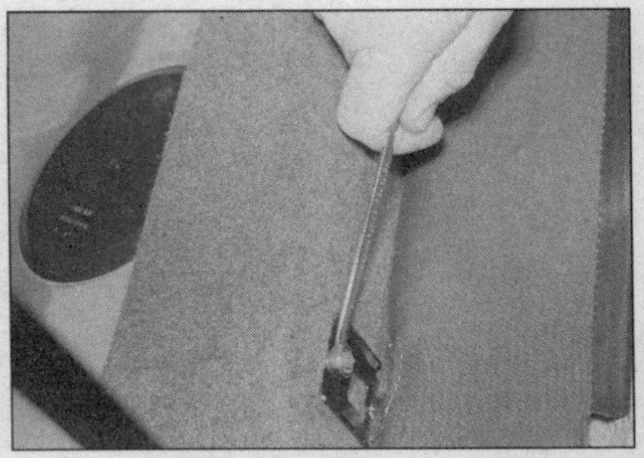

24.14 Removing one of the seat cushion hinge nuts

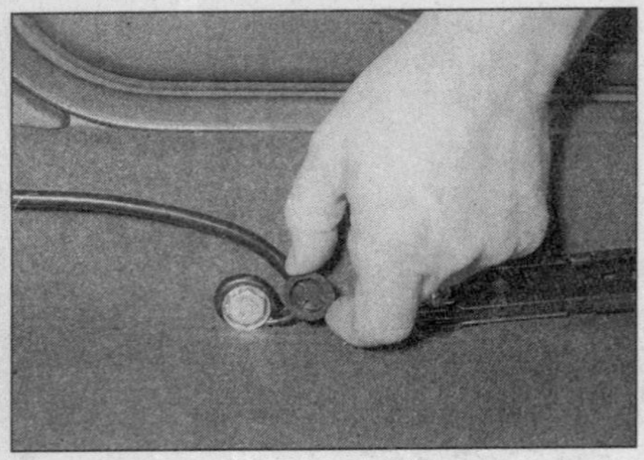

25.2a Prise off the trim cap . . .

and remove the cushion and hinges from the car. If preferred, the cushion can be unhooked from the hinges by pulling the cushion upwards; we found, however, that hooking the cushion back in place was rather awkward.

Refitting

15 Refitting is a reversal of removal.

25 Seat belt components - removal and refitting

Front seat belt - 3-door models

Removal

1 Remove the rear passenger compartment side trim panel, as described in Section 26.

2 Prise off the trim cap from the lower belt anchorage bolt. Remove the bolt, washer and

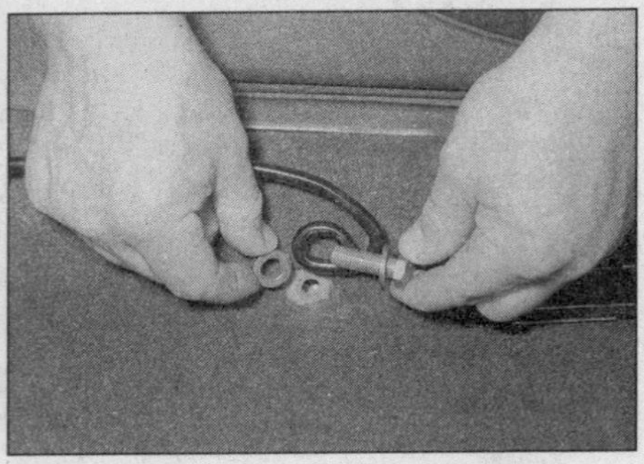

25.2b . . . then remove the seat belt lower anchorage bolt, washer and spacer

spacer, then pull out the anchorage bar, and free the seat belt from the bar **(see illustrations)**.

3 Prise the trim cap from the seat belt upper mounting bolt, then unscrew the bolt, and release the seat belt mounting plate. Note the location of the spacer **(see illustration)**.

4 Feed the seat belt and the upper mounting plate through the aperture in the trim panel.

5 Remove the inertia reel securing bolt **(see illustration)**, and withdraw the seat belt from the vehicle.

Refitting

6 Refitting is a reversal of removal. Ensure that all washers and spacers are positioned as noted before removal, and tighten all mounting bolts to the specified torque.

Front seat belt - 5-door models

Removal

7 Prise off the trim cap, then remove the lower belt anchorage bolt, and recover the washer.

8 Similarly, remove the upper anchor bolt.

9 Remove the two securing screws, then unclip the centre pillar trim panel from the body.

10 Remove the inertia reel securing bolt, then withdraw the seat belt assembly from the vehicle.

Refitting

11 Refitting is a reversal of removal. Tighten the mounting bolts to the specified torque.

Front seat belt stalk and tensioner

Removal

Warning: The front seat belt stalks are fitted with seat belt tensioners which contain a small explosive charge. Do not handle the assembly roughly, or expose it to high temperatures, while it is removed from the car. Before removing the front seat belt stalks, disconnect the battery and wait at least 10 minutes to allow the system capacitors to discharge.

12 Remove the front seat as described in Section 24.

13 Remove the screw securing the trim panel over the seat belt stalk, and unclip the trim panel **(see illustrations)**.

14 Unclip the wiring plug retaining clip, then disconnect the wiring plug from the seat belt tensioner **(see illustrations)**. Ensure that the wiring harness for the seat belt tensioner has

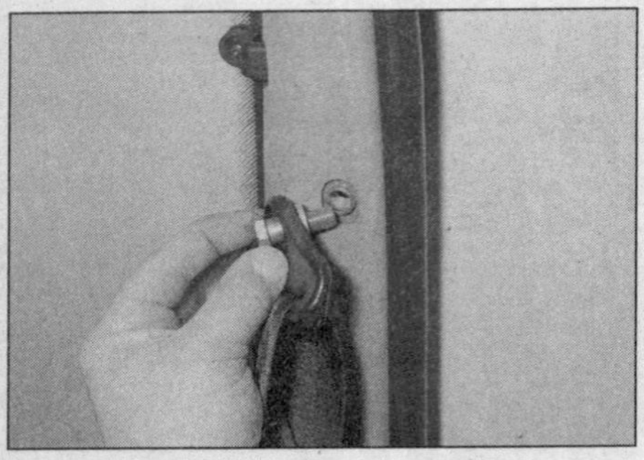

25.3 Removing the seat belt upper mounting bolt, mounting plate and spacer

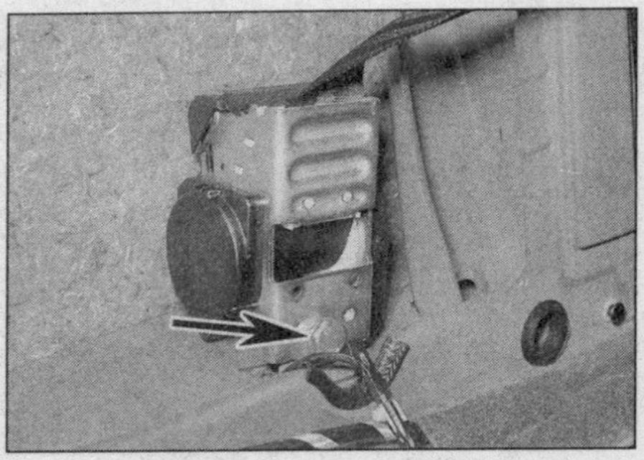

25.5 Front seat belt inertia reel securing bolt (arrowed)

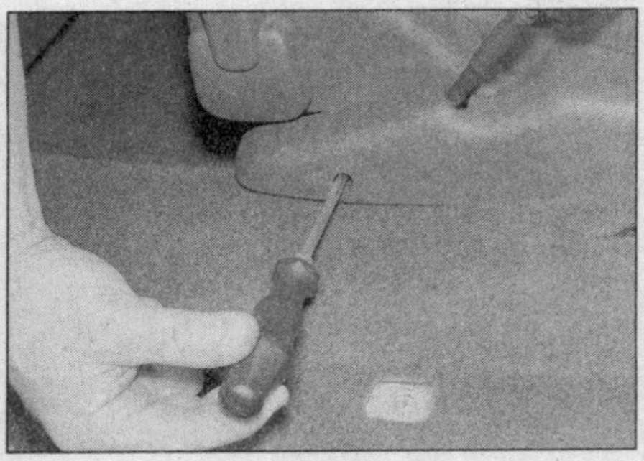

25.13a Remove the trim panel screw . . .

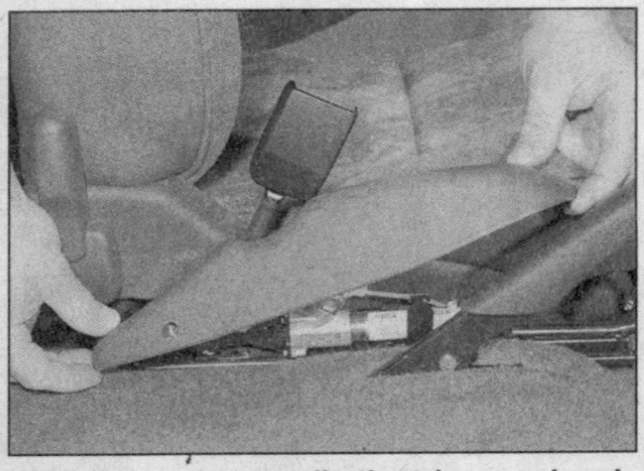

25.13b . . . then unclip the trim panel and remove it

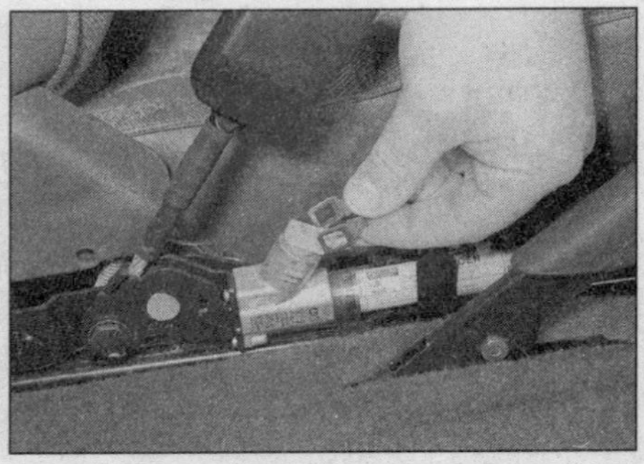

25.14a Remove the clip from the seat belt tensioner wiring plug . . .

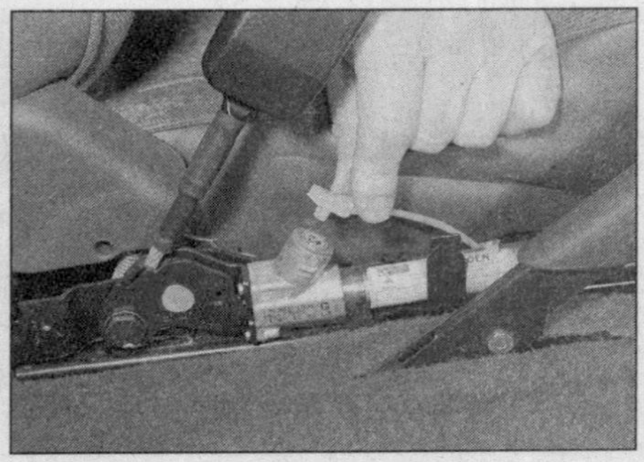

25.14b . . . then disconnect the plug

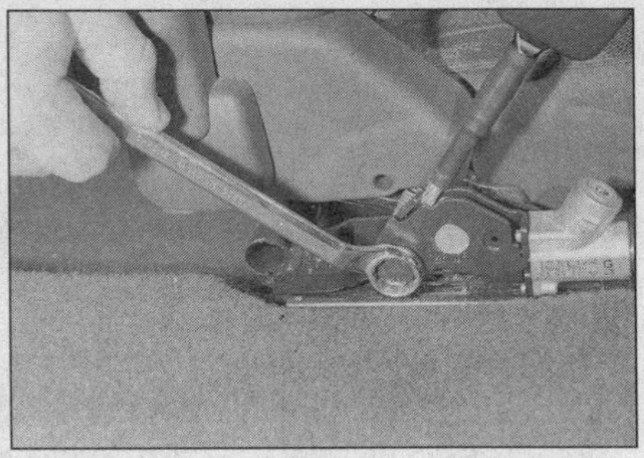

25.15 Removing the seat belt stalk securing bolt

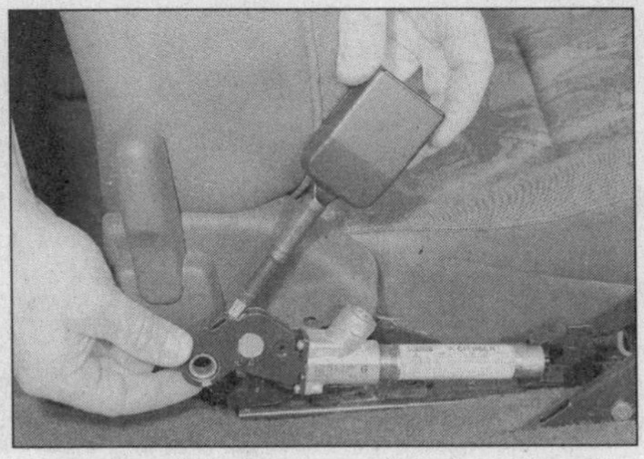

25.16 Removing the seat belt stalk and tensioner

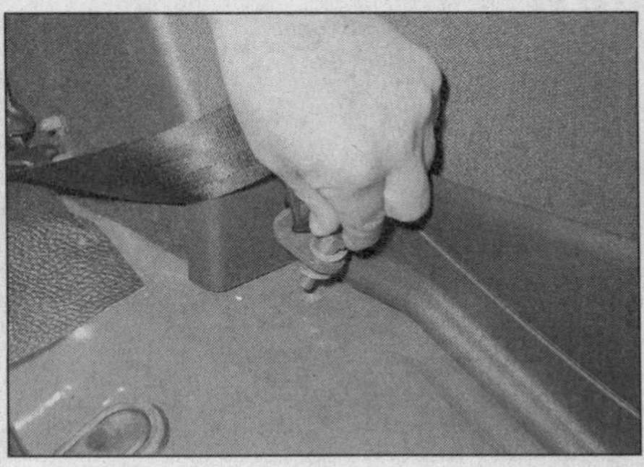

25.20 Removing the rear seat belt lower mounting plate

been completely unclipped from under the seat cushion and from the tensioner barrel, so that it can be removed with the seat belt stalk.

15 Unscrew the bolt securing the stalk assembly to the seat frame **(see illustration)**.

16 Withdraw the assembly from the seat **(see illustration)**. Handle the assembly by holding the tensioner barrel, or the buckle - **do not** hold the assembly by the stalk.

Refitting

17 Refitting is a reversal of removal, bearing in mind the following points:

a) *Ensure that the wiring for the seat belt tensioner is routed as noted on removal, and is clipped securely to the base of the seat cushion.*

b) *Tighten the stalk mounting bolt to the specified torque.*

c) *Refit the seat as described in Section 24.*

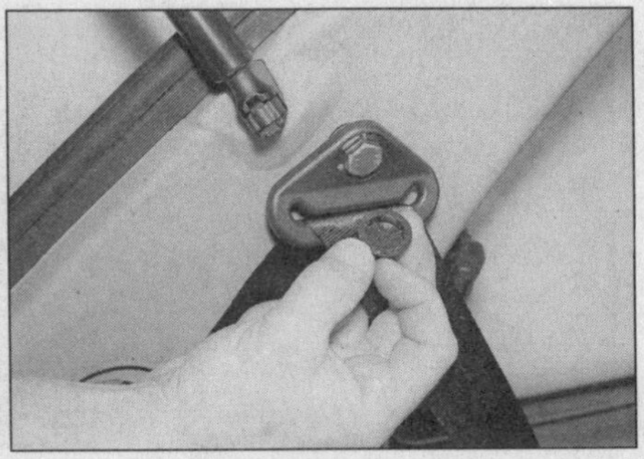

25.21a Prise off the trim cap . . .

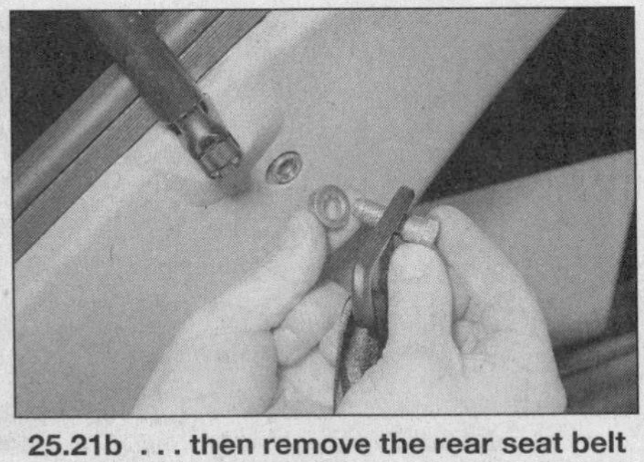

25.21b . . . then remove the rear seat belt upper mounting bolt, mounting plate and spacer

Rear seat belt

Removal

18 Remove the parcel shelf support panel as described in Section 26.

19 Fold the rear seat cushion forwards to expose the lower seat belt anchorage.

20 Unbolt the seat belt lower mounting plate from the floor panel. Note the locations of any washers and spacers on the bolt **(see illustration)**.

21 Prise off the trim cap, and unbolt the seat belt upper anchorage from the body. Again, note the locations of the washer and spacer **(see illustrations)**.

22 Remove the bolt securing the inertia reel assembly to the body **(see illustration)**, and remove the seat belt assembly from the vehicle.

Refitting

23 Refitting is a reversal of removal. Ensure that all washers and spacers are positioned as noted before removal, and tighten all mounting bolts to the specified torque.

Rear belt buckles

Removal

24 The assemblies can simply be unbolted from the floor panel, after folding the rear seat cushion forwards **(see illustration)**. Note the locations of any washers and spacers, to ensure correct refitting.

Refitting

25 Refitting is a reversal of removal. Ensure that all washers and/or spacers are positioned as noted before removal, and tighten all mounting bolts to the specified torque.

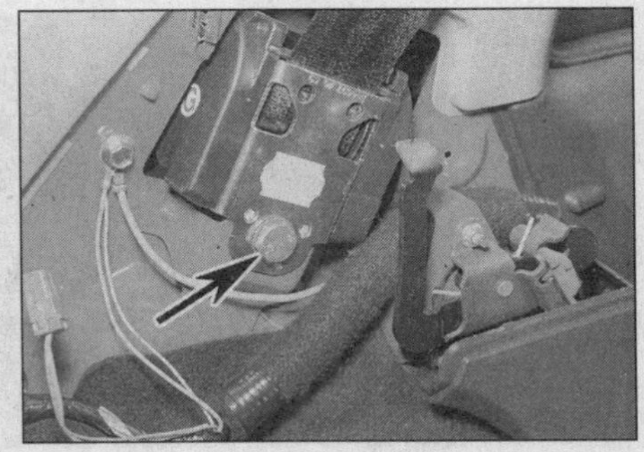

25.22 Rear seat belt inertia reel mounting bolt (arrowed)

26 Interior trim - removal and refitting

Door trim panels

1 Refer to Section 12.

Rear passenger compartment side trim panel - 3-door models

Removal

2 Remove the rear parcel shelf support panel, as described later in this Section.

3 Remove the rear seat cushion, with reference to Section 24, and fold the seat back fully forwards.

4 Open the front door, and carefully pull away the rubber seal from the front door aperture, in the area in front of the side trim panel. Similarly, open the side window and pull up the rubber seal from the bottom of the window aperture.

5 Carefully pull the panel from the body to release the five securing clips (three at the front edge, one each near the rear corners).

6 Lift the panel away from its location. Where

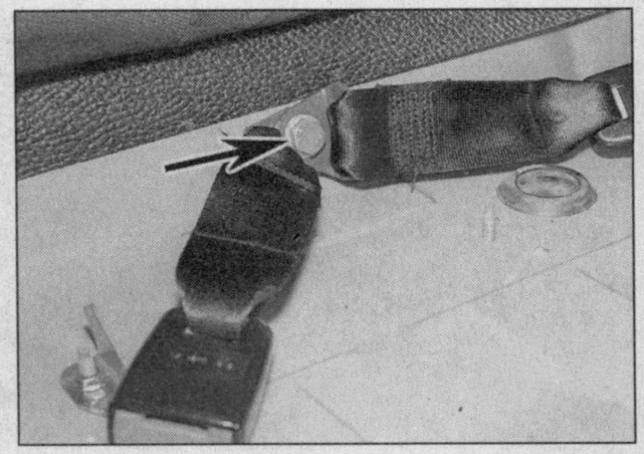

25.24 Rear seat belt buckle mounting bolt (arrowed)

26.6a Pull the rear side trim panel away from the car . . .

26.6b . . . and disconnect the rear speaker wiring (where applicable)

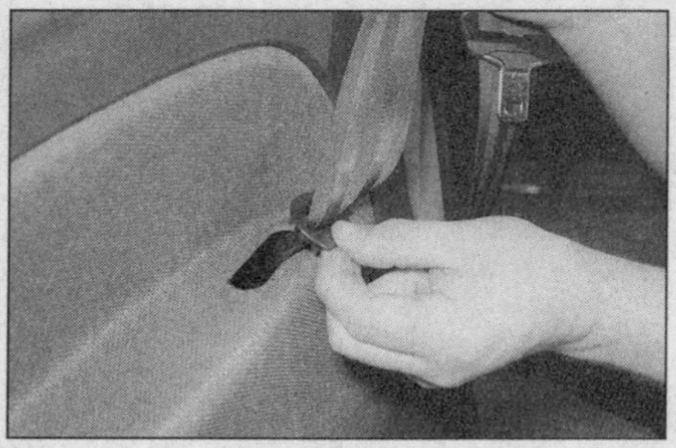

26.7 Prise out the seat belt guide from the panel, and withdraw the seat belt through the aperture

applicable, disconnect the wiring from the speaker **(see illustrations)**.

7 Unbolt the seat belt upper and lower anchor brackets, with reference to Section 25. Remove the plastic belt guide from the panel, and feed the seat belt and anchor brackets through the aperture in the trim panel **(see illustration)**. Withdraw the trim panel from the vehicle.

Refitting

8 Refitting is a reversal of removal, bearing in mind the following points:

a) Tighten the seat belt mountings to the specified torque.

b) Refit the rear parcel shelf support panel as described later in this Section.

Rear parcel shelf support panel

Removal

9 Open the tailgate, remove the rear parcel shelf, and fold the rear seat back forwards.

10 Remove the two securing screws, then pull the knob from the seat back release lever, and pull the weatherstrip from the rear edge of the panel **(see illustrations)**.

11 Where applicable, disconnect the battery negative lead, and prise the luggage compartment light and the switch from the trim panel **(see illustrations)**.

12 Lift and manoeuvre the panel away from the body to release the securing clips at the front, and withdraw the panel **(see illustration)**.

Refitting

13 Refitting is a reversal of removal, but ensure that the seat belt webbing is routed over the top of the panel, and is not trapped behind the panel.

Windscreen pillar trim panel

Removal

14 Carefully prise the weatherstrip from the edge of the trim panel.

15 Starting at the top, pull the panel away from the pillar to release the securing clips, and withdraw the panel.

Refitting

16 Refitting is a reversal of removal.

Centre pillar trim panel(s)

17 The panel is in two halves on 5-door models, with only the top section being fitted on 3-door models.

26.10a Remove the screw from the front . . .

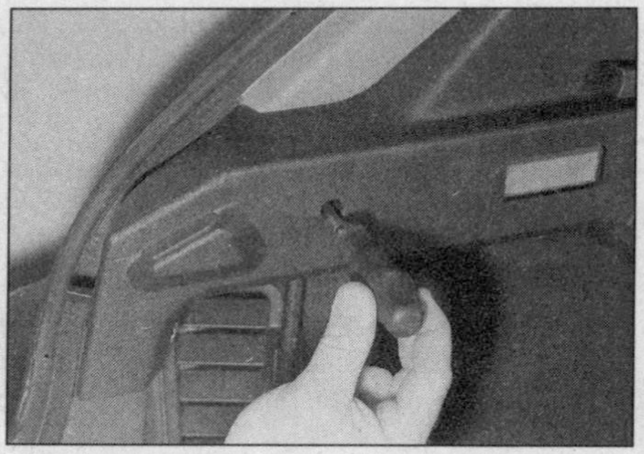

26.10b . . . and the one at the rear . . .

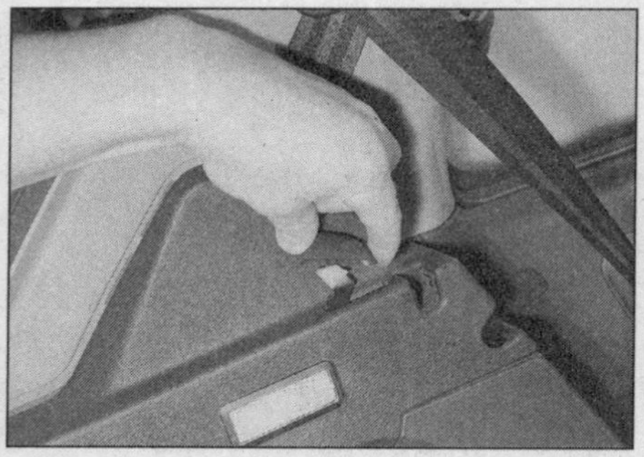

26.10c . . . then pull the knob from the seat back release lever

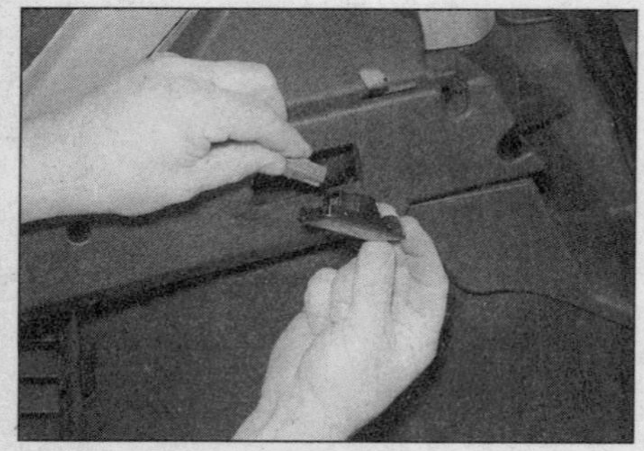

26.11a Where applicable, remove the light unit . . .

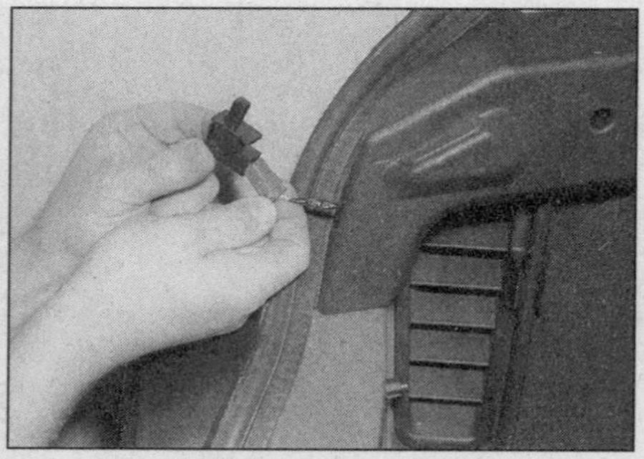

26.11b . . . and disconnect the light switch

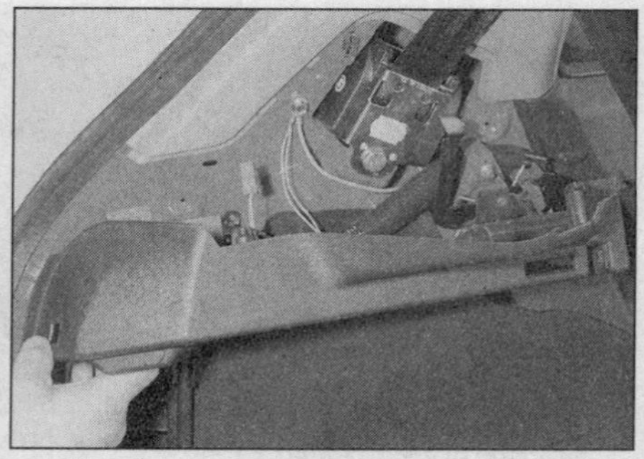

26.12 Removing the parcel shelf support panel

Upper panel - 3-door models

18 Open the front door, and carefully peel away the rubber seal from the door aperture, in the area in front of the trim panel.
19 Prise off the trim cap and unbolt the seat belt upper mounting, noting the fitted position and order of all washers and spacers, and lower the mounting out of the way.
20 Work around the panel, releasing it from its retaining clips and from the surrounding trim, and remove it from the car **(see illustration)**.
21 Refitting is a reversal of removal. Where applicable, tighten the seat belt anchor bolt to the specified torque.

Upper panel - 5-door models

22 To remove the upper panel, first remove the lower panel, then remove the securing screw from the bottom of the upper panel.
23 Prise off the trim cap and unbolt the seat belt upper mounting, noting the fitted position and order of all washers and spacers, and lower the mounting out of the way.
24 Unclip and withdraw the panel.

Lower panel - 5-door models

25 Open the front door and rear doors on the side concerned, and carefully peel away the rubber seal from the front door aperture, in the area in front of the trim panel.
26 Remove the two securing screws, then unclip the panel.
27 Refitting is a reversal of removal.

Rear pillar trim panel

28 Open the tailgate, and carefully peel away the rubber seal from the tailgate aperture, in the area behind the trim panel. On 5-door models, open the rear door on the side concerned, and peel the rubber seal from the door aperture, in front of the trim panel.
29 On 3-door models, open the rear window. Carefully peel away the rubber seal from the window aperture, in front of the trim panel.
30 Remove the rear parcel shelf support panel as described previously in this Section.
31 Prise off the trim cap and unscrew the rear seat belt upper anchor bolt.
32 Unclip the panel from the body, and remove it from the car.

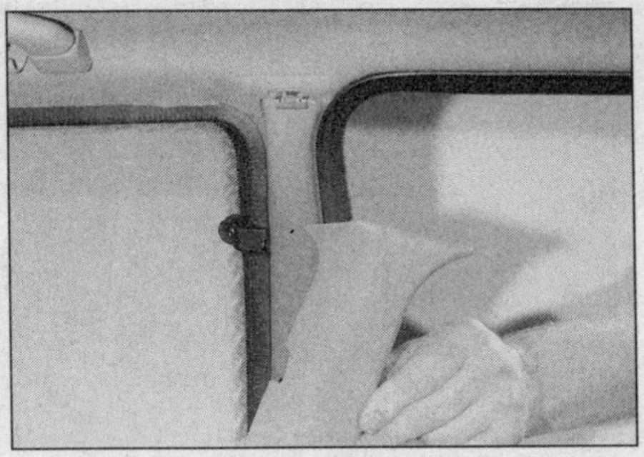

26.20 Centre pillar trim panel is clipped into place

Rear wheel arch trim panel - 5-door models

33 Open the rear door, and prise the rubber seal from the edge of the panel.
34 Release the panel from the securing clips, then release the panel from the rear parcel shelf support panel, and withdraw the wheel arch trim panel.

Carpets

35 The passenger compartment floor carpet is in one piece, and is secured at its edges by screws or various types of clips.
36 Carpet removal and refitting is reasonably straightforward, but time-consuming, due to the fact that all adjoining trim panels must be removed first, as must components such as the seats and centre console.

Headlining

37 The headlining is clipped to the roof, and can be withdrawn only once all fittings such as the grab handles, sun visors, sunroof (if fitted), windscreen, centre and rear pillar trim panels, and associated panels have been removed. The door, tailgate and sunroof aperture weatherstrips will also have to be prised clear.
38 Note that headlining removal requires considerable skill and experience if it is to be carried out without damage, and is therefore best entrusted to an expert.

Glovebox

Conventional glovebox - models without a passenger airbag

39 On the project vehicles seen in the workshop, the glovebox could not be removed, and was integral with the facia panel. This despite the fact that there are two screws visible with the glovebox lid open, which did not appear to serve any purpose when removed.
40 To remove the glovebox lid, open the glovebox, then remove the securing screws along the base of the lid and withdraw the glovebox lid **(see illustration)**.
41 Refitting is a reversal of removal.

Upper glovebox - high-specification models, and those with a passenger airbag

42 On models with a passenger airbag, the airbag unit is fitted where the glovebox would normally be. As a result, an upper glovebox is fitted to the top of the passenger side of the facia (this glovebox also appears on some high-specification models without the passenger airbag).
43 To remove the glovebox, open the lid and prise the glovebox out of the top of the facia panel, releasing the three clips along the front edge of the glovebox. Take care not to mark the finish.
44 Refitting is a reversal of removal.

Roof console

45 Prise out the interior light, and disconnect the wiring plug.
46 Fully close the sunroof, then mark the position of the sunroof handle in relation to the roof console for refitting. Remove the screw from the sunroof handle, and pull the handle from its splines **(see illustrations)**.
47 According to model, prise out the map

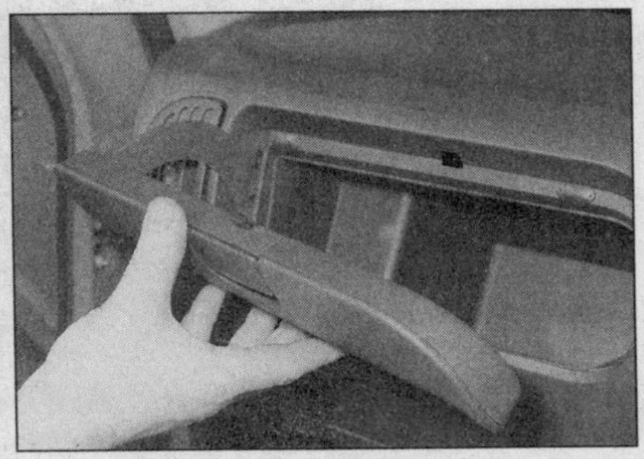

26.40 Removing the glovebox lid

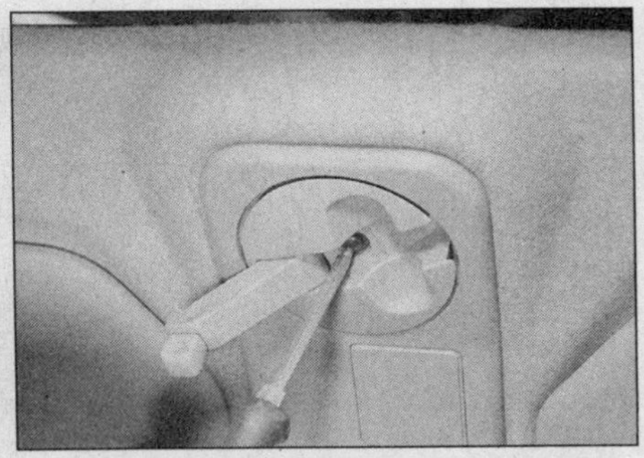

26.46a Remove the screw securing the sunroof handle . . .

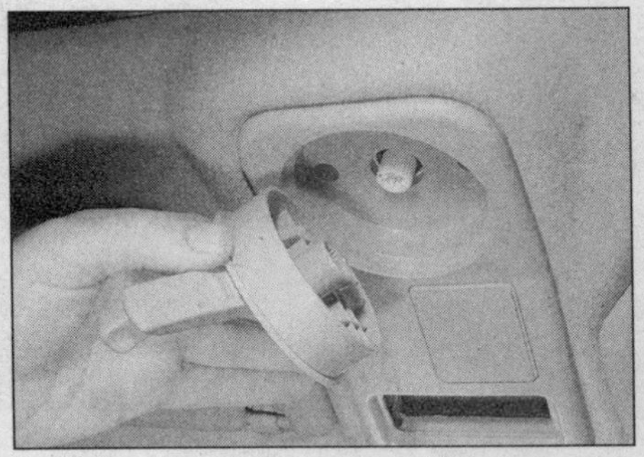

26.46b . . . then pull the handle from its splines

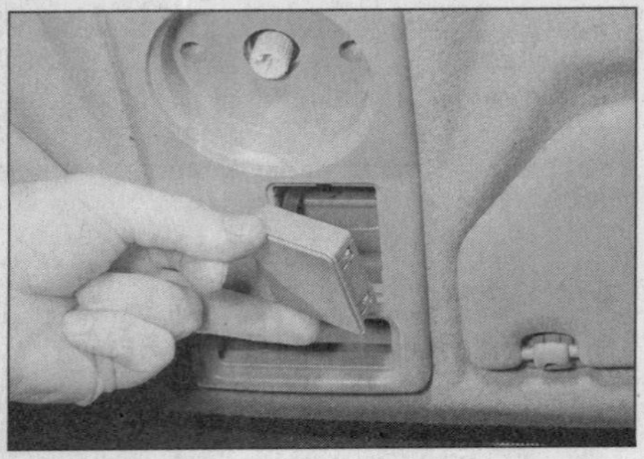

26.47 Removing the blanking plate (on this model)

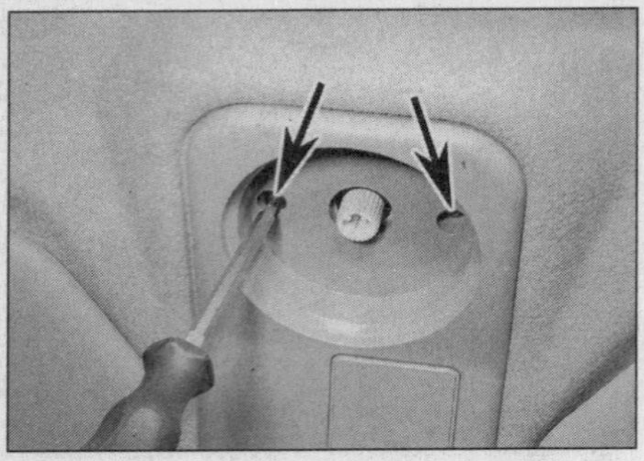

26.48a Remove the two screws from the sunroof handle aperture . . .

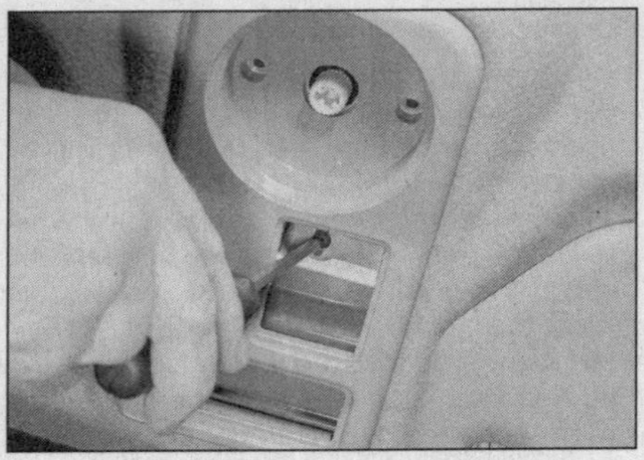

26.48b . . . and the screw behind the blanking plate . . .

reading light or the blanking plate **(see illustration)**.

48 Remove the three roof console securing screws, and lower the console from the headlining, disconnecting any further wiring (for instance, from the remote central locking receiver) as applicable **(see illustrations)**.

49 Refitting is a reversal of removal.

27 Centre console - removal and refitting

Removal

1 Where applicable, prise out the anti-theft immobiliser keypad and surround from the front of the console. The keypad surround is secured by five clips (two each side, one at the front), which are released by inserting a slim flat-bladed screwdriver in through the cut-outs provided, and pressing inwards while prising the surround upwards. Take care not to mark or damage the plastic. Withdraw the keypad and surround, and disconnect the wiring plug **(see illustrations)**.

2 On models with electric windows, prise out the window switches from the centre console; disconnect the wiring plugs, noting their locations.

Manual transmission models

3 Carefully prise the gear lever gaiter from the centre console.

4 Remove the single Torx screw behind the gear lever **(see illustration)**.

Automatic transmission models

5 Remove the two screws (one each side) securing the selector lever knob to the selector lever.

6 Carefully lift the knob approximately 10 mm, then turn it gently to the rear by a quarter-turn, and lift it up a further 7 mm.

7 Press in the detent button and hold it, then turn the knob gently back to the front through a quarter-turn. Lift the knob off the top of the selector lever.

8 Prise out the selector cover from the top of the console, and remove it over the selector lever.

9 Remove the two screws in front of the selector lever.

All models

10 Pull the console to the rear to disengage the locating clip, then remove it upwards over the gear/selector lever **(see illustration)**.

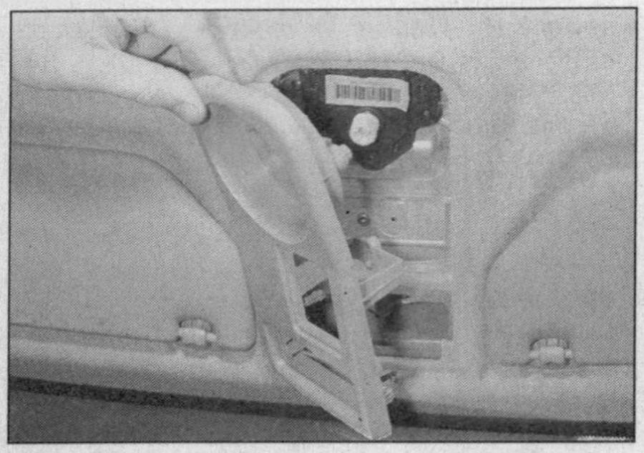

26.48c . . . and remove the roof console

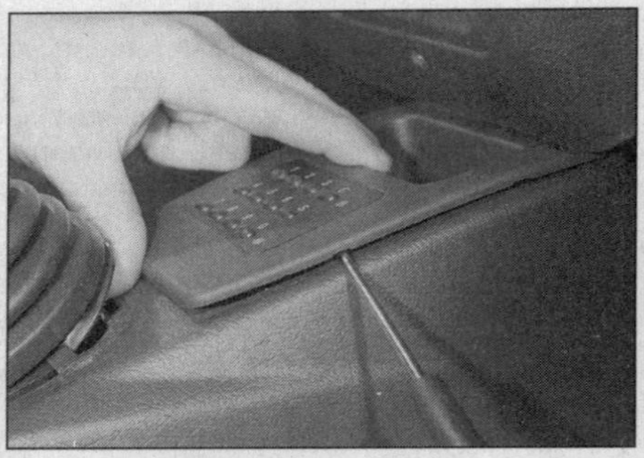

27.1a Release the keypad clips by pressing inwards and upwards . . .

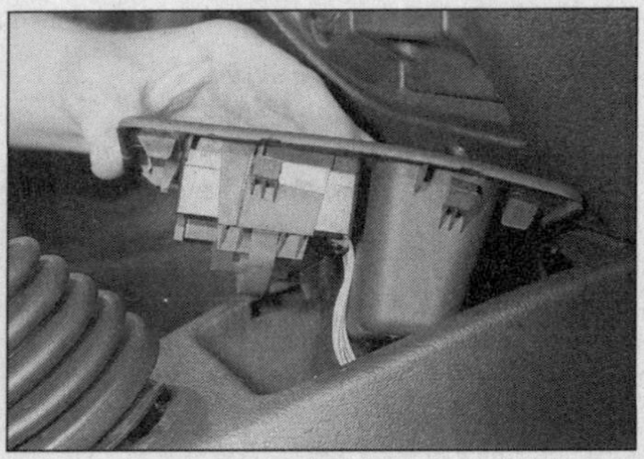

27.1b . . . then withdraw the keypad from the centre console . . .

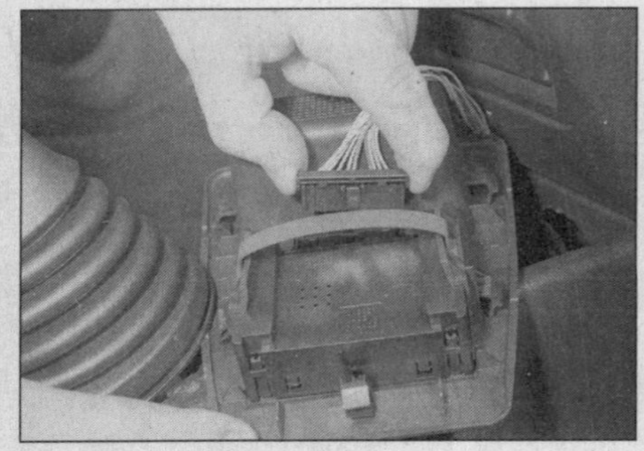

27.1c . . . and disconnect the wiring plug

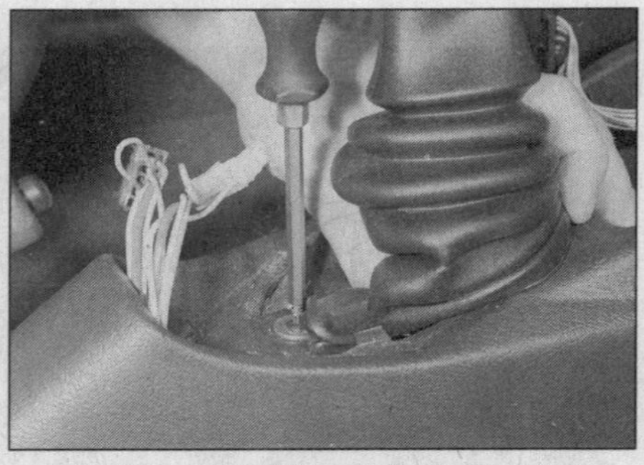

27.4 On manual transmission models, remove the Torx screw from behind the gear lever

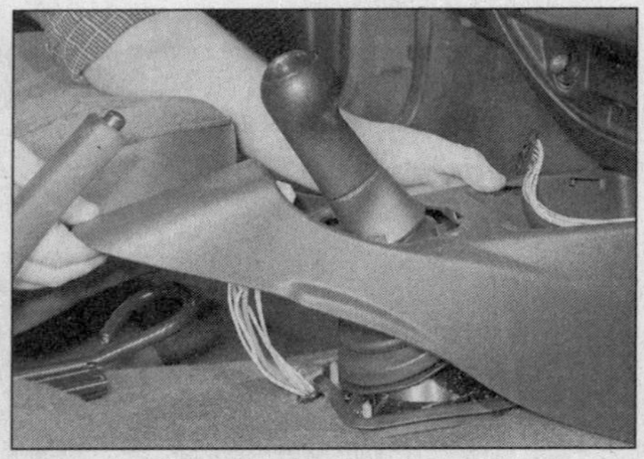

27.10 Lift the centre console over the gear lever to remove

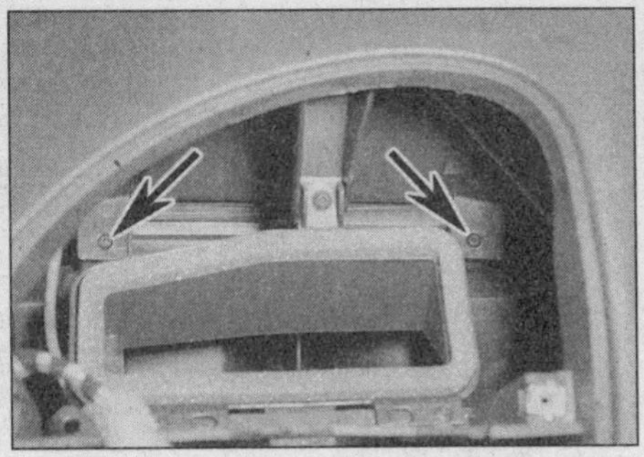

28.7 Remove these two screws (arrowed) from inside the heater control panel aperture

Refitting

11 Refitting is a reversal of removal, but the selector lever knob on automatic transmission models must be refitted as follows.

12 Press in the detent button, and hold it. Align the knob over the lever in its normal fitted direction, then slide it carefully down the lever until resistance is felt.

13 Still holding the detent button in, turn the knob gently a quarter-turn to the rear, and slide it down approximately 7 mm.

14 Release the detent button, then gently turn the knob a quarter-turn back to the front.

15 Ensure that the detent button is facing the driver's side of the car, then refit the screw either side of the knob and tighten securely.

16 Check for correct operation of the detent button on completion.

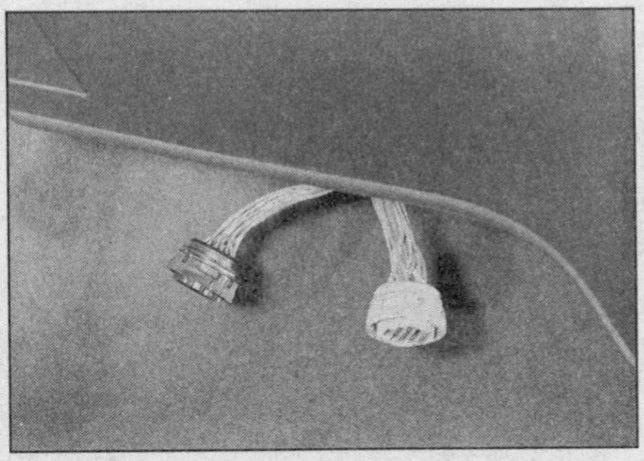

28.9 The facia harness connectors are removed by twisting their locking collars

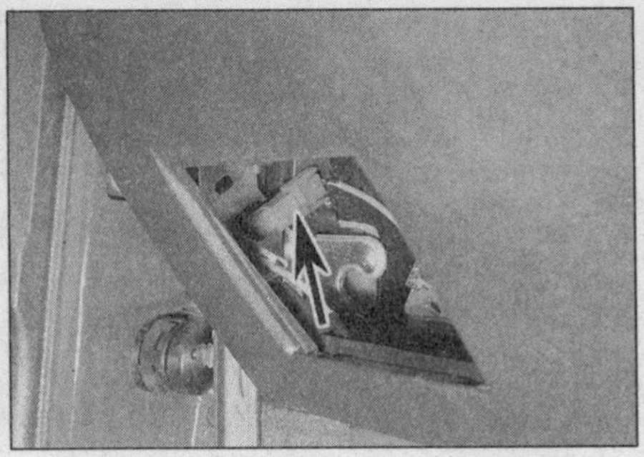

28.8 Disconnect the airbag/seat belt tensioner wiring plug (arrowed)

28 Facia assembly - removal and refitting

Removal

Right-hand-drive models

1 Disconnect the battery negative lead, and wait at least 10 minutes before proceeding.

2 On models with a passenger airbag, it is recommended to remove the airbag unit as described in Chapter 12. However, if care is taken to avoid knocking the unit as the facia panel is removed, the airbag can be left in place, provided the wiring is disconnected.

3 Remove the steering column, as described in Chapter 10.

4 Remove the instrument panel, windscreen wiper motor assembly and headlight adjuster switch as described in Chapter 12.

5 Remove the centre console as described in Section 27.

6 Remove the heater control panel as described in Chapter 3.

7 Working through the heater control panel aperture, remove the two screws nearest the bulkhead **(see illustration)**.

8 Remove the access panel for the fusebox. Inside, disconnect the wiring connector for the airbag/seat belt tensioner system **(see illustration)**.

HAYNES HiNT

A mirror is useful in locating the facia harness connectors (arrowed) behind the panel

9 The facia harness connector plugs are located behind the facia panel, and cannot therefore be seen - if a mirror (and torch) is available, they can be viewed more readily **(see Haynes Hint)**. Reach up under the passenger's side of the facia, and disconnect the facia harness connector plugs by twisting their locking collars **(see illustration)**. Note the location of each connector for refitting.

10 The various fasteners securing the facia panel must now be removed. Enlist the help of an assistant to support the facia as the fasteners are loosened.

11 Working in each front footwell in turn, remove the bolts and washers from the lower front corners of the facia panel **(see illustrations)**.

12 Remove one screw under the facia panel, directly below the heater control panel aperture.

13 With an assistant inside the car supporting the facia panel, move to the engine compartment and unscrew the three facia mounting nuts visible below the windscreen. Do not remove the bolt which secures the heater/ventilation housing **(see illustrations)**.

14 Inside the car, pull the facia panel carefully away from the bulkhead, with the help of your assistant. Make a final check that all fasteners have been removed, and that all

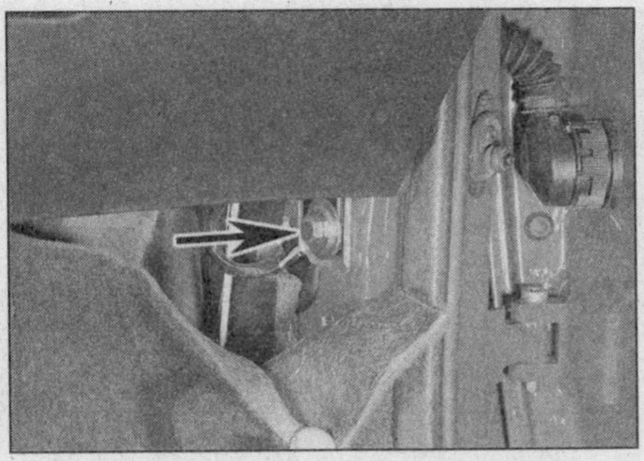

28.11a Remove the bolt (arrowed) from each lower front corner of the facia panel . . .

28.11b . . . and recover the washer

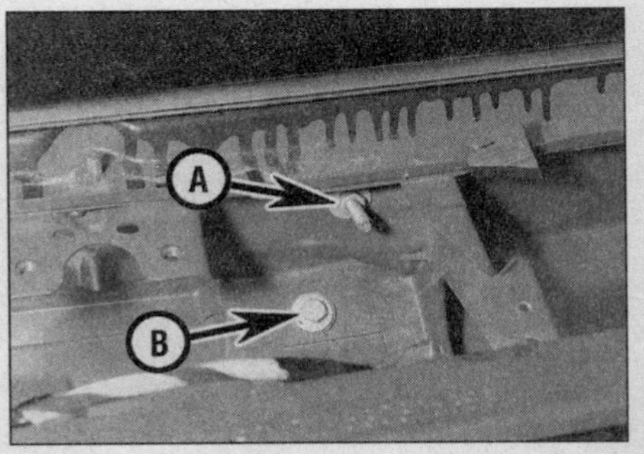

28.13a One of the facia panel securing nuts (A) below the windscreen. Bolt (B) retains the heater housing and should not be removed

...g has been moved aside so that it does ...hinder removal. Remove the facia panel ...m the car **(see illustration)**.

Left-hand-drive models

15 The procedure is identical to that described above for right-hand-drive models, with the following exception. The facia harness connectors mentioned in paragraph 9 are below the steering column, and there are three of them - note their locations carefully.

Refitting

16 Refitting is a reversal of removal, bearing in mind the following points:

a) Before pushing the facia into position, make sure that the ventilation ducts which supply the facia-end vents are in place. The ducts are pushed onto the heater/ventilation housing, and are suspended at the vent end by rubber bands.

b) Ensure that all the fasteners are securely tightened, and that the facia harness connectors are re-connected to their original locations.

c) Refit the heater control panel as described in Chapter 3.

d) Refit the centre console as described in Section 27.

e) Refit the instrument panel, windscreen wiper motor and headlight adjuster as described in Chapter 12.

f) Refit the steering column as described in Chapter 10.

g) Refit the passenger airbag (if removed) as described in Chapter 12.

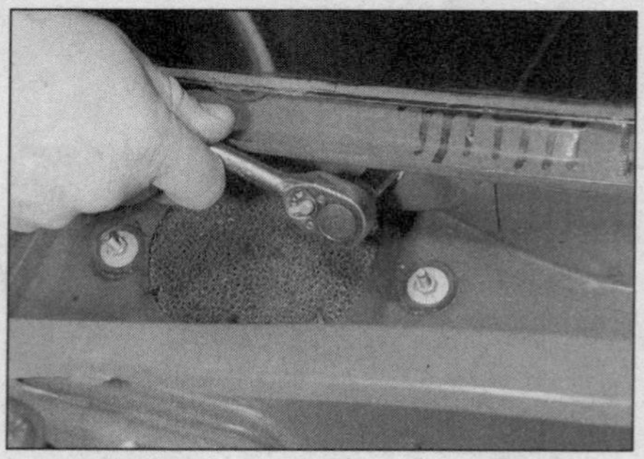

28.13b Unscrew the securing nuts while an assistant supports the facia inside the car

28.14 Removing the facia panel

Chapter 12
Body electrical system

Contents

Degrees of difficulty

Easy, suitable for novice with little experience	**Fairly easy,** suitable for beginner with some experience	**Fairly difficult,** suitable for competent DIY mechanic	**Difficult,** suitable for experienced DIY mechanic	**Very difficult,** suitable for expert DIY or professional

Specifications

Bulbs	**Wattage**
Direction indicator side repeater light	5
Front direction indicator light	21
Front driving/foglight (H1 type bulb)	55
Front sidelight	5
Headlight (H4 type bulb)	60/55
High-level stop-light (five bulbs)	5
Interior lights	5
Rear direction indicator light	21
Rear foglight	21
Rear number plate light	5
Reversing light	21
Stop-light/tail light	21/5

Torque wrench setting	**Nm**	**lbf ft**
Driver's airbag retaining screws	8	6

1 General information and precautions

General information

The body electrical system consists of all lights, wash/wipe equipment, interior electrical equipment, and associated switches and wiring.

The electrical system is of the 12-volt negative earth type. Power to the system is provided by a 12-volt battery, which is charged by the alternator (see Chapter 5A).

The engine electrical system (battery, alternator, starter motor, ignition system - petrol engine models, pre-heating system - diesel engine models, etc) is covered separately in Chapter 5.

Precautions

Warning: Before carrying out any work on the electrical system, read through the precautions given in "Safety first!" at the beginning of this manual, and in Chapter 5.

Caution: If the radio/cassette player fitted to the vehicle has an anti-theft security code (as does the standard unit fitted), refer to the information given in the Reference section of this manual before disconnecting the battery.

Prior to working on any component in the electrical system, the battery negative lead should first be disconnected, to prevent the possibility of electrical short-circuits and/or fires.

2 Electrical fault-finding - general information

Note: *Refer to the precautions given in "Safety first!" and in Section 1 of this Chapter before starting work. The following tests relate to testing of the main electrical circuits, and should not be used to test delicate electronic circuits (such as anti-lock braking systems), especially not those where an electronic control unit is used.*

General

A typical electrical circuit consists of an electrical component, any switches, relays, motors, fuses, fusible links or circuit breakers related to that component, and the wiring and connectors which link the component to both the battery and the chassis. To help to pinpoint a problem in an electrical circuit, wiring diagrams are included at the end of this Chapter.

Before attempting to diagnose an electrical fault, first study the appropriate wiring diagram, to obtain a more complete understanding of the components included in the particular circuit concerned. The possible sources of a fault can be narrowed down by noting whether other components related to the circuit are operating properly. If several components or circuits fail at one time, the problem is likely to be related to a shared fuse or earth connection.

Electrical problems usually stem from simple causes, such as loose or corroded connections, a faulty earth connection, a blown fuse, a melted fusible link, or a faulty relay (refer to Section 3 for details of testing relays). Visually inspect the condition of all fuses, wires and connections in a problem circuit before testing the components. Use the wiring diagrams at the end of this Chapter to determine which terminal connections will need to be checked, in order to pinpoint the trouble-spot.

The basic tools required for electrical fault-finding include a circuit tester or voltmeter (a 12-volt bulb with a set of test leads can also be used for certain tests); a self-powered test light (sometimes known as a continuity tester); an ohmmeter (to measure resistance); a battery and set of test leads; and a jumper wire, preferably with a circuit breaker or fuse incorporated, which can be used to bypass suspect wires or electrical components. Before attempting to locate a problem with test instruments, use the wiring diagram to determine where to make the connections.

To find the source of an intermittent wiring fault (usually due to a poor or dirty connection, or damaged wiring insulation), a "wiggle" test can be performed on the wiring. This involves wiggling the wiring by hand, to see if the fault occurs as the wiring is moved. It should be possible to narrow down the source of the fault to a particular section of wiring. This method of testing can be used in conjunction with any of the tests described in the following sub-Sections.

Apart from problems due to poor connections, two basic types of fault can occur in an electrical circuit - open-circuit, or short-circuit.

Open-circuit faults are caused by a break somewhere in the circuit, which prevents current from flowing. An open-circuit fault will prevent a component from working, but will not cause the relevant circuit fuse to blow.

Short-circuit faults are caused by a "short" somewhere in the circuit, which allows the current flowing in the circuit to "escape" along an alternative route, usually to earth. Short-circuit faults are normally caused by a breakdown in wiring insulation, which allows a feed wire to touch either another wire, or an earthed component such as the bodyshell. A short-circuit fault will normally cause the relevant circuit fuse to blow.

Finding an open-circuit

To check for an open-circuit, connect one lead of a circuit tester or voltmeter to either the negative battery terminal or a known good earth.

Connect the other lead to a connector in the circuit being tested, preferably nearest to the battery or fuse.

Switch on the circuit, bearing in mind that some circuits are live only when the ignition switch is moved to a particular position.

If voltage is present (indicated either by the tester bulb lighting or a voltmeter reading, as applicable), this means that the section of the circuit between the relevant connector and the battery is problem-free.

Continue to check the remainder of the circuit in the same fashion.

When a point is reached at which no voltage is present, the problem must lie between that point and the previous test point with voltage. Most problems can be traced to a broken, corroded or loose connection.

Finding a short-circuit

To check for a short-circuit, first disconnect the load(s) from the circuit (loads are the components which draw current from a circuit, such as bulbs, motors, heating elements, etc).

Remove the relevant fuse from the circuit, and connect a circuit tester or voltmeter to the fuse connections.

Switch on the circuit, bearing in mind that some circuits are live only when the ignition switch is moved to a particular position.

If voltage is present (indicated either by the tester bulb lighting or a voltmeter reading, as applicable), this means that there is a short-circuit.

If no voltage is present, but the fuse still blows with the load(s) connected, this indicates an internal fault in the load(s).

Finding an earth fault

The battery negative terminal is connected to "earth" - the metal of the engine/transmission and the car body - and most systems are wired so that they only receive a positive feed, the current returning via the metal of the car body. This means that the component mounting and the body form part of that circuit. Loose or corroded mountings can therefore cause a range of electrical faults, ranging from total failure of a circuit, to a puzzling partial fault. In particular, lights may shine dimly (especially when another circuit sharing the same earth point is in operation), motors (eg wiper motors or the radiator cooling fan motor) may run slowly, and the operation of one circuit may have an apparently-unrelated effect on another. Note that on many vehicles, earth straps are used between certain components, such as the engine/transmission and the body, usually where there is no metal-to-metal contact between components, due to flexible rubber mountings, etc.

To check whether a component is properly earthed, disconnect the battery, and connect one lead of an ohmmeter to a known good earth point. Connect the other lead to the wire or earth connection being tested. The resistance reading should be zero; if not, check the connection as follows.

If an earth connection is thought to be faulty, dismantle the connection, and clean back to bare metal both the bodyshell and the wire terminal or the component earth connection mating surface. Be careful to remove all traces of dirt and corrosion, then use a knife to trim away any paint, so that a clean metal-to-metal joint is made. On reassembly, tighten the joint fasteners securely; if a wire terminal is being refitted, use serrated washers between the terminal and the bodyshell, to ensure a clean and secure connection. When the connection is remade, prevent the onset of corrosion in the future by applying a coat of petroleum jelly or silicone-based grease, or by spraying on (at regular intervals) a proprietary ignition sealer.

3 Fuses and relays - general information

Fuses

1 Fuses are designed to break a circuit when a predetermined current is reached, in order to protect the components and wiring which could be damaged by excessive current flow. Any excessive current flow will be due to a fault in the circuit, usually a short-circuit (see Section 2).

2 The main fuses are located in the fusebox behind a panel below the glovebox on right-hand-drive models, or behind a panel in the driver's side facia on left-hand-drive models.

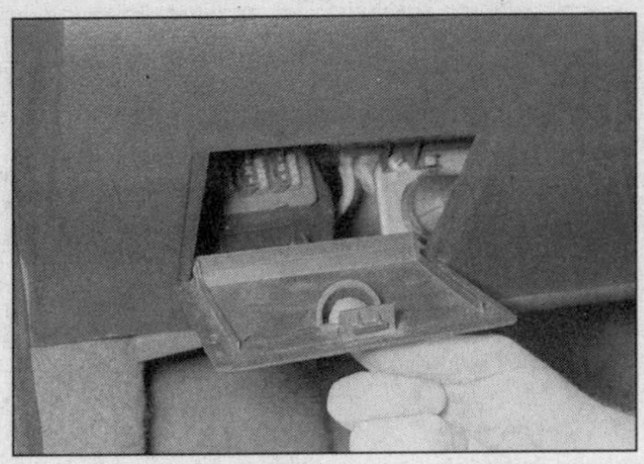

3.3 Prise out the fusebox cover panel for access to the fuses

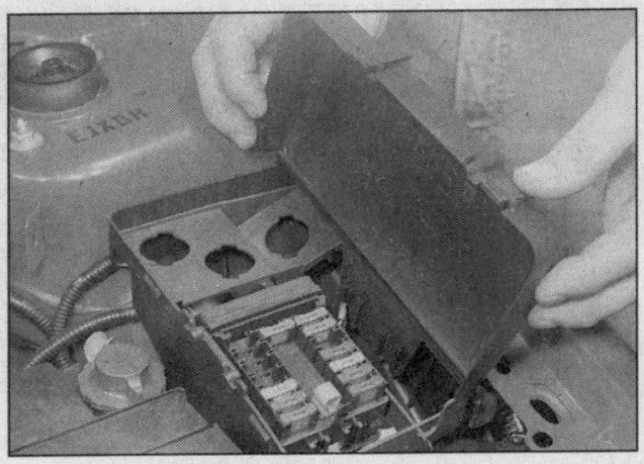

3.4 Removing the fusebox lid for access to the engine compartment fuses

3.5 The fusible links are housed in a small fusebox next to the suspension strut turret

3 For access to the fuses, prise the fusebox cover panel from the facia **(see illustration)**.

4 Additional fuses are located in an auxiliary fusebox in the engine compartment, next to the battery **(see illustration)**.

5 Further high-current fusible links are located in a smaller engine compartment fusebox, clipped to the left-hand suspension strut turret **(see illustration)**. If one of the fusible links blows, this indicates an extremely serious wiring fault, and the problem should be referred to a Citroën dealer.

6 A blown fuse can be recognised from its melted or broken wire.

7 To remove a fuse, first ensure that the relevant circuit is switched off.

8 Using the plastic tool provided in the fusebox, pull the fuse from its location **(see illustration)**.

9 Before renewing a blown fuse, trace and rectify the cause, and always use a fuse of the correct rating. Never substitute a fuse of a higher rating, or make temporary repairs using wire or metal foil; more serious damage, or even fire, could result.

10 Note that the fuses are colour-coded as follows. Refer to the wiring diagrams for details of the fuse ratings and the circuits protected:

Colour	Rating
Orange	5A
Red	10A
Blue	15A
Yellow	20A
Clear or White	25A
Green	30A

11 The radio/cassette player has an in-line fuse located in the wiring behind the unit.

Relays

12 A relay is an electrically-operated switch, which is used for the following reasons:

a) *A relay can switch a heavy current remotely from the circuit in which the current is flowing, allowing the use of lighter-gauge wiring and switch contacts.*

b) *A relay can receive more than one control input, unlike a mechanical switch.*

c) *A relay can have a timer function - for example, the intermittent wiper relay.*

13 Depending on model and equipment level, a few relays may be located in the engine compartment fusebox next to the battery, but the main relays are located behind the facia, above the fusebox **(see illustration)**.

14 If a circuit or system controlled by a relay develops a fault, and the relay is suspect, operate the system. If the relay is functioning, it should be possible to hear it "click" as it is energised. If this is the case, the fault lies with the components or wiring of the system. If the relay is not being energised, then either the relay is not receiving a main supply or a switching voltage, or the relay itself is faulty. Testing is by the substitution of a known good unit, but be careful - while some relays are identical in appearance and in operation, others look similar but perform different functions.

15 To remove a relay, first ensure that the relevant circuit is switched off. The relay can then simply be pulled out from the socket, and pushed back into position.

4 Switches - removal and refitting

Note: *Disconnect the battery negative lead before removing any switch, and reconnect the lead after refitting the switch.*

Ignition switch/ steering column lock

1 Refer to Chapter 10.

3.8 Using the plastic tool provided, pull out the fuse

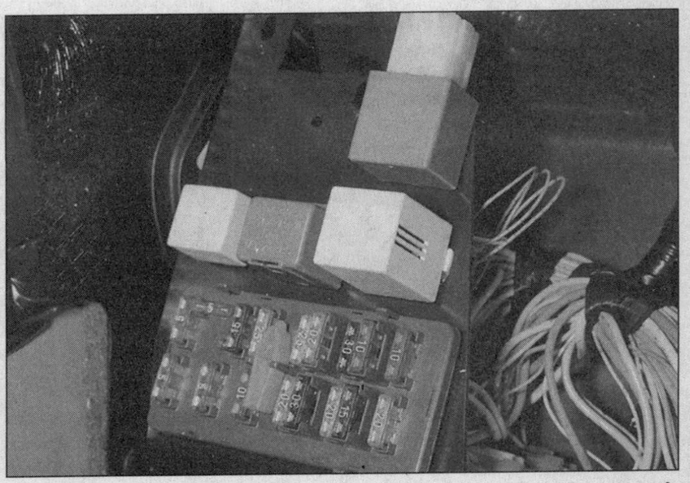

3.13 The fuse and relay panel seen with the facia panel removed

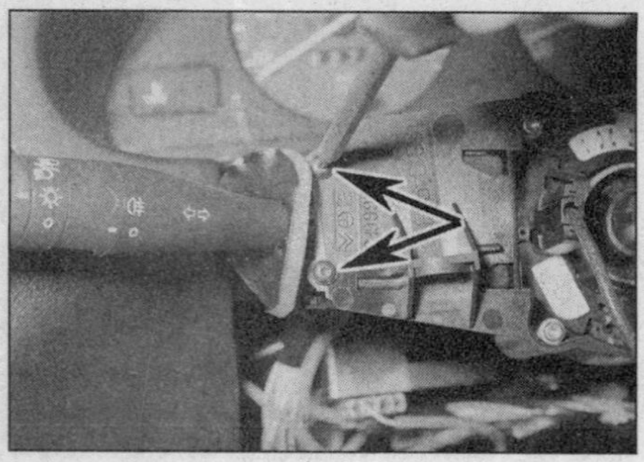

4.5a Remove the two small Torx screws (arrowed) . . .

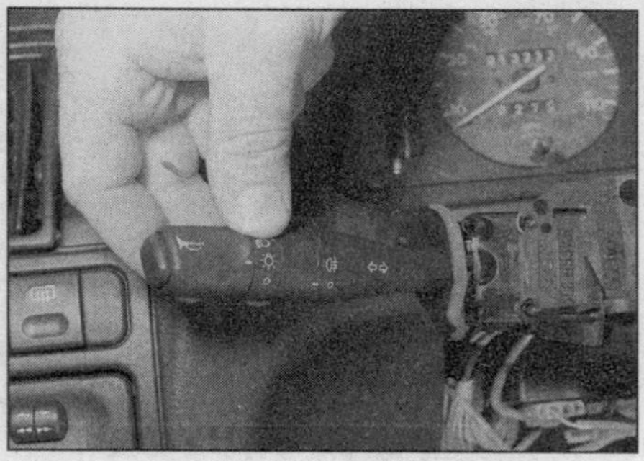

4.5b . . . and partially slide the switch out to the side

4.6a Remove the three screws (arrowed) . . .

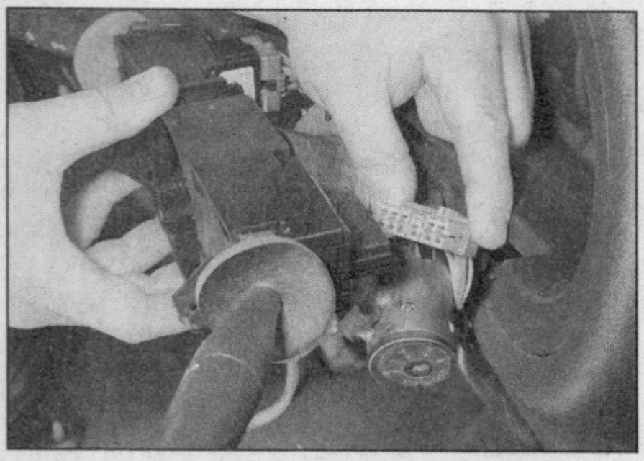

4.6b . . . disconnect the wiring plug from the right-hand switch . . .

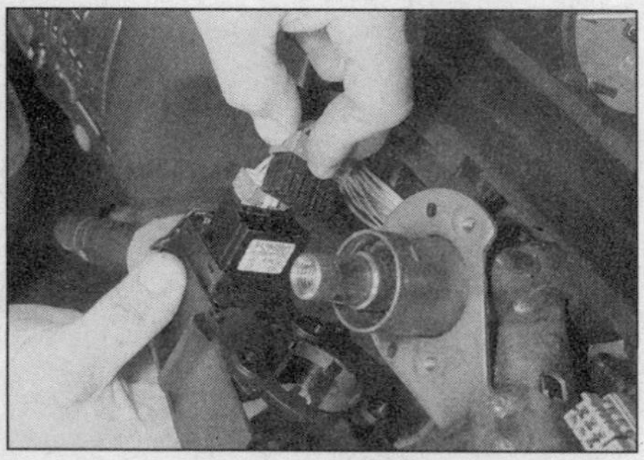

4.6c . . . and from the left-hand switch, and remove the assembly

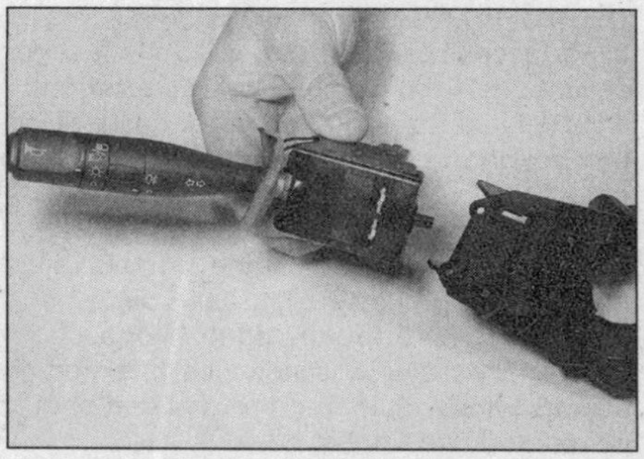

4.7 Slide the switch out of the main housing

Steering column combination switches

2 Remove the steering wheel as described in Chapter 10.

4.9a Prise out the blank switch next to the one to be removed . . .

3 Working under the steering column, remove the two steering column shroud Torx screws (T20). Unclip and lift off the upper shroud, then withdraw the lower shroud. Disconnect the wiring plug from the instrument lighting rheostat.

4 On models with a driver's airbag, remove the rotary contact switch as described in Section 24.

5 Remove the two small Torx screws from the left-hand switch, and partially slide the switch out of position **(see illustrations)**.

6 Remove the three securing screws, disconnect the wiring plugs from the rear, and withdraw the switch assembly from the housing on the steering column **(see illustrations)**.

7 If not already done, remove the two small Torx screws and slide the switch out of the main housing **(see illustration)**.

8 Refitting is a reversal of removal. Refit the airbag contact switch as described in Section 24, and the steering wheel as described in Chapter 10.

Facia-mounted pushbutton switches

9 Using a slim flat-bladed screwdriver, prise out one or two of the "blank" switches next to the switch to be removed **(see illustrations)**.

10 Working through the aperture, carefully press the relevant switch out through the front of the facia, and disconnect the wiring plug **(see illustrations)**.

11 Refitting is a reversal of removal.

Heater blower motor switch

12 Remove the radio/cassette unit as described in Section 19. On models without a radio, prise out the blanking plate from the radio aperture.

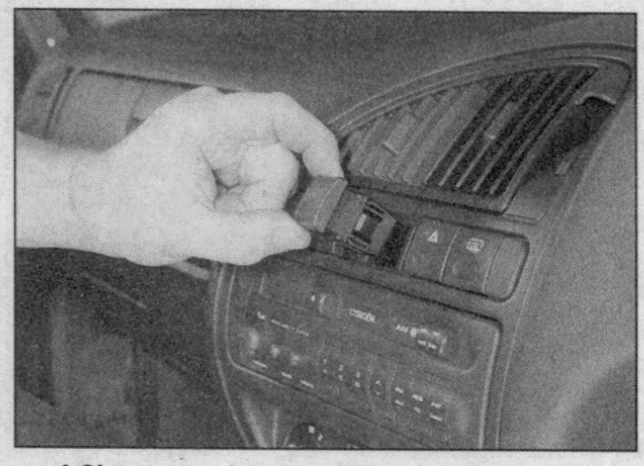

4.9b . . . and remove it from the panel

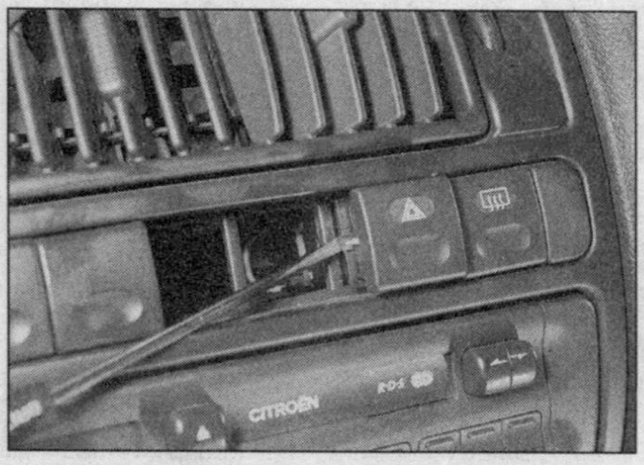

4.10a Prise the switch out of the panel . . .

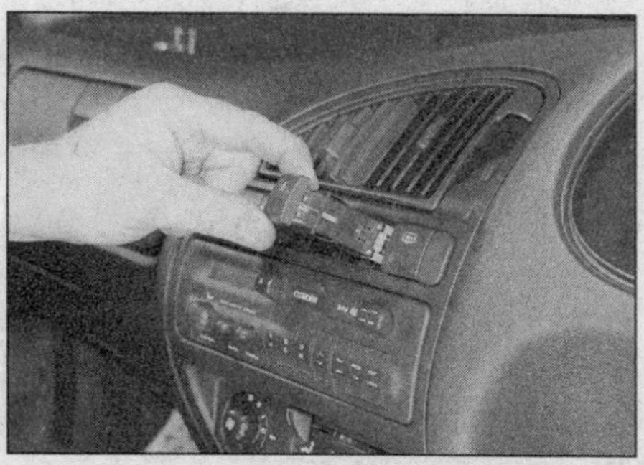

4.10b . . . withdraw it from the facia . . .

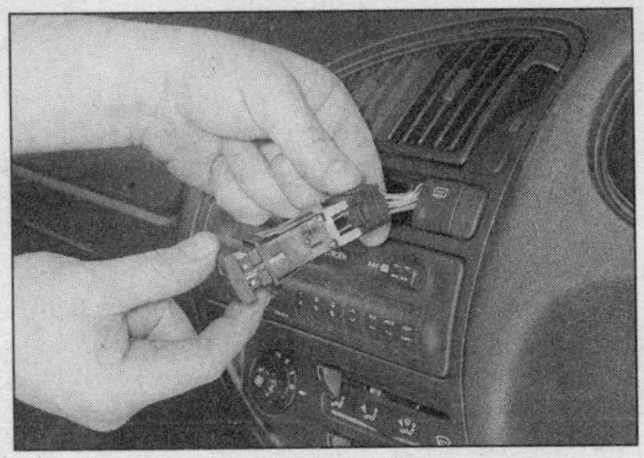

4.10c . . . and disconnect the wiring plug

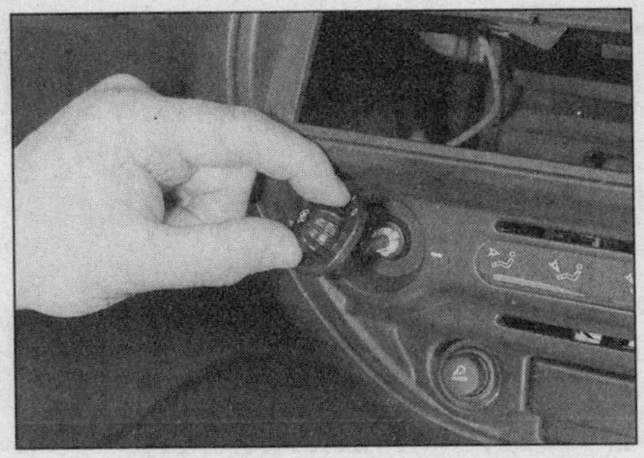

4.13 Pull off the blower motor control knob

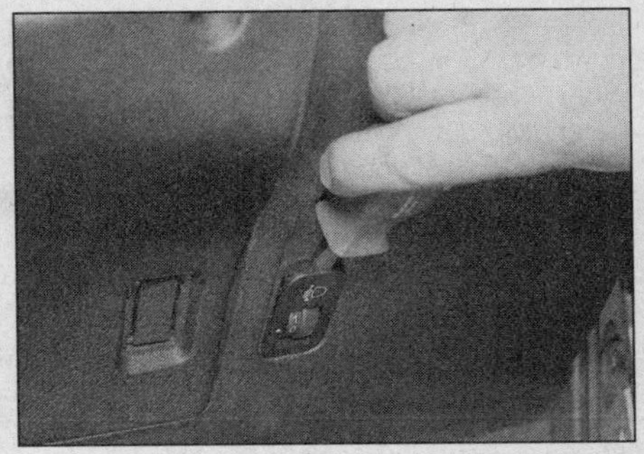

4.17a Prise up the headlight adjustment switch . . .

13 Carefully pull off the blower motor control knob **(see illustration)**. If necessary, use a pair of pliers, with thin card wrapped round the jaws to protect the switch. Take care that the metal inserts in the control knob do not fall out.
14 Reach in through the radio aperture, and disconnect the wiring plug from the rear of the switch.
15 At the front of the switch, squeeze together the legs which secure the switch in the facia, then withdraw the switch to the rear, through the radio aperture.
16 Refitting is a reversal of removal.

Headlight adjustment and instrument light dimmer switches

17 Using a suitable flat-bladed screwdriver, carefully prise the relevant switch out of the facia, taking great care not to mark either the panel or the facia. Tilt the switch forward to remove it, and disconnect the wiring connector **(see illustrations)**.
18 Refitting is a reversal of removal.

Door courtesy light switches

19 Open the door, then remove the securing screw, and withdraw the switch from the door pillar. Disconnect the wiring connector as it becomes accessible **(see illustrations)**.

> **HAYNES HiNT** *Tape the wiring to the door pillar, to prevent it falling back into the door pillar. Alternatively, tie a piece of string to the wiring, to retrieve it.*

20 Refitting is a reversal of removal, but ensure that the rubber gaiter is correctly seated on the switch and in the door pillar.

Luggage compartment light switch

21 Open the tailgate, then carefully prise the switch from its location and disconnect the wiring connector **(see illustrations)**.
22 Refitting is a reversal of removal.

Centre console-mounted switches

23 Using a suitable flat-bladed screwdriver, carefully prise the switch from the centre console **(see illustration)**.
24 Disconnect the switch wiring connectors, and remove the switch **(see illustration)**. In the case of electric window switches, if both are being removed, note which connector serves which switch.
25 Refitting is a reversal of removal.

Electric door mirror adjustment switch

26 Carefully prise the switch from the door trim panel, and disconnect the wiring plug.

4.17b . . . then withdraw it from the facia, and disconnect the wiring plug

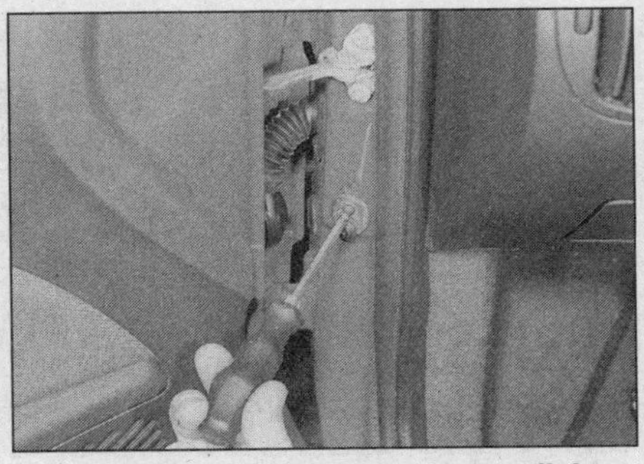

4.19a Remove the door courtesy light switch screw . . .

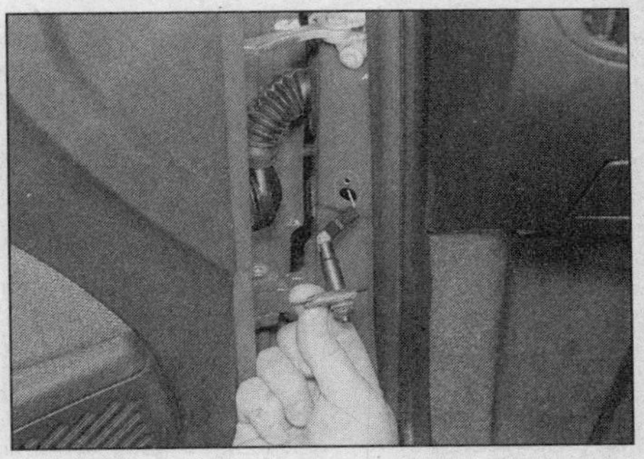

4.19b . . . and withdraw it from the door pillar for access to the wiring plug

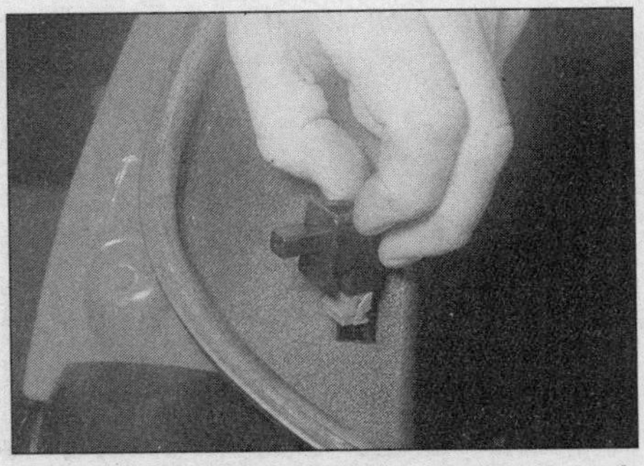

4.21a Prise out the luggage compartment light switch . . .

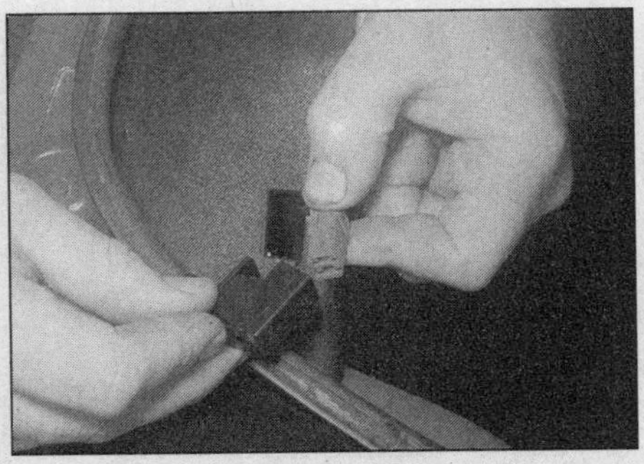

4.21b . . . and disconnect the wiring connector

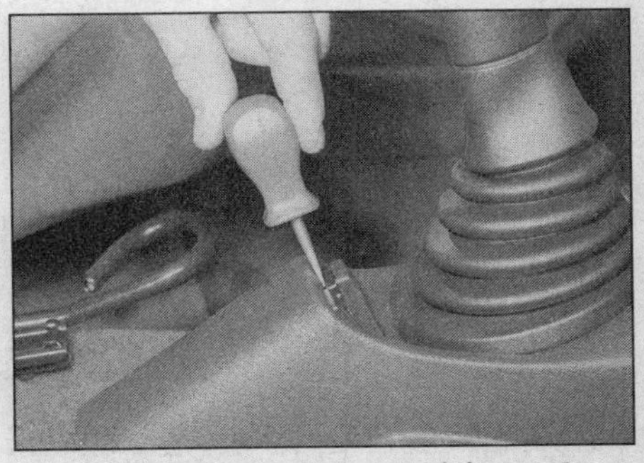

4.23 Prise the switch out of the centre console

Note that on some models, the switch wiring connector may be located inside the door, in which case it will be necessary to remove the inner trim panel and the sealing sheet for access, as described in Chapter 11.

27 Refitting is a reversal of removal. Where applicable, refit the door inner trim panel with reference to Chapter 11, and use a new sealing sheet.

Stop-light switch

28 See Chapter 9.

Handbrake-on warning light switch

29 See Chapter 9.

5 Bulbs (exterior lights) - renewal

General

1 Whenever a bulb is renewed, note the following points:

a) Disconnect the battery negative lead before starting work.

b) Remember that, if the light has just been in use, the bulb (and its holder) may be extremely hot.

c) With certain bulbs, the bulb may have stopped working because it has worked loose in its holder, or because its wiring plug is not securely or cleanly fitted. Always check that any suspect bulb has in fact blown before purchasing a new one.

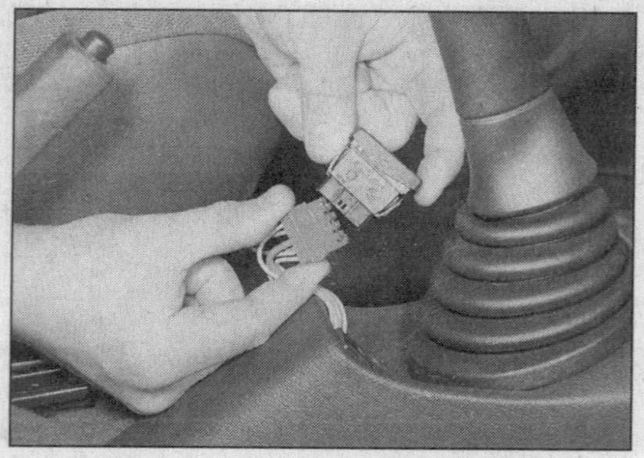

4.24 Disconnect the wiring plug from the rear of the switch

d) Always check the bulb contacts and holder, ensuring that there is clean metal-to-metal contact between the bulb and its live contact(s) and earth. Clean off any corrosion or dirt before fitting a new bulb.

e) Wherever bayonet-type bulbs are fitted, ensure that the live contact(s) bear firmly against the bulb contact.

f) Always ensure that the new bulb is of the correct rating, and that it is completely clean before fitting it; this applies particularly to headlight/foglight bulbs (see following paragraphs).

g) Where it is possible and safe to do so, it is worth checking that a newly-fitted bulb works before refitting any trim removed for access.

Headlight

2 Open the bonnet, then working at the rear of the headlight assembly, disconnect the main wiring plug from the rear of the headlight bulb **(see illustration)**.

3 Peel off the rubber cover from the rear of the headlight **(see illustration)**.

4 Press together the looped ends of the bulb retaining clip, and release it from the rear of the light **(see illustration)**.

5 Withdraw the bulb **(see illustration)**.

6 When handling the new bulb, use a tissue or clean cloth, to avoid touching the glass with the fingers; moisture and grease from the skin can cause blackening and rapid failure of this type of bulb.

> **HAYNES HiNT** ***If the headlight glass is accidentally touched, wipe it clean using methylated spirit.***

7 Install the new bulb, ensuring that its locating tabs are correctly located in the light unit cut-outs. Secure the bulb in position with the retaining clip.

8 Fit the headlight rear cover, ensuring that it is correctly seated on the rear of the light unit.

9 Reconnect the wiring plug.

Front sidelight

10 Open the bonnet, then identify the sidelight bulbholder to one side of the rubber cover on the rear of the headlight assembly. Twist the sidelight bulbholder a quarter-turn and withdraw it from the rear of the headlight **(see illustration)**.

11 Pull the wedge-type bulb from the bulb-holder **(see illustration)**. Before condemning the old bulb, check its condition. Sidelight

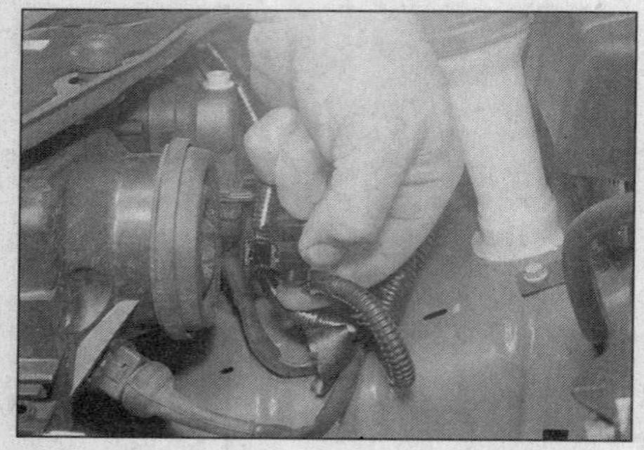

5.2 Disconnect the wiring plug from the rear of the headlight bulb

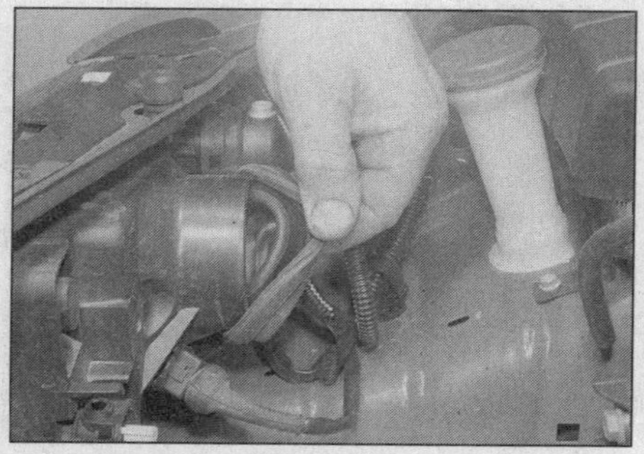

5.3 Peel the rubber cover from the rear of the headlight

5.4 Press together the looped ends (arrowed) of the bulb retaining clip - headlight removed for clarity

5.5 Withdrawing the bulb from the headlight

5.10 Twist and remove the sidelight bulb-holder from the rear of the headlight . . .

5.11 . . . and pull out the bulb

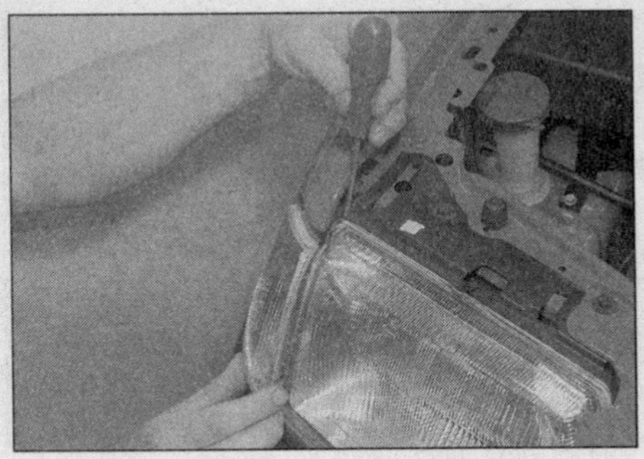

5.13 Using a screwdriver to release the indicator locating clip . . .

bulbs which have stopped working are often found to be loose in their holders, rather than blown.

12 Press the bulb fully into position, then check that the rubber seal is in place on the bulbholder. Fit the bulbholder to the rear of the headlight, twisting it a quarter-turn to secure.

Front direction indicator - models up to September 1999

13 Open the bonnet, and working between the direction indicator light and the headlight, release the indicator light unit retaining clip by pressing it down gently with a flat-bladed screwdriver **(see illustration)**.

14 Withdraw the light unit forwards from the front wing **(see illustration)**.

15 Twist the bulbholder anti-clockwise to release it from the rear of the light unit.

16 The bulb is a bayonet fit in the bulbholder, and can be removed by pressing it and twisting in an anti-clockwise direction **(see illustration)**.

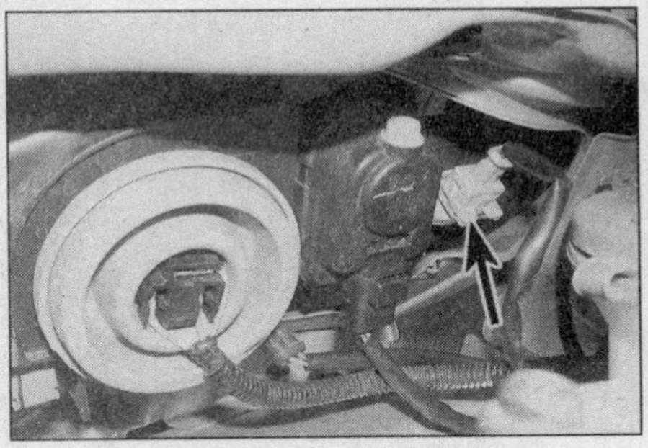

5.18 The indicator bulb holder

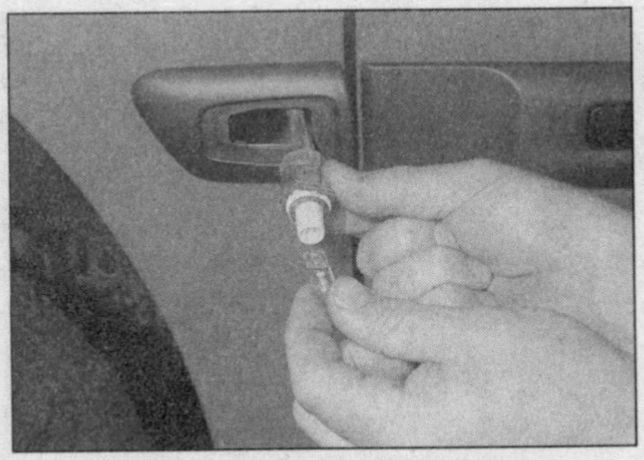

5.22b . . . and pull out the bulb

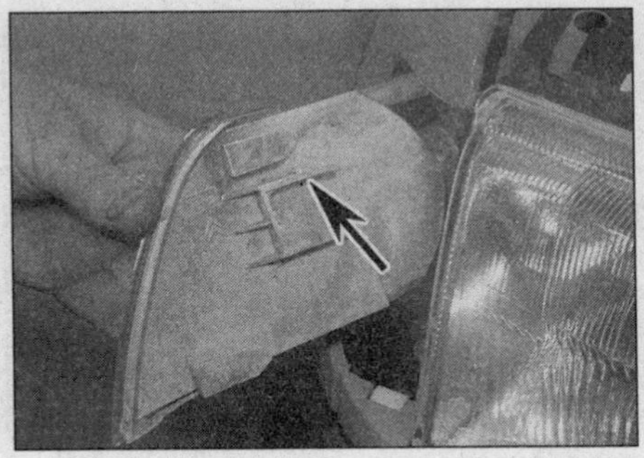

5.14 . . . which can more easily be seen (arrowed) with the unit removed

17 Refitting is a reversal of removal, bearing in mind the following points:

a) Ensure that the bulbholder sealing ring is in good condition.

b) When refitting the light unit, ensure that the light unit retaining clip and slide engage correctly, and that the light unit wiring does not get trapped.

Front direction indicator - models from October 1999

18 On this later model the indicator light is an integral part of the headlight **(see illustration)**. Working to the rear of the headlight, twist the bulbholder anti-clockwise to release it from the rear of the light unit.

19 The bulb is a bayonet fit in the bulbholder, and can be removed by pressing it and twisting in an anti-clockwise direction.

20 Refitting is a reversal of removal

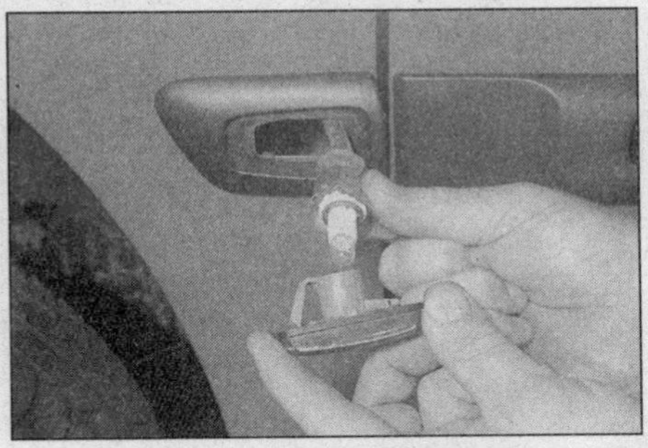

5.22a Remove the bulbholder from the repeater light unit . . .

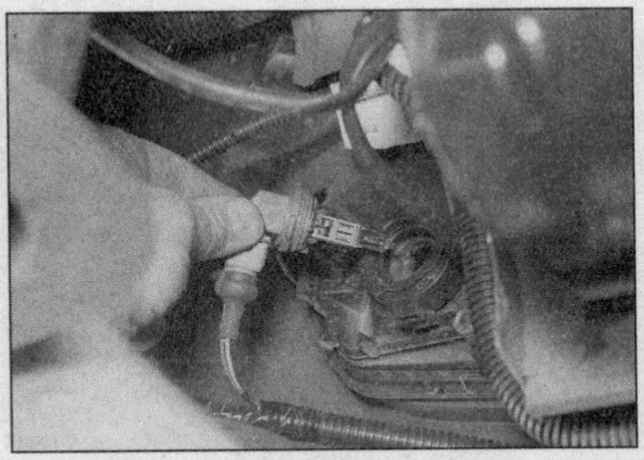

5.25 Twist the bulbholder anti-clockwise to remove it

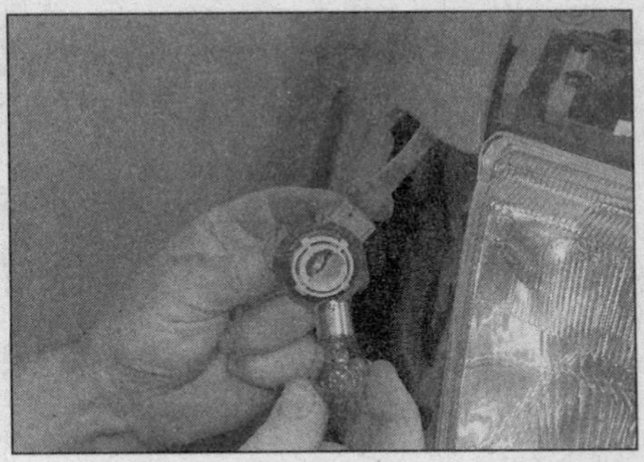

5.16 Twist the bulbholder from the light unit, and remove the bulb

Front direction indicator side repeater

21 Remove the light unit, as described in Section 7.

22 Twist and pull the bulbholder from the rear of the light unit. The bulb is a push fit in the bulbholder **(see illustrations)**.

Front driving lights/foglights

23 To improve access, apply the handbrake, then jack up the front of the car and support on axle stands (see *"Jacking and vehicle support"*).

24 Removing the wheel arch liner as described in Chapter 11 will further improve access, but is not essential.

25 Working from below and to the rear of the light unit, twist the bulbholder anti-clockwise and withdraw it from the light unit **(see illustration)**. Disconnect the bulbholder wiring connector, if necessary.

26 Pull the bulb out of the bulbholder.

27 When handling the new bulb, use a tissue or clean cloth, to avoid touching the glass with the fingers; moisture and grease from the skin can cause blackening and rapid failure of this type of bulb. If the glass is accidentally touched, wipe it clean using methylated spirit.

28 Refitting is a reversal of removal.

Rear light cluster

29 Remove the light unit as described in Section 7.

30 Release the two plastic retaining clips - one at the side, one at the bottom - and withdraw the bulbholder from the rear of the light unit **(see illustrations)**.

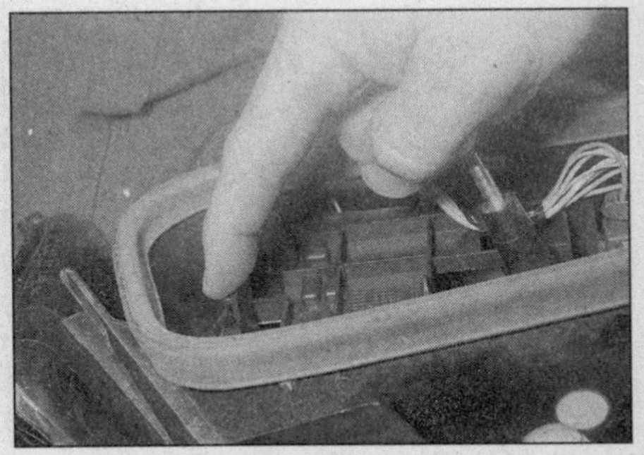

5.30a Release the bulbholder retaining clips . . .

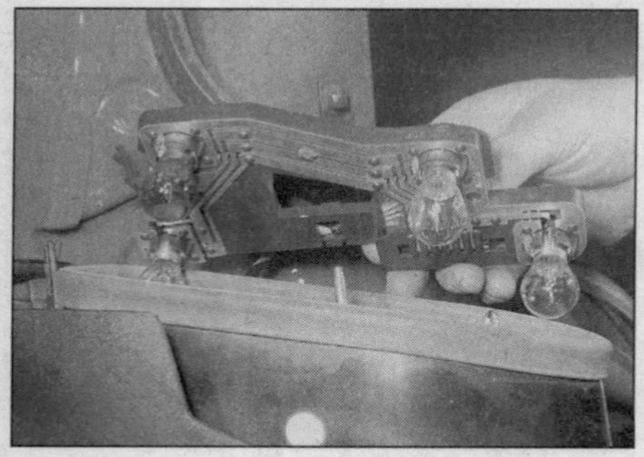

5.30b . . . and withdraw the bulbholder from the rear light

31 The bulbs are a bayonet fit in the bulbholder, and can be removed by pressing and twisting anti-clockwise **(see illustration)**. Note that the stop/tail light has offset pins, to ensure correct installation.

32 Note that, on some models, only one rear foglight bulb is fitted at the factory. If wished, a bulb can be installed to the other rear light unit.

33 Refitting is a reversal of removal, ensuring that the bulbholder is clipped back into position. Refit the light unit with reference to Section 7.

Rear number plate light

34 To improve access, open the tailgate.

35 On early models, remove the single cross-head screw, then unhook the tab on the light lens **(see illustrations)**. On later models, a lens securing screw is not fitted, and the lens must be carefully prised off with a small flat-bladed screwdriver.

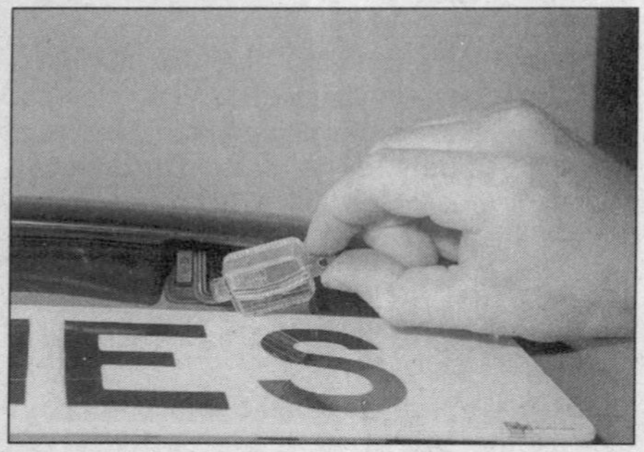

5.35b . . . then unhook the lens tab and remove

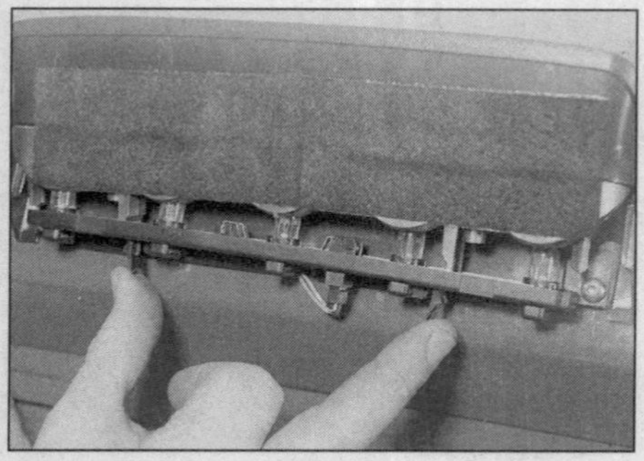

5.39 Squeeze together the bulbholder retaining clips, and remove

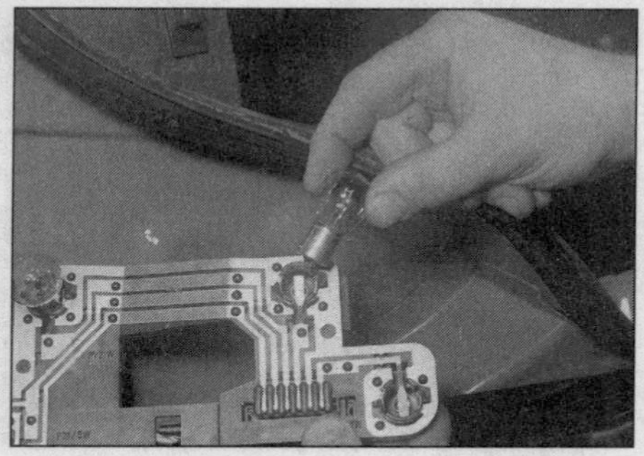

5.31 The rear light cluster bulbs are all bayonet-fitting

36 The bulb is a push fit in the light unit, but it proved to be awkward to remove.

> **HAYNES HiNT** ***We used the plastic filler tube from a gearbox oil bottle fitted over the top of the bulb, and pressed on to achieve a good fit. The tube is then used to extract the bulb***

37 Refitting is a reversal of removal.

High-level stop-light

38 Open the tailgate, then use a flat-bladed screwdriver to release the light unit cover retaining tab at either side. Remove the cover from the light unit **(see illustrations)**.

39 Press together the bulbholder retaining clips at the base of the light unit, and withdraw the bulbholder. If wished, the wiring plug can be disconnected **(see illustration)**.

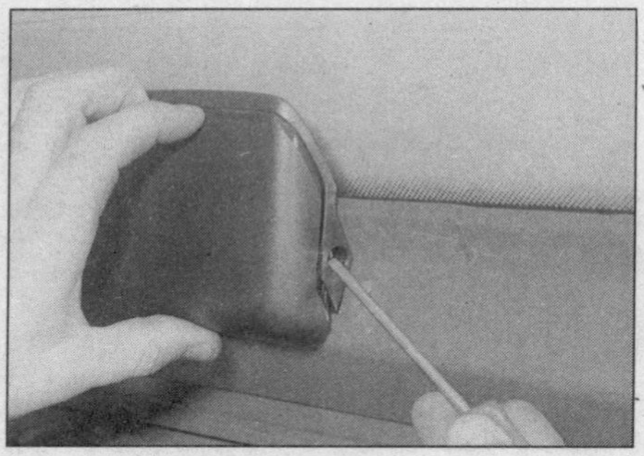

5.38a Depress the light cover tabs . . .

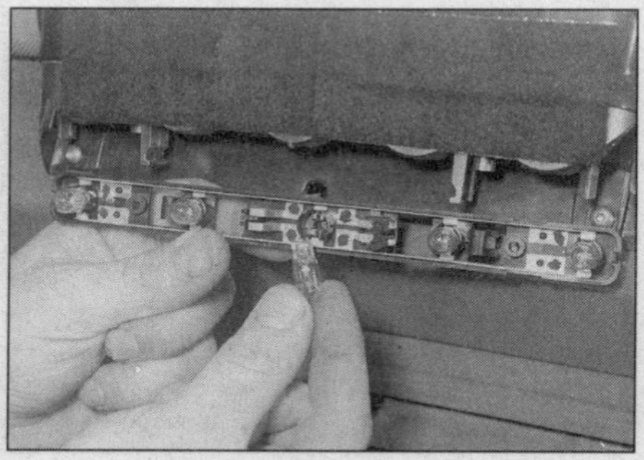

5.40 The five bulbs are all a push-fit

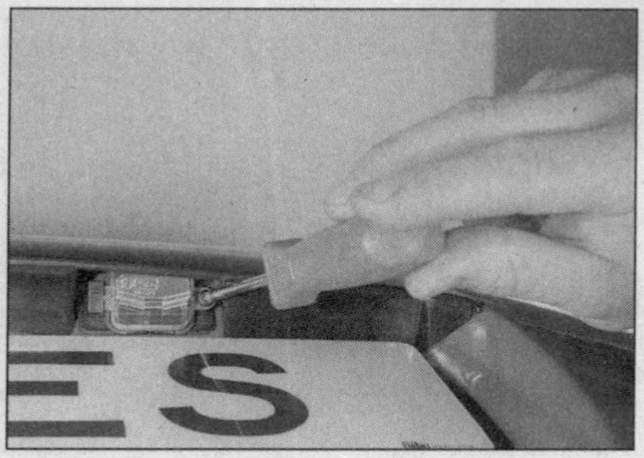

5.35a Remove the lens securing screw . . .

40 Each of the five bulbs is a push fit in the bulbholder **(see illustration)**.

41 Refitting is a reversal of removal.

6 Bulbs (interior lights) - renewal

General

1 Refer to Section 5, paragraph 1.

Courtesy light

2 Carefully prise the light unit from its location in the roof console, then twist the bulbholder anti-clockwise, and pull the bulb from the bulbholder **(see illustrations)**.

3 Refitting is a reversal of removal.

Luggage compartment light

4 Carefully prise the light unit from its location,

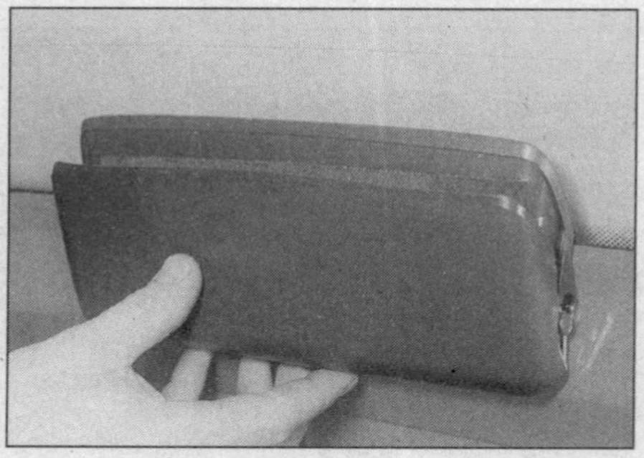

5.38b . . . and remove the cover for access to the bulbholder

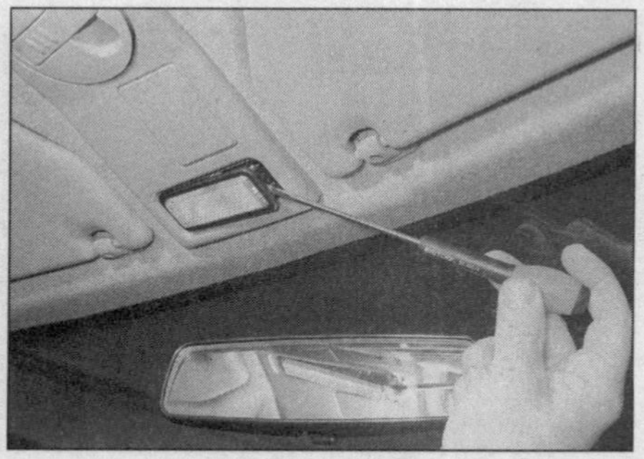

6.2a Prise out the interior light . . .

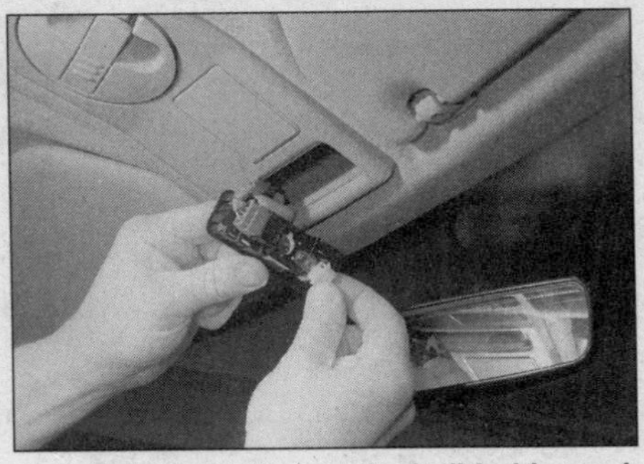

6.2b . . . then twist out the bulbholder and remove the bulb

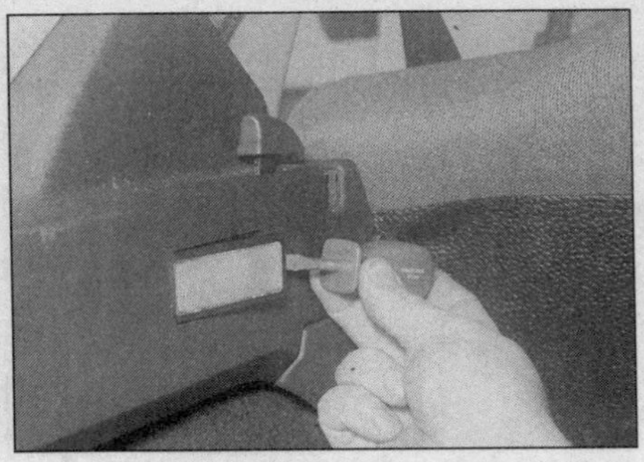

6.4a Prise out the luggage compartment light . . .

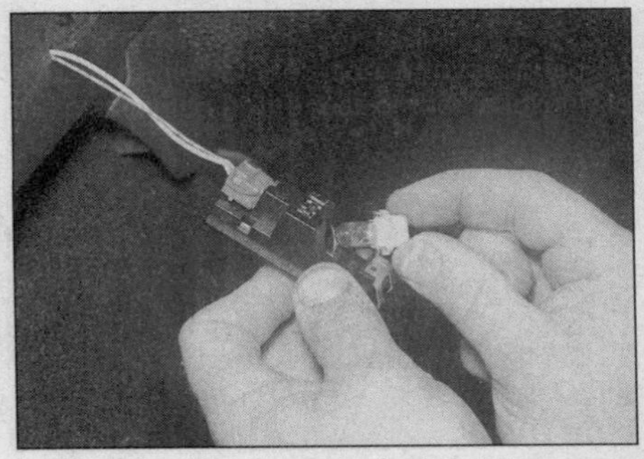

6.4b . . . twist out the bulbholder . . .

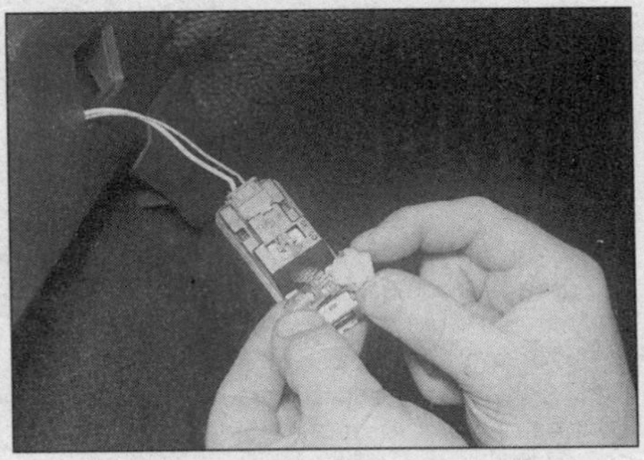

6.5 . . . and pull out the bulb

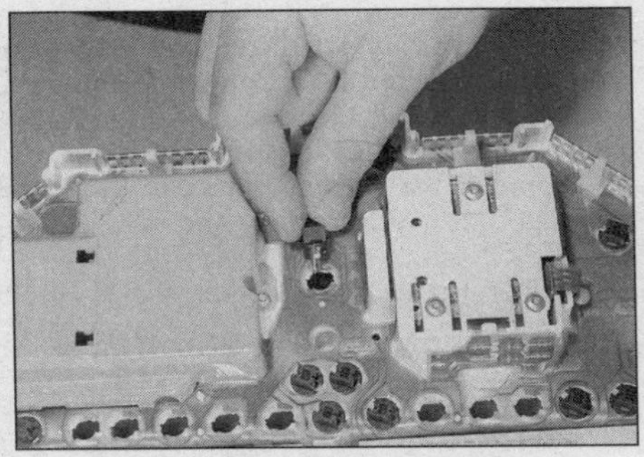

6.12 Removing an instrument panel bulbholder

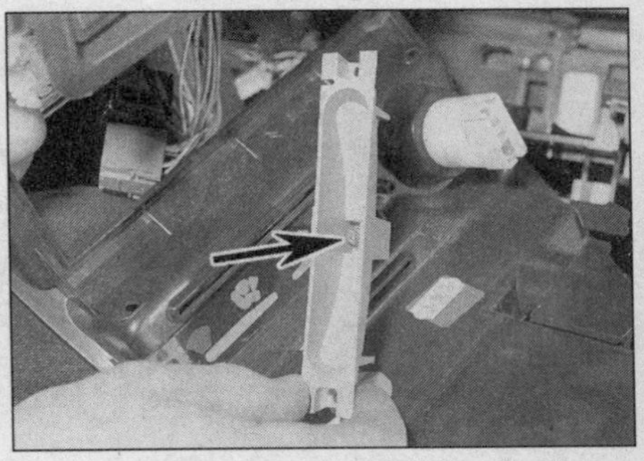

6.16 Heater control panel illumination bulbholder removed for access to the bulb (arrowed)

then twist the bulbholder to remove it from the rear of the light unit **(see illustrations)**.

5 The bulb is a push fit in the bulbholder **(see illustration)**.

6 Refitting is a reversal of removal.

Map reading light

7 Carefully prise the light unit from its location in the roof console.

8 Twist the bulb anti-clockwise to remove it from the light unit.

9 The bulb is integral with the bulbholder.

10 Refitting is a reversal of removal.

Instrument panel lights

11 Remove the instrument panel as described in Section 9.

12 Twist the relevant bulbholder anti-clockwise, and withdraw it from the rear of the panel **(see illustration)**.

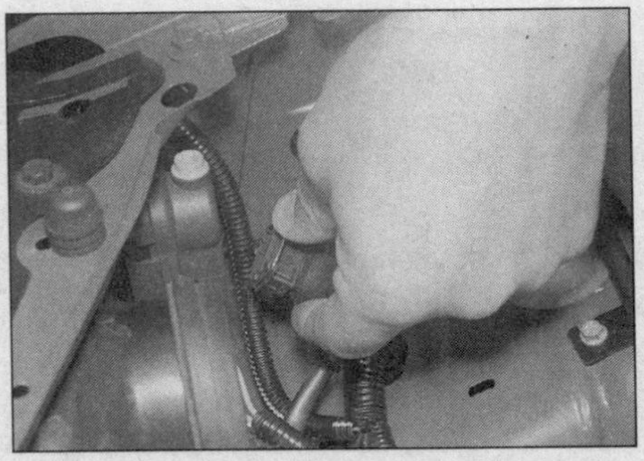

7.2 Disconnecting the headlight adjuster motor wiring plug

13 All bulbs are integral with their holders.

14 Refit the bulbholder to the rear of the instrument panel, then refit the instrument panel as described in Section 9.

Heater control panel illumination bulb

15 Remove the heater control panel as described in Chapter 3.

16 Unclip the illumination bulbholder from the rear of the panel **(see illustration)**.

17 The illumination bulb is a push fit in the bulbholder.

18 Fit the new bulb using a reversal of the removal procedure, then refit the heater control panel as described in Chapter 3.

Cigar lighter illumination bulb

19 The bulb is integral with the surround - refer to Section 12.

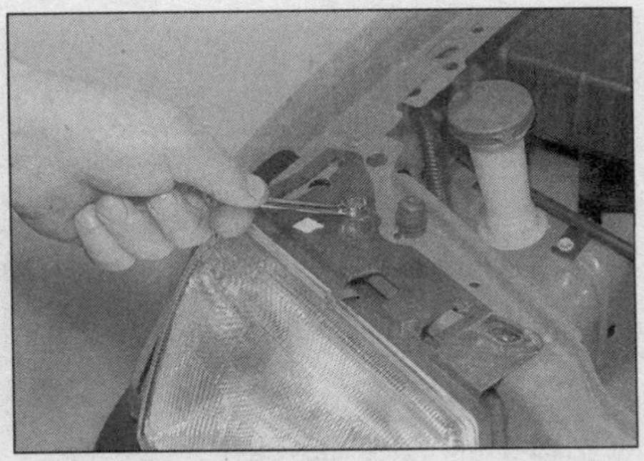

7.3a Remove the headlight mounting bolt from the top . . .

Switch illumination bulbs

20 All of the switches are fitted with illuminating bulbs, and some are also fitted with a bulb to show when the circuit concerned is operating. The bulbs are an integral part of the switch assembly, and cannot be obtained separately. Bulb renewal will therefore require renewal of the complete switch assembly.

7 Exterior light units - removal and refitting

Note: *Disconnect the battery negative lead before removing any light unit, and reconnect the lead after refitting the light.*

Headlight - models up to September 1999

1 Remove the radiator grille/headlight surround as described in Chapter 11, Section 23.

2 Working at the rear of the headlight assembly, disconnect the main wiring plug from the headlight bulb. Twist the sidelight bulbholder through a quarter-turn, and withdraw it from the rear of the headlight. Where applicable, disconnect the wiring plug from the headlight adjustment motor **(see illustration)**.

3 Remove the retaining bolt from the top and bottom of the headlight unit **(see illustrations)**.

4 Using a flat-bladed screwdriver, prise up the plastic flap at the rear of the headlight, to

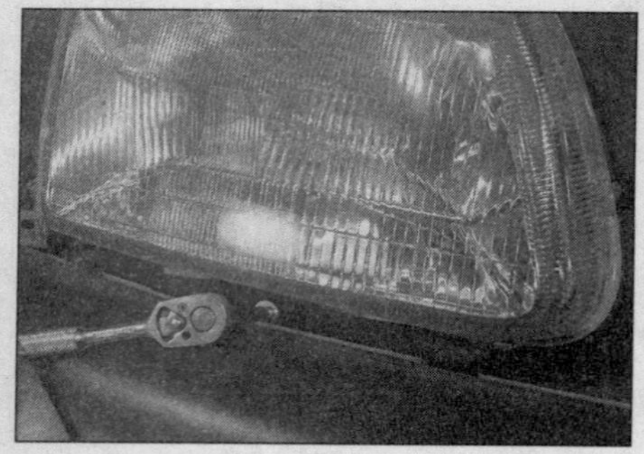

7.3b . . . and from below the headlight

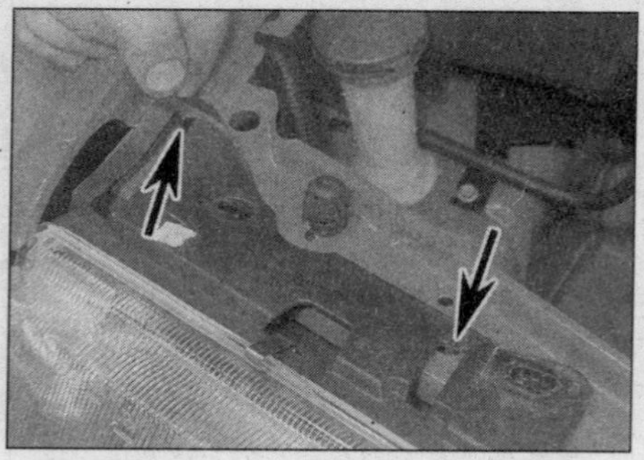

7.4 Pull up the plastic flap to release the two retaining lugs (arrowed)

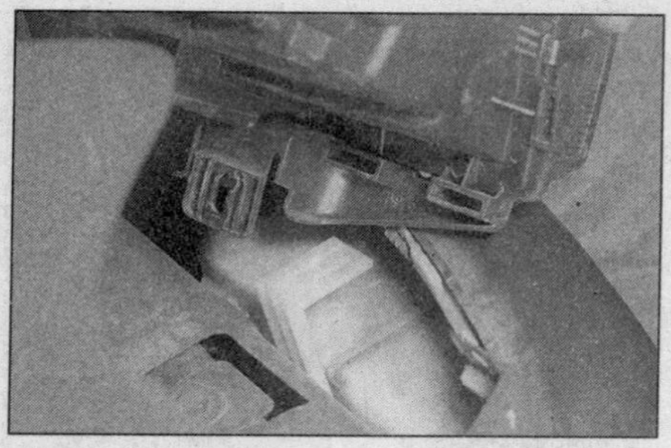

7.5 Showing the L-shaped headlight retaining clip, and the slot on the base of the headlight in which it fits

release the two retaining lugs from the body **(see illustration)**.

5 Pull the headlight unit forwards to release the L-shaped clip at the base of the unit **(see illustration)**, and withdraw it from the car.

6 Refitting is a reversal of removal.

7 We had difficulty aligning the L-shaped clip at the base of the headlight unit, and found it could only be achieved if an assistant guided the clip and the slot in the light unit together, using a screwdriver through the direction indicator light aperture.

8 Refit the radiator grille/headlight surround as described in Chapter 11, Section 23.

Headlight - models from October 1999

9 Remove the headlight surround as described in Chapter 11, Section 23

10 Remove the front bumper as described in Chapter 11, Section 6.

11 Working at the rear of the headlight assembly, disconnect the main wiring plug from the headlight bulb, indicator and side light. Where applicable, disconnect the wiring plug from the headlight adjustment motor.

12 Remove the 3 retaining bolts from the headlight **(see illustration)** and remove the headlight.

13 Refitting is the reverse of removal.

Front direction indicator light

14 Removal and refitting of the direction indicator light is described in Section 5.

Front direction indicator side repeater light

15 Push the light unit towards the front of the car, and unhook the rear of the unit from the wing panel **(see illustration)**.

16 Withdraw the light unit from the wing panel, and disconnect the wiring plug **(see illustration)**. Tape the wiring to the wing panel, to prevent it falling back into the hole.

17 Refitting is a reversal of removal. Push the light unit towards the rear of the car until it locks into position.

Front driving light/foglight

18 To improve access, apply the handbrake, then jack up the front of the car and support on axle stands (see *"Jacking and vehicle support"*). Remove the wheel arch liner.

19 Working from below and to the rear of the light unit, disconnect the bulbholder wiring connector (refer to Section 5).

20 Remove the two upper retaining bolts, and one at the base of the unit, then withdraw the light unit from the bumper.

21 Refitting is a reversal of removal.

Rear light cluster

22 Open the tailgate.

23 Support the light unit, then unscrew and remove the plastic "wing nut" inside the luggage compartment **(see illustration)**.

24 Partially withdraw the light unit from the car **(see illustration)**.

25 Release the bulbholder from the rear of the light unit as described in Section 5, or disconnect the multi-plug connector from the rear of the bulbholder **(see illustration)**.

26 Refitting is a reversal of removal, but check the condition of the seals on the rear of the light assembly.

Rear number plate light

27 Open the tailgate.

28 Remove the three screws (one at each side, one in the pull handle) securing the tailgate trim panel, then release the securing

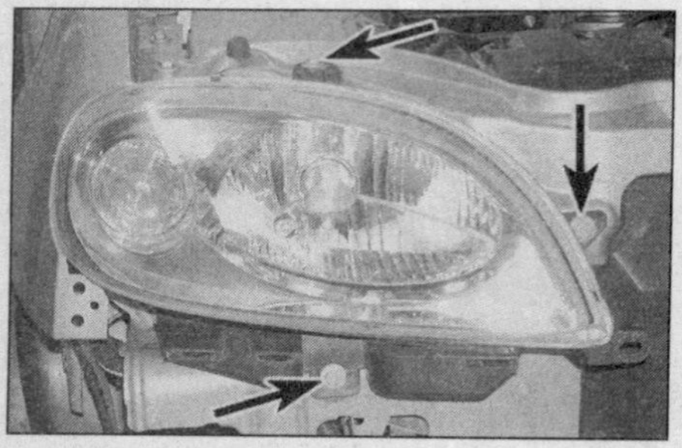

7.12 Headlight retaining bolts (arrowed)

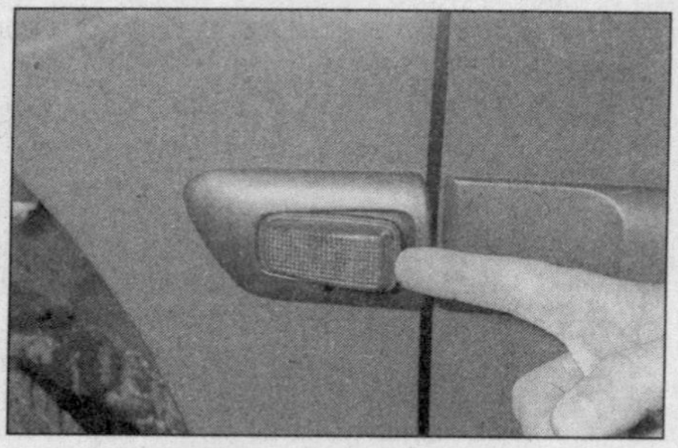

7.15 Push the light unit forwards, and unhook it at the rear

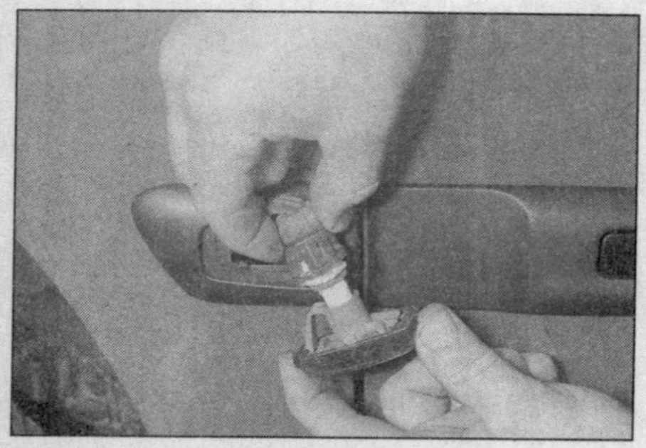

7.16 Disconnect the wiring plug from the bulbholder, and remove the light unit

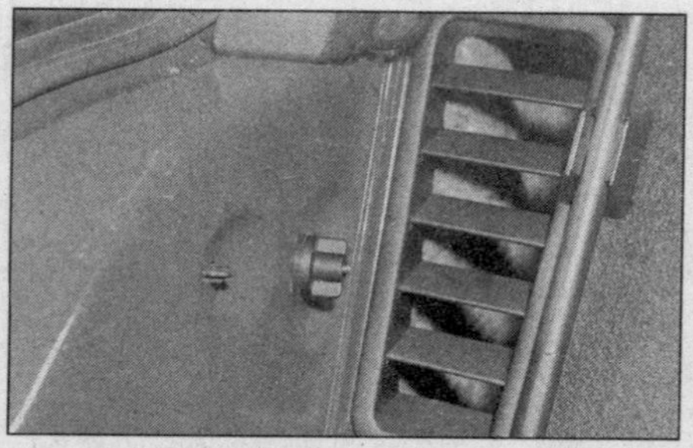

7.23 To remove the rear light cluster, unscrew the "wing nut" in the luggage compartment

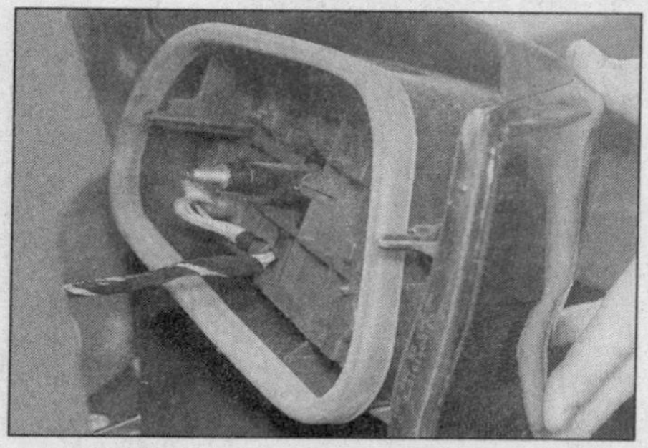

7.24 Withdraw the light unit to the rear

7.25 Disconnect the wiring plug from the bulbholder

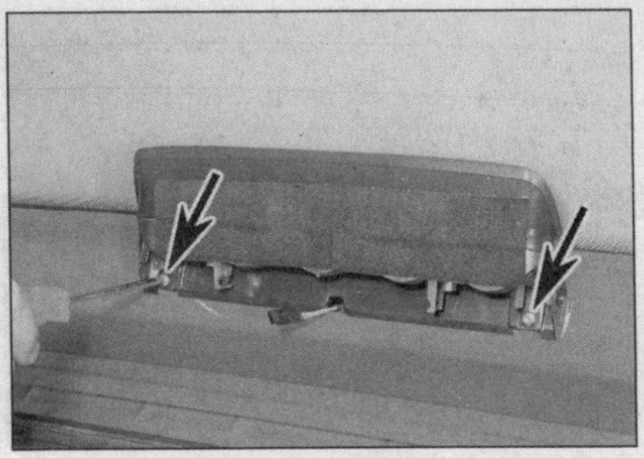

7.34a Remove the two screws (arrowed) . . .

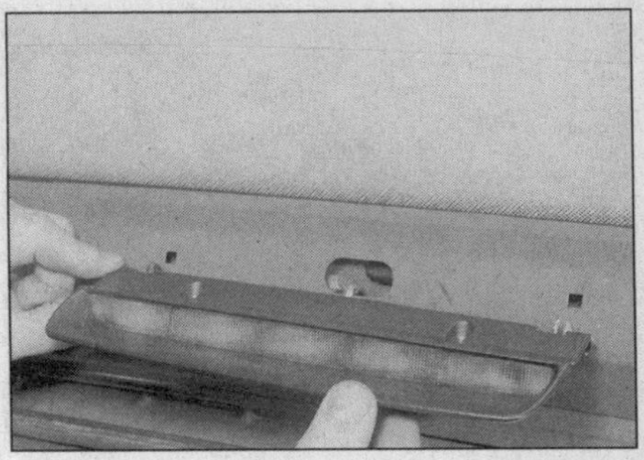

7.34b . . . then withdraw the high-level stop-light from the tailgate

clips and withdraw the panel from the tailgate (see Chapter 11, Section 16).

29 Working inside the tailgate, remove the nuts securing the number plate light shroud, and lift the shroud off the outside of the tailgate.

30 Prise the light unit out of its location in the tailgate, and disconnect the wiring plug.

31 Refitting is a reversal of removal.

High-level stop-light

32 Remove the bulbholder from the rear of the light unit, as described in Section 5.

33 Disconnect the wiring plug from the bulbholder. Tape the wiring to the tailgate, to prevent it from disappearing back into the hole.

34 Unscrew and remove the two Torx retaining screws, and withdraw the light unit from the tailgate **(see illustrations)**.

35 Refitting is a reversal of removal.

8 Headlight beam alignment - general information

1 Accurate adjustment of the headlight beam is only possible using optical beam-setting equipment, and this work should therefore be carried out by a Citroën dealer or suitably-equipped workshop.

2 All models are equipped with a headlight beam adjustment switch, which allows the aim of the headlights to be adjusted to compensate for the varying loads carried in the vehicle. Certain models have a switch on the facia, which enables beam adjustment via electric adjuster motors located in the rear of the headlight assemblies. Models not equipped with electric headlight adjusters have levers located on the rear of the headlight units (in the outer top corner) in the engine compartment. The switch or levers, as applicable, should be positioned as follows according to the load being carried in the vehicle:

Position 0 Unloaded (front seats only occupied)
Position 1 Lightly loaded (front seats occupied, luggage compartment full)
Position 2 Half-loaded (front and rear seats occupied)
Position 3 Fully-loaded (front and rear seats occupied, luggage compartment full)

9 Instrument panel - removal and refitting

Removal

1 Disconnect the battery negative lead.

2 Remove the steering wheel as described in Chapter 10.

3 Remove the steering column switches as described in Section 4.

4 Remove the two securing screws from the lower edge of the instrument panel surround, then remove the two upper surround securing screws. Withdraw the surround from the facia panel **(see illustrations)**.

5 Remove the three retaining screws (one at the top, two at the bottom), and pull the instrument panel from its location **(see illustrations)**.

6 Pull the instrument panel forwards sufficiently to disconnect the wiring plugs

9.4a Remove the two lower screws (arrowed) . . .

9.4b . . . and the two upper screws . . .

9.4c . . . then withdraw the instrument panel surround

9.5a Remove the three instrument panel screws (arrowed) . . .

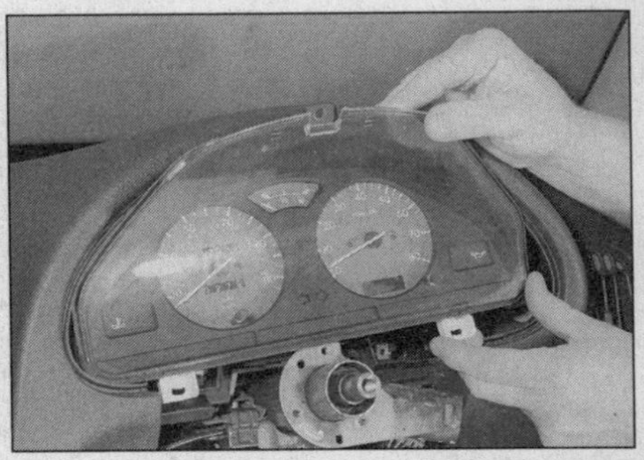

9.5b . . . then withdraw the panel from its location in the facia

9.6a Pull the instrument panel forwards . . .

(note their locations), then carefully withdraw the panel from the facia **(see illustrations)**.

Refitting

7 Refitting is a reversal of removal, bearing in mind the following points:

- a) *Ensure that the wiring plugs are connected as noted on removal.*
- b) *Refit the steering column switches as described in Section 4, and the steering wheel as described in Chapter 10.*

10 Instrument panel components - removal and refitting

General

1 Remove the instrument panel as described in Section 9, then proceed as described under the relevant sub-heading.

Speedometer

2 Working at the rear of the instrument panel, remove the two screws securing the lens assembly.

3 Using a flat-bladed screwdriver, carefully release the lens assembly securing clips (three at the top, three at the bottom), then withdraw the lens assembly.

4 Working at the front of the speedometer, unscrew the two securing screws. If necessary, pull off the knob for the trip meter reset button.

5 Remove the screws securing the rear cover **(see illustration)**, then unscrew the nuts and

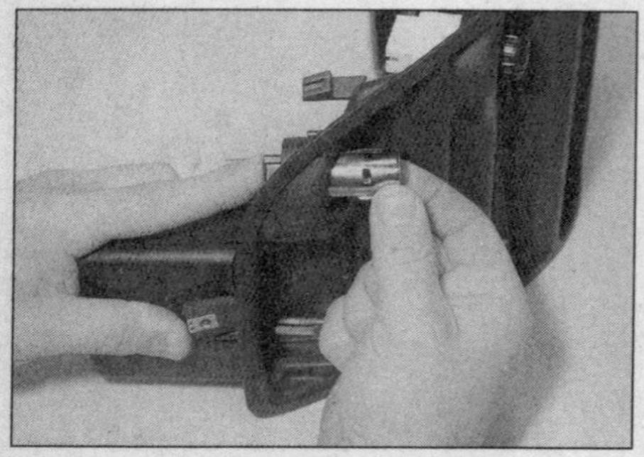

12.2 The cigar lighter can be pushed out of the heater panel

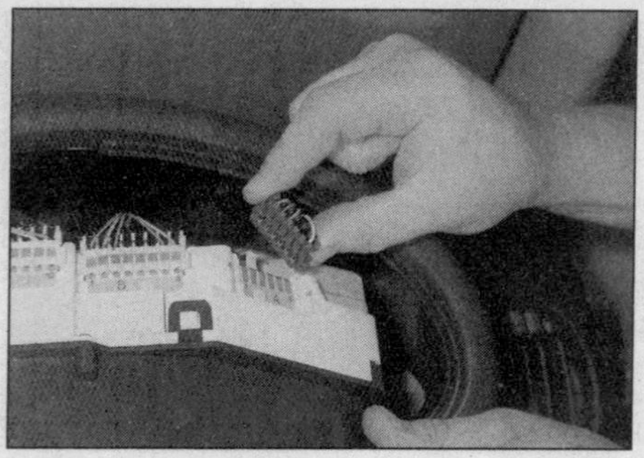

9.6b . . . in order to disconnect the wiring plugs

withdraw the speedometer from the instrument panel.

6 Refitting is a reversal of removal.

Tachometer

7 Proceed as described in paragraphs 1 to 3.

8 Working at the front of the tachometer, remove the securing screws. If necessary, pull off the knob from the digital clock reset button.

9 Remove the screws securing the rear cover, then unscrew the nuts and withdraw the tachometer from the instrument panel.

10 Refitting is a reversal of removal.

Analogue clock

11 Proceed as described in paragraphs 1 to 3.

12 Working at the front of the clock, remove the securing screws. If necessary, pull off the knob for the clock setting button.

13 Remove the screws securing the rear cover, then unscrew the nuts and withdraw the clock from the instrument panel.

Digital clock

14 Remove the tachometer as described previously in this Section.

15 Carefully unclip the clock from the instrument panel.

16 Refitting is a reversal of removal.

Fuel gauge, temperature gauge and oil level gauge

17 Proceed as described in paragraphs 1 to 3.

18 Working at the front of the gauge, remove the securing screw(s).

19 Working at the rear of the gauge, remove the securing nut(s), then withdraw the gauge from the instrument panel.

12.3 The cigar lighter can be removed with its surround, if required

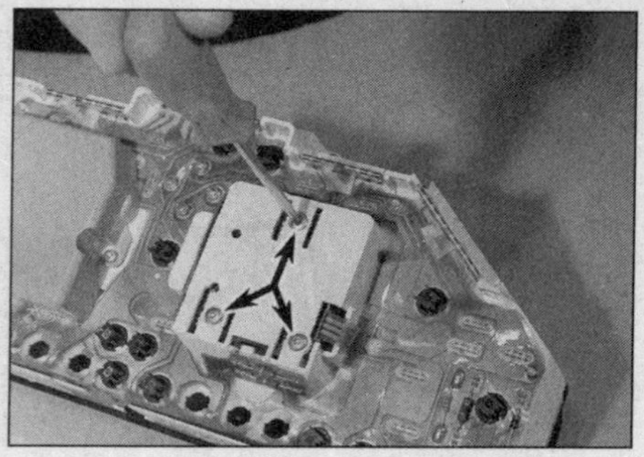

10.5 Removing the speedometer rear cover screws (arrowed)

Printed circuit

20 Remove all the instruments as described previously in this Section.

21 Remove all the bulbholders from the rear of the instrument panel, by twisting them in an anti-clockwise direction. Slacken and remove all the circuit securing screws, then release the printed circuit from the retaining pins, and remove it from the rear of the instrument panel.

22 Refitting is a reversal of removal, ensuring that the circuit tracks are not damaged, and that the circuit is correctly located on all the retaining pins.

11 "Lights on" warning system - general information

Most vehicles covered by this manual are fitted with a "lights-on" warning system. The purpose of this system is to inform the driver that the lights have been left switched on, once the ignition switch has been turned off - the buzzer will sound when a door is opened. The system consists simply of a buzzer unit which is connected to the door courtesy light switches.

The buzzer unit is located with the relays behind the facia, above the passenger compartment fusebox (see Section 3).

12 Cigar lighter - removal and refitting

Removal

1 Disconnect the battery negative lead.

2 Reaching in around the back of the facia panel, disconnect the wiring from the cigar lighter, and push it out forwards from the panel **(see illustration)**. Alternatively, to improve access, remove the radio/cassette player (Section 19) and work through the radio aperture in the facia to remove the cigar lighter.

3 If required, the cigar lighter surround can also be pressed out of the panel **(see illustration)**. The illumination bulb is integral with the surround.

Refitting

4 Refitting is a reversal of removal.

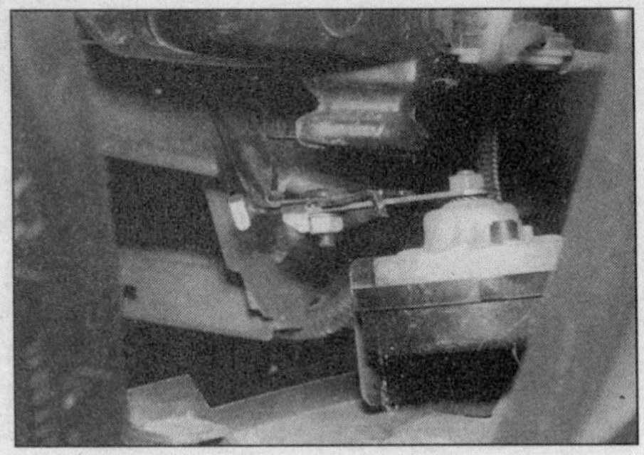
13.1 Horn location - seen through the wheel arch

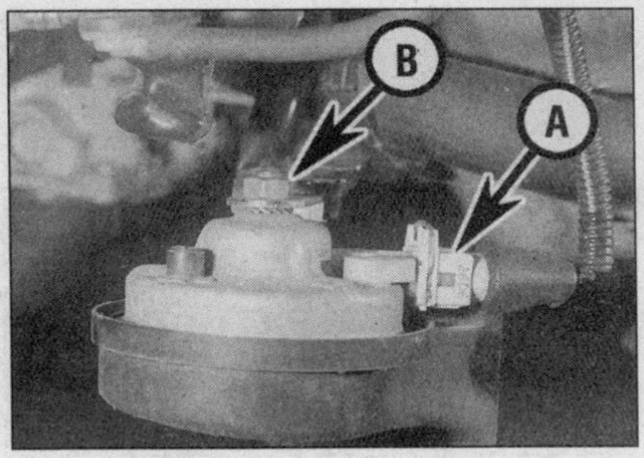

13.5 Horn unit wiring plug (A) and securing nut (B)

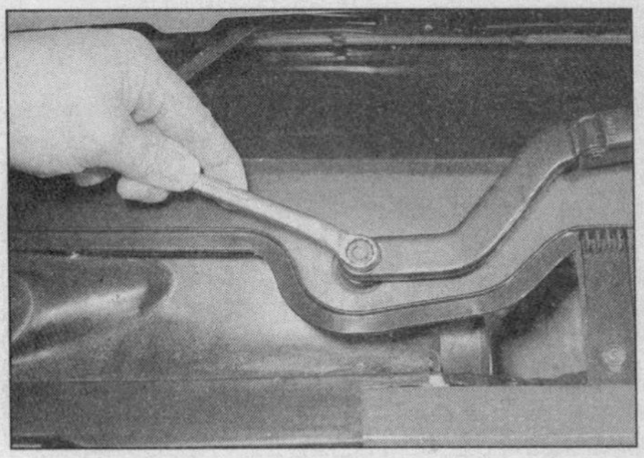
15.3a Unscrew the windscreen wiper spindle nut . . .

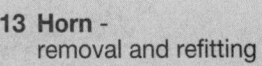

13 Horn - removal and refitting

Removal

1 The horn is located at the front of the driver's side wheelarch, behind the front bumper **(see illustration)**. One or more horn units may be fitted, depending on model.

2 Disconnect the battery negative lead.

3 If desired to improve access, apply the handbrake, then jack up the front of the vehicle and support securely on axle stands (see *"Jacking and vehicle support"*). Remove the relevant roadwheel.

4 Remove the screw under the bumper end which secures the wheel arch liner, then prise out the liner securing clips, and move the wheel arch liner to expose the horn.

5 Disconnect the horn wiring plug, then unscrew the horn securing nut **(see illustration)**, and withdraw the horn from the vehicle.

Refitting

6 Refitting is a reversal of removal.

14 Speedometer drive - general

The Saxo range is equipped with an electronic speedometer, driven by a transducer fitted into the transmission. Refer to Chapter 7 for removal and refitting details.

15 Wiper arms - removal and refitting

Removal

1 Operate the wiper motor, then switch it off so that the wiper arm(s) return to the at-rest ("parked") position.

2 Stick a piece of tape along the edge of the wiper blade(s), to use as an alignment aid

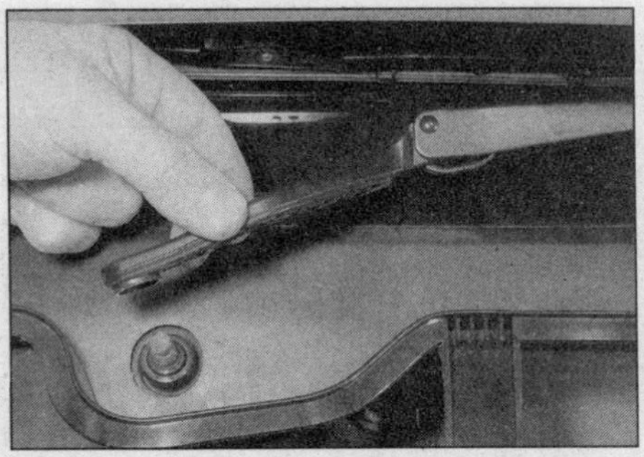
15.3b . . . then pull the wiper arm from the splines

when refitting. If both windscreen wiper arms are removed, note their locations, as different arms are fitted to the driver's and passenger's sides.

3 Where applicable, lift up the wiper arm spindle nut cover, then slacken and remove the spindle nut. Lift the blade off the glass, and pull the wiper arm off its spindle **(see illustrations)**. If necessary, the arm can be levered off the spindle using a suitable flat-bladed screwdriver.

Refitting

4 Ensure that the wiper arm and spindle splines are clean and dry, then refit the arm to the spindle, aligning the wiper blade with the tape fitted before removal. If both windscreen wiper arms have been removed, ensure that the arms are refitted to their correct positions as noted before removal.

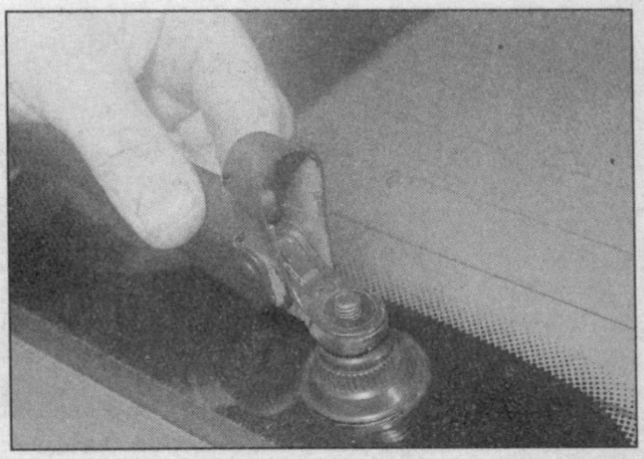
15.3c Removing the tailgate wiper arm

5 Refit the spindle nut, tighten it securely, and where applicable, clip the cover back into position.

16 Windscreen wiper motor and linkage - removal and refitting

Removal

1 Disconnect the battery negative lead.

2 Remove the windscreen wiper arms as described in Section 15.

3 If not already done, open the bonnet.

4 Remove the central Torx screw and the Torx nut at either end, and withdraw the windscreen cowl panel from the scuttle. Note that the panel is clipped around the edge of the windscreen and the front wings **(see illustrations)**.

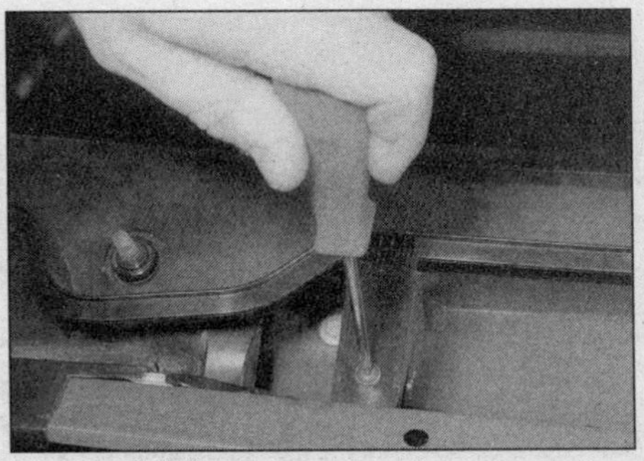
16.4a Remove the Torx screw in the centre . . .

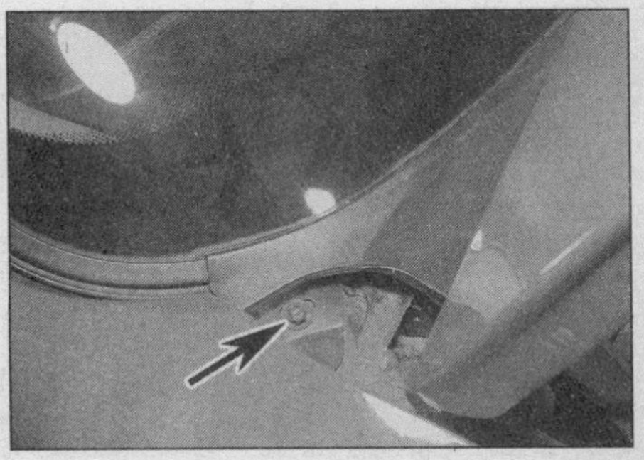
16.4b . . . and the Torx nut at either end (arrowed) . . .

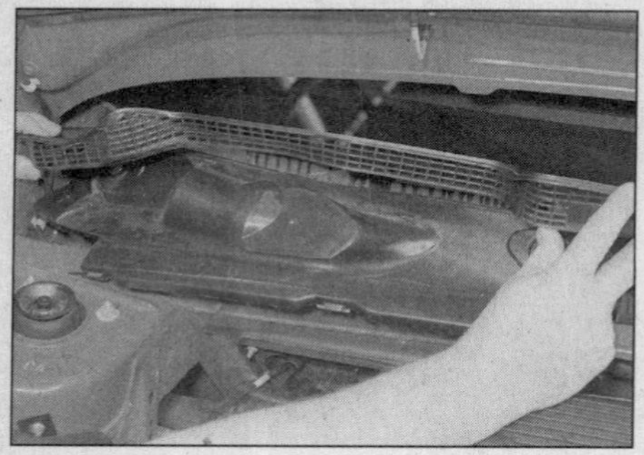

16.4c . . . then unclip and remove the windscreen cowl panel

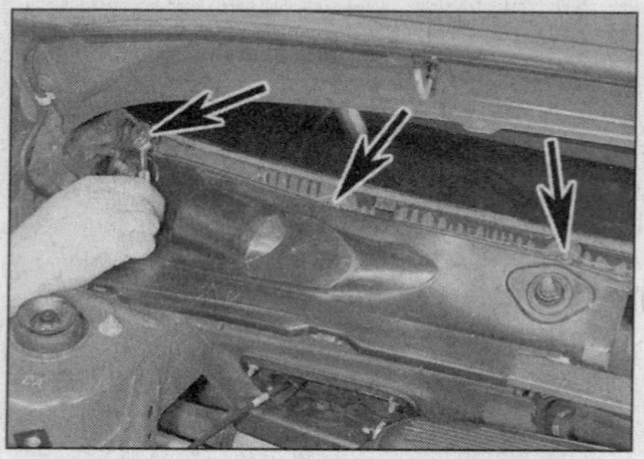

16.5a Remove the three upper nuts (arrowed) . . .

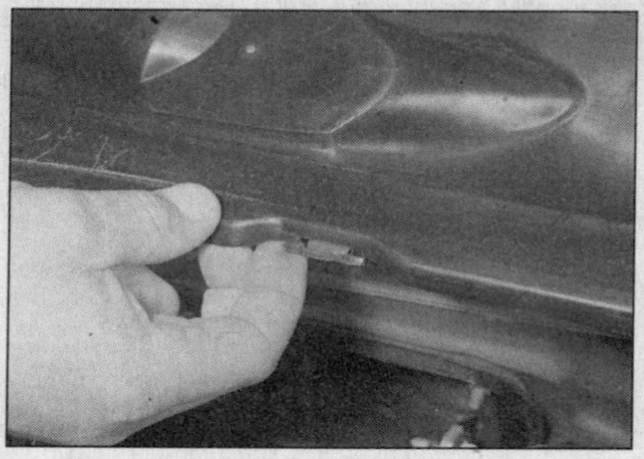

16.5b . . . release the front clips . . .

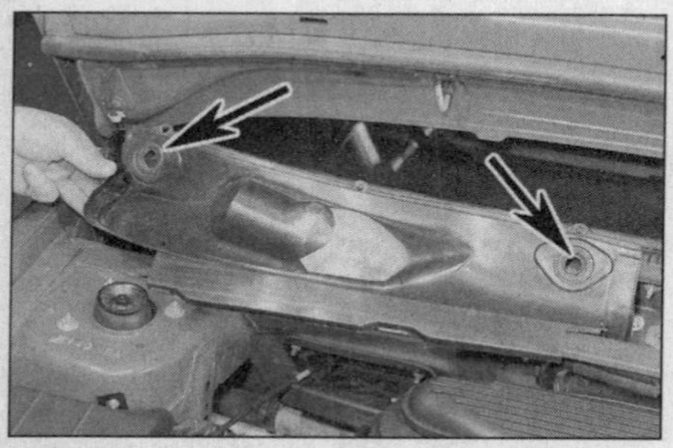

16.5c . . . and remove the wiper motor cover panel, noting the locations of the spindle grommets (arrowed)

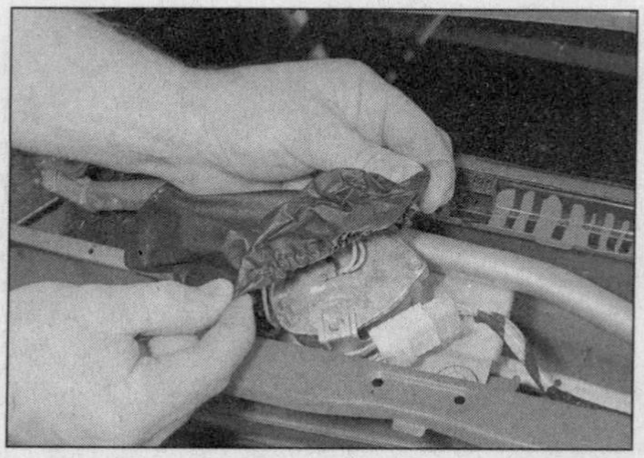

16.6 Removing the elasticated cover from the wiper motor

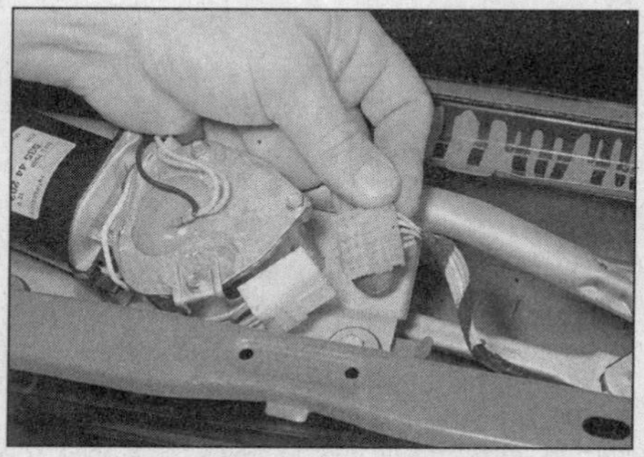

16.7 Disconnecting the wiper motor wiring plug

5 Remove the three upper nuts, then release the two clips at the front of the wiper motor cover panel, and remove the panel. Make sure that the rubber grommets for the wiper spindles are removed with the panel **(see illustrations)**.

6 Where applicable, pull the elasticated cover from the wiper motor assembly **(see illustration)**.

7 Disconnect the wiring plug from the motor **(see illustration)**.

8 Unscrew the six mounting bolts (recover the washers, where applicable), and withdraw the wiper motor and linkage assembly from the scuttle **(see illustrations)**.

9 To separate the motor from the linkage, unscrew the nut securing the crank arm to the motor shaft, then unscrew the three motor securing bolts, and withdraw the motor from the linkage.

Refitting

10 Refitting is a reversal of removal, bearing in mind the following points:

a) Ensure that the windscreen cowl panel is correctly engaged with the windscreen and the wing panels.

b) Refit the windscreen wiper arms as described in Section 15.

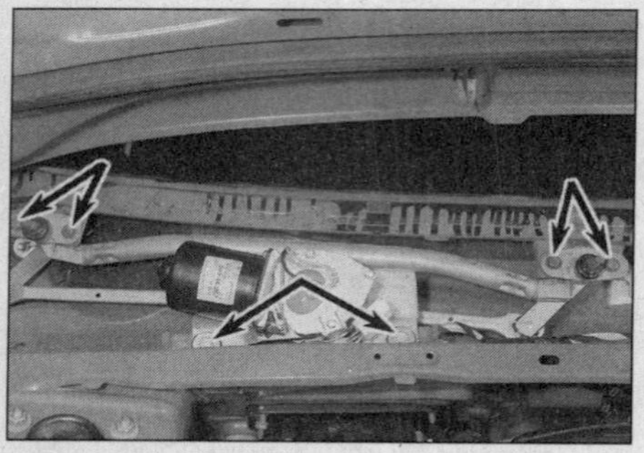

16.8a Remove the wiper motor assembly bolts (arrowed) . . .

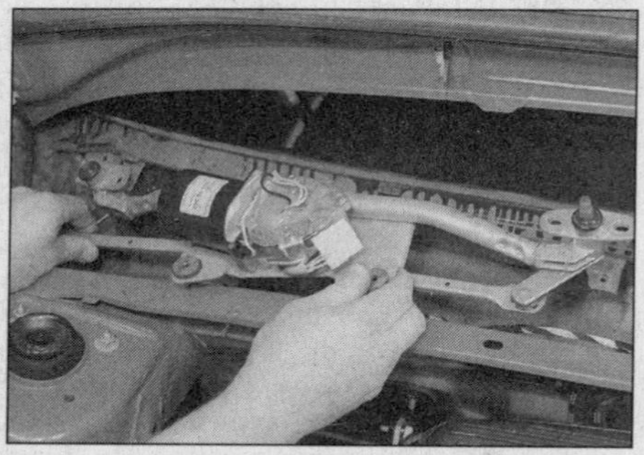

16.8b . . . and remove the assembly from the car

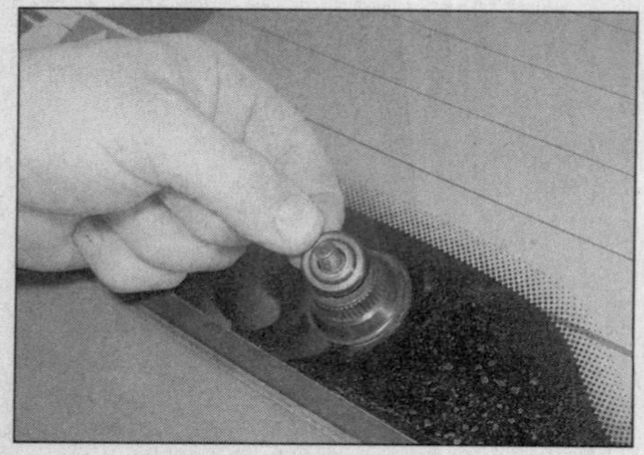

17.3a Remove the tailgate wiper spindle dust cover . . .

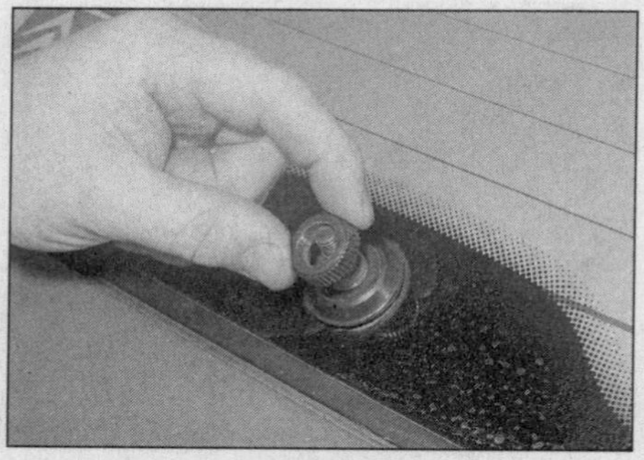

17.3b . . . unscrew the trim disc . . .

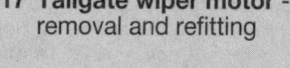

17 Tailgate wiper motor - removal and refitting

Removal

1 Disconnect the battery negative lead.

2 Remove the tailgate wiper arm, as described in Section 15.

3 Recover the spindle dust cover, then unscrew the trim disc and lift off the grommet cover **(see illustrations)**.

4 Open the tailgate.

5 Remove the three screws (one at each side, one in the pull handle) securing the tailgate trim panel, then release the securing clips and withdraw the panel from the tailgate.

17.3c . . . and lift off the grommet cover

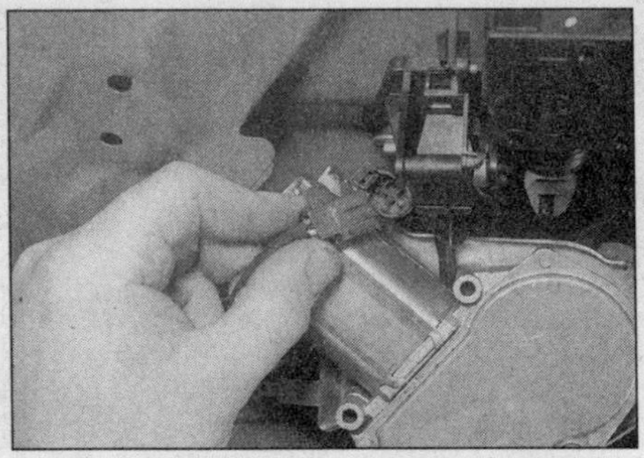

17.6 Disconnecting the tailgate wiper motor wiring plug

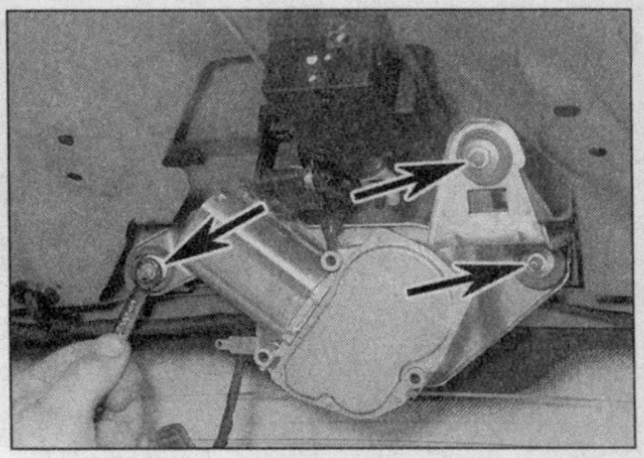

17.7a Unscrew the three tailgate wiper motor nuts (arrowed) . . .

6 Disconnect the wiper motor wiring connector **(see illustration)**.

7 Unscrew the three motor securing nuts, and withdraw the assembly from the tailgate **(see illustrations)**.

8 If required, the wiper motor can be removed from the assembly and renewed separately, after unscrewing the three retaining bolts **(see illustration)**.

Refitting

9 Refitting is a reversal of removal, bearing in mind the following points:

a) Before refitting the assembly, check the condition of the wiper spindle grommets, and renew if necessary.

b) Refit the wiper arm with reference to Section 15.

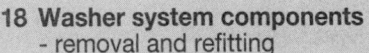

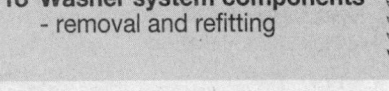

18 Washer system components - removal and refitting

Washer fluid reservoir

Removal

1 Disconnect the battery negative lead.

2 Working in the engine compartment, unscrew the filler neck from the top of the reservoir **(see illustration)**.

3 Apply the handbrake, then jack up the front of the vehicle and support securely on axle stands (see *"Jacking and vehicle support"*). If the screen washer reservoir is being removed, remove the right-hand roadwheel; to remove

17.7b . . . and remove the motor assembly from the tailgate

the headlight washer reservoir, remove the left-hand roadwheel.

4 Remove the screw securing the front of the wheel arch liner to the bumper, then release the securing clips (which are a push fit), and withdraw the liner from under the wheel arch.

5 Release the securing strap from the reservoir, then lower the reservoir from the wheel arch.

6 Disconnect the washer pump wiring plug(s). Disconnect the fluid hose(s) from the pump(s) - be prepared for fluid spillage - then withdraw the reservoir.

Refitting

7 Refitting is a reversal of removal.

Washer pump(s)

Removal

8 Remove the fluid reservoir as described previously in this Section.

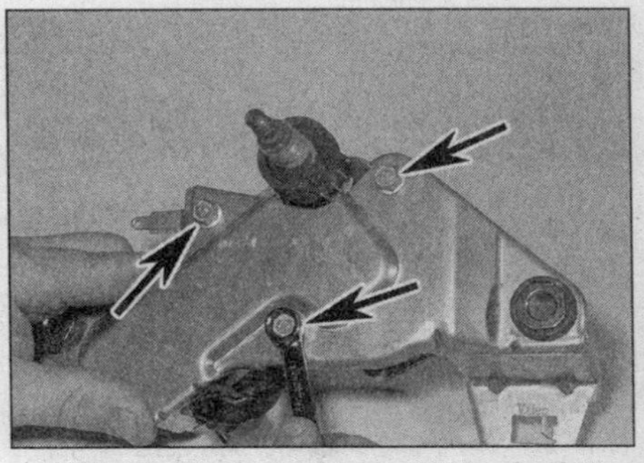

17.8 To separate the motor, undo the three bolts (arrowed)

9 The washer pump(s) is/are a push fit in the reservoir **(see illustration)**.

Refitting

10 Refitting is a reversal of removal, but check the condition of the mounting grommet in the reservoir, and renew if necessary.

Windscreen washer jet

11 Carefully prise the washer nozzle from the bonnet (take care not to damage the paintwork), and disconnect the fluid hose.

12 Refitting is a reversal of removal.

Tailgate washer jet

13 Carefully prise the washer jet from the tailgate, taking care not to damage the paintwork. Alternatively, remove the high-level stop-light as described in Section 7, and push the jet out from inside, through the aperture in the tailgate **(see illustrations)**.

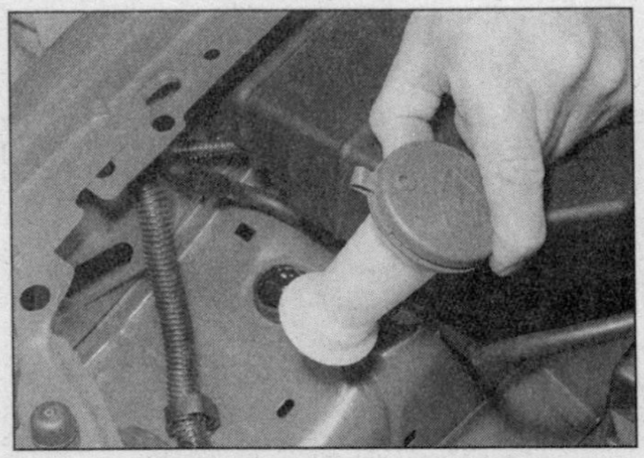

18.2 The washer reservoir filler neck can be unscrewed and removed

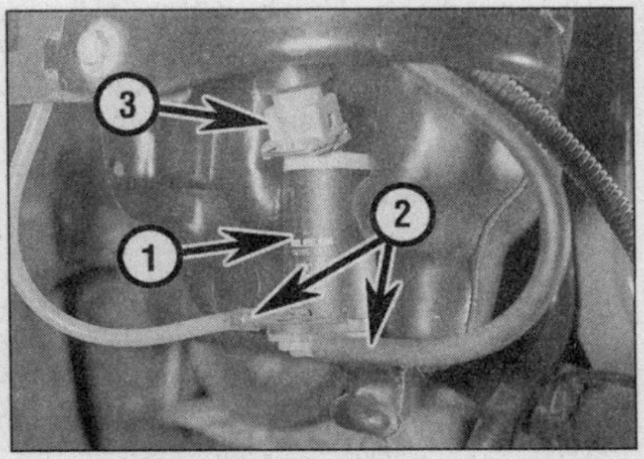

18.9 Windscreen washer pump (1), fluid hoses (2) and wiring plug (3)

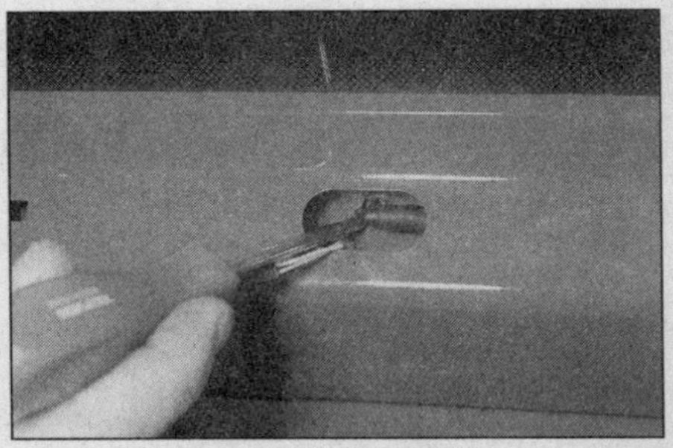

18.13a Working through the high-level stop-light aperture, press out the washer jet . . .

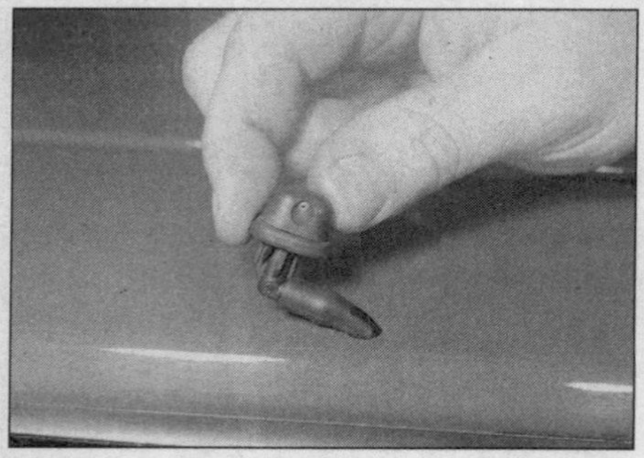

18.13b . . . and withdraw it from the top of the tailgate

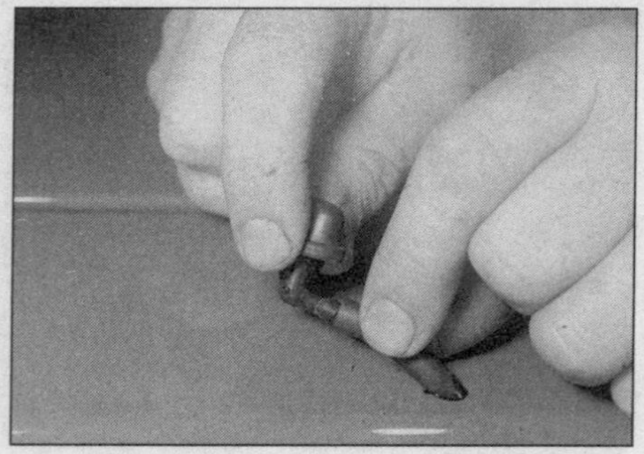

18.14 Disconnecting the fluid hose from the tailgate washer jet

19.2 Prise off the radio/cassette end caps

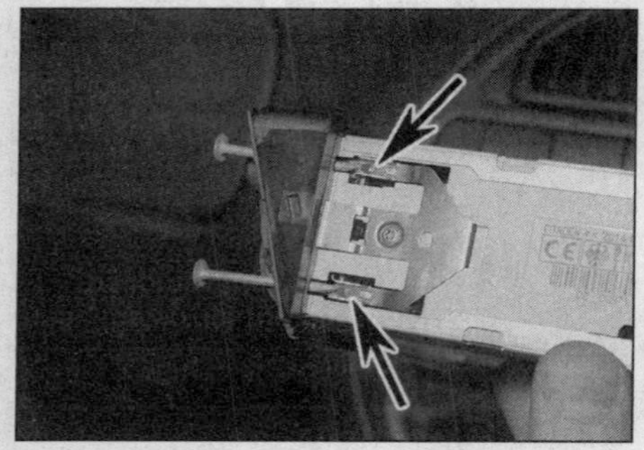

19.3 Radio/cassette removed to show locking mechanism (arrowed)

19.5 In the absence of special tools, this radio/cassette can be removed as shown

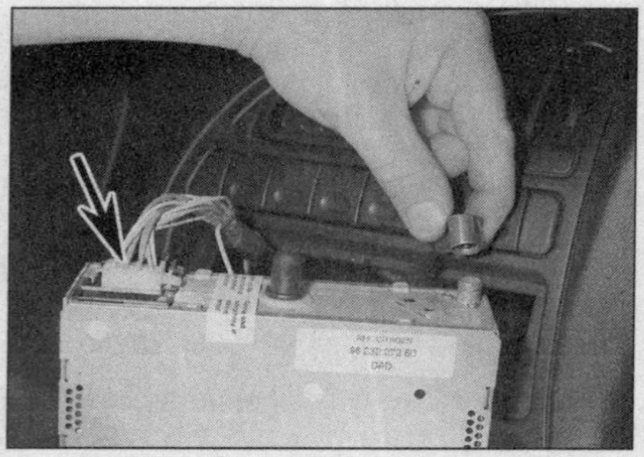

19.6 Disconnect the wiring plug (arrowed) and the aerial lead

14 Disconnect the fluid hose from the jet **(see illustration)**. Take care not to allow the hose to drop back into the tailgate - tape it to the tailgate if necessary.
15 Refitting is a reversal of removal.

Headlight washer jet

16 Apply the handbrake, then jack up the front of the vehicle and support securely on axle stands (see *"Jacking and vehicle support"*).
17 Working from below and behind the front bumper, reach up and disconnect the washer supply tube from the jet.
18 Carefully prise the jet from the bumper, taking care not to mark the finish.
19 Refitting is a reversal of removal.

19 Radio/cassette player - removal and refitting

Note: *The following applies only to radio/cassette units fitted as standard equipment. Refer to "Radio/cassette unit anti-theft system - precaution" in the Reference section of this Manual before proceeding.*

Removal

1 Disconnect the battery negative lead.
2 Where applicable, prise off the end caps which cover the access holes for the removal tools **(see illustration)**.
3 The radio/cassette player is normally removed using special tools to release the locking mechanism which locates the unit in the facia. The tools required will vary according to the exact unit fitted, but are typically thin metal strips or rods with specially-shaped ends to engage the locking mechanism. **Note:** *These tools should be provided with the car, if the unit was fitted as standard, or can be obtained from your Citroën dealer or an in-car entertainment specialist.* Trying to remove the unit without these tools may result in damage to the unit or to the facia. However, we found that the locking mechanism in our project car could be released using four 1.5-inch nails, as shown **(see illustration)**.
4 Slide the tools into position, until the slots in the tools are felt to engage with the radio/cassette player securing clips.
5 If the proper tools are used, push the tools forwards to release the clips, then use the tools to pull the unit from the facia. Otherwise, release the locking mechanism and carefully prise the unit from the facia, taking care not to damage the plastics **(see illustration)**.
6 Disconnect the wiring plug(s) and the aerial lead, and withdraw the unit **(see illustration)**.

Refitting

7 Reconnect the wiring and the aerial lead to the rear of the unit, then push the wiring into position at the rear of the radio/cassette player aperture. Ensure that the wiring is positioned correctly behind the radio/cassette player, to allow space for the unit to be pushed into position.
8 Push the unit into position until the locking mechanism engages on both sides.

20 Speakers - removal and refitting

Front or rear door speakers

1 Disconnect the battery negative lead.
2 Using a suitable screwdriver, carefully unclip the speaker grille panel, taking care not to mark the trim panel **(see illustration)**.
3 Remove the securing screws, then withdraw the speaker from the door, and disconnect the wiring plug **(see illustrations)**. Note the routing of the wiring, and any markings on the speaker to indicate direction of fitting.

20.2 Unclip the speaker grille panel

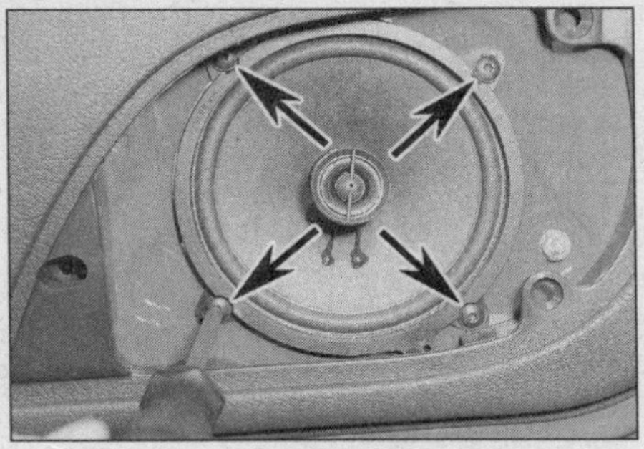

20.3a Remove the four Torx screws (arrowed) . . .

20.3b . . . withdraw the speaker from the door . . .

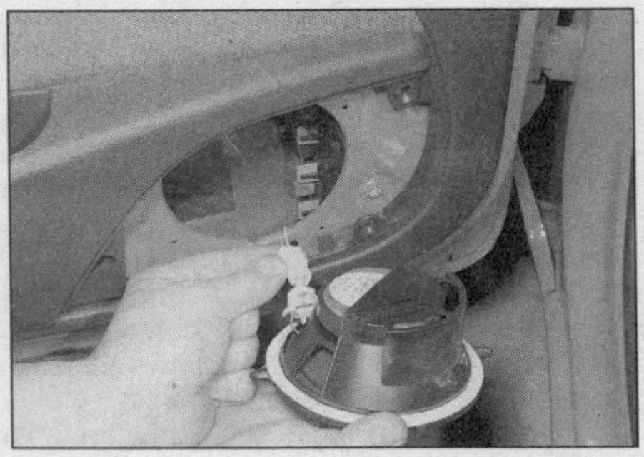

20.3c . . . and disconnect the wiring plug

20.6 Speaker retaining screws (arrowed) - rear trim panel speaker

4 Refitting is a reversal of removal.

Rear trim panel speakers

5 Remove the rear trim panel as described in Chapter 11, Section 26.
6 Remove the two securing screws **(see illustration)**, then remove the speaker from the panel.
7 Refitting is a reversal of removal.

21 Radio aerial - removal and refitting

Aerial mast

1 Note that the aerial mast can be unscrewed from the mounting on the roof **(see illustration)**, and is available as a separate component. To remove the complete assembly, proceed as follows.
2 Carefully prise the courtesy light from the roof panel, and disconnect the wiring plug **(see illustration)**. To improve access further, remove the roof console as described in Chapter 11, Section 26.
3 Pull the suppressor can from the bottom of the aerial, where applicable.
4 Unscrew the aerial mounting nut **(see illustration)**, then disconnect the aerial lead from the stud, and pull the aerial from the roof.
5 Refitting is a reversal of removal.

Upper aerial lead

6 Disconnect the lead from the aerial mast as described in paragraphs 2 to 4.
7 Check to see the routing of the aerial lead, then carefully pull the appropriate windscreen pillar trim panel from the pillar to expose the aerial lead. Take care not to break the trim panel securing clips.
8 If working in the driver's footwell, prise out the two push-in clips and remove the carpet trim panel above the foot pedals.
9 Reach up behind the facia panel, and trace the aerial lead to the lower aerial connector. Where applicable, pull the insulation from the connector.
10 Separate the two halves of the connector, then tie a length of string to the top of the aerial lead.
11 Release the lead from the clips on the body pillar, then carefully pull the lead down through the roof lining, pillar and facia. Untie the string from the end of the lead, and leave it in place to aid refitting.
12 Refitting is a reversal of removal, bearing in mind the following points:

a) *Use the string to pull the lead up through the facia, body pillar and roof panel.*
b) *Make sure that the lead is securely clipped to the body pillar.*

Lower aerial lead

13 Remove the radio/cassette player as described in Section 19.
14 Separate the two halves of the aerial connector as described in paragraphs 8 to 10.
15 Tie a length of string to the upper end of the lead, then pull the lead down into the footwell. Untie the string, and leave it in place in the facia to aid refitting.
16 Commence refitting by using the string to pull the lead back into position. With the lead correctly routed, untie the string.
17 Reconnect the lead connector, then refit the carpet panel and, where applicable, the trim panel.
18 Refit the radio/cassette player as described in Section 19.

22 Anti-theft alarm and immobiliser system - general information

Note: *This information is applicable only to the anti-theft alarm system fitted by Citroën as standard equipment.*

Immobiliser

All models are fitted with an anti-theft immobiliser, which cuts the ignition circuit (or, on diesel versions, holds the stop solenoid closed), preventing the engine from being started. Models up to 1998 had a keypad

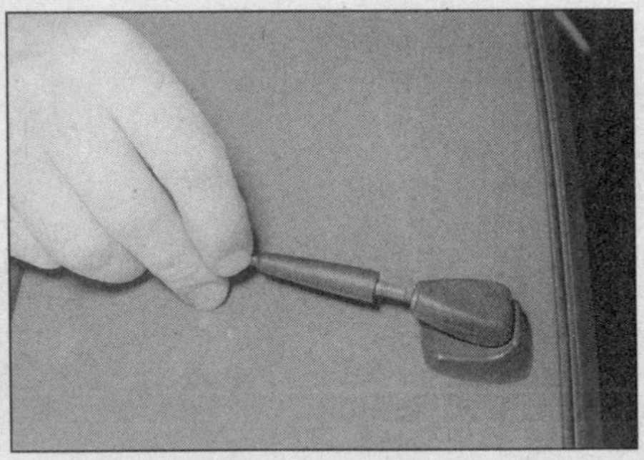

21.1 The aerial mast can be unscrewed from the roof mounting

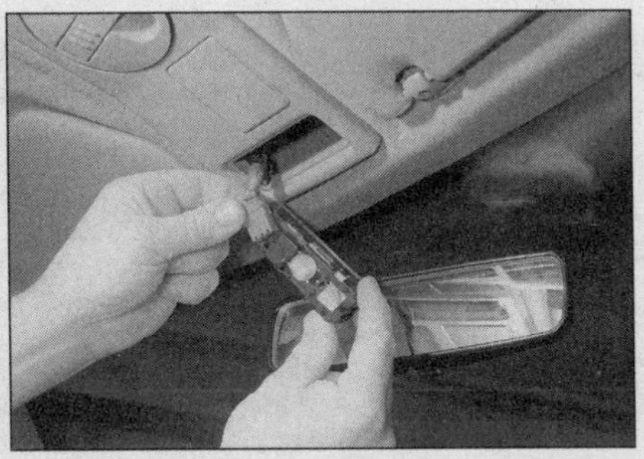

21.2 Disconnect the wiring plug from the courtesy light

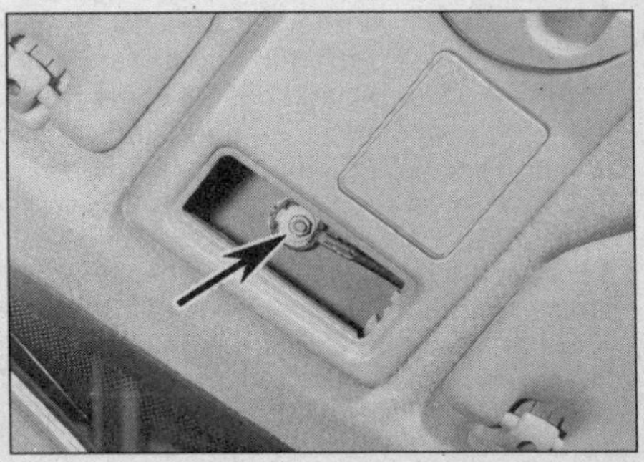

21.4 Aerial mounting nut (arrowed) seen with the courtesy light removed

immobiliser; after this date, the keypad was replaced by an ignition key transponder system.

Keypad immobiliser

A four-digit code has to be entered before the engine will start. This code can be changed by the owner to one which is easiest to remember - details are given in the vehicle handbook. Also, the immobiliser can be set in "service" mode, intended for when the car is left at a garage for servicing; this mode could also be selected if the car is on loan. Details on how to select the service mode are given in the vehicle handbook.

Make sure that the four-digit code is one which can easily be remembered, and that this code is passed on when the car is sold. If the code is lost or forgotten, it may result in the engine management ECU or the diesel injection pump having to be replaced, at great expense.

Removing the keypad is described as part of the centre console removal in Chapter 11.

Transponder immobiliser

The transponder immobiliser is a "passive" system, in that no action is required on the owner's part to deactivate the immobiliser, beyond inserting the ignition key into the lock. The head of the ignition key contains a transponder micro-chip, and the ignition lock contains a reader coil. When the key enters the lock, the reader coil recognises the signal from the micro-chip, and de-activates the immobiliser.

It is essential that a record is kept of the key number (this will be supplied with the car when new). Any duplicate keys will have to be obtained from a Citroën dealer, who will need the key number to supply a duplicate - any keys cut elsewhere will work the door locks, but will not contain the transponder chip necessary to de-activate the immobiliser and allow the engine to be started.

Alarm system

Some models in the range are fitted with an anti-theft alarm system as standard equipment. The alarm is automatically armed and disarmed using the remote central locking transmitter (where applicable). When the system is activated, the alarm indicator light, located on the facia, will flash continuously.

Note that if the doors are operated using the key, the alarm will not be armed or disarmed (as applicable). If for some reason the remote central locking transmitter fails whilst the alarm is armed, the alarm can be disarmed using the key. To do this, open the door with the key, then enter the vehicle, noting that the alarm will sound as the door is opened, and switch on the ignition switch whilst depressing the alarm switch (details of the alarm switch location are given in the vehicle handbook). Note that the ignition switch must be turned on and the alarm switch depressed within 10 seconds of opening the door.

The alarm system has switches on the bonnet, tailgate and each of the doors. It also has ultrasonic sensing, which detects movement inside the vehicle, via sensors mounted on either side of the vehicle interior. If required, the ultrasonic sensing facility can be switched off, whilst retaining the switched side of the system. To switch off the ultrasonic sensing, refer to the information in the vehicle handbook. This facility is useful, as it allows you to leave the windows/sunroof open, and still arm the alarm. If the windows/sunroof are left open with the ultrasonic sensing not switched off, the alarm may be falsely triggered by a gust of wind.

Should the alarm system become faulty, the vehicle should be taken to a Citroën dealer for examination.

23 Airbag system - general information and precautions

Warning: Before carrying out any operations on the airbag system, disconnect the battery negative terminal and wait at least 10 minutes to allow the system capacitors to discharge. When operations are complete, make sure no one is inside the vehicle when the battery is reconnected.

Note that the airbag(s) must not be subjected to temperatures in excess of 90°C (194°F). When the airbag is removed, ensure that it is stored the correct way up to prevent possible inflation.

Do not allow any solvents or cleaning agents to contact the airbag assemblies. They must be cleaned using only a damp cloth.

The airbag(s) and control unit are both sensitive to impact. If either is dropped or damaged they should be renewed.

Disconnect the airbag control unit wiring plug prior to using arc-welding equipment on the vehicle.

1 A driver's airbag was fitted as standard to all models but the most basic in the Saxo range; a passenger's side airbag was available as an optional extra. Models fitted with a driver's side airbag have the word AIRBAG stamped on the airbag unit, which is fitted to the centre of the steering wheel. Models also equipped with a passenger's side airbag also have the word AIRBAG stamped on the passenger's end of the facia, in place of the main glovebox (a smaller glovebox is fitted to the top of the facia on these models). The airbag system comprises of the airbag unit (complete with gas generator), an impact sensor, the control unit and a warning light in the instrument panel.

2 The airbag system is triggered in the event of a heavy frontal impact above a predetermined force; depending on the point of impact. The airbag is inflated within milliseconds, and forms a safety cushion between the driver and the steering wheel or (where applicable) the passenger and the facia. This prevents contact between the upper body and the wheel/facia, and therefore greatly reduces the risk of injury. The airbag then deflates almost immediately.

3 Every time the ignition is switched on, the airbag control unit performs a self-test. The self-test takes approximately 6 seconds, and during this time the airbag warning light on the facia is illuminated. After the self-test has been completed, the warning light should go out. If the warning light fails to come on, remains illuminated after the initial 3-second period, flashes, or comes on at any time when the vehicle is being driven, there is a fault in the airbag system. The vehicle should then be taken to a Citroën dealer for examination at the earliest possible opportunity.

4 The airbag system works in conjunction with the seat belt tensioners described in Chapter 11. If an impact of sufficient force is detected by the impact sensor, the airbag and seat belt tensioner systems will be triggered.

5 Citroën state that, after a period of ten years from first registration, the airbag unit(s) and seat belt tensioners should be replaced, to avoid problems caused by the deterioration of the explosive charges used to operate the systems. This will clearly be an expensive exercise - consult your Citroën dealer for advice.

24 Airbag system components - removal and refitting

Note: *Refer to the warnings in Section 23 before carrying out the following operations.*

1 Disconnect the battery negative terminal (see Section 1), and wait at least 10 minutes to allow the system capacitors to discharge.

Driver's side airbag

Note: *New airbag retaining screws will be required on refitting.*

Removal

2 Slacken and remove the two Torx screws from the rear of the steering wheel, rotating the wheel as necessary to gain access to the screws **(see illustration)**.

3 Return the steering wheel to the straight-

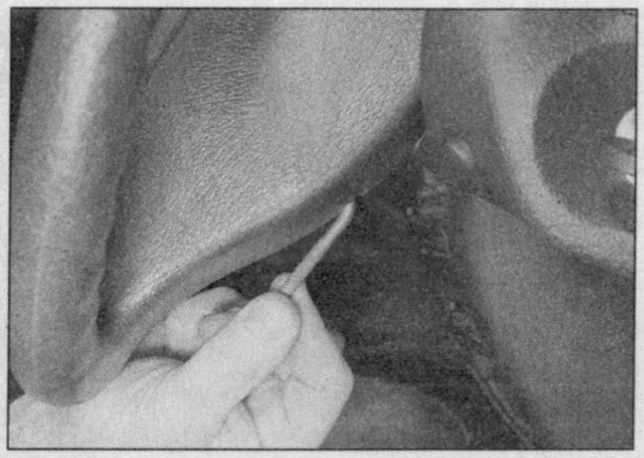

24.2 Removing the airbag securing screws from behind the steering wheel

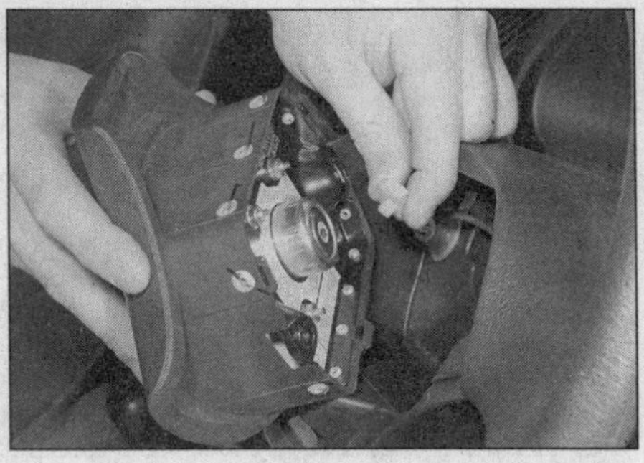

24.3 Unplug the wiring connector from the airbag unit

ahead position, then carefully lift the airbag assembly away from the steering wheel and disconnect the wiring connector from the rear of the unit **(see illustration)**. All airbag wiring is typically orange in colour, to aid identification. Note that the airbag must not be knocked or dropped, and should be stored the correct way up with its padded surface uppermost.

Refitting

4 Make sure that the steering wheel is in the straight-ahead position.

5 Reconnect the wiring connector and seat the airbag unit in the steering wheel, ensuring that the wire does not become trapped. Fit the new retaining screws, and tighten them to the specified torque.

6 Making sure that no-one is inside the car, reconnect the battery negative lead. Keeping your face away from the steering wheel, switch on the ignition and check the operation of the airbag warning light (see Section 23).

Passenger's side airbag

Removal

7 The passenger airbag is secured by four nuts (one at each corner). Remove the upper glovebox as described in Chapter 11, Section 26 for better access - otherwise, the nuts must be removed by reaching in behind the facia from below.

8 Support the airbag unit from the front, and remove the securing nuts.

9 Disconnect the airbag wiring connector, and remove the airbag unit from the front of the facia. All airbag wiring is typically orange in colour, to aid identification. Note that the airbag must not be knocked or dropped, and should be stored the correct way up with its padded surface uppermost.

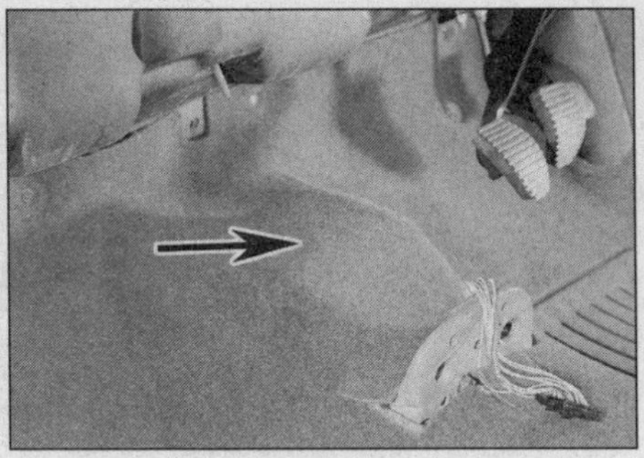

24.11 The airbag control unit (location arrowed) is completely covered by the carpet

Refitting

10 Refitting is a reversal of removal. Make sure that no-one is inside the car, then reconnect the battery negative lead. Keeping your face away from the facia, switch on the ignition and check the operation of the airbag warning light (see Section 23).

Airbag control unit

11 The airbag control unit is fitted in the centre of the car, beneath the facia in front of the centre console. The unit is completely covered by the carpet **(see illustration)**, which will have to be cut or folded back for access.

12 Remove the centre console as described in Chapter 11.

13 Cut the carpet for access to the control unit. The carpet is secured at the front by a number of clips, and by large plastic plate nuts, which can be unscrewed and removed. However, the proximity of the facia panel means that only limited access will be gained by releasing the carpet fasteners, as the carpet cannot be folded back sufficiently.

14 Release the securing catch and disconnect the wiring plug from the side of the unit **(see illustration)**.

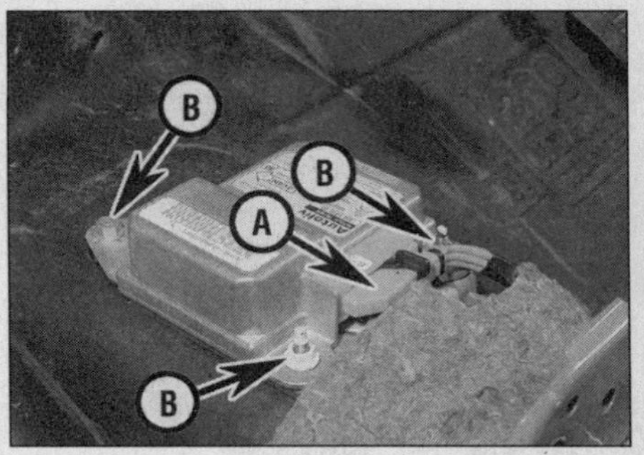

24.14 Airbag control unit wiring plug (A) and securing nuts (B) - seen with facia panel removed

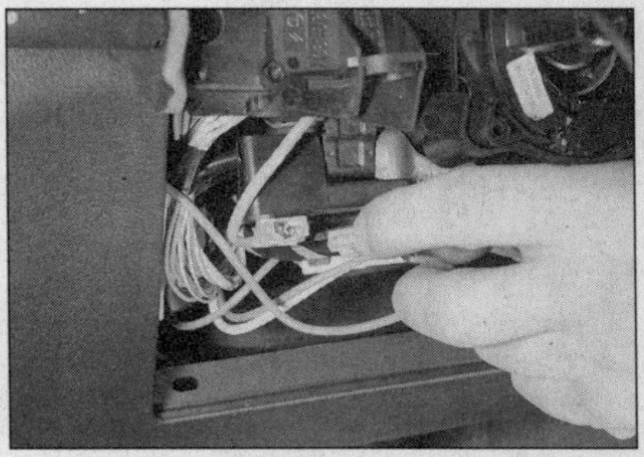

24.18 Disconnecting the airbag contact unit wiring plug

15 Undo the securing nuts and remove the control unit from the car.

16 Refitting is a reversal of removal.

Airbag wiring rotary contact unit

17 Remove the airbag unit as described above, and the steering wheel as described in Chapter 10.

18 Disconnect the contact unit wiring connector from under the steering column **(see illustration)**. All airbag wiring is typically orange in colour, to aid identification.

19 Taking care not to rotate the contact unit, undo the three retaining screws and remove it from the steering column **(see illustrations)**.

20 Once the unit is removed, line up the two orange arrow markings, then tape up the unit to prevent unnecessary rotation **(see illustration)**.

21 Before refitting, remove the tape, where

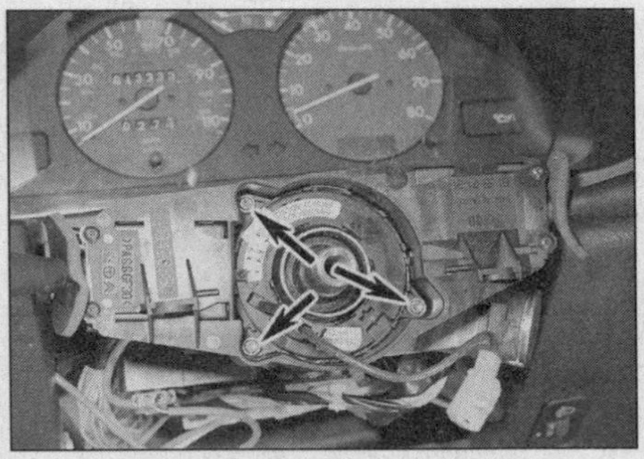

24.19a Remove the three screws (arrowed) . . .

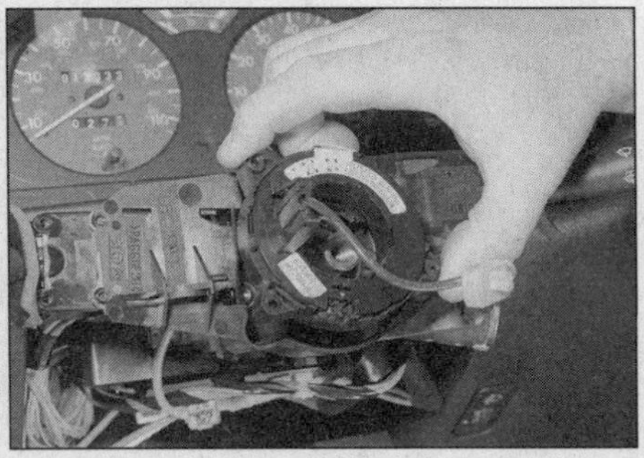

24.19b . . . and withdraw the airbag contact unit

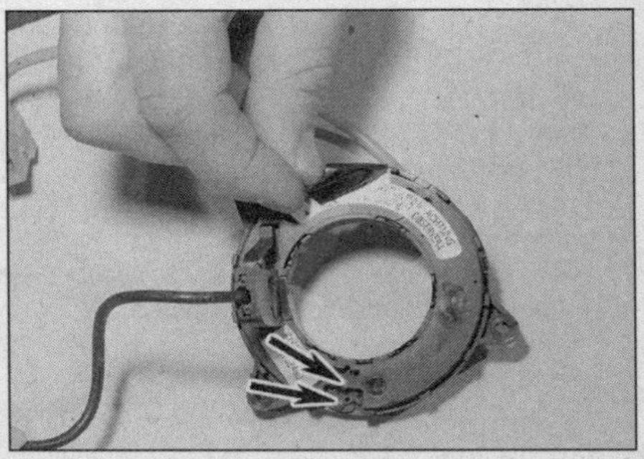

24.20 With the orange arrows aligned (arrowed), tape up the contact unit to prevent rotation

applicable. If a new contact unit is being fitted, cut the cable-tie which is fitted to prevent the unit accidentally rotating.

22 Fit the unit to the steering column and securely tighten its retaining screws.

23 Refit the steering wheel as described in Chapter 10, and the airbag unit as described above.

25 Inertia switch - general information, removal and refitting

General information

1 All models except later diesel engine versions are equipped with a fuel cut-off inertia switch, mounted in the rear corner of the engine compartment **(see illustration)**. The purpose of the switch is to prevent fuel spillage in the event of an accident.

2 The switch consists of a steel ball mounted in a conical housing - the steel ball is normally held in place by a magnet. When an impact of greater than 8g occurs (equivalent to hitting a wall at around 15 mph), the switch activates. On petrol models, the switch cuts the supply to the fuel pump relay, while on diesels, the switch activates the injection pump stop solenoid.

3 It is not unknown for these switches to operate in conditions other than in an accident situation - for example, if the car receives a severe enough jolt, the switch might be triggered, leading to the engine suddenly cutting out.

25.1 Inertia switch location

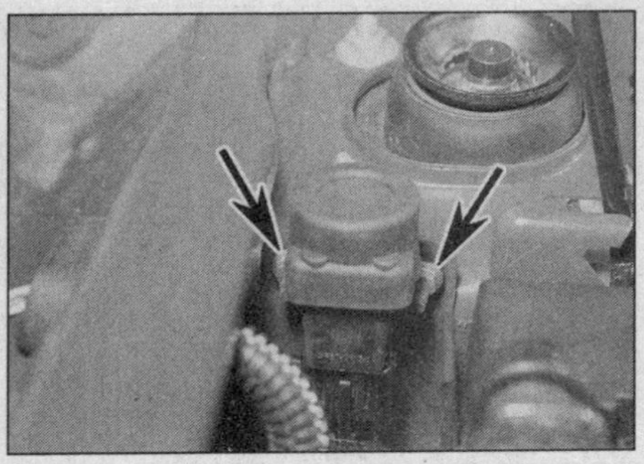

25.5 Inertia switch securing nuts (arrowed)

4 The switch can be reset by depressing the pushbutton on top of the switch. This should restore normal fuel system operation.

Removal

5 Unscrew and remove the two securing nuts **(see illustration)**, then disconnect the wiring plug from below, and remove the switch from the engine compartment.

Refitting

6 Refitting is a reversal of removal. Given the safety-related nature of the switch, it would be useful to have its operation checked by a Citroën dealer, if possible.

26 Heated front seat components - general information

Certain models may be equipped with heated front seats. The seats are heated by electrical elements built into the seat cushions.

For access to the heating elements, the seats must be dismantled; this work should be entrusted to a Citroën dealer.

The heated seat switches are mounted in the centre console. Removal and refitting details are given in Section 4.

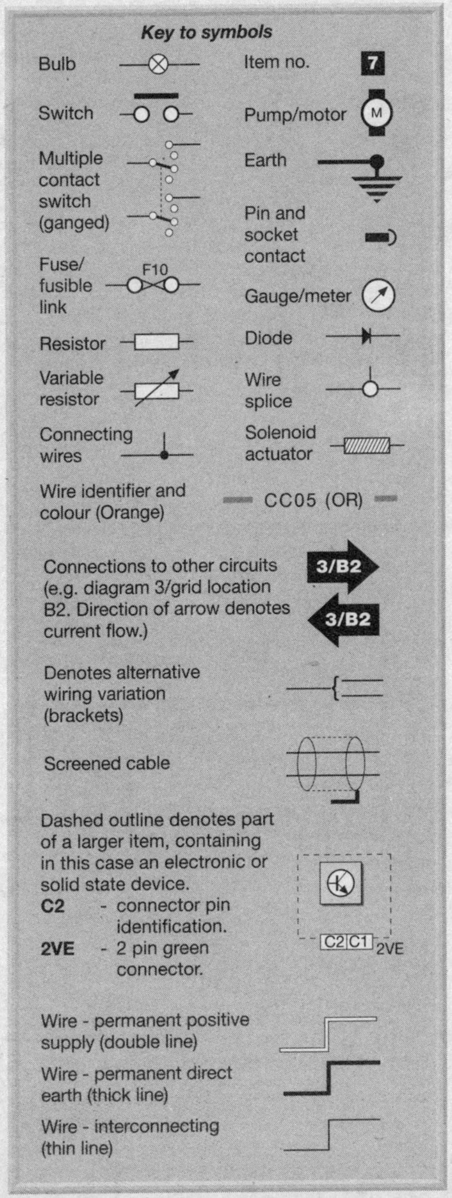

Passenger fusebox - up to 1998

Fuse	*Rating*	*Circuit protected*
F1	5A	Instrument panel, cat.control unit, tacho, air. cond. and auto. trans.
F2	25A	Heater blower, heated mirrors and rear screen
F3	25A	Heated screen/mirrors
F4	10A	Map reading light, lights-on buzzer, no charge warning light, electric mirrors and windows, radio, direction indicators
F5	20A	Horn, cigar lighter
F6	10A	Hazard warning lights
F7	15A	Stop and reversing lights
F8	20A	Luggage compartment and interior light, radio, clock, diagnostic socket, central locking
F9	20A	Front/rear wash/wipe
F10	30A	Electric windows
F11	5A	Rear fog lights
F12	5A	Front side lights, RH tail light, lights-on buzzer, illumination
F13	5A	LH tail and number plate light

Fuse variation - from 1998

Fuse	*Rating*	*Circuit protected*
F1	25A	Heated rear window and mirrors
F2	25A	Air cond. blower, heated mirrors, heated rear window, relay high pressure pump
F3	5A	Instrument panel, tachometer, diagnostic socket, auto. trans. relay, alarm

Fuses **F4** *to* **F13** *as above*

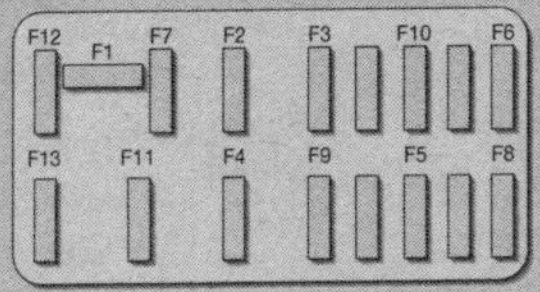

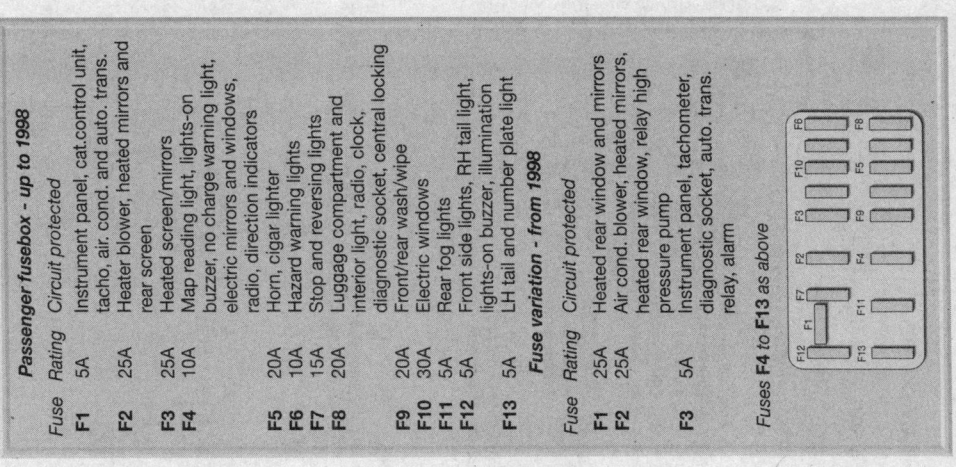

Standard terminal identification (typical)

15	Ignition switch 'ignition' position
30	Battery +ve
31	Earth
85	Relay winding input
86	Relay winding earth
87	Relay output
87a	Relay output

Engine fusebox

Fuse	*Rating*	*Circuit protected*
F1	15A	Injection
F2	30A	Anti-lock brakes
F3	30A	Fan
F4	30A	Anti-lock brakes
F5	30A	Fan
F6	15A	Front fog lights, alarm
F7	-	-
F8	-	-
F9	10A	Fuel pump
F10	20A	Injection relay, anti-lock brakes, pre-post heating relay, automatic transmission relay
F11	5A	Oxygen sensor
F12	10A	LH main beam
F13	10A	RH main beam
F14	10A	LH dipped beam
F15	10A	RH dipped beam

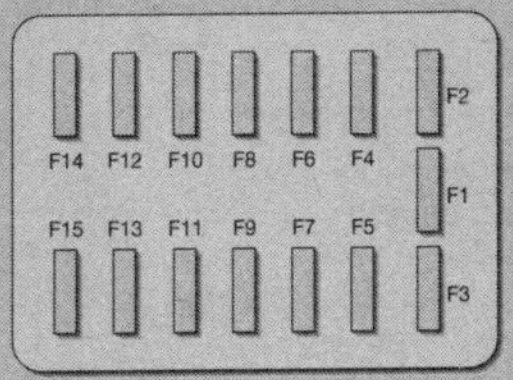

Earth locations

E1	Near battery
E2	Base of LH 'A' pillar
E3	On gearbox
E4	Engine bay, LH front inner wing
E5	Near cooling fan
E6	Engine bay, RH front inner wing
E7	On gearbox
E8	RH 'C' pillar
E9	On gearbox
E10	LH 'C' pillar
E11	LH 'C' pillar
E12	Base of LH 'A' pillar
E13	Transmission tunnel
E14	Dashboard

H31045/a

Diagram 1 : Information for wiring diagrams

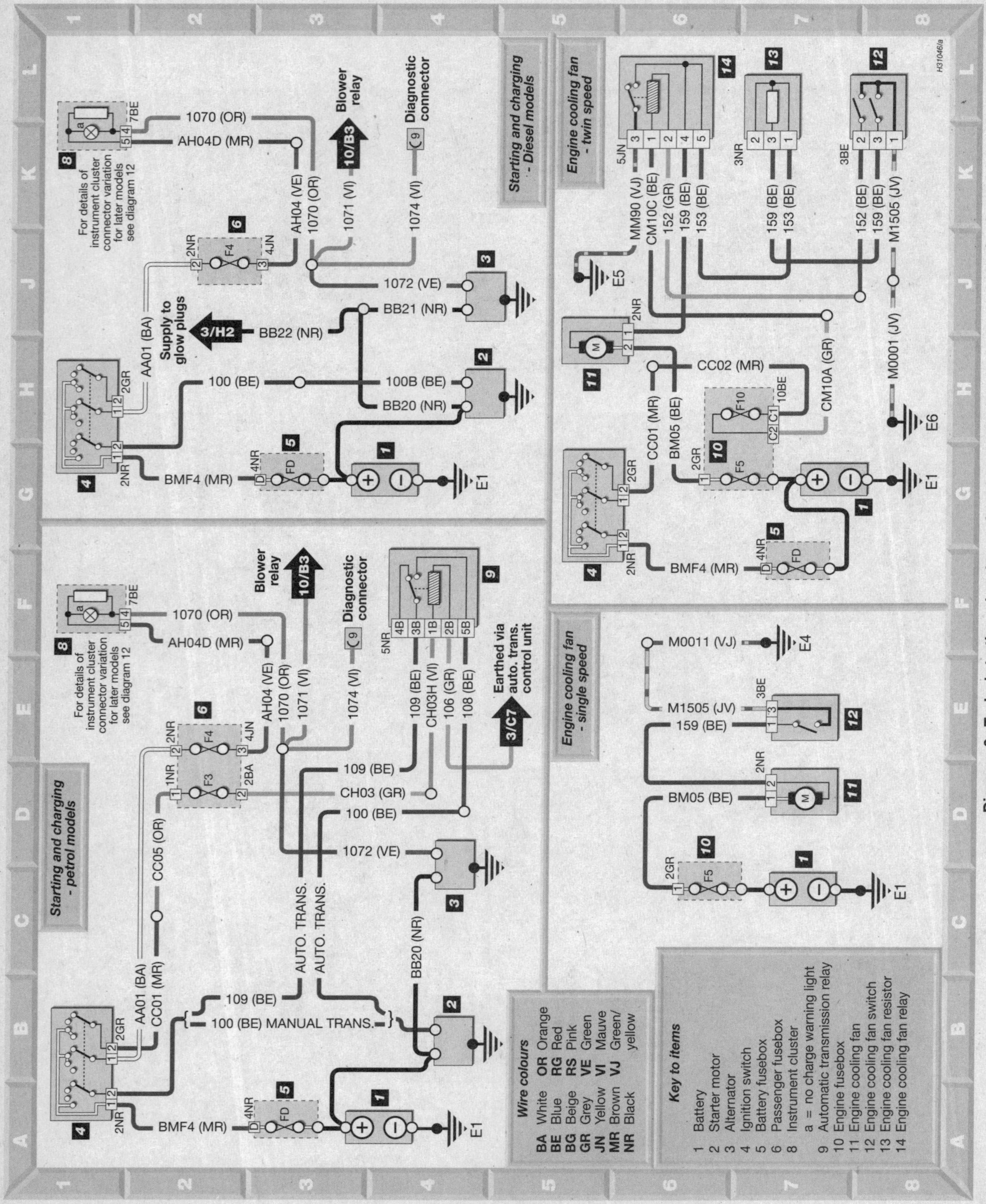

Diagram 2 : Typical starting, charging and engine cooling fan

Wire colours

BA White	**OR** Orange		
BE Blue	**RG** Red		
BG Beige	**RS** Pink		
GR Grey	**VE** Green		
JN Yellow	**VI** Mauve		
MR Brown	**VJ** Green/yellow		
NR Black			

Key to items

1 Battery
2 Starter motor
3 Alternator
4 Ignition switch
5 Battery fusebox
6 Passenger fusebox
8 Instrument cluster
a = no charge warning light
9 Automatic transmission relay
10 Engine fusebox
11 Engine cooling fan
12 Engine cooling fan switch
13 Engine cooling fan resistor
14 Engine cooling fan relay

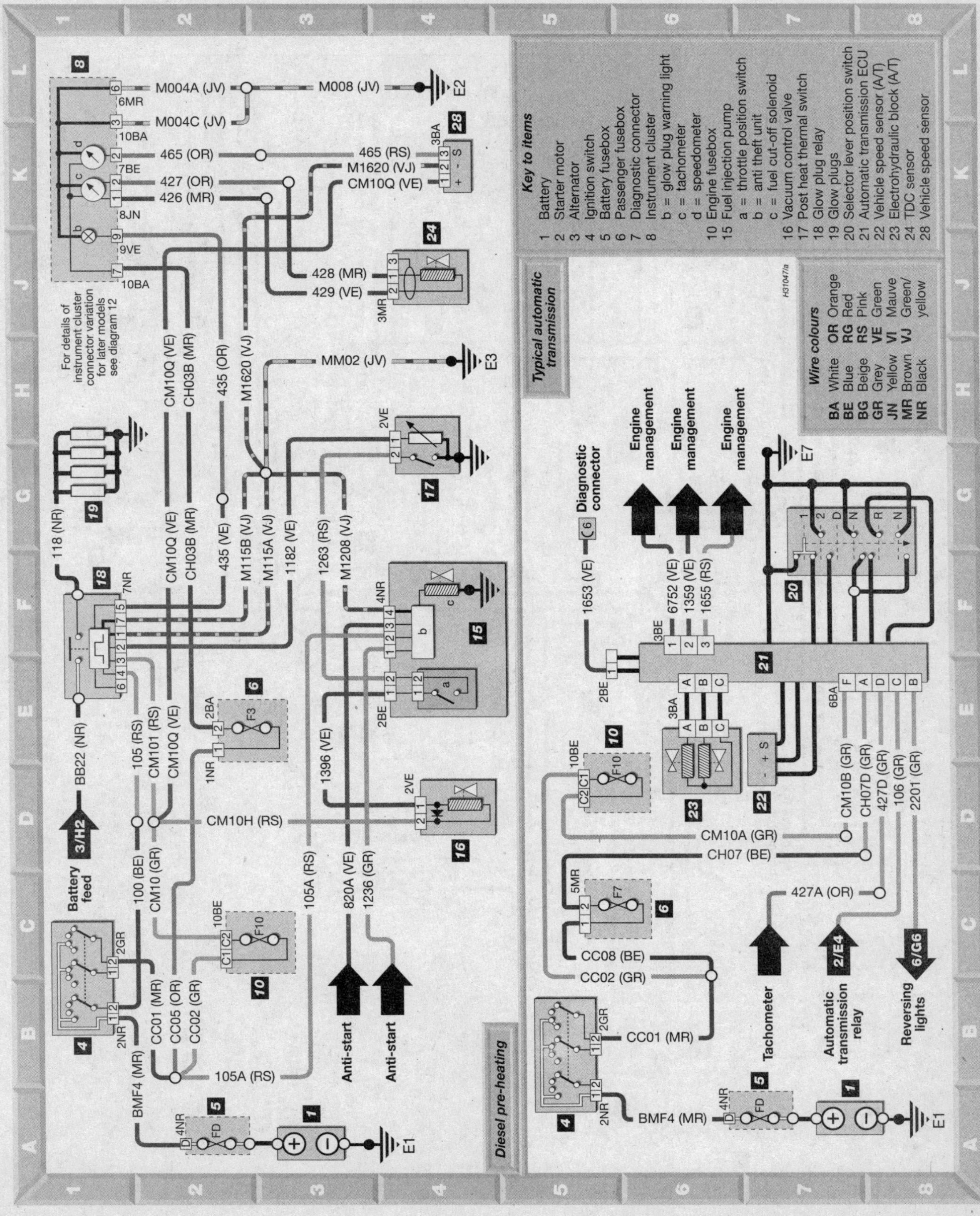

Diesel pre-heating
Typical automatic transmission
Key to items
1 Battery
2 Starter motor
3 Alternator
4 Ignition switch
5 Battery fusebox
6 Passenger fusebox
7 Diagnostic connector
8 Instrument cluster
b = glow plug warning light
c = tachometer
d = speedometer
10 Engine fusebox
15 Fuel injection pump
a = throttle position switch
b = anti theft unit
c = fuel cut-off solenoid
16 Vacuum control valve
17 Post heat thermal switch
18 Glow plug relay
19 Glow plugs
20 Selector lever position switch
21 Automatic transmission ECU
22 Vehicle speed sensor (A/T)
23 Electrohydraulic block (A/T)
24 TDC sensor
28 Vehicle speed sensor
Wire colours
BA White
BE Blue
BG Beige
GR Grey
JN Yellow
MR Brown
NR Black
OR Orange
RG Red
RS Pink
VE Green
VI Mauve
VJ Green/yellow
H31047/a

Diagram 3 : Typical Diesel pre-heating and automatic transmission

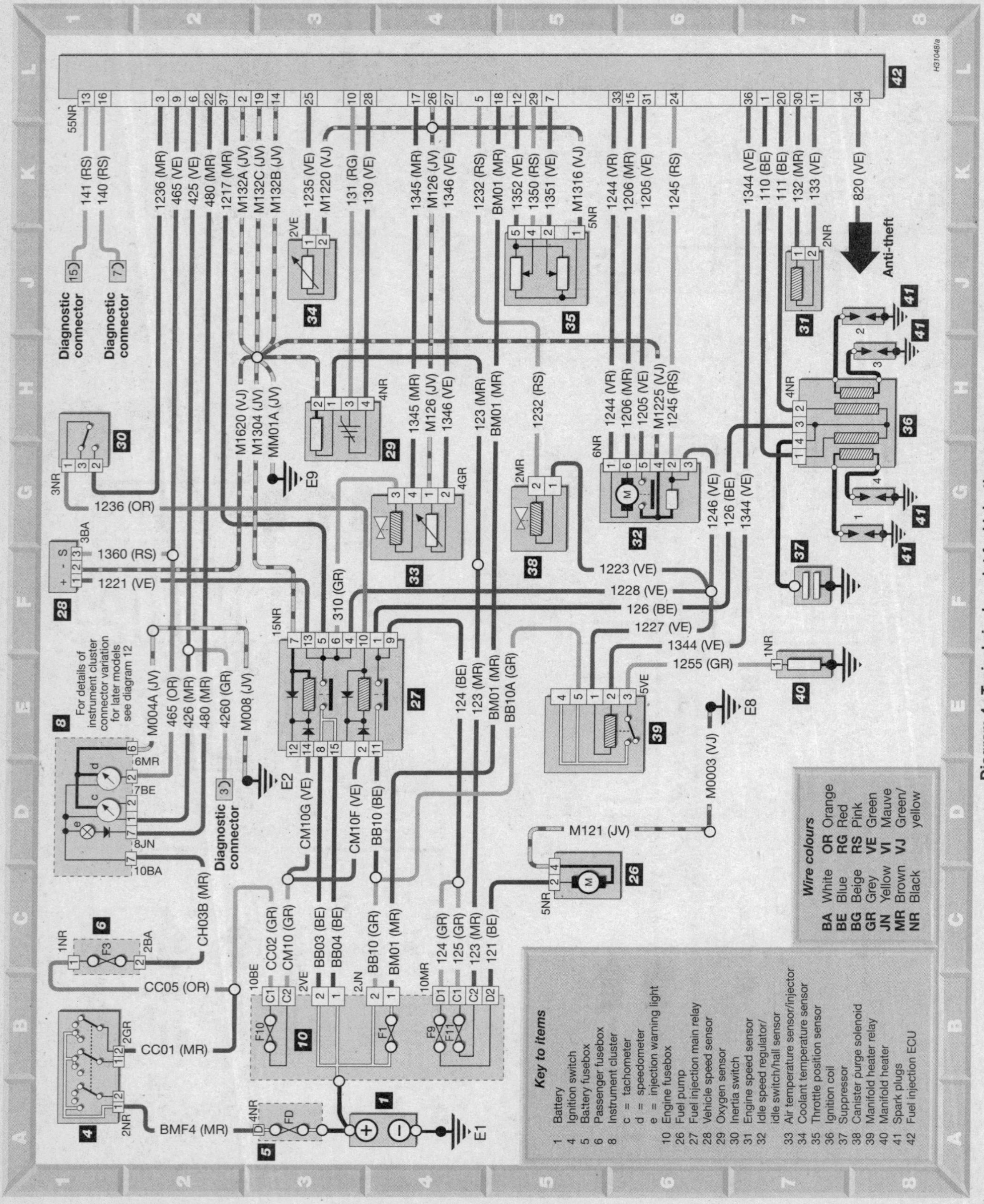
Key to items
1 Battery
4 Ignition switch
5 Battery fusebox
6 Passenger fusebox
8 Instrument cluster
c = tachometer
d = speedometer
e = injection warning light
10 Engine fusebox
26 Fuel pump
27 Fuel injection main relay
28 Vehicle speed sensor
29 Oxygen sensor
30 Inertia switch
31 Engine speed sensor
32 Idle speed regulator/idle switch/hall sensor
33 Air temperature sensor/injector
34 Coolant temperature sensor
35 Throttle position sensor
36 Ignition coil
37 Suppressor
38 Canister purge solenoid
39 Manifold heater relay
40 Manifold heater
41 Spark plugs
42 Fuel injection ECU
Wire colours
BA White
BE Blue
BG Beige
GR Grey
JN Yellow
MR Brown
NR Black
OR Orange
RG Red
RS Pink
VE Green
VI Mauve
VJ Green/yellow
Diagnostic connector
Anti-theft
For details of instrument cluster connector variation for later models see diagram 12
H31048/a

Diagram 4 : Typical single-point fuel injection system

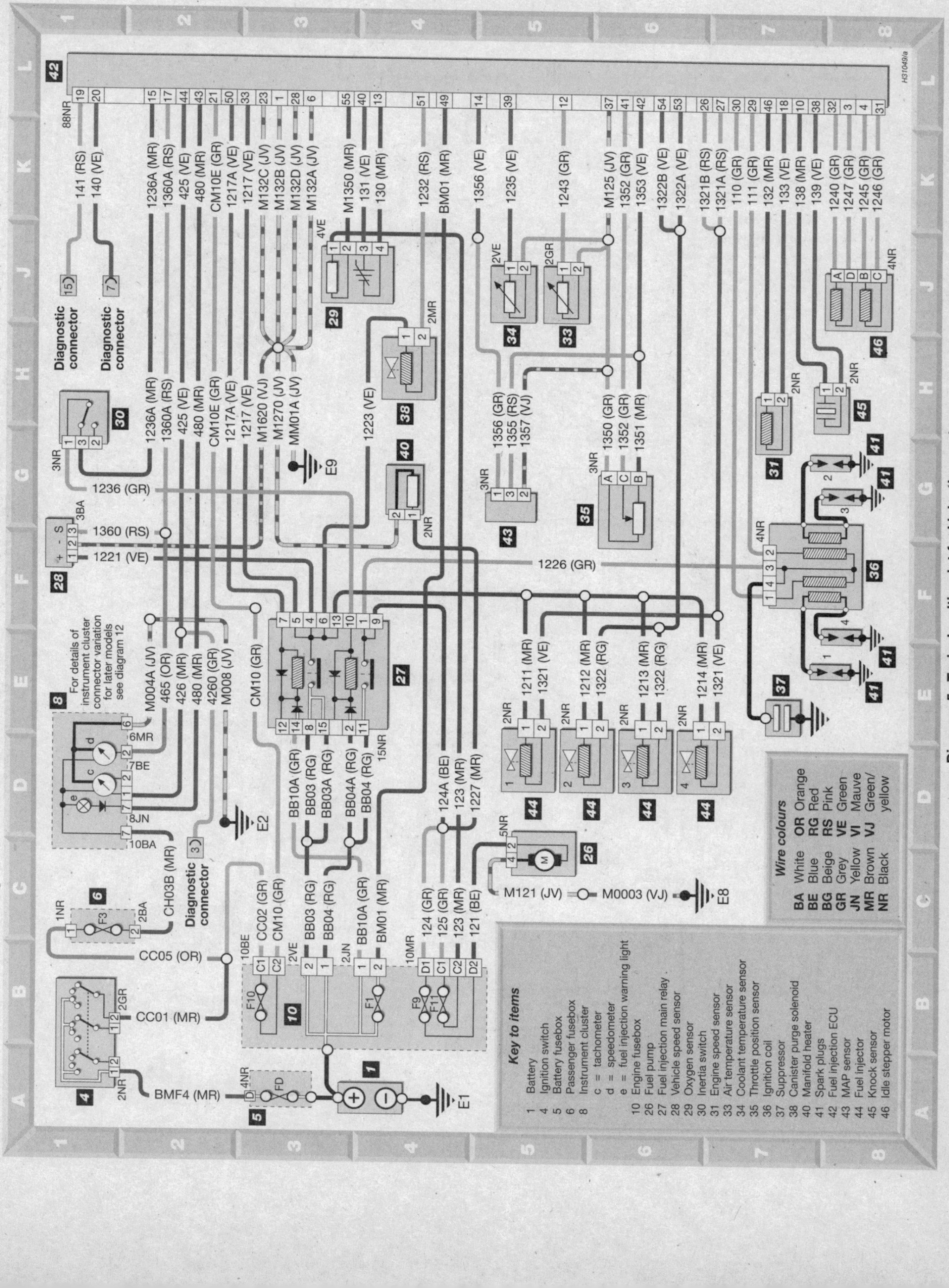

Diagram 5 : Typical multi-point fuel injection system

Key to items

1 Battery
4 Ignition switch
5 Battery fusebox
6 Passenger fusebox
8 Instrument cluster
c = tachometer
d = speedometer
e = fuel injection warning light
10 Engine fusebox
26 Fuel pump
27 Fuel injection main relay
28 Vehicle speed sensor
29 Oxygen sensor
30 Inertia switch
31 Engine speed sensor
33 Air temperature sensor
34 Coolant temperature sensor
35 Throttle position sensor
36 Ignition coil
37 Suppressor
38 Canister purge solenoid
40 Manifold heater
41 Spark plugs
42 Fuel injection ECU
43 MAP sensor
44 Fuel injector
45 Knock sensor
46 Idle stepper motor

Wire colours

BA	White	OR	Orange
BE	Blue	RG	Red
BG	Beige	RS	Pink
GR	Grey	VE	Green
JN	Yellow	VI	Mauve
MR	Brown	VJ	Green/ yellow
NR	Black		

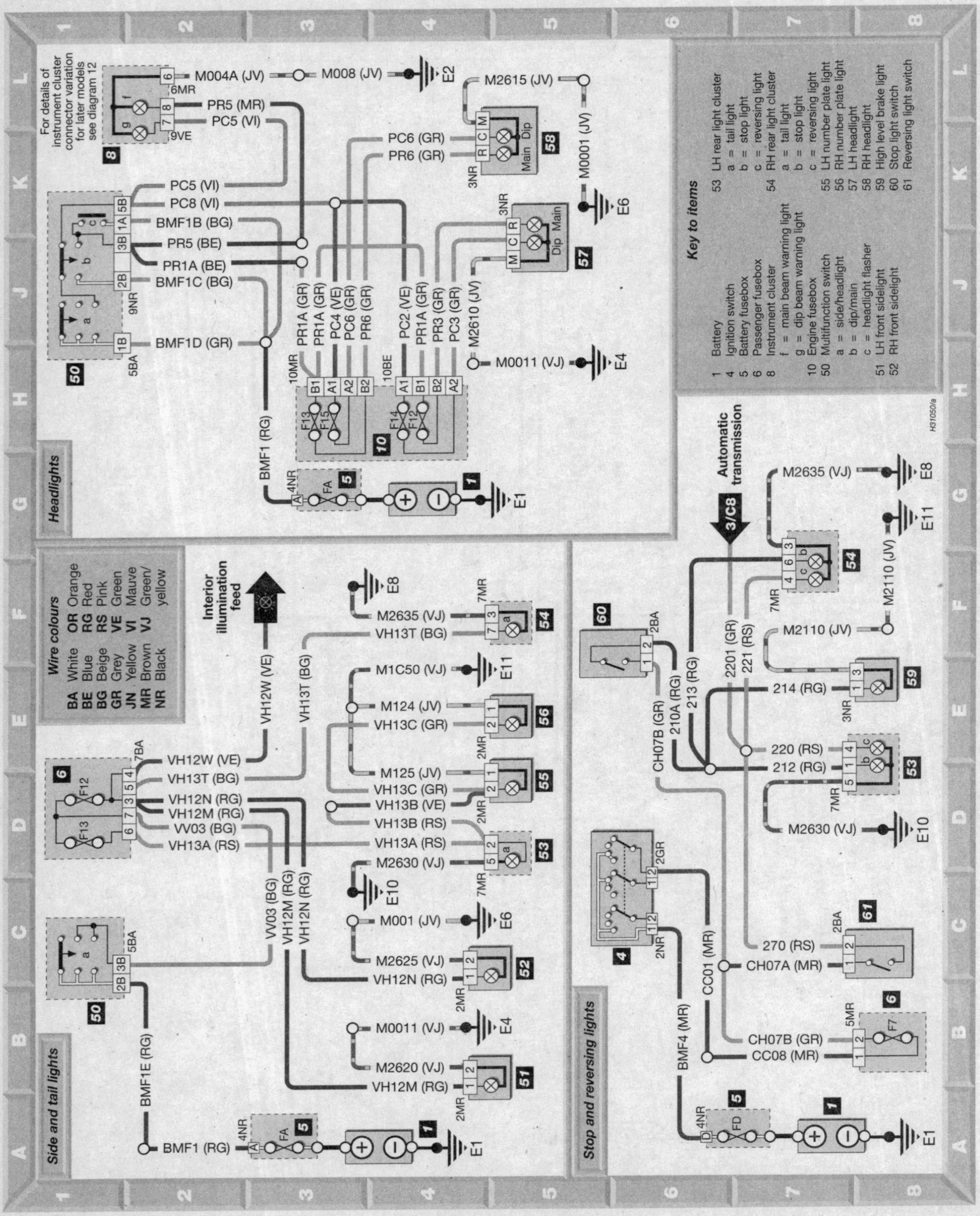

Diagram 6 : Typical side, tail, stop, reversing and headlights

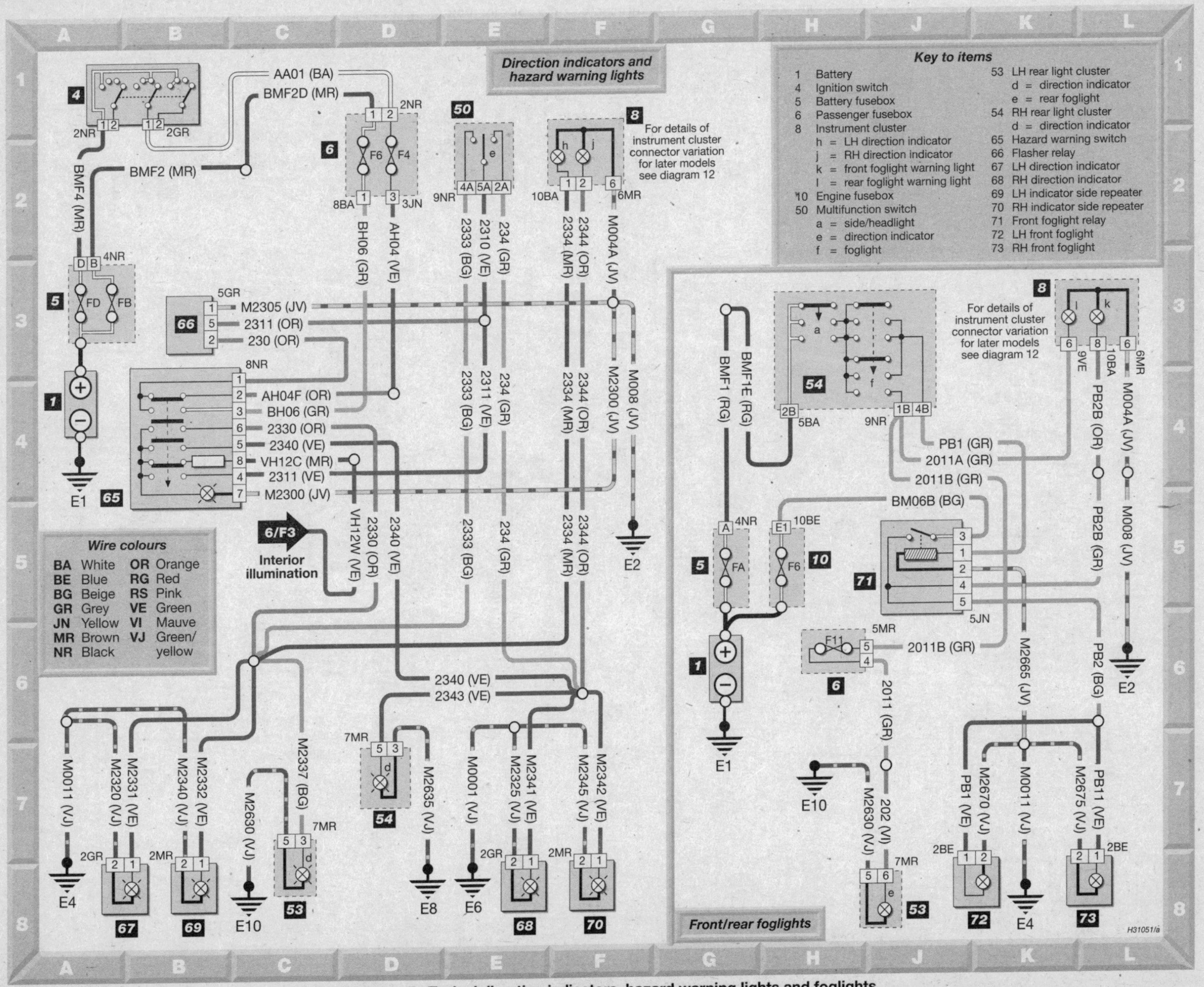
Direction indicators and hazard warning lights
Front/rear foglights
Key to items
1 Battery
4 Ignition switch
5 Battery fusebox
6 Passenger fusebox
8 Instrument cluster
h = LH direction indicator
j = RH direction indicator
k = front foglight warning light
l = rear foglight warning light
10 Engine fusebox
50 Multifunction switch
a = side/headlight
e = direction indicator
f = foglight
53 LH rear light cluster
d = direction indicator
e = rear foglight
54 RH rear light cluster
d = direction indicator
65 Hazard warning switch
66 Flasher relay
67 LH direction indicator
68 RH direction indicator
69 LH indicator side repeater
70 RH indicator side repeater
71 Front foglight relay
72 LH front foglight
73 RH front foglight
Wire colours
BA White
BE Blue
BG Beige
GR Grey
JN Yellow
MR Brown
NR Black
OR Orange
RG Red
RS Pink
VE Green
VI Mauve
VJ Green/yellow
For details of instrument cluster connector variation for later models see diagram 12
6/F3 Interior illumination
H31051/a

Diagram 7 : Typical direction indicators, hazard warning lights and foglights

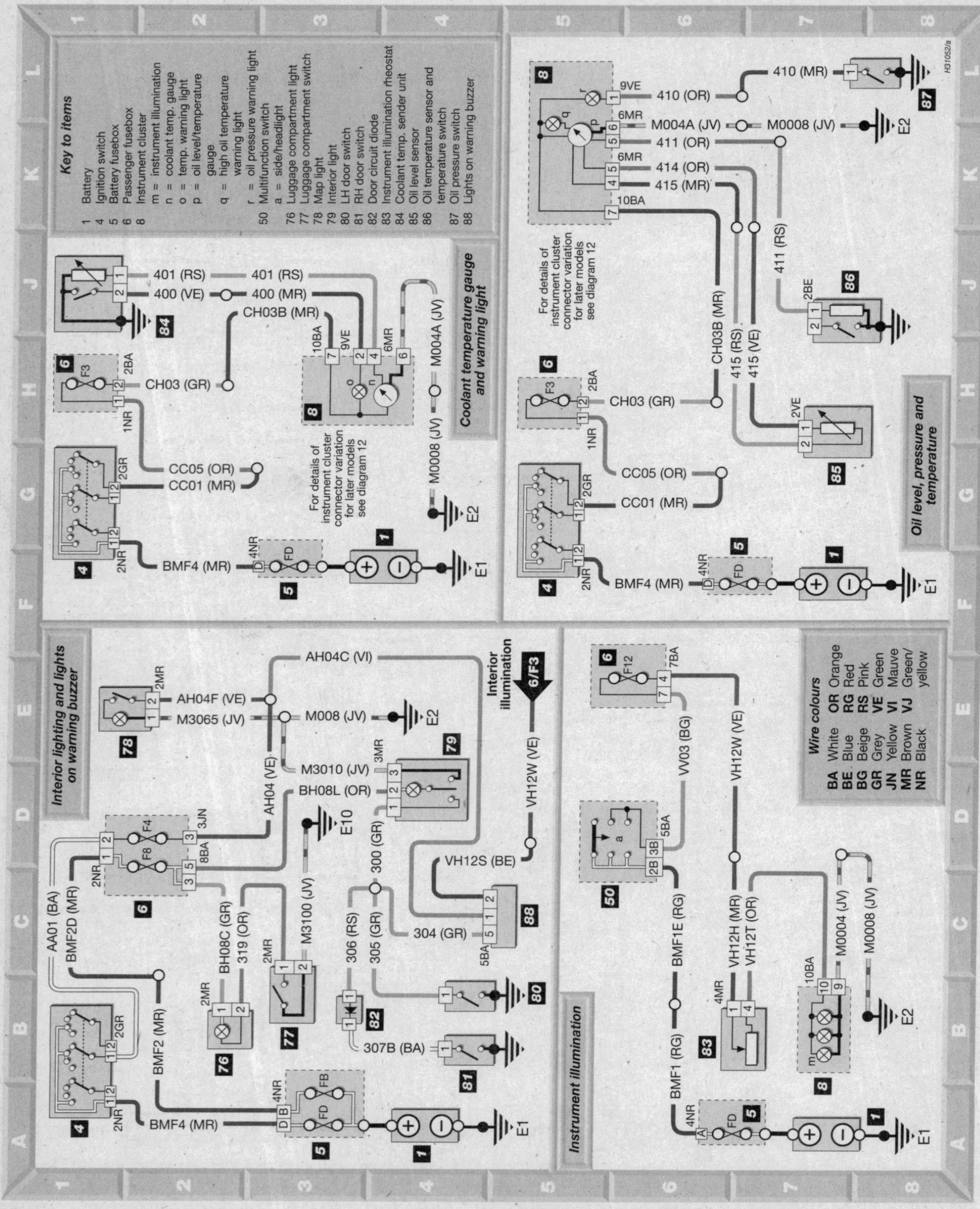

Interior lighting and lights on warning buzzer
Coolant temperature gauge and warning light
Instrument illumination
Oil level, pressure and temperature
Key to items
1 Battery
4 Ignition switch
5 Battery fusebox
6 Passenger fusebox
8 Instrument cluster
m = instrument illumination
n = coolant temp. gauge
o = temp. warning light
p = oil level/temperature gauge
q = high oil temperature warning light
r = oil pressure warning light
50 Multifunction switch
a = side/headlight
76 Luggage compartment light
77 Luggage compartment switch
78 Map light
79 Interior light
80 LH door switch
81 RH door switch
82 Door circuit diode
83 Instrument illumination rheostat
84 Coolant temp. sender unit
85 Oil level sensor
86 Oil temperature sensor and temperature switch
87 Oil pressure switch
88 Lights on warning buzzer
Wire colours
BA White
BE Blue
BG Beige
GR Grey
JN Yellow
MR Brown
NR Black
OR Orange
RG Red
RS Pink
VE Green
VI Mauve
VJ Green/yellow
For details of instrument cluster connector variation for later models see diagram 12
Interior illumination 6/F3
H31052/a

Diagram 8 : Typical interior lighting, illumination, warning lights and gauges

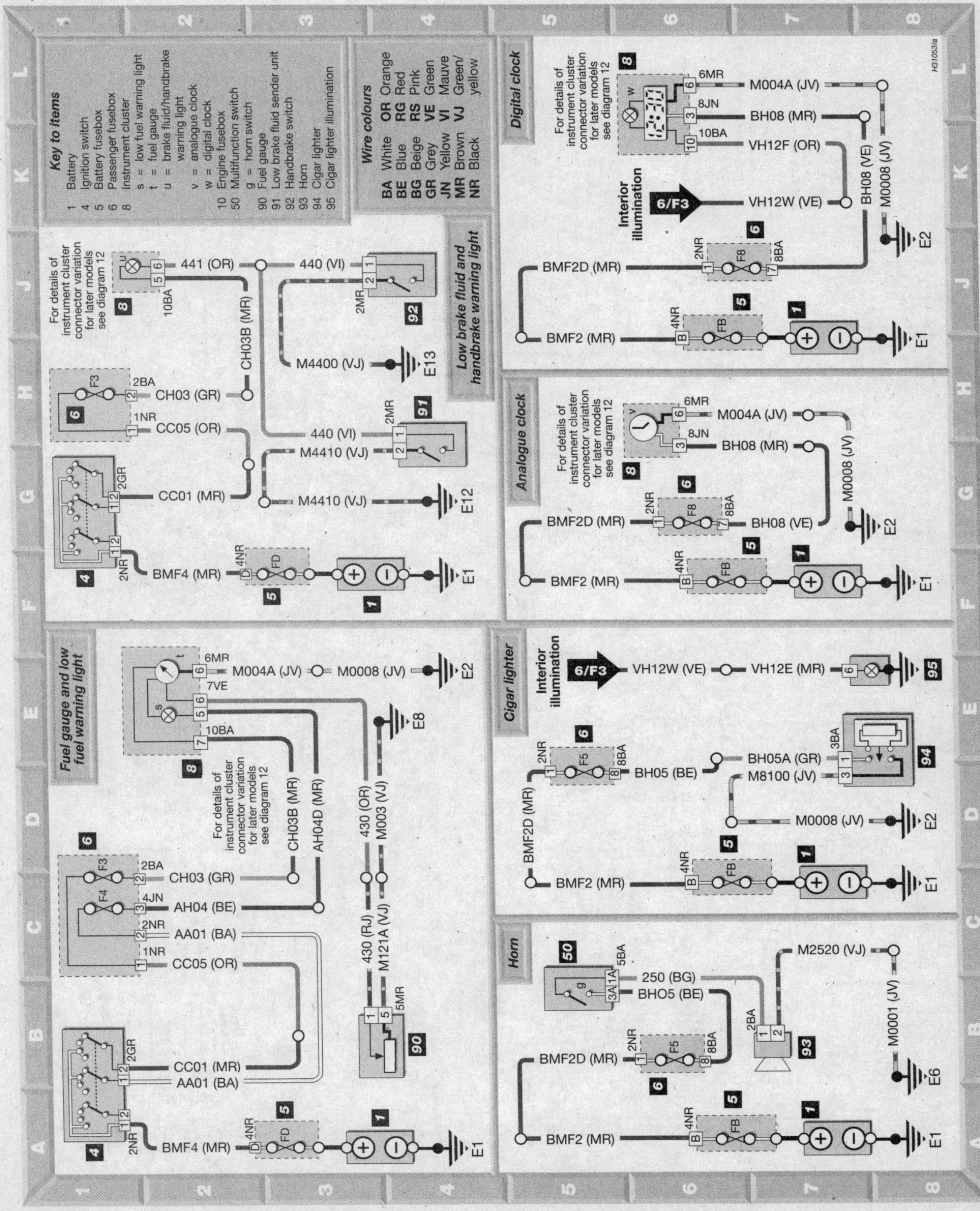

Diagram 9 : Typical warning lights and gauges continued, horn, cigar lighter and clock

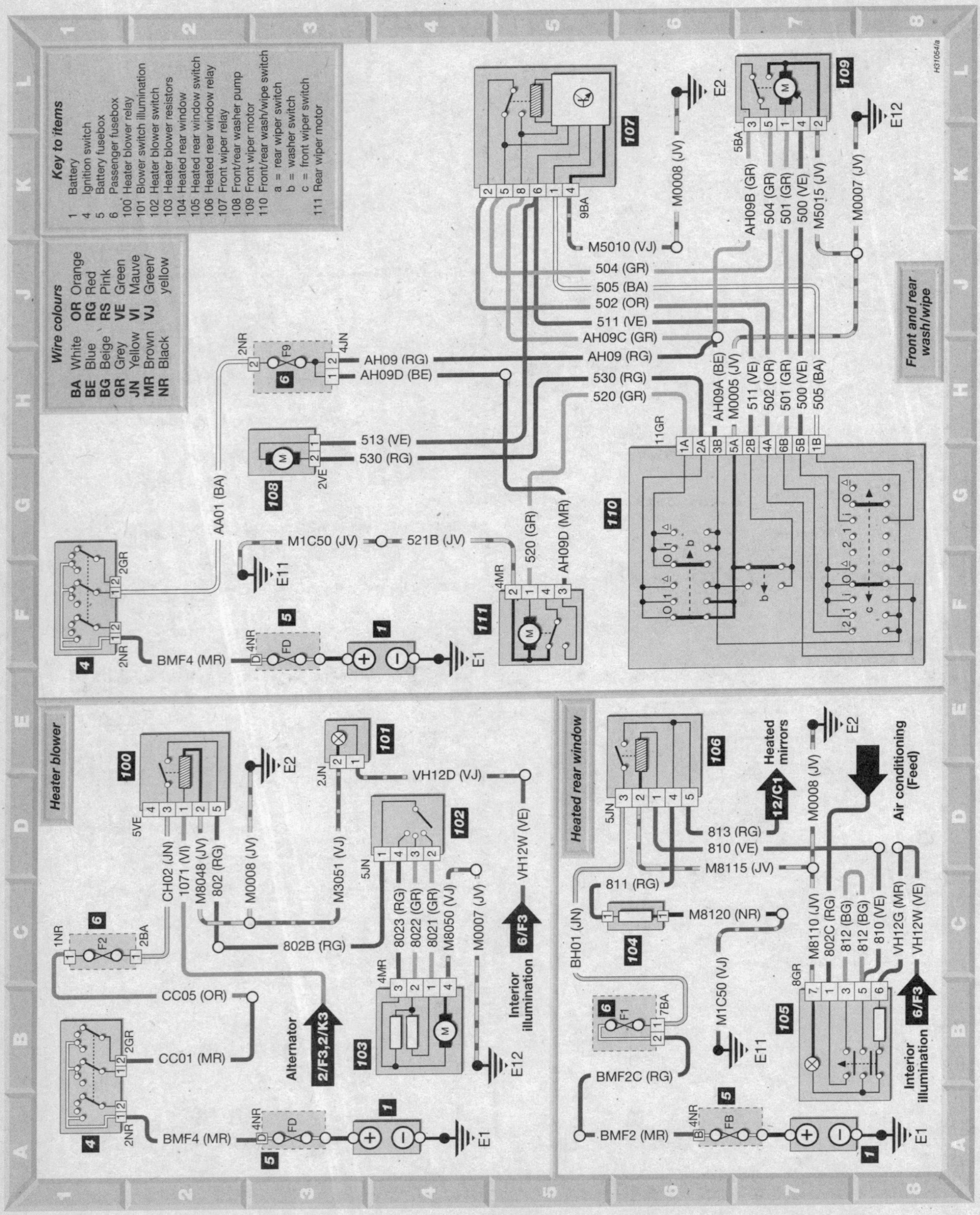

Diagram 10 : Typical heater blower, heated rear window, front and rear wash/wipe

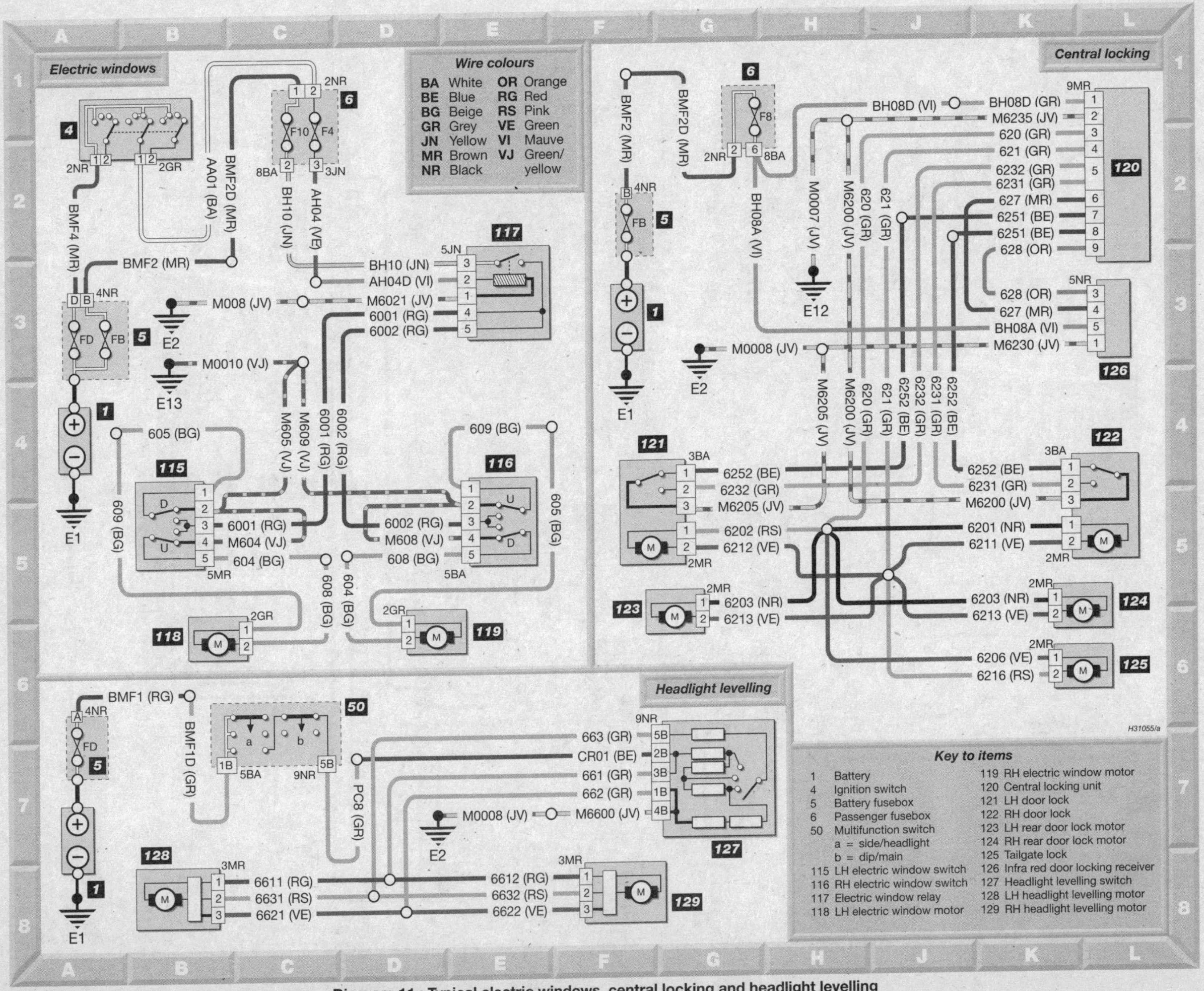
Electric windows
Central locking
Headlight levelling
Wire colours
BA White
BE Blue
BG Beige
GR Grey
JN Yellow
MR Brown
NR Black
OR Orange
RG Red
RS Pink
VE Green
VI Mauve
VJ Green/ yellow
H31055/a
Key to items
1 Battery
4 Ignition switch
5 Battery fusebox
6 Passenger fusebox
50 Multifunction switch
a = side/headlight
b = dip/main
115 LH electric window switch
116 RH electric window switch
117 Electric window relay
118 LH electric window motor
119 RH electric window motor
120 Central locking unit
121 LH door lock
122 RH door lock
123 LH rear door lock motor
124 RH rear door lock motor
125 Tailgate lock
126 Infra red door locking receiver
127 Headlight levelling switch
128 LH headlight levelling motor
129 RH headlight levelling motor

Diagram 11 : Typical electric windows, central locking and headlight levelling

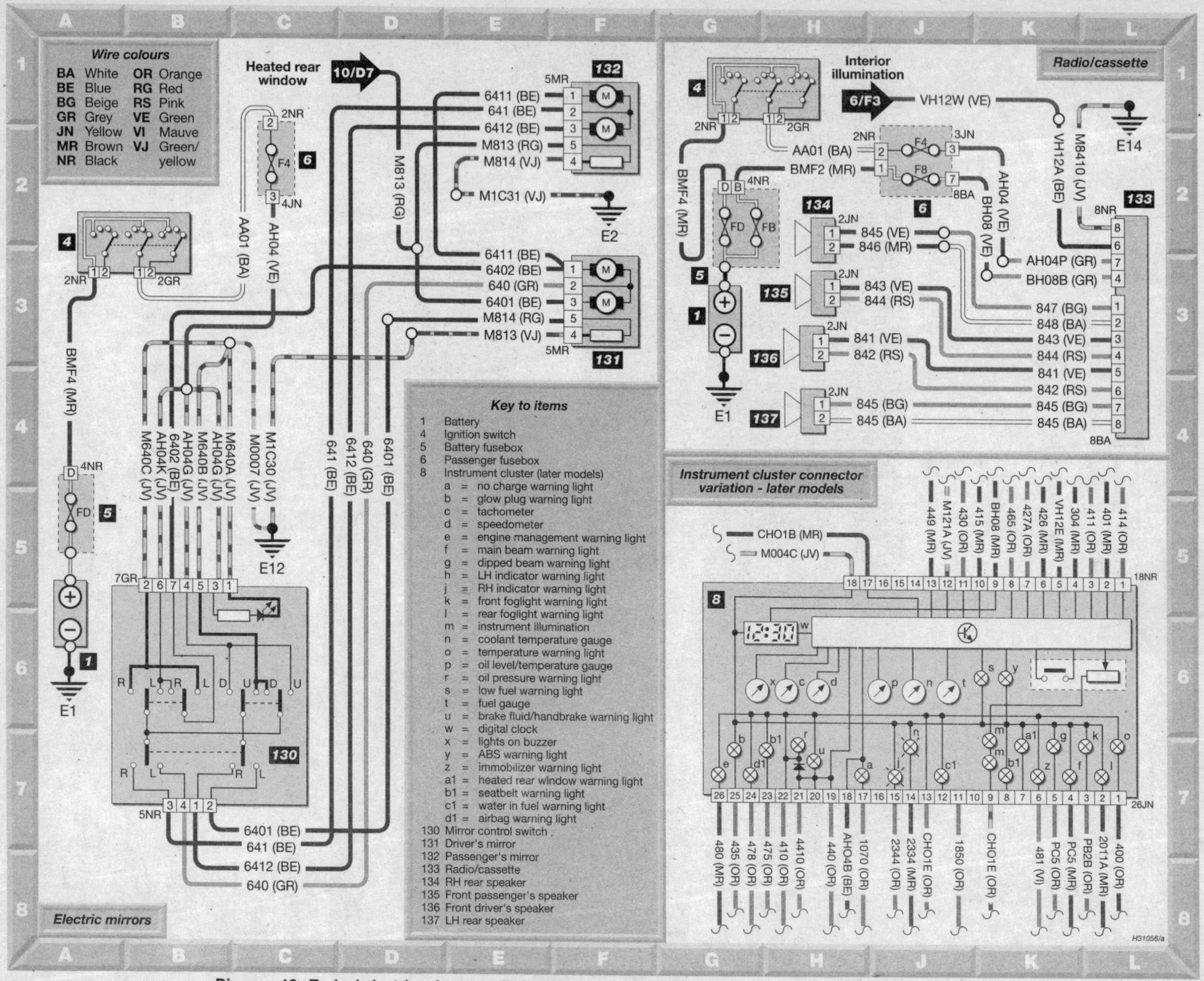
Wire colours
BA White
BE Blue
BG Beige
GR Grey
JN Yellow
MR Brown
NR Black
OR Orange
RG Red
RS Pink
VE Green
VI Mauve
VJ Green/yellow
Heated rear window
Electric mirrors
Interior illumination
Radio/cassette
Instrument cluster connector variation - later models
Key to items
1 Battery
4 Ignition switch
5 Battery fusebox
6 Passenger fusebox
8 Instrument cluster (later models)
a = no charge warning light
b = glow plug warning light
c = tachometer
d = speedometer
e = engine management warning light
f = main beam warning light
g = dipped beam warning light
h = LH indicator warning light
j = RH indicator warning light
k = front foglight warning light
l = rear foglight warning light
m = instrument illumination
n = coolant temperature gauge
o = temperature warning light
p = oil level/temperature gauge
r = oil pressure warning light
s = low fuel warning light
t = fuel gauge
u = brake fluid/handbrake warning light
w = digital clock
x = lights on buzzer
y = ABS warning light
z = immobilizer warning light
a1 = heated rear window warning light
b1 = seatbelt warning light
c1 = water in fuel warning light
d1 = airbag warning light
130 Mirror control switch
131 Driver's mirror
132 Passenger's mirror
133 Radio/cassette
134 RH rear speaker
135 Front passenger's speaker
136 Front driver's speaker
137 LH rear speaker
H31056/a

Diagram 12 : Typical electric mirrors, radio/cassette and instrument cluster connector variation (later models)

Dimensions and weights

Note: *All figures are approximate, and may vary according to model. Refer to manufacturer's data for exact figures.*

Dimensions	Except VTR, VTS	VTR, VTS
Overall length	3720 mm	3740 mm
Overall width (including mirrors)	1900 mm	1900 mm
Overall height (unladen)	1370 mm	1360 mm
Wheelbase	2390 mm	2390 mm

Weights	
Kerb weight	805 to 950 kg*
Maximum gross vehicle weight	1220 to 1400 kg*
Maximum roof rack load	50 kg
Maximum towing weight (braked trailer)	500 to 700 kg*
Maximum trailer nose weight	50 kg*

**Depending on model and specification.*

Conversion factors

Length (distance)

Inches (in)	x 25.4	= Millimetres (mm)	x 0.0394	= Inches (in)
Feet (ft)	x 0.305	= Metres (m)	x 3.281	= Feet (ft)
Miles	x 1.609	= Kilometres (km)	x 0.621	= Miles

Volume (capacity)

Cubic inches (cu in; in^3)	x 16.387	= Cubic centimetres (cc; cm^3)	x 0.061	= Cubic inches (cu in; in^3)
Imperial pints (Imp pt)	x 0.568	= Litres (l)	x 1.76	= Imperial pints (Imp pt)
Imperial quarts (Imp qt)	x 1.137	= Litres (l)	x 0.88	= Imperial quarts (Imp qt)
Imperial quarts (Imp qt)	x 1.201	= US quarts (US qt)	x 0.833	= Imperial quarts (Imp qt)
US quarts (US qt)	x 0.946	= Litres (l)	x 1.057	= US quarts (US qt)
Imperial gallons (Imp gal)	x 4.546	= Litres (l)	x 0.22	= Imperial gallons (Imp gal)
Imperial gallons (Imp gal)	x 1.201	= US gallons (US gal)	x 0.833	= Imperial gallons (Imp gal)
US gallons (US gal)	x 3.785	= Litres (l)	x 0.264	= US gallons (US gal)

Mass (weight)

Ounces (oz)	x 28.35	= Grams (g)	x 0.035	= Ounces (oz)
Pounds (lb)	x 0.454	= Kilograms (kg)	x 2.205	= Pounds (lb)

Force

Ounces-force (ozf; oz)	x 0.278	= Newtons (N)	x 3.6	= Ounces-force (ozf; oz)
Pounds-force (lbf; lb)	x 4.448	= Newtons (N)	x 0.225	= Pounds-force (lbf; lb)
Newtons (N)	x 0.1	= Kilograms-force (kgf; kg)	x 9.81	= Newtons (N)

Pressure

Pounds-force per square inch (psi; lbf/in^2; lb/in^2)	x 0.070	= Kilograms-force per square centimetre (kgf/cm^2; kg/cm^2)	x 14.223	= Pounds-force per square inch (psi; lbf/in^2; lb/in^2)
Pounds-force per square inch (psi; lbf/in^2; lb/in^2)	x 0.068	= Atmospheres (atm)	x 14.696	= Pounds-force per square inch (psi; lbf/in^2; lb/in^2)
Pounds-force per square inch (psi; lbf/in^2; lb/in^2)	x 0.069	= Bars	x 14.5	= Pounds-force per square inch (psi; lbf/in^2; lb/in^2)
Pounds-force per square inch (psi; lbf/in^2; lb/in^2)	x 6.895	= Kilopascals (kPa)	x 0.145	= Pounds-force per square inch (psi; lbf/in^2; lb/in^2)
Kilopascals (kPa)	x 0.01	= Kilograms-force per square centimetre (kgf/cm^2; kg/cm^2)	x 98.1	= Kilopascals (kPa)
Millibar (mbar)	x 100	= Pascals (Pa)	x 0.01	= Millibar (mbar)
Millibar (mbar)	x 0.0145	= Pounds-force per square inch (psi; lbf/in^2; lb/in^2)	x 68.947	= Millibar (mbar)
Millibar (mbar)	x 0.75	= Millimetres of mercury (mmHg)	x 1.333	= Millibar (mbar)
Millibar (mbar)	x 0.401	= Inches of water (inH_2O)	x 2.491	= Millibar (mbar)
Millimetres of mercury (mmHg)	x 0.535	= Inches of water (inH_2O)	x 1.868	= Millimetres of mercury (mmHg)
Inches of water (inH_2O)	x 0.036	= Pounds-force per square inch (psi; lbf/in^2; lb/in^2)	x 27.68	= Inches of water (inH_2O)

Torque (moment of force)

Pounds-force inches (lbf in; lb in)	x 1.152	= Kilograms-force centimetre (kgf cm; kg cm)	x 0.868	= Pounds-force inches (lbf in; lb in)
Pounds-force inches (lbf in; lb in)	x 0.113	= Newton metres (Nm)	x 8.85	= Pounds-force inches (lbf in; lb in)
Pounds-force inches (lbf in; lb in)	x 0.083	= Pounds-force feet (lbf ft; lb ft)	x 12	= Pounds-force inches (lbf in; lb in)
Pounds-force feet (lbf ft; lb ft)	x 0.138	= Kilograms-force metres (kgf m; kg m)	x 7.233	= Pounds-force feet (lbf ft; lb ft)
Pounds-force feet (lbf ft; lb ft)	x 1.356	= Newton metres (Nm)	x 0.738	= Pounds-force feet (lbf ft; lb ft)
Newton metres (Nm)	x 0.102	= Kilograms-force metres (kgf m; kg m)	x 9.804	= Newton metres (Nm)

Power

Horsepower (hp)	x 745.7	= Watts (W)	x 0.0013	= Horsepower (hp)

Velocity (speed)

Miles per hour (miles/hr; mph)	x 1.609	= Kilometres per hour (km/hr; kph)	x 0.621	= Miles per hour (miles/hr; mph)

Fuel consumption*

Miles per gallon, Imperial (mpg)	x 0.354	= Kilometres per litre (km/l)	x 2.825	= Miles per gallon, Imperial (mpg)
Miles per gallon, US (mpg)	x 0.425	= Kilometres per litre (km/l)	x 2.352	= Miles per gallon, US (mpg)

Temperature

Degrees Fahrenheit = (°C x 1.8) + 32

Degrees Celsius (Degrees Centigrade; °C) = (°F - 32) x 0.56

** It is common practice to convert from miles per gallon (mpg) to litres/100 kilometres (l/100km), where mpg x l/100 km = 282*

Spare parts are available from many sources, including maker's appointed garages, accessory shops, and motor factors. To be sure of obtaining the correct parts, it will sometimes be necessary to quote the vehicle identification number. If possible, it can also be useful to take the old parts along for positive identification. Items such as starter motors and alternators may be available under a service exchange scheme - any parts returned should always be clean.

Our advice regarding spare part sources is as follows.

Officially-appointed garages

This is the best source of parts which are peculiar to your car, and which are not otherwise generally available (eg badges, interior trim, certain body panels, etc). It is also the only place at which you should buy parts if the vehicle is still under warranty.

Accessory shops

These are very good places to buy materials and components needed for the maintenance of your car (oil, air and fuel filters, spark plugs, light bulbs, drivebelts, oils and greases, brake pads, touch-up paint, etc). Components of this nature sold by a reputable shop are of the same standard as those used by the car manufacturer.

Besides components, these shops also sell tools and general accessories, usually have convenient opening hours, charge lower prices, and can often be found not far from home. Some accessory shops have parts counters where the components needed for almost any repair job can be purchased or ordered.

Motor factors

Good factors will stock all the more important components which wear out comparatively quickly, and can sometimes supply individual components needed for the overhaul of a larger assembly (eg brake seals and hydraulic parts, bearing shells, pistons, valves, alternator brushes). They may also handle work such as cylinder block reboring, crankshaft regrinding and balancing, etc.

Tyre and exhaust specialists

These outlets may be independent, or members of a local or national chain. They frequently offer competitive prices when compared with a main dealer or local garage, but it will pay to obtain several quotes before making a decision. When researching prices, also ask what "extras" may be added - for instance, fitting a new valve and balancing the wheel are both commonly charged on top of the price of a new tyre.

Other sources

Beware of parts or materials obtained from market stalls, car boot sales or similar outlets. Such items are not invariably sub-standard, but there is little chance of compensation if they do prove unsatisfactory. In the case of safety-critical components such as brake pads, there is the risk not only of financial loss but also of an accident causing injury or death.

Second-hand components or assemblies obtained from a car breaker can be a good buy in some circumstances, but this sort of purchase is best made by the experienced DIY mechanic.

Vehicle identification

Modifications are a continuing and unpublicised process in vehicle manufacture, quite apart from major model changes. Spare parts manuals and lists are compiled upon a numerical basis, the individual vehicle identification numbers being essential to correct identification of the component concerned.

The VIN plate is located on the inside rear edge of the luggage compartment

When ordering spare parts, always give as much information as possible. Quote the car model, year of manufacture, body and engine numbers as appropriate.

The *Vehicle Identification Number (VIN)* plate is located in the luggage compartment, next to the tailgate striker, and can be viewed once the tailgate is open **(see illustration)**. The plate carries the VIN and vehicle weight information, as well as paint and trim colour codes.

The *chassis number* is stamped into the body, along the top edge of the bulkhead at the rear of the engine compartment, and can be viewed with the bonnet open **(see illustration)**. On some models, the chassis number may also be etched into the windscreen and window glass.

The *engine number* is situated on the left-hand end of the front face of the cylinder block. On models with an aluminium cylinder block, the number is stamped on a plate which is riveted to the block **(see illustration)**; on models with a cast-iron cylinder block, the number is stamped on a machined surface on the cylinder block, at the flywheel end. The first part of the engine number gives the engine code - eg "HDZ".

The *paint code* is stamped onto the left-hand suspension turret (first three letters only) **(see illustration)**.

The chassis number appears on the top of the bulkhead at the rear of the engine compartment

The engine number on aluminium-block engines appears on a plate riveted to the block

The paint code is stamped on the left-hand suspension turret

Whenever servicing, repair or overhaul work is carried out on the car or its components, observe the following procedures and instructions. This will assist in carrying out the operation efficiently and to a professional standard of workmanship.

Joint mating faces and gaskets

When separating components at their mating faces, never insert screwdrivers or similar implements into the joint between the faces in order to prise them apart. This can cause severe damage which results in oil leaks, coolant leaks, etc upon reassembly. Separation is usually achieved by tapping along the joint with a soft-faced hammer in order to break the seal. However, note that this method may not be suitable where dowels are used for component location.

Where a gasket is used between the mating faces of two components, a new one must be fitted on reassembly; fit it dry unless otherwise stated in the repair procedure. Make sure that the mating faces are clean and dry, with all traces of old gasket removed. When cleaning a joint face, use a tool which is unlikely to score or damage the face, and remove any burrs or nicks with an oilstone or fine file.

Make sure that tapped holes are cleaned with a pipe cleaner, and keep them free of jointing compound, if this is being used, unless specifically instructed otherwise.

Ensure that all orifices, channels or pipes are clear, and blow through them, preferably using compressed air.

Oil seals

Oil seals can be removed by levering them out with a wide flat-bladed screwdriver or similar implement. Alternatively, a number of self-tapping screws may be screwed into the seal, and these used as a purchase for pliers or some similar device in order to pull the seal free.

Whenever an oil seal is removed from its working location, either individually or as part of an assembly, it should be renewed.

The very fine sealing lip of the seal is easily damaged, and will not seal if the surface it contacts is not completely clean and free from scratches, nicks or grooves. If the original sealing surface of the component cannot be restored, and the manufacturer has not made provision for slight relocation of the seal relative to the sealing surface, the component should be renewed.

Protect the lips of the seal from any surface which may damage them in the course of fitting. Use tape or a conical sleeve where possible. Lubricate the seal lips with oil before fitting and, on dual-lipped seals, fill the space between the lips with grease.

Unless otherwise stated, oil seals must be fitted with their sealing lips toward the lubricant to be sealed.

Use a tubular drift or block of wood of the appropriate size to install the seal and, if the seal housing is shouldered, drive the seal down to the shoulder. If the seal housing is unshouldered, the seal should be fitted with its face flush with the housing top face (unless otherwise instructed).

Screw threads and fastenings

Seized nuts, bolts and screws are quite a common occurrence where corrosion has set in, and the use of penetrating oil or releasing fluid will often overcome this problem if the offending item is soaked for a while before attempting to release it. The use of an impact driver may also provide a means of releasing such stubborn fastening devices, when used in conjunction with the appropriate screwdriver bit or socket. If none of these methods works, it may be necessary to resort to the careful application of heat, or the use of a hacksaw or nut splitter device.

Studs are usually removed by locking two nuts together on the threaded part, and then using a spanner on the lower nut to unscrew the stud. Studs or bolts which have broken off below the surface of the component in which they are mounted can sometimes be removed using a stud extractor. Always ensure that a blind tapped hole is completely free from oil, grease, water or other fluid before installing the bolt or stud. Failure to do this could cause the housing to crack due to the hydraulic action of the bolt or stud as it is screwed in.

When tightening a castellated nut to accept a split pin, tighten the nut to the specified torque, where applicable, and then tighten further to the next split pin hole. Never slacken the nut to align the split pin hole, unless stated in the repair procedure.

When checking or retightening a nut or bolt to a specified torque setting, slacken the nut or bolt by a quarter of a turn, and then retighten to the specified setting. However, this should not be attempted where angular tightening has been used.

For some screw fastenings, notably cylinder head bolts or nuts, torque wrench settings are no longer specified for the latter stages of tightening, "angle-tightening" being called up instead. Typically, a fairly low torque wrench setting will be applied to the bolts/nuts in the correct sequence, followed by one or more stages of tightening through specified angles.

Locknuts, locktabs and washers

Any fastening which will rotate against a component or housing during tightening should always have a washer between it and the relevant component or housing.

Spring or split washers should always be renewed when they are used to lock a critical component such as a big-end bearing retaining bolt or nut. Locktabs which are folded over to retain a nut or bolt should always be renewed.

Self-locking nuts can be re-used in non-critical areas, providing resistance can be felt when the locking portion passes over the bolt or stud thread. However, it should be noted that self-locking stiffnuts tend to lose their effectiveness after long periods of use, and should then be renewed as a matter of course.

Split pins must always be replaced with new ones of the correct size for the hole.

When thread-locking compound is found on the threads of a fastener which is to be re-used, it should be cleaned off with a wire brush and solvent, and fresh compound applied on reassembly.

Special tools

Some repair procedures in this manual entail the use of special tools such as a press, two or three-legged pullers, spring compressors, etc. Wherever possible, suitable readily-available alternatives to the manufacturer's special tools are described, and are shown in use. In some instances, where no alternative is possible, it has been necessary to resort to the use of a manufacturer's tool, and this has been done for reasons of safety as well as the efficient completion of the repair operation. Unless you are highly-skilled and have a thorough understanding of the procedures described, never attempt to bypass the use of any special tool when the procedure described specifies its use. Not only is there a very great risk of personal injury, but expensive damage could be caused to the components involved.

Environmental considerations

When disposing of used engine oil, brake fluid, antifreeze, etc, give due consideration to any detrimental environmental effects. Do not, for instance, pour any of the above liquids down drains into the general sewage system, or onto the ground to soak away. Many local council refuse tips provide a facility for waste oil disposal, as do some garages. If none of these facilities are available, consult your local Environmental Health Department, or the National Rivers Authority, for further advice.

With the universal tightening-up of legislation regarding the emission of environmentally-harmful substances from motor vehicles, most vehicles have tamperproof devices fitted to the main adjustment points of the fuel system. These devices are primarily designed to prevent unqualified persons from adjusting the fuel/air mixture, with the chance of a consequent increase in toxic emissions. If such devices are found during servicing or overhaul, they should, wherever possible, be renewed or refitted in accordance with the manufacturer's requirements or current legislation.

OIL CARE
FOLLOW THE CODE

OIL BANK LINE
0800 66 33 66
www.oilbankline.org.uk

Note: It is antisocial and illegal to dump oil down the drain. To find the location of your local oil recycling bank, call this number free.

The jack supplied with the vehicle tool kit should only be used for changing the roadwheels - see "*Wheel changing*" at the front of this manual. When carrying out any other kind of work, raise the vehicle using a hydraulic (or "trolley") jack, and always supplement the jack with axle stands positioned under the vehicle jacking points.

When using a hydraulic jack or axle stands, always position the jack head or axle stand head under, or adjacent to, one of the relevant jacking points. Use a shaped block of wood on the jack head or axle stand if necessary, to prevent denting or scratching the underside of the sill. The jacking points are between two horizontal flanges in the lower sill - there are two jacking points on each side of the car, one behind the front wheel, and one in front of the rear wheel. On models where a body kit is fitted, the jacking points are indicated by small arrowhead-shaped indentations in the sill moulding **(see illustration)**.

To raise the front of the vehicle, Citroën recommend the use of a special lifting crossmember, which locates across the car between the mounting points at the rear of the suspension arms. Assuming that this tool is not available, raise one side at a time using axle stands positioned behind each front wheel **(see illustration)**. **Do not** jack the vehicle under the sump, or any of the steering or suspension components.

To raise the rear of the vehicle, remove the spare wheel from its cradle, and ensure that the cradle is positioned out of the way. Position the jack head under the rear crossmember, making sure that it is located as centrally as possible. Otherwise, raise one side at a time using axle stands positioned in front of each rear wheel; depending on the axle stands used, it may be necessary to fit a piece of wood between the stand and the jacking point, to prevent damage to the base of the sill **(see illustration)**. **Do not** attempt to raise the vehicle with the jack positioned underneath the spare wheel, as the vehicle floor will almost certainly be damaged.

Never work under, around, or near a raised vehicle, unless it is adequately supported in at least two places.

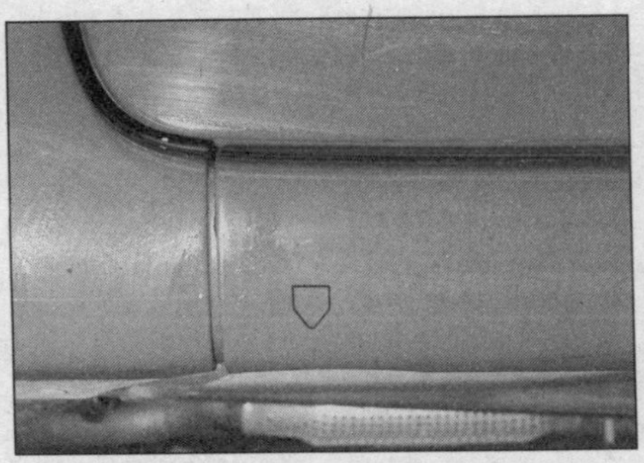

Models with a body kit have arrowhead markings to indicate the jacking point locations

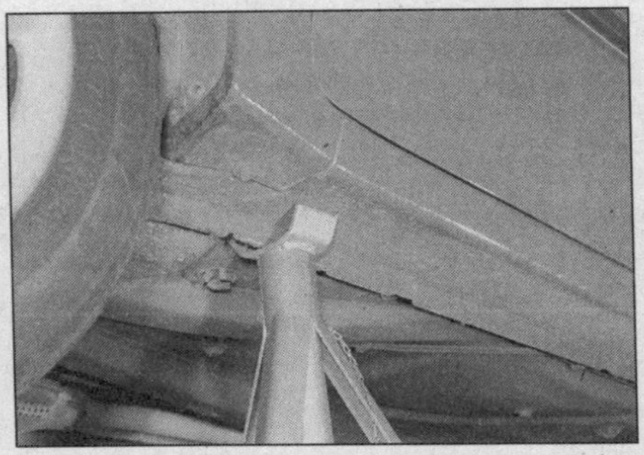

Axle stand positioned under a front jacking point

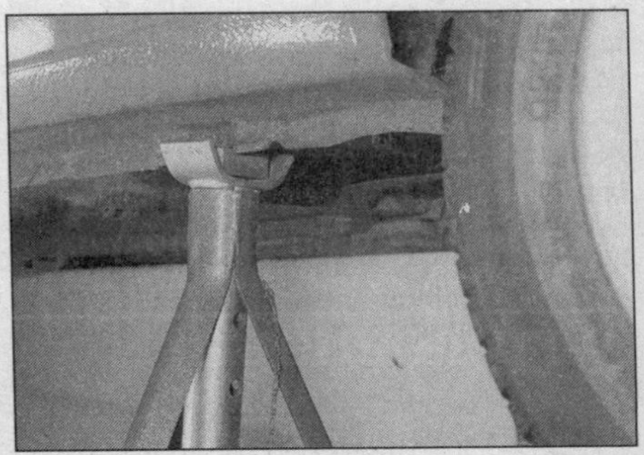

Axle stand and block of wood in use under a rear jacking point

Radio/cassette unit anti-theft system - precaution

The radio/cassette unit fitted by Citroën may be equipped with a built-in security code, to deter thieves. If the power source to the unit is cut, the anti-theft system will activate. Even if the power source is immediately reconnected, the unit will not function until the correct security code has been entered. Therefore, if you do not know the correct code, DO NOT disconnect the battery negative lead, or remove the radio/cassette unit from the vehicle. The exact procedure for reprogramming a unit which has been disconnected from its power supply varies from model to model. Consult the radio booklet which should have been supplied with the vehicle for specific details. On production of proof of ownership, a Citroën dealer (or possibly, an in-car entertainment specialist) should be able to enter the code.

Introduction

A selection of good tools is a fundamental requirement for anyone contemplating the maintenance and repair of a motor vehicle. For the owner who does not possess any, their purchase will prove a considerable expense, offsetting some of the savings made by doing-it-yourself. However, provided that the tools purchased meet the relevant national safety standards and are of good quality, they will last for many years and prove an extremely worthwhile investment.

To help the average owner to decide which tools are needed to carry out the various tasks detailed in this manual, we have compiled three lists of tools under the following headings: *Maintenance and minor repair, Repair and overhaul*, and *Special*. Newcomers to practical mechanics should start off with the *Maintenance and minor repair* tool kit, and confine themselves to the simpler jobs around the vehicle. Then, as confidence and experience grow, more difficult tasks can be undertaken, with extra tools being purchased as, and when, they are needed. In this way, a *Maintenance and minor repair* tool kit can be built up into a *Repair and overhaul* tool kit over a considerable period of time, without any major cash outlays. The experienced do-it-yourselfer will have a tool kit good enough for most repair and overhaul procedures, and will add tools from the *Special* category when it is felt that the expense is justified by the amount of use to which these tools will be put.

Maintenance and minor repair tool kit

The tools given in this list should be considered as a minimum requirement if routine maintenance, servicing and minor repair operations are to be undertaken. We recommend the purchase of combination spanners (ring one end, open-ended the other); although more expensive than open-ended ones, they do give the advantages of both types of spanner.

- ☐ *Combination spanners:*
Metric - 8 to 19 mm inclusive
- ☐ *Adjustable spanner - 35 mm jaw (approx.)*
- ☐ *Spark plug spanner (with rubber insert) - petrol models*
- ☐ *Spark plug gap adjustment tool - petrol models*
- ☐ *Set of feeler gauges*
- ☐ *Brake bleed nipple spanner*
- ☐ *Screwdrivers:*
Flat blade - 100 mm long x 6 mm dia
Cross blade - 100 mm long x 6 mm dia
Torx - various sizes (not all vehicles)
- ☐ *Combination pliers*
- ☐ *Hacksaw (junior)*
- ☐ *Tyre pump*
- ☐ *Tyre pressure gauge*
- ☐ *Oil can*
- ☐ *Oil filter removal tool*
- ☐ *Fine emery cloth*
- ☐ *Wire brush (small)*
- ☐ *Funnel (medium size)*
- ☐ *Sump drain plug key (not all vehicles)*

Repair and overhaul tool kit

These tools are virtually essential for anyone undertaking any major repairs to a motor vehicle, and are additional to those given in the *Maintenance and minor repair* list. Included in this list is a comprehensive set of sockets. Although these are expensive, they will be found invaluable as they are so versatile - particularly if various drives are included in the set. We recommend the half-inch square-drive type, as this can be used with most proprietary torque wrenches.

The tools in this list will sometimes need to be supplemented by tools from the *Special* list:

- ☐ *Sockets (or box spanners) to cover range in previous list (including Torx sockets)*
- ☐ *Reversible ratchet drive (for use with sockets)*
- ☐ *Extension piece, 250 mm (for use with sockets)*
- ☐ *Universal joint (for use with sockets)*
- ☐ *Flexible handle or sliding T "breaker bar" (for use with sockets)*
- ☐ *Torque wrench (for use with sockets)*
- ☐ *Self-locking grips*
- ☐ *Ball pein hammer*
- ☐ *Soft-faced mallet (plastic or rubber)*
- ☐ *Screwdrivers:*
Flat blade - long & sturdy, short (chubby), and narrow (electrician's) types
Cross blade – long & sturdy, and short (chubby) types
- ☐ *Pliers:*
Long-nosed
Side cutters (electrician's)
Circlip (internal and external)
- ☐ *Cold chisel - 25 mm*
- ☐ *Scriber*
- ☐ *Scraper*
- ☐ *Centre-punch*
- ☐ *Pin punch*
- ☐ *Hacksaw*
- ☐ *Brake hose clamp*
- ☐ *Brake/clutch bleeding kit*
- ☐ *Selection of twist drills*
- ☐ *Steel rule/straight-edge*
- ☐ *Allen keys (inc. splined/Torx type)*
- ☐ *Selection of files*
- ☐ *Wire brush*
- ☐ *Axle stands*
- ☐ *Jack (strong trolley or hydraulic type)*
- ☐ *Light with extension lead*
- ☐ *Universal electrical multi-meter*

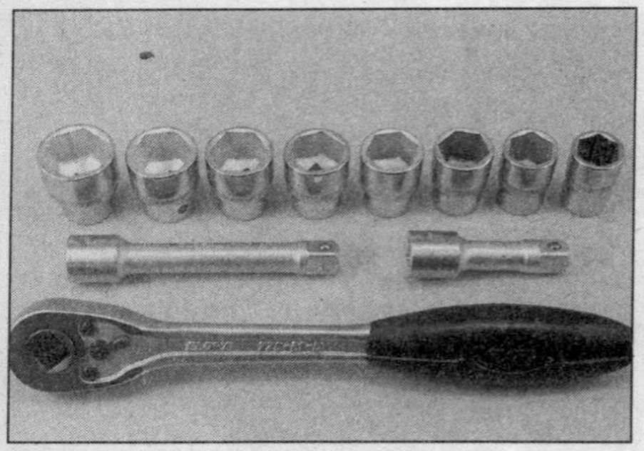

Sockets and reversible ratchet drive

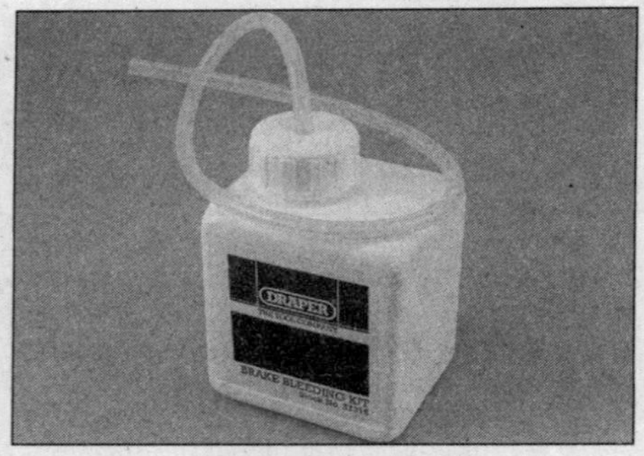

Brake bleeding kit

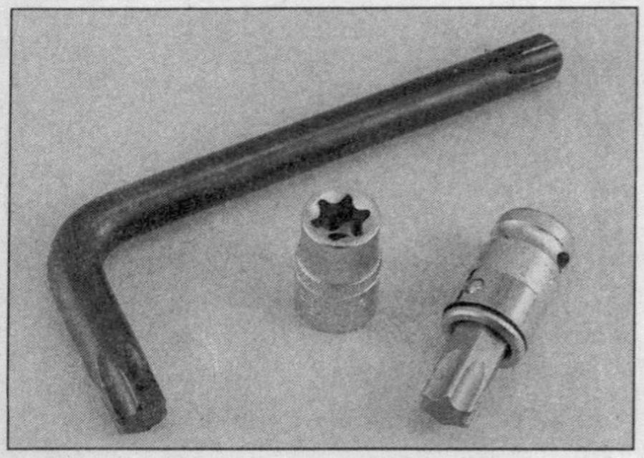

Torx key, socket and bit

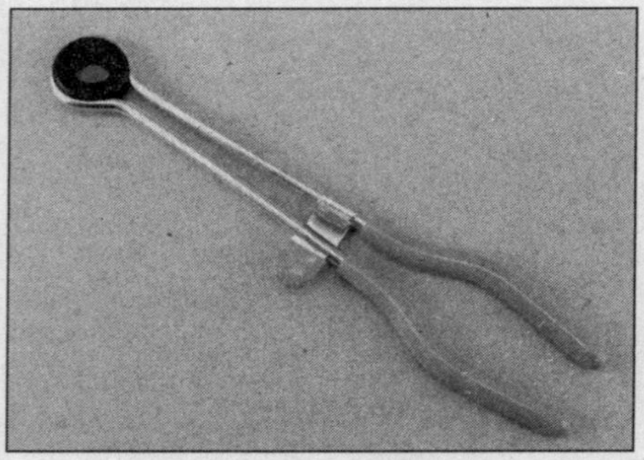

Hose clamp

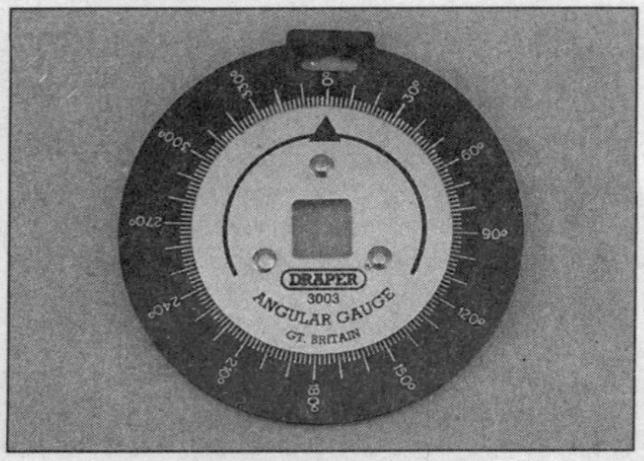

Angular-tightening gauge

Special tools

The tools in this list are those which are not used regularly, are expensive to buy, or which need to be used in accordance with their manufacturers' instructions. Unless relatively difficult mechanical jobs are undertaken frequently, it will not be economic to buy many of these tools. Where this is the case, you could consider clubbing together with friends (or joining a motorists' club) to make a joint purchase, or borrowing the tools against a deposit from a local garage or tool hire specialist. It is worth noting that many of the larger DIY superstores now carry a large range of special tools for hire at modest rates.

The following list contains only those tools and instruments freely available to the public, and not those special tools produced by the vehicle manufacturer specifically for its dealer network. You will find occasional references to these manufacturers' special tools in the text of this manual. Generally, an alternative method of doing the job without the vehicle manufacturers' special tool is given. However, sometimes there is no alternative to using them. Where this is the case and the relevant tool cannot be bought or borrowed, you will have to entrust the work to a dealer.

- ☐ *Angular-tightening gauge*
- ☐ *Valve spring compressor*
- ☐ *Valve grinding tool*
- ☐ *Piston ring compressor*
- ☐ *Piston ring removal/installation tool*
- ☐ *Cylinder bore hone*
- ☐ *Balljoint separator*
- ☐ *Coil spring compressors (where applicable)*
- ☐ *Two/three-legged hub and bearing puller*
- ☐ *Impact screwdriver*
- ☐ *Micrometer and/or vernier calipers*
- ☐ *Dial gauge*
- ☐ *Stroboscopic timing light*
- ☐ *Dwell angle meter/tachometer*
- ☐ *Fault code reader*
- ☐ *Cylinder compression gauge*
- ☐ *Hand-operated vacuum pump and gauge*
- ☐ *Clutch plate alignment set*
- ☐ *Brake shoe steady spring cup removal tool*
- ☐ *Bush and bearing removal/installation set*
- ☐ *Stud extractors*
- ☐ *Tap and die set*
- ☐ *Lifting tackle*
- ☐ *Trolley jack*

Buying tools

Reputable motor accessory shops and superstores often offer excellent quality tools at discount prices, so it pays to shop around.

Remember, you don't have to buy the most expensive items on the shelf, but it is always advisable to steer clear of the very cheap tools. Beware of 'bargains' offered on market stalls or at car boot sales. There are plenty of good tools around at reasonable prices, but always aim to purchase items which meet the relevant national safety standards. If in doubt, ask the proprietor or manager of the shop for advice before making a purchase.

Care and maintenance of tools

Having purchased a reasonable tool kit, it is necessary to keep the tools in a clean and serviceable condition. After use, always wipe off any dirt, grease and metal particles using a clean, dry cloth, before putting the tools away. Never leave them lying around after they have been used. A simple tool rack on the garage or workshop wall for items such as screwdrivers and pliers is a good idea. Store all normal spanners and sockets in a metal box. Any measuring instruments, gauges, meters, etc, must be carefully stored where they cannot be damaged or become rusty.

Take a little care when tools are used. Hammer heads inevitably become marked, and screwdrivers lose the keen edge on their blades from time to time. A little timely attention with emery cloth or a file will soon restore items like this to a good finish.

Working facilities

Not to be forgotten when discussing tools is the workshop itself. If anything more than routine maintenance is to be carried out, a suitable working area becomes essential.

It is appreciated that many an owner-mechanic is forced by circumstances to remove an engine or similar item without the benefit of a garage or workshop. Having done this, any repairs should always be done under the cover of a roof.

Wherever possible, any dismantling should be done on a clean, flat workbench or table at a suitable working height.

Any workbench needs a vice; one with a jaw opening of 100 mm is suitable for most jobs. As mentioned previously, some clean dry storage space is also required for tools, as well as for any lubricants, cleaning fluids, touch-up paints etc, which become necessary.

Another item which may be required, and which has a much more general usage, is an electric drill with a chuck capacity of at least 8 mm. This, together with a good range of twist drills, is virtually essential for fitting accessories.

Last, but not least, always keep a supply of old newspapers and clean, lint-free rags available, and try to keep any working area as clean as possible.

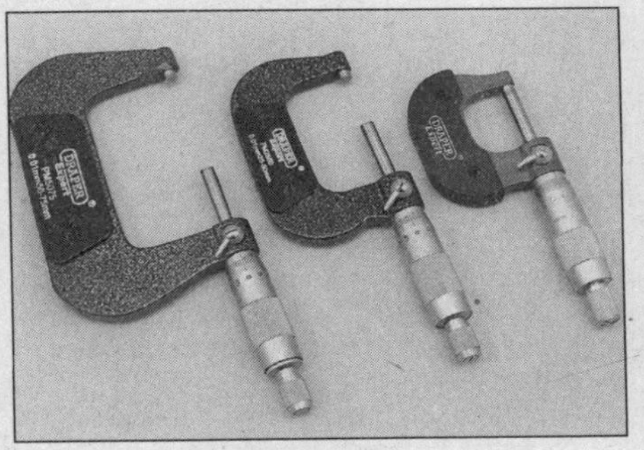

Micrometers

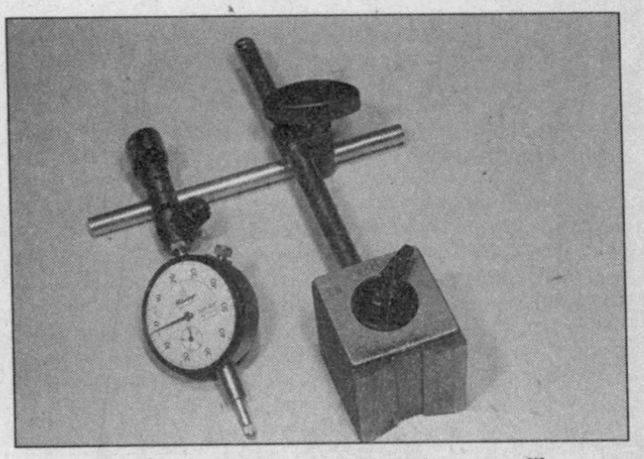

Dial test indicator ("dial gauge")

Strap wrench

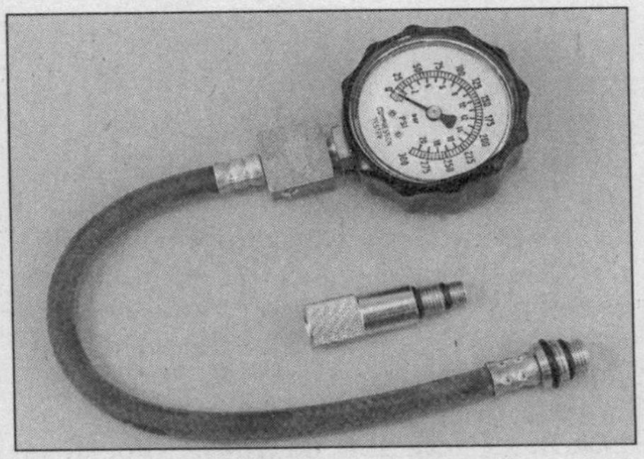

Compression tester

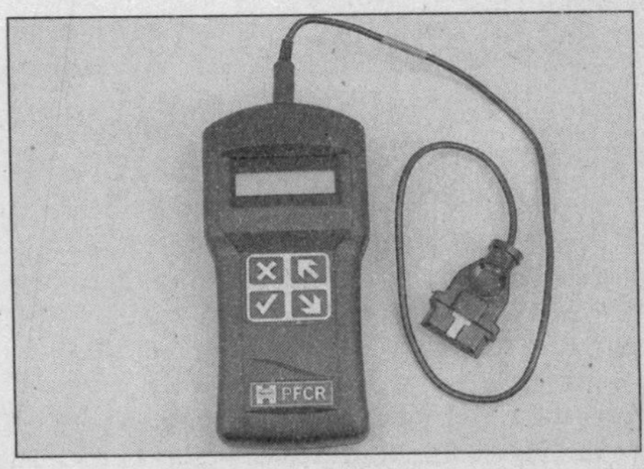

Fault code reader

This is a guide to getting your vehicle through the MOT test. Obviously it will not be possible to examine the vehicle to the same standard as the professional MOT tester. However, working through the following checks will enable you to identify any problem areas before submitting the vehicle for the test.

Where a testable component is in borderline condition, the tester has discretion in deciding whether to pass or fail it. The basis of such discretion is whether the tester would be happy for a close relative or friend to use the vehicle with the component in that condition. If the vehicle presented is clean and evidently well cared for, the tester may be more inclined to pass a borderline component than if the vehicle is scruffy and apparently neglected.

It has only been possible to summarise the test requirements here, based on the regulations in force at the time of printing. Test standards are becoming increasingly stringent, although there are some exemptions for older vehicles.

An assistant will be needed to help carry out some of these checks.

The checks have been sub-divided into four categories, as follows:

1 Checks carried out **FROM THE DRIVER'S SEAT**

2 Checks carried out **WITH THE VEHICLE ON THE GROUND**

3 Checks carried out **WITH THE VEHICLE RAISED AND THE WHEELS FREE TO TURN**

4 Checks carried out on **YOUR VEHICLE'S EXHAUST EMISSION SYSTEM**

1 Checks carried out FROM THE DRIVER'S SEAT

Handbrake

☐ Test the operation of the handbrake. Excessive travel (too many clicks) indicates incorrect brake or cable adjustment.

☐ Check that the handbrake cannot be released by tapping the lever sideways. Check the security of the lever mountings.

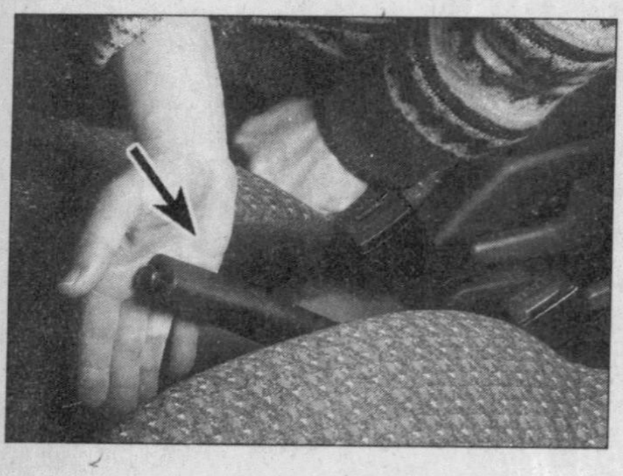

Footbrake

☐ Depress the brake pedal and check that it does not creep down to the floor, indicating a master cylinder fault. Release the pedal, wait a few seconds, then depress it again. If the pedal travels nearly to the floor before firm resistance is felt, brake adjustment or repair is necessary. If the pedal feels spongy, there is air in the hydraulic system which must be removed by bleeding.

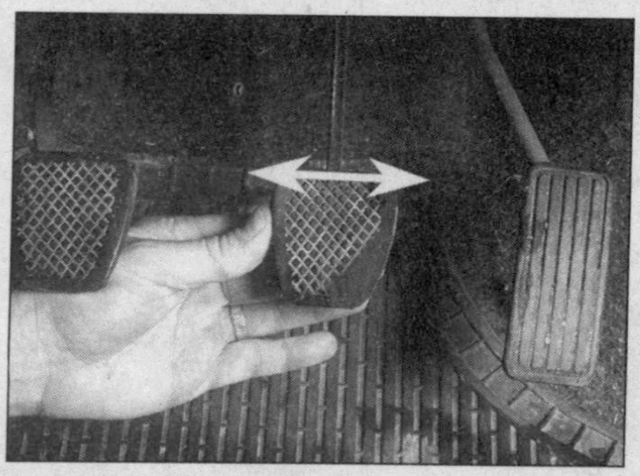

☐ Check that the brake pedal is secure and in good condition. Check also for signs of fluid leaks on the pedal, floor or carpets, which would indicate failed seals in the brake master cylinder.

☐ Check the servo unit (when applicable) by operating the brake pedal several times, then keeping the pedal depressed and starting the engine. As the engine starts, the pedal will move down slightly. If not, the vacuum hose or the servo itself may be faulty.

Steering wheel and column

☐ Examine the steering wheel for fractures or looseness of the hub, spokes or rim.

☐ Move the steering wheel from side to side and then up and down. Check that the steering wheel is not loose on the column, indicating wear or a loose retaining nut. Continue moving the steering wheel as before, but also turn it slightly from left to right.

☐ Check that the steering wheel is not loose on the column, and that there is no abnormal

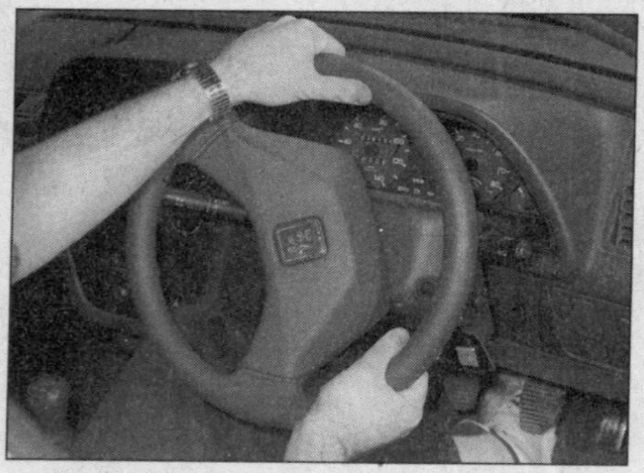

movement of the steering wheel, indicating wear in the column support bearings or couplings.

Windscreen, mirrors and sunvisor

☐ The windscreen must be free of cracks or other significant damage within the driver's field of view. (Small stone chips are acceptable.) Rear view mirrors must be secure, intact, and capable of being adjusted.

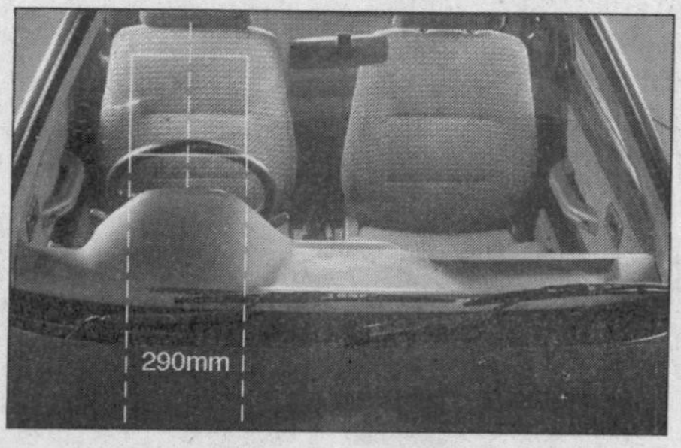

☐ The driver's sunvisor must be capable of being stored in the "up" position.

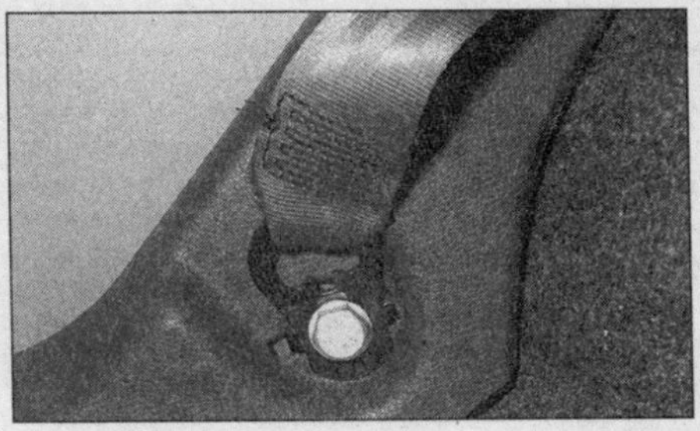

Seat belts and seats

Note: *The following checks are applicable to all seat belts, front and rear.*

☐ Examine the webbing of all the belts (including rear belts if fitted) for cuts, serious fraying or deterioration. Fasten and unfasten each belt to check the buckles. If applicable, check the retracting mechanism. Check the security of all seat belt mountings accessible from inside the vehicle.

☐ Seat belts with pre-tensioners, once activated, have a "flag" or similar showing on the seat belt stalk. This, in itself, is not a reason for test failure.

☐ The front seats themselves must be securely attached and the backrests must lock in the upright position.

Doors

☐ Both front doors must be able to be opened and closed from outside and inside, and must latch securely when closed.

2 Checks carried out WITH THE VEHICLE ON THE GROUND

Vehicle identification

☐ Number plates must be in good condition, secure and legible, with letters and numbers correctly spaced – spacing at (A) should be at least twice that at (B).

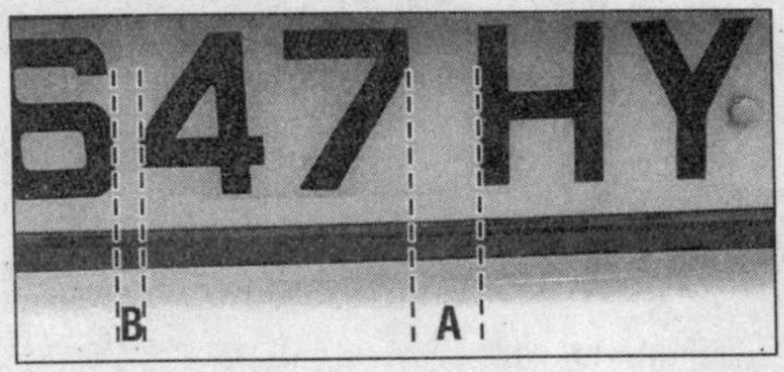

☐ The VIN plate and/or homologation plate must be legible.

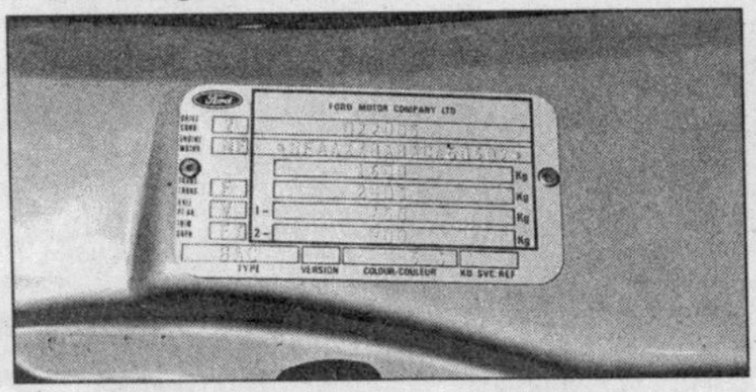

Electrical equipment

☐ Switch on the ignition and check the operation of the horn.

☐ Check the windscreen washers and wipers, examining the wiper blades; renew damaged or perished blades. Also check the operation of the stop-lights.

☐ Check the operation of the sidelights and number plate lights. The lenses and reflectors must be secure, clean and undamaged.

☐ Check the operation and alignment of the headlights. The headlight reflectors must not be tarnished and the lenses must be undamaged.

☐ Switch on the ignition and check the operation of the direction indicators (including the instrument panel tell-tale) and the hazard warning lights. Operation of the sidelights and stop-lights must not affect the indicators - if it does, the cause is usually a bad earth at the rear light cluster.

☐ Check the operation of the rear foglight(s), including the warning light on the instrument panel or in the switch.

☐ The ABS warning light must illuminate in accordance with the manufacturers' design. For most vehicles, the ABS warning light should illuminate when the ignition is switched on, and (if the system is operating properly) extinguish after a few seconds. Refer to the owner's handbook.

Footbrake

☐ Examine the master cylinder, brake pipes and servo unit for leaks, loose mountings, corrosion or other damage.

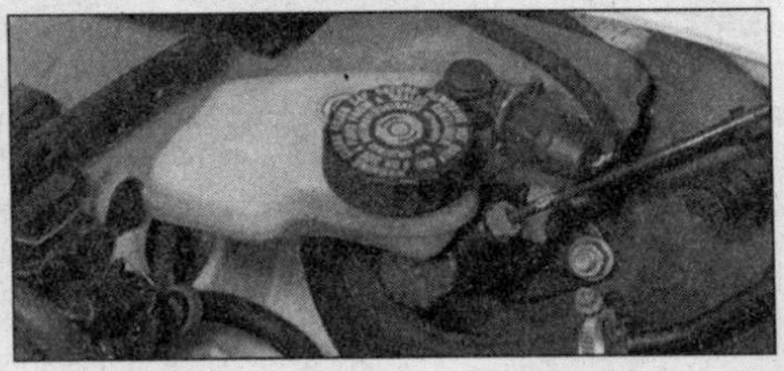

☐ The fluid reservoir must be secure and the fluid level must be between the upper (**A**) and lower (**B**) markings.

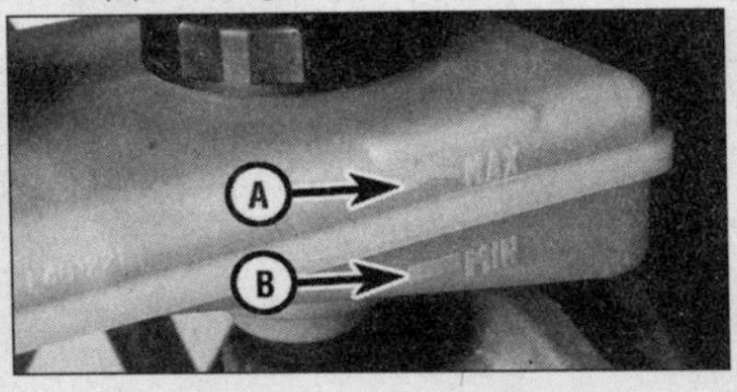

☐ Inspect both front brake flexible hoses for cracks or deterioration of the rubber. Turn the steering from lock to lock, and ensure that the hoses do not contact the wheel, tyre, or any part of the steering or suspension mechanism. With the brake pedal firmly depressed, check the hoses for bulges or leaks under pressure.

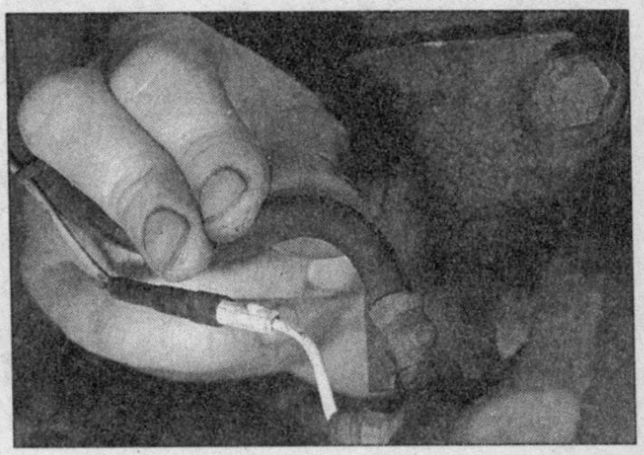

Steering and suspension

☐ Have your assistant turn the steering wheel from side to side slightly, up to the point where the steering gear just begins to transmit this movement to the roadwheels. Check for excessive free play between the steering wheel and the steering gear, indicating wear or insecurity of the steering column joints, the column-to-steering gear coupling, or the steering gear itself.

☐ Have your assistant turn the steering wheel more vigorously in each direction, so that the roadwheels just begin to turn. As this is done, examine all the steering joints, linkages, fittings and attachments. Renew any component that shows signs of wear or damage. On vehicles with power steering, check the security and condition of the steering pump, drivebelt and hoses.

☐ Check that the vehicle is standing level, and at approximately the correct ride height.

Shock absorbers

☐ Depress each corner of the vehicle in turn, then release it. The vehicle should rise and then settle in its normal position. If the vehicle continues to rise and fall, the shock absorber is defective. A shock absorber which has seized will also cause the vehicle to fail.

Exhaust system

□ Start the engine. With your assistant holding a rag over the tailpipe, check the entire system for leaks. Repair or renew leaking sections.

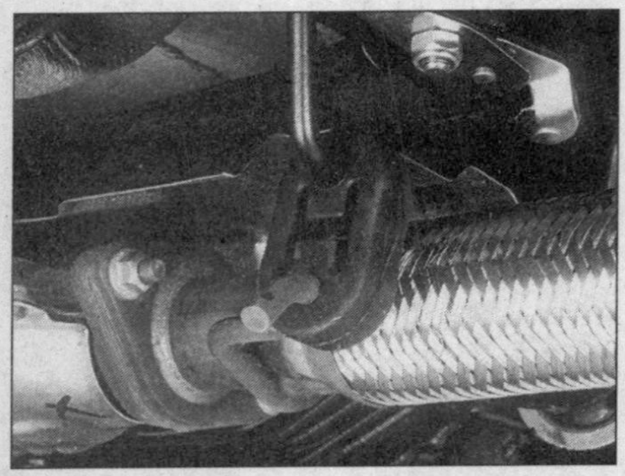

3 Checks carried out WITH THE VEHICLE RAISED AND THE WHEELS FREE TO TURN

Jack up the front and rear of the vehicle, and securely support it on axle stands. Position the stands clear of the suspension assemblies. Ensure that the wheels are clear of the ground and that the steering can be turned from lock to lock.

Steering mechanism

□ Have your assistant turn the steering from lock to lock. Check that the steering turns smoothly, and that no part of the steering mechanism, including a wheel or tyre, fouls any brake hose or pipe or any part of the body structure.

□ Examine the steering rack rubber gaiters for damage or insecurity of the retaining clips. If power steering is fitted, check for signs of damage or leakage of the fluid hoses, pipes or connections. Also check for excessive stiffness or binding of the steering, a missing split pin or locking device, or severe corrosion of the body structure within 30 cm of any steering component attachment point.

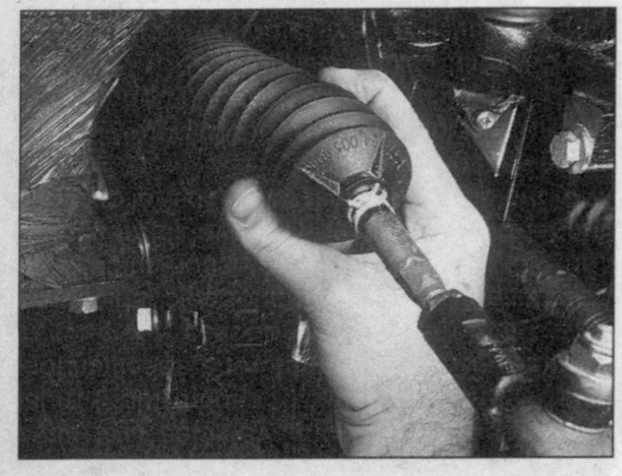

Front and rear suspension and wheel bearings

□ Starting at the front right-hand side, grasp the roadwheel at the 3 o'clock and 9 o'clock positions and rock gently but firmly. Check for free play or insecurity at the wheel bearings, suspension balljoints, or suspension mountings, pivots and attachments.

□ Now grasp the wheel at the 12 o'clock and 6 o'clock positions and repeat the previous inspection. Spin the wheel, and check for roughness or tightness of the front wheel bearing.

□ If excess free play is suspected at a component pivot point, this can be confirmed by using a large screwdriver or similar tool and levering between the mounting and the component attachment. This will confirm whether the wear is in the pivot bush, its retaining bolt, or in the mounting itself (the bolt holes can often become elongated).

□ Carry out all the above checks at the other front wheel, and then at both rear wheels.

Springs and shock absorbers

□ Examine the suspension struts (when applicable) for serious fluid leakage, corrosion, or damage to the casing. Also check the security of the mounting points.

□ If coil springs are fitted, check that the spring ends locate in their seats, and that the spring is not corroded, cracked or broken.

□ If leaf springs are fitted, check that all leaves are intact, that the axle is securely attached to each spring, and that there is no deterioration of the spring eye mountings, bushes, and shackles.

□ The same general checks apply to vehicles fitted with other suspension types, such as torsion bars, hydraulic displacer units, etc. Ensure that all mountings and attachments are secure, that there are no signs of excessive wear, corrosion or damage, and (on hydraulic types) that there are no fluid leaks or damaged pipes.

□ Inspect the shock absorbers for signs of serious fluid leakage. Check for wear of the mounting bushes or attachments, or damage to the body of the unit.

Driveshafts (fwd vehicles only)

□ Rotate each front wheel in turn and inspect the constant velocity joint gaiters for splits or damage. Also check that each driveshaft is straight and undamaged.

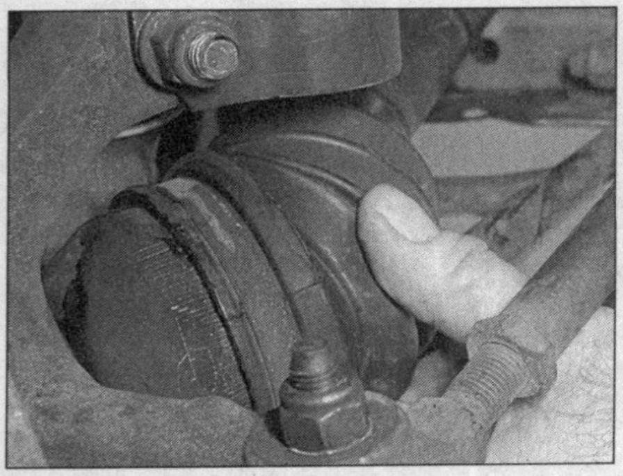

Braking system

□ If possible without dismantling, check brake pad wear and disc condition. Ensure that the friction lining material has not worn excessively, (A) and that the discs are not fractured, pitted, scored or badly worn (B).

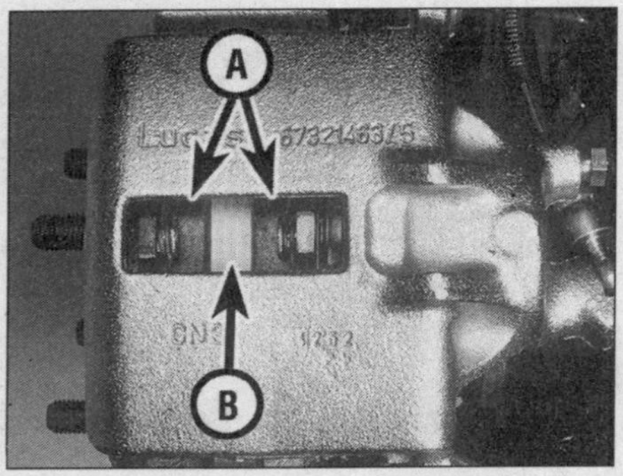

□ Examine all the rigid brake pipes underneath the vehicle, and the flexible hose(s) at the rear. Look for corrosion, chafing or insecurity of the pipes, and for signs of bulging under pressure, chafing, splits or deterioration of the flexible hoses.

□ Look for signs of fluid leaks at the brake calipers or on the brake backplates. Repair or renew leaking components.

□ Slowly spin each wheel, while your assistant depresses and releases the footbrake. Ensure that each brake is operating and does not bind when the pedal is released.

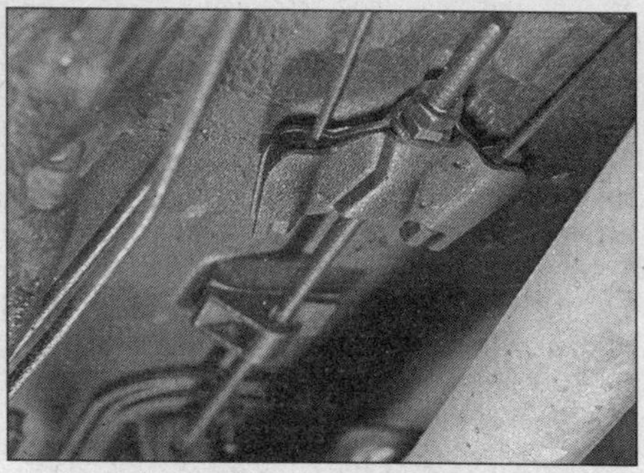

☐ Examine the handbrake mechanism, checking for frayed or broken cables, excessive corrosion, or wear or insecurity of the linkage. Check that the mechanism works on each relevant wheel, and releases fully, without binding.

☐ It is not possible to test brake efficiency without special equipment, but a road test can be carried out later to check that the vehicle pulls up in a straight line.

Fuel and exhaust systems

☐ Inspect the fuel tank (including the filler cap), fuel pipes, hoses and unions. All components must be secure and free from leaks.

☐ Examine the exhaust system over its entire length, checking for any damaged, broken or missing mountings, security of the retaining clamps and rust or corrosion.

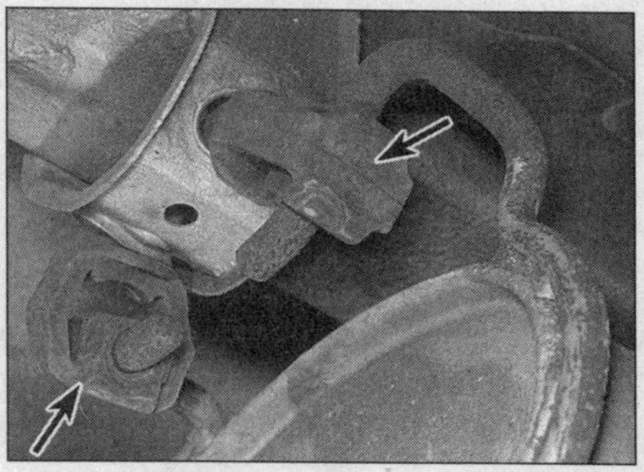

Wheels and tyres

☐ Examine the sidewalls and tread area of each tyre in turn. Check for cuts, tears, lumps, bulges, separation of the tread, and exposure of the ply or cord due to wear or damage. Check that the tyre bead is correctly seated on the wheel rim, that the valve is sound and properly seated, and that the wheel is not distorted or damaged.

☐ Check that the tyres are of the correct size for the vehicle, that they are of the same size and type on each axle, and that the pressures are correct.

☐ Check the tyre tread depth. The legal minimum at the time of writing is 1.6 mm over at least three-quarters of the tread width. Abnormal tread wear may indicate incorrect front wheel alignment.

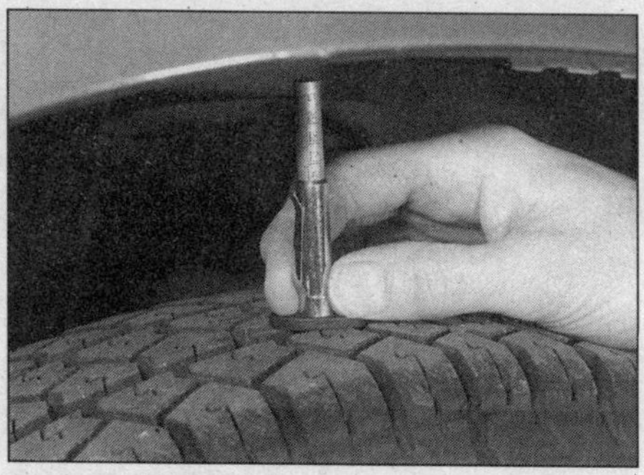

Body corrosion

☐ Check the condition of the entire vehicle structure for signs of corrosion in load-bearing areas. (These include chassis box sections, side sills, cross-members, pillars, and all suspension, steering, braking system and seat belt mountings and anchorages.) Any corrosion which has seriously reduced the thickness of a load-bearing area is likely to cause the vehicle to fail. In this case professional repairs are likely to be needed.

☐ Damage or corrosion which causes sharp or otherwise dangerous edges to be exposed will also cause the vehicle to fail.

4 Checks carried out on **YOUR VEHICLE'S EXHAUST EMISSION SYSTEM**

Petrol models

☐ Have the engine at normal operating temperature, and make sure that it is in good tune (ignition system in good order, air filter element clean, etc).

☐ Before any measurements are carried out, raise the engine speed to around 2500 rpm, and hold it at this speed for 20 seconds. Allow the engine speed to return to idle, and watch for smoke emissions from the exhaust tailpipe. If the idle speed is obviously much too high, or if dense blue or clearly-visible black smoke comes from the tailpipe for more than 5 seconds, the vehicle will fail. As a rule of thumb, blue smoke signifies oil being burnt (engine wear) while black smoke signifies unburnt fuel (dirty air cleaner element, or other carburettor or fuel system fault).

☐ An exhaust gas analyser capable of measuring carbon monoxide (CO) and hydrocarbons (HC) is now needed. If such an instrument cannot be hired or borrowed, a local garage may agree to perform the check for a small fee.

CO emissions (mixture)

☐ At the time of writing, for vehicles first used between 1st August 1975 and 31st July 1986 (P to C registration), the CO level must not exceed 4.5% by volume. For vehicles first used between 1st August 1986 and 31st July 1992 (D to J registration), the CO level must not exceed 3.5% by volume. Vehicles first used after 1st August 1992 (K registration) must conform to the manufacturer's specification. The MOT tester has access to a DOT database or emissions handbook, which lists the CO and HC limits for each make and model of vehicle. The CO level is measured with the engine at idle speed, and at "fast idle". The following limits are given as a general guide:

At idle speed -
CO level no more than 0.5%
At "fast idle" (2500 to 3000 rpm) -
CO level no more than 0.3%
(Minimum oil temperature 60°C)

☐ If the CO level cannot be reduced far enough to pass the test (and the fuel and ignition systems are otherwise in good condition) then the carburettor is badly worn, or there is some problem in the fuel injection system or catalytic converter (as applicable).

HC emissions

☐ With the CO within limits, HC emissions for vehicles first used between 1st August 1975 and 31st July 1992 (P to J registration) must not exceed 1200 ppm. Vehicles first used after 1st August 1992 (K registration) must conform to the manufacturer's specification. The MOT tester has access to a DOT database or emissions handbook, which lists the CO and HC limits for each make and model of vehicle. The HC level is measured with the engine at "fast idle". The following is given as a general guide:

At "fast idle" (2500 to 3000 rpm) -
HC level no more than 200 ppm
(Minimum oil temperature 60°C)

☐ Excessive HC emissions are caused by incomplete combustion, the causes of which can include oil being burnt, mechanical wear and ignition/fuel system malfunction.

Diesel models

☐ The only emission test applicable to Diesel engines is the measuring of exhaust smoke density. The test involves accelerating the engine several times to its maximum unloaded speed.

Note: *It is of the utmost importance that the engine timing belt is in good condition before the test is carried out.*

☐ The limits for Diesel engine exhaust smoke, introduced in September 1995 are:

Vehicles first used before 1st August 1979:
Exempt from metered smoke testing, but must not emit "dense blue or clearly visible black smoke for a period of more than 5 seconds at idle" or "dense blue or clearly visible black smoke during acceleration which would obscure the view of other road users".
Non-turbocharged vehicles first used after 1st August 1979: 2.5m^{-1}
Turbocharged vehicles first used after 1st August 1979: 3.0m^{-1}

☐ Excessive smoke can be caused by a dirty air cleaner element. Otherwise, professional advice may be needed to find the cause.

1 Engine

- ☐ Engine fails to rotate when attempting to start
- ☐ Engine rotates, but will not start
- ☐ Engine difficult to start when cold
- ☐ Engine difficult to start when hot
- ☐ Starter motor noisy or excessively-rough in engagement
- ☐ Engine starts, but stops immediately
- ☐ Engine idles erratically
- ☐ Engine misfires at idle speed
- ☐ Engine misfires throughout the driving speed range
- ☐ Engine hesitates on acceleration
- ☐ Engine stalls
- ☐ Engine lacks power
- ☐ Engine backfires
- ☐ Oil pressure warning light illuminated with engine running
- ☐ Engine runs-on after switching off
- ☐ Engine noises

2 Cooling system

- ☐ Overheating
- ☐ Overcooling
- ☐ External coolant leakage
- ☐ Internal coolant leakage
- ☐ Corrosion

3 Fuel and exhaust systems

- ☐ Excessive fuel consumption
- ☐ Fuel leakage and/or fuel odour
- ☐ Excessive noise or fumes from exhaust system

4 Clutch

- ☐ Pedal travels to floor - no pressure or very little resistance
- ☐ Clutch fails to disengage (unable to select gears)
- ☐ Clutch slips (engine speed increases, with no increase in vehicle speed)
- ☐ Judder as clutch is engaged
- ☐ Noise when depressing or releasing clutch pedal

5 Manual transmission

- ☐ Noisy in neutral with engine running
- ☐ Noisy in one particular gear
- ☐ Difficulty engaging gears
- ☐ Jumps out of gear
- ☐ Vibration
- ☐ Lubricant leaks

6 Automatic transmission

- ☐ Fluid leakage
- ☐ Transmission fluid brown, or has burned smell
- ☐ General gear selection problems
- ☐ Transmission will not downshift (kickdown) with accelerator pedal fully depressed
- ☐ Engine will not start in any gear, or starts in gears other than Park or Neutral
- ☐ Transmission slips, shifts roughly, is noisy, or has no drive in forward or reverse gears

7 Driveshafts

- ☐ Clicking or knocking noise on turns (at slow speed on full-lock)
- ☐ Vibration when accelerating or decelerating

8 Braking system

- ☐ Poor brake performance
- ☐ Vehicle pulls to one side under braking
- ☐ Noise (grinding or high-pitched squeal) when brakes applied
- ☐ Excessive brake pedal travel
- ☐ Excessive brake pedal effort required to stop vehicle
- ☐ Judder felt through brake pedal or steering wheel when braking
- ☐ Brakes binding

9 Suspension and steering

- ☐ Vehicle pulls to one side
- ☐ Wheel wobble and vibration
- ☐ Excessive pitching and/or rolling round corners, or during braking
- ☐ Wandering or general instability
- ☐ Excessively-stiff steering
- ☐ Excessive play in steering
- ☐ Lack of power assistance (where applicable)
- ☐ Tyre wear excessive

10 Electrical system

- ☐ Battery will not hold a charge for more than a few days
- ☐ Ignition/no-charge warning light stays on with engine running
- ☐ Ignition/no-charge warning light fails to come on
- ☐ Lights inoperative
- ☐ Instrument readings inaccurate or erratic
- ☐ Horn inoperative, or unsatisfactory in operation
- ☐ Windscreen/tailgate wipers inoperative, or unsatisfactory in operation
- ☐ Windscreen/tailgate washers inoperative, or unsatisfactory in operation
- ☐ Electric windows inoperative, or unsatisfactory in operation
- ☐ Central locking system inoperative, or unsatisfactory in operation

Introduction

The vehicle owner who does his or her own maintenance according to the recommended service schedules should not have to use this section of the manual very often. Modern component reliability is such that, provided those items subject to wear or deterioration are inspected or renewed at the specified intervals, sudden failure is comparatively rare. Faults do not usually just happen as a result of sudden failure, but develop over a period of time. Major mechanical failures in particular are usually preceded by characteristic symptoms over hundreds or even thousands of miles. Those components which do occasionally fail without warning are often small and easily carried in the vehicle.

With any fault-finding, the first step is to decide where to begin investigations. Sometimes this is obvious, but on other occasions, a little detective work will be necessary. The owner who makes half a dozen haphazard adjustments or replacements may be successful in curing a fault (or its symptoms), but will be none the wiser if the fault recurs, and ultimately may have spent more time and money than was necessary. A calm and logical approach will be found to be more satisfactory in the long run. Always take into account any warning signs or abnormalities that may have been noticed in the period preceding the fault - power loss, high or low gauge readings, unusual smells, etc - and remember that failure of components such as fuses or spark plugs may only be pointers to some underlying fault.

The pages which follow provide an easy-reference guide to the more common problems which may occur during the operation of the vehicle. These problems and their possible causes are grouped under headings denoting various components or systems, such as Engine, Cooling system, etc. The Chapter and/or Section which deals with the problem is also shown in brackets.

Whatever the fault, certain basic principles apply. These are as follows:

Verify the fault. This is simply a matter of being sure that you know what the symptoms are before starting work. This is particularly important if you are investigating a fault for someone else, who may not have described it very accurately.

Don't overlook the obvious. For example, if the vehicle won't start, is there petrol in the tank? (Don't take anyone else's word on this particular point, and don't trust the fuel gauge either!). If an electrical fault is indicated, look for loose or broken wires before digging out the test gear. Establish what work (if any) has recently been carried out - any job which has not been done properly will sometimes lead to puzzling side-effects.

Cure the disease, not the symptom. Substituting a flat battery with a fully-charged one will get you off the hard shoulder, but if the underlying cause is not attended to, the new battery will go the same way. Similarly, changing oil-fouled spark plugs (petrol models) for a new set will get you moving again, but remember that the reason for the fouling (if it wasn't simply an incorrect grade of plug) will have to be established and corrected.

Don't take anything for granted. Particularly, don't forget that a "new" component may itself be defective (especially if it's been rattling around in the boot for months), and don't leave components out of a fault diagnosis sequence just because they are new or recently-fitted. When you do finally diagnose a difficult fault, you'll probably realise that all the evidence was there from the start.

1 Engine

Engine fails to rotate when attempting to start

- ☐ Battery terminal connections loose or corroded ("Weekly checks").
- ☐ Battery discharged or faulty (Chapter 5A).
- ☐ Broken, loose or disconnected wiring in the starting circuit (Chapter 5A).
- ☐ Defective starter solenoid or switch (Chapter 5A).
- ☐ Defective starter motor (Chapter 5A).
- ☐ Starter pinion or flywheel ring gear teeth loose or broken (Chapters 2A, 2B, and 5A).
- ☐ Engine earth strap broken or disconnected (Chapter 5A).

Engine rotates, but will not start

- ☐ Fuel tank empty.
- ☐ Battery discharged (engine rotates slowly) (Chapter 5A).
- ☐ Battery terminal connections loose or corroded (*"Weekly checks"*).
- ☐ Ignition components damp or damaged - petrol models (Chapters 1A and 5B).
- ☐ Broken, loose or disconnected wiring in the ignition circuit - petrol models (Chapters 1A and 5B).
- ☐ Worn, faulty or incorrectly-gapped spark plugs - petrol models (Chapter 1A).
- ☐ Preheating system faulty - diesel models (Chapter 5C).
- ☐ Fuel injection system fault - petrol models (Chapter 4A or 4B).
- ☐ Stop solenoid faulty - diesel models (Chapter 4C).
- ☐ Air in fuel system - diesel models (Chapter 4C).
- ☐ Major mechanical failure (eg camshaft drive) (Chapter 2A, 2B or 2C).
- ☐ Anti-theft immobiliser fault (Chapter 12).
- ☐ Inertia switch in operation - reset (Chapter 12).

Engine difficult to start when cold

- ☐ Battery discharged (Chapter 5A).
- ☐ Battery terminal connections loose or corroded (*"Weekly checks"*).
- ☐ Worn, faulty or incorrectly-gapped spark plugs - petrol models (Chapter 1A).
- ☐ Preheating system faulty - diesel models (Chapter 5C).
- ☐ Injection pump timing incorrect - diesel models (Chapter 4C)
- ☐ Fuel injection system fault - petrol models (Chapter 4A or 4B).
- ☐ Other ignition system fault - petrol models (Chapters 1A and 5B).
- ☐ Fast idle valve incorrectly adjusted - diesel models (Chapter 4C).
- ☐ Low cylinder compressions (Chapter 2A or 2B).
- ☐ Engine management system in "limp-home" mode (engine check warning light illuminated) - petrol models (Chapter 4A or 4B).

Engine difficult to start when hot

- ☐ Air filter element dirty or clogged (Chapter 1A or 1B).
- ☐ Fuel injection system fault - petrol models (Chapter 4A or 4B).
- ☐ Low cylinder compressions (Chapter 2A or 2B).

Starter motor noisy or excessively-rough in engagement

- ☐ Starter pinion or flywheel ring gear teeth loose or broken (Chapters 2A, 2B and 5A).
- ☐ Starter motor mounting bolts loose or missing (Chapter 5A).
- ☐ Starter motor internal components worn or damaged (Chapter 5A).

Engine starts, but stops immediately

- ☐ Loose or faulty electrical connections in the ignition circuit - petrol models (Chapters 1A and 5B).
- ☐ Vacuum leak at the throttle body or inlet manifold - petrol models (Chapter 4A or 4B).
- ☐ Blocked injector/fuel injection system fault - petrol models (Chapter 4A or 4B).

Engine idles erratically

- ☐ Air filter element clogged (Chapter 1A or 1B).
- ☐ Vacuum leak at the throttle body, inlet manifold or associated hoses - petrol models (Chapter 4A, 4B or 4D).
- ☐ Worn, faulty or incorrectly-gapped spark plugs - petrol models (Chapter 1A).
- ☐ Uneven or low cylinder compressions (Chapter 2A or 2B).
- ☐ Camshaft lobes worn (Chapter 2A or 2B).
- ☐ Timing belt incorrectly tensioned (Chapter 2A or 2B).
- ☐ Blocked injector/fuel injection system fault - petrol models (Chapter 4A or 4B).
- ☐ Engine management system in "limp-home" mode (engine check warning light illuminated) - petrol models (Chapter 4A or 4B).
- ☐ Faulty injector(s) - diesel models (Chapter 4C).

Engine misfires at idle speed

- ☐ Worn, faulty or incorrectly-gapped spark plugs - petrol models (Chapter 1A).
- ☐ Faulty spark plug HT leads - petrol models (Chapter 1A).
- ☐ Vacuum leak at the throttle body, inlet manifold or associated hoses - petrol models (Chapter 4A, 4B or 4D).
- ☐ Blocked injector/fuel injection system fault - petrol models (Chapter 4A or 4B).
- ☐ Faulty injector(s) - diesel models (Chapter 4C).
- ☐ Uneven or low cylinder compressions (Chapter 2A or 2B).
- ☐ Disconnected, leaking, or perished crankcase ventilation hoses (Chapter 4D).

Engine (continued)

Engine misfires throughout the driving speed range

- ☐ Fuel filter choked (Chapter 1A or 1B).
- ☐ Fuel pump faulty, or delivery pressure low (Chapter 4A or 4B).
- ☐ Fuel tank vent blocked, or fuel pipes restricted (Chapter 4A, 4B or 4C).
- ☐ Vacuum leak at the throttle body, inlet manifold or associated hoses - petrol models (Chapter 4A or 4B).
- ☐ Worn, faulty or incorrectly-gapped spark plugs - petrol models (Chapter 1A).
- ☐ Faulty spark plug HT leads - petrol models (Chapter 1A).
- ☐ Faulty injector(s) - diesel models (Chapter 4C).
- ☐ Faulty ignition coil - petrol models (Chapter 5B).
- ☐ Uneven or low cylinder compressions (Chapter 2A or 2B).
- ☐ Blocked injector/fuel injection system fault - petrol models (Chapter 4A or 4B).

Engine hesitates on acceleration

- ☐ Worn, faulty or incorrectly-gapped spark plugs - petrol models (Chapter 1A).
- ☐ Vacuum leak at the throttle body, inlet manifold or associated hoses (Chapter 4A or 4B).
- ☐ Blocked injector/fuel injection system fault - petrol models (Chapter 4A or 4B).
- ☐ Faulty injector(s) - diesel models (Chapter 4C).

Engine stalls

- ☐ Vacuum leak at the throttle body, inlet manifold or associated hoses - petrol models (Chapter 4A, 4B or 4D).
- ☐ Fuel filter choked (Chapter 1A or 1B).
- ☐ Fuel pump faulty, or delivery pressure low - petrol models (Chapter 4A or 4B).
- ☐ Fuel tank vent blocked, or fuel pipes restricted (Chapter 4A, 4B or 4C).
- ☐ Blocked injector/fuel injection system fault - petrol models (Chapter 4A or 4B).
- ☐ Faulty injector(s) - diesel models (Chapter 4C).
- ☐ Perished diaphragm in hand-priming pump - diesel models (Chapter 4C)
- ☐ Engine management system in "limp-home" mode (engine check warning light illuminated) - petrol models (Chapter 4A or 4B).

Engine lacks power

- ☐ Timing belt incorrectly fitted or tensioned (Chapter 2A or 2B).
- ☐ Fuel filter choked (Chapter 1A or 1B).
- ☐ Fuel pump faulty, or delivery pressure low - petrol models (Chapter 4A or 4B).
- ☐ Uneven or low cylinder compressions (Chapter 2A or 2B).
- ☐ Worn, faulty or incorrectly-gapped spark plugs - petrol models (Chapter 1A).
- ☐ Vacuum leak at the throttle body, inlet manifold or associated hoses - petrol models (Chapter 4A or 4B).
- ☐ Blocked injector/fuel injection system fault - petrol models (Chapter 4A or 4B).
- ☐ Faulty injector(s) - diesel models (Chapter 4C).
- ☐ Injection pump timing incorrect - diesel models (Chapter 4C).
- ☐ Perished diaphragm in hand-priming pump - diesel models (Chapter 4C).
- ☐ Brakes binding (Chapters 1 and 9).
- ☐ Clutch slipping (Chapter 6).

Engine backfires

- ☐ Timing belt incorrectly fitted or tensioned (Chapter 2A).
- ☐ Vacuum leak at the throttle body, inlet manifold or associated hoses - petrol models (Chapter 4A or 4B).
- ☐ Blocked injector/fuel injection system fault - petrol models (Chapter 4A or 4B).

Oil pressure warning light illuminated with engine running

- ☐ Low oil level, or incorrect oil grade (*"Weekly checks"*).
- ☐ Faulty oil pressure warning light switch (Chapter 5A).
- ☐ Worn engine bearings and/or oil pump (Chapter 2C).
- ☐ High engine operating temperature (Chapter 3).
- ☐ Oil pressure relief valve defective (Chapter 2A or 2B).
- ☐ Oil pick-up strainer clogged (Chapter 2A or 2B).

Engine runs-on after switching off

- ☐ Excessive carbon build-up in engine (Chapter 2C).
- ☐ High engine operating temperature (Chapter 3).
- ☐ Fuel injection system fault - petrol models (Chapter 4A or 4B).
- ☐ Faulty stop solenoid - diesel models (Chapter 4C).

Engine noises

Pre-ignition (pinking) or knocking during acceleration or under load

- ☐ Ignition timing incorrect/ignition system fault - petrol models (Chapters 1A and 5B).
- ☐ Incorrect grade of spark plug - petrol models (Chapter 1A).
- ☐ Incorrect grade of fuel (Chapter 4A or 4B).
- ☐ Vacuum leak at the throttle body, inlet manifold or associated hoses - petrol models (Chapter 4A or 4B).
- ☐ Excessive carbon build-up in engine (Chapter 2C).
- ☐ Blocked injector/fuel injection system fault - petrol models (Chapter 4A or 4B).

Whistling or wheezing noises

- ☐ Leaking inlet manifold or throttle body gasket - petrol models (Chapter 4A or 4B).
- ☐ Leaking exhaust manifold gasket or pipe-to-manifold joint (Chapter 4D).
- ☐ Leaking vacuum hose (Chapter 4A, 4B, 4C, or 4D).
- ☐ Blowing cylinder head gasket (Chapter 2A or 2B).

Tapping or rattling noises

- ☐ Worn valve gear or camshaft (Chapter 2A or 2B).
- ☐ Ancillary component fault (coolant pump, alternator, etc) (Chapters 3, 5A, etc).

Knocking or thumping noises

- ☐ Worn big-end bearings (regular heavy knocking, perhaps less under load) (Chapter 2C).
- ☐ Worn main bearings (rumbling and knocking, perhaps worsening under load) (Chapter 2C).
- ☐ Piston slap (most noticeable when cold) - engine worn (Chapter 2C).
- ☐ Ancillary component fault (coolant pump, alternator, etc) (Chapters 3, 5A, etc).

2 Cooling system

Overheating

- ☐ Insufficient coolant in system (*"Weekly checks"*).
- ☐ Thermostat faulty (Chapter 3).
- ☐ Radiator core blocked, or grille restricted (Chapter 3).
- ☐ Electric cooling fan or thermoswitch faulty (Chapter 3).
- ☐ Pressure cap faulty (Chapter 3).
- ☐ Ignition timing incorrect/ignition system fault - petrol models (Chapters 1A and 5B).
- ☐ Inaccurate temperature gauge sender unit (Chapter 3).
- ☐ Airlock in cooling system (Chapter 1A or 1B).

Overcooling

- ☐ Thermostat faulty (Chapter 3).
- ☐ Inaccurate temperature gauge sender unit (Chapter 3).

External coolant leakage

- ☐ Deteriorated or damaged hoses or hose clips (Chapter 1A or 1B).
- ☐ Radiator core or heater matrix leaking (Chapter 3).
- ☐ Pressure cap faulty (Chapter 3).
- ☐ Water pump seal leaking (Chapter 3).
- ☐ Boiling due to overheating (Chapter 3).
- ☐ Core plug leaking (Chapter 2C).

Internal coolant leakage

- ☐ Leaking cylinder head gasket (Chapter 2A or 2B).
- ☐ Cracked cylinder head or cylinder bore (Chapter 2A, 2B or 2C).

Corrosion

- ☐ Infrequent draining and flushing (Chapter 1A or 1B).
- ☐ Incorrect coolant mixture or inappropriate coolant type (*"Lubricants and fluids"* and Chapter 1A or 1B).

3 Fuel and exhaust systems

Excessive fuel consumption

- ☐ Air filter element dirty or clogged (Chapter 1A or 1B).
- ☐ Fuel injection system fault - petrol models (Chapter 4A or 4B).
- ☐ Faulty injector(s) - diesel models (Chapter 4C).
- ☐ Ignition timing incorrect/ignition system fault - petrol models (Chapters 1A and 5B).
- ☐ Tyres under-inflated (*"Weekly checks"*).

Fuel leakage and/or fuel odour

- ☐ Damaged or corroded fuel tank, pipes or connections (Chapter 4A, 4B, 4C or 4D).

Excessive noise or fumes from exhaust system

- ☐ Leaking exhaust system or manifold joints (Chapters 1 and 4D).
- ☐ Leaking, corroded or damaged silencers or pipe (Chapters 1 and 4D).
- ☐ Broken mountings causing body or suspension contact (Chapter 1A or 1B).
- ☐ Faulty injector(s) - diesel models (Chapter 4C).
- ☐ Injection pump timing incorrect - diesel models (Chapter 4C).

4 Clutch

Pedal travels to floor - no pressure or very little resistance

- ☐ Broken clutch cable (Chapter 6).
- ☐ Incorrect clutch cable adjustment (Chapter 6).
- ☐ Broken clutch release bearing or fork (Chapter 6).
- ☐ Broken diaphragm spring in clutch pressure plate (Chapter 6).

Clutch fails to disengage (unable to select gears)

- ☐ Incorrect clutch cable adjustment (Chapter 6).
- ☐ Clutch disc sticking on gearbox input shaft splines (Chapter 6).
- ☐ Clutch disc sticking to flywheel or pressure plate (Chapter 6).
- ☐ Faulty pressure plate assembly (Chapter 6).
- ☐ Clutch release mechanism worn or incorrectly assembled (Chapter 6).

Clutch slips (engine speed increases, with no increase in vehicle speed)

- ☐ Incorrect clutch cable adjustment (Chapter 6).
- ☐ Clutch disc linings excessively worn (Chapter 6).
- ☐ Clutch disc linings contaminated with oil or grease (Chapter 6).
- ☐ Faulty pressure plate or weak diaphragm spring (Chapter 6).

Judder as clutch is engaged

- ☐ Clutch disc linings contaminated with oil or grease (Chapter 6).
- ☐ Clutch disc linings excessively worn (Chapter 6).
- ☐ Clutch cable sticking or frayed (Chapter 6).
- ☐ Faulty or distorted pressure plate or diaphragm spring (Chapter 6).
- ☐ Worn or loose engine or gearbox mountings (Chapter 2A or 2B).
- ☐ Clutch disc hub or gearbox input shaft splines worn (Chapter 6).

Noise when depressing or releasing clutch pedal

- ☐ Worn clutch release bearing (Chapter 6).
- ☐ Worn or dry clutch pedal bushes (Chapter 6).
- ☐ Faulty pressure plate assembly (Chapter 6).
- ☐ Pressure plate diaphragm spring broken (Chapter 6).
- ☐ Broken clutch disc cushioning springs (Chapter 6).

5 Manual transmission

Noisy in neutral with engine running

- ☐ Input shaft bearings worn (noise apparent with clutch pedal released, but not when depressed) (Chapter 7A).*
- ☐ Clutch release bearing worn (noise apparent with clutch pedal depressed, possibly less when released) (Chapter 6).

Noisy in one particular gear

- ☐ Worn, damaged or chipped gear teeth (Chapter 7A).*

Difficulty engaging gears

- ☐ Clutch faulty (Chapter 6).
- ☐ Worn or damaged gear linkage (Chapter 7A).
- ☐ Incorrectly-adjusted gear linkage (Chapter 7A).
- ☐ Worn synchroniser units (Chapter 7A).*

Jumps out of gear

- ☐ Worn or damaged gear linkage (Chapter 7A).
- ☐ Incorrectly-adjusted gear linkage (Chapter 7A).
- ☐ Worn synchroniser units (Chapter 7A).*
- ☐ Worn selector forks (Chapter 7A).*

Vibration

- ☐ Lack of oil (Chapter 1A or 1B).
- ☐ Worn bearings (Chapter 7A).*

Lubricant leaks

- ☐ Leaking differential output oil seal (Chapter 7A).
- ☐ Leaking housing joint (Chapter 7A).*
- ☐ Leaking input shaft oil seal (Chapter 7A).*

**Although the corrective action necessary to remedy the symptoms described is beyond the scope of the home mechanic, the above information should be helpful in isolating the cause of the condition, so that the owner can communicate clearly with a professional mechanic.*

6 Automatic transmission

Note: *Due to the complexity of the automatic transmission, it is difficult for the home mechanic to properly diagnose and service this unit. For problems other than the following, the vehicle should be taken to a dealer service department or automatic transmission specialist. Do not be too hasty in removing the transmission if a fault is suspected, as most of the testing is carried out with the unit still fitted.*

Fluid leakage

- ☐ Automatic transmission fluid is usually dark in colour (typically, red). Fluid leaks should not be confused with engine oil, which can easily be blown onto the transmission by airflow.
- ☐ To determine the source of a leak, first remove all built-up dirt and grime from the transmission housing and surrounding areas using a degreasing agent, or by steam-cleaning. Drive the vehicle at low speed, so airflow will not blow the leak far from its source. Raise and support the vehicle, and determine where the leak is coming from. The following are common areas of leakage:
  - *a) Fluid pan or "sump" (Chapter 1A or 7B).*
  - *b) Dipstick tube (Chapter 1A or 7B).*
  - *c) Transmission-to-fluid cooler pipes/unions (Chapter 7B).*

Transmission fluid brown, or has burned smell

- ☐ Transmission fluid level low, or fluid in need of renewal (Chapter 1A).

General gear selection problems

- ☐ The selector cable is self-adjusting, and should not normally require attention. The following problems could be caused by a malfunction in the control system electronic components described in Chapter 7B (or by a faulty or poorly-fitted cable):
  - *a) Engine starting in gears other than Park or Neutral.*
  - *b) Indicator panel indicating a gear other than the one actually being used.*
  - *c) Vehicle moves when in Park or Neutral.*
  - *d) Poor gear shift quality or erratic gear changes.*

Transmission will not downshift (kickdown) with accelerator pedal fully depressed

- ☐ Low transmission fluid level (Chapter 1A).
- ☐ Transmission control system component failure (Chapter 7B).

Engine will not start in any gear, or starts in gears other than Park or Neutral

- ☐ Transmission multi-function switch faulty or poorly-fitted (Chapter 7B).
- ☐ Selector cable faulty or poorly-fitted (Chapter 7B).

Transmission slips, shifts roughly, is noisy, or has no drive in forward or reverse gears

- ☐ There are many probable causes for the above problems, but the home mechanic should be concerned with only one possibility - fluid level. Before taking the vehicle to a dealer or transmission specialist, check the fluid level and condition of the fluid as described in Chapter 1A. Correct the fluid level as necessary, or change the fluid and filter if needed. If the problem persists, professional help will be necessary.

7 Driveshafts

Clicking or knocking noise on turns (at slow speed on full-lock)

- ☐ Lack of constant velocity joint lubricant, possibly due to damaged gaiter (Chapter 8).
- ☐ Worn outer constant velocity joint (Chapter 8).

Vibration when accelerating or decelerating

- ☐ Worn inner constant velocity joint (Chapter 8).
- ☐ Bent or distorted driveshaft (Chapter 8).

8 Braking system

Note: *Before assuming that a brake problem exists, make sure that the tyres are in good condition and correctly inflated, that the front wheel alignment is correct, and that the vehicle is not loaded with weight in an unequal manner. Apart from checking the condition of all pipe and hose connections, any faults occurring on the anti-lock braking system should be referred to a Citroën dealer for diagnosis.*

Poor brake performance

- ☐ Air in hydraulic system - bleed the brakes (Chapter 9).
- ☐ Brake fluid contaminated - change fluid (Chapter 1A or 1B).
- ☐ Seized or partially-seized brake caliper piston(s) (Chapter 9).
- ☐ Brake pads incorrectly fitted (Chapters 1A or 1B and 9).
- ☐ Incorrect grade of brake pads fitted (Chapters 1A or 1B and 9).
- ☐ Brake pads "glazed" - replace (Chapter 9).
- ☐ Automatic adjustment mechanism on rear brake shoes seized (Chapter 9).
- ☐ Brake pedal-to-servo linkage incorrectly adjusted - right-hand-drive models (Chapter 9).
- ☐ Brake pads or linings contaminated with oil or brake fluid (Chapters 1A or 1B and 9).

Vehicle pulls to one side under braking

- ☐ Worn, defective, damaged or contaminated brake pads on one side (Chapters 1A or 1B and 9).
- ☐ Seized or partially-seized front brake caliper piston (Chapters 1A or 1B and 9).
- ☐ A mixture of brake pad lining materials fitted between sides (Chapters 1A or 1B and 9).
- ☐ Brake caliper mounting bolts loose (Chapter 9).
- ☐ Worn or damaged steering or suspension components (Chapters 1A or 1B and 10).
- ☐ Primary or secondary hydraulic circuit failure (Chapter 9).

Noise (grinding or high-pitched squeal) when brakes applied

- ☐ Brake pad friction lining material worn down to metal backing (Chapters 1A or 1B and 9).
- ☐ Excessive corrosion of brake disc (may be apparent after the vehicle has been standing for some time) (Chapters 1A or 1B and 9).
- ☐ Foreign object (stone chipping, etc) trapped between brake disc and shield (Chapters 1A or 1B and 9).

Excessive brake pedal travel

- ☐ Automatic adjustment mechanism on rear brake shoes seized (Chapter 9).
- ☐ Brake pedal-to-servo linkage incorrectly adjusted - right-hand-drive models (Chapter 9).
- ☐ Air in hydraulic system - bleed the brakes (Chapter 9).
- ☐ Brake fluid contaminated - change fluid (Chapter 1A or 1B).
- ☐ Brake fluid leak - check especially fluid unions and bleed screws (Chapter 9).

Excessive brake pedal effort required to stop vehicle

- ☐ Primary or secondary hydraulic circuit failure (Chapter 9).
- ☐ Seized brake caliper piston(s) (Chapter 9).
- ☐ Brake pads incorrectly fitted (Chapters 1A or 1B and 9).
- ☐ Incorrect grade of brake pads fitted (Chapters 1A or 1B and 9).
- ☐ Brake pads linings contaminated (Chapters 1A or 1B and 9).
- ☐ Brake pedal-to-servo linkage binding - right-hand-drive models (Chapter 9).

Judder felt through brake pedal or steering wheel when braking

Note: *On models equipped with ABS, vibration felt through the brake pedal under heavy braking is a sign that the anti-lock system is in operation, and this does not normally indicate a fault.*

- ☐ Excessive run-out or distortion of discs (Chapters 1A or 1B and 9).
- ☐ Brake pad linings worn (Chapters 1A or 1B and 9).
- ☐ Brake caliper mounting bolts loose (Chapter 9).
- ☐ Wear in suspension or steering components or mountings (Chapters 1A or 1B and 10).

Brakes binding

- ☐ Seized brake caliper piston(s) (Chapter 9).
- ☐ Incorrectly-adjusted handbrake mechanism (Chapter 1A or 1B).

9 Suspension and steering

Note: *Before diagnosing suspension or steering faults, be sure that the trouble is not due to incorrect tyre pressures, mixtures of tyre types, or binding brakes.*

Vehicle pulls to one side

- ☐ Defective tyre (*"Weekly checks"*).
- ☐ Excessive wear in suspension or steering components (Chapters 1A or 1B and 10).
- ☐ Incorrect front wheel alignment (Chapter 10).
- ☐ Accident damage to steering or suspension components (Chapter 1A or 1B).

Wheel wobble and vibration

- ☐ Front roadwheels out of balance (vibration felt mainly through the steering wheel) ("*Weekly checks*" and Chapter 10).
- ☐ Rear roadwheels out of balance (vibration felt throughout the vehicle) ("*Weekly checks*" and Chapter 10).
- ☐ Roadwheels damaged or distorted ("*Weekly checks*" and Chapter 10).
- ☐ Faulty or damaged tyre ("*Weekly checks*").
- ☐ Worn steering or suspension joints, bushes or components (Chapters 1A or 1B and 10).
- ☐ Wheel bolts loose.

Excessive pitching and/or rolling round corners, or during braking

- ☐ Broken suspension component (Chapters 1A or 1B and 10).
- ☐ Worn or damaged anti-roll bar or mountings (Chapter 10).

Wandering or general instability

- ☐ Incorrect front wheel alignment (Chapter 10).
- ☐ Worn steering or suspension joints, bushes or components (Chapters 1A or 1B and 10).
- ☐ Roadwheels out of balance ("*Weekly checks*" and Chapter 10).
- ☐ Faulty or damaged tyre ("*Weekly checks*").
- ☐ Wheel bolts loose.

Excessively-stiff steering

- ☐ Lack of steering gear lubricant (Chapter 10).
- ☐ Seized track-rod end balljoint or suspension balljoint (Chapters 1A or 1B and 10).
- ☐ Incorrect front wheel alignment (Chapter 10).
- ☐ Steering rack or column bent or damaged (Chapter 10).

Suspension and steering (continued)

Excessive play in steering

- ☐ Worn steering column intermediate shaft universal joint (Chapter 10).
- ☐ Worn steering track-rod end balljoints (Chapters 1A or 1B and 10).
- ☐ Worn rack-and-pinion steering gear (Chapter 10).
- ☐ Worn steering or suspension joints, bushes or components (Chapters 1A or 1B and 10).

Lack of power assistance (where applicable)

- ☐ Low power steering fluid level (*"Weekly checks"*).
- ☐ Air in power steering system - bleed (Chapter 10).
- ☐ Power steering pump wiring disconnected or damaged (Chapter 10).
- ☐ Power steering pump fuse blown, or other wiring fault (Chapter 12).
- ☐ Fluid leak (Chapter 10).
- ☐ Power steering pump or steering gear defective (Chapter 10).

Tyre wear excessive

Tyres worn on inside or outside edges

- ☐ Tyres under-inflated (wear on both edges) (*"Weekly checks"*).
- ☐ Incorrect camber or castor angles (wear on one edge only) (Chapter 10).
- ☐ Worn steering or suspension joints, bushes or components (Chapters 1A or 1B and 10).
- ☐ Excessively-hard cornering.
- ☐ Accident damage.

Tyre treads exhibit feathered edges

- ☐ Incorrect toe setting (Chapter 10).

Tyres worn in centre of tread

- ☐ Tyres over-inflated (*"Weekly checks"*).

Tyres worn unevenly

- ☐ Tyres/wheels out of balance ("*Weekly checks*").
- ☐ Excessive wheel or tyre run-out ("*Weekly checks*").
- ☐ Faulty tyre (*"Weekly checks"*).

10 Electrical system

Note: *For problems associated with the starting system, refer to the faults listed under "Engine" earlier in this Section.*

Battery will not hold a charge for more than a few days

- ☐ Battery defective internally (Chapter 5A).
- ☐ Battery terminal connections loose or corroded ("*Weekly checks*").
- ☐ Auxiliary drivebelt worn or incorrectly adjusted ("*Weekly checks*").
- ☐ Alternator not charging at correct output (Chapter 5A).
- ☐ Alternator or voltage regulator faulty (Chapter 5A).
- ☐ Short-circuit causing continual battery drain (Chapters 5A and 12).

Ignition/no-charge warning light stays on with engine running

- ☐ Auxiliary drivebelt broken, worn, or incorrectly adjusted (Chapter 1A or 1B).
- ☐ Alternator brushes worn, sticking, or dirty (Chapter 5A).
- ☐ Alternator brush springs weak or broken (Chapter 5A).
- ☐ Internal fault in alternator or voltage regulator (Chapter 5A).
- ☐ Broken, disconnected, or loose wiring in charging circuit (Chapter 5A).

Ignition/no-charge warning light fails to come on

- ☐ Warning light bulb blown (Chapter 12).
- ☐ Broken, disconnected, or loose wiring in warning light circuit (Chapter 12).
- ☐ Alternator faulty (Chapter 5A).

Lights inoperative

- ☐ Bulb blown (Chapter 12).
- ☐ Corrosion of bulb or bulbholder contacts (Chapter 12).
- ☐ Blown fuse (Chapter 12).
- ☐ Faulty relay (Chapter 12).
- ☐ Broken, loose, or disconnected wiring (Chapter 12).
- ☐ Faulty switch (Chapter 12).

Instrument readings inaccurate or erratic

Instrument readings increase with engine speed

- ☐ Faulty voltage regulator in instrument panel (Chapter 12).

Fuel or temperature gauges give no reading

- ☐ Faulty gauge sender unit (Chapters 3 and 4A, 4B or 4C).
- ☐ Wiring open-circuit (Chapter 12).
- ☐ Faulty gauge (Chapter 12).

Fuel or temperature gauges give continuous maximum reading

- ☐ Faulty gauge sender unit (Chapters 3 and 4A, 4B or 4C).
- ☐ Wiring short-circuit (Chapter 12).
- ☐ Faulty gauge (Chapter 12).

Horn inoperative, or unsatisfactory in operation

Horn operates all the time

- ☐ Horn push either earthed or stuck down (Chapter 12).
- ☐ Horn wire to horn push earthed (Chapter 12).

Horn fails to operate

- ☐ Blown fuse (Chapter 12).
- ☐ Wiring connections loose, broken or disconnected (Chapter 12).
- ☐ Faulty horn (Chapter 12).

Horn emits intermittent or unsatisfactory sound

- ☐ Wiring connections loose (Chapter 12).
- ☐ Horn mountings loose (Chapter 12).
- ☐ Faulty horn (Chapter 12).

Windscreen/tailgate wipers inoperative, or unsatisfactory in operation

Wipers fail to operate, or operate very slowly

- ☐ Wiper blades stuck to screen, or linkage seized or binding (Chapter 12).
- ☐ Blown fuse (Chapter 12).
- ☐ Wiring connections loose, broken or disconnected (Chapter 12).
- ☐ Faulty relay (Chapter 12).
- ☐ Faulty wiper motor (Chapter 12).

Wiper blades sweep over too large or too small an area of the glass

- ☐ Wiper arms incorrectly positioned on spindles.
- ☐ Excessive wear of wiper linkage (Chapter 12).
- ☐ Wiper motor or linkage mountings loose or insecure (Chapter 12).

Wiper blades fail to clean the glass effectively

- ☐ Wiper blade rubbers worn or perished (*"Weekly checks"*).
- ☐ Wiper arm tension springs broken, or arm pivots seized (Chapter 12).
- ☐ Insufficient windscreen washer additive to adequately remove road film (*"Weekly checks"*).

Windscreen/tailgate washers inoperative, or unsatisfactory in operation

One or more washer jets inoperative

- ☐ Blocked washer jet (Chapter 1).
- ☐ Disconnected, kinked or restricted fluid hose (Chapter 12).
- ☐ Insufficient fluid in washer reservoir (*"Weekly checks"*).

Washer pump fails to operate

- ☐ Broken or disconnected wiring or connections (Chapter 12).
- ☐ Blown fuse (Chapter 12).
- ☐ Faulty washer switch (Chapter 12).
- ☐ Faulty washer pump (Chapter 12).

Washer pump runs for some time before fluid is emitted from jets

- ☐ Faulty one-way valve in fluid supply hose (Chapter 12).

Electric windows inoperative, or unsatisfactory in operation

Window glass will only move in one direction

- ☐ Faulty switch (Chapter 12).

Window glass slow to move

- ☐ Regulator seized or damaged, or in need of lubrication (Chapter 11).
- ☐ Door internal components or trim fouling regulator (Chapter 11).
- ☐ Faulty motor (Chapter 11).

Window glass fails to move

- ☐ Blown fuse (Chapter 12).
- ☐ Faulty switch or relay (Chapter 12).
- ☐ Broken or disconnected wiring or connections (Chapter 12).
- ☐ Faulty motor (Chapter 11).

Central locking system inoperative, or unsatisfactory in operation

Complete system failure

- ☐ Blown fuse (Chapter 12).
- ☐ Faulty relay (Chapter 12).
- ☐ Broken or disconnected wiring or connections (Chapter 12).
- ☐ Faulty control unit (Chapter 11).

Latch locks but will not unlock, or unlocks but will not lock

- ☐ Broken or disconnected latch operating rods or levers (Chapter 11).
- ☐ Faulty relay (Chapter 12).
- ☐ Faulty control unit (Chapter 11).

One solenoid/motor fails to operate

- ☐ Broken or disconnected wiring or connections (Chapter 12).
- ☐ Faulty solenoid/motor (Chapter 11).
- ☐ Broken, binding or disconnected latch operating rods or levers (Chapter 11).
- ☐ Fault in door latch (Chapter 11).

A

ABS (Anti-lock brake system) A system, usually electronically controlled, that senses incipient wheel lockup during braking and relieves hydraulic pressure at wheels that are about to skid.

Air bag An inflatable bag hidden in the steering wheel (driver's side) or the dash or glovebox (passenger side). In a head-on collision, the bags inflate, preventing the driver and front passenger from being thrown forward into the steering wheel or windscreen.

Air cleaner A metal or plastic housing, containing a filter element, which removes dust and dirt from the air being drawn into the engine.

Air filter element The actual filter in an air cleaner system, usually manufactured from pleated paper and requiring renewal at regular intervals.

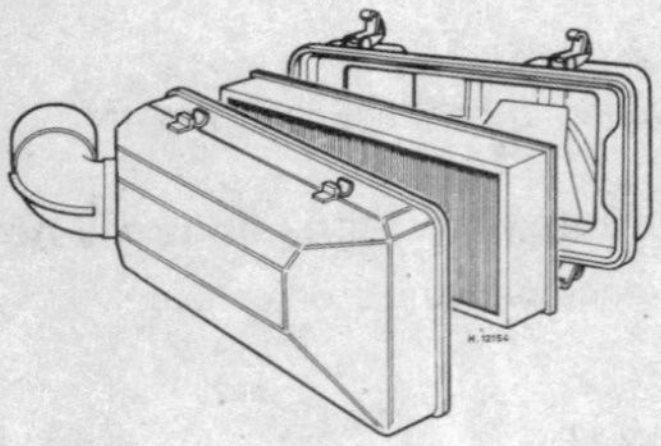

Air filter

Allen key A hexagonal wrench which fits into a recessed hexagonal hole.

Alligator clip A long-nosed spring-loaded metal clip with meshing teeth. Used to make temporary electrical connections.

Alternator A component in the electrical system which converts mechanical energy from a drivebelt into electrical energy to charge the battery and to operate the starting system, ignition system and electrical accessories.

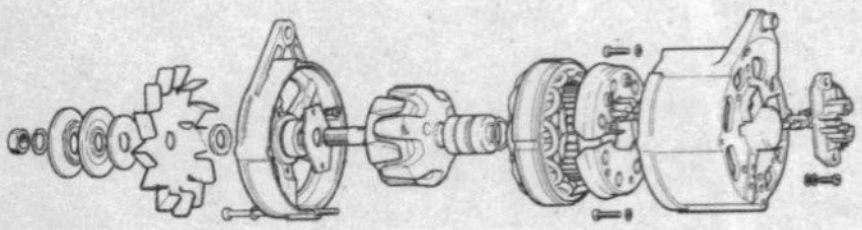

Alternator (exploded view)

Ampere (amp) A unit of measurement for the flow of electric current. One amp is the amount of current produced by one volt acting through a resistance of one ohm.

Anaerobic sealer A substance used to prevent bolts and screws from loosening. Anaerobic means that it does not require oxygen for activation. The Loctite brand is widely used.

Antifreeze A substance (usually ethylene glycol) mixed with water, and added to a vehicle's cooling system, to prevent freezing of the coolant in winter. Antifreeze also contains chemicals to inhibit corrosion and the formation of rust and other deposits that would tend to clog the radiator and coolant passages and reduce cooling efficiency.

Anti-seize compound A coating that reduces the risk of seizing on fasteners that are subjected to high temperatures, such as exhaust manifold bolts and nuts.

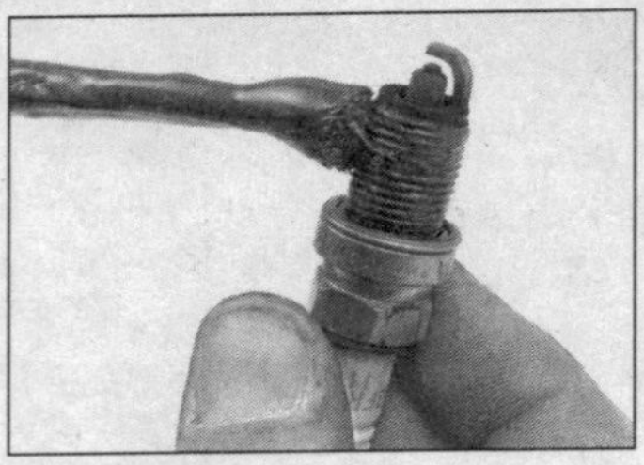

Anti-seize compound

Asbestos A natural fibrous mineral with great heat resistance, commonly used in the composition of brake friction materials. Asbestos is a health hazard and the dust created by brake systems should never be inhaled or ingested.

Axle A shaft on which a wheel revolves, or which revolves with a wheel. Also, a solid beam that connects the two wheels at one end of the vehicle. An axle which also transmits power to the wheels is known as a live axle.

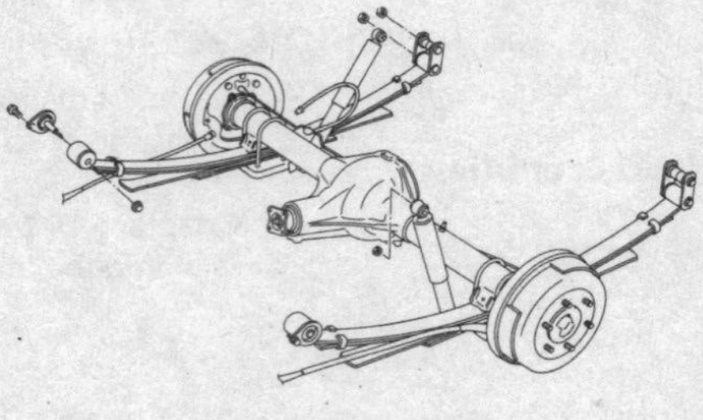

Axle assembly

Axleshaft A single rotating shaft, on either side of the differential, which delivers power from the final drive assembly to the drive wheels. Also called a driveshaft or a halfshaft.

B

Ball bearing An anti-friction bearing consisting of a hardened inner and outer race with hardened steel balls between two races.

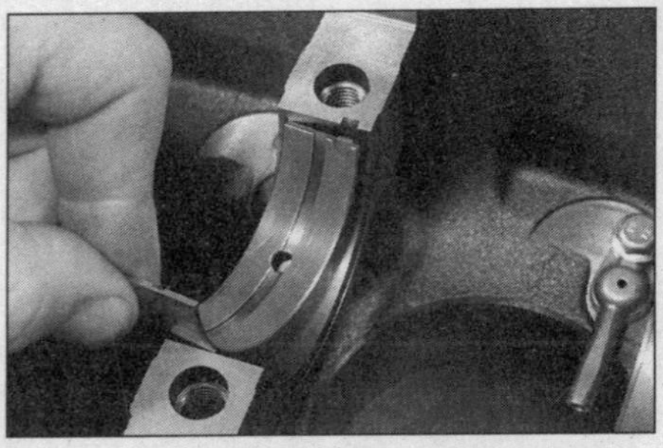

Bearing

Bearing The curved surface on a shaft or in a bore, or the part assembled into either, that permits relative motion between them with minimum wear and friction.

Big-end bearing The bearing in the end of the connecting rod that's attached to the crankshaft.

Bleed nipple A valve on a brake wheel cylinder, caliper or other hydraulic component that is opened to purge the hydraulic system of air. Also called a bleed screw.

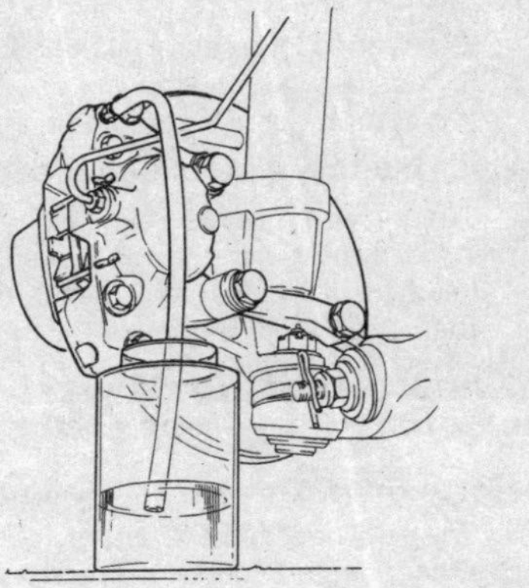

Brake bleeding

Brake bleeding Procedure for removing air from lines of a hydraulic brake system.

Brake disc The component of a disc brake that rotates with the wheels.

Brake drum The component of a drum brake that rotates with the wheels.

Brake linings The friction material which contacts the brake disc or drum to retard the vehicle's speed. The linings are bonded or riveted to the brake pads or shoes.

Brake pads The replaceable friction pads that pinch the brake disc when the brakes are applied. Brake pads consist of a friction material bonded or riveted to a rigid backing plate.

Brake shoe The crescent-shaped carrier to which the brake linings are mounted and which forces the lining against the rotating drum during braking.

Braking systems For more information on braking systems, consult the *Haynes Automotive Brake Manual*.

Breaker bar A long socket wrench handle providing greater leverage.

Bulkhead The insulated partition between the engine and the passenger compartment.

C

Caliper The non-rotating part of a disc-brake assembly that straddles the disc and carries the brake pads. The caliper also contains the hydraulic components that cause the pads to pinch the disc when the brakes are applied. A caliper is also a measuring tool that can be set to measure inside or outside dimensions of an object.

Camshaft A rotating shaft on which a series of cam lobes operate the valve mechanisms. The camshaft may be driven by gears, by sprockets and chain or by sprockets and a belt.

Canister A container in an evaporative emission control system; contains activated charcoal granules to trap vapours from the fuel system.

Canister

Carburettor A device which mixes fuel with air in the proper proportions to provide a desired power output from a spark ignition internal combustion engine.

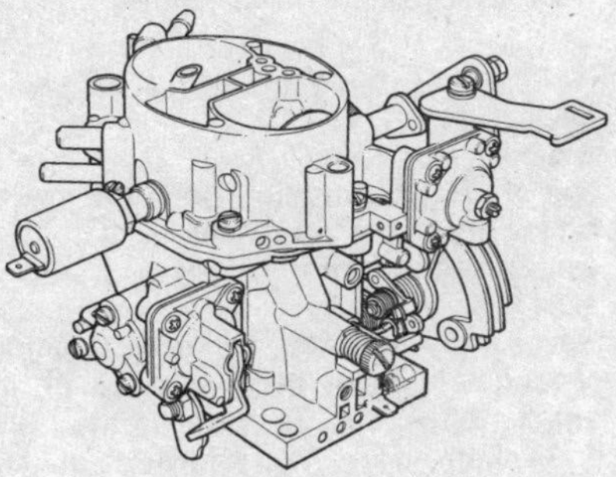

Carburettor

Castellated Resembling the parapets along the top of a castle wall. For example, a castellated balljoint stud nut.

Castellated nut

Castor In wheel alignment, the backward or forward tilt of the steering axis. Castor is positive when the steering axis is inclined rearward at the top.

Catalytic converter A silencer-like device in the exhaust system which converts certain pollutants in the exhaust gases into less harmful substances.

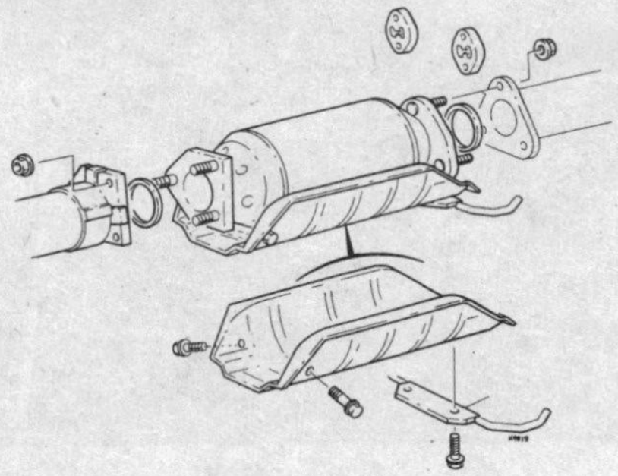

Catalytic converter

Circlip A ring-shaped clip used to prevent endwise movement of cylindrical parts and shafts. An internal circlip is installed in a groove in a housing; an external circlip fits into a groove on the outside of a cylindrical piece such as a shaft.

Clearance The amount of space between two parts. For example, between a piston and a cylinder, between a bearing and a journal, etc.

Coil spring A spiral of elastic steel found in various sizes throughout a vehicle, for example as a springing medium in the suspension and in the valve train.

Compression Reduction in volume, and increase in pressure and temperature, of a gas, caused by squeezing it into a smaller space.

Compression ratio The relationship between cylinder volume when the piston is at top dead centre and cylinder volume when the piston is at bottom dead centre.

Constant velocity (CV) joint A type of universal joint that cancels out vibrations caused by driving power being transmitted through an angle.

Core plug A disc or cup-shaped metal device inserted in a hole in a casting through which core was removed when the casting was formed. Also known as a freeze plug or expansion plug.

Crankcase The lower part of the engine block in which the crankshaft rotates.

Crankshaft The main rotating member, or shaft, running the length of the crankcase, with offset "throws" to which the connecting rods are attached.

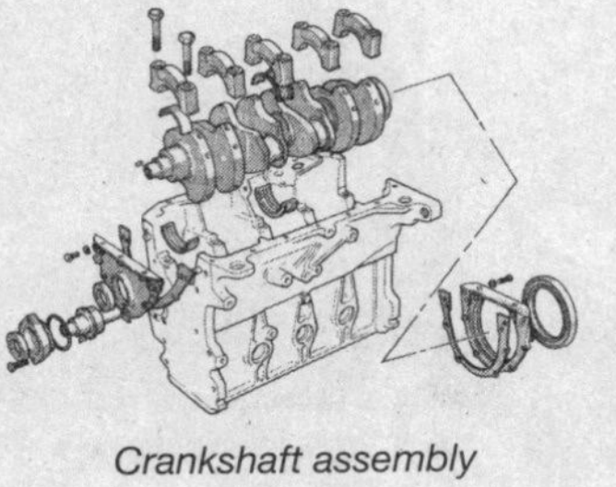

Crankshaft assembly

Crocodile clip See Alligator clip

D

Diagnostic code Code numbers obtained by accessing the diagnostic mode of an engine management computer. This code can be used to determine the area in the system where a malfunction may be located.

Disc brake A brake design incorporating a rotating disc onto which brake pads are squeezed. The resulting friction converts the energy of a moving vehicle into heat.

Double-overhead cam (DOHC) An engine that uses two overhead camshafts, usually one for the intake valves and one for the exhaust valves.

Drivebelt(s) The belt(s) used to drive accessories such as the alternator, water pump, power steering pump, air conditioning compressor, etc. off the crankshaft pulley.

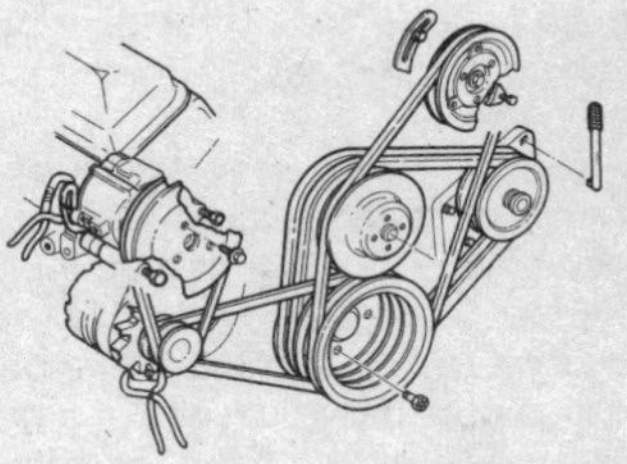

Accessory drivebelts

Driveshaft Any shaft used to transmit motion. Commonly used when referring to the axleshafts on a front wheel drive vehicle.

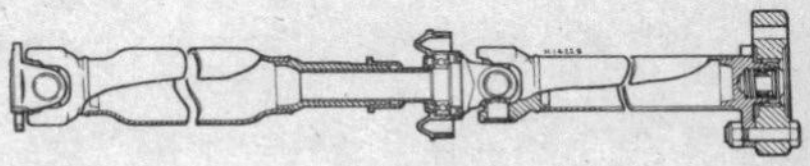

Driveshaft

Drum brake A type of brake using a drum-shaped metal cylinder attached to the inner surface of the wheel. When the brake pedal is pressed, curved brake shoes with friction linings press against the inside of the drum to slow or stop the vehicle.

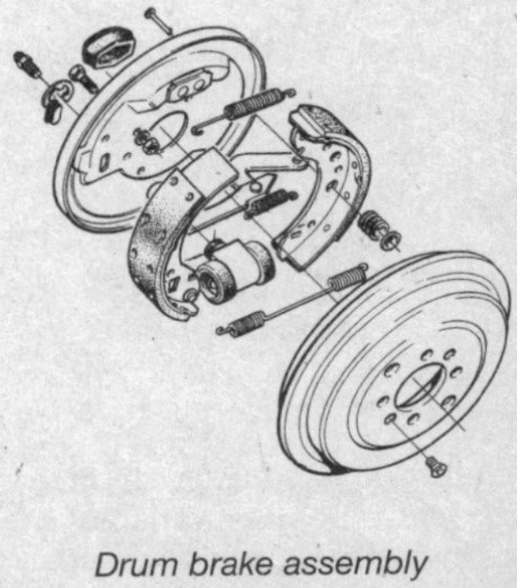

Drum brake assembly

E

EGR valve A valve used to introduce exhaust gases into the intake air stream.

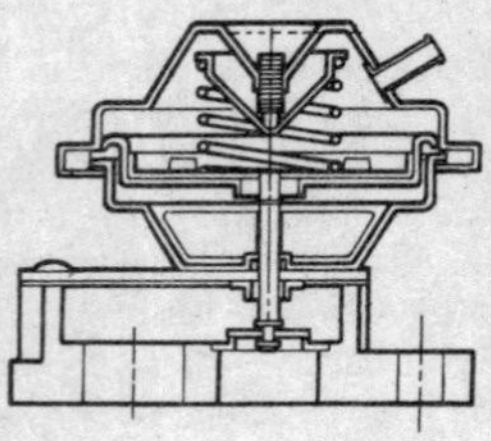

EGR valve

Electronic control unit (ECU) A computer which controls (for instance) ignition and fuel injection systems, or an anti-lock braking system. For more information refer to the *Haynes Automotive Electrical and Electronic Systems Manual.*

Electronic Fuel Injection (EFI) A computer controlled fuel system that distributes fuel through an injector located in each intake port of the engine.

Emergency brake A braking system, independent of the main hydraulic system, that can be used to slow or stop the vehicle if the primary brakes fail, or to hold the vehicle stationary even though the brake pedal isn't depressed. It usually consists of a hand lever that actuates either front or rear brakes mechanically through a series of cables and linkages. Also known as a handbrake or parking brake.

Endfloat The amount of lengthwise movement between two parts. As applied to a crankshaft, the distance that the crankshaft can move forward and back in the cylinder block.

Engine management system (EMS) A computer controlled system which manages the fuel injection and the ignition systems in an integrated fashion.

Exhaust manifold A part with several passages through which exhaust gases leave the engine combustion chambers and enter the exhaust pipe.

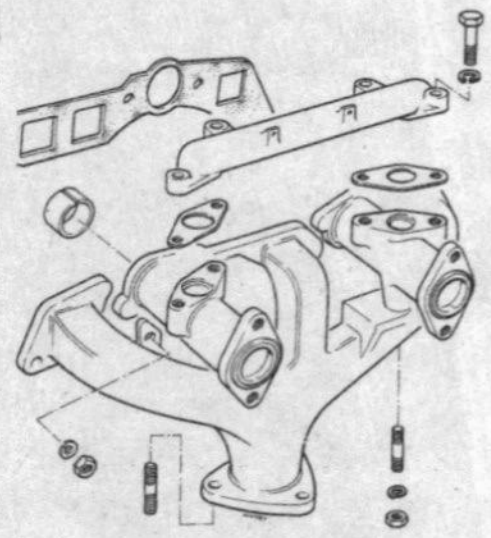

Exhaust manifold

F

Fan clutch A viscous (fluid) drive coupling device which permits variable engine fan speeds in relation to engine speeds.

Feeler blade A thin strip or blade of hardened steel, ground to an exact thickness, used to check or measure clearances between parts.

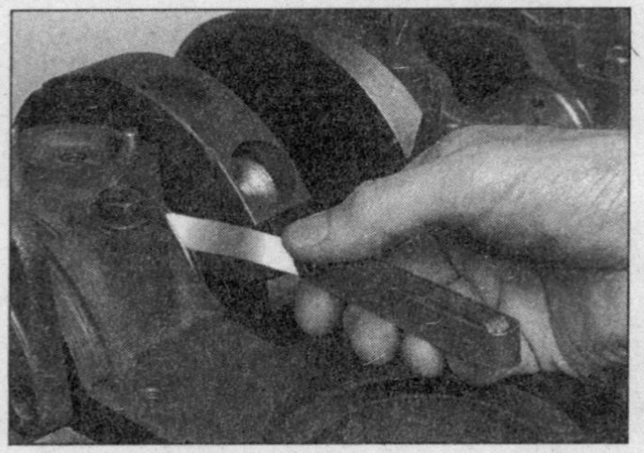

Feeler blade

Firing order The order in which the engine cylinders fire, or deliver their power strokes, beginning with the number one cylinder.

Flywheel A heavy spinning wheel in which energy is absorbed and stored by means of momentum. On cars, the flywheel is attached to the crankshaft to smooth out firing impulses.

Free play The amount of travel before any action takes place. The "looseness" in a linkage, or an assembly of parts, between the initial application of force and actual movement. For example, the distance the brake pedal moves before the pistons in the master cylinder are actuated.

Fuse An electrical device which protects a circuit against accidental overload. The typical fuse contains a soft piece of metal which is calibrated to melt at a predetermined current flow (expressed as amps) and break the circuit.

Fusible link A circuit protection device consisting of a conductor surrounded by heat-resistant insulation. The conductor is smaller than the wire it protects, so it acts as the weakest link in the circuit. Unlike a blown fuse, a failed fusible link must frequently be cut from the wire for replacement.

G

Gap The distance the spark must travel in jumping from the centre electrode to the side electrode in a spark plug. Also refers to the spacing between the points in a contact breaker assembly in a conventional points-type ignition, or to the distance between the reluctor or rotor and the pickup coil in an electronic ignition.

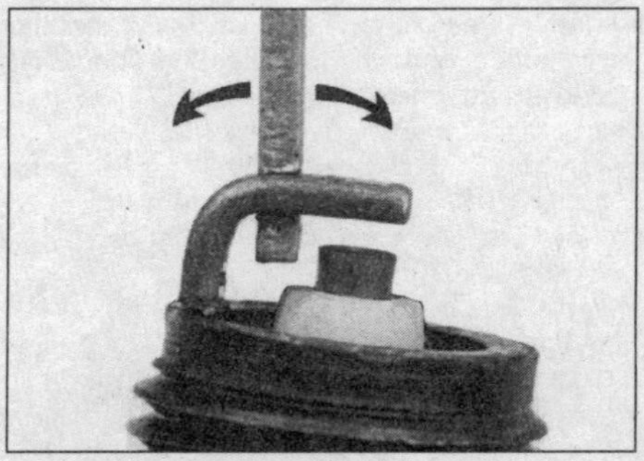

Adjusting spark plug gap

Gasket Any thin, soft material - usually cork, cardboard, asbestos or soft metal - installed between two metal surfaces to ensure a good seal. For instance, the cylinder head gasket seals the joint between the block and the cylinder head.

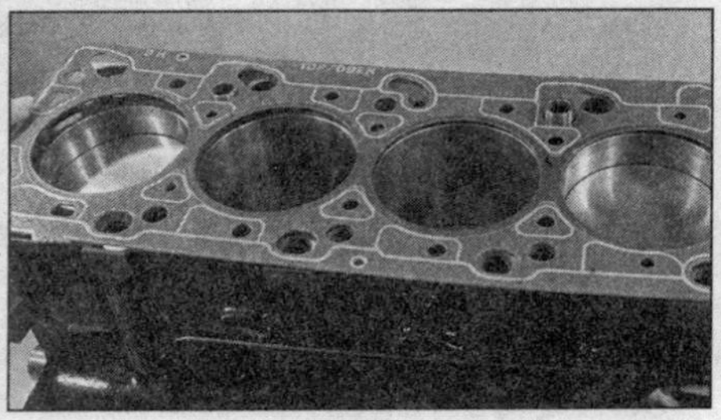

Gasket

Gauge An instrument panel display used to monitor engine conditions. A gauge with a movable pointer on a dial or a fixed scale is an analogue gauge. A gauge with a numerical readout is called a digital gauge.

H

Halfshaft A rotating shaft that transmits power from the final drive unit to a drive wheel, usually when referring to a live rear axle.

Harmonic balancer A device designed to reduce torsion or twisting vibration in the crankshaft. May be incorporated in the crankshaft pulley. Also known as a vibration damper.

Hone An abrasive tool for correcting small irregularities or differences in diameter in an engine cylinder, brake cylinder, etc.

Hydraulic tappet A tappet that utilises hydraulic pressure from the engine's lubrication system to maintain zero clearance (constant contact with both camshaft and valve stem). Automatically adjusts to variation in valve stem length. Hydraulic tappets also reduce valve noise.

I

Ignition timing The moment at which the spark plug fires, usually expressed in the number of crankshaft degrees before the piston reaches the top of its stroke.

Inlet manifold A tube or housing with passages through which flows the air-fuel mixture (carburettor vehicles and vehicles with throttle body injection) or air only (port fuel-injected vehicles) to the port openings in the cylinder head.

J

Jump start Starting the engine of a vehicle with a discharged or weak battery by attaching jump leads from the weak battery to a charged or helper battery.

L

Load Sensing Proportioning Valve (LSPV) A brake hydraulic system control valve that works like a proportioning valve, but also takes into consideration the amount of weight carried by the rear axle.

Locknut A nut used to lock an adjustment nut, or other threaded component, in place. For example, a locknut is employed to keep the adjusting nut on the rocker arm in position.

Lockwasher A form of washer designed to prevent an attaching nut from working loose.

M

MacPherson strut A type of front suspension system devised by Earle MacPherson at Ford of England. In its original form, a simple lateral link with the anti-roll bar creates the lower control arm. A long strut - an integral coil spring and shock absorber - is mounted between the body and the steering knuckle. Many modern so-called MacPherson strut systems use a conventional lower A-arm and don't rely on the anti-roll bar for location.

Multimeter An electrical test instrument with the capability to measure voltage, current and resistance.

N

NOx Oxides of Nitrogen. A common toxic pollutant emitted by petrol and diesel engines at higher temperatures.

O

Ohm The unit of electrical resistance. One volt applied to a resistance of one ohm will produce a current of one amp.

Ohmmeter An instrument for measuring electrical resistance.

O-ring A type of sealing ring made of a special rubber-like material; in use, the O-ring is compressed into a groove to provide the sealing action.

O-ring

Overhead cam (ohc) engine An engine with the camshaft(s) located on top of the cylinder head(s).

Overhead valve (ohv) engine An engine with the valves located in the cylinder head, but with the camshaft located in the engine block.

Oxygen sensor A device installed in the engine exhaust manifold, which senses the oxygen content in the exhaust and converts this information into an electric current. Also called a Lambda sensor.

P

Phillips screw A type of screw head having a cross instead of a slot for a corresponding type of screwdriver.

Plastigage A thin strip of plastic thread, available in different sizes, used for measuring clearances. For example, a strip of Plastigage is laid across a bearing journal. The parts are assembled and dismantled; the width of the crushed strip indicates the clearance between journal and bearing.

Plastigage

Propeller shaft The long hollow tube with universal joints at both ends that carries power from the transmission to the differential on front-engined rear wheel drive vehicles.

Proportioning valve A hydraulic control valve which limits the amount of pressure to the rear brakes during panic stops to prevent wheel lock-up.

R

Rack-and-pinion steering A steering system with a pinion gear on the end of the steering shaft that mates with a rack (think of a geared wheel opened up and laid flat). When the steering wheel is turned, the pinion turns, moving the rack to the left or right. This movement is transmitted through the track rods to the steering arms at the wheels.

Radiator A liquid-to-air heat transfer device designed to reduce the temperature of the coolant in an internal combustion engine cooling system.

Refrigerant Any substance used as a heat transfer agent in an air-conditioning system. R-12 has been the principle refrigerant for many years; recently, however, manufacturers have begun using R-134a, a non-CFC substance that is considered less harmful to the ozone in the upper atmosphere.

Rocker arm A lever arm that rocks on a shaft or pivots on a stud. In an overhead valve engine, the rocker arm converts the upward movement of the pushrod into a downward movement to open a valve.

Rotor In a distributor, the rotating device inside the cap that connects the centre electrode and the outer terminals as it turns, distributing the high voltage from the coil secondary winding to the proper spark plug. Also, that part of an alternator which rotates inside the stator. Also, the rotating assembly of a turbocharger, including the compressor wheel, shaft and turbine wheel.

Runout The amount of wobble (in-and-out movement) of a gear or wheel as it's rotated. The amount a shaft rotates "out-of-true." The out-of-round condition of a rotating part.

S

Sealant A liquid or paste used to prevent leakage at a joint. Sometimes used in conjunction with a gasket.

Sealed beam lamp An older headlight design which integrates the reflector, lens and filaments into a hermetically-sealed one-piece unit. When a filament burns out or the lens cracks, the entire unit is simply replaced.

Serpentine drivebelt A single, long, wide accessory drivebelt that's used on some newer vehicles to drive all the accessories, instead of a series of smaller, shorter belts. Serpentine drivebelts are usually tensioned by an automatic tensioner.

Serpentine drivebelt

Shim Thin spacer, commonly used to adjust the clearance or relative positions between two parts. For example, shims inserted into or under bucket tappets control valve clearances. Clearance is adjusted by changing the thickness of the shim.

Slide hammer A special puller that screws into or hooks onto a component such as a shaft or bearing; a heavy sliding handle on the shaft bottoms against the end of the shaft to knock the component free.

Sprocket A tooth or projection on the periphery of a wheel, shaped to engage with a chain or drivebelt. Commonly used to refer to the sprocket wheel itself.

Starter inhibitor switch On vehicles with an automatic transmission, a switch that prevents starting if the vehicle is not in Neutral or Park.

Strut See MacPherson strut.

T

Tappet A cylindrical component which transmits motion from the cam to the valve stem, either directly or via a pushrod and rocker arm. Also called a cam follower.

Thermostat A heat-controlled valve that regulates the flow of coolant between the cylinder block and the radiator, so maintaining optimum engine operating temperature. A thermostat is also used in some air cleaners in which the temperature is regulated.

Thrust bearing The bearing in the clutch assembly that is moved in to the release levers by clutch pedal action to disengage the clutch. Also referred to as a release bearing.

Timing belt A toothed belt which drives the camshaft. Serious engine damage may result if it breaks in service.

Timing chain A chain which drives the camshaft.

Toe-in The amount the front wheels are closer together at the front than at the rear. On rear wheel drive vehicles, a slight amount of toe-in is usually specified to keep the front wheels running parallel on the road by offsetting other forces that tend to spread the wheels apart.

Toe-out The amount the front wheels are closer together at the rear than at the front. On front wheel drive vehicles, a slight amount of toe-out is usually specified.

Tools For full information on choosing and using tools, refer to the *Haynes Automotive Tools Manual.*

Tracer A stripe of a second colour applied to a wire insulator to distinguish that wire from another one with the same colour insulator.

Tune-up A process of accurate and careful adjustments and parts replacement to obtain the best possible engine performance.

Turbocharger A centrifugal device, driven by exhaust gases, that pressurises the intake air. Normally used to increase the power output from a given engine displacement, but can also be used primarily to reduce exhaust emissions (as on VW's "Umwelt" Diesel engine).

U

Universal joint or U-joint A double-pivoted connection for transmitting power from a driving to a driven shaft through an angle. A U-joint consists of two Y-shaped yokes and a cross-shaped member called the spider.

V

Valve A device through which the flow of liquid, gas, vacuum, or loose material in bulk may be started, stopped, or regulated by a movable part that opens, shuts, or partially obstructs one or more ports or passageways. A valve is also the movable part of such a device.

Valve clearance The clearance between the valve tip (the end of the valve stem) and the rocker arm or tappet. The valve clearance is measured when the valve is closed.

Vernier caliper A precision measuring instrument that measures inside and outside dimensions. Not quite as accurate as a micrometer, but more convenient.

Viscosity The thickness of a liquid or its resistance to flow.

Volt A unit for expressing electrical "pressure" in a circuit. One volt that will produce a current of one ampere through a resistance of one ohm.

W

Welding Various processes used to join metal items by heating the areas to be joined to a molten state and fusing them together. For more information refer to the *Haynes Automotive Welding Manual.*

Wiring diagram A drawing portraying the components and wires in a vehicle's electrical system, using standardised symbols. For more information refer to the *Haynes Automotive Electrical and Electronic Systems Manual.*

Note: *References throughout this index are in the form* ***"Chapter number"•"page number"***

E

F

G

H

S

T

U

V

W

Haynes Manuals – The Complete List

Title	Book No.
ALFA ROMEO Alfasud/Sprint (74 - 88) up to F *	0292
Alfa Romeo Alfetta (73 - 87) up to E *	0531
AUDI 80, 90 & Coupe Petrol (79 - Nov 88) up to F	0605
Audi 80, 90 & Coupe Petrol (Oct 86 - 90) D to H	1491
Audi 100 & 200 Petrol (Oct 82 - 90) up to H	0907
Audi 100 & A6 Petrol & Diesel (May 91 - May 97) H to P	3504
Audi A4 Petrol & Diesel (95 - Feb 00) M to V	3575
AUSTIN A35 & A40 (56 - 67) up to F *	0118
Austin/MG/Rover Maestro 1.3 & 1.6 Petrol (83 - 95) up to M	0922
Austin/MG Metro (80 - May 90) up to G	0718
Austin/Rover Montego 1.3 & 1.6 Petrol (84 - 94) A to L	1066
Austin/MG/Rover Montego 2.0 Petrol (84 - 95) A to M	1067
Mini (59 - 69) up to H	0527
Mini (69 - 01) up to X	0646
Austin/Rover 2.0 litre Diesel Engine (86 - 93) C to L	1857
AUSTIN HEALEY 100/6 & 3000 (56 - 68) up to G *	0049
BEDFORD CF Petrol (69 - 87) up to E	0163
Bedford/Vauxhall Rascal & Suzuki Supercarry (86 - Oct 94) C to M	3015
BMW 316, 320 & 320i (4-cyl) (75 - Feb 83) up to Y *	0276
BMW 320, 320i, 323i & 325i (6-cyl) (Oct 77 - Sept 87) up to E	0815
BMW 3- & 5-Series Petrol (81 - 91) up to J	1948
BMW 3-Series Petrol (Apr 91 - 96) H to N	3210
BMW 3-Series Petrol (Sept 98 - 03) S-reg. on	4067
BMW 520i & 525e (Oct 81 - June 88) up to E	1560
BMW 525, 528 & 528i (73 - Sept 81) up to X *	0632
BMW 1500, 1502, 1600, 1602, 2000 & 2002 (59 - 77) up to S *	0240
CHRYSLER PT Cruiser Petrol (00 - 03) W-reg. on	4058
CITROËN 2CV, Ami & Dyane (67 - 90) up to H	0196
Citroën AX Petrol & Diesel (87 - 97) D to P	3014
Citroën BX Petrol (83 - 94) A to L	0908
Citroën C15 Van Petrol & Diesel (89 - Oct 98) F to S	3509
Citroën CX Petrol (75 - 88) up to F	0528
Citroën Saxo Petrol & Diesel (96 - 01) N to X	3506
Citroën Visa Petrol (79 - 88) up to F	0620
Citroën Xantia Petrol & Diesel (93 - 98) K to S	3082
Citroën XM Petrol & Diesel (89 - 00) G to X	3451
Citroën Xsara Petrol & Diesel (97 - Sept 00) R to W	3751
Citroën Xsara Picasso Petrol & Diesel (00 - 02) W-reg. onwards	3944
Citroën ZX Diesel (91 - 98) J to S	1922
Citroën ZX Petrol (91 - 98) H to S	1881
Citroën 1.7 & 1.9 litre Diesel Engine (84 - 96) A to N	1379
FIAT 126 (73 - 87) up to E *	0305
Fiat 500 (57 - 73) up to M *	0090
Fiat Bravo & Brava Petrol (95 - 00) N to W	3572
Fiat Cinquecento (93 - 98) K to R	3501
Fiat Panda (81 - 95) up to M	0793
Fiat Punto Petrol & Diesel (94 - Oct 99) L to V	3251
Fiat Punto Petrol (Oct 99 - July 03) V-reg on	4066
Fiat Regata Petrol (84 - 88) A to F	1167
Fiat Tipo Petrol (88 - 91) E to J	1625
Fiat Uno Petrol (83 - 95) up to M	0923
Fiat X1/9 (74 - 89) up to G *	0273
FORD Anglia (59 - 68) up to G *	0001
Ford Capri II (& III) 1.6 & 2.0 (74 - 87) up to E	0283
Ford Capri II (& III) 2.8 & 3.0 V6 (74 - 87) up to E	1309
Ford Cortina Mk III 1300 & 1600 (70 - 76) up to P*	0070
Ford Escort Mk I 1100 & 1300 (68 - 74) up to N*	0171
Ford Escort Mk I Mexico, RS 1600 & RS 2000 (70 - 74) up to N *	0139
Ford Escort Mk II Mexico, RS 1800 & RS 2000 (75 - 80) up to W *	0735
Ford Escort (75 - Aug 80) up to V *	0280
Ford Escort Petrol (Sept 80 - Sept 90) up to H	0686
Ford Escort & Orion Petrol (Sept 90 - 00) H to X	1737
Ford Escort & Orion Diesel (Sept 90 - 00) H to X	4081
Ford Fiesta (76 - Aug 83) up to Y	0334
Ford Fiesta Petrol (Aug 83 - Feb 89) A to F	1030
Ford Fiesta Petrol (Feb 89 - Oct 95) F to N	1595
Ford Fiesta Petrol & Diesel (Oct 95 - 01) N-reg. on	3397
Ford Fiesta (02 - 04) 02-reg. onwards	4170
Ford Focus Petrol & Diesel (98 - 01) S to Y	3759
Ford Focus Petrol & Diesel (01 - 04) Y-reg. on	4167
Ford Galaxy Petrol & Diesel (95 - Aug 00) M to W	3984
Ford Granada Petrol (Sept 77 - Feb 85) up to B	0481
Ford Granada & Scorpio Petrol (Mar 85 - 94) B to M	1245
Ford Ka (96 - 02) P-reg. onwards	3570
Ford Mondeo Petrol (93 - Sept 00) K to X	1923
Ford Mondeo Petrol & Diesel (Oct 00 - Jul 03) X to 03	3990
Ford Mondeo Diesel (93 - 96) L to N	3465
Ford Orion Petrol (83 - Sept 90) up to H	1009
Ford Sierra 4-cyl Petrol (82 - 93) up to K	0903
Ford Sierra V6 Petrol (82 - 91) up to J	0904
Ford Transit Petrol (Mk 2) (78 - Jan 86) up to C	0719
Ford Transit Petrol (Mk 3) (Feb 86 - 89) C to G	1468
Ford Transit Diesel (Feb 86 - 99) C to T	3019
Ford 1.6 & 1.8 litre Diesel Engine (84 - 96) A to N	1172
Ford 2.1, 2.3 & 2.5 litre Diesel Engine (77 - 90) up to H	1606
FREIGHT ROVER Sherpa Petrol (74 - 87) up to E	0463
HILLMAN Avenger (70 - 82) up to Y	0037
Hillman Imp (63 - 76) up to R *	0022
HONDA Accord (76 - Feb 84) up to A	0351
Honda Civic (Feb 84 - Oct 87) A to E	1226
Honda Civic (Nov 91 - 96) J to N	3199
Honda Civic Petrol (Mar 95 - 00) M to X	4050
HYUNDAI Pony (85 - 94) C to M	3398
JAGUAR E Type (61 - 72) up to L	0140
Jaguar MkI & II, 240 & 340 (55 - 69) up to H *	0098
Jaguar XJ6, XJ & Sovereign; Daimler Sovereign (68 - Oct 86) up to D	0242
Jaguar XJ6 & Sovereign (Oct 86 - Sept 94) D to M	3261
Jaguar XJ12, XJS & Sovereign; Daimler Double Six (72 - 88) up to F	0478
JEEP Cherokee Petrol (93 - 96) K to N	1943
LADA 1200, 1300, 1500 & 1600 (74 - 91) up to J	0413
Lada Samara (87 - 91) D to J	1610
LAND ROVER 90, 110 & Defender Diesel (83 - 95) up to N	3017
Land Rover Discovery Petrol & Diesel (89 - 98) G to S	3016
Land Rover Freelander Petrol & Diesel (97 - 02) R-reg. onwards	3929
Land Rover Series IIA & III Diesel (58 - 85) up to C	0529
Land Rover Series II, IIA & III 4-cyl Petrol (58 - 85) up to C	0314
MAZDA 323 (Mar 81 - Oct 89) up to G	1608
Mazda 323 (Oct 89 - 98) G to R	3455
Mazda 626 (May 83 - Sept 87) up to E	0929
Mazda B-1600, B-1800 & B-2000 Pick-up Petrol (72 - 88) up to F	0267
Mazda RX-7 (79 - 85) up to C *	0460
MERCEDES-BENZ 190, 190E & 190D Petrol & Diesel (83 - 93) A to L	3450
Mercedes-Benz 200 D, 240 D, 240 TD, 300 D & 300 TD 123 Series Diesel (Oct 76 - 85) up to C	1114
Mercedes-Benz 250 & 280 (68 - 72) up to L	0346
Mercedes-Benz 250 & 280 123 Series Petrol (Oct 76 - 84) up to B *	0677
Mercedes-Benz 124 Series Petrol & Diesel (85 - Aug 93) C to K	3253
Mercedes-Benz C-Class Petrol & Diesel (93 - Aug 00) L to W	3511
MGA (55 - 62) *	0475
MGB (62 - 80) up to W	0111
MG Midget & Austin-Healey Sprite (58 - 80) up to W	0265
MITSUBISHI Shogun & L200 Pick-Ups Petrol (83 - 94) up to M	1944
MORRIS Ital 1.3 (80 - 84) up to B	0705
Morris Minor 1000 (56 - 71) up to K	0024
NISSAN Almera Petrol (95 - Feb 00) N to V	4053
Nissan Bluebird (May 84 - Mar 86) A to C	1223
Nissan Bluebird Petrol (Mar 86 - 90) C to H	1473
Nissan Cherry (Sept 82 - 86) up to D	1031
Nissan Micra (83 - Jan 93) up to K	0931
Nissan Micra (93 - 99) K to T	3254
Nissan Primera Petrol (90 - Aug 99) H to T	1851
Nissan Stanza (82 - 86) up to D	0824
Nissan Sunny Petrol (May 82 - Oct 86) up to D	0895
Nissan Sunny Petrol (Oct 86 - Mar 91) D to H	1378
Nissan Sunny Petrol (Apr 91 - 95) H to N	3219
OPEL Ascona & Manta (B Series) (Sept 75 - 88) up to F	0316
Opel Ascona Petrol (81 - 88) *(Not available in UK see Vauxhall Cavalier 0812)*	3215
Opel Astra Petrol (Oct 91 - Feb 98) *(Not available in UK see Vauxhall Astra 1832)*	3156
Opel Astra & Zafira Diesel (Feb 98 - Sept 00) *(See Vauxhall/Opel Astra & Zafira Diesel Book No. 3797)*	
Opel Astra & Zafira Petrol (Feb 98 - Sept 00) *(See Vauxhall/Opel Astra & Zafira Petrol Book No. 3758)*	
Opel Calibra (90 - 98) *(See Vauxhall/Opel Calibra Book No. 3502)*	
Opel Corsa Petrol (83 - Mar 93) *(Not available in UK see Vauxhall Nova 0909)*	3160
Opel Corsa Petrol (Mar 93 - 97) *(Not available in UK see Vauxhall Corsa 1985)*	3159
Opel Corsa Diesel (Mar 93 - Oct 00) *(See Vauxhall/Opel Corsa Diesel Book No. 4087)*	
Opel Corsa Petrol (Apr 97 - Oct 00) *(See Vauxhall/Opel Corsa Petrol Book No. 3921)*	
Opel Corsa Petrol & Diesel (Oct 00 - Sept 03) *(See Vauxhall/Opel Corsa Petrol & Diesel Book No. 4079)*	
Opel Frontera Petrol & Diesel (91 - 98) *(See Vauxhall/Opel Frontera Book No. 3454)*	
Opel Kadett Petrol (Nov 79 - Oct 84) up to B	0634
Opel Kadett Petrol (Oct 84 - Oct 91) *(Not available in UK see Vauxhall Astra & Belmont 1136)*	3196
Opel Omega & Senator Petrol (Nov 86 - 94) *(NA in UK see Vauxhall Carlton & Senator 1469)*	3157
Opel Omega (94 - 99) *(See Vauxhall/Opel Omega Book No. 3510)*	
Opel Rekord Petrol (Feb 78 - Oct 86) up to D	0543

* Classic reprint